THE LETTERS, WRITINGS, AND SPEECHES
OF OLIVER CROMWELL

THE LETTERS, WRITINGS, AND SPEECHES OF
Oliver Cromwell

General Editor
JOHN MORRILL

Volume 1
14 October 1626 to 29 January 1649

Volume Editors
ANDREW BARCLAY
TIM WALES
JOHN MORRILL

OXFORD
UNIVERSITY PRESS

Great Clarendon Street, Oxford, OX2 6DP,
United Kingdom

Oxford University Press is a department of the University of Oxford.
It furthers the University's objective of excellence in research, scholarship,
and education by publishing worldwide. Oxford is a registered trade mark of
Oxford University Press in the UK and in certain other countries

© Andrew Barclay, Tim Wales, and John Morrill, 2022

The moral rights of the authors have been asserted

First Edition published in 2022

All rights reserved. No part of this publication may be reproduced, stored in
a retrieval system, or transmitted, in any form or by any means, without the
prior permission in writing of Oxford University Press, or as expressly permitted
by law, by licence or under terms agreed with the appropriate reprographics
rights organization. Enquiries concerning reproduction outside the scope of the
above should be sent to the Rights Department, Oxford University Press, at the
address above

You must not circulate this work in any other form
and you must impose this same condition on any acquirer

Published in the United States of America by Oxford University Press
198 Madison Avenue, New York, NY 10016, United States of America

British Library Cataloguing in Publication Data
Data available

Library of Congress Control Number: 2021942655

ISBN 978–0–19–958788–9

Printed and bound by
CPI Group (UK) Ltd, Croydon, CR0 4YY

Links to third party websites are provided by Oxford in good faith and
for information only. Oxford disclaims any responsibility for the materials
contained in any third party website referenced in this work.

CONTENTS

Chronological List of Letters, Writings and Reported Speech	vii
Acknowledgements	xxiii
Editorial Conventions	xxv
Abbreviations	xxix
General Introduction to Volumes 1–3	xxxv
Introduction to Volume 1	li
EDITED TEXTS	1
List of Omissions	653
Index of Biblical Citations	657
General Index	661

VOLUME 1: CHRONOLOGICAL LIST OF LETTERS, WRITINGS AND REPORTED SPEECH

1626

1626 10 14	Letter from Oliver Cromwell to Henry Downhall (14 October 1626).	3

1629

1629 02 11	Speech by Oliver Cromwell to the grand committee for religion of the House of Commons (11 February 1629).	4

1631

1631 04 01	Letter from Oliver Cromwell to [John Newdigate] (1 April 1631).	6

1636

1636 01 11	Letter from Oliver Cromwell to [James] Storye (11 January 1636).	8

1638

1638 09 13	Letter from Oliver Cromwell to John Hand (13 September 1638).	13
1638 10 13	Letter from Oliver Cromwell to Mrs St John (13 October 1638).	14

1640

1640 05 14	Certificate from Oliver Cromwell (14 May 1640).	17
1640 12 30	Speech by Oliver Cromwell to the House of Commons (30 December 1640). On annual Parliaments.	19

1641

1641 02 09	Speeches of Oliver Cromwell to the House of Commons (9 February 1641). On the Root and Branch petition.	20
1641 04 10	Speech by Oliver Cromwell to the House of Commons (10 April 1641). On observing the Sabbath.	21
1641 04 21	Speech by Oliver Cromwell to the House of Commons (21 April 1641). On victims of Laudian persecution.	22
1641 04 30[?]	Letter from Oliver Cromwell to George Willingham (late April or early May 1641).	22

CHRONOLOGICAL LIST OF LETTERS, WRITINGS AND REPORTED SPEECH

1641 05 03	Speech by Oliver Cromwell to the House of Commons (3 May 1641). On the need for an oath of Association.	25
1641 05 09[?]	Letter from Oliver Cromwell and John Lowry to the mayor and aldermen of Cambridge (n.d. [but between 7 and 11 May 1641]).	26
1641 05 11	Speech by Oliver Cromwell to the House of Commons (11 May 1641). On the future funding of cathedrals.	28
1641 05 22a	Speech by Oliver Cromwell to the House of Commons (22 May 1641). On a matter of parliamentary privilege.	28
1641 05 22b	Speech by Oliver Cromwell to the House of Commons (22 May 1641). On fen drainage.	30
1641 06 01	Speech by Oliver Cromwell to the House of Commons (1 June 1641). On a matter of privilege.	31
1641 06 04	Speech by Oliver Cromwell to the House of Commons (4 June 1641). Presenting a petition from Cambridge.	32
1641 06 09	Speech by Oliver Cromwell to the House of Commons (9 June 1641). On fen drainage.	33
1641 08 09a	Speech by Oliver Cromwell to the House of Commons (9 August 1641). On Anglo-Scottish relations.	34
1641 08 09b	Speech by Oliver Cromwell to the House of Commons (9 August 1641). On Crown appointments.	35
1641 08 12	Speech by Oliver Cromwell to the House of Commons (12 August 1641). On the expulsion of bishops from the House of Lords.	36
1641 08 16	Speech by Oliver Cromwell to the House of Commons (16 August 1641). On putting the Kingdom into a 'Posture of Defence'.	36
1641 08 24	Speech by Oliver Cromwell to the House of Commons (24 August 1641). On the disbandment of the Scottish army.	37
1641 09 01	Speech by Oliver Cromwell to the House of Commons (1 September 1641). Against the Book of Common Prayer.	38
1641 09 08	Speech by Oliver Cromwell to the House of Commons (8 September 1641). On preaching.	39
1641 10 26	Speech by Oliver Cromwell to the House of Commons (26 October 1641). On the bishops in the House of Lords.	40
1641 10 27	Speech by Oliver Cromwell to the House of Commons (27 October 1641). On the result of a by-election.	41
1641 10 29	Speech by Oliver Cromwell to the House of Commons (29 October 1641). On the King's nomination of new bishops.	42
1641 11 04	Speech by Oliver Cromwell to the House of Commons (4 November 1641). Prisoners in the Tower.	43
1641 11 06	Speech by Oliver Cromwell to the House of Commons (6 November 1641). Defence of the realm.	44
1641 11 27	Speech by Oliver Cromwell to the House of Commons (27 November 1641). On royalist sentiment in London.	45

CHRONOLOGICAL LIST OF LETTERS, WRITINGS AND REPORTED SPEECH

1641 12 06	Speech by Oliver Cromwell to the House of Commons (6 December 1641). On by-elections.	46
1641 12 10	Speech by Oliver Cromwell to the House of Commons (10 December 1641). Influence of peers in parliamentary elections.	46
1641 12 11	Speech by Oliver Cromwell to the House of Commons (11 December 1641). Defence of the Palace of Westminster.	47
1641 12 28	Speech by Oliver Cromwell to the House of Commons (28 December 1641). Against the earl of Bristol.	48
1641 12 29	Speech by Oliver Cromwell to the House of Commons (29 December 1641). On an Irish appointment.	49

1642

1642 01 14	Speech by Oliver Cromwell to the House of Commons (14 January 1642). For the Kingdom to be put in 'a Posture of Defence'.	50
1642 01 17	Speech by Oliver Cromwell to the House of Commons (17 January 1642). On the drift to civil war.	51
1642 01 20	Speech by Oliver Cromwell to the House of Commons (20 January 1642). Against a royalist JP.	52
1642 01 26a	Speech by Oliver Cromwell to the House of Commons (26 January 1642). Rate of pay for soldiers going to Ireland.	53
1642 01 26b	Speech by Oliver Cromwell to the House of Commons (26 January 1642). Against a royalist JP.	53
1642 02 02	Speech by Oliver Cromwell to the House of Commons (2 February 1642). For a burning of a book.	54
1642 02 07a	Speech by Oliver Cromwell to the House of Commons (7 February 1642). On a petition for reform of church government.	55
1642 02 07b	Speech by Oliver Cromwell to the House of Commons (7 February 1642). On the discharge of an Irish officer	56
1642 02 07c	Speech by Oliver Cromwell to the House of Commons (7 February 1642). Commissioning a response to Sir Edward Dering's book on episcopacy.	57
1642 02 16	Speech by Oliver Cromwell to the House of Commons (16 February 1642). How to respond to the Irish Rebellion.	58
1642 03 02	Speech by Oliver Cromwell to the House of Commons (2 March 1642). For the interrogation of Will Murray.	58
1642 03 08	Speech by Oliver Cromwell to the House of Commons (8 March 1642). Seditious words in Covent Garden.	59
1642 03 16	Speech by Oliver Cromwell to the House of Commons (16 March 1642). Presenting Cambridge petition.	60
1642 03 22	Speech by Oliver Cromwell to the House of Commons (22 March 1642). Election of a master at Emmanuel College, Cambridge.	61
1642 03 29	Speech by Oliver Cromwell to the House of Commons (29 March 1642). Catholic plots in Monmouthshire.	62

ix

CHRONOLOGICAL LIST OF LETTERS, WRITINGS AND REPORTED SPEECH

1642 03 31a   Speech by Oliver Cromwell to the House of Commons
(31 March 1642). Investigating opposition to the Militia Ordinance.   63

1642 03 31b   Speech by Oliver Cromwell to the House of Commons
(31 March 1642). Addition to a committee.   64

1642 04 28   Speeches of Oliver Cromwell to the House of Commons
(28 April 1642). Reporting from a conference with the Lords.   64

1642 05 03   Speech by Oliver Cromwell to the House of Commons
(3 May 1642). Expulsion of Catholics from Dublin.   65

1642 05 04   Speech by Oliver Cromwell to the House of Commons
(4 May 1642). Supporting a petition against a 'Laudian' minister.   66

1642 05 16   Speech by Oliver Cromwell to the House of Commons
(16 May 1642). Funding the campaign in Ireland.   67

1642 05 23   Speech by Oliver Cromwell to the House of Commons
(23 May 1642). Querying bail conditions.   67

1642 05 24   Speech by Oliver Cromwell to the House of Commons (24 May
1642). Delivering a petition about the appointment of a lecturer.   69

1642 05 26   Speeches of Oliver Cromwell to the House of Commons (26 May
1642). Report from conference with the Lords about Ireland.   69

1642 05 27a   Speech by Oliver Cromwell to the House of Commons
(27 May 1642). Delays in delivering Ireland from the rebels.   70

1642 05 27b   Speech by Oliver Cromwell to the House of Commons
(27 May 1642). Problems with the Irish expedition.   71

1642 05 28a   Speech by Oliver Cromwell to the House of Commons
(28 May 1642). The arms held by London livery companies.   72

1642 05 28b   Speech by Oliver Cromwell to the House of Commons
(28 May 1642). Raising volunteers for Ireland.   72

1642 05 30   Speech by Oliver Cromwell to the House of Commons
(30 May 1642). Implementing the Militia Ordinance.   73

1642 06 01a   Speech by Oliver Cromwell to the House of Commons
(1 June 1642). Disputes over the Militia Ordinance.   74

1642 06 01b   Speech by Oliver Cromwell to the House of Commons
(1 June 1642). Naval defence of Newcastle upon Tyne.   74

1642 06 01c   Speech by Oliver Cromwell to the House of Commons
(1 June 1642). Preventing the import of arms.   75

1642 06 01d   Speech by Oliver Cromwell to the House of Commons (1 June 1642).
Cromwell presents a petition from Scots troops in Ulster.   76

1642 06 03   Speech by Oliver Cromwell to the House of Commons
(3 June 1642). Investigation of riots.   77

1642 06 04   Speech by Oliver Cromwell to the House of Commons
(4 June 1642). Naval support for the Irish expedition.   77

1642 06 11   Speech by Oliver Cromwell to the House of Commons (11 June
1642). In support of voluntary loans on the propositions.   78

1642 06 15a   Speech by Oliver Cromwell to the House of Commons
(15 June 1642). Disarming of Papists.   79

CHRONOLOGICAL LIST OF LETTERS, WRITINGS AND REPORTED SPEECH

1642 06 15b	Speech by Oliver Cromwell to the House of Commons (15 June 1642). Organising loans on the propositions.	80
1642 06 15c	Speech by Oliver Cromwell to the House of Commons (15 June 1642). Appointment of some deputy lieutenants.	80
1642 06 17	Speech by Oliver Cromwell to the House of Commons (17 June 1642). Report from a conference with the Lords.	81
1642 06 20	Speech by Oliver Cromwell to the House of Commons (20 June 1642). Queries about proposition money.	82
1642 06 22	Speech by Oliver Cromwell to the House of Commons (22 June 1642). Procedural motion.	82
1642 06 24	Speech by Oliver Cromwell to the House of Commons (24 June 1642). Issues arising from the surrender of Galway to the Irish rebels.	83
1642 06 25	Speech by Oliver Cromwell to the House of Commons (25 June 1642). The expulsion of Papists from Dublin.	84
1642 06 27a	Speech by Oliver Cromwell to the House of Commons (27 June 1642). Report on a conference with the Lords.	85
1642 06 27b	Speech by Oliver Cromwell to the House of Commons (27 June 1642). Payment of army officers in Ireland.	86
1642 07 15	Speech by Oliver Cromwell to the House of Commons (15 July 1642). Organising the defence of Cambridgeshire.	86
1642 07 16	Speech by Oliver Cromwell to the House of Commons (16 July 1642). Report on conference with the Lords about Ireland.	87
1642 07 18	Speech by Oliver Cromwell to the House of Commons (18 July 1642). Militia disputes.	88
1642 07 19a	Memorandum by Oliver Cromwell about purchase of arms (19 July 1642).	89
1642 07 19b	Speech by Oliver Cromwell to the House of Commons (19 July 1642). Report on conference with the Lords.	90
1642 07 21	Speech by Oliver Cromwell to the House of Commons (21 July 1642). Irish affairs.	91
1642 07 22a	Speech by Oliver Cromwell to the House of Commons (22 July 1642). Matters relating to the impeachment of the lord mayor of London.	92
1642 07 22b	Speech by Oliver Cromwell to the House of Commons (22 July 1642). Irish affairs.	93

1643

1643 01 16	Receipt signed by Oliver Cromwell for arms received from Sir John Hewett (16 January 1643).	93
1643 01 23	Letter from Oliver Cromwell to Robert Barnard, recorder of Huntingdon (23 January 1643).	95
1643 01 26[?]	Letter from Miles Sandys, Torrell Jocelyn, Francis Russell, William Marche, Oliver Cromwell, Edward Clenche, James Thompson, Thomas Symons, Robert Clerke to Sir John Hobart, Sir Thomas Richardson, Sir John Potts, Sir John Palgrave, John Spelman and the rest of the Norfolk deputy lieutenants (written between 24 and 27 January 1643).	97

CHRONOLOGICAL LIST OF LETTERS, WRITINGS AND REPORTED SPEECH

1643 01 27	Letter from Miles Sandys, Thomas Martin, Oliver Cromwell, Francis Russell, Torrell Jocelyn, William Marche[?], Edward Clenche, Thomas Symons [Symon Sr?], Robert Clerke, James Thompson to Sir John Hobart, Sir Thomas Richardson, Sir John Potts, Sir John Palgrave, Sir John Spelman, knights and baronets (27 January 1643).	99
1643 03 08	Order from Oliver Cromwell and 23 members of the Committee at Cambridge to all and every inhabitant of Fen Drayton in the hundred of Papworth, Cambridgeshire (8 March 1643).	103
1643 03 10	Letter from Oliver Cromwell to the deputy lieutenants of Suffolk (10 March 1643).	105
1643 03 23	Letter from Oliver Cromwell to the mayor of Colchester [Thomas Lawrence] and Captain John Langley (23 March 1643).	108
1643 03 28	Receipt signed by Oliver Cromwell and Captain Sir Thomas Martyn issued to John Annis of Landbeach, Cambs. (28 March 1643).	110
1643 04 04	Pass signed by Cromwell and three others for Abraham Wheelock (4 April 1643).	110
1643 04 07	Letter from Oliver Cromwell and 28 others to 'the inhabitants' of Cambridge or some parts of Cambridgeshire (7 April 1643).	111
1643 04 10	Letter from Oliver Cromwell to Sir John Burgoyne (10 April 1643).	114
1643 04 17	Oliver Cromwell to Robert Bernard [Barnard] (17 April 1643).	115
1643 05 03	Letter from Oliver Cromwell to the Lincolnshire County Committee (3 May 1643).	116
1643 05 13	Letter from Oliver Cromwell to Sir Miles Hobart (13 May 1643).	119
1643 05 28	Letter from Oliver Cromwell to [? the mayor and aldermen of Colchester] (28 May 1643).	121
1643 06 02	Letter from John Hotham; Sir John Gell; Oliver Cromwell; Sir Miles Hobart; Thomas Grey, Baron Grey of Groby to Ferdinando Fairfax, second Lord Fairfax of Cameron (2 June 1643).	123
1643 06 13	Letter from Oliver Cromwell to the Commissioners for the Eastern Association (13 June 1643).	126
1643 07 22	Letter from Oliver Cromwell to the committee at Cambridge (22 July 1643).	130
1643 07 29	Letter from Sir Edward Ayscough, Oliver Cromwell and John Broxolme to [William Lenthall, Speaker of the House of Commons] (29 July 1643).	132
1643 07 30	Letter from Oliver Cromwell to Sir John [Hobart] (30 July 1643).	137
1643 07 31a	Letter from Oliver Cromwell to Sir Edmund Bacon, Sir William Spring, Sir Thomas Barnardiston and Maurice Barrowe, esq. (31 July 1643).	143
1643 07 31b	Letter from Oliver Cromwell to the committee at Cambridge (31 July 1643).	147
1643 08 01	Letter from Oliver Cromwell to the deputy lieutenants of Essex (1 August 1643).	151
1643 08 02	Letter from Oliver Cromwell to [? the mayor of Norwich] (2 August 1643).	152
1643 08 04	Letter from Oliver Cromwell and others to the deputy lieutenants of Essex (4 August 1643).	154

CHRONOLOGICAL LIST OF LETTERS, WRITINGS AND REPORTED SPEECH

1643 08 06a	Letter from Oliver Cromwell to the committee at Cambridge (6 August 1643).	156
1643 08 06b	Letter from Oliver Cromwell to the deputy lieutenants of Essex (6 August 1643).	158
1643 08 08	Letter from Oliver Cromwell to the Cambridge Committee (8 August 1643).	160
1643 08 29a	Letter from Oliver Cromwell and eight members of the Cambridge Committee to the deputy lieutenants of Essex (29 August 1643).	162
1643 08 29b	Letter from Oliver Cromwell to the deputy lieutenants of Essex (29 August 1643).	163
1643 08 30[?]	Letter from Oliver Cromwell to Sir William Spring and Maurice Barrowe (late August 1643).	164
1643 09 11	Letter from Oliver Cromwell to Oliver St John (11 September 1643).	168
1643 09 28	Letter from Oliver Cromwell to Sir William Spring and Mr [Maurice] Barrow (28 September 1643).	171
1643 10 03	Warrant addressed by Oliver Cromwell to Robert Brown, deputy treasurer of Ely (3 October 1643).	176
1643 10 06	Letter from Oliver Cromwell to Sir Thomas Barrington (6 October 1643).	177

1644

1644 01 06	Order from Oliver Cromwell to Dr [William] Staine (6 January 1644).	179
1644 01 10a	Letter from Oliver Cromwell to the Committee of the Isle of Ely (10 January 1644).	180
1644 01 10b	Letter from Oliver Cromwell to William Hitch (10 January 1644).	181
1644 01 19	Warrant signed by Oliver Cromwell and Miles Sandys to [William?] Edwards (19 January 1644).	183
1644 01 21	Letter from Oliver Cromwell to [the Committee of the Eastern Association at Cambridge] (21 January 1644).	184
1644 01 22	Speech by Oliver Cromwell to the House of Commons (22 January 1644).	185
1644 01 30	Letter from Oliver Cromwell to the Committee of Ely (30 January 1644).	186
1644 03 08	Letter from Oliver Cromwell to Sir Samuel Luke (8 March 1644).	187
1644 03 09	Letter from Oliver Cromwell to Sir Samuel Luke (9 March 1644).	188
1644 03 10	Letter from Oliver Cromwell to Sergeant Major General Lawrence Crawford (10 March 1644).	189
1644 03 28	Warrant signed by Edward Montagu, second earl of Manchester and Oliver Cromwell to the Committee at Cambridge (28 March 1644).	192
1644 04 11	Warrant from Oliver Cromwell and others to Robert Browne, deputy treasurer of the Isle of Ely (11 April 1644).	193
1644 04 13	Warrant from Oliver Cromwell and others to Dr [Richard] Staine, treasurer for the Isle of Ely (13 April 1644).	194
1644 04 22	Letter from Oliver Cromwell to Sir Henry Vane the younger (22 April 1644).	195
1644 07 05	Letter from Oliver Cromwell to Valentine Walton (5 July 1644).	196

xiii

CHRONOLOGICAL LIST OF LETTERS, WRITINGS AND REPORTED SPEECH

1644 09 01	Letter from Oliver Cromwell to the Committee for the Isle of Ely (1 September 1644).	200
1644 09 05	Letter from Oliver Cromwell to Valentine Walton (5 or 6 September 1644).	202
1644 10 05	Warrant from Oliver Cromwell to [unspecified persons] about sick soldiers (5 October 1644).	204
1644 10 06	Letter from Oliver Cromwell to Sir Samuel Luke (6 October 1644).	205
1644 10 08	Letter from Oliver Cromwell to Sir Samuel Luke (8 October 1644).	206
1644 11 15	Letter [drafted by Cromwell?] and signed by the earl of Manchester; William Balfour; William Waller; Philip Skippon to the Committee of Both Kingdoms (15 November 1644).	207
1644 11 25a	Speech by Oliver Cromwell to the House of Commons (25 November 1644).	210
1644 11 25b[?]	'Lieutenant General Cromwell's Narrative Concerning the Earl of Manchester' (on or after 25 November 1644).	214
1644 11 27[?]	Clerk's summary of Cromwell's narrative concerning the earl of Manchester (late November 1644, but after 25 November).	241
1644 12 02[?]	Cromwell's words recollected by the earl of Manchester in a written testimony to the House of Lords (2 December 1644).	242
1644 12 04a	First examination of Oliver Cromwell taken by the Committee of the House of Commons examining Cromwell's allegations against the earl of Manchester (4 December 1644).	245
1644 12 04b	An overheard conversation involving Oliver Cromwell, contained in the examination of James Pitsum (alias Pitson), Scoutmaster General to Sir William Waller (4 December 1644).	246
1644 12 04c	Speech by Oliver Cromwell to the House of Commons (4 December 1644).	247
1644 12 06	Conversation between Oliver Cromwell and the earl of Manchester as reported by Sir Arthur Heselrige (6 December 1644).	248
1644 12 09a	Speech by Oliver Cromwell to the House of Commons (9 December 1644). Self-Denial.	249
1644 12 09b	Speech (perhaps) made by Oliver Cromwell to the House of Commons (9 December 1644). Self-Denial.	251
1644 12 09c	Speech by Oliver Cromwell to the House of Commons (9 December 1644). Self-Denial.	253
1644 12 10	Lieutenant General Cromwell's second examination [before the committee of the House of Commons chaired by Zouch Tate] (10 December 1644).	254

1645

1645 01 10	Reported speech by Cromwell in the House of Commons (10 January 1645). Army petition.	256
1645 01 17	Letter from Oliver Cromwell to the sequestrators for the Isle of Ely (17 January 1645).	258

CHRONOLOGICAL LIST OF LETTERS, WRITINGS AND REPORTED SPEECH

1645 02 22	Speech by Oliver Cromwell to the House of Commons (22 February 1645). Mutinies.	259
1645 04 09a	Letter from Oliver Cromwell to Sir Thomas Fairfax (9 April 1645).	259
1645 04 09b	Letter from Oliver Cromwell to Edward Whalley (9 April 1645).	261
1645 04 25a	Letter from Oliver Cromwell to Sir Thomas Fairfax (25 April 1645).	262
1645 04 25b	Letter from Oliver Cromwell to the Committee of Both Kingdoms (25 April 1645).	265
1645 04 28	Letter from Oliver Cromwell to the Committee of Both Kingdoms (28 April 1645).	268
1645 04 29a	Letter from Oliver Cromwell to Roger Burgess, deputy [or lieutenant] governor of Faringdon (29 April 1645).	272
1645 04 29b	Letter from Oliver Cromwell to Roger Burgess, deputy [or lieutenant] governor of Faringdon ([29] April 1645).	273
1645 04 30	Letter from Oliver Cromwell to Roger Burgess, deputy [or lieutenant] governor of Faringdon (30 April 1645).	274
1645 05 04	Letter from Oliver Cromwell to Sir Peter Wentworth MP (4 May 1645).	275
1645 05 09	Letter from Oliver Cromwell to William Lenthall, Speaker of the House of Commons (9 May 1645).	278
1645 05 20a	Letter from Oliver Cromwell to Sir Samuel Luke (20 May 1645).	279
1645 05 20b	Letter from Oliver Cromwell to Sir Samuel Luke (20 May 1645).	280
1645 06 04	Letter from Oliver Cromwell to Sir Thomas Fairfax (4 June 1645).	281
1645 06 06a	Order from eleven members of the Eastern Association Committee to the deputy lieutenants of Suffolk (6 June 1645).	283
1645 06 06b	Letter from Oliver Cromwell to Captain Francis Underwood (6 June 1645).	285
1645 06 14	Letter from Oliver Cromwell to William Lenthall, Speaker of the House of Commons (14 June 1645).	286
1645 06 15	Letter from Oliver Cromwell to Sir Samuel Luke (15 June 1645).	289
1645 07 10	Letter from Oliver Cromwell to [unnamed MPs] (10 July 1645).	290
1645 07 11 [?]	Letter from Oliver Cromwell to an unnamed MP (July 1645, sometime between 10 and 23 July).	291
1645 08 04	Letter from Oliver Cromwell to Sir Thomas Fairfax (4 August 1645).	294
1645 08 05	Report of a speech made by Oliver Cromwell to Clubmen captured on Hambledon Hill (5 August 1645).	299
1645 09 03	Letter from Sir Thomas Fairfax, Oliver Cromwell and twenty-four other officers to Alexander Leslie, first earl of Leven (3 September 1645).	300
1645 09 08	Letter from Thomas Fairfax and Oliver Cromwell to the High Sheriff of Cornwall and 'the wellaffected Gentry, & Inhabitants of that Countie' (8 September 1645).	303
1645 09 14a	Letter from Oliver Cromwell to William Lenthall, Speaker of the House of Commons (14 September 1645).	305

xv

CHRONOLOGICAL LIST OF LETTERS, WRITINGS AND REPORTED SPEECH

1645 09 14b	Letter from Oliver Cromwell to William Lenthall, Speaker of the House of Commons (14 September 1645).	315
1645 09 22	Articles of Surrender sent by Oliver Cromwell to Sir Charles Lloyd, the governor of Devizes (22 September 1645).	317
1645 09 28	Letter from Oliver Cromwell to the [William Longland], mayor of Winchester (28 September 1645).	318
1645 10 06	Letter from Oliver Cromwell to William Lenthall, Speaker of the House of Commons (6 October 1645).	319
1645 10 14	Letter from Oliver Cromwell to William Lenthall, Speaker of the House of Commons (14 October 1645).	322
1645 10 16	Letter from Oliver Cromwell to Sir Thomas Fairfax (16 October 1645).	326
1645 10 17a	Letter from Oliver Cromwell to William Lenthall, Speaker of the House of Commons (17 October 1645).	328
1645 10 17b	Warrant from Oliver Cromwell to Thomas Herbert, Commissioner of Parliament for the Army (17 October 1645).	331
1645 12 10	Letter from Oliver Cromwell to [Colonel Thomas Ceely], governor of Lyme Regis (10 December 1645).	332

1646

1646 01 27[?]	Summary of speech by Oliver Cromwell to 3,000 'recruits' in Devon (January 1646 probably between 24 and 29 January).	334
1646 04 24	Speech by Oliver Cromwell to the House of Commons (24 April 1646). On funding the war in the south-west.	335
1646 04 25	Speech by Oliver Cromwell to the House of Commons (25 April 1646). Demanding no peace before outright victory.	336
1646 06 16	Letter from Oliver Cromwell to John Holles, earl of Clare (16 June 1646).	338
1646 07 08[?]	Speech by Oliver Cromwell to the House of Commons (before 10 July 1646). A retrospective version of Cromwell's speech against the earl of Manchester of November 1644.	339
1646 07 14	Speech by Oliver Cromwell to the House of Commons (14 July 1646). Defending the honour of Fairfax's army.	341
1646 07 26	Letter from Oliver Cromwell to Thomas Knyvett (26 July 1646)	341
1646 07 31	Letter from Oliver Cromwell to Sir Thomas Fairfax (31 July 1646)	344
1646 08 10	Letter from Oliver Cromwell to Sir Thomas Fairfax (10 August 1646)	345
1646 08 20	Speech by Oliver Cromwell to the House of Commons (20 August 1646). Honouring the terms of the Oxford articles of surrender.	348
1646 08 26	Letter from Oliver Cromwell to John Rushworth (26 August 1646).	349
1646 09 17	Speech by Oliver Cromwell to the House of Commons (17 September 1646). On the appointment of a new lord lieutenant of Yorkshire.	350
1646 10 06	Letter from Oliver Cromwell to Sir Thomas Fairfax (6 October 1646).	351
1646 10 09	Speech by Oliver Cromwell to the House of Commons (9 October 1646). During a heated debate on renewing assessment taxes.	353
1646 10 25	Letter from Oliver Cromwell to his daughter Bridget Ireton (25 October 1646).	353

xvi

CHRONOLOGICAL LIST OF LETTERS, WRITINGS AND REPORTED SPEECH

1646 10 29	Letter from Oliver Cromwell to Robert Jenner MP (undated but probably 29 October 1646).	356
1646 10 31 [?]	Recalled conversation between Oliver Cromwell and Edmund Ludlow (n.d. but no earlier than 12 October 1646 and possibly as late as spring 1647).	358
1646 12 21	Letter from Oliver Cromwell to Sir Thomas Fairfax (21 December 1646).	360

1647

1647 01 23	Certificate signed by Oliver Cromwell and sent to the House of Commons committee for petitions (23 January 1647).	362
1647 01 24	Certificate of service of Edward Whalley, signed by Oliver Cromwell (24 January 1647).	364
1647 02 10	Certificate signed by Cromwell and sent to the House of Commons committee for petitions (10 February 1647).	365
1647 03 07	Letter from Oliver Cromwell to Sir Thomas Fairfax (7 March 1647, but just possibly 3 March 1648).	365
1647 03 19	Letter from Oliver Cromwell to Sir Thomas Fairfax (19 March 1647).	368
1647 03 23	Letter from Oliver Cromwell to Edward Howard, Lord Escrick (23 March 1647).	370
1647 03 30	Letter from Oliver Cromwell to Sir Dudley North (30 March 1647).	372
1647 03 31	Letter from Oliver Cromwell to Henry Darley and John Gurdon (31 March 1647).	373
1647 03 31[?]	Letter from Oliver Cromwell to Sir Thomas Fairfax (some time in March 1647 or later in 1647).	374
1647 05 03a	Letter from Philip Skippon, Oliver Cromwell and Henry Ireton to the 'Colonels or chief officers of the respective regiments' (3 May 1647).	377
1647 05 03b	Letter from Philip Skippon, Oliver Cromwell and Henry Ireton to William Lenthall, Speaker of the House of Commons (3 May 1647).	379
1647 05 08	Letter from Philip Skippon, Oliver Cromwell, Henry Ireton, Charles Fleetwood to William Lenthall, Speaker of the House of Commons (8 May 1647).	380
1647 05 09	Letter from Philip Skippon and Oliver Cromwell to the eight regiments of horse who had petitioned them on 28 April 1647 (9 May 1647).	382
1647 05 15	Oliver Cromwell's contributions to the New Model Army Debate at Saffron Walden (15 May 1647).	384
1647 05 16	Oliver Cromwell's contributions to the New Model Army Debate at Saffron Walden (16 May 1647).	386
1647 05 17	Letter from Philip Skippon, Oliver Cromwell, Henry Ireton, Charles Fleetwood to William Lenthall, Speaker of the House of Commons (17 May 1647).	388

CHRONOLOGICAL LIST OF LETTERS, WRITINGS AND REPORTED SPEECH

1647 05 20a	Letter from Philip Skippon, Oliver Cromwell, Henry Ireton, Charles Fleetwood to William Lenthall, Speaker of the House of Commons (20 May 1647).	390
1647 05 20b	Heads of a report signed by Philip Skippon, Oliver Cromwell, Henry Ireton, Charles Fleetwood and which Cromwell delivered to the House of Commons on 21 May 1647 (20 May 1647).	391
1647 05 21	Speech by Oliver Cromwell to the House of Commons (21 May 1647). Report on the proceedings of the Army Council at Saffron Walden.	397
1647 06 10	Letter from Sir Thomas Fairfax and other officers to the lord mayor, aldermen and common council of the city of London (10 June 1647).	399
1647 06 25	Letter from Oliver Cromwell and John Hewson to Colonel Edward Whalley (25 June 1647).	402
1647 06 29	Warrant from Thomas Grey, Oliver Cromwell, Henry Mildmay, Denis Bond, William Ashhurst, F Rous, Thomas Hoyle to Thomas Fauconbridge, receiver general of the revenue (29 June 1647).	405
1647 07 12	Conversation between Oliver Cromwell and Sir John Berkeley (12 July 1647).	406
1647 07 15	Conversation between Oliver Cromwell and Sir John Berkeley (15 July 1647).	409
1647 07 16	Oliver Cromwell's contributions to the New Model Army Debate at Reading (16 July 1647).	410
1647 07 17	Oliver Cromwell's contributions to the New Model Army Debate at Reading (17 July 1647)	422
1647 07 31[?]	Letter from Oliver Cromwell to Sir Thomas Fairfax (31 July 1647)	423
1647 08 20	Speech by Oliver Cromwell to the House of Commons (20 August 1647). On the aftermath of the Army's occupation of London.	425
1647 09 01	Letter from Oliver Cromwell to John Williams, archbishop of York (1 September 1647).	426
1647 09 14	Letter from Oliver Cromwell to Colonel Michael Jones (14 September 1647).	428
1647 09 15	Instructions for William Rowe issued by Oliver Cromwell and nine other members of the Committee of Lords and Commons at Derby House for Irish Affairs (15 September 1647).	429
1647 10 13	Letter from Oliver Cromwell to Sir Thomas Fairfax (13 October 1647).	432
1647 10 22	Letter from Oliver Cromwell to Sir Thomas Fairfax (22 October 1647).	433
1647 10 28	Oliver Cromwell's contributions to the New Model Army Debate at Putney (28 October 1647).	435
1647 10 29	Oliver Cromwell's contributions to the New Model Army Debate at Putney (29 October 1647).	453
1647 11 01	Oliver Cromwell's contributions to the New Model Army Debate at Putney (1 November 1647).	463
1647 11 08	Oliver Cromwell's contributions to the New Model Army Debate at Putney (8 November 1647).	473

xviii

CHRONOLOGICAL LIST OF LETTERS, WRITINGS AND REPORTED SPEECH

1647 11 11a	Oliver Cromwell's contributions to the New Model Army Debate at Putney (11 November 1647).	475
1647 11 11b	Letter from Oliver Cromwell to Colonel Edward Whalley (11 November 1647).	476
1647 11 11c	Letter from Oliver Cromwell to [William Lenthall, Speaker of the House of Commons] (11 November 1647).	478
1647 11 19	Speech by Oliver Cromwell to the House of Commons (19 November 1647). 'An Account of the Proceedings at the Rendesvous of the Army'.	479
1647 11 23a	Speech by Oliver Cromwell to the House of Commons (23 November 1647). For severe measures against troublemakers in the Army.	483
1647 12 23b	Letter from Oliver Cromwell to Thomas Hill, master of Trinity College, Cambridge (23 December 1647).	484
1647 12 26[?]	Letter from Oliver Cromwell to Robert Hammond (undated but probably 25 or 26 December 1647).	486

1648

1648 01 03a	Speech by Oliver Cromwell to the House of Commons (3 January 1648). Debating the Vote of No Addresses.	489
1648 01 03b	Letter from Oliver Cromwell to Robert Hammond (3 January 1648).	490
1648 02 25	Oliver Cromwell to Richard Norton (25 February 1648).	493
1648 03 07	Letter from Oliver Cromwell to Sir Thomas Fairfax (7 March 1648 but more likely 7 March 1647).	495
1648 03 21	Letter from Oliver Cromwell to the Committee at Derby House (21 March 1648).	497
1648 03 28	Letter from Oliver Cromwell to Colonel Richard Norton (28 March 1648).	499
1648 04 03a	Letter from Oliver Cromwell to Colonel Richard Norton (3 April 1648).	502
1648 04 03b	Warrant signed by members of the Committee for the Affairs of Ireland at Derby House: from Robert Rich, earl of Warwick; Arthur Annesley; William Pierrepont; Oliver Cromwell; Sir John Temple; Sir Gilbert Gerard to Sir Adam Loftus (3 April 1648).	505
1648 04 06	Letter from Oliver Cromwell to Colonel Robert Hammond (6 April 1648).	506
1648 04 14	Receipt signed by Oliver Cromwell for one month's pay (14 April 1648).	508
1648 04 18	Letter from Oliver Cromwell to Colonel William Kenricke (18 April 1648).	509
1648 05 09a	Letter from Oliver Cromwell to Thomas Fairfax, (now) Lord Fairfax (9 May 1648).	511
1648 05 09b	Instructions from Oliver Cromwell to Captain Thomas Roberts and others (9 May 1648).	513

xix

CHRONOLOGICAL LIST OF LETTERS, WRITINGS AND REPORTED SPEECH

1648 05 16	Letter from Oliver Cromwell to Captain [John] Crowther, vice admiral of the Irish Seas (16 May 1648).	515
1648 06 09	Letter from Oliver Cromwell to the Committee of Carmarthenshire (9 June 1648).	516
1648 06 14	Letter from Oliver Cromwell to [? William Lenthall as Speaker or to some other member of the Long Parliament] (14 – or possibly 16 – June 1648).	518
1648 06 17	Letter from Oliver Cromwell to Major Thomas Saunders (17 June 1648).	520
1648 06 18	Letter from Oliver Cromwell to [the Hon. Richard Herbert] (18 June 1648).	523
1648 06 26	Letter from Oliver Cromwell to Colonel Thomas Hughes (26 June 1648).	524
1648 06 27	Letter from Oliver Cromwell to the Derby House Committee (27 June 1648).	525
1648 06 28	Letter from Oliver Cromwell to Thomas Fairfax, Lord Fairfax (28 June 1648).	526
1648 07 10	Letter from Oliver Cromwell to John Poyer, governor of Pembroke (10 July 1648).	529
1648 07 11a	Letter from Oliver Cromwell to William Lenthall, Speaker of the House of Commons (11 July 1648).	530
1648 07 11b	Articles of Surrender of Pembroke signed by Cromwell and David Poyer (11 – just possibly 10 – July 1648).	532
1648 07 12	Cromwell's comments written on a letter sent by Roger, Samson and John Lort to the mayor and aldermen of Haverfordwest (12 July 1648).	534
1648 07 14	Oliver Cromwell to the mayor and aldermen of Haverfordwest (14 July 1648).	535
1648 08 02	Overheard conversations involving Oliver Cromwell recorded by Major Robert Huntington (2 August 1648).	536
1648 08 04[?]	Letter from Oliver Cromwell to the people of Bristol (4 August 1648 or later, but before 18 August 1648).	542
1648 08 14	Letter from Oliver Cromwell to [unknown] (14 August 1648).	544
1648 08 17	Letter from Oliver Cromwell to the Lancashire County Committee in Manchester (17 August 1648).	545
1648 08 20a	Letter from Oliver Cromwell to Sir Henry Cholmley and Sir Edward Rodes (20 August 1648).	549
1648 08 20b	Letter from Oliver Cromwell to William Lenthall, Speaker of the House of Commons (20 August 1648).	551
1648 08 23a	Letter from Oliver Cromwell probably to the Committee at York (23 August 1648).	560
1648 08 23b	Letter from Oliver Cromwell to the Committee at Derby House (23 August 1648).	562
1648 09 01	Letter from Oliver Cromwell to Oliver St John (1 September 1648).	565

xx

CHRONOLOGICAL LIST OF LETTERS, WRITINGS AND REPORTED SPEECH

1648 09 02	Letter from Oliver Cromwell to Philip Wharton, Lord Wharton (2 September 1648).	568
1648 09 07	Letter from Oliver Cromwell to Colonel Charles Fairfax (7 September 1648).	570
1648 09 08	Declaration (or remonstrance and resolution) of Lieutenant General Oliver Cromwell relating to Scottish prisoners of war (8 September 1648).	571
1648 09 11	Letter from Oliver Cromwell to Thomas Fairfax, Lord Fairfax (11 September 1648).	573
1648 09 14	Letter from Oliver Cromwell to [possibly William Armyne MP] (14 September 1648).	575
1648 09 15	Letter from Oliver Cromwell to Ludovic Lesley, governor of Berwick (15 September 1648).	577
1648 09 16a	Letter from Oliver Cromwell to the Scottish Committee of Estates (16 September 1648).	578
1648 09 16b	Letter from Oliver Cromwell to Archibald Campbell, marquis of Argyll, 'and the rest of the well affected lords, gentlemen, ministers and people now in armes in the kingdome of Scotland' (16 September 1648).	580
1648 09 18	Letter from Oliver Cromwell to John Campbell, earl of Loudon, Lord Chancellor of Scotland (18 September 1648).	581
1648 09 20a	Proclamation by Oliver Cromwell as lieutenant general of the Army in the Scottish Borders (20 September 1648).	585
1648 09 20b	Letter from Oliver Cromwell to the Committee at Derby House (20 September 1648).	586
1648 09 21	From Oliver Cromwell to the Scottish Committee of Estates (21 September 1648).	589
1648 09 23[?]	Precis of letter from Oliver Cromwell to Archibald Campbell, marquis of Argyll (written sometime between 21 and 25 September 1648).	591
1648 10 02a	Letter from Oliver Cromwell to William Lenthall, Speaker of the House the Commons (2 October 1648).	592
1648 10 02b	Letter from Oliver Cromwell to Thomas Fairfax, Lord Fairfax (2 October 1648).	595
1648 10 05	Letter from Oliver Cromwell to the Committee of Estates of Scotland (5 October 1648).	597
1648 10 08	Letter from Oliver Cromwell to William Lenthall, Speaker of the House of Commons (8 October 1648).	599
1648 10 09	Letter from Oliver Cromwell to William Lenthall, Speaker of the House of Commons (9 October 1648).	601
1648 10 28	Letter from Oliver Cromwell to William Lenthall, Speaker of the House of Commons (28 October 1648).	603
1648 11 02	Letter from Oliver Cromwell to Charles Fairfax (2 November 1648).	605
1648 11 06a	Letter from 'Heron's brother' (quite possibly Oliver Cromwell) to Robert Hammond (6 November 1648).	606

xxi

CHRONOLOGICAL LIST OF LETTERS, WRITINGS AND REPORTED SPEECH

1648 11 06b	Letter from Oliver Cromwell to Charles Fairfax (6 November 1648).	613
1648 11 09	Letter from Oliver Cromwell to John Morris, governor of Pontefract Castle (9 November 1648).	614
1648 11 10	Letter from Oliver Cromwell to Colonel Charles Fairfax (10 November 1648).	615
1648 11 11a	Letter from Oliver Cromwell to Charles Fairfax (11 November 1648).	617
1648 11 11b	Letter from Oliver Cromwell to Charles Fairfax (11 November 1648).	617
1648 11 13	Annotation by Oliver Cromwell to a letter from Charles Fairfax (letter dated on or after 13 November 1648).	618
1648 11 15	Letter from Oliver Cromwell to the Derby House Committee (15 November 1648).	619
1648 11 20a	Letter from Oliver Cromwell to Thomas Fairfax, Lord Fairfax (20 November 1648).	622
1648 11 20b	Letter from Oliver Cromwell to Robert Jenner and John Ashe (20 November 1648).	624
1648 11 25a	Letter from Oliver Cromwell to Robert Hammond (25 November 1648).	626
1648 11 25b	Letter from Oliver Cromwell to Thomas St Nicholas (25 November 1648).	633
1648 11 27	Letter from Oliver Cromwell to [Philip Wharton, Lord Wharton] (27 November 1648).	634
1648 11 30[?]	Letter from Oliver Cromwell to Thomas Fairfax, Lord Fairfax (written between 25 November and 1 December 1648).	635
1648 12 02	'A *LETTER* from *Lieut. Generall* CRUMWELL To the Citizens of London, Concerning the King's Majesty the Parliament, the City, Army and Kingdome' (2 December 1648).	637
1648 12 08	Certificate signed by Oliver Cromwell (8 December 1648).	639
1648 12 18	Letter from Oliver Cromwell to the master and fellows of Trinity Hall, Cambridge (18 December 1648).	640
1648 12 22a	Letter from Oliver Cromwell and Henry Ireton to Thomas Harrison (22 December 1648).	641
1648 12 22b	Letter from Oliver Cromwell and Henry Ireton to Colonel Christopher Whichcott, governor of Windsor Castle (22 December 1648).	643

1649

1649 01 04	Protection issued by Oliver Cromwell to all officers and soldiers whom it may concern (4 January 1649).	645
1649 01 06	Summary of speeches by Oliver Cromwell in the Council of the Army (6 January 1649).	646
1649 01 08	Warrant appointing the meeting of the High Court of Justice to try the King, signed by Oliver Cromwell and thirty-three others (8 January 1649).	647
1649 01 29	Death warrant of Charles I (Oliver Cromwell is one of 59 signatories) (29 January 1649).	650

ACKNOWLEDGEMENTS

The following are thanked for their financial assistance: The Leverhulme Trust for a Major Research Grant of £204,337 (2011–13); The AHRC/IRCHSS for a joint grant of £30,000 for resesarch workshops; British Academy for a Small Research Grant (for a scoping exercise 2010–11); Trinity College Dublin for support throughout the project and especially for the support of its High Performing Computing group in managing a tailored Virtual Research Environment (VRE), with particular thanks to Vikas Sahni and the late Shay Lawless and Pat Carty; The University of Cambridge Faculty Board of History for conference funding and supporting the VRE in 2014–15; Nottingham Trent University for Conference Support.

The following Libraries are thanked for providing digitised images of Cromwell material in their collections and for advice: Beinecke Library, Yale University; Bodleian Library (and especially Mike Webb); British Library; Cambridge University Library; Cheshire Archives and Local Studies; Christ Church, Oxford; Clarke Library, Worcester College, Oxford; Cromwell Museum (and especially John Goldsmith and Stuart Orme); FDR Presidential Library; Fitzwilliam Museum, Cambridge; Friends House London; Gloucestershire Archives; Harry Ransom Center (and especially Eva Griffiths); Huntington Library, California; Huntingdon Archives; Kent History and Library Centre; Lambeth Palace Library (and especially Krystzof Adamiec); Leicestershire RO; Library of Congress; London Metropolitan Archives; Longleat House; Marsh's Library Dublin (and especially Jason McElligott); Massachusetts Historical Society; Museum of London (and especially Hazel Forsyth); National Archives of Scotland; National Library of Scotland; National Library of Wales; National Maritime Museum; New York Public Library; Northampton RO; Orkney RO; Parliamentary Archives, Westminster; Pembrokeshire Archives Service (David Llewellyn); Pierpont Morgan Library (and especially Bonnie Lee); Society of Antiquaries London; Special Collections Library at Franklin and Marshall College; Surrey Historical

ACKNOWLEDGEMENTS

Centre; The National Archives; Trinity College Cambridge (and especially Nicolas Bell); University of Virginia; Warwickshire RO.

Kevin Frostick is thanked for sending us an image of a previously unknown letter in his personal possession; and the Trustees of the Chequers Trust for granting us access to their normally closed archive.

The following staff at a number of auction houses are thanked for help with accessing Cromwell material that passed through their hands and especially Luke Batterham and Sarah Lindes at Bonhams (London); Rhiannon Knol at Christie's (London).

Stephen Roberts is thanked for granting us access, well ahead of publication, to the draft biographical entries in *The History of Parliament: the Commons 1640–1660*.

The following are thanked for assistance with gathering material from remote locations, with carrying out checks for us (e.g. on sales catalogues across the twentieth century) and for drawing material to our attention: David Brown, Ian Campbell, John Collins, Liesbeth Corens, Jon Fitzgibbons, Tim Gray, Anna Groundwater, Graham Hart, Ineke Huysman, Jason McElligott, Brid McGrath, Steve Murdoch, Joan Redmond, Stephen Roberts, LeeAnn Saw, Paul Seaward, Jennifer Smyth, Christopher Thompson, Lucy Underwood, Malcolm Wanklyn, Mark Williams and Ben Woodford.

The preparation of the Index of Biblical Citations was greatly assisted by Olivia Saunders as part of her student work-experience with the project.

A GUIDE TO TRANSCRIPTION CONVENTIONS

1. Transcription layout:
   - The transcriptions reproduce the original documents in content, but not in lay-out (except that line endings have been retained in the case, and only in the case, of holographs).
   - The first line of a paragraph is indented when the intention of a paragraph is clear in the text.
   - Endorsements are placed at the end of the transcription.
   - Wrap-around text written down the side or at the top of a page is not preserved in that form. Nor is text written along the side or at the top reproduced in that form, unless (and only in the case of holographs) it is crucial to interpreting the document.

2. Spelling, capitalisation, punctuation, and paragraphing follow the original text.
   - Where spelling, capitalisation, punctuation, or paragraphing is ambiguous in the original text, we have provided the transcription that offers the clearest meaning. Alternative readings are provided in notes where necessary, and especially when the meaning could be affected. Ambiguities as regards to capitalisation, full stops, etc. are dealt with practically and follow modern usage.
   - Non-Cromwell scribal practice/ambiguity is not commented on unless it affects the sense of the scribe's version.
   - Implied punctuation is provided in square brackets[.] where necessary.

3. Commonplace or self-evident contractions and abbreviations have been silently expanded to prevent over-cluttering of the text. For example:
   'ye aforesd dept went wth'
   Is transcribed as: 'the aforesaid deponent went with'
   Rather than: 'the afores[ai]d dep[onen]t went w[i]th'

xxv

A GUIDE TO TRANSCRIPTION CONVENTIONS

- '-con' endings are represented as '-cion' when they appear with a tilde, and as '-con' when without a tilde.
- For 'honoʳ', and the like, there is no addition of a 'u', but merely lower the superscript 'r' silently.

4. Words that have been run together have been left as they appear.

5. All original numeration has been transcribed.

6. Superscripts:
   - Superscripts for dates are left as they appear; for example: '20th'.
   - Superscripts for monetary values (li-s-d) are given in regular text, followed by a full stop whenever it appears in the original, thus: 20 li. or Xl li. or 10 s.

7. Marginalia are transcribed within angle brackets: < >.
   - They are inserted in the transcript in the place at which they appear on the original document, unless they relate to a whole paragraph or longer section of a text rather than to a part of it, in which case they are placed at the end of the relevant section.

8. Italic type is used for italic type where it appears in the text.
   - When a printed text is primarily in italics, we reversed italicisation, preserving existing straight/italic contrasts.

9. Interlinear words are transcribed using\/to indicate the start and end of the interlineation.

10. Round or wavy brackets are used only as they appear in the original text.

11. Illegible words appear in square brackets: [].
    - No attempt has been made to represent the space occupied by illegible words.
    - Plausible suggested readings are included within the square brackets, followed by a question mark: '[enimie?]'; or,
    - Footnotes are used to suggest other possible readings, including partial readings (i.e. specific known letters), or the number of illegible words.

12. The loss of words or parts of words due to binding or damage is indicated by square brackets: [].

A GUIDE TO TRANSCRIPTION CONVENTIONS

- The source for any supplied text is given in footnotes. Major or consistent editorial additions are discussed in document introductions rather than through repeated footnoting.

13. Deletions have been transcribed where possible and crossed out.
    - They have been left in the text where they appear in the original.
    - Illegible deletions are indicated by square brackets, crossed out: [].
    - Words already deleted which are later crossed out again appear both with a line through them and underlined e.g., 'like ~~this~~'

14. Malformed words can be clarified in footnotes. For example:
    'eninie⁴'
    '⁴ Read "enimie".'

15. A blank space in the transcript indicates a blank space within the text.

16. Dates in the text have not been altered.

17. Preserving printers' conventions:
    - When a printer uses 'vv' for 'w', or 'f' for 's', etc., the intended letter is given here ('w' and 's' in these instances).
    - Pictograms are indicated by the word '[symbol]', with footnote explanations where necessary.
    - Extra capital letters for the opening word of a paragraph or document are not preserved: for example, 'WHereas' has been transcribed as 'Whereas'.
    - Individual italic letters are not preserved when context suggests they are due to available type. Italic words are preserved.

ABBREVIATIONS

The following abbreviations occur regularly in footnotes:

A&O	*Acts and ordinances of the interregnum, 1642–1660,* 3 vols., eds. C. H. Firth and R. S. Rait (London: Wyman and Sons, Limited, 1911)
Abbott, *Writings and Speeches*	W. C. Abbott, ed., *The Writings and Speeches of Oliver Cromwell,* 4 vols. (Cambridge, MA: Harvard University Press, 1937–47)
Al. Cantab.	*Alumni Cantabrigienses: A biographical list of all known students, graduates and holders of office at the University of Cambridge from the earliest times to 1900,* 6 vols., ed. John Venn (Cambridge: Cambridge University Press, 1922–54), also https://venn.lib.cam.ac.uk/
Al. Oxon.	*Alumni Oxonienses: The members of the University of Oxford, 1500–1714,* 4 vols., ed. Joseph Foster (Oxford: Oxford University Press, 1891)
Aylmer, *State's Servants*	Gerald Aylmer, *The State's Servants. The Civil Service of the English Republic, 1649–1660* (London, 1973)
BL	The British Library
Bodl.	Bodleian Library, Oxford
Burrows, *Register of the Visitors*	M. Burrows, ed., *The Register of the Visitors of the University of Oxford* (Camden Society, n.s., 39, 1881)
Burton, *Diary*	*Diary of Thomas Burton, Esq. Member in the Parliaments of Oliver and Richard Cromwell, from 1656 to 1659: Now First Published from the Original Autograph Manuscript with an Introduction Containing an Account of Parliament of 1654,* 4 vols., ed. John Towill Rutt, (London: H. Colburn, 1828)
Calamy Rev.	*Calamy Revised: Being a revision of Edmund Calamy's Account of the ministers and others ejected and silenced, 1660–1662,* ed. A. G. Matthews (Oxford: Oxford University Press, 1934)
Cal. Clarendon St. Pap.	*Calendar of the Clarendon State Papers preserved in the Bodleian Library,* 5 vols., eds. O. Ogle, et al. (Oxford: Clarendon Press, 1872–1970)
Cal. Inner Temple Records	*A Calendar of the Inner Temple Records,* 5 vols., ed. F. A. Inderwick (London, 1896)
Carlyle-Lomas	Thomas Carlyle, ed., *The Letters and Speeches with Elucidations by Thomas Carlyle/Oliver Cromwell; edited in three volumes, with notes, supplement and*

xxix

ABBREVIATIONS

	enlarged index by S. C. Lomas; with an introduction by C. H. Firth, 3 vols. (London: Methuen, 1904)
CCCD	*Calendar for the Committee for Compounding with Delinquents*
CCED	Clergy of the Church of England Database, https://theclergydatabase.org.uk/
Clarke Papers	*The Clarke Papers. Selections from the Papers of William Clarke, Secretary to the Council of the Army, 1647–1649, and to General Monck and the Commanders of the Army in Scotland, 1651–1660*, 4 vols., ed. C. H. Firth (London: Camden Society, 1891–1901)
CPM	Committee for Plundered Ministers
CSP	*State Papers Collected by Edward, Earl of Clarendon*, ed. Richard Scrope and Thomas Monkhouse, 3 vols. (Oxford: Clarendon Press, 1767–86)
CSPD	*Calendar of State Papers Domestic Series*
CSPI	*Calendar of State Papers Irish Series*
CSPV	*Calendar of State Papers Venetian Series*
CUL	Cambridge University Library
DIB	*Dictionary of Irish Biography*
Dunlop, *Commonwealth*	Robert Dunlop, ed., *Ireland under the Commonwealth: Being a Selection of Documents Relating to the Government of Ireland from 1651 to 1659*, 2 vols. (Manchester: Manchester University Press, 1913)
DWB	*Dictionary of Welsh Biography*
DWL	Doctor Williams's Library, London
ESTC	English Short Title Catalogue
EUL	Edinburgh University Library
Firth and Davies, *Regimental History*	C. H. Firth and G. Davies, *The Regimental History of Cromwell's Army*, 2 vols. (Oxford: Clarendon Press, 1940)
fl.	*floruit* (active life)
Furgol, *Covenanting Armies*	Edward Furgol, *A Regimental History of the Covenanting Armies, 1639–1651* (Edinburgh: J. Donald, 1990)
Gardiner, *C&P*	Samuel Rawson Gardiner, *History of the Commonwealth and Protectorate*, 4 vols. (London: Longmans, Green, 1903)
Gaunt, *Gazetteer*	Peter Gaunt, *The Cromwellian Gazetteer* (Gloucester: A. Sutton, 1987). PDFs of this are freely available on the Cromwell Association website: http://www.olivercromwell.org/wordpress/wp-content/uploads/2018/04/gazetteer%201.pdf
Gaunt, *Henry Cromwell Corresp.*	Peter Gaunt, ed., *The Correspondence of Henry Cromwell, 1655–1659: British Library Lansdowne Manuscripts* (Camden Society, 5th series, 31, 2007)

ABBREVIATIONS

GEC, *Baronetage*	G. E. Cokayne, *Complete Baronetage*, 6 vols. (Exeter: William Pollard and Co., 1900–09)
GEC, *Peerage*	G. E. Cokayne, *The Complete Peerage of England, Scotland, Ireland, Great Britain, and the United Kingdom*, 8 vols. (London: G. Bell and Sons, 1887–98); new edn., 14 vols. in 15, eds. V. Gibbs and others (London: St Catherine's Press and Stroud, Sutton 1910–98); microprint repr. (1982) and (1987)
Gilbert, Contemporary History	J. T. Gilbert, ed., *A Contemporary History of Affairs in Ireland from History 1641 to 1652: now for the first time published, with an appendix of original letters and documents*, 3 vols (Dublin: Irish Archaeological and Celtic Society, 1879–80)
Greaves and Zaller, *BDBR*	R. L. Greaves and R. Zaller, *Biographical Dictionary of British Radicals in the Seventeenth Century*, 3 vols. (Brighton: Harvester Press, 1982)
HMC	Historical Manuscript Commission Reports
HoP Commons, 1604–1629	*The House of Commons 1604–1629*, 6 vols., eds. Andrew Thrush and John P. Ferris (Cambridge: Cambridge University Press, 2010); available online at: www.historyofparliamentonline.org
HoP Commons, 1640–1660	*The House of Commons 1640–1660*, ed. Stephen Roberts (forthcoming)
HoP Commons, 1660–1690	*The House of Commons 1660–1690*, 3 vols., ed. Basil Duke Henning (London: Secker and Warburg, 1983); available online at: www. historyofparliamentonline.org
IMC	Irish Manuscript Commission
JHC	*Commons Journals*
JHL	*Lords Journals*
Johnston, *Diary*	*Diary of Sir Archibald Johnston of Wariston*, 3 vols., eds. David Hay Fleming and James D. Ogilvie (Edinburgh: Scottish History Society, 1911–40)
LPL	Lambeth Palace Library
Ludlow, *Memoirs*	*The Memoirs of Edmund Ludlow, Lieutenant-General of the Horse in the Army of the Commonwealth of England, 1625–1672*, 2 vols., ed. C. H. Firth (Oxford: Clarendon Press, 1894)
Middle Temple Admissions	*Register of Admissions to the Honourable Society of the Middle Temple*, 2 vols. (London, 1978)
MS	manuscript
MS Add.	Additional manuscript
N&S	Carolyn Nelson and Matthew Seccombe, *British Newspapers and Periodicals, 1641–1700: A Short–Title Catalogue of Serials Printed in England, Scotland, Ireland and British America: With a Checklist of Serials*

xxxi

ABBREVIATIONS

	Printed, 1701–March 1702 (New York: Modern Language Association of America, 1987)
NAS	National Archives Scotland
Nickolls, *Original Letters*	*Original Letters and Papers of State Addressed to Oliver Cromwell*, ed., John Nickolls (London: J. Whiston, 1743)
Nicoll, *Diary*	*A Diary of Public Transactions and Other Occurrences, Chiefly in Scotland, from January 1650 to June 1667*, ed. D. Laing (Edinburgh, The Bannatyne Club, 1836)
NLI	National Library of Ireland
NLS	National Library of Scotland
NLW	National Library of Wales
NMM	National Maritime Museum, Greenwich
ODNB	*Oxford Dictionary of National Biography*
OED	*Oxford English Dictionary*
Online Directory of Parliamentarian Officers	*The Cromwell Association Directory of Parliamentarian Army Officers*, ed. Stephen K Roberts (2017); British History Online http://www.british-history.ac.uk/no-series/cromwell-army-officers
PA	House of Lords, Parliamentary Archives
Rawl.	Rawlinson manuscripts
RCGA	*Records of the Commission of the General Assembly*, 3 vols., eds. A. F. Mitchell and James Christie (Edinburgh: Scottish History Society, 1890–1909)
RIA	Royal Irish Academy
RO	Record Office
RPS	Records of the Parliament of Scotland to 1707: https://www.rps.ac.uk/
SP	State Papers
SR	*A Transcript of the Registers of the Worshipful Company of Stationers from 1640–1708*, 3 vols., eds. G. E. Briscoe Eyre and C. R. Rivington, (London, 1913)
Stainer	Charles L. Stainer, ed., *Speeches of Oliver Cromwell* (London: Henry Frowde, 1901)
SU	Sheffield University
TCD	Trinity College Dublin
Thomason	George Thomason's collection of pamphlets in the British Library, dated according to his purchase or receipt of the text. For a chronological catalogue, see *Catalogue of the Pamphlets, Books, Newspapers, and Manuscripts Relating to the Civil War, the Commonwealth, and Restoration, Collected by George Thomason, 1640–1661*, 2 vols. (London: [British Museum], 1908)

ABBREVIATIONS

TNA	The National Archives
TSP	*A Collection of the State Papers of John Thurloe*, 7 vols., ed. T. Birch (London: for the executors of F. Gyles, 1742)
Wanklyn, *Reconstructing*	Malcolm Wanklyn, *Reconstructing the New Model Army*, 2 vols. (Solihull: Helion and Company, 2015–16)
Whitelocke, *Diary*	*The Diary of Bulstrode Whitelocke 1605–1675*, ed. Ruth Spalding (Oxford: Published for the British Academy by Oxford University Press, 1990)
Whitelocke, *Memorials*	Bulstrode Whitelocke, *Memorials of the English affairs: or, an historical account of what passed from the beginning of the reign of Charles the First, to Charles the Second his happy restauration. Containing the publick transactions, civil and military; together with the private consultations and secrets of the cabinet* (London, 1682); 4 vols. (Oxford: Oxford University Press, 1853)
Whitelocke, *Swedish Embassy*	Bulstrode Whitelocke, *A journal of the Swedish embassy in the years Embassy 1653 and 1654: Impartially written by the Ambassador Bulstrode Whitelocke*, 2 vols., ed. Dr Charles Morton (London: Longman, Brown, Green and Longmans, 1855)
Wing (2nd ed.)	D. G. Wing, *Short-Title Catalogue of Books Printed in England, Scotland, Ireland, Wales, and British America, and of English Books Printed in Other Countries, 1641–1700*, 3 vols. (New York: Columbia University Press, 1945–51)
Wing	*Wing Short-Title Catalogue, 1641–1700* (Chadwyck-Healey: Modern Language Association of America, 1996)
Wood, *Athenae*	Anthony Wood, *Athenae Oxonienses*, 4 vols. (London: F. C. and J. Rivington, 1813–20)
Woolrych, *Commonwealth to Protectorate*	Austin Woolrych, *Commonwealth to Protectorate* (Oxford: Clarendon Press, 1982)
Worden, *Rump*	Blair Worden, *The Rump Parliament, 1648–1653* (Cambridge: Cambridge University Press, 1974)

GENERAL INTRODUCTION
John Morrill

Some time in 2008, OUP asked twelve early modern historians whether they thought a new edition of Oliver Cromwell's writings and speeches was desirable and they unanimously replied that they considered it a high priority. The Press then approached the author of this introduction to see if he was interested. He was—because the existing editions were not fit for purpose and because the rapid advance of Digital Humanities made it possible to envisage a new kind of edition. He also immediately realised that this needed to be a collaborative project and that he should recruit a team of scholars to work together and to find external funding. This was the germ of the idea that has now, many years later, resulted in this new edition. This introduction seeks to explain *why* a new edition is necessary, *how* we have produced it and *what* we have produced (and what we have not produced).

WHY

The need for a new edition of Cromwell's recorded words, searchable and reliable, has long been recognised. There have been two editions of his writings and recorded speeches, and a third just of his speeches. It is hoped this new edition meets the current and future expectations of the scholarly community and of wider publics.

The first attempt to gather Cromwell's words together was famously that of the radical Romantic Thomas Carlyle.[1] His 1845 edition in two volumes contained

---

[1] Thomas Carlyle, *The Letters and Writings of Oliver Cromwell*, 2 vols. (1845). It was continuously in print until the 1940s in a wide range of formats. There are a number of excellent analyses of the relationship between the historical Cromwell and Thomas Carlyle: the best are Blair Worden, 'Thomas Carlyle and Oliver Cromwell', *Proc. Brit. Ac.* 105 (1999), pp. 131–70 (and, extended, in Blair Worden, *Roundhead Reputations: The English Civil Wars and the Passions of Posterity* (2001), pp. 264–96); Perez Zagorin, 'Thomas Carlyle and Oliver Cromwell', in Anthony Grafton and John Salmon, eds., *Historians*

XXXV

225 letters and eighteen speeches, but such was the effect of its publication that many people sent him material he had not found for himself, and subsequent editions in the period down to 1859 added a further seventy-five letters which appeared, albeit not integrated into the chronological flow of his text but as an appendix.[2] Unhappily some of the materials newly sent to Carlyle at this point were shown to be forgeries[3] which had to be omitted from later editions and this created its own chaos. This probably mattered little to the wider publics who owned a copy of the work—in various editions in one, two, three or five volumes. But it caused a good deal of inconvenience to the more informed and scholarly readers. Of course Carlyle, while not oblivious to scholarly standards, was careless with them. Accessibility not accuracy was what mattered to him. He added words and phrases to clarify meaning, sometimes but by no means always in brackets, he modernised spelling, imposed what was very much his own punctuation and paragraphing, and famously he interpolated in italics a highly idiosyncratic running diatribe. This was aimed not at Cromwell himself, but at an imaginary Dryasdust, a desiccated scholar uninterested in getting into Cromwell's heart as well as his head.[4] Where different versions of a text survived, especially Cromwell's speeches to Parliament, Carlyle's decisions about which version to rely on as a proof text can perhaps best and most generously be described as quixotic. All this was very fully and quite ruthlessly explored by Sir Charles Firth in his introduction to the version we will turn to next (and usually known as Carlyle-Lomas), and it was also explored much more patiently and charitably by Sophia Lomas.[5]

Carlyle's *Letters and Speeches of Oliver Cromwell* had been a literary sensation and it transformed public perceptions of Cromwell: from distaste and shame to hero, from flawed to the mainly unflawed. To give one crude but not misleading set of figures. In 1929, as a preliminary to undertaking his own edition, Wilbur Cortez Abbott produced his magisterial *Bibliography of Oliver Cromwell* which listed year by year from 1597 to 1927 everything that 'seems to bear immediately on his

---

and Ideologues, (Rochester, NY, 2001), pp. 231–58; Ivan Roots, 'Carlyle's Cromwell' in Roger Richardson, ed., *Oliver Cromwell: Essays for and by Roger Howell* (Manchester, 1993), pp. 74–95.

[2] The best history of how Carlyle produced and developed his text is David Trela, *A History of Carlyle's Oliver Cromwell's Letters and Speeches* (1992).

[3] Most obviously 'the Squire Letters', for which see Carlyle-Lomas, 1:xlii–xliii. But Sophia Lomas gives other examples (ibid, 1:xli–xlii).

[4] The first chapter of the introduction is entitled 'Anti-Dryasdust'. See the comments of Blair Worden, 'Thomas Carlyle and Oliver Cromwell', *Proc. Brit. Ac.* 105 (1999), pp. 131–70 at pp. 137–8.

[5] Carlyle-Lomas, 1:xxi–lii (Firth) and liii–lxii (Lomas).

GENERAL INTRODUCTION

career, his character, his opinions, his acts and policies'.[6] For the period from 1700 to 1844, Abbott recorded an average of four items per year; for the period between the appearance of Carlyle's two volumes in 1845 and the tercentenary of Cromwell's birth in 1899, the average was above twenty. To put it in another way: in the 150th anniversary of Cromwell's birth (1749) and again on the bicentennial (1799), there were four items, on the 250th anniversary (1849) fifteen and the tercentenary (1899) seventy-four items. Historians attribute this largely to Carlyle.

Still, with the rise of professional history, the grossly unsatisfactory aspects of Carlyle's edition, despite its joie-de-vivre and quirky polemical brilliance, demanded a new edition, and Sir Charles Firth, who had spent much of the 1890s editing texts central to any understanding of the English or Puritan Revolution, found the perfect collaborator in Sophia Lomas.[7] She was very well qualified for the post. She came from an academic family and she was the niece of Mary Everett Green, the veteran editor of the Calendar of State Papers, a job she inherited when Mrs Green died. She had also edited a number of volumes for the Historical Manuscripts Commission, including some with important Cromwell connections.[8] She was sufficiently admired to be invited, in 1902, to give a paper to the Royal Historical Society.[9] She was highly respected both by Firth and by S. R. Gardiner.[10]

Together Firth and Lomas made many small but cumulatively good decisions, and several very bad ones—all based on an exaggerated respect for the ghost of Thomas Carlyle. They—principally Lomas—went back to the originals and re-transcribed them to a much higher standard. This often meant going back to manuscripts where Carlyle had used later print versions of poor quality;[11] it

---

[6] W. C. Abbott, *Bibliography of Oliver Cromwell* (Cambridge, MA, 1929).

[7] These included his editions of the *Clarke Papers*, of the so-called memoirs of Edmund Ludlow, of Lucy Hutchinson's life of her husband and his editions of the papers relating to Cromwell's Scottish campaigns.

[8] For example, she had edited for the Historical Manuscripts Commission the Leyborne-Popham manuscripts (1899) with their important strays from the Clarke papers, and even more pertinently she had edited the Frankland-Russell-Astley manuscripts at Chequers Court (1900) with many Cromwell family papers, especially relating to Oliver's youngest daughter Frances, who had married a Russell.

[9] S. C. Lomas, 'The State Papers of the Early Stuarts and the Interregnum', published in the *TRHistS*, n.s., 16 (1902), pp. 97–132.

[10] For all this, see the very positive evaluation of her career and achievement in David L. Smith, 'Mrs S. C. Lomas: Cromwellian Editor', *Cromwelliana*, 3rd series, 1 (2012), pp. 79–94.

[11] The prime example given by Lomas is her replacement of Carlyle's transcription from the *Thurloe State Papers*, ed. Thomas Birch (1742) with her own from the original manuscript copies in Thurloe's papers in the Rawlinson Manuscripts in the Bodleian Library (Carlyle-Lomas, 1:liii).

xxxvii

GENERAL INTRODUCTION

meant removing some of his idiosyncratic decisions on stylistic matters; and it meant adding massively to the footnotes. The result was by far the best and most reliable edition of the letters thus far, albeit with spelling and punctuation modernised. However, the edition of the speeches is much less satisfactory. Indeed Lomas wrote in her preface that 'these volumes being only [only: sic!] a new edition of Carlyle's *Cromwell*, the speeches have been for the most part left as he printed them.'[12] So all she did was to tidy them up a little but with all his interjections, all his italics for emphasis and all his inattentiveness over the choice of version unchallenged. It is possible that she was inhibited by the near simultaneous appearance of Stainer's edition of the speeches to which we will turn shortly. She could not plagiarise him, and the thoroughness of his versions would leave anything she did trailing behind. Safer to hide behind Carlyle's name.

Sophia Lomas did however seek out and add 185 additional items—145 letters, nineteen speeches and twenty-one miscellaneous declarations, grants and passes etc. Most of the additions are very minor in significance, but three letters to Robert Hammond, and Cromwell's speeches to the Army Council on 27 February 1657 and 6 February 1658, were really important, and the incorporation of Firth's edition of Cromwell's speeches at the Reading and Putney Debates was really useful. The 180 new items appear by themselves as a 'supplement', not integrated even with Carlyle's 'Appendix'. So the reader always has three places to search— the texts of the 1845 edition, 105 pages of Carlyle's own appendices and 206 pages of her own supplement.

Alas, as reviewers from the outset made clear, the deference to Carlyle in the new work was a major error. What Lomas and Firth had done was to upgrade most of Carlyle's transcriptions and to add additional writings and speeches. But by far the greater part of Carlyle's interjections in the text and most of his linking narrative and notes were left. It is an enhanced version of Carlyle's conception. It therefore retained good things, not least the ease of use, with excellent lists of contents in each of the three volumes, with a clear numbering of items and with brief summaries of the main element in each item. But it also contained all the dross. Because it did cut out palpable errors and excesses it is less useful to those interested in Carlyle than the various earlier editions; but because of its deference to the shape and form of the 1845 edition and its recensions, it was a lot less useful to those interested in Cromwell than it could have been.

---

[12] Carlyle-Lomas, 1:xlix.

GENERAL INTRODUCTION

Carlyle-Lomas was published in 1904, three years after a new and extended version of the *Speeches of Oliver Cromwell*, 'collected and edited' as the title page puts it, by Charles L. Stainer of Christ Church Oxford, published by a small private press and distributed by Oxford University Press.[13] Who he was is a bit of a mystery. He is not in the list of Oxford (or Cambridge) matriculands and apart from his edition of Cromwell's speeches he appears only to have written one other book,[14] to have edited another to which he did not contribute,[15] and to have written at least two historical plays.[16] In his preface to his *Speeches*, he thanks just one scholar, once more Sir Charles Firth. His *Speeches* contains a seven-page preface; 403 pages of text with light annotation, principally textual; and eighty pages of commentary on the fifty-five speeches, some of which are not in Carlyle-Lomas. Although he did not add to or rearrange the texts, Stainer did modernise both spelling and punctuation. And he did include, in endnotes, some (only some) of the major textual differences between discreet versions of the same speech. There are however (in addition to modernisation) major problems. Stainer never explains why he uses a particular version as his proof text and sometimes—most seriously in his version of the speech to the Nominated Assembly in July 1653— he produces hybrid texts drawn from more than one surviving version. And although few of his explications are wrong, his evident lack of detailed knowledge of the period makes the selection of matters for comment very erratic. It is, in the end, a worthy but amateurish version, and it went out of print very quickly, overwhelmed by the appearance of Carlyle-Lomas three years later.

Much later, in 1989, Stainer's texts of the Protectoral speeches, without any apparatus except for a list of Stainer's sources, formed the basis of Ivan Roots' edition published in the Everyman Classics.[17] There is an entertaining introduction which tells us something about Cromwell, but it does not engage at all with the difficulties of relating different surviving versions of a speech with one another. What it does offer is a powerful evocation of Cromwell's speaking style:

> One fact is clear: on almost every occasion, Cromwell spoke extempore. He may have had a few notes and obviously had in his head—and one may perhaps add, heart—an idea of the basic structure of his oration, and of the topics upon which he intended to

[13] Charles L. Stainer, *Speeches of Oliver Cromwell 1644–1658* (1901).

[14] C. L. Stainer, *Oxford Silver Pennies, 925–1272* (Oxford Historical Society, 1904).

[15] C. L. Stainer, ed., *Studies in Oxford History, Chiefly in the Eighteenth Century: a series of papers* (Oxford Historical Society, 1901).

[16] *Thomas Blood* (Oxford, 1933) and *Overbury* (Oxford, 1934), the latter a play about the murder of Sir Thomas Overbury in 1613.

[17] *Speeches of Oliver Cromwell*, edited and introduced by Ivan Roots (1989).

xxxix

touch and the line to take on them…It is clear to the reader, and must have been to his listeners, that with him the wind blew where it listed. The man was thinking on his feet, groping for the words to express the ideas that flashed or drifted into his mind. The phrases were tumbling out even before they were formed. One thing led, directly or circuitively, to another, and sometimes, but not always, back again.[18]

Roots also explains how on the tercentenary of Cromwell's speeches to the first Protectorate parliament, a professional actor had delivered the speeches of 4 and 12 September 1654 on what was then the Third Programme on the radio.

> The results were illuminating. Where Oliver breaks off in mid-sentence the mind of the reader manages to finish it off for him, much as we find happens in our own conversations. The performance brought out acceptable nuances and emphases on particularly pregnant words or phrases that set the speaker off on a new tack or brought him back to an old.[19]

This testimony reinforces the sense of those of us editing the texts anew. They are much easier to follow when read aloud. While some scholars have doubted that there is much connection between what Cromwell said and what stenographers recorded him as having said, these testimonies suggest what we are printing here is actually likely to be very close to the words of the man himself in full flow. Seventeenth-century shorthand was up to the job: it would have been even better if the record had been made with biros not quills.

Stainer, especially in its original form, is better than Carlyle-Lomas and certainly far better than Abbott, but it is not a good version of what contemporaries recorded Cromwell as having said.

The unsatisfactory nature of the Carlyle, Carlyle-Lomas and Stainer is what drove Wilbur Cortez Abbott, Professor of History first at Yale and then Harvard, to make his assault on this literary Everest. He spent many years laying the foundations and credits the assistance of one scholar for all four volumes and of a second one for the last two of the four volumes.[20] The project was however blighted by the rise of Adolf Hitler.[21] Firstly the war with Hitler prevented Abbott

---

[18] *Speeches*, ed. Roots, pp. xiii–xiv.   [19] *Speeches*, ed. Roots, p. xvii.

[20] *The Writings and Speeches of Oliver Cromwell with an introduction, Notes and a Sketch of His Life by Wilbur Cortez Abbott with the assistance of Catherine Crane and Madeleine R. Gleason.* 4 vols. *Volume 1 1599–1649* (1937); *Volume 2 1649–1653* (1939); *Volume 3 1653–1655* (1945); *Volume 4 1655–1658* (1947). Madeleine Gleason joined the team as second assistant for vol. 3 and was named as first assistant for vol. 4.

[21] See David L. Smith, 'W.C. Abbott and the historical reputation of Oliver Cromwell', *Cromwelliana*, 3rd ser. 2 (2013), pp. 42–58.

GENERAL INTRODUCTION

from being able to get to Europe after 1939 and forced him to rely on copies made earlier and from what he could see in the libraries at Harvard; and secondly Cromwell turned into a mini-Hitler, as much an anti-hero to Abbott as he had been a super-hero to Carlyle. Abbott seems to have fallen out of love with Cromwell and also with editing Cromwell. Each volume is less thoughtful and reflective than the one before, and each volume throws in more and more undigested material. Abbott added more than 700 items to what was in Carlyle-Lomas. But the vast majority was not written *by* Cromwell but *for* him, pro-forma warrants, passes, protections and so on, orders and proclamations issued in his name but without any evidence of input from him, together with a whole host of correspondence to foreign rulers, once again emanating from his office but not his person. Abbott also reconstructed many documents from calendars or other short-form records[22] and he was undiscriminating in including examples of Cromwell being ventriloquised long after the event or by those not present when speeches or conversations took place. So the result is tired and unreflective. Even worse is Abbott's editorial practice. Especially, but not exclusively, in the case of speeches, when faced by more than one version of a text, Abbott produced hybrid versions, taking bits from two or more versions without giving the reader any indication about what came from where. As he became old, tired and fed up with the man and the project, this became ever more of a problem.

And if that was not bad enough, the edition is really hard to negotiate. Bizarrely, Abbott's commentary is in a larger typeface than the texts themselves (and both are too small for comfort). There is no guide to the contents, only chapter titles—and his fifty chapters average about seventy pages in length. Although scrupulously chronological, there are no running heads so finding particular writings or speech acts can take a great deal of time, especially if you are looking for a particular letter and are unsure about the date. Using the list of contents and the much more user-friendly index in Carlyle-Lomas, it is possible to find most things in less than thirty seconds; it can take many minutes with Abbott (and to add to the chaos, there is an index to volumes 1–2 at the end of volume 2 and of volumes 3 and 4 at the end of volume 4). Abbott's intentions were excellent; but he was defeated by the project's challenges.[23]

---

[22] Examples are Abbott 2:309, 341, 428.

[23] For a fuller analysis of the failings of the edition, see John Morrill, 'Textualising and Contextualising Cromwell', *The Historical Journal*, 33:3 (1990), pp. 629–39.

xli

GENERAL INTRODUCTION

HOW?

Once the author of this introduction had been asked to take on the task of creating a new edition of the writings and speeches of Oliver Cromwell, he knew it had to be a collaborative project. He was just emerging from another funded project[24] involving scholars from three universities and working closely with three (and later more than three) funded research associates and he knew how such projects could be more than the sum of their parts. Although Abbott's edition was in four volumes and ran to more than 3,600 pages, a new edition did not need all the padding and digressions that had drowned the texts. If there were to be three volumes (one ending at the Regicide, the second with the establishment of the Protectorate and the third with Cromwell's death) then it seemed sensible to find for each volume two senior scholars as editors and an externally funded research associate. The first decisions therefore were to choose the six editors, including the general editor[25] and an advisory board of scholars[26] who knew a lot about Cromwell and/or about the problems of editing early modern lives and letters. In addition to the three volumes of edited texts there would be one or two companion volumes to be written principally by the editors of the other three volumes.

This done, the next stage was to get funding for a scoping exercise and for a pilot, and to hold some workshops including established scholars and graduate students. That preliminary funding was secured:[27] two research assistants were appointed and three workshops were held. Tim Wales, based in London, was appointed to undertake a scoping exercise. Using Abbott as a starting point, he analysed how many 'items' there were, how many holographs, autographs, early copies of missing originals, later copies of originals not easily available, how many in early print etc. Ian Campbell, based in Dublin, was appointed to analyse surviving material from Cromwell's time in Ireland, which was a large enough sample for our purposes. Since almost all Cromwell's letters from Ireland survive only because they were published, sometimes in several newsbooks and pamphlets,

---

[24] The edition of the 8,000+ depositions of survivors of the violence accompanying the rebellion or rising first in Ulster and then across Ireland in and after the winter of 1641/2 and now available online at www.1641.tcd.ie and in twelve volumes published by the Irish Manuscripts Commission.

[25] Andrew Barclay and myself (vol. 1); Micheál Ó Siochrú and Jason Peacey (vol. 2); Patrick Little and David Smith (vol. 3).

[26] Martyn Bennett, Jan Broadway, Colin Davis, Peter Gaunt, Clive Holmes, Ann Hughes, Laura Knoppers and Blair Worden.

[27] The funding for the scoping exercise and one of the workshops was a grant funded jointly by the UK Arts and Humanities Research Council and the Irish Research Council for Humanities and Social Science.

xlii

GENERAL INTRODUCTION

we wanted to measure the scale of the problem and how easy it would be to establish one as a base or proof text.[28] Workshops at Nottingham Trent University, Trinity College Dublin and Selwyn College Cambridge, involving the editors, members of the advisory board and lots of graduate students, addressed questions of inclusion and exclusion, core editorial practice (modernisation of spelling and punctuation, nature and extent of contextual material) and matters thrown up by the scoping and pilot exercises.

All this led to a successful bid for a Major Leverhulme Trust award for the appointment of the three research associates who were duly appointed. It was envisaged that their role would be to track down all holographs and autographs and to list all other versions of material to be considered for inclusion, and after consultation with their volume editors to acquire digital images (wherever possible) for later transcription, or, where digital photography was not permitted,[29] to transcribe on site. All transcriptions would be made by one of the research associates and checked by one (or more) of the editors. The research associates would attach notes to assist the editors in producing introductory headnotes and footnotes, most importantly about the provenance and transmission histories of all texts being considered for inclusion. In practice, the tasks of editors and research associates bled into one another so much that a decision was made within months that the research associates would be included as full editors in their volumes.

A number of tasks were delegated to graduate students—such as trawling through the catalogues of appropriate auction houses, checking translations from Law French or Dutch and imaging documents in archives remote from Cambridge.

Meanwhile, all 'strategic decisions' having been made, the advisory board was stood down. But apart from the general editor's almost daily contact with the research associates (and monthly meetings with agendas), and in addition to the regular interactions of the volume teams, there were six-monthly meetings of what were soon the nine editors. This was to monitor progress and to ensure as much consistency as possible. But the work of identifying all possible items,

---

[28] See the discussion towards the end of this introduction.

[29] By the time we started, in 2011, most major libraries were allowing digital images to be created. The major exceptions at the time were the British Library and the Bodleian Library. Sometimes—as with the Clarke manuscripts in Worcester College Oxford—transcription was made from microfilms and later checked against the original. Some transcriptions in archives remote from Cambridge were delegated to trusted doctoral students and post-doctoral researchers and almost always checked by a member of the editorial team later.

xliii

GENERAL INTRODUCTION

resolving issues of inclusion and exclusion and getting as much consistency as we have achieved, all these required the kind of help that only advances in IT make possible.

At its simplest, this meant the creation of a large database of digital images of as many items as possible—some 12,000 by the end of the project—and making them available to all members of the team. The combination of the images we created ourselves or which were created for us by some exceptionally helpful librarians around the world, notably in the United States, together with immediate access (principally via the Early English Books Online database) to all those of Cromwell's words that survive in contemporary pamphlets and newspapers, gave us a great start. The fact that by 2010–11 so many of the relevant libraries had put their catalogues online was another immense help, as was the rapid increase in libraries allowing digital imaging, which was happening as we worked. As a result mainly of this, and a lot of leg-work going through sales' catalogues, we were able to reduce the number of writings which in previous editions were only known from later copies, rather than from holographs or autographs or from contemporary manuscript or print copies, from around 40 per cent to less than 15 per cent. We are confident that most of the residue no longer exists.

But how to stabilise the huge amount of data we were gathering and allow each of the teams to keep abreast of what everyone else was doing? The answer was to create a dedicated Virtual Research Environment for the project. An early attempt to create one from scratch failed, but we were then able to acquire and to modify an existing commercially available VRE, Alfresco, for our own purposes.[30]

This can be imagined both as a warehouse and an intranet social networking site. All nine editors could see everything that had been done and that was in the process of being done. Crucial to the 'warehouse' dimension was the creation for each item of a folder in Microsoft Word with its own unique eight-digit number based on its date: year, month, day. So a document written on 29 July 1643 would be **1643 07 29**. In the minority of cases where there was more than one item in a single day, an alphabetical signifier was added (thus **1643 07 29** but **1643 07 31a** and **1643 07 31b**). This had the great advantage of putting them into a continuously updating chronological order. Within the folder created for each

---

[30] This required exceptionally generous assistance from members of the I.T. and Computing team at TCD, especially Pat Carty and more especially the late and much-missed Shay Lawless.

xliv

item, there were sub-folders for any or all images, for transcriptions, for notes and for the various stages of the editing process. It was exceptionally easy to navigate and search.

The reconfigured Alfresco was also a kind of social networking site. Any member of the team could contact any one or more of the others. Some of us had particular skills (e.g. knowledge of obscure military terms or obscure biblical or other religious references) and could be targeted. If an editor came across an issue not addressed in our style guides, everyone could be asked for a view. The ability to hold and process so much information within Alfresco, hosted from Dublin, was exceptionally important and contributed to making the outcome as consistent as it is. Funds were found from Cambridge to keep it 'alive' for two years after the Leverhulme Grant had expired. Transferring all the data (which took most of our PCs fifteen hours to upload) was one of the great times of stress. But if communication between members within Alfresco ceased in 2016, at least all members had all the data for the whole project as it stood at that time—that is 96 per cent of all the digitised images and almost all of the transcriptions, if not of the fully edited texts.

When the Leverhulme Grant expired the edition was stabilised and almost all items had been fully transcribed. It did take longer than had been intended for the further editing and checking to bring us to this point.

WHAT

The current edition is focused tightly on what Oliver Cromwell said and wrote. It includes a significant amount of material that will not be found in any of the editions discussed above. It includes everything that is in Carlyle-Lomas and in Stainer, but it omits a good deal that is in Abbott. That is because we have excluded items that we believe were written for Cromwell to sign, and where there is no evidence of authorial intent. We have discovered a number of items that were unavailable to previous editors and we have found a much larger number of original autograph and holograph letters that have previously been printed from often very poor eighteenth- or nineteenth-century transcripts. We have included the admittedly very much abbreviated accounts of speeches Cromwell made in the Long Parliament between 1640 and 1648, some of them previously unpublished, and we have produced a new and much more accurate transcription of his contributions to the army debates of the summer and autumn of 1647. We have excluded a number of items which we are confident are

xlv

GENERAL INTRODUCTION

forgeries[31] and we have left in, but with very heavy warnings, items where the evidence of Cromwell's authorship is reasonable but short of conclusive. The two most dramatic of these are the document Cromwell presented to the committee of the House of Commons in late November 1644 denouncing his commander, the earl of Manchester, for not wanting to win an outright victory over the King;[32] and the letter to Robert Hammond dated 6 November 1648 signed by 'Heron's Brother' and ascribed a little too hastily by Sir Charles Firth to Cromwell.[33]

At an early stage of proceedings we decided that the edition should seek to give us 'Cromwell's voice'. We would print all holographs and autographs and all speeches which only survive in single versions (as with his speeches at the Putney Debates) in their raw state with no changes to spelling or punctuation and with all marks on the manuscript (crossings-out, additions etc.) indicated. We would not offer (as our predecessors all did) 'interpretations' by additions and substitutions. For example, the much-used edition of the Putney Debates by Sir Charles Firth adds words, rearranges sentences and even changes the order of sentences to improve what he believed to be the speakers' meaning. Our edition may be harder to follow at times, but it leaves the user able and free to make their own interpretation.

Where no holograph or autograph has survived and where there are different surviving copies (most typically in near-contemporary newsbooks and pamphlets) we have always made a careful choice of which to make our proof text and have always explained our choice in the headnote. We found it easier than we expected to make these decisions for two reasons. The first was that it was frequently the case that we could readily establish when one version was clearly a

---

[31] We had workshops including all the editors and groups of graduate students in various institutions to debate the most difficult cases. Ones that were finally admitted include **1648 11 06a** and **1657 12 04**. Amongst those excluded, and representative of the difficulties is a purported speech by Cromwell before he left for Ireland, dated late June 1649 and published as a pamphlet: *A most learned, conscientious, and devout-exercise; held forth the last Lords-day, at Sir Peter Temples, in Lincolnes-Inne-Fields;/by Lieut.-General Crumwell. As it was faithfully taken in characters by Aaron Guerdon*. (Wing/C7117A). The case for it being a hostile account of an actual event, with much satire in the early pages, but a serious and plausible political analysis in the later pages, is outweighed by the lack of any external evidence that the event took place. For a discussion of the content, see John Morrill, 'Cromwell and his Contemporaries', in *Oliver Cromwell and the English Revolution* (1990), pp. 265–7, and Aaron Guerden (*c*.1602–76?), physician and master of the mint in *ODNB*. The uploaded paper on Academia.edu makes a strong case for the piece as a royalist satire: Nicholas Poyntz, 'A Most Learned, Conscientious and Devout Exercise: anti-Cromwellian satire in 1649' (https://www.academia.edu/545378/).

[32] See **1644 11 25b**.   [33] See **1648 11 06a**.

xlvi

GENERAL INTRODUCTION

deteriorated copy of another. The other reason was that it was often possible to determine which printer at any given time was the preferred printer of material that either the army leadership or more usually the Parliament wanted to see in the public domain. These two principles almost always reinforced one another. This did, however, involve a decision to privilege an 'intentionalist' version over a 'social' version: that is, a version which gets us closer to what Cromwell wrote or said rather than a version which had more impact at the time or in the subsequent historiography. The best example of this is the text known in all previous editions as 'A Declaration of the Lord Lieutenant of Ireland. For the undeceiving of deluded and seduced People', printed in London on 21 March 1650. This is the version which appeared in Carlyle, Carlyle-Lomas and Abbott and has been the basis of all debate at the time and since. But that London printing was itself a modified version of an earlier text published first in Cork and then in Dublin which has a different title and includes within it the decrees of the Catholic clergy gathered at Clonmacnoise in December 1649, to which it is a response. Detailed investigation shows that it was unlikely Cromwell authorised or oversaw the London printing, so the Irish printings are likely to be much closer to the words he committed to paper. It is the Cork printing which is used in this edition, with the changes made for the London edition clearly indicated.[34]

Every item is encased in supporting materials. Each letter has its own item number and we have given each item a title, identified our source and provided it with an introduction. That introduction has two functions. The first is to stabilise the history of the text: its provenance, authenticity and—whenever multiple copies of a lost or non-existing original survive—an explanation of why we have selected one particular version as a proof text; and where necessary to clarify and secure the date on which the document was created. The second is to offer guidance on the historical context within which the writing was created or the speech act occurred. This is not to offer an interpretation so much as to clarify how and why the document came into being.

Every item is annotated. In the significant number of cases where we have more than one version of an item, we have noted differences between them whenever there is any possibility of a difference of meaning. It would be impractical to include all variations of spelling or punctuation—especially since this would be exploring differences amongst third parties—but we have erred on the side of caution when it comes to including variants that might make even small

---

[34] See **1650 01 99**.

xlvii

GENERAL INTRODUCTION

differences to the sense of the text. Our transcription conventions, reproduced before this introduction, were designed to ensure that we recorded all corrections, deletions, additions (in the same or a different hand), the existence of gaps, marginalia and other physical characteristics that affect how we consider the content (e.g. signs of illness or exhilaration). In the case (and only in the case) of holograph letters, we have retained line-endings as in the original text (since this gives some important clues to Cromwell's writing practices). We have reproduced what was on the page we have transcribed except for the conversion of absolutely standard short-forms (e.g. tails on the letter 'p' indicating 'pro' 'pre' or 'per' have been expanded).

The second purpose of the notes is to clarify meaning. We have added a note for every proper name—person, place, event. Occasionally a person has eluded our searches, but the vast majority of proper names have been identified. Where the spelling in the original is not self-evident, we have given the accepted spelling in the footnote. For people, we started by checking, as appropriate, *The Oxford Dictionary of National Biography, the Dictionary of Irish Biography, the Dictionary of Welsh Biography* and the standard biographical guides to royalist and parliamentarian army officers and the specialist guides to officers in the New Model Army. We have also cited, as appropriate, the databases for identifying clergy and the matriculation records of Oxford and Cambridge. When all those were insufficient we looked as widely as we could. We have given all places their modern spelling and county and, whenever appropriate, distances from other places of relevance to the matter in hand. Over and above identifying people, places and events referred to by name, we have sought to identify others that are referred to obliquely or indirectly and we have also defined words that are no longer in use or that have period-specific meanings. Particular attention has been paid to military terminology. Cromwell cited very little other than the books of the Bible and wherever possible we have identified biblical quotations or allusions.

We hope that the result is an edition of Cromwell's words that is much closer to what he actually wrote and said than in previous editions. Cromwell is so central to the history of England, Scotland, Ireland and Wales and to their interactions, so central to the history of religious pluralism and to Western notions of 'liberty', so disruptive a force in the history of constitutionalism and discretionary power, so inspiring to many, so loathsome to others, that a reliable edition of his surviving words is essential. Cromwell spoke from the heart as much as from the head and he has drawn hundreds of scholars to write about him and his impact not only on his own times but on all history since his times. In one recent

xlviii

GENERAL INTRODUCTION

poll, his image was more recognisable than that of all but three monarchs before Elizabeth II, and more recognisable than all but two non-royals from before 1950. What he actually wrote, and what he actually said, matters.

SIGNIFICANCE

This edition contains 1,077 separate items—555 letters, 211 speeches,[35] forty-three conversations reported by others (and thought by the editors to have a prospect of being based on clear recollection),[36] fifteen declarations (issued while Cromwell was on campaign), ten reports from parliamentary committees and another 248 writings, mainly pro-forma orders, certificates, commissions, warrants, passes, protections etc.—a cross-section of many more pro-forma documents chosen as exempla, or because he personalised them in some way, or because they contain important information about a person or event of particular significance. A list of similar pro-formas appears in the form of appendices to each volume. One further small, distinctive group is included to demonstrate Cromwell's central role in the unfolding of the Commonwealth and Protectorate—the King's death warrant in which Cromwell's signature is so emphatic and highly placed; the oaths he took (and modified) at his first institution as Lord Protector in December 1653 and then, significantly modified, in June 1657; and his extempore prayer as he lay dying at Whitehall in September 1658.

One thousand and seventy-seven items. This is more than double the number in the Carlyle-Lomas edition which included 329 letters and sixty speeches and a small number of other writings. It is a lot less than in Abbott's, but for what we believe are good reasons.[37] Abbott did not add significantly to the number of letters and speeches but he overloaded his edition with documents Cromwell certainly did not write, and in many cases may well not have read, and indeed he manufactured a lot of writings from second-hand minutes of meetings. This edition contains far more evidence of Cromwell's 'voice' and of his mind at work—perhaps 30 per cent more—and, just as important, it has restored the authority

---

[35] This counts separately the numerous interventions recorded in the debates in the General Council of the Army in 1647. As in Carlyle-Lomas, each day's debate is a single item in our list of contents, but Cromwell spoke several or many times on these days.

[36] No conversations are included in Carlyle-Lomas. Abbott has many more than are included here, but many of them are of very dubious provenance and those we have excluded.

[37] No attempt has been made to calculate the number of items in Abbott, *Writings and Speeches*, because of the chaotic layout of his four volumes, his inclusion of much material that is neither a writing nor a speech and the many artificially created items.

xlix

of the texts. Sophia Lomas did a very good job of tracking down holographs and autographs, but already by the 1890s many had disappeared into private collections and public libraries without published catalogues. We had the benefit of producing this edition just as all the world's great libraries were putting their manuscript catalogues online, and many of them, especially in North America, were generous in providing us with high-resolution digital images. A large number of the letters in this edition have only previously been published from later transcripts and not as here from holographs or autographs. Although Sophia Lomas added only eighty-five letters to Carlyle's 244, she improved the text of many included in Carlyle's first and third editions. But because she modernised spelling and punctuation, omitted corrections to be found in the originals and was a little cavalier in confirming detail such as the identity of unnamed recipients, she introduced a lot of misleading information. And she was far too deferential in accepting Carlyle's quixotic editions of the letters. Abbott rarely produced an edition of a letter that was an improvement on Carlyle-Lomas and, as already explained, he made catastrophic, unacceptable decisions about how to present the main speeches by creating hybrids of very different versions.

So this edition claims to be a much better canon of Cromwell's recorded words. It also claims to be arranged in a way that will make it far easier to use in hard copy or online. It is arranged in strict chronological order so far as that can be determined. It forefronts issues of provenance and of transmission history. It offers a comprehensive, itemised list of contents and a single, integrated index. Every person, place and event has an identifying footnote (less than 2 per cent have eluded identification). It settles, far more clearly than ever before, problems of authenticity.[38] By clarifying the canon—extending it and de-cluttering it, by providing authoritative annotated editions of the best surviving texts, by paying much more attention to how the texts reflect Cromwell's mood—including issues of transparency, deceit and religious fervour—and by setting out to contextualise much more than to explain, this edition seeks to be one that can much more securely form the basis for historical writing about the central figure in a series of events central to English, archipelagic and global history.

---

[38] For example, it challenges the assumption that the assault on the reputation of the earl of Manchester presented in Cromwell's name in late November 1644 was actually prepared by Cromwell (**1644 11 25b[?]**) and it completely transforms our understanding of Cromwell's *Declaration for the undeceiving of deluded and seduced people* by privileging not a later printing issued in London many weeks later (as in all former editions), but the original version printed and published in Cork with other documents two months earlier (**1650 01 31[?]**).

INTRODUCTION TO VOLUME 1 (1626–1649)

Andrew Barclay, Tim Wales and John Morrill

This volume traces the life of Oliver Cromwell from his birth to the climacteric of 30 January 1649, the day on which King Charles I was executed for treason against his people. It traces that life through all the surviving words that Cromwell was recorded as having spoken, and all those written words that can reliably be thought to have been written or dictated by him.

It was a life in two parts: of provincial obscurity until his forty-second year and then a life of mounting public prominence and controversy. The hinge was his election to Parliament as member for Cambridge in 1640. He quickly became recognised as a radical voice in Parliament, engaged in forthright, emotionally wrought criticism of the Crown's secular and religious policies. From the summer of 1642—when all too many colleagues were sitting on their hands waiting to see what might happen—he became an activist in raising volunteers to fight for Parliament in his home area; and from late 1642 until the Regicide he was engaged in two theatres, intermittently as an MP in Westminster, and more usually as a soldier in the field—as a colonel in a cavalry regiment by the spring of 1643, lieutenant general of a regional army by the end of that year, and lieutenant general of the New Model Army from June 1645—the most prominent of the very small number of men exempted from the Self-Denying Ordinance which had as a central purpose the separation of those who served in Parliament and those who served in the armies.

Few if any Englishmen have generated so many biographies.[1] His hundreds of letters and dozens of speeches along with the lustre and the controversy attached to his career make him an attractive proposition. He has attracted biographies by

---

[1] By our calculation no more than six to 1840 and no less than 150 since then, including biographies originally published in all the major European languages as well as many translated into those languages from English. If he is not the most biographied of Britons, it is hard to think who has had more biographies, even amongst the monarchs.

INTRODUCTION TO VOLUME 1 (1626–1649)

a former president of the United States, a governor general of Canada, a French prime minister and a UK cabinet minister.[2] All rely heavily on one or more editions of his writings and speeches, specifically Thomas Carlyle's *Letters and Speeches of Oliver Cromwell* (1845) and W. C. Abbott's *Writings and Speeches of Oliver Cromwell* (1937–47). But this creates a problem: he has not been well served by his editors. The nature and problems with previous editions of his writings and speeches are explored in the general introduction to this project. In what follows, we will simply summarise the nature and significance of what has survived for the period down to 1649 and note and comment on some of the significant gaps in the archive and on the ways this edition remedies the frailties of its predecessors.

There is no Cromwell archive. If he kept copies of his incoming or outgoing correspondence before his fiftieth birthday in April 1649 no part of it survives. What we have is a lot of material generated by Cromwell that other people kept and which subsequent generations preserved. John Goldsmith, in discussing the survival of material objects linked to Oliver Cromwell suggests that that depends on *inertia, continuity* and *awareness*.[3] No-one got round to destroying William Clarke's papers when his son, in a fit of pique with his own Oxford college, gave them to the newly founded Worcester College, where they were stored, forgotten, until discovered in the 1890s. Some families stored Cromwell material with other papers and cherished or more often neglected or forgot about them. But damp, neglect or a desire to make space caused a lot of material that survived into the eighteenth or early nineteenth century to be burnt or binned during that period. There is little evidence of destruction, by wilfulness or inadvertence, since Thomas Carlyle's edition of his letters and speeches appeared in 1845. At that point 'awareness' clicked in.

This affects what has survived and what we can be very clear must have vanished. And the asymmetrical patterns of survival must affect our view of Cromwell. We will examine patterns of survival later, but one thing is most obvious: we have very little evidence of his words—speech acts or writings—before 1640 and then more and more, as he emerged as a public figure.

---

[2] Theodore Roosevelt, *Oliver Cromwell, the Story of his Life and Work* (NY, 1906), was President of the USA from 1901 to 1909. John Buchan, *Oliver Cromwell* (London, 1934) was governor general of Canada from 1935 to 1940. Francois Guizot, *Histoire de la république d'Angleterre et de Cromwell*, 2 vols. (Paris, 1854) was foreign minister under the July Monarchy from 1840 to 1847 and prime minister 1847–8. John Morley, *Oliver Cromwell* (London, 1900), was the cabinet minister responsible for Ireland (1886 and 1892–5), for India (1905–10) and Lord President of the Council (1910–17).

[3] John Goldsmith, 'Does Cronwelliana exist? A review of personalia association with Oliver Cromwell', in Jane Mills, ed., *Cromwell's Legacy* (2012), pp. 33–56 at p. 34.

INTRODUCTION TO VOLUME 1 (1626–1649)

Let us deal with the period down to the autumn of 1640 very quickly. Oliver Cromwell was born into a family that rose from near-rags to riches as a result of the Reformation, Oliver's great-great-grandfather, Morgan Williams, had the good fortune to marry the sister of Thomas Cromwell, chief minister of Henry VIII in the 1530s, a happy event that occurred before Thomas's rise. Brought up in Thomas's household alongside the latter's son Gregory,[4] Oliver Cromwell's great-grandfather Richard, who changed his name from Williams to Cromwell, received the lands of a wealthy nunnery in Huntingdon, the Cistercian Abbey at Sawtry just three miles north of Huntingdon and the lands of Ramsey Abbey, the third wealthiest and third most highly ranked Benedictine Abbey in England.[5] Cromwell continued until the end of his life to use the form 'Oliver Cromwell alias Williams' on many private legal documents and his awareness that before they gained a fortune in East Anglia they had come from South Wales guided his choice of lands when he was handsomely rewarded for his success in war by the grant of lands of defeated royalists.[6]

Oliver was the eldest son of a younger son, and so only received a minor part of this inheritance, most going to his (royalist) cousins. He was born in Huntingdon, a small county town on the Great North Road, and stayed there—except for a year studying at Cambridge and just possibly a period studying law in London—until a series of misfortunes caused him to sell up what properties he had in and around Huntingdon and to move six miles to St Ives where he became a tenant farmer. The death of a childless brother of his mother brought him a substantial income as the manager of the lands of the cathedral at Ely and a substantial townhouse close by. It was there that his wife and children lived, he periodically with them, until they—mother, wife, children (at least each child until they married)—moved to London in the summer of 1646, to a property in Drury Lane (i.e. Covent Garden).

Cromwell has left enough traces in the record to have generated a book-length study of several aspects of that life as a man of limited local importance, but

---

[4] The best discussion of the link between the Cromwell family and the Williams family who become 'Cromwells' can be found in Diarmaid MacCulloch, *Thomas Cromwell: a Life* (London, 2018), pp. 19–20, 38, 47–9, 482–3 and *passim*; and Lloyd Bowen, 'Oliver Cromwell (alias Williams) and Wales', in Patrick Little, ed., *Oliver Cromwell: New Perspectives* (Basingstoke, 2009), pp. 168–94.

[5] It was worth £1,731 p.a. in 1535; and its abbot ranked third behind Glastonbury and St Albans amongst the mitred abbots in late medieval parliaments: Charles Herbermann, ed., *The Catholic Encyclopoedia* (1906); William Page and Granville Proby, eds., assisted by H. E. Norris, *V. C. H. Huntingdonshire* (1926), 1:377–85.

[6] Bowen, 'Oliver Cromwell (alias Williams) and Wales', pp. 168–94.

liii

INTRODUCTION TO VOLUME 1 (1626–1649)

hardly an actor on the national stage. But his records of what he said and wrote down to 1640 are very meagre. He was born in 1599 but we have no word of his before a letter inviting an old Cambridge college friend to stand as godfather at the baptism of his son Richard in October 1626. Between then and 1640 we have three more letters and an account of a speech he made in the House of Commons in 1628. This is a meagre amount but from clues afforded by these few letters, it has been possible to flesh out very full accounts of Cromwell's life at least from the late 1620s.[7] One letter, from January 1636, demonstrates Cromwell's links with a godly network based in London[8] and East Anglia; another, from October 1638, shows his links into leading figures amongst the major gentry families of Essex.[9] A simple letter to the radical George Willingham takes us to the heart of the godly milieu of London in the early 1640s and even to John Lilburne, flogged and imprisoned for his activities in the late 1630s.[10] It has been suggested that Cromwell was involved in an underground conventicle in St Ives in the mid-1630s and that that in turn helps to explain his election as an MP in 1640.[11]

That said, this volume is concerned in effect with the period from the calling of the Long Parliament in October 1640 to the Regicide in January 1649 and during that time we have 186 letters together with often very abbreviated versions of 110 interventions in Parliament and forty-five much fuller accounts of speeches in the Council of the Army in 1647.[12]

Almost all the speeches survive in original versions: all the speeches from the Army Debates (in Churches at Saffron Walden in Essex in May 1647, at Reading in Berkshire in July and at Putney in October and November) survive in transcripts made by William Clarke from his own shorthand notes and from those of his colleagues, those transcripts being made at some point between 1647 and Clarke's death in 1665. Almost all the parliamentary speeches from 1640–4 and 1647–8 survive in the hands of the MPs who wrote down, in summary (often *very*

---

[7] Andrew Barclay, *Electing Cromwell: the Making of a Politician* (London, 2011); John Morrill, 'The Making of Oliver Cromwell' in John Morrill, ed., *Oliver Cromwell and the English Revolution* (1990), pp. 19–48; Simon Healy, '1636: The Unmaking of Oliver Cromwell?', in Patrick Little, ed., *Oliver Cromwell: New Perspectives* (Basingstoke, 2009), pp. 20–37.

[8] See **1636 01 11**.

[9] See **1638 10 10**.

[10] See **1641 04 99** (and also **1640 11 09, 1641 08 09a**).

[11] Barclay, *Electing Cromwell*, ch. 5.

[12] In addition, this edition includes seventeen other writings to which he attached his name—very varied in type from warrants and military passes to the order establishing the High Court of Justice in January 1649 and the King's death warrant, in which Cromwell's signature appears third, after those of John Bradshawe, President of the High Court, and Thomas Lord Grey of Groby.

liv

INTRODUCTION TO VOLUME 1 (1626–1649)

summary) form, what Cromwell said. The major exceptions are three speeches delivered on 9 December 1644 during the crisis that led to the Self-Denying Ordinance and the New Model Ordinance, one of which survives in the weekly diurnal *Perfect Occurrences*, another in Rushworth's *Historical Collections* and the third in Clarendon's *History* (**1644 12 09a–c**).

The letters are a more diverse collection. Of the 187 surviving letters, sixty come down to us in holograph (ie in Cromwell's own hand) and another thirty-nine in the hands of one of his clerks but with his signature (and often traces of his seal), and many of these contain corrections that are in Cromwell's hand. Another twenty-seven survive in near-contemporary transcriptions, most notably letters internal to the Army transcribed by William Clarke and in his papers, and others that were copied into letter books kept by Sir Samuel Luke, who was governor of Newport Pagnell from 1642 to 1644. Another thirty-five exist only in print form in pamphlets and newspapers, occasionally in several published more or less simultaneously. The remaining twenty-six letters only survive in later transcriptions made in the eighteenth or nineteenth century. This represents only 15 per cent of the total. In comparison, the Carlyle-Lomas and Abbott editions present 40 per cent of the letters in often poor eighteenth- or nineteenth-century transcriptions.

It is impossible to know how representative this material is of what Cromwell wrote. Is what survives likely to be a representative cross-section of what he wrote? Surely Cromwell wrote regularly to his close family? Before 1649, we have no letters to his wife, one to just one of his children, none to his sisters. There are a few letters, quite personal in nature, that were written to relations by blood or marriage, most notably his deeply moving letter of condolence to Valentine Walton (who had married his sister Margaret) about the death of their son and his nephew, also Valentine, at the battle of Marston Moor (see **1644 07 05**). But there are no letters before 1649 to Henry Ireton, his son-in-law and closest political ally in and after 1646, only one to Henry Vane with whom we have independent evidence of a close personal friendship (at least down to Pride's Purge in December 1648). Cromwell spent less and less time at home between 1640 and 1646. He was in Ely for two six-week periods in August/September 1641 and towards the end of 1642 (when he was rushing around whipping up support for the parliamentary war effort). He was next certainly at home for a couple of days in September 1643, for a fortnight in January 1644 and perhaps occasionally during the periods of intense activity (about fifty nights in all) when he was based in Cambridge or Huntingdon (17 and 23 miles from Ely respectively). Surely there were letters

lv

between Oliver and his immediate family—mother, wife, children—during the 80 per cent of the time he was in London or on campaign? In the summer of 1646, his household moved up from Ely to a house in Drury Lane in Covent Garden, where they lived until Cromwell became Head of State and moved into quarters in Whitehall Palace and Hampton Court. Once again Cromwell was absent from London more than he was at home: but no family correspondence survives.

What about his letters about war and politics? Let us look at a diagram of his surviving letters from the years 1643–8:

	Jan	Feb	Mar	Apr	May	Jun	Jul	Aug	Sep	Oct	Nov	Dec	TOTAL
1643	3		3	3	3	2	4	9	2	1			30
1644	4		4	1		1			2	4			16
1645	1			7	4	4	2	4	2	5			29
1646						1	3	2	3	1			10
1647			6		7	1			2	2	2	2	22
1648	1	1	3	4	3	7	5	6	14	6	14	3	70

With the obviously exceptional case of November 1648, when Cromwell was in Scotland and then at the siege of Pontefract in Yorkshire, there are very few surviving letters written in the months of November to February (twelve in the years 1643–7 inclusive) compared with forty-six written in the months May to August. The reason is principally that he wrote more during campaigning seasons than when the Army was in winter quarters. It is war, not politics, that generated most of his letters. Similarly, he wrote three times as many letters in the months when he was not in London than in the months when he was in London. We have little evidence of political meetings with friends and allies when he was in Westminster, although surely he had them. We can never place him in church once the war began, except perhaps at the marriage of his daughter Elizabeth in 1646. Many of his letters from East Anglia and from his campaigning across England (between 1642 and 1648 he led troops into thirty-three of the forty English counties)[13] were written to London—to the Speaker of the House of Commons, to the Committee of Both Kingdoms or more occasionally to other parliamentary committees, to individual members of one or both houses. But there is no trace of the letters he surely wrote *from* London to his friends and allies in East Anglia and elsewhere.

---

[13] Calculated from 'A Cromwellian Itinerary' in Peter Gaunt, *The Cromwellian Gazetteer* (1987), pp. 224–6.

lvi

INTRODUCTION TO VOLUME 1 (1626–1649)

Overwhelmingly, the thirty-two letters printed at the time were letters sent to Parliament and printed by order of the House of Commons. So this represents a category of letters with a very high 'survival' rate. Cromwell's letters to the Speaker, which the House of Commons ordered to be printed, fall into two main groups: twelve in 1645 and twenty in 1648. These were, of course, the years in which he was most frenetically involved in active campaigning. But no letters from Cromwell to the Speaker were published until Naseby in June 1645, a measure of his lack of public visibility until that date. The handful of earlier letters were published without authority and had been written to individuals: a letter reporting the battle of Belton in Lincolnshire (May 1643) was written to Sir Miles Hobart, a Norfolk gentleman who commanded regiments of foot and of dragoons in the army of the Eastern Association, and a pamphlet describing the battle of Gainsborough (July 1643) which was the last of a series of letters Cromwell wrote about the battle, this one to the Committee of the Eastern Association in Cambridge, and which was the first of several to be censored prior to publication.[14]

Finally, in the spring of 1645, allies in Parliament arranged for the publication of a letter he had written to Fairfax about the capture of Bletchingdon House in Oxfordshire and Cromwell's exchange of letters with the governor of Faringdon. This was of course between the end of his old commission with the Eastern Association and his formal appointment to the New Model. Only with that appointment as lieutenant general of the New Model do his letters to the Speaker begin regularly to appear in print. Then, with his return to Westminster in the late winter of 1645/6, his writings disappear from print, although his profile as a general was maintained in a series of publications,[15] such as a series of chronicles of the war by John Vicars in and after 1644, culminating in *Magnalia Dei Anglicana. Or, Englands Parliamentary chronicle* (1646),[16] and *England's worthies under whom all the civill and bloudy warres since anno 1642 to anno 1647 are related* (1647)[17] and

---

[14] See the letters from Naseby (**1645 06 14**) and Bristol (**1645 09 14a**).

[15] For a general discussion, see John Morrill, 'Cromwell and his Contemporaries' in J. Morrill, ed., *Oliver Cromwell and the English Revolution* (1990), pp. 260–5.

[16] *Magnalia Dei Anglicana. Or, Englands Parliamentary chronicle. Containing a full and exact narration of all the most memorable Parliamentary mercies, and mighty (if not miraculous) deliverances, great and glorious victories, and admirable successes,... from the yeer, 1640. to this present year, 1646... Collected cheifly for the high honour of our wonder working God; and for the unexpressible comfort of all cordiall English Parliamentarians./By the most unworthy admirer of them, John Vicars. Burning-bush not consumed Burning-bush not consumed,* Imprinted at London: for J. Rothwell, at the Sun & Fountain, in Pauls Church-yard, and Tho. Vnderhill, at the Bible in Woodstreet., 1646. (Wing/V319; Thomason/E.348[1])

[17] *England's worthies under whom all the civill and bloudy warres since anno 1642 to anno 1647 are related,* London: Printed by J. Rothwell, 1647. (Wing/V304)

lvii

INTRODUCTION TO VOLUME 1 (1626–1649)

Joshua Sprigge's *Anglia Rediviva* (1647).[18] In 1646, only one piece of writing ascribed to him was published (Thomason noted that he received his copy on 10 July) and it may well have been unauthorised by him and indeed put words into his mouth. It has not been noticed in previous Cromwell editions. It was a single-sheet broadside headed *The summe of the charge given in by Lieutenant Generall Cromwel against the Earle of Manchester*, a 20-line summary of Cromwell's charge against Manchester's opposition to ending the war by force of arms, followed by a gloss which refers to John Lilburne's *England's Birth-right justified* which had been published in October 1645. No printer or publisher took responsibility for the publication but it served to remind all who read it of the importance of Cromwell in bringing about the total military defeat of the King.[19]

It is important that in 1647 Cromwell was voiceless in print but was the subject of prolonged vilification from London radicals and Leveller leaders, most obviously by his former lieutenant colonel, John Lilburne.[20] So the long series of printed letters in 1648 defending his actions in war, in reaching agreement with those in Scotland who had opposed the Engagement with the King and the Scottish 'invasion' of England, and his commitment to protecting civilian populations from abuses by troops, can be seen at one level as an attempt to restore his reputation from attacks from both Presbyterians and radicals. A study of Cromwell based only on what was said by him and about him in print would show him as a beleaguered figure riding roughshod over a welter of criticisms of social insurgency, dangerous religious libertarianism—and with a streak of Machiavellian duplicity.

This view is modified once we include a consideration of the letters than we possess in manuscript which are a much more varied group, and survival here appears to be arbitrary. The pre-1642 letters all survive, with one exception, from antiquarian collections made some time after Cromwell's death. The exception is

[18] *Anglia rediviva Englands recovery being the history of the motions, actions, and successes of the army under the immediate conduct of His Excellency Sr. Thomas Fairfax, Kt., Captain-General of all the Parliaments forces in England/compiled for the publique good by Ioshua Sprigge*..., London: Printed by R.W. for Iohn Partridge..., 1647. (Wing/S5070)

[19] *The Summe of the Charge given in by Lieutenant Generall Crumwel, against the Earle of Manchester* (London, s.n. 1646) [Thomason/669.f.10(69)]. The reference is to *England's birth-right justified against all arbitrary usurpation, whether regall or parliamentary, or under what vizor soever... and in other things of high concernment to the freedom of all the free-born people of England; by a well-wisher to the just cause for which Lieutenant Col. John Lilburne is unjustly im-prisoned in New-gate*, printed by Richard Overton, October 1645. [Thomason/E.304(17)]. The cross-reference given in *The Summe of the Charge* is 'the 35. page' but this seems an error for the 32 page.

[20] Jason Peacey, 'John Lilburne and the Long Parliament', *Historical Journal*, 43:3 (2000), pp. 625–46.

lviii

INTRODUCTION TO VOLUME 1 (1626–1649)

a minor letter kept in the archives of the recipient's family.[21] Thereafter there are many letters to colleagues in the Army and to a lesser extent in the Parliament, to county committees and others engaged in regional government; a few to royalists often relating to their pleas for leniency.[22] There are a small number of family letters, including one to his daughter Bridget fretting about the religious soundness of her sister Elizabeth, and there is a string of letters between early 1648 and early 1649 in the protracted negotiations to find a bride for his eldest surviving son, Richard.[23] Although the letters throw a great deal of light on his military activities and indeed his religious proclivities and on his preference for godly men over mere gentlemen, they shed less light on his political activity and political beliefs. It is from his speeches, not from his letters, that we get some evidence of his changing attitude to the King and to the fateful decision to push for his trial and execution. The letters certainly appear to demonstrate the sincerity of his religious beliefs and his growing commitment to a broad measure of religious liberty, and this edition throws new light on this and on the dramatic way in which his pleas for religious toleration were regularly censored by the House of Commons as the House of Lords ordered that parts were cut out of the letters they ordered to be published. But beyond that, it is not possible to find much evidence of the kind of political settlement he wanted.

The lack of epistolary material on the crisis in the Army in the late spring and early summer of 1647, and indeed the lack of any personal or public letters in the months either side of the Putney Debates, is notable. And the almost complete absence of personal correspondence between his arrival back in London at the beginning of December 1648 and his departure for Ireland nine months later is striking. Is this just chance? Did he exercise a great deal of self-censorship? Or did those who received highly charged letters at the time decide then or later to get rid of them before they got the recipients into trouble for collusion? At any rate, any interpretation of Cromwell needs to take more account of the *silences* in the archive than has been customary.[24]

---

[21] See **1631 04 01**, a letter to John Newdigate and still in the Newdegate papers in the Warwickshire Record Office.

[22] See for example **1648 07 27**, where he calls in a favour from having helped Sir Thomas Knyvett escape from imprisonment and sequestration for a borderline case of delinquency.

[23] See **1648 02 25, 1648 03 28, 1648 04 03, 1649 02 01, 1649 02 12, 1649 02 26, 1649 03 08** and four more in March and April 1649. (See also **1649 07 19**.)

[24] For some preliminary thoughts on this, see John Morrill, 'Rewriting Cromwell: A Case of Deafening Silences', *Canadian Journal of History*, 38:3 (2003), pp. 553–78.

lix

INTRODUCTION TO VOLUME 1 (1626–1649)

The lack of letters on the nitty-gritty of politics may be partly the result of the fact that he did not need to write letters to his political allies in Parliament when he was actively engaged at Westminster. We have already noted the comparative dearth of letters written while he was in London or Westminster.

For the period down to the Regicide we have sixty holograph letters and thirty-six autograph letters as well as the twenty-seven letters that survive in near-contemporary and twenty-six letters in later (post-1700) transcriptions. There is no reason to think the contemporary copies, made by the clerks of the recipients, are anything but reliable. Many of the later transcriptions are almost certainly unreliable, for this edition has retrieved a good many holograph and auto-graph letters not seen for a century or more and where we compare these with previous editions of Cromwell's letters/writings and speeches we find not only sometimes significant variations of spelling and punctuation, but serious tran-scriptions of words and especially proper names.[25] If that is true of the letters transcribed here for the first time, then it is surely true of those where the original appears now to be lost. In this edition, scrupulous attention has been paid (for the first time) to Cromwell's habit of making corrections in his own hand to letters he had written and to those written by the small number of clerks he employed in and after 1644. One of Cromwell's characteristics whenever he is writing discursively, especially to friends and allies, is for him to use up all the space on the page and to cram the last part of a letter with text, often in the form of postscripts into tiny spaces. We have sought to indicate where and how he does this. It speaks to his temperament, and to his level of agitation at particular times.

Although the ratio of holographs to autographs remains fairly constant across the years 1643–7 at a ratio of 2.5:1, there was a levelling up in 1648, where we have eighteen surviving holographs and eighteen surviving autographs. One thing stands out from 1645 on: Cromwell's signed letters to Sir Thomas (later Lord) Fairfax are all holographs. Excluding the letters to William Lenthall in his cap-acity as Speaker of the House of Commons, his sixteen letters to Fairfax prior to the Regicide are the largest single group of letters to any individual, the next most common being his six surviving letters to his cousin Robert Hammond, while he was the King's custodian on the Isle of Wight, all but one of which survive only because they were printed by Thomas Birch in 1764. Indeed the sixth letter, signed

---

[25] For a good example, see the notes on **1643 07 30**.

lx

INTRODUCTION TO VOLUME 1 (1626–1649)

not by Cromwell but by 'Heron's Brother' but ascribed to Cromwell by Sir Charles Firth, may not be by Cromwell at all.[26]

That leaves us with the speeches. Cromwell was a member of the Parliament of 1628–9 and there survives what looks like a fairly full summary of a speech he made while the House was in a Committee of the Whole House (a distinctly fiery speech on false religion and the bishops). He was a member of the Short Parliament (April to May 1640) but is not recorded as having spoken.[27] And he was a member of the Long Parliament from 1640–53. There are nine diaries (some fragmentary)—some for all and some for part of the period down to the outbreak of war, after which most of them dry up.[28] Once war broke out, Sir Simonds D'Ewes kept a much less full journal of debates and three other (new) diarists record debates for long periods during the years 1643–7. Between them they give us glimpses of Cromwell's intervention on fourteen occasions. A recruiter MP, John Boys, took up the challenge in 1647–8 but what has survived is a few fragments, although his summaries, above all of Cromwell's speeches, are fuller than those of any MPs hitherto. We are offering here the entries in the diaries of seven MPs, a total of ninety interventions in the years 1640–2 and eighteen in the period 1643–8.[29] These are often so abbreviated that they give little sense of his language or style. They rarely give any indication of length. But they do certainly indicate the subjects that Cromwell (and others) addressed and that in itself is helpful: his preoccupation with religious reform is not a surprise, but his close involvement with the crisis in Ireland in 1641–2 and Parliament's legislative and administrative response to it is more unexpected. In an attempt to weigh the significance of his role in Parliament, we have added an additional heading to our editing of

---

[26] See below **1648 11 06a**. There is a lengthy introduction which explores the complicated issues of authorship.

[27] The diary of Sir Thomas Aston is relatively full, the others much more fragmentary: see Judith D. Maltby, *The Short Parliament (1640) Diary of Sir Thomas Aston*, Camden Society, 4th series, 35 (1988); Esther S. Cope and W. H. Coates, *Proceedings of the Short Parliament of 1640*, Camden Society, 4th series, 19 (1977).

[28] Maija Jansson, ed., *Proceedings in the Opening Session of the Long Parliament, House of Commons* (Woodbridge: 7 vols., 2000–2007). There is a discussion of all the surviving diaries in the introduction to vol. 1.

[29] Of these 108 recorded interventions, seventy-nine are recorded by Sir Simonds D'Ewes (1640–5), and all but five of those are unique to him. In comparison, John Moore records seven interventions (1640–2), Framlingham Gawdy three (1641–2), the anonymous author of BL, Add. MS 5047 records four (1641–2), Lawrence Whitaker five (1644–6), Sir John Harington seven (1646–7) and John Boys three (1647–8). Five diarists in the period 1640–2 and one in the period 1642–6 record no Cromwell interventions. D'Ewes is the fullest and longest, but this disproportion might be evidence of his obsession with 'fiery spirits', amongst whom he very obviously numbered Cromwell.

lxi

INTRODUCTION TO VOLUME 1 (1626–1649)

these speeches—'outcomes'. As well as seeking to contextualise Cromwell's interventions, what happened *before* he rose to speak (taking this as broadly as is necessary), we have indicated whether there is any evidence of the effectiveness, ineffectiveness or counter-productiveness of his contributions.

Far fuller and far more dramatic is the evidence of Cromwell's role in the deliberations of the General Council of the Army in 1647. By the spring of that year, a deeply divided Parliament was confronted by a king who would not face up to defeat and ducked and weaved his way through negotiations, and both the Long Parliament and the New Model were faced by a rapidly worsening economic and fiscal crisis—a collapse of trade, a run of terrible harvests, a mountain of debate and tens of thousands of men in arms it could not pay.[30] A majority of MPs tried to ease their own burdens and those of a disillusioned population by sending part of the New Model to Ireland, and disbanding the rest of the Army without payment of the massive and mounting arrears and without the indemnity for things done *in loco et tempore belli* that the Army was demanding. The result was the Army Revolt which began in May 1647 and lasted until the end of the year. For several months, the general officers, regimental commanders and 'agitators' or 'agents' elected or selected from amongst the junior officers and from the rank and file met weekly as a 'General Council of the Army', and at three points, in mid-May, mid-July and for two weeks straddling the end of October and early November, William Clarke and a team of stenographers took shorthand notes on what was said at these meetings, which were transcribed by Clarke himself some years later.[31]

The first recorded meetings were those held at Saffron Walden in May, where various sets of demands prepared by different regiments were discussed. Cromwell only made two inconsequential interventions. The second recorded meetings were at Reading and unfortunately cover only the first two days, just before the proposals generated from within the Army (and most notably by Cromwell's son-in-law Henry Ireton), viz the Heads of the Proposals, were laid before the Council. Many agitators were pressing for an immediate advance of

---

[30] Ian Gentles, 'The Arrears of Pay of the Parliamentary Army at the End of the First Civil War', *Bulletin of the Institute of Historical Research*, 48 (1975), pp. 52–63.

[31] See Frances Henderson, 'Reading, and Writing, the Text of the Putney Debates', in Michael Mendle, ed., *The Putney Debates of 1647: The Army, the Levellers and the English State* (Cambridge, 2001), pp. 36–50; and Frances Henderson, '"Swifte and Secrete Writings" in Seventeenth-Century England, and Samuel Shelton's Brachygraphy', *The Electronic British Library Journal* (2008), pp. 1–13 and the introductions to the transcriptions below of the Army Debates, which follow her arguments.

lxii

INTRODUCTION TO VOLUME 1 (1626–1649)

the Army to London to force Parliament to expel eleven MPs who were perceived as opponents of the Army and for several other demands.[32] Cromwell was the most prominent speaker at these debates, strongly opposing precipitate action— memorably telling the agitators not to 'quarrel with every dogg in the streete that barkes at us & suffer the Kingdome to bee lost with such a fantasticall thinge'. He also, surely very revealingly, tells them to refocus: 'That's the Question,' he said of the agitators' friends in London, 'whats for their good not what pleases them.'[33] In all, Cromwell made ten recorded speeches at Reading, including three of the five longest. If Fairfax chaired the Council, Cromwell ran it.

Then, more famously, came his contributions to the Putney Debates between 28 October and 11 November. Clarke appears to have fully transcribed his own and his stenographers' notes for three of the days (28 and 29 October, and 1 November), quite probably giving fuller accounts, close to full transcripts, for the interventions of the Grandees than for other speakers. But even on those days Clarke came in late to debates, most importantly for the prayer meeting on 29 October, and for the committee meeting at which agreement was reached by all groups within the Army over the arrangements for future elections, including the franchise. He also preserved only fragments of the very important debates that stretched from 2 to 11 November, giving us tantalising glimpses about debates on the future of the King, including the interventions of Cromwell. In the surviving material more than forty men are recorded as speaking, but four men contributed more than 80 per cent of the recorded words—Henry Ireton having sixty-six recorded speeches, Thomas Rainborowe thirty-six, Oliver Cromwell twenty-nine and John Wildman twenty-six. Cromwell chaired the first day and his contributions are principally concerned to keep order and focus. He made very little contribution to the committee debate on the franchise on 29 October, but became fully engaged in the debate on the future powers of the King, and indeed on the future of Charles I, on 1 November, including three of the longest, in which he reveals more of his political philosophy than at any time before his speeches in Parliament as Lord Protector. The case for seeing his contributions to the Army debates—in contrast to what is recorded of his parliamentary debates

---

[32] 1. To expel the eleven impeached Members from the House. 2. To restore the London militia to Independent hands. 3. to obtain a declaration against the inviting-in of foreign forces. 4. to release John Lilburne and other radicals from prison. 5. to secure Army pay on an equal basis with those who had deserted them (see the summary and gloss in Ian Gentles, *The New Model Army in England Ireland and Scotland, 1645–1651* (Oxford, 1991), p. 181).

[33] See **1647 07 16**.

lxiii

down to 1649—as being very full and close to his actual words is explored in the introductions to each day's debates. At any rate, they represent an excellent counter-balance to the military preoccupations in his surviving letters.

We are left with a very incomplete account of what Cromwell did and how he thought. We certainly cannot claim that what survived is a representative cross-section of his writings or of his public utterances. What we can claim is that what is offered here is the most complete, considered and fully contextualised edition of what has come down to us, and it is presented here in the hope that we can *hear* this most contentious—revered and detested—of Englishman more precisely and accurately than ever before.

EDITED TEXTS

14 OCTOBER 1626

1626 10 14

Letter from Oliver Cromwell to Henry Downhall

Date: 14 October 1626

Source: Thomas Hearne, ed. *Liber niger Scaccarii. E codice, calamo exarato, sibique ipsi à Rochardo Gravesio Mickletoniensi donato* (Oxford, 1728), 1:261n–2n (later print)

Cromwell's eventual successor as Lord Protector, his third son, Richard,[1] was born at Huntingdon on 4 October 1626. His baptism required godparents, whose selection was always a matter of importance in early modern England. So ten days later Cromwell wrote to Henry Downhall[2] inviting to him to become his son's godfather. As the brief letter indicates, this would be a favour by Downhall which Cromwell would want to repay in due course. Downhall was a fellow of St John's College, Cambridge, and the vicar of Toft, a parish about seven miles to the west of Cambridge. Why Cromwell chose him is not clear. The letter leaves no doubt that the two men were already friends. How they had become so is the mystery. Downhall was not related to him, he was originally from Northamptonshire, he must have been some years older, he had gone up to Cambridge eight years before Cromwell, he had attended different colleges (Trinity and St John's rather than Sidney Sussex) and his parish was some distance from Huntingdon. Whether he was seen as a clerical high-flyer is also unclear. His advancement in the years that followed depended on the patronage of the bishop of Lincoln, John Williams,[3] another St John's man. In 1630 Williams appointed Downhall as the vicar of St Ives in place of the troublesome Job Tookey and then in 1631 he appointed him as one of the prebendaries of Lincoln Cathedral. Downhall later became a royalist army chaplain. Cromwell's friendship with Downhall strengthens the later claim that Williams as bishop had known of Cromwell.[4] Richard's baptism went ahead as planned on 19 October 1626 at St John's, Huntingdon.

———

Loving Sir,

Make me so much your servant by being Godfather unto my Child. I would my selfe have come over unto you, to have made a more formall invitation, but my occasions would not permitt, & therefore hold me in that excused. The day of

---

[1] Richard Cromwell (1626–1712), Lord Protector of England, Scotland and Ireland. See *ODNB*.

[2] Henry Downhall (d. 1669), fellow of St John's College, Cambridge, and vicar of Toft, Cambs.; later vicar of St Ives 1630–43 and archdeacon of Huntingdon 1667–9. Venn, 2:54; Matthews, *Walker Revised*, p. 79; Clergy of the Church of England database; John Morrill, 'The Making of Oliver Cromwell', in John Morrill, ed., *Oliver Cromwell and the English Revolution* (1990), pp. 19–48. 'Making', at p. 34.

[3] John Williams (1582–1650), archbishop of York. See *ODNB*.

[4] John Hacket, *Scrinia Reserata* (London, 1693), pt. 2, p. 212.

your Trouble is Thursday next.⁵ Let me intreate your company on Wednesday. By this tyme it appeares I am more apt to incroch upon you for new favours, then to shew my thankefullness for the love I have already found; but I know your patience, and your goodness cannot be exhausted by

Your Freind & servant
Oliver Cromwell

Hunt. this 14
October 1626

To his approved good Freind Mr. Henry Downhale,
att his Chamber in St. John's Colledge theise⁶
5 March 1659/60⁷

1629 02 11

Speech by Oliver Cromwell to the grand committee for religion of the House of Commons

Date: 11 February 1629
Sources: [A] TNA, SP 16/134, fo. 20, Diary of Edward Nicholas. Printed in Wallace Notestein and Francis Relf, eds., *Commons Debates for 1629* (Minneapolis, 1921), p.139. [some words are written in shorthand. They have here been expanded and shown in italics.] (reported speech). [B] Anonymous diary ('True Relation'), *The Diurnall Occurrences of every dayes proceeding in Parliament since the beginning thereof, being Tuesday the twentieth of January, which ended the tenth of March. Anno Dom. 1628* (1641), p. 40. Text collated with other known versions printed in *Commons Debates for 1629*, p. 59 (reported speech)

Cromwell was elected as an MP for the first time in 1628 when he sat for Huntingdon. During this Parliament he made just one recorded speech. It however provides one of the earliest indications as to his developing religious views. On 11 February 1629 the House of Commons sat as the grand committee for religion with John Pym, MP for Tavistock

---

⁵ 19 October 1626.
⁶ Evidently endorsement on the original. Not printed in black letter in copy text.
⁷ '59' written over '60'. The text printed by Hearne included the following annotation. 'I copied this (saith Mr. Ashmole) from the Originall, being then in the said Mr. Downhall's hands. The Child above mentioned was named Richard, who came to be Lord Protector 1658'. Ashmole was Elias Ashmole (1617–1692), astrologer and antiquary. See ODNB.

11 FEBRUARY 1629

(Devon),[1] in the chair. Christopher Sherland, MP for Northampton, a regular critic of Arminian clergymen,[2] reported from a subcommittee. In doing so, he made various allegations against the bishop of Winchester, Richard Neile.[3] That prompted Cromwell to speak up with an allegation of his own against Neile. Between 1614 and 1617 Neile had been bishop of Lincoln. During that time William Alabaster,[4] a clergyman who had converted from the Church of England to Roman Catholicism and back again, preached a sermon in London at St Paul's Cross. Thomas Beard,[5] warden of St John's Hospital, Huntingdon, had then, with the encouragement of Nicholas Felton, future bishop of Bristol and Ely, preached a sermon against Neile criticising him as a not-so-crypto-Papist. Whether Beard did so immediately following Alabaster or on some other occasion is not clear. For this, Beard was reprimanded by Neile, his local bishop. The point that Cromwell was therefore making was that Neile had suppressed justified criticisms of preaching that had been too overtly Catholic. Cromwell made it clear that his source for this information was Beard. That was someone Cromwell knew well because Beard, the master of the Huntingdon grammar school, was his old schoolteacher. Although not the most recent allegation against Neile, Cromwell's information seemed well-authenticated and so was a convenient addition to the list of misdeeds by Neile being compiled by the Commons to use against him. Neile's critics probably hoped to impeach him. For such purposes, any dirt supported by credible witnesses could be put to use.

[A] TNA, SP 16/134, fo. 20, Diary of Edward Nicholas. Printed in Wallace Notestein and Francis Relf, eds., *Commons Debates for 1629* (Minneapolis, 1921), p.139

Mr Cromwell saith that Dr Beard tould him that one Dr Allabaster did att *the* Spittle[6] preach \in/ a sermon tenets of popery & Beard being to repeate the same, the *now* Bpp of Winton (the Bpp of lincolne) did send *for* Dr Bearde & did charge him as being *his* diocessen not *to* preach any doctryne contrary to *that* which Allabaster had dl, & whn Dr Beard did *by the* advice of Bpp felton [7] preach agt Dr Allabasters sermon & person, Dr Neale thn Bpp *of* Winton did reprhend him *the* sd Beard for it.

---

[1] John Pym (1584–1643), politician. See *ODNB*.
[2] Christopher Sherland (1594–1632), lawyer and politician. See *ODNB*.
[3] Richard Neile (1562–1640), archbishop of York. See *ODNB*.
[4] William Alabaster (1568–1640), Church of England clergyman and writer. See *ODNB*.
[5] Thomas Beard (c.1568–1632), Church of England clergyman and author. See *ODNB*.
[6] The outdoor pulpit at St Mary Spital, Spitalfields, London. This and St Paul's Cross were the two major sites for outdoor preaching in London. But it would seem that Alabaster's sermon was delivered at St Paul's Cross.
[7] Nicholas Felton (1556–1626), bishop of Ely. See *ODNB*.

THE LETTERS, WRITINGS, AND SPEECHES OF OLIVER CROMWELL

[B] Anonymous diary ('True Relation'), *The Diurnall Occurrences of every dayes proceeding in Parliament since the beginning thereof, being Tuesday the twentieth of January, which ended the tenth of March. Anno Dom. 1628* (1641), p. 40

Master Cromwell saith, he had by relation from one Doctor Beard, that Beard said, that Doctor Alabaster had preached flat Popery at Pauls Crosse. The Bishop of Winchester commanded him, as he was his Diocessan, that he should preach nothing to the contrary.

Outcome: Pym reported back to the House from this committee. The Commons then ordered that the Speaker, Sir John Finch,[8] should write to Beard instructing him to come to London to testify against Neile. That letter was to be delivered to Beard via Cromwell.[9] The intermittent adjournments and then the dissolution on 10 March prevented the Commons pursuing this any further.

1631 04 01
Letter from Oliver Cromwell to [John Newdigate][1]

Date: 1 April 1631
Source: Warwickshire County RO, CR 136/B/3 (Newdegate of Arbury papers) (holograph)

This is a holograph letter and written by Cromwell after he had left Huntingdon and moved to St Ives. At first sight this seems no more than a routine letter between two country gentlemen about a stray hawk. One of Cromwell's neighbours had lost a hawk and, as it had a Cromwell name tag on it, John Newdigate had got in touch with Cromwell to say that the hawk had been found. But there are a few indirect clues in it about Cromwell's status in the early 1630s. The letter does not in itself confirm that Cromwell hunted with hawks. All it says is that someone else was using a hawk with his name tag. The most obvious explanation would be that the hawk had formerly belonged to Cromwell. The letter

---

[8] John Finch, Baron Finch of Fordwich (1584–1660), Speaker of the House of Commons and judge. See *ODNB*.
[9] *JHC*, 1:929.

[1] As the address is now missing, the identity of the recipient is uncertain. However, the endorsement in a seventeenth-century hand indicates that it had been sent to 'my uncle JN'. Anne Emily Newdigate-Newdegate, who published this letter for the first time, identified this later hand as that of Sir Richard Newdigate, 2nd Bt. (1644–1710). *Cavalier and Puritan in the Days of the Stuarts* (1901), pp. 5–6. The recipient can therefore be assumed to have been Sir Richard's uncle, John Newdigate of Arbury, Warws., MP for Liverpool in 1628. In 1631 he was mainly living at Ashtead, Surr. (John Newdigate [1600–42], gentleman and diarist. See *ODNB*.)

1 APRIL 1631

also reveals that Cromwell did not have a servant he could spare to travel to recover the hawk. There are hints here of the ambiguity of Cromwell's social position; he owned or had owned hawks, an undoubted mark of gentility, but employed only a limited number of male servants. Hawking may have been one pleasure which his reduced financial circumstances had forced him to give up. He is however known to have hunted with hawks later in life.[2] This letter is the only documented contact between Cromwell and the Newdigates.

Sir, I must with all thankfullnesse acknow=
ledge the curtesye you have intended me
in keepinge this hawke so longe to
your noe smale trouble, and although
I have noe intrest in her, yett if ever
it fall in my way, I shalbe ready to doe
you service, in the like, or any other kinde
I doe confesse I have neglected you in
that I have receaved 2 letters from
you with out sendinge you any answare
but I trust you \will/ passe by it and accept
of my true and reasonable excuse, this
poore man the owner of the hawke
whoe livinge in the same towne with
me made use of my varvells,[3] I did
daly expect to have soner returned
from his jorney then indeed he did
\which/ was the cause whie I protracted time
and deferred, to send unto you, untill I
might make him the messinger ⊢⊣
whoe was best able to give ~~an acc~~ \ac=/
count as alsoe fittest to ~~send~~ fetch her
I my selfe beinge utterly desti=
tute of a falconer att this present,
\and not havinge any man/ hom I durst venter to carrie a
hawke ⊢⊣ of that kinde soe farr.

---

[2] Patrick Little, 'Cromwell and falconry', *Cromwelliana*, series II, 5 (2008), pp. 70–2.

[3] Varvel: 'A metal ring (freq. of silver with the owner's name engraved on it) attached to the end of a hawk's jess and serving to connect this with the leash' (*OED*).

THE LETTERS, WRITINGS, AND SPEECHES OF OLIVER CROMWELL

This is all I can apologuise. I be=
seech you command me and I shall
rest
Your servant.
Oliver Cromwell.

Huntingto 10
Appr: 1631

my Cozen Cromwell of
Grayes Inn[4] was the
first that told me
of her

1636 01 11

Letter from Oliver Cromwell to [James] Storye

Date: 11 January 1636
Source: BL, Sloane MS 2035 B, fos 3–4v (holograph)

This letter is in Cromwell's own hand and bears his signature.

The future of clerical lectures was an important issue for Cromwell during the 1630s. Lectures were endowed sermons in a parish church. Their most obvious purpose was to provide additional preaching beyond the regular Sunday sermons offered by the parish priest. They also furnished modest financial support to able preachers without a parish of their own. To the godly, they were an effective means of encouraging more and better preaching. But they could also be a source of tension. Some, not least the parish priest himself, might see the lecturer as a rival. Rights of nomination could also be used to appoint men whom the local bishop might otherwise be disinclined to favour. Not everyone during the 1630s thought that more sermons were the best solution to the problems of the Church of England.

Conflict over the lectures at Huntingdon and the neighbouring parish of Godmanchester were the context for this letter. In about 1631 Cromwell had moved away from Huntingdon following disagreements over the provision of lectures. Richard Fishbourne, a wealthy London merchant who had been born in Huntingdon, had left a

---

[4] Presumably Cromwell's first cousin, Henry Cromwell (b. 1608), eldest son of Sir Philip Cromwell of Ramsey, Huntingdonshire. He had been admitted as a student at Gray's Inn on 26 May 1620. John Newdigate had likewise been admitted there just five weeks later, although he had subsequently transferred to the Inner Temple.

11 JANUARY 1636

charitable bequest of £2,000 to the town. Members of the town corporation, including Cromwell, then disagreed over whether some of that money should be used to endow a new lecture or merely used to fund the existing one. Fishbourne's own London livery company, the Mercers, strongly favoured the former. Cromwell almost certainly did so as well. Their preferred candidate as lecturer, Robert Proctor, was appointed only after an unsatisfactory deal had been agreed by which the rival candidate, Cromwell's old schoolmaster, Thomas Beard, had received financial compensation. Animosities over the issue became so bitter that the corporation was reformed with the grant of a new royal charter. One consequence of that was that Cromwell lost his position as a common councillor on the corporation.[1]

Five years later those quarrels still rankled with Cromwell and his fears for the future of those lectures had grown. He therefore initially thought of turning to one of his old allies in the Mercers' Company to encourage them to continue their support. The 'Mr Basse' to whom he had considered writing was Edward Basse,[2] who, as a prominent member of the company, had been involved in the dispute over the Fishbourne bequest.[3] The immediate concern now was the Godmanchester lecture, which is known to have been held by Dr Walter Welles, a Leiden graduate who had previously corresponded with Samuel Hartlib and John Dury.[4] It may be significant that by 1643 at the latest Basse is known to have been closely associated with Stephen Marshall,[5] the celebrated preacher and vicar of Finchingfield, Essex, who was originally from Godmanchester. [6]

But fearing that Basse would be too busy to respond, Cromwell instead wrote to 'Mr Storie'. Who he was has previously been rather uncertain. The favoured theory in recent decades has been that he was George Story.[7] He was the 'young merchant of London' who emigrated to Massachusetts Bay and who this same year became involved in the dispute between Robert Keayne and Elizabeth Sherman over the killing of a pig in Boston which led to a celebrated legal case.[8] But there is a much more plausible

---

[1] Morrill, 'Making', pp. 26–33; Ian Doolittle, *The Mercers' Company 1579–1959* (London, 1994), pp. 47–54.

[2] Edward Basse (d. 1665), mercer, of Cheapside, London. Supplier of lace to Charles I and Henrietta Maria. J. R. Woodhead, *The Rulers of London 1660–1689* (London, 1965), p. 25; W. J. Harvey ed. *List of the Principal Inhabitants of the City of London 1640* (1886, reprinted Bath, 1969), p. 14; TNA, SP 63/319, fo. 51.

[3] Morrill, 'Making', p. 40.   [4] Morrill, 'Making', pp. 38–40.

[5] Stephen Marshall (1594/5?–1655), Church of England clergyman. See *ODNB*.

[6] TNA, SP 28/8, fo. 199; SP 18/153, fo. 13.

[7] Morrill, 'Making', p. 40; Andrew Barclay, *Electing Cromwell* (2011), pp. 66, 67; Ian Gentles, *Oliver Cromwell: God's Warrior and the English Revolution* (2011), p. 86. Both Morrill and Barclay erroneously assumed that George Story was a member of the Mercers' Company. But no one called 'Storie' (or its variants) was a member of the Company in this period. https://www.londonroll.org/.

[8] Richard S. Dunn, James Savage and Laetitia Yeandle, eds., *The Journal of John Winthrop 1630–1649* (Cambridge, Mass. and London, 1996), pp. 395–8, 451–4 (quote at p. 396); *Records and Files of the Quarterly Courts of Essex County, Massachusetts* (Salem, Mass. 1911–75), 1:28; John Noble, ed., *Records of the Court of Assistants of the Colony of Massachusetts Bay 1630–1692* (Boston, Mass. 1901–28), 2:117, 119.

candidate.[9] James Storye (1588–1660) was a London haberdasher.[10] He lived in St Benet Fink, the parish immediately to the north-east of the Royal Exchange.[11] In 1640 he would be described as an 'exchanceman', that is an 'exchange-man', probably implying that he traded from the Exchange.[12] It therefore makes sense that Cromwell should have addressed this letter to him there. But equally telling is that he was originally from St Ives, the Huntingdonshire town where Cromwell had lived since leaving Huntingdon.[13] Storye had been baptised at St Ives on 27 December 1588 and his father, Walter Storye (d. 1639), a tailor, still lived there. Until as recently as 1634, when he had transferred his lease to his younger brother, James had also been a tenant of one of the local manors.[14] St Ives was only about five miles from Huntingdon and Godmanchester. When Cromwell spoke of 'our cuntrie men' and 'our cuntrie', he was explicitly appealing to their shared local loyalties. Storye is also known to have had dealings with one of Cromwell's less obvious relatives. Edward Lynne (1570–1655) was the younger brother of William Lynne (d. 1589), who had been the first husband of Cromwell's mother. On being appointed as the rector of Abington Pigotts in Cambridgeshire in 1633, Edward Lynne had borrowed money from Storye and Storye's son-in-law, Thomas Starkey, to pay his first fruits.[15] James Storye later became one of the trustees for the sale of bishops' lands.[16]

To my very lovinge freind
Mr. Storie, att the Signe

[9] A third candidate ought to be noted. Robert Story (d. 1652), a linen draper, was a near neighbour of Basse in the parish of St Mary Magdalen Milk Street. He was originally from Chesterton, Cambridgeshire. A. W. Hughes Clarke, ed., *The Registers of St Mary Magdalen Milk Street 1558–1666 and St Michael Bassishaw London 1538–1625* (Harleian Society, 72, 1942), pp. 28–32, 46–8, 50, 54; T. C. Dale, ed., *The Inhabitants of London in 1638* (1931), p. 137; W. J. Harvey, ed., *List of the Principal Inhabitants of the City of London 1640* (1886, reprinted Bath, 1969), p. 14; TNA, PROB 11/233/37, will of Robert Story, 20 Sept. 1652; Joseph Jackson Howard and Joseph Lemuel Chester, eds., *The Visitation of London, Anno Domini 1633, 1634 and 1635* (Harleian Society, 15, 17, 1880–3), 2:268; John Bedells, ed., *The Visitation of the County of Huntingdon 1684* (Harleian Society, n.s., replacement volume 13, 2000), p. 114.

[10] TNA, PROB 11/302/147, will of James Storye, 18 Oct. 1660. He had been a freeman of the Haberdashers' Company since 1611. London Metropolitan Archives, CLC/L/HA/C/007/MS15857/001, fos 163v, 191v, 215v, 239.

[11] Dale, ed., *Inhabitants of London in 1638*, p. 39. He had been living there since at least 1614, when his daughter, Elizabeth, had been baptised. London Metropolitan Archives, St Benet Fink parish register 1538–1720, fos 12, 54.

[12] Harvey, ed., *List of the Principal Inhabitants*, p. 5; See also 'Exchange', definition 10a in *OED*.

[13] Howard and Chester, eds., *Visitation of London*, 2:268; Huntingdonshire Archives, Huntingdon, HP72/1/1/1, St Ives All Saints parish register, 1561–1653; AH16/1639/109, will of Walter Storye, 1 May 1639. Walter Storye was one of the brothers of Robert Storey of Chesterton and thus the uncle of Robert Story of St Mary Magdalen Milk Street. TNA, PROB 11/164/562, will of Robert Storey, 22 Mar. 1632.

[14] Huntingdonshire Archives, KHMR/17/1, manor of St Ives court book, 1632–61, fo. 29v.

[15] William Graham F. Pigott ed. *The Parish Registers of Ablington Pigotts* (Norwich, 1890), pp. 144–5.

[16] *A&O*, 1:880–1. Based solely on this appointment, Thomas Carlyle guessed that James Storye might be the recipient of this letter. Carlyle-Lomas, 1:80.

11 JANUARY 1636

of the dogg in the
Royall exchange[17] London
dlr. theise

[fo. 3r]
Mr. Storie amongst the Catalogue of those good
workes which your fellowe cityzenes and our
cuntrie men have donn, this will not be ~~recon~~
reckoned for the least that ~~you~~ \they have/ provided for
the ~~the~~ feedinge of Soules: Buildinge of hospi
talls provides for mens bodyes, \to/ build ~~of~~ ma=
teriall temples is judged a worke of pietye
but they that procure [-] Spirituall food, they that
builde up Spirituall temples,[18] they are the
men truly ~~and~~ charitable, trulye pious. Such
a worke as this was your erectinge the lec
ture in our cuntrie ~~over~~ \in/ the which you
placed Dr wellss[19] a man for goodnesse and industrie
and abilitie to doe good every way: not short
of any I knowe in England, and I am perswa
ded that Sithence his cominge the Lord by him
hath wrought much good amongst us. It only
remaines now that he whoe first moved you
to this, put you forward to the continewance
therof, it was the Lord, and therfore to him
lift we up our harts[20] that he would perfect itt
And surely mr. Storie it were a piteous thinge
to See a lecture fall in the hands off soe
manie able and godly men as I am per=
swaded the founders of this are, in theise

---

[17] The Royal Exchange was the market founded by Sir Thomas Gresham at Cornhill in the City and opened in 1570. A petition submitted to the Lord Mayor's Court in 1682 made reference to 'the Dog Tavern on the back side of the Exchange', although any building from 1636 would not have survived the Great Fire. Michael Scott, ed., *Apprenticeship Disputes in the Lord Mayor's Court of London 1573–1723* (British Record Society, cxxxii–cxxxiii, 2016), 1:368. The 'dogg' was more probably just Storye's shop sign in the Exchange.

[18] 1 Peter 2:5.   [19] As written, but surely 'Welles' was intended.

[20] Lamentations 3:41.

times wherin wee see they are Suppressed with
too much hast, and violence by the enemies
of God his truth, farr be it that soe much
guilt should sticke to your hands whoe
live in a citye soe renowned for the clere
shininge light of the Gospell. You knowe mr.
Storie, to withdrawe the pay is to \lett/ fall ~~downe~~ \the/
lecture, for whoe goeth to war fare att his
owne cost.[21] I beseech you therfore in the bowells
of christ Jesus,[22] putt it forward, and lett the good man have his pay.
the soules of god his children will blesse you for it: And soe shall I
and ever rest
Your lovinge freind in the Lord
Oliver Cromwell.

commend my harty love to mr. Basse, mr. Bradly,[23] and
my other good freinds, I would have written to mr.
Basse, but I was loath to trouble him with a longe
letter, and I feared I should not receave an answere
from him, from you I expect one, soe soone as
conveniently you may. vale.[24] St Ives[25] 11th. of Jan. 1635

---

[21] 1 Corinthians 9:7.   [22] Philippians 1:8.

[23] John Bradley (*fl.* 1626–1665), haberdasher, of London. Uncle of Edward Basse (TNA, PROB 11/316/613). Importer of tobacco from Virginia. Captain in the London trained bands by 1639. Strong supporter of Parliament in the City during the early 1640s. Later a captain in the army of the earl of Essex. Robert Brenner, *Merchants and Revolution* (Cambridge, 1993), pp. 183n, 338, 343, 435; Valerie Pearl, *London and the Outbreak of the Puritan Revolution* (Oxford, 1961), p. 120; Ian W. Archer, *The History of the Haberdashers' Company* (Chichester, 1991), p. 152; Keith Lindley, *Popular Politics and Religion in Civil War London* (Aldershot, 1997), pp. 20, 32–3, 172–3, 222; the *Online Directory Parliamentarian Army Officers*, available on British History Online at https://www.british-history.ac.uk/no-series/cromwell-army-officers.

[24] *Vale* = Latin for 'farewell' (*OED*).

[25] St Ives, Huntingdonshire, where Cromwell had been living as a working farmer since 1631.

1638 09 13

Letter from Oliver Cromwell to John Hand[1]

Date: 13 September 1638

Source: Oliver Cromwell, *Memoirs of the Protector, Oliver Cromwell* (1820), p. 230 (later transcription)

Following the death of his uncle, Sir Thomas Steward, in 1636, Cromwell succeeded him as the largest tenant of the dean and chapter of Ely Cathedral. He was now the most significant lay resident of Ely. That new status was recognised with his appointment in August 1636 as one of the feoffees of Parsons Charity. Ely had no borough corporation, so Parsons Charity, which dated from the fifteenth century, was the city's principal secular public body. It had been granted a royal charter as recently as 1634 as part of a redefinition of its role to enable it to build a workhouse. This letter, written to the Charity's treasurer, presumably concerns a payment to be made by the feoffees for medical assistance to an Ely inhabitant. The patient for whom the payment was being made was William Benson. The feoffees had made two earlier payments totalling £3 2s 4d to assist him.[2]

Cromwell's descendant, Oliver Cromwell,[3] printed this letter from the records of Parsons Charity in 1820. This letter was however among a number of documents that had already gone missing from the Charity's archives when C. H. Cooper drew the attention of Thomas Carlyle to those archives in 1846. Those documents remain missing from the Charity's archives, which are now on loan to the Ely Museum.

Mr Hand;

I doubt not but I shall be as good as my word for your monie. I desier you to deliver 40s. of the town monie to this bearer, to pay for the phisicke for Benson's cure. If the gentlemen will not allow it at the tyme of account, keep this noat, and I will pay it out of my own purse. Soe I rest

Your lovinge friend,

Oliver Cromwell.

Sept. 13. 1638.

---

[1] John Hand, prominent Ely resident and treasurer of Parsons Charity. In 1636 he had witnessed the will of Cromwell's uncle, Sir Thomas Steward, and in 1640 and 1641 he became the tenant of some of the lands formerly leased to Cromwell by the dean and chapter of Ely Cathedral. Barclay, *Electing Cromwell*, pp. 100, 102, 106.

[2] Reg Holmes, *Cromwell's Ely* (Ely 1975, 1982), p. 15.

[3] Oliver Cromwell (c.1742–1821), biographer and lawyer. See ODNB.

THE LETTERS, WRITINGS, AND SPEECHES OF OLIVER CROMWELL

1638 10 13
Letter from Oliver Cromwell to Mrs St John

Date: 13 October 1638
Source: Bodl. MS Rawl. A 1, pp. 1–4 (holograph)

Much has been made of this letter by Cromwell's biographers since it first appeared in print in 1742. More than any of the earlier letters, it seems to give some real sense of his personality. Written in his own hand, Cromwell describes at length how he had overcome past doubts to find a strong religious faith. This he does mostly by quoting, adapting and imitating passages from the Bible, thus anticipating the style of so many of his later letters and speeches. He is already recognisably the man who would over the next two decades assert his faith in the public realm and who would do so as much by words as by the sword.

The identity of the recipient has caused much confusion. The easy step is to realise that she must have been the wife of Cromwell's cousin, Oliver St John.[1] The previous year St John had acted as counsel for another of their cousins, John Hampden,[2] in the famous Exchequer Chamber case on the legality of the ship money writs. But was Cromwell writing to St John's first or second wife? Both women were related to Cromwell. St John's first wife, Joanna Altham, daughter of Sir James Altham, was a cousin once removed to both St John and Cromwell, being a granddaughter of their aunt, Joan, Lady Barrington.[3] She was also the stepdaughter of Sir William Masham,[4] to whose house this letter was addressed. St John's second wife, Elizabeth Cromwell, was another of their cousins, being the daughter of their late uncle, Henry Cromwell of Upwood, Huntingdonshire.[5] She was thus also Lady Barrington's niece. Aged just thirteen when her father died in 1630, Elizabeth had probably then been brought up by Cromwell's sister, Margaret, and her husband, Valentine Walton.[6] Everything therefore depends on when the first Mrs St John died and when the second married. That second marriage is recorded in the High Laver parish register. Unfortunately, the date of the entry can be read as either 'Jan 21 1638' (that is, 21 January 1639) or 'Jun 21 1638'.[7] A draft of the marriage settlement survives, but unhelpfully

---

[1] Oliver St John (1598–1673), lawyer and politician. See *ODNB*.

[2] John Hampden (1595–1643), politician. See *ODNB*.

[3] Joan Barrington, [née Williams or Cromwell] Lady Barrington (*c.*1558–1641], noblewoman. See *ODNB*. She was a formidable godly matriarch, patron of clergy and arranger of marriages for her large extended family.

[4] Sir William Masham (1591–1656), MP for Maldon (Essex) 1624, 1625 and 1626, for Colchester in 1628 and the Short Parliament and for Essex in the Long Parliament and 1654. His wife, Elizabeth Barrington, was one of Cromwell's first cousins.

[5] Mark Noble, *Memoirs of the Protectoral House of Cromwell* (2 vols., 1787), 1:29–30.

[6] Valentine Walton (1593–1661), parliamentarian army officer and regicide. See *ODNB*. The lands left by Henry Cromwell to his two daughters, Elizabeth and her younger sister, Anna, were administered for them by Walton. BL, Add. Ch. 53667–53668.

[7] Essex Record Office, D/P 111/1/1, High Laver parish register, 1593–1812.

13 OCTOBER 1638

the day and the month are left blank, with only the regnal year, 14 Chas. I (27 March 1638–26 March 1639), being given.[8] Consistent with the second marriage taking place on 21 June 1638 would be for the first wife to have been the 'Mrs St John wife of Mr Oliver St John' who had been buried at Romford, Essex, on 31 December 1636.[9] On balance, it seems slightly more likely that Cromwell was writing to the second Mrs St John four months after her marriage.

The first marriage may nevertheless provide the letter's immediate context. One of St John's sons, Oliver, had been buried at High Laver on 18 September 1638, less than four weeks before Cromwell was writing.[10] This was probably the boy who had been baptised at Romford on 4 December 1636.[11] Indeed, if his mother was the woman buried there four weeks later, she could well have died of postnatal complications. One might also wonder whether Cromwell had been his godfather. Although the name Oliver was common in the St John family, the boy could have been named after him. That would then alter how one reads the letter. It is obviously one of consolation. But the death possibly meant more to Cromwell than it did to the new Mrs St John, who would thus have been young Oliver's stepmother for only a few months. The tone of the letter otherwise reads rather oddly. At no point does it directly acknowledge any loss suffered by Mrs St John. Its main theme is instead Cromwell's own faith and his confidence that God had forgiven him for his past sins. It is, in the end, mostly about himself, which is, of course, why it is so fascinating.

One indication of the letter's importance is that Cromwell seems to have made an effort to write it as neatly as possible. The letter survives among the papers of John Thurloe,[12] who in 1638 was employed by St John as one of his clerks. Few knew Cromwell as well as Thurloe or had handled more letters by him. That he preserved it could suggest that Thurloe considered this letter to be of special significance.

––––––

[p. 4]
to my beloved Cozen mrs
St Johns att Sir William
Masham his house called
Oates[13] in Essex present
theise.

[8] Huntingdon Library and Archives, DDMB 6/1.
[9] Essex Record Office, D/P 346/1/2, Romford parish register, 1610–1732.
[10] Essex Record Office, D/P 111/1/1.
[11] Essex Record Office, D/P 346/1/2.
[12] John Thurloe (1616–68), government official. See *ODNB*. Oliver Cromwell's secretary of state during the Protectorate.
[13] Otes at High Laver, Essex. Oliver St John was steward of the manor of Otes.

[p. 1]

Deere Cozen,

I thankfully acknowledge your love in your kind remembrance of mee upon this oportunitye, alas you doe too highlye prize my lines, and my companie, I may bee ashamed to owne your expressions, consideringe how unproffitable I am, and the ~~little~~ \meane/ improvement of my tallent. Yett to honour my God, by declaringe what Hee hath done for my soule, In this I am confident,[14] and I will bee soe, ⊢trulye then this I finde, that Hee giveth Springes in a drye and barren wildernesse, where noe water is.[15] I live (you knowe where) in mesheck which they say signifies prolonginge, in Kedar which signifieth blacknesse,[16] yett the Lord forsaketh mee not. though Hee doe prolonge, yett Hee will (I trust) bringe mee to his Tabernacle, to his restinge place, my soule is with the congregation of the first borne,[17] my body rests in hope,[18] and if heere I may honour my God either by doeinge, or Sufferinge I shalbe most glad. Truly noe poore cre= ature hath more cause to putt forth himselfe in the cause of his god then I I have had \plentifull/ wadges before hand, And I am suer I shall never earn the least mite. the Lord accept mee in his Sonn, and give mee to walke in the light, and give us to walke in the light, as hee is in the light.[19] Hee it is that inlightneth our blacknesse, our darknesse,[20] I dare not say hee hydeth his face from mee,[21] he giveth mee to see light in his light, one beame in a darke place hath exceedinge much refreshment in it, blessed bee his name for shininge over soe darke a hart as mine, you knowe what my manner of life hath bene, O I lived in, and loved darknesse, and hated the light,[22] I was a cheife, the cheife of sinners,[23] this is true, I hated godlinesse yett God had mercy onn mee, O the riches of his mercy. praise him for mee. pray for mee that Hee whoe hath begunn a good worke would perfect it to the day of christ.[24] Salute all my good freinds in that family wherof you are yett a member, I am much bound unto them for ther love. I blesse the Lord for them, and that my Sonn by there procurement is soe well,[25] lett him have your prayers, your councell, lett mee have them. Salute your husband

---

[14] Psalm 27:3. [15] Psalm 63:1.

[16] Psalm 120:5. Meshech had been the son of Japheth, so Psalm 120 was referring to the city or territory occupied by his descendants. That location has often been thought to have been in Cappadocia. Kedar referred to the descendants of Kedar, a son of Ishmael. They had settled in Arabia. The Psalmist used them as figurative examples of remote, forbidding locations.

[17] = the firstborn of the Father, Jesus Christ. See Hebrews 12:23. [18] Psalm 16:9.

[19] John 1:7–9. [20] 2 Samuel 22:29; John 1:5. [21] Psalm 10:11.

[22] John 3:19. [23] 1 Timothy 1:15. [24] Philippians 1:6.

[25] High Laver was about ten miles from Felsted, Essex, where Cromwell's sons attended school.

14 MAY 1640

and Sister from mee, hee is not a man of his word, hee promised to
write about Mr. Wrath of Epinge[26] but he as yett I receaved noe letters.
putt him in minde to doe what with conveniency may bee donn for
the, poore cozen, I did sollicit him about. Once more fare=well the
Lord bee with you. soe prayeth
Your truly lovinge Cozen
Oliver Cromwell
Ely. 13th. of
Octobr. 1638
my wives service and
love presented to all her
freinds

1640 05 14
Certificate from Oliver Cromwell

Date: 14 May 1640
Source: TNA, SP16/453 fo. 74 (holograph)

This certificate was hand-written by Cromwell and bears his signature.

Some of English equity law courts, such as Chancery and Exchequer, received evidence
from witnesses only in writing. Arrangements therefore had to be made for written
depositions to be taken from those witnesses unable to travel to Westminster. The usual
procedure was for a commission of local gentlemen to be appointed by the court to
receive evidence under oath at a location convenient for the witnesses. Those depositions
were then sealed and forwarded to London. Alternatively, the commissioners could sometimes be given powers to resolve the dispute without referring it back to the court. From
the present document, it would appear that Cromwell served as such a commissioner in
the autumn of 1639 in a case involving members of the Kirby family. The men chosen to
act as commissioners were often justices of the peace. That was true of Cromwell by this
date, although only for the Isle of Ely rather than Huntingdonshire. The Kirbys were from

---

[26] Schoolmaster at Epping, Essex. Two students admitted to Cambridge University almost a
decade later are known to have attended school at Epping under a 'Mr Wroth'. They were
Thomas Smithsby, later a fellow of All Souls, Oxford, who matriculated at St John's, Cambridge
in about 1646, and John Stapleton (son of Sir Philip Stapleton (1603–47), the recently deceased
MP for Boroughbridge, Yorkshire), who was admitted at Christ's, Cambridge in 1647. Venn,
4:115; John Peile, *Biographical Register of Christ's College, 1505–1905* (Cambridge, 1910–13), 1:516.
Epping was about six miles to the south-west of the Mashams' house at High Laver. Even more
suggestively, the Wroths of Durants lived at Enfield, Middlesex, about nine miles from Epping
in the opposite direction. But none of them can plausibly be identified with the schoolmaster.

Upton, which was just six miles from Huntingdon, which helps explain why Cromwell was appointed as a commissioner. However, for reasons unknown, the hearings had been held at Oundle across the county border in Northamptonshire. No record of this case has so far come to light in the records of either Chancery or the Exchequer. Cromwell may well have attended to this question from William Kirby on his return from London, where he had been sitting as MP for Cambridge in the Short Parliament.

What little is known about the Kirbys of Upton suggests that they were of borderline gentry status. In 1607 Thomas Kirby of Upton, conceivably the father mentioned in this document, had been considered for appointment as an escheator for Cambridgeshire and Huntingdonshire, but at the heraldic visitation of Huntingdonshire held six years later he was found to be using the title of 'gentleman' without justification.[1] In 1629 a man of that name and claiming the rank of gentleman joined with Richard Packerell and Richard Godrey to acquire lands at Ramsey, Huntingdonshire from Cromwell's uncle, Sir Oliver Cromwell.[2] So it would seem that they were among those able to take advantage of the growing financial difficulties of the senior line of the Cromwell family.

May the 14th 1640.
Beinge ~~demanded~~ \desired/ by william Kirbye of Upton
in the Countye of Huntington gent. to certi=
fie my knowledge of what passed att the spee=
dinge of a Commission betweene Thomas Kirbye
the Father, and Thomas Kirbye the Sonn
sate upon att Oundel in the Countye
of Northampton about michelmas last past
I beinge one amongst \and with/ others authorised
to execute the same, I doe heereby testi
fie, and affirme. that by the and with the
consent of both the said parties, and
upon a full, and final, agreement then
had, and made, betweene the said Father
and Sonn, of the matters then in diffe
rence. to the searchinge out the truth
of which the said commission tended, It was
then and there agreed, and consented unto

---

[1] *HMC Sackville*, 1:320; John Bedells, ed., *The Visitation of the County of Huntingdon 1684* (Harleian Society, n.s., replacement volume 13, 2000), p. 126.

[2] Jan Broadway, Richard Cust and Stephen K. Roberts, eds., *A Calendar of the Docquets of Lord Keeper Coventry 1625–1640* (List and Index Society, special series, xxxiv–xxxviii, 2004), 3:595.

by both the said parties, that farther
~~examination~~ \execution of the said commission/, and returne of depositions should cease, and that the same should be
suppressed {} which accordingly was donn. And
that this was soe and is true I doe by theise
presents testifie under my hand

Oliver Cromwell

1640 12 30

Speech by Oliver Cromwell to the House of Commons

Date: 30 December 1640
Source: BL, Harl. MS 162, fo. 103, Diary of Sir Simonds D'Ewes. Printed in *Procs. LP*, 2: 63–4 (reported speech)

On 24 December William Strode,[1] MP for Bere Alston (Devon), introduced a bill for annual Parliaments. This was one possible constitutional reform often suggested in this period. Those proposing it usually saw this as a revival of the lapsed legislation on the subject dating back to the reign of Edward III (4 Edw. III, c. 14 and 36 Edw. III c. 10). Cromwell now moved that Strode's bill should receive a second reading.

Then Mr Cromwell moved that the bill touching the holding of a Parliament everie yeare, whether the King sends out his writt or not wch Mr Stroud preferred might bee read the second time & soe it was.

Outcome: There followed a long debate on the subject, after which the Commons agreed to send it to committee stage. Cromwell was included on that committee.[2] This bill was subsequently amended to extend the maximum interval between Parliament to three years and in that form was passed into law as the 1641 Triennial Act (16 Car. I c. 1).

---

[1] William Strode (bap. 1594, d. 1645), politician. See ODNB.   [2] JHC, 2:60.

1641 02 09

Speeches of Oliver Cromwell to the House of Commons

Date: 9 February 1641

Source: BL, Harl. MS 162, fos 209–210, Diary of Sir Simonds D'Ewes. Printed in Maija Jansson, ed., *Proceedings in the Opening Session of the Long Parliament: the House of Commons* (7 vols., Rochester NY and Woodbridge, 2007), 2:398–9 (reported speech)

On 11 December 1640 the Commons had received the London petition calling for the abolition of episcopacy (the 'Root and Branch petition'). A remonstrance from clergymen throughout England had also been presented to the House on 23 January 1641. Now on 9 February Isaac Penington,[1] MP for London, spoke in the Commons in defence of the London petition. Some MPs supported him and called for a vote on the future of the bishops. However, Sir John Strangways,[2] MP for Weymouth and Melcombe Regis (Dorset), objected, implying that the abolition of the bishops would be a step towards social equality.

Mr Cromwell stood upp next & saied Hee knew noe reason of those suppositions & inferences wch the gentleman had made that last spake upon this divers interrupted him & called him to the barre.

Outcome: Others, including D'Ewes, spoke at length.

Soe after I had spoaken Mr Cromwell went on & saied he did not understand why the gentleman that last spake should make an inference of paritie from the Church to the Commonwealth: nor that ther was anie necessitie of the great revennues of Bpps Hee was moore convinced touching the irregularitie of Bpps then ever before, because like the Romane Hierarchie, they would not endure to have ther condition come to a triall.

Outcome: Some MPs evidently supported Cromwell as they tried to move that any MP who called for another MP to be called to the bar without good reason should be fined.[3] Penington's wish that the Commons should act on the London petition was successful. That petition and the clergymen's remonstrance were referred to the committee of twenty-four on the state of the kingdom.[4]

[1] Isaac Penington (c.1584–1661), local politician and regicide. See ODNB.
[2] Sir John Strangways (1584–1666), politician. See ODNB.
[3] JHC, 2:81.   [4] JHC, 2:81.

1641 04 10

Speech by Oliver Cromwell to the House of Commons

Date: 10 April 1641

Source: [A] BL, Harl. MS 164, fo. 162, Diary of Sir Simonds D'Ewes. Printed in *Procs. LP*, 3:496 (reported speech). [B] BL, Harl. MS 1601, fo. 55, Anonymous diary. Printed in *Procs. LP*, 3:500 (reported speech)

Several statutes, including, most recently, a 1625 law on the subject (1 Car. 1 c. 1), forbade many activities on Sundays. Cromwell now sought to have those laws enforced in London.

[A] BL, Harl. MS 164, fo. 162, Diary of Sir Simon D'Ewes. Printed in *Procs. LP*, 3:496 (reported speech)

Mr Cromwells motion. Divers spake to it. about Ls day how it was profaned heere in London by \sportes &/ gaming and by selling of severall commodities.

[B] BL, Harl. MS 1601, fo. 55, Anonymous diary. Printed in *Procs. LP*, 3:500 (reported speech)

Mr Crom[1] a good law all ready for the better keepinge of the Lord day this uppon the Continnuance of the Statute to be inlarged ordered that the Aldermen and Citizen of this house shall give intemation to the Ld maior that the statute made for the better keepinge of the Lords day be put in operation

---

Outcome: The Commons ordered that the London MPs were to tell the lord mayor that the existing statutes were to be enforced. Similar instructions were to be issued to the justices of the peace throughout England and Wales.[2]

---

[1] That this word reads 'Crom' is not at all certain.   [2] *JHC*, 2:118.

THE LETTERS, WRITINGS, AND SPEECHES OF OLIVER CROMWELL

1641 04 21

Speech by Oliver Cromwell to the House of Commons

Date: 21 April 1641
Source: BL, Harl. MS 164, fo. 182, Diary of Sir Simonds D'Ewes. Printed in *Procs. LP*, 4:39 (reported speech)

The Commons now returned to the case of Alexander Leighton which they had referred to a committee on 9 November. That was the same committee to which Cromwell had got John Lilburne's case referred and to which he had then been added. Francis Rous,[1] MP for Truro (Cornwall), informed the Commons of the committee's recommendations. Those recommendations were that the punishments inflicted on Leighton had been illegal and that he should be granted compensation for his sufferings. Cromwell then spoke to reinforce Rous's comments.

———

Mr Cromwell spake to shew the crueltie

———

Outcome: The Commons accepted the committee's recommendations.[2]

———⊗⊗⊗———

1641 04 30[?]

Letter from Oliver Cromwell to George Willingham[1]

Date: n.d. [late April or early May 1641]
Source: BL, Sloane MS 2035B, fos 5–5v (holograph)

This holograph letter was sent to George Willingham (d. 1651), a painter-stainer, of St Swithin's parish in the City of London.

The King had agreed an interim truce with the Scots, whose army was occupying the north of England, in October 1640, shortly before the Long Parliament had assembled. But the Scots and the new English Parliament wanted a more permanent settlement and so had entered into negotiations for an Anglo-Scottish treaty. The immediate concern for many English MPs was to reach an agreement that would bring about the withdrawal of the Scottish army. Both sides were however also keen that the treaty address the major

---

[1] Francis Rous (1580/1–1659), religious writer and politician. See *ODNB*.
[2] *JHC*, 2:124.

———

[1] Edward Town, 'A biographical dictionary of London painters, 1547–1625', *Walpole Society*, 76 (2014), p. 191.

30 APRIL 1641[?]

constitutional issues between the two kingdoms. In particular, those in England and Scotland who wanted a church settlement in England more akin to that in Scotland saw this as an opportunity to seek common religious uniformity on both sides of the border.

The two sets of commissioners appointed to conduct the negotiations had made sufficient progress that provisional agreement on the first seven of the Scots' demands had been reached by early February 1641. The Scottish commissioners had however been vague about what their eighth article would contain. This was so that the more controversial issues could be dealt with only during the later stages of the negotiations. Indeed, the Scots themselves disagreed about exactly what they should propose. The result was that peers and MPs at Westminster discovered the contents of this eighth article only on 14 April. Reporting on behalf of the English commissioners, the first earl of Bristol[2] was then able to give the House of Lords a rough outline of what the Scots intended to include. Prominent among those demands was that there should be uniformity of religion between the two kingdoms. A conference between the two Houses took place the following day so that Bristol could repeat this information to MPs.[3] The Commons however did not rush its response. MPs did not formally debate the subject until 15 May and the resolution they finally agreed two days later confined itself to the rather lukewarm statement that 'this House doth approve of the Affection of their Brethren of Scotland in their Desire of a Conformity, in Church Government between the Two Nations'.[4] The likelihood is therefore that Cromwell wrote this letter at some point between 15 April and 15 May in the expectation that the Commons would soon debate this issue. If however he was seeking information from Willingham with the intention of taking part in those debates, he may not in the end have done so; none of the parliamentary diarists mentions him as speaking during the debates on either 15 May or 17 May. The negotiations with the Scots were not completed until the following August. Cromwell certainly spoke in the Commons on this subject at that point.

George Willingham is best known as the recipient of letters written by his servant, Nehemiah Wharton,[5] while serving in the army of the earl of Essex in 1642.[6] But other aspects of his career are equally well-documented. He was a member of the Painter-Stainers' Company, was its upper warden in 1641 and would serve as its master in 1644–5.[7] In 1640 he was described as a gilder.[8] Many letters from his brother-in-law and agent,

---

[2] John Digby, first earl of Bristol (1580–1653), diplomat and politician. See *ODNB*.

[3] *JHL*, 4:216, 217, 218; *JHC*, 2:120, 121.

[4] *Procs. LP*, 4:395–6, 399, 400, 401, 416–17, 418, 421; *JHC*, 2:148; Peter Donald, *An Uncounselled King* (Cambridge, 1990), pp. 301–2.

[5] Nehemiah Wharton (*fl.* 1641–9), parliamentarian soldier and letter writer. See *ODNB*.

[6] H. Ellis, ed., 'Letters of a subaltern officer', *Archaeologica*, 35 (1853), pp. 310–34.

[7] W. A. D. Englefield, *The History of the Painter-Stainers Company of London* (London, 1923), pp. 110–12; Alan Borg, *The History of the Worshipful Company of Painters otherwise Painter-Stainers* (Huddersfield, 2005), pp. 50, 210; Edward Town, 'A biographical dictionary of London painters, 1547–1625', *Walpole Society*, 76 (2014), p. 191.

[8] W. J. Harvey, ed., *List of the Principal Inhabitants of the City of London 1640* (1886, reprinted Bath, 1969), p. 18.

THE LETTERS, WRITINGS, AND SPEECHES OF OLIVER CROMWELL

Prestwick Eaton, from San Sebastián in Spain reporting on his trading activities between 1631 and 1642 survive among the State Papers. There is also good reason to link Willingham to the London godly. That he was a friend and neighbour of Thomas Hewson, John Lilburne's former master, has already been mentioned. Moreover, when two of the leading victims of the activities of the court of high commission, Henry Burton[9] and William Prynne,[10] were released from prison in November 1640, Burton made his hero's entry into London in Willingham's coach.[11] Later, as a member of the London sequestration committee, Willingham would also have friendly dealings with John Bastwick,[12] as well as with Burton and Prynne.[13]

Willingham's friendship with Hewson may explain why Cromwell assumed that he would be well-informed about Scottish affairs. Hewson's son-in-law, Daniel Butler, who lived on Cannon Street at the corner with St Swithin's Lane, had visited Scotland on business in November 1638. Some months later his contact in Edinburgh, William Symontoun, had sent him some clandestine letters and a Scottish prayer book. Those were then seized by government officials in a raid on Butler's house in February 1639.[14] That two years later Cromwell was writing to Willingham for information about the Scots is consistent with the impression that Willingham was a man with particularly extensive commercial, religious and political contacts.

[fo. 5v]

[address]

To his lovinge Freind

Mr Willingham att his house

in ~~Wood streete~~ Swithins lane[15]

[fo. 5r]

Sir I desier you to send mee the

Resons of the Scotts to inforce

---

[9] Henry Burton (bap. 1578, d. 1647/8), Independent minister and religious controversialist. See *ODNB*.

[10] William Prynne (1600–69), pamphleteer and lawyer. See *ODNB*.

[11] Henry Burton, *A Narration of the Life of Mr. Henry Burton* (1643), p. 4: (Thomason / E.94[10]).

[12] John Bastwick (1593–1654), religious controversialist and pamphleteer. See *ODNB*.

[13] BL, Sloane MS 2035B, fos 9r–12r; Keith Lindley, *Popular Politics and Religion in Civil War London* (Aldershot, 1997), p. 331.

[14] TNA, SP 16/409, fo. 333; SP 16/412, fos 215–217; SP 16/413, fos 101, 239–239v; 241; SP 16/414, fo. 123; SP 16/417, fo. 101.

[15] St Swithin's Lane was a street in the City running between Lombard Street and Cannon Street. Wood Street, which Cromwell originally put as the address, lay about quarter of a mile to the west. Willingham had lived in the parish of St Swithin London Stone since the mid-1620s and his business was based at the Sign of the Golden Anchor on St Swithin's Lane. Town, 'Biographical dictionary', p. 191.

3 MAY 1641

ther desier of uniformity in Religion
expressed in ther 8 Article,[16] I meane
that which I had before of you,
I would peruse itt against wee
fall upon that debate which wilbe
Speedily.
yours Ol: Cromwell

1641 05 03

Speech by Oliver Cromwell to the House of Commons

Date: 3 May 1641
Source: BL, Harl. MS 477, fo. 28, Diary of John Moore. Printed in *Procs. LP*, 4:181 (reported speech)

Proceedings in Parliament during the spring of 1641 were dominated by the impeachment and attainder of the former Lord Deputy of Ireland, the first earl of Strafford.[1] Fears that the King's supporters planned to save Strafford by organising a military coup seemed to be justified by the discovery of the First Army Plot.[2] Moreover, on 3 May the King sent a force of armed men to try to seize the Tower of London. This was viewed as an attempt by him to free Strafford now that it looked as if the House of Lords were about pass the attainder bill that would condemn the earl to death. As with the Army Plot revelations, John Pym, MP for Tavistock and leading figure in the opposition to the King's policies, saw this news as an opportunity to build the case that those around the King could not be trusted. His speech to the Commons that same day repeated his earlier claims that there was a Catholic plot in the army and at court against Parliament. Those who spoke after him mostly agreed. Henry Marten,[3] MP for Berkshire, seems to have been the first to propose an association. The allusion, which others were quick to pick up on, was to the Elizabethan bond of association of 1584 following the Throckmorton Plot. What Marten was therefore

---

[16] Almost certainly a reference to the paper on 'unity in religion and uniformity of church government' which the Scottish commissioners had prepared in March 1641 and which had not been printed *Procs. LP*, 3:xxxiv, 4:421–7.

---

[1] Thomas Wentworth, first earl of Strafford, lord lieutenant of Ireland. See *ODNB*.
[2] Conrad Russell, 'The first army plot of 1641', *Transactions of the Royal Historical Society*, 5th ser., 38 (1988), pp. 85–106.
[3] Henry Marten (1601/2–1680), politician and regicide. See *ODNB*.

proposing was a collective oath for their mutual self-preservation.[4] Cromwell joined in with the general enthusiasm for this idea.

Mr Cromwell. Hee for an oath of associacon

Outcome: A committee was appointed to draft a suitable oath without delay. What they produced was the Protestation. This declared the willingness of the swearer to defend the doctrines of the Church of England, the person of the King, the privileges of Parliament and the peace of England, Scotland and Ireland. Most MPs who were present in the House, including Cromwell, swore this oath later that same day.

1641 05 09[?]
Letter from Oliver Cromwell and John Lowry to the mayor[1] and aldermen of Cambridge

Date: n.d. [but between 7 and 11 May 1641]
Source: Cambridgeshire Archives, Cambridge Corporation common day book, 1610–46 (contemporary copy)

The other Cambridge MP, John Lowry,[2] did not take the Protestation until 7 May.[3] Not that he is likely to have been reluctant to do so; it seems more likely that he had simply not attended the Commons since 3 May. Meanwhile, on 5 May the Commons had ordered that the Protestation was to be printed. It also ordered that MPs should send that printed text to all sheriffs, justices of the peace, cities and boroughs, explaining 'with what Willingness the Members of this House made this Protestation; and as they justify the Taking of it in themselves, so they cannot but approve it in them that shall likewise take it'.[4] Cromwell and Lowry obeyed that instruction by writing to the Cambridge corporation. The letter was read at the next meeting of the aldermen on 11 May. All those present followed its advice and took the Protestation. The text of the letter survives only because it was then copied into the corporation's common day book. Other examples of corporations receiving such letters are known.[5] But this seems to be a unique example where there is a record

---

[4] John Walter, *Covenanting Citizens* (Oxford, 2017), pp. 11–21.

[1] The mayor was Robert Robson (d. 1659) who had presided over the election of Cromwell and Lowry as the town's MPs the previous October.

[2] John Lowry (d. 1699). See *HoP Commons, 1640–1660*. Lowry was a chandler in Cambridge and a prominent member of the city corporation.

[3] *JHC*, 2:137.

[4] *JHC*, 2:135.   [5] John Walter, *Covenanting Citizens* (Oxford, 2017), pp. 82, 123, 125.

of the actual text of the letter. The meeting on 11 May was notable for another reason. A vacancy had arisen among the aldermen and they chose to fill it by promoting Lowry. This shifted the balance of power within the corporation towards the more godly faction allied to Cromwell.[6]

[p. 332]
To the right wohsp the Maior & Aldermen of Cambridge with the rest of that Bodie prsent these Gentlemen
Wee hartily salute you and herewith (according to the direccon of the howse of Comons in this prsent Parliament assembled) send unto you A protestacon by them lately made the Contents whereof will best appeare in the thing it selfe the Preamble therewith printed doth declare the weighty reasons inducing them in their owne persons to begin Wee shall only lett you know that with Alacritie and willingnesse the members of that Bodie entred thereinto It was in them a iust honle & necessary Act no unworthy yor Imitacon. you shall hereby as the Bodie represented avow the practice of the representative the Conformitie is in it selfe praise worthy and wilbe by them approved The result may (through the Almighties blessing) because stabilitie & securitie to the whole kingdome Coniunction carryes strength with it its dreadfull to adversaries especially when its in order to the dutie wee owe to God to the Loyaltie wee owe to or King & Soveraigne

[p. 333]
and to the affection due to or Countrie and Libties the manie Ends of this protestation wee herewith sent you Wee say noe more But Comitt you to the protection of him whoe is able to save you desireing yor prayers for the good successe of or present affaires and Indeavors which indede are not ors But the Lords, and yors whome wee desire to serve in Integritie & Bidding you
hartily farewell rest
yor Loveing freinds to be comanded
Oliver Cromwell
John Lowrye

---

[6] Barclay, *Electing Cromwell*, pp. 147–9.

1641 05 11

Speech by Oliver Cromwell to the House of Commons

Date: 11 May 1641
Source: BL, Harl. MS 164, fo. 208, Diary of Sir Simonds D'Ewes. Printed in *Procs. LP*, 4:320 (reported speech)

On this day the Commons resolved that £400,000 should be raised 'for the great affairs of the kingdom'.[1] George Peard,[2] MP for Barnstaple (Devon), took advantage of this to propose a scheme which would fund part of that sum while, at the same time, undermining the rights of the cathedral chapters. Peard's argument was that the lands of the cathedral deans and chapters currently brought in £28,400 per annum, but that improved management of those estates could raise this to £200,000 per annum and that, if converted into fee farm grants, this could raise £900,000 immediately. The implication was either that the cathedral chapters would be stripped of most of their wealth or that they would be abolished outright. This was a matter in which Cromwell had direct personal experience. Between 1636 and 1640 he had been the principal tenant of the chapter of Ely Cathedral. He also had good reason to think that some such grants were undervalued, as those Ely leases had been made to him on very favourable terms.[3] He now became the one MP to voice support for Peard's proposal.

~~Divers~~ Mr Perd & Mr Cromwell spake againe to this matter.

Outcome: This idea however received no other support and the House moved on to other business.

1641 05 22a

Speech by Oliver Cromwell to the House of Commons

Date: 22 May 1641
Source: BL, Harl. MS 163, fo. 218, Diary of Sir Simonds D'Ewes. Printed in *Procs. LP*, 4:525 (reported speech)

Sir Thomas Thynne of Longleat, Wiltshire, had died in August 1639. Since then the various members of his family had been squabbling over his inheritance. The main problem was that Sir Thomas had married twice and had left sons from both marriages. The eldest son

---

[1] *JHC*, 2:143.   [2] George Peard (bap. 1594, d. 1644/5), politician. See *ODNB*.
[3] Barclay, *Electing Cromwell*, pp. 98–102.

from the first marriage, Sir James Thynne, felt that the share of lands which had been bequeathed to his half-brother, Henry Frederick Thynne, the only surviving son from the second marriage, was too generous. As a further complication, Sir Thomas's widow, Henry Frederick's mother, was expected to surrender some of her dower lands to make up the share allocated to Sir James. Both sides had, in consequence, quickly become entangled in a series of messy lawsuits in the court of Star Chamber and the court of Wards.[1] Sir James's election as the Long Parliament MP for Wiltshire in 1640 gave him a crucial advantage, as MPs enjoyed immunity from arrest in civil suits. In January 1641 Sir James invoked his parliamentary privilege to block the case which had been brought against him by his half-brother in the court of Wards.[2] Only the Commons itself could overturn this. Cromwell now asked for clarification. His reasons for doing so are unclear. Sir James Thynne was married to Lady Isabella Rich, daughter of the first earl of Holland,[3] so it is just possible that Cromwell was raising this as a favour to the Rich family. If so, it backfired. It can however just as plausibly be assumed that Cromwell thought that Sir James was abusing his position as an MP.

A motion \was/ made by Mr Crumwell concerning Sr James Thinne a member of this howse & his brother Mr Henry ffredericke Thinne who had been ~~shew~~\su/ed by his brother James who being a member of this howse tooke an order wch made for his good, but when another was made rather against him then otherwise then hee pleaded his priviledge of this howse and desired to know the resolucon of this howse in this case but it was laid aside till Sr Thomas[4] Thinne came to the howse.

Outcome: The Commons made no order or resolution at all on the case at this point.[5] Cromwell would raise this matter again on 1 June.

---

[1] *HoP Commons, 1604–1629*, 6:523; Mary Frear Keeler, *The Long Parliament* (Philadelphia, 1954), pp. 360–1.
[2] *Procs. LP*, 4:525n.
[3] Henry Rich, first earl of Holland (bap. 1590, d. 1649), courtier. See ODNB.
[4] Presumably an error by D'Ewes for 'James'. Sir James Thynne did have a younger brother, Thomas, the other surviving son by their father's first marriage, but Thomas was not knighted until the following year.
[5] *JHC*, 2:154–5.

1641 05 22b
Speech by Oliver Cromwell to the House of Commons

Date: 22 May 1641
Source: BL, Harl. MS 163, fos 223v–224, Diary of Sir Simonds D'Ewes. Printed in *Procs. LP*, 4:533 (reported speech)

In 1631 a group of investors, the Bedford Level Adventurers, headed by the fourth earl of Bedford,[1] had been granted the right to drain the Great Level of the Isle of Ely. Those drainage works had since then encountered sustained opposition from the local inhabitants.[2] Exactly what Cromwell, who owned land in the area, thought about this remains uncertain.[3] The latest disorders had taken place at Somersham, Huntingdonshire. The principal local landowner was the queen, Henrietta Maria. In early 1641 some of the Somersham inhabitants had petitioned Parliament and on 19 February that petition had been referred by the Commons to its committee on the queen's jointure.[4] Other locals however opposed those protests. Their leaders were probably Viscount Mandeville (the future second earl of Manchester)[5] and the queen's surveyor-general, Sir Thomas Hatton. Lobbying to the House of Lords rather than to the House of Commons produced a series of orders commanding that the queen's tenants were to be left unmolested and that the rioters were to desist.[6] Mandeville and Hatton now sought to obtain similar orders against disturbances at St Ives, Holywell and Needingworth, all of which were immediately to the south of Somersham. Their petition was presented to the Commons on 22 May by Denzil Holles,[7] MP for Dorchester (Dorset). Cromwell was probably the first speaker to respond.

Divers spake to this busines. Mr Cromwell showed this much concerned the priviledge of this howse & of all the Commons of England for after the petition by the inhabitants of the saied towne preferred heere & that it was in hearing before a committee of this howse: the Lords made an order in the howse of Peers to settle the possession wch made the people to committ this outrage wch hee did not approve nor desire to justifie: & that since they had made another order to settle the possession againe by the sheriffe & by force of armes wth the trained bands.

---

[1] Francis Russell, fourth earl of Bedford (bap. 1587, d. 1641), politician. See *ODNB*.
[2] Keith Lindley, *Fenland Riots and the English Revolution* (London, 1982), pp. 41–4, 83–6, 92–105.
[3] Barclay, *Electing Cromwell*, pp. 75–96.   [4] *JHC*, 2:89.
[5] Edward Montagu, second earl of Manchester (1602–71), politician and parliamentarian army officer. See *ODNB*. Until his father's death in 1642, Montagu held the courtesy title of Viscount Mandeville. Since 1626 he had sat in the Lords by virtue of his father's title as Baron Kimbolton.
[6] *JHL*, 4:204, 227, 236, 252.   [7] Denzil Holles (1598–1680), politician. See *ODNB*.

1 JUNE 1641

Outcome: Other unnamed MPs then also spoke, but this debate was interrupted when Sir John Hotham,[8] MP for Beverley (Yorkshire), returned from a conference with the House of Lords about the latest messages from the commissioners from the Scottish Parliament. The House subsequently returned to their discussion of the petition from Mandeville and Hatton. From D'Ewes's account of that later debate, it would appear that MPs accepted Cromwell's argument that the Lords had violated the Commons' privileges by issuing orders on a matter that had been under consideration by the other House. The Commons therefore decided not to act on this latest petition for the time being.[9]

1641 06 01

Speech by Oliver Cromwell to the House of Commons

Date: 1 June 1641

Sources: [A] BL, Harl. MS 163, fo. 249, Diary of Sir Simonds D'Ewes. Printed in *Procs. LP*, 4:675 (reported speech). [B] BL, Harl. MS 477, fo. 117, Diary of John Moore. Printed in *Procs. LP*, 4:681 (reported speech).

Sir James Thynne had failed to appear in the Commons since Cromwell had raised his privilege case on 22 May. That tends to confirm that Cromwell was not acting on Sir James's behalf. This time Cromwell was able to secure a formal order from the House.

[A] BL, Harl. MS 163, fo. 249, Diary of Sir Simonds D'Ewes. Printed in *Procs. LP*, 4:675 (reported speech)

Upon Mr Cromwells motion it was ordered that Sr James Thinne should bee here upon ffriday next to shew cause concerning his Brother.

[B] BL, Harl. MS 477, fo. 117, Diary of John Moore. Printed in *Procs. LP*, 4:681 (reported speech)

Upon Mr Cromwells motion it was ordered tht Sr James Thine should be here upon Friday next to shew cause concerning his brother.

---

[8] Sir John Hotham (1589–1645), parliamentarian army officer. See *ODNB*.
[9] *JHC*, 2:155.

THE LETTERS, WRITINGS, AND SPEECHES OF OLIVER CROMWELL

Outcome: Strictly speaking, the order made by the Commons did not instruct Sir James Thynne to appear; all that it did was to say that the case would be considered by the House at 9 a.m. on 4 June.[1] But the case was one that other MPs thought important and the House debated it in detail on 20 July. Eventually, on 17 August, the Commons ruled that Sir James Thynne could not claim privilege.[2]

———— ⊗⊗⊗ ————

1641 06 04

Speech by Oliver Cromwell to the House of Commons

Date: 4 June 1641
Source: BL, Harl. MS 163, fo. 263, Diary of Sir Simonds D'Ewes. Printed in *Procs. LP*, 4:717–18 (reported speech)

This is the first instance of Cromwell raising a matter in the Commons on behalf of his constituency. The Cambridge corporation wished to submit a petition to the Commons. It is known to have been delivered to London by one of the Cambridge common council-men, James Blackley.[1] The petition evidently complained about the revenues collected by two Chancery officials, the clerks of the parcels. The fines collected by them were small and irregular. That made them a trivial yet tiresome nuisance. Cromwell raised this at the start of the day's proceedings.

\After Praiers/ Upon Mr Cromwels motion it was ordered that the office of \the Clarke/ ~~Parcels~~ of the Parcels in the Exchequer should bee referred to the same Committee that was appointed to consider of the Fines \given/ of the \for/ original writts in the Chancerie[2] & the saied Committee is to consider what benefitt accrues by it to the King & what loose & damage to the subject. Divers spake to this matter as well as Mr Cromwell ~~& shewed~~ beforre it was referred & & shewed that this office had formerlie been questioned in parliament & the execution of it superseded for some time & that it was a grievance to the subject.

————

[1] *JHC*, 2:162.   [2] *JHC*, 2:261.

[1] James Blackley (d. 1666), baker and Cambridge common councilman. Originally from Ramsay, Hunts. Linked to the group on the Cambridge corporation who had supported Cromwell's elections as the town's MP in 1640. Later he was the town's leading Quaker. Barclay, *Electing Cromwell*, pp. 50, 138, 140–1, 147.

[2] The date when this committee had been created is not clear. Several MPs were added to it three days later. *JHC*, 2:169 (reported speech).

Outcome: This committee may have been responsible for drafting two separate bills introduced in the Commons on 6 July 1641. Those bills hoped to reduce the fees imposed on sheriffs or paid to officials in the law courts. It is possible that one of those bills addressed the issue raised by the Cambridge petition.[3] But neither of those bills was ever passed.

1641 06 09
Speech by Oliver Cromwell to the House of Commons

Date: 9 June 1641
Source: BL, Harl. MS 163, fo. 303*, Diary of Sir Simonds D'Ewes. Printed in *Procs. LP*, 5:68 (reported speech)

This revived the matter that Cromwell had previously raised on 22 May. The inhabitants of Somersham had submitted a second petition complaining about the legal proceedings which had been brought against them by Viscount Mandeville's father, the first earl of Manchester.[1]

Mr Cromwell moved tht the Earle of manchester hath sent forth 60 ~~peticons~~ writts against the poore inhabitants in huntingtonsher, & desyrs that the comittie for the queenes Joynture might be renewed & tht this peticon may be ~~deliver~~ considered of by it. wch is soe ordered.

Source: BL, Harl. MS 478, fo. 46, Diary of John Moore. Printed in *Procs. LP*, 5:72 (reported speech)

Mr Cromwell moved tht the Earle of manchester hath sent forth 60 writts against the poore inhabitants in huntingtonshire for pullinge downe some inclosures, & desyred tht the committee for the queenes Joynture might be renewed, & tht this peticon may be considered of by it, wch is soe ordered.

Outcome: As D'Ewes and Moore indicate, the petition was referred to the committee on the queen's jointure.[2] According to its chairman, Edward Hyde,[3] MP for Saltash (Cornwall), Cromwell vigorously pressed the petitioners' claims at subsequent meeting of this committee.[4]

---

[3] *JHC*, 2:200.

[1] Henry Montagu, first earl of Manchester (c.1564–1642), politician and parliamentarian army officer. See ODNB.
[2] *JHC*, 2:172.
[3] Edward Hyde, first earl of Clarendon (1609–74), politician and historian. See ODNB.
[4] *The Life of Edward, Earl of Clarendon* (Oxford, 1857), 1:73–4.

1641 08 09a

Speech by Oliver Cromwell to the House of Commons

Date: 9 August 1641
Source: BL, Harl. MS 5047, fo. 60, Anonymous diary. Printed in *Procs. LP*, 6:321 (reported speech)

Negotiations with the Scots had made slow progress over the summer. One of the Scottish demands was that the King should visit Scotland regularly and so Charles pressed ahead with the idea that he travel to Edinburgh as soon as possible. MPs at Westminster were however wary. Many worried that now that it was no longer needed as protection against the Scots, the English army in the north would be used by Charles to carry out a military coup against them and that his journey northwards was just a cover for this scheme. On 9 August, just one day before the King intended to set out, the Scots reached agreement with him. Charles therefore sent a message to Parliament assuring them that he would be back by the end of September at the latest. He also asked that the bills confirming the Anglo-Scottish treaty and making arrangements during his absence be passed at once. The Commons proceeded to give the first of those bills its first and second readings.[1] Later that same morning they debated which other bills should be passed before the King departed. Sir Arthur Hesilrige,[2] MP for Leicestershire, however sought to widen the discussion by questioning the proposed appointment of commissioners with powers to grant the royal assent to bills while the King was in Scotland. Speaking in support of Hesilrige, Cromwell questioned whether the King needed to go to Scotland at all.

_____

Mr Cromw. not satisfied wth reasons offered by his Maty
  1. the necessity of his going
  2. his owne particular occasion
to the first. if we can give the Scots satisfacon we disingaged fr the tye of publicke faith. wch may be done by an ample Comm: for passing there acts[3]
to 2d. if we can propose consideracons equivalent. if not satisfie yet will acquitt us. danngers to his person going through the Armyes & faction stird up in Scotland,
damages in this kingdome if he go infinite

_____

[1] *JHC*, 2:247.
[2] Sir Arthur Heselrige [Haselrig], second baronet (1601–61), army officer and politician. See *ODNB*.
[3] Cromwell was here alluding to the proposals for religious uniformity which he had mentioned in his letter to George Willingham the previous spring and from which the Commons had since distanced itself.

Outcome: A third speaker, Sir Henry Anderson, MP for Newcastle-upon-Tyne (Northumberland), raised further concerns. The House took note and agreed to return to this subject that afternoon.[4] The treaty was eventually passed by Parliament as the Act for the Pacification between England and Scotland (16 Car. 1 c. 17), which received the royal assent on 10 August 1641.

1641 08 09b
Speech by Oliver Cromwell to the House of Commons

Date: 9 August 1641

Source: BL, Harl. MS 5047, fo. 61v, Anonymous diary. Printed in *Procs. LP*, 6:322 (reported speech)

Cromwell spoke again that afternoon when, as agreed, the House resumed its discussion about the King's proposed absence. In what was probably a coordinated move, several MPs saw this as an opportunity for them to propose that their favoured peers be appointed to key court offices. The result was two resolutions asking the King to appoint the earl of Salisbury[1] as lord high treasurer and, if the post became vacant, the earl of Pembroke[2] as lord steward of the household. Cromwell then intervened with a suggestion of his own. The King was about to grant custody of the Prince of Wales[3] to his tutor, the marquis of Hertford.[4] Cromwell thought that Hertford should be joined by two other peers.

Mr Cromwell. Concerning the Prince that Lo: Bedford[5] & Lo. Say[6] be added to him, not seconded.

Outcome: Cromwell seems to have failed to arrange for other MPs to support him. Had this been a spontaneous idea? The commission granting custody of the prince to Hertford alone was issued the following day.[7] The King started his journey northwards on 11 August.

---

[4] *JHC*, 2:247.

[1] William Cecil, second earl of Salisbury (1591–1668), politician. See *ODNB*.
[2] Philip Herbert, first earl of Montgomery and fourth earl of Pembroke (1584–1650), courtier and politician. See *ODNB*.
[3] Charles II (1630–85), king of England, Scotland and Ireland. See *ODNB*.
[4] William Seymour, first marquis of Hertford and second duke of Somerset (1587–1660), politician and royalist army officer. See *ODNB*.
[5] Francis Russell, fourth earl of Bedford (1593–1641), politician. See *ODNB*.
[6] William Fiennes, first Viscount Saye and Sele (1582–1662), politician. See *ODNB*.
[7] Thomas Rymer, *Foedera* (The Hague, 1739–45), 9 (pt. 2): 76–7.

1641 08 12

Speech by Oliver Cromwell to the House of Commons

Date: 12 August 1641
Source: BL, Harl. MS 5047, fo. 63v, Anonymous diary. Printed in *Procs. LP*, 6:382 (reported speech)

Since the spring the Commons had been slowly gathering evidence against the ringleaders of the Army Plot, Sir John Suckling,[1] Henry Percy[2] and Henry Jermyn.[3] Only now, on 12 August, did the Commons finally get round to discussing whether to charge all three with high treason. But before they could do so, Cromwell tried to tie this to another, even more controversial issue. On 4 August the Commons had agreed to impeach thirteen of the bishops. The bishops' political status was therefore highly topical. Whether they could vote in capital cases was disputed. Cromwell's call for them to be expelled from the Lords could be interpreted simply as a way of removing a bloc that could be expected to support Suckling, Percy and Jermyn. But it was also unmistakably a general attack on the power of the bishops.

Mr Cromwell to remeove the Bps out of the Lds house before we proceed in this

Outcome: MPs ignored Cromwell's suggestion. But that was just because they did not want to be distracted from the chance to discuss the Plotters' crimes. The idea that the bishops should be removed from the Lords had been raised before in this Parliament and it was revived the following October when the bill to prevent clergymen exercising temporal powers was introduced. That became law in February 1642 (16 Car. I c. 27).

1641 08 16

Speech by Oliver Cromwell to the House of Commons

Date: 16 August 1641
Source: BL, Harl. MS 5047, fo. 74v, Anonymous diary. Printed in *Procs. LP*, 6:441 (reported speech)

The Anglo-Scottish treaty still had to be ratified by the Scottish Parliament and there were a number of matters that the treaty avoided addressing. The two Houses had agreed on 10

---

[1] Sir John Suckling (bap. 1609, d. 1641?), poet. See *ODNB*.
[2] Henry Percy, Baron Percy of Alnwick (c.1604–59), royalist army officer. See *ODNB*.
[3] Henry Jermyn, earl of St Albans (bap. 1605, d. 1684), courtier and government official. See *ODNB*.

24 AUGUST 1641

August that a commission should be sent to Edinburgh to complete these negotiations. The question now arose whether such a commission could be issued under the Great Seal. This was a delicate issue as it could seem that Parliament was asserting control over the use of the Great Seal. The five MPs who spoke before Cromwell expressed a variety of opinions on how to proceed. Cromwell introduced a new point by linking this issue with that of their desire, as expressed on 10 August, of 'putting the Kingdom into a Posture of Defence'.[1] He seemed to be suggesting that they might wish to appoint other commissioners at some point in the near future without consulting the King.

Mr Cromwell. the putting of seale wilbe as necessary for Comm to put kingdom to a posture as in this. desires a Comittee of Long robe[2] may Consider it.

Outcome: Cromwell's specific suggestion was not pursued, but a conference with the Lords was held to discuss the appointment of the commissioners.[3] In the end, the commissioners were appointed by a warrant from the King.[4]

1641 08 24

Speech by Oliver Cromwell to the House of Commons

Date: 24 August 1641
Source: BL, Harl. MS 164, fo. 57v, Diary of Sir Simonds D'Ewes. Printed in *Procs. LP*, 6:541 (reported speech)

An essential feature of the deal with the Scots was that both the armies in the north of England were to be disbanded. That required money. Parliament had previously granted a poll tax. On the morning of 24 August the Commons passed a resolution ordering the sheriffs of eight counties (Norfolk, Cambridgeshire, Huntingdonshire, Leicestershire, Northamptonshire, Rutland, Warwickshire and Worcestershire) to pay the money raised from this directly to the treasurer of the army, Sir William Uvedale, at York. It was agreed that the Lords' approval would also be sought. Later that day an order confirming the original resolution was approved.[1] After other business had intervened, Cromwell made sure that no more time was lost in seeking the Lords' agreement.

---

[1] *JHC*, 2:249.
[2] A committee of judges ('the gentlemen of the long robe') attending the House of Lords as legal advisers.
[3] *JHC*, 2:258.   [4] *JHC*, 2:264.

[1] *JHC*, 2:269, 270.

Mr Cromwell moved that wee might send upp a message to the Lords to desire a conference by a committee of both howses touching the speedie sending of monie to,² for the disbanding of the Armies. And hee was appointed to goe with it.

Outcome: This had the intended effect. On returning, Cromwell was able to report that the Lords had agreed to an immediate conference in the Painted Chamber. After the conference, the Lords returned to their chamber and passed the joint order.³

1641 09 01

Speech by Oliver Cromwell to the House of Commons

Date: 1 September 1641
Source: BL, Harl. MS 164, fo. 84, Diary of Sir Simonds D'Ewes. Printed in *Procs. LP*, 6:635 (reported speech)

On 31 August the Commons debated the subject of the re-ordering of chancels. A resolution was passed instructing churchwardens to move communion tables from the east end of chancels and to remove altar rails and altar steps. Later that same day a committee was appointed to discuss extending this policy to the chapels of university colleges and the inns of court. That committee was also told to consider 'all other Matters of Innovation'.¹ This committee acted without delay and the following day John Pym was able to report back to the Commons on a long list of draft orders which they were recommending should be accepted. The Commons accepted those orders with only minor amendments.² There then followed a prolonged discussion on other possible reforms. One speaker, Sir John Colepeper,³ MP for Kent, proposed that they balance their condemnation of innovations with a condemnation of those who criticised the Book of Common Prayer. Cromwell was one of several MPs who countered by arguing that such criticism was justified.

Sr Tho: Barrington⁴ Mr Crombwell and others spake agt the Common prayer booke it selfe that was established by act of Parliament shewing that there were

---

² There is an illegible deletion here.   ³ *JHC*, 2:270; *JHL*, 4:375.

¹ *JHC*, 2:278.   ² *JHC*, 2:279.
³ John Colepeper, first Baron Colepeper (bap. 1600, d. 1660), politician. See *ODNB*.
⁴ Sir Thomas Barrington, second baronet (c.1584–1644), politician. See *ODNB*.

many passages in it which divers grave learned & wise divines could not submit unto and practice

---

Outcome: A division was then held on Colepeper's idea. MPs voted by 55 votes to 37 in favour of it. Barrington's Essex friends, Sir Henry Mildmay[5] and Sir William Masham,[6] were the teller for the noes. The previous committee was therefore told to prepare an additional order.[7] There was much debate on 6 September when the committee returned with its draft for that additional order. The Commons finally passed those orders in their original form without the addition defending the Book of Common Prayer on 8 September.[8]

1641 09 08
Speech by Oliver Cromwell to the House of Commons

Date: 8 September 1641
Source: BL, Harl. MS 164, fo. 101, Diary of Sir Simonds D'Ewes. Printed in *Procs. LP*, 6:688 (reported speech)

The Commons had much business to transact on this day as it planned to rise the following day for the recess. Cromwell nevertheless managed to slip through an important order concerning preaching. The order itself was relatively anodyne, as few could object to the principle of more sermons and no one in the House seems to have queried what Cromwell was proposing. There was however a subtle agenda involved, as the order undermined the rights of bishops to regulate parish lectures. Cromwell was almost certainly motivated in part by his experiences in Ely. Complaints about non-preaching clergymen had been among those made by some of the Ely inhabitants in a petition they had submitted to the House of Lords three months earlier.[1]

Upon Mr Cromwells motion it was ordered that Sermons should be in the afternoone in all parishes of England in the afternoone at the charge of the inhabitants of those parishes where ther are no sermons in the afternoone which order was afterwards printed: & the libertie of Lecture to be set upp on weeke dayes added to it.

---

[5] Henry Mildmay (c.1594–1644/5), politician and courtier. See *ODNB*.
[6] William Masham (c.1592–1656). See *HoP Commons, 1640–1660*. He had recently been elected as knight of the shire for Essex.
[7] *JHC*, 2:279.   [8] *JHC*, 2:283.

[1] Barclay, *Electing Cromwell*, pp. 98–9.

Outcome: The Commons ordered that parishioners could appoint a lecturer to preach if there were no sermons preached on Sundays and that they could also do so on a week day if there was no existing weekly lecture.² As D'Ewes mentions, this order was printed.³

1641 10 26

Speech by Oliver Cromwell to the House of Commons

Date: 26 October 1641

Source: BL, Harl. MS 162, fo. 41v, Diary of Sir Simonds D'Ewes. Printed in Willson Havelock Coates, ed., *The Journal of Sir Simonds D'Ewes from the First Recess of the Long Parliament to the Withdrawal of King Charles from London* (New Haven and London, 1942), p. 40 (reported speech)

Parliament reassembled as planned on 20 October. The following day the bill to prevent clergymen exercising secular offices was re-introduced and received its first and second readings. Its provisions included the removal of the bishops from the House of Lords. This was passed by the Commons on 23 October. Its supporters now sought to link this to the existing impeachment proceedings against thirteen of the bishops for their role in the decision by the Convocation to approve the 1640 Canons. They argued that these thirteen bishops should be prevented from voting at all and that the other bishops should be prevented from voting on this bill. That neatly reinforced the idea that the bishops could not be trusted to exercise secular powers as members of the House of Lords. Several MPs, led by Sir Henry Vane the younger,[1] set out reasons why the Lords should be asked to bar the bishops from voting.

Mr Cro\m/well gave this reason for it because wee did but suspend their voices for a time only, till this bill was passed, and others gave other resons none of wch gave mee any Satisfaction which made mee stand upp and speake in effect following.

Outcome: D'Ewes argued against the proposed motion. He made the obvious point that it was all very well for MPs (such as Cromwell) to argue that this was only a temporary suspension of the bishops' rights but that what they would be prevented from voting on was a bill that would remove those rights permanently. The Commons however resolved that

---

² JHC, 2:677.

³ *An order Made by the House of Commons for the Establishing of Preaching Lecturers, throughout England and Wales*: (Wing / E2640; Thomason / E172[1]).

¹ Sir Henry Vane the Younger (1613–62), politician and author. See ODNB.

a joint conference should be held with the Lords to make these requests.² The Lords deliberately took their time over this bill, which was not finally passed by them until 5 February 1642.

1641 10 27

Speech by Oliver Cromwell to the House of Commons

Date: 27 October 1641
Source: BL, Harl. MS 162, fo. 43v, Diary of Sir Simonds D'Ewes. Printed in Coates, *Journal*, p. 42 (reported speech)

On 26 August 1641 a by-election had been held for a new Hertfordshire MP following the elevation of Arthur Capel[1] to the peerage as Baron Capel of Hadham. The successful candidate was Sir Thomas Dacres.[2] Cromwell seems to have raised this matter immediately after John Pym had reported to the House on the reasons that would be offered to the Lords at the planned joint conference on whether the bishops should be allowed to vote on the bill to prevent clergymen holding secular offices.

Mr Cromwelle moved about the \late\ Election of a knight of the shire in Hartfordshire

---

Outcome: What point Cromwell was trying to make is unclear. The result had been questioned in the Commons on 30 August, although D'Ewes's notes on that occasion are equally uninformative as to the grounds for the challenge.[3] Dacres would later during the Civil War become a strong supporter of the peace party in Parliament, but previously he had quarrelled with William Laud (then bishop of London) about prosecutions for Sabbath drinking and he had also been reluctant to support the King's campaigns against the Scottish Covenanters.[4] So as yet there was no obvious reason for Cromwell to have disapproved of his election. The Commons did not pursue Cromwell's motion.

---

[2] *JHC*, 2:295.

[1] Arthur Capel, first Baron Capel of Hadham (1604–49), royalist army officer and politician. See *ODNB*.
[2] Sir Thomas Dacres (1587–1668). See *HoP Commons, 1603–1629* and *HoP Commons, 1640–1660*.
[3] *Procs. LP*, 6:610.   [4] *HoP Commons, 1640–1660*.

1641 10 29

Speech by Oliver Cromwell to the House of Commons

Date: 29 October 1641
Source: BL, Harl. MS 162, fo. 52v, Diary of Sir Simonds D'Ewes. Printed in Coates, *Journal*, pp. 52, 53 (reported speech)

The King's decision to make appointments to five vacant bishoprics was a provocative move at a time when the political role of the bishops was such a hot topic. In fact, the five men nominated by Charles—John Prideaux,[1] Henry King,[2] Ralph Brownrigg,[3] Thomas Winniffe[4] and Richard Holdsworth[5]—were ones intended to reassure his critics. But those most hostile to episcopacy wanted no appointments to be made at all. On 28 October the Commons had debated whether to submit a petition to the King condemning the influence of evil councillors. Speaking in that debate, Sir Simonds D'Ewes had queried these new episcopal appointments.[6] The proposal was made the following day that the two Houses should write to the King to ask that the appointments be suspended.

Mr Cromwell renewed againe the motion which had been first moved by my selfe yesterday and ~~now~~ \was this day/ renewed againe by Sr Walter Earle[7] touching a Conference with the Lords for the staying of the investiture of the five new Bissopps that were to bee made and did speake somewhat bitterly against Doctor Howlsworth...

Outcome: Others, including D'Ewes, then spoke. In his speech D'Ewes defended 'one of these five persons \that is/ to be made a Bpp (viz. Dr Houlesworth) \against/ whome the gentleman on the other side ~~did alle~~ (viz. Mr Cromwelle) did alledge divers particulars...' (fo. 53v). It would therefore seem that Cromwell had criticised Holdsworth, who was the current vice-chancellor of Cambridge University and the master of Emmanuel College. The motion that they should ask the Lords to join with them in writing to the King was put to the vote. MPs voted by 71 to 53 to do so. Cromwell and D'Ewes then headed the list of MPs appointed as the committee to prepare the agenda for the joint conference with the Lords on this subject.[8] These moves were however overtaken by the news from Ireland. The appointments of the five bishops went ahead several weeks later.

[1] John Prideaux (1578–1650). See ODNB—as bishop of Worcester.
[2] Henry King (1592–1669). See ODNB—as bishop of Chichester.
[3] Ralph Brownrigg (1592–1659). See ODNB—as bishop of Exeter.
[4] Thomas Winniffe (1576–1654). See ODNB—as bishop of Lincoln.
[5] Richard Holdsworth (1590–1649), church of England clergyman and college head. See ODNB—he declined the see of Bristol.
[6] Coates, *Journal*, pp. 44–7.
[7] Sir Walter Erle [Earle] (1586–1665), politician. See ODNB.
[8] JHC, 2:298.

1641 11 04

Speech by Oliver Cromwell to the House of Commons

Date: 4 November 1641
Source: BL, Harl. MS 162, fo. 86v, Diary of Sir Simonds D'Ewes. Printed in Coates, *Journal*, p. 80 (reported speech)

William Ashburnham,[1] MP for Ludgershall (Wiltshire), Henry Wilmot,[2] MP for Tamworth (Staffordshire), Hugh Pollard,[3] MP for Bere Alston (Devon), and Sir John Berkeley[4] had all been accused of involvement in the First Army Plot. Ashburnham, Wilmot and Pollard had been imprisoned by the Commons on 14 June 1641 but all three had since been released on bail.[5] After they had surrendered themselves, Berkeley and Daniel O'Neill had been sent to the Tower of London on 20 October.[6]

Mr Cromwell shewed that Mr Ashburnham who had been accused heere of the late designe had visited Sir John Barklay in the Tower being ther a prisoner for the same & therfore hee desired that the saied Mr Ashburnham Mr Wilmot & Mr Pollard should noe longer goe upon baile but be remannded to prison.

Outcome: Arthur Goodwin,[7] MP for Buckinghamshire, spoke in support of Cromwell's motion, but Edward Hyde and Sir Simonds D'Ewes spoke against. The matter was then left unresolved. Ashburnham, Wilmot and Pollard were however all expelled as MPs on 9 December.[8]

---

[1] William Ashburnham (1604/5–1679), army officer and politician. See ODNB. Important adviser to Charles I in his final years.
[2] Henry Wilmot, first earl of Rochester (bap. 1613, d. 1658), royalist army officer. See ODNB. Royalist army officer.
[3] Sir Hugh Pollard, second baronet (1603–66), royalist army officer and court official. See ODNB. Royalist army officer.
[4] Sir John Berkeley, first baron of Stratton (bap. 1607, d. 1678), royalist army officer and courtier. See ODNB. Important adviser to Charles I in his final years.
[5] JHC, 2:175–6, 194, 203.   [6] JHC, 2:290.
[7] Arthur Goodwin (d. 1643), politician. See ODNB.   [8] JHC, 2:337.

1641 11 06

Speech by Oliver Cromwell to the House of Commons

Date: 6 November 1641
Source: BL, Harl. MS 162, fo. 106v, Diary of Sir Simonds D'Ewes. Printed in Coates, *Journal*, pp. 97–8 (reported speech)

The outbreak of the rebellion in Ireland heightened concerns at Westminster about military security in England. John Hotham,[1] MP for Scarborough (Yorkshire), was now sent by the Commons to the Lords to seek a joint conference on the safety of the kingdom. Among the topics to be discussed was one that was proposed by Cromwell. Three months earlier, before departing for Scotland, the King had appointed the third earl of Essex[2] as the commander of the military forces in southern England. Cromwell now suggested that Essex should be given command of the militia trained bands there as well.

Another head of the conference was added upon Mr Cromwells mo.[3] tion that wee should desire ~~that~~ \the/ Lords that an ordinance of Parliament might passe to give the Earle of Essex power to assemble at all times the trained bands of the kingdome for the on this side Trent[4] for the defence ther of till further order weere taken by Parliament

---

Outcome: Cromwell's suggestion was adopted and the Commons resolved that this should be raised at the joint conference.[5] Denzil Holles repeated this suggestion on 15 November. But later that same month the King dismissed Essex from his existing command. Underlying these moves was the idea that Parliament should place the militia into the hands of a commander it could trust. This would recur again and again over the months that followed and would in the end result in the passage of the Militia Ordinance.

---

[1] John Hotham (1610–45), parliamentarian army officer. See ODNB.
[2] Robert Devereux, third earl of Essex (1591–1646), parliamentarian army officer. See ODNB.
[3] Illegible deletion.
[4] The river Trent, which runs through Staffordshire, Derbyshire, Leicestershire, Nottinghamshire, Lincolnshire and Yorkshire, was the traditional administrative boundary between southern and northern England.
[5] JHC, 2:306.

1641 11 27

Speech by Oliver Cromwell to the House of Commons

Date: 27 November 1641
Source: BL, Harl. MS 162, fo. 191v, Diary of Sir Simonds D'Ewes. Printed in Coates, *Journal*, p. 202 (reported speech).

On 25 November the King entered London on his return journey from Scotland, The lord mayor, Richard Gurney,[1] made sure that the corporation of London gave him the warmest possible welcome. But there were some in the City who felt that the King's reception was excessive.[2] Those tensions were reflected in the information that Cromwell reported to the Commons two days later.

Mr Cromwell brought in a Testimoniall of one James Best dwelling in Pater Noster row;[3] by wch hee witnessed that one (\whome/ hee named not least he should withdraw himselfe) had saied: That this howse was offended that the cittie of London gave the King such great entertainment & that the said howse did send to the saied cittie not to intertaine him. It was therupon ordered after the Clarke had read it that the saied Best should be sent for to the howse to witnes the same.

Outcome: It would seem that Best knew of someone who had suggested that Parliament disapproved of the City's actions and that it had specifically ordered that the King should not be welcomed. The first of those suggestions may have been true enough but Parliament had been careful to refrain from saying so and no order had been sent to the London corporation. So the potential offence was that this unnamed individual had been spreading false rumours about Parliament. To act however the Commons needed the name of that individual and so they ordered that Best should attend on them in person.[4] Nothing more was heard of this.

---

[1] Sir Richard Gurney, baronet (bap. 1587, d. 1647), mayor of London. See *ODNB*.
[2] John Adamson, *The Noble Revolt* (London, 2007), pp. 438–40.
[3] Paternoster Row, the street to the north of St Paul's Cathedral that was the centre of the London book trade. The Journals describe Best as living 'at the Sign of the Death's Head in the Old Bailey'. *JHC*, 2:325. That is not inconsistent with D'Ewes's statement, as the Old Bailey and Paternoster Row were close to each other. Best is otherwise unidentifiable.
[4] *JHC*, 2:325.

1641 12 06
Speech by Oliver Cromwell to the House of Commons

Date: 6 December 1641
Source: BL, Harl. MS 162, fo. 213v, Diary of Sir Simonds D'Ewes. Printed in Coates, *Journal*, p. 236 (reported speech)

At least one of the parliamentary seats in the Sussex constituency of Arundel had become vacant, as one of the MPs, Henry Garton, had died. There was also a possibility that a second vacancy would arise as the other MP, Sir Edward Alford, wanted to sit instead for Tewkesbury, which was however the subject of an ongoing election dispute. The writ for the by-election to replace Garton had been moved on 12 November.[1] The town's dominant electoral patron was the earl of Arundel,[2] who proceeded to nominate his preferred candidate, his own secretary, Nicholas Harman. Cromwell sought to challenge this in Parliament by making it an issue about the improper interference by peers in parliamentary elections.

Mr Cromwell moved that the Earle of Arundel had \written/ ~~written~~ Lres to the Burrough of Arundel in Sussex for the election of a new Burgesse ther; & desired that the Speaker would write a lre to them to make a free election.

Outcome: The Commons responded by appointing a committee, including Cromwell, to consider such abuses, in general and with specific reference to the Arundel by-election.[3] Cromwell reported back to the House from that committee four days later (see 10 December 1641).

1641 12 10
Speech by Oliver Cromwell to the House of Commons

Date: 10 December 1641
Source: BL, Harl. MS 162, fo. 226v, Diary of Sir Simonds D'Ewes. Printed in Coates, *Journal*, p. 260 (reported speech)

Cromwell reported back from the committee created four days earlier to consider the influence of peers in parliamentary elections (see 6 December 1641).

---

[1] JHC, 2:313.
[2] Thomas Howard, fourteenth earl of Arundel, fourth earl of Surrey and first earl of Norfolk (1585–1646), art collector and politician. See ODNB.
[3] JHC, 2:333.

11 DECEMBER 1641

Mr Cromwell made reporte ~~touching~~ \from/ the Committee appointed to consider of the Earle of Arundels lre written to the Burrough of Arundel for the choice of Mr Harman[1] his secretarie: brought in an order wch the committee had drawn to prevent that election & all others of the same kinde. wch after it had been a little alt\e/red was allowed by the howse & ordered accordinglie.

Outcome: The order approved by the Commons condemned letters of nominations from peers as a violation of the Commons' privileges and instructed voters to ignore them. Constituencies were also instructed to inform the Speaker of the contents of any such letters.[2] Despite this, Harman did not withdraw his candidacy and, as there was a double return, he was named in one of the two indentures resulting from the poll on 20 December. The Commons however accepted the election of the other candidate, John Downes.[3]

1641 12 11

Speech by Oliver Cromwell to the House of Commons

Date: 11 December 1641
Source: BL, Harl. MS 164, fo. 227, Diary of Sir Simonds D'Ewes. Sentence in cipher. Printed in Coates, *Journal*, p. 269n. (reported speech)

On 10 December the Commons had expressed concerns about the troops which had been ordered to assemble around the Palace of Westminster. Those were ostensibly guards for Parliament's protection but could equally be viewed as an armed force with which the King might overawe Parliament. The Commons had therefore asserted that guards could be stationed around Westminster only with its consent.[1] Now on 11 December the Commons questioned some of the Middlesex justices of the peace about their roles in the events of the previous day. MPs then debated whether to take action against one of the justices, George Long. D'Ewes spoke to argue that Long had violated Parliament's privilege. D'Ewes's notes do not make it clear whether, in speaking after him, Cromwell agreed or disagreed.

---

[1] i.e. Nicholas Harman, secretary to the earl of Arundel. See **1641 12 06.**
[2] *JHC*, 2:337.   [3] John Downes (bap. 1609, d. in or after 1666), regicide. See *ODNB*.

[1] *JHC*, 2:338.

I spake. &c. Mr Cromwell. Lord Falkland² tooke exception.

Outcome: The Commons agreed that Long had violated its privileges and so sent him to the Tower.³

1641 12 28
Speech by Oliver Cromwell to the House of Commons

Date: 28 December 1641
Source: BL, Harl. MS 162, fo. 288v, Diary of Sir Simonds D'Ewes. Printed in Coates, *Journal*, p. 357 (reported speech)

The first earl of Bristol had been the British ambassador to Spain between 1622 and 1624, when he had taken a leading role in the efforts to secure a Spanish marriage for the Prince of Wales and when Prince Charles and the first duke of Buckingham[1] had visited Madrid in person in the hope of completing that deal. The Hispanophile Bristol had remained a supporter of a Spanish alliance after Charles and Buckingham turned hostile to the idea. On 20 January 1626 Charles, by then king, had written to Bristol accusing him of having encouraged Charles to convert to Catholicism while in Spain.[2] That same year the King promoted proceedings against Bristol in the Lords in the hope of discouraging the rival proceedings against Buckingham. However, by 1641 Bristol was back in royal favour; he was readmitted to the privy council and by the end of the year he was one of the King's more active supporters in the Lords. Some in the Commons therefore saw him as an easy target. On 27 December Walter Long,[3] MP for Ludgershall (Wiltshire), denounced him. Sir Gilbert Gerard,[4] MP for Middlesex, and Sir John Hotham,[5] MP for Beverley (Yorkshire), were then sent to obtain copies of the evidence which had been gathered against the earl in 1626.[6] The next day Hotham presented the Commons with copies of the 1626 letter and other supporting documents. Sir Simonds D'Ewes seems to have spoken first on the question as to whether these documents should be referred to a committee.

After I had spoken there ensued silence againe for a while till Mr Cromwell moved that hee conceived it fitt for this howse to desire the Lords to ioine with them in

---

[2] Lucius Cary, second Viscount Falkland (1609/10–1643), politician and author. See *ODNB*.
[3] *JHC*, 2:339.

[1] George Villiers, first duke of Buckingham (1592–1628), royal favourite. See *ODNB*.
[2] *JHL*, 3:544.   [3] Sir Walter Long, first baronet (1589–1645), politician. See *ODNB*.
[4] Sir Gilbert Gerard, first baronet (1587–1670), politician. See *ODNB*.
[5] Sir John Hotham, first baronet (1589–1645), parliamentarian army officer. See *ODNB*.
[6] *JHC*, 2:358.

29 DECEMBER 1641

moveing his Matie that the said Earle of Bristow[7] might bee removed from his Counsell who had thus perswaded his Matie to putt the saied Armie into a posture, wch could have noe ordinarie meaning in it, but because the saied was then in its due posture of lying still.

Outcome: What Cromwell was insinuating was that Bristol had advised the King to use the army in England against Parliament. Other MPs, led by William Strode,[8] supported Cromwell, but others defended Bristol on the grounds that those claims were unsubstantiated. In the end, no further action was taken.

1641 12 29

Speech by Oliver Cromwell to the House of Commons

Date: 29 December 1641
Source: BL, Harl. MS 162, fo. 290v, Diary of Sir Simonds D'Ewes. Printed in Coates, *Journal*, pp. 359–60 (reported speech)

On 22 October 1641 Owen O'Connolly,[1] a servant of Sir John Clotworthy,[2] MP for Maldon (Essex), had revealed the existence of the plot for an uprising in Ireland to one of the lords justices, Sir William Parsons.[3] He had then been sent to London with this news. O'Connolly was thus the man who had broken the news of the Irish rebellion to the authorities in both Dublin and London. On receiving this news on 1 November, the Commons had agreed that O'Connolly should receive a reward of £500 and a pension of £200, and that the lord lieutenant of Ireland, the second earl of Leicester,[4] should be asked to find a position for him in Ireland.[5] Cromwell now presented the petition from O'Connolly reminding the Commons of the last part of that promise.

---

[7] John Digby, first earl of Bristol (1580–1653), diplomat and courtier. See *ODNB*.
[8] William Strode (bap. 1594, d. 1645), politician. See *ODNB*.

[1] Owen O'Connolly (d. 1649), plot discloser and parliamentarian army officer. See *ODNB*.
[2] Sir John Clotworthy, first Viscount Masareene (d. 1665), politician. See *ODNB*. Clotworthy was a major planter-landowner in Ulster and the most important single resident of Ireland to secure a seat in the House of Commons in 1640 and to promote the problems of Ireland and the existence of a 'popish plot' in the early 1640s.
[3] Sir William Parsons, baronet (*c*.1570–1650), political administrator and promoter of the plantation of Ireland. See *ODNB*.
[4] Robert Sidney, second earl of Leicester (1595–1677), diplomat and landowner. See *ODNB*.
[5] *JHC*, 2:300.

THE LETTERS, WRITINGS, AND SPEECHES OF OLIVER CROMWELL

Mr Cromwel shewed that the Lord Leiftenant of Ireland had not yet bestowed upon Owen Occonelle a captaines place over a companie of Dragoones. His petition was read wheerein hee desired ~~againe~~ to have some place of preferment in Ireland in the Province of Munster to serve in the Warrs against the Rebels wee had formerlie voted that hee should have some place of preferment in the armie. Soe ~~Mr~~ the saied \Mr Cromwell and/ Mr Hotham[6] weere appointed to goe to the Lord Leiftenant to desire in the name of this howse that the saied Occonelle might be preferred to a captaines place under a companie of Dragoons.

Outcome: Cromwell and Hotham were ordered to inform Leicester that O'Connolly ought to be given the command of a troop of dragoons.[7] O'Connolly was subsequently appointed to a position in Clotworthy's regiment.

1642 01 14
Speech by Oliver Cromwell to the House of Commons

Date: 14 January 1642
Source: BL, Harl. MS 162, fo. 328v, Diary of Sir Simonds D'Ewes. Printed in Private Journals 3 Jan.–5 Mar. 1642, p. 67 (reported speech)

On 4 January 1642 Charles I arrived in person at Westminster and tried to arrest the Five Members. Six days later Charles withdrew from the capital. Even more so than previously, Parliament distrusted the King's intentions and so began to take steps for their own protection. On 14 January the two Houses each sought a joint conference to discuss the latest developments. The Lords wanted one to inform the Commons of the contents of a letter that the King had sent to the lord keeper, Lord Littleton,[1] while the Commons wanted one to discuss suspicious troop movement in the Windsor area. These specific concerns assisted Cromwell when, on MPs' return from that joint conference, he moved that a committee be created to discuss the military situation.

Upon our returne from our conference Mr Cromwell moved that a Committee might be named to consider of meanes to putt the kingdome in a \posture of/

---

[6] John Hotham (1610–45), parliamentarian army officer. See ODNB. He is the son of Sir John Hotham (for whom see **1641 12 28**).

[7] JHC, 2:360–1.

---

[1] Edward Littleton, Baron Littleton (1589–1645), judge and politician. See ODNB.

50

17 JANUARY 1642

defence: wch after two or three moore had spooken to it was done. to meete in Court of Wards[2] toomorrow at 7 of the clocke

Outcome: The committee's specific purpose was to prepare proposals on how the kingdom could be put into a posture of defence. The eight MPs named as this committee did not include Cromwell.[3] William Pierrepont,[4] MP for Much Wenlock (Shropshire), reported back from that committee the following day. Their recommendation was that lists should be prepared of possible candidates to be appointed as lords lieutenant. This represented an assertion by Parliament of the right to control the county militias and so was a major step towards the subsequent Militia Ordinance.

1642 01 17

Speech by Oliver Cromwell to the House of Commons

Date: 17 January 1642
Source: BL, Harl. MS 480, fo. 35, Diary of John Moore. Printed in *Private Journals 3 Jan.–5 Mar. 1642*, p. 101 (reported speech)

The information that Cromwell now reported to the Commons reflected the growing and justified fears that the divisions between the King and Parliament had become so bad that armed conflict between them was a realistic possibility.

Mr Cromwell declared that there was a gent in their county[1] whoe said that if the King & pl. Should be devided there was never a gent in England that would take the pl: parte. & that the King should have 10000 forth of ffrance & then he would be harde enough for the pl: & that those that tooke the Kings parte should have all the others lands for their service. & tht he knew by the first proceeding of pl: it would be noe better. after a long debate whether he should be named, or noe, & thn ~~see~~ to be sent for as a delinqueint, but it was ordered upon Mr Cromwell & Mr Waltons[2] informacon that they should goe to

---

[2] The court of wards met in a room at the southern end of Westminster Hall, leading off the Commons lobby. It was regularly used for meetings by parliamentary committees.

[3] *JHC*, 2:379–80.

[4] William Pierrepont (1607–78), politician. See *ODNB*.

---

[1] i.e. Huntingdonshire.

[2] Valentine Walton (1593/4–1661), parliamentarian army officer and regicide. See *ODNB*. Walton was MP for Huntingdonshire.

Mr Speaker,³ & deliver up the gent. his name, & to be sent for up & to be ~~kept~~ brought up in saffe custody.

Outcome: The Commons ordered that the Speaker should issue a warrant for the arrest of the individual named to him by Cromwell and Walton.⁴ That individual was clearly James Ravenscroft, whose case Cromwell raised again three days later.

1642 01 20

Speech by Oliver Cromwell to the House of Commons

Date: 20 January 1642

Source: BL, Harl. MS 162, fo. 337v, Diary of Sir Simonds D'Ewes. Printed in *Private Journals 3 Jan.–5 Mar. 1642*, p. 114 (reported speech)

This entry must be assumed to be a continuation of the case that Cromwell and Valentine Walton had raised on 17 January. The crucial detail that could now be revealed was that their complaint was against a 'Mr Ravenscroft', a Huntingdonshire justice of the peace. That is identifiable as James Ravenscroft.¹

\A little after 4 of the clocke in the afternoon ~~about~~ to be Mr Cromwell moved/ ~~Upon Mr Cromwells motion it was ordered~~ that Mr Ravenscroft a justice of peace in Huntingdonshire might be bailed who was sent for upp & kept in the serieants² custodie but not as a delinquent: It had been witnessed against him under a ministers hand that he had said. That if the King & Parliament should differ, the most of the gentrie would be for the King, & that hee had 10.000 readie to assist him. Divers spake against it for the present but upon my seconding it this afternoone againe as followeth afterwarde it was ordered accordinglie.

---

³ William Lenthall, appointed Lord Lenthall under the Protectorate (1591–1662), lawyer and Speaker of the House of Commons. See *ODNB*.

⁴ *JHC*, 2:386.

¹ TNA, SP 16/352, fo. 82, Huntingdonshire justices of the peace to privy council, 6 April 1637; SP 16/357, fo. 249, privy council to Huntingdonshire justices of the peace, 31 May 1637. This appears to have been James Ravenscroft of Alconbury Weston, Huntingdonshire, who was a Roman Catholic: see the entry on his son, George Ravenscroft (1632/3–1683), the noted glass manufacturer, in *ODNB*.

² John Hunt, the serjeant at arms to the House of Commons.

Outcome: The Commons agreed to bail Ravenscroft.[3] Cromwell would raise this case again a few days later (see **1642 01 26b**).

1642 01 26a
Speech by Oliver Cromwell to the House of Commons

Date: 26 January 1642
Source: BL, Harl. MS 480, fo. 62, Diary of John Moore. Printed in *Private Journals 3 Jan.– 5 Mar. 1642*, p. 180 (reported speech)

That this entry refers to Cromwell is most uncertain. The name of the MP who tried to get the motion laid aside has sometimes been read as 'Cromwell'. But it reads more like 'Stowell'. However, the only MP with a surname similar to that was Sir John Stawell,[1] MP for Somerset, and he would not have been referred to as 'Mr Stowell'. The motion in question related to the rates of pay for the officers in the army to be sent to Ireland. The Commons passed a series of resolutions fixing the pay for the different ranks. 'Stowell' seems to have queried the proposal that the pay for the two commissaries should be set at five shillings per diem.

2 deputy comissaries for the field–vs apeece per die. but upon Mr Stowells motion it was laid asyde but after voted.

Outcome: The Journals confirm that their pay was set at five shillings after all.[2]

1642 01 26b
Speech by Oliver Cromwell to the House of Commons

Date: 26 January 1642
Source: BL, Harl. MS 162, fo. 354, Diary of Sir Simonds D'Ewes. Printed in *Private Journals 3 Jan.–5 Mar. 1642*, pp. 177–8 (reported speech)

Cromwell continued to pursue the Huntingdonshire justice of the peace, James Ravenscroft (see **1642 01 20**).

---

[3] JHC, 2:388.

[1] Sir John Stawell (1599/1600–1662), royalist army officer. See ODNB. Stawell later served in the royalist army.

[2] JHC, 2:397.

Upon Mr Cromwels motion it was ordered that the \two/ witnesses wch weere come about the accusation put in against Mr Ravenscroft sho a Justice of peace in Huntingdonshire touching words by him spoaken should be referred to the Committee for Intelligence to examine.

Outcome: The matter was referred to the recently formed committee of examinations.[1] The Commons dismissed Ravenscroft from the Huntingdonshire commission of the peace on 2 February.[2]

1642 02 02

Speech by Oliver Cromwell to the House of Commons

Date: 2 February 1642

Sources: [A] BL, Harl. MS 162, fo. 366v, Diary of Sir Simonds D'Ewes. Printed in *Private Journals 3 Jan.–5 Mar. 1642*, p. 255 (reported speech). [B] BL, Harl. MS 480, fos 91v–92, Diary of John Moore. Printed in *Private Journals 3 Jan.–5 Mar. 1642*, p. 257 (reported speech). [C] BL, Add. MS 14827, fo. 26, Diary of Framlingham Gawdy. Printed in *Private Journals 3 Jan.–5 Mar. 1642*, p. 264 (reported speech)

In January 1642 Sir Edward Dering,[1] MP for Kent, published *A Collection of Speeches* (1642), which brought together in print the speeches he had delivered to the Long Parliament. The previous May he had introduced the 'root and branch' bill against episcopacy, but he had since opposed the Grand Remonstrance and so was viewed by some of his colleagues as being inconsistent. This edition of his speeches was intended by him to clarify his actual views. Some however interpreted it as a further attack by him on the policies now being advocated by Parliament.

[A] BL, Harl. MS 162, fo. 366v, Diary of Sir Simonds D'Ewes. Printed in *Private Journals 3 Jan.–5 Mar. 1642*, p. 255 (reported speech)

Upon Mr Cromwells motion Sr Edward Derings booke was ordere to be burnt on friday next,[2] & the sheriffs of London & Middlesex.[3]

---

[1] JHC, 2:397. [2] JHC, 2:409.

[1] Sir Edward Dering, first baronet (1598–1644), antiquary and religious controversialist. See ODNB.
[2] 6 February 1642.   [3] Sir George Garret and Sir George Clarke.

7 FEBRUARY 1642A

[B] BL, Harl. MS 480, fos 91v–92, Diary of John Moore. Printed in *Private Journals 3 Jan.–5 Mar. 1642*, p. 257 (reported speech)

Mr Cromwell moved against the booke put forth against by Sr Ed: Deareinge, wch he conceaves to be against the honor of the house & conceaves to be a great breach of the privi. of this house, & nominats some members to bringe th in disrespecte. of the contrary pte & desyres that it may be refered to a comitte to ex it.

[C] BL, Add. MS 14827, fo. 26, Diary of Framlingham Gawdy. Printed in *Private Journals 3 Jan.–5 Mar. 1642*, p. 264 (reported speech)

Mr Cromwell desyre a booke that Syr Edward deerings booke sett forthe by hymselfe full of \impertynences/ Indypencies, and many other thyngs as that If the bill agaynst bishops had passed he yntended to have desyred leave to have protested agaynst thtt. he desyre itt may be reserved to a committe.

Outcome: Cromwell's motion was successful. The Commons ordered that Dering's Collection of Speeches was to be burned by the common hangman at Westminster, Cheapside and Smithfield, that Dering be expelled as an MP and that he be sent to the Tower of London.[4]

1642 02 07a

Speech by Oliver Cromwell to the House of Commons

Date: 7 February 1642
Source: BL, Harl. MS 480, fo. 113, Diary of John Moore. Printed in *Private Journals 3 Jan.–5 Mar. 1642*, pp. 302–3 (reported speech)

The crisis over the Five Members and the ongoing debates about the reform of church government prompted the submission of numerous petitions from throughout England and Wales during the early months of 1642. The Monmouthshire petition was therefore just one of many.

Mr Cromwell delivered a peticon from Ed: Hollister, Robt Jones & others[1] in the county of monmouth who for want of preaching ministers have gone from the parish church,

---

[4] *JHC*, 2:411.

---

[1] The Journals mention 'Sisley Rumsey, Edward Harry, David Kenkins, and divers others': *JHC*, 2:419.

THE LETTERS, WRITINGS, AND SPEECHES OF OLIVER CROMWELL

where there is noe preachinge & are therefore psented at the assyeys[2] tht a reference may be made to[3] Walter Rumsey,[4] Mr Harbart[5] & Mr Morgell[6] Justices of peace in tht county or to any two of th & in the meanetyme all suits to be staied against th.

———

Outcome: As Moore notes, three of the local justices of the peace, Walter Rumsey, William Herbert and Edward Morgan, were asked to investigate and the assizes cases were suspended.[7]

———⦇⦈———

1642 02 07b
Speech by Oliver Cromwell to the House of Commons

Date: 7 February 1642
Source: BL, Harl. MS 480, fo. 114, Diary of John Moore. Printed in *Private Journals 3 Jan.–5 Mar. 1642*, p. 304 (reported speech)

Theobald Taaffe, second Viscount Taaffe of Corren, later first earl of Carlingford,[1] had been one of the officers in the Irish army who had been appointed to transport the disbanded Irish soldiers abroad. Although his own role in the uprising was (and remains) unclear, some of his troops had since joined the Irish rebellion in late 1641.[2] In early 1642 he had evidently been arrested in England.

———

Mr Cromwell moved tht colonell Taaf[3] might be dischardged, soe it is ordered tht Mr Pim[4] shall ex it, tht soe he may either be chardged or disc.[5]

———

[2] Illegible deletion.   [3] Illegible deletion.
[4] Walter Rumsey (1584–1651). See *HoP Commons, 1640–1660*. He was second justice of the Brecon circuit 1631–47, MP for Monmouthshire in the Short Parliament, 1640.
[5] (Probably) William Herbert (*c*.1593–1651). See *HoP Commons, 1603–1629*. He was from Coldbrook, Abergavenny, Monmouthshire and had been MP for Monmouthshire in 1626.
[6] At *JHC*, 2:419 he is Edward Morgan, either way he has not been identified.
[7] *JHC*, 2:419.

[1] Theodore Taaffe, first earl of Carlingford (d.1677), army officer and politician. See *ODNB*.
[2] Evidence of his activity with the rebels can be found in many of the 1641 depositions: see especially within www.1641.tcd.ie, MS831 fos 216–217, deposition of Ismay Darby; MS810, fos 358–363, deposition of Brien O'Neill, MS836, fos 127–138.
[3] Partly smudged. Taaffe had only very recently succeeded his father as the second viscount. *Complete Peerage*, 12(2): 595. The Commons Journals also describes him only as 'Colonel Taffe': *JHC*, 2:419.
[4] John Pym (1584–1643), politician. See *ODNB*.   [5] *JHC*, 2:419.

Outcome: The Commons Journals confirm that John Pym was ordered to review Taaffe's examination. Taaffe remained in custody for the time being, but escaped in June 1642.

1642 02 07C

Speech by Oliver Cromwell to the House of Commons

Date: 7 February 1642

Source: BL, Harl. MS 162, fo. 373, Diary of Sir Simonds D'Ewes. Printed in *Private Journals 3 Jan.–5 Mar. 1642*, p. 293 (reported speech)

The Commons now returned to the subject of Sir Edward Dering (see **1642 02 02**), possibly at Cromwell's instigation.

Mr Cromwel moved that Sr Edward Derings booke latelie sett out by him had many dangerous and scandalous passages in it by which many might bee deceived and ledd into an ill opinion concerning the proceedings of this howse and therfore desired that some able member of the howse might bee appointed to make a short confutation of the same and then nominated mee which made mee presently stand upp and answer

Outcome: Sir Simonds D'Ewes responded by pointing out that as it was now almost 7 p.m., it was inappropriately late for such a matter to be raised. He then argued that there were other more important subjects on which he might wish to publish and so suggested that Cromwell himself should write the reply to Dering. The Speaker, William Lenthall, expressed the hope that D'Ewes might publish the other works he had mentioned. D'Ewes's account implies that the Commons then adjourned until the following morning. However, the Journals show that the Commons ordered that Dering hand over his papers as chairman of the House's committee for printing.[1] It is not clear whether this was ordered before or after Cromwell had moved his motion.

[1] *JHC*, 2:419.

1642 02 16

Speech by Oliver Cromwell to the House of Commons

Date: 16 February 1642
Source: BL, Harl. MS 162, fo. 388v, Diary of Sir Simonds D'Ewes. Printed in *Private Journals 3 Jan.–5 Mar. 1642*, p. 395 (reported speech)

The Commons this day received a report from Sir Walter Erle from the sub-committee of the committee for Irish affairs on proposals for the suppression of the rebellion in Ireland. Erle gave details of how money could be raised to fund that campaign and of how lands could be confiscated from the rebels. This plan was what would become the Irish Adventure.[1] Cromwell correctly discerned that one of the key figures behind these plans was Sir John Clotworthy.[2] He therefore proposed that Clotworthy should be discouraged from departing for Ireland as soon as possible.

Mr Cromwell moved that Sr John Clatworthie had done great service for setling these propositions at the Committee & soe desired that some time might be allowed him to stay still & not yet goe into Ireland for the furtherance of this particular busines.

Outcome: The Commons did not formally take up Cromwell's suggestion. Perhaps it was felt to be enough that Cromwell and others were able to praise Clotworthy for his efforts in this matter.

1642 03 02

Speech by Oliver Cromwell to the House of Commons

Date: 2 March 1642
Source: BL Add. MS 14827, fo. 57v, Diary of Framlingham Gawdy. Printed in *Private Journals 3 Jan.–5 Mar. 1642*, p. 496 (reported speech)

One of the grooms of the bedchamber, William Murray,[1] had known the King since childhood and was considered to be one of his closest confidants. It was believed that he had leaked the news of the King's plan to arrest the Five Members to Lord Digby,[2] MP for Dorset. On 2 March Cromwell was sent by the Commons to the Lords to request that a

---

[1] *JHC*, 2:435. See Karl Bottigheimer, *English Money and Irish Land: the 'Adventurers' in the Cromwellian Settlement of Ireland* (Oxford, 1971), ch. 2.
[2] Sir John Clotworthy, first Viscount Massereene (d. 1665), politician. See *ODNB*.

[1] William Murray, first earl of Dysart (d. 1655), courtier. See *ODNB*.
[2] George Digby, second earl of Bristol (1612–77), politician. See *ODNB*.

joint committee be appointed to examine Murray about this. Cromwell now returned to report that the Lords had agreed to such a meeting.[3]

Mr Cromwell a report from the lords that they have appoynted att 5 a clocke to examyn Mr William murrey concerning my Lord dygbye.

1642 03 08
Speech by Oliver Cromwell to the House of Commons

Date: 8 March 1642
Source: BL, Harl. MS 163, fo. 23v, Diary of Sir Simonds D'Ewes. Printed in Vernon F. Snow, Anne Steele Young, eds., *The Private Journals of the Long Parliament, 1 June to 17 September 1642* (New Haven and London, 1992), p. 8 (reported speech)

The case of Colonel Francis Edmonds[1] involved seditious words allegedly spoken by him on 5 March at the Balcony Tavern in Covent Garden. Three days later Cromwell raised the case in the Commons.

Mr Cromwel enformed that dangerous words had been spoaken by a Colonel latelie & that the witnesses weere at the doore who could testifie it. viz. Mr Crant & Mr Parker.[2]

Outcome: The two witnesses, Thomas Crant and George Parker, then testified to the House. Crant claimed that Edmonds had said that the King had been right to give no reply to Parliament's militia bill, that he was happy if the King and Parliament continued to disagree, and that the King would 'dispatch' William Strode, John Pym and John Hampden. Parker confirmed this and also accused Sir Piers Crosby,[3] 'Mr Baily'[4] and others. Parker also claimed that Edmonds was a Roman Catholic. A prominent figure in Irish politics, Crosby had played a leading role in the proceedings against the first earl of Strafford. The Commons therefore summoned Edmonds, Crosby and Baily to appear before them.[5] Crosby subsequently sided with the Irish Confederates.

---

[3] JHC, 2:465; JHL, 4:472.

[1] Probably the same Francis Edmonds who later served as a royalist army officer: Newman, *Royalist Officers*, no. 473.
[2] Not identified.   [3] Sir Piers Crosby (1590–1646). See *DIB*.
[4] Not identified.   [5] JHC, 2:471.

THE LETTERS, WRITINGS, AND SPEECHES OF OLIVER CROMWELL

1642 03 16
Speech by Oliver Cromwell to the House of Commons

Date: 16 March 1642
Source: BL, Harl. MS 163, fo. 35, Diary of Sir Simonds D'Ewes. Printed in *Private Journals 7 Mar.–1 June 1642*, p. 47 (reported speech)

Parliament continued to receive large numbers of petitions from throughout the kingdom. The one collected in Cambridgeshire expressed its support for Parliament and, among other things, called for the reform of the universities, action against Roman Catholics, reform of probate, the abolition of the bishop of Ely's secular jurisdiction, a single sheriff for Cambridgeshire and Huntingdonshire and the implementation of the Militia Ordinance.[1] The text of the related petition, which was just from the town of Cambridge, does not survive. When both groups of petitioners came to deliver them to Parliament, it was natural that they should ask Cromwell to arrange this for them.

———

The messengers being withdrawen upon Mr Cromwels motion \divers of/ the gentlemen of Cambridgeshire & some inhabitants of the towne of Cambridge weere admitted in with a pe & Sr Thomas \Martin/[2] in the name of the rest delivered in a petition from the Countie of Cambridge to this howse: & ther petition alsoe wch they weere to preferre to the the Lords,[3] with a very short preface in which hee was almost out, then[4] delivered in a Petition from the Towne of Cambridge and soe they withdrewe out of the howse. The Petition of the County of Cambridge to the howse of Commons was first read which contained little matter differing from other Petitions formerly delivered in by other Counties. The next was read the Petition they were to preferre to the Lords not.

———

Outcome: The Speaker, William Lenthall, thanked the petitioners. His comments to the Cambridge petitioners reveal something of that petition's content, because he told them, 'That as to the Particular concerning the Lecture, that when they shall nominate one to the House, That they hold fit to be a Lecturer, that they will give Order for Erecting of a Lecture, and establishing a Lecturer'.[5] It is just possible that this was a reference to the existing town lecture at Holy Trinity, Cambridge. John Ellis,[6] a distant kinsman of Cromwell and a

---

[1] *The humble Petition of the Knights, Esquires, Gentry and Commons, Inhabitants of the County of Cambridgeshire* (1641).

[2] Insertion in a different hand. Martin was subsequently one of the leading Cambridgeshire parliamentarians.

[3] At this point, a new hand takes over.   [4] Gap as in the original manuscript.

[5] *JHC*, 2:480.

[6] John Ellis (d. 1681), Church of England clergyman and religious controversialist. See *ODNB*.

close associate of the group of Cambridge townsmen who had supported Cromwell's election in 1640, was probably appointed as the Holy Trinity lecturer at about this time.[7] But there is no record of Ellis being appointed to that position by the Commons, and Lenthall's comment implies that the petitioners wanted to create a new lectureship. It may however be that Ellis's appointment to the existing lectureship removed the pressure for a new one.

1642 03 22

Speech by Oliver Cromwell to the House of Commons

Date: 22 March 1642
Source: BL Harl. MS 163, fo. 41v, Diary of Sir Simonds D'Ewes. Printed in *Private Journals 7 Mar.–1 June 1642*, p. 71 (reported speech)

Since its foundation in 1584, Emmanuel College, Cambridge, had maintained a reputation for godly Protestantism.[1] Elsewhere in Cambridge significant numbers of Laudian clerics had gained college fellowships. Those who disapproved therefore feared that the composition of the fellowship at Emmanuel might change in the same way. Much depended on the existence of a clause in the college statutes which required fellows of Emmanuel to resign their fellowships within one year of receiving a doctoral degree. This was raised in Parliament in December 1640 and a bill confirming that requirement had been introduced in June 1641. In the meantime, the most recent election of a fellow, Thomas Hodges, was challenged on the grounds that three of the fellows who had voted for him held their fellowships in contravention of this rule. Disputing this election was also a means of embarrassing the university's vice-chancellor, Richard Holdsworth, as he was the college's master.[2] On 21 October 1641 the Commons had intervened to suspend Hodges's election pending further investigations.[3] Now on 22 March 1642 Peregrine Pelham, MP for Kingston upon Hull (Yorkshire), reported from the Commons committee on the subject. The committee recommendation was that Hodges's election was invalid. The Commons agreed.[4] Cromwell then intervened to make a supplementary point.

---

[7] Barclay, *Electing Cromwell*, pp. 50–1.

[1] Sarah Bendall, Christopher Brooke and Patrick Collinson, eds., *A History of Emmanuel College Cambridge* (Woodbridge, 2000), chs. 1–2.
[2] John Twigg, *The University of Cambridge and the English Revolution* (Woodbridge, 1990), pp. 55–6.
[3] JHC, 2:291, 351, 427.   [4] JHC, 2:492.

THE LETTERS, WRITINGS, AND SPEECHES OF OLIVER CROMWELL

Mr ~~Will~~ Cromwell shewed that Mr Worlington[5] had then the maior part of voices & was dulie elected, & desired that the same might be voted but because Mr Pelham had made no report of it, it was laied aside.

***

Outcome: What Cromwell was attempting to do was to persuade the Commons to appoint the losing candidate, John Worthington, but as the committee had made no recommendations on that point, no decision was taken. A week later Pelham was able to report back from the committee on this. The Commons then resolved that Worthington should be appointed.[6]

1642 03 29

Speech by Oliver Cromwell to the House of Commons

Date: 29 March 1642
Source: BL, Harl. MS 163, fo. 54, Diary of Sir Simonds D'Ewes. Printed in *Private Journals 7 Mar.–1 June 1642*, p. 104 (reported speech)

This intervention by Cromwell involved him informing the House of the contents of a letter from three Monmouthshire clergymen about possible Catholic plots in Monmouth. It is revealing that Cromwell should have been one of the three MPs to whom those clergymen addressed their letter. This suggests that he was already well-known as an MP who would be willing to raise concerns about suspicious activities by Catholics.

***

Mr Cromwell then delivered in a certificate from Mr Symonds[1] & three other Ministers of Monmouthshire directed to Sr Arthur Haslerigg[2] himselfe & Mr Pym[3] bearing date Mar. 23. 1641 by wh they shewed ~~Mar. 23. 1641~~ that the strength of papists was soe great about \the towne of/ Monmouth as they feared if some speedie course weere not taken it would be in as great danger shortlie as Ireland.

---

[5] John Worthington (bap. 1618, d. 1671), Church of England clergyman, translator and editor of philosophical works. See *ODNB*.
[6] *JHC*, 2:504.

---

[1] Richard Symonds (b. 1609, d. in or after 1658), independent minister. A native of Monmouthshire, Symonds was a separatist clergyman who had formerly been the schoolmaster to the Harleys of Brampton Bryan. He had only recently been appointed by the Commons as the lecturer at Andover, Hampshire. *JHC*, 2:440.
[2] Sir Arthur Hesilige (1601–61), army officer and politician. See *ODNB*.
[3] John Pym (1584–1643), politician. See *ODNB*.

Outcome: The Speaker, William Lenthall, then informed the Commons that he had received a letter of the same date from the mayor of Monmouth refusing to obey a previous order that the town magazine be moved from Monmouth to Newport. The Commons therefore reiterated its former order for the removal of the magazine, while also ordering that the Monmouthshire recusants were to be disarmed and that the mayor was to be summoned before them.[4]

1642 03 31a

Speech by Oliver Cromwell to the House of Commons

Date: 31 March 1642
Source: BL, Harl. MS 163, fo. 56v, Diary of Sir Simonds D'Ewes. Printed in *Private Journals 7 Mar.–1 June 1642*, p. 112 (reported speech)

Parliament had passed the Militia Ordinance on 5 March. Its assertion of parliamentary control over the militia was a challenge to the King's authority that he was never likely to accept quietly. In the several declarations he issued in the weeks that followed, he had made it clear that he would not consent to the Ordinance's contents. He moreover began to send orders to the sheriffs instructing them to publish these declarations. One of the sheriffs who received such an order was the sheriff of Kent. The issue as to whether he should obey it then became entangled with the Kentish petition promoted by Sir Edward Dering and other local gentlemen. Among other things, that petition condemned the Militia Ordinance. By late March the Commons was keen to investigate who had promoted this petition. On 31 March it asked its committee on that subject to prepare a general order against such instructions from the King.[1] This was evidently done at Cromwell's suggestion.

Upon Mr Cromwels motion it was ordered that some order should be prepared to inhibit the sherifs of England to publish anie Declaration from his Matie agst the Militia.

Outcome: Another committee to prepare an order against such instructions from the King to the sheriffs was created on 5 April.[2] Over the coming months the Commons would issue numerous orders against the publication of declarations and proclamations from the King.

---

[4] *JHC*, 2:503.

[1] *JHC*, 2:506. [2] *JHC*, 2:512.

1642 03 31b
Speech by Oliver Cromwell to the House of Commons

Date: 31 March 1642
Source: BL, Harl. MS 163, fo. 56v, Diary of Sir Simonds D'Ewes. Printed in *Private Journals 7 Mar.–1 June 1642*, p. 113 (reported speech)

Alexander Carew,[1] MP for Cornwall, had apparently been appointed to the committee on the Kentish petition, although there is no actual record of this in the Journals. He had since been granted leave of absence on 29 March.[2] Cromwell now secured the agreement of the Commons that Sir Henry Vane the younger[3] should take Carew's place on that committee.[4]

Upon Mr Cromwels motion Sr Henry Fane the yonger was added to the Committee for the petition of Kent in the roome of Mr Alexander Carew gone into the Cuntrie.

1642 04 28
Speeches of Oliver Cromwell to the House of Commons

Date: 28 April 1642
Source: BL, Harl. MS 164, fo. 255v, Diary of Sir Simonds D'Ewes. Printed in *Private Journals 7 Mar.–1 June 1642*, p. 237 (reported speech)

Cromwell is not recorded as speaking at all in the four weeks between 31 March and 28 April although there is no evidence he was away from Westminster. But then begins a period of intense activity in the House: nearly thirty recorded interventions over the next two months.

On 23 April Sir John Hotham as the town's governor had refused to allow the King to enter Kingston upon Hull. Now, on 28 April, the Commons sent Cromwell to the Lords to

---

[1] Sir Alexander Carew, second baronet (1608–44), politician and army officer. See *ODNB*. He was an active parliamentarian (and served as an army officer) during the first year of the war, but changed sides in the high summer of 1643.

[2] *JHC*, 2:503.

[3] Sir Henry Vane the younger (1613–62), politician and author. See *ODNB*. The younger Vane was the radicalised son of a man who had been Charles I's secretary of state from 1639 to 1641.

[4] *JHC*, 2:506.

3 MAY 1642

ask that they continue sitting as they had important information about that event. He returned to report that the Lords would sit that afternoon.[1]

Mr Crumwell reported that the Lords had appointed to sitt againe at 2 of the clocke & thereupon the same Mr Hollis[2] mooved that Mr Crumwell might bee sent up againe to Desire their Lordshipps that they would sitt awhile for wee had somewhat to communicate to them touching the petition of Kent wch concerned the safetie of the kingdome whereupon Mr Crumwell went againe instantly to the Lords with the said message…

Outcome: Cromwell's message had interrupted the interrogation of John Best of Allington, Kent, a Gray's Inn lawyer who had information about the Kentish petition. The interrogation of Best therefore resumed after Cromwell had been sent back to the Lords. MPs were debating the implications of Best's testimony when Cromwell returned.

Then Mr Cromwell returned and made report that the Lords would sitt as wee had desired.

Outcome: Sir Henry Vane the younger was then sent to the Lords to request a joint conference on the subject of the Kentish petition.[3]

1642 05 03

Speech by Oliver Cromwell to the House of Commons

Date: 3 May 1642
Source: BL, Harl. MS 163, fo. 104, Diary of Sir Simonds D'Ewes. Printed in *Private Journals 7 Mar.–1 June 1642*, p. 268 (reported speech)

The Irish rebels had failed to take control of Dublin. But to nervous Protestants the presence of large numbers of Irish Catholics there seemed a security threat. Cromwell now voiced those fears in the Commons.

Mr Crumwell moved that wee might take some course to turne the papists out of Dublin: others seconded him.

---

[1] *JHL*, 5:25; *JHC*, 2:545.
[2] Denzil Holles, first Baron Holles (1598–1680), politician. See *ODNB*.
[3] *JHC*, 2:545.

65

Outcome: Sir Simonds D'Ewes spoke against the idea on the grounds that this was better left to the lords justices in Dublin. He also thought that if the Catholic inhabitants were a real threat, they would already have seized the city. The matter was then referred to the committee for Irish affairs.[1] D'Ewes interpreted that as meaning that the Commons had followed his advice, although that perhaps says more about his own sense of self-importance.

1642 05 04
Speech by Oliver Cromwell to the House of Commons

Date: 4 May 1642
Source: BL, Harl. MS 163, fo. 106v, Diary of Sir Simonds D'Ewes. Printed in *Private Journals 7 Mar.–1 June 1642*, p. 275 (reported speech)

John Manby,[1] the rector of Cottenham,[2] Cambridgeshire, had a reputation as a firm Laudian. His parishioners, with Cromwell's support, now petitioned Parliament seeking the appointment of alternative preachers.

Mr Cromwell preffered in a petition for the inhabitants of the towne of Codenham in the County of Cambridge wherein they complained that one Dr Manlie was their ~~Mr Cromwell moved to Codenham Dr Manlie~~ Minister who neglected to preach and soe desired that some fellowes of the Colledges of Cambridge might bee authorized by this howse to preach there each Lords day which was ordered accordingly.

~~Mr Cr~~

Outcome: The Commons agreed to appoint eight Cambridge dons, including Benjamin Whichcote,[3] John Sadler[4] and Ralph Cudworth,[5] to preach in Manby's place at Cottenham. Several of the eight clergymen appointed, such as the Ellis brothers, John and Thomas, and John Almond, probably knew Cromwell personally.[6]

---

[1] *JHC*, 2:545.

---

[1] *Walker Rev.*, pp. 83–4.
[2] Cottenham was and is a fen-edge village five miles north of the city of Cambridge.
[3] Benjamin Whichcote (1609–84), theologian and moral philosopher. See *ODNB*.
[4] John Sadler (1615–74), political theorist and reformer. See *ODNB*.
[5] Ralph Cudworth (1617–88), philosopher and theologian. See *ODNB*.
[6] Barclay, *Electing Cromwell*, pp. 49, 50, 55.

16 MAY 1642

1642 05 16

Speech by Oliver Cromwell to the House of Commons

Date: 16 May 1642

Source: BL, Harl. MS 163, fo. 123, Diary of Sir Simonds D'Ewes. Printed in *Private Journals 7 Mar.–1 June 1642*, p. 327 (reported speech)

Any military campaign in Ireland would require money, so the Commons had been seeking loans from the merchants of the City of London. The Merchant Adventurers of London, as one of the wealthier mercantile companies, remained one potential source of funding. A year earlier Cromwell had been sceptical of the offer of a loan from them (see **1641 05 29**). He now however took a different line and pressed for the efforts to obtain a new loan to be pursued. Perhaps it made all the difference that this money was to be used against the Irish rebels.

Upon Mr Cromwells motion it was ordered that Sr Henry Mildmay[1] & the other gentlemen formerlie appointed should againe attend the marchant adventurers about monie to be borrowed of them

Outcome: The Commons ordered that some members of its existing committee to seek a loan from the Merchant Adventurers should meet with the company.[2]

1642 05 23

Speech by Oliver Cromwell to the House of Commons

Date: 23 May 1642

Sources: [A] BL, Harl. MS 163, fo. 130, Diary of Sir Simonds D'Ewes. Printed in *Private Journals 7 Mar.–1 June 1642*, p. 361 (reported speech). [B] BL, Add. MS 14827, fo. 113, Diary of Framlingham Gawdy. Printed in *Private Journals 7 Mar.–1 June 1642*, p. 363 (reported speech)

The former Army Plotters, Henry Wilmot and William Ashburnham, had been released on bail the previous year (see **1641 11 04**). The King had since summoned them to join him at York. Viscount Mandeville (the future second earl of Manchester)[1] had stood bail for

---

[1] Sir Henry Mildmay (1593–1668), see *HoP Commons, 1640–1660*.   [2] *JHC*, 2:572.

[1] Edward Montagu, second earl of Manchester (1602–71), parliamentarian army officer and politician. See *ODNB*.

one of them—it is not clear for which—and so wanted this to be waived if they now violated their bail by obeying that summons. Cromwell was presumably acting on Mandeville's behalf when he raised the issue.

[A] BL, Harl. MS 163, fo. 130, Diary of Sir Simonds D'Ewes. Printed in *Private Journals 7 Mar.–1 June 1642*, p. 361 (reported speech)

A little after eleven of the clocke I returned into the Howse & Mr Cromwell had newlie moved that Mr Wilmot ~~Pullard~~[2] & Colonel Ashburnham for ~~whom~~ \ whose appearance/ the Lord Mandevill was bound baile might bee sommoned to come in & appeare that soe the baile might bee discharged which was ordered accordingly
~~L. Mandevill ther baile.~~

[B] BL, Add. MS 14827, fo. 113, Diary of Framlingham Gawdy. Printed in *Private Journals 7 Mar.–1 June 1642*, p. 363 (reported speech)

Mr Cromwell that the king hath sent for Mr Willmott and Mr Will: asburnham. Therefore my lo: mandevyll that ths bayle for one them desyre that he may be dyschardged and that new bayle may be putt in.

Ordered that Mr Willmott and Mr Ashburnham be summoned to appeare heere to morrow mornyng. and the bayle to have notyce.

Outcome: As noted by Gawdy, Wilmot and Ashburnham were summoned to appear the following morning.[3] No one can have been too surprised when they failed to obey that order.

[2] Hugh Pollard. Pollard had also been an Army Plotter back in May 1641, so D'Ewes's initial assumption that Pollard was involved here as well as Wilmot and Ashburnham is an understandable mistake.
[3] JHC, 2:583.

24 MAY 1642

1642 05 24

Speech by Oliver Cromwell to the House of Commons

Date: 24 May 1642
Source: BL, Harl. MS 163, fo. 132v, Diary of Sir Simonds D'Ewes. Printed in *Private Journals 7 Mar.–1 June 1642*, p. 368 (reported speech)

On 30 April 1642 the Commons had ordered that Ambrose Mostyn should be appointed as the lecturer of Pennard, Glamorganshire.[1] That had presumably been intended to weaken the influence of the vicar, William Edwards. The parishioners now submitted a new petition complaining that Edwards had refused to accept that order.

Mr Cromwell delivered in the \in a petition in the name of the/ parishoners of the parish of Pennh\a/rd in the Countie of Glamorgan; where wee had setled a Lecturer against one William Edwards a clergieman who opposed the same order & had spoaken verie disgracefullie of this: wch was read; & then a witnes being brought in who avowed it hee was sent for as a delinquent.

Outcome: The Commons ordered that Edwards should be summoned before them as a delinquent.[2]

⚬∞∞⚬

1642 05 26

Speeches of Oliver Cromwell to the House of Commons

Date: 26 May 1642
Source: BL, Harl. MS 163, fo. 133v, Diary of Sir Simonds D'Ewes. Printed in *Private Journals 7 Mar.–1 June 1642*, p. 372 (reported speech)

The planned expedition to Ireland would require ships to transport that army. The new concern was that there would be too few sailors to man those ships. A bill to recruit soldiers for that purpose had been sent by the Commons to the Lords. Cromwell was now sent to the Lords to encourage them to pass it. He also took with him an order for the appointment of Sir Richard Samuel as a deputy lieutenant for Northamptonshire.[1]

---

[1] *JHC*, 2:551.
[2] *JHC*, 2:586.

---

[1] *JHL*, 5:85.

Mr Cromwell was sent upp to the Lords to desire them to hasten the[2] raising of 1000. men by authoritie of both howses for the shipps that weere to go into \Ireland./

Outcome: On receiving the message from Cromwell, the Lords agreed to approve the order for Samuel's appointment. They however told Cromwell that the bill to recruit soldiers was in the hands of a peer who was ill, although they promised to send a reply as soon as they could.[3]

Mr Cromwell returned from his message alsoe & shewed that hee received the Lords answeare from the Earle of Leicester[4] \who was now the Speaker/ ~~wch was that the~~ in the Lords Howse, that ther Lor.pps ~~did concurre~~ would doe as wee had desired.

Outcome: The entry in the Commons Journals is incomplete and ambiguous, while D'Ewes's account oversimplifies what the Lords had told Cromwell.[5]

1642 05 27a

Speech by Oliver Cromwell to the House of Commons

Date: 27 May 1642
Source: BL, Harl. MS 163, fo. 133v, Diary of Sir Simonds D'Ewes. Printed in *Private Journals 7 Mar.–1 June 1642*, p. 375 (reported speech)

Claiming that the King was obstructing the preparations for the expedition to Ireland was a useful way of insinuating that he could not be trusted to oversee the efforts to suppress the Irish rebellion.

Mr Cromwell moved that a Committee might be appointed to draw a Poclamation to shew the severall delaies had proceeded from his Matie of late in de hinderance of the supplies for Ireland. Soe himselfe & some others weere appointed a committee to withdraw presentlie & prepare such a declaration.

---

[2] Illegible deletion.   [3] *JHL*, 5:85.
[4] Robert Sidney, second earl of Leicester (1595–1677), diplomat and landowner. See *ODNB*.
[5] *JHC*, 2:588; *JHL*, 5:85.

Outcome: Contrary to what D'Ewes states, Cromwell was not listed in the Journals as one of the six MPs appointed as this committee.[1] No such declaration by Parliament was ever issued.

1642 05 27b
Speech by Oliver Cromwell to the House of Commons

Date: 27 May 1642
Source: BL, Harl. MS 163, fo. 133v, Diary of Sir Simonds D'Ewes. Printed in *Private Journals 7 Mar.–1 June 1642*, p. 375 (reported speech)

Later that day Cromwell returned to the subject of the problems being encountered in the preparations for the Irish expedition.

Mr Cromwell delivered in a Lre sent from Mr Charles Walleigh[1] dated at Chester May. 23. 1642. to Mr Adam Loftis,[2] in wh hee shewed that divers troupes lay at Chester who had received ther pay & had a faire winde to passe & yet neglected.

Outcome: The Commons ordered Sir John Corbett, first baronet, MP for Shropshire, to travel to Chester to investigate. Cromwell was not one of the three MPs asked to prepare instructions for Corbett.[3]

---

[1] *JHC*, 2:588.

[1] Charles Walley, innkeeper and alderman of Chester, MP for the town in 1654. Walley was regularly involved in the shipment of military supplies to Ireland throughout this period. Probably inclined more towards the royalists during the Civil War and, as mayor of Chester 1644–6, he cooperated with the royalist forces occupying the city. A. M. Johnson, 'Politics in Chester during the Civil Wars and the Interregnum', in *Crisis and Order in English Towns 1500–1700: Essays in Urban History*, ed. P. Clark and P. Slack (1972), pp. 213–14.

[2] D'Ewes appears to have slightly confused this name. Either Sir Adam Loftus of Rathfarnham, County Dublin (d. 1651), vice-treasurer and treasurer at war for Ireland, or his brother, Nicholas Loftus (1592–1666), his deputy as treasurer at war (for both see *DIB*).

[3] *JHC*, 2:588. And Sir John Corbett (d. 1665). See *HoP Commons, 1640–1660*.

1642 05 28a

Speech by Oliver Cromwell to the House of Commons

Date: 28 May 1642
Source: BL, Harl. MS 163, fo. 136v, Diary of Sir Simonds D'Ewes. Printed in *Private Journals 7 Mar.–1 June 1642*, p. 382 (reported speech)

Now that a civil war seemed a real possibility, the demand for armour and weapons soared. Cromwell seems to have realised that one way of checking who might be stockpiling arms would be to monitor the output of the relevant London livery companies, the Armourers and Brassiers, the Gunmakers and the Saddlers.

Upon Mr Cromwels motion seconded by others, it was ordered that the wardens of the companies of Armorers gunn- ~~makers~~ smiths & sadlers should certify Sr Thomas Barrington[1] & Sr Walter Earle[2] of it weekelie & that the Serjeant should instantlie send

Outcome: The wardens and officers of those companies were ordered to make weekly reports to Barrington and Erle on their production of saddles, arms and muskets.[3]

1642 05 28b

Speech by Oliver Cromwell to the House of Commons

Date: 28 May 1642
Source: BL, Harl. MS 163, fo. 136v, Diary of Sir Simonds D'Ewes. Printed in *Private Journals 7 Mar.–1 June 1642*, p. 382 (reported speech)

D'Ewes's notes on this occasion are difficult to reconcile precisely with the Commons Journals. One of them seems to have been slightly confused. But the basic point seems clear enough. On this day the Lords sent back an amended version of the bill to recruit soldiers for the Irish expedition. This was the bill about which Cromwell had been sent to the Lords two days earlier to encourage them to pass (see 26 May 1642). The Commons immediately agreed to the single, minor amendment that the Lords had made. It was evidently at this point that Cromwell moved this related motion.

---

[1] Sir Thomas Barrington (*c.*1585–1644), politician. See ODNB.
[2] Sir Walter Erle or Earle (1586–1665), politician. See ODNB.
[3] *JHC*, 2:590.

30 MAY 1642

Mr Rigbie[1] upon Cromwells motion was appointed to draw an order for raising voluntiers, according to the Ordinance now brought downe.

Outcome: There is however no record of this in the Journals.[2] But such an order was certainly drawn up and was approved by the Commons on 30 May. That gave permission to the officers for the Irish expedition to recruit soldiers throughout England and Wales. Cromwell was then appointed to carry it to the Lords.[3]

1642 05 30

Speech by Oliver Cromwell to the House of Commons

Date: 30 May 1642
Source: BL, Harl. MS 163, fo. 139v, Diary of Sir Simonds D'Ewes. Printed in *Private Journals 7 Mar.–1 June 1642*, p. 389 (reported speech)

William Purefoy,[1] MP for Warwick, wished to obtain permission to return to Warwickshire to assist in the implementation of the Militia Ordinance. Cromwell moved the necessary motion.[2]

Upon Mr Cromwels motion Mr Purefoy one of the Deputie Leiftenants of Warwickshire had licence to goe into the cuntrie &c. I went out of the House a little after one of the clocke in the afternoone & the Howse rose awhile after.

Outcome: Over the coming months Purefoy was one of the leading figures in mobilising Warwickshire on behalf of Parliament.

---

[1] Alexander Rigby (bap. 1594, d. 1650), politician and parliamentarian army officer. See ODNB.
[2] *JHC*, 2:591.   [3] *JHC*, 2:594; *JHL*, 5:92.

[1] William Purefoy (*c*.1580–1659), politician and regicide. See ODNB.   [2] *JHC*, 2:595.

73

THE LETTERS, WRITINGS, AND SPEECHES OF OLIVER CROMWELL

1642 06 01a

Speech by Oliver Cromwell to the House of Commons

Date: 1 June 1642

Source: BL, Harl. MS 163, fo. 141v, Diary of Sir Simonds D'Ewes. Printed in *Private Journals 7 Mar.–1 June 1642*, p. 398 (reported speech)

Some of Parliament's supporters in Hertford had organised themselves as a volunteer military force under the authority of the Militia Ordinance. Their captain, a local grocer, William Turner, complained however that the town's recorder, John Kelyng,[1] and its mayor, Andrew Palmer, had presented charges against them at the Hertfordshire quarter sessions.[2] Cromwell now arranged for Turner to appear before the Commons to give evidence on the matter.

Mr Cromwell shewed that some persons in the towne of Hartford to the number of about 80. had exercised themselves

---

Outcome: After Turner had set out his claims, the Commons ordered that Kelyng and Palmer were to be summoned to appear before them. The Commons also ordered that the joint committee with the Lords on the militia was to prepare an order indemnifying those who took up arms in accordance with the Militia Ordinance.[3] The complaints against Kelyng were referred to the committee of examinations on 3 June.[4] He was imprisoned by Parliament early the following year.

1642 06 01b

Speech by Oliver Cromwell to the House of Commons

Date: 1 June 1642

Source: BL, Harl. MS 163, fo. 141v, Diary of Sir Simonds D'Ewes. Printed in *Private Journals 7 Mar.–1 June 1642*, p. 399 (reported speech)

One concern was that the King might receive shipments of military supplies via the northern ports, such as Newcastle upon Tyne. Cromwell called for action to prevent this.

---

[1] Sir John Kelyng (bap. 1607, d. 1671), judge and politician. See *ODNB*.

[2] Alan Thomson, ed., *The Impact of the Civil War on Hertfordshire 1642–1647* (Hertfordshire Record Society, 23, 2007), pp. xxi–xxii.

[3] *JHC*, 2:597.   [4] *JHC*, 2:602.

Mr Cromwell moved that the Lords might be ~~appointed~~ \desired to/ send some \two/ shipps to guard the Tyne mouth leading upp to Newcastle: to stay \all shipps that come out of denmarke or the low cuntries/

Outcome: The Commons responded by sending Denzil Holles[1] to ask the lord high admiral, the tenth earl of Northumberland,[2] to send two ship to prevent arms, ammunition or money being landed at Tynemouth or Newcastle upon Tyne.[3]

1642 06 01C

Speech by Oliver Cromwell to the House of Commons

Date: 1 June 1642
Source: BL, Harl. MS 163, fo. 142v, Diary of Sir Simonds D'Ewes. Printed in *Private Journals 7 Mar.–1 June 1642*, p. 399 (reported speech)

Later that same day Thomas Toll, MP for King's Lynn (Norfolk), repeated the concerns expressed by Cromwell about military supplies being shipped to the northern ports. He moved that officials in those ports should stop any ships bringing arms and money from Denmark and the Low Countries.

Mr Cromwell seconded it, & was sent up with it.

Outcome: The Commons did indeed agree that officials in the northern ports should be ordered to conduct searches for arms, ammunition and money. But this order was carried to the Lords not by Cromwell but by Denzil Holles.[1]

---

[1] Denzil Holles (1599–1680), politician. See *ODNB*.
[2] Algernon Percy, tenth earl of Northumberland (1602–68), politician. See *ODNB*.
[3] *JHC*, 2:598.

---

[1] *JHC*, 2:598.

1642 06 01d
Speech by Oliver Cromwell to the House of Commons

Date: 1 June 1642

Source: BL, Harl. MS 163, fo. 143, Diary of Sir Simonds D'Ewes. Printed in *Private Journals 7 Mar.–1 June 1642*, pp. 400–1 (reported speech)

Following the outbreak of the Irish rebellion some of the Protestant settlers in the Laggan, County Donegal, had organised their own army under the command of Sir William Stewart.[1] They were currently engaged in fighting against the rebels under Sir Phelim Roe O'Neill[2] for control of those territories. Cromwell now presented the petition from them to Parliament.

Mr Cromwell delivered in a petition from Colonell Steward[3] and others in behalfe of themselves and about 3500. Scotts who had long maintained themselves together against the Rebells in the Province of Ulster in which petition being read it appeared that they had long maintained themselves in two Barronies of that Province against the Rebells without any Supply of Armes, Victualls or money from hence and therfore being in great want of Armes and victualls Mr Cromwell delivered in a petition from Colonel Steward & others in be halfe of themselves 3500 Ulster[4] they now desired some supply from hence The Petition being read Mr Cromwell shewed that they had all this while had but a thousand Armes amongst them and that there were certaine Marchants that did now offer to furnish the howse with victuals and Armes to releive the said Scots and to give 6. moneths time for the payment of the same

Outcome: The petition was referred to the committee for Irish affairs.[5]

[1] Sir William Stewart or Stuart (d. 1647), See *DIB*. Also Kevin Forkan, 'Army List of the Ulster British Forces, 1642–1646', *Achivum Hibernicum*, 59 (2005), pp. 60–1.
[2] Sir Phelim Roe [Felim Ruadh] O'Neill (1603–53), landowner and insurgent. See *ODNB*.
[3] See n. 1.   [4] Deleted words in a different hand.   [5] *JHC*, 2:599.

1642 06 03
Speech by Oliver Cromwell to the House of Commons

Date: 3 June 1642
Source: BL, Harl. MS 163, fo. 144v, Diary of Sir Simonds D'Ewes. Printed in *Private Journals 1 June–17 Sept. 1642*, p. 8 (reported speech)

This was not the first time that Peter Scott, one of the constables of St Martin-in-the-Fields, had petitioned Parliament. Earlier this year the landlord of the Mermaid Tavern had brought a prosecution at the Old Bailey against Scott in connection with his efforts to deal with riotous behaviour by some apprentices. On 15 February, in response to a petition from Scott, the Commons had ordered that the case be suspended.[1] Scott now petitioned the Commons about his latest troubles.

Mr Cromwel delivered into the petition of Peter Scott a Constable of St Martins who had done severall services for the Howse, & was now severall times arrested by the cavaliers & others of who goe away to Yorke and never declare against him. soe it was referred to the committee of information,[2] of which I was

Outcome: As well as referring the petition to the committee of examinations, the Commons ordered that Scott was to have its protection against any such prosecutions.[3]

1642 06 04
Speech by Oliver Cromwell to the House of Commons

Date: 4 June 1642
Source: BL, Harl. MS 163, fo. 146, Diary of Sir Simonds D'Ewes. Printed in *Private Journals 1 June–17 Sept. 1642*, p. 14 (reported speech)

Cromwell continued to take a close interest in the preparation for the expedition to Ireland.

---

[1] JHC, 2:382; *Private Journals 3 Jan.–5 Mar. 1642*, p. 293.
[2] Also known as the committee of examinations.
[3] JHC, 2:603.

THE LETTERS, WRITINGS, AND SPEECHES OF OLIVER CROMWELL

Mr Cromwell delivered in a list of the names of the sea captaines \&other officers/ wch weere to goe ~~to the~~ wth the 13. shipps to the sea-coasts of Ireland against the Rebells of wch fleete Robert Lord Brooke[1] was to be commander in cheife: wch names weere all read & allowed.

Outcome: There is no reference to this in the Journals. The Commons however did order that the commissioners for Irish affairs should send a total of £36,000 to Ireland. It also ordered that Cromwell should brief the committee to send corn to Ireland on what progress had been made in that matter.[2]

1642 06 11

Speech by Oliver Cromwell to the House of Commons

Date: 11 June 1642
Source: BL, Harl. MS 163, fo. 157v, Diary of Sir Simonds D'Ewes. Printed in *Private Journals 1 June–17 Sept. 1642*, p. 61 (reported speech).

On 10 June Parliament approved a set of propositions to allow private individuals to lend money, plate or horses to Parliament to counter the military mobilisation by the King.[1] Among those MPs who that same day offered to contribute was Cromwell, who promised to give £500.[2] The willingness or otherwise of individual MPs to contribute could now be used as a test of loyalty.

Mr ~~Denzel~~[3] Cromwel moved that the Committee appointed to take the answeare of such gentlemen of the Howse as would contribute to the propositions might have power to receive the saied answeares or anie two of them: wch was ordered accordinglie.

Outcome: The propositions had named committees of both Houses to receive subscriptions from peers and MPs. This new order subtly altered the presumption behind that

---

[1] Robert Greville, second Baron Brooke of Beauchamps Court (1607–43), parliamentarian army officer and religious writer. See *ODNB*. Brooke had been appointed as the commander of the expedition.
[2] *JHC*, 2:604–5.

[1] *JHC*, 2:618–19; *JHL*, 5:123.   [2] *Private Journals 1 June–17 Sept. 1642*, p. 472.
[3] Presumably Denzil Holles corrected by D'Ewes to Cromwell.

provision by giving the Commons committee the power to seek answers from those MPs who had failed to subscribe.[4]

1642 06 15a
Speech by Oliver Cromwell to the House of Commons

Date: 15 June 1642

Source: BL, Harl. MS 163, fo. 161v, Diary of Sir Simonds D'Ewes. Printed in *Private Journals 1 June–17 Sept. 1642*, p. 80 (reported speech)

One major aspect of the military preparations being undertaken throughout the country was the disarming of Catholic recusants. The attempts to do so in Yorkshire were particularly sensitive as the King was now based at York and so might well look to the gentry of that county as key supporters in any forthcoming conflict. The order that Cromwell proposed was therefore intended to protect those local officials who had been carrying out such confiscations on Parliament's behalf.

Mr Oliver Cromwell moved that an order might be made that the Justices armes papists trained bands Yorkshire rdered of peace in Yorkshire who had any of the Armes of the Papists of that County in their custodie should not deliver them to any person whatsoever but by authoritie from his Ma:tie signified unto them by both howses of Parliament and that no[1] freeholders armes who was not a papist ought to bee taken from them without their consent all which was ordered accordingly.

Outcome: The order as passed authorised those Yorkshire justices of the peace and other officials who had confiscated arms to retain them unless ordered otherwise by Parliament. The trained bands were also given permission to retain their arms.[2]

---

[4] JHC, 2:619.

[1] Illegible deletion.   [2] JHC, 2:625.

1642 06 15b
Speech by Oliver Cromwell to the House of Commons

Date: 15 June 1642

Source: BL, Harl. MS 163, fo. 162, Diary of Sir Simonds D'Ewes. Printed in *Private Journals 1 June–17 Sept. 1642*, p. 81 (reported speech)

The loans on the propositions (see 11 June 1642) were conceived as a national collection. The propositions envisaged that collections would be made in each county by persons nominated by the local MPs and approved by Parliament. One obvious group to organise those collections would be the local deputy lieutenants, many of whom had been newly appointed by Parliament. But what if the deputy lieutenants were unsupportive? Keen to see these collections succeed, Cromwell proposed an alternative solution.

Upon Mr Cromwels motion it was ordered that the Committee for the Propositions should consider whether it weere not fitt to give the Justices of peace powers to take the subscription in those Counties wheere ther weere no Deputie Leiftenants who had under-written to the same propositions.

Outcome: An order to this effect does not appear in the Journals, although there are other inconsistencies between the Journals and D'Ewes's diary for this day, suggesting that one of them was confused. The other available diary, that by Framlingham Gawdy, does not help clarify this point.[1]

1642 06 15c
Speech by Oliver Cromwell to the House of Commons

Date: 15 June 1642

Source: BL, Harl. MS 163, fo. 162, Diary of Sir Simonds D'Ewes. Printed in *Private Journals 1 June–17 Sept. 1642*, p. 82 (reported speech)

Later that same day Cromwell and Sir Thomas Barrington secured the appointments of two deputy lieutenants.

---

[1] JHC, 2:625; *Private Journals 1 June–17 Sept. 1642*, pp. 81–2, 84.

\Upon Mr Cromwells motion that/ Mr John Brograve.[1] ~~Mr Timothie Middelton[2]~~ i (of Alburie lodge in the Countie of Hartford Esquire) af might be recommended from this Howse as a Deputie Leiftenant for Hartfordshire; it was after some debate, ordered accordinglie.

Outcome: The Commons agreed to appoint Brograve as a Hertfordshire deputy lieutenant. D'Ewes's confusion over Timothy Middleton's appointment was because, as the next item of business, Barrington got Middleton appointed as a deputy lieutenant for Essex.[3]

1642 06 17
Speech by Oliver Cromwell to the House of Commons

Date: 17 June 1642
Source: BL, Harl. MS 163, fo. 183v, Diary of Sir Simonds D'Ewes. Printed in *Private Journals 1 June–17 Sept. 1642*, p. 94 (reported speech)

On this day Cromwell was sent as a messenger to the Lords regarding various pieces of business. He was to encourage them to pass the bill for the additional forces by sea, to ask about their progress on the bills for the loans on the propositions and for an assembly of divines, to deliver the order for Timothy Middleton's appointment as an Essex deputy lieutenant (see **1642 06 15**) and to seek their agreement to the proposal that the new Devon militia should take effect on 1 July.[1] Later that same day he was able to report back from the Lords.

Mr Cromwell made report of message That take consideration of ordinance

Outcome: The full details of the message were that the Lords would expedite the bill for the additional forces by sea, that they approved the order for Middleton's appointment, that they would send their own answers concerning the bills for the loans on the propositions and for an assembly of divines, and that they agreed that the new Devon militia should take effect from 1 July.[2]

---

[1] John Brograve (1596–1670) of Albury, Hertfordshire. Brograve was a kinsman of D'Ewes, as his wife, Hanna, was the aunt of D'Ewes's first wife and the D'Eweses had lived with the Brograves at Albury following their marriage in 1626. J. Sears McGee, *An Industrious Mind: the Worlds of Sir Simonds D'Ewes* (Stanford, Calif., 2015), pp. 115, 171, 211.
[2] Timothy Middleton (d. 1655) of Stansted Mountfichet, Essex.   [3] JHC, 2:625.

---

[1] JHC, 2:629; JHL, 5:142.
[2] JHC, 2:629.

81

1642 06 20

Speech by Oliver Cromwell to the House of Commons

Date: 20 June 1642
Source: BL, Harl. MS 163, fo. 196v, Diary of Sir Simonds D'Ewes. Printed in *Private Journals 1 June–17 Sept. 1642*, p. 106 (reported speech)

On 10 June Henry Darley,[1] MP for Northallerton (Yorkshire), had offered to lend £200 to Parliament on the propositions.[2] He now wanted to supply four horses instead.

Upon Mr Cromwells motion Mr Darlie who had promised 200£ did offer instead therof to maintaine 4 horses wch was allowed.

Outcome: There is no reference to this in the Journals, presumably because they did not usually record individual subscriptions by MPs.[3]

1642 06 22

Speech by Oliver Cromwell to the House of Commons

Date: 22 June 1642
Source: BL, Harl. MS 163, fo. 204v, Diary of Sir Simonds D'Ewes. Printed in *Private Journals 1 June–17 Sept. 1642*, p. 116 (reported speech)

Prompted by Cromwell, the Commons agreed that no committees were to meet that afternoon.[1] This was usually intended as a way of increasing attendance in the House. The main issue discussed later that day was probably the state of the defences of Kingston upon Hull, which continued to be one of the major sources of tension between Parliament and the King.

Upon Mr Cromwels motion it was ordered that no private Committee should sitt in the afternoon

---

[1] Henry Darley (c.1596–1671), politician. See ODNB.
[2] *Private Journals 1 June–17 Sept. 1642*, p. 467. On 9 June, Parliament had passed an Ordinance 'for bringing in Plate, Money, and Horses' which came to be known as 'on the propositions'. Reluctant to raise taxes without royal assent, the Houses opted for loans at 8 per cent per annum. See *A&O*, 1:6–8.
[3] *JHC*, 2:634.

[1] *JHC*, 2:634.

1642 06 24
Speech by Oliver Cromwell to the House of Commons

Date: 24 June 1642
Source: BL, Harl. MS 163, fo. 214v, Diary of Sir Simonds D'Ewes. Printed in *Private Journals 1 June–17 Sept. 1642*, p. 126 (reported speech)

Although a Roman Catholic, the fifth earl of Clanricarde[1] had opposed the rebellion in Ireland. As its governor, he had initially been able to retain control of Galway for the King, but in April 1642 he was forced to surrender the town to the forces of the Irish confederacy. The terms of that surrender had now become the subject of controversy at Westminster because Clanricarde had agreed that the townspeople of Galway could worship as Catholics. Directly challenging Clanricarde (who was the third earl of Essex's half-brother) was risky, because, as earl of St Albans, he was a member of the English House of Lords, as well as an English privy counsellor.

…and in the issue upon Mr Cromwells motion that the whole matter of the debate might be referred to a committee; & upon Mr \it was upon/ the motion of Sr Henry Fane the elder,[2] it referred to the commissioners for the affaires of Ireland who weere appointed the committee to whome this should be referred.

Outcome: In other words, Vane the elder had outmanoeuvred Cromwell. Cromwell's proposal was that the issue should be referred to a new committee. Vane however countered this with the proposal that it be referred to a committee comprising the commissioners for Irish affairs (all of whom were MPs). That had the advantage of being a known group of individuals. The Commons however supplemented that committee by also appointing Vane himself and Sir Henry Mildmay as additional members.[3] MPs may have seen Vane's proposal as the more judicious option.

---

[1] Ulick Burke, marquis of Clanricarde, landowner and politician. See ODNB. He was the half-brother of the Earl of Essex.
[2] Sir Henry Vane the elder (1589–1655), administrator and diplomat. See ODNB.
[3] JHC, 2:638.

1642 06 25

Speech by Oliver Cromwell to the House of Commons

Date: 25 June 1642
Source: BL, Harl. MS 163, fo. 231v, Diary of Sir Simonds D'Ewes. Printed in *Private Journals 1 June–17 Sept. 1642*, p. 134 (reported speech)

Seven weeks earlier Cromwell had voiced concerns about the number of Roman Catholics living in Dublin and had called for their expulsion (see 3 May 1642). He now returned to that subject.

Upon Mr Cromwels motion it was ~~desired that wee~~ \ordered that the commissioners/ ~~require should~~ for Ireland should consider what course might be taken wth the papists in Dublin there being above 10000 of them there ~~by which~~ \for hee shewed that by that/ meanes they are not only inforced to keepe a constant garrison of 10000 men in the said Citty but also all their designes and Counsells are revealed by the said papists to the enemy soe as the other day when some forces should have gone into the Province of Connot[1] for the assistance of the Lord President[2] there the very draught horses that should have drawne the carriages being neare upon the number of 300 were taken away from the walls of Dublin the very night preceeding that day on which the said forces should have gone in the same expedition.

Outcome: This was referred to the commissioners for Irish affairs, who were told 'to take some speedy Resolution upon it'.[3]

---

[1] Connacht.
[2] The lord presidency of Connacht was held jointly by Sir Charles Wilmot, first Viscount Wilmot of Athlone (1570/71–1644), army officer and administrator. See *ODNB*; and Roger Jones, first Viscount Ranelagh (d. 1644). See *DIB*. This is more probably a reference to the latter.
[3] *JHC*, 2:640.

1642 06 27a
Speech by Oliver Cromwell to the House of Commons

Date: 27 June 1642

Source: BL, Harl. MS 163, fo. 235, Diary of Sir Simonds D'Ewes. Printed in *Private Journals 1 June–17 Sept. 1642*, p. 137 (reported speech)

On 25 June John Barker,[1] MP for Coventry (Warwickshire), wrote to Parliament's lord lieutenant of Warwickshire, Lord Brooke,[2] informing him that the King's lord lieutenant, the earl of Northampton,[3] had been attempting to raise forces for the King at Coventry.[4] That letter was read to the Commons on 27 June. Cromwell was then sent as a messenger to the Lords with the letter.[5] On 3 June the Lords had issued an order for the earl of Lindsey,[6] the King's lord lieutenant of Lincolnshire, to be summoned as a delinquent.[7] Cromwell was therefore asked to request that the Lords issue a similar order against Northampton. He also took with him an order for the appointment of Sir Robert Lytton and Clement Throckmorton as deputy lieutenants for Warwickshire and a set of instructions to be sent to Warwickshire. On receiving this message, the Lords agreed to all these requests.[8] Cromwell now returned to inform the Commons of this.[9]

Mr Cromwell returned & shewed that the Lords had agreed to our instructions for Warwickshire; and had resolved to send for the Earle of Northampton in the same meanes by wch they had sent for the Earle of Lindsey.

Outcome: Northampton ignored this summons and so on 20 July 1642 the Commons presented the Lords with articles of impeachment against him and eight other peers.[10]

---

[1] John Barker (*fl.* 1624–70). See *HoP Commons, 1640–1660*.
[2] Robert Brooke, second Baron Brooke of Beauchamps Court (1607–43), parliamentarian army officer and religious writer. See *ODNB*.
[3] Spencer Compton, second earl of Northampton (1601–43), army officer. See *ODNB*.
[4] *JHL*, 5:164–5.   [5] *JHC*, 2:641.
[6] Robert Bertie, first earl of Lindsey (1582–1642), naval officer and royalist army officer. See *ODNB*.
[7] *JHL* 5:102–3.   [8] *JHL*, 5:163.   [9] *JHC*, 2:641.
[10] *JHL*, 5:222–3.

THE LETTERS, WRITINGS, AND SPEECHES OF OLIVER CROMWELL

1642 06 27b

Speech by Oliver Cromwell to the House of Commons

Date: 27 June 1642

Source: BL, Harl. MS 163, fo. 235v, Diary of Sir Simonds D'Ewes. Printed in *Private Journals* 1 June–17 Sept. 1642, p. 140 (reported speech)

Cromwell's intervention secured this order that the officers for the army to be sent to Ireland were paid. Once again, he showed that he was keen to see that this army was properly paid and supplied.

Upon Mr Cromwels motion the quarter masters who weere to be sent into Ireland by the Adventurers wth the armie weere to have a months pay.

Outcome: D'Ewes's notes underplayed the significance of this order as it applied not just to the pay for the quartermasters but to that for all the officers.[1]

1642 07 15

Speech by Oliver Cromwell to the House of Commons

Date: 15 July 1642

Source: BL, Harl. MS 163, fo. 273, Diary of Sir Simonds D'Ewes. Printed in *Private Journals* 1 June–17 Sept. 1642, pp. 219–20 (reported speech)

This entry is one of the first indications that Cromwell was taking the lead in organising the military preparations on Parliament's behalf in Cambridgeshire. He had evidently already arranged for a consignment of arms to be sent there, so on this day the Commons ordered that he should be reimbursed £100 for the cost of doing so. This was to be paid to him by Sir Dudley North,[1] MP for Cambridgeshire and one of the deputy lieutenants of the county, from money North had received from the former sheriff of Cambridgeshire, John Crane.[2] This was the balance on the sums collected for coat and conduct money. Crane (1571–1652), who had been sheriff during the past year, was a wealthy Cambridge

---

[1] *JHC*, 2:642.

[1] Dudley North, fourth Baron North (1602–77), politician and author. See *ODNB*.
[2] *JHC*, 2:674; TNA, SP16/491 fo. 176; Barclay, *Electing Cromwell*, p. 157.

16 JULY 1642

apothecary of royalist sympathies.[3] North's actions ensured that Crane would not use it on behalf of the King, which now made it possible to use it on behalf of Parliament.

Mr Cromwell moved that wee might make an order to allow the townesmen of Cambridge to raise two companies of volunteers, & to appoint of 100 men apece & to appoint captains over them: wh was iust upon ordering: but I stood upp & moved[4]

Outcome: As his notes are incomplete, what D'Ewes moved is not known. What is known is that the Commons did accept Cromwell's motion. It ordered that the lord lieutenant of Cambridgeshire, Lord North,[5] was to authorise the townsmen of Cambridge to begin military training.[6]

1642 07 16

Speech by Oliver Cromwell to the House of Commons

Date: 16 July 1642
Source: BL, Harl. MS 163, fo. 274, Diary of Sir Simonds D'Ewes. Printed in *Private Journals*
1 *June–17 Sept.* 1642, p. 222 (reported speech)

On this day Robert Reynolds,[1] MP for Hindon (Wiltshire), reported to the Commons from the committee for Munster. The House then accepted the recommendation of that committee that some of the military forces in Ulster and Leinster should be moved to Munster.[2] That was in response to the rebels' seizure of the castle at Limerick several weeks earlier. Sir Henry Mildmay was now appointed to go to the Lords to seek a joint conference about Irish affairs, presumably to discuss this same matter.[3] But it seems to have been Cromwell, not Mildmay, who delivered that message. The Lords duly agreed to hold a conference that afternoon at 3 p.m. on 'some important Business concerning Ireland'.[4] Cromwell evidently then returned to the Commons to report this.

---

[3] Laurence Martin, 'John Crane (1571–1652); the Cambridge apothecary and philanthropist', *Medical History*, 24 (1980), pp. 432–46.

[4] Followed by a blank space.

[5] Dudley North, third Baron North (bap. 1582, d. 1666), nobleman and poet. See *ODNB*. He was father of Dudley North MP.

[6] *JHC*, 2:674.

[1] Sir Robert Reynolds (1600/01–1678), lawyer and politician. See *ODNB*.

[2] *JHC*, 2:675. [3] *JHC*, 2:675. [4] *JHL*, 5:214.

87

Mr Cromwell made reporte from the Lords that they would give us a meeting at 3: of the clocke in the afternoone in the painted chamber.

Outcome: This is not recorded in the Journals, but it is known that the conference did take place that afternoon and that the Commons used it to present their proposals concerning Munster to the Lords.[5]

1642 07 18

Speech by Oliver Cromwell to the House of Commons

Date: 18 July 1642
Source: BL, Harl. MS 163, fo. 277v, Diary of Sir Simonds D'Ewes. Printed in *Private Journals 1 June–17 Sept. 1642*, p. 231 (reported speech)

On 27 May Charles I had issued a proclamation forbidding any members of the trained bands from obeying the Militia Ordinance or any other orders from Parliament concerning the militia.[1] For local officials to whom that proclamation had been sent, the decision as to whether to publish it or not was an important test of loyalty. On 15 July the Commons summoned the undersheriff of Middlesex to answer the accusation that he had published the proclamation.[2] Three days later it was Cromwell who moved that he be called in.

Upon Mr Cromwells motion Mr Frend the Undersherife of Middlesex was called in, & questioned for publishing the kings proclamation against the militia; who confessed that hee kept it by him 4 dayes before hee read it, & was at last soe terrified that hee read it. soe hee withdrew & then wee agreed that he should onlie be reprehended; wch the Speaker did accordinglie upon his second calling in.

Outcome: The biggest uncertainty in this is the name of the undersheriff. The man D'Ewes called 'Mr Frend' is called 'Mr Prinne' in the Journals. Either way, he remains unidentified. That the entry in the Journals is incomplete has led some to assume incorrectly that this man was an MP. However, that wording, 'notwithstanding that he was advised to the contrary…a Member of this House', should instead be interpreted as meaning that the

---

[5] JHC, 2:676.

---

[1] *A Proclamation forbidding all His Majesties Subjects belonging to the Trained Bands or Militia of this Kingdom* (1642): (Wing / C2647).
[2] JHC, 2:674.

88

undersheriff had been advised not to read the proclamation by an MP. The House reprimanded the undersheriff and warned him not to make the same mistake again.[3]

1642 07 19a
Memorandum by Oliver Cromwell

Date: 19 July 1642
Source: TNA, SP16/491, fo. 177 (no. 71.I) (holograph)

This note (in Cromwell's own hand) records the action taken by Cromwell in response to the order he had obtained from the Commons on 15 July. As instructed, Sir Dudley North,[1] MP for Cambridgeshire, had paid the £100 to Cromwell as payment for the arms which Cromwell had sent to Cambridge. This note served as North's receipt for the payment of that money. North subsequently submitted it in 1645 to Parliament's committee for taking the accounts of the kingdom (the committee of accounts) as part of the auditing of his military expenses.

[fo. 117r, no. 71.I]
Julij 19o. 1642
memorandum the day and yeare above written, that I Oliver
Cromwell Have receaved \att the hands of Sir Dudly North/ one hundred pounds lawfull
monie of England. In satisfaction of divers Armes by
mee sent down to mr. Blackly[2] of Cambridge, one of
the high constables for the sayd Countye which sayd Armes
are to bee kept by the sayd mr Blacklye, u\untill they/ bee
disposed of by the Leiueten \Right/ honble. the Lord North
Ld Leiuetennant of the sayd Countye, for the
use and benefitt of the said Countye, the sayd
hundred pounds havinge bin receaved by the sayd
Sir Dudly North, from mr. Crane, late high sherrif
of the sayd County, And ordered to be payed Inn
to mee by the house of Commons

---

[3] *JHC*, 2:679.

[1] Sir Dudley North, fourth Baron North (1602–77), politician and author. See *ODNB*.
[2] James Blackley. See **1641 06 04**.

by mee Oliver Cromwell
[Beneath this, same folio, 71.II]
'The Accompt of Sir Dudley North for one hundred
poundes which he recd the 13th of June 1642 of Wm Crane[3]
of East Smithfeild[4] Gent. by the appointmt of John
Crane of Cambridge Esqr.

Paid all the said Hundred poundes to Oliver Cromwell
Esqr one of the members of the house of Commons for Armes
and as is exprest by his acquittance above expressed the
Same payment being likewise warranted \& directed/ by order of the house
of Comons bearing date the 15th of July 1642 hereunto annexed.

Dud. Northe

[same folio, 71.III]
on the 22th of Aprill 1645 the said
Sir Dudley North delivered his Accompt
upon oath

Jno. Gregorie
Lawr: Brinley[5]

1642 07 19b

Speech by Oliver Cromwell to the House of Commons

Date: 19 July 1642
Source: BL, Harl. MS 163, fo. 278v, Diary of Sir Simonds D'Ewes. Printed in *Private Journals 1 June–17 Sept. 1642*, p. 235 (reported speech)

On this day Cromwell was sent as a messenger to the Lords with several pieces of business. Three of them related to Ireland: an order that the deputy treasurer at war for Ireland,

---

[3] Just possibly John Crane's cousin once removed, William Crane (1608–73), who had been a fellow of Trinity College, Cambridge 1633–9, later of Woodrising, Norf. Venn, 1:413; Laurence Martin, 'John Crane (1571–1652); the Cambridge apothecary and philanthropist', *Medical History*, 24 (1980), pp. 433, 434, 437.

[4] This is the area immediately to the east of the Tower of London.

[5] These are the autographs of John Gregory and Lawrence Brinkley, two members of the committee for taking the accounts of the kingdom.

Nicholas Loftus, was to be paid £10,000, an order that Sir John Clotworthy was to be paid £1,000 for his expenses in Ireland and the request that the Lords take a speedy decision on their request that troops be sent to Munster (see **1642 07 16**). He also took with him an order to indemnify military volunteers in Shrewsbury and Hertfordshire.[1] Cromwell duly delivered these messages to the Lords and then returned.[2]

Mr Cromwell made reporte of the Lords answere to his message.

Outcome: Cromwell reported that the Lords had agreed to the orders indemnifying volunteers in Shrewsbury and Hertfordshire. Immediately before this, the Lords' own messengers had informed the Commons that the Lords agreed to the orders concerning Loftus and Clotworthy.[3]

1642 07 21

Speech by Oliver Cromwell to the House of Commons

Date: 21 July 1642
Source: BL, Harl. MS 163 fo. 284v, Diary of Sir Simonds D'Ewes. Printed in *Private Journals* 1 June–17 Sept. 1642, p. 245 (reported speech)

Its governor, Lord Esmonde of Limerick,[1] held the fort at Duncannon, County Wexford, against the Irish rebels. Cromwell now arranged for Parliament to order the lords justices of Ireland to send troops to reinforce him.[2]

Mr Cromwell brought in a \copie of/ lre to be sent by the Speaker to the Lords Justices of Ireland touching the assistance of the Lord Esmond who commanded the fort of Dungannon; wch was allowed by the Howse.

---

[1] JHC, 2:679–80.   [2] JHL, 5:218, 221–2.   [3] JHC, 2:681.

[1] Laurence Esmonde, Baron Esmonde of Limerick (c.1570–1645), army officer and landowner. See ODNB.
[2] Elaine Murphy, 'Siege of Duncannon Fort in 1641 and 1642' in E. Darcy, A. Margey and E. Murphy, eds., *The 1641 Depositions and the Irish Rebellion* (2012), pp. 143–54.

Outcome: Cromwell was appointed to carry this order to the Lords for their agreement. He did so the following day (see 22 July 1642).[3]

1642 07 22a

Speech by Oliver Cromwell to the House of Commons

Date: 22 July 1642
Source: BL, Harl. MS 163, fo. 288v, Diary of Sir Simonds D'Ewes. Printed in *Private Journals 1 June–17 Sept. 1642*, p. 249 (reported speech)

The Commons seems to have spent time soon after assembling debating a declaration, possibly a response to the King's latest message concerning Kingston upon Hull. Cromwell seems then to have interrupted this to make a separate but urgent point. The lord mayor of London, Sir Richard Gurney,[1] had been increasingly displaying royalist sympathies and had even gone so far as to attempt to publish the King's commission of array. The Commons had therefore impeached him on 11 July. His trial was due to commence on this day. Mindful of this, Cromwell proposed that the committee which had been appointed to present the Commons' case at the trial should withdraw to prepare themselves.

Mr Cromwell moved whilst the declaration was in reading that the Committee wch was to draw the \this day to/ manage the Evidence against the Lord Mayor might withdraw & prepare themselves for it; wch Serjeant Wilde[2] & the rest of them did accordinglie

Outcome: Cromwell's suggestion was a timely one, as soon after this messengers from the Lords arrived to say that the committee was expected in the Lords.

---

[3] JHC, 2:684; JHL, 5:229–30.

[1] Sir Richard Gurney, baronet (bap. 1578, d. 1647), mayor of London. See *ODNB*.
[2] John Wilde (1590–1669), barrister and politician, MP for Worcestershire. See *ODNB*. JHC, 2:685.

1642 07 22b
Speech by Oliver Cromwell to the House of Commons

Date: 22 July 1642

Source: BL, Harl. MS 163, fo. 288v, Diary of Sir Simonds D'Ewes. Printed in *Private Journals 1 June–17 Sept. 1642*, p. 250 (reported speech)

Having been sent the previous day to secure the Lords' consent to the letter to be written to the lord justices of Ireland for reinforcement to support Lord Esmonde at Duncannon (see **1642 07 21**), Cromwell did so this day.[1] He then returned to the Commons to inform them that the Lords would reply using their own messengers.[2]

Mr Cromwell made report that hee had carried upp the message yesterday touching the Lre to be sent to the Justices touching the sending of forces to the aid of the Lord Esmon: that th hee had delivered the saied Lre, & that the Lords answeare was that they would send an answeare by messengers of ther owne

Outcome: The Lords meanwhile agreed the text of the letter, altering it only to clarify that the troops to be sent by the lord justices were to be 'of sufficient Force' rather 'a complete Company'. The Lords' messengers, Sir Robert Rich and Thomas Heath, then returned it to the Commons, which agreed to accept this amendment.[3]

1643 01 16
Receipt for arms received from Sir John Hewett

Date: 16 January 1643

Source: Cromwell Museum, Huntingdon, HUTCM: L4 (holograph)

This receipt for a small consignment of arms is in Cromwell's own hand and bears his signature. The endorsement is in a separate hand.

This is the first time we hear Cromwell's voice since the brief summary of a report he made to the House of the Commons almost six months earlier (**1642 07 22b**). At some point after this, and no later than 8 August, he left Westminster and returned to East Anglia, first to his constituency of Cambridge where he raised some volunteers and occupied the main roads out of Cambridge north of the river Cam, thus preventing the Cambridge colleges from sending their silver to the King at York. A week later he was in

---

[1] *JHL*, 5:229–30. [2] *JHC*, 2:685. [3] *JHL*, 5:230, 245; *JHC*, 2:685.

Huntingdon and stayed there for three weeks, probably including a visit to his family in Ely. During this time he raised a company of eighty cavalrymen from in and around Huntingdon. After a quick visit to London around 6 September, he set off to join the army opposing the King and took a small part in the first major but indecisive battle of the Civil War, the battle of Edgehill (22/23 October). He can be placed at Warwick (24 October), Northampton (2 November), St Albans (5 November) and he was with Essex at the important stand-off between the King and Parliament's main forces at Turnham Green (Brentford), six miles west of the Palace of Westminster, on 13 November. It is likely—but not certain—that he returned to Ely fairly soon after 13 November and remained there until early January 1643 when he was present at, but not recorded as speaking in, Parliament on 6 January. And then back to Cambridge. And about this time he was commissioned to be a full colonel and asked to create a regiment of 500 cavalry. Already an exceptionally hectic and forceful pattern of commitment to his duties as MP and soldier was established. And this document begins the story of his war in his own words.

January 16th. 1642
Receaved att the hands of Sir John Hewett[1] to the
use of the Parliament, and of his Excellence the
Earle of Essex Lord Generall of the Armie,[2]
Eleven musketts, one Blunderbusts,[3] three pay{e}r o{f}[4]
pistolls and a halfe with holsters \one Carbine/,[5] I say re=
ceaved as aforesayd by me
Oliver Cromwell.

16 Jan: 1642
O Cromwell Rect. for
Armes

---

[1] Almost certainly the Sir John Hewet, bart, who had been sheriff of Huntingdonshire in 1637–8: T. H. McKenny and M. C. Hughes, *Cambridgeshire* (1909), pp. 313–14.
[2] Robert Devereux, third earl of Essex.
[3] Blunderbuss: 'A short gun with a large bore, firing many balls or slugs, and capable of doing execution within a limited range without exact aim' (*OED*). The earliest usage of the word in *OED* is 1654, so this is something of a neologism for Cromwell.
[4] Parts of letters in brackets are visible but parts are lost.
[5] Carbine: 'A kind of firearm, shorter than the musket, used by the cavalry and other troops' (*OED*).

23 JANUARY 1643

1643 01 23
Letter from Oliver Cromwell to Robert Barnard, recorder of Huntingdon

Date: 23 January 1643
Source: *New York Times*, 21 April 1912 (facsimile of a holograph)

This letter was up for sale in 1912 and a facsimile was published in the *New York Times* with a comment that it was being sold as part of the estate of a C. J. Toovey.[1] Carlyle had seen it in the 1830s, and he recorded that 'my Copy, two Copies, of this Letter I owe to kind friends, who have carefully transcribed it from the Original at Lord Gosford's. The present Lady Gosford is "granddaughter to Sir Robert Barnard", to whose lineal ancestor the Letter is addressed.'[2] The *New York Times* did not copy the verso, so we have to rely on Carlyle for the address: 'To my assured friend Robert Barnard, Esquire: Present these'.[3] It is very evidently written and signed by Cromwell, and his seal was still evident in 1912. We believe the original is now in the possession of the duke of Rutland at Belvoir Castle, but we do not have permission to cite it.

What is most striking about this letter is its studied courtesy and acid tone. Cromwell was convinced that Bernard was a furtive supporter of the King, but his hands were tied because Bernard enjoyed the patronage of the earl of Manchester. (See **1643 04 17**.)

———

Mr Bernard,[4] its most true my Leiftennant,[5] with
some other souldiers of my Troope were att
your house, I deale freely to inquier
after you, the reason was, because I
have heard you \reported/ active, against the pro=
ceedings of Parliament, for those alsoe

[1] It can be found online at http://query.nytimes.com/mem/archive-free/pdf?_r=1&res=9E02 EEDD1E3CE633A25752C2A9629C946396D6CF. It appeared in the *New York Times* on 21 April 1912.

[2] Carlyle-Lomas, 1:115–16.   [3] Carlyle-Lomas, 1:115.

[4] Robert Bernard, since 1625 the Recorder of Huntingdon and a close ally of the Montagus of Hinchingbrooke, by 1643 specifically Edward Montagu, second earl of Manchester. He was MP for Huntingdon in the Short but not in the Long Parliament. There is evidence of longstanding animus between Cromwell and Bernard, see John Morrill, 'The Making of Oliver Cromwell', in John Morrill, ed., *Oliver Cromwell and the English Revolution* (1990), pp. 29–36. There is a rounded account of the life of Robert Bernard of Huntingdon (1600–66) in *HoP Commons, 1640–1660*, which suggests Cromwell may have got it wrong. See also **1643 04 17**.

[5] Possibly James Berry (d. 1691), parliamentarian army officer and major general, who was to rise to great heights alongside Cromwell in the New Model Army. See *ODNB*.

that disturbe the peace of this
cuntrie, and the Kingdom, with those
of this Countye, whoe have had meetings
not a few, to intents, and purpose, too
too full of Suspect, Its true Sir I knowe
you ~~are~~ \have beene/ warie in your carrages, bee not
too confident therof, Subtilty may de=
ceave you, integritie never will. with
my hart I shall desier that your iudg
ment ~~were~~ \may/ alter, and your practise,
I come only to hinder men from increa
singe the rent,[6] from doeinge hurt,
but not to hurt any man, Nor shall
I you [—]⁷ \ I hope you will/ give noe cause,
if you doe, I must bee pardoned ~~wt~~ what
my relation to the publike calls for,
If your good parts bee disposed that
way, Knowe mee for your servant

Oliver Cromwell
January 23
1642

bee assured, fayer words from
mee, shall neither deceive you
of your houses, nor ~~of~~ your
libertye.[8]

[verso]
To my assured friend
Robert Bernard esqr
present theise.

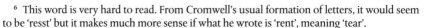

---

[6] This word is very hard to read. From Cromwell's usual formation of letters, it would seem to be 'resst' but it makes much more sense if what he wrote is 'rent', meaning 'tear'.
[7] Several words are very heavily crossed out here: the first seems to be 'Good'.
[8] This postscript is written in the margin.

1643 01 26[?]

Letter from Miles Sandys, Torrell Jocelyn, Francis Russell, William Marche, Oliver Cromwell, Edward Clenche, James Thompson, Thomas Symons, Robert Clerke to Sir John Hobart, Sir Thomas Richardson, Sir John Potts, Sir John Palgrave, John Spelman and the rest of the Norfolk deputy lieutenants

Date: January 1643 [written between 24 and 27 January]
Source: Bodl., MS Tanner 64, no. 124, fos 116r–117v (autograph)

Previous editors have confidently dated this letter as 26 January 1643, but there is no evidence that that was the date of composition.[1] It is clearly written before **1643 01 27** and 26 January is possible, but it could be any date between 24 and 27 January. In **1643 01 27** it is described as having been prepared before the Committee received a letter from the Norfolk deputy lieutenants, and that they are now sending it with **1643 01 27**. Sophia Lomas also thought that it was in Cromwell's hand;[2] while Wilbur Abbott thought that it contained 'corrections in Cromwell's hand'.[3] In our view, Lomas is clearly mistaken but Abbott may be correct. At any rate, he did sign his name to the letter.

As far back as the early autumn of 1642, deputy lieutenants in Norfolk, Suffolk and Cambridgeshire had talked of cooperation and a commitment to support one another in the event of a royalist attack. Then in late November Parliament had proposed the integration of the resources of those three counties with those of Essex and Hertfordshire but this had been strongly resisted in Parliament and in the counties. It took the threat of a Catholic rising and of the possible arrival of Prince Rupert to persuade the leaders to organise a joint meeting of the original three counties at Mildenhall. This in turn led to a meeting at Bury St Edmunds of representatives of all five counties on 9 February, at which a committee made up of delegates of each county (the 'Eastern Association Committee') was agreed.[4] This letter represents a key moment in that process.[5]

---

[1] Carlyle-Lomas 3, appendix 4; Abbott, *Writings and Speeches*, 1:211.
[2] Carlyle-Lomas, appendix 4.   [3] Abbott, *Writings and Speeches*, 1:211 at fn. 22.
[4] All this is fully explored in Clive Holmes, *The Eastern Association in the English Civil War* (1974), pp. 62–9.
[5] The role of all these prominent Norfolk landowners in the formation of the parliamentarian party (from which Sir Thomas Richardson was soon to defect) is discussed by Holmes, *The Eastern Association*, ch. 3 and *passim*. John Spelman esq of Narborough is not to be confused with John Spelman of Hunstanton, who had been knighted in December 1641 and had by the time of this letter defected to the King in Oxford.

[fo. 117v]

To our Noble freinds Sir John Hobart, Sir Thomas Richardson Sir John Potts, Sir John Palgrave Knights & Barronetts, John Spelman Esqr and the rest of the Deputie Leiftennants for the Countye of Norfolke præsent

theise

[fo. 116r]

Gentlemen

The Parliament and the Lord generall[6] have taken into their care the peace and protection of these Eastern partes of the kingdome and to that end have Sent downe hither some parte of their forces as likewise a commission with certeine instructions to us and others directed, all which doe highly concerne the peace and Safety of your County,[7] therefore we intreate that some of you would give us the \a/ meeteing at Millnall[8] in Suffolke on tuesday the 31th of this instant January and in the meane time that you would make all possible speed to have in readines against \any/ notice shalbe given) a considerable force of horse and foote to joyne with us to keepe any enemyes force from breaking in uppon your yet peaceable County: for we have certeine intelligence that some of Prince Rupers[9] forces are come as farre as Wellingborrow[10] in Norhamptonshire and that the Papists in Norfolke[11] are Solicited to rise presently uppon you; thus presenting all our Neighbourely and loveing respects; we rest Your respective friends to serve you

Miles Sandys
Franc: Russell

---

[6] Robert Devereux, third earl of Essex (1590–1646), parliamentarian army officer. See *ODNB*.

[7] There are no orders about this in the Journals of either the Commons or the Lords, but Cromwell had recently arrived from London with a small force raised in London and that may be what is referred to here.

[8] Mildenhall, a market town close to where Cambridgeshire, Suffolk and Norfolk meet. It is also close to the main road from Cambridge (and London) to Norwich.

[9] Rupert, prince and count Palatine of the Rhine and duke of Cumberland (1619–82), royalist army and naval officer. See *ODNB*.

[10] Wellingborough, a borough in Northamptonshire 49 miles west of Cambridge.

[11] For the leading Catholic families of Norfolk at this time, see John Morrill, 'East Anglian Catholics in the Seventeenth Century', in Francis Young, ed., *Catholic East Anglia: a History of the Catholic faith in Norfolk, Suffolk, Cambridgeshire and Peterborough* (Leominster, 2016), pp. 61–92.

Torrell Jocelyn
William Marche   Oliver Cromwell
Edw: Clenche
James Thompson   Thomas Symons

                                            Robt Clerke[12]

1643 01 27
Letter from Miles Sandys, Thomas Martin, Oliver Cromwell, Francis Russell, Torrell Jocelyn, William Marche[?], Edward Clenche, Thomas Symons [Symon Sr?], Robert Clerke, James Thompson to Sir John Hobart, Sir Thomas Richardson, Sir John Potts, Sir John Palgrave, Sir John Spelman, knights and baronets

Date: 27 January 1643
Source: Bodl., MS Tanner 64, no. 139, fos 128r–129v (holograph)

This letter from ten parliamentary commissioners in Cambridgeshire and sent to five deputy lieutenants of Norfolk is in Cromwell's own hand and the fact that it was originally written in the first person singular and then changed to the first person plural suggests it was very much his idea and his formulation. It is a companion piece to **1643 01 26[?]**, written a day or two earlier, and the two letters were despatched together. There were nine signatories to the previous letter, and they signed again, with a tenth signature (that of Thomas Martin being added). The five named recipients are the same except that in this second letter John Spelman esq is called Sir John Spelman. This is surely a mistake by Cromwell. *Sir* John Spelman of Hunstanton had now defected to the royalists at Oxford, whereas John Spelman of Narborough was to remain an active member of the Norfolk parliamentarian war effort.

    The previous letter had called for a meeting of representatives of the several East Anglian counties and had suggested in vague terms that there was a planned Catholic Rising in conjunction with a royalist 'invasion' of the Eastern Counties. This letter repeats that fear, now given urgency by a report coming from the parliamentarian Scoutmaster

---

[12] This is a gathering of Cambridge and Cambridgeshire men, not an embryonic gathering of the Committee for the Eastern Association.

General, Sir Samuel Luke. Major, or Captain, Gawdy—probably Edward Gawdy—had slipped through the lines to pass on information (Cromwell's calling him a 'prisoner' seems rather a generous description). He warned of the King's intention to send his cavalry into East Anglia, commissioning Gawdy major in a regiment of horse and giving him a commission to raise a troop of horse in Norfolk, 'and to this purpose hee had his Majesties letters and commission to divers gentlemen whoe had sent word the horses were ready'.[1] The news was sent back to the Parliamentarian HQ at Windsor, and from there on 25 January Sir Philip Stapleton,[2] Cromwell's fellow-MP and a senior figure to the earl of Essex, wrote to Cromwell, urging him to seize the royalist messenger (evidently Gawdy himself) as he passed though Cambridge and, if it was too late for that, for the Norfolk authorities to seize Gawdy and Sir Henry Bedingfield.[3]

[fo. 129v]

To our Worthy Frends
Sir Jhon Hobard Sir
Tho: Rychardson Sir Jhon
Potts Sir Jhon Palgrave
Sir Jhon Spelman[4] Knights
and Baronetts present
these

[fo. 129r]

Gentlemen, the grounds of your Jealosies are
real: they concurr with our intelligences from Windsor[5]

---

[1] I. G. Philip, ed., *Journal of Sir Samuel Luke*, 3 vols., Oxfordshire Rec. Soc., 3 vols., 29, 31, 33 ([1950–3]), pp. 1:10–11. Luke's dating is a bit haywire here, the Gawdy entry appearing between entries for 22 January and 19 February, but there is little doubt that this is the incident to which Luke is referring.

[2] Sir Philip Stapleton (bap. 1603, d. 1647). See *ODNB*. Stapleton was captain of the earl of Essex's lifeguard and colonel of his regiment of horse.

[3] D. Turner, ed., 'Letter from Sir Philip Stapleton to Oliver Cromwell, and Four Letters from Oliver Cromwell Himself', *Norfolk Archaeology*, 2 (1849), pp. 43–60 [the letter is on pp. 44–5]. If Gawdy was telling something near the truth to Luke, the reason Cromwell's scouts could not find him was probably that he either never set off or never intended to go into Norfolk. He claimed that he had thrown up his commission after Edgehill and had only stayed with the royalist army 'because hee was afraid hee should not get home quietly'. Now, faced with an unpleasant and dangerous mission behind enemy lines pushed on him, his leaking the information to Luke looks like an attempt to sabotage it before it even began, Philip, *Luke*, p. 1:11.

[4] Presumably a mistake: not Sir John Spelman of Hunstanton, by now an active royalist, but John Spelman esquire of Narborough, an addressee of the previous letter **1643 01 26[?]**.

[5] Windsor, Berkshire, a royal borough dominated by the King's castle, and in the winter of 1642–3 headquarters of the main parliamentarian army under the earl of Essex.

27 JANUARY 1643

the Summ whereof wee give unto you: From a pri=
soner taken by Sir Samuell Luke[6] (one mr Gau=
dy, a Capt. of Dragooners)[7] this confession was
drawen, that the Papists by direction from
Oxford should rise in Norfolke, whereupon itt
was desired from thence, that Sir Henry Benning
feild,[8] and mr Gaudye, their persons should
bee seized, and that ~~I~~ \we/[9] should doe ~~my~~ \our/ indeavors
to make stay of the \person and/ letter which conteyned this
incoragment to them, hee beinge described by
his horse and clothes, but wee beleive was
past us, before wee had notice, for our Scouts
could not light onn him, as for the other con=
sideration of his Maties forces beinge invited into
theise parts wee have confirmation thereof
from all hands, and there is this reason to
doubt itt wilbe soe because his Matie is ~~wear~~ \weary/[10]
of Oxford, there beinge little in those parts
left to Sustaine his armie, and suerly the full
nesse of theise parts, and fitnesse of them
for horse, are too too good arguments to
invite ~~them~~ \him/ heither, thus wee agree in the ~~groun~~ \grounds/
of our doubt, and feare. The next thought is
of remidi[e], and in this wee account itt, our hap
pinesse to consult with you of common Saftye \to bee had/ , ei=

---

[6] Sir Samuel Luke (bap. 1603, d. 1670), parliamentarian army officer, see *ODNB*. A Bedfordshire man, he served as a captain at the battle of Edgehill and was commissioned by Essex as a colonel to raise a regiment of dragoons on 4 January 1643. He was appointed Scoutmaster General on 14 January 1643, Philip, *Luke*, p. 1:vii.

[7] Probably Edward Gawdy, who served in the royalist army at Edgehill and was wounded. He was in the dragoons. This is consistent with the Major Gawdy who fed the information to Luke, described in the latter's journal as formerly a captain of dragoons shot in the thigh at Edgehill. See Newman, *Royalist Officers*, no. 590.

[8] Sir Henry Bedingfield (1581/2–1657) of Oxburgh Hall, Norfolk, was at the heart of a network of Catholic families: Bedingfield [Bedingfeld] family (per. 1476–1760), gentry. See *ODNB*.

[9] The 'we' is added on the same line as the crossed-out 'I' (whereas the 'our' later in the same line is written above the crossed-out 'my'). The former suggests he changed pronouns as he wrote, not once he realised that he wanted or needed to co-author it with the other signatories.

[10] Cromwell here tried to cram 'weary' into the end of a line and failed. So he crossed it out and wrote the whole word above the crossed-out 'wear'.

THE LETTERS, WRITINGS, AND SPEECHES OF OLIVER CROMWELL

ther by t[h]e association you speake off,[11] or by

any[12] other consideration, by communication of assistance accordinge to necessitye, wherein

I hope you shall finde

all readinesse, and cheerfullnesse in us, to assist you to breake any strength ~~may~~ \shall/ bee

gathered, or to prevent it if

desired, havinge timely notice given from you thereof. the way wilbe best settled if you give

us a meetinge

accordinge to our desier by a letter perticularly prepared, ~~and di~~ before wee receaved yours,

and now sent unto

you for that purpose together with theise. This is all wee can say for the present, but that wee

are

Your freinds, and servants.

Miles Sandys

[fo. 128r]

Thoms Martin

Oliver Cromwell.	Franc: Russell	Torrell Jocelyn
Willm Marche		Tho: Symons:
Edw: Clenche		Robt Clerke
		James Thompson[13]

[fo. 129r]

Wee sent to Sir Willm Spring[14] to offer him our assistance for the apprehendinge Sir H.

---

[11] See **1643 01 26**[?].

[12] From hereon, the letter is written down the left-hand margin at right angles to the main text.

[13] Three of these ten men are briefly mentioned in A. Barclay, *Electing Cromwell: the Making of a Politician* (2011) pp. 105–6 and *passim*. The three are Myles Sandys, William Marsh and Thomas Simmonds. Thomas Martin of Barton was sheriff of Cambridgeshire in 1643–4. McKenny and Hughes, *Cambridgeshire*, p. 14.

[14] For Sir William Spring of Pakenham (1613–54), see his life in HoP *Commons, 1640–1660*. See John Walter, *Understanding Popular Violence in the English Revolution: the Colchester Plunderers* (Cambridge, 1999) and *passim*, for his part in the searches of Catholic homes in 1642. See also **1643 07 31a, 1643 08 29, 1643 08 30**[?].

Benningfeild ~~and~~ &c.

wee have not yett receaved any answare. wee knew[15] not how to address our selves to you

its our desire to assist you in that or any other publike service.[16]

[fo. 128r]
Cambridge the 27th. of Jan: 1642.

1643 03 08

Order from Oliver Cromwell and 23 members of the Committee at Cambridge to all and every inhabitant of Fen Drayton in the hundred of Papworth, Cambridgeshire

Date: 8 March 1643
Source: C. H. Cooper, *Annals of Cambridge*, 5 vols. (1842), 3:340 (later copy)

Cromwell is the first named of twenty-four commissioners writing to Fen Drayton and presumably to many other townships and parishes in the Cambridge area firmly requesting a 'free-will offering' to help to pay for defence works around the city of Cambridge. According to Cooper, 'in the parish of Fendrayton fifteen persons contributed £1.19s.2d which was paid to Wm Willbore'.[1]

The original has now disappeared, but it was transcribed by the reliable C. H. Cooper in the early 1840s, apparently with original spelling. Carlyle and Abbott include it, but as usual with modernised spelling and punctuation.[2]

Cromwell may well have been the author of the letter as well as the first signatory.

---

[15] 'Know' or 'knew'—either is a possible reading here.
[16] This postscript is also in Cromwell's distinctive hand but in much smaller characters to fit into the remaining space in the left margin.

---

[1] C. H. Cooper, *Annals of Cambridge*, 5 vols. (1842), 3:340 quoting Bowtell MS ii (otherwise unknown). Welbore was a member of the common council of Cambridge and had many links to Cromwell and to his mother, for which see Barclay, *Electing Cromwell*, esp. pp. 43–50.
[2] Carlyle-Lomas, 1:117, Abbott, *Writings and Speeches*: 1:217.

THE LETTERS, WRITINGS, AND SPEECHES OF OLIVER CROMWELL

To all & every the Inhabitants of Fendrayton in the Hundred of Papworth[3] COM. CANT. WHEREAS, we have been inforced by apparent grounds of approaching daunger to begin to fortifie the towne of Cambr. for preventing the enemies inroade, and the better to maineteine the peace of this County, havinge in parte seen your good affeccions to the cause & now standing in need of your Further assistance to the perfecting of the Fortificacions which will cost at the least Two thousand pounds: WEE are incouraged as well as necessitated to desire a free will offering of a liberal Contribucion from you, for the better enabling of us to obtaine our desired ends, viz., the preservation of our County, Knowing that every honest and well affected man, considering the vast expences wee have already been at, & our willingnes to do according to our ability, wil be ready & willing to contribute his best assistance to a worke of soe high concernment & soe good an end. Wee doe therefore desire that what shal be by you freely given & collected, may with all convenient speed be sent to the Commissioners at Cambridge to be imployed to the use aforesaid, and so you shall further ingage us to be

Yours ready to serve[4]

OLIVER CROMWELL   ROBERT TWELLS, Maior [c]   THO. MARTIN [b]
THO. ATKINSON   TERRELL JOCELYN [a]   SAML. SPALDING [c]
THO.DUCKETT [c]   ROBERT HUDSON   ROBT CASTELL [c]
EDWARD ALMOND [c]   ROBT CLARKE [ab]   WILLM. GRAVE
EDW.CLENCHE [ab]   JAMES BLACKLEY [c]   JAMES THOMPSON
[ab]   WILLIAM WELBOR [c]   THOMAS BUCKLEY   STEPHEN
FORTUNE   NICHOLAS WEST   ROBT. IBBET [c]   RICH. PETTIT [c]
RICHARD TIMES [c]   GEORGE FELSTEED
THO. BERT   WILLM. BURTON

---

[3] Fen Drayton is a village and parish 13 miles north-west of the city of Cambridge. 'The hundred of Papworth extends along the former western boundary of Cambridgeshire between the river Ouse on the north and the road from Cambridge to St. Neots on the south', see A. P. M. Wright and C. P. Lewis, eds., *A History of the County of Cambridge and the Isle of Ely: Volume 9, Chesterton, Northstowe, and Papworth Hundreds* (London, 1989), pp. 267–8. Available at British History Online http://www.british-history.ac.uk/vch/cambs/vol9/pp267-8.

[4] Most of the readily identifiable of these men were from the city of Cambridge, and were councillors there. Those marked [a] and [b] had co-signed with Cromwell letters six weeks earlier (see, for [a], **1643 01 26[?]** and for [b] **1643 01 27**); or they were personally involved with Cromwell over fen drainage or over Cromwell's elections as MP in 1640. These links are discussed in Barclay, *Electing Cromwell*, and can be found via the index and are marked [c] below.

Cambridge this 8th of March, 1642

Note, what shal be by you gather, deliver to Tho: Noris[5] this bearer. Deliver this wrighting to the Churchwardings, who are to deliver the same unto the Minister or Curate to be published in the parish Church the next Sunday after the receipt theireof and what shal be by you collected lett it be endorced on the back side heireof, together with a declaration of what is given by every particular person, & then delivered to Thomas Norris the bearer heirof.

1643 03 10
Letter from Oliver Cromwell to the deputy lieutenants of Suffolk

Date: 10 March 1643
Source: NLS, MS 592, fos 118r–119v (holograph)

This is a holograph letter that survives in a random collection of autographs collected by a Mr Watson. The address as well as the contents of the letter itself are in Cromwell's hand.

A month had passed since the meetings at Mildenhall discussed in **1643 01 26[?]** and **1643 01 27**. The agreement of the Eastern Counties to associate for mutual assistance had advanced considerably. The 'Catholic' Rising and the 'invasion' by Prince Rupert had not taken place but there were royalist discontents across Norfolk in early April and these would result in a purge of the Norwich corporation on and after 2 March. On 13 March Cromwell with a detachment of horse swept by Norwich and arrived at Lowestoft where royalists had succeeded in blocking up the town.[1]

[fo. 118r]

Gentlemen, I am sorrie I should soe often trouble
you about the businesse of monie, it's noe pleasan[t][2]

---

[5] Not identified.

[1] See R. W. Ketton-Cremer, *Norfolk in the Civil War* (1969), pp. 173–87, for the discontents in Norfolk in March: the purging of the mayor of Norwich and several aldermen (the mayor was arrested on 2 March and taken prisoner to Cambridge); other royalist sympathisers were taken at Augustine Holl's house at Heigham on 7 March, and also sent to Cambridge. Cromwell was in Norwich by 13 March, when he went to Lowestoft against the royalist blocking-up of the town there.

[2] There are two other end-of-line letters supplied in brackets which are lost in the binding of the manuscript.

THE LETTERS, WRITINGS, AND SPEECHES OF OLIVER CROMWELL

Subject to bee too frequent upon. But such is
Captaine Nelsons[3] occasion for want thereof that
Hee hath not wherewith to Satisfie for the
billett of his Souldiers, and soe this businessse
for Norfolke soe hopefull to sett all right
there may fayle, Truly hee hath borrowed
monie from mee, else hee could not hav{e}
payed to discharge this Towne att his depar
ture, it's pittye a gentleman of his affection{s}
should bee discoraged, wherfore I earnestly
beseech you to consider him, and the cause.
It's honorable that you doe soe, what
you can help him too, bee pleased to send
into Norfolke, hee hath not wherwith to
pay a Troope one day, as Hee tells mee,.
lett your returne bee Speedy to Norwich
Gentlemen Command your servant.

Oliver Cromwell

Mar. 10 1642
Cambridge

I hope to serve you in
my returne, with your con=
junction wee shall quickly
putt an end to theise businesses
The Lord assistinge

---

[3] There is no officer of that name in the *The Cromwell Association Online Directory of Parliamentarian Army Officers*, available on British History Online at https://www.british-history.ac.uk/no-series/cromwell-army-officers. Henceforth: *Online Directory of Parliamentarian Army Officers*. But he is presumably the 'John Nelson' who signs a receipt at the end of the letter. On 31 January 1643 the Suffolk deputy lieutenants order that 'Captaine Nellsonn shall remayne in the Countye with the troope of horse that he have raysed for the safety of the Countye, to be imployed upon such service as wee shall see needful for the peace of the Countye' (Alan Everitt, *Suffolk and the Great Rebellion, 1640–1660*, Suffolk RS (1960), 3:38–9) and he may well be that Captain Nelson.

10 MARCH 1643

[fo. 118v]

March 11th 1642

Res of Mr Jacob Caley[4] the Somme of One
hundred pownds for the use of Captaine
Nelson per the appointmt of the deputy Leiuetenantes
of the ~~Cap~~ County of Suffs I say Rec   }   100 li.

John Nelson

[fo. 119v]

Marche 10th 1642.

Mr Caley pay to the bearer heereof for the use
of Captayne Nelson One hundred poundes
& it shalbe allowed you upon your Accompt[5]

Ed[??] Bacon[6]
Wllm: Spring[7]
Nath: Bacon[8]

[fo. 119v]

To my honoured freinds
The Deputie Leiftennants
for the County off
Suffolke present.[9]

---

[4] This is presumably the Jacob Caley who was a member of the Nominated Assembly in 1653 and was from Suffolk. See *HoP Commons, 1640–1660*. See also Alan Everitt, ed., *Suffolk and the Great Rebellion*, Suffolk RS (1969), 3:132, 130. Caley was portman of Ipswich, and a committeeman for Suffolk 1649–57, and for Ipswich 1643, 1649–57.

[5] This short postscript is in a clerk's hand.

[6] This is very hard to read. The forename looks most like 'Evs' or just possibly 'Eds', with a strange giant thorn between it and 'Bacon'. Not that it particularly looks like Edmund, but of the Bacons around, that is by far the most plausible. If so, he is Sir Edmund Bacon of Redgrave, Suffolk committeeman 1642–9.

[7] See **1643 01 27**.

[8] Nathaniel Bacon of Shrubland was committeeman for both Ipswich and the county (1643–60) and became chair of the Association Committee at Cambridge (Holmes, *Eastern Association*, pp. 123–5. (There is another Nathaniel Bacon, of Friston, Suffolk committeeman, 1642–4.)

[9] This is in Cromwell's own hand.

107

Warrant
for pay of C li. to Capt
Nelson & his receipt.[10]

1643 03 23
Letter from Oliver Cromwell to the mayor of Colchester [Thomas Lawrence] and Captain John Langley

Date: 23 March 1643
Source: Essex Record Office, D/Y 2/7/49 (Morant papers), pp. 177–80 (178, 179, 181, 182 are blank) (holograph)

This holograph letter, complete with Cromwell's signature and seal, has a clear provenance although a number of words are underlined, probably not by Cromwell but by someone later—see fn. 3. This is an early example of Cromwell supporting 'religious' (i.e. zealous) men of lower social status for commissions.

[p. 180]
To my worthy freinds
the Maior of Colchester[1]
and Captaine John
Langley[2] present
theise

[p. 177]
Gentlemen, upon the cominge downe of your townsmen to Cambridge, Capt Langlie not knowinge how to dispose of ab them, desired mee to nominate a fitt Captaine,[3] which

---

[10] This is in a different and unrecognised seventeenth-century hand.

[1] The mayor in the year 1643 was Thomas Lawrence.
[2] For Captain John Langley, see Walter, *Colchester Plunderers*, pp. 107–10 and *passim*; and the *Online Directory of Parliamentarian Army Officers*.
[3] The underlinings (three over two lines) may be by Cromwell but seem more likely to have been added later as was a comment in the margin. In the margin, next to this 'fitt captain', in a later, italic, hand is written 'Captn Dodsworth appointed Captain of the Colchester Troop'. Both the underlinings and the marginalia are probably the work of the antiquary Philip Morant, who edited the letter for his eighteenth-century *The History and Antiquities of Colchester* (1748), Book 1, 55–6 fnn.

23 MARCH 1643

I did, an honest, <u>religious</u>, <u>valliant</u> Gentleman, Capt
Dodsworth[4] the bearer heereof, Hee hath diligently attended
the service, and much improved his men in their exer=
cise, But hath beene unhappie beyond others, in not recea=
vinge \any/ pay, for himselfe, and what Hee had for his sould
iers, is out longe agoe. Hee hath by his prudence
what with fayer, and winninge carriage, what with
monie borrowed kept them together, Hee is able to
doe soe noe longer, they will presently disband if
a course bee not taken, it's pittye itt should bee soe, for
I beleive they are brought into as good order as most
cumpanies in the Armie. {-} [5]\beside/ att this instant there
is great neede to use them, I havinge receaved \{-}/ [6]~~the~~
a speciall command from my Lord Generall to advance with
what force wee cann, to putt an end (if itt may bee)
to this worke (God soe assistinge) from whome all helpe
cometh. I beseech you therfore consider this gentleman,
and the souldiers, and if itt bee possible, make up his cum=
panie, a hunderd, \and twentye/ and send them away with what expedition
is possible, itt may (thorough Gods blessings) prove very
happie, one months pay, may prove all your trouble.
I speake to wise men, God direct you, I ~~am~~ \rest/,
Yours to serve you
Oliver Cromwell

March. 23

---

[4] Not in the *Online Directory of Parliamentarian Army Officers* and not otherwise identified.
[5] Illegible erasure. It looks as if it may have been intended as the beginning of a sentence, a full stop probably, followed by a capital letter, which looks like a 'P'.
[6] Illegible erasure, one or two letters; looks as if written to replace next erasure.

1643 03 28

Receipt signed by Oliver Cromwell and Captain Sir Thomas Martyn issued to John Annis of Landbeach, Cambs.

Date: 28 March 1643
Source: BL, Harl. MS 6988, fo. 224 (autograph)

This is one of the pro-forma receipts issued by Cromwell to those who made loans or gifts to the parliamentary cause. This one, not in Cromwell's hand but bearing his signature, was a loan made on the 'propositions'—i.e. all ratepayers who had not lent voluntarily before the end of November 1642 had become liable to a forced loan equivalent to one fifth of their annual income or one twentieth of the value of their property, and these 'Propositions' were administered by the Committee for the Advance of Money sitting at Haberdashers' Hall.[1] John Annis got his 'voluntary' loan in just before the committee was becoming effective.

[fo. 224r]

No. 1

28 march 1643

Recd of ~~John~~ John Annis[2] of Landbeach[3] in the County of Cambridge for the Use of the King and parliamt the Sum of Five pounds to be repd according to the propositions of parliamt   5 li. 00 s. 00 d. Tho: Martyn[4]   Oliver Cromwell

1643 04 04

Pass signed by Cromwell and three others for Abraham Wheelock

Date: 4 April 1643
Source: Carlyle-Lomas, 3:227 (appendix 3) (later transcription)

This is an example of one of the courtesies of war, allowing civilians to move safely around war zones. This one is remarkable for having survived pasted onto the fly-leaf of an Arabic

---

[1] See M. A. Everitt Green, ed., *Calendar of the Committee for Advance of Money*, 3 vols. (1888) and the helpful review by C. H. Firth in *English Historical Review*, 5:20 (Oct. 1890), pp. 791–2.
[2] Not identified.   [3] Landbeach, a village six miles north of Cambridge.
[4] Sir Thomas Martyn led a troop of horse raised in Cambridgeshire and was on the Cambridge county committee. Holmes, *East Anglia*, p. 81 notes that he illegally seized a horse from a papist for use on his own farm.

edition of one of the works of Robert Bellarmine SJ published in Rome in 1627.[5] This small volume, small enough to fit into a pocket, must have been a constant companion[6] to Abraham Wheelock, successively Professor of Arabic and then of Anglo-Saxon at the University of Cambridge as well as University Librarian.[7]

Carlyle, who inspected the book in the 1840s when it was owned by a Dr Lee, believed the pass or warrant to be written in Cromwell's own hand.[8]

On the same fly-leaf, and issued a year later on 27 February 1644, was a renewal of the pass signed by the earl of Manchester, who was by then the general commanding the forces of the Eastern Association.

4th April 1643

Suffer the Bearer hereof, Mr Abraham Whelocke, to pass your guards so often as he shall have occasion, into and out of Cambridge, towards Little Shelford[9] or any other place; and this shall be your warrant.

THO. COOKE   OLIVER CROMWELL
EDW. CLENCHE   JAMES THOMPSON[10]

1643 04 07

Letter from Oliver Cromwell and 28 others to 'the inhabitants' of Cambridge or some parts of Cambridgeshire

Date: 7 April 1643
Source: BL, Stowe MS 807, fos 117v–118r ('Cambridge collections containing the monuments in all the parish churches, and chapels in the said town with all the arms in & about the colleges with a short historical acct. of each college collected by Fra: Blomefield student in Caius col. 1724') (later transcription)

---

[5] Cardinal Robert Bellarmine SJ (1542–1621). So this translation into Arabic was a posthumous publication. Bellarmine was a major figure in promoting post-Tridentine Catholicism.
[6] 'A thin duodecimo, in white hogskin binding...size handy for the smallest coat-pocket' (Carlyle-Lomas 3:227).
[7] Abraham Wheelocke, (c.1593–1653), linguist and librarian. See *ODNB*.
[8] Carlyle-Lomas: 3.227–8, note.
[9] Little Shelford is a village 5.6 miles from Cambridge. Wheelocke's connection with it is unclear. He was not, for example, ever the incumbent or curate or lecturer there.
[10] Cromwell plus three members of the county committee of Cambridgeshire.

THE LETTERS, WRITINGS, AND SPEECHES OF OLIVER CROMWELL

This letter only survives in an eighteenth-century transcription, apparently transcribed in 1724 by Francis Blomefield, then a student at Gonville and Caius College. Many of the signatories are Cambridge councillors or aldermen (including the top two names on the right (Robert Twells was the mayor and Sam[uel] Spalding the town clerk)—and see **1643 03 08**—but the content of the letter suggests that more of them were inhabitants of the hundreds to the west of Cambridge, facing 'invasion' by royalists from the north and west.

[fo. 117v][1]

To the Inhabitants Whereas we have beene inforced by apparent grounds of approaching danger to begin to fortifie the Castle & towne of Cambr for preventing of the enemies in roade And the better to mainetaine the peace & Safety of ┼┼[2] this & all the associated Counties haveing in pt Seene Your good affection to the Cause And now Standing in pnte neede of your further assistance to the perfecting of the Said fortificacons being of great concernmt for a place of Retreate and randevouz in any pressing danger and likewise takeing it into our consideracons That there must be a further charge for the preservacon of the associated Counties as namely for to make Some provision for secureing of all the passages upon the river Owes[3] into our Counties as namely Huntington bridges St Ives bridg offord mills[4] & Some other The which charges with our fortificacons of the Castle & towne of Cambr will cost att leat[5] five thousand pounds by estimacon We are in couraged as well as necessitated to desire a free will offering of a liberall contribucon from You for the better enabling of us to attaine our desired ends viz the preservacon of your & our wished peace not doubting But everie honest & well affected person considering the vast expences we have beene at already & our willingness not to doe according to but beyond our abilities Wil be ready & willing to contribute his best assistance to a worke of Soe high concernmt to all the said united Counties And we doe there fore desire That what shalbe collected & freely given may with all convenient Speed be paid unto either of these bearers

---

[1] In the margin beside the head of the text are written the words 'Papyr penes me'.

[2] A crossed-out word, perhaps meant to reproduce the original: possibly 'Yr', though 'the' (possibly with a capital thorn) is more likely.

[3] = the river Ouse, which rises in the Midlands and was navigable from Bedford to King's Lynn with major road-crossing points at Huntingdon, St Ives and Ely.

[4] Offord Mills were situated on the east bank of the river Great Ouse between Saint Neots and Huntingdon.

[5] In the margin and by this line, and presumably because of this, Blomefield has written 'ita.'.

112

7 APRIL 1643

Robt Newton or John Vicars to be Sent unto the Commissioners at Cambr to be im ploied by them to the use aforesaid And soe you shall further ingage us to be

Yours ready to Serve you
dat. 7. April 1643

		Robert Gwells major
Oliver Cromwell	Tho Cooke	Saml Spalding
Tho: Hugan.	Tho Barnardiston	Robt Robson
Tho Martin	Mathew Peckover	Edw: Almond
Tho Symons	Ad Washington	Wm Grayne
Maurice Barrowe		Wm Welber
Johes King		James Blackley
Edw: Clench		Tho Bert
Robt Clarke	Jo Raven	Wm Burton
James Thompson	James Persevall	Israell Harrison
	Tho Buckley.	James Andrewes
		Edwd Potter
		Robt Ibbot

[fo. 118r]
in dorso predict
papyr

[fo. 118r]
Deliver this Wrighting unto the Church wardens who are to deliver the Same unto the Minister or Curate to be published In the parish Church the next Sundaie after the receipt hereof And what Shall be Collected lett it be indorced on the back Side hereof together with a declaracon what is given by everie particular perspon and wee require you to return unto us the names of all them that are rated to the poore that refuse or doe not give towards So goode a worke, And then deliver it to the within named Robt Newton & John Vicars or to either of them
Tho: Bendish   Jo: Eillistone.   Tho: Cooke   Tho: Gaudie James Hobart James Thompson   Thom: Wright   Mathew Linsey   Jo: Scroggs:

THE LETTERS, WRITINGS, AND SPEECHES OF OLIVER CROMWELL

1643 04 10

Letter from Oliver Cromwell to Sir John Burgoyne

Date: 10 April 1643

Source: 'Facsimile of a Letter addressed to Sir John Burgoyne, by Oliver Cromwell, in the Year 1643', reprinted in Montague Burgoyne, *A Letter to the Churchwardens of the Diocese of Lincoln, by Montagu Burgoyne, Esq., with reference to a letter addressed to them last year on the subject of Dr. Free, late Rector of Sutton, in the County of Bedford, In the letter now addressed to them, his reasons are given for declining the churchwardenship, though requested by the Rector to act in that capacity. In this publication is inserted a Facsimile of a Letter addressed to Sir John Burgoyne by Oliver Cromwell* (London, 1831), p. 14 (later copy)

In 1831 Montague Burgoyne was locked in a bitter dispute with Dr Edward Drax Free, minister of Sutton, about subscriptions for a local school of industry and over allotments for the poor.[1] Feeling himself traduced, Burgoyne published a long and rambling defence of himself and of his longstanding commitment to Reform and Reformation. In the midst of all this, he included a transcript of this letter from Cromwell to his ancestor, Sir John Burgoyne.[2] Its reliability is strengthened by a quite separate version of the same letter (very similar but not identical). The transcriber of that second version, a Bedfordshire clergyman, Thomas Orlebar Marsh (someone who may well have known the Burgoynes), tried to mimic the original hand in the first four lines and in the signature, date and address. For the rest of the letter it lurches into a later hand.[3] It seems safer to follow the 1831 version.

In early April Cromwell was assembling a large force to meet what he believed to be an imminent royalist threat when his superior officer, Lord Grey of Wark, marched off with 5,500 men from the Eastern Association to join the earl of Essex at the siege of Reading, leaving Cromwell with, he tells us, six or seven troops of horse. This letter is to Sir John Burgoyne, a landowner with estates in Bedfordshire (and Warwickshire) who had Cambridgeshire connections through his mother, Margaret Wendy of Haslingfield.[4]

[p. 14]

Sir

theise plunderers drawe neere I thinke itt will doe well if you can afford us any assistance of Dragooners to helpe in this great exigence, wee have heere about

---

[1] The dispute is described in Edward Drax Free (1764–1843), Church of England clergyman in *ODNB*.

[2] At the end of the transcript, Burgoyne adds a note: 'It is, I hope, unnecessary to say, that though my Ancestor, Sir John Burgoyne, was willing to assist in opposition to the illegal and tyrannical acts of Charles the First, he had no concern in punishing these acts by the execution of this unfortunate Monarch.'

[3] BL, Add. MS 23205 (correspondence of Rev. Thomas Orlebar Marsh, 1787–1828).

[4] Burgoyne was baptised at Haslingfield in 1592.

17 APRIL 1643

six or seaven troopes of horse, such I hope as will fight, it's happie to resist such beginninges betimes iff you can contribute any thinge to our ayde lett us speedilie participate thereof, In the meane tyme and ever comand Your humble Servant

O Cromwell

Ap 10 1643

Hunt.[5]

To Sir John Burgoyne, Bart.

1643 04 17
Oliver Cromwell to Robert Bernard [Barnard]

Date: 17 April 1643
Source: The Gentleman's Magazine, 61.i (1791), p. 44 (later transcription)

By mid-April 1643 Cromwell was stationed in Huntingdon. Three months earlier, Cromwell had written a letter to Robert Bernard letting him know he was aware of his furtive royalism (**1643 01 23**).[1] Bernard left the town, evidently for London. He appealed for protection to Edward Montagu, earl of Manchester, whose family had grown powerful at the expense of the Cromwell family, and whose father had backed Bernard (his nominee as town clerk of Huntingdon) and the new corporation against Cromwell in 1630; Bernard had recognised Montagu patronage by christening one child 'Manchester Bernard'. On 18 February the Lords granted Bernard a protection as he was, 'employed in the Affairs of the Earl of Manchester ... to keep him, his House and Goods, from Plundering'.[2]

This letter, two months later, is Cromwell's response to appeals from Bernard and from the earl, as the former faced the threat of financial penalties for his alleged delinquency. There is surely a lot of sarcasm at the end of this letter. Bernard seems to have escaped punishment for his alleged disaffection. By the late 1640s his accommodations saw him

---

[5] i.e. Huntingdon.

[1] Robert Bernard, since 1625 the Recorder of Huntingdon and a close ally of the Montagus of Hinchingbrooke, by 1643 specifically Edward Montagu, second earl of Manchester. He was MP for Huntingdon in the Short but not in the Long Parliament. There is evidence of longstanding animus between Cromwell and Bernard, see John Morrill, 'The Making of Oliver Cromwell', in John Morrill, ed., *Oliver Cromwell and the English Revolution* (1990), pp. 29–36. The best account is Robert Bernard of Huntingdon (1600–66) in *HoP Commons, 1640–1660*, which suggests Cromwell might have got it wrong. See also **1643 01 23**.

[2] *JHL*, 5:610.

appointed as a serjeant-at-law in 1648 and as steward and judge of the court in the Isle of Ely the following year.

This letter was printed in *The Gentleman's Magazine*, probably with some reshuffling of format to fit eighteenth-century conventions, but with an attempt to retain original spelling.

April 17, 1643

SIR, I have receaved two letters, the one from my Lord of Manchester,[3] the other from yourselfe, much to the same effect; I hope, therefore, one answare will serve them both; which is in short this, that we know you are disaffected to the Parliament; and truelye, if the Lords or any friends may take you off from a reasonable contribution, for my part I should be glad to be commanded to any other employment. Sir, you may (if you will) come freely into the cunterie about your occasions; for my part, I have protected you in your absence, and shall doe soe to you. This is all, but that I am ready to serve you, and rest your loving friend,

OLIVER CROMWELL.

To his very loving friend, Robert Barnard, *Esq. Present these.*

1643 05 03

Letter from Oliver Cromwell to the Lincolnshire County Committee

Date: 3 May 1643
Source: Bodl., MS Tanner 62/1A, fos 94r–95v (holograph)

This holograph letter found its way from its original recipients into the papers of William Lenthall, Speaker of the House of Commons. Did someone on the Lincolnshire committee think the Commons should see something of Cromwell's tart comments about Lord Grey of Groby?

Cromwell had left Huntingdon on or about 20 April and had moved via Peterborough to take the strongly defended Crowland, an important crossing point of the river Welland, which had kept Lincolnshire forces at bay, but succumbed to his men. He had been asked by the earl of Essex to link up with Lord Grey and with Sir John Gell to reduce the pressure

---

[3] Edward Montagu, second earl of Manchester (1602–71), parliamentarian army officer and politician. See *ODNB*.

3 MAY 1643

on parliamentarians in the East Midlands, and he was frustrated by the lack of response from those other commanders.[1]

[fo. 95v]

May 3 [? tio][2] 1643

To the Right Honoble the
Lords and others the Comittee's
at Lincolne these
present

from Mr Cromwell[3]
3 May 1643

[fo. 94r]
My Lords and Gentlemen.

I must needes be hardly thought on because I am still the
messenge of unhappy tideings and delayes concerninge you
though I know my heart is to assist you with all expedition, my
Lord Grey[4] hath now againe failed me of the Rendevous at
Stamford[5] notwithstandinge that both he and I received letters \from his Excellency/[6]
comanding us both to meete, and together with Sir John Gell,[7]
and the Nottingham forces to joyne with you, my Lord Grey
sent Sir Edward Hartop[8] to me to let me know he could
not meete me at Stamford according to our agreement, feareing

---

[1] Clive Holmes, *Seventeenth-century Lincolnshire* (1980), pp. 163–7.

[2] Very unclear what Cromwell attempted to write here. It does not look like '3rd'.

[3] This is faintly written and in another contemporary hand.

[4] Thomas Lord Grey of Groby (1621–57), regicide. See *ODNB*. He was major general of the Midlands Association from January 1643 and a member of the House of Commons (and he was the eldest son of the earl of Stamford).

[5] An important market town on the Great North Road in South Lincolnshire.

[6] Robert Devereux, third earl of Essex (1591–1646).

[7] Sir John Gell first baronet (bap. 1593, d. 1671), parliamentarian army officer. See *ODNB*. He had recently (on the death of Lord Brooke) been appointed commander of Parliament's forces in Derbyshire (his home county), Staffordshire and Warwickshire.

[8] Sir Edward Hartopp, first baronet (1572–1655), of Buckminster, Leics., see *HoP Commons, 1604–1629*.

the exposeing of Liester[9] to the forces of Mr Hastings[10] and Some
other Troopes draweing that way, beleeve it, it were better in my
poore opinion Lester were not, then that there should not be
an imediate takeing of the feild by our forces to accomplishe the
common end wherein I shall deale as freely with him when I meete
him as you can desire, I perceive Ashby de la Zouch[11] sticks much
with him, I have offered him now an other place of meeteing, to
come to which I suppose he will not deny me and that to be
too morrow, if you shall therefore thinke fitt to send one over
unto us to be with us at night, you doe not know how farre
we may prevaile with him to draw speedily to a head with Sir
John Gell and the other forces where we may all meete at
a generall Rendevous to the end you know of and then you shall
receive full Satisfaction concering[12] my integrity, and if noe man
shall helpe you, yet will I not be wanting to doe my duety,
God assisting me, if we could unite those forces and with them
speedily Make Grantham[13] the generall Rendevous both of yours and
ours I thinke it would doe well I shall bend my endeavours that
way; your concurence by Some able instrument to Solicite
this might probably exceedingly hasten it especially haveing
Soe good a foundation to worke uppon as my Lord Generalls commands
our Norfolke forces which will not prove soe many as you may
imagine by Sixe or Seaven hundred men will Lie conveniently
at Spalden[14] and I am confident be ready to ~~advance to~~ \meete at/
Grantham as the generall Rendevous I have noe more to
Trouble you, but [a] begging of god to take away the impediments
that hinder our conjunction and to prosper our designes take leave

---

[9] = Leicester, the county town of Leicestershire.

[10] Henry Hastings, second son of the earl of Huntingdon and one of the King's most active and effective commanders in the East Midlands. See Newman, *Royalist Officers*, no. 691.

[11] Ashby-de-la-Zouche, a market town in Leicestershire. Its castle was at the heart of the Hastings family lands and interest.

[12] This is the best rendering of very unclear penstrokes.

[13] Grantham, another town on the Great North Road in Lincolnshire. No nearer to Leicester than Stamford and therefore no easier for Grey of Groby but 25 miles closer to Gell's heartland.

[14] Spalding, a borough in mid-Lincolnshire, well to the east of the Great North Road.

13 MAY 1643

your faithfull servant
Oliver Cromwell

3th. May 1643

1643 05 13
Letter from Oliver Cromwell to Sir Miles Hobart[1]

Date: 13 May 1643

Source: *A true relation of a great victory obtained by the Parliament forces in Lincolnshire, under the command of the Lord Willoughby, Colonel Hobart, Colonel Cromwell, Lieutenant Generall Hotham.* (London, printed for Benjamin Allen, in Pope's Head Alley, 27 May 1643), pp. 1–2 (Wing / T2883A; Thomason / E.104[12]) (several contemporary printings)

This is a difficult text to stabilise. Cromwell's letter was printed three times in 1643, and the differences are numerous, although few affect the meaning. The earliest and fullest is the one used as the proof text here. It was published on 27 May, whereas the second, in *A perfect diurnall* covering events from 22–29 May,[2] includes the letter as having arrived on 25 May, and the third, *God on the mount, or a continuation of Englands parliamentary chronicle*, written by John Vicars,[3] was only received by Thomason on 27 October 1643.[4]

A True Relation is the only version that gives an addressee (Col. [Miles] Hobart), and a salutation and a place from which it is written ('Shasten').[5] *A perfect diurnall* is quite similar but omits what look like two lines of manuscript text, implying compositor error. Vicars's account is later and adds to what is in the *True Relation*, especially strengthening the providentialist strain and modifying the conclusion. But because of its late printing, and despite the real possibility that Vicars had access to the original, it seems prudent to rely on the first printing and to refer to the significant changes in the other versions in the notes. As usual in this edition, the many small differences in spelling, punctuation and use of italics are not included.

---

[1] For Sir Miles Hobart, see the *Online Directory of Parliamentarian Army Officers.*
[2] [S. Pecke, ed.] *A Perfect Diurnall of the Passages in Parliament: from the 22 of May to the 29 of May*, no. 50 sig. Ddd3v (N&S, 513.50: Thomason / E.249[10]).
[3] John Vicars (1580–1652), chronicler and poet. See *ODNB*. He had strong connections in various radical political and religious factions.
[4] John Vicars, *God on the mount, or a continuation of Englands parliamentary chronicle* (1643), p. 336. (Wing / V319; Thomason / E.73[4]).
[5] Cromwell spent the night after the battle at Syston Park, which was three miles north of Grantham on the road to Lincoln.

THE LETTERS, WRITINGS, AND SPEECHES OF OLIVER CROMWELL

The letter is a graphic account of the battle at Belton[6] in Lincolnshire, another important step in Cromwell's growth in confidence as a commander. In the preliminaries of the skirmish, two or three troops of Lord Willoughby of Parham's were surprised by the royalists of Charles Cavendish. In the battle itself, Cromwell's success in routing the royalist left wing was later contrasted at the trial of John Hotham with the latter's failure: either that he had failed to charge the royalist right or, as he claimed, that he had charged, but ineffectually.[7] Although his cavalry routed the royalists, his Lincolnshire allies failed to make progress and the battle (really a skirmish) did not lead to any further parliamentarian advances.[8]

[p. 1] A Letter from Collonell Cromwell
to Collonell Hobart from Shasten.

Noble[9] Sir,

The god of glory[10] hath given us this evening a glorious victory over our enemies, they were as we are enformed one and twentie Colours of horse troopes, and three or foure of dragoones: it was late in the evening when we drew out, they came and faced us within two miles of the town, so soon as we had the alarum[11] we drew out our forces, consisting of about twelve troops, whereof some of them so poore and broken that you shall seldome see worse; with this handfull it pleased God to cast the scale,[12] for after we had stood a little above musket shot the one body from the other, and the Dragooners having fired on both sides for the space of halfe an houre or more, they not advan- [p. 2] cing towards us we agreed (being therunto enabled by the great God of heaven)[13] to charge them, and advancing the body[14] after many shootes on both sides,[15] came[16] with our

---

[6] Belton is two miles north of Grantham and one mile south of Syston. There is a good brief account of the battle in Gaunt, *Cromwellian Gazetteer*, p. 104. See also A. C. E. Welby, 'Belton Fight' *Lincolnshire Notes and Queries: a Quarterly Journal*, 13 (1915), pp. 38–47.

[7] J. Rushworth, *Historical Collections*, 5:745–7.

[8] Holmes, *The Eastern Association in the English Civil War*, p. 73 and more particularly p. 259 at n. 19.

[9] *Perfect Diurnall* [henceforth PD] omits 'Noble'. Vicars, *God on the Mount* [henceforth JV] omits 'Noble Sir'.

[10] PD and JV omit 'the' and 'of glory' and so read 'God hath given us'.

[11] JV omits 'we drew out, they came and faced us within two miles of the town, so soon as we had the alarum'.

[12] JV adds 'of victorie on our side'.   [13] PD and JV omit the phrase in brackets.

[14] JV has 'our whole body'.

[15] After 'on both sides', JV adds '(but it pleased God that their bullets still flew over our heads and did us no harm)'.

[16] JV expands 'came' to 'we came on'.

28 MAY 1643

troopes a pretty round trot, they standing firme to receive us,[17] and our men chargeing feircely upon them,[18] they were imediately rowted and rann all away, and wee had the execution of them two or three miles; I beleive some of our souldiers did kill two or three men a pece,[19] my youngest corporall killed foure with his owne hand give glory to God, give glory, let all that know God, say, the Lord be praysed;[20] we have gotten some of their officers, and some of their Colors, but what the number of dead is, or what the prisoners, wee know not,[21] but great is the goodnes of God to us.[22]

Shasten, &c.

1643 05 28

Letter from Oliver Cromwell to [? the mayor and aldermen of Colchester]

Date: 28 May 1643

Source: Essex Record Office, D/Y 2/7/50, pp. 183–5 'Collection made by Revd Philip Morant of letters to Borough of Colchester.' ([probably] a contemporary copy)

In 1748 Philip Morant published a series of letters addressed to the Mayor and/or the Corporation of Colchester.[1] The originals, which he kept in his own papers, are in a hand very similar to, but not identical with, Cromwell's, and the same can be said for the

---

[17] JV (after 'us') adds 'but after almost half an houre in that posture, and some great shot spent on both sides, our men most valiantly and resolutely marched up,'.

[18] Between 'them' and 'they' JV adds 'whereupon by Gods providence, their hearts instantly failed them, a spirit of trembling, it seemed, came upon them, and'.

[19] JV adds 'in the pursuit'.

[20] PD omits the whole of 'my youngest corporall killed foure with his owne handgive glory to God, give glory, let all that know God, say, the Lord be praysed'.

[21] PD replaces 'wee knowe not' by 'for the present we have not time to inquire into'.

[22] JV replaces the whole of the final section from 'my youngest corporall killed . . .' by the following: 'the true number of men slain we are not certain of, but by credible report and estimate of our soldiers, and by what I my self saw, there were very little lesse then an hundred slain and mortally wounded, and we lost but two men at the most on our side. We took 45 prisoners besides divers of their horse and armes, and rescued many prisoners whom they had lately taken of ours, and we tooke foure or five of their Colours, and so marched away to Lincoln.'

---

[1] P. Morant, *The History of Colchester* (London, 1748), Book 1, 56n. Morant is mostly accurate in reproducing the original spelling and punctuation.

THE LETTERS, WRITINGS, AND SPEECHES OF OLIVER CROMWELL

signature.[2] Given the provenance, the addressees are surely the mayor and corporation, although with no endorsements surviving, we cannot be sure.[3] Nor can we say where Cromwell was when he wrote it. Abbott, without saying why he thinks so, dates it as from Nottingham and the usually cautious Peter Gaunt appears to concur.[4]

The letter concerns a daring storm of the town of Wakefield by the Yorkshire forces of Ferdinando Lord Fairfax (father of Sir Thomas). Wakefield had been garrisoned by the royalists at the start of the war, but they had abandoned it in January 1643 and then repossessed it in April. The assault referred to in this letter had taken place on 21 May, a week before Cromwell wrote. He uses this good news to push the parliamentarians in Essex (and perhaps other East Anglian authorities in non-surviving letters) to send reinforcements. Give us the tools and we will complete the task was a refrain in Cromwell's letters down to the very end of his time as a soldier.

[p. 183]

Gent

I thought it my duty once more to write unto yow for some more strengts to be speedily sent unto us for this great Service; I must Suppose yow heare of the great defeat geven by my L: Fairfax[5] to the Newcast:[6] Forces at Wakefield:[7] it was a great mercy of god to us, & had it not bin bestoone upon us at this very present, my Lo Fairfax had not knowne how to have Subsisted: we assure yow, should the force WE have miscarry, expect nothing but a speedy march of the enemy up unto yow; why yow should not strengthen us to make us to subsist, judg yow the danger of the neglect, & How inconvenient this improvidence or unthrifty it may be to yow; I shall never write but according to my Judgment, I tell yow againe it concernes yow exceedingly to be perswaded by me: My Lor: Newcastle is neer 6000 foot & \about/ 60[8] troopes of horse: my Lo: Fairfax is about 3000 foot & 9 troopes of horse;[9] & we have about 24 troopes of horse & Draggooners: The

---

[2] Some of the letters look very similar (lower case 'd' and 'e', for instance), but the lower-case 's', the capital 'I' and the capital 'G' all look off, in the first two cases very much so.

[3] Abbott, *Writings and Speeches*, 1:232.

[4] Abbott, *Writings and Speeches*, 1:232; Gaunt, *Cromwellian Gazetteer*, p. 224.

[5] Ferdinando, second Lord Fairfax of Cameron (1584–1648). See *ODNB*.

[6] William Cavendish, earl (later marquis, duke) of Newcastle (bap. 1593, d. 1676). See *ODNB*.

[7] A large market town in West Yorkshire, 10 miles from Leeds. For the context see Gaunt, *Cromwellian Gazetteer*, p. 169.

[8] The '6' looks as if it has been written in as an alteration: it is out of alignment. The 'o' is a changed number. It is just conceivably a '2' now, but most likely a 'o', but with a line underneath which is not an underlining so much as an erasure.

[9] Indeed, four weeks later, on 30 June, at the battle of Adwalton Moor just outside Bradford, Newcastle's 10,000 troops heavily defeated Fairfax with half the number.

2 JUNE 1643

Enemy drawes more to the Lo: Fairfax: Our motion & yours must be exceeding speedy, or else it will doe yow noe good at all; if yow send let your men come to Boston.[10] I beseech yow hasten the supply to us: forgett not monie I presse not hard, though I doe soe need that I assure yow the foot & Draggoonrs are ready to mutiny: lay not too much upon the back of a poore Gentl who desires without much noyse to lay doune his life, & bleed the last dropp to serve the cause & yow;[11] I aske not your monie for my selfe, if that were my end & hope (viz: the pay of my place) I would not open my mouth at this time: I desire to deny my selfe, but others will not be satisfyed: I beseech yow hasten Supplies forget not your prayers. Gent I am Yours Ol: Cromwell

May: 28. 1643.

[p. 184 endorsement, in another hand]

'G. Essex

Ol. Cromwell's Lett.'

1643 06 02

Letter from John Hotham; Sir John Gell; Oliver Cromwell; Sir Miles Hobart; Thomas Grey, Baron Grey of Groby to Ferdinando Fairfax, second Lord Fairfax of Cameron

Date: 2 June 1643
Source: BL, Add. MS 18979, fo. 141 (a probable forged letter)

This letter has been identified by Andrew Hopper as in the handwriting of John Hotham.[1] The letter represents a downright rejection of Lord Fairfax's request for the forces at Nottingham to come to his aid against the King's northern army under the earl of Newcastle in Yorkshire, with what was evidently a draft of Fairfax's own angry response written on the back. The rejection is all the more striking as the various forces had gathered

---

[10] Boston, an inland port in Lincolnshire.
[11] The passage 'lay not...& yow' is underlined, and there is a tick in the margin, which suggests that it and the underlining were added later. Place names earlier in the letter are also underlined.

---

[1] Andrew Hopper edited the letter, with modernised spelling and punctuation, in *The Papers of the Hothams, Governors of Hull during the Civil War* (Camden Society, 5th series, 2011), pp. 102–3. He also identifies the seal on the letter as Hotham's.

THE LETTERS, WRITINGS, AND SPEECHES OF OLIVER CROMWELL

at Nottingham to aid Fairfax.[2] Our view is that Cromwell did not sign this in person, possibly because someone signed for him in his absence, but much more probably because Hotham was forging his consent.

Cromwell's signature does not look right: neither in the way the letters are formed nor in spelling ('Oli:' is unusual for him; he uses 'Crumwell' never). The 'e' and 'r' in Cromwell's and Hobart's signatures look suspiciously alike, and were probably written by the same person. Given the way Hotham does 'w's (basically the first loop is an 'n'), which matches the 'w' in Cromwell's signature, it could well be that Hotham has written Cromwell's signature.

Certainly it seems likely that three of the five signatures on the letter were forged. The other Eastern Association officer was Sir Miles Hobart.[3] Hobart's signature, like Cromwell's, looks neither like his hand nor indeed how he spelt his own name (Mi: Hoobertt here rather than his own Miles Hobarte).[4] A very similar 't' to that in the signature of Sir Miles Hobart appears sometimes in the body of the text and in the address. Hobart's and Cromwell's signatures are almost certainly in the same hand, which is probably Hotham's. The signature of Sir John Gell, parliamentarian commander in Derbyshire, also looks to be a fake.[5] The only signature which might be authentic—apart from Hotham's own—is that of Thomas Grey, Baron Grey of Groby. Despite his youth, Grey was commander-in-chief of the Midlands Association and senior military commander in Leicestershire.[6] The most one can say is that Grey's and Gell's signatures are not, or rather not necessarily, the same hand as Cromwell and Hobart—but probably the same hand as each other.[7]

The Fairfaxes and the Hothams—John Hotham and his father Sir John, governor of Hull—were the leading parliamentarian gentry in Yorkshire; their relationship had been deteriorating since the beginning of the war.[8] Already, the tensions between the two families—and doubts about the Hothams—were coming into the open: on 22 April a letter from Lord Fairfax complaining that Hotham had disobeyed and deserted him was read in the House of Commons. It was also perhaps a deliberate attempt to discredit a series of senior parliamentarian commanders in the eyes of, at the very least, Lord Fairfax. Hotham was coming under suspicion of being a double agent, having had private interviews with

---

[2] C. Holmes, *The Eastern Association in the English Civil War* (Cambridge, 1974), pp. 73–4. Holmes, accepting the authenticity of the letter, posits the danger of a royalist domination of the East Midlands by the royalists of Gainsborough and Newark.

[3] For Sir Miles Hobart, see *The Online Directory of Parliamentarian Army Officers.*

[4] The spelling of Hobart's name—like Cromwell's—is probably a phonetic spelling of the name.

[5] Sir John Gell, first baronet (bap. 1593, d. 1671), parliamentarian army officer, see *ODNB.* Gell was the General for Parliament's forces in the North Midlands. See also *The Online Directory of Parliamentarian Army Officers.*

[6] Thomas Grey, Baron Grey of Groby. See also *The Online Directory of Parliamentarian Army Officers.*

[7] For the signatures, see BL, Egerton MS 2643, fo. 19r (Hobart); TNA, SP 16/316 fo. 15r (Gell) and TNA, SP 46/109, fo. 73r (Grey).

[8] A. Hopper, ed., *The Papers of the Hothams*, pp. 14–21.

2 JUNE 1643

Queen Henrietta Maria when she had landed in North Yorkshire in February. 'Early in April Hotham led his forces into Lincolnshire, where his kinsmen, the Wrays, had secured him the generalship of the county's forces. Once in Lincolnshire he endeavoured to subvert the local parliamentarian leaders, and by the end of May had begun a "private treaty" with the queen at Newark. He also allowed his men to plunder indiscriminately, informing Colonel John Hutchinson that "he fought for liberty and expected it in all things".'

The upshot of the letter is unclear. Certainly, Fairfax received no aid from Nottingham—perhaps more in response to other military preoccupations—and on 30 June 1643 was badly defeated by Newcastle at Adwalton Moor. Nevertheless, if the angry words that Fairfax evidently wrote on the back of this letter are indeed the draft of a letter sent to Nottingham, it can hardly have helped Hotham. Three weeks after this letter, suspecting that he was disloyal, Cromwell and Hutchinson obtained a parliamentary order for Hotham's arrest, and on 22 June he was seized and imprisoned in Nottingham Castle on charges of plundering Parliament's supporters, desertion in battle, and maintaining correspondence with the enemy. Hotham escaped to Hull, where he and his father were imprisoned; they were subsequently put on trial and beheaded for treason in January 1645.[9]

The case for seeing this letter as Hotham's letter, with forged signatures, including Cromwell's, is very strong.

[fo. 142v]

For the right Honourd Ferdinando Lord Fayrfax generall of the northern forces these present att Leedes

2 June.
the Lo: Grey Capt Hotham &c[10]

after I had concluded this lre I recd: yours dated. 2. Junij & do notwith standing all the objeccons & difficultyes therein represented desire that as you tender the publique safety you draw downe this way with all the forces you have and joyne with me to suppress this popish army here, which else (whatsoever report gives it out be) is of power without gods myraculous deliverance to distroy our forces & so by degrees to ruyne the Kingdom[11]

---

[9] The quotations are from David Scott's entry for John Hotham (1610–45), parliamentarian army officer in *ODNB*. Much of this relies on the memoirs of Colonel John Hutchinson, ventriloquised by his wife Lucy. See also the *Online Directory of Parliamentarian Army Officers*. For Grey's hostility by the time of the arrest, see Hopper, *Papers of the Hothams*, pp. 21–2; Holmes, *Eastern Association*, p. 74.

[10] This is a contemporary endorsement, and it comes below the broken seals. For Grey see below n. 10 and for Hotham, see above, n. 4.

[11] This further note has been identified by Andrew Hopper (see fn.1) as probably being in the hand of Ferdinando Lord Fairfax and representing a draft reply.

[fo. 141r]

May itt please your Lordsh:

Wee were even ready to march with all the forces here, to attend you when wee had certayn intelligence of the state of my Lord Newcastles army soe weake and in such a distraction that wee conceive itt far unfit to force your Lordsh: in your quarters, wee had certayn notice likewise That a good strenth of horse and foot were marched from him to Newarke f to face and attend the moving of the forces that are here, upon Tewsday last there was towards 40 troopes of horse and dragooners appeared in a body some 4 miles from this place, and wee heare behind them stood their foot wee drew out to fight them but they had chosen such a ground as wee could not come to them without great disadvantage att night they drew away and are still within 6 or 7 miles hoverin\g/ up and downe the country, untill wee see what these people intend or which way my Lord Newcastle will move wee thinke itt best to stay here and \not/ to draw downe into Yorkshire to eat up that small remayn der of provisions that is left and by that meanes doe your Lordsh. more prejudice then the enimy can doe this wee thought fitt to offer to your consideration, and if notwithstanding all this you shall \thinke/ fitt for us to move towards you, itt shall be readily done by

Your Lordshs humble servants

John Gell   Oli: Crumwell   Mi: Hoobertt   Tho: Grey   John Hotham
Notingham

June 2$^{d.}$
1643

1643 06 13

Oliver Cromwell to the Commissioners for the Eastern Association

Date: 13 June 1643

Source: J. Gwenogvryn Evans, 'Cromwell on Sir John Palgrave', *The Athenaeum*, no. 4032, 4 Feb. 1905, p. 145 (much later transcription)

This letter has been twice and independently transcribed from an original that has been missing from some time between 1926 (when it was included in a *Calendar of the Wynn Papers*)[1] and 1941 when the papers of the Thomas Pennant, the eighteenth-century traveller

---

[1] *Calendar of Wynn (of Gwydir) Papers, 1515–1690*, in the National Library of Wales and elsewhere (Aberywystwyth, Cardiff and London, 1926), p. 280 [no 1722A].

13 JUNE 1643

writer and antiquarian[2] reached the National Library of Wales. There is a very early photocopy which was the basis of the later transcription.[3] There are no differences of any significance between the version in *The Atheneum* and the one in the *Calendar* except that the former includes examples of things crossed out and corrected, and it does include an address and date.

In editing the letter in 1905, J. Gwenogvryn Evans tells us that the letter had become detached from the Pennant papers and was in the possession of a Mrs Anne Gough of Geliwig in Caernafsonshire. In 1941, the Pennant papers came to the NLW with many of the papers that had been diverted to Mrs Gough; but this was not one of them.

There is no need to question the authenticity of the letter, but just to note its chequered history.

The subject matter is more straightforward. The internal tension amongst the east-of-England parliamentarians was reaching the first of several peaks. Following his victory at Belton on 13 May Cromwell had spent nearly three weeks in Nottingham. No later than 4 June (just after his name was probably taken in vain by John Hotham), Cromwell had headed south, sweeping through Leicestershire, Lincolnshire and Nottinghamshire intending to drive the royalists out of Newark (only to find they had already gone). This provides some of the context for the warrant procured three weeks later by Cromwell and Colonel John Hutchinson charging Hotham with treason.

There was the further anxiety in these weeks of the progress of Queen Henrietta Maria, marching through the East Midlands with men and supplies for the King at Oxford. These continued bursts of energy made him very frustrated with those regiments in the Eastern Association which just sat around defending areas with unnecessary strength and in this letter he demands that one such regiment, Sir John Palgrave's Norfolk Regiment of Foot—with or without its commander—be required to move north to strengthen his forces.

Palgrave's lieutenant colonel was Sir Edward Astley (not, as Cromwell miscalled called him, Ashley). A series of letters that he wrote to his wife provide a counterpoint to Cromwell's complaints.[4] Cromwell's complaint of Palgrave's foot-dragging is confirmed: when Astley was ordered to Wisbech to command three companies on 22 May, he heard that the rest of the regiment was supposed to be joining Cromwell in Lincolnshire[5]—which it evidently did not. Nevertheless, the problems were not all with the commander: on 17 June Astley complained 'of the condition of our Regiment, which is very ill at present,

---

[2] Thomas Pennant (1726–98), naturalist, traveller, and writer, see *ODNB*.

[3] It is in the NLW and is listed as Ms 9105F. The Library was unable to provide us with a copy. An archivist at the NLW confirmed that 'the transcript of the letter in the Calendar is a near exact copy, apart from the fact it does not reproduce the long "S" used in words such as "because" in the opening line'.

[4] Sir Edward Astley [Asteley] (1603–54). See R. W. Ketton-Cremer, *Three Generations* (privately printed, 1958). Astley's letters to his wife are reprinted, pp. 9–18. Astley was great-nephew and son-in-law of the royalist general Sir Jacob Astley.

[5] Ketton-Cremer, *Three Generations*, 9.

THE LETTERS, WRITINGS, AND SPEECHES OF OLIVER CROMWELL

the soldiers doing what they list, having the power in theyre owne handes'.[6] Nevertheless, Cromwell's complaints seem to have had some effect; on 20 June—a week after Cromwell's letter—Astley told his wife that, 'We are to drawe up all our Forces in these partes by to morrow night', including more trained bands, to Bourne in Lincolnshire to rendezvous with Cromwell: 'itt is conceived all the Forces in this County, the Ile of Ely, Cambridgeshire and Huntinton are to joyne with the Nottingham Army to impeach the Quenes advance unto Oxforde.'[7] By 1 July he had advanced to Peterborough and was preparing to march to Rockingham to join with Cromwell and Baron Grey of Groby.[8]

To my honourd freinds the Commissioners for the Association present theisse att Cambridge June the 13

Collonell Cromwells letter 13 Junij 1643

Gentlemen, because I understood s[r] John Palgrave[9] was resolved to come to you, and knowinge Hee is very much mistaken in my Lord Generalls meaninge concerninge the comeinge of his Regiment, to the Armie,[10] and findinge too too many delayes therein, excuses sometimes[11] putt upon the Lief[tnt] Collonell,[12] sometimes upon the Captaines, sometimes upon want of monie, upon Leif[tnt] Hotham[13] and my selfe, upon misunderstanding his Excellency, by all w[ch] the service is neglected and delayed, and the kingdome indangered. least you upon his comeinge should bee ledd allsoe into mistakes upon pretences, I make this short addresse to you, desiringe you to beleive mee itt exceedingly imports the kingdom the Association, and you all that Hee hasten to us. lett noe words whatsoever leade your resol[u]tions any other way, I maintaine and affirme to you. as I would deale faythfully with you, and love the Association, two or three-hundred men in those parts are enowe. Holland[14] is fron teen[15] to itt. Horsea bridge[16]

---

[6] Ketton-Cremer, *Three Generations*, 10.　　[7] Ketton-Cremer, *Three Generations*, 11.

[8] Ketton-Cremer, *Three Generations*, 12.

[9] Sir John Palgrave of Barningham Norwood, Norfolk (1605–72): see his life in *HoP Commons, 1640–1660*; *The Online Directory of Parliamentarian Army Officers*.

[10] Lord General = Robert Devereux third earl of Essex (1591–1646).

[11] The three 'sometimes' in the *Atheneum* version are all transcribed in the *Calendar* version as 'somtimes'.

[12] Sir Edward Astley. See n. 4.

[13] *Online Directory of Parliamentarian Army Officers*. Hotham was lieutenant general of the parliamentarian forces in Lincolnshire, or would be until his arrest on 22 June.

[14] Holland was the name of an administrative district (equivalent to a hundred or wapentake) in south-east Lincolnshire.

[15] The Calendar version, surely correctly, has 'fronteer'.

[16] Horsea Bridge, over the river Nene just south of Peterborough.

128

over the river out of Huntington sheire beinge ~~walled~~ made a draw bridge makes the advance theither altogether ~~impossi~~ fearelesse. If the enimies horse advance to Stamford[17] what can they doe. nothinge att all as to that place, if wee bee stronge in the feild, you are very well secured, and bee assured if the enimie advance towards you, wee shall followe him in the heeles. for s[r] miles Hobart[18] and my selfe doubt not, wee shall not bee soe unfaythfull to you, to give the enimie leave to march into the Association, and tarrie behinde. my Lord Generalls expresse command is, that wee all advance if Hee drawe towards the south with his Armie. His care is for you, soe wee trust shall our faythfullnesse. lett noe words therfore from S[r] John Palgrave prevaile but command him to march up wth all the volunteers, both the two cumpanies w[ch] you send, and all the rest of the volunteers. if Hee cannott bee spared lett S[r] Edward Ashlye bringe them. lett him not keepe a volunteer at wisbeach I beseech you doe not. Hee hath a minde to this cumpanie and the other cumpanie, to please himselfe in composinge his Regiment. this is not a time to picke and choose for pleasure. service must bee donn, command you, and bee obeyed, the Queene[19] is marchinge with 1200 horse, and 3000 foote. wee are [~~but~~?] much under that number. wee trust to indevor our dutyes wth theise wee have, but it will not bee good to lose the use of any force god gives us, by negligence. The Lord give you, and us zeale, I take leave and rest

Your faythfull servant
Oliver Cromwell

I besseech you informe your selves fully of the numbers of your men. att wisbech, and send what you thinke may well be spared. you need few when wee are in the feild, whereof doubt not when his comes up to us.

---

[17] Stamford: a market town in south Lincolnshire strategically placed on the Great North Road.
[18] Sir Miles Hobart: see The *Online Directory of Parliamentarian Army Officers*.
[19] Queen Henrietta Maria [Princess Henrietta Maria of France] (1609–69), queen of England, Scotland and Ireland, consort of Charles I. See *ODNB*.

THE LETTERS, WRITINGS, AND SPEECHES OF OLIVER CROMWELL

1643 07 22
Letter from Oliver Cromwell to the committee at Cambridge

Date: 22 July 1643

Source: Privately owned (by Mr Kevin Frostick of North Runcton, Norfolk and published with his consent and assistance) (contemporary copy)

This letter was written at a crucial moment in the struggle for control of north Lincolnshire. Although a parliamentarian garrison had been established in Gainsborough at the outset of the war, the town had been captured by a royalist raiding party from Newark in January 1643. It gave the King control of all the major crossing points on the river Trent and broke links between the parliamentarian heartland and its garrisons in Yorkshire, not least Hull. Its recapture had therefore been a priority and a combination of Lord Fairfax and Lord Willoughby had stormed the town on 20 July. This letter makes it clear that the royalists were expected to make an immediate attempt to retake it.

Cromwell was down in the south of the county, 68 miles from Gainsborough on 19 July when he captured Burghley House (outside Stamford), home of the Cecil earls of Exeter.[1] He had then set off to support the Lincolnshire forces now garrisoning Gainsborough. This letter seems to have been written from Syston Park, just a few miles north of Grantham, midway between Stamford and Gainsborough, where he had bivouacked in mid-May at the time of the siege of Grantham and the battle of Belton.[2] From there he wrote at least one letter, printed here. It was almost certainly sent to the parliamentarian committee at Cambridge, for they referred to the precise content of this letter in one of their own which they sent, together with a copy of Cromwell's letter to them, to Sir Thomas Barrington[3] and other deputy lieutenants in Essex asking for men and money to be hurriedly despatched and confirming that they had sent the two companies under their captains that Cromwell had requested. That letter was sent from Cambridge on 23 July, the following day.[4] They *may* have sent another copy together with a separate cover letter to the House of Commons. The Journal of the House of Commons reports receiving 'A Letter from Sir Edw. Aiscough,[5] from Colonel Cromwell to the Committee of Cambridge; and a Letter from the Committee at Cambridge, relating the good Success it has pleased to bless the Lord Willoughby of Parham, in taking of Gainsborough'.[6] It is certainly attractive to think the letter from Cambridge was the letter printed here. But this is reported on the morning of 24 July so the time to receive Cromwell's 22 July letter in Cambridge, to copy

---

[1] Stamford (Lincolnshire) changed hands frequently during the Civil War, and Burghley House was the great prodigy house built by Lord Burghley, chief minister to Elizabeth I. See Gaunt, *Cromwellian Gazetteer*, p. 108.

[2] Clive Holmes, *Seventeenth-Century Lincolnshire* (Lincoln, 1980), pp. 166–9.

[3] Sir Thomas Barrington (*c.*1585–1644). See *ODNB*.   [4] BL, Egerton MS 2647 fo. 51r.

[5] Sir Edward Ayscough was MP for the county of Lincolnshire in the Long Parliament, and an active parliamentarian (*HoP Commons, 1640–1660*; Holmes, *Lincolnshire*, p. 143). See also **1643 07 29**.

[6] *JHC*, 3:180.

130

22 JULY 1643

it and to forward it to Westminster and have it presented the next morning is very tight.[7] Perhaps Cromwell wrote directly to the House of Commons at the same time that he wrote to Cambridge. At any rate, whatever the Commons received was destroyed in the great Westminster fire of 1834.

The letter presented here is in an unknown hand. It is not Cromwell's signature (and there is no evidence he had a clerk to write down his letters before mid-1644). There is no reason to doubt that it is a very early copy. It is written in an outdated secretary hand, more likely that of a gentleman than of a trained scribe and it has two slightly worrying things in it. The first is that Cromwell is made to write 'it seemeth' twice and that is an outdated idiom he does not use. The other is the opening phrase 'Goeing back to Shilton'. There is no such place within 50 miles of Burghley House, where Cromwell can be firmly placed on 19 July, or en route to Gainsborough which he reached a week later. It is surely a mistake for Syston, three miles north of Grantham. Syston is 26 miles north of Stamford and 40 miles south of Gainsborough, so the timings make sense and if it is Syston then he is 'goeing back' to somewhere he had spent time two months earlier. It is a careless transcription but not something to challenge the basic authority of the letter.

Since the Cambridge letter makes it clear Cromwell did write a letter on the matters contained in this letter, and because it contains really esoteric names—the very obscure captains Poe and Patterson—we can be confident that this is a very early copy of a genuine Cromwell letter, a copy made in a hurry with careless but minor errors. When read alongside the four accounts of the battle of Gainsborough Cromwell despatched a week later, it is an important letter.

[recto]

Gent

Goeinge backe to Shilton,[8] I mett there with lettres shewinge the great dainger of Gainsborough, which it seemeth is in some distresse, The place is of very great concernment, and in noe sort to bee neglected: My Lo: Newcastle[9] it seemeth is ingaged to doe what in him lyeth to bringe off the Earle of Kingstone,[10] which makes it probable, that all the ingagement of the North is likelye to come to an

---

[7] BL, Add. MS 31116, p. 129 (Lawrence Whittaker's diary) reports that 'news was brought this day into the House by Sir Christopher Wray of a victory obtained in Gainsborough in Lincolnhire'. Wray was another Lincolnshire MP and so may have only introduced Ayscough's letter; the Journal entry suggests all three were presented together.

[8] Probably Syston Park, near Grantham. See above in the introduction to this item.

[9] William Cavendish, William, first duke of Newcastle upon Tyne (bap. 1593, d. 1676) and Charles I's commander of all armies north of the river Trent from the beginning of the civil wars until after his defeat at Marston Moor (July 1644), when he went into voluntary exile in France.

[10] Robert Pierrepont, first earl of Kingston upon Hull (1584–1643), nephew of Newcastle and since May 1643 lieutenant general of the King's forces in Lincolnshire, Cambridgeshire, Huntingdonshire, Norfolk and Rutland. He was killed by 'friendly fire' three days after this letter was written. See *ODNB*.

yssue in those parts. Therefore it wilbee exceding necessaie for yow to send what strength you can both of horse and Foote, leave none behind, All yours is concened in this buisnes, I pray yow send us what Foote Companies yow can spare but especially Captaine Poes[11] and Captaine Pattersons[12] troopes, I beseeche you lett noe excuse hinder, Butt strictly charge Obedience to your Comands & hasten them away, If I marche towards Gainsborough, which wilbee somwhat farr, I haveing noe considerable summes of mony, what shall I doe, I must addresse myself to you, I beseech you send with your Horse what mony can bee spared, or soddainly after, Gentlemen I am July 22°: 1643
Your Humble servant
Oliver Cromwell

You may know our intelligence is that the Lo; Newcastle will advance his Army upp presently; And that some of his Horse is come to Gainsborough, and therefore it wilbee necessary to hasten with all possible speede to get upp what force you can, loose no tyme

[verso]
July the 22th
From Collonell Crumwell[13]

1643 07 29

Letter from Sir Edward Ayscough, Oliver Cromwell and John Broxolme to [William Lenthall, Speaker of the House of Commons]

Date: 29 July 1643
Source: Bodl., MS Tanner 62/1B, fos 194r–195v (no. 98) (autograph)

This is the first of four letters in which Cromwell describes and comments on his victory over the royalists at the battle of Gainsborough on 28 July. Or perhaps more accurately, the

---

[11] William Poe was Captain of a troop in Oliver Cromwell's regiment of horse in the Eastern Association Army from the raising of that troop in Suffolk in February 1643 until February 1645.

[12] Robert Patterson. He was a captain in Cromwell's own regiment by early 1644 but nothing is known of him before that. Poe and Patterson are both in the *Online Directory of Parliamentarian Officers*.

[13] This looks authentic. Many contemporaries—and few later—address him as 'Crumwell' which is presumably closer to how he pronounced his name than Cromwell.

29 JULY 1643

first of four letters describing the victory at Gainsborough to which Cromwell put his name. This is the official letter of the Parliamentarian commanders to the Speaker of the House of Commons and survives in Speaker Lenthall's own papers. It is written by a clerk but bears what is almost certainly Cromwell's own signature together with those of Sir Edward Ayscough of South Kelsey, Lincolnshire, MP for Lincolnshire[1] and John Broxolme of Lincoln and Barrow, Lincolnshire MP for the city of Lincoln.[2] The letter pays due attention to Cromwell's crucial role in the fighting—and apart from the similarity of the accounts in all four letters, in terms of what it describes of the military action, it indeed makes most sense that Cromwell indeed had, unsurprisingly, a significant input into the letter. But it is probably better treated as *jointly* authored. The very first paragraph is clearly written from the perspective of the Lincolnshire commanders: 'We' had solicited a joining of forces, and had been joined at a rendezvous by Cromwell. This, therefore, is most safely seen as the joint letter of the Lincolnshire commanders and Cromwell, all MPs (but not of the other senior officer, the Scottish professional Sir John Meldrum).

The letter is dated 29 July, and was followed by three more: one written on 30 July, to Sir John Hobart, a Norfolk baronet, and two written on 31 July to the deputy lieutenants of Suffolk and to the Committee in Cambridge [see **1643 07 30**, **1643 07 31a**, **1643 07 31b**].

Gainsborough was the most important crossing point on the river Trent north of Newark, had been occupied by the royalists in January 1643 and had been captured by Lord Willoughby of Parham[3] for Parliament on 20 July but the royalists in Newark (25 miles to the south) were determined to retake it quickly and sent a force under Charles Cavendish[4] to besiege it. Willoughby issued a plea for help and 1,200 men, drawn equally from the garrison in Nottingham with Sir John Meldrum[5] in command and 600 cavalry and dragoons under Cromwell rushing north after the successful capture of Burghley House (just outside Stamford on the Great North Road in South Lincolnshire). The four letters together give us a close narrative of the subsequent engagement and of the defeat and death of Charles Cavendish. But in following up their victory, Cromwell came face to face with the arrival of the main force of the royalist Northern Army under the Earl of Newcastle. Cromwell himself oversaw a brilliantly staged withdrawal of his forces in a retreat initially to Lincoln, but the victory on 28 July, important though it was for Cromwell's military self-assurance, proved to be pyrrhic: on 31 July, coming under

---

[1] Sir Edward Ayscough (bap. 1596. d. in or by 1654) had also been MP for Lincoln in 1621 and 1628. See *HoP Commons, 1604–1628*; *HoP Commons, 1640–1660*.

[2] John Broxolme (bap. 1583, d. 1647). See *HoP Commons, 1640–1660*, and Clive Holmes, *Seventeenth-Century Lincolnshire* (1980), pp. 140, 143, 180.

[3] For Francis Willoughby, fifth Baron Willoughby of Parham (bap. 1614, d. 1666), colonial governor, see *ODNB*. Willoughby was, until stood down six weeks later, commander of all parliamentarian forces in Lincolnshire.

[4] Charles Cavendish (1620–43), royalist army officer. See *ODNB*. He was a nephew of the earl of Newcastle and he was destined to die at the end of the battle.

[5] Sir John Meldrum (b. before 1584? d. 1645), parliamentarian army officer. See *ODNB*.

THE LETTERS, WRITINGS, AND SPEECHES OF OLIVER CROMWELL

sustained artillery attack, Willoughby surrendered Gainsborough to the Earl of Newcastle.[6] Moreover, the appearance of the King's Northern Army south of the Trent placed the whole Eastern Association in great danger.

———

[fo. 195v]

Lincolne Julij 29th 1643 A true Relation of the Pursuite of Colonell Cromwell & others att Gainsborough against the Earle of Newcastles forces.[7]

[fo. 194r]

Noble Sir

Wee haveing sollicited a Conjunction of Forces towardes the raising of the seige of Gainsborough did appoint a generall Rendevous at North Scarle[8] to be upon thursday the 27th of July. To the which place Sir John Meldrum[9] with about 300 horse & Dragooneres & Colonell Cromwell with about six or 7 troopes of horse & about 100 dragoon's came with these they marched towardes Gainsborough & meeting with a good partie of the Enimy about a myle from the towne, beat them backe but, not with any Comendacons to our Dragoon's, wee advanced still towardes the Enimy all along under the Cony warren[10] which is uppon a high hill above Gainsborough. The Lincolne troops had the Van, two North Hampton[11] & three small troups of Nottingham the Battaile,[12] and Colonell Cromwell the Reere, the Enimy in the meane time with his body keeping the topp of the hill. Somme of the Lincolne troops beganne to advance upp the hill which were opposed by a force of the Enimy, but our men repelled them untill all our whole body was gott upp the hill The Enimy kept his grownd which he chose for his

---

[6] There are several excellent short accounts of the battle and its aftermath: John West, *Oliver Cromwell and the Battle of Gainsborough* (Boston, 1992), pp. 9–14, has the advantage of the clearest battlefield plan which helps make sense of Cromwell's account in these four letters. See also Ian Beckwith, *Gainsborough during the Great Civil War* (1969), pp. 9–16; Clive Holmes, *Seventeenth-Century Lincolnshire* (1980), pp. 167–70; Martyn Bennett, *Oliver Cromwell* (2006), pp. 64–7.

[7] This endorsement (there is no address) is in a different hand, but a clearly mid-seventeenth-century hand. For William Cavendish, first earl, later duke, of Newcastle upon Tyne (bap. 1593, d. 1676), writer, patron and royalist army officer, see *ODNB*.

[8] North Scarle, a small village on the Lincolnshire/Nottinghamshire border and about 15 miles due south of Gainsborough.

[9] See n. 5.   [10] Cony warren = rabbit warren, and therefore very uneven ground.

[11] i.e. troops from Northamptonshire—these were the men under Meldrum's immediate command.

[12] That is, the main body of the Army (see *OED*).

134

29 JULY 1643

best advantage with a body of horse of about 3 Regimentes of horse & a reserve behind them consisting of ~~Leiuetennt~~ Genrall Cavendish his Regiment which was a verie full Regiment. Wee presentlie put our horse in Order which wee could hardlie doe by reason of the Cony holes & the difficult ascent upp the Hill, the Enimy being with in musquett shott of us and advanceing towardes us before wee could gett our selves into any good Order, But with those troups wee could gett upp wee charged the greater bodie of the Enimy, came upp to the swordes point & disputed it soe a little with them, that our men pressing heavilie upon them they could beare it but all their body ranne away some on the one side of their reserve others on the other, divers of our troops pursueing, had the chase about six miles, Genrall Cavendish with his Regimt standing firme, all the while, and faceing some of our troops that did not follow the Chase, Colonell Cromwell with his Major Whaley[13] & one or two troops more were following the Chase & were in the Reere of that Regiment, when they saw the body stand unbroken endeavored with much adoe to gett into a bodie those 3 or 4 troops which were divided which when they had donne perceiving the Enimy to Charge two or [fo. 94v] Three of the Lincolne Scattered troops and making them retyre by reason of their being many more then they in number, \& the rest being elswhere ingaged & following the chase/ Colonell Cromwell with his three troops follow ed them in the reere brake this Regiment & forced their Generall with diveres of their men into a quagmire in the bottome of the hill, where one of \Collonell Cromwell/ his men cutt him in the head by reason whereof he fell of his horse; and his Captaine Leiuetennt thrust him into the side wherof within two hours he dyed;[14] the rest Chasing his Regiment quite out of the feild having execucon of them soe that the feild was left whollie unto us not a man appearing. Upon this div[e]rs of our men went into the towne carrying in to my Lord willoughbie somme of the Ammunition wee brought for him beleiving our worke was at an end, saving to take care how to bring further provisions into the towne to enable it to Stand a Seige in case my Lo: Newcastle \Should draw upp/ with his Army to attempt it, Whilst wee were considering of these things word was brought us that there was a Small remainder of the Enimies Force not yett medled with about a myle beyond Gainsbrough with some foot & two peeces of Ordnance. Wee haveing noe foot

---

[13] Edward Whalley, appointed Lord Whalley under the Protectorate (d. 1674/5), regicide and major general. See *ODNB*. He was not only major in Cromwell's regiment but his first cousin. See also the *Online Directory of Parliamentarian Army Officers*.

[14] This man is identified in **1643 07 30** as being captain-lieutenant James Berry.

135

desired to have some out of the towne which my Lo: willughby graunted & sent us about 600 foot, with these wee advanced towardes the Enimy when wee came thither to the topp of the hill wee beat diveres troops of the Enimies horse backe but at the bottome wee saw a Regimt of foot, after that another, My Lord Newcastles owne Regiment consisting of 19 Colours appearing allsoe and many horse, which indeed was his Army. Seing these there soe unexpectedlie wee advised what to doe, Colonell Cromwell was Sent to commaund the Foot to retire and to draw of the horse, by the time he came to them the Enimy was marching upp the hill, the Foot did retire disorderly into the towne which was not much above a qu'ter of a mile from them upon whome the Enimys horse did somme small execu tion, the horse allsoe did retire in some disorder about halfe a mile untill they came to the end of a feild [fo. 195r] Where a passage was whereby the endeavor of Colonell⸗ Cromwelles Major Whaley & Captaine Ayscoghe[15] a body was drawne upp, with these wee forced the Enimy staid their pursuit & opposed them with about 4 troops of Colonell Cromwelles & 4 Lincolne troops, the Enimies bodie in the meane time increasing verie much from the Army: But such was the goodnes of god giveing Courage and valour to our men & officers, That whilst Major Whaley & Captaine Ayscoghe somtimes the one with 4 troops faced the Enimy somtimes the other to the exceeding glorie of god bee it spoken, And the great honour of those two gentlem they with this handfull forced the Enimy soe and dared them to their teeths, in at the least 8 or 9 Severall Removes, the Enimy following at thier heels and they though their horses were exceed inglie tired retreated in this Order neare Carbine shott of the Enimy whoe thus followed them, fireing upon them Colonell Cromwell gathering upp the maine bodie and faceing them behind these two lesser bodies that in dispite of the Enimy wee brought of our horse in this Order without the losse of two men, Thus have yw a true Relation of this notable service wherin god is to have all the glorie and Care must be taken speedily to releive this Noble Lord from his and the States Enimyes by a speedy force Sent unto us, & that without any delay or else he will be lost & that Important towne and all these parts & way made for this Army instantly to advance into the South. Thus resting uppon your Care in speeding present Succours hither wee humbly take our Leaves and Remaine

---

[15] Edward Ayscough (bap. 1618, d. 1668) was a captain in Lord Willoughby's regiment of horse, having previously served in Essex's army. He was the eldest son of Sir Edward Ayscough. See *Online Directory of Parliamentarian Army Officers*; A. R. Maddison, ed., *Lincolnshire Pedigrees*, 4 vols. (Harleian Society, 50, 51, 52, 55, 1902–6), 1:66.

Your humble servts
Edw. Ayscoghe   Jo: Broxolme   Olliver Cromwell

Lincolne July 29th 1643 at six a clocke at night

1643 07 30
Letter from Oliver Cromwell to Sir John [Hobart], knight and baronet

Date: 30 July 1643

Source: 'Letter from Sir Philip Stapleton to Oliver Cromwell and four letters from Oliver Cromwell himself', Dawson Turner, ed., *Norfolk Archaeology*, 2 (1849), pp. 46–50 (later transcription)

The original of this letter, in Cromwell's hand and with his signature,[1] exists but is in private hands and the current editors do not have permission to reproduce it. They have, however, had an opportunity to view it and can confirm that the nineteenth-century transcript relied on here is accurate in many respects. It reproduces the spelling if not the punctuation of the original (as a close comparison of the Dawson Turner transcription and the photograph of the third of four pages of the letter contained in the 2018 auction catalogue confirms).[2] The current editors had already concluded that the passage included by Dawson Turner as a postscript was in fact a passage that belonged to the end of page 1 of the letter, Cromwell (as was his wont) turning the paper by 90 degrees to write additional matter in the margin. The name of the intended recipient had been so heavily crossed out that Dawson Turner could not work out the surname. Carlyle, Lomas, Abbott and others all thought the letter had most probably been directed to Sir John Wray, a prominent Lincolnshire MP and baronet. For reasons explored in the appendix to this document, it is clear that the recipient must have been Sir John Hobart of Blickling in Norfolk.[3] This too is consistent with what the inspection of the original indicates.

This letter was written two days after the battle and the day after the letter by Cromwell and others to the Speaker of the House of Commons (**1643 07 29**). It is a day before the two letters to the deputy lieutenants of Suffolk and to the Committee at Cambridge. It therefore

---

[1] As claimed by Dawson Turner and confirmed from the image of page 3 referred to in n. 2 below.

[2] Sales Catalogue for Sale of Fine Books and Manuscripts at Bonhams, Knightsbridge (London) on 21 March 2018, item 11 (image on p. 11).

[3] Sir John Hobart, second baronet (1593–1647). See *HoP Commons, 1604–1628* and *HoP Commons, 1640–1660*.

THE LETTERS, WRITINGS, AND SPEECHES OF OLIVER CROMWELL

incorporates part of the story of the aftermath of the battle on 28 July which was to lead to the surrender of Gainsborough to the royalists on 31 July. It was also a letter written under particular strain as Cromwell retreated south down the length of Lincolnshire: at Gainsborough on 28 July, at Lincoln on the evening of the 29th and in Huntingdon on the 31st, the day after this letter. For a discussion of the sequence of events see **1643 07 29**.

———

To my noble friend Sir John [Hobart],[4] Knight and Baronett, present theise.

Sir,

The perticular respects I have receaved att your hands doe much oblige me, but the great affection you beare to the publike much more: for that cause, I am bould to acquaint you with some late passages wherein it hath pleased God to favor us, which, I am assured, wilbee welcome to you. After Burlye house[5] was taken, wee went towards Gaynsbrowe, to a generall rendevouze, where mett us Lincolnesheire troopes, soe that we were nineteene or twentye troopes, when wee were together, of horse, and about three or foure troupes of dragooners: wee marched with this force to Gainsbrowe: upon fryday morninge, being the 28th day of July, wee mett with a forlorne hope of the enimie, and with our men brak it in: wee marched onn to the townes end, the enimie beinge upon the top of a very steepe hill over our heads, some of our men attemted to march up that hill: the enimie oposed: our men drove them up, and forced their passage: by that tyme wee came up, wee saw the enimie well sett in two bodyes; the former a large fayre body, the other a reserve, consisting of six or seaven brave troopes: before wee could gett our force into order, the great body of the enimie advanced: they were with in muskett shott of us when wee came to the pitch of the hill: wee advanced likewise towards them; and both charged, each upon other: thus advancinge, wee came to pistoll and sword's point both in that closse order, that it was disputed very strongly whoe should breake the other; but, our men pressinge a little heavilye upon them, they begun to give backe, which our men perceavinge, instantly [p. 48] forced them, brake that whole body: some of them flyinge on this side, some on the other side of the reserve: our men pursuinge them in great disorder had the execution about 4 or, some say, 6 miles with much

---

[4] In the appendix to this item, the case is made from internal evidence that the intended recipient was in fact Sir John Hobart of Blickling in North Norfolk.

[5] Burghley House was the home of the Cecils, earls of Exeter, by the 1640s the (royalist) third earl, from a cadet branch of the family. Cromwell captured it between 16 and 21 July (see **1643 07 31a**, note 2).

30 JULY 1643

a doe *I stayed two of my owne troupes, and my major stayed his, in all three: there were in the front of the enimies reserve three or four of the Lincolne troupes yett unbroken: the enimie charged those troupes, utterly broake and chased them; soe that none of the troupes on our part stood but my three: whilst the enimie was followinge our flyinge troupes, I charged him on the reere with my three troupes, drove him downe the hill, brake him all to peices, forced Leiuetennant General Cavendish[6] into a bogg, whoe fought in this reserve: one officer cutt him on the head; and, as hee lay, my Capt Leuietennant Berry thrust him into the short ribbs, of which hee dyed about two hours after in Gainsbrowe.*[7] this donn, and all their force beinge goun, not one man standinge, but all beaten out of the field, wee drew up our body together, and kept the field; the half of our men beinge well worne in the chase of the enimie. Upon this wee indeavored the businesse wee came for, which was the releife of the towne with ammunition: wee sent in some powder, which was the great want of that towne; which doun, word was brought us that the enimie had about 6 troupes of horse and 300 foote a little onn the other side of the towne, and with our body of horse marched towards them: wee saw two troupes towards the mill, which my men drove downe into a little village att the bottom of the hill: when wee came with our horse to the top of that hill, wee sawe, in the bottom, a whole regiment of foote, after that, another and another; and, as some counted, about 50 colours of foote, with a great body of horse, which indeed was my Lord Newcastle's Armie,[8] with which hee now beseiges Gainsbrowe. My Lord Willoghby[9] commanded mee to bringe off the foote and horse, which I endeavoured; but the foote (the enimie pressinge onn with the armie) retreated in some disorder into the towne, beinge of that garrison: our horse, also beinge wearied, and unexpectedly pressed by this new force, soe great, gave off, not beinge able to brave the charge; but with some difficulty wee gott our horse into a body, and with them

---

[6] Charles Cavendish, a nephew of the earl of Newcastle.

[7] The text between the two asterisks (127 words in length) appears in the Dawson Turner transcript as a postscript at the end of the text. But it much more logically appears at what can be worked out to be the end of the first page. We had already conjectured that it was written as a long marginal comment before we were allowed to see (but not to reproduce) the manuscript in private hands. We saw nothing that changed our view that this passage belongs at this point in the letter.

[8] i.e. the royalist army of the North under William Cavendish, first duke of Newcastle upon Tyne.

[9] Francis Willoughby, fifth Baron Willoughby of Parham (bap. 1614, d. 1666), colonial governor. See ODNB. Willoughby was, until stood down six weeks later, commander of all parliamentarian forces in Lincolnshire.

THE LETTERS, WRITINGS, AND SPEECHES OF OLIVER CROMWELL

faced the enimie, and retraited in such order, that, though the enimie followed hard, yett they were not able to disorder us, but wee gott them off safe to Lincolne from this fresh force, and lost not one man: the honor of this retraite, æqual to any of late tymes, is due to Major Whalye[10] and Captaine Ayscough,[11] next under God: this relation I offer you for the honor of God, to whome be all the praise; as also to lett you know you have some servants [p. 49] faythfull to you, to incite to action. I beseech you, lett this good successe quicken your cuntrimen to this ingagement: its great evidence of God's favor: lett not your businesse be starved. I know if all bee of your minde we shall have an honorable return; its your owne businesse: a reasonable strength, now raised speedilie, may doe that which much more will not doe after sometime. Undoubtedly, if they succeed heere, you will see them in the bowells of your Association. For the tyme, you will have itt from your noble kinesman and Colonell Palgrave:[12] if wee bee not able in ten days to releive Gainsbrowe, a noble Lord wilbe lost, many good foote, and a considerable passe over trent into theise parts: the Lord prosper your indeavors and ours. I beseech you present my humble service to the High honble Lady.[13] Sir, I am your faythfull servant

Oliver Cromwell

July 30th 1643.

Appendix to 1643 07 30:
The identity of the addressee of Cromwell's Gainsborough letter of 30 July 1643

Dawson Turner was unable to make out the surname heavily scored out on the manuscript. Carlyle in a later edition of his *Letters and Speeches* (reinforced by

---

[10] Edward Whalley was not only the major in Cromwell's regiment but his first cousin. See also the *Online Directory of Parliamentarian Army Officers*.

[11] Edward Ayscough (bap. 1618, d. 1668) was a captain in Lord Willoughby's regiment of horse, having previously served in Essex's army. See the *Online Directory of Parliamentarian Army Officers*; A. R. Maddison, ed., *Lincolnshire Pedigrees*, 4 vols., Harleian Society 50, 51, 52, 55 (1902–6), 1:66.

[12] For Colonel Sir John Palgrave, a Norfolk man who raised a regiment in his own county and served as governor of Wisbech and then served with Fairfax at the siege of Hull, see the *Online Directory of Parliamentarian Army Officers*.

[13] Frances Lady Hobart (d. 1664), daughter of John Egerton, first earl of Bridgwater, whom Sir John had married as his second wife in 1622. *HoP Commons, 1604–1628* describes her as a 'pious woman of strong puritan convictions … [who] reformed his character, broke his habit of swearing, and managed his affairs, reducing his debts by £6,000'.

30 JULY 1643

Sophia Lomas in her 1904 rescension of Carlyle),[14] in adding this letter in modernised spelling expressed confidence that the recipient was Sir John Wray.[15] Abbott[16] and others accept this uncritically. That cannot be the correct identification. We are confident, a confidence confirmed by seeing the original letter, that we do not have permission to transcribe, that the addressee is in fact Sir John Hobart of Blickling, Norfolk.

Sir John Wray of Glentworth, Lincolnshire was MP and Commissioner for Lincolnshire, and his house was, Carlyle opined, within 'sight and sound of these transactions' who 'for many reasons', may 'fitly hear a word' of the battle and its aftermath 'while we rest from our march'. He took as 'your noble kinsman' the earl of Manchester (Wray's mother was a Montagu of Boughton, a remote relative of the Montagu earls of Manchester).[17]

The much more likely identity of the addressee rests on the words in bold in this passage:

> it's your owne businesse, a reasonable strength, now raised speedilie, may doe that which much more will not doe after some time, undoubtedly, if they succeed **heere,** you will see them in **the bowells of your Association.** For the tyme, you will have itt from **your noble kindsman, and Colonell Palgrave**

The letter is clearly addressed to somebody living within the bounds of the Eastern Association (which did not include Lincolnshire [which at that time was in no Association at all]) and it suggests that there was a threat of an invasion of 'your Association' by Newcastle's royalist army (which *was* in Lincolnshire). 'Heere' in the letter means Lincolnshire, and whoever the Sir John is, he has to be somebody within the Eastern Association, which at that point was composed of Norfolk, Suffolk, Cambridgeshire, Hertfordshire, Essex and Huntingdonshire. So the recipient cannot be Sir John Wray.

In fact, for two reasons it is surely Sir John Hobart. Firstly, the recipient is almost certainly a Norfolk man since Cromwell states that the recipient can expect also to receive a letter about the military situation from Sir John Palgrave and from 'a noble kindsman' and they can be identified as Norfolk gentlemen who also happen to be commanding infantry regiments from that county and in

---

[14] Carlyle-Lomas, III:233.

[15] Sir John Wray, second baronet (bap. 1586, d. 1655), politician. See *ODNB*.

[16] Abbott, *Writings and Speeches*, I:242.

[17] Carlyle-Lomas, 3:233. Abbott, *Writings and Speeches*, 1:242, follows Carlyle, who also (incorrectly on two scores) identified Manchester as sergeant major of the Eastern Association.

South Lincolnshire. Sir Miles Hobart and Sir John Palgrave had been serving on the fenland boundaries of the Eastern Association and beyond in the summer of 1643. Palgrave had been stationed at Wisbech, and in July had defended Peterborough and seems to have been present at the taking of Burghley House mentioned in **1643 07 29**. Meanwhile Hobart had captured Crowland on 28 April.[18] So these were Norfolk officers guarding, or likely to find themselves guarding again, the northern boundary of the Association

If the recipient is a Norfolk baronet, then it has to be Sir John Hobart. He is the only possible 'Sir John, baronet' in Norfolk at this time. By the summer of 1643 there were only two baronets called Sir John who were active parliamentarians in Norfolk, of whom one was Sir John Palgrave, the other Sir John Hobart. Hobart was not an MP at this point, but, as has been noted on his appointment in the parliamentary ordinance establishing the Association Committee on 13 August 1643, Hobart was 'a respected and influential figure...whose name had been in the forefront of all the county committees from their inception'.[19] And the recipient was a knight and baronet: Sir John Hobart was knighted at the age of eighteen in 1611, and he acceded to his father's baronetcy when the latter died in 1625. Reinforcing this, Sir Miles Hobart is a much closer 'noble kinsman' to Sir John Hobart than the earl of Manchester is to Sir John Wray, for Sir Miles Hobart of Plumstead, Norfolk, was Palgrave's fellow infantry colonel in the region while Manchester spent the whole of July 1643 in the House of Lords where he was Speaker.[20] Sir John Hobart's father was the second son of Thomas Hobart of Plumstead (d. 1560). Miles is the great-grandson of the same Thomas through the latter's eldest son Miles, and his father would be Sir Thomas Hobart of Plumstead, who was knighted in 1603.[21] John and Miles were second cousins.[22] This is a letter addressed to Sir John Hobart.

---

[18] Gaunt, *Cromwellian Gazetteer*, p. 106.
[19] R. W. Ketton-Cremer, *Norfolk*, p. 288. The two baronets who head the list for Norfolk in the Ordinance establishing the expanded Association are Hobart and Palgrave; see An Ordinance for naming a Committee for the Associated Counties, of Norfolke, Suffolke, Essex, Cambridge, Hertford, and Huntingdon (A&O 1:242–5). For letters from Cromwell and the other Cambridgeshire committeemen to the Norfolk Deputy Lieutenants, of whom Hobart was one, see **1643 01 26[?]** and **1643 01 27**.
[20] *JHL*, 6:152–3 where Manchester is named as presiding as Speaker on 28 and 29 July.
[21] W. A. Shaw, *The Knights of England*, 2 vols. (1906), II:109, 163.
[22] *The visitacon of Norffolk: made and taken by William Harvey, Clarencieux king of arms, anno 1563, enlarged with another visitacion made by Clarenceux Cooke, with many other descents; and also the visitation made by John Raven, Richmond, anno 1613.* (Edited by Walter Rye, Harleian Society, 32, 1891), pp. 165–6.

31 JULY 1643A

1643 07 31a

Letter from Oliver Cromwell to Sir Edmund Bacon, Sir William Spring, Sir Thomas Barnardiston and Maurice Barrowe, esq.

Date: 31 July 1643

Sources: [A] Maggs Brothers Catalogue, no. 365 (Spring 1918): *Autographs Letters, Signed Documents and Manuscripts, etc.* Plate V, facing p. 65. [B] *Letters selected from the collection of autographs in the possession of William Tite, Esq., M.P., V.P.S.A.*, Camden Miscellany, Volume the Fifth, Camden Society, o.s. 87 (1864), pp. 8–12 (part holograph, part later transcription)

The autograph version of this letter was sold at auction in 1918 and the auctioneers included photographs of the first page and of the top part of the final page (which contained the autograph) in their catalogue. But they did not offer photographs of the middle two pages. Two independent scholars transcribed the whole letter in the mid-nineteenth century. Comparing their transcriptions with the original opening and closing of the letter reveals that they were fairly reliable in copying the original spelling but made no attempt to reproduce the original punctuation. One of the two is slightly more interventionist but he is also slightly more accurate, and so it this version in a Camden Society volume listed above, and not the one by Dawson Turner,[1] which is relied on here for the transcription of pages 2 and 3 and for the postscript.

This letter is one of two written on 31 July which are very similar to one another and it is not clear which is written first. They are also very similar to the letters describing the battle of Gainsborough written on the two previous days (above **1643 07 29** and **1643 07 30**). The letters written on 31 July were addressed respectively to the deputy lieutenants of Suffolk and to the Eastern Association Committee in Cambridge and they give a bit more detail about the horrid shock of encountering the whole of the earl of Newcastle's army as Cromwell chased the troops he had defeated at the battle, but otherwise are substantially the same. They seem to have been written early in the day, since they make no reference to Lord Willoughby's enforced surrender that afternoon of the town of Gainsborough to the royalists (see the introduction to **1643 07 29**).

Gentlemen, noe man desires more to præsent you with incoragment then my selfe, be- cause of the forwardnesse I finde in you (to your honor bee it spoken) to promote this

---

[1] 'Letter from Sir Philip Stapleton to Oliver Cromwell, and four Letters from Oliver Cromwell himself', Dawson Turner, ed., *Norfolk Archaeology*, 2 (1849), pp. 51–4.

THE LETTERS, WRITINGS, AND SPEECHES OF OLIVER CROMWELL

great cause, and truly God followes you with incoragments, whoe is the God of blessinges, and I beseech you lett him not loose his blessings upon us, they come in Season and with all the advantages of hartninge, As if God should say up and bee doeinge, and I will helpe you, and stand by you, there is nothinge to bee feared, but our owne sinn, and sloath.

It hath pleased the Lord, to give your servant, and Souldiers, a notable vic= torie now att Gainsbrowe. I marched after the takinge of Burlye house[2] upon wedensday to Grantham[3], where mett mee about 300. Horse and Dragoones [—] \of/ Notingham,[4] with theise, by agreement with the Linconers wee mett att North Scarle which is about tenn[5] miles from Gainsbrowe upon Thursday in the eveninge, where wee tarried untill two of the clocke in the morninge, and then with our whole body advanced towards Gainsbrowe, about a mile and halfe from the towne wee mett a forlorne hope of the enimie of neere 100. horse, our Dragoones labored to beate them backe, but not alightinge off their horses, the enimie charged them, and beate \some 4. or five of/ them off their horses, our horse charged them, and made them retyer unto their ~~toward~~ \maine/ body, wee advanced, and came to the bottom of a steepe hill, upon which the enimie stood, // [6]

Wee could not well gett up but by some tracts, which our men assayinge to doe, a body of the enimie indeavored to hinder, wherein wee prævailed, and gott the top of the hill. This was donn by the Linconers, whoe had the vantgaurd. When wee all recovered the top of the hill, wee saw a great body of the enimies horse facinge of us att about muskitt shott or lesse distance, and a good reserve of a full regiment of horse behinde itt. Wee indeavored to putt our men into as good order as wee could, the enimie in the meane tyme advancinge towards us to take us att disadvantage, but in such order as wee were wee charged their great body. I havinge the right winge, wee came up horse to horse, where we disputed itt

[2] i.e. Burghley House outside Stamford, home of the third earl of Exeter (see **1643 07 30**, note 4).

[3] This must have been Wednesday 22 July.

[4] These are the troops led by Sir John Meldrum—see **1643 07 29**.

[5] North Scarle is on the Lincolnshire/Northamptonshire border, 8.5 miles south-west of Lincoln and 8.5 miles north of Newark on the Great North Road. Gainsborough is not ten but 16 miles north of North Scarle.

[6] Here this edition switches from source [A] to source [B]—from the photograph in the Maggs catalogue to the nineteenth-century transcript in the *Camden Miscellany*.

with our swords and pistolls a pretty tyme, all keepinge close order, soe that one could not breake the other. Att last they a little shrinkinge, our men perceavinge itt pressed in upon them, and immediately routed this whole body, some flyinge on one side, others on the other, of the enimies reserve, and our men persuinge them had chase and execution about 5. or 6. miles. I perceavinge this body, which was the reserve, standinge still unbroken, kept backe my maior Whaley[7] from the chase, and with my owne troupe and one other of my regiment, in all beinge 3. troupes, wee gott into a body. In this reserve stood Generall Cavendish,[8] whoe one while faced mee, another while faced 4. of the Lincolne troupes, which were all of ours that stood upon the place, the rest beinge ingaged in the chase. Att last the Generall charged the Linconers, and routed them. I immediately fell on his reere with my three troupes, which did soe astonish him that he gave over the chase, and would fayne have delivered himselfe from mee, but I pressing onn forced them downe a hill, havinge good execution of them, and belowe the hill drove the generall with some of his souldiers into a quagmier, where my Capt. Leiuetennant[9] slew him with a thrust under his short ribbs. [p. 10] The rest of the body was wholly routed, not one man stayinge upon the place. Wee then, after this defeat, which was soe totall, releived the towne[10] with such powder and provisions as wee brought; which donn, wee had notice that there were 6. troupes of horse and 300. foote on the other side of the towne, about a mile off us. Wee desired some foote of my Lord Willoghby,[11] about 400, and with our horse and theise foote marched towards them. When wee came towards the place where their horse stood, wee beate backe with my troupes about 2. or 3. troupes of the enimie, whoe retyred into a smale village att the bottom of the hill. When wee recovered the hill, wee sawe in the bottom, about a quarter of a mile from us, a regiment of foote, after that another, after that Newcastles[12] owne regiment, consistinge in all of about 50. foote colours, and a great body of horse, which indeed was Newcastles armie, which cominge soe unexpectedlye putt us to new

[7] Edward Whalley. He was not only major in Cromwell's regiment but his first cousin. See also the *Online Directory of Parliamentarian Army Officers*.

[8] Charles Cavendish, nephew of the earl of Newcastle, was destined to die at the end of the battle.

[9] Identified in **1643 07 30** as James Berry, for whom see the *Online Directory of Parliamentarian Army Officers*.

[10] i.e. Gainsborough.

[11] Francis Willoughby, fifth Baron Willoughby of Parham (bap. 1614, d. 1666), colonial governor. See *ODNB*.

[12] William Cavendish, first earl, later duke, of Newcastle upon Tyne.

THE LETTERS, WRITINGS, AND SPEECHES OF OLIVER CROMWELL

consultations. My Lord Willoghby and I, beinge in the towne, agreed to call off our foote. I went to bringe them off; but before I returned diverse of the foote were ingaged, the enimie advancinge with his whole body. Our foote retraited in some disorder, and with some losse gott the towne, where now they are. Our horse alsoe came off with some trouble, beinge wearied with the longe fight, and their horses tyred; yett faced the enimies fresh horse, and by severall removes got off without the losse of one man, the enimie followinge in the reere with a great body. The honor of this retrait is due to God, as alsoe all the rest. Maior Whaley did in this carry himselfe with all gallantrie becominge a gentleman and a Christian. Thus have you this true relation, as short as I could. What you are to doe upon it is next to bee considered. If I could speake words to peirce your harts, with the sence of our and your condition, I would. If you will raise 2000. foote att the present, to encounter this armie of Newcastles, to raise the seige, and to inable us to fight him, wee doubt not by the grace of God but that wee shalbe able to relieve[13] //

the towne,

and beate the enimie onn the other side Trent,
whereas if Somwhat bee not donn in this, you will see Newcastle
Armie march up into your \bowells, / beinge now as it is on this side Trent.
I know it wilbe difficult, to raise thus many in soe short tyme, but let
mee assuer you its necessarie, and therfore to bee donn, att least doe
what you may, with all possible expedition, I would I had
the happinesse to speake with one of you, truly I cannott come
over, but must attend my charge, our enimie is vigilant,
The Lord direct you what to doe, Gentlemen I am
your faythfull servant
Oliver Cromwell.
July 31
1643
Huntington
Give this gentleman credence. Hee is worthy to bee trusted. Hee knowes the urgency of our affaires better then my selfe. If hee give you intelligence in point of tyme of hast to bee made, beleive him. Hee will advise for your good.[14]

---

[13] At this point this edition switches back from source [B] to source [A], from the nineteenth-century transcript for the Camden Society to the photograph of the original in the Maggs catalogue.

[14] This postscript only survives in the nineteenth-century transcripts.

To my noble friend's Sir Edmon Bacon, kt. & barronet,[15] Sir Will'm Springe,[16] knights and barronetts, Sir Thomas Bernardiston, kgt.,[17] Maurice Barrowe esq,[18] present. theise.[19]

———— ∞∞ ————

1643 07 31b
Letter from Oliver Cromwell to the committee at Cambridge

Date: 31 July 1643

Sources: [A] *The Copy of a letter written by Colonel Cromwel, to the committee at Cambridge. Dated on Monday last being the 31 of July. Concerning the raising of the siege at Gainsborough* (Printed for *Edward Blackmore*, at the Angell in *Pauls* Church-Yard. *August* the 3. 1643). Wing / C7051; Thomason / E.63[12] (contemporary print). [B] [John Vicars], *Gods arke overtopping the worlds waves, or The third part of the Parliamentary chronicle.* London: Printed by M. Simons, and J. Macock, 1646 [i.e. 1645]. Wing / V309; Thomason / E.312[3] (contemporary print)

This letter exists in two forms: as a short six-page pamphlet published on 3 August 1643 and as incorporated in a history of the war put together by John Vicars and published in late 1645 (George Thomason annotated his copy as being received on 17 December 1645). There are many differences of spelling[1] and punctuation and a few small but significant changes in the later version. The differences of spelling in particular do not suggest that Vicars was using the 1643 printing, but the earlier one seems the safer one to use as the proof text, with any changes that could affect the meaning from the Vicars' text noted below.

---

[15] Presumably Sir Edmund Bacon of Redgrave (1569–1649), second baronet. Second but eldest surviving son of Sir Nicholas Bacon (*c.*1543–1624). See https://landedfamilies.blogspot.com/2017/09/306-bacon-of-redgrave-hall-gorhambury_72.html.

[16] See **1643 01 27**, **1643 08 29** and **1645 06 06**. The main source is the life of Spring in *HoP Commons, 1640–1660*.

[17] Sir Thomas Barnardiston, first baronet (*c.*1618–69), politician. See *ODNB*.

[18] See **1643 01 27**, **1643 08 29** and **1645 06 06**. The main source is the life of Barrowe in *HoP Commons, 1640–1660*.

[19] Tite (and Dawson Turner) place this at the head of their transcriptions. But it is not on the Maggs catalogue photograph and so presumably in the original is on the verso, written after the document was folded and sealed.

---

[1] e.g. [A] Gainsborow, Burley house, Gratham, North-Scarle where [B] has Gainesborough, Burleigh-House, Grantham, North-Scarl.

THE LETTERS, WRITINGS, AND SPEECHES OF OLIVER CROMWELL

There are striking similarities between this version and **1643 07 31a** and both 31 July letters allow a greater reflectiveness about the whole of the battle and its aftermath, but it is written in apparent ignorance that Lord Willoughby had surrendered Gainsborough on the day of this letter.

The body of the text is printed in black-letter. The text reverts to normal type at Cromwell's signing off and the address.

The letter is entered in normal type; where words within the printed letter are rendered as normal type, they appear here in italics.

[p. 1]

The Coppy of a Letter written by Colonel Cromwel, to the Committee at Cambridge,[2] the 31 of July, 1643.

GENTLEMEN,

It[3] hath pleased the Lord, to give your Servant and Souldiers a notable Victory now at *Gainsborow*; I marched after the taking of *Burley* house upon Wednesday to *Gratham*, where I met about *300*. Horse[4] and Dragoneers of *Nottingham*, with these by agreement with the Lincolneers, we met at *North- Scarle*, which is about ten miles from *Gainsborow* upon Thursday in the evening, where we tarried untill two of the clocke in the morning, and then with our whole body, advanced towards *Gainsborow*, about a mile and a halfe from the Towne. We met a forlorne hope[5] of the Enemy, of neere a *100*. Horse, out Dragoneers laboured to beat them back, but [p. 2] not a lighting[6] of their Horses, the Enemy charged them, and beat some foure or five of them of their off their Horse, our Horse charged them,[7] and made them retire unto their maine body: Wee advanced, and came to the bottome of a steepe hill, upon which the Enemey stood, we could not well get up but by some tracts, which our men assaying to doe, the body of the Enemy endeavoured to hinder, wherein we prevailed, and got the top of the hill, this was

---

[2] Presumably the Committee of the Eastern Association rather than the county committee of Cambridge.

[3] From here on the letter is almost entirely printed in black-letter until the end of the body of the text.

[4] The text is very hard to read here and it looks more like 500 than 300, but [B] has 300 and the figure is more consistent with **1643 07 31a**.

[5] = advance party.

[6] [B] clarifies here with 'not alighting'.

[7] [B] is much clearer here: 'beat some four or five of them off their horse; then our horse came up and charged them'.

31 JULY 1643B

done by the Lincolneers, who had the Vanguard when we all recovered the top of the hill, we saw a great body of the Enemies horse, facing of us at about a Muskets shot or lesse distance, and a good reserve of a full Regiment of Horse behind it,[8] we endeavoured to put our men into as good order as we could, the Enemy in the meane time advanced towards us, to take us at dis-advantage, but in such order as we were, we charged their great body. I having the right wing, we came up Horse to Horse, [p. 3] where we disputed it with our Swords and Pistols a pretty time, all keeping close order, so that one could not breake the other: at last they a little shrinking our men, perceiving it, pressed in upon them, and immediately routed this whole body,[9] some flying on one side, others on the other of the Enemies reserve, and our men persuing them, had chase and execution about five or six miles. I perceiving this body which was the reserve, standing still unbroken, kepte backe my Major *Whaley*[10] from the chace,[11] and with mine owne Troope and the other of my Regiment, in all being three Troopes, we got into a body, in this reserve stood Generall *Cavendish*,[12] who one while faced me, another while faced foure of the *Lincolne* Troopes, which was all of ours stood upon the place, the rest being ingaged in the chace, at last the Generall charged the Lincolneers and routed them, I immediately fell on his reare with my three Troopes, which did so astonish him [p. 4] that he gave over the chace, and would faine have delivered himselfe from me, but I pressing on, forced them done a a hill, having good execution of them, and below the hill drove the General with some of his Souldiers into a Quagmire, where my Captaine Lieutenant[13] slew him, with a thrust under his short ribs, the rest of the body was wholly routed, not one man staying upon the place. Wee after the defeate which was so totall releived the Towne, with such powder and provision as we brought, which done we had notice that there were 6. Troops of Horse and 300 foote on the other side of the Towne, about a mile of us, we desired some foote of my Lord *Willoughbyes*,[14] about 400. And with our Horse and their Foote marched

---

[8] i.e. Charles Cavendish's regiment, for which see below.

[9] [B] is clearer here, not least in the spelling: 'at last, they a little shrinking, and our men perceiving it, and pressing in upon them, immediately we routed this whole bodie'.

[10] Edward Whalley was not only major in Cromwell's regiment but his first cousin. See also the *Online Directory of Parliamentarian Army Officers*.

[11] [B] surely more accurately has not 'chace' but 'charge'   [12] Charles Cavendish.

[13] Identified in **1643 07 30** as James Berry, for whom see the *Online Directory of Parliamentarian Army Officers*.

[14] Francis Willoughby, fifth Baron Willoughby of Parham (bap. 1614, d. 1666), colonial governor. See *ODNB*.

THE LETTERS, WRITINGS, AND SPEECHES OF OLIVER CROMWELL

towards them, when we came towards the place where their Horse stood, wee beat back with my Tropes about 2 or 3 Troops of the Enemies, who retired into a small village, at the bottome of [p. 5] the hill, when wee recovered the hill, we saw in the bottome about a quarter of a mile from us, a Regiment of Foote, after that another,[15] after that *NewCastles*[16] owne Regiment, consisting in all, of about fifty Foote Colours, and a great body of Horse which indeed was, *NewCastles* army: which coming so unexpectedly, put us to new consultations: My Lord *Willoughby* and I being in the Towne, agreed to call of our Foote, I went to bring them off, but before I returned, divers of the Foote were engaged, the Enemy advancing with his whole body, our Foote retreated in some disorder, and with some losse[17] got the Towne,[18] where now they are, our Horse also came off, with some trouble being wearied with the long fight[19] and their Horses tired yet faced the Enemies fresh Horse and by severall removes got off, without the losse of one man, the Enemy following the Reare with a great body, the honour of this retreat is due to God, [p. 6] as also all the rest, Major *Whalley*, did in this carry himselfe withall gallantly becomming a Gentleman and a Christian. Thus have you this true Relation as short as I could, what you are to do upon it is n w[20] to be considered, the Lord direct you what to doe. Gentlemen I am Your faithfull servant

Oliver Cromwell.

Huntington.

July, 31. 1643.

[p. 6]

A List of those that were slaine and taken at the raysing of the Seidge at Gainsborow, on Friday last, by Colonell Cromwell.

---

[15] [B] has 'after that another, and then also Newcastles own regiment'.

[16] William Cavendish, first earl, later duke, of Newcastle upon Tyne (bap. 1593, d. 1676), writer, patron and royalist army officer. See *ODNB*.

[17] [B] adds 'yet' here.   [18] i.e. Gainsborough.

[19] [B] has 'their former long fight'.

[20] This is the best reading of a smudge in the manuscript. The 'n' is clear, the rest isn't. [B] has 'next' which could be what is lost here.

1 AUGUST 1643

General King slaine, as is supposed.[21] General Cavendish certainly slaine.[22] Colon Beton, slaine.[23] A Lieutenant Colonel, slaine:[24] A Serjeant Major, slaine,[25] Captaine Hussey, slaine.[26] 100 Dead upon the place. 150. Prisoners taken. A total defeate not ten men being seene stand in a body. 200. slaine in the persute of them.

FINIS.

1643 08 01

Letter from Oliver Cromwell to the deputy lieutenants of Essex

Date: 1 August 1643
Source: BL, Egerton MS 2643 (Barrington papers, 1629–43), fos 11r–12v (autograph)

Three days after his victory at Gainsborough, Cromwell was back in Huntingdon. This letter bears his signature but does not appear to be in his own hand. He is clearing up some housekeeping matters, but why he was asking the deputy lieutenants of Essex rather than the Association Committee at Cambridge for money to repay a loan is not clear. The reference to 'your counties' suggests he may have been asking each of the counties and not just Essex, but a puzzle remains.

[fo. 12v]

For My Lovinge frinds the Deputy Leuitenants of the Countye of Essex

[fo. 11r]

Gentlemen

---

[21] [B] omits this entry, presumably because Lt Gen James King, who commanded Newcastle's infantry, was not killed, a fact known to Vicars by 1645. For King, see Newman, *Royalist Officers*, no. 829, and James King, Lord Eythin (1589–1652), royalist army officer, in *ODNB*,

[22] For Cavendish, see above, n. 12.

[23] For Sigismund Beaton see Newman, *Royalist Officers*, no. 94.   [24] Not identified.

[25] Not identified.   [26] Not identified.

151

The time I was absent from Notingham,[1] this[2] bearer[3] was forced to borrow of the Maior of Notingham[4] 100 l for the payment of the three Companies belonginge to your Counties, besides shoues stockings shirts and Billett money which I promised should be repaied, I Receivinge no money out of your Countyes wherewithall to doe itt, I can but Re= fer it to your Considerations, for I thinke it is not expected I should pay your Soulders out of my owne purse; This is the Sume of his desire whoe Rests Your truly Lovinge frind
Oliver Cromwell

Huntington
August 1. 1643

I desire yow would Recruite your two Companies, and send them up with as much hast as may be that they may helpe on in the publique Service.

1643 08 02
Letter from Oliver Cromwell to [? the mayor of Norwich]

Date: 2 August 1643
Source: R. Bell, ed., *Memorials of the Civil War... forming the concluding volumes of the Fairfax correspondence*, 2 vols. (1849), 1:56–7 (later transcription)

The whereabouts of this letter is unknown. This is the only complete version, published in 1849. Robert Bell modernised spelling and punctuation but is generally a careful editor. Two years later, in 1851, the letter was put on sale and there is a transcription with what purports to be original spelling in the sale catalogue. But this contains less than half of the letter. There is not a single instance where that part-transcription affects the meaning of Bell's modernised reading, except that while Bell dates the letter as '2nd August, 1643, from Huntingdon', the sales catalogue gives it as '[Huntingdon], August 2, 1643', implying that the place of writing is not on the document but was assumed by Bell.[1]

---

[1] i.e., mid-May to early June, or 3–16 July 1643.
[2] The original word was 'the' and it was changed to 'this' by overwriting the 'e'.
[3] This bearer is unidentified and unknown.   [4] William Nix, mayor 1643–5.

---

[1] A partial transcript in a sales catalogue for 1851 is identical and may therefore be cribbed from Bell's version. See the *Catalogue of highly interesting and valuable autograph letters and historical manuscripts, being the well-known collection of Monsr. A. Donnadieu... which will be sold by auction, by Messrs. Puttick and Simpson... on Tuesday, July 29th, 1851, and 4 following days*, p. 43.

2 AUGUST 1643

There is nothing in either transcription to indicate the addressee of the letter, but Sophia Lomas very plausibly argued that it must have been one or more persons in authority in Norwich, and very possibly the mayor. Bell's own heading is positively unhelpful: 'COLONEL CROMWELL'S LETTER TO THE BACHELORS AND MAIDS, 2ND AUGUST, 1643'. Certainly the context is the forming of Cromwell's 'Ironside' regiment which came together in the first half of August and there is no doubt that the letter refers to the 'Maidens' troop' raised in Norwich at exactly this time, and commanded by Captain Robert Swallow.[2]

[p. 56]

Sir,

I understand by these gentlemen the good affections of your young men and maids, for which God is to be [p. 57] praised. I approve of the business, only I desire to advise you that your foot company may be turned into a troop of horse, which, indeed, will (by God's blessing) far more advantage the cause than two or three companies of foot, especially if your men be honest, godly men, which by all means I desire. I thank God for stirring up the youth to cast in their mite, which I desire may be employed to the best advantage; therefore my advice is, that you would employ your twelve-score pounds to buy pistols and saddles, and I will provide four-score horses; for 400*l.* more will not raise a troop of horse. As for the muskets that are bought, I think the country will take them of you. Pray raise honest, godly men, and I will have them of my regiment. As for your officers, I leave it as God shall or hath directed to choose, and rest, Your loving friend,

Oliver Cromwell.

August 2nd., 1643.

---

[2] Alfred Kingston, *East Anglia and the Great Civil War* (1902), pp. 129–30; Carlyle-Lomas 1:145 n. 2; and more generally C. H. Firth, 'The Raising of the Ironsides', *TRHS* n.s., 13 (1899), pp. 17–73.

THE LETTERS, WRITINGS, AND SPEECHES OF OLIVER CROMWELL

1643 08 04

Letter from Oliver Cromwell and others to the deputy lieutenants of Essex

Date: 4 August 1643
Source: BL, Egerton MS 2643 (Barrington papers, 1629–43), fos 15r–16v (part holograph)

This is an unusual letter. Three separate men have written passages: Oliver Cromwell, William Harlakenden and Miles Corbett in a single folio letter. However, on the verso there are three addresses, to the deputy lieutenants (in Cromwell's hand), to Tymothy Mydelton and the other deputy lieutenants at Stansted Mountfitchet (probably not in Cromwell's hand); to Sir Thomas Barrington in London; and a covering note by Jo: Kendall which plausibly glosses the address to Barrington.

[fo. 16v]
From Mr Cromwell & Mr Harlackenden 4° Augustij[1] To my honored freinds the Deputie Leiuetennts of the County of Essex present theise[2]

To Tymothy Midleton esqr[3]
& the other Deputy
Leuietennts

at Stanceted Munfitchett in
Essex next Elsnam.[4]

To Sir Tho: Barrington[5] at the
upper end of Queenes
Streete neare Lincolns
Inne Fields.[6]

[fo. 16v]
Sir,

---

[1] This endorsement is in an unrecognised seventeenth-century hand.
[2] This endorsement is in Cromwell's hand.   [3] The current sheriff of Essex.
[4] This endorsement is in an unrecognised seventeenth-century hand. Stansted Mountfitchet and Elsenham are in the north-west corner of Essex.
[5] Sir Thomas Barrington, second baronet (*c.*1585–1644). See ODNB. He was leader of the Essex puritan gentry before and during the civil wars.
[6] This final endorsement is in probably in the hand of Jo: Kendall.

154

4 AUGUST 1643

this letter came this Morneing from Sir Richard Everard[7] & my Mr being att London & like to meet yow to Morrow at Rumford,[8] I am bold to send it your worship. because it requires a Speedy answere.

Jo: Kendall[9]

[fo. 15r]

Gentlemen, I beinge att Cambridge, and meetinge there
with some monies which came from you, some doubt
was made whether that monie was intended to
bee your proportion of the 3000li. assigned
mee by the house of Commons towards the
payment of my Troopes, If it bee in per=
suance of their Order I beseech you send
word, Your letters make itt Cleere to mee
but yett because doubt is made therof,
none beinge able to resolve it better then
~~yourselues~~ \You/, I should be very glad to have
it from your selves, and rest
Your humble servant
Oliver Cromwell[10]

August the 4[th.]
1643.

[fo. 15r]

Jentlemen, I being in want of monyes, this two hundred pounds being almost spent that I received of Sir Thomas Barrington our fower Companyes of Essex forces being now to martch a way to Huntington & soe to Stamford, I beseech you speedely send me monyes to Cambridge least our forces returne for want of monyes whoe alread[y] have begunn to mutiny, & many of them are at [this?] instant running whome most of Captaine Geo[...] Company if this be suffered the kingdome will so[on?] be under your humble servant in all duty & service to be Commanded William Harlakenden[11]

---

[7] Sir Richard Everard of Much Waltham, Essex, Brother-in-law of Sir Thomas Barrington.

[8] Romford, Essex. [9] Presumably a household officer of Sir Thomas Barrington.

[10] This section of the letter is in Cromwell's own hand and signature.

[11] William Harlakenden, younger son in an important Essex puritan family in Earls Colne and at this time paymaster of the Essex forces stationed at Cambridge. See Holmes, *Eastern Association*, pp. 128–9 and *passim*.

August the 4th 1643.

the great discontent of the souldiers is, because they haue but 8d. per day. almost all the board are gonn now to fetch them back againe.[12]

[fo. 15r]

Gentelmen

I am desird by this Com:tee to desire you to tak mor care thet the Companies heer may bee recruited & such as hav not apered or ar run awey may be sent to this plac So as the companies may be full by Your Servant

Miles Corbett[13]

1643 08 06a
Letter from Oliver Cromwell to the committee at Cambridge

Date: 6 August 1643

Source: Bodl., MS Tanner 62/1B, fo. 229r (no. 117) (contemporary copy)

This letter and an enclosure have been copied at the time and forwarded, it would seem, to William Lenthall, Speaker of the House of Commons, amongst whose papers these copies have survived from the 1640s to the present.[1] They lack endorsements or addresses.

There is no direct evidence that Cromwell's letter was directed to the Committee at Cambridge. It was first so surmised by Thomas Tanner (1674–1735), bishop of St Asaph and noted antiquary, and accepted by Carlyle, Lomas and Abbott. Since internal references rule out Norfolk, Suffolk and Essex and probably Huntingdonshire, we are in fact left with Cambridgeshire.

The letter demonstrates the sense of crisis that was causing Cromwell to pull together a new regiment of horse that came to be known as the Ironsides, and for which see **1643 08 02**. The first week of August saw all the gains made at the battle of Gainsborough lost as the earl of Newcastle moved the main body of his army south, forcing Lord Willoughby to abandon first Gainsborough (1 August) and then Lincoln. Abandoning all his artillery

---

[12] In Harlackenden's hand. A tear make some words impossible or difficult to make out.

[13] Miles Corbett (1594/5–1662). See *ODNB*. Corbett, from Sprowston in Norfolk, was an MP in the Long Parliament.

---

[1] These letters may be connected to another letter Willoughby sent to the earl of Essex, also on 5 August—see Bodl., MS Tanner 62/3 (art 119, fo. 232).

6 AUGUST 1643A

train, Willoughby pulled back to Boston, and it was from there, on 5 August, that he wrote a panicky note to Cromwell, and Cromwell in turn called on the Eastern Association for a major push to raise more men and more money.[2]

[fo. 229r]

[Willoughby to Cromwell]

Noble Sir

Since the busines at Gainsborough[3] the hearts of our men have beene so deaded, as we have lost most of them by running away, so as we were forced to leave Lincolne upon a suddaine, and if I had not done it, then I should have beene left alone in it so as now I am at Boston, where wee are Very poore in strength, so that without some speedy supply I feare wee shall not hold this long neither my Lord Generall I perceive hath Write to you, to draw all the forces togeather, I should be glad to see it, for if that will not be, theire can be noe good expected If you will endeavoure to stopp my Lord of Newcastle[4] you must presently draw them to him and fight him, for without wee be masters of the feild, we shall all be pulled out by the eares one after another, the foote if they will come on may march very securely to Boston[5] which to me will be very considerable to your assotiation for if they gett that Towne which is now very weake for defence for want of men, I beleive they will not be long out of Norfolke and Suffolke: I cann say no more but desire you to hasten and rest Francis Willowby[6]

Boston the 5th of
August: 1643

[Cromwell to Cambridge Committee]

Gent

You see by this inclosed how sadly your affaires stand, its noe longer disputing but out instantly all you cann, rayse all your bands send them to Huntington, get

---

[2] For this, see Holmes, *Eastern Association*, pp. 91–4.
[3] i.e. the victory in which Cromwell and Willoughby fought side-by-side, on 28 July.
[4] William Cavendish, earl and later first duke of Newcastle upon Tyne.
[5] Boston, Lincolnshire, an inland port in east-central Lincolnshire.
[6] Francis Willoughby, fifth Baron Willoughby of Parham (bap. 1614, d. 1666), colonial governor. See *ODNB*.

up what Volunteers you cann, hasten your horses send theise Letters to Suffolke Norfolke & Essex without delay, I beseech you spare not but be expeditious and industrious, allmost all our foote have quitted Stamford there is nothing to interrupte an enimy but our horse that is considerable you must acte lively, doe it without distraction neglect noe means, I am your faithfull servant
Oliver Cromwell
Huntington this
6th of August

1643 08 06b
Letter from Oliver Cromwell to the deputy lieutenants of Essex

Date: 6 August 1643
Source: BL, Egerton MS 2643 (Barrington papers, 1629–43), fos 15r–16v (holograph)

This holograph letter is very much of a piece with **1643 08 06a**. The promised enclosure no longer survives but could well have been a copy of the letter from Lord Willoughby of Parham enclosed with that letter.

[fo. 18v]
To the Deputye
Leiuetennants of
Essex theise
hast hast
post hast

[fo. 17r]
Gentlemen, you see by this inclosed the necessi
tye of goeinge out of our ould pace, you
sent indeed your part of the 2000. foote
but when they came they as soone
returned, is this the way to save
a Kingdom, where is ~~your~~ \the\ doctreine
of some of your Countye, concerninge

the trayned bands \and other forces/ not goeinge out
the Association, I wish your forces
may bee ready to meete with the
enimie, when Hee is in the Association,
hast what you cann, not your part
only of 2000. foote, but I hope 2000.
foote att least, \Ld/ Newcastle[1] will ad=
vance into your bowells, better joyne
when others will joyne, and cann joyne
with you, then stay till all bee lost hasten
to our helpe, the enemie in all probability
wilbe in our bowells else in tenn dayes.
his Armie is powerfull, see your men
come,[2] and some of your ~~Good~~ \Gentle/[3] men and ministers come along
with them, that soe they may bee delivered over to those
shall command them otherwise they will returne att pleasure.
If we have them att our Armie wee can keepe them.

I rest your faythfull servant.
Oliver Cromwell
Aug. 6° 11 of the clocke
1643.

---

[1] William Cavendish, earl and later first duke of Newcastle upon Tyne.
[2] From hereon the letter continues down the left-hand margin.
[3] 'Gentle' written over erased 'Good'. No attempt made to make one word of 'Gentlemen' rather than two.

THE LETTERS, WRITINGS, AND SPEECHES OF OLIVER CROMWELL

1643 08 08

Letter from Oliver Cromwell to the Cambridge Committee

Date: 8 August 1643

Source: R. Bell, ed., *Memorials of the Civil War… forming the concluding volumes of the Fairfax correspondence*, 2 vols. (1849), pp. 1.58–9 (later transcription)

This letter survives only in a nineteenth-century transcription, with spelling and punctuation modernised. A fragment is preserved with the original spelling in a sales catalogue published in 1851.[1]

[p. 58]

TO MY HONOURED FRIENDS THE COMMISSIONERS AT CAMBRIDGE, THESE PRESENT.

GENTLEMEN, Finding our foot much lessened at Stamford,[2] and having a great train and many carriages, I held it not safe to continue there, but presently after my return from you, I ordered the foot to quit that place and march into Holland,[3] which they did on Monday last. I was the rather induced so to do because of the letter I received from my Lord Willoughby,[4] a copy whereof I sent you. I am now at Peterborough, whither I came this afternoon. I was no sooner come but Lieutenant Colonel Wood[5] sent me word, from Spalding,[6] that the enemy was marching with twelve flying colours of horse and foot within a mile of Swinstead,[7] so that I hope it was a good providence of God that our foot were at Spalding; it much concerns your association and the kingdom that so strong a place as Holland is be not possessed by them; if you have any foot ready to march, send them away to us with all speed. I fear lest the enemy should press in upon

---

[1] See *The Catalogue of… valuable Autograph Letters and Historical Manuscripts, being the well-known collection of… A. Donnadieu. Compiled by Messrs. Puttick and Simpson* (London, 1851), p. 43 (available for reading online through Googlebooks).

[2] Stamford, a market town on the Great North Road in south-west Lincolnshire.

[3] An administrative district in south and south-east Lincolnshire.

[4] Francis Willoughby, fifth Baron Willoughby of Parham; and see **1643 08 06a**.

[5] Difficult to trace. We do have evidence of a [ ] Woods who was a lieutenant colonel in charge of a company in Sir Miles Hobart's regiment of foot in the Eastern Association Army by January 1644 and still there in summer 1644, though he seems to have left the regiment around that time, but he is otherwise not traceable. See the *Online Directory of Parliamentarian Army Officers*.

[6] Spalding: a market town in mid-Lincolnshire.

[7] Swinstead, a Lincolnshire village nine miles north of Stamford.

our foot; he being thus far advanced towards you, I hold it very fit that you should hasten your horse at Huntingdon and what you can speedily raise at Cambridge unto me. I dare not go into Holland with my horse, lest the enemy should advance with his whole body of horse this way into your association, but am ready endeavouring to get my Lord Gray's[8] and the Northamptonshire horse to me, that so, if we be able, we may fight the enemy, or retreat unto you with our whole strength. I beseech you hasten your leavers,[9] what you can, especially those of foot; quicken all our friends with new letters upon this occasion, which I believe you will find to be a true alarm; the parti- [p. 59] culars I hope to be able to inform you speedily of more punctually, having sent in all haste to Colonel Wood for that purpose. The money I brought with me is so poor a pittance when it comes to be distributed amongst all my troops that, considering their necessity, it will not half clothe them, they were so far behind; if we have not more money speedily they will be exceedingly discouraged. *I am sorry you put it to me to write thus often, it makes it seem a needless importunity in me; whereas, in truth, it is a constant neglect of those that should provide for us. Gentlemen, make them able to live and subsist that are willing to spend their blood for you.*[10] I say no more, but rest

Your faithful servant,
OLIVER CROMWELL.

August 8th, 1643.

---

[8] Thomas Grey, Baron Grey of Groby (1622–57), regicide. See *ODNB*.
[9] Presumably he means 'levies'.
[10] The sentence that runs between the asterisks is the one contained in *the Catalogue of... valuable Autograph Letters and Historical Manuscripts... Compiled by Messrs. Puttick and Simpson*, p. 43. That extract, which claims to reproduce the original spelling and punctuation, runs: 'I am sorry you put me to it to wright thus often, it makes it seems a needles importunity in me, whereas in truth it is a constant neglect of those that should provide for us. Gentlemen, make them able to live and subsist that are willing to spend their bloods for you.'

THE LETTERS, WRITINGS, AND SPEECHES OF OLIVER CROMWELL

1643 08 29a

Letter from Oliver Cromwell and eight members of the Cambridge Committee to the deputy lieutenants of Essex

Date: 29 August 1643
Source: BL, Egerton MS 2643 (Barrington papers, 1629–43), fos 26r–27v (autograph)

This is the first of two letters despatched from Cambridge on 29 August 1643 to the deputy lieutenants of Essex. This, the first, is from the Committee of the Association with Cromwell just one of nine signatories; the second is from Cromwell alone.

The letter is not in Cromwell's hand and he does not seem to be the first to sign. The version published by Abbott is seriously defective.[1]

———

[fo. 27v]
From the Comittee att
Cambridg to the
Deputy Leiuetents
of Essex. August
29°: 1643[2]

[fo. 27v]
To our honorable frends Sir Tho: Barrington,[3] & the rest off the Deputy Lieutenants off Essex.

[fo. 26r]
Gentlemen
Divers off your companyes ariving here at Cambridg, make demand to us off armes & as they informe us by your directions, which wee beleeve to be a mistake, knowing your wisdome & care in a business off so greate a consequence to be such, that you coulde not omitt a provision, without which all your other preparations in that kinde, wilbe vaine, & useless; wee beseech you therfore (to prevent all further inconveniencyes which in default theroff may arise to the service, now intended) to give some spedy, & certain order for the supply off this want, that so they may be fitt for action; & are

---

[1] Abbott, *Writings and Speeches*, 1:255. It relies on a poor calendar entry.

[2] This endorsement is in a different hand from the letter itself.

[3] Sir Thomas Barrington, second baronet (*c*.1585–1644), politician. See *ODNB*. Barrington was perhaps the leading figure other than the Earl of Warwick amongst the Essex parliamentarian leaders.

162

Your loving frends & associatts

W: Rowe[4]	Oliver Cromwell	O: Winche[5]	Tho: Martyn[6]
Tho: Duckett[7]	Henry Meautys[8]	Ral Freman[9]	
Edm: Harvey[10]	Willm Harlakenden[11]		

Cambridge 29th August,1643

1643 08 29b
Letter from Oliver Cromwell to the deputy lieutenants of Essex

Date: 29 August 1643
Source: BL, Egerton MS 2643 (Barrington papers, 1629–43), fos 25r–v (holograph)

This letter in Cromwell's own hand and bearing his signature was sent on the same day as a letter from him and from the Commissioners at Cambridge and was received by, amongst others, Sir Thomas Barrington,[1] who placed the original in his own letter folder. The earl of Manchester had just, earlier in August, been appointed instead of Lord Grey of Warke[2] as major general of the army of the Eastern Association, and whatever the difficulties of his relationship with Cromwell before and after this date (and Cromwell's with him), Cromwell clearly had no difficulty in invoking Manchester's new authority in a peremptory way. The letter mentions an attached order which no longer survives.

---

[4] Sir William Rowe of Higham Hall, Essex, a member of the Committee of the Eastern Association at this time. See Holmes, Eastern Association, pp. 101–4. See also J. A. Sharpe, '"William Holcroft his booke": Local Office-holding in Late Stuart Essex'. Essex Historical Documents no. 2, Essex Record Office Publication no. 90 (1980), p. 107.
[5] Not identified.
[6] Co-signatory with Cromwell of two previous letters, **1643 01 27** and **1643 03 27**.
[7] Not identified.
[8] Henry Meautys (MP for St Albans in 1621, for whom see History of Parliament: House of Commons 1603–29), was the brother of the government official who was Cromwell's fellow MP for Cambridge in 1640 (Barclay, Inventing Cromwell, pp. 119–27).
[9] Not identified.
[10] Edmund Harvey (c.1601–73), regicide. See ODNB. Harvey was receiver general of all moneys in Suffolk as well as a deputy lieutenant serving on the Cambridge Committee.
[11] Harlackenden was a Commissary General in Manchester's army, and a younger son in a prominent Essex family based in Earls Colne. See Holmes, Eastern Association, and passim but esp. pp. 128–9.

---

[1] See **1643 08 27a** fn. 3.
[2] William Grey, first Baron Grey of Warke (1593/4–1674), politician. See ODNB.

[fo. 25v]
To my Noble freinds
the Deputy Leiuetnts
of the Countye of
Essex present theise

[fo. 25r]
Gentlemen I thought it my dutye to send
unto you this Order from my Lord of Man=
chester,[3] you will see what it purports, And
I beseech you to cause all your horse,
and Dragoones, immediately to repaire to
mee to Huntington, this Order of his Lordps
beares date since any Hee sent you,
and therfore superseades them, Not doubtinge of
your favor heerein I take leave and rest

Your most humble serv[ant]
Oliver Cromwell
Aug. 29[th.]
1643

1643 08 30[?]

Letter from Oliver Cromwell to Sir William Spring and Maurice Barrowe

Date: late August 1643
Source: Franklin Delano Roosevelt Presidential Library, Hyde Park, NY, Historical Manuscripts Collection, no. 373 (holograph)

Cromwell's preference for 'a plaine russett coated captaine, that knowes what Hee fights for, and loves what Hee knowes, then that which you call a Gentleman and is nothinge else' makes this one of his most famous and widely quoted letters. Previous editions have

---

[3] Edward Montagu, second earl of Manchester (1602–71), politician and parliamentarian army officer. See ODNB.

30 AUGUST 1643[?]

relied on a very imperfect 1849 transcription.[1] Our version is based on Cromwell's holograph letter that also still contains his seal.

The date is not certain. Sophia Lomas argued that it must be between 27 August and 1 September but it is difficult to be more precise. William Harlackenden,[2] writing to Cromwell's cousin Sir Thomas Barrington[3] about Cromwell's movements, places him in Cambridge from 27 August and we know that he signed letters from Cambridge, including one jointly with the Cambridge committeemen, on 29 August. But he does *not* sign a letter from those same committeemen, updating the Essex deputy lieutenants about the Essex troop and dated 31 August and we know that not later than 4 September he was heading north and did not return to Cambridge until late October.[4]

The letter is to two or three prominent members of the Suffolk Committee, although one name has been erased so thoroughly as to be illegible. Cromwell had already written an earlier letter to Sir William Spring,[5] and Maurice Barrow[6] (**1643 07 31**), would write another a month later (**1643 09 28**), and would be co-signatory to another nearly two years later (**1645 06 04**). But 'Sir William' is written above a heavily crossed out (and unreadable) name that might have been a wrong name or someone Cromwell very purposefully wanted, on reflection, to omit.

The hand is calm and authoritative for the most part. But the content from the beginning is disjointed and agitated. And having reached the bottom of the page Cromwell writes the remainder of the letter (from 'that is soe indeed') at 90 degrees in the left margin and in a smaller hand with much narrower gaps between the lines, clearly to leave space for two postscripts. One of them runs from the top of the page to halfway down and in smaller writing still, and the second runs from midway to nearer the bottom, written

---

[1] 'Letter from Sir Philip Stapleton to Oliver Cromwell, and four Letters from Oliver Cromwell himself', Dawson Turner, ed., *Norfolk Archaeology*, 2 (1849), pp. 43–60: this letter is at pp. 59–60. The letter was auctioned, with many other of Dawson Turner's books and manuscripts, in 1859, and next surfaced in the possession of Austin Taylor (1858–1955). Taylor, a shipowner, was a militant Protestant in the sectarian politics of Edwardian Liverpool. See P. J. Waller, *Democracy and Sectarianism: A Political and Social History of Liverpool, 1868–1939* (Liverpool, 1981), esp. 127, 174, 178–80, 183–6, 188–91. 195–6, 201, 203, 210, 226–7, 243. In 1944 he presented it to Theodore Roosevelt for his part in turning the tide of war and it is now in his memorial library.

[2] For Harlackenden, see **1643 08 29b**.   [3] For Barrington, see **1643 08 29b**.

[4] Carlyle-Lomas, 1:154 n. 1; BL, Egerton MS 2647 fo. 229; Gaunt, *Cromwellian Gazetteer*, p. 224.

[5] Sir William Spring of Pakenham, first baronet (1613–17 December 1654) was head of a family that had made a fortune in the wool trade in late medieval Lavenham, a once-prosperous town in south Suffolk. Spring was the most active of all the Suffolk county gentry in the Suffolk war effort and in making Suffolk the most effective of all the associated counties. He became a recruiter MP for Bury St Edmunds in 1645. See Alan Everitt, *Suffolk and the Great Rebellion 1640–60*, Suffolk Record Society, 3 (1960), 16, 27, 40, 43, 52, 60, 67–9, 72–3, 79, 84. Cromwell wrote just to Spring and Barrow on this occasion and one other (**1643 09 28**) and he wrote to them and just two others on **1643 07 31**.

[6] Maurice Barrow of Barningham, sheriff of Suffolk 1644–5 and recruiter MP for Eye from 1645, was closely associated with Sir William (they lived on either side of the main road from Bury St Edmunds to Diss). See Everitt, *Suffolk and the Great Rebellion*, 39–40, 52, 59–60, 69, 79, 84.

around the signature, which is positioned right up to bottom right, and crammed into very little area and only just finishing in the last millimetre of space. The writing of this postscript, the passionate plea on behalf of Ralph Margery, becomes at least as agitated as the content. It was a plea he had to repeat in a later letter to Spring and Barrow a month later (**1643 09 28**).

Ralph Margery was a farmer from Walsham-le-Willows, Suffolk, his family sometimes called yeomen and sometimes gentlemen. Margery and his wife had been excommunicated in 1638 and were clearly outspoken opponents of Bishop Wren and Archbishop William Laud. He was quick to volunteer once the war started and had gained notoriety for exceeding orders in the arbitrary seizure of horses from suspected royalists. Both his religious enthusiasm and his freedom in implementing orders against delinquents made the county committee distrust him. In the event, he served as captain of the troop in Oliver Cromwell's regiment of horse in the Eastern Association Army, and through the absorption of the troop in Colonel Pye's regiment of horse in the New Model Army; Margery continued to serve as captain in that regiment (by then under Rich) until his death in 1653 or 1654.[7]

This is a letter in which Cromwell pits the claims of the godly above the claims of social rank, and the claims of a notorious religious radical and bishop-baiter who had conducted illegal searches of Catholic homes above a strict adherence to law. It was a letter that reverberated.

[verso]

To my noble freind's ⊢⊣ \Sir/
⊢⊣ \Willm Springe, knight
and Barronett and Maurice
Barrowe Esqr &c. present
theise[8]

Gentlemen, I have beene nowe two dayes att
Cambridge, in expectation to have the fruite of
your indeavors in Suffolke, towards the
publike Assistance, beleive itt you will here
of a storme in few dayes, you have noe
infantrie, att all considerable, ~~Sir~~ Hasten[9] your

---

[7] See Ralph Margery in the *Online Directory of Parliamentarian Army Officers*; Wanklyn, *Reconstructing*, 1:53, 63, 74, 83, 95, 108, 126 and 2:52, 68–9; R. and J. Lock, 'Captain Raphe Margery, a Suffolk Ironside', *Proceedings of the Suffolk Institute of Archaeology and History*, 36 (1987), pp. 207–18.

[8] For the persons mentioned in this address, see above in the introduction to this letter.

[9] The 'Sir' is not so much crossed out as overwritten with a bold capital 'H'.

30 AUGUST 1643[?]

horses, a few howers may undoe You, neg
lected. I beseech you bee carefull what
captaines of horse You choose, what
men bee mounted, a few honest men
are better then numbers, some tyme
they must have for exercise. If you choose
Godly honest men to bee captaines of
horse, honest men will followe them
and they will bee carefull to mount
such, the Kinge is exceedinge stronge
in the west, If you bee able to
foyle a force att the first cominge
of itt, you will have reputation, and \that/ th[ ]
is of great advantage in our affaires, God
hath given itt to our handfull, lett us
indeavor to keepe itt. I had rather have
a plaine russett coated captaine, that knowes
what Hee fights for, and loves what Hee
knowes, then that which you call a Gentleman
and is nothinge else, I honor a Gentleman[10]
that is soe indeed,[11] I understand mr Margery[12] hath honest men will follow him,
if soe
\bee pleased to/ make use of him, it
much concernes your good, to have conscientious men: I understand that there
is an Order,
for mee to have 3000 li,[13] out of the
Association E̶ Essex hath sent their partt or neere itt. I assuer you wee neede
exceedinglye. I

[10] The rest of the letter, from this point, is written at right angles to the main text, in the left-hand margin.

[11] The word 'indeed' is strictly redundant here, but if Cromwell wrote or intended 'in deed' (i.e. two separate words) then it would radicalise what he meant. He would be saying that he could only honour a gentleman who was 'in deed' like a plain russet-coated captain. In the holograph, there is a small gap been 'in' and 'deed' (bigger than in 'understand' two words later, but not enough to allow it to be transcribed as two words. Probably enough, but probably not quite enough.

[12] For Margery, see the discussion in the introduction to this letter.

[13] It is not clear what order this is. But what is clear is that Cromwell was unclear about it himself; but that by 11 September he was fully in possession of the facts (see **1643 09 11**).

hope to finde your

favor and respect, I protest ~~my body of~~ \if it were/[14] for my selfe I would not move you. This is

all from

Your faythfull servant
Oliver Cromwell

If you send such men as Essex hath
sent, it wilbe to little purpose, bee
pleased to take care of theire march
and that such may come along with them
as wilbe able to bringe them to the mayne body and then I doubt not but wee shall keepe
them, and make good use of them

I beeseech you give countenance to mr. Margery,
helpe him in raisinge the[15] troope, lett him not
want your favor, in whatsoever is needfull
for promotinge his worke and command your servant,
if Hee can raise the horses from malignants,[16] lett him have your
warrant it wilbe a speciall service

1643 09 11

Letter from Oliver Cromwell to Oliver St John

Date: 11 September [1643]
Source: BL, Add. MS 5015*, fos 6r–7v (holograph)

This is a holograph letter, slightly damaged. For several weeks Cromwell had been bombarding deputy lieutenants and commissioners from the Associated Counties with

---

[14] 'If it were' is written over the previous words, which are difficult to make out.
[15] This is either 'this' overwritten as 'the' or vice versa. It is difficult to be sure which.
[16] Parliament distinguished between those royalists who would be fined for their action (delinquents) and those who would forfeit all their property (malignants). Of course, it was for Parliament or its designated committeemen not for a junior army officer to decide who was in which category.

11 SEPTEMBER 1643

demands for supplies in the face of imminent royalist threats. This letter, to an old friend and longstanding ally, might be one of several sent at about this time as he changed from pleading with local leaders to lobbying Members of Parliament.

What had changed since the end of August was that Cromwell had taken all the troops he had at his disposal and headed north, still expecting the earl of Newcastle to head south through Lincolnshire towards the Association. On 4 September he had been at Ely, where he dined with members of the Eastern Association Committee, with them assuring him of the belated despatch of new troops from Essex, and he telling them that his men were on the march towards Lincoln and that he would follow them the following day 'for his scouts brought word of 8,000 of the Earl of Newcastle's forces appeared'.[1]

[fo. 7v]

To my honored freind
Oliver St John Esqr[2]
~~sollicitor~~[3] theise
present[4]
Lincolns Inn

[fo. 6v]

Oliver Cromwell
to
Oliver St. John[5]

[fo. 6r]

Sir of all men I should not trouble you with mo
nie matters, did \not/ the heavie necessityes my Troupes are
in, presse mee beyond measure. I am neglected excee=
dinglye, I am [ ][6] now ~~upon~~ \ready for/ my march towards ~~Hull~~ \the/
enemie whoe hath intrenched himselfe over against

---

[1] William Harlackenden to Sir Thomas Barrington, 4 September 1643, BL, Egerton MS 2647 fo. 229.

[2] Both Oliver St John's wives were second cousins to Cromwell, and the two men had been friends for years (see **1638 10 13**).

[3] He had been appointed Solicitor General by Charles I in 1641 and he retained that office and status throughout the 1640s.

[4] This is in Cromwell's hand.   [5] This is in another seventeenth-century hand.

[6] A word of probably two letters, the second, probably 'y', has been erased here.

THE LETTERS, WRITINGS, AND SPEECHES OF OLIVER CROMWELL

Hull,[7] my L Newcasl.[8] haveinge beseiged the tow[n]e.[9]
Many of my Ld. of Manchesters[10] Troupes are
come to mee, very bad, and mutenus, not to
bee confided in, they payed to a weeke almost,
mine ~~men []~~[11] \noe wayes/ provided for to support them,
except by the poor Sequestrations[12] of the
County of Hunt.[13] my Troupes increase, I have
a lovely cumpanie, you would respect them did
you knowe them, they are no Anabapt.[14] they are
honest sober Christians, they ~~greive~~ \expect/ to be used
as men. If tooke pleasure to write to the house[15]
in bitternesse I have occasion, the 3000 li. allotted
mee,[16] I cannot gett the part of Norfolke, nor
Hartfordsheire, it was gonn before I had itt,
I have minded your service, to forgetfullnesse
of my owne and souldiers necessityes, I desier
not to seeke my selfe, I have little monie of
my owne to helpe my souldiers, my estate is
little, \I tell/ you ~~know~~ the businesse of Ireland and
England hath had of mee in monie betweene
eleven and 1200 pounds,[17] therfore my private can

---

[7] Kingston upon Hull on the river Humber in south-east Yorkshire, a major parliamentarian garrison town.

[8] William Cavendish, earl and later first duke of Newcastle upon Tyne, commander in chief of the King's northern armies ('North of Trent') until the catastrophic defeat at Marston Moor on 5 July 1644 following which he went into exile.

[9] A small hole in the document obliterates what must be an 'n'.

[10] Edward Montagu, second earl of Manchester. Montagu had been appointed major general for the Eastern Association the previous month.

[11] Heavily crossed out. Both 'men' and 'are' are possible readings.

[12] Sequestrations. The process by which those deemed to be royalists by committees of parliamentarians set up in each county could have their lands seized and profits deployed for the parliamentarian cause for the duration of the war.

[13] i.e. Huntingdonshire.

[14] 'Anabaptist' is a term tightly defined as those who believed in believers' (i.e. adult) baptism, but in the 1640s more generally for those who were separatists, members of gathered churches made up only of 'saints', the elect.

[15] i.e. House of Commons. He is of course writing to a prominent member and close ally.

[16] Cf **1643 08 30**[?].

[17] 'The businesse of Ireland' was the rebellion which broke out in late November 1641 and which led to the Adventurers Act of March 1642, by which Parliament sought to borrow a

28 SEPTEMBER 1643

doe little to helpe the publike, you have had

my monie, I hope in God, I desier to venter my

skinn, soe doe mine, lay waite upon their patience

but[18] betake itt not, thinke of that which may be a real helpe, I beleive ~~[ ] 5000~~

~~li. is due~~

if you lay aside the thought of mee and my letter, I expect noe helpe. pray for

Your true freind and servant

Oliver Cromwell

Sept. 11th.

~~I am confident there bee of the~~

There is noe care taken how to maintaine that force of horse

and foote raised and a raisinge: by my Ld of Manchester, He hath

not one able to putt onn, the force will fall if some help not, weake

councells and weak actings undoe all [   ][19] come, or all wilbee lost if God

help not

remember whoe tells you

⸺⊶∞⊷⸺

1643 09 28

Letter from Oliver Cromwell to Sir William Spring
and Mr [Maurice] Barrow

Date: 28 September 1643

Source: Museum of London, Tangye MS 643 (holograph)

This is a holograph letter on a single sheet, folded. The text starts on the right-hand page, then into left margin of that page (at right angles to original text) and then carries on to the

million pounds to finance an army that would protect those not yet massacred and avenge those who had been. Cromwell lent £850 for this cause (Karl Bottigheimer, *English Money and Irish Land: the 'Adventurers' and the Cromwellian Settlement of Ireland* (1971), pp. 70, 179, 201. The 'business of England' was the system of voluntary loans raised by Parliament before it became willing to vote taxation without royal assent. These voluntary (in fact increasingly involuntary) loans were known as the 'Propositions' and presumably Cromwell donated something like £300.

[18] This is where he begins to write in the left-hand margin.

[19] Two words here are illegible, a longer one and a short one probably ending in 'o'. The first word just may be 'donne' as in v.2.

THE LETTERS, WRITINGS, AND SPEECHES OF OLIVER CROMWELL

left-hand page. The letter finishes about a third of the way down; then carries on to the bottom as a PS which leaves a wide space to the left of the signature which it curves around and below. Some punctuation, clearly added in pencil after the event, has been omitted here.

Since he wrote to St John on 11 September, Cromwell had stayed mainly around Boston while Newcastle's advance had faltered and then been abandoned. Although Cromwell had even made a two-day probing advance as far as Hull on the Yorkshire/Lincolnshire border, by the time he wrote this letter he was back in Boston. But the situation remained fluid. The following week Cromwell made a flying visit to Cambridge via King's Lynn and Ely but he was back in Boston on 4 November and by the end of that week he was joining up for the first time with Sir Thomas Fairfax for the long-deferred battle with Newcastle's forces at Winceby, near Horncastle in the Lincolnshire Wolds. It was an important parliamentary victory with a third of the royalist force killed or captured and Newcastle forced to call off the siege of Hull, the last parliamentarian stronghold in Yorkshire.

Cromwell was surely right to emphasise the need for greater urgency from the associated counties, but even more striking is the close repetition of his call for bold appointments of godly men and his repeated support for the widely distrusted Ralph Margery. But he is writing to two men who, at any rate a year later, would head a list of seven leading Suffolk commissioners in writing to the Committee of Both Kingdoms, arguing that the real danger in Suffolk was not the threat of royalism but the upsurge in 'antinomians and anabaptists'. Cromwell is unlikely here to be preaching to the converted.[1]

――――――

[verso]

To his honoured friend Sir Willm
Springe[2] & Mr [Maurice] Barrow[3] these present
    H   H
       H[4]

[recto]

Gentlemen

It hath pleased God to bring of Sir Thomas Fairefax[5]
his horse over the river from Hull, being about one

---

[1] See below, nn. 2 and 3, and University of Chicago, Bacon Collection, item 4552.

[2] See **1643 01 27**, **1643 07 31**, **1643 08 29** and **1645 06 06**. The main source is the life of Spring in *HoP Commons, 1640–1660*.

[3] See **1643 01 27**, **1643 07 31**, **1643 08 29** and **1645 06 06**. The main source is the life of Barrowe in *HoP Commons, 1640–1660*.

[4] These could be an alternative to his more usual 'haste, haste, haste' when he is agitated.

[5] Thomas Fairfax, third Lord Fairfax of Cameron (1612–71), parliamentarian army officer. See *ODNB*.

28 SEPTEMBER 1643

and twenty troopes of horse & Dragoonrs the Lincolne
shire horse laboured to hinder this worke being about
thirty foure coullours of horse and Dragoonrs, we marched
up to their landing place and the Lincolne shire horse
retreated after they were come over we all marched
towards Holland and when we came to our last quarter
upon the Edge of Holland[6] the Enemy quartered
within foure miles of us and kept the field all night
with his whole body his intendment as we conceive
was to fight us or hopeing to interpose betwixt us and
our retreate, haveing received to his 34 coulours [?of][7]
horse twenty fresh troopes ten companies of D[?ragoonrs]
and about a thousand foote being generall Kings ow[?n]
regiment with these he attempted our guards and our
quarters and if god had not beene mercifull had
ruined us before we had knowne of it the five troopes
we Set to keepe the watch faileing much of their
duty, but we got to horse and retreated in good order
with the Safety of all our horse of the Association
not looseing foure of them that I heare of and we
got five of their's and for this we are exceedingly bound to
the goodnes of god who brought our troopes of with Soe little
losse, I write unto you to acquaint you with this the
rather that God may bee acknowledged and that you
may help forward in Sending Such force away unto us as
lye unproffitably in your countrey and especially that troope
of Capt Margerie's[8] which Surely would not be wantinge
now we Soe much neede it the enemy may teach us
that wisdome who is not wanting to himselfe in makeing
up his best Strenght for the accomplishmt of his designes.

---

[6] Holland, an administrative district in south-eastern Lincolnshire.

[7] There is a tear on the right side of the paper that affects this and the next two lines. The words in brackets are conjectural.

[8] For Cromwell's passionate support for Ralph Margery, see **1643 08 30[?]** (introduction and postscript to the letter).

THE LETTERS, WRITINGS, AND SPEECHES OF OLIVER CROMWELL

I heare there hath beene much exception taken to Capt
Margery & his officers for takeing of horses. I am Sorry
you Should discountenance those (who (not to make benefitt to
themselves but to Secure their countrey) are willing to
venture their lives and to purchase to themselves
the displeasure of bad men that t⫫ they may doe a
publique benefitt. I undertake not to justify all Captaine
Margerie's actions, but his owne conscience knowes whether
he hath taken the horses of any but malignants[9] and it were
Somewhat too hard to put it upon the consciences of your fellow deputy
Lieftenants whether they have not
freed the horses of knowne malignants, a fault not lesse considering the Sad
estate of this Kngdome
then to take a horse from a knowne honest man, the offence being against the
publique which is a considerable
aggravation. I know not the measu{r}e that every one takes of Malignants, I
thinke it is not fitt Capt. Margery
should be the judge but if he in this{ } takeing of horses hath observed the
parliamt ⊢—⫤[10] charecter of
a malignant and cannot be Charged for our horse otherwise taken, it had beene
better that Some of the bitternes
wherewith he and his have beene followed had been Spared, the horses that his
Coronett Boallry[11] tooke he will put
himselfe upon that issue for them all, if these men be accounted troublesome to
the countrey I shalbe glad you would
Send them all to me Ile bid them welcome and when they have fought for you and
indured Some other
difficulties of warre which your honester men will hardly beare I prayou then let
them your for honest men

---

[9] For malignants, see **1643 08 30**[?].

[10] A word here is heavily crossed out but appears to be 'made' or 'make'.

[11] Coronet Boallry. Not identified except that a cornet Samuel Boally signed one of the regimental petitions to Fairfax at Saffron Walden in May 1647 (he was a member of Charles
Fleetwood's regiment at that time). It may just be the same man (anon., *A perfect and true copy of
the severall grievances of the army under his Excellencie, Sir Thomas Fairfax*, May 1647, penultimate page
(Wing / P1472; Thomason / E390[3]) Wanklyn, *Reconstructing*, 1:168n.28. This gives us Boally as
being in the '4th regiment' which on 31 May 1647 was Fleetwood's (ibid., pp. 167, 82). Fleetwood's
was an Eastern Association regiment in 1643.

28 SEPTEMBER 1643

I professe you many of t{he/ho?}se[12] men which are of your countreys choos-
einge under Capt Johnson[13] are Soe

farre from Serving you that were it not that I have honest troopes to maister
them, althoughe they be well

payd yet they are Soe mutinous that I may justly feare they would cut my throate,
Gentlemen it may

be it provokes Some spiritts to See Such plaine men made Captaines of horse I
~~assure you~~ it had beene well

that men of honour and birth had entred into these imployments but why doe
they not appeare, who would

have hindered them? but Seeing it was necessary the worke must goe on, better
plaine men then none

but[——][14] best to have men patient of wants faithfull and conscientious in the
imploymt. and Such I hope

these will approve themselves to be, let them therefore if I be thought worthy of
any favoure leave

your countrey with your good wishes and a blessing I am confident they wilbe
well bestowed and I beleeve

before it be longe you wilbe in their debte and then it will not be hard to quit
Scores, what armes you

can furnish them withall I beseech you do it I have ever hitherto found your
kindnes great to me I know

not what I have done to loose it I love it Soe well and price it Soe highe that I
would doe my best

to gaine more, you have the assured affection of

Your most humble & faithfull
servant
Oliver Cromwell

---

[12] Two letters are lost here; what is left is 'th—e' so the word must surely be 'these' or 'those'.

[13] Captain Johnson: probably the William Johnstone [Johnson] who was captain of a company in Lawrence Crawford's regiment of foot in the Eastern Association Army, although he is
only known as a captain from 15 July 1644. So he is also possibly Thomas Johnson, initially a
cornet in, but then a lieutenant of, Ralph Knight's troop in the earl of Manchester's regiment of
horse in the Eastern Association Army, he too became a captain at some point: *Online Directory
of Parliamentarian Army Officers*.

[14] The 'ut' are heavily imposed over what Cromwell originally wrote, which was probably
'better'.

28th. Sep. 1643

I understand there were Some exceptions taken at a horse that was sent to me which was ceized out of the hands of one mr Goldsmith of Wilby,[15] if he be not by you judged a malignant and that you doe not approve of my haveing of the horse I shall as willingly returne him againe as you shall desire and therefore I prayou Signify your pleasure to me herein under your hands, not that I would for ten thousand horses have the horse to my owne private benefitt, Saveing to make use of him for the publique for I will most gladly returne the vallue of him to the State, if the Gentle man stand cleere in your judgments, I beg it as a Speciall favour that if the Gent be freely willinge to let me have him for my money, let him Set his owne price. I shall very justly returne him the money or if he be unwilling to part with him but keepes him for his pleasure be pleased to Send me an answeare thereof: I shall instantly returne him his horse and doe \it/ with a great deale more Satisfaction to my Selfe, then keepe him, therfore I beg it of you to Satisfy my desire in this last request, it shall exceedingly oblige me to you, if you doe it not, I shall rest very unsatisfied and the horse wilbe a burthen to me So long as I shall keep him

1643 10 03

Warrant from Oliver Cromwell to Robert Brown, deputy treasurer of Ely

Date: 3 October 1643
Source: C. H. Firth, 'The Raising of the Ironsides', *Transactions of the Royal Historical Society*, n.s. 13 (1899), p. 35 n. 2 (modern transcription)

Charles Firth found this document 'amongst the papers of the Ely Committee', and it is not traceable 120 years later. It marks an early appearance of Cromwell's key ally and future son-in-law Henry Ireton. Firth added these words to his transcription: 'the letter is

---

[15] Mr Goldsmith of Wilby: Wilby was a small village in mid-Suffolk, east of Eye but 'Mr Goldsmith' has not been identified.

endorsed with a receipt showing the money was paid on October 6. It is only signed by Cromwell and apparently written by Ireton.'

These are to require you forthwith out [of] the treasure in your hands to pay to Sarj.-Maj. Henry Ireton[1] the summe of seventye pounds upon accompt towards the paye of his troope and officers, and also the summe of thirtye pounds to be by him payd over to Capt. Gervase Lomax[2] upon accompt towards the pay of his foote company and officers; Hereof fayle not at your perill, and this shall be your warrant.

Given under my hand this 3rd daye of October 1643.

OLIVER CROMWELL

To Robert Brown,[3] Deputy Treasurer of Ely.

1643 10 06
Letter from Oliver Cromwell to Sir Thomas Barrington

Date: 6 October 1643
Source: Carlyle-Lomas, *Letters and Speeches*, 3:317 [Supplement No. 5] (modern transcription)

This holograph letter was in the possession of the great collector Alfred Morrison when it was seen by Sophia Lomas as she revised Carlyle's *Letters and Speeches*. Its whereabouts since the dispersal of the Morrison collection at auction in 1918 is unknown.[1] Lomas was a very accurate reader of Cromwell's hand, but she followed Carlyle in modernising spelling and punctuation.

Cromwell is writing from east-central Lincolnshire as he moved north to meet up with Sir Thomas Fairfax in readiness to confront a probe by 3,000 royalist troops. In the event there was to be a significant encounter—and a significant parliamentarian success at Winceby [in the Lincolnshire Wolds, five miles east of Horncastle]—just five days later on 11 October.

His ongoing concerns about supplies, especially from Essex, were a recurring theme of his letters through the campaigning season of 1643. Here he is probably trying to get a

---

[1] Henry Ireton (bap. 1611, d. 1651). See *ODNB*.
[2] See the entries for Gervaise Lomax and Jarvis Lomax (surely the same man) in the *Online Directory of Parliamentarian Army Officers*. He was a Nottinghamshire man who had served in the same regiment as Ireton and come over to the Eastern Association a month or two earlier.
[3] Not otherwise identified.

---

[1] Its sale is recorded in *Autograph Prices Current* 1.265, fn. 171.

more rapid response to the parliamentary ordinance of 6 September 1643, which had empowered the deputy lieutenants and committeemen of the Eastern Association counties to raise a special regular assessment.[2]

To Sir Thomas Barrington[3]
Boston, October 6th. 1643.
SIR,
It is against my will to be too troublesome to my friends. I had rather suffer under some extremities, were it my particular; but that which I have to offer concerns those honest men under my command, who have been, who are in straits; if want of clothes, boots, money to fix their arms, to shoe their horses be considerable,[4] such are theirs not in an easy degree, truly above what is fit for the state to suffer. Sir, many may complain they are many weeks behind of pay, many who can plunder and pillage, they suffer no want. But truly mine (though some have stigmatised them with the name of Anabaptists), are honest men, such as fear God, I am confident the freest from unjust practices of any in England, seek the soldiers where you can. Such imputations are poor requitals to those who have ventured their blood for you. I hear there are such mists cast to darken their services. Take no care for me, I ask your good acceptance, let me have your prayers, I will thank you; truly I count not myself worthy to be employed by God; but for my poor men, help them what you can, for they are faithful. The last ordinance hath provided for me, but paper pays not, if not executed. I beg your furtherance herein. Sir, know you have none will more readily be commanded by you, than your cousin and humble servant,

OLIVER CROMWELL.

---

[2] A&O, 1:273.

[3] For his dominant position in civil-war Essex, see Sir Thomas Barrington, second baronet (c.1585–1644), politician, in *ODNB*.

[4] As previous letters had shown, Cromwell was particularly frustrated at the sluggish response of Essex more than any other county. Barrington, the son of his formidable aunt Joan Barrington (née Cromwell), was one of the few Essex commissioners he believed he could rely on.

6 JANUARY 1644

1644 01 06

Order from Oliver Cromwell to Dr [William][1] Staine

Date: 6 January 1644

Source: C. H. Firth, 'The Raising of the Ironsides', *Transactions of the Royal Historical Society*, n.s. 13 (1899), p. 66 (modern transcription)

Sir Charles Firth transcribed this document from within what he called 'the Exchequer Manuscripts in the Record Office' (now known as TNA, SP28). It has not been possible to find it within the 356 volumes and bundles that make up that class.

This is the first communication from Cromwell to survive since his letter to Sir Thomas Barrington on 6 October 1643. He had spent the rest of October and November strengthening parliamentarian defences in north Lincolnshire and as far north as Newark. In early December he was at Sleaford in mid-Lincolnshire. He returned to winter quarters at Ely around 12 December and remained there until 17 January when returned to Westminster for the first time for just over one year. He took his place in the House of Commons and remained there for around one month.

This document is not quite a letter but its personal appeal to Staine makes it more than a pro-forma order. He in turn forwarded it (with the signature 'W.Stane') to Commissary General Harlackenden and payment was then authorised by Manchester, Nathaniel Bacon and Brampton.[2]

Dr Staines[3]

I desire you doe me the favour to let the bearer have five pounds of my money for his Captain, Captain Coleman,[4] his want is great and I should be loathe he should be sent away to him empty. You must not fayle me herein.

I rest,

---

[1] No Christian name is given and Firth almost certainly incorrectly got the wrong brother and wrote 'Dr Richard Staines. For Richard and William see below, **1644 01 06** fn 3. For Richard, see below **1644 04 13**.

[2] Carlyle-Lomas, 3:319.

[3] There are two 'Dr Stanes' in and around Cambridge and Ely in the 1640s and 1650s, and Firth gets them confused. There is an admirable note by Sophia Lomas which sorts them out: Richard is treasurer of the Isle of Ely and not William in late 1643 (who served first as physician to the earl of Manchester)—from the time of Manchester's appointment as major general of the Eastern Association—served as auditor general and treasurer first of Manchester's army and later of the New Model Army (Carlyle-Lomas, 3:318–20). For William, see Holmes, *Eastern Association*, pp. 128–30, 157, 216.

[4] Almost certainly Captain Henry Coleman, an Essex man serving in the army of the Eastern Association, for whom see the *Online Directory of Parliamentarian Army Officers*.

Your very loving father,[5]
Oliver Cromwell
Jan.6

1644 01 10a
Letter from Oliver Cromwell to the Committee of the Isle of Ely

Date: 10 January 1644
Source: C. H. Firth, 'The Raising of the Ironsides', *Transactions of the Royal Historical Society*, n.s. 13 (1899), p. 66 (modern transcription)

Cromwell can be securely placed (at home) in Ely from 12 December to 16 January, using the time to make the town that rose from the surrounding flooded fenland militarily more secure. This is the second of a series of short letters, orders really, that he fired off in the second week of January 1644. This version is a copy of a transcript made by the reliable Sir Charles Firth in the late nineteenth century. He tells us that the original is 'from the Exchequer Manuscripts in the Record Office' [i.e. TNA, SP28] but not where it is within the 356 bundles in that class.

Gentlemen, there is a boate framinge for the defence of theise parts, I believe it's of consequence, I therefore desire you to let the officer that directs the framing of itt[1] to have twenty markes[2] for the perfectinge of itt and I shall rest
Your true servant,
Oliver Cromwell
Jan.10, 1643[4]
To my very noble friends the Committee of the Isle of Ely present these.

[5] This is a curious and unusual usage. Some light be thrown on it by a letter from Cromwell in 1651 endorsed 'To my dear Sister Mrs. Elizabeth Cromwell, at Doctor Richard Stane his house at Ely'. See **1651 12 15**.

[1] Firth identified this officer (he does not say how) as 'Lieutenant Thomas Selby'. There was a Lieutenant John Selby in Colonel Francis Russell's regiment (TNA SP28/27 fo.288) who went on to serve in Charles Fleetwood's regiment in the New Model Army and was killed at Naseby. If Firth was right to see a Lieutenant Selby as the man in charge of the new boat, then it is surely this John Selby. See the *Online Directory of Parliamentarian Army Officers*, and Wanklyn, *Reconstructing*, 1: 51, 61, 72.

[2] 20 Marks at 13s 4d per mark is £13 6s 8d.

1644 01 10b
Letter from Oliver Cromwell to William Hitch

Date: 10 January 1644

Source: *Isographie des hommes célèbres ou collection de fac-simile de lettres autographes et de signatures*, ed. S. Bérard, H. de Chateaugiron, J. Duchesne aîné, Trémisot.-Supplément…dressé par Étienne Charavay, 5 vols. (Paris, 1828–80), vol. 1 (unfol.). (lithographic reproduction of holograph)

This letter survives as a lithographic reproduction of a Cromwell holograph letter. Previous editions have not attempted to reproduce crossed-out material, but the condition is poor, making this task now difficult.

Cromwell is writing to William Hitch (b. *c.*1590), a vicar choral at Ely Cathedral and since 1615 curate of Holy Trinity Church, which was a parish community that gathered in the Lady Chapel of the Cathedral.[1]

It has been claimed by many historians that Cromwell wrote this letter telling Hitch (whom he must have known) to desist from holding choral services and that when Hitch went ahead, Cromwell and his troops put an end to the service and began a spate of iconoclasm, specifically pulling out the organ pipes. But it has recently been convincingly demonstrated that there was spontaneous action by some soldiers on 9th January and that Cromwell's letter on the 10th was an attempt to restore order and to prevent any further undisciplined actions by his troops. Cromwell almost certainly favoured an end to formal worship, but this letter does not represent support for intimidation or iconoclasm here or elsewhere.[2] It is also surely significant that Hitch was not removed from his position. Although the dean and chapter of the Cathedral was dissolved, Hitch stayed on as vicar of Holy Trinity parish,[3] meeting for prayer and sermons in the Lady Chapel until his death in October 1658, indeed with an 'augmentation' of his income (a supplement paid out of the revenues from impropriations surrendered by convicted royalists).[4] In fact Cromwell's daughter Elizabeth was married to John Claypole of Northborough,

---

[1] Hitch matriculated as a sizar at Queens' College Cambridge in 1606 taking his MA in 1614 (venn.lib.cam.ac.uk/cgi-bin/search-2018.pl?sur=hitch&suro=w&fir=William). He then moved to Ely where he was both the curate of Holy Trinity (1615–58) and schoolmaster at the college in the Cathedral close from 1619 (CUL, EDR B2/37 fo.21v–22r). From 1635 he was also vicar of St Andrew's Church next to the market square in Cambridge. See Hitch,Willimo in http://db.the-clergydatabase.org.uk/jsp/search/index.jsp, CCEd Person ID: 28086. He was also quite a substantial landowner around Ely and held the manor of Ketton in Rutland (CUL, 8A/1/22 fo.4). From no later than 1649 he was living in the Archdeacon's lodgings in the Cathedral Close (CUL, Add. MS 41 fo.50r) and was the lessee of the Swann Inn in Ely (CUL, Add. MS 41 fo.61r). We are grateful to William Franklin for his assistance.

[2] Graham Hart, 'Oliver Cromwell, Iconoclasm and Ely Cathedral', *Historical Research* 87, no. 236 (2014), pp. 270–6.

[3] See also **1646 10 25**.

[4] A. G. Matthews, *Walker Revised: being a revision of being a revision of John Walker's 'Sufferings of the clergy during the Grand Rebellion, 1642–60'* (1948), p. 82.

Northamptonshire in Holy Trinity, presumably by Hitch, on 13 January 1646. This allows us to hear a very different tone in Cromwell's letter from an assumed menacing of a 'ceremonialist' minister.[5]

Mr. Hich, least the Souldiers should in any
tumultuarie, or disorderly way attempt the Refor=
mation of your Cathedrall church, I requier
you to forbeare altogether your Quire service[6]
soe unedifyinge, and offensive, and this
as you will answere it, if a{ny}[?contention] \disorder/
should arise thereupon.

I advise you to ~~chattechise~~ cattechise and
reade, and expound the Scriptures to the
people, not doubtinge but the Parlnt
with the advise of the Assemblie \of Divines/[7] will
in due tyme direct you \farther/ [-].[8]

I desier the sermons may bee [-][9] where usually
they have beene, but more frequent,
Your lovinge freind
Oliver Cromwell
Jan. 10th 1643:

---

[5] Cambridgeshire Archives, P67/1/2, Composite register of baptisms, weddings and burials, 1627–84, unfol.

[6] i.e. sung services following the Book of Common Prayer.

[7] i.e. the Westminster Assembly of Divines, which had been meeting in Westminster Abbey since 1 July 1643.

[8] 'farther' was written over a now-illegible crossed out word. It is just possible that 'direct you further' was originally 'direct your management'.

[9] 'where' written over successfully obliterated two letters: 'as'? in'?

1644 01 19

Warrant signed by Oliver Cromwell and Miles Sandys to [William?] Edwards

Date: 19 January 1644
Source: TNA, SP16/539, Part 2, fo. 124 (no. 175) (autograph)

This is an exemplum of a number of pro-forma warrants signed by Cromwell at about this time. On the same sheet, for example, there are shorter warrants to Richard Stane, Treasurer for the Isle of Ely, for payments to Henry Ireton's troop and dates 20 April and 8 May 1644.

Mr. Edwards[1]
You being Trear for Wisbich[2] and North wichford hundred[3] of such moneys as are rai[s]ed within the same by authority of Parliamt. for such Soldyers as are for the defence of the Isle of Eely, These are to authorise and requyre you to pay unto Major Dodson,[4] the somme of ~~eight~~ \Six/ hundred poundes with all possible speed You cann, which hee is to have in part of his arreares untill his Accompt can bee taken, and the remainder payd him, that soe hee may have wherewith to satisfy the poore people, which Quartereth his Souldyers and soe March away to his Charge under Collonell Pickering[5]
London this 19th of Januarij 1643

Miles Sandys[6]
Oliver Cromwell

---

[1] Abbott, *Writings and Speeches*, 1:192n draws attention to a James Edwards, son and heir of William Edwards of Wisbech, who was to matriculate as a fellow commoner at Peterhouse, Cambridge in 1650 and serve as bailiff of Wisbech either side of the Restoration (Venn, *Alumni Cantabrigienses*). It is entirely plausible to think William is the recipient of this letter.
[2] Wisbech is a market town on the river Nene in the far north of Cambridgeshire fenland.
[3] This hundred lay south and west of Wisbech, including the towns of Chatteris and March.
[4] William Dodson. See Clive Holmes, 'The Identity of the Author of the "Statement by an Opponent of Cromwell", *English Historical Review*, 129 no. 541 (2014), pp. 1371–82.
[5] For Colonel John Pickering (d. 1645), see the *Online Directory of Parliamentarian Army Officers*.
[6] Miles Sandys of Wilburton (with extensive lands west of Ely). He and his father Sir Miles were prominent Cambridge committeemen.

1644 01 21

Letter from Oliver Cromwell to [the Committee of the Eastern Association at Cambridge] (modern copy)

Date: 21 January 1644
Source: C. H. Firth, 'The Raising of the Ironsides', *Transactions of the Royal Historical Society*, n.s. 13 (1899), p. 54.

This is at once a straightforward letter of support for a soldier, George Frane—an otherwise unidentified trooper in his own regiment—broken by war, and is remarkable in its sense of personal commitment and in its hesitancy to command the civil authorities to carry out a command. The tone here is surely instructive.

There is a separate but connected warrant, dated 25 January 1644, for 'George Frane, trooper in Lieutenant General Cromwells owne troope', to be paid 'upon the Lieutenant General's accompt'.[1]

Sir Charles Firth included it in his article on the raising of the Ironsides and indicates that it was to be found in what nowadays is TNA SP28 (Commonwealth Exchequer Papers). But it has not been possible to find it during our research.

Gentlemen, - This soldier of mine (Mr Frane) is a man whoe on my knowledge hath very faithfully served you, his arreers are great, his sickness much and longe, by occasion whereof hee is brought to great lownesse, and is much indebted. If now upon my recommendation of his person and condition unto you, you will be please to help him with some competent sum of monie to discharge his debt, and relieve himselfe, I shall take it for a great favour, and bee ready to repay such a respect with a thankfull [acknow] ledgment and ever [be]
                    Your real and faythfull friend
Oliver Cromwell
Jan.21, 164[4], London

---

[1] Firth, 'Ironsides', p. 55.

22 JANUARY 1644

1644 01 22

Speech by Oliver Cromwell to the House of Commons

Date: 22 January 1644
Source: BL, Harl. MS 165, fo. 280v, Diary of Sir Simonds D'Ewes

Cromwell had spent much of late 1643 on campaign in and around Lincolnshire. On returning to Westminster in mid-January 1644, he took the opportunity to criticise one of the senior officers he had been serving under, the fifth Lord Willoughby of Parham.[1] This arose from the power struggle between Willoughby and his main rival on the parliamentarian side, the second earl of Manchester. During the early stages of the war Willoughby had been the leading parliamentarian commander in Lincolnshire, but his independence was undermined in September 1643 when the county was added to the Eastern Association, which seemed to imply that Manchester, as the Association's major general, had authority over that county. The two peers had since worked together uneasily. Manchester's powers over all seven associated counties, including Lincolnshire, had been strengthened by an ordinance approved by Parliament as recently as 20 January.[2] Now, two days later, Cromwell sought to get Manchester formally confirmed as the major general for Lincolnshire. He did so mainly by disparaging Willoughby's military record.

———

During my absence Cromwell \stood upp & desired that the/ L. Willoughby of Parham who had commanded in Lincolnshire as serjeant maior generall of the forces ther might be ordered to stay heere & to goe no moore thither, & that the Earle of Manchester might be made serjeant maior generall of that countie as well \as/ of the other associated counties. out area. That the Lord Willoughby quitted Gainsborow when hee was not farr offe with forces to releive him that hee quitted the cittie of Lincoln &c. & left powder match & armes ther & 7 great peices mounted with all the carriages wch the enemie made use offe against the Parliaments forces.[3] That hee had verie loose & profane commanders under him, one of them sending out a warrant to Constable &c. in the end to bring him in some wenches for his turne &c.

———

[1] Francis Willoughby, fifth Baron Willoughby of Parham.
[2] A&O, 1:368–71.
[3] A reference to the fact that Willoughby had captured Gainsborough in Lincolnshire on 20 July 1643 and that Cromwell had come to his assistance on 28 July, but that Willoughby had allowed the town to be recaptured by the royalists on 31 July.

185

Outcome: Such criticism, coming from the most distinguished officer of the Eastern Association sitting the Commons, could not be ignored. Sir Christopher Wray, MP for Great Grimsby (Lincolnshire), did attempt to defend Willoughby, but he conceded almost everything by admitting that Willoughby was prepared to agree not to return to Lincolnshire. Cromwell's proposal therefore prevailed, with the Commons ordering the lord general, the earl of Essex, to grant a commission to Manchester as the major general for Lincolnshire. Essex was also told that he could decide how many of Willoughby's cavalry units should be allowed to remain in Lincolnshire.[4] In what may not have been a coincidence, Cromwell was probably now promoted to the rank of lieutenant general. His salary for that position was paid from this date.

1644 01 30
Letter from Oliver Cromwell to the Committee of Ely

Date: 30 January 1644
Source: C. H. Firth, 'The Raising of the Ironsides', *Transactions of the Royal Historical Society*, n.s. 13 (1899), p. 67 (modern copy)

This short letter is notable for its tone and Cromwell's apparent willingness to allow a group of civilians to make a decision on a primarily military matter. The letter is in fact an endorsement on a petition submitted to him by John Disbrowe. This is the petition:

'To the Right Honourable Leiftenant Generall Cromwell the petition of John Disbrowe, showeth

That whereas he was commanded by the Lord of Manchester to conduct a company of prest men[1] out of the Isle of Ely into Lincolne with the promise of satisfaction for the said service which he never could obtaine, he hath since repayred to the Committee of the Isle of Ely for pay for the said service. But they informed him they could pay nothing without expresse order from your Honour May it therefore please you to order the said Committee herein, and your petitioner shall upon all occasions be ready to serve you.'

Disbrowe had married Cromwell's sister Jane in 1636 and had been a captain in Cromwell's own regiment of horse since April 1643.[2]

---

[4] *JHC*, 3:373.

---

[1] The first parliamentary ordinance for the conscripting men to fight had been passed on 10 August 1643: see *A&O*, 1:241.
[2] Jane Disbrowe, née Cromwell, see https://www.geni.com/people/Jane-Desborough/6000000002831254906 and http://www.olivercromwell.org/faqs1.htm.

Gentlemen, I desire you take this petition into consideration, and to do therein as to your judgments shall seeme meete, and what you please to doe heerein shall content mee.

Jan 30th, 1644
To the Committee for the Isle of Ely.

Your servant
OLIVER CROMWELL

1644 03 08
Letter from Oliver Cromwell to Sir Samuel Luke

Date: 8 March 1644
Source: BL, Egerton MS 785, fo. 10v (Letter Book of Sir Samuel Luke, 1643–45) (contemporary copy)

This letter was copied by Sir Samuel Luke or his clerk as soon as it arrived or soon afterwards. Cromwell returned from Westminster to his command sometime in mid-February 1644 and his route from Cambridge to the environs of Oxford at the very end of February would take him close to Newport Pagnell where Luke was governor.[1] He and Luke joined forces to drive back a royalist raiding party from Oxford which had, amongst other things seized and garrisoned Hillesden House, just south of Buckingham. On 4 March 1644 Cromwell and Luke led 2,000 men to Hillesden House, 20 miles south-west of Newport Pagnell, overrunning some newly made trenches around it and expelling a small royalist detachment from the church. As the parliamentarians prepared to assault the fortified manor house, the governor surrendered and the building was then burnt to the ground.[2] Cromwell then returned to Cambridge, arriving on 8 March. He presumably wrote this letter to Luke from there.

[fo. 10v]

Noble Sir[3]

I beseech you cause 300 Foote undr 3: Capt. to march to Buckingham upon Monday morning, there to quarter with 400 Foote of Northampton which Mr Crew[4] sends thither upon monday next: there willbee the Major Generall[5] to Command

---

[1] By 2019, Newport Pagnell was part of Milton Keynes.
[2] Gaunt, *Cromwellian Gazetteer*, p. 11.
[3] Sir Samuel Luke (bap. 1603, d. 1670). See *ODNB*, and also the *Online Directory of Parliamentarian Army Officers*.
[4] Possibly John Crew of Steane, Northamptonshire and MP for Northamptonshire in the Long Parliament. For John Crew, first Baron Crew (1597/8–1679), see *ODNB*.
[5] Presumably this is a reference to Major General Lawrence Crawford, the Scottish veteran and third in command of the army of the Eastern Association, with whom Cromwell was soon

them, I am goeing for 1000: Foote more at Least to bee sent from Cambridge, & out of the assotiacone if my man bee come to you from Cambridge I beseech you send him to mee to Bedford, with all speed, let him stay for mee at the Swan[6], Sir I am Your humble servt
Oliver Cromwell
March the 8th

Present my humble Service to Coll Aylife[7] & tell him hee promised me his Coate of male

1644 03 09
Letter from Oliver Cromwell to Sir Samuel Luke

Date: 9 March 1644
Source: BL, Egerton MS 785, fo. 12r (Letter Book of Sir Samuel Luke, 1643–45) (contemporary copy)

Cromwell wrote to Luke upon his return to Cambridge from the sack of Hillesden House (**1644 03 08**) and this seems to be an afterthought sent the next day and self-explanatory. As with its predecessor, this letter survives as a copy made by or for Luke.

[fo. 12r]
Sir
Its my Lords[1] pleasure that the Prisoners[2] bee hasted to Cambridge, pardon this hast Your humble Servant
   Oll[3] Cromwell

---

to be in bitter dispute. Lawrence Crawford (1611–45), parliamentarian army officer, see *ODNB*. For the beginnings of the bitter dispute, see **1644 04 10**.

[6] An inn on the Great Ouse in the centre of the county town of Bedford.
[7] Colonel Thomas Ayloffe, an Essex man, and governor of Boston and later Newport Pagnell. See the *Online Directory of Parliamentarian Army Officers*.

[1] Presumably 'my Lord's' means his commanding officer, Edward Montagu, second earl of Manchester.
[2] Presumably prisoners taken at the capture of Hillesden House and Church, for which see **1644 03 08**.
[3] There is a stroke across 'll'. Luke seems originally to have written 'Coll', then turned the 'C' to an 'O', and tried to obscure the 'O'.

10 MARCH 1644

1644 03 10

Letter from Oliver Cromwell to Sergeant Major General Lawrence Crawford

Date: 10 March 1644
Source: NLS, Acc. 5003 (contemporary copy)

This letter is not in Cromwell's hand and it is not his signature—although it is very similar to his, it is not identical. It is almost certainly a copy of a letter sent by Cromwell as lieutenant general of the cavalry in the army of the Eastern Association to Lawrence Crawford, sergeant major general of the infantry in the same army. There is a strong case for thinking that it is a copy made by or on behalf of Crawford and forwarded to the overall commander, the earl of Manchester. The endorsement, possibly in the same hand as the body of the letter, gives the recipient as Manchester. But the matter of the letter makes it quite clear that it is addressed to Crawford and it is a very acidic complaint about his treatment of religiously radical officers.[1]

There are many reasons why Cromwell and Crawford did not get on. One was constant bickering about resources, and who should get priority in the disbursement of scarce funds. Another, the one stressed here, is Cromwell's commitment to employing men whether or not they had taken the Covenant and were committed to a godly confessional church and state. And behind that is surely Cromwell's distrust of a soldier who had not only been a mercenary for many years in Swedish, Danish and German armies, but more recently in Ormond's royalist army in Ireland, defecting in December 1643 presumably unhappy with Ormond's truce with the Catholic Confederates. Within six weeks, and at the behest of the Scottish Parliament, Manchester had given him the post of sergeant major general of the infantry in the army of the Eastern Association. This was timed to coincide with Crawford presenting to the House of Commons a denunciation of the marquis of Ormond for his dealings with Irish Catholics, with his attempt to impose an oath on all his officers binding them 'with the hazard of my life [to] maintaine and defend the true Protestant Religion established in the Church of England' and to fight for Charles I (and his successors) against those 'now under the conduct of the Earle of Essex'.[2] This may

---

[1] The letter as now presented was bought by the National Library of Scotland in 1970 when it was sold by the then duke of Manchester, descendant of Edward Montagu, second earl of Manchester and commanding officer of both Cromwell and Crawford. It is the copy seen by Sophia Lomas when she revised the version in Carlyle's *Letters and Speeches*. Her version, modernised in spelling and in punctuation, appears in Carlyle-Lomas I:170–1. Abbott, *Writings and Speeches*, 1:277–8 simply uses Sophia Lomas's modernised transcription.

[2] For Crawford's remonstrance to the House of Commons, see *JHC*, 5:386–7. This was then published on the authority of the House as *Ireland's Ingratitude to the Parliament of England or A Remonstrance of Colonell Crawfords, shewing the Jesuiticall plots against the Parliament which was the onely cause he left his imployment there*, 1644 (Wing/C.6864; Thomason/E33[28]). Thomason received his copy on 20 February 1644. This was a thirteen-page pamphlet and the oath is printed on p. 6.

189

THE LETTERS, WRITINGS, AND SPEECHES OF OLIVER CROMWELL

have predisposed Manchester to him, but if he had seen some private letters from Crawford and from Sir William Vaughan to Ormond, he would have seen that he was taking on a prickly thin-skinned man and a rigid Presbyterian.[3]

Much of this would have predisposed Cromwell to distrust him, and so Crawford's attempt to dismiss Lieutenant Colonel Henry Warner as an Anabaptist (which he wasn't) and to replace him with another Scot previously in Ormond's service (Major William Hamilton)[4] must have stuck in Cromwell's craw. It would appear that at this moment Manchester backed Cromwell and Warner, but it opened a festering wound between Cromwell and Crawford that was to return on a much bigger scale in November and December 1644 and form part of the backdrop to the Self-Denying Ordinance (see **1644 II 25b**).[5]

[fo. 1r]

Sir

The Complaints yow preferred to my Lord[6] against your lieftenant Collonell[7] both by Mr Lee[8] & your owne letters have occasioned his stay heare, my Lord being imployed in regard of many occasions which are upon him, that he hath not beene at leasure to here him make his defence, which in Justice ought to be graunted him or any man before a judgement be past upon him, dureing his aboade here & absence from yow, he hath accquainted mee what a griefe it is to him to be absent from his chardge, especially now the regiment is called forth to accon, & therefore askeing of mee my oppinion, I advised him speedily to repaire unto yow, and thought good by him thus to write unto yow, surely yow are not well advised thus to turne of one soe faithfull to the cause, & soe able to serve yow as this man is, give me leave to tell yow I cannot be of your Judgement that if A

---

[3] The letters are in Bodl., MS Carte 7/4 fos 606r–607v and fos 623r–624v.

[4] For whom see William Hamilton in the *Online Directory of Parliamentarian Army Officers*.

[5] There is an extensive account of Crawford in the *Online Directory of Parliamentarian Army Officers*. Also Lawrence Crawford (1611–45), parliamentarian army officer. See *ODNB*. Also see the discussion in Holmes, *Eastern Association*, pp. 147, 162, 164, 177, 199–204.

[6] Edward Montagu, second earl of Manchester.

[7] Henry Warner, see the *Online Directory of Parliamentarian Army Officers*. It is also worth noting that just five days later the earl of Manchester names Warner to be on the Cambridgeshire Committee for Scandalous Ministers (Graham Hart, ed., *The Cambridgeshire Committee for Scandalous Ministers 1644–45* (Cambridge Record Society, 24 (2017), p. 149.

[8] Samuel Lee, Rector of Burton Pedwardine, Lincs, and chaplain to Colonel Edward King. According to Edmund Calamy, he earned the nickname King's 'Confessor and Chaplain' (*Calamy Rev.*, p. 321). John Lilburne names him as one of King's two chaplains, and blames him and the other one, Mr Garter, for setting King against him (he called them 'the firebrands of dissention' and nicknames him 'Bishop Lee' (John Lilburne, *Innocency and Truth Justified* (1645[/46], p. 42).

10 MARCH 1644

man notorious for wickednes, for oaths, for drinking hath as great a share in your affeccion as one that feares an oath, that feares to sin that this dothe commend your eleccion of men to serve as fitt instruments in this worke. I[9] but the man is an Anabaptist are yow sure of that? admitt he be, shall that render him incapeable to serve for the publique? he is indiscreete; it may be soe, in some things, we have all humane infirmities, I tell yow if yow had none but such indiscreete men about yow & would be pleased to use them kindly yow would find as good afence[10] to yow, as any yow have yett chosen. Sir the state in choosing men to serve them takes noe notice of theire opinions if they be willing faithfully to serve them, yt satisfies, I advised yow formerly to beare with men of different minds from your selfe, if yow had done it when I advised yow to it, I thinke yow would not have had soe many stumbling blockes in your way, it may be it yow judge otherwise but I tell yow my minde, I desire yow would receive this man int[o] your favour & good opinion, I beleeve if he followe my councell he will deserve noe other but respect from yow, take heede of being sharpe or too easily sharpened by others against those to whome yow can object litle but that they square not with yow in every opinion concerning matters of religion, if there be any other offence to be charged upon him that must in a judiciall receive a determinacion, I knowe yow will not thinke it fitt my Lord should dischardge & an officer of the field, but in a regulate way, I question whether either yow or I have any president for that,[11] I have not further to trouble yow, but rest

your humble servant

Oliver Cromwell

March 10 Cambridge

To the right honourable

---

[9] Carlyle, plausibly, transcribes as 'Ay' (Carlyle-Lomas, 1:171).

[10] Previous transcribers have read this as two words ('a fence') and indeed there are examples in the letter of an indefinite article being run into a noun ('ajudiciall', adetermination', 'aregulate'). But it is also quite possible that the word intended would be the modern 'affiance', meaning 'trust or faith' or 'confidence in oneself or one abilities' (see mid-seventeenth usages in *OED*).

[11] Around this time Cromwell also complained about Crawford's attempt to imprison and cashier Lieutenant William Packer. Within weeks Cromwell had promoted him to a captain. We know about this episode from Crawford's own account: see *The Quarrel between the Earl of Manchester and Oliver Cromwell: an episode of the English Civil War. Unpublished documents relating thereto collected by J. Bruce, with fragments of a historical preface by Mr. Bruce, annotated and completed by D. Masson.* (Camden Society, 1875), p. 59. Also, William Packer (*fl.* 1644–62), army officer and deputy major general. See *ODNB*.

the Earle of Manchester
these humbly
present
[Seal][12]

1644 03 28

Warrant signed by Edward Montagu, second earl of Manchester and Oliver Cromwell to the Committee at Cambridge

Date: 28 March 1644
Source: TNA, SP16/539, Part 2, fo. 140 (autograph)

The poignant aspect of this brief warrant is that the twenty-six horses were to be delivered to 'captain' John Browne, who had been promoted to his position as captain just ten days earlier to replace Oliver who was Cromwell's second-born son and namesake (and at the time of his death oldest son) who had died of smallpox at Newport Pagnell.[1] The order was signed both by Cromwell and his commander and Cromwell's signature looks odd and strained. But war, like life, had to go on.

[fo. 140r]
Deliver to Mr Allexander Akehurst for Captayne Brownes[2] troope theese twentie Six horses lately come to Cambridge heerof fayle not xxviii[th]. of March 1644

To the Comittee at Cambridge
Manchester
Oliver Cromwell

---

[12] The seal itself has gone, but there are traces of wax where it once was.

[1] *Parliament Scout* no. 39 for 15–22 March 1644, pp. 329–30 (N&S, 485.39, Thomason / E.38[18]).

[2] 'Captaine Browne' = John Browne: see the *Online Directory of Parliamentarian Army Officers*. Browne remained in the Ironsides until after the creation of the New Model Army, when he transferred to the cavalry regiment of Sir Thomas Fairfax.

1644 04 11
Warrant from Oliver Cromwell and others to Robert Browne, deputy treasurer of the Isle of Ely

Date: 11 April 1644

Source: C. H. Firth, 'The Raising of the Ironsides', *Transactions of the Royal Historical Society*, n.s. 13 (1899), p. 67 (modern transcription)

An exemplum of a pay warrant. The company in question was part of the Ely garrison, stationed at 'the Hermitage'.[1]

April 11th, 1644

Mr Browne,[2] what monies you have in hands of the last three months tax.[3] I desire you to pay to Leiftnt Bolton,[4] to Captaine Wests[5] uses for the payment of his cumpanie, which I now order him to receive upon account. If you have not soe much yet let him have what is in your hands. And soe doeinge this shall be your warrant. Given under my hand this day and yeare above written.

                              OLIVER CROMWELL

William Marche[6]   Miles Sandys[7]

---

[1] The Hermitage is the name of a medieval hospital, dissolved at the Reformation.

[2] Robert Brown was deputy treasurer of the Isle of Ely.

[3] Almost certainly a reference to the Ordinance of 20 January 1644 'for the Recruiting, maintaining, and regulating of the Forces of the seven Associated Counties, under the Command of Edward Earle of Manchester, *A&O*, 1:368–71.

[4] Probably Robert Bolton, a lieutenant in the company of Captain Nicholas West in a regiment of foot which served under Oliver Cromwell and later under Colonel Francis Russell in their capacity as governors of the Isle of Ely—see the *Online Directory of Parliamentarian Army Officers*.

[5] For Nicholas West, see the *Online Directory of Parliamentarian Army Officers*.

[6] An active member of the Cambridge county committee. A Thomas Marsh of Swaffham Prior was sheriff of Cambridgeshire in 1648 and may be a relation.

[7] Miles Sandys of Wilburton (with extensive lands west of Ely). He and his father Sir Miles were prominent Cambridge committeemen.

1644 04 13

Warrant from Oliver Cromwell and others to Dr [Richard] Staine,[1] treasurer for the Isle of Ely

Date: 13 April 1644
Source: C. H. Firth, 'The Raising of the Ironsides', *Transactions of the Royal Historical Society*, n.s. 13 (1899), p. 67 (modern transcription)

This is written in the first person singular but countersigned by two close allies on the Cambridge committee. It is not clear what the 'extraordinary charges' were. Is Cromwell getting Staine to pay his wife Elizabeth enough money to settle his parliamentary taxes? No similar payment to any commander in any of Parliament's armies has been discovered. It is almost certainly the document referred to by Lieutenant Colonel William Dodson in his attack on Cromwell's personal integrity in December 1644 (see **1644 11 25b**, at fn. 233). Dodson claimed: 'I see at Ely, upon the fial of letters to that Committee [for the Isle] a letter from Colonell Cromwell to them that they should pay his wife £5 per weeke towards her extraordinaryes, which hath benn duly payd her a great while, I am sure there is noe ordinance of Parliament for that.'[2]

Dr Stane,[3] I do hereby require you to pay my wife[4] 5*l*. a weeke to beare the extraordinary charges. This will be your warrant. Take her hand in your noates.

Oliver Cromwell
Miles Sandys
William Marche[5]

---

[1] Firth, as in **1644 01 06**, gets the wrong brother and attributes this warrant as being addressed to William. See n. 3 below.
[2] Bruce and Masson, *Quarrel*, p. 74.
[3] For Drs William and Richard Staine, two physicians and for which is which in documents addressed to 'Dr Stane', see **1644 01 06**. This one is addressed to the 'Treasurer of the Isle of Ely' and that is Richard. In December 1651 he wrote a letter to 'my dear Sister, Mrs Elizabeth Cromwell, at Dr Richard Stane his house at Ely (see **1651 12 15**).
[4] Elizabeth Cromwell ([née Bourchier] (1598–1665), lady protectress of England, Scotland, and Ireland, consort of Oliver Cromwell. See *ODNB*. She remained in their pre-war house close to the west front of Ely Cathedral throughout the First Civil War.
[5] For Marche and Sandys, see **1644 04 11**.

22 APRIL 1644

1644 04 22

Letter from Oliver Cromwell to Sir Henry Vane the younger

Date: 22 April 1644
Source: BL, Facs. MS Suppl. VII (q), 2 (facsimile of holograph)

Both the text of this letter and the address are in Cromwell's hand. In it, he urged his friend and political ally in Parliament and on the Committee of Both Kingdoms, Sir Henry Vane the younger,[1] to use his influence in the filling of officer vacancies, whilst also pressing the cause of Richard Norton, colonel of a regiment of horse and governor of Southampton.[2] All the regiments named were under Sir William Waller's command in the South-Eastern Association army.[3] One context of the letter was the need to fill the gaps left by death and casualty after Waller's victory at Cheriton on 29 March (when, for instance, the Colonel Thomson of the letter—George Thomson— had lost his leg).[4] There may have been other issues: on 10 April Thomson's regiment was reported by the Committee of Both Kingdoms to be marching home to London against orders.[5]

Surviving letters between Cromwell and Vane are rare, but the distinctive use of brotherly language and nicknames between them is to be found elsewhere: in a letter to Cromwell of 2 August 1651 Vane addresses Cromwell as Brother Fountaine and describes himself as Brother Heron, whilst Cromwell calls Vane Brother Heron in a letter to Robert Hammond of 6 November 1648.[6]

For Sir Henry Vane the
Younger   theise
My deere brother
I beseech you in this ~~vacancye~~ \fallinge off of Officers/ to improve your uttmost in gettinge good ones in the roome of them, Coll Thomsons Reg[ime]nt of horse is very good, the best of all Sir Willm Wallers, there bee 320.[7] men in itt, very

---

[1] Sir Henry Vane the younger (1613–62). See *ODNB*.
[2] Richard Norton [nicknamed Idle Dick] (1615–91). See *ODNB*.
[3] L. Spring, *The Regiments of Sir William Waller's Southern Association* (2007), pp. 133–6 (George Thomson's Regiment of Horse), pp. 139–43 (Sir William Waller's Regiment of Horse); pp. 101–3 (Richard Norton's Regiment of Horse).
[4] George Thomson (bap. 1607, d. 1691). See *ODNB*.
[5] Spring, *Southern Association Army*, p. 139.
[6] See **1648 11 06a**, where Cromwell's authorship is doubted but finally, on balance, accepted.
[7] The '2' has been heavily written over the original digit, probably 'o'.

THE LETTERS, WRITINGS, AND SPEECHES OF OLIVER CROMWELL

many, very honest, and a most choice major, a precious man.[8] I beseech you to Gett Norton[9] men; You knowe him not so well as I doe, Hee is a most choyce man, fitt for the feild, I pittye Hee should bee buried in a hole, you must gett him men, his Reg[ime]nt is 400. or thereabouts[.] Noe more but my service to my sister,[10] I begg your prayers

Your faythfull Brother Fountaine

Apl. 22.

1644 07 05
Letter from Oliver Cromwell to Valentine Walton

Date: 5 July 1644
Source: Chequers Collection Library, Bookcase 6 Shelf F (holograph)

This is one of Cromwell's most famous letters, long lost to view but now rediscovered in the collection held at the Prime Minister's country retreat at Chequers.[1]

This is a holograph letter and includes Cromwell's only account of the battle of Marston Moor.[2] In fact, it is one of only two surviving letters between early March 1644 and a letter to the Committee of the Isle of Ely on 1 September 1644. In those months he not only played a decisive role in the largest and arguably most decisive battle of the First Civil War,

---

[8] Between March and October 1644 the major was Thomas Roe. The regiment was raised in London, and Roe was very possibly a kinsman of Owen Rowe (1592/3–1661), merchant and regicide. See *ODNB*. He is very possibly the Thomas Rowe, admitted to the Society of the Artillery Garden on 20 August 1635. Roe was apparently reduced to the rank of captain but remained in the regiment under Thomson and then under Edward Popham until at least 16 August 1645. See Spring, *Waller's Army*, p. 136.

[9] For Norton and his close friendship with Cromwell, see Richard Norton [nicknamed Idle Dick] (1615–1691), army officer and politician, in *ODNB*.

[10] Vane's wife was Frances (1623/4–79), daughter of Sir Christopher Wray of Ashby, Lincolnshire.

[1] The history of the survival of this letter is told in Carlyle-Lomas: 1.177n and Abbott, *Writings and Speeches*: 1:288. It was sold at Sotheby's in 1869 and in 1876 it became part of the Morrison Collection and when that was dispersed by auction in 1917 it was acquired by the Chequers Trust and this edition is published with permission of the Chequers Trustees.

[2] There are many accounts of this battle: the clearest are, perhaps, Austin Woolrych, *Battles of the English Civil War* (1961), ch. 3; Peter Newman, *The Battle of Marston Moor* (1981); and P. R. Newman and P. R. Roberts, *Marston Moor 1644: The Battle of the Five Armies* (2003). Also important is I. Roy and J. Macadam, 'Why Did Prince Rupert Fight at Marston Moor?' *Journal of the Society for Army Historical Research*, 86:347 (2008), pp. 236–57.

5 JULY 1644

at Marston Moor outside York in early July, but was also engaged in a series of tough sieges in Yorkshire (Knaresborough, Tickhill, Doncaster) and also in Lincolnshire (around Belvoir and Lincoln in April and early June and Lincoln again for most of August and Sleaford in early September). Marston Moor was a battle of five armies: on the royalist side, the armies of Prince Rupert and the marquis of Newcastle, numbering perhaps 20,000, against the Allied force made up of the Yorkshire army of the Fairfaxes, the Eastern Association Army, and probably making something over half the force of 28,000 men, the Earl of Leven's Scottish army. Cromwell commanded the left wing of the parliamentarian cavalry: two lines of his Eastern Association cavalry backed by a third line of Scottish cavalry; and three regiments commanded by Major General David Leslie.[3] Cromwell's letter conveys something of the intense experience of the battle, in which he received a flesh wound. His wing's breaking of the opposing cavalry and the pressing on the royalist infantry on its flank and rear was essential to the completeness of the victory: indeed, in Cromwell's Biblical-sounding but not Biblical phrase 'made the latter stubble to their swords'.[4]

The letter is perhaps most famous as an astonishingly powerful and moving letter of condolence to Valentine Walton,[5] who was married to Cromwell's sister Margaret. Valentine Walton's second but eldest surviving son, also Valentine, was killed at Marston Moor. It was just three months since Cromwell's second son Oliver, the eldest surviving son, and the one who shared his name, had died while serving as a captain in the garrison at Newport Pagnell.[6] This adds great poignancy to Cromwell's frank, unvarnished account of Valentine's agonising death, a death in a just and victorious cause for he was, as Cromwell puts it, 'a precious young man, fit for God'.

---

[3] Estimates vary as to the size of the wing: Newman and Roberts, *Marston Moor*, suggest 3,000 Eastern Association cavalry, 1,000—probably more lightly mounted—Scottish cavalry in the third line, and some 800 Scottish dragoons on the flanks. Elsewhere Newman suggests Cromwell's wing—English and Scots—amounted to 5,000 (Newman, *Marston Moor*, 73). Woolrych, *Battles*, 71, suggests that Cromwell's first and second lines of Eastern Association horse were not far short of 2,500 strong, with about 800 Scots in their three regiments, 'much under strength'. In short, the numbers and weight of the charge came from the Eastern Association cavalry, but Cromwell's perception of 'some few Scots' downplays the third line.

[4] Newman and Roberts, *Marston Moor*, 124, estimates 'at least 4,000 and probably nearer 6,000' royalists dead or dying by the end of a battle which lasted some ninety minutes. They also write how, 'Cromwell's cavalry, squeezing the rear of the Royalist lines, would have been sword-happy from the beginning, riding down their opponents and slashing at them as they passed' (p. 104).

[5] Valentine Walton (1593/4–1661), parliamentarian army officer and regicide. See *ODNB*. Walton came from a prominent Huntingdonshire gentry family. He had been the ward of Cromwell's grandfather Sir Oliver Cromwell at Hinchingbrook (Huntingdon) and therefore well known to Oliver long before Walton married Margaret, who was just 18 months younger than Oliver, in 1617.

[6] See **1644 03 28**.

THE LETTERS, WRITINGS, AND SPEECHES OF OLIVER CROMWELL

Deere Sir its our own duty to Sympathize
in all mercyes, that wee may praise
the Lord together, in chastisements,
or tryalls, that soe wee may Sorrowe
together. Truly England, and the
Church of God hath had a great[7]
favor from the Lord in this great
victorie given unto us, such as the like,
never was since this warr begunn,
itt had all the evidences of an ab=
solute victorie, obtained by the Lords
blessinge upon the godly partye prin
cipally, wee never charged but wee
routed the enimie, the \[ ]/ winge which
I commanded beinge our owne horse,
savinge a few scotts in our reere,
beat all the Princes[8] horse, God
made them as stubble to our Swords,
wee charged their Regiments of foote
with our horse, routed all wee charged.
the perticulars I cannot relate now
but, I beleive of 20000. the prince
hath not 4000. left. Give glory, all
the glory to God. Sir God hath taken
away your eldest Sonn by a cannon shott,
itt brake his legg, wee were necessitated
to have itt cutt off, wherof Hee died. Sir you know my tryalls this way, but the
Lord supported mee, with this that the Lord tooke him into the happinesse wee
all pant
after, and live for. There is your precious child, full of Glory, to know Sinn

---

[7] There is blotting over this word (and some blotting on the lines above and below.
Speculatively the blotting over 'great' is consistent with drops of water, and even more speculatively (as of course even if it is due to water drops there could be a number of reasons), it is possible that these are the teardrops of Cromwell or Walton over what is so much a letter of condolence.

[8] Rupert, prince and count palatine of the Rhine.

5 JULY 1644

nor Sorrow any more. Hee was a gallant younge man, exceedinge gracious
god give you his comfort, before his death Hee was soe full of comfort, that
to Franke Russell[9] and my selfe Hee could not expresse itt, itt was
soe great above his paine \this hee said to us/ , indeed itt was admirable, a[10] little
after
Hee sayd one thinge lay upon his Spirit, I asked him what that was
was, Hee told mee, that it was, that God had not Suffered him
to bee \noe more/ the executioner of his enemies, Att his fall, his horse beinge
killed with the bullett and as I am enformed 3 horses more,
I am told, Hee bid them open to the right, and left, that
Hee might see the Rouges runn. Truly Hee was exceedingly
beloved in the Armie of all that knew him, but few knew
him, for Hee was a precious younge man, fitt for God, you have
cause to blesse the Lord, Hee is a glorious Sainct in heaven.
wherin you ought exceedingly to rejoyce, lett this drinke up
your sorrowe, ~~because~~ \seinge/ theise are not fayned words to com=
fort you, but the thinge is soe real and undoubted a truth,
you may doe all thinges by the strength of christ, seeke that,
and you shall easily beare your tryall ~~draw~~ \lett/ this publike mercy
to the church of God make you to forgett your private
sorrowe, the Lord bee your strength soe prayes
your truly faythfull and lovinge
Brother
Oliver Cromwell

July 5th
1644

my love to your
Daughter[11] and [ ] my

---

[9] Francis Russell, for whom see the *Online Directory of Parliamentarian Army Officers.*
[10] This is best reading of an erasure. It is possibly a 't' crossed out and 'a' written over, but this
seems doubtful.
[11] Almost certainly Anna Walton (1622–61). See www.geni.com/family-tree/index/
6000000000076296522

Cozen Percevall[12] sister
Disbrowe[13] and all freinds with you[14]

1644 09 01
Letter from Oliver Cromwell to the Committee for the Isle of Ely

Date: 1 September 1644
Source: Museum of London, Tangye MS 659 (holograph)

This is the first letter of Cromwell's to come down to us since his letter to Valentine Walton about the death of Walton's son at what he describes as the great victory at Marston Moor (see **1644 07 05**). Since then Cromwell had been campaigning hard in Yorkshire, Nottinghamshire and Lincolnshire and this letter was written from Lincoln where he was based from 6 August to 2 September 'kicking his heels while Manchester did nothing'.[1] His frustration shows in this letter.

This letter is certainly not in Cromwell's hand and although the signature is similar to his, it is not identical. In all other respects it seems to be a genuine contemporary copy.

It is stern reprimand to the committee for authorising the release of prisoners who had been incarcerated by three of his junior officers. His irritation is very evident.

[verso]
For my noble friends the
Committee for the Isle of
Ely present these

[recto]
Gentlemen
I understand that yow have lately released some person[s]
Committed by Major Ireton[2] & Captaine Husbandes[3] & one

---

[12] Not identified.
[13] Jane Disbrowe (1606–56), sister to Oliver and wife of John Disbrowe, a Cambridgeshire gentleman who served as a captain in Cromwell's own regiment of horse throughout 1644.
[14] There is no address or endorsement. Cromwell remained in North Yorkshire after the battle of Marston Moor, and this letter was written three days after the battle.

---

[1] Gaunt, *Cromwellian Gazetteer*, p. 107.
[2] Henry Ireton (bap. 1611, d. 1651), parliamentarian army officer and regicide. See ODNB.
[3] Azariah Husbands, captain in Francis Russell's regiment, see Spring, *Eastern Association*, 2:99.

1 SEPTEMBER 1644

Committed by Captaine Castell[4] all upon cleere and
necessary groundes as they represented ~~unto~~ me
rendring them as very enemyes as any we have
& asmuch requiring to have them contynued secured
I have given order to Captaine Husbandes to see them
recommitted to the handes of my Marshall Richard White[5]
And I much desire yow (for future) not to entrench
upon me soe much as to release them or any committed
in the like case by my selfe or my deputy and
Comannders in the Garrison untill my selfe or some
superior authority be satisfied in the cause, & doe
give Order in allowance for their enlargemt.
For I professe I wilbe noe Governor nor engage any
other under me to undertake such a charge upon such
weake termes. I am soe sensible of the neede we have
to improove the present opportunity of our being
Mrs[6] in the feild and haveing noe enemy nere the
Isle to spare what charge may be towardes the
makeing of those Fortificacons which may make it more
defensible hereafter if we shall have more ~~d~~ neede
as I shall desire you for that end to ease the Isle
& Tresury from the superfluous charge of twoe
severall Committees for the severall partes of the Isle
And that one Committee setled at March[7] may serve
for the whole Isle. Wherefore I wishe that
one of your number may in your courses attend &
appeare at that Committee to mannage & uphold
it the better for all partes of the Isle Resting upon
your care herein I remayne

---

[4] Thomas Castle—by August 1643 he was captain of a company in a regiment of foot which served under Oliver Cromwell and later under Colonel Francis Russell in their capacity as governors of the Isle of Ely and which probably originated as an auxiliary regiment of the Cambridgeshire militia. See the *Online Directory of Parliamentarian Army Officers*.

[5] Not identified.   [6] Mrs = masters.

[7] March, a fenland town within the Isle of Ely. The distance between March and Ely is about 20 miles.

Your friend to serve yo[u]
Oliver Cromwell

from Lincolne
this 1st. of Sept.
1644

1644 09 05
Letter from Oliver Cromwell to Valentine Walton

Date: 5 or 6 September 1644
Source: BL, RP 522 (holograph)

This letter is dated by Cromwell himself 'Sept. 6 or 5th' so perhaps written late at night. It is a holograph, edited here from a photograph retained by the British Library under the terms of an export licence in 1966 when the original was purchased and went abroad to an undisclosed destination.[1]

The British Library only photographed the letter itself, recto, not verso, though the way the letter is folded the address probably is not verso. The sheet is folded in two. The letter starts on the right-hand page; then continues on the left margin of that page but then flows onto the left-hand page, remaining at right angles to the first part of the letter.

The letter itself is dated from Sleaford in Lincolnshire (an independent report places Cromwell as arriving there on 3 September) and he moved to Peterborough on 6 September, but the name of the recipient is not given on the British Library photograph. For that we have to rely on a 1798 transcription.[2] This letter talks in veiled terms of the escalating rift between Cromwell and Manchester about the urgency of heading west to shore up the parliamentarian position after the earl of Essex's humiliating surrender at Lostwithiel, which led to the loss of most of his infantry and artillery. This was to lead to the full-blown 'Quarrel with Manchester' at the end of the year. As the letter develops, the pent-up anger becomes more and more evident.

Sir wee doe with greife of hart resent
the sadd condition of our Armie in the

---

[1] Before this turned up, the only source was W. Seward, *Anecdotes of distinguished persons, chiefly of the present and two preceding centuries*, 4 vols. (4th ed., 1798), 1:364, which is the version edited in Carlyle-Lomas, 1:181–2. This seems to have been itself a copy of a copy.
[2] See above, n. 1.

5 SEPTEMBER 1644

west,[3] and of Affaires there. That busi=
nesse hath our hartes with itt, and truly
had wee winges wee would flye theither,
Soe soone as ever my Lord,[4] and the \foote/
sett mee loose, there shall bee noe
want in mee, to hasten what I cann
to that service, for indeed all other
considerations are to bee layed aside,
and to give place to itt, as beinge of
farr more importance, I hope the
Kingdom shall see that in the mide{ }[5]
of our necessities, wee shall serve the{?m}[6]
without dispute, wee hope to forge{tt} o{u}r [7]
wants, which are exceedinge great, and
ill cared for, and desier to referr the
many slaunders heaped upon us by false
tongues, to God, whoe will in due tyme
make itt apeare to the world, that wee
studye the Glory of God, the honor, and
libertye of the Parliament, for which wee
unannimously fight, without seekinge our
owne Interests, Indeed wee finde our men never soe cheerfull as when
there is worke to doe, I trust you will alwaies heere soe of them, the
Lord is our strength, and in him all our hope, pray for us, present my
love to my freinds, I begg their prayers, The Lord still blesse you, wee
have some some amongst us much slowinge action, If we could all intend
our owne ends lesse, and our ease too, our businesses in this Armie

---

[3] This is a reference to the battle of 'Lostwithiel' (30 miles west of Plymouth in southern Cornwall), which was in fact a number of engagements with long standoffs, beginning on 21 August. On 31 August, the earl of Essex's cavalry broke through royalist lines and got away to Plymouth. The earl of Essex himself escaped by sea. On 2 September, 6,000 parliamentarian infantry together with the Army's guns and train surrendered. For all this see Richard Holmes, *Civil War Battles in Cornwall, 1642 to 1646* (1989).

[4] Edward Montagu, second earl of Manchester.

[5] The edge of the page is damaged. The fourth letter looks pretty definitely 'e'. Seward (see n. 1) has 'middest' but there does not seem enough room for 'st' in what is left.

[6] Lost to damage. 'Them' in Seward seems preferable to 'then' or 'there'.

[7] The paper is again damaged but Seward's readings seem secure.

THE LETTERS, WRITINGS, AND SPEECHES OF OLIVER CROMWELL

would goe onn wheeles for expedition: Because some of us are eni=
mies to rapine, and other wickednesses, wee are sayd to bee factious,
to seeke to maintaine our opinions \in Religion/ by force, which we detest, and
abhorr, I professe I could never Satisfie my selfe of the justnesse
of this warr but from the Authoritye of the Parliament
to maintaine itt, in itts rights, and in this cause I hope to
approve my selfe an honest man, and single harted, pardon
mee that I am thus troublesom, I write but seldom, ~~then~~ \Itt/
gives me a little ease to poure my minde, in the middest
of callumnies, into the bosom of a freind, Sir noe man
more truly loves you then

Your Brother and servant
Oliver Cromwell

Sept. 6 or 5th.
Sleeford.[8]

<hr/>

1644 10 05

Warrant from Oliver Cromwell to [unspecified persons] about sick soldiers

Date: 5 October 1644
Source: TNA, SP16/539, Part 2, fos 192a (autograph)

In the month since the previous surviving letter from Sleaford, Cromwell had been in London for one week (11–16 September) and had then been sent west to join his troops who had headed there for the campaign that culminated in the (second) battle of Newbury (27 October 1644). On 5 October he was near or at Reading.

This tantalising warrant, in a clerk's hand but with Cromwell's signature, has no address or endorsement except to say that an 'Elizabeth Okey' and unnamed others were paid to look after sick soldiers. It is tempting to think she is related to John Okey, later to command the dragoons in the New Model Army. But he was a Londoner who was serving with the earl of Essex in 1644 and his biographer mentions no 'Elizabeth' in his close family.[1]

<hr/>

[8] Sleaford, a market town in east-central Lincolnshire, due west of Boston.

<hr/>

[1] H. G. Tibbutt, *Colonel John Okey, 1606–1662*, Beds. HRS 35 (1955); also, John Okey (bap. 1606, d. 1662), parliamentarian soldier and regicide. See *ODNB*.

6 OCTOBER 1644

Sir

I would desire you to let these Sick Soldiars have Convenient Quarter in Your towne untill they be Recovered of their Sicknes

Oliver Cromwell

Octob: 5th:

1644

pd. Eliz. Okey & others for

quartering these Souldiers   1 – 12 – o.

1644 10 06

Letter from Oliver Cromwell to Sir Samuel Luke

Date: 6 October 1644

Source: BL, Stowe MS 190, fo. 42v (Letter Book of Sir Samuel Luke, 1644–45) (contemporary copy)

This is a copy in the hand of Luke or of his clerk. Following the great royalist success in forcing the earl of Essex to surrender all his infantry and much of his artillery at Lostwithiel in Cornwall, Charles I and his nephews Rupert and Maurice hastened to exploit the parliamentarian disarray by heading east. To prevent catastrophe, Parliament ordered its three main remaining armies, those of the Southern Association (Waller), Eastern Association (Manchester and Cromwell) and the London militia (Skippon) to intercept them. The result was to be the inconclusive second battle of Newbury on 27 October. As he gathered as many of his forces as he could from East Anglia, Cromwell frantically wrote this letter on to Sir Samuel Luke. governor of Newport Pagnell in Buckinghamshire on the Great North Road.

Noble Sir.

I thanke you for your Letters I have sent them both to the E: of Manchester I mett heere with a commaund to send mee back againe to intend this businesse at Banbury[1] I march that way this evening wee must still desire the continuance of

---

[1] Banbury, a market town 20 miles north of Oxford. The town itself had been seized by troops under Colonel John Fiennes in August 1644, but the castle was still holding out despite parliamentarian artillery pounding the castle walls from the churchyard. Cromwell was sent to reinforce the siege, but in the event the town was relieved by a force sent out from Oxford on the eve of the battle of Newbury, and was to hold out until May 1645.

your assistance in this businesse, I hope Sir that if you heare of the Kings advanceing neere to these parts or to Oxford, wee shall have timely notice from you ; It will behoove us to bee vigilant, because the King horseth his Foote Sir noe man is more yours then Your humble servant.

Oliver Cromwell.

Octob: 6.

Potscr. Sir I expect 2 of my Troopes Capt Horsmans[2] & Capt. Porters[3] to come up to mee If yu heare of them, I pray yu send them up towards Banbury I feare least they should march towards Aylesbury.[4]

1644 10 08

Letter from Oliver Cromwell to Sir Samuel Luke

Date: 8 October 1644

Source: BL, Stowe MS 190, fo. 57r (Letter Book of Sir Samuel Luke, 1644–45) (contemporary copy)

This letter from Cromwell is transcribed into his letter book either by Luke or by his clerk. Cromwell was writing from Syresham (Northamptonshire), a village close to Brackley and 12 miles east of Banbury. He knows he cannot require Luke to leave the troop of horse under his command, but he makes clear his desire for Luke to so oblige him. We do not know what Luke decided.

Sir[1]

I beleeve you are assured I take noe pleasure in keepeing your Troope heere its only for that end to which it was commaunded hither at the first by the Committee of both Kingdomes I was very loath to detayne it, & leave it wholy

---

[2] There were two Horsmans who were captains in the army of the Eastern Association at this time: Edward and Robert. Edward is marginally the more likely to be the one referred to here: he was a captain in Cromwell's own regiment of horse. Both can be found in the *Online Directory of Parliamentarian Army Officers*.

[3] For Captain Samuel Parker who commanded a troop in Cromwell's own troop, see the *Online Directory of Parliamentarian Army Officers*.

[4] Aylesbury, a market town in Buckinghamshire, 23 miles east of Oxford and 37 miles southeast of Banbury.

---

[1] Sir Samuel Luke (bap. 1603, d. 1670).

15 NOVEMBER 1644

to your selfe, either continue or dismisse it only Col: Fiennes[2] sent mee word early this morneing that about a 1000 of the enemyes Horse were gathering together about Evesham[3] & endeavoring to mount as many Muskettees as they could upon which And to draw nearer to the rest of our Horse I have a Randevouz this morneing at Sougrave[4] Sir not haveing more to trouble you I rest

Yor humble servant.

Oliver Cromwell.

Octob: 8th 1644.

Siseham.[5]

I doubt the drawing a way of your Troope may occasion the Aylesbury[6] Troopes to longe to bee goeing alsoe.

1644 II 15

Letter [drafted by Cromwell?] and signed by the earl of Manchester; William Balfour; William Waller; Philip Skippon to the Committee of Both Kingdoms

Date: 15 November 1644
Source: TNA, SP 21/17, pp. 126–7 (see below)

This is a problem letter. It is not in Cromwell's hand and he is not even a signatory. But it is quite possible that he is the draftsman. The four officers whose names are attached are the most senior officers in the combined force made up principally of what was left of the armies of the Eastern Association and the Southern Association.

The case for Cromwell's authorship rests upon a clear statement by his old opponent Lawrence Crawford, who wrote that Cromwell had articulated the views of all the senior officers after the second battle of Newbury that a major reorganisation of the armies and of their funding was necessary (of course they had different views on how this should be done but they could agree to tell the politicians at Westminster that they, the politicians,

---

[2] Almost certainly Colonel John Fiennes, third son of Viscount Saye and Sele. See the *Online Directory of Parliamentarian Army Officers*.
[3] Evesham, a market town in Worcestershire, 40 miles west of Banbury.
[4] Sulgrave, a village in Northamptonshire, five miles north of Brackley.
[5] Syresham (Northamptonshire), a village close to Brackley and 12 miles east of Banbury.
[6] Aylesbury, a major market town in Buckinghamshire and a parliamentarian stronghold.

THE LETTERS, WRITINGS, AND SPEECHES OF OLIVER CROMWELL

did not understand the logistical crisis faced by all commanders). The Council of War 'thought fit that there should bee a letter drawne and sent to the Committee of Both Kingdomes representing the whole condition of the army, which was referred to Leif,-Generall Cromwell which accordingly was done'.[1] Crawford was writing this very soon after the event. Samuel Gardiner carefully considered the evidence and found the content consistent with Cromwell's authorship.[2] There is nothing in the content that would suggest Crawford would want to invent this story. The case against Cromwell being entrusted with this task is the implausibility of Manchester and Balfour being willing to delegate this task to Cromwell at this stage, just ten days before Cromwell's bitter and lethal denunciation of Manchester and the Scottish officers in the House of Commons.[3] The balance of evidence seems just to favour this letter's inclusion in an edition of Cromwell's own words.

[p. 126]

15° Nov: 1644

E of Manchester & the rest. Newberry

15° Novemb 1644

My Lords & Gent: For the Committee of both Kingdomes &c.

According to your Comands Wee shall endeavor: to keepe the forces together and with them to make the best advantage upon the Enemy that tyme and oportunity shall afford Us. Wee shall use our best dilligence also in preventing the releife of Basing house,[4] and in every thing approve our selves faithfull in dischargeing the Trust reposed in Us, And therefore Wee hold it our duty to represent the State of the Army, and also the nature of the service you require. The Army is much weakened both in the horse & foote. The horse are very unable for marchings, or watchings, haveing now for soe long tyme been tried[5] out with hard duty in such

---

[1] John Bruce and David Masson, eds., *The Quarrel between the Earl of Manchester and Oliver Cromwell: an Episode in the English Civil War* (Camden Society, 1875), p. 69.

[2] Gardiner, *GCW*, 2:60 and fnn. 1–3 and p. 61 and fnn. 1–3.

[3] The version printed in *The Quarrel between the Earl of Manchester and Oliver Cromwell* (pp. 55–6) is said to be signed only by Manchester, Waller and Balfour. But the original in The National Archives and used here also includes Philip Skippon as a signatory.

[4] Basing House, the massively fortified and strongly defended home of the Catholic marquis of Winchester in Hampshire. Parliamentarian assaults were driven back in 1643 and in the autumn of 1644 and it finally fell when Cromwell took it by storm on 14 October 1645.

[5] Presumably a copyist's error for 'tired'.

15 NOVEMBER 1644

extreamitie of weather, as hath beene seldome seene, Soe that if much more be required at their hands, you will quickly see your Cavalry ruined, without fighting. The foote are not in better Case, besides the lessening of their numbers through cold and soe[6] duty; Wee finde Sicknesse to encrease soe much upon them, that Wee cannot in duty conceale it from You, nor indeed with that Christian Consideracion which wee owe to them, whose extreame sufferings wee dayly looke upon, not with a little sorrow: The places wee are in not affording fireing, food, or covering for them; Nor is the Condition of the people lesse to be pittied, who both in our horse and foote Quarters are soe exhaust, that they have soe little left for themselves, that wee may justly feare a famine will fall upon them haveing represented these things unto you. Wee are notwithstanding ready to obey what you shall command Us to undertake to prevent the Enemyes releiveing of Basing house Wee finde but two wayes, the one is by guards with the halfe of our horse upon it night & day, which will undoubtedly destroy our body of horse soe weakened as before. The other is by marching our whole Army thither, who must lye from under [p. 127] Covert, there being not one place to shelter them and that soe long untill the house be famished whose provisions wee doubt will last longer then is imagined. How certainely this would breake our Army and cause all the Foote to leave Us, that wee humbly submitt to your Judgmt: If any Inconvenience comes to the State by not keeping such Castles and houses from releife, Wee conceive the Error: lies in the first undertaking such Sieges and the loose prosecution of them; Wee hope nothing of that can bee laid to our Charge. Wee have represented what the waiting upon this place this Season is like to cost you; wherein Wee shall be ready to observe your Comands, if yow please to let Us know them. For the present to that force that is already there wee send this day one of the Cittie Regimts. of Foote, and 3 of the Earle of Manchesters to quarter in Basingstoke.[7] Wee have alsoe appointed all the horse to severall Rendezvous this day that soe wee may quarter them conveniently neere Basing, and be ready with them to prevent releife. But wee desire you to remember what wee said before that wee can lye soe but a very little tyme for want of Provision both for horse and man, If what is here represented give not your Lops. satisfaccion and that you would have anything more done either in relation to that place or the Enemy

---

[6] Presumably a clerical error, missing an 'r' out of 'sore'.
[7] Basingstoke, the substantial market town in Hampshire quite close to Basing House.

upon the signification of your pleasure it shall be obeyed by. E Manchester[8]
W Balfour[9]   William Waller[10]   Ph: Skippon[11]
Newberry
15°: Nov: 1644

1644 II 25a
Speech by Oliver Cromwell to the House of Commons

Date: 25 November 1644
Source: See below, separate short newspaper reports

These are five very short accounts of the lengthy speech that Cromwell delivered on 25 November and that was then written up (and very probably massively changed) and presented to an investigative Committee and delivered sometime over the next few days and that is printed below with a lengthy commentary as **1644 II 25b**.

This was a moment of the highest political drama. The complaints that many in the army had about what they viewed as the many failings of the second earl of Manchester now got the fullest possible airing in Parliament. What had until then been private arguments would be set out in detail to the Commons. On 22 November the Committee for Both Kingdoms asked Waller and Cromwell to report to the Commons on the events at Donnington Castle (which Manchester had failed to take in mid-October) and on the siege of Basing House.[1] The following day the Commons ordered that these reports were to be heard on 25 November. Waller and Cromwell were told that they would be expected to reveal 'their whole Knowledge and Informations of the particular Proceedings of the Armies, since their Conjunction'.[2] Waller spoke first on 25 November, arguing that Manchester had been too cautious during and after the second battle of Newbury

---

[8] The 'E.' here is written over the 'M'. Edward Montagu, second earl of Manchester.
[9] William Balfour: a veteran Scottish cavalry officer, in mercenary service from the 1590s, he had served as a brigade commander under the earl of Essex and Sir William Waller in 1643–4, commanding Waller's cavalry at the second battle of Newbury on 27 October 1644. See the *Online Directory of Parliamentarian Army Officers*.
[10] Sir William Waller (bap. 1598?, d. 1668). See ODNB. In 1643–4 he was major general of the Southern Association (Hampshire, Sussex, Surrey and Kent).
[11] Philip Skippon, appointed Lord Skippon under the Protectorate (d. 1660). See ODNB. He had commanded the London trained bands at the beginning of the war, and he had been with the earl of Essex's infantry until forced to surrender at the battle of Lostwithiel. He commanded the infantry at the second battle of Newbury.

---

[1] TNA, SP 21/8, p. 8.   [2] JHC, 3:703.

25 NOVEMBER 1644A

(27 October).[3] But it was Cromwell's speech following him that made the real impact. Three eyewitness accounts survive of what Cromwell said on 25 November—two by Sir Simonds D'Ewes[4] and one by Laurence Whitaker.[5] A fourth account by the London diarist, Thomas Juxon,[6] is probably the least authoritative, as it cannot have been first-hand. It is however the most vivid. It is possible that it derives from a newspaper account (source [E]) which first appeared on 29 or 30 November. But Juxon was writing up his journal in real time and not in arrears so these might be independent testimonies that the emphasis of Cromwell's speech was rather different from the written version he subsequently handed over to Zouch Tate's committee.

———

[A] BL, Harl. MS 483, fos 117–117v, Diary of Sir Simonds D'Ewes

Consessum parum ante ii. repetii. Oliverum Cromwellum perorantem reperi contra Edwardu Montagurum Mancastriae comitem, quasi in causa esset quod comitiales exercitus nihil effecerant Newberiae[7] et Aldermashae[8] etc. Res subdelegatis ad examinandum concredita etc.

I went back into the House a little before 11 o'clock. I found Oliver Cromwell speaking vehemently against Edward Montagu, earl of Manchester, as though he were on trial because the Armies of Parliament had achieved nothing at Newbury and Aldermaston. The matter was passed to the committee to examine.

[B] BL, Harl. MS 166, fo. 156, Diary of Sir Simonds D'Ewes

Returned parum ante 11. Cromwell perorans cum inegressus sum &c de miscarriage at Newberie & Aldmarst &c.[9] laide all on Earle of Manchester &c accused him alsoe for miscarriages in the North. Waller had before my

---

[3] No version of Waller's words has survived.

[4] For D'Ewes as a parliamentary diarist, see his entry in *HoP Commons, 1640–1660*.

[5] For Whitaker as a parliamentary diarist, see his entry in *HoP Commons, 1640–1660*.

[6] Thomas Juxon (1614–72), parliamentarian activist and diarist. See *ODNB*.

[7] A reference to the second battle of Newbury, fought on 27 October 1644. Newbury is in Berkshire. For more details, see **1644 11 25b**.

[8] Aldermaston, Berkshire, lies about seven miles to the east of Newbury. Its significance in this context is not clear. There had been a minor skirmish there in early September 1644 and, in advance of the second battle of Newbury, the parliamentarian army had approached Newbury from that direction. But here it may simply be a reference to the fact that during that battle Manchester commanded the parliamentarian forces to the east of Newbury close to the road to Aldermaston. See **1644 11 25b**.

[9] Translation: *I returned to the House before 11 o'clock. Cromwell speaking as I entered &c about the miscarriage at Newbury and Aldermanston &c.*

THE LETTERS, WRITINGS, AND SPEECHES OF OLIVER CROMWELL

comming in read out of a paper &c Debate after Cromwell had done what to doe. many spake &c.

[C] BL, Add. MS 31116, fos 175v–176, Diary of Laurence Whitaker

This day Sr Wm Waller & Lieut: Gen: Cromwell, made theire reports of what had passed in the Army since the conjuncon of the forces of the Lo: Genll, & the Ea: of Manchester; And Sr Will Waller & Lieut: Gen: Cromwell, Lay'd the Blame upon the Ea: of Manchester tht he would not Assent, to fight wth the K. when the Parliamts forces were not much Inferior to the K. & the Soldiers very dessierous of fight & tht some of his comanders did dishearten them, & put them On to dessier to goe home & he allsoe related the like Carriage of the Ea: of Manchester in Lincolnsheire when he was required to send some of his forces into the west;[10] And upon a dessier of a Brother of the Earles whoe is a Member of the ho: & said he believed not tht wch was reported of his Brother,[11] to be true the further Examinacon thereof was referred to the Cottee wch was for the Ld Genll's Army.

[D] Doctor Williams's Library, London, MS 24.50, fos 31–31v, printed in Keith Lindley and David Scott, eds., *The Journal of Thomas Juxon 1644–1647* (Camden Society, 5th series, 13, 1999), p. 67

Hee layd the whole blame or ye grtest pte one Ld Manchr.
Hee did Confess his judgmt ws for Independencie, & And soe were most of them under his Comand: & it might bee some wr Annabaptst: but he tould them twas not for that: that hee chose them, but because they wr honest & gallant men: men that wr faithfull in yr dutys, & would fight And where as there ws a Reporte that hee and they hd a designe to bee the Head of a partie and to carie one yr desires by force: He did sollemly Protest: that twas by Comande & fro the Authoritie of the Howse that hee first tooke upp Armes: & twas for the prservatio of them & the Kdome with yr Liberties: wch if it should please God to bless wth success: And that they had once hated the Q in Poynte of discipline: did not doubte but as Gd had given them hartes to be Active for him: soe if they could not submitt: He would give them to bee Passive: But they wr resolved never to take upp Armes for yr Religeon:

---

[10] In September 1644 Manchester had failed to obey the orders that he march from Lincolnshire to assist the earl of Essex in the south-west. See **1644 II 25b**.

[11] i.e. George Montagu, MP for Huntingdon, for whom see the biography in *HoP Commons, 1640–1660*.

[E] *Perfect Occurrences of Parliament*, no. 16 for 22–29 November 1644, pp. 2–3 (N&S, 465.1023; Thomason / E.252[36])

This day the House of Commons spent much time about the businesse of the Armies not fighting at Dunnnington, and Generall Crumwell spake very worthily (as also Sir William Waller) Generall Crumwell in his speech, certified as followeth.
The heads of Generall Crumwell's speech.
Whereas it is reported that the Independents would not fight, that it was a scandall put upon them, and that none can say, but that they every man of them were very desirous to fight, and whereas some fear that the independents would be troublesome when the Presbytery was setled (that he beleeved) that they would live under their lawes quietly, and be obedient either actively or passively: And for those who were charged to be the cause why they did not fight, it being referred to examination, it is not thought fit to name any person of honour untill the businesse be further examined. This afternoon the Committee met about it, and in short space of time, something will be done about it.[12]

Outcome: According to Juxon, Cromwell's speech was delivered with 'soe much cleareness and ingenuitie yt the howses Rested sattisfied yr wth'.[13] He also stated that it was 'Runge' throughout the City. The information presented by Waller and Cromwell was referred by the Commons to its committee on the lord general's army, chaired by Zouch Tate,[14] MP for Northampton.[15]

---

[12] Henry Walker (*fl.* 1638–60), journalist and preacher. See *ODNB*. If Thomas Juxon's account of the speech was not taken from this published version (which it might have been, although it appears to have written in his diary before Walker's newspaper came out on 29 November), then that gives two accounts of the speech, which emphasises Cromwell's religious convictions which are absent from the full version we are about to consider. See source [D].
[13] Doctor Williams's Library, London, MS 24.50, fos. 31–31v (*Journal of Thomas Juxon*, pp. 66, 67).
[14] Zouch Tate (1606–50), politician. See *ODNB*. See also **1644 11 25a** and **1644 12 09a**.
[15] *JHC*, 3:704.

1644 11 25b[?]

'Lieutenant General Cromwell's Narrative Concerning the Earl of Manchester' (not holograph or autograph but with probable Cromwell holograph additions)

Date: [on or after 25] November 1644
Sources: [A] TNA, SP16/503 fos 108r–113r (draft copy). [B] TNA, SP16/503 fos 114r–119v (fair copy)

Cromwell's relationship the Montagus was poor from the time the latter acquired Hinchingbrooke House from Cromwell's uncle and played their part in driving Cromwell out of his home town.[1] Relations may have been better with the second earl, despite Cromwell's clear unhappiness—during the winter of 1642–3—that Manchester had placed under his protection an old foe of Cromwell's in Huntingdon—the Recorder, Robert Bernard (or Barnard)—for which see **1643 01 23** and **1643 04 17**. That said, there is evidence that they worked together to secure the removal of the first major general of the Eastern Association, Lord Willoughby, and Manchester clearly went along with, and quite likely supported, Cromwell's promotion to be lieutenant general of horse in the army Manchester now commanded. But relations seem to have deteriorated from no later than the battle of Marston Moor on 2 July 1644, and perhaps sooner. Quite possibly to balance the appointment of Cromwell as lieutenant general of horse, Manchester had appointed Lawrence Crawford to command his infantry. Crawford was a professional soldier, and a veteran of the Thirty Years War, fighting as a mercenary. More to the point—and this would not have won Cromwell's approval—in 1642 and 1643 he had served in Ireland as part of the marquis of Ormond's royalist army. Above all, he was as vehemently anti-sectarian as Cromwell was vehemently in favour of the promotion of godly men including known sectaries. He and Cromwell had clashed as early as March 1644 (see **1644 03 10**) when Cromwell prevented Crawford from cashiering an alleged Baptist, Lieutenant Colonel Henry Warner. But Manchester blocked Cromwell's attempts to have Crawford himself removed.[2] Scots resentment at the way Cromwell had claimed and been accorded in the press and public opinion primary responsibility for the victory at Marston Moor added to the animus. Meanwhile, the failure of the parliamentarians to gain full advantage of that great victory on 2 July, and indeed the crushing reverse represented by the earl of Essex's defeat and the loss of most of his infantry at Lostwithiel in Cornwall two months later, led to plenty of recrimination.[3] This was compounded by the failures of the joint force

---

[1] John Morrill, *Oliver Cromwell and the English Revolution* (1990), pp. 29–33, 38.

[2] For the clearest account of Cromwell's feud with Crawford, see Holmes, *Eastern Association*, pp. 199–204.

[3] The foundational—and very broad—analysis of the background to the December crisis and to the subsequent Self-Denying Ordinance and New Model Ordinance was presented with

25 NOVEMBER 1644B[?]

headed by the armies of Waller and Manchester that had operated in the area to the west and north of Oxford in the nine weeks from 17 September. Cromwell himself, writing to his friend Valentine Walton on 5 September, mournfully reported: 'wee have some amongst us much slowinge action, If we could all intend our owne ends lesse, and our ease too, our businesses in this Armie would goe onn wheeles for expedition' [see **1644 10 06**]; and two weeks later the Scots minister Robert Baillie, a member of the Westminster Assembly, wrote that 'Manchester's army is more pitifully divided' even than Essex's and Waller's, and he wrote that Manchester, 'a sweet, mild man', allowed Cromwell to walk all over him 'to guide all the army at his pleasure' and to vilify Baillie's fellow Scot, Major General Lawrence Crawford.[4] From that point on, things got steadily worse, as mistrust, antipathy and underlying ideological differences, reinforced by military disappointment, took their toll. At some point, probably before the battle of Newbury, Manchester, finding the dissention getting out of control, 'brought to London two persons of my army that were most concerned in these differences' (Crawford presumably one of them), 'and did represent to the Committee of both kingdomes the danger and prejudice that might thereby arise'. The committee thought it 'unfitt at that time to take them into considera-tion' and 'directed mee to endeavour that they should be composed or at least laide aside till further leasure in the time of our winter quarters. But this hath not satisfied the aimes of some who I heare…doe fixe upon me the character of being a discountancer of honest and godly men.'[5]

This is the background to the attack by Sir William Waller and by Cromwell on the earl of Manchester which began with their return to Parliament on 25 November. It is certain that Cromwell knew that Manchester and the Scots were spreading rumours about *his* failings, but that in turn might be the result of their anticipation of his attacks on them. In other words, both sides seem to have wanted to get their retaliation in first.[6]

---

magisterial sweep and authority in Gardiner, *GCW*, 2:20–41, 76–83. Almost all scholars since Gardiner (whose account first appeared in 1889) have taken Cromwell's charges more or less at face value, but Malcolm Wanklyn has presented a powerful counter-narrative, much more sympathetic to Manchester. Of his various accounts, the most relevant here is 'A General Much Maligned: the Earl of Manchester in the Second Newbury Campaign (July to November 1644)', *History*, 14:2 (2007), pp. 133–56.

[4] Cited in John Bruce and David Masson, eds., *The Quarrel between the Earl of Manchester and Oliver Cromwell* (Camden Society, 1875), pp. lx–lxi.

[5] 'A letter from the Earl of Manchester to the House of Lords' ed. S. R. Gardiner, *Camden Miscellany VIII* (Camden Society, n.s. 36, 1883), p. 1 (the Miscellany contains a number of items, of which this is no. 5, each document with a separate pagination). It is dated as 4 December 1644.

[6] It is also worth adding that, as Bruce and Masson noted, the Commons had been making repeated requests to the Committee of Both Kingdoms over the previous fortnight to send a report on what they knew of recent setbacks, especially the failure to take Donnington Castle (see Bruce and Masson, *Quarrel*, pp. lxvi–lxvii, citing the *JHC* from 13, 14, 19, 22 and 23 November). For more on the blame game and on the initiative of the Committee of Both Kingdoms on 19 November ordering a review of the condition of *all* parliamentary armies, see David Como, *Radical Parliamentarians and the English Civil War* (Oxford, 2018), pp. 279–80, 284–5.

Characteristically Cromwell, coming up from Reading on horseback got back to London three days before Manchester, almost certainly travelling by coach, and by the time Manchester took his seat in the Lords, Cromwell had levelled his charges against Manchester, although precisely what these were is, as we shall see, far from clear. The stage was set for one of the defining moments in Cromwell's life. Manchester launched a cold-angered, haughty counter-attack and the two Houses took sides behind their respective members. We have added an 'outcome' section to this item, looking at what happened after this text was generated. At this point it is enough to say that the major historiographical issues which remain unresolved are as follows:

1. What was Cromwell's purpose in launching this attack—to what extent was it pre-emptive and to what extent was it based on sheer frustration and anger?[7]
2. How much collusion was there amongst the war-party generals and politicians and how far was this Cromwell's own initiative?[8]
3. How far was the text that has come down to us a text that Cromwell himself prepared and how far was it written for him. We will see that he certainly had a hand in revising a draft, but was it his own draft?[9]
4. How far was his purpose to see the removal of the earl of Manchester and how far was he already aware of, and complicit in, the plan that was to emerge on and after 9 December 1644, with the Self-Denying Ordinance and the New Model Ordinance?[10]
5. Insofar as was an advocate for those, how far did he believe that to get rid of incompetent commanders he would need to surrender his own command?

With these questions in mind, let us look at the highly problematic text that emerged from the speech Cromwell delivered in the House of Commons on 25 November.

1644 II 25b has traditionally been dated 25 November 1644 as a version of Cromwell's speech on that day. But was it? The contemporary reports of that speech and the evidence of Manchester's response to what he was told had been said both suggest that Cromwell's line of attack on 25 November and the content of **1644 II 25b** are far apart.

Cromwell returned from the autumn campaign on 23 November 1644 and on that day he and Sir William Waller were 'enjoined' to appear two days later to 'declare unto the House their whole Knowledge and Informations of the particular Proceedings of the Armies, since their Conjunction'. They duly did so and Waller, speaking first, made a detailed complaint about the conduct of the Newbury campaign and the earl of Manchester's failures of leadership. That account has not survived. He was followed by Cromwell and we have five very

---

[7] For evidence of a press campaign building against Cromwell in the previous weeks, see A. N. B. Cotton, 'Cromwell and the Self-Denying Ordinance', *History*, 62:205 (1977), pp. 211–31, mainly at 217–22; Como, *Radical Parliamentarians*, pp. 279 et seq.

[8] John Adamson. 'Oliver Cromwell and the Long Parliament', in Morrill, ed., *Oliver Cromwell and the English Revolution*, pp. 60–4.

[9] See below within this introduction to **1644 II 25b**.

[10] The issues are neatly encapsulated in the arguments presented by Adamson (pp. 63–5) and Woolrych (pp. 102–3) in Morrill, ed., *Cromwell and the English Revolution* (pp. 63–5. 102–3). See below, in the 'outcome' section at the end of this item.

25 NOVEMBER 1644B[?]

short summaries of Cromwell's speech (see **1644 II 25a**). These focus not only Manchester's failings as a general and someone with no stomach for a fight, but on his commitment to the godly cause and on a defence of himself against the charge that he was as opposed to Presbyterianism as he was to prelacy. There is not a whiff of this, nor any reference of any kind to religion in the text that has come down to as **1644 II 25b.**

After Waller and Cromwell had spoken on 25 November, the Commons ordered that Waller's and Cromwell's allegations 'concerning divers Passages and Proceedings of the Armies, be referred to the Examination of the Committee formerly appointed for my Lord General's Army, where Mr. Tate has the Chair:[11] With Power to send for Parties, Witnesses, Papers, Records; and to examine Sir Wm. Waller, Lieutenant General Cromewell, and Sir Arthur Hasilrigge,[12] in this Business, if Occasion shall be; and with Power to send to the Committee of both Kingdoms, for Copies of such Letters as have been written upon Occasion of this Business; and they are to bring in a Report with all convenient Speed: And all the Members of this Committee are enjoined to meet this Afternoon.'

The Committee set to work and took more than twenty witness statements over the next six weeks. Significantly the first of these was on 30 November, by which time they had drawn up a list of witnesses and linked them to specific charges levelled by Cromwell in [A]. That surely means that [A] was in their hands by 30 November and most probably on one of 27, 28 or 29 November. At 5,700 words it could surely not have written up earlier.[13]

That committee was to meet on many days over the next six weeks and to examine many army officers nominated by both Waller and Cromwell (an equal number from each of their armies). It was twice ordered to maintain total secrecy of its proceedings. Waller appears never to have submitted a text of his allegations, but Cromwell certainly did, and that is what we now know as Cromwell's narrative. It was a committee completely dominated by hard-line war-party members although its chair, Zouch Tate, MP for Northampton, was fiercely anti-toleration as well as a believer in a fight-to-the-end strategy.[14] But the committee as a whole was made up of war-party Independents.[15]

---

[11] This Committee, made up entirely of members of the Commons, had been set up on 26 February 1644 to review all the officers in the many depleted regiments of Essex's army and to nominate officers for thirteen reconstituted and expanded regiments (seven of infantry and six of cavalry) and a strengthened train of artillery (*JHC* 3:408). It had reported three times on this matter on 11, 13 and 18 March but had never been wound up, and it continued to advise on officer lists for the various armies, and in a rather desultory fashion to investigate the aftermath of Essex's defeat/surrender at Lostwithiel.

[12] Heselrige was Skippon's second-in-command and commanded his own regiments both of horse and foot and he was with Waller throughout the autumn campaigns of 1644, fighting at Newbury. He sat in the Commons as knight of the shire for Leicestershire: Sir Arthur Hesilrige [Haselrig], second baronet (1601–61), See *ODNB*. See also the *Online Directory of Parliamentarian Army Officers*.

[13] See below, **1644 II 25b** fns 227 and 228.   [14] Zouch Tate (1606–50), politician. See *ODNB*.

[15] Those who are listed as attending meetings of the Committee in December 1644 were William Ashurst, John Blakiston, Sir John Curzon, John Gurdon, Sir Henry Heyman, Thomas Hodges, Cornelius Holland, John Lisle, Edmund Prideaux. Nathaniel Stephens, Zouch Tate and Sir Peter Wentworth.

THE LETTERS, WRITINGS, AND SPEECHES OF OLIVER CROMWELL

How different is the document submitted to the Committee from what we can glean was said in the House of Commons? And, in addition, why are there two, quite different versions of the Narrative in the State Papers in the National Archives? The fact that they are in the State Papers and not in the parliamentary archives must mean that they remained with the committee and were not held by the Commons. One is a rough draft covered in corrections in several hands and was clearly the working copy; the other is a pristine copy whose purpose would seem *not* to be the one used by the committee but prepared for a different purpose. It is shorter and significantly toned down. The rough and much-corrected draft, used here, is more than 5,700 words in length and contains more than 500 corrections, albeit most of them to punctuation. Significantly, many of the corrections were removed again from the final version. The version edited here is the rough draft as amended.[16]

The working text is the product of several hands. The original text was produced by one of Cromwell's regular clerks—for example it is the same clerk who wrote the letter describing the storm and capture of Bristol the following year (see **1645 09 14a**). And that clerk made some of the subsequent emendations. But other corrections are in Cromwell's own hand: those which are clearly his own corrections are indicated in the notes; and, based on the characteristic darkness of his ink, there may well be more where there is not enough calligraphic evidence to be certain. But we can be sure that the important paragraph headings given in the margins as well as some of the corrections, and certainly some of the underlinings in the text, were made by the clerk of Zouch Tate's committee to whom the document was submitted. Certainly they are in the same hand as scribal copies of the statements by made some of the officers who testified to that committee (e.g. those of Lt Col John Lilburne and Captain John Hooper).[17] This would indicate that Tate's committee relied on, and worked through [A], the rough copy, with corrections on the face of the document, and not [B], the fair copy.

The precise purpose of the fair copy [B] is less clear. [B] is shorter than the draft [A], omitting the preamble and with various shorter cuts. But most striking is the change of voice from the first person in [A] to the third person in [B], the result of which is to make it less personal. No words were attributed to Cromwell and so no charges could be brought against him for words said. This change of voice involved more than one hundred changes.

---

[16] Following the conventions of the whole edition, changes to spelling or punctuation with no possible effect on the meaning of the text are not noted. This applies both to changes within version [A], and changes between [A] and [B]. All differences that affect the sense are, of course noted.

[17] TNA, SP16/503 fo.125r/v., 127r/v. These are two of the twenty-six examinations of witnesses (all army officers) who appeared before Zouch Tate's Committee between 30 November 1644 and 6 January 1645. All were broadly supportive of the charges levelled by Cromwell and Waller. Indeed, they are prefaced by a list of the specific allegations contained in **1644 11 25b** together with marginal lists of witnesses willing to testify to each of those charges. So those quietly dropped from [B] are those for whom no witnesses had been identified. This document, together with very full (modernised) transcribed transcripts can be conveniently found in *CSPD: 1644–5*, pp.148–60.

25 NOVEMBER 1644B[?]

This fair copy [B] is in a different hand from any to be found in [A]. To understand its purpose, we need to look at what happened once Manchester heard about Cromwell's criticisms of him.

From the moment that he returned to the House of Lords on 26 November, Manchester counter-attacked and amongst his demands was to be shown the text of Cromwell's attack on him. Claiming privilege, the Commons consistently ignored or rejected his demands but the pressure on them to hand over Cromwell's text was severe. Is it possible that [B], the tidied-up—and markedly softened—text was prepared by those assisting the Zouch Tate Committee as a sanitised version to be given to the earl of Manchester in the event that the committee was ever required by the Commons to hand over a copy of what Cromwell's had submitted to them?

Cromwell clearly 'owned' the content of [A] and less certainly [B] but was he the author of [A]? When the document was given its only previous editing,[18] for a Camden Society volume in 1875, the two editors took opposite sides: the original editor, John Bruce, thought it a multi-authored construction;[19] David Masson, completing the work after Bruce's death and contributing the introduction, disagreed and thought it Cromwell's own words and close to what he actually said.[20] Almost all those discussing the matter since 1875 have taken their lead from Bruce or Masson or have sat on the fence.

Is it possible to cast further light on this? One intriguing suggestion (in one of Lilburne's tracts)[21] is that Cromwell was staying during the early parts of this crisis with the journalist John Dillingham[22] and that during the furore created by Cromwell's narrative, there were meetings in 'Cromwell's owne chamber in Dillinghams house' to discuss what to

[18] Neither [A] nor [B] appears in Carlyle-Lomas. The version in Abbott, *Writings and Speeches*, I:302–11 is copied (text and notes) from Bruce and Masson, *Quarrel*, pp. 78–95. There has hitherto been no discussion of the relationship between the draft copy and the fair copy.

[19] 'This narrative may or may not correspond exactly with the charge of Cromwell in the House. Probably it differs in many particulars. It is quite unlike the usual style of Cromwell. This document is compiled with great care and skill and is remarkable for terseness and perspicuity; and is also notable for the absence of scriptural language and allusions common to most of Cromwell's speeches and letters. It may be the work of several hands. Probably Waller and Hasilrigg had something to do with it. A question might arise as to whether Vane, who was no doubt very active in the "Independent Plot", may not have had a chief hand in the compilation'. Bruce and Masson, *Quarrel*, p. 95.

[20] 'It is doubtless the reduction to writing immediately by Cromwell himself, in consultation with his friends, of those parts of his speech [made in the Commons on 25 November] which the House required to have in that shape for further proceedings', Bruce and Masson, *Quarrel*, p. lxviii.

[21] John Lilburne, *Jonahs Cry out of the Whales Belly* (1647), pp. 8–9 (Wing / L2122).

[22] John Dillingham (*fl.* 1639–49), journalist. See *ODNB*. Until 1644, Dillingham had been close to Manchester, but their relations had become badly strained and Manchester had Dillingham imprisoned for defamation in December 1644 and henceforth he became a New Model loyalist and advocate. Anthony Cotton maintained that he led a campaign to 'bury' Cromwell's radicalism during the crisis of December 1644 and January 1645, A. N. B. Cotton, 'Cromwell and the Self-Denying Ordinance', *History*, 62:205 (1977), pp. 216–22.

THE LETTERS, WRITINGS, AND SPEECHES OF OLIVER CROMWELL

do—meetings at which Cromwell, Lilburne, and army officers and Dillingham were involved. Could this have been where the final version of the narrative had been hammered out? And could Dillingham have used his journalistic skills to produce a document that avoided the neuralgic issues of religion and focused, as Cromwell so rarely did, on purely military matters? Manchester's rebuttal of Cromwell's attacks on him focus precisely on Cromwell's supposed sectarian intolerance and on his disparagement of aristocracy, but there is not a trace of those to be found in [A] let alone [B]. And yet two of the five accounts of Cromwell's speech on 25 November made at the time (three made by his fellow-MPs, one by a well-informed London activist and one by Henry Walker, the most pro-Independent of all the diurnal editors active at this time) offer summaries of what Cromwell said that indicate that he did parade his commitment to religious radicals. Indeed as these two accounts—those of Thomas Juxon and Henry Walker—both seem to indicate that Cromwell was intent on getting his retaliation in first, and certainly Manchester's response on 2 December looks more like a reply to Walker's summary than to [A] or [B].[23] Anticipating this, what was prepared for the committee by Cromwell or in his name may have had a quite different emphasis from what he said in the House itself.

The consequences of whatever Cromwell said in the House and of the paper he delivered to the Committee will be explored in the 'outcome' section after the text and in the introductions to Cromwell's next three reported speeches (**1644 12 09a, b** and **c**).

[fo. 109r]

An accompt of the Effect and Substance of my narrative made to this house, for soe much thereof as concern'd the Earle of Manchester.[24]

Being Commaunded by the house to give an accompt concerning the many opportunityes lost and advantages given to the enemy since the late Conjunction of our Arrmyes[25] (Which Seemed to be by Some miscarriage or neglect in the conduct of the armyes) and, espetially, of our not prosecuteing the victory at Newbery[26] in time to prevent the King's rallying, Of our Suffering him (after he had Recollected and gott to an heade againe) to releive Denington Castle[27]; and

---

[23] See **1644 11 25a** Source [D], the journal of Thomas Juxon; and Source [E], an account in the *Perfect Weekly Account*, a diurnal edited by Henry Walker.

[24] Everything down to fo. 109v, at 'That at our Coming from Yorke…' is omitted from [B].

[25] i.e. the army of the Southern Association under Sir William Waller and of the Eastern Association under the earl of Manchester, with some of the remaining troops of the earl of Essex, who was unwell and *hors de combat* in more senses than one.

[26] The second battle of Newbury, which was fought on 27 October 1644. The best modern account is by Malcolm Wanklyn, *Decisive Battles of the English Civil War* (Barnsley, 2006), pp. 136–58. The first battle of Newbury had been fought on 20 September 1643.

[27] Donnington Castle, a massive fourteenth-century three-storey castle that straddled the intersection of the London to Bath and the Oxford to Portsmouth roads and of great strategic significance. It was held by the royalists from the beginning of the war until 1 April 1646, withstanding sieges in every year of the war.

220

fetch off his Ordnance (with all hee had left there) in the face of our armyes, and to goe off without fighting, Of our quitting of Newberry afterwards, and withdraweing the Seige from Basing,[28] I <u>did in my narrative</u>[29] of the Story, freely declare, that I thought the Earle of Manchester was most in fault, for most of those <u>miscarriages</u>, and the ill Consequences of them; And because I had a greate deale of reason to thinke, that his Lopps miscarriage in those particulers, was neither through Accidents (which could not be helped) nor through his improvidence onely, But <u>through his backwardnes to all Action</u>; and had Some reason to conceive that this backwardnes was not (meerely) from dulnes or indisposednes to ~~fighting~~ \engagement/,[30] but (with all) from Some principle of ⊞[31] unwillingnes in his Lopp to have this warre prosecuted unto a full victory, <u>and a designe or</u> ⊞[32] <u>desire</u> to have it ended by accommodacon (and that) on Some Such termes, to which it might be disadvantagious to bring the King too lowe; To the Ende therefore ~~To the end therefore~~ that (if it were Soe) the State might not be further deceived in theire expectations from theyr Army, I did (in the faithfull discharge of my duty to the parliament and kingdome) freely discover those my apprehensions and what grounds I had for them: And, to that purpose,

I did, not onely in the accompt of the particulers in question (Since the Conjunction of the armyes) but alsoe, in many precedent carriages upon former opportunityes Since our coming from Yorke[33] (whereof I had been a wittnesse) declare his Lopps contin<u>ued backwardnes to all Action, his aversenes to engagement</u>, or what tended thereto, his neglecting of opportunityes and declineing to take or pursue advantages upon the enemy, And this, (in many particulers) contrary <u>to advice given him, contrary to commaunds received</u>. And when there had been noe impediment or other imployment for his army.

2 I did likewise declare how his Lop had (both in words and actions) expre̦ssed <u>much contempt and Scorne of Commaunds from the parliament,</u> or the

---

[28] Basing House, close to Basingstoke, Hampshire and home of the Catholic marquis of Winchester. It consisted of an 'old house'—medieval buildings clustered round a Norman motte and bailey—and a fortified 'new house' in five storeys with strong towers and turrets. Semi-continuously besieged from early in the war, it was finally taken and destroyed by Cromwell in a brutal assault on 14 October 1645.

[29] The ink used in the underlinings is the same as that used by the clerk of the army committee.

[30] The word 'fighting' is heavily crossed out and 'engagement' written in what is almost certainly Cromwell's own hand.

[31] Almost illegible. Bruce and Masson, *Quarrel*, p. 79 thought 'great' but 'some' seems more likely.

[32] This may be ('a'?) crossed out, or just a blot. (Bruce, p. 79, thinks 'a').

[33] i.e. following the victory of Marston Moor, ten miles due west of York, on 2 July 1644.

221

THE LETTERS, WRITINGS, AND SPEECHES OF OLIVER CROMWELL

Committee of both Kingdomes, which have required his advanceing with or employment of his army, espetially those for advanceing westwards, and his desires and endeavours to have his Army drawne back into his Assotiation,[34] to lye idle there, while the businesse of the Kingdome hath needed it, and the aforesaid Commaunds, required it, to be employed elsewhere,

3 I did alsoe declare in diverse circumstances of the said omissions and miscarriages what Shuffleing pretences and Evasions his Lop had used Sometimes to delay and put off (till twas too late) Sometimes, to deny and avoyde things propounded to him, tending to Action or engagement, when th'advantage and Security of the Same hath been Clearely urged upon him; In which he had Seemed, Studiously, to decline the gayneing of such advantages upon the enemy, and sometimes to designe the draweing of the army off from the advantages it hath had, into a posture of lesse advantage

4 I did alsoe declare Some Such speaches and expressions uttered by his Lop concurrent with the Said Series of his Actions and carryages, whereby hee hath declared his dislike to the present warre, or the prosecution thereof, and his unwillingesse to have it prosecuted unto a victory, or ended by the Sword and desire to make up the Same with Some Such a peace as himself best fancyed.

~~Of these heads, The particulers of the first and third, which I \either/ toucht upon, or related more at large in my narrative, are breifly these.~~ [fo. 109v]

Of these heads the particulers of the first and third, which I either toucht upon, or related more at large in my narrative, are breifely these.

⟨July⟩[35]

⟨The neglect of blocking up of Newarke⟩[36]

---

[34] i.e. the Eastern Association of Cambridgeshire, Essex, Hertfordshire, Huntingdonshire, Lincolnshire, Norfolk and Suffolk.

[35] The marginalia alongside most of the following paragraphs are normally but not always at the head of the paragraph to which they belong, but occasionally they are placed closer to a particular passage (both physically and in terms of content). The marginalia are in a different hand from the text: it is almost certainly the same hand as took down the testimonies of John Lilburne and Captain John Hooper against Manchester.

[36] Newark: small market town but of great significance since it was the major crossing point of the river Trent and on the Great North Road. It was held for the King from the beginning of the war until May 1646 and it tied down a besieging Scots army for many months. Its medieval defences were in ruins and so it was protected by the most extensive earthworks and sconces built anywhere in Britain in the early modern period.

25 NOVEMBER 1644B[?]

[37]That at our Coming from Yorke (which was about the middle of July last) his Lop haveing many advantages represented to him, and time enough, to have taken or blockt up Newarke before he was comaunded into the South, and haveing then noe other employment or impediment to hinder his Army from th'attempt thereof, did lye idle, first, with his whole army, Eight or Ten dayes about Doncaster,[38] and afterwards, with the greatest part of it, about Lincolne,[39] for a month or more, without attempting any thing either to reduce Newarke, or Secure the country against it,

⟨Tickhill Castle⟩[40]

[41]That lyeing at Doncaster, and Tickhill Castle being hard by, and Welbeck house,[42] with Sheffeild[43] and Bolsover Castle[44] not farre off, he was very unwilling to the Summoning of Tickhill Castle, and exprest much anger and threates against him, that (being Sent to Quarter in the Towne) did Summon it, though upon the bare Summons it was Surrendred, And whereas, while he lay thereabouts, he might, in that time, have taken in those other garrisons alsoe, Soe as to have had his army intire to march with him in good time against Newarke Hee would not be perswaded to Send any party against any of them, till he marcht from Doncaster, and then, Sending a party against Sheffeild and afterwards (with much difficulty), giveing way for the Same party in their returne to attempt Bolsover, and Wingfeild Mannor,[45] Hee made that Serve for an excuse for that greater part of his army which went with him into Lincolnshyre to lye idle there,

[37] [B] begins abruptly at this point and it omits all the marginal summaries.

[38] Doncaster: a market town in South Yorkshire besieged by Cromwell and the army of the Eastern Association from c.25 July to 5 August 1644, so a little less than a month.

[39] Lincoln: the county town of Lincolnshire and therefore back within the Association, where Cromwell was based from 6 August to 2 September 1644.

[40] Tickhill Castle, on the Yorkshire/Nottinghamshire border, held for the King from the outset of the war, but which surrendered to Lt Col John Lilburne on 26 July 1644.

[41] The whole of this paragraph is omitted from [B].

[42] Welbeck Abbey, Nottinghamshire, was one of the two major homes of the royalist earl of Newcastle. It was a heavily fortified Tudor/Jacobean mansion that was besieged and taken by the earl of Manchester in August 1644 but subsequently retaken by royalist troops from Newark.

[43] Sheffield, South Yorkshire. It changed hands several times during the war. In July 1644 the town itself was overrun by Major Lawrence Crawford's infantry but the medieval castle held out for two more weeks after a botched attempt to mine the walls.

[44] Bolsover Castle in north-east Derbyshire: the earl of Newcastle's cultural castle built in the previous thirty years. It was captured by Major General Crawford on 12 August 1644.

[45] Wingfield Manor or Wingfield House was a sprawling late medieval house first built by Ralph Lord Cromwell, Treasurer of England, in the early fifteenth century and then developed by the Catholic earls of Shrewsbury in the sixteenth century. It was in Derbyshire and the Pennines, and the nearest town was Alfreton.

THE LETTERS, WRITINGS, AND SPEECHES OF OLIVER CROMWELL

till the returne of the other, without attempting of any thing against Newarke, Belvoyr,[46] Wereton,[47] or Shelford,[48]

⟨Newarke Belvoyr & othr places neglected⟩[49]

That, in his way to Lincolne, hee was very backward and hardly perswaded to march reare[50] Welbeck, to induce the Surrender of that house.

⟨Proposicons for Newarke⟩

[51]That, at Lincolne, his Lop being much prest by some of his officers to certaine proposicons for the takeing or blocking up of Newarke; although the forces he had there with him all the while, were Sufficient for the Service propounded, yet his Lop first put off the Consideration thereof till the returne of that party from Sheffeild, pretending that then hee would advise upon it.

⟨Newarke still neglected⟩

But when that party was returned he further deferred the consideration of it, till, at last, (through importunity) a Councell being cald, his Lop labouring with various objections to avoyde the Service, made the time lost by those delayes a mayne argumt against it, And when (notwithstanding all)[52] the Councell did conclude and his Lop thereupon Seemed to agree to drawe downe to quarter about Newarke, and doe what we could while we had time,[53] yet his Lop, after this, put it off againe with other pretences and at last did noething at all. to agree to drawe downe to quarter about Newarke, yet his Lopp. after this put it off againe with other pretences and at last did nothing at all

⟨Lres to the E. to send some horse to Chesshire⟩[54]

---

[46] The clerk originally wrote 'Bolsover' and then changed it 'Belvoir'. Belvoir Castle is in Leicestershire and is eight miles due west of Grantham. It was the ancestral home of the Manners, earls of Rutland, and the eighth earl was a prominent parliamentarian. However, the castle was captured by the royalists in the summer of 1643 and remained in their hands until January 1646.

[47] Wereton, a fortified house in North Staffordshire.

[48] Shelford House, just south of Newark, Nottinghamshire, was held for the King from the beginning of the war until November 1645, protected by half-moon earthworks thrown up to protect the main approaches.

[49] This and most (not all) of the marginal summaries may be in Cromwell's hand.

[50] This is surely a scribal error for 'neare'.   [51] [B] resumes here (see n. 40).

[52] [B] omits 'notwithstanding all'.

[53] [B] omits 'and doe what we could while we had time'.

[54] 'Cheshire', or more particularly Chester, where Sir William Brereton was engaged in a long siege of a city which was seen as a bridgehead for the long-anticipated invasion by Irish Catholic troops. See Bruce and Masson, *Quarrel*, pp. 9–12.

25 NOVEMBER 1644B[?]

That dureing the Suspense of those propositions His Lop. haveing letters from the Comittee (soone after his coming to Lincolne) to march into Cheshire, was very angry and much displeased thereat, Sent up reasons against it,[55] pretending a necessity of doeing something against Newarke to Secure those parts before he could march Soe farre thence, and in the answer thereto,[56] being left to follow the Service of those parts with his army, and required only to send some horse into Cheshire, Hee was utterly against that alsoe and (notwithstanding many letters out of Cheshire pressing him thereto, and Signifying the great need and danger of those parts, yet) he would not nor ever offred to Send any till after that resolucon taken against Newarke as before; and then (though, by later letters thence, he was advertised, that their danger was past, and their need lesse then before, yet) he pretended that he must needs send horse thither and thereupon broke of [fo. 110r] the resolucon against Newarke, yet (that being soe putt off) there went none. That he caused his army (while it lay about Lincolne) to quarter up on our[57] freinds, in the more Secured parts of the Country, leaveing the other partes free ~~from~~ \for/[58] the Enemy to Range in, rather then he would allow a Sufficient part thereof to drawe downe towards Newarke, to Quarter upon the enemy and to Straiten and Keep them in.

⟨Neglecting of Belvoyr Wereton, & Shelford:⟩[59]
That though his Lop., while he thus lay idle about Lincolne (to avoyde the Consideracons against Newarke) did, Sometimes, pretend he would attempt the lesser garrisones about it (Belvoyre, Wereton, and Shelford) and was much desired thereto, in case he would not meddle against Newarke, Yet haveing put of the one, he did nothing against the other, not soe much, as to Secure the Country against any of them That by the Said neglects thereof, while he had time, Hee was occasioned for secureing of the Country (whcn he was cal'd Southward) to leave much the more force behinde, out of his feild army, besides the forces of the Country, which, otherwise \by themselves/ might have Served to Secure it, and the Country Soe cleared (as it might have been in that time) might have rayesed and maintayned a greate Accession \of Force/[60] to our[61] feild armyes All which

---

[55] See Bruce and Masson, *Quarrel*, p. 14. See also, pp. 18–20.
[56] The 't' at the start of the word is added later.
[57] [B] replaces 'our' by 'the Parliament's'.
[58] Written over struck-out word, possibly in Cromwell's hand.
[59] This marginal note is not in Cromwell's hand but that of the committee clerk.
[60] This addition appears to be in the hand of the committee clerk.
[61] [B] replaces 'our' by 'the'.

THE LETTERS, WRITINGS, AND SPEECHES OF OLIVER CROMWELL

(with much more, of thadvantages of that Service, and disadvantage by the neglect) was timely and often foretold and urged to his Lop by his officers while he lay idle as before, But his Lop, from the time he came from York (which was about July the fifteenth) till his coming from Lincolne (which was about September the Third) Did not vouchsafe to call his Councell of warre, to advise on any action or employmt for his army, Saveing that one Councell, before menconed, upon the proposicons against Newarke, when, indeed,[62] the best opportunity and advantages for that Service, were lost, by the former delayes.

⟨July 15⟩

⟨The E. came from Y. about July the 3ᵈ from Linc: towards the west[63]

7b: 3ᵈ ⟩

⟨Unwillingnes to march Westwrd:⟩[64]

That though, when (before any reall danger in the South appeared) these things were propounded for the cleareing and Secureing of his Assotiation, and that, expressly, to th'end his army might be the more free to leave those parts for the Southerne Service, if there should be need \his Ldpp:/, then (to avoyde these Services) his Lp would, sometimes, pretend the keeping of his army free and ready to advance into the west if he should be required, yet when he Saw a reall danger and need of him in the west, being cald up, and commaunded thitherwards,[65] Hee was then much displeased thereat and[66] averse thereunto, pretending that he must provide for his the Security of his Assotiation, That that was his propper busines, and, accordingly, his Lop hath shewed himselfe both extream backward to be drawne from his Assotiation towards the west,[67] and (being with much reluctance drawne but a little that way) he was averse to all good Service thereabouts, and desireing and endeavouring to be drawne back to his Assotiation agayne, As may appeare by what followes.

⟨13ᵗʰ 7ber the Army comes to St Albans⟩[68]

The first letters for his advance from Lincolne, comeing about the end of August, hee made it Septemb 13ᵗʰ. ere his army got to St Albans lyeing, by the way, about

---

[62] [B] omits ', indeed,'.

[63] Another marginal summary added by the clerk to the committee.

[64] Marginal comment: almost certainly in the hand of the committee's clerk—actually quite a long way down the paragraph, beside the line with contemporary underlining, 'displeased thereat and'.

[65] The Committee of Both Kingdoms' orders switched from ordering the earl of Manchester to Chester to ordering him to the west around 1 September (Bruce and Masson, *Quarrel*, p. 22).

[66] Contemporary underlining (and beside which the marginal note above has been put).

[67] It must be said this is not borne out by Manchester's letters to the Committee of Both Kingdoms at this time—see Bruce and Masson, *Quarrel*, pp. 24–8.

[68] St Albans, Hertfordshire. His initial commitment was to take a stand at Abingdon.

25 NOVEMBER 1644B[?]

Peterborrough[69] and Huntingdon fower nights \or/ more; though he was in that time quickened by fresh letters and desired to hasten by his cheife officers, whom he threatened to hang for such advice.

⟨The Armyes stay att St A: 8 or 9 dayes⟩
At St Albans he caused the army to lye Still 8 or 9 dayes and then, marching slowly to Redding,[70] he Stay'd there till about October 16th And then advanced not westwards \directly/ to Sir Willm Waller, but Southwards to Basingstoke,[71] notwithstanding a desire from this house, an ordinance [fo. 110v] ⟨The E. advanceth to Basing, wn commanded to march Westw: & desired by Sir W: W: lres⟩ of both houses, and many letters from the Comittee of both Kingdomes, all requireing his speedy advance westward to Sir Willm Waller, and Sir William Wallers earnest desires in frequent letters to that purpose, There being, this while, nothing justly to hinder, but that his army might have advanced directly to Sir William Waller, and the Ld Generalls,[72] & the Citty foote might soe have marched Securely after them to have had the Conjunction about Salisbury.[73]
4. This might have been Securely \done by/[74] ⧉ the Earle of Manchesters foot, with his owne, and Sir William Wallers Draggoones, being then above 6000nd. (without the Lord Generalls, and the Citty Regimts) and the Kings not soe many, And their horse, with the Lord Generalls, much Superior to the Kings; ⊢⊣ And if his Lop had advanced \thither/ accordingly, The King could not (in probability) have passed Salisbury River[75], or the plaines, for this winter
⟨Advantages if the E. had marched Westw:⟩

---

[69] The cathedral city of Peterborough was where the road from Lincoln joined the Great North Road which he would follow for 60 miles via Huntingdon before turning left, probably at Hatfield, for the seven-mile march to St Albans.

[70] Reading, Berkshire. Cromwell rode on from St Albans to London, arriving on 11 September and only left Westminster six days later. He was then based not at Reading but at Banbury until early October. His time in London is unexplained but may be important. The only reference in the parliamentary records to his presence in the House over that week is this entry on 13 September: 'Mr. Speaker, by Command of the House, gave Thanks to Lieutenant General Cromwell, for his Fidelity in the Cause in hand; and in particular for the faithful Service performed by him in the late Battle near York, where God made him a special Instrument in obtaining that great Victory over Prince Rupert's and the Marquis of Newcastle's Armies there.' (*JHC*, 3:626–7).

[71] Basingstoke, Hampshire, within Waller's Southern Association.

[72] i.e. the troops of the Lord General, the third earl of Essex.

[73] Salisbury, a cathedral city in Wiltshire. It had no defensive walls but had a small royalist force defending the cathedral close.

[74] [B] replaces 'securely done by' with 'secured by'.

[75] [B] omits 'river'. Since four rivers—Nadder, Ebble, Wylye and Bourne—have their confluence at Shrewsbury, this is not one of his more helpful descriptions.

THE LETTERS, WRITINGS, AND SPEECHES OF OLIVER CROMWELL

And ~~Soe~~ \soe/ the Seiges of Denington, Basing, and Banbury[76] Castles, had been Secured, and those places ours ere now[77], and the King by this time, not had a foot on this Side Salisbury, (except Oxford \Winchester Castle/[78] Wallingford)[79] and those, distressed by our quarters.

⟨The E. resolution to goe to Odiam[80] but diswaded⟩

That, by neglect hereof, Sir William Waller being forced to give back to Andover[81] and from thence to his Lop. and the King coming on, His Lop, being then at Basing Stoke, the Citty Regiments then with him, & the Lord Generalls within Seaven miles, and the King not \come/ much nearer then Andover, His Lop drew out his army, in all haste, to retreate to Odiam \(leaving Basing and the beseigers exposed to the Enemy)/ had not Sir William Waller, and Sir Arthur Haslerig,[82] coming in the nicke, diswaded him from the dishonor of it

⟨The slownes of the march to New: & inconveniences attending it⟩

That, after this Conjunction, we[83] being at Basing neare [12000] \12000/[84] foote and about 8000 horse and dragoones, and the King (with not above 10000 horse and foote) marching by Kingscleare[85] to Newberry,[86] on Tuseday October

---

[76] Banbury had been held for the King since the beginning of the war. The town fell to the parliamentarians under John Fiennes in August 1644 but the castle held out until relieved by the earl of Northampton in late October 1646. Town and castle then remained in royalist hands until May 1646.

[77] [B] replaces 'ours ere now' by 'the Parliament's'.

[78] Winchester, the cathedral city in Hampshire, changed hands several times early in the war, but by this time was held for the King and was to remain until Cromwell bombarded it into submission in October 1645. Winchester Castle was owned by Sir William Waller himself.

[79] Wallingford on the Thames, about 15 miles south of Oxford and guarding the southern approaches to the King's headquarters. It only surrendered on 27 June 1646.

[80] Odiham, Hampshire, a small town with a medieval keep, mid-way between Basingstoke and Farnham, a parliamentarian stronghold throughout the Civil War and the scene of a fierce skirmish on the night of 31 May/1 June 1644, when royalist troops from Basing House were repelled by Colonel Richard Norton's garrison troops.

[81] Andover, Hampshire, on a main route from London to the south-west. Waller's retreat was the result of his 3,000 horse being surprised by the main body of Goring's royalist western army.

[82] See n. 10.   [83] [B] replaces 'we' with 'the forces'.

[84] Inserted in a different hand and ink; possibly 11000, which is the preferred reading of Bruce and Masson, *Quarrel*, p. 85. It is blotted, and the insertion above is to clarify, but quite possibly—more plausibly—that it was another digit: but it could be a 2, 3 or 5. Masson read it as 11000, but perhaps the most likely reading of the pen-strokes is 12000. However, [B] clearly reads it as '11000'.

[85] Kingsclere, Hampshire, a village midway between Basingstoke and Newbury.

[86] Newbury, Berkshire, and the site of major battles on 20 September 1643 and 27 October 1644.

25 NOVEMBER 1644B[?]

the 21th, It being agreed (as we[87] thought) to march towards him, or to interpose betwixt him and Redding, about Alder-Marston Heath,[88] And our horse marching before to the Heath, Our foot Struck downe to Swallowfeild,[89] and thence, next day, to Redding, as if wee[90] had declined to fight, And thus makeing fower dayes march from Basing Stoke to Newberry (which might have been little more then one th'other way) wee[91] gave the King opportunity to have got cleare to Oxford (if Hee[92] would) without, fighting, and (not [n]ng[93] \stayinge there/)[94] he had \thereby/ time to fortify himselfe against our approaches to Newberry, and by our coming that way wee gave him th'advantage of Denington River[95] interposed betwixt him and us[96], the passes whereof, he soe comanded, by the Castle[97] & Dolmans house,[98] as put us[99] to the hazard of divideing, and the difficulty of marching about by Boxford[100] to come upon them \him/ by Speene,[101] which tooke two dayes more; whereas, by a direct march from Basing, on betwixt us[102] and Newberry but the Towne open & naked to us,[103] and neither the Castle nor the horse to annoy us[104] (as they did) in our[105] falling on. And our[106] horse, being thus, for \these/[107] six dayes and two before, kept together out of quarter wayteing for that Service (which \th'other way/ might have been dispatch't in two

---

  [87] [B] replaces 'we had it' by 'twas had'.

  [88] Aldermaston Heath. Aldermaston was a village nine miles east of Newbury.

  [89] Swallowfield, a village in Berkshire close to the Hampshire border. It was five miles south of Reading and 23 miles east of Newbury.

  [90] [B] replaces 'wee' by 'they'.

  [91] [B] has 'we gave the King \had/ opportunity', revealing a momentary inadvertence by the scribe.

  [92] This has been changed from 'we', possibly later.

  [93] Heavily crossed through and no longer legible.

  [94] This insertion is very probably in Cromwell's own hand.

  [95] Denington River is properly the river Lambourn, a tributary of the Kennet which is itself a tributary of the Thames. At the second battle of Newbury, the centre of the royalist position was at the confluence of the Lambourn and the Kennet.

  [96] [B] replaces 'us' with 'the Parliament's Army'.

  [97] i.e. Donnington Castle, just outside Newbury.

  [98] Dolman's House: otherwise known as Shaw's House, this was an Elizabethan prodigy house on the northern side of Newbury and Charles I's quarters during the battle of Newbury.

  [99] [B] replaces 'us' by 'the Army'.

  [100] Boxford, Berkshire, a village on the east bank of the Lambourn, about four miles (6.4 km) north-west of Newbury

  [101] Speen, Berkshire, a village two miles north-west of Newbury.   [102] [B] 'the army'

  [103] [B] 'us' to 'them', a strange switch.

  [104] [B] 'us' to 'them'—pronouns in disarray hereabouts in [B].

  [105] [B] replaces 'our' by 'their'.   [106] [B] replaces 'our' by 'the'.

  [107] [B] omits 'these'.

THE LETTERS, WRITINGS, AND SPEECHES OF OLIVER CROMWELL

\dayes)/) were both lessen'd & disabled for the Service when they came to it, and from pursueing the victory, when we[108] had it.

[fo. 111r]

⟨The E keepes not the agreemt to fall on att Shawe wn the othr forces wr engaged att Speene⟩

That, on Saturday \Oct: 26/ when we[109] came up to Redhill[110] feild within shot of Shawe, and found the passes of the River soe possest against us[111], It was agreed, that the Lord Generalls and the Citty foote, with the greatest parte of the horse should march about, by Boxford, and attempt to breake in upon the enemy on that Side by Speene, and that his Lop, with his own foote & about 1500 horse, should stay behinde on Shawe Side and fall on there at the same instant that he should perceive the other part to fall on at Speene (which was clearely in his viewe) yet that other part falling on upon Spene side about two a Clock next day (though he had notice of our engagement by the first fireing of Cannon on both parts, and saw the enemy retreateing from hedge to hedge in disorder, and was much importuned to fall on by diverse about him, and his men likewise all the while within shot of Shawe) yet his Lop would not Suffer the men to fall on, but commanded the Contrary, till allmost halfe an houre after Sunsett, about which time we, on the other side (haveing gayned most of the hedges towards Newberry feild) \did cease and drawe our men[112] together, to avoyd confusion in the darke/[113] by that scattred way of fighting; And his Lop going on soe late, his men, presently fell fowle one upon another and were put to assault Dolmans house on that onely side where it was inaccessible

⟨The E men fall fowle one on the othr in the darke: loose 2 peeces⟩

(whereas twas open on the other) by which meanes he lost two peices of Ordnance and many gallant men; whereas, had he falne on by day light and according to agreement, he might, on the open side, have taken that house ~~which~~ \with/ the men and ordnance in it[114] and (if soe) we[115] had betwixt our two bodyes in probability ruined the enemy, who had then had noe free passe over that River \to gett away/ nor ground to stand on, betwixt it and Newberry, not comaunded by us.[116]

---

[108] [B] replaces 'we' by 'the Army'.   [109] [B] replaces 'we' by 'the Army'.
[110] Redhill/ Redhill Field: not identified.   [111] [B] replaces 'us' with 'them'.
[112] [B] replaces 'our men' with 'the Army'.
[113] This insertion is almost certainly in Cromwell's own hand.   [114] [B] omits 'in it'.
[115] [B] replaces 'we' by 'the Army'.   [116] [B] replaces 'us' by 'the Army of the Parliament'.

25 NOVEMBER 1644B[?]

⟨The E[117] Suffrs those {in} Dolmans house {g}oe away⟩ That the enemy flying away in the night, his Lops body lying close by Dolmans house on that side of the River to which they fled, Suffred them to passe over the river and goe by \him/ without prosecution, yea Suffred those in Dolmans house, which was on the same side the River soe neare him, to goe cleare away with their owne, and his advance,[118] The next morneing, being munday Octo. 28th, All the horse on Speen ~~hill~~ Side marching after the enemy, His Lop with all the foot Stay'd at Newberry, And, the horse coming to Blewberry[119] late that night, the enemy being got cleare over the River at Wallingford,[120] many houres before, and we[121] haveing noe passe to follow them nearer then ~~Wallingford~~ \Abbinton/,[122] and our[123] horse being tyred out with Eight or nyne dayes continued hard duty without ☐ \any/ quarters, (as before), It was thought fit, to let them goe to quarters that night, but something close together; And, upon consultacon, It was ~~thought~~ \judged/ both hazardous and uselesse to pursue further with the horse alone and intangle them amongst rivers, and woodlands, without foote; Whereupon Sir William Waller Sir Arthur Haslerig and myselfe[124] (meeting by the way, a letter from the Earle of Manchester to desire our returne to Newberry) did goe back thither, to get some foot, to enable the horse for further pursuite; There we[125] prest earnestly
⟨Te E. refuseth to send foote to pursue the enimy⟩
first to have the whole army march speedily into the quarters beyond Oxford (about Wittney,[126] Burford,[127] and Woodstock)[128] where the enemy began to rally, and, that being denyed, To have 2 or 3000nd. foot sent with the horse; But neither would be granted, [fo. 111v] his Lop expresssing extreame unwillingnesse \thereto/, makeing many excuses and delayes, speakeing for his <u>returne into his assotiation and much for peace</u>; neither would he be perswaded to stirre, till the Satturday following \ Novemb: 2:/ and then marching but to Harwell (Eleaven miles towards Abbington)[129]

---

[117] i.e. the earl of Manchester.   [118] [B] replaces 'advance' by 'ordinance'.
[119] Blewbury is a village at the foot of the Berkshire section of the North Wessex Downs about four miles south of Didcot, 16 miles north of Newbury.
[120] i.e. the river Thames.   [121] [B] replaces 'we' by 'the ~~Army~~ \horse/'.
[122] Abingdon, a parliamentary borough, was in Berkshire. It is 18 miles north of Newbury on the road to Oxford, nine miles to the north.
[123] [B] replaces 'our' by 'the'.   [124] [B] replaces 'myself' by 'Leuitenant Cromwell'.
[125] [B] omits 'we prest'.
[126] Witney, Oxfordshire, a market town on the river Windrush, 12 miles west of Oxford.
[127] Burford, Oxfordshire, a small market town on the river Windrush, 18 miles west of Oxford.
[128] Woodstock, Oxfordshire, a good-sized market town eight miles north-west of Oxford.
[129] Harwell, Oxfordshire, a village 13 miles south of Oxford, close to Abingdon and the road from Newbury.

THE LETTERS, WRITINGS, AND SPEECHES OF OLIVER CROMWELL

in two dayes (which at his returne hee disptach't in one) he Stop't there, and would advance noe further at all; some excuses being found, but, especially, unpassablenesse of the wayes to Abbington and beyond (though they were indeed good enough and proved both before and since to be passable for the enemy though not for us,[130] And at this time, ere we[131] went away, his Lop allowed them passable to Abbington for the heavy carriages of his victualls all which he sent thither,) And the Lord ⟨Ld Warestone & Mr Crewe⟩ Warreston[132] and Mr Crewe[133] goeing from Harwell to London possest with that and other Suggestions against advanceing[134] and for our draweing back His Lop engaged himselfe, by promise to them, not to stirre thence, till he received from them, the directions of both Kingdomes; and made that \promise/ serve while hee stayed at Harwell, to Stop their mouthes that moved for advanceing further

⟨Advantages of Marching forward towards Oxon: et contra⟩

And whereas (as it was timely represented to his Lop) our[135] timely marching into those quarters about Oxford and soe forward would have forced the enemy westward, prevented his recollecting, occasioned his broken forces (in frequent and hasty mocons) to droppe \off/ and to discipate still more, Had hindred the Conjunction with Ruparts,[136] and Garretts[137] forces; and kept the King from reenforceing his army to appeare any more in the feild for this yeare. By our Neglect[138] thereof By our neglect thereof The King gathers to head againe, with Ruparts and Garretts forces, and others out of garrisons, getts all to Oxford and thence reinforceth the trayne (and (the old being left at Denington) resolves to fetch it thence and releive that place, And in order thereto, ere we[139] came from Harwell, hee drew fort thorowe Oxford, Had a Rendezvous, or two att Bullington green,[140] yet drewe

---

[130] [B] replaces 'us' by 'his Lordshipps Army'.

[131] [B] replaces 'at this time, we' by 'at that tyme ere they'.

[132] Sir Archibald Johnston, Lord Wariston (bap. 1611, d. 1663). See *ODNB*. He was one of the commissioners travelling with the Army as representatives of the Committee of Both Kingdoms. He was a Scot.

[133] John Crewe, MP for Northamptonshire, and one of the commissioners travelling with the Army as representatives of the Committee of Both Kingdoms. See Bruce and Masson, *Quarrel*, p. 52.

[134] [B] omits 'further'.   [135] [B] replaces 'our' by 'the'.

[136] Rupert, prince and count palatine of the Rhine, was now the King's most senior general.

[137] Charles Gerard, first earl of Macclesfield (*c*.1618–94), royalist army officer. See *ODNB*.

[138] [B] replaces 'our' by 'the'.   [139] [B] replaces 'we' with 'the army'.

[140] Bullingdon Green, Oxfordshire. A hamlet three miles to the north of the city of Oxford.

25 NOVEMBER 1644B[?]

in againe, not dareing to come on that w{ay}[141] till wee,[142] draweing back to Newberry, gave him the way cleare by Do{r}chester and Wallingford, as followes;[143] Wee[144] being thus brought to the defensive part againe, while wee[145] lay {at}[146] Harwell, Some of us[147] thought our[148] present posture or some other there abou{ts} very good for ~~lye well~~ \lyinge/ in the Kings way to fight, ere he got over those pla{ynes} Others propounded to Crosse the Rivers to Dorchester,[149] to possesse th{at} towne and passe, and to quarter on this Side the Rivers, (for more Secur{e} quarter, and nearer interposition in the Kings way to Denington & to prevent all other hazards of his impressions[150] towards London, or other parts on this

⟨The E. marcheth backe to Newbury {ag}t advise⟩[151]

Side Thames) All were against draweing back to Newbury, that I know or heard, Save his Lop onely; The inconveniencyes of that, and the greate advantages of the other postures were represented to his Lop. But those that were for any advance beyond Harwell, his Lop. silenced with prete{nces} of his promise not to remove till the directions came; yet the day before they came, he did \on tuesday Nov: 5:/ appoint a Rendezvous for next morneing at Compton, 4 or 5 miles back towards Newberry,[152] without any Councell[153] that I or[154] those that were for the other postures know of; But (to Stopp our mouthes) hee pretended he would have a Councell ~~there~~ \at the Randevous/, before he would resolve whither to dispose the Army from thence; Yet, his Lop, goeing earely to the Rendezvous, when we[155] came thither found the Army ordred before to Newberry, in such haste as (I beleeve)[156] the Vanne was ~~then~~ \by noone at or/ neare Newberry; and this before

---

[141] All the missing letters in brackets at the end of this and the next eight lines (where the paper is worn away) are provided from [B].

[142] [B] replaces 'wee' by 'the Army'.   [143] [B] deletes 'as follows'.

[144] [B] replaces 'wee' by 'the Army'.   [145] [B] replaces 'wee' by 'it'.

[146] All the missing letters in brackets at the end of this and the next five lines (where the paper is worn away) are provided from [B].

[147] [B] replaces 'us' by 'the officers'.   [148] [B] replaces 'our' by 'its'.

[149] Dorchester-on-Thames, Oxfordshire, a village eight miles south-west of Oxford and close to Wallingford.

[150] This does not read right, and the 'im' at the beginning are not as usually formed by this clerk (and there is no 'dot' on the 'i'). But alternative readings eluded Bruce and Masson and elude us.

[151] This is another of the marginal summaries which looks convincingly to be in Cromwell's hand.

[152] Compton, Berkshire, a village in the river Pang valley in the Berkshire Downs about 11 miles north of Newbury and 21 miles south of Oxford.

[153] [B] adds 'of Warre' here.   [154] [B] omits 'or I'.

[155] [B] replaces 'we' by 'the officers'.   [156] [B] replaces '(I believe) with '(as was believed)'.

233

THE LETTERS, WRITINGS, AND SPEECHES OF OLIVER CROMWELL

any Councell met; his Lop (when they were \come/ together) alledginge for <u>what was donne, that</u> he had there received the letters from the Committee <u>of both Kingdomes, comm</u>aunding his returne to Newberry.[157]

From this Rendevous, all the victualls,(which were come up by water for the army were Sent, by his Lop, to Abbington), to excuse his not goeing beyond the river nor staying thereabouts to Secure it. [fo. 112r] And that Sending away of our victualls Served afterwards for an occasion to necessitate the army to drawe homewards the Sooner.

⟨The drawing backe to Newb. caused the losse of Denington⟩

That our[158] draweing back to Newberry, was the cheife or onely cause of our[159] losse of the busines of Denington, gieveing the King a cleare advantage to releive it, & putting us,[160] allmost, out of possibility to hinder him, For ꝉꞇ haveing thus left the King the way cleare by Dorchester, ~~and~~ \to/ Wallingford, and a large Secure quarter in that Corner, on the North Side of Thames, close by his passe at Wallingford (beyond which we[161] could not come to disturbe or discover him And by which hee could come to annoy or discover us[162] even to our[163] quarters, and beate in Small guards at pleasure) In this case, if wee[164] at Newberry (upon every party appearing to drawe over to Wallingford; and beate in our[165] Scoutes) should have drawne our[166] horse together, The King might lye quiet with his body beyond the River, till wee[167] had been forced to dismisse them back to quarters weary and faint, and then might he have taken th'opportunity to drawe Speedily over, and be at the Castle before we[168]could recall them; soe as there was noe end of our[169] draweing our[170] horse together, till certaine notice that the Kings \mayne/ body was drawne over at Wallingford; And, Staying for that (Since the notice could not come to us[171] till three hours after, or more,) hee might, in that time, be got over the plaines, and Consequently (before wee[172] could possibly, after that, drawe our[173] horse together, \or/ ~~and~~ get our[174] foote to interpose) he might be at the Castle, and have donne his businesse.

---

[157] See Bruce and Masson, *Quarrel*, pp. 52, 53, letters of 5 and 6 November 1644.

[158] [B] replaces 'our' by 'the Army's'.   [159] [B] replaces 'our' by 'the'.

[160] [B] replaces 'us' by 'the Army'.   [161] [B] replaces 'we' by 'the Army'.

[162] [B] replaces 'us' by 'the Ea: Army' = the earl [of Manchester]'s army.

[163] [B] replaces 'our' by 'the'.   [164] [B] replaces 'wee' by 'the Army'.

[165] [B] replaces 'our' by 'the'.   [166] [B] replaces 'our' by 'Ea:' = the earl's.

[167] [B] replaces 'wee' by 'the Army'   [168] [B] replaces 'we' by 'the Army.

[169] [B] replaces 'our' by 'the Ea:' = the earl's.   [170] [B] replaces 'our' by 'his'.

[171] [B] replaces 'us' by 'the Earle'.   [172] [B] replaces 'wee' by 'the Horse'.

[173] [B] just deletes 'our' here.   [174] [B] replaces 'our foote' by 'and the foote'.

25 NOVEMBER 1644B[?]

And this being foretold, and demonstrated before his Lop, upon the first Intelligence of a party drawne out from Wallingford, the day after we[175] came to Newberry (which after drew in againe) and it being therefore moved to remove thence, with our[176] whole army to some better posture of Interposition, his Lop was content indeed, to have had our[177] horse drawne together if we[178] would (which the King would soone have made us[179] weary of, as before) but would not hearken to drawe the foot thence, till the King should come on; alledging that he might not quit Newberry; neither would he, ~~as yet~~ \as yett/ seeme to acknowledge, but that (lying still ~~there~~ \, till the King came on)/) we[180] might well enough prevent the releife of the Castle. ⟨{ }4⟩ On the Fryday after \Nov: 8:/ the King draweing over in earnest, about two a Clock advanced forward and, about five, \certayne/ word was brought us,[181] by a fugitive (Sooner then we[182] could otherwise expect): wee sent orders[183] immediately for our horse to meet att Redhill feild; But, a Councell being called, It was then found infeisible to drawe out time enough to interpose, and concluded, that we must give[184] them Castle for releived,[185] and should onely stand upon our guard till the enemy retreated But then to fall on; And, upon this, the Rendevous for ~~all~~ the horse was altred to Newberry washe on the South Side of the towne, and River The Castle, and the enemy being on the North Side. The next morneing (our[186] horse being come together before day, and the King contrary to expectacon, Staying all night at Ilsley, 6 miles short of the Castle,)[187] It was then urged by diverse that we[188] might drawe out, but the debate being held long, till wee[189] could not doe it time enough to interpose, The former resolucon stood, His Lop in these debates being most ready to finde the danger or infeisibility of draweing out to interpose, most earnest against it and (in that last dispute) to protract time.

---

[175] [B] replaces 'we' by 'the Army'.   [176] [B] replaces 'our' by 'the Army'.

[177] [B] deletes 'indeed' and replaces 'our' by 'the'.   [178] [B] replaces 'we' by 'they'.

[179] [B] replaces 'us' by 'them'.   [180] [B] replaces 'we' by 'they'.

[181] [B] deletes 'us'.

[182] [B] replaces 'sooner then we could otherwise expect' by 'sooner than could otherwise be expected'.

[183] [B] replaces 'wee sent orders' by 'orders were sent'.

[184] [B] replaces 'we must give the Castle for relieved' by 'the Castle must be given relief'.

[185] [B] deletes 'we must give' and changes 'the Castle for relieved' by 'the Castle must be given relief.'

[186] [B] replaces 'our' by 'the'.

[187] East and West Ilsley, Berkshire, are two villages 10 and 11 miles due north of Newbury.

[188] [B] replaces 'we' by 'the Army'.   [189] [B] replaces 'wee' by 'they'.

THE LETTERS, WRITINGS, AND SPEECHES OF OLIVER CROMWELL

The enemy came on, Releived the Castle, drew downe into Newberry feild, braved us at our workes,[190] and (that while draweing their ordinance and carriages out of the Castle)[191] in the evening, they retreated up to the Castle & the Heath beyond it; upon intelligence that they continued their retreate in the night, It was concluded that our[192] horse should be drawne over into Shawe feild by three in the morninge, to pursue the enemy & endeavour to put them to a stand, till our[193] foote could come up, which were to follow by breake of day; By light day, we[194] discovered the enemy not gone but drawne up on winterburn Heath;[195] And, whereas before (while we[196] thought they would be gone), we[197] Seemed forward to fight and regaine our lost honor, being now[198] prest to hasten out [fo. 112v] the foote, there appeared much backwardnesse thereto espetially in his Lop (the foote, with much importunity, being nott got \out/ into Shawefeild[199] till about Eleaven a clock) And the enemy being not yet gone (soe as we[200] might fight if we[201] would and have the advantage (before pretended to be lookt for) (of a retreateing enemy) His Lop haveing now noe further Evasion left, to shift it off under another name, playnely declared himself against fighting, And haveing spent much time in vieweing the enemy, while they drewe off, and preparatory Discourses, A Councell being calld, Hee made it the question, whether t'were prudent to fight; with all earnestnesse and Solliscitousnesse he urged all discouragemts against it, opposed all that was said for it; And amongst other things, It being urged that if now we let the King goe off with such honor. It would give him reputacon both at home and abroade to drawe assistance to him, ~~espetially~~ espetially from France, where (we[202] heard) endeavours were to get ayde for him But if wee beate him[203] now, it would loose him every where, And therefore it concern'd us, now to attempt it, before such ayde came his Lop replyeing, told the Councell he could assure them, there was noe Such thing; Adding (with vehæmence) this principle against fighting That if we beate the king 99 times, he would be King Still and his posterity, and we Subjects still, But if he beate us but once, we should be hang'd, and our posterityes be undonne; Thus t'was concluded not to fight,

---

190 [B] replaces 'us at our workes' by 'the Army at the workes'.
191 Donnington Castle which was on the road from the Ilsleys to Newbury.
192 [B] replaces 'our' by 'the'.   193 [B] replaces 'our' by 'the'.
194 [B] replaces ', we' by 'the enemy'.
195 Winterbourne Heath, between Newbury and Donnington, a bit closer to Newbury.
196 [B] replaces 'we' by 'twas'.   197 [B] replaces 'wee' by 'the Army'.
198 [B] replaces 'now' by 'then'.   199 Not identified.
200 [B] replaces 'we' by 'the Army'.   201 [B] replaces 'we' by 'they'.
202 [B] replaces 'we' by 'twas'.   203 [B] replaces 'if wee beate him' by 'if he were beaten'.

25 NOVEMBER 1644B[?]

the King Suffred to march off unfought, (being within a mile of us)[204] ~~re~~ and wee,[205] retreated into Newberry

The King (thus encouraged) retires not back, towards Oxforde, but goes to Marleborough;[206] hovers there, for an opportunity, to releive Basing alsoe; The Earle of Manchester \(the while)/ hangs homewards to be gone into his Assotiation, his agentes endeavour (Some) to procure command for it (others) to stirre up the Soldiers mindes to it; for both,[207] extremityes are needlessly put upon the Soldiers and pretended to be greate where they are not; His Lops Treasurer telling the Soldiers (when they complayn'd of their wants) that they should have neither money nor clothes till they came into the Assotiation, but there they should have both, And whereas (for our[208] coming back to Newberry \from Harwell/) twas Sometimes pretended by his Lop That Newberry must be fortifyed for a winter quarter, yet when we came there, noe order was taken for it; (And though the importance of that place (espetially in referrence to the Seige of Basing)[209] was by the former \Councel/[210] Judged to be greate, and t'was readily apprehended by his Lop, as a reason to avoid{?e} our marching out to fight the King, least he should wheele about into Newberry, and soe releive Basing. Yet afterwards (the King Staying at Marlebrough for an opportunity to releive Basing) The Earle of Manchester was very forward to quitt Newberry, and at last, upon intelligence of a greate party drawne out from Marleborowe, to goe to Basing another way wee did drawe out[211] ~~another way~~ from Newberry; But, then, it was pretended to the Councell that we[212] should goe to Kingscleare for a more direct interposico{n} in the Kings way to Basing and that there we[213] might fight with him upon the Downes, if he came that way, and lye ready (if he should bend towards Newberry) to repossesse it before him; And on those grounds onely and to that end, was our[214] remove agreed to, in a full Councell; But, being thus got out, and upon our[215] way to Kingscleare, haveing intelligence that the King was

---

[204] [B] replaces 'us' by 'the Army'.   [205] [B] replaces 'wee,' by 'thus'.

[206] Marlborough, Wiltshire, a borough 20 miles due west of Newbury.

[207] [B] replaces 'both' by 'such'.

[208] [B] deletes 'whereas' and replaces 'our' by 'the Army'.

[209] The eight words in parenthesis are omitted in [B].

[210] The second 'c' has a tell-tale shape that strongly suggests it was made by Cromwell's usual clerk.

[211] [B] replaces 'wee did drawe out' by 'the Army was drawne out'.

[212] [B] replaces 'we' by 'they'.   [213] [B] replaces 'we' by 'they.'

[214] [B] replaces 'our' by 'the'.   [215] [B] replaces 'our' by 'the'.

coming \on/ by Hungerford[216] towards Newberry, his Lop would \then/ neither go on to Kingscleare, nor returne into Newberry; But, upon new pretences (without the Councell of warre) turn'd his course to Aldermarston (which was five miles homewards from Newberry, and Seaven miles nearer home than Kingscleare) And though Kingscleare was the knowne direct Roade to Basing yet he pretended to turne to Aldermarston, with intent to goe directly to Basing [fo. 113r] And that he would fight the King there which way soever he should come,[217] if he attempted to releive it; This gave some Satisfaction for present, but from Aldermarston, his Lop would not be got to Basing (making many excuses) But with much adoe being got out next day to Mortimer heath,[218] he would not be perswaded to goe on any further, alledging that many of the Soldiers were run to Redding, and more would goe thither (being got soe neare it) Thus[219] (\when/ he pretended for Basing) draweing the Army to Aldermarston (which was cleare out of the way) he brought the Soldiers soe neare Redding, that they would be runing thither; And then made their runing thither an occasion to avoyde goeing to Basing at all, and at last to drawe all to Redding; & withdrew the Seige {fr}om Basing.

Outcome: It is striking how *invisible* Cromwell is during the period from 25 November to 9 December, the date on which Zouch Tate suggested and Cromwell enthusiastically supported the principle of the Self-Denying Ordinance [see **1644 12 09a-c**], that all MPs should resign their commissions in Parliament's armies and resume their places at Westminster.

According to *The Parliament Scout*, edited by John Dillingham with whom Cromwell may well have been staying,[220] Cromwell made a speech on 4 December in which he 'made answer to every part' of Manchester's charges against him that had been delivered to the Commons, but there is no reference to the delivery of the charges, let alone any rebuttal, in the Journals of either the House of Commons or the House of Lords.[221] And *Parliament Scout* gave no details at all of what Cromwell said. It was a report designed to dampen not fan rumours.[222] Otherwise the only reference to Cromwell in the parliamentary records

[216] Hungerford, Berkshire, a market town midway between Newbury and Marlborough.
[217] [B] replaces 'come' by 'remove'.
[218] Mortimer Heath or Common, Berkshire, adjacent to a village 14 miles east of Newbury.
[219] [B] replaces 'Thus' by 'That'.   [220] See above at n. 21.
[221] On 2 December the Lords had voted to have Manchester's charges delivered to the Commons at a joint conference, and the Commons had agreed to consider such a conference. But there is no record of it having taken place. See below.
[222] *The Parliament Scout*, no. 76 for 28 November–5 December 1644), pp. 610–11 (N&S, 485:76). Because Early English Books Online (at the time of going to press) has digitised the wrong pamphlet in place of *The Parliament Scout* no. 76, the version checked here is the one from the online '17th and 18th century Burney collection newspapers' website. See also *JHC*, 3:713.

25 NOVEMBER 1644B[?]

for the three weeks after 25 November is a reference on 28 November to an order for reparations to a woman from Shaw (near Newbury) for damage caused by parliamentary troops 'according to an Information given in to this House by Lieutenant General Cromwell'.[223] His name was also kept, especially by diurnal editors favourable to his cause, out of the newspapers except for the vaguest of references to the dispute between the Houses. Meanwhile Zouch Tate's committee, commanded to keep the tightest secrecy on their deliberations,[224] were taking witness statements from officers nominated by Cromwell and Waller as being able to support their testimony. The first such dated examination was on 30 November and in total more than twenty army officers were examined—general officers, colonels, majors, two captains and a lieutenant, two scoutmasters, a quartermaster, and a judge advocate (for martial law trials)—over the period down to 6 January, about half[225] before 9 December. The deponents were drawn fairly indiscriminately from Waller's and Manchester's armies and the number with close relationships to Cromwell was quite small (Ireton, Disbrowe, Lilburne and Norton). Their testimony consistently supported that of Waller and Cromwell. So within the committee that would report to the Commons, the case was building. But nothing they were doing leaked into the public domain. Manchester certainly seems to have been aware of what was being said about him, presumably through one or more friends on the committee.[226]

If Cromwell was keeping a low profile and letting his accusations gather momentum within Zouch Tate's Committee, Manchester was making a point of being the centre of attention. He arrived back in Westminster on 26 November and immediately announced his desire to reject that which he believed he was being accused of by Waller and Cromwell. He made a 'a large narrative' to the Lords on 28 November and this in turn was presented as a written document on 2 December, following which the Lords resolved to call for a conference of both houses at which Lord Wharton and Lord North would read out Manchester's statement. The Commons promised a reply and then did nothing, and it was only indirectly that the Lords discovered that the Commons had set up a Committee under John Lisle to examine whether the Lords request represented a breach of privilege.[227] This committee was to be chaired by John Lisle, MP for Winchester and one of the most hawkish of all MPs, and even at this stage, noted for anti-monarchical views, to look into the question of privilege and to find the longest of long grass.[228] And so trench warfare began.

Manchester's narrative survives in two parts, the first a rebuttal of Cromwell's claims and the allegation that it was Cromwell who had consistently been insubordinate in

---

[223] JHC, 3:707.

[224] 'Resolved, &c. That the Protestation of Secrecy shall be continued upon the Committee where Mr. Tate has the Chair (to whom is referred the Examination of the Narrative made by Sir Wm. Waller and Lieutenant General Cromwell), as to the Business of that whole Narrative. Resolved, &c. That all Orders, that give Power to fewer than eight of this Committee to act, shall be revoked'—JHC, 3:713.

[225] Several are undated.   [226] TNA, SP16/503 fos 122–135.

[227] JHL, 7:79–81. JHC, 3:711. The membership of the Lisle Committee, a distinctly radical group, is given at JHC, 3:714.

[228] John Lisle (1609/10–64), regicide. See ODNB.

thwarting Manchester's commands and failing in his duty, and the second a haughty and seething assault on Cromwell specifying his contempt for the peerage and for the Westminster Assembly and his 'animositie against the Scottish nation'.[229]

The Lords set up their own committee, made up of seven peers, to investigate his claims,[230] and that was predictably as much on Manchester's side as Zouch Tate's and John Lisle's committees were on Cromwell's side. To support his claims Manchester got two substantial testimonies from close allies. A narrative of the Newbury campaign through a Mancunian rather than Cromwellian lens was provided by Major General Lawrence Crawford,[231] and a character assassination by 'an opponent' now identified as Lt Col William Dodson, a local man who knew all about Cromwell as an allegedly tyrannical figure in the Isle of Ely, that portrays Cromwell as 'a dangerously subversive radical' and denounces his 'attack on the nobility, his promotion of Independents, often "common men, pore and of meane parentage", while cashiering those who did not subscribe to his religious principles, and his fierce antipathy to the Scots'.[232]

And so both Houses dug in behind their own member. Cromwell's narrative existed only as a document held close by Zouch Tate's committee, while John Lisle's committee refused to engage with the Lords over matters of privilege. Cromwell stayed silent and did not put anything into the public domain. Manchester meanwhile, perhaps in an attempt to get Cromwell to respond in print, got his chaplain, Simeon Ashe, to rush out into print a tendentious account of the Newbury campaign.[233]

Perhaps the most dramatic evidence of the strength of feeling generated by Cromwell's attack on Manchester came at some point between 28 November and 2 December when a cluster of peers, the Scots commissioner in London and prominent lawyers with seats in the Commons met at the earl of Essex's London home to plot Cromwell's ruin, by impeaching him or bringing a charge of *scandalum magnatum* against him. In the end, it was not the legal arguments of the lawyers that dissuaded them; it was the pragmatic political one—

---

[229] The defence of himself is in Rushworth, *Historical Collections* III:ii, pp. 733–6; the assault on Cromwell as a contemnor of the peerage, of the Westminster Assembly and to the Scots is in S. R. Gardiner, ed., 'A Letter from the Earl of Manchester to the House of Lords', in *Camden Miscellany VIII* (Camden Society, n.s. 36, 1883), pp. 1–3. There is a shorter version in the Huntingdon Archives and Local Studies Office, Manchester Papers, 32/5/1.

[230] There is a convenient collation of all the House of Lords actions on the quarrel between Manchester and Cromwell in the period down to 4 December in Bruce and Masson, *Quarrel*, pp. lxxi–lxxiii.

[231] Bruce and Masson, *Quarrel*, pp. 59–70. The original is in private hands and is not available to scholars. Clive Holmes saw it in the 1960s when it was on loan at the old Public Record Office and assures us that the transcription in *Quarrel* is a good one. C. Holmes, 'The Identity of the Author of the "Statement by an Opponent"', *EHR*, 129:541 (2014), fn. 13.

[232] Holmes, 'The Identity of the Author of the "Statement by an Opponent"', p. 1373. The text of Dodson's 'Statement' is printed in Bruce and Masson, *Quarrel*, pp. 71–7. The original is in Huntingdon Archives and Local Studies Office, Manchester Papers, M80/ Acc.3343.

[233] Simeon Ashe, *A true relation, of the most chiefe occurrences, at, and since the late battell at Newbery*, London: Printed by G.M. for Edward Brewster at the signe of the Bible at Fleete-Bridge, M.DC.XLIV [1644] (Wing / A3968; Thomason / E.22[10]).

they did not have the votes to make the charges stick.[234] Indeed, the argument that it was *Cromwell* not Manchester who was on the defensive is a strong one.[235] What was clear was that the Commons were determined to believe Cromwell and the Lords to believe Manchester. This was not absolutely foreseeable, but it certainly became an impasse. And it was to break that impasse that Zouch Tate rose to make his report on 9 December 1644. It is unlikely that the Self-Denying Ordinance lay behind Cromwell's narrative; it is certain that it was its unintended consequence.

1644 11 27[?]
Clerk's summary of Cromwell's narrative concerning the earl of Manchester

Date: Late November, but after 25 November 1644
Source: TNA, SP16/503 fo. 121r (contemporary record)

This document was drawn up by a clerk to the army committee investigating Cromwell's and Waller's allegations against the earl of Manchester. It is not clear that Cromwell had any say in its composition, but it does represent a summary of his 5,600-word report to the committee (**1644 11 25b**). It is worth noting that the clerk first called it an 'examination' and this was then changed, perhaps by a different person, to 'narrative'. It was retained in the State Papers and is placed immediately after the rough and fair copies of Cromwell's report but before the examinations of the many witnesses, for which see the 'outcome' section of **1644 11 9a**.

The examination of Lieutenant Generall Cromwell [————] that is the substance of it[1]

Three generall heads conteyning the substance of Lieutenant Generall Cromwells Examination \narrative/ concerning the Earle of Manchester.

The first generall head

That by his Lordshipp \by/ constant backwardness to action and unwillingness to ingage with the Enemy [————][2] hath lost many advantages and opportunityes

---

[234] Holmes, *The Eastern Association*, pp. 209–11 gives the sources and a very balanced account. The key source is Bulstrode Whitelocke, *Memorials of the English Civil Wars* (1682), pp. 111–12.
[235] Cotton, 'Cromwell and the Self-denying Ordinance', pp. 211–31.

---

[1] This is in the margin to the left of the 'first general head' and is heavily crossed out and only partly readable.
[2] This is too heavily crossed out to be legible.

THE LETTERS, WRITINGS, AND SPEECHES OF OLIVER CROMWELL

against the Enemy and hath neglected the direccons of the house of Comons and Committee of both kingdomes in matters of importance to the greate disservice of the Parliament and kingdome.

The second generall head.

That there is good reason to conceive that This backwardness and neglect in his Lordshipp to to take advantage against the Enemy was out of a designe, or desire not to prosecute the war to a full victory.

The third generall head.

That his Lordshipp hath not onley neglected the direction of the house of Comons and Committee of both kingdomes as aforesaid but even when his Lordshipp hath received those direccons, And also at other tymes his Lordshipp hath expressed contempt and scorne of the parliament, and Committee of both Kingdomes.

1644 12 02[?]

Cromwell's words recollected by the earl of Manchester in a written testimony to the House of Lords

Date: 2 December 1644
Source: Bodl., MS Tanner 61 fos 205r–206v

On 26 November 1644, the day after Cromwell launched his assault on the military and political competence of the earl of Manchester in the House of Commons, the House of Lords received a letter from the earl of Manchester in which he 'signified to this House' a desire to give his account of recent 'events' in the army that he led and he was asked by the Lords to give his account forty-eight hours later, on Thursday 28 November.[1] This he did and, in the words of the Journal of the Lords, he 'made to the House a large Narrative of the Carriage of the Affairs of the Army at Newbery, and of some Speeches spoken by Lieutenant Colonel Cromwell, which concerns much the Honour of this House, and the Peers of England, and the Good and Interest between the Two Kingdoms of England and Scotland'.[2] The Lords then asked him to write up his defence of his honour and that of the peers and his allegations against Cromwell and to deliver it to the House. This he did on 2

---

[1] *JHL*, 7:73.
[2] *JHL*, 7:76. The fullest surviving account of what he said on 28 November is in Rushworth, *Historical Collections*, 3: pt 2, 733–6. That is an account of how Manchester, unlike Cromwell, followed his orders from the Houses and from the Committee of Both Kingdoms. He does not offer any version of Cromwell's words in that document.

242

2 DECEMBER 1644[?]

December.[3] The Lords set up their own enquiry and requested a joint conference with the Commons to discuss the matters raised. On 4 December Lords North and Wharton read out Manchester's charges, and having informed the Commons that the Lords had nominated a Committee of Seven, 'they desired this House to appoint a proportionable Number, to examine that Business'.[4] The Commons refused to do so and set up a committee to examine breaches of privilege committed by the Lords in seeking to investigate the actions of a member of the Commons. The result was the impasse only broken, and then only partially, by the events of 9 December 1644 (see below).

There are two documents which are relevant to this story. The first, in the papers of William Lenthall, Speaker of the House of Commons, is clearly the document brought down and handed over by the members of the Lords on 4 December as Manchester's report and is annotated by a clerk of the Commons as 'Concerning Leiutenant Generall Cromwell referred xber. 40 1644'.[5] But there is another version, in the papers of the earl of Manchester himself.[6] This has a completely different opening page and then follows the other version very closely except for an important rewriting of the section on Cromwell's hostility to the Scots. The status of this version is difficult to establish. It is just possible that it is the text Manchester delivered orally on 28 November. It is more likely to be an early draft of what he submitted to the Lords on 2 December which was then significantly changed, perhaps with advice from others. The third possibility is that the version in Manchester's papers is what he delivered on 2 December and that it was further developed before it was handed over to the Commons on 4 December. Since our concern here is only with Manchester's recall of conversations with Cromwell and that the text of that section is—with the exception of a single sentence and some spelling and punctuation, we cannot speculate further here. This edition is based on the version in Lenthall's papers of the alleged words of Cromwell, with the variation in the version in Manchester's own papers in the notes.

The first 400 of the 1,400 words in the version in the Lenthall papers focuses on how the divisions within his army had been allowed to fester—when he had sent complaints about Cromwell to the Committee of Both Kingdoms, he had been ordered that because of the 'necessitie of putting the Armies into present Action against the Common enemie' he should try to prevent further escalation until after the army was in winter quarters. This replaces the much shorter introduction in the version in Manchester's papers which is an appeal to the Lords to vindicate his honour and loyalty against 'so high a slaunder'. The two versions then come together to substantiate Cromwell's dishonesty and misplaced zeal.

There then follows the section that comments on Cromwell's public and private comments on the nobility, on the Westminster Assembly and on the Scots which is

---

[3] JHL, 7:79.   [4] JHC, 3:713–14.

[5] Mysteriously and a little disturbingly, the text delivered to the House of Lords and referred to in the Lords Journal, is not in the Main Papers of the House of Lords for that or any subsequent date.

[6] Huntingdon Library and Archives, Manchester Papers DDM 32/5/1.

243

reproduced below; and both versions end with the very similar 166/160 words in which Manchester records how he 'did not Communicate my Councells to him [i.e. Cromwell] with that Freedom that formerly I had done', denies the claim that he was 'an enemie to Godly men' but rather that 'my affeccions are still set upon such as love Christ in sincerity'.

...and indeed I grew Jealouse that his designes were not as he made his professions to mee; For his Expressions were sometimes agt. the Nobillitie, That he hoped to live to see never a Noble man in England, and he loved such better then others because they did not love Lordes, he hath further expressed himselfe with contempt of the Assembly of Divines, to whom I pay a Reverence, as to the most learned and godly Convention that hath bin this many ages, yett these he termed persecutors And that they persecuted honester men than themselves, his Animositie agt. the Scottish Nation, *whome I affect as joined with us in solemne league & Covent. and honor as joyntly Instrumentall with us in the Common Cause,*[7] yett agt. these his Animositie wassuch as he told mee, That in the way [fo. 206r] they now caried them selves, pressing for their discipline, he could as soone draw his sword agt. them as against any in the kings Army. And he grew soe pressing for his designes as he told mee that he would not deny, but that he desired to have none in my Army but such men as were of the Independt. Judgmt. giving mee these reasons That in case there should be Proposicions for Peace or any Conclusion of a Peace such as might not stand with those endes that honest men should aime at this Army might prevent such a mischeife.

I must confess these speeches some of them spoken publiquely others privately yett soe as I had saw they had a publique Influence on the Army made mee jealous of his Intencions...

---

[7] The version in Manchester's papers replaces the words between the asterisks added here with this: 'whome I confess next under the over ruling Providence of God, I acknowledge to be the preservers of this Kingdome from Tiranny & prelacy.'

4 DECEMBER 1644A

1644 12 04a

First examination of Oliver Cromwell taken by the Committee of the House of Commons examining Cromwell's allegations against the earl of Manchester

Date: 4 December 1644
Source: TNA, SP16/503, fos 130r–v (no. 56.vii) (autograph)

After Cromwell and Waller lodged their complaints about the earl of Manchester (see **1644 11 25b**), the Commons referred the matter to the committee that was chaired by Zouch Tate. Cromwell and Waller had nominated witnesses to support their allegations, and they were called before the committee over several weeks from 4 December. Cromwell was called before the committee twice, on 4 and 10 December. His responses were recorded by the unnamed clerk of the committee. What survive appear to be rough notes. There are tears in the manuscript that make it difficult to read in places. Importantly the notes bear Cromwell's own signature. See also **1644 12 10**.

[fo. 130v]

Leuitenent Generall Crumwell his examination

[fo. 130r]

Wednesday 1ober. 4th 1644.

Generall Crumwell Sayth.

That after ~~the Commands from the~~ Comtee of bothe kingdoms ~~Signifyed to th~~ \had directed the/ Earl of Manchester to advance with the army into the west whilst his army {} himself wer at Huntington leiutenant Generall Hamond {}th this Examinant Came to him to desire his lordshippe that he {?wou}ld hasten his march in obedience to the Commands he {h}ad received to the which he replyed that he would hang him \or them/ that Should advise him to move with his army into the west; or words to th effect;

Oliver Cromwell

Present att the Examination. Sir Henry Hamond mr. Prideaux. Sir John Curson. Sir Peter Wentworth. mr. Ashurst mr. Hodges mr. Stevens mr. Holland Mr Lisle.

THE LETTERS, WRITINGS, AND SPEECHES OF OLIVER CROMWELL

1644 12 04b

Examination of James Pitsum (alias Pitson), Scoutmaster General to Sir William Waller

Date: 4 December 1644
Source: TNA, SP 16/503, fo. 131r (no. 56.viii) (overheard conversation)

As the committee charged with investigating Cromwell and Waller's case against the earl of Manchester got into its stride, it began to call the witnesses identified by the two generals as being able to support the allegations they had made. One of the first to be called was Waller's Scoutmaster General who testified that he had been present at the Council of War before the battle of Newbury six weeks earlier and that he could remember a particular exchange between Manchester and Cromwell.

The examination bears Pitsum's signature. There is a tantalising extension to what he originally remembers Manchester as saying which is crossed out in the manuscript but by whom and why is unclear.

Wednesday 10ber. 4th. 1644

James Pitsum[1] Scoutmaster generall to Sir William Waler Sayth…\that/ att this Councell of warr ther were words spoken by the Earl of Manchester \in the hearing of this examinant/ to this effect videll: ~~the~~ He was assured that wee need not feare the french or any forraigne nation to Come in the \next/ spring, & sayth that he heard the earl of Manchester say att the same Councell of warre that wee must tak heed of fighting for if wee beat the kings \army never soe many times if a hundred times/ yet he is king still \& soe will his posterity be after ~~& sayth that all our armys are heer present, & that it was of a most dangerus Consequence to the kingdome to engage them if they shold be beaten~~ but if he beat us once then wee ar every one of us undonne, & besides wee shall loose our necks & our posterity \will bee/ made bondslaves ~~as long they live~~ or ~~words to that effect.~~ To which Leutenant Generall Crumwell replyed, That his lordshipp had as good have \ sayd/ that wee ar resolved to have peace upon any termes in the world as to have sayd thus for by that same argument wee should never have fought with ~~them~~ \ kings army/ ~~as long as wee had lived; & sayd that the king~~

per me Ja Pitsom

----

[1] James Pitsum (or Pitson) was scoutmaster to Sir William Waller in 1644 (see the *Online Directory of Parliamentarian Army Officers*) and is probably the man who went on to serve as a captain in Fairfax's own regiment of foot in the New Model Army (Wanklyn, *Reconstructing*, 1:76, 85, 97, 2:43). He left the Army early in 1651.

246

4 DECEMBER 1644C

Present att the examination. Sir Peter wentworth. Sir Henry Hamond. mr. Steevens mr. Hodges mr. Prideaux. mr: Ashurst mr: Holland. mr: Lisle.

— ◦◦◦ —

1644 12 04C

Speech by Oliver Cromwell to the House of Commons

Date: 4 December 1644
Source: [A] BL, Harl. MS 483, fo. 120, Diary of Sir Simonds D'Ewes. [B] BL, Add. MS 31116, fo. 178, Diary of Laurence Whitaker

On this day the Commons heard the earl of Manchester's answer to the accusations against him. Cromwell replied to defend himself against the counter-accusations which Manchester had made against him.[1]

[A] BL, Harl. MS 483, fo. 120, Diary of Sir Simonds D'Ewes

Interfui circa 9 precibus in consessu &c. Res maxime agitata, quod subdelegati secrete examinarunt Cromwelli accusationes contra Mancastrium et Mancastrii comitis defensio et contra Cromwellum accusatio publice lecta &c. Defendere se parans Cromwellus exii parum ante 12, nec denuo redii &c. Ipse omnia capita absolute negebat &c. Tum dissertatio orta au privilegia nostri consessus temerata a Mancastrio &c. post acrem dissertationem subdelegati tandem constituti qui de hoc inquirerent &c. Surrexerunt parum ante 4 &c.

At around 9 am I was present in the House for prayers. The chief subject of discussion was that the committee had examined Cromwell's charge against Manchester in private, and the earl of Manchester's defence and his charge against Cromwell were read in open session. Cromwell was preparing to defend himself when I left, slightly before 12 o'clock and did not return. Cromwell absolutely denied all the articles. Then a discussion arose as to whether the House's privileges had been defiled by Manchester. After a fierce debate a committee was at length appointed to enquire into the matter &c. The House arose shortly before 4pm.

[B] BL, Add. MS 31116, fo. 178, Diary of Laurence Whitaker

…unto both wch papers Lieut: Gen: Cromwell Gave a very Large Answer in the ho:…

————

[1] *Parliament Scout*, no. 76 for 28 November–5 December 1644), p. 611 (N&S, 485.76; Thomason / E.21[3]). *Perfect Diurnall*, no. 71 for 2–9 December 1644), p. 565 (N&S, 504:071; Thomason / E.256[45]).

Outcome: The Commons referred the Lords' documents not to the Committee chaired by Zouch Tate which was taking statements from witnesses nominated by Waller and Essex but to a new committee chaired by the radical John Lisle. See **1644 11 25b**[2]

1644 12 06

Conversation between Oliver Cromwell and the earl of Manchester as reported by Sir Arthur Heselrige

Date: 6 December 1644

Source: TNA, SP16/503. fos 132r–v (no. 56.ix), examination of Sir Arthur Heselrige before Zouch Tate's Committee (reported conversation)

Sir Arthur Heselrige's examination before the committee investigation into the allegations of Cromwell and Waller against the earl of Manchester contains the best known version of the words Manchester is alleged to have used implying a reluctance to engage the King in battle. Heselige also gives—at a distance of six weeks—what he remembers as being Cromwell's response. These are underlined in the transcript below.[1]

This examination, recorded by the same clerk as was going to take Cromwell's second examination (see **1644 12 10**), contains Heselrige's autograph signature.

[fo. 132v]

Sir Arthur Haslerigges Examination.

[fo. 132r]

Fryday 10ber 6th 1644.

Sir Arthur Haslerigge Sayth that he was present att the Councell of warre Sitting in a little howse att the Same time when the {-} Parlements army was drawne out upon Shawfeild & the kings army was drawne forthe upon winterborne heath & Marching away, & Sayth that he well remembreth that it was there urged among other arguments as a motive for present fighting & engaging with the kings army That if the kings army were now beaten it would prevent the bringing over of the French or of any foreigne force which was the present designe in hand whereunto the earle of Manchester answered & Sayd these words or to this effect, Upon my creditt You need not feare the Comming in of the French I know there is noe Such thing

---

[2] *JHC*, 3:713.

[1] Sir Arthur Heselige, second baronet (1601–61), army officer and politician. See *ODNB*.

9 DECEMBER 1644A

And the earle of Manchester Sayd afterwards there ~~with the most earnestnesse & in the hearing of this examinante~~, That if wee beate the king ninety & nine times yet he is king Still, & Soe will his posterity bee after him, but if the kinge beate us once wee Shall bee all hanged & our posterity \made/ Slaves. These \weere the very/ words as this Exmainant remembreth, but he is Sure words to this effect the earle of Manchester there used ~~with Much earnestnesse~~ as a motive against present engaging whereuppon <u>Leiutenant Generall Crumwell replyed My lord if this be Soe why did wee take up armes att first, this is against fighting ever heereafter if Soe lett us make peace bee it never Soe base.</u>

Art. Hesilrige

Present at this Committee. Sir Henry Hamond Sir Peter Wentworth. mr. Stevens mr. Holland mr. Ashurst Sir John Curson mr. Blackston mr. Gurdon mr. Lisle

---

1644 12 09a

Speech by Oliver Cromwell to the House of Commons

Date: 9 December 1644

Source: John Rushworth, *Historical Collections of Private Passages of State*, 8 vols. (London, 1722) VI:4, available online at https://www.british-history.ac.uk/rushworth-papers/vol6/pp1–23

This is the first of three Cromwell speeches that have come down to us as having been delivered on 9 December 1644. It only survives as printed from the papers of John Rushworth and his source is not known. It comes early in a chapter headed 'Chap. I. Containing the Proposals, Debates, and perfecting of the New Model of the Parliament's Army under Sir Thomas Fairfax, Commander in Chief: And the State of the King's Affairs and Strength, as also the Parliament's, at that time', and it immediately follows an account, drawing on Bulstrode Whitelocke's *Memorials*, of the meeting at Essex House on 3 December where the Earl of Essex met with his allies in the Commons and with the Scottish Commissioners to plot Cromwell's downfall.[1] The specific context of this and the following speeches (**1644 12 09b** and **1644 12 09c**) is the report by the committee chaired by Zouch Tate[2] given responsibility on 25 November to consider the charges brought by Cromwell against the earl of Manchester. This is how Rushworth introduces Cromwell's speech: 'so it was, that on the 9th of December 1644 ... the House of Commons took into consideration the sad Condition

---

[1] Bulstrode Whitelocke, *Memorials of the English affairs, or an historical account of what passed from the beginning of the reign of King Charles the First to King Charles the Second his happy restauration* ... (1732), p. 116.

[2] Zouch Tate (1606–50), politician. See ODNB.

of the Kingdom in reference to its Grievances by the Burthen of the War in case the Treaty for a Peace, which was then propounded (and of the successless Issue of which we have before in the former Volume given an account) should not take effect, nor the War be effectually prosecuted. After a long Debate of this matter, the House Voted themselves into a Grand Committee, where there was a general silence for a good space of time, many looking one upon another, to see who would break the Ice, and speak first in so tender and sharp a Point: Amongst whom Oliver Cromwell stood up, and spake shortly to this effect.'[3]

Opinions are sharply divided about Cromwell's motivations in this and in the immediately succeeding speeches. Was he feeling the relentless pressure from the House of Lords to make him answer for the insubordination contained in his narrative (**1644 II 25b**)? Was he rather wanting to find some way out of the deadlock created in the aftermath of the accusations he had hurled at Manchester and that Manchester had hurled at him? Was he persuaded that it was a price worth paying for him to surrender his own command if it meant that the generals he held responsible for the failures of 1644 would also have to stand down? Had he foreseen that he might be able to claim an exemption for the self-denying proposal laid before the House? There are almost as many opinions about this as there are historians.[4] His speeches on 9 December, assuming he did indeed make them all, represent some of the greatest riddles of his life.

That it was now a time to speak, or for ever to hold the tongue: The important occasion being no less than to save a Nation out of a bleeding, nay, almost dying condition, which the long continuance of the War had already brought it into; so that without a more speedy vigorous and effectual prosecution of the War, casting off all lingering proceedings like Soldiers of Fortune beyond Sea, to spin out a War, we shall make the Kingdom weary of us, and hate the Name of a Parliament. For what do the Enemy say? Nay, what do many say that were Friends at the beginning of the Parliament? Even this, that the Members of both Houses have got great Places and Commands, and the Sword into their hands, and what by Interest in Parliament, and what by power in the Army, will perpetually continue themselves in Grandeur, and not permit the War speedily to end, lest their own power should determine with it. This I speak here to our own Faces, is but what others do utter abroad behind our Backs. I am far from reflecting on any, I know the worth of those Commanders, Members of both Houses, who are yet in power; but if I may speak my Conscience without reflection upon any, I do

---

[3] Gardiner, *GCW*, 3:82–4, 86–91 remains the clearest narrative laying out the background to these speeches.

[4] Almost every biographer of Cromwell has addressed the issues of when Cromwell came to support the principle of Self-Denial and whether he had a plan to be exempted from it. There are a broad spectrum of views. Historians even within a single volume can disagree, as John Adamson and Austin Woolrych do in John Morrill, ed., *Oliver Cromwell and the English Revolution* (1990), pp. 60–4 and 102–4 which also footnote a range of views.

9 DECEMBER 1644B

conceive if the Army be not put into another Method, and the War more vigorously prosecuted, the People can bear the War no longer, and will enforce you to a dishonourable Peace. But this I would recommend to your Prudence not to insist upon any Complaint or Over-sight of any Commander in Chief upon any occasion whatsoever; for as I must acknowledge my self guilty of Over-sights, so I know they can rarely be avoided in Military Affairs; therefore waving a strict inquiry into the Causes of these things, let us apply our selves to the Remedy which is most necessary: And I hope, we have such true English Hearts, and zealous Affections towards the General Weal of our Mother-Country, as no Members of either House will scruple to deny themselves and their own private Interests for the Publick Good, nor account it to be a dishonour done to them whatever the Parliament shall resolve upon in this weighty matter.

Outcome: After one (or perhaps more) speeches—and this looks highly orchestrated—Zouch Tate rose again. According to Rushworth 'the first that moved expressly to have all Members of Parliament Excluded from Commands and Offices was Mr. Zouch Tate; wherein he was seconded by Sir Henry Vane Jun. and others. The Debate lasted long, but in conclusion the Grand Committee came to this Resolution, "That no Member of either House of Parliament shall during the War Enjoy or Execute any Office or Command Military or Civil, and that an Ordinance be brought in to that purpose."'

1644 12 09b
Speech (perhaps) made by Oliver Cromwell to the House of Commons

Date: 9 December 1644
Source: Edward Hyde, earl of Clarendon, manuscript of his 'History of the Rebellion and Civil Wars in England': Bodl., MS Clarendon 123, pp. 279–80 (reported speech)

There are major difficulties in accepting this as an actual Cromwell speech. It comes from part of Clarendon's 'Life and Continuation of the History' which he wrote in 1669 when he was in exile and far from his notes and papers.[1] It is not clear on what basis he attributed

---

[1] The principal modern edition of Clarendon's *History* contains this text, with modernised spelling and modified punctuation and paragraphing, but otherwise a very careful and accurate translation from the manuscript: Edward Hyde, first earl of Clarendon, *The History of the Rebellion and Civil Wars in England*, 6 vols. (Oxford, 1888), III, book 8, paras 195–6.

THE LETTERS, WRITINGS, AND SPEECHES OF OLIVER CROMWELL

these precise words to Cromwell. The words attributed to Cromwell are consistent with what is known of his views and it is compatible with the apparently more authentic **1644 12 09a** (recorded by Cromwell's long-time acquaintance and ally John Rushworth) and **1644 12 09c** (a contemporary newsbook, which at one point it resembles closely). We include it here but with heavy reservations.

When the ice was thus broke, Oliver Cromwell, who had not yett arryved at the faculty of speakinge with decency and temper, commended the preachers[2] for havinge dealte plainely and impartially, and told them of ther faultes, which they had bene so unwillinge to heare of: that thr were many thinges upon which he had never reflected before, yett, upon revolving what he had bene sayd, he could not but confesse that all was very true, and till ther were a perfecte reformacon in those particulars which had bene recommended to them, nothing would prosper that they tooke in hande; that the Parliament had done very wisely in the entrance into this warr, to ingage many members of their owne in the most daungerous parts of it, that the nacon might see that they did not intend to imbarke them in perills of warr whilst themselves sat securely at home out of gunnshott, but would march with them, where the daunger most threatned; and those Honble persons who had exposed themselves this way had merited so much of thr coun-try that thr memoryes should be held in perpetuall veneracon, and whatsoever should be well done after them, should be alwayes imputed to thr example; but that God had so blessed their Armyes, that thr had growne up with it and under it very many excellent officers who were fit for much greater charges than they were now possessed of; and desyred them not to be terrifyed with an imagina-con, that if the highest offices were vacant they would not be able to putt as fitt men into them, for, besydes that it was not good to putt so much trust in any arme of flesh, as to think such a cause as thers depended upon any one man, he did take upon him to assure them, that they had officers in their Armyes who

---

[2] 9 December was a Monday and there had been no Fast Sermons or other sermons directed to members of the Commons since 27 November when neither George Gipps nor Benjamin Pickering had touched on matters germane to Cromwell's speech here. Perhaps Cromwell was speaking about sermons in Westminster Abbey or St Margaret's the previous day. So this may be evidence that the whole of this speech is manufactured. (There was a special Fast Day arranged for 18 December when Obadiah Sedgwick and Stephen Marshall dealt with the issues of self-denying and new modelling head-on, and in ways so politically sensitive that these sermons were never printed.) See J. F. Wilson, *Pulpit in Parliament* (1969), pp. 81–2.

9 DECEMBER 1644C

were fitt to be Generalls in any enterprise in Christendom. He sayd, he thought nothinge so necessary as to purge and vindicate the Parliament from the partiality towards ther owne members; and made a profer to laye down his commission of commaunde in the Army; and desyred that an ordinance might be prepared, by which it might be made unlawfull for any member of ether House of Parliament to hold any office or commaund in the Army, or any place or imployment of profitt in the state; and so concluded, with an inlargement upon the vices and corrupcons which were gotten into the Army, the prophanenesse and impiety and absence of all religion, the drinkinge and gaminge, and all manner of license and lazinesse; and said playnely that till the whole army were new modelled and governed under a stricter disciplyne, they must not expecte any notable successe in any thing they went aboute.

1644 12 09c

Speech by Oliver Cromwell to the House of Commons

Date: 9 December 1644

Source: *Perfect Occurrences of Parliament and Chief Collections of Letters*, no. 18 (6–13 December 1644), unpaginated, but third page (N&S, 465:2018; Thomason / E.258[1]) (reported speech)

All the newspapers commented on the debates of 9 December and on the introduction of the Self-Denying principle, but only *Perfect Occurrences* names any of the speakers, and it only names one speaker, Oliver Cromwell. The preceding three pages cover the events of 6 and 7 December and then coverage of Monday 9 December begins as follows: 'THis day the Parliament Voted that the Vote to take off all Members of either House from all Offices and places, Civill and Martiall, which in a full House, about 200 it was carried very cleere, as wee shall shortly see by the Ordinance. Indeed some opposed it and said, *That it would prove the breaking of our Armies; and we should be all undone by it*. And divers others oppositions was made against it by some, and by others it was excellently pleaded for Amongst the rest, Lieuetant Generall Cromwell said to the this effect.'

MR. SPEAKER,

I am not of the minde that the calling of the Members to sit in Parliament will break, or scatter our armies; I can speake this for my owne souldiers, that they look not upon me, but upon you, and for you they will fight and live and die in your cause, and if others be of that minde that they are of, you need not feare

253

THE LETTERS, WRITINGS, AND SPEECHES OF OLIVER CROMWELL

them, they do not Idolize me, but looke upon the Cause they fight for. you may lay upon them what commands you please: they will obey your Commands in that icause [sic], they fight for.[1]

———

Outcome: *Perfect Occurrences* concludes its account as follows: 'With many other most admirable expressions which he and divers other members of the house had, farre more full and satisfactory, than I can heere expresse; so that the businesse was carried very clear, and the Ordnance is speedily to be drawn up.' It continues by some discussion of events outside the House and then moves on to other matters.

———✎———

1644 12 10

Lieutenant General Cromwell's second examination [before the committee of the House of Commons chaired by Zouch Tate]

Date: 10 December 1644
Source: TNA, SP16/503, fos 133r–v (no. 56.x) (autograph)

Six days after his first examination at the committee chaired by Zouch Tate and investigating his allegations about the conduct of the earl of Manchester, Cromwell appeared before the committee again and the examination was recorded by the same clerk and ends with Cromwell's own signature.

The hand looks surprisingly similar to Cromwell's in some ways (certainly the 'e'), but is quite clearly the clerk who wrote down the examinations of several others (Hesilrige, fo. 132r. Pickering 134r–135v) and we think others either in a faster, looser, hand, including Cromwell's first examination. The signature is Cromwell's. Several other examinations bear down on the episode and on Manchester's alleged comment about the consequences of defeating or being defeated by the King. The best known version ('that if we beate the King ninety & nine times yet he is king still, & so will be his posterity be after him, but if

---

[1] This displays ignorance, insouciance or insincerity. When three weeks later Cromwell's regiment heard that they were to be placed under a Scottish colonel, they were reported to have threatened mutiny. Richard Cockraine, deputy governor of Newport Pagnell added a postscript to a letter to Sir Samuel Luke, the governor, on 12 January 166/45: 'Sr: I hard that there was a greate mutinie at Cambr[idge] by Col: Cromwells Regim[en]t wch[struck out] who was to bee putt under another Col: wch is a Scotch man but they are resolved not to lay downe their Armes, till as they say have vindicated Col; Cromwell', BL, Stowe MS 190 fo. 104b, A modernised version is published in H. G. Tibbutt, ed., *The Letter Books of Sir Samuel Luke 1644–45*. HMC JP4 (1963), no. 106 on p. 420.

254

10 DECEMBER 1644

the king beat us once wee shall be all hanged and our posteritie made slaves') comes from the examination of Sir Arthur Hesilrige.[1]

The note at the bottom is a rough jotting, but almost certainly in the same clerk's hand.

––––––

[fo. 133v]

[endorsement]

Leiutenant Generall

Cromwells 2^{d} Examina

tion

[fo. 133r]

Tuessday 10^{ber}. 10th. 1644

Leiutenant Generall Cromwell Sayth.

That the Kings armie marching from Dunnington Castle & being drawen up on winterborne heath The army belonging to the Parlement drew out of the towne of newberry & newberry feild into Shawfeild about a mile from the kings army & the earle of manchester with diverse of the Cheife officers having viewed the Same did a little after repayer into a Cottage in or neere the Sayd feild Consult what to doe & amongst other debates it was urged by this examinante that if wee Should beate the kings army it would hinder his affayres in France & might prevent the Comming of french forces which into this Kingdome which wee heard was indeavoured to which his lordshippe gave answer that he did assure them meaning the Councell of warre then present there was noe Such thing as any forces to be brought from France which undertaking of his lordshippe this examinante wondered at Consideringe whatt he this examinante had heard Concerning endeavours of that nature, & this examinante Still pressing towards engagement His lordshippe Sayd forther that he was against fighting giving this as his reason & Saying that if wee Should beate the king never Soe often yet he would be king Still & his posterity, but if hee Should beate us but once wee must be hanged & our posterity undonne or words to that effect to which this examinante replyed that if this principle was true it Condemned all our former fighting as foolish & was an argument against fighting for the future & a ground for making a peace how dishonorable Soever.

––––––

[1] See the examinations of Sir William Waller (TNA, SP16/503, fos 124r, 152r–153v, 154r–155r); John Pitsom, Scoutmaster General (fo. 131r); Leon Watson (fos 138r–140v) and Henry Ireton (fos 156r–158r). The Hesilrige examination is TNA, SP16/503 fo. 132r.

Oliver Cromwell

Present att the examination. Sir Peter Wentworth. Mr Hodges ~~Mr S~~ Mr Stevens' Mr Holland. Mr Lisle.

1645 01 10
Reported speech by Cromwell in the House of Commons

Date: 10 January 1645
Source: Two versions, source given before each transcription

By late 1644 the soldiers from the army of the Eastern Association serving as a garrison at Henley-on-Thames, Oxfordshire, had become discontented. Two of the officers had already been removed.[1] Its governor, Colonel Robert Sterling, had also evidently refused to allow some of his men to join the army being assembled for the campaign in the south-west. Underlying this discontent was opposition to the proposed reorganisation of the parliamentarian armies. Those plans threatened to subsume the Eastern Association's army into a single national force. Moreover, moves to bar peers and MPs from holding military commissions, if implemented, would remove the earl of Manchester as their commander. Such concerns were, of course, inescapably bound up with the dispute between Cromwell and the earl. Cromwell wanted Manchester removed anyway. Those calling for Manchester to remain on as commander were therefore openly siding with the earl against Cromwell. In early January 1645 the pro-Manchester members of the Henley garrison attempted to submit a petition to Parliament. Their ringleaders included Sterling and one of the captains, Moses O'Neale.[2] But Cromwell was one step ahead of then.

[A] BL, Harl. MS 483, fo. 134, Diary of Sir Simonds D'Ewes

Consessum inter 9 et 10 ingressus, inter alia Oliveri Crowelli querelam audivi, quod ordinum ductores in comitis Mancastrii exercitu libellu supplicem oblaturi erant, ut ille contra nostri consessus plebiscitu supremum ipsorum continuaretur

---

[1] F. R. Harris, *The Life of Edward Montagu, K.G. First Earl of Sandwich* (London, 1912), 1:52.

[2] TNA, SP 14/506, fos 27–33. Both Sterling and O'Neale were officers in Manchester's regiment of foot. Laurence Spring, *The Regiments of the Eastern Association* (Bristol, 1998), 1:61–2 (the entries in the *Online Directory of Parliamentarian Army Officers* just repeat information that is in Spring).

10 JANUARY 1645

Imperator. hoc ad examinandum subdelegatis concreditum &c. Exii circa 12 nec denuo reversus sum &c. Surrexerunt circa 1 &c.

I entered the House between 9 and 10 am, and, amongst other things, I heard Oliver Cromwell complain that some officers in the earl of Manchester's army were about to present a petition that he [Manchester], contrary to the latest votes of the House, might continue as their commander. This was passed to the Committee of Examinations. I left at about 12 o'clock and did not go back. They rose at about 1 o'clock.

[B]   BL, Add. MS 31116, fo. 185v, Diary of Laurence Whitaker

This day the ho: was Inform'd by Coll: Cromwell tht he had sent Advertizmt,[3] tht One Capt Oneale was Come to Towne wth a peticon subscribed by 40 of the Officers of the Ea: of Manchesters Armey, wherein they dessier tht the Ea: of Manchester might still Continue Genll of tht Army they feareing tht it would Else breed a Greate Confussion amongst them by reason, of the difference Betweene the Presbiterians & Independants whome the Ea: favored not: And allso tht Lieut: Coll Sterling whoe is Govrner of Henly being required to draw Out his forces to assist Sr Will Waller refus'd to doe it until he had heard the Successe of tht Peticon, soe it was Ordered tht Capt Oneale, should be sent for in Safe Custody & his papers searched & tht Lieut: Coll Sterling should allso be sent for

---

Outcome: The Commons summoned O'Neale and Sterling to appear before them. The committee on the lord general's army was also asked to investigate the circumstances in which the petition had been organised.[4] That same day Sterling was replaced as governor by Edward Montagu,[5] a loyal ally of Cromwell against his kinsman, Manchester. Montagu's appointment however failed to solve the problem. The Henley garrison mutinied six weeks later.

---

[3] Advertisement = the action or an act of informing or notifying. See *OED*.
[4] *JHC*, 4:15–16.
[5] For Edward Montagu, see the *Online Directory of Parliamentarian Army Officers*.

1645 01 17

Letter from Oliver Cromwell to the sequestrators for the Isle of Ely

Date: 17 January 1644[/45] (London)
Source: TNA. SP16/539, Part 3, fos 7r–8v (no. 3) (autograph)

This letter is in a clerk's hand and signed by Cromwell but lacks a seal. Cromwell, as governor of Ely, is writing to the sequestrators appointed under the Ordinance of 11 October 1643[1] giving the earl of Manchester extensive powers over the Eastern Association.

[fo. 8v]
To the Sequestrators of the Isle of Ely these.

[fo. 7r]
Gentlemen.
If I have sound[2] any respect or favour from you, Or may any wayes Seeme to deserve any: I intreate yow most earnestly, and as for my selfe, that you will pay to Doctor Wells,[3] and to Mr William Sedgwick[4] the money which the Earle of Manchester hath given them a warrant to receive. I am inform'd that moneyes are not very plentifull with yow, Howbeit I intreate yow to doe this for my sake and for their sakes that should have it. for let me speake freely whatsoever the world may judge they doe fully deserve what I desire for them. I have not been often troublesome to yow, I have Studyed to deserve the good opinion of honest men, amongst which number, As I have cause to account yow Soe I hope I have the like esteeme with yow which I desire yow to testify by fulfilling this my request giveing yow the assurance of his unfained freindship, who is Your very loveing freind

Oliver Cromwell

London
Jan 17th 1644.

[1] A&O, 1:309.   [2] Definitely 'sound' in the manuscript but surely 'found'?
[3] Almost certainly Dr Walter Welles whom Cromwell had supported in his ministry at Godmanchester in the 1630s, perhaps now a preacher at Ely Cathedral. See John Morrill, 'The Making of Oliver Cromwell' in J. Morrill, ed., *Oliver Cromwell and the English Revolution* (Harlow, 1990), pp. 38–42.
[4] William Sedgwick, (bap. 1609, d. 1663/4). See *ODNB*.

1645 02 22
Speech by Oliver Cromwell to the House of Commons

Date: 22 February 1645
Source: BL, Harl. MS 166, fo. 179, Diary of Sir Simonds D'Ewes (reported speech)

On 15 January 1645 Sir William Waller had been appointed as the commander of the army to be sent to gain control of the south-west. It was envisaged that this army would be partly composed of men transferred from the existing armies commanded by the earls of Essex and Manchester. The plan was that they would rendezvous at Alresford, Hampshire. By mid-February however some units which had been ordered to join Waller's army had begun to mutiny. Most were reluctant to march until they had been paid. Among those that refused to march were some of Manchester's cavalry soldiers.[1] D'Ewes arrived in the Commons halfway through a debate on the subject.

I came into the Howse about 12 of the clocke & found them in debate about the mutinies of some of the Earle of Manchesters forces & Colonel Cromwell moved that some monie to pay part of ther arreares might be sent unto them &c.

Outcome: The Commons did not accept Cromwell's proposal, but it did agree to refer the issue to the committee on the lord general's army chaired by Zouch Tate.[2]

1645 04 09a
Letter from Oliver Cromwell to Sir Thomas Fairfax

Date: 9 April 1645
Source: BL, Harl. MS 166, fo. 189r (diary of Sir Simonds D'Ewes from 13 February 1643 to 3 November 1645) (reported speech)

On 12 April 1645 Fairfax wrote to the House of Commons about recent military developments (a letter that has not survived), but enclosing two letters he had received from senior

---
[1] John Adair, *Roundhead General: the campaigns of Sir William Waller* (Stroud, 1997), pp. 223–7.
[2] JHC, 4:59.

THE LETTERS, WRITINGS, AND SPEECHES OF OLIVER CROMWELL

military commanders in the field;[1] Sir Simonds D'Ewes MP[2] made copies of them and they appear, in his handwriting, in his diary. Cromwell's letter is the first of the two. The second (fo.189r & v) was from Edward Massey to Fairfax (and is dated from Gloucester on 9 April) noting the composition and movements of Rupert's army. Massey, who had been governor of Gloucester since June 1643, had been forced to withdraw out of the Forest of Dean[3] by their advance there. The House referred Fairfax's letter and its enclosures, to the Committee of the Army.

[fo. 189r]

For the Right honoble Sir Thomas Fairfax Generall of the Army. hast hast[4] theise at Windsor

Sir

Upon Sunday[5] last we marched towardes Bruton[6] in Sommersettsheire which was Genl Gorings[7] head Quarter, but hee would not stand us, but marched away upon our approach, to Wells,[8] and Glastenburye,[9] whether we held itt unsafe to follow him, least we should ingage our body of Horse too farr into that inclosed Cuntrie, not having Foot enowe to stand by them, and partly because we doubted the advance of Prince Rupert with his force, to joyne with Goringe having some notice from Coll: Masseye[10] of the Prince his Coming this way. Genll Goringe hath Greenvill[11] in a neere posture to joyne with ~~them~~ him, Hee hath all their guarrisons in Devon Dorsett and Somersettsheeire to make an Addition to him, whereupon Sir William Waller[12] haveing a very poore Infantry of about 1600 men, least they being soe inconsiderable, should engage our Horse, wee came from Shaftsburye[13] to Salisburye[14] to secure our Foot to prævent \the/ ~~our~~ being necessitated to ~~a~~ a too unæquall ingagement, and to be nearer a Conjunction

---

[1] JHC, 4:108.   [2] Sir Simonds D'Ewes, first baronet (1602–50). See ODNB.
[3] The Forest of Dean: the deeply wooded area of western Gloucestershire between the rivers Severn and Wye.
[4] i.e. haste, haste.
[5] i.e. 8 April. On Monday 9 April he was in Salisbury and on Tuesday 10th at Wilton, seat of the earl of Pembroke and 30 miles from Bruton.
[6] Bruton, a small market town in south-east Somersetshire.
[7] George Goring, Baron Goring (1608–57). See ODNB.
[8] Wells, Somerset, a cathedral city 12 miles north-west of Bruton.
[9] Glastonbury, Somerset, a town 15 miles due west of Bruton.
[10] Sir Edward Massey (1604x9–74), parliamentarian and royalist army officer. See ODNB.
[11] Sir Richard Grenville, baronet (bap. 1600, d. 1659), royalist army officer. See ODNB.
[12] Sir William Waller (bap. 1598? d. 1668), parliamentarian army officer. See ODNB.
[13] Shaftesbury, a parliamentary borough in Dorset.
[14] Salisbury, cathedral city in Wiltshire.

with our Freindes. Since our coming heither wee heare Prince Rupert is come to Marshfeild[15] a market Towne not farre from Trubridge,[16] If the Enemy advance altogether, how farre wee may bee indangerd, that I humbly offer to you, intreating you to take care of us, and to send us with all speed such an assistance to Salisbury as may inable us to keepe the Feild, and to repell the Enemye if God assist us, at least to secure and Countenance us soe, as that wee bee not put to the shame & hazard of a retreat, which will loose the Parliament many Freinds in theise parts, whoe will thinke themselves abandoned, upon our departure from them. Sir I beseech you send what Foot and Horse you can spare towardes Salisbury by the way of Kinges Cleere[17] with what convenient expedicon may bee, truly wee looke to be attempted upon every day, Theise things beinge humbly represented to your knowledg and Care, I subscribe my selfe Your most humble servant
Oliver Cromwell
April 9th tenn a Clocke att night. 1645.

1645 04 09b
Letter from Oliver Cromwell to Edward Whalley

Date: 9 April 1645
Source: Jones' Views of the Seats, Mansions, Castles, &c. of noblemen and gentlemen in England, Wales, Scotland, and Ireland, 6 vols. ([1829]–1830), vol. 2 [second series: comprising the western counties, 1829], sig. x2 (later copy)

This letter only exists in a nineteenth-century copy and is undated. The nineteenth-century editor states confidently that it was 'an original letter in the hand-writing of Oliver Cromwell', and that it was at that time in the 1820s at Melbury, Dorset, the seat of the earl of Ilchester.

Since Cromwell was writing from Salisbury and is only known to have been there on 9 April,[1] and since the letter appears to cohere with the other surviving letter he wrote that

---

[15] Marshfield, 16 miles north of Trowbridge on the Wiltshire/Gloucestershire border.
[16] Trowbridge, a market town in Wiltshire.
[17] Kingsclere, Hampshire, a village at the bottom of a big southern loop from army headquarters in Windsor to Salisbury.

[1] Gaunt, *Cromwellian Gazetteer,* p. 225.

THE LETTERS, WRITINGS, AND SPEECHES OF OLIVER CROMWELL

evening (**1645 04 09a**), the dating of 9 April seems secure.[2] Cromwell is writing to Edward Whalley, who was by then colonel of a newly formed cavalry regiment of the New Model Army, having previously been Lt Col in Cromwell's own regiment in the army of the Eastern Association.[3] He was also Cromwell's first cousin.

———

For the hble Coll: Edward Whalley at his quarters haste these.

Sir,

I desire you to be with all my troopes and Collonell Fines[4] his troopes alsoe, at Wilton[5] at a Rendevous by break of day to morrow morneing, for we heare the enemy has a designe upon our quarters to morrow. – morning.

Sir I am

Your Cozen & Servant

Oliver Cromwell.

Sarum,[6] Wednesday

night at 12 o'clock.

———⊗———

1645 04 25a
Letter from Oliver Cromwell to Sir Thomas Fairfax

Date: 25 April 1645

Source: *An abstract of a letter from Lieutenant-Generall Crumwell to Sir Thomas Fairfax command-er in chiefe of the forces raised for the defence of the kingdome. Dated April 26. 1645…Published by authority.* London: Printed for Francis Coles in the Old-baily, 1645 (Wing / C7039; Thomason / E.279[7]) (contemporary print)

This letter survives only in print, in a pamphlet and in a newspaper, the second quite possibly a loose transcription of the former.[1] The version used here is certainly the basis

———

[2] When J. L. Sanford republished the letter in his *Studies and Illustrations of the Great Rebellion* (1858), at p. 623, he too dates it to 9 April but without explanation. 9 April 1645 was a Wednesday, and Wednesday is given as the day of the week on which Cromwell was writing.

[3] Wanklyn, *Reconstructing* 1:53.

[4] John Fiennes, appointed Lord Fiennes under the Protectorate (d. in or before 1710), parlia-mentarian army officer and politician. See *ODNB*. For his military career to this point, see the *Online Directory of Parliamentarian Army Officers.*

[5] Wilton House, just outside Salisbury, was the seat of the earls of Pembroke.

[6] Sarum = Salisbury, a cathedral city in Wiltshire.

———

[1] *The Weekly Account, containing certain special and remarkable passages*, no. 17 for 23–29 April 1645, under Saturday 26 April (N&S, 671:271; Thomason / E.279[12]).

for other newspaper accounts[2] of the skirmish at Islip[3] and the surrender of Bletchingdon House.[4] This letter needs to be read alongside the letter written on the same day to the Committee of Both Kingdoms (see **1645 04 25b**). Cromwell's swift action was designed to disrupt the reinforcement of Oxford, especially with big guns, hence the emphasis on rounding up every horse he could find so as to immobilise the guns Prince Maurice had with him.

The pamphlet also contains the articles of surrender of Bletchingdon. These are also contained in Cromwell's letter to the Committee of Both Kingdoms (**1645 04 25b**) and they can be found there rather than in his second-hand copy.

[p. 1]

AN ABSTRACT Of the Letter, sent from Generall *Crumwell*, to Sir *Thomas Fairfax*, Commander in chiefe of the Forces raised for the defence of the Kingdome.

Right Honourable:

I met at my Randezvous at *Notingham*,[5] on Wednesday last, where I staid somewhat long for the comming up of the Bodie of Horse, which Gods Honour[6] was pleased to give mee command of: After the comming whereof I marched with all expedition to *Wheatly*-Bridge,[7] having sent before to Major Generall *Browne*,[8] for what Intelligence he could afford me of the state of affaires in *Oxford*, I being not so well acquainted in those parts, and the condition and number of the

---

[2] Both *The Kingdomes Weekly Intelligencer* no. 97 for 22–29 April (N&S, 241.096; Thomason / E.279[11]) and *Perfect Passages* no. 27 for 23–29 April (N&S, 523.27; Thomason / E.260[25]), cite Cromwell's letter to Fairfax as their authority for the events of this week and indeed draw heavily on its text, both under 26 April.

[3] Islip, Oxfordshire, seven miles due north of Oxford.

[4] Bletchingdon House, three miles further north, was a medieval manor house completely rebuilt in the 1630s by Sir Thomas Coghill and in April 1645 had a royalist garrison of about 200 men (*VCH Oxfordshire*, 6:56–71).

[5] Almost certainly 'Nottingham' in both printed versions is a mistranscription of Watlington, which is a few miles south-east of Oxford and on a direct route from Reading (which Cromwell left on 21 April) to Islip (where he fought this skirmish three days later). It is also confirmed by **1645 04 25b**.

[6] Both printed versions use the phrase 'God's Honour'. Sophia Lomas suggests this is a mistranscription of 'Your Honour', surely correctly: Carlyle-Lomas, 3:327.

[7] Wheatley is a village midway between Watlington and Oxford and suggests that Cromwell was sweeping to the east of Oxford on his way to the encounters at Islip and Bletchingdon, well to the North.

[8] Sir Richard Browne, first baronet (*c*.1602–69), parliamentarian army officer and lord mayor of London. See *ODNB*. He was major general in the South Midlands Association of Berkshire, Buckinghamshire and Oxfordshire.

THE LETTERS, WRITINGS, AND SPEECHES OF OLIVER CROMWELL

Enemy in *Oxford*, as him- [p. 2] selfe informed me by Letters; That Prince *Maurice*[9] his Forces were not in *Oxford*, (as I suppos'd), and that as he was informed by foure very honest and faithfull Gentlemen, that came out of *Oxford* to him a little before the Receipt of this Letter,[10] that there were Twelve Peeces of Ordnance, with their Carriages and Waggons, readie for a March, and in another place Five more Peeces, with their Carriages, another[11] readie to Advance with their Convoy: After I received this satistaction from Major Generall *Browne*, I advanced this Morning, being Thursday,[12] the Twenty fourth of *Aprill*, neere *Oxford*, then I lay before the Enemie perceiving it at *Oxford*, and[13] they being in readinesse to advance, sent out a partie of Horse against me, part of the Queenes Regiment,[14] part of the Earle of *Northamptons*[15] Regiment, and part of the Lord *Wilmotes*[16] Regiment, who made an Infall[17] upon mee whereupon your Honours Regiment (lately mine owne) I drew forth against the Enemie (who had drawne themselves into severall Squadrons,[18] to be readie for Action) and your Honours owne Troope therein, I commanded to Charge a Squadron of the Enemie, who performed it so gallantly, that after a short fiering they entred the whole Squadron, and put them to a Confusion, and the rest of my Horse presently entring after them, they made a Totall Roote[19] of the Enemie, and had the Chace of them three or foure Miles, and killed Two Hundred, tooke as many Prisoners, and about Foure Hundred Horse, and the Queenes Colours Richly Embrodered with the

---

[9] Maurice, prince palatine of the Rhine (1621–1652), royalist army officer and naval officer. See *ODNB*.

[10] Not identified.

[11] The version in *The Weekly Account* has 'five more Peeces and their Cariages, ready to advance'.

[12] The version in *The Weekly Account* omits 'this Morning, being Thursday'. But 24 April 1645 was a Monday not a Thursday. If Cromwell wrote 'this day' then he began it on the Monday and completed it on Thursday 25 April (as he dates it at the end) which would mean that the printer mis-transcribed Tuesday as Thursday.

[13] The version in *The Weekly Account* replaces 'then I lay before the Enemie perceiving it at Oxford, and' with 'which the enemy perceiving, and'.

[14] For the Queen's Regiment in the Civil War, see bcw-project.org/royalist/horse-regiments/the-queen. The commander at this time was Lt Col Sir John Cansfield (for whom see Newman, *Royalist Officers*, no. 240).

[15] For the military career of James Compton, earl of Northampton, see Newman, *Royalist Officers*, no. 322.

[16] Henry Wilmot, first earl of Rochester (bap. 1613, d. 1658). See *ODNB*.

[17] Infall = according to *OED*, 'attack, incursion, or descent upon an army, town, etc.'.

[18] Squadron = a small group of horsemen consisting of men chosen from more than one company but a lot less than a regiment.

[19] The version in *The Weekly Account*, presumably more accurately, has 'rout'.

25 APRIL 1645B

Crowne in the midst, and Eighteene Flower- [p. 3] Deluces[20] wrought about all in Gold, with a Golden Crosse on the Top: many escapt to *Oxford*, and divers were drowned, parte of them likewise betooke themselves to a strong House in *Bletchington*, where Colonell *Windebanke*[21] kept a Garrison with neere Two Hundred Horse and Foote therein, which after surrounded I summoned, but they seemed very delatory in their Answer, at last they sent out Articles to me of Surrender (which I have sent your Honour inclosed) and after a large Treatie thereupon, the Surrender was agreed upon betweene us, they left behind them between two and Three Hundred Musquets, Seventy Horses, besides other Armes and Ammunition: I Humbly rest Your Honours Humble Servant
Oliver Crumwell
25 of Aprill, 1645.

⊗⊗⊗

1645 04 25b
Letter from Oliver Cromwell to the Committee of Both Kingdoms

Date: 25 April 1645
Source: Parliamentary Archives, HL, PO/JO/1/34: Journal of the House of Lords, 24 April to 25 July 1645 (unfol.) (contemporary copy)

Having written about his latest military successes to Fairfax. Cromwell then sent a more circumspect letter to the Committee of Both Kingdoms. It was passed by the Committee to the House of Lords,[1] who ordered it to be fully entered in their Journals and then passed on to the Commons, who entered it in more summary form into their Journal. The original was then copied into the Main Papers of the Lords. It is striking that it is Cromwell's letter to Fairfax, not this version, which was released for publication (**1645 04 25a**).

---

[20] 'Flowers Deluces', presumably fleurs de lis. The fleur de lis was an ornamental lily which formed part of the heraldic arms of the French Crown/royal family and thereafter appropriate for the French queen of Charles I to have on her colours (see *OED*).

[21] Francis Windebank, younger son of Sir Francis Windebank (d. 1646), former secretary of state to Charles I: see Newman, *Royalist Officers*, no. 1591. For surrendering Bletchington so easily, Windebank was court-martialled and shot.

---

[1] JHL, 7:339–41. It is preceded with this note: 'Next a lre was reported to this house from the Com{mittee}of both Kingdomes, written from Lt Generall Cromwe{ll} with the Articles betweene him & Coll Wyndebanke, Ap{ril} the 24th. 1645.'

265

THE LETTERS, WRITINGS, AND SPEECHES OF OLIVER CROMWELL

My Lords and Gentlemen

According to your Lopps appointments I have attended your service in these parts, and have not had soe fitt an opportunity to give you account as now, Soe soone as I received your Commaunds I appointed a Rendezvous at Watlington[2] The body being come upp I marched to wheatly bridge haveing sent before to Major Generall Browne[3] for intelligence And it being Markett day at Oxford from whence I ~~hoped~~ likewise hoped by some of the Markett people to gaine notice where the Enemy was, toward night I received certaine notice from Major G: Browne that the Carryages[4] were not stirred, that Prince Maurice[5] was not here; And by fower Oxford Schollers[6] with their carriages & Waggons ready and in annother place five all (as conceived) fitt for a march I received notice alsoe that the Earle of Northtones[7] Regimt: was quartered at Islip,[8] In the evening I marched that way hopeing to have surprized them, but by mistake, and fayling of the forlorne hope[9] they had an alarum there and to all their Quarters, and soe escaped. By meanes whereof they had tyme to drawe ~~altogether~~ all together, I kept my body all night at Islipp, and in the morning a part of the earle of Northtons Regiment the Lord Wilmotts[10] and the Queenes[11] came to make an infall upon me, Sir Thomas Fairefax Regiment was the first that tooke the feild the rest drewe out with all possible speed, and that which is the Generalls Troope charged a whole squadron[12] of the Enemy presently brake it, and our other Troopes commeing seasonably on, the rest of the Enemy were presently put into a confusion soe that wee had the Chase of them three or fower Miles, wherein wee killed many and tooke neere 200 prisonrs: and aboute 400 Horse, many of them

---

[2] Watlington, a village south-east of Oxford.

[3] Sir Richard Browne, first baronet (c.1602–69), parliamentarian army officer and lord mayor of London. See *ODNB*. He was major general in the South Midlands Association of Berkshire, Buckinghamshire and Oxfordshire.

[4] Carryages = gun carriages.   [5] Maurice, prince palatine of the Rhine.

[6] Not identified.

[7] James Compton, third earl of Northampton: see Newman, *Royalist Officers*, no. 322.

[8] Islip, Oxfordshire, seven miles due north of Oxford.

[9] 'forlorn hope'—an advance party sent to sound out enemy positions.

[10] Henry Wilmot, first earl of Rochester (bap. 1613, d. 1658), royalist army officer. See *ODNB*.

[11] For the Queen's Regiment in the Civil War, see bcw-project.org/royalist/horse-regiments/the-queen. The commander at this time was Lt Col Sir John Cansfield (for whom see Newman, *Royalist Officers*, no. 240).

[12] Squadron = a small group of horsemen consisting of men chosen from more than one company but a lot less than a regiment.

escaped towards Oxford, and Woodstocke[13] divers were drowned, and diverse gott into a strong House in Bletchington[14] belonging to Sir Thomas Coggin,[15] wherein Coll: Windebancke[16] kept a Garrison with neere two hundred, whome I presently summoned and after long Treaty he went out aboute 12 at night with these Termes here inclosed leaveing us betweene .2. and 300. Musketts besides Horse Armes and other Amunicion And aboute three score and Eleven Horses more This was the mercy of God, and nothing more due then a reall acknowledgmt And though wee have had greater mercyes, yet none cleerer, because in the first God brought them to our hands when wee looked not for them, and layed a reasonable designe which wee carefully endeavored in It appeares in this alsoe that I did much doubt the storming of the House it being strong and well manned, I having few dragoons ~~and~~ and this not being my busines, and yet wee gott it, I hope you will pardon me if I say God is not enough owned wee looke to much to men and visible helps, this hath much hindred our successe but I hope God will direct all to acknowledge him alone in all

Your most humble servant

Oliver Cromwell.

Bletchington
April. 25. 1645

Articles of Agreement upon the surrender of Bletchington House betweene Liuetennt Generall Cromwell, and Colonell Wyndebanke Aprill 24th 1645

1° First it is agreed that all officers of Horse of Commission of the Garrison shall march away with their Horse, sword, and Pistoll.

2° That the Colonell and the Major are to march with their Horse, swords and Pistolls, and the Captaines of Foote to march with their Horse and Swords,

---

[13] Woodstock, a market town eight miles north-west of Oxford.

[14] Bletchingdon House, three miles further north, was a medieval manor house completely rebuilt in the 1630s and in April 1645 had a royalist garrison of about 200 men (*VCH Oxfordshire*, 6:56–71).

[15] Sir Thomas Coghill, who had rebuilt Bletchingdon House in the 1630s. For his background (London mercantile wealth) see https://armorial.library.utoronto.ca/stamp-owners/COG002.

[16] Francis Windebank, see Newman, *Royalist Officers*, no. 1591. For surrendering Bletchington so easily, Windebank was court-martialled and shot.

3° That all the Souldiers in the Garrison are to march a way leaving their Armes Colours and drumms behind them, and for such officers of Horse, as retreate hither for safety, they are to march a way with their swords

4° That Mr Hutchinson,[17] Mr Ernly,[18] Mr Edes, and Mr Pitts[19] being gentlemen that came to visit the Colonell & not engaged, shall march a way with their horses swords and Pistolls.

5° That all other Armes and Amunicion shall be delivered upp immediatly to Luietennt Generall Cromwell without imbezling except above mencioned

6° That a ~~salfe~~ safe Conduct bee graunted by the Liuetennt Generall for all the abovemencioned to Oxford.

7° That the Colonells wife his two servants and Chapline[20] March a way a long with the Colonell with their Horses

8 That the Lady of the House shall enjoy her goods as before without plunder and all her family.

Subscribitur
Windebanke.

1645 04 28

Letter from Oliver Cromwell to the Committee of Both Kingdoms

Date: 28 April 1645
Source: Parliamentary Archives, HL/PO/JO/10/1/185, fos 187r–188v (House of Lords Main Papers, 28 April 1645) (contemporary transcription)

The original of this letter has not survived. Cromwell had written from the siege of Faringdon to the Committee of Both Kingdoms and the committee sent this copy to the two Houses of Parliament, where it is noticed in the Lords Journal and a little more fully in

---

[17] A Lt Col Hutchinson (Christian name not given) is listed in Newman, Royalist Officers, no. 793 as having been cashiered by the King for his part in the surrender of Bletchington.
[18] Major Richard Earnley is listed in Newman, Royalist Officers, no. 468. He too was subsequently cashiered.
[19] Masters Eddes and Pitts have not been identified.
[20] Chaplain not identified (for example he cannot be traced through Matthews, Walker Revised; or www.theclergydatabase.org.uk/).

28 APRIL 1645

the *Commons Journal*.[1] It continues the story of Cromwell's campaign around Oxford and specifically his letter to the Committee of Both Kingdoms three days earlier (**1645 04 25b**). It records more success, a keen sense of strategy and it bristles with confidence and energy.

———

[fo. 187r]

Copie

My Lords & Gent:

Since my last it has pleased God to blesse me with more Successe in your Service. In pursuance of your Comands I marched from Bletchington[2] to Middleton Stonnie,[3] and from thence towards Witny,[4] as privately as I could, beleiving that, to be a good place for interposing betweene the King & the West, whether he intended, Goring,[5] & Greenevill[6] or the two Princes,[7] In my march I was enformed of a body of Foote which were marching towards Faringdon[8] (which ~~intended~~ indeed were a comanded Party of 300. which came a day before from Faringdon, under Col. Rich: Vaughan[9] to Strengthen Woodstocke[10] against mee, & were now returning) I understood they were not above 3. howers march before me. I sent after them, my forlorne overtooke them as they had gotten into Inclosures not farr from Brampton Bush,[11] skirmished with them, they Killed

[1] *JHL*, 7:345 for 1 May 1645: 'Letters from Colonels Cromwell and Massey. The Lord Wharton reported divers Letters from the Committee of both Kingdoms, which were read; One from Colonel Cromwell, another from Colonel Massey.' *JHC*, 4:127: 'The Copy of a Letter from Lieutenant-General Cromwell, of April is 28 1645, relating the Taking of some Ninescore Prisoners, besides Officers, and some Two hundred Horse, was this Day read.'

[2] Bletchingdon, Oxfordshire, five miles from Oxford. For Cromwell's taking of Bletchington House on terms, see **1645 04 25a** and **1645 04 25b**.

[3] Middleton Stoney, Oxfordshire, five miles from Bletchingdon.

[4] Witney, Oxfordshire, 16 miles west of Middleton Stoney.

[5] George Goring, Baron Goring (1608–57), royalist army officer. See *ODNB*; also Newman, *Royalist Officers*, no. 627.

[6] Sir Richard Grenville, baronet (bap. 1600, d. 1659), royalist army officer. See *ODNB*; also Newman, *Royalist Officers*, no. 637.

[7] i.e. Charles, Prince of Wales and Prince Maurice of the Palatinate.

[8] Faringdon, Oxfordshire, 12 miles south of Witney and 18 miles west of Oxford.

[9] Colonel Richard Vaughan. The only man of that name recorded by Newman, *Royalist Officers*, no. 1481 was serving, apparently, in South Wales and in any case was by then ennobled. Cromwell may have confused him with Lt Col Henry Vaughan (Newman, *Royalist Officers*, no. 1478) who was in the Oxford area at the time. But note the reference to 'Sir Richard Vaughan', apparently the same man, later in the letter. So a puzzle.

[10] Woodstock, a market town 10 miles north of Oxford.

[11] Brampton (historically Brampton-in-the-Bush) is an Oxfordshire village just four miles from Cromwell's last resting place at Witney and midway between Witney and Faringdon.

THE LETTERS, WRITINGS, AND SPEECHES OF OLIVER CROMWELL

some of my horses, nine Killed & got some of them, but they recovered the Towne before my body came up, & my forlorne[12] not being strong enough was not able to doe more then they did, the Enemy presently barricadoed up the Towne got ~~pe~~ a pretty strong house, my body comeing up about Eleven in the night. I sent them a Summons: they Slighted it, I put my Selfe in a posture that they should not escape mee, hopeing to deale with them in the morning, my men charged them up to their [fo. 187v] Barricadoes[13] in the night but truely they were of soe good resolution that wee could not force them from it, and indeed they Killed Some of my horses and I was forced to waite untill the morning besides they had got a passe over a brooke, in the night they Strengthened themselves as well as they could in the Store house. In the morning I sent a Drum to them, but their answere was they would not quitt except they might march out upon honoble. Tearmes. the tearmes I offered were to Submitt all to mercy, they refused with anger. I insisted upon them, & prepared to Storme, I sent them word to desire them to deliver out the Gent. & his family which they did, for they must expect extremity, if they put me to a Storme. after some tyme Spent all was yeilded to mercy. Armes I tooke Musquettes neare 200: besides other Armes about 2 Barrelles of Powder, Souldieres & Officeres neare 200: Ninescore besides Officers, the rest being Scattered & killed before: The Chiefe Prisonrs. were Colonell Sir Rich: Vaughan Lieutent: Coll: Littleton[14] & Major: Lee,[15] 2 or 3. Captaines & other Officers. As I was upon my march I heard of some horse of the Enemy which crossed me towards Evesham,[16] I sent Colonell Fiennes[17] after them, whom God soe blessed, that he tooke about 30. Prisonrs. 100 horse & three horse Colours, truely his dilligence was great & this I must testifie that I finde noe man more ready to all Services then himselfe I would say soe if I did not finde it, if his men [fo. 188r] were at all considered I should hope you might expect very S reall Service from them; I speake this the rather because I finde him a Gentleman of that fidelity to you & so conscientious that he would all his Troups were as Religious & Civill as any, & make it a great pare of his Care to gett them Soe. In this march my men

---

[12] 'forlorn' = forlorn hope: a picked body of men, detached to the front to begin the attack; a body of skirmishers (see *OED*).

[13] 'Barricadoes' = hastily formed ramparts of barrels, wagons, timber, stones, household furniture, or any other materials readily available, thrown up to obstruct the advance of an enemy (see *OED*).

[14] Lt Col Edward Littleton, see Newman, *Royalist Officers*, no. 899.   [15] Not identified.

[16] Evesham, Worcestershire.

[17] Colonel John Fiennes, see the *Online Dictionary of Parliamentarian Army Officers*.

28 APRIL 1645

alsoe got me of the Quenes Troopers[18] & of them & others about 100. horses. This morning Col. John ~~Fiend~~ Fiennes Sent me in the Gent.[19] that waites upon the Lord Digbie[20] in his Chamber, who was goeing to Genll: Goring about exchange of a Prisoner ~~he~~ he tells me the King's forces were drawen out the last night to come to releive Sir Rich Vaughan,[21] And Leg[22] comande them, they were about 700 horse & 500. Foote, but I beleive they are gone backe, he saith many of the Horse were Voluntiers, Gent: for I beleive I have left him few others here, I looked upon his letters & found them directed to Marlorough.[23] Hee tells mee Goring is about the Devises,[24] I asked him what further Orders he had to him, he tells me he was onely to bid him follow further Orders I pressed him to know, what they were, and all that I could get was that it was to hasten with all he had up to the King to Oxford He Sayth he has about 3000. horse & 1000. Foote, that he is discontented that Prince Rupert comanded away his Foote. I am now quartered up to Farringdon. I [fo. 188v] shall have an eye towards him. I have that which was my Regimt. & a part of Colonell Sydneys[25] 5 Troops more recreuted & a part of Col: Vermudens[26] and 5 Troopes of Col: Fiennes 3. whereof & Sir John[27] & Capt: Hamonds[28] I sent with the first Prisonrs. to Aylesbury[29] Its great pitty wee want dragoones I beleive most of their petty Guarrisons might have beene taken in & other Services done for the Enemy is in high feare, God does terrifie them. its good to take the Season, & surely God delights that you have endeavoured to reforme your Armyes, & I begg it may be done more & more, bad men & discontented Say its faction, I wish to be of the faction that desires to avoyd the oppression of the poore people of this miserable Nation, upon whom who can looke

[18] For the Queen's Regiment in the Civil War, see http://wiki.bcw-project.org/royalist/horse-regiments/the-queen

[19] Not identified.

[20] George Digby, second earl of Bristol (1612–77), politician. See *ODNB*.

[21] See above, n. 9.

[22] William Legge (1607/8–70), royalist army officer. See *ODNB*. He was governor of Oxford at this time. See also Newman, *Royalist Officers*, no. 869.

[23] Marlborough is a market town in Wiltshire.

[24] Devizes, another market town in Wiltshire.

[25] For Algernon Sidney's military career to this point, see the *Online Dictionary of Parliamentarian Army Officers*. For his career in full: Algernon Sidney [Sydney], (1623–83), political writer. See *ODNB*.

[26] For Colonel Bartholemew Vermuyden's pre-New Model career, see his entry in the *Online Dictionary of Parliamentarian Army Officers*.

[27] Not identified.

[28] For Captain Thomas Hammond, see the *Online Dictionary of Parliamentarian Army Officers*.

[29] Aylesbury, Berkshire.

without[30] a bleeding heart, truely it greives my Soule Our men should still be upon free Quarters as they are. I beseech you helpe it what & as Soone as you can My Lords pardon me this boldnesse, it is because I finde in these things wherein I serve you, that Hee doe's all, I professe his very hand has led me, I preconsulted none of these things My Lords & Gent: I waite your farther pleasure Subscribing my Selfe

Oliver Cromwell.

Aprill 28th. 1645

1645 04 29a
Letter from Oliver Cromwell to Roger Burgess, deputy [or lieutenant] governor of Faringdon

Date: 29 April 1645

Source: *Mercurius Aulicus, communicating the intelligence, and affaires of the court to the rest of the kingdome*, 27 April–4 May 1645 (N&S, 275.314 / Thomason / E.285[14]), p. 1570) (contemporary print)

Cromwell arrived at Faringdon on the Oxford/Berkshire border and at the head of the Vale of the White Horse sometime during 28 April. Faringdon was a small market town, but within it was a 'large and straggling habitation of Elizabethan or early Jacobean design' that had been acquired by Sir Robert Pye, Remembrancer of the Exchequer since 1621. It had a garrison of perhaps 200 men. During the following day (29 April) Cromwell exchanged letters with the governor, Sir Roger Burgess,[1] who refused to surrender. Reinforced by men from the South Midlands Association, Cromwell attempted to storm the town at 3am on the morning of 30 April but was driven back with an unknown number of casualties and at least three officers were taken prisoner. In a further letter later that day, Cromwell thanked Burgess for returning the bodies and offered an exchange of prisoners. He then abandoned the siege and headed westwards, reaching Newbury on 2 May.[2] Cromwell's three letters from Faringdon, **1645 04 29a**, **1645 04 29b** and **1645 04 30** only

---

[30] Possibly two words, 'with out'.

[1] Roger Burgess, for whose career see Newman, *Royalist Officers*, no. 211.

[2] There is a full account of the siege and its context in C. H. Hartman, *Faringdon in the Civil War*, available online at http://www.faringdon.org/uploads/1/4/7/6/14765418/ faringdon_in_ the_civil_war_ hartman.pdf.

29 APRIL 1645B

survive as part of a narrative gloating at his failure in the very unreliable royalist newsbook *Mercuries Aulicus*. They must be treated with some caution but they show no signs of having been written or re-written by Sir John Berkenhead or others involved in the editing of *Mercurius Aulicus*.[3]

Also included here are the letters of Burgess and some editorial comments by Berkenhead to give more context to Cromwell's letter. Here is the first of the three letters. It claims to have been despatched at 4pm on 29 April.

Sir,

I summon you to deliver into my hands the house wherein you are and your ammunition with all things else there, and persons to be disposed of as the Parliament shall appoint, which if you refuse to doe you are to expect the uttermost extremities of warre. I rest

Your Servant

Oliver Cromwell

April 29. 1645

To the Governour of the Garrison in Farringdon.

1645 04 29b

Letter from Oliver Cromwell to Roger Burgess, deputy [or lieutenant] governor of Faringdon

Date: [29] April 1645

Source: *Mercurius Aulicus, communicating the intelligence, and affaires of the court to the rest of the kingdome*, 27 April–4 May 1645 (N&S, 275.314; Thomason / E.285[14]), p. 1571) (contemporary print)

The date is not given but can be inferred from its following the summons issued on 29 April (see above **1645 04 29a**). It also clearly precedes the failed assault on the House at 3am on 30 April. *Mercurius Aulicus* prints Lt Col Burgess's reply to the summons ('That the King had entrusted them to keepe that Garrison, and without speciall order from His Majesty Himselfe they could not deliver it'), it says that Cromwell brought his men up

---

[3] The fullest account of the editorial reliability of *Mercurius Aulicus* is in P. W. Thomas, *Sir John Berkenhead 1617–1679: a Royalist Career in Politics and Polemics* (Oxford, 1969), chs. 2–4 and (with particular emphasis on military coverage in 1645), pp. 67–72.

THE LETTERS, WRITINGS, AND SPEECHES OF OLIVER CROMWELL

closer and then issued this second, and more menacing, summons together with the governor's defiant response:

—————

Sir, I understand by 40 or 50 poore men whom you forced into your house that you have many still there whom you cannot arme, and who are not serviceable to you: if these men should perish by your meanes it were great inhumanity, surely honour and honesty re- quires this, and though you be prodigall of your owne lives, yet be not of theirs, if God give you into my hands I will not spare a man of you if you put me to a storme.

Oliver Cromwell.

This particular of forcing men into the Garrison was Crom well's meer pretence whereon to ground another Summons, for he was willing (if possible) to word it onely; but the brave Lieutenant Governour did hope Cromwell was now engaged to fight, & therefore instantly disptacht him this answer. Sir, We have forced none into our Garrison, we would have you know you are not now at Blechington:[1] the guiltlesse bloud that shall be spilt God will require at your hands that have caused this unnaturall warre. We feare not your Storming, nor will have any more Parlies. your Servant.

Roger Burges.

—————⟨⟩—————

1645 04 30

Letter from Oliver Cromwell to Roger Burgess, deputy [or lieutenant] governor of Faringdon.

Date: 30 April 1645
Source: *Mercurius Aulicus, communicating the intelligence, and affaires of the court to the rest of the kingdome,* 27 April–4 May 1645 (N&S, 275.314; Thomason / E.285[14]), p. 1572) (contemporary print)

This letter follows on, with narrative passages, from Cromwell's summonses to the governor of Faringdon and after a failed attempt to storm the town at 3am on 30 April. Cromwell lost fourteen men in the assault, and more who were wounded or taken prisoner and he had been driven back.[1] Before abandoning the siege and moving off to pursue royalists in

—————

[1] For the surrender of Bletchingdon (and the consequences for its royalist defenders) see **1645 04 25b**.

—————

[1] There is a full account of the siege and its context in C. H. Hartman, *Faringdon in the Civil War*, only available online at http://www.faringdon.org/uploads/1/4/7/6/14765418/faringdon_in_the_civil_war_hartman.pdf.

274

the west, Cromwell wrote this letter thanking Burgess[2] for returning the bodies of those of his men who had been killed, and suggesting an exchange of prisoners. This particular letter, set as it is amidst some gloating from the royalist *Mercurius Aulicus*, is less likely than the earlier letters to have been doctored.

Sir, There shall be no interruption of your viewing and gathering together the dead bodies,[3] and I doe acknowledge it as a favour, your willingnesse to let me dispose of them. Captaine Cannon[4] is but a Captaine, his Major is Smith[5] so farre as I knowe, but he is a stranger to me, I am confident he is but a Captaine, Master Elmes[6] but an Ancient, I thanke you for your civility to them, you may credit me in this, I rest
Your servant
Oliver Cromwell
April 30.
If you accept of equall exchange I shall performe my duty.

1645 05 04

Letter from Oliver Cromwell to Sir Peter Wentworth MP

Date: 4 May 1645
Source: BL, Egerton MS 2042 (a miscellaneous collection of holograph letters dated 1645–1736), fos 1r–2v (holograph)

Cromwell's holograph letter is to one of the most radical MPs in the Commons. Parliament had not yet agreed to agree who should be lieutenant general and commander of the cavalry in the New Model Army, and there was no guarantee or indeed likelihood that it would be Cromwell, given the hostility of many, especially in the Lords, to him. So he is in the final days of his existing commission. This letter would seem to be his plea on behalf of an officer for whom he had a high regard and who had not been commissioned into the New Model but who Cromwell believed could still be useful to the cause. He asks

---

[2] See **1645 04 29a**.
[3] There were fourteen men killed including an unnamed captain sent over from Abingdon to assist Cromwell.
[4] This was Captain Henry Cannon, for whom see the *Online Directory of Parliamentarian Army Officers*.
[5] No Major Smith who could have been in this regiment at this time has been found.
[6] Not identified.

THE LETTERS, WRITINGS, AND SPEECHES OF OLIVER CROMWELL

Wentworth to assist in getting Major Purbeck Temple appointed as governor of Newport Pagnell.

Sir Samuel Luke (a fierce Presbyterian and anti-sectarian) was MP for Bedford and he was therefore required under the Self-Denying Ordinance to give up the position as governor of Newport Pagnell he had held since October 1643. He had recommended his deputy Lt Col Richard Cockraine[1] to replace him and the parliamentary committee that had been appointed in 8 April[2] to make nominations to garrison governorships vacated under the Self-Denying Ordinance had supported Cockraine's appointment.[3] Wentworth was on that committee and when the recommendation came to the floor of the House five days after Cromwell wrote this letter and about three days after we can be confident that Wentworth received it, Wentworth acted as a teller *against* Cockraine's appointment.[4] In the event Cockraine's appointment was voted down by 60 votes to 53. Intriguingly on 3 May, the day before this letter was written (but after Cromwell could have heard the news), it was Wentworth who had brought in the nomination of Cromwell's friend Francis Russell as Cromwell's relief as governor of the Isle of Ely.[5] What is more, on 1 May Wentworth had been appointed to draft a letter of thanks to be sent by the Speaker to Cromwell for his recent successes in the Oxford area. So in seeking a new favour from Wentworth, Cromwell was writing to a kindred spirit.

It took several months to resolve the dispute over the governorship of Newport Pagnell, and the eventual decision (in August) was to appoint neither Cockraine nor Temple, but Charles Doyley, a nominee of Sir Thomas Fairfax.[6]

[fo. 2v]

[Three seals, one fairly intact]
For my honoured freind
Sir Peter Wentworth[7] Knt
of the Bath[8]

      these

Lt: Gen: Cromwell 4 May 1645
concerning Major Temple[9]
in London

---

[1] Richard Cockraine. See the *Online Directory of Parliamentarian Army Officers*. There are many entries to Cockraine in Luke's letter books.

[2] JHC, 4:104. [3] Tibbutt, *Letter Books of Sir Samuel Luke*, p. 517. [4] JHC, 4:136.

[5] JHC, 4:128.

[6] JHC, 4:164, 235, 239; TNA SP28/7 fo.117, SP28/121B, SP28/127 part 1, fos 7v–8r; Tibbutt, *Letter Books of Sir Samuel Luke*, and *passim*.

[7] Sir Peter Wentworth (1592–1675). See *ODNB*; and his entry in *HoP Commons, 1640–1660*.

[8] This endorsement is not in Cromwell's hand.

[9] This is a separate endorsement in a different hand and 'in London' is clearly added later.

4 MAY 1645

Lt: Generall Cromwell
4 May 1645[10]

[fo. 1r]
Sir Peter wentworth, although I never
had the honor to have a word from you,
yett I hope you have not cast mee out
of your favor, Ile trye you, Major
Temple[11] it seemes has had some re=
commendation from maior Generall
Skippon[12] to the government of Newport
Pagnell,[13] if itt lye in your way
to shew him any favor heerein
or any of my friendes, I beleive
the gentleman is very right, for=
ward, and noble, [—] therfore (ex=
cept you bee præingaged) I begg
your assistance to him heerin. I
shall ever say ditur digniori.[14]
Sir no man is more yours then

Your humble servant
Oliver Cromwell

May 4th.
1645

[10] A further endorsement in yet another seventeenth-century hand.
[11] Purbeck Temple, major in Colonel John Fiennes regiment and left in charge of Bletchington after Cromwell took it three weeks earlier. He was later appointed to be governor of Henley: the *Online Directory of Parliamentarian Army Officers*.
[12] Philip Skippon, appointed Lord Skippon under the Protectorate (d. 1660), parliamentarian army officer. See *ODNB*. He had recently been appointed sergeant major general of the New Model.
[13] Newport Pagnell, Buckinghamshire, an important garrison town on the Great North Road. Since its capture by Essex in October 1643, the governor had been Sir Samuel Luke, who had a distinguished military career but who differed fundamentally from Cromwell on matters of religion.
[14] An error by Cromwell: he surely meant *datur digniori* ('it is [or may it be] given to the more worthy').

THE LETTERS, WRITINGS, AND SPEECHES OF OLIVER CROMWELL

1645 05 09

Letter from Oliver Cromwell to William Lenthall, Speaker of the House of Commons

Date: 9 May 1645

Source: Bernard Alsop, ed., *The Weekly Account* no. 19 for 7–14 May, Under Saturday 10 May (N&S, 671.219; Thomason / E.284[5]) (contemporary print copy)

After Cromwell's withdrawal from the siege of Faringdon House (see **1645 04 30**) he swept in an arc to the west of Oxford, down to Newbury and then back to Abingdon, Dorchester and Burford before returning to block the movement of royalist troops heading from Oxford in the direction of Worcester. He wrote this letter on Friday 9 May, explaining where he was and asking for pay for his men and ammunition for their guns. It was read the next day and the response of the House of Commons was very striking: the House ordered that 'the Committee of the Army do take care for Providing of Monies and Ammunition for those Horse and Foot, that are within the new Model, and now under the Command of Lieutenant General Cromwell, and Major-General Browne'. Even more strikingly, rather than reminding him that his commission had now lapsed under the Self-Denying Ordinance and that he should return to his place in the House, the House ordered that 'WHereas Lieutenant-General Cromwell is now in the actual Service of the Parliament, and in Prosecution of the Enemy; It is this Day Ordained, by the Lords and Commons, That he shall continue in the Employment he is now in, for Forty Days longer; notwithstanding the late Ordinance, or any Clause therein, that discharges the Members of either House from having any Office or Command, Military or Civil.' The Lords swiftly concurred.[1]

The letter was printed in one of the newsbooks of the week. Other newsbooks commented on the letter having been received and read, but they do not comment on its contents or consequences.[2]

Letters this day from Lieutenant-Generall *Cromwel*, directed to the Speaker of the House of commons, to this effect.

SIR,

Upon Information that His Majestie was marched out of Oxford, *my self and Major Generall* Brown,[3] *drew towards* Hinton,[4] *and are resolved to follow them (for its thought) they will advance to* Worcester, *and so for the relief of* Chester. *We desire some money, for the better*

---

[1] *JHC*, 4:137–8.

[2] Richard Collinges, ed., *The Kingdomes Weekly* Intelligence, r no. 99, p. 795 (N&S, 214.099; Thomason / E.284[2]); Samuel Pecke, ed., *A Perfect Diurnall of Some Passages in Parliament*, no. 93 for 5–12 May, p. 734 (*recte* 742) (N&S, 511.93; Thomason / E.260[35]]).

[3] Major General Sir Richard Browne, first baronet (*c.*1602–69). See *ODNB*.

[4] Hinton = Hinton Waldrist, Oxfordshire, a village 13 miles from Oxford.

incouragment of the Souldiers, and a proportionable measure of Ammunition, for our persuing after the Enemy.

Subscribed,
OLIVER CROMWEL.

May the 9th.
1645.

1645 05 20a
Letter from Oliver Cromwell to Sir Samuel Luke

Date: 20 May 1645
Source: BL, Egerton MS 3514, fo. 30r (Letter Book of Sir Samuel Luke, 1644–45) (contemporary copy)

This is a copy[1] made by Sir Samuel Luke,[2] the governor of Newport Pagnell, or by his clerk, of a curt (rather than courteous) letter to him from Cromwell, seeking to ensure that when he sent a captain and troopers to collect money sent to his men by the Treasurers of War, it was handed over without delay. It may be remembered that two weeks earlier Cromwell had asked a political ally at Westminster to block Luke's own preference to replace Luke as governor of Newport Pagnell and secure the appointment of an officer Cromwell admired (see **1645 05 04**).

[fo. 30r]

Sir

I understand by Lres from the Comttee of both Kingdomes, that there is some mony for this Army sent downe to your Garr:[3] I have according to their Order appointed a convoy to rec' it there & convoy it to the Army. Capt Tomlinson[4] who commands the party will bee with yu I suppose before to morrow

---

[1] The short forms used in this version are uncharacteristic of Cromwell's holograph letters and those prepared by his clerks. Perhaps Luke abbreviated words in making his copies.

[2] Sir Samuel Luke had been governor of Newport Pagnell since the town was captured by Parliament in October 1643. See more particularly the introduction to Tibbutt, *The Letter Books of Sir Samuel Luke, 1644–45*.

[3] Newport Pagnell, a large market town and a strategically significant garrison town on the Great North Road in Buckinghamshire.

[4] Matthew Tomlinson [Thomlinson], appointed Lord Tomlinson under the Protectorate (bap. 1617, d. 1681), parliamentarian army officer and politician. See *ODNB*.

THE LETTERS, WRITINGS, AND SPEECHES OF OLIVER CROMWELL

morneing, I desire yu that assoone as hee cometh The Trer or his deputy who has the charge of the mony may [come] bee appointed to come away with the Treasure, along with the Convoy to Brackley[5] where the Army will bee to morrow night, & from thence towardes Oxford after the Army if it bee removed from Brackley before they gett thither, I pray let this inclosed be delivered to the party that hath the charge of the mony, And yu shall hereby much ingage

Your most humble servant

Oliver Cromwell

Daventree.[6] May. 20th

1645

1645 05 20b

Letter from Oliver Cromwell to Sir Samuel Luke

Date: 20 May 1645

Source: BL, Egerton MS 3514, fo. 30r (Letter Book of Sir Samuel Luke, 1644–45) (contemporary copy)

This is a follow-up to the letter earlier the same day [**1645 05 20a**] about the money sent from London for Cromwell's men and which had been sent to Newport Pagnell.[1] After despatching his first letter, Cromwell received one from Luke and this is his updated and rather peremptory reply.

This is what Luke wrote to Cromwell: 'I have received the Originall of this inclosed coppy[2] and could not but lett you understand that there is mony here for you at Newport and I have afforded it quarter according to the Order of the Comtee of both Kingdomes but for a Convoy I am not able to furnish you with such a sufficient One as such a charge will deserve. And therefore have putt it to your particuler care therein and rest Yours in any serviceable respects commandable. S: L: May. 19. 1645.'[3]

---

[5] Brackley, a market town in Northamptonshire, is 22 miles west of Newport Pagnell and 25 miles due south of Daventry, whence Cromwell is writing this letter.

[6] Daventry, a market town in Northamptonshire.

[1] For details of Luke, Newport Pagnell and Daventry, see **1645 05 20a**.

[2] i.e. a letter from the Committee of Both Kingdoms to Luke that is not in his papers.

[3] BL, Egerton MS 3514, fo. 70r.

[fo. 30r]
Sir

I received yours & a Coppy of Lres from the Comttee of both Kingdomes, wherein your assistance is desired to helpe the mony to us, which I beseech yu with a convoy to doe, but to Grafton,[4] where it shall be recd. Sir I am
Your humble servant
Oliver Cromwell
May. 20th 1645

1645 06 04
Letter from Oliver Cromwell to Sir Thomas Fairfax

Date: 4 June 1645
Source: John Rushworth, *Historical Collections*, 4 parts in 7 vols. (1659–1701), 4.i:37 (later transcription)

This letter, addressed to Fairfax, survives in the printed papers of John Rushworth, Fairfax's kinsman and fellow Yorkshireman. A clerk of the Parliament since 1640, he became secretary to the new lord general and to the army's council of war from the formation of the New Model Army. This letter was subsequently published in the Rushworth's *Collections* from the original that was subsequently destroyed or lost. It demonstrates Cromwell's huge energy in preparing the Eastern Association to withstand an assault by the King's main armies at that time gathering in the midlands (they sacked Leicester on 30 May). Ten days later the threat was completely removed by Fairfax and Cromwell's comprehensive victory at the battle of Naseby. But as this and other letters from early June make clear, Cromwell took the threat very seriously.

SIR,

I most humbly beseech you to pardon my long Silence: I am conscious of the fault, considering the great Obligations lying upon me. But since my coming into these parts I have been busied to secure that part of the Isle of *Ely*,[1] where I conceived most danger to be. Truly, I found it in a very ill posture, and it is yet but

---

[4] Grafton, Oxfordshire, is only three miles from Farringdon, and 40 miles south and west of the previous delivery point of Brackley.

[1] The Isle of Ely was the semi-autonomous northern fenland part of Cambridgeshire dominated by the cathedral city of Ely.

weak without Works, Ammunition or Men, considerable, and of Money least; and then I hope you will easily conceive of the defence; and God has preserv'd us all this while to a Miracle. The party under *Vermuyden*[2] waits the King's Army, and is about *Deeping*,[3] has a command to Joyn with Sir *John Gell*[4] if he commands him, so the *Nottingham*-Horse. I shall be bold to present you with Intelligence as it comes to me: We heard you were marching towards us, which was matter of rejoycing to us. I am bold to present this as my humble suit, That you would be pleased to make Captain *Rawlins*[5] this Bearer, a Captain of Horse; He has been so before, was nominated to the Model, is a most Honest Man: Col. *Sidney*[6] leaving his Regiment, if it please you to bestow his Troop on him, I am confident he will serve you faithfully; so by God's Assistance, will Your most Humble Servant,
Oliver Cromwell.

June 4th, 1645,

[2] Colonel Bartholomew Vermuyden served first under Sir John Gell in Derbyshire and then in the army of the Eastern Association. He served briefly as a colonel in the New Model, but soon withdrew and went to fight on the Continent. See the *Online Directory of Parliamentarian Army Officers*.

[3] There are a number of villages with 'Deeping' in their names along the river Welland, north of Peterborough, and therefore guarding the route into East Anglia from the north. The likeliest place mentioned here (because of its ancient bridge) is Deeping St James.

[4] Sir John Gell was the dominant military and political figure for the Parliament in Derbyshire and was also MP for the shire. For his military career, see Sir John Gell, first baronet (bap. 1593, d. 1671) in the *Online Directory of Parliamentarian Army Officers*.

[5] This is almost certainly the Thomas Rawlins who was a captain in Nathaniel Fiennes's regiment of horse in 1643, for whom see the *Online Directory of Parliamentarian Army Officers*. That man was a favourite of Cromwell's and a firebrand who had given testimony against the earl of Manchester on Cromwell's behalf in December 1644. Sometime within a week of the despatch of this, Fairfax gave him a troop in Pye's regiment in the New Model, replacing Algernon Sidney, and he served at Naseby ten days after this letter,

[6] i.e. Algernon Sidney, younger son of the earl of Leicester: Algernon Sidney [Sydney] (1623–83), political writer. See *ODNB*.

6 JUNE 1645A

1645 06 06a

Order from members of the Committee of the Eastern Association meeting in Cambridge (Henry Mildmay, William Heveningham, Timothy Middleton, William Spring, Maurice Barrow, Nathaniel Bacon, Francis Russell, Oliver Cromwell, Humphrey Walcot, Isaac Puller, [and possibly ?Edward Clench]) to the deputy lieutenants of Suffolk

Date: 6 June 1645
Source: Carlyle-Lomas, 1:199–200 (later copy)

Carlyle tells us that in 1849 the original was in the possession of a Norwich newspaper editor,[1] but there is no record of it having been seen since, so we are left just with his (modernised) version. It is Carlyle, not the original, who gives as the recipients of the letter the deputy lieutenants of Suffolk, but this seems probable. Carlyle's gloss on the letter is worth repeating: 'the Original, a hasty, blotted Paper, with the Signatures in two unequal columns, and with the Postscript crammed hurriedly into the corner, and written from another ink-bottle as is still apparent, - represents to us an agitated scene in the old Committee-rooms at Cambridge that Friday.'[2]

[p. 199]

Cambridge, 6th June 1645.

GENTLEMEN,

The cloud of the enemy's army hanging still upon the borders, and drawing towards Harborough,[3] make some supposals that they aim at the Association.[4] In regard whereof, we having information that the army about Oxford was not yesterday advanced, albeit it was ordered so to do, we thought meet to give you intelligence thereof, - and therewith earnestly to propound to your consideration, That you will have in readiness what Horse and Foot may be had, that so a proportion may be drawn forth for this service, such as may be expedient. And because we conceive that the exigence may require Horse and Dragoons, we desire that all your Horse and Dragoons may hasten to Newmarket;[5] where they

---

[1] His footnote reads, 'Original, long stationary at Ipswich, is now (Jan. 1849) the property of John Wodderspoon, Esq., Mercury Office, Norwich.'
[2] Carlyle-Lomas, I:200 fn.
[3] Harborough = Market Harborough, a market town in Leicestershire just seven miles north of Naseby.
[4] i.e. the Eastern Association. For the background, see Holmes, *Eastern Association*, ch. 6.
[5] Newmarket, Suffolk—this is what makes the recipient of this letter most likely to the deputy lieutenants of Suffolk.

THE LETTERS, WRITINGS, AND SPEECHES OF OLIVER CROMWELL

will receive orders for farther advance, according as the motion of the enemy and of our army shall require. And to allow both the several troops of Dragoons and Horse one week's pay, to be laid down by the owner; which shall be repaid out of the public money out of the county; the pay of each trooper being 14 shillings per week, and of a dragoon 10s. 6d. per week.

Your servants,

H. MILDMAY,[6]   W. SPRING,[7]
W. HEVENINGHAM,[8]   MAURICE BARROW,[9]
TI. MIDLTON,[10]   NATHANIEL BACON,[11]
                                 FRANCIS RUSSELL,[12]
                                 OLIVER CROMWELL,
                                 HUM. WALCOT,[13]
                                 ISAAC PULLER,[14]
                                 ED [   ][15]

The Place of Rendezvous for the Horse and Dragoons is to be at Newmarket; and for the Foot Bury.[16] Since the writing hereof, we received certain intelligence that

[6] Sir Henry Mildmay (c.1594–1664/5?), politician and courtier. See *ODNB*. Mildmay was from Essex.

[7] William Spring of Pakenham (1613–54), a prominent member of the Suffolk Committee. From a very wealthy and godly Suffolk family (the greatest of all the Lavenham wool merchants) and recruiter MP for Bury St Edmunds from later in 1645. The main source is the life of Spring in *HoP Commons, 1640–1660*.

[8] William Heveningham MP (1604–78), regicide. See *ODNB*. Heveningham was a Norfolk gentleman (from Ketteringham). He was MP for Stockbridge (Dorset).

[9] Maurice Barrowe of Westhorpe and Barningham (1597–1666) was a prominent and very wealthy Suffolk committeeman and recruiter MP for the Suffolk borough of Eye from the autumn of 1645. The main source is the life of Barrowe in *HoP Commons, 1640–1660*.

[10] Timothy Middleton was an Essex gentleman from Stansted Mountfitchet: see Alan Everitt, ed., *Suffolk and the Great Rebellion, 1640–1660*, Suffolk Record Society, 3 (1960), p. 136.

[11] Nathaniel Bacon (bap. 1593, d. 1660), politician and author. See *ODNB*. He was from Coddenham on the Suffolk/Essex border and MP for Cambridge University from November 1645. He chaired the committee at this time (see Holmes, *Eastern Association*, pp. 123–5).

[12] Francis Russell of Chippenham, Cambridgeshire and recruiter MP for Cambridgeshire from November 1645. See *HoP Commons, 1640–1660*.

[13] Humphrey Walcott was a Lincolnshire man from Boston and MP for Lincoln during the Protectorate. See Holmes, *Eastern Association*, pp. 125–6.

[14] Isaac Puller was a Hertfordshire man and MP for Hertford during the Protectorate.

[15] Although Carlyle noted that the last signatory is illegible, he did give the first two letters of a Christian name ('Ed…') from which Sophia Lomas, with access to papers of the Cambridge Committee, deduced the likely signatory was Edward Clench. He is referred to in Everitt, ed., *Suffolk and the Great Rebellion*, p. 132. See also, Holmes, *Eastern Association*, p. 125.

[16] i.e. Bury St Edmunds, Suffolk.

the enemy's body, with 60 carriages,[17] was p. 200] upon his march towards the Association, 3 miles on this side Harborough, last night at 4 of the clock.

1645 06 06b
Letter from Oliver Cromwell to Captain Francis Underwood

Date: 6 June 1645
Source: Cromwell Museum Huntingdon, HU TCM 313 (holograph)

Writing to one of the original officers of his Ironside regiment in the Isle of Ely, now stationed at his home town of Huntingdon, Cromwell issued specific instructions for strengthening a defensive line. The bridge at Huntingdon represented a crucial crossing point of the Great Ouse into East Anglia.

A not-very-good modernised version of the holograph letter was published by Carlyle in later editions of his *Letters and Speeches*.[1] The document, previously in the Bristol Baptist College, has now been acquired by the Cromwell Museum in Huntingdon.

Captain Underwood,[2] I desiere the
Guardes may be very well
strengthened and looked unto,
lett a new brestworke[3] bee
made about the gravell and
a newe worke halfe musket
shott[4] behinde the ould worke att
stounground staff,[5] desire Col.

---

[17] Carriages = gun carriages for artillery.

---

[1] Carlyle-Lomas, 3:244.

[2] Francis Underwood served in a regiment of foot which Oliver Cromwell and later Colonel Francis Russell commanded in their capacity as governors of the Isle of Ely and which probably originated as an auxiliary regiment of the Cambridgeshire militia. See the *Online Directory of Parliamentarian Army Officers*.

[3] A breastwork is a hastily created earthwork thrown up to breast height to provide protection to defenders firing over it from a standing position.

[4] The range of a civil-war musket was up to 300 yards. So Cromwell is asking for a second defensive earthwork about 150 yards/metres behind the existing one.

[5] It is not clear what this refers to. There is some speculation that it refers to a mound with a flagstaff on it close to a gravel pit close to Ely, and Sophia Lomas thinks that two encircling works, one outside the other, may be what is left of these breastworks, but it was and is highly

Fothergell[6] to take care of
keepinge stronge guardes, not
havinge more, I rest
Yours
Oliver Cromwell
June 6. 1645
Huntingdon

1645 06 14
Letter from Oliver Cromwell to William Lenthall, Speaker of the House of Commons

Date: 14 June 1645
Source: BL, Add. MS 5015*, fos 12r–13r (holograph)

On 8 June 1645 Sir Thomas Fairfax and his senior officers wrote to Parliament asking that Cromwell be appointed to the still-vacant position of lieutenant general of horse in the New Model Army. The letter was read in both Houses on 10 June. The Commons (but not the Lords) voted their agreement and a letter was sent to Fairfax under Speaker Lenthall's hand confirming the appointment.[1] Cromwell rode into camp on the morning of 13 June, and the following day the battle of Naseby was fought. This letter was written in the immediate aftermath of the battle and the ensuing pursuit.

The letter was read in both Houses two days later, on Monday 16 June, alongside other letters: the report on the battle by Fairfax's secretary John Rushworth; an account by the commissioners with the Army, the MPs Harcourt Leighton and Thomas Herbert; a brief letter from Fairfax himself to accompany the verbal report that his chaplain Edward Bowles was to make to Parliament, and a list of the prisoners taken. Both Houses concurred in ordering a day of thanksgiving and that the letters be published.[2]

---

speculative (see Carlyle-Lomas, 3:244 fn). More likely is that it may refer to the earthwork sconce fort at Horsey Hill near Peterborough, which is by the village of Stanground—then known as Stoneground—which was securing the route to Ely. Given the scare that there had been at the end of May that the Royalists might retake Peterborough, this seems the likelier explanation. We are grateful to Stuart Orme from the Cromwell Museum for this suggestion.

[6] Probably John Fotheringay [Fothergill] who by autumn 1643 was captain in Francis Russell's regiment of horse in the Eastern Association Army. There is no evidence of when he became a Colonel. See the *Online Directory of Parliamentarian Army Officers*. He was certainly a colonel, however, by the 1650s, see http://wiki.bcw-project.org/parliamentarian/foot-regiments/fothergill.

---

[1] JHC, 4:169–70; JHL, 7:421.   [2] JHC, 4:175–6; JHL, 7:432–6.

14 JUNE 1645

Two pamphlets followed, both containing versions of Cromwell's letter. *Three letters, From the right honourable Sir Thomas Fairfax, Lieut. Gen. Crumwell, and the Committee residing in the Army* dated by Thomason as 17 June, was authorised by the Lords and printed by John Wright.[3] It sandwiched Cromwell's letter between those of Fairfax and the commissioners, with the letters followed by the list of prisoners. A copy of the pamphlet was subsequently pasted into the *Lords Journal* for 16 June (Parliamentary Archives, HL/PO/JO/1/34). *An ordinance of the Lords and Commons assembled in Parliament* authorised by the Commons and printed by their publisher Edward Husband on the same day, comprised Cromwell's letter and Rushworth's account (attributed to a 'a Gentleman of publike employment').[4]

The Commons-authorised pamphlet gives a greater prominence to Cromwell's letter than that of the Lords: it takes up the first page of text and acts as a rousing prelude to Rushworth's account. Yet it also drastically alters the balance of the letter, by omitting the end of the letter from 'Honest men served you...' onwards. It ends not with the fidelity of the soldiery and the demand for liberty of conscience, but with the valour of the general.[5] By contrast, *Three Letters* printed Cromwell's letter in full.[6] It is impossible to be certain of the reasons for the difference, but George Thomason recognised the political charge that the difference embodied. As a Presbyterian who did not yet want to acknowledge Cromwell's radicalism, he got which was the more authentic version the wrong way round, inscribing on the title-page of *An Ordinance*, 'this is Crumwells owne trew letter over the leafe'. On *Three Letters*, he noted that Cromwell's letter there 'is a false Letter in the Conclusion of it', and he marked up the offending passage with the comment 'all this is added and not his owne'.

The original letter, along with those of Fairfax and the commissioners, was evidently retained in the Lords' archives until 1758, when they were presented by its assistant clerk to the British Museum.

Over time the letter has become slightly torn and damaged down the right-hand side of the page. Most of the missing letters are obvious but have been confirmed from the pamphlets. In both cases where parts of place-names were lost, it is clear that Cromwell must have been using abbreviations: these have been expanded below.

[fo 13r]

Sir beinge Commanded by you to this service, I thinke my Selfe bound to acquaint you with the good hand of God
towards you, and us. Wee marched yesterday

---

[3] *Three letters, from the Right Honourable Sir Thomas Fairfax, Lieut. Gen. Crumwell and the committee residing in the army. Wherein all the particulars of the great uictory* [sic] *obtained by our forces against His Majesties, is fully related, fought the 14 of Iune, 1645.* (Thomason / E.288[27])

[4] *An ordinance of the Lords and Commons assembled in Parliament, for Thursday next to be a day of thanksgiving within the lines of communication. And throughout the whole kingdome the 27. of this instant Iune, for the great victory. Obtained against the Kings forces, nere Knasby in Northampton-shire the four-teenth of this instant Iune.* (Wing / E2072; Thomason / E.288[26]).

[5] *An ordinance*, p. 1.   [6] *Three letters*, pp. 2–3.

THE LETTERS, WRITINGS, AND SPEECHES OF OLIVER CROMWELL

after the Kinge whoe went before us
from Daventree[7] to Haverbrowe,[8] and quartered about Six miles from him, this day
wee marched towards him, Hee drew out
to meete us, both Armies engaged, wee
after 3. howers fight, very doubtful
att last routed his Armie, killed and
tooke about 5000. very many officers
but of what quallitye wee yett know
not, wee tooke alsoe about 200. carrag
all hee had, and all his gunns, beinge
12. in number, wherof 2. were Demi
cannon, 2 demmie Culveringes, and (I
thinke) the rest Sacers,[9] wee persued
[the] enimie from three miles short of Ha[verbrowe]
to nine beyond, even to sight of Leice[ster]
whether the Kinge fled. Sir this is non[e]
other but the hand of God, and to him
aloane belongs the Glorie, wherin no
are to share with him, The Generall[10]
served you with all faythfullnesse, in honor,
and the best commendations I ca[n] give him is, th[a]t I d[are][11] say Hee attributes
all to God, and would rather perish then assume to himselfe,
which is an honest, and \a/ thrivinge way, and yett as much for bravery may
bee given to him in this action, as to a man. *Honest men served you faythfully
in this action. Sir they are trustye, I beseech you in the name of God not to
discorage them. ~~If this act~~[12] I wish this action may begett thankfullnesse, and
    humilitye
in all that are concerned in itt, Hee that venters his life for the libertye of his cuntrie,
I wish Hee trust God for the libertye of his conscience, and you

---

   [7] Daventry, a market town in Northamptonshire.

   [8] Market Harborough, a market town in Leicestershire.

   [9] Cromwell lists the artillery taken in order of size downwards: demi-cannon, demi-culverin and saker (*OED*).

   [10] Sir Thomas Fairfax (1612–71) was commander-in-chief of the New Model Army, February 1645–June 1650.

   [11] There is a small tear in the manuscript. This word has been completed from *Ordinance* and *Three letters*.

   [12] This is obscured by heavy crossing-out and this seems the best reading.

288

for the libertye Hee fights for,*[13] In this Hee rests whoe is
your most humble servant
Oliver Cromwell

June 14th. 1645
Haverbrowe.[14]

[fo. 12r]
For the Honble. Willm Lenthall Speker of Commons house of Parliament theise

1645 06 15
Letter from Oliver Cromwell to Sir Samuel Luke

Date: 15 June 1645

Source: BL, Egerton MS 786, fo. 54r (Letter Book of Sir Samuel Luke, 1643–45) (contemporary transcript)

Writing to Sir Samuel Luke, governor of Newport Pagnell following the great victory at Naseby, Cromwell is very matter of fact, perhaps because of his antipathy for Luke, perhaps because he is a great hurry.[1] Luke or his clerk copied the (lost) original into Luke's letter books.

S^r

I doubt not but yu heare before this tyme of the greate Goodnesse of God to this poore nation, for wch wee have all cause to reioyce The Generall commaunded mee to desire yu to conuoy the Trer[2] to Northton[3] where Col: Cox will rec it & discharge yo^u this is desired may speedily bee done

S^r I am
Yo^r humble seruant
Oliver Cromwell

June 15th 1645

---

[13] The text between the asterisks is the text omitted from the version of the letter authorised to be printed by the House of Commons, but restored in the version authorised by the House of Lords.

[14] Presumably Market Harborough, seven miles due north of Naseby.

[1] For Cromwell's recent dealings with Sir Samuel Luke, see **1645 05 20a** and **1645 05 20b**. See also the introduction to Tibbutt, *The Letter Books of Sir Samuel Luke, 1644–45*.

[2] 'Trer' has an abbreviation mark at the end, so is the full word 'Treasure', i.e. valuables seized from the royalist army after the battle of Naseby?

[3] Presumably Northampton.

THE LETTERS, WRITINGS, AND SPEECHES OF OLIVER CROMWELL

1645 07 10
Letter from Oliver Cromwell to [unnamed MPs]

Date: 10 July 1645

Source: John Lilburne, *The copy of a letter from Lieutenant-Colonell John Lilburne, to a freind*, sig. C2v: (Wing L2090A; Thomason / E.296[5]) (contemporary copy)

Lilburne's pamphlet was published in early August 1645 (George Thomason dated his copy 9 August), and it is preceded with an explanation by Lilburne about how he had never received the financial compensation he had been promised for his brutal flogging and imprisonment in the late 1630s after conviction in Star Chamber.[1] He claimed to have tried in vain to get the Speaker to take up his petition and had handed copies of his petition to 150 MPs but in vain. Finally, he had travelled to see 'my honoured Freind, Lieutenant Generall Cromwell, who had formerly taken compassion on me in my bands, and under God, was the principall instrument to get me my liberty from my long Captivity by the Bishops'. Cromwell had, he said, given him the letter he now printed, and he had handed the original and copies of it to divers Members of the House. Alas, Lilburne had also been busy alienating many other MPs or those with friends who were MPs, and on 19 July he was imprisoned for allegedly slandering the Speaker, Lenthall, and he was to languish in prison, although never charged, until his friends made their first effort to get him released in early October.[2] Unsurprisingly Cromwell's letter fell on deaf parliamentary ears.

[sig. C 2 v.]

Here followeth a true Copy of Lieutenant Generall Cromwells Letter.

Gentlemen, Being at this distance from Lon. *I am forced to trouble you in a busines, which I would have done my self, had I been there; it is for Lie. Col. Lilburne, who hath done you & the Kingdom good service, otherwise I should not have made use of such freinds, as you are:*[3] *he hath a long time attended the House of Com. with a Petition, that he might have repairation according to their Votes, for his former sufferings and losses, and some satisfaction for his Arrears for his service of the State, which hath been a long time due unto him; To this day he cannot get his Petit. read; his attendance hath proved very expensive, and hath kept*

---

[1] John Lilburne (1615?–57), Leveller. See *ODNB* which describes his sufferings in the 1630s and offers some background to this pamphlet and this letter.

[2] Jason Peacey, 'John Lilburne and the Long Parliament', *The Historical Journal*, 43:3 (2000), pp. 625–46.

[3] Given the feud between Lilburne and Colonel Edward King, which touched on all the neuralgic issues that divided politicians as much as army officers, this is a thick-skinned endorsement. See Clive Holmes. 'Colonel King and Lincolnshire Politics, 1642–6', *The Historical Journal*, 16 (1973), pp. 451–84.

11 JULY 1645[?]

him from other imployment, & I beleeve that his former losses, and late services (which have been very chargeable) considered; he doth find it a hard thing in these times, for himself and his family to subsist; Truly it is a grief to see men ruine themselves through their affection & faithfulnes to the Publick, and so few lay it to heart: It would be an honor to the Parl. & an encouragement to those that faithfully serve them (if provisions were made for the comfortable subsistence of those, who have lost all for them.) And I can assure you, that this neglect of those that sinceerly serve you, hath made some already quit their Commands in this Army, who hath observed oftentimes their wives & children have begged, who have lost their limbs and lives in the Kingdoms service: I wish it were looked to betimes; That which I have to request of you is, that you give him your best assistance to get his Petition read in the House, and that you will doe him all lawfull favor & justice in it; know he will not be unthankfull, but adventure himself as freely in the service of the Kingdom, as hitherto he hath done. Hereby you shall lay a special Obligation upon your servant,

Oliver Cromwell. July the 10, 1645.

1645 07 11[?]
Letter from Oliver Cromwell to an unnamed MP

Date: July 1645 (between 10 and 23 July)
Source: *Good nevves out of the vvest, declared in a letter sent from Lieutenant Generall Cromwel, to a worthy member of the House of Commons... Published by authority*: (Wing / C7089; Thomason / E.293[18]) (contemporary print)

This letter survives only in pamphlet form. It is an account of the battle of Langport[1] (Somerset) on 10 July 1645 and was addressed (according to the pamphlet) to 'a worthy Member of the House of Commons'. It does not seem to have been read in the House of Commons but does claim to be 'published by authority'. It was obviously written after the battle of Langport on 10 July and early enough to be published in London on 23 July. From the tone and content of the last two pages of the letter, it seems that the most likely dates are 11 or 12 July.

After Naseby, the largest forces loyal to the King were concentrated in the west and the strongest of the parliamentarian strongholds was Taunton. Re-taking Taunton was a

---

[1] For a succinct account of the battle of Langport with maps, see the Battlefield Trust website at http://www.battlefieldstrust.com/resource-centre/civil-war/battlepageview.asp?pageid=685; or Malcolm Wanklyn and Frank Jones, *A Military History of the English Civil War* (Harlow, 2005), pp. 253–63.

THE LETTERS, WRITINGS, AND SPEECHES OF OLIVER CROMWELL

major royalist objective, and the relief of Taunton was a major parliamentary objective, and Fairfax and Cromwell headed west meeting up with a major royalist force initially spread out along 12 miles defending the crossing points of the Wagg Rhyne (something between a stream and a river). As the New Model advanced, George Goring pulled back to create a strong defensive line on a ridge with a bog in front of it, hoping to get his artillery clear of the area before Fairfax and Cromwell could seize them. Cromwell's letter describes what happened next.

[sig. Ar.]

THE
COPY OF LIEUTENANT
GENERALL
CROMWEL
HIS LETTER TO
To a worthy Member of the House of
COMMONS.

Dear Sir,

I have now a double advantage upon you, through the goodnesse of God, who still appeares with us. And as for us, we have seen great things in this last mercy: It is not inferior to any we have had, as followeth: Wee were advanced to *Long-Sutton*,[2] neere a very strong Place of the Enemies, called *Lamport*,[3] farre from our owne Garrisons, without [sig. Av.] much Ammunition, in a place extreamly wanting in provisions, the malignant Club-men[4] interposing, who are ready to take all advantages against our parties, and would undoubtedly take them against our Armie, if they had opportunity. *Goring*[5] stood upon the advantage of strong passes, staying untill the rest of his retreats came up to his Army, with a resolution not to engage, untill *Greenvill*[6] and Prince CHARLES[7] his men were come up to him. We could not well have necessitated him to an Engagement, nor have

---

[2] Long Sutton, Somerset, about midway between Bristol and Exeter, and 14 miles east of Taunton.

[3] Lamport = Langport, Somerset, four miles west of Long Sutton.

[4] Clubmen: armed groups determined to limit the impact of the war on their region. See John Morrill, *Revolt in the Provinces* (1999), ch. 3; David Underdown, 'The Chalk and the Cheese: contrasts among the English clubmen', *Past and Present*, 85 (1979), pp. 25–48. For a report on Fairfax's and Cromwell's problems with the Clubmen, see **1645 08 04**.

[5] George Goring, Baron Goring (1608–57), royalist army officer. See *ODNB*.

[6] Sir Richard Grenvile, baronet (bap. 1600, d. 1659), royalist army officer. See *ODNB*.

[7] Charles, Prince of Wales. In March 1645, Charles I sent his fifteen-year-old eldest son to take control of his armies in the West of England, and he stayed in the west until his flight into exile in early 1646. For his part in this campaign: Charles II (1630–85), King of England, Scotland and Ireland. See *ODNB*.

11 JULY 1645 [?]

stayed one day longer without retreating to our Ammunition, and to conveniency of victuall. In the morning word was brought us, That the enemy drew out. He did so, with a resolution to send most of his Cannon and Baggage, to *Bridgewater*,[8] which he effected: But with a resolution not to fight; but trusting to his ground, thinking he could march away at pleasure. The passe was strait between him and us, he brought two Cannons to secure his, and laid his Muskettiers strongly in the hedges: wee beat off his cannon, fell down upon his Muskettiers, beat them off from their strength; and where our horse could scarcely passe two a breast, I commanded Major *Bether*[9] to charge them with two Troops of about an hundred and twenty Horse, which he performed with the greatest gallantry imaginable, beat back two bodies of the enemies Horse, being *Gorings* owne Brigade, brake them at Swords point. The enemy charged him with neer four hundred fresh Horse. He set them all going, untill oppressed with multitudes, he brake through them with the loss not of above three or foure men. Major *Desborough* seconded him with some other of those Troops, which were about three, *Bether* faced about, & they both ranted as[10] swords point, a great body of the enemies Horse, which gave such an unexpected terror to the enemies Army, that set them all a running. Our Foot in the mean time coming on bravely, and beating the enemy from their strength, we presently had the chase to *Lamport* and *Bridgewater*. We took and killed about 2000, brake all his Foot: We have taken very many Horse, and considerable prisoners; what are slain we know not, we have the Lieutenant Generall of the Ordnance, Col: *Preston*,[11] Colonel *Heveningham*,[12] Colonel *Slingsbey*,[13] we know of: besides very many other Officers of quality. All Major Generall *Massies*[14] party was with him 7 or 8 miles from us, and about 1200 of our Foot, and 3 Regiments of our Horse: so that we had but 7

---

[8] Bridgewater, Somerset, 12 miles north-west of Langport.

[9] Major Bether = Christopher Bethell, major in Edward Whalley's regiment of horse. He was to be killed in the final stages of the siege of Bristol two months later (Wanklyn, *Reconstructing the New Model*, pp. 53, 63).

[10] This looks like a misprint. Carlyle silently changes 'ranted at' to 'routed at' which makes a lot more sense and may well be what the lost original said (Carlyle-Lomas, 3:246).

[11] Not identified (not in Newman, *Royalist Officers*).

[12] Arthur Heveningham of Heveningham, Suffolk. He was sent up to London from Langport and imprisoned there until he was released and allowed to compound in September 1646.

[13] Probably one of the three Slingsby brothers, sons of Sir Guilford Slingsby of Bifrons in Kent. Since two of them were in the siege of Bristol in Aug/Sept 1645, the likeliest is Arthur Slingsby (d. 1666) (see Newman, *Royalist Officers*, no. 1322). But perhaps Robert or Walter (Newman, *Royalist Officers*, nos. 1321 and 1327) were released and made their way to Bristol.

[14] Major General Edward Massey, commander of the Western Association and strong opponent of Cromwell's political and religious programme. He was to change sides in 1647: Edward Massey (1604x9–1674), parliamentarian and royalist army officer. See *ODNB*.

Regiments with us. Thus you see what the Lord hath wrought for us: Can any creature ascribe any thing to it selfe? Now can we give all the glory to God, and desire all may doe so: for it is all due unto him. Thus you have *Long-Sutton* mercy added to *Naesby*[15] mercy: And to see this, is it not to see the face of God? You have heard of *Naesby*, it was a happy victory: As in this, so in that, God was pleased to use his servants; and if men will be malicious, and swell with envy, we know who hath said, If they will not see, yet they shall see and be ashamed for their envy at his people. I can say this of *Naesby*, that when I saw the enemy drew up, and march in gallant order towards us, and we a company of poore ignorant men to seek how to order our battell: The Generall having commanded mee to order all the Horse, I could not (riding alone about my businesse) but smile out to God in praises, in assurance of victory, because God would by things that are not, bring to nought things that are, of which I had great assurance, and God did it. Oh that men would therefore praise the Lord, and declare the wonders that he doth for the children of men. I cannot write more particulars now, I am going to the Rendevouz of all our Horse, 3 miles from *Bridgewater*, we march that way. It is a seasonable mercy; I can better tell you then write, that God will goe on. We have taken two Guns, three Carriages of Ammunition in the Chase. The enemy quitted *Lamport*: when they ran out at one end of the town, we entred the other: they fiered that at which we should chase, which hindered our pursuit, but wee over-took many of them. I beleeve we got neere fifteen hundred horse. Sir, I beg your Prayers: Beleeve and you shall be established, I rest, *Your Servant*. FINIS

1645 08 04

Letter from Oliver Cromwell to Sir Thomas Fairfax

Date: 4 August 1645
Source: Bodl., MS Tanner 60/1, fos 236r–v (holograph)

This is a holograph letter without an address or endorsement. But the contents make it clear that it is addressed to Fairfax, and seven separate print copies all confirm this. Sir Thomas Fairfax forwarded it to his father who read it out in the Commons on

---

[15] i.e. Battle of Naseby, 14 June 1645.

4 AUGUST 1645

8 August,[1] together with a letter from Sir Thomas about the taking of Bath. One of the pamphlets, in printing both letters, also records Sir Thomas telling his father that 'I desire Your Lordship would acquaint the House with it'.[2] Clearly having done so, he handed the letter to the Speaker, amongst whose papers it has survived into the present.

After its victory over Goring at Langport, the New Model spent ten days besieging Bridgwater, before turning back to recruit some reinforcements and to take Bath. Fairfax undertook the latter but sent Cromwell to tackle the Clubmen, the 'third partie' as Cromwell called them, armed groups determined to prevent plundering, new taxes or conscription in their area. He gave assurances to one group who then disbanded but he was forced into a sharp encounter with another group on Hambledon Hill near Blandford Forum in Dorset. A handful of Clubmen were killed and fifty-one taken prisoner.[3]

Sir I marched this morninge towards
Shaftsbury,[4] in my way I found a
[—] partie of clubmen[5] gathered to=
gether about 2. miles on that side of
the towne towards you,[6] and one Mr.
Newman[7] in the head of them, whoe
was one of those that did attend
you att Dorchester[8] with mr. Hollis,[9]
I sent to them to ~~kn~~ knowe the

[1] JHC, 4:134: 'The Lord Fairfax acquainted the House, That he had received Letters from his Son Sir Thomas Fairfax; and a Letter of 4 Augusti 1645, written to Sir Thomas from Lieutenant-General Cromwell; and also a List of the Country Gentlemen and Ministers, called the Leaders of the Clubmen, for the Counties of Wiltes, Dorset, and Somerset, surprised at Shaftsbury, and brought Prisoners to Sherborne: Which were all read.'

[2] *Two letters: the one, sent to the Right Honorable, the Lord Fairfax, from Sir Tho: Fairfax his son, commander in chief of the Parliaments forces; concerning his besieging Sherborn. The other sent to Sir Tho: Fairfax, from Lieutenant Generall Cromwell; concerning the late fight at Shaftesbury... Ordered by the Commons in Parliament, that these letters be forthwith printed and published: H: Elsynge, Cler. Parl. D. Com., London: Printed for Edward Husband, printer to the Honorable House of Commons., Aug. 9. 1645*, p. 4 (Wing / F252. Thomason / E.296[7]).

[3] The list mentioned by Lord Fairfax in his report to the Commons is included in several of the print accounts including *Two Letters*, p. 8. Cromwell's letter is on pp. 5–7.

[4] Shaftesbury, Dorset.

[5] See John Morrill, *Revolt in the Provinces* (1999), ch. 3; David Underdown, 'The Chalk and the Cheese: contrasts among the English clubmen', *Past and Present*, 85 (1979), pp. 25–48.

[6] Fairfax was on his way from the capture of Bath to the capture of Sherborne, in North Dorset. Cromwell was 16 miles east of Sherborne.

[7] Richard Newman of Fifehead Magdalen, http://www.thedorsetpage.com/history/Dorset_Clubmen/Dorset_Clubmen.htm.

[8] Dorchester, the county town of Dorset.

[9] The list of prisoners in *Two Letters* includes a Mr Robert Holles.

THE LETTERS, WRITINGS, AND SPEECHES OF OLIVER CROMWELL

cause of their meetinge, mr. Newman
came to mee, and tould mee that the
Clubmen in Dorsett and wilts to the
number of tenn thousand were to meete
about their ⊟ men which were taken
away att Shaftsburye, and that
their intendment was to Secure them
selves from plunderinge. To the
first I tould them, that although
noe account was due to them,
yett I knewe the men were taken
by your Authoritye, to be tryed
~~for rai~~ judicially for raisinge a
third partie in the Kingdom, and
If they should bee found guiltye they must Suffer acccording
to the nature of their offence, If innocent I assured \them/ you
would acquitt them, upon this they sayd, if they have
deserved punishment they would not have any thinge
to doe with them, and soe were quieted as to that point
For the other I asured them that it was your
great care not to Suffer them in the least to
bee plundered, ~~with~~ and that they should defend them
selves from violence and bringe to your Armie such
as did them any wronge, where they should bee
punished with all severitye. upon this very quietly
and peaceablie they marched away to their
houses, beinge very well Satisfied, and contented,
wee marched onn to Shaftsburye, where wee
heard a great body of them was drawen
together about Hammilton Hill,[10] where indeed
neere 2000. were gathered, I sent a forlorne[11]
of about 50. horse, whoe cominge very civilly
to them they fired upon them, and they desiring

[10] Hambleton Hill six miles south of Shaftesbury, a steep hill crowned by the remains of a Neolithic hill fort.

[11] = Forlorn hope, or advance party.

4 AUGUST 1645

some of them to come to mee, were refused, with
disdayne. They were drawen into one of the Old
Rom [12] Camps upon a very high Hill, I ~~des~~ [13] sent
One Mr Lee[14] to them to certifie the peaceablenesse
of my intentions, and to desier them to peaceablenesse
and to submitt to the Parliament, they refused and

[fo. 236v]

fyred att us, I sent him a second
tyme to lett them knowe that if
they would lay downe theire Armes
noe wronge should be donn them
they still (thorough the Annimation
of their leaders, and especially 2
vile ministers) refused, I commanded
your Capt. Leifnt.[15] to draw up to
them, to bee in readinesse to charge,
and if upon his fallinge onn they
would lay downe Armes to accept
them, and Spare them,When Hee
came neere they refused his offer
and lett flye att him, Killed ~~seve~~ \about/
\two/ of his men, and att least 4 horses,
and passage not beinge for above
three a brest kept them out wherupon
Major Desburgh[16] wheeled about, got
in the reere of th

---

[12] The original word (no longer legible) has been written over and changed very clumsily. The middle letter might be an 'a', but also looks like an 'o'; it might just be a crossing-out, but that does not fit the 'R' , or indeed the middle letter. Perhaps Cromwell thought the Neolithic hill fort was a Roman construction. None of the printed versions offers a word, but they do all construe the sentence differently. For example, *Two letters* (see n. 2) has 'one of the old camps' and *A perfect diurnal* no. 106 (for 4–11 August) has 'one of the camps'.

[13] Uncertain reading: only the 'd' is certain.

[14] Not identified.

[15] John Gladman was captain-lieutenant in Fairfax's cavalry regiment, William Fortescue was captain-lieutenant in his infantry regiment (Wanklyn, *Reconstructing*, 1:61, 43).

[16] John Disbrowe was major in Fairfax's regiment of cavalry (Wanklyn, *Reconstructing the New Model*, 1:50).

THE LETTERS, WRITINGS, AND SPEECHES OF OLIVER CROMWELL

em, \beat them from the worke/ and did some
smale execution upon them ⊣⊢ \I beleive/
killed not twelve of them, but cutt
very manye, and have taken about 300.
many of which a poore sillye creatures,
whome if you please to lett mee send
home, they promise to bee very duty
full for tyme to come, and wilbe hang
ed before they come out againe.

The ringleaders which wee have I hope
to bringe to you, They had taken
diverse of the Parliament Souldiers
prisoners, besides Col Fienes[17] his m{en}
and used them most barbarouslye,
Bragginge they hoped to see my
Lord Hopton,[18] that Hee ~~was~~ \is/ to
command them, they expected from
wilts great store, and gave
out they meant to raise the
seige att Shafte[19] Sherburne
when they were all mett. wee
have gotten good stoare of their
Armes and they carried few or
none home. wee Quarter about
tenn miles off & purpose to draw
our Quarters neere to you to morrow
Your most humble servant
Oliver Cromwell

---

[17] Presumably the remnants of Colonel John Fiennes' regiment, which had served with Cromwell in his Oxfordshire campaign of the late spring and early summer but had not been absorbed into the New Model. See the *Online Directory of Parliamentarian Army Officers*.

[18] Ralph Hopton, Baron Hopton (bap. 1596, d. 1652). See *ODNB*.

[19] 'Shafte' looks to be erased and it does not appear in any of the printed versions. Cromwell presumably started to write 'Shaftesbury' and then realised he mean 'Sherburne' (= Sherborne, Dorset).

August 4th
1645

[20]Read 8º
Augusti
1645

1645 08 05
Report of a speech made by Oliver Cromwell to Clubmen captured on Hambledon Hill

Date: 5 August 1645
Source: Joshua Sprigg, *Anglia rediviva; Englands recovery: being the history of the motions, actions, and successes of the army under the immediate conduct of His Excellency Sr. Thomas Fairfax* (1647), p. 81 (Wing / S5070) (near contemporary copy)

This letter links closely to the preceding one (**1645 08 04**) and it adds an account by Joshua Sprigg[1] of a speech Cromwell made the following day to prisoners taken on Hambledon Hill. Sprigge was a chaplain to the New Model and a member of Fairfax's secretariat and was quite possibly an ear-witness to the speech. He wrote a comprehensive defence of the New Model from its foundation to the crisis of 1647 and we do not know whether he made notes at the time or reconstructed the speech from memory two years later.

After the examination [of the leaders], the Lieutenant-Gen. spake to them, giving them liberty to defend themselves against plunderings; only forbidding any such meetings, which they protested against, and freely consented, that if any of them (whose names were in the paper) were taken again opposing the Parliament, or in any such assembly, they deserved to be hanged, whereupon they were dismissed,

---

[20] The following annotation is in another hand, and the other way up, in space between the two pages.

[1] Joshua Sprigg [Sprigge] (bap. 1618, d. 1684), Independent minister: see ODNB. Sprigg was the Independent (pro-tolerationist) minister in the parish of St Pancras, Soper Lane, London from 1640 until he was hand-picked by Fairfax to be his chaplain and part of the secretariat of the New Model Army and he was by Fairfax's side from the foundation of the New Model until the end of the fighting.

to their very good satisfaction, and confessed they saw themselves misled by their leaders, who by a pretence to save their goods, indangered both their goods and lives, and so ours parted with them

1645 09 03

Letter from Sir Thomas Fairfax, Oliver Cromwell and twenty-four other officers to Alexander Leslie, first earl of Leven

Date: 3 September 1645
Source: Joshua Sprigg, *Anglia rediviva; Englands recovery: being the history of the motions, actions, and successes of the army under the immediate conduct of His Excellency Sr. Thomas Fairfax* (1647), pp. 96–7 (Wing / S5070) (early print copy)

This letter was signed by twenty-five senior officers of the New Model Army on the same day that they met as a Council of War to draw up plans (which they executed seven days later) to storm the city of Bristol, the capture of which was a further major step towards to end of the English Civil War. But in Scotland the royalists under Montrose[1] were running amok, winning major victories at Alford in early July and at Kilsyth in mid-August, news of which only reached western England a few days before this letter. Little did they know that three days after the seizure of Bristol, Montrose's army was to be overwhelmed at Philiphaugh. Fearing that Montrose's successes were making the Covenanting Army uneasy and at some risk of heading back north making a royalist resurgence in the north possible, the officers entered into a new joint commitment.

The letter, which does not seem to have been shared with the Houses of Parliament or with the Committee of Both Kingdoms, survives only in the subsequent history of the Army written by Joshua Sprigg, one if its chaplains and a member of the Army secretariat, and was published in the second half of 1647.

[p. 95]
May it please your Excellency,[2] *and the rest, honoured Freinds, and beloved Brethren*, We have, not without much grief, received the sad report of your affairs in *Scotland*; how far God, for his best and secret ends, hath been pleased to suffer the Enemy to prevaile there: And are (we speak unfainedly) not lesse sensible of your evils, then you have been and are of ours, nor then we are of our own. And the greater

---

[1] James Graham, first marquis of Montrose (1612–50), royalist army officer. See ODNB.
[2] Alexander Leslie, first earl of Leven (c.1580–1661), army officer. See ODNB.

3 SEPTEMBER 1645

cause of sympathie have we with you, and the more do our bowels earn[3] towards you, because whatever you now suffer your selves in your own Kingdom, are chiefly occasioned by your assisting us in ours, against the power that was risen up against the Lord himself, and his Anointed ones.[4] Wherefore we cannot forget your labour of love, but thought good at this season, even amongst our many occasions, to let you know, that when the affairs of this Kingdom will possibly dispense with us, the Parliament allowing, and your accepting of our assistance; We shall be most willing, if need so require, to help and serve you faithfully in your own Kingdom, and to engage our selves to suppresse the Enemy there, and to establish you again in peace. In the mean time we shall endeavour to help you by our prayers, and to wrestle with God for one blessing upon both Nations; between whom, besides many other strong relations and engagements, We hope the *Unity of Spirit* shall be the surest *Bond of Peace*.[5] And this, whatever suggestions or jealousies may have been to the contrary, we desire you would believe, as you shall ever really find to proceed from integrity of heart, a sense of your sufferings, and a full purpose to answer any call of God to your assistance, as become *Your Christian friends, and servants in the Lord,*

[p. 97]

Thomas Fairfax.	*Robert Pye.*[6]
Oliver Cromwell.	*Thomas Rainsborough.*[7]
Thomas Hamond.[8]	*Thomas Sheffield*[9]
Henry Ireton.[10]	*Charles Fleetwood.*[11]

[3] A common variant of 'yearn' (used thus by Shakespeare and Ben Jonson, and by the army chaplain Peter Sterry in 1652) and meaning 'To be affected with poignant grief or compassion' (*OED*). See for example, the grief-stricken mother in the parable of Solomon forcing two women to divide a child they both claimed as their own 'then spake the woman whose the liuing childe was, vnto the king, (for her bowels yerned vpon her sonne) and she said, O my lord, giue her the liuing childe, and in no wise slay it: But the other said, Let it be neither mine nor thine, but diuide it' (*KJV*, 1 Kings 3:26).

[4] The reference to Kings as 'the Lord's anointed' appears many times in the Old Testament. For some examples in the *KJV* see Samuel 24:6; 1 Chronicles 16:22; Psalms 105:15; and perhaps best Psalms 2:2 'The kings of the earth set themselves, and the rulers take counsel together, against the LORD, and against his anointed...'

[5] Ephesians 4:3: 'Endeuouring to keepe the vnitie of the Spirit in the bond of peace.'

[6] Robert Pye (*c*.1622–1701), Exchequer official and politician. See *ODNB*.

[7] Thomas Rainborowe [Rainborow] (d. 1648), parliamentarian army officer and leveller. See *ODNB*.

[8] Thomas Hammond (*c*.1600–58), parliamentarian army officer and regicide. See *ODNB*.

[9] Thomas Sheffield, colonel, see Wanklyn, *Reconstructing*, I:1; C. H. Firth and G. Davies, *The Regimental History of Cromwell's Army*, 2 vols. (Oxford, 1940), 1:175–8.

[10] Henry Ireton (bap. 1611, d. 1651), parliamentarian army officer and regicide. See *ODNB*.

[11] Charles Fleetwood, appointed Lord Fleetwood under the Protectorate (*c*.1618–92), army officer. See *ODNB*.

Edward Montague.[12]
Richard Fortescue.[14]
Richard Inglesby.[16]
John Pickering.[18]
Hardresse Waller[20]
William Herbert.[22]
Robert Hamond.[24]
James Gray.[26]
Thomas Pride[28]

Ralph Welden.[13]
John Raymond.[15]
Leon Wattson.[17]
Arthur Evelin.[19]
Richard Dean.[21]
Thomas Jackson.[23]
John Desborough.[25]
Christopher Bethel.[27]

[12] Edward Montagu [Mountagu], first earl of Sandwich (1625–72), army and naval officer and diplomat. See ODNB.
[13] Weldon, Ralph (bap. 1606, d. 1676), parliamentarian army officer. See ODNB.
[14] Richard Fortescue (d. 1655), parliamentarian army officer. See ODNB.
[15] John Raymond, not identified.
[16] Sir Richard Ingoldsby, appointed Lord Ingoldsby under the Protectorate (bap. 1617, d. 1685), army officer and regicide. See ODNB.
[17] Leon Watson, Scoutmaster General of the Army, see Gentles, New Model Army, pp. 182, 187, 197.
[18] John Pickering (bap. 1615, d. 1645), parliamentarian army officer. See ODNB.
[19] Arthur Evelyn, a captain in Colonel James Sheffield's regiment from April 1645 until he left the Army in June 1646, see Wanklyn, Reconstructing, 1:51, 61, 72, 82; Firth and Davies, Regimental History, 1:175, 177, 179.
[20] Sir Hardress Waller (c.1604–66), parliamentarian army officer and regicide. See ODNB.
[21] Richard Deane, (bap. 1610, d. 1653), army and naval officer and regicide. See ODNB.
[22] William Herbert who had recently taken over as colonel of the 11th regiment of foot after the death of Colonel Walter Lloyd at the siege of Taunton. See Wanklyn, Reconstructing, 1:59; Firth and Davies, Regimental History, 1:385–6.
[23] Thomas Jackson, Lt Col. of Fairfax's regiment of foot, see Wanklyn, Reconstructing, 1:43; Firth and Davies, Regimental History, 1:317–25.
[24] Robert Hammond (1620/1–54), parliamentarian army officer. See ODNB.
[25] Disbrowe [Desborough], John (bap. 1608, d. 1680), parliamentarian army officer and politician. See ODNB.
[26] James Gray, Lt Col in William Herbert's regiment of foot, see Wanklyn, Reconstructing, 1:59.
[27] Christopher Bethell, major of Whalley's regiment of horse, Firth and Davies, Regimental History, 1:209–13; Wanklyn, Reconstructing, 1:63.
[28] Thomas Pride, appointed Lord Pride under the Protectorate (d. 1658), parliamentarian army officer and regicide. See ODNB.

8 SEPTEMBER 1645

1645 09 08

Letter from Thomas Fairfax and Oliver Cromwell to the High Sheriff of Cornwall[1] and 'the wellaffected Gentry, & Inhabitants of that Countie'

Date: 8 September 1645
Source: Bodl., MS Clarendon 25, fos 127r–128v (autograph)

By 8 September Fairfax and Cromwell were in the final stages of planning their assault on Bristol, but they needed to bear in mind that despite their successes in Somerset and Devon in previous weeks, they had made no progress in securing Cornwall. So they took time out to write to those they hoped might take matters down there into their own hands.

The letter survives only in the papers of Edward Hyde, later first earl of Clarendon, secretary of state to Charles, who had been sent down with Charles, Prince of Wales, earlier in 1645 to strengthen royalist power in the south-west. Although this letter, written in the hand of Cromwell's normal clerk and bearing the autographs of both Fairfax and Cromwell, was intended for anti-royalists, it clearly fell into hostile hands.

———

[fo. 127r]

Whereas besides the greate and frequent Supplyes of men monye and other aydes to the enimye which have beene raised out of your Countye above others, to the Sadd continuation & often reinforceing of the unaturall warr against the Parliamt. Wee are given to understand, that the restless enimyes of your and our and the kingdomes peace, being (through godes late retorning mercyes to us all, and the blessing of the forces of the Parliamt.) driven almost out of all other partes of the kingdome, and destitute of all clere Supplyes from elswhere Save that little angle which yow possesse) doe yet persist by all the wayes of art and violence, to draw out from amonst yow Some fresh Supplyes & reinforcemt. of their broken forces, whereby they may once againe appeare in the feild to disturbe the peace of the kingdome, and continue & renew the miseryes of it by a further warr we being æqually carefull to prevent (if possible) your ruine or further Sufferings as the kingdomes further troubles, have thought good to admonish yow and declare to yow, as followeth

———

[1] The sheriff from 15 July 1644 to 1 December 1646 was John St Aubyn—see A. Hughes, *List of Sheriffs for England and Wales from the Earliest Times to A.D. 1831* (London, 1898), p. 23. He had served as a colonel in the garrison of Plymouth for much of the war as well as on various committees. See the *Online Directory of Parliamentarian Army Officers*.

THE LETTERS, WRITINGS, AND SPEECHES OF OLIVER CROMWELL

Wee desire yow would bee, & wee pray god to make yow once at last Sensible of the interest of Religion, & of the rightes & libertyes of your Selves and the rest of the people of England, of which the power & authority of Parliamts. hath beene in former ages and is ever like to be (under god) the best conservatory & Support, and which by this unnaturall warr against the Parliament (& that) ~~from~~ in \a greate/ [————] degree by the aydes your Country hath afforded thereunto, have beene Soe much endangered; And if now at last yow Shall appeare Sensible thereof, wee Shall be willing to beleeve of yow, and be gladd wee may have occasion Soe to represent yow to the Parliament and kingdome. That the greate aydes yow have formerly afforded the Enimy against them, have beene onely forced or drawne from yow by violence or deceipt of those that god has Suffered hitherto to be possessed of the power over yow. As wee beleeve yow have had by this tyme Sufficyent Sense & experience of the violence & oppressions (besides all other wickednes) of that party, Soe we advise yow tymely to consider how unlike yow are in humane probability to beare & mainteyne theire warr [fo. 127v] alone against the rest of the kingdome, that is now by godes blessing almost cleared to the Parliamt., how heavie the burthen is like to be to yow in the prosecution of Such a warr alone, and how great Calamity may befall yow in the issue of it. If god Shall See good to Sett those Consideracions home upon your heartes and incline yow to endeavor the freeing of your Selves from the yoake yow have beene under, from the burden of dangers that may befall yow, and from the guilt of Soe much mischeife & trouble to the kingdome as the prolonging of Such a warr, when otherwise likely to be happily ended. And if upon these Considerations yow Shall apply yourselves to drive the remainder of the Enimy out of your Country, if yow Shall call home, and (asmuch as in yow lies) withdraw from the Enimy the forces which yow have Sent them, and forbeare for future to afford them any more aydes or contribution, but Stand upon your guarde to defend your Selves & Country from any further oppressions, plunderings or invasions, yow shall not onely be allowed therein, but countenanced and assisted, as yow Shall desire, by the Parliamtes. Partye; and be Secured from any invasion or incursions of the Parliamtes. forces, unles yow Shall desire any of them for your assistance. Yow Shall likewise have free trading and Commerce by Sea & land to all places, & with all persons that are not in hostility against the Parliamt., and shall have for mony what Supplyes of Armes or Amunition yow Shall neede for your Said defence. But if notwithstanding this offer, yow Shall persist to ayde the Enimy any further, yow must expect & be assured when god shall give leasure and oportunity (as your Selves thereof will give occasion) for the Parliamtes.

304

forces to come downe amongst yow, that yow Shall be accompted & delt withall in the Seveerest way of warr as the most Eminent & obstinate disturbers and reterders of the kingdomes peace, now by godes mercy in a faire way to be Speedyly Setled. Yet hopeing better of yow for the future (which we shall be gladd to heare of) we remayne

Your assured frends

Tho Fairfax
Oliver Cromwell

From before Bristoll
Sept. 8: 1645.

[fo. 128v]
For the Highe Sheriffe of the Countie of Cornwall and the wellaffected Gentry, & Inhabitants of that Countie.[2]
Fayrefax & Cromwell to the High Shriefe of Cornewall.[3]

1645 09 14a
Letter from Oliver Cromwell to William Lenthall, Speaker of the House of Commons

Date: 14 September 1645
Source: Bodl., MS Nalson 4, no. 80, fos 168r–169v (autograph)

This original text of this letter, written down by Cromwell's usual clerk and bearing his signature, still exists, and a shortened version of it was ordered to be printed by the Commons and it was duly printed by Parliament's most usual printer.[1] The part suppressed by the Commons was then separately published (see **1645 09 14b**). So this is a letter with a very contentious history.

Cromwell—apparently at Fairfax's instruction—wrote a long and detailed account of the storm and capture of Bristol and dated it 14 September. It was read in the Commons on the morning of Sunday 17 September and the Commons ordered it to be printed and to be

---

[2] This is in a different hand, but one characteristic of the mid-seventeenth century.
[3] This is another hand again, but also characteristic of the mid-seventeenth century.

[1] *Lieut: Generall Cromwells letter to the House of Commons, of all the particulars of taking the city of Bristoll and the manner of P: Ruperts marching to Oxford.... London: printed for Edward Husband, printer to the Honorable House of Commons, Sept. 22. 1645.* (Wing / C7114 or C7114A).

THE LETTERS, WRITINGS, AND SPEECHES OF OLIVER CROMWELL

read in all London churches the following Sunday (24 September).[2] What the order of the Commons does not say, however, is that the final paragraph in which Cromwell made a plea for religious freedom was to be omitted from the official printed version[3] and from a shortened version for reading in the churches.[4] However, an anonymous printer/publisher then published a broadside (**1645 09 14b**) which Thomason recorded as having been received on 22 September, and to which he added the following note: 'this was printed by the Independent partie and Scattered up and downe the streets last night but expresly omitted by order of the House.'[5] This is the second time one of Cromwell's letters had been censored before it was published and the second time his friends ensured that what he had written was put into the public domain. On the previous occasion, after Naseby, it was the Lords who put out a full-length printing of the whole letter restoring the parts censored by the Commons.[6] This time it was only the censored parts in an anonymous broadside.

The original letter survives in the Nalson Papers in the Bodleian, having been 'borrowed' in the late 1670s by John Nalson from William Lenthall's papers as he prepared his riposte to the *Historical Collections* of John Rushworth, published in 1659.[7] It is in Cromwell's clerk's hand with many corrections in a darker ink, some of which are certainly in Cromwell's hand, and all of which are likely to be in his hand. The suppressed final part has been crossed out or underlined in another ink and we can presume that was done by the person overseeing the printing of the letter. All the printed versions follow the manuscript closely other than for spelling, punctuation and writing out of some numbers as numbers not in words.

There are a few tears in the manuscript so a few letters or words are difficult to read. Where we have confirmed a word from the print version (see n. 1), we have done so silently. When we have to provide it we have used square brackets.

[fo. 169v]

Lre from Bristoll of 14°: of

[2] *JHC*, 4:277. Fairfax himself wrote separately to the House of Lords. They did not sit on 17 or 18 September so it was read early on the 19th. Fairfax was thanked but there was no order to print his letter—*JHL*, 7:583.

[3] See below, the marked section at the end of the text. In all, this removed 184 words from a letter of just under 2,200 words.

[4] *The Kingdomes Weekly Intelligencer* for 16–23 September 1645, p. 946 (N&S, 214.118; Thomason / E.302[23]).

[5] *The conclusion of Lieuten: Generall Cromwells letter to the House of Commons, concerning the taking of Bristoll which was contained in the originall, (signed by himselfe) but omitted in the printed copy* (1647) (Wing / C7050).

[6] See **1645 06 14**.

[7] John Nalson's *An Impartial Collection of the Great Affairs of State*, 2 vols. (1682–3), was a fragment of a much larger work envisaged but prevented by his death at the age of 48. Nalson had however gathered a great deal of material for the later period covered by Rushworth. John Nalson, (bap. 1637, d. 1686). See *ODNB*. Nalson added at the top of the manuscript: 'Printed in Rushworth. Vol. 6. p. 85 with Some Variations not Material.'

14 SEPTEMBER 1645A

Septembr: 1645 from
Colonell Cromwell.[8]

[fo. 168r]
Sir,

It hath pleased the Genll: to give me in Charge to represent unto you
a particular accompt of the takeing of Bristoll,[9] the which I gladly undertake.

After the finishing of that service at Sherborne,[10] it was disputed att a
Councell of warr whether wee should march into the West or to Bristoll,
amongst other Argumtes, the leaving soe considerable an enemy at our backes
to march
into the heart of the Kingdome, the undoeing of the Country about Bristoll,
which was exceedingly harrassed by the Prince[11] his being but a fortnight thereaboutes,
the Correspondence he might hold with Wales, the possibility of uniting the
enemies forces where they please, & especially the drawing to an head the
disaffected Clubmen of Somersett, Wilts, & Dorsett,[12] when once our backes
were
towardes them; these Consideracons together with takeing soe important a
place, soe advantageous for the opening of trade to London, did sway the
baleance,
& begatt that Conclusion: When wee came within fower miles of the Citty wee
had
a new debate whether wee should endeavor. to block itt up or make a regular
seidge,
the latter being over ruled Col. Welden[13] with his Brigade marched to Pilehill
on the

---

[8] Seventeenth-century endorsement.
[9] Bristol, a major port in the west of England, held by Parliament at the outset of the war and captured by the royalists in July 1643, now the largest city in royalist hands.
[10] Sherborne, a market town in Dorset.
[11] Prince Rupert of the Rhine, nephew of Charles I, who had led the capture of Bristol in July 1643.
[12] See above, **1645 08 04**.
[13] Colonel Ralph Weldon, who commanded a regiment of foot from the creation of the New Model until he resigned in July 1647 and was replaced by Robert Lilburne. See Wanklyn, *Reconstructing*, 1:58; and Ralph Weldon (bap. 1606, d. 1676). See *ODNB*.

307

South side of the Citty being within Musquett shott thereof, where in a few dayes they made a good Quartr. over lookeing the Citty, upon our advance, the Enemy fired

Bedminster,[14] Clifton,[15] & some other villages, & would have fired the Countrey thereaboutes, if our unexpected Comming had not hindered. The Generall caused

some horse & dragoonrs. under Commissary genrll Ireton[16] to advance over Avon to

keepe in the Enemy on the north side of the Towne,[17] untill the foote could

come upp, & after a day the Generall with Colonell Mountagues[18] and Colonell Rainsborowes[19] Brigades marched over att Keynsham[20] to Stapleton[21] where he quartered

that night, the next day Colonell Mountague haveing his Post assigned with his Brigade was to secure all betweene Froome[22] & Avon,[23] he came up to Lawfordes

Gate,[24] within Musquett shott thereof; Colonell Rainsborowe's Post was neare to Durdham downe, where the dragoonrs. & three Regimtes. of horse made good a post

upon the downe, betweene him & the River Avon on his right hand, and from Colonell Rainsborowes quartr. to Froome river on his left; A part of Colonell Birch,[25] & Maior Gnrll. Skippons Regimt.[26] were to ~~have~~ [27] mainteyne that post

---

[14] Bedminster is a village on the south side of Bristol (it had been sacked by Prince Rupert's soldiers in 1644).

[15] A village on the outskirts of seventeenth-century Bristol.

[16] Henry Ireton (bap. 1611, d. 1651), parliamentarian army officer and regicide. See *ODNB*.

[17] The north side was protected by a ring of forts and by the river Frome.

[18] Edward Montagu, a colonel first in the army of the Eastern Association and now of the New Model. He resigned six weeks later, on 27 October 1645, and was replaced by John Lambert. See Wanklyn, *Reconstructing*, 1:48, 58, 59n.

[19] Thomas Rainborowe [Rainborow] (d. 1648), parliamentarian army officer and Leveller. See *ODNB*.

[20] Keynsham, Somerset, a village five miles south east of Bristol.

[21] Stapleton, Somerset, a village nine miles due north of Keynsham.

[22] Frome, Somerset is a market town 22 miles south-east of Bristol.

[23] The river that forms the Somerset/Gloucestershire boundary and enters the sea at Bristol.

[24] For Lawford's Gate, see www.fortified-places.com/bristol.html

[25] Colonel John Birch, not in the New Model but the leading military figure in Gloucestershire during the Civil War. See the *Online Directory of Parliamentarian Army Officers*.

[26] Philip Skippon, appointed Lord Skippon under the Protectorate (d. 1660), parliamentarian army officer and politician. See *ODNB*.

[27] This crossing out is in the same ink that is used later when we can be fairly sure the pen/ quill is in Cromwell's hand. See nn. 54, 55 and 61.

14 SEPTEMBER 1645A

these Postes being thus settled our horse were forced to be upon exceeding great
duty to stand by the foote, least the foote beeing soe weake in all their postes
might receive an affront, and truly herein wee were very happy, that wee
should receive soe little losse by sallyes, Considering the paucity of our men to
make good there postes, & the strength of the enemy within. ~~by~~ By sallyes (which
were three or fower) I know not that wee lost thirty men in all the time of
our Seidge. Of Officrs. of quallitye, onely Colonell Okey[28] was taken, by mistake goeing to
the Enemy, thinking them to be freinds, & Capt. Guilliams[29] slayne in a charge,
wee tooke Sir Bernard Asteley,[30] & kild Sir Richard Crane,[31] men very Considerable
with the Prince; We had a Councell of warr Concerning the storming of the
Towne, about 8 dayes before wee tooke it,[32] & in that there appeared great
unwillingnesse to the worke, through the unseasonablenesse of the weather and
other apparant difficulties: Some inducemt. to bring us thither was the report of
the good affeccon of the Townesmen to us, but that did not answer expectation,
Upon a second Consideracon, It was over-rul'd for a storme, which no sooner Concluded
but difficulties were removed; & all things seemed to favor the designe, & indeed
there hath beene seldome the like cheerfullnesse in officrs. & souldiers to any
worke like to this after it was once resolved on. Tha\e/t[33] day & houre of our Storme
was appointed to be Wednesday Morning \the 10ᵗʰ f/[34] about. 1. of the Clock, wee chose to
{[35]} early, because wee hoped thereby to surprise the enemy, with this

---

[28] John Okey (bap. 1606, d. 1662), parliamentarian soldier and regicide. See *ODNB*.

[29] Captain William Gwilliam had been a major in the dragoons, but had transferred as a captain to Henry Ireton's regiment of horse before this time. See Wanklyn, *Reconstructing*, 1:50, 64, 74.

[30] Sir Bernard Astley, fourth son of the major general, Jacob Astley, served in Ireland (1642–3) and then in England, taking part in the storm and siege of Leicester and in the battle of Naseby. He was wounded before he was captured on 10 September and he died of those wounds on 16 September. He was knighted in 1644. See Newman, *Royalist Officers*, no. 38.

[31] Newman, *Royalist Officers*, no. 368.

[32] See **1645 09 03**.

[33] Originally written 'That'. Changed in another hand (probably Cromwell's) to 'The'.

[34] Insertion with a caret in a darker hand and looks probably to be Cromwell's. In the erasure, the 'f' is clear; possibly 'o' in front, but cannot be seen and it may well be only one letter.

[35] Words lost at the foot of the page—the words given in version 2 are: 'act it so'.

309

THE LETTERS, WRITINGS, AND SPEECHES OF OLIVER CROMWELL

{[36]}on also, (to avoyde Confucion, & falling fowle upon one another, (that

[fo. 168v]

when we had recovered the Line, & forte upon it, wee would not to advance

further untill day. The Generall's signall unto the storme was the fireing of Straw
& discharging fower peece of Canon att Prior hill forte,[37] the signall was very
well perceived by all, & truly the men went on with great resolution, and very
presently recovered the line, makeing way for the horse to enter, Col:
Mountague,[38]

& Colonell Pickering[39] who Storme[40] d att Lawfords gate, where was a double
worke well

fild with men & Canon presently entred, & with great resolution beate the Enemy
from their workes, & possessed their Canon, their expedicon was such that they
forced the enemy from their advantages, without any Considerable losse to
themselve

they layd downe the bridges for the horse to enter, Major Desborowe[41]
Commaunding

the horse, who very gallantly seconded the foote, then our foote advanced to the
Citty walls, where they possessed the gate against the Castle Streete, whereinto
were putt an hundred men who made it good. Sir Hardresse Waller[42] with his
& the

Generalls Regimt. with no lesse resolucon entred on the other side of Lawfordes
gate

towardes Avon river, & putt themselves into an imediate Conjunccon with the rest
of the Brigade. During this Col: Rainborow[43] & Col: Hamond[44] attempted Prior

---

[36] Word lost at the foot of the page—the word given in version 2 is: 'resolution'.

[37] For which, see www.fortified-places.com/bristol.html   [38] Above, n. 17.

[39] John Pickering, a colonel in the Eastern Association and then in the New Model who was
to die of 'a new disease' during the siege of Exeter a few months later (Firth and Davies, *Regimental
History*, 2:405; Wanklyn, *Reconstructing*, 1:48, 60.

[40] One word erased: the darker ink suggests by another hand (Cromwell's). The word crossed
out is illegible and there is no word in version 2.

[41] John Disbrowe [Desborough] (bap. 1608, d. 1680), parliamentarian army officer and politician. *See ODNB*.

[42] Sir Hardress Waller (*c*.1604–66), parliamentarian army officer and regicide. *See ODNB*.

[43] Thomas Rainborowe [Rainborow] (d. 1648), parliamentarian army officer and Leveller.
See ODNB.

[44] Colonel Thomas Hammond, see Wanklyn, *Reconstructing*, 1:58 and Thomas Hammond
(*c*.1600–58). *See ODNB*.

14 SEPTEMBER 1645A

hill fort, & the line downewardes towardes Froome, Col. Birch[45] & the Maior genlls[46]

Regimt being to Storme towardes Froome river;[47] Col: Hamond possessed the Line

imediately, & beating the Enemy from it, made way for our horse to enter:

Col. Rainborowe who had the hardest taske of all att Prior hill forte

attempted it, & fought neare three houres for it, & indeed there was great

despaire of carrying the place, it being exceeding high, a ladder of thirty round

scarce reaching the topp thereof, but ⊢—⊣[48] his resolucon was such that

notwithstanding the inaccessiblenesse & difficulty he would not give it over.

The enemy had fower peece of Canon upon it, which they plⱧyed with round &

Case shott upon our men, his Lt. Colonell Bowen[49] & others were two houres att push

of pike, standing upon the Pallisadoes,[50] but could not enter, Colonell Hamond

being entred the line, & Capt. Ireton[51] with a forlorne[52] of Col: Riche's Regimt.[53]

interposeing with his horse, between the enemies horse & Col: Hammond, received

a shott with two pistoll bullettes, which brake his Arme, by meanes ~~whereof~~ \his entrance/ [54] Col:

Hamond did storme the fort on that part, which was inward. By which meanes

Colonell Rainborowe & Col: Hamondes men entred the fort, & \imediately[55]/ putt to the

Sword allmost all in it, & as this was the place of most difficulty, soe of

---

[45] See above, n. 24.   [46] i.e. Major Generall Philip Skippon (see n. 25).

[47] For the (21-mile) course of the river Frome, see www.somersetrivers.co.uk/index.php?module=Content&func=view&pid=13

[48] There is a word here so heavily scored through that it is now unreadable.

[49] Henry Bowen was lieutenant colonel in Thomas Rainborowe's regiment: Wanklyn, *Reconstructing*, 1:46–7.

[50] Pallisado: any kind of defensive wall, especially but not necessarily a thick hedge; see *OED*.

[51] Formerly a captain in Cromwell's Eastern Association regiment and now a captain in Nathaniel Rich's New Model regiment of horse. He was Commissary General Henry Ireton's youngest brother.

[52] 'Forlorn hope' = advance party.

[53] Nathaniel Rich, eldest son of the second earl of Warwick and a colonel both in the Eastern Association army and the New Model. See the *Online Directory of Parliamentarian Army Officers*.

[54] The crossing-out and insertion is in another hand and darker ink: probably Cromwell himself.

[55] The addition is almost certainly in Cromwell's hand.

THE LETTERS, WRITINGS, AND SPEECHES OF OLIVER CROMWELL

most losse to us on that side, & of very great honor. to the undertakers. The horse did second them with great resolution, & indeed[56] both those Colonells doe acknowledge that their interposicon between the enemies horse and their foote was a great meanes of obtaining this strong fort, without which all the rest of the line to Froome river would have done us little good, and indeed neither horse nor foote, would have stood in all that way, in any manner of security, had not the fort been taken.

Major. Bethels[57] were the first horse entered the line, who did behave himselfe very gallantly, and was shott in the thigh, had one or two shottes more, & his horse kill'd under him.

Colonell Birch with his men, and the Maior. Genrlls Regimt., entred with very good

resolucon, where their post was, possessing the enemies guns, & turning them upon them.

By this all the lyne from Prior hill fort to Avon which was a full mile with all the fortes Ordinance & bullwarkes were possessed by us, but one wherein there were about. 120. men of the enemy, which the Generall summoned, & all t}he men submitted to mercy

[fo. 169]

The Sucesse on Colonell Weldens[58] side did not answer with this, and allthough the Colonells, & other the Officrs & Souldiers both horse and foote testified very much resolution as could be expected, Col: Welden, Col: Ingoldsby,[59] Col: Herbert[60] & the rest of the Colonells and Officrs, \both of horse and foote/ [61] doeing what could be well looked for, from

men of honur, yett what by reason of the height of the workes, which proved higher then report made them, & the shortnesse of the Ladders, they were repulsed with the losse of about. 100. men, Col: Fortescues Lt. Colonell[62] was

---

[56] Erasure may be by Cromwell: darker ink.

[57] For Christopher Bethel, major in Edward Whalley's regiment, who died of the wounds described here, see Wanklyn, *Reconstructing*, 1:53 and 63.

[58] Colonel Ralph Weldon, see Wanklyn, *Reconstructing*, 1:25, 47, 58, and n. 138.

[59] Sir Richard Ingoldsby, appointed Lord Ingoldsby under the Protectorate (bap. 1617, d. 1685), parliamentarian army officer and regicide. See *ODNB*.

[60] Colonel William Herbert, newly promoted after the death of Col. Walter Lloyd at the siege of Taunton. See Wanklyn, *Reconstructing*, 1:59, 70.

[61] Insertion with a caret in a darker ink and different hand, probably Cromwell's.

[62] Severinus Dursey had only recently been promoted from the rank of major to lieutenant colonel in Richard Fortescue's regiment when the previous lieutenant colonel, Jeffrey Richbell, was killed at the siege of Taunton. Wanklyn, *Reconstructing*, 1:56.

14 SEPTEMBER 1645A

kill'd, Maior: Cromwell dangerously shott,[63] & two of Col: Ingoldsbyes brothers[64] hurt with some Officrs.

Being possessed of thus muche as hath beene related, the Towne was fired in three places by the enemy, which wee could not putt out, & this begatt a great trouble to the Generall, & us all, fearing to see, soe famous a Citty burnt to ashes before our faces, whiles wee were viewing so sad a spectacle, & Consulting which way to make further advantage of our successe, the Prince sent a Trumpett to the Genll: to desire a treaty for the surrender of the Towne, to which the Generall agreed, & deputed Col: Mountague, Colonell Raniborow, & Col: Pickering for that service, Authorizing them with Instruccons to treate & Conclude the Articles, ~~wh~~[65] are these enclosed,[66] for performance whereof, hostages were mutually given on Thursday about 2. of the Clocke in the afternoone. The Prince marched out having a Convoy of two Regimtes of horse from us & makeing eleccon of Oxford for the place he would goe to, which he had liberty to doe by his Articles.

The Canon which we have taken are about. 140. mounted, about. 100. barrells of powder allready Come to our handes with a good quantity of Shott, Ammunicon & Armes, wee have found allready betweene 2000. &. 3000. Musquettes the royall fort had in it, victualls for 150. men for. 320. dayes, the Castle victuall'd for neare halfe soe long: The Prince had foote of the Garrison as the Maior. of the Citty informed me. 2500 \2500/ [67]. & about. 1000 horse, besides the trayned bandes of

---

[63] Major Richard Cromwell shortly afterwards died of his wounds: Wanklyn, *Reconstructing*, 1:57. His relationship to Oliver Cromwell is not clear, but he was not a son or nephew or first cousin.

[64] These are almost certainly Oliver Ingoldsby (a captain in Fortescue's regiment who was to die at the siege of Pendennis in March 1646) and Henry Ingoldsby, a captain in his brother's regiment (Wanklyn, *Reconstructing*, 1:56–7, 68, 78, 88).

[65] Best reading: there may be another letter. Not clear who crossed it out, but probably the clerk.

[66] For the articles of surrender, see *An exact relation of Prince Rupert his marching out of Bristoll, the 11. of this instant Septemb. 1645. according to articles of agreement made betweene him and the Right Honourable, Sir Thomas Fairfax*, which were 'published by authority' on 18 September 1645 (Wing E3678).

[67] The first number was originally written with a different first digit—not clear whether it was a '1' or '3', but it was changed (in a darker ink) to '22', so '2500'. The second number written over the first, in the same darker ink and different hand (Cromwell's?)

THE LETTERS, WRITINGS, AND SPEECHES OF OLIVER CROMWELL

the towne, & Auxiliaries of. 1000.[68] Some Say. 1500. I heare but
one man hath died of the ~~plack~~ \plague/[69] in all our Army, although wee
have quartered amongst & in the midst of infected persons and
places, wee, had not kill'd of ours in this Storme, nor all this
seidge. 200. men.
Thus I have given you a true but not a full Account of this great
busines, wherein he that runns may read that all this is none
other then the worke of God, he must be a very Atheist that doth not
acknowledge it.
It may be thought that some praises \are/ due to these gallant men,
of whose valor. so much mention is made, their humble suit to you.
& all that have an interest in this blessing is, that in remembrance
of Godes prayses they may be forgotten: It'es their joy that they are
Instrumtes. to Godes glory, & their Countreys good, it's their honor. that God
vouchsafes to use them: ~~loe~~ \Sir/[70] they that have been imployed, in this

[fo. 169v]
Service knowe, that faith and prayer obteyned this Citty for you. I ~~doubt~~ \doe/ [71]not
say ours
onely, but of the people of God with you, & all England over, who have ~~waited~~
\wrastled/[72]
~~on~~ \with/[73] God for a blessing in this very thing: Our desires are that God may bee
glorified by the same spiritt of faith by which wee asked all our sufficiency, &
haveing received it, it's meete that he have all the praise. ~~Presbiterians~~ [74]
Independentes all had here the same spiritt of faith & prayer, the ~~y~~ same pretence
& answer, they agree here, ~~th~~ know no names of difference, pitty it is, it
should be otherwise, any where, All that beleive have the reall unitie,
which is most glorious, because inward & spirituall in the body & to the head,

---

[68] The number as written could be 1000 or 1200, but the printed version (see n. 1), has 1000.

[69] Written in darker ink in another hand (probably Cromwell's).

[70] Insertion with caret; darker ink; another hand (probably Cromwell's).

[71] 'doe' inserted over struck out 'doubt': darker ink; different hand.

[72] Not in *OED*, but that is clearly what is written although versions 2 and 3 have 'wrastled' and 'wrasteled'. Most likely what is intended is 'wrestled'.

[73] 'with' written over erased 'on': darker ink, almost certainly Cromwell's hand.

[74] This is where the censorship starts. The last sentences are underlined—or more precisely 'Presbiterians', the last word on one line, has been crossed out; the next three lines (starting with 'Independents') are fully underlined. The remaining lines have the beginning of the line underlined, and all the underlined lines are bracketed together with a line down the left margin. Underlining here is functionally a crossing-out.

14 SEPTEMBER 1645B

as for being united in formes, Commonly called uniformity, every Christian will for peace take studdy and doe as farr as Conscience will permitt, and from brethren in the[75] things of the minde, we looke for no Compulsion, but that of light and reaason. In other things, God hath putt the sword into the Parliamtes. handes, for the terror. of evill doers, & the praise of them that doe well, if any plead exemption from it, he knowes not the Gospell, if any would wring it out of your handes or steale it from you, under what pretence soever, I hope they shall doe it wwithout effect, that god will mainteyne it in your hand, & direct you: in the use thereof, is the prayer of

Your humble Servant
Oliver Cromwell

From Bristoll the 14th
of September. 1645.

***

1645 09 14b

Letter from Oliver Cromwell to William Lenthall, Speaker of the House of Commons

Date: 14 September 1645

Source: *The conclusion of Lieuten: Generall Cromwells letter to the House of Commons, concerning the taking of Bristoll which was contained in the originall, (signed by himselfe) but omitted in the printed copy, which is authorized by the House of Commons, (though there was a whole page left blanke in that sheete): whereby the world may know, how both truth it selfe, and that worthy gentleman are wronged (as well as other men) either by the printer or some others* [London : s.n., 1645]: (Wing / C70500; Thomason / 669.f.10[38]) (print copy)

This broadside prints the passage from Cromwell's letter recounting the capture of Bristol that was omitted (excised) from the official version (**1645 08 14a**), which had been printed on 18 September.

When George Thomason collected his copy, he was very explicit about how this broadside was a challenge to parliamentary censorship. It is of course a challenge to Parliament's plans to replace one (episcopal) system of church government by another (Presbyterian) form.

---

[75] Unclear who made the erasure: presumably Cromwell.

THE LETTERS, WRITINGS, AND SPEECHES OF OLIVER CROMWELL

It was published again as an appendix to another tolerationist tract which Thomason received on 10 October 1645. It is identical in spelling and punctuation.[1]

7bre. 22. this was printed by the Independent partie and Scatterd up and downe the Streets last night but expresly omitted by order of the howse vide the 4° 7bre. 18. 1645[2]

THE CONCLUSION OF Lieuten: Generall *Cromwells* Letter to the House of Commons, concerning the taking of *BRISTOLL*: Which was contained in the Originall, (signed by himselfe) but omitted in the Printed Copy, which is Authorized by the House of Commons, (though there was a whole Page left blanke in that sheete): Whereby the World may know, how both Truth it selfe, and that worthy Gentleman are wronged (as well as other men,) either by the Printer or some others. Presbiterians, Independents, all had here the same Spirit of Faith and prayer, the same presence and answer, they agree here, know no names of difference; pitty it is, it should be otherwise any where: All that beleeve havethe[3] reall Unity which is most glorious, because inward and spirituall in the body and to the head. As for being united in formes (commonly called uniformity) every Christian will for Peace sake, study and doe as far as Conscience will permit; And from brethren in things of the mind, we looke for no cumpulsion, but that of Light and reason. In other things God hath put the sword into the Parliaments hands, for the terrour of Evill dooers, and the praise of them that doe well; if any plead exemption from it, he knowes not the Gospel. If any would wring it out of your hands, or steale it from you, under what pretence so ever, I hope they shall doe it without effect, That God will maintaine it in your hands and direct you in the use thereof, is the prayer of Your humble servant,

Oliver Cromwell.

From *Bristoll*, this 14th. of

Septemb. 1645.

---

[1] *Strong motives, or Loving and modest advice, vnto the petitioners for presbiterian government. That they endeavour not the compulsion of any in matters of religion, more then they wish others should endeavour to compell them. But with all love, lenitie, meekenesse, patience, & long-suffering to doe unto others, as they desire others should doe unto them. Whereunto is annexed the conclusion of Lieuten. Generall Cromwells letter to the House of Common tending to the same purpose.* [no printer or publisher is given] (Wing / S6016; Thomason / E.304[15]).

[2] This is a handwritten note added by George Thomason to his copy of the printed text.

[3] Printed without a space between the words.

1645 09 22

Articles of Surrender sent by Oliver Cromwell to Sir Charles Lloyd, the governor of Devizes

Date: 22 September 1645

Source: Joshua Sprigge, *Anglia Rediviva; England's Recovery: being the History of the Motions, Actions and Successes of the Army under the Immediate Conduct of His Excellency Sr. Thomas Fairfax* (1647), pp. 123–4 (Wing / S5070) (slightly later print version)

Fairfax and Cromwell spent four days in Bristol consolidating their hold on the city. Fairfax then sent Cromwell with a brigade of four regiments with orders to take Devizes[1] which blocked one of the main routes between London and the West Country. Cromwell's attempts to take the town with musket fire and grenades failed but once his heavy artillery was in place, the governor of Devizes, Sir Charles Lloyd,[2] offered to treat but asked for time to consult with the King for permission to surrender. Cromwell brushed this aside and within 24 hours the terms he offered in this despatch were accepted.

The Lieutenant-general sent two Captains into them, and about eleven of the clock the Lieutenant-general sent them in these Propositions following, viz.

1. That all Commanders and Gentlemen should march to any garrison the King had within thirty miles, with their horse and armes; and that all private souldiers should march away leaving their armes behinde them, but not to go to the same garrisons the Commanders marched to.
2. That all Gentlemen in the Castle should have liberty to go to their own homes or beyond the seas.
3. That all souldiers that have been formerly in the Parliament service, should be delivered up to the Lieutenant-general; and all souldiers that would take up armes in the Parliament service should be entertained.

To these Propositions the Lieutenant-general desired his speedy answer.

---

[1] Devizes, a medieval market town and important road crossing in mid-Wiltshire, at the north end of the Salisbury Plain.

[2] Sir Charles Lloyd was the King's chief military engineer and quartermaster. He is not included in Newman, *Royalist Officers*, but see www.devizesheritage.co.uk/devizescastle.html

THE LETTERS, WRITINGS, AND SPEECHES OF OLIVER CROMWELL

1645 09 28

Letter from Oliver Cromwell to the [William Longland], mayor of Winchester

Date: 28 September 1645

Source: *The History and Antiquities of Winchester, setting forth its original constitution, government, manufactories, trade, commerce and navigation*, 2 vols. (1773), 2:127 (later transcription)

After taking Bristol on 10 September and settling a garrison there, Fairfax headed back to Devon and he sent Cromwell—before going into winter quarters—to take out the ring of fortified houses and towns that could hinder supply lines for the full-scale siege of Oxford that he saw as a top priority for the next campaign. As Joshua Sprigg explained (in 1647): 'Winchester,[1] Basing,[2] Dennington,[3] Farrington,[4] and Wallingford,[5] which together with Oxford, like Vipers in the bowels infested the midland parts'. After leaving Bristol, Cromwell then headed for Devizes,[6] and it took him eight days to take that town and the castle. Then he moved on to the important cathedral town of Winchester and its castle, arriving on 28 September. This letter is his initial summons to the mayor, William Longland. Longland said he was powerless to do so, but offered to plead with the governor of the castle (and town's MP), Sir William Ogle, to surrender.[7] Cromwell ignored this response and immediately blew out the city gates and occupied the town, although the castle was to hold out for another week.[8]

———

To the mayor of the Cittie of Winchester

Sir, I Come not to this cittie but with a full resolution to save itt and the inhabitants thereof from ruine. I commanded the soldyers upon payne of death, that noe wronge bee done, which I shall strictly observe,[9] only I expect you give mee

---

[1] Winchester, a Cathedral city in Hampshire.

[2] Basing House, Hampshire, one mile east of the town of Basingstoke, Hampshire and seat of the Catholic marquis of Winchester. For Cromwell's violent seizure and destruction of this highly fortified house, see **1645 10 14**.

[3] Dennington = Donnington Castle, near Newbury, Berkshire. It held out until April 1646.

[4] Faringdon, Oxfordshire. Cromwell had failed to take this back in the spring (see **1645 04 29 a & b**, **1645 04 30**) and it held out for the King until 24 June 1646.

[5] Wallingford town and castle, Oxfordshire, held out for the King until 27 June 1646.

[6] Devizes, Wiltshire. Cromwell arrived on 15 September 1645 and quickly occupied the town, but it took him until 23 September (after seven days of bombardment) to persuade the governor to surrender.

[7] *History and Antiquities of Winchester*, 2:128.

[8] For an account of all this, see Joshua Sprigg, *Anglia Rediviva* (1647), pp. 141–4 (Wing / S5070). See also **1645 10 06**.

[9] See **1645 10 06**, n. 17.

318

entrance into the cittie, without necessitateing me to force my way, which yf I doe, then it will not be in my power to save you or yt. I expect your answer within half and houre, and rest,

Sept.28   Your humble servant
5 o'clock at night   OLIV.CROMWELL

1645 10 06

Letter from Oliver Cromwell to William Lenthall, Speaker of the House of Commons

Date: 6 October 1645
Source: Bodl., MS Nalson 4, fos 224r–225v (autograph)

This letter is in the hand of Cromwell's usual clerk with interlineations in the same hand. It bears Cromwell's signature and fragments of his seal. It was 'borrowed' from Speaker Lenthall's papers by John Nalson in the late 1670s and never returned (see **1645 09 14b**).

After occupying the town (and cathedral) of Winchester on the evening of 28 September, Cromwell spent a week bombarding the castle walls. The governor, having rejected two offers of terms, immediately sued for terms once a breach was achieved. Cromwell despatched this letter on 6 October and it was read the next day in the House of Commons (but not in the House of Lords). There were two attachments, both absent from this manuscript original: the list of provisions seized from Winchester Castle was included in a newspaper republication of Cromwell's letter a few days later,[1] but the articles of surrender were not published until eighteen months later when they appear in Joshua Sprigg's history of the New Model down to the crisis of spring 1647.[2]

[fo. 225v]
6 ° Octobr. 1645
Letter from Coll Cromwell

---

[1] *Perfect Occurrences of Parliament, and chief collections of letters… Number 42, 3rd–10th October 1645*, unpag. (N&S, 465.3042: Thomason / E.264[25]).

[2] J. Sprigg, *Anglia rediviva; Englands recovery*, p. 131 (Wing / S5070). This also reproduced the list of goods taken. The main terms were that the garrison would leave the town the next morning and would march under armed guard to Woodstock. It would abandon almost all its arms, ammunition and equipment, the governor, William Ogle (see below, n. 9), being permitted to keep his own colours, a lightly armed bodyguard and six carriages for himself and his senior officers and their personal effects.

from Winton 6 Oct

For the honourable William Lenthall Esqr Speaker of the House of Commons these

read. Oct. 7° 1645

[fo. 224r]

Sir

I came to Winchester on the Lords day being the 28th of Septemb. with Collonell Pickering[3] comaunding his owne, Collonell Muntagues,[4] and Sir Hardres Wallers[5] Regiments. After some dispute with the Governor, wee entred the towne, I summoned the Castle, was denyed, whereupon wee fell to prepare our batteries, which wee could not perfect (some of our gunns being out of order) untill fryday following our battry was Six gunns which being finished after one firing of them round I sent him a Second Summons for a treaty which hee refused, whereupon wee went onn with our worke and made a breach in the wall neare the black tower, which after about 200. shott wee thought Stormable, and purposed on Munday[6] morneing to attempt it, on sunday night about ten of the clock, The Governor[7] beate a parlie, desireing to treate, I agreed unto it, and Sent Coll. Hammond[8] and Major Harrison[9] in to him, who agreed upon these enclosed articles. Sir This is the addition of another mercy, you See God is not weary in doeing yow good. I confesse Sir his favour to you is as visible when hee comes by his power upon the hearts of your enemyes makeing them quitt places of strength to yow, as when he gives courage to your Soldiers to attempt hard things, his goodnesse in this is much to be acknowledged. For the Castle was well mannd with 680 foote and horse there being neare 200 gentlemen, officers and their servants well victualld, with very greate store of wheate \& beare/, 15000 waite of cheese, and beare neare 20 barrells, of powther, 7 peice of Cannon, the workes were exceeding good and strong, Its very likely it would have cost

---

[3] John Pickering, who was to die three weeks later at Ottery St Mary and be replaced by his lieutenant colonel John Hewson. See Wanklyn, *Reconstructing*, 1:59.

[4] Edward Montagu, who was to resign three weeks later and be replaced by John Lambert. See Wanklyn, *Reconstructing*, 1:58–9.

[5] Sir Hardress Waller (*c*.1604–66), parliamentarian army officer and regicide. See *ODNB*.

[6] The 'M' here overwrites an 'S'.

[7] Sir William Ogle (created Viscount Ogle in the Irish peerage by Charles during his time as governor). He was MP for Winchester in the Short and Long Parliaments. He had served in the 'English' Army in Ireland 1642–4. See Newman, *Royalist Officers*, no. 1067.

[8] Robert Hammond (1620/21–54), parliamentarian army officer. See *ODNB*.

[9] Thomas Harrison (bap. 1616, d. 1660), parliamentarian army officer and regicide. See *ODNB*.

6 OCTOBER 1645

much blood to have gained it by storme, wee have not lost twelve men This is repeated to you that God may have all the praise, for its all his due, Sir I rest
Your most humble servant
Oliver Cromwell

Winton octob the 6th 1645

Sir I understand exceptions are taken at my giving a passe to Mr Chichley[10] to come into Cambridgeshyre[11] to see his Lady,[12] truely Sir I did it upon the Suggestion of his ladyes being very ill, and much desireing to See him, she being (as I beleive you will heare) a vertuous woman and sister to a true Servant of yow, Coll. Russells,[13] I thought it to be an act of humanity, I shall not hereafter presume, I can say I have donne you service by some civilityes, nor have I taken liberty this way I hope I never shall, but out of Judgmt to serve yow If it offend the house I aske their pardon, and had rather be chidden by yow then accused by them, from whome, I have not deserved any jealousie of me, who truely beare an upright heart to the publique, and am sorry I need this apologie. Sir Mr Peeters[14] is to wayte upon you with some considerations concerneing the Army which it may be are not Soe fitt to be comitted to writeing,[15]

---

[10] Thomas Chicheley (1614–99), politician and administrator. See *ODNB*.

[11] His home was at Wimpole, six miles west of Cambridge.

[12] Sarah Chicheley, née Russell (d. 1654), daughter of Sir William Russell of Chippenham, Cambridgeshire.

[13] Francis Russell, see the *Online Directory of Parliamentarian Army Officers*. For his service in Parliament during the periods 1645–53, 1654–5 and 1656–8, see his entry in *HoP Commons, 1640–1660*. His daughter married Cromwell's younger surviving son Henry on 10 May 1653.

[14] Hugh Peter [Peters] (bap. 1598, d. 1660). See *ODNB*. Peter was later one of Cromwell's chaplains, especially during the Irish campaign of 1649 50.

[15] This is almost certainly a reference to the trial of six of his soldiers and execution of one of them for looting (see **1645 09 28**). In the words of Joshua Sprigg (*Anglia Rediviva*, 133–4): 'I cannot but observe a remarkable peece of Justice done in satisfaction to the Enemy, for some injury they had su|stained at their marching forth of Winchester, by Plunder, contrary to the Articles, which was done by some Troopers; who being apprehended, were afterwards tried by a Councel of war, and condemned to die; and after lots cast for their lives (being six of them) he whose lot it was to die, was brought to the place of execution, where with a demonstration of great penitence (so far as the beholders did judge) he suffered death for his offence; which exemplary justice made a good impression upon the Souldiery: The other five were sent with a Convoy to Oxford, (together with a full account of this proceeding, to the Governour there, Sir Tho. Glemham) to be delivered over as prisoners, and to be put to death, or otherwise punished as he should think fit: Which was so well received by the Enemy (to see so much right was done them) that Sir Thomas Glemham returned the prisoners back again, with an acknowledgement of the Lieutenant-Generals Noblenesse, in being so tender in breach of Articles.'

yet very fitt yow should seasonably be acquainted with them wherein I beseech yow to heare him.

1645 10 14
Letter from Oliver Cromwell to William Lenthall, Speaker of the House of Commons

Date: 14 October 1645

Source: [A] *Lieut: Generall Cromwells Letter to the Honorable, William Lenthall Esq; Speaker of the House of Commons; of the storming and taking Basing-House* (1645), pp. 3–7 (Wing / C7108C) (contemporary copies)

This letter, sent to the Speaker of the Commons on 14 October, was published in four different pamphlets and diurnalls over the next week. The proof text here is the only one to be published at the orders of House of Commons and its publication date is 16 October,[1] just two days after he wrote the letter.

Cromwell proceeded straight from Winchester to Basing House (19 miles to the southwest) and he took it by storm after a five-day siege on 14 October. Basing was the seat of the marquis of Winchester,[2] and he and many of those defending Basing were Catholics. Basing consisted of a medieval motte and bailey with many later-medieval buildings within the bailey ('the Old House') alongside a substantial fortified mansion in five storeys with a substantial tower at the north corner and with substantial defence works around it ('the New House').[3] Two previous sieges had failed, but Cromwell had better siege guns this time which ravaged the walls for five successive days. More than one hundred of the garrison were killed and another two hundred taken prisoner as Cromwell overran the whole site. He permitted extreme plunder and subsequently the complete destruction of both Houses.[4]

The original of Cromwell's letter has not been preserved in the parliamentary archives or in the papers of Speaker Lenthall in the Bodleian Library. But there are surviving four

---

[1] 'Ordered by the Commons assembled in Parliament, that this letter and order be forthwith printed and published: H: Elsynge, Cler. Parl. D. Com. London: printed for Edward Husband, printer for the honorable House of Commons.'

[2] For John Paulet, fifth marquis of Winchester (1598?–1675), royalist nobleman. See *ODNB*.

[3] For an archived English Heritage website describing the House at this time, see https://web.archive.org/web/20121022153801/http://www.imagesofengland.org.uk/details/default.aspx?pid=1&id=138833.

[4] The fullest and best account is by Wilfrid Emberton, *'Love Loyalty': the close and perilous siege of Basing House 1643–1645* (Basingstoke, 1972); and the best analysis of the 'massacre' is Inga Volmer, 'A Comparative Study of Massacres during the Wars of the Three Kingdoms', University of Cambridge, PhD thesis, 2006, pp. 92–103.

14 OCTOBER 1645

contemporary or near contemporary copies, each of which seems to have been a copy of the lost original. The one presented below is the earliest and probably the most careful copy.

The other contemporary or near-contemporary versions are:

[B] *Liuetenant Generall Cromwels letter Sent to the Honorable William Lenthall Esq; Speaker of the honourable house of Commons, concerning the Storming and taking of Basing House, with the Marquesse of Winchester, Sir Robert Peake, and divers other Officers of quality.* (Wing / C7108)

[C] *A Perfect Diurnall of Some Passages in Parliament, Numb.* 116 (13–20 Oct. 1645), p. 923 (N&S, 504.116; B.L., Thomason / E.266[5])

[D] J. Sprigg, *Anglia rediviva; Englands recovery: being the history of the motions, actions, and successes of the army under the immediate conduct of His Excellency Sr. Thomas Fairfax, Kt. Captain-General of all the Parliaments forces in England. Compiled for the publique good by Ioshua Sprigge. M.A. London, printed by R.W. for Iohn Partridge, and are to be sold at the Parot in Pauls Church-yard, and the Cock in Ludgate-streete),* pp. 137–9 (Wing / S5070)

Cromwell's letter was read the following day—15 October—in the Commons and the proposals made in his letter were fully endorsed. The Commons also ordered that 'on the next Lord's Day, publick Thanks be given unto Almighty God, for his great Mercies and Blessings upon the Parliament's Forces under Lieutenant-General Cromwell, and under Colonel Dalbeere,[5] in taking Winchester-Castle and Basinge-House, in all Churches and Chapels of London and Westminster, and within the Lines of Communication'.[6] Strikingly, Cromwell's letter was *not* read in the Lords. Instead the Lords received a letter from the county committee of Hampshire with a short account of the capture of Basing House (an account in which Cromwell is only mentioned in passing).[7] Is it possible that the Lords (with the earl of Manchester in the chair) were unwilling to receive letters from Cromwell and certainly unwilling to offer him their thanks?

[p. 3]

Lieutenant Generall Cromwels *Letter to the Honorable* William Lenthall *Esq; Speaker to the Honorable house of Commons.*

SIR,

I thank God I can give you a good account of *Basing;* After our Batteries placed, we setled the severall posts for the storm, Col: *Dalbier*[8] was to be on the North side of the house next the Grange, Col. *Pickering*[9] on his left hand, and Sir *Hardres*

------

[5] John Dalbier (d. 1648). See ODNB.   [6] JHC, 4:309.   [7] JHL, 8:646.

[8] See above, n. 4.

[9] Wanklyn, *Reconstructing*, I:48, 60; John Pickering (bap. 1615, d. 1645), parliamentarian army officer. See ODNB.

323

THE LETTERS, WRITINGS, AND SPEECHES OF OLIVER CROMWELL

Wallers,[10] and Col: *Mountagues*[11] Regiments next him. We Stormed this morning after six of the Clock: The signall for falling on, was the firing four of [p. 4] our Canon; which being done, our men fell on with great Resolution and cheerfulnesse: We took the two houses without any considerable losse to our selves: Col: *Pickering* Stormed the new house, passed through, and got the gate of the old house; whereupon, they Summoned a Parley, which our men would not hear: In the mean time, Col: *Mountagues*, and Sir *Hardres Wallers* Regiments, assaulted the strongest works, where the Enemy kept his Court of Guard,[12] which with great resolution they recovered, beating the enemy from a whole culverin,[13] & from that Work; which having done, they drew their Ladders after them, and got over another Work and the house wall, before they could enter in this:[14] Sir *Hardres Waller* performing his duty with honour and diligence, was shot on the arm, [p. 5] but not dangerous: We have had little losse; many of the Enemy our men put to the Sword, and some Officers of quality, most of the rest we have Prisoners, amongst which the Marques and Sir *Robert Peake*,[15] with divers other Officers, whom I have Ordered to be sent up to you. We have taken about ten piece of Ordnance, much Ammunition, and our Souldiers a good encouragment. I humbly offer to you to have this place slighted,[16] for these Reasons; It will ask Eight hundred men to man[17] it, it is no frontier, the Countrey is poor about it, the place exceedingly ruined by our Batteries and Morter-pieces,[18] and a fire which fell upon the place since our taking it. If you please to take the Garrison at *Farnham*,[19]

[10] Sir Hardress Waller (*c*.1604–66), parliamentarian army officer and regicide. See *ODNB*.

[11] Edward Montagu [Mountagu], first earl of Sandwich (1625–72), army and naval officer and diplomat. See *ODNB*.

[12] 'court of guard' = *corps de garde*: 'The post or station occupied by a small military guard; a guard-room or guard-house' (see *OED*) and so used again by Cromwell in **1648 II 15**.

[13] A culverin was a piece of artillery whose barrel was very long in proportion to its bore (most usually in the range of 10 to 13 ft., with a bore 5.0 to 5.5 inches in diameter) and firing shot of 17 to 20 lbs. Here it presumably means that the royalists were driven back from around such a culverin (see *OED*).

[14] [C] and [D] have here '…could enter: in this Sir Hardress Waller…'.

[15] Sir Robert Peake (*c*.1605–67), printseller and royalist army officer. See *ODNB*.

[16] 'slight' = 'To level with the ground; to raze (a fortification, etc.)' (see *OED* which also notes that this obsolete usage was common only in the period 1640–80).

[17] [C] has 'men to manage it'.

[18] Mortar pieces = 'A short piece of artillery with a large bore…trunnions on the breech, used to discharge missiles, in later use esp. explosive shells, at high angles' (*OED*).

[19] Farnham, a market town (with castle) just on the Surrey side of the Surrey/Hampshire border and 14 miles from Basing. It was a parliamentarian stronghold, where the artillery train for the bombardment of Basing was assembled.

14 OCTOBER 1645

some out of *Chichester*,[20] and a good part of the Foot which were here under *Dalbier*, and [p. 6] make a strong quarter at *Newbery*[21] with three or four Troops of horse: I dare be confident, it would not only be a curb to *Dennington*,[22] but a security and a Frontier to all these parts, inasmuch as *Newbery* lies upon the River,[23] and will prevent any incursion from *Dennington*, *Wallingford*,[24] or *Farringdon*[25] into these parts, and by lying there will make the Trade most secure between *Bristoll* and *London* for all Carriages; And I believe the Gentlemen of *Sussex* and *Hantshire* will with more cheerfulnes contribute to maintain a Garrison on the Frontier, then in their bowels,[26] which will have lesse safety in it. Sir I hope not to delay. but march towards the West to-morrow, and to be as diligent as I may in my expedition thither: I must speak my judgment to you, that if you intend to have your work ca- [p. 7] ried on, recruits of Foot must be had, and a course taken to pay your Army; else believe me Sir, it may not be able to answer the work you have for it to do. I entreated Coll: *Hamond*[27] to wait upon you, who was taken by a mistake whilest we lay before this Garrison, whom God safely delivered to us, to our great joy, but to his losse of almost all he had which the Enemy took from him. The Lord grant that these mercies may be acknowledged with all thankfulnesse; God exceedingly abounds in his goodnesse to us, and will not be weary, untill righteousnesse and peace meet, and that he hath brought forth a glorious work, for the happinesse of this poor Kingdom, wherein desires to serve God and you with a faithfull heart,[28]

Your most humble Servant,

OLIVER CROMWEL.

---

[20] Chichester, a cathedral city in Sussex.   [21] Newbury, a market town in Berkshire.

[22] Donnington Castle, just north of Newbury. Captured by the royalists after the first battle of Newbury (20 September 1643), it withstood long sieges between the late summer of 1644 and its surrender in April 1646.

[23] River Kennet.

[24] Wallingford, a market town and castle in Oxfordshire. An important royalist garrison from 1642 to 1646, guarding the south-easterly approaches to Oxford.

[25] Faringdon, a market town in the Vale of the White Horse on the Berkshire/Oxfordshire border, which had withstood a siege and attempted storm by Cromwell earlier in the year (see **1645 04 29a, 1645 04 29b, 1645 04 30**).

[26] A modern equivalent would be 'at the heart of their territory'.

[27] Robert Hammond (1620/1–54), parliamentarian army officer. See *ODNB*.

[28] [A] and [D] have 'faithful heart', [B] and [C] have 'faithful hand'.

Basingstoke, Octo-
ber, 14. 1645.

Octobr. 15. 1645.

Ordered by the Commons in Parliament assembled, That the next Lords day publique thanks be given unto Almighty God for his great mercies and blessings upon the Parliaments Forces under Lieutenant Generall *Cromwell,* and Col. *Dalbier,* for taking in *Winchester* Castle and *Basing house,* in all Churches and Chappels in the Cities of *London* and *Westminster,* and within the Lines of Communication; and Alderman *Pennington* and Colonell *Venn* are appointed by this House to desire the Lord Major[29] to give timely notice hereof to the Ministers of the Churches and Chappels within the Lines of Communication. *Hen. Elsynge Cler. Parl. D. Com.*

1645 10 16
Letter from Oliver Cromwell to Sir Thomas Fairfax

Date: 16 October 1645
Source: BL, Sloane MS 1519, fos 127r–128v (autograph)

The text is in the hand of Cromwell's usual clerk but the address and postscript are in an unrecognised hand. However, the signature is certainly Cromwell's. On 14 October 1645 Cromwell had written to the Speaker of the Commons about the taking of Basing House (see **1645 10 14**). That letter was read in the Commons the following day, and the House had resolved that 'a Letter be forthwith sent to Lieutenant General Cromwell, to give him Thanks for his good Services to the Parliament; for approving of his Opinion to slight the Garison and Works of Basing; and to recommend to his Care and Consideration the Taking in of Dennington-Castle, if it may not be prejudicial to his other Designs: And Mr. Sollicitor and Mr. Whitelock are to prepare this Letter: And Mr. Speaker is to sign the same.'[1] That letter was sent early on 16 October and arrived in time for Cromwell to receive it and to despatch this letter to Fairfax that evening. He also replied to Speaker Lenthall and that letter in turn was read in the Commons on

---

[29] All the other versions have 'Lord Mayor'.

[1] *JHC,* 4:309. The letter itself appears not to have survived.

16 OCTOBER 1645

17 October[2] (see **1645 10 17a**). It was at this critical juncture that the Commons voted a further forty-day extension to Cromwell's commission as lieutenant general in despite of the Self-Denying Ordinance.[3]

———

[fo. 128v]

To the Right hble. Sir Thomas Fairfax Genll of the parliamts army haste these.

[fo. 127r]

Sir

In two dayes march I came to Wallup,[4] 20 miles from Basing towards you That night I received this enclosed from the Speaker of the house of Commons, which I thought fitt to send you and to which I returned \an/ ~~this~~ answer a Copie whereof I have alsoe sent enclosed to you. I perceive it's the desire to have the place taken in. But truely I could not doe other {than let}[5] them know \what/ the condition of affaires in the West are and submitte the businesse to them and you. I shalbe at Langford[6] tomor{row}[7] night if God please. I hope the worke will not be long. If it should I will rather leave a small part of the force (if that will not be Sufficient to take it in,) then be detayned from obeying such Comaunds as I shall receive. I humbly beseech you to be confident that noe man hath a more faithfull heart to serve you then my selfe nor shalbe more strict to observe your comaunds then Your most humble servant

Oliver Cromwell

---

[2] *JHC*, 4:312: 'A Letter from Lieutenant-General Cromwall, from Wallop, of Octobris 16 1645, was this Day read: And It is Ordered, &c. That Sir Henry Vane junior do forthwith send to Lieutenant-General Cromwall the Order, this Day made, concerning the General and Lieutenant-General's disposing their Forces.' The order alluded to, which was made earlier that day, was: 'That the General and Lieutenant-General be left free to dispose of their Forces in such manner as they shall think most advantageous for the Commonwealth, in relation to the Affairs of the West; and to a competent Number of Force for the Safety of these Parts; notwithstanding any former Order of this House: And that the Committee of both Kingdoms do send this Order to the General and Lieutenant-General, with all convenient Speed.'

[3] *A Perfect Diurnall* no. 116 for 13–20 October 1645, p. 925 (N&S, 504.116; Thomason / E.266[5]).

[4] Nether, Middle and Over Wallop are three villages spread over two miles near Stockbridge near the Hampshire/Wiltshire border.

[5] This is the reading by Carlyle and repeated in the Carlyle-Lomas edition at 1:229. The fading and dirt of the document make it not quite clear. The first of the words is either 'than' or 'then' but the next word is unclear. Perhaps it was easier to read 180 years ago.

[6] Longford Castle was an Elizabethan prodigy house with strong defences, located two miles beyond Salisbury on the river Avon (and 16 miles from the Wallops, where Cromwell was as he wrote this letter).

[7] The final letters are too faded to be read, but the word must be 'tomorrow'.

Wallup this 15th of Octob 1645

Sir

I beseech you to let me have your resolution in this businesse with all the possible speed that may be because whatsoever I be design'd to, I wish I may speedily endeavour it time being soe pretious for action in this Season.

1645 10 17a
Letter from Oliver Cromwell to William Lenthall, Speaker of the House of Commons

Date: 17 October 1645
Source: *Severall letters from Col. Gen. Poyntz. Lieu. Gen. Cromwell. and Col. Hutchison. Col. Whitt. of the late great victory neere Sherborne in the north, with some other happy successes in the west*, pp. 4–5 (Wing / S2771) (contemporary print copy)

No manuscript version survives in the parliamentary archives or in Lenthall's papers in the Bodleian Library. It was included with other military letters in a pamphlet approved for publication by both Houses.[1] It was also printed in one of the weekly newsbooks.[2] Both versions of the letter, which are almost identical, also include the surrender articles from Langford House, which are fairly generous and may indicate Cromwell's sense of urgency. The version in *The Weekly Account* is printed separately from the letter and although very similar overall, is arranged quite differently. The version here seems likely to be closer to the original. The slightly peremptory tone at the end is also worthy of note.

Langford House was the home of Hugh Hare, first Lord Coleraine and had been a royalist stronghold since 1642, withstanding a siege undertaken by Waller and Cromwell the previous April. *The Moderate Intelligencer* had reported on 7 October that 'they say there will be Wagers laid, that Bazing is taken before Langford. When both are taken, then the way is open, and passage for Trade cleare: which is worth a little more than thanks.'[3]

---

[1] 'Printed according to the originall, together with an order of both Houses for thanksgiving for the same. Die Sabbathi 25. Octob. 1645. Ordered by the Lords assembled in Parliament, that these letters, with the order for the thanksgiving, be forthwith printed and published. Joh. Brown Cler. Parliamentorum.'
[2] *The Weekly Account*, no. 42 for 18–22 October 1642, unpag., *sub* Saturday 15 October 1645 (N&S, 671.42; Thomason / E.305[19]).
[3] *The Moderate Intelligencer*, no. 32, p. 155 (N&S, 417.32; Thomason / E.304[11]).

17 OCTOBER 1645A

For the Honourable William Lenthall *Esq. Speaker of the Commons House of Parliament, these.*

SIR:

I gave you an accompt the last night of my marching to *Langford-house:*[4] whether I came this day, and immediatly sent them in a Summons; the Governour[5] desired I should send two Officers to treat with them, and I accordingly appointed Lieutenant Colonell *Hewson,*[6] and Major *Kelsey*[7] thereunto: the Treaty produced the agreement which I have here enclosed to you. The Generall I heare is advanced as farre west as *Columpton,*[8] and hath sent some Horse and Foot to *Teverton,*[9] it is earnestly desired that those Foot might march up to him, it being convenient that we stay a day for our Foot that are behind and comming up. I waite your Answer to my Letter last night from *Wallop,*[10] I shall desire that your pleasure may be speeded to me, and rest, Sir;

Your humble servant

Oliver Cromwell.

Salisbury Octo. 17. at 12. at night.

[p. 5]

17. October 1645.

Articles of agreement made between Sir *Bartholomew Pell* Knight, and Major *Edmond Uvedale,*[11] Commanders in chief of *Langford* Garrison, and Lieu. Col. *Hewson,* and Major *Tho. Kelsey* on the behalf of *Oliver Cromwell,* Lieu. Generall to Sir *Tho. Fairfax* Army.

---

[4] For Longford (or Langford) House, see **1645 10 16**.

[5] Sir Bartholomew Pell (d. 1671), a Nottinghamshire man who had been a royalist officer since 1642 and had taken part in the royalist capture of Bristol in 1643 and perhaps at Naseby, see Newman, *Royalist Officers*, no. 1108.

[6] John Hewson, appointed Lord Hewson under the Protectorate (*fl.* 1630–60), army officer and regicide. See *ODNB*.

[7] Thomas Kelsey (d. in or after 1676), parliamentarian army officer and major general. See *ODNB*.

[8] Cullompton, a village in mid-Devon, on the river Cull and 13 miles north-east of Exeter.

[9] Tiverton, a market town six miles north-east of Cullompton. The town and church were occupied on 15 October by troops of the Western Brigade led by Major General Edward Massey but the castle held out until Fairfax arrived and bombarded it for 24 hours. Fairfax then made it his winter quarters as he prepared for the siege of Exeter.

[10] See **1645 10 16**.

[11] See Newman, *Royalist Officers*, no. 1471.

First, That the said Commanders in chiefe of the said Garrison shall surrender the said House and Garrison to the said Lieutenant Generall Cromwell to morrow by twelve of the clock, being the eighteenth of October instant.

2. That all Armes and Amunition in the said Garrison be then delivered to the use of the Parliament without any imbesiling of it.
3. That the said Commanders in chief with 15 Gent. of the said Garrison shall march away with Horse and Armes, and the private Souldiers without Armes to Oxford within ten daies, and to have a Troop of Horse for their Guard the first day, and a Trumpet, with a Passe the rest of the way.
4. That the rest of the Gentlemen, not exceedinge more, shall march with their Swords and Pistols, and Horses, if they can lawfully procure them.
5. That the said Commanders in chief shall have a Cart or Waggon allowed them to carry their goods to Oxford.
6. That if any Gentleman of the said Garrison have a desire to goe to any other Garrison, or Army of the Kings, they shall have Passes to that purpose.
7. That the goods remaining in the said Garrison shall be delivered to the severall Owners thereof upon demand, with- in two daies next following the date hereof.
8. That Lieutenant Col. Bowles[12] and Major Fry[13] be left Hostage untill these Articles be performed.

John Hewson.   Bartho. Pell.
Thomas Kelsey.   Edm. Uvedale

---

[12] Lt Col Richard Bolles (or Bolle), from Salisbury. He was later executed for his part in Penruddock's Rising in 1655. See Newman, *Royalist Officers*, no. 150.

[13] Not identified.

1645 10 17b
Warrant from Oliver Cromwell to Thomas Herbert, Commissioner of Parliament for the Army

Date: 17 October 1645
Source: TNA, SP 16/511, fo. 35 (autograph)

This warrant and the endorsements were written by Cromwell's usual clerk and bear Cromwell's own signature.

[fo. 35r]
Forasmuch, as a gratuity of five shillings was promist each foot souldier of the Army as were at the taking of Winchester Castle;[1] our being speedily to ingage upon other the Enemies Guarrisons, I desire yw for their better incouragemt (out of such moneys as the Comttee. of Hampshire shall give for the provisions gayned from the Enemy & now in Winchester Castle) to pay Unto a feild (or other cheife) officer comanding the regiments, such a somme as may be distributed amongst the private soldyers according to that proportion. for which this togeather with their Receipts shall be your Warrant.
Dated at Sarum[2] the 17th of October 1645.

O Cromwell

For Coll Tho. Herbert[3] Commissioner of Parlt. for the Army

[fo. 35v]
Winchester gratuity Warrt. from the Lt. Gen who commanded there.

---

[1] Winchester, the recently captured cathedral city of Hampshire.
[2] Salisbury, the cathedral city in Wiltshire.
[3] Sir Thomas Herbert, first baronet (1606–82), traveller and government official. See *ODNB*. Herbert, a client of Philip Herbert, fifth earl of Pembroke, was a parliamentary commissioner accompanying the earl of Essex (1644–5) and the New Model (1645–7). He was never a colonel, as surely Cromwell would have known, so perhaps this is a slip by the clerk, addressing the letter after Cromwell had signed it.

THE LETTERS, WRITINGS, AND SPEECHES OF OLIVER CROMWELL

1645 12 10

Letter from Oliver Cromwell to [Colonel Thomas Ceely], governor of Lyme Regis

Date: 10 December 1645
Source: Bodl., MS Clarendon 91 fo. 17r (holograph)

By early December, Cromwell was in winter quarters, with his own headquarters in Tiverton. Many of the infantry in his brigade were quartered around Ottery St Mary and with the onset of a wet winter, half of those infantrymen were incapacitated by influenza, with an unknown number dying from it. One of those who died was Colonel John Pickering.[1] Pickering (and his brother Gilbert, a close ally of Cromwell's in the Commons) came from Northamptonshire but John had become a key player as commissary and then colonel in the army of the Eastern Association, and his advanced religious views (and reputation as a lay preacher) caused considerable delay in the Lords when Fairfax nominated him to command a regiment in the New Model. He died on 24 November in Ottery St Mary,[2] and this letter from Cromwell, possibly to the governor of Lyme Regis, specifies Sir Gilbert's wishes for his brother's funeral and burial. It is not clear why Lyme Regis was chosen.[3]

The letter was presented to the Bodleian Library[4] by Montagu Montagu, a collector of autographs in the mid- to late nineteenth century and was included in a supplementary volume of the Clarendon Manuscripts. Before reaching the Bodleian it was seen by Carlyle, who included it in the third edition of *The Letters and Speeches of Oliver Cromwell* (1850) and it was later seen by Sophia Lomas and a generally reliable modernised transcription was included in Carlyle-Lomas.[5]

There is no contemporary evidence that the letter was address to Colonel Thomas Ceely but in a much later hand it is said to be addressed to him, in proof of which ownership is rather unconvincingly traced back to a daughter of Colonel 'Ciely'.

Colonel Thomas Ceely was a Cornishman who had (before the Civil War) married the daughter of a prominent Lyme Regis townsman and he played an important part in the siege and capture of Lyme Regis (April–June 1644) and had served as mayor there until his appointment as governor. In December 1645 he became recruiter MP for Bridport.[6]

---

[1] John Pickering (bap. 1615, d. 1645), parliamentarian army officer, and Sir Gilbert Pickering, first baronet, appointed Lord Pickering under the Protectorate (1611–68), politician. See *ODNB*.

[2] Wanklyn, *Reconstructing*, 1:60n.

[3] Ottery St Mary is 18 miles from Lyme Regis.

[4] There are lots of puzzles about exactly when it arrived and why the Bodleian miscatalogued it but, in essence, it was given to the library by the descendants of Montagu Montagu and very possibly was then detached from the rest of the collection. We are grateful to Dr Michael Webb, Curator of Early Modern Archives and Manuscripts at the Bodleian, for his assistance.

[5] Carlyle-Lomas 3:243, appendix 8. Abbott simply copied Lomas's version without seeing the original, giving an out-of-date Bodleian reference.

[6] For Ceely's earlier career, see the *Online Directory of Parliamentarian Army Officers*, For his career as a whole, see *HoP: Commons 1640–1660*.

332

10 DECEMBER 1645

To Colonel Ceely at Lyme Regis Castle: These
SIR,
Its the desier of Sir Gilbert
Pickeringe that his deceased Brother,
Colonel Pickeringe, should bee
enterred in your guarrison. And to the
end his funeral may be sollemnised
with as much Honor as his me-
morie calls for, you are desired
to give all possible assistance therein, the particulars wilbe offered
to you by his maior, maior Jubbs,[7]
with whome I desier you to concur herein, and beleive it sir
you will not only lay a huge
obligation upon my self and
all the officers of this armie,
But I dare assure you the
General himselfe will take itt
for an especial favor, and
will not lett it goe without
a full acknowledgment, But
what neede I prompt him to soe
honorable action whose owne
ingenuitye wilbe argument sufficient herein; whereof rests
assured Your humble servant,
10th December 1645   Oliver Cromwell
Teverton

---

[7] John Jubbes (*fl.* 1643–49), parliamentarian army officer. See *ODNB*. See also Wanklyn, *Reconstructing*, 1:49, 59, 71, 81, 91.

1646 01 27[?]
Summary of speech by Oliver Cromwell to 3,000 'recruits' in Devon

Date: January 1646 (probably between 24 and 29 January)
Source: *The Moderate Intelligencer: impartially communicating martiall affaires to the kingdome of England* no. 48 for 29 January–4 February 1646, p. 280 (N&S, 419.048; Thomason / E 320[11])

Only one letter and indeed no other written document by or attributed to Cromwell survives for the period from 17 October 1645 to 16 June 1646, a period of eight months, by far the longest period between the meeting of the Long Parliament and his death in 1658. He was in Devon and Cornwall for most of that period, first in winter quarters and then mopping up royalist garrisons.

There is just one oblique account of his words via a newspaper report in late January 1646 and two brief summaries by others of speeches in the House of Commons for April 1646. The New Model led by Fairfax and Cromwell were quartered in Devon from 24 October 1645 to 23 February 1646, Cromwell himself being principally quartered in Crediton. At some point in late January 1646 Fairfax called for local volunteers to enlist in his army and, at least according to *The Moderate Intelligencer*, 3,000 did so. When they were assembled, Cromwell, who had travelled to their gathering point at Totnes, is said to have addressed them as below. After offering this account of Cromwell's speech, the newsbook concluded that '[t]he Country men exprest much joy, and profest all willingnesse to serve every man, and to quit their Princely Cage for old English Country Liberty'; and that just one thousand were then recruited and made into a garrison for Totnes while Fairfax concentrated on the siege of Exeter. The precise date is not known: Abbott, without explanation, says 24 January;[1] news reached London in time for inclusion in a diurnal published on 4 February but not in time to appear in one that went to print on 28 January. So a date within the range 24–29 January is probable. (There is no reference to any of this in any of the other newspapers published in late January/early February.)

When they were come together, the *Lieutenant-General* made a short speech to them, telling them, They were come to set them (if possible) at liberty from their Task masters, and by setling Peace, bring Plenty to them again: In which designe God had blest them hitherto, and from thence they took hopes in short time to free them of all Swords that should any way discourage them, in their Trade or dealing oppresse them, or tyrannize over soule or body, or to this effect.

---

[1] Abbott, *Writings and Speeches*, 1:395.

1646 04 24
Speech by Oliver Cromwell to the House of Commons

Date: 24 April 1646
Source: BL., Add. MS 10114, fo. 14, Diary of John Harington. (Printed in Margaret Stieg, ed., *The Diary of John Harington, M.P., 1646–53: with notes for his charges*. Somerset Record Society 74 (1977), p. 22) (reported speech)

In late April 1646 Cromwell returned to London for the first time since March 1645. On 23 April he appeared in the Commons and was formally thanked by the House.[1] The following day Edmund Prideaux, MP for Lyme Regis, reported from the committee for the west. The issue at stake was how much of a military presence was required in the south-west now that those counties had been secured for Parliament. It was probably during this debate that Cromwell spoke on the more immediate issue of the money owed to the soldiers currently stationed there.

Lieutent genal Cromwell declared tht it greatly imported to send money to the soldiers in Devon & Cornwal for the genal[2] had bin vy careful to win their harts, the taken of free quartr[3] would alienat their minds from us

---

Outcome: No specific order was made on the point raised by Cromwell. However, the Commons agreed that the forces stationed in the south-west should be reduced and so asked the committee of the west to prepare detailed proposals to effect this.[4]

---

[1] JHC, 4:520.
[2] i.e. the Lord General of the (new) New Model Army, Sir Thomas Fairfax.
[3] Free quarter. The right of soldiers to billet themselves on civilians without charge. Soldiers were understandably opposed to any suggestion that this right should be removed as otherwise they would be required to pay for their own lodgings.
[4] JHC, 4:521.

THE LETTERS, WRITINGS, AND SPEECHES OF OLIVER CROMWELL

1646 04 25
Speech by Oliver Cromwell to the House of Commons

Date: 25 April 1646
Source: Two reported versions, itemised and discussed below

In the spring of 1646, following the surrender of the royalist forces in the south-west, Henry Ireton and his regiment of horse were transferred to Oxfordshire to join the forces besieging Oxford. On 23 April he wrote to Cromwell. That letter was now presented by Cromwell to the Commons.[1] The information it contained had the potential to be sensational. Ireton reported that late on 22 April two royalists had left Oxford, crossed the parliamentarian lines and made their way to his quarters at Woodstock, Oxfordshire. They had been able to do so because they were among the forty royalist officers who had been granted passes to go abroad by Sir Thomas Fairfax under the terms by which Exeter had surrendered on 13 April. The officers had told Ireton that the King was minded to reach a peace settlement with Parliament. According to them, Charles would be willing to disband his army in return for assurances that he could remain on as king. Ireton had then refused to allow the two officers to return to Oxford, with or without any reply from him. Cromwell viewed the information from Ireton as a problem. Many at Westminster thought any possible peace overtures, however dubious, as being worth exploring. But others, including Cromwell, wanted a decisive military victory of the sort that seemed increasingly realistic. That the prospect of defeat might make the King more willing to negotiate was not so improbable. That however might make for a messier political outcome.[2] Cromwell probably took the view that any talk at all of a settlement was a serious distraction until a complete victory had been achieved. His decision to reprimand Ireton so publicly was less an attack on his future son-in-law and more a warning to other officers against dabbling in such matters.

[A] BL, Add. MS 10114, fo. 14, Diary of John Harington. Printed in *Diary of John Harington*, p. 23.

Colonel Iarton comander in cheif by Oxford. 2 soldiers tht by articles at Exiter were to go to the King & then to have a pass to go beyond sea acquait Col: Iarton tht the King having divs designes pposed resolvd to refuse al & to delvr up himself freely to be disposed of at the pleasure of the Parle. So tht he might continue King only he desired to have the company of Du of Lennox[3] Marqs

---

[1] JHC, 4:523.

[2] Henry Cary, ed., *Memorials of the Great Civil War in England* (2 vols., London, 1842), 1:1–4.

[3] James Stuart, fourth duke of Lennox and first duke of Richmond (1612–55), nobleman. See *ODNB*. These five names are the individuals whom Ireton had named in his letter as the individuals whom the King wished would be allowed to remain in attendance on him.

336

25 APRIL 1646

Hartford[4] Earles of \Southampton[5] & Lindsay[6] / Aspnday[7] &c. to converse with & required not tht they should have any authority or power required a sudden answer els being hopeles he should be forced on other courses Al the English Lords wth him agreed on tht offer to Parl: Iarton shewed them the declaration of the Parl: detained them prisoners sent at this report to Lieut: genal Cromwel. He acquaint the hous of comms comending Col: Iarton in al his other deportmts only in this he had don weakly.

[B] BL, Add. MS 31116, fo. 266v, Diary of Laurence Whitaker

Also, this day Lieut: Gen: Cromwell aquainted the ho: tht he had recd a Letter from Coll: Ayreton from Woodstock informing him tht 2: of the 40 K: Collonells tht had Sr Tho: ffairefax his passe Out of Cornwall to goe beyond Seas Came to him to his quarters & told him tht the K was now Content to Come in & to render himselfe to the Parliamt into wt place soev they should appoint him, soe as the Parliamt would not depose him But Suffer him to Continue K still: for sending wch Letter Lt. Gen: Cromwell sayd he Conceived he deserved a reproofe…

Outcome: A six-man committee, including Cromwell, was appointed to consider this.[8] Later that same day one of the members of the committee, Henry Marten, MP for Berkshire,[9] reported back to the House. The Commons then resolved that if Sir Thomas Fairfax received any peace overture from the King, he was to pass it on to Parliament and that no other soldier was to receive such overtures. Cromwell was ordered to forward copies of these orders to Fairfax and Ireton.[10] The settlement for the marriage between Ireton and Cromwell's daughter, Bridget, was probably signed the following day.[11]

---

[4] William Seymour, first marquis of Hertford and second duke of Somerset (1587–1660), politician and royalist army officer. See ODNB.
[5] Thomas Wriothesley, fourth earl of Southampton (1608–67), politician. See ODNB.
[6] Montague Bertie, second earl of Lindsey (1607/8–66), royalist nobleman and army officer. See ODNB.
[7] Mangled spelling of the name Ashburnham. Reference to John Ashburnham (1602/3–71), courtier and politician, elder brother of William Ashburnham. See ODNB.
[8] JHC, 4:523.
[9] Henry [Harry] Marten [Martin] (1601/2–80), politician and regicide. See ODNB.
[10] JHC, 4:523.
[11] David Farr, *Henry Ireton and the English Revolution* (Woodbridge, 2006), p. 54.

THE LETTERS, WRITINGS, AND SPEECHES OF OLIVER CROMWELL

1646 06 16
Letter from Oliver Cromwell to John Holles, earl of Clare

Date: 16 June 1646
Source: HMC, *Portland Manuscripts* (1893), 2:137 (later copy)

Apart from the brief report on a speech Cromwell is reported to have made in late January 1646 (for which see **1646 01 27[?]**) only one letter by Cromwell survives for the period from 17 October 1645 to 16 June 1646, a period of eight months, by far the longest period between the meeting of the Long Parliament and his death in 1658. He spent the time from late October to 1645 to mid-April 1646 in Devon and Cornwall. After the surrender of Exeter, he rode up to London, arriving on 22 April but he then soon left for the last great action of the First Civil War, the siege and capture of Oxford, which finally took place on 20 June. The King meanwhile had slipped out of Oxford on 26 April and surrendered to the Scots at Newark a week later.

The first letter to survive after this long apparent silence was to John Holles, second earl of Clare. He was a very hesitant parliamentarian, having defected to the King at Oxford (June to August 1642) and again in the autumn of 1643. On both occasions he returned to London and was pardoned, but from April 1644 he was barred from his seat in the House of Lords. His brother Denzil was one of Cromwell's most persistent opponents in the Commons. This requires us to read Cromwell's comments on the virtues of Major Charles White as being bitterly ironic.[1]

This letter was seen at Welbeck Abbey in 1893 when it was edited for the Historical Manuscripts Commission. In 1989 the volume was acquired by the British Library where it is now BL, Add. MS 70499, containing a collection of letters of the de Vere and Cavendish families. This letter was at fos. 218–219 but it disappeared from the collection at some point between 1893 and 1989, with a gap in the current foliation between 217 and 220. The *HMC* version given here appears to follow original spelling, but the uncharacteristic use of apostrophes suggests some tidying up.

[1646, June 16. Oxford]

Noe command from your Lordship[2] will finde mee disobedient to observe you. In that which I last received I have a double obligation. I doe admire your

---

[1] White was a key opponent of John Hutchinson, at this stage of the wars an ally of Cromwell's—see Neil Keeble, ed., *Memoirs of the Life of Colonel Hutchinson: With a Fragment of Autobiography (of the Life of Lucy Hutchinson)* (London, 1995), pp. 103–4, 111, 116, 122, 129, 144, 147, 154, 161, 164, 169, 172–3, 174, 187, 189, 192, 193, 199, 200, 201, 203, 209, 210, 211, 216, 217, 232, 236, 253. See also Gladwyn Turbutt, *A History of Derbyshire* (4 vols., Cardiff, 1999), 3:1058–64, 1097, 1397.

[2] John Holles, second earl of Clare (1595–66), aristocrat. See *ODNB*.

338

8 JULY 1646[?]

Lordship's caracter of Major White,[3] it's to the life. I cann with some confidence speake itt, beinge noe stranger to him. Hee is of a right stamp in this that hee would have the honestest men disbanded first, the other beinge more suitable to his and the common designe. The General[4] will instantly order the Nottingham horse to Worcester, wherein I shalbe your Lordship's remembrancer to him.

1646 07 08[?]
Speech by Oliver Cromwell to the House of Commons (near contemporary print)

Date: Shortly before 10 July 1646
Source: *The Summe of the Charge Given in by Lieutenant Generall CRUMWEL. Against the Earle of MANCHESTER* (Wing / L2012; Thomason / 669.f.10 [67]) (re-issued and shortened)

This single-sheet broadside was almost certainly not written or authorised by Cromwell, but it is included here because it bears a sufficient ressemblance to the charges laid by Cromwell against the earl of Manchester (see **1644 11 25**) which launched the crisis leading to the Self-Denying and New Model Ordinances. Although published in July 1646, the 'svmme of the Charge' contains no matter that can be dated later than November 1644, although the suffix to the Cromwell material relates to the consequences of Cromwell's charge and contains a reference to John Lilburne's[1] *England's Birthright Justified*, published in October 1645.[2] So the pamphlet is part of Lilburne's vendetta against the earl of Manchester which had seen him, in June 1646, in Newgate prison for showing disrespect to a peer. In a feud with a former army colleague, Colonel Edward King, Lilburne had

---

[3] Major Charles White was commissioned as a captain of dragoons in 1642 despite humble birth. He was a fierce puritan but an equally fierce opponent of separatists and hence one of the main opponents in Nottinghamshire of Colonel John Hutchinson, during the First Civil War an admirer of Cromwell's. See the *Online Directory of Parliamentarian Army Officers*.
[4] Sir Thomas Fairfax.

---

[1] John Lilburne (1615?–57), Leveller. See ODNB.
[2] John Lilburne, *England's birth-right justified against all arbitrary usurpation, whether regall or parliamentary, or under what vizor soever*...London: Larner's Press at Goodman's Fields, Printed Octob. 1645, p. 17 (Wing / L2125; Thomason / E.304[17]). The passage alluded to is given as 'the 35. Page' but is in fact on p. 17: 'And yet notwithstanding, although Lieutenant Generall Cromwell, according to his duty long since, revealed the Earl of Manchesters treachery and basenesse at Dennington Castle, and other places, and proved it punctually by unquestionable witnesses before a Com|mittee of the House of Commons, and before hee could perfect his charge, he was sent upon an unhopefull designe with Sir William Waller to relieve Taunton with Horse, although it be an exceeding close inclosed Country, where a hundred foot may deale with a thousand horse.'

published *A Just Man's Justification*,[3] which took a side-swipe at the earl of Manchester. On 10 June 1646 he was summoned to appear before the Lords, and having refused to show any repentance, was committed to Newgate. From there he wrote and published *A Freeman's Freedom vindicated* which repeated all Cromwell's charges against Manchester from the winter of 1644–5.[4] He appealed to the Commons on 16 June but got no support and the Lords condemned him, on 11 July, to a fine of £2,000 and imprisonment at the pleasure of the House, in the Tower.[5]

A further possible reason for the timing of the publication (George Thomason noted that he received his copy on 10 July 1646) was that Manchester was a leading commissioner in the framing of the 'Newcastle Propositions' for a 'presbyterian' peace settlement, despatched to the King on 6 July. Cromwell was no more a fan of those propositions than were Lilburne and his London allies.[6]

THE SVMME OF THE Charge Given in by Lieutenant Generall CRUMWEL. Against the Earle of MANCHESTER

THAT he the Earle of MANCHESTER, hath alwaies been indisposed, and backward to ingagements. And against the ending of the Warre by the sword; And for such a peace to which a Victory would be a disadvantage; and this declared by principles exprest to that purpose: And a continued series of cariages answerable. And since the taking of *York*,[7] (as if the Parliament had now advantage full enough) He hath declined what ever tended to further advantage upon the Enemy; neglected and Studiously shifted off all opportunityes to that purpose, as if he thought the *King* too low, and the Parliament to high, especially at *Dennington* Castle.[8] He hath drawne the Army too, and detained them in such a posture, as to give the Enemy fresh advantages; and this before his conjunction with other Armies, by his owne absolute will, against, or without. his Councell, against many Commands from the Committee of both Kingdome; with contempt, &

---

[3] John Lilburne, *The iust mans iustification: or a letter by way of plea in barre* (1646) (Wing / L2125; Thomason / E.340[12]). Thomason dated his receipt of this pamphlet as 10 June 1646 and it was burnt by the common hangman in the Old Exchange on 13 July 1646 by order of the House of Lords.

[4] *The free-mans freedome vindicated. Or A true relation of the cause and manner of Lievt. Col. Iohn Lilburns present imprisonment in Newgate* (1646) (Wing / L2111; Thomason / E.341[12]). Thomason annotates his copy as having been received on 23 June 1646.

[5] Gardiner, *GCW*, 3:124–5; Clive Holmes, 'Colonel King and Lincolnshire Politics, 1642–6', *The Historical Journal*, 16 (1973), pp. 451–84.

[6] Gardiner, *GCW*, 3:126–7.

[7] York surrendered to the parliamentarians, including Manchester, on 16 July 1644, in the wake of the battle of Marston Moor.

[8] i.e. Donnington Castle. The failure of Cromwell to take this following the second battle of Newbury (it was only finally taken by the parliamentarians in April 1646) was one of the major matters of dispute between Cromwell and Manchester in November-December 1644.

vilifying of the Commands. And since the conjunction, somtimes against Councells of War, and somtimes perswarding, and deluding the Councell, to neglect one opportunity, with another, and againe with a third, and at last when no other pretence would serve; by perswading that it was not fit to fight at all.

1646 07 14
Speech by Oliver Cromwell to the House of Commons

Date: 14 July 1646
Source: BL, Add. MS 31116, fo. 277v, Diary of Laurence Whitaker (reported speech)

Whitaker gives almost no indication as to the context of this speech. The likelihood is that Cromwell delivered it during the debate on the future of the Exeter garrison. Anthony Nicoll, MP for Bodmin, had reported on this from the joint committee of the Lords and Commons on the Western Association. Its recommendation was that the garrison should be reduced to just 200 men and that the city's fortifications be demolished. The Commons agreed and proceeded to make various orders for payments to the garrison.[1] MPs speaking in this debate might well have made comments about the conduct of the soldiers in Fairfax's army to which Cromwell felt it necessary to respond.

Also: Lieut Gen: Cromwell made a Long Speech in vindication of Sr Tho: Fairfax his Army from an Aspersion Cast upon it.

1646 07 26
Letter from Oliver Cromwell to Thomas Knyvett

Date: 26 July 1646
Source: BL, Add. MS 42,153, fos 171r–172v (holograph)

Three years earlier Cromwell had helped the royalist Thomas Knyvett[1] in his attempts to avoid the sequestration of his estates. In March 1643 Cromwell had taken Knyvett prisoner when he swept down on Lowestoft to prevent a suspected attempt to seize the town by a

---

[1] JHC, 4:617.

---

[1] Thomas Knyvett (1596–1658) of Ashwellthorpe, Norfolk. See B. Schofield, ed., *The Knyvett Letters, 1620–1644*. Norfolk RS, vol. 20 (1949), Introduction; *HoP Commons, 1640–1660*.

THE LETTERS, WRITINGS, AND SPEECHES OF OLIVER CROMWELL

group of royalist sympathisers who were gathered there. Knyvett claimed he was only there to take ship for Holland. A few days later, imprisoned at Cambridge, Knyvett wrote to his wife asking that she write to Elizabeth Hampden, Cromwell's aunt, 'praye let it be only to use her Interest to Corronell Cromwell that I may be fayerly treated hear 'till we shalbe releast'.[2] Some months later Cromwell did indeed speak up for him, assuring the earl of Manchester that 'Mr Knyvett did voluntarily yield himselfe without making any resistance, being not otherwise armed then with his sword hee ordinarily wore'.[3] A year later, now a prisoner in Windsor Castle, Knyvett wrote of Cromwell's 'courteous testimony', though he feared a report that he had disclaimed it, 'saying I put a tricke upon him at Leistolff'.[4]

What survives in Knyvett's papers is Cromwell's holograph letter asking for a favour in return, on behalf of 'your honeste poore Neighbors of Hapton'. Hapton, a village nine miles south of Norwich and some two and a half miles from Knyvett's home at Ashwellthorpe, was (or was shortly to become) the site of an Independent congregation, which was active in the late 1640s and 1650s.[5]

Knyvett's reply to Cromwell's letter does not survive, but the comments on a draft by his friend, Henry Elsyng, clerk of the House of Commons, do. He advised that Knyvett remove the words 'clandestine' and 'divinity' from the letter. This was if Knyvett wished to give 'so large an Account of what hath concerned you in your carriage towards these People of Hapton, which his letter to you doeth not seeme cleerely to invite, nor doeth he touch upon any compl[ain]ts against you, onely desires you to use your interest with one Robt. Browne, your Tenant, that those Poore people may by him receive noe Trouble & that you would protect them from Injury and Oppression'. Elsyng thought a more general reply, satisfying Cromwell over Browne and promising 'such Proteccion as your condition can afford them' would suffice.[6]

Sir I cannott prætend to any Interest in
you, for any thinge I have donn, nor aske
any favor for any service I may doe you,
but because I am conscious to my selfe
of a readinesse to serve any Gentleman
in all possible civillityes, I am bold

---

[2] Schofield, *Knyvett Letters*, p. 109.

[3] Schofield, *Knyvett Letters*, p. 36 (quoting Bodl., MS Tanner 62, fo. 317).

[4] Schofield, *Knyvett Letters*, pp. 135–6.

[5] The congregation first appears, in the records of the Great Yarmouth Congregational Book, on 1 February 1648, which record anxieties about the admission of a member who rejected the baptism of infants. Norfolk RO, FC 31/1 (Great Yarmouth Congregational Church, Church Book, 1642–1855), unfol. In January 1656 the Norwich Independent Church wrote to the Hapton congregation advising on its proposed dissolution, Norfolk RO, FC 19/1 (Norwich Old Meeting Congregational Church, Church Book, 1642–1839), unfol.

[6] Schofield, *Knyvett Letters*, pp. 41–2 [original Bodl., MS Tanner 58, fo. 695]. Robert Browne has not otherwise been identified.

to bee before hand with you to aske your favor
onn the behalfe \of\ your honeste poore
Neighbors of Hapton, whoe as I am informed are in some trouble, and are
like to bee putt to more, by one Robert
Browne your tennant,[7] whoe not welpleased
with the way of those men, seekes their
disquiett all hee may. Truly nothinge
moves mee to desier this more then
the pittie I beare them in respect of
their honesties, and the trouble I here
they are like to suffer for their consciences, and however the world inter-
pretts itt, I am not ashamed to solicit
for such as are any where under a
pressure of this kinde, doeinge herein
as I would bee donn by. Sir this is a
quarrelsome age, and the anger seemes
to mee to bee the worse where the
ground is, thinges of ~~difference in~~ opinion
which to cure, to hurt men in their names
persons or estates, will not bee found an apt remedie. Sir it will
not repent you to protect those poore men of Hapton from in-
jurie, and oppression, which that you would, is the effect of this letter
Sir you will not want the gratefull acknowledgment, not utmost
endeavors of requitall from Your most humble servant
Oliver Comwell
1646. July 27. London.

[fo. 172v]

For my Noble Freind Thomas Knevett, Esqr att his house att Ashwell Thorpe
Norfolke, theise

[7] No more is known of Browne than is in the text. In 1635/36 the money paid by Knyvett for the lands occupied by himself and the farmers who leased from him formed by far the largest proportion of the poor rate in the small village of Hapton, 9s. 11d. out of the total amount of 24s. (Norfolk RO, NAS 1/1/2/133, Hapton overseers' account, 1635/36).

1646 07 31[?]

Letter from Oliver Cromwell to Sir Thomas Fairfax.

Date: 31 July 1646
Source: BL, Sloane MS 1519, fos 144r–145v (autograph)

This letter seems straightforward enough, but it is full of riddles. It appears in this edition both as **1646 07 31** and as **1647 07 31**.

It is in the hand of Cromwell's usual clerk and has Cromwell's own signature and his seal is still attached. There is an endorsement in an unknown hand. Both the letter and the endorsement are very clearly dated 31 July 1646. But…

Cromwell is asking Fairfax to support the petition 'of Adj. Flemming' for assistance in an unstated cause. Christopher Flemming had served as a captain under the earl of Essex from the beginning of the wars. By 2 September 1644 he was adjutant of horse, and continued as both captain and adjutant until at least 21 October 1644.[1] He transferred to the New Model, the only officer in his regiment to do so[2] and has been identified as an 'adjutant general' in the New Model at some unspecified point.[3] He left the Army in June 1647 (1647, not 1646, note), at the time of the mass resignations over the Army's defiance of Parliament's will[4] but he was reappointed as governor of Pembroke Castle in early 1648.[5] There is also evidence that he was very seriously wounded in hand-to-hand combat on 24 May 1645 and 'shot his enemy, yet received a wound himself, conceived then to be mortal'.[6]

So a complicated story. The one year in which it seems unnecessary for Cromwell to write on his behalf is 1646. And yet that is what the letter clearly gives as its date. So why do we find this entry in the Journal of the House of Lords for 24 August 1647 (yes, 1647): 'Adj. Fleming recommended for an Employment. A Letter from Sir Thomas Fairefax was read, recommending Adjutant Fleming for to have some such Employment conferred upon him as he is capable of, inregard, by his Wounds for the Service of the Parliament, he is disabled from his Service to the Parliament in that Way he is in'?[7]

Because of these complexities, this letter is appearing twice in this edition, first under the date given on the face of the letter, and again under the far more likely actual date.

———

For his Excie: Sir Thomas Fairfax, Generall of the parliaments forces theise

Lt. Gen: Cromwell.

July. 31. 1646

---

[1] See 'Christopher Flemming [Fleming]' in the *Online Directory of Parliamentarian Army Officers*.
[2] Wanklyn, *Reconstructing*, 1:151.   [3] Wanklyn, *Reconstructing*, 1:164.
[4] As did his colonel (Richard Graves) and all but one of the captains. The major, Adrian Scroop, took over as colonel and the one surviving captain, Nathaniel Barton, was promoted to major—Wanklyn, *Reconstructing*, 1:84.
[5] Wanklyn, *Reconstructing*, 1:84, fn. 331.   [6] Firth and Davies, *Regimental History*, 1:103.
[7] *JHL*, 9:401.

[Seal]

Sir

I was desired to write a letter to you by Adjutant Flemming.[8] The end of it is, to desire your letter in his recommendation. Hee will acquaint you with the Summe thereof more particulerly what the business is. I most humbly Submitt to your better judgment when you heare it from him. Craving pardon for my boldness in putting yow to this trouble I rest
Your most humble servant

1646 08 10
Letter from Oliver Cromwell to Sir Thomas Fairfax

Date: 10 August 1646
Source: BL, Sloane MS 1519, fos 131r–132v (holograph)

This is one of the very few holograph letters from the post-war period, and so perhaps a sign of the importance of the confidentiality of the content. It fills the whole page and is completed with writing down the left-hand margin. The two postscripts are added at the top. The first to be written appears second, but the tiny handwriting of the second PS indicates it was written second and squeezed into the space. We have edited them here in the order in which we are convinced that they were written and intended.

Cromwell had by now returned to London and was reporting to his superior officer still in the field. This is an important letter for Cromwell's political priorities in 1646. He had now been in Parliament for just over a month since he had returned to London following the surrender of Oxford on 24 June. On 13 July Parliament had sent to the King (who since 5 May had been in Scottish custody) 'the Newcastle Propositions', an amalgam of the Nineteen Propositions of 1642 and the obligations entered into in by the Solemn League and Covenant with the Scots (1643). Six commissioners from Parliament had reached the King in Newcastle on 30 July, the very day that the marquis of Ormond, Charles's lord lieutenant in Ireland, had promulgated what is known as the 'First Ormond Peace' that opened the way to Irish Catholic intervention in Britain. Montrose, the King's lieutenant general in Scotland was also still free and with the residue of his army in the Highlands of Scotland. The King's first answer to the Newcastle Propositions,

---

[8] Christopher Flemming (or Fleming), who had served in Waller's army as a captain of horse; he subsequently served in the New Model Army as a captain in the regiment of Richard Graves (1645–7), replaced by Adrian Scrope (1647); and he was killed in a skirmish near Carmarthen in 1648 (See the *Online Directory of Parliamentarian Army Officers*.)

a wide-ranging rejection of them, was read in Parliament on 12 August, two days after this letter was sent.[1]

———

For his Excellencye
Sir Thomas Fairfax
the Generall
               theise

[Seal]

Lt. G. Cromwell.[2]

Ag. 10. <u>1646</u>

Sir hearinge you were returned
from Ragland[3] to the Bathe,[4] I take
the boldnesse to make this addresse
unto you. Our Commissioners[5] sent to
the Kinge came this night to Londo[n.][6]
I have Spoken with two of them,
and cann only learne theise general[s][7]
that there appeares a good inclina
tion \in the Scotts/ to the rendition of our Towne[8]
and to their march out of the
Kingdom, when they bringe in their
papers, wee shall knowe more. Argil[e][9]

---

[1] For political context, see Gardiner, *GCW*, 3: chs. XLII–XLIV and David Scott, *Politics and the War in the Three Stuart Kingdoms, 1637–49* (Basingstoke, 2004), pp. 110–29.

[2] This endorsement is in a different seventeenth-century hand.

[3] Raglan (Monmouthshire). The strong medieval castle was one of the very last places to hold out for the King. It finally surrendered on terms to Fairfax on 19 August 1646, so Cromwell may be misinformed that Fairfax was already heading back to London.

[4] Presumably Bath (Somerset).

[5] The six commissioner-MPs named on 6 July were the earls of Pembroke and Suffolk and Sir Walter Erle, Sir John Hippesley, Robert Goodwyn and Luke Robinson (*JHC*, 4:607).

[6] Part of the 'n' and a putative full stop are lost at the worn edge of the page.

[7] Most of the last letter is lost on the edge of the page, but not enough space for more than one letter—there is not enough space, for example, for it to be 'generallie'.

[8] Newcastle-upon-Tyne, occupied by the Scots from 1644 to 1647.

[9] Archibald Campbell, fifth marquis of Argyll (1605x7–61), nobleman and politician. See *ODNB*. A key member of the Scottish Committee of Estates, he was one of those sent to Westminster with the King's Answer to the Newcastle Propositions.

10 AUGUST 1646

~~and~~ the Chancellor,[10] and Dunfarlin,[11]
are come up, Duke Hamilton is
gonn from the Kinge into Scotland.[12]
I heere that Montrosse[13] his men
are not disbanded. The Kinge gave
a very General answare, thinges are
not well in Scotland, would they
were in England. wee are full of
faction, and worse: \I heere for certaine that Ormond[14] hath concluded a peace/
with the
\Rebells/[15] Sir I beseech you
command the Sollicitor[16] to come away
to [-] \us/, his helpe would be welcome,
Sir I hope you have not cast mee
off, Truly I may say noe more affec
tionately honors, nor loves you,
You, and yours are in my daylie prayers, you have
donn enough to command the uttermost of

[10] John Campbell, first earl of Loudoun (1598–1662), Lord Chancellor of Scotland, and one of the Scottish commissioners to the Parliament of England 1644–50. See *ODNB*.

[11] Charles Seton, second earl of Dunfermerline (1615–72), politician and army officer. See *ODNB*. In August 1646 he was one of the Scottish Committee of Estates, a commissioner to attend the New Model Army and he was one of those sent to Westminster with the King's Answer to the Newcastle Propositions.

[12] James Hamilton, first duke of Hamilton, (1606–49), politican. See *ODNB*. A former chief adviser to Charles I on Scottish affairs, he was imprisoned for disloyalty in Pendennis Castle in Cornwall for more than two years. He was released after the capture of Pendennis by Fairfax, and returned to Scotland to urge the King to accept the Newcastle Propositions.

[13] James Graham, first marquis of Montrose (1612–50), royalist army officer. See *ODNB*.

[14] James Butler, marquis (later first duke) of Ormond (1610–88), lord lieutenant of Ireland. See *ODNB*.

[15] A reference to the treaty published on 30 July 1646 as between the King's lord lieutenant in Ireland, the marquis of Ormond, and the leaders of the Catholic Confederation of Kilkenny. There had been a truce between these parties since the autumn of 1643, but this 'First Ormond Peace' promised to place a large and mostly Catholic army at Charles's disposal. Its potency was quickly wrecked by the papal nuncio, Archbishop Gianbattista Rinuccini, who excommunicated all those Irish Catholics who subscribed to it. The best account of the treaty and its British context is by Micheál Ó Siochrú, 'Catholic Confederates and the Constitutional Relationship between Ireland and England 1641–1649' in C. Brady and J. Ohlmeyer, eds., *British Interventions in Early Modern Ireland* (Cambridge, 2005), pp. 207–29.

[16] i.e. the Solicitor General, Oliver St John.

347

THE LETTERS, WRITINGS, AND SPEECHES OF OLIVER CROMWELL

your faythfullest, and most obedient
servant

Oliver Cromwell

August the 10th:
1646. London

I beseech you my humble
service may be presented
to your Lady.[17]

The monie for disbandinge
massies[18] men is gotten, and you
will Speedily heere directions
about them, from the Commons house,

1646 08 20

Speech by Oliver Cromwell to the House of Commons

Date: 20 August 1646

Source: BL, Add. MS 10114, fo. 17v, Diary of John Harington. Printed in *Diary of John Harington*, p. 33 (reported speech)

As its royalist governor, Sir Thomas Glemham[1] had surrendered Oxford to Parliament on 24 June 1646. He was now being sued by his creditors, who had managed to get him arrested by the sheriffs of London and Middlesex. He was being held in the Fleet prison. The complication was that Glemham was covered by the general immunity from arrest granted in the articles of surrender he had agreed when surrendering Oxford. Cromwell seems now to have intervened in the Commons on his behalf.

---

[17] Anne Fairfax [née Vere], Lady Fairfax (1617/18–65), noblewoman. See *ODNB*.

[18] Sir Edward Massey (1604x9–74), parliamentarian and royalist army officer. See *ODNB*. He had been governor of Gloucester 1642–5 and was general commanding the forces of the Western Association 1645–7. A political and religious Presbyterian, Cromwell's allies had been striving to get parliamentary orders for the disbandment of his brigade since May 1646, but Cromwell's confidence here was misplaced. His troops were only disbanded in October 1646. See Mark A. Kishlansky, *The Rise of the New Model Army* (Cambridge, 1979), pp. 112–17 and Ian Gentles, *The New Model Army in England, Ireland and Scotland, 1645–1653* (Oxford, 1992), pp. 143–4.

---

[1] Sir Thomas Glemham (1595–1649), royalist army officer. See *ODNB*.

the Governor of Oxford arrested upon an action of debt prest by L:[2] Cromwel tht he should be dischargd by the Articles. put of.

Outcome: The Commons agreed to hear a report on the matter the following day.[3] On 21 August Thomas Chaloner, MP for Richmond,[4] made that report. The Commons then resolved that Glemham was indeed covered by the immunity and so should be released.[5]

1646 08 26
Letter from Oliver Cromwell to John Rushworth

Date: 26 August 1646
Source: BL, Sloane MS 1519, fos 146r–147v (autograph)

This letter is in the hand of one of Cromwell's regular clerks, with some highly characteristic quirks, such as an acute accent over the letter 'c'. The signature is certainly Cromwell's. It is a letter of recommendation for John Lilburne's younger brother, addressed to Rushworth as Secretary to General Fairfax, and surely intended for the latter.

For John Rushworth Esqr Secretary to his Excie. at Bathe. these.

Lt. Generall Cromwell.
Aug. 26. 1646.[1]

[Seal]

Mr Rushworth

I must needs intreate a favour on the behalfe of Major Lilburne,[2] who has a long time wanted employmt. and by reason thereof his necessityes may grow upon

---

[2] Presumably an abbreviation for lieutenant, as in lieutenant general.
[3] JHC, 4:668.   [4] Thomas Chaloner (1595–1660), politician and regicide. See *ODNB*.
[5] JHC, 4:651.

[1] Seventeenth-century endorsement.
[2] This must be Henry Lilburne, younger brother of John Lilburne, the Leveller. Henry was a major from 1644 to 1645, but his last recorded pay claim was for the period ending 24 June 1645 (Firth and Davies, *Regimental History*, 1:264), whereas Robert was a colonel and John a lieutenant colonel. Their cousin Thomas was still a captain (Firth and Davies, *Regimental History*, 1:264). See the *Online Directory of Parliamentarian Army Officers*. The following year, Henry was to marry Rushworth's sister: T. C. Wales and C. P. Hartley, eds., *The Visitation of London begun in 1687* (Harleian Society, n.s., 2 vols., 16 and 17, 2004), 2:490–1, 495.

him, You should doe very well to move the Generall to take him into favourable thoughts, I know a reasonable employment will content him. As for his honesty and Courage I neede not speake much of. Seeing he is soe well knowne both to the Genll. and your selfe. I desire yow answer my expectation herein soe farre as you may. You shall very much oblige
Sir
Your reall freind & servt.
Oliver Cromwell

the house
Aug: 26

1646 09 17

Speech by Oliver Cromwell to the House of Commons

Date: 17 September 1646
Source: BL, Add. MS 10114, fo. 19, Diary of John Harington. Printed in *Diary of John Harington*, p. 37 (reported speech)

The third earl of Essex died on 14 September 1646. One office that he had still held at the time of his death was that of lord lieutenant of Yorkshire. Both Houses moved quickly to fill the vacancy, although the evidence as to the sequence in which they did so is confused. In his diary John Harington recorded that the Commons met the following day and agreed that the second Lord Fairfax of Cameron[1] should be appointed to succeed Essex in that position.[2] But the *Commons Journals* contain no record of the decision to appoint Fairfax.[3] To confuse matters further, the entry below states that the Commons had made that decision not on 15 September (the Tuesday) but on 14 September (the Monday), which was a day on which the Commons had not sat.[4] Less uncertainty surrounds the Lords' decision. On 16 September they ordered that the tenth earl of Northumberland was to be appointed to the position.[5] They informed the Commons of this the following day.[6]

A message from the Lords tht they appointed the Earle of Northumb: Lo: Lieuten: of Yorkshire we on Munday last had agreed on my Lord Farfax Lei: Gen: Cromwel

---

[1] Ferdinando Fairfax, second Lord Fairfax of Cameron (1584–1648), parliamentarian army officer. See *ODNB*.
[2] BL, Add. MS 10114, fo. 18v; Diary of John Harington, p. 36.   [3] JHC, 4:668–70.
[4] JHC, 4:668.   [5] JHL, 8:491.   [6] JHC, 4:671.

6 OCTOBER 1646

& Mr Denzil Hollis[7] in some heat upon it Sr Ph: Stapleton[8] & Sr Le. Dives prs for the Earle[9] ag: the Lo: Farfax we defer this

---

Outcome: The result of this stalemate was that the position of lord lieutenant of Yorkshire was left vacant.

1646 10 06

Letter from Oliver Cromwell to Sir Thomas Fairfax

Date: 6 October 1646
Source: BL, Sloane MS 1519, fos 148r–149v (holograph)

This letter is a holograph and it also has Cromwell's seal but the endorsement is in a different hand from the letter.

Throughout the autumn of 1646, Cromwell was busy in Parliament. This letter shows his continuing efforts to keep Fairfax in the picture about his work to protect the New Model Army's interests in a frequently hostile House of Commons. No evidence contemporary with this letter has been found to throw light on the 'desiers' of the 'Stafford shiere gentlemen'. But the 'businesse of your Armie' that was to come before the Commons on 7 October is clear. On that day the Commons voted to bring in an Ordinance to extend the assessment (land tax) for a further six months, and they also sent Sir William Armyne to the Lords to expedite a decision to extend the lives of the Committee of the Army and of the Treasurers at War. As a context, note that on 2 October 1646, the Commons has expedited the disbandment of Massie's Western Brigade and had paid off some of the Reformadoes[1] in London and gave extended attention to the sending of English forces to Ireland.

[fo. 149v]

For his Excie: Sir Thomas
Fairfax   these
Lt. Generall Cromwell.
October. 6. 1646

---

[7] Denzil Holles first Baron Holles (1598–1680), politician. See *ODNB*.
[8] Sir Philip Stapleton (bap. 1603, d. 1647), politician and army officer, MP for Boroughbridge. See *ODNB*.
[9] That this reads 'Sr Le. Dives' is far from certain and it cannot refer to Sir Lewis Dyve. It is transcribed in Diary of John Harington as 'Sir La: Lues' but that does not seem correct either. Whatever the exact reading, this is most likely to be a reference to Sir William Lewes, MP for Petersfield, for whom see the biography in *HoP Commons, 1640–1660*.

---

[1] Reformadoes were discharged, but not yet disbanded, troops, awaiting the payment of the substantial arrears owed to them.

351

[fo. 148r]

Sir I should be loath to
trouble you with any thinge
but indeed the Stafford sheire
Gentlemen came to mee this
day, \and/ with more then ordinarie
importunity did presse mee to
give their desiers furtheran[ce][2]
to you, their letter will she[w][3]
what they intreat of you,
Truly Sir it will not bee
amisse to give them what
ease may welbe afforded \and the sooner the better especially att this tyme/,[4]
I have noe more att præsent
but to lett you knowe the
businesse of your Armie is
like to come onn to morrow,
You shall have account of
that businesse, soe soone as
I am able to give itt.[5] I
humblie take leave and rest
your Excellencies most humble
servant

Oliver Cromwell

Octobr. 6. 1646

[2] Part of the 'c' and all of the 'e' are missing because of wear to the page.
[3] 'w' missing because of wear to the page.
[4] For a background to conflict amongst the Staffordshire parliamentarians, see Donald Pennington and Ivan Roots, eds., *The Committee at Stafford 1643–1645* (Staffordshire Record Society, 1957), pp.lxxiv-lxxxiii, and for the heavy costs incurred to the county in the successful sieges at Dudley, Tutbury and Lichfield in 1645-6, see Ian Atherton, ed., *The Civil War in Staffordshire in the Spring of 1646: Sir William Brereton's Letter Book, April–May 1646* (Staffordshire Record Society, 4th series, vol. 21, 2007), pp. 1–62, esp. pp. 58–60.
[5] If that account was written and despatched, it has not survived.

1646 10 09
Speech by Oliver Cromwell to the House of Commons

Date: 9 October 1646
Source: BL, Add. MS 10114, fo. 20v, Diary of John Harington. Printed in *Diary of John Harington*, p. 42 (reported speech)

These brief notes by Harington may relate to the debate on the bill to continue the assessments. The previous assessment grant had expired on 1 October. On 8 October the Commons had resolved that the extension would be for just six months.[1] The assessments were the main means by which the Army was funded, and many MPs felt that, now that the war was over, the Army should not continue at its current size. This was also an issue on which Cromwell was bound to side with the army.

Some heat about the army LG Cromwell plede for them & for charity I intended to have spoken but did not

---

Outcome: The Commons ordered that the bill for that purpose was to be introduced on 12 October. This bill however was not passed by the Commons until early December and was never passed by the Lords.[2] Only in March 1647 was a new assessment grant approved.

1646 10 25
Letter from Oliver Cromwell to his daughter Bridget Ireton

Date: 25 October 1646
Source: Yale University, Beinecke Rare Book and Manuscript Library, Osborn fb67/7 (holograph)

The original of this letter (long lost) was rediscovered in the 1920s and acquired by James Osborn. He in turn donated it to Yale University. It is in an album facing a print of Cromwell's daughter Elizabeth, with the later addition 'this letter I had from my mother

---

[1] JHC, 4:687.   [2] JHC, 4:688.

THE LETTERS, WRITINGS, AND SPEECHES OF OLIVER CROMWELL

Sittington[1] who had it fro[m   ][2] who liv'd with Oliver Cromwell's daughter (presumably Elizabeth).'

The manuscript is very worn and stained and at times difficult to read. It has therefore been checked against an eighteenth-century transcript (BL, Harl. MS 6988 fo. 225), a transcript which also contains the address, now lost.

Cromwell is writing to his eldest daughter (and third of nine children) Bridget, and he is discussing with her the spiritual difficulties of his third daughter (and sixth child) Elizabeth. It provides insight into his own religious views, and those of his children, at this time.

_____

Deere daughter,[3]
I write not to thy husband,[4]
partly to avoid trouble, for one line
of mine begitts many of
his which I doubt makes him sitt
up too late, partly because I am
my selfe indisposed att this
tyme, havinge some other considerations
Your freinds att Ely[5] are well,
your Sister Clapole[6] is (I trust in
mercye) exercised with some perplex
ed thoughts, shee sees her owne vanitye, and carnal minde, bewailing
itt, shee seekes after (as I hope
alsoe) that which will satisfie, and

[1] Not identified.   [2] Illegible.

[3] Bridget Fleetwood [née Cromwell; *other married name* Ireton], Lady Fleetwood under the Protectorate (bap. 1624, d. 1662), daughter of Oliver Cromwell. See *ODNB*. She married her first husband, Henry Ireton, a close military associate of Cromwell in the Isle of Ely, on 15 June 1646 in Holton, Oxfordshire, where Ireton was based at the end of the siege of Oxford. The marriage was conducted by Fairfax's domestic chaplain.

[4] Henry Ireton.

[5] Ely (Cambridgeshire) where Bridget had lived with her parents since 1636.

[6] Elizabeth Claypole [Cleypole, Claypoole] née Cromwell (bap. 1629, d. 1658), daughter of Oliver Cromwell. See *ODNB*. She married the Northamptonshire gentleman John Claypole on 13 January 1646 in Holy Trinity Church, Ely. Her *ODNB* entry (which incorrectly gives the date of the marriage as 13 January 1645) chronicles how she remained a favourite of Cromwell's despite her 'being cozened with worldly vanities'. For details of the marriage, see Cambridgeshire Archives, P67/1/2, the composite register of baptisms, weddings and burials 1627–84 for Holy Trinity parish, Ely.

thus to bee a seeker, is to bee
of the best sect, next a finder,
and such an one shall very fayth
full humble seeker, bee, in the end.
Happie seeker, happie finder
whoe ever tasted that the Lord
is gracious, without some sence of
selfe vanitye and badnesse &[7] whoe
ever tasted that graciousnesse of
his, and could goe lesse in desire
\lesse then/ pressinge after full enjoyment.
deere hart presse onn, lett not husband, lett not any thinge Coole
thy affections after christ, I hope Hee wilbe an occasion to inflame them.
that which is best worthy of love in thy husband, is that of the Image of
christ hee beares, looke on that, and love itt best, and all the rest for that,
I pray for thee, and him doe soe for mee, my Service and deere affections
to the generall, and generallesse,[8] I Heere shee[9] is very kind to thee, it adds to all
other obligations, my love to all, I am thy deere Father
Oliver Cromwell
For my beloved daughter
Bridgett Ireton att
Cornbury[10] the Generall's Quarters theise[11]

Octobr.25
1646.
London

[7] The manuscript is very smudged here. The eighteenth-century transcript has a question mark after 'badnesse'; it may be a comma with a smudge over it; but the likeliest intention is an added ampersand.

[8] Sir Thomas and Lady Anne Fairfax.

[9] The eighteenth-century transcript has 'shee' and there is a very indistinct mark in the original which could well be a very faded 's'. But it is not certain whether Cromwell is saying that Fairfax or his wife was being very kind to Bridget Ireton.

[10] Cornbury House, in Oxfordshire was the family home of Henry Danvers, first earl of Danby (d. 1643) and was in late 1646 the headquarters of Sir Thomas Fairfax and his army.

[11] This endorsement is included in the eighteenth-century transcript of the letter but is not on the original at Yale. There is no reason to doubt its authenticity.

1646 10 29

Letter from Oliver Cromwell to Robert Jenner MP

Date: n.d. but endorsement in a different hand '29 October 1646'
Source: TNA, SP23/78 pp. 479–82 (autograph)

Cromwell's letter is addressed to Robert Jenner,[1] an active member of the Committee for Compounding with Delinquents, and he is writing on behalf of a very remote relative, the Lords Cromwell having six generations of separation from him. Thomas, fourth Lord Cromwell (1594–1653)[2] was an active royalist facing a very heavy fine for his active support of the King. Cromwell seeks a reduction of the fine on Lord Cromwell, whose father (who died in 1607) had played a prominent part in the Irish campaigns of the second earl of Essex and who continued those Irish interests, acquiring lands in County Down (Ulster) and acquiring an Irish title as Viscount Lecale in 1624,[3] and the earldom of Ardglass in 1645.[4] His military service in the 1640s, serving as colonel of a cavalry regiment under the King's lord lieutenant, the marquis of Ormond, was entirely in Ireland but his English lands were still sequestered. Those lands included those he had inherited from his father in Leicestershire, Rutland and Wiltshire and those referred to in the letter in Staffordshire and Derbyshire which came to him by marriage. Two days after Cromwell's letter, Lord Cromwell got his way, with a significant reduction of his fine.[5]

———

p. 482]

Lord Cromwell[6]

To my very loveinge frend mr Joinner[7] at Gouldsmith halle thes.

---

[1] Robert Jenner (1584–1651), MP for Cricklade, was a London merchant and London goldsmith: see his entry in *HoP Commons, 1640–1660*.

[2] There is a short entry for Thomas Lord Cromwell contained within the longer one for his father: Cromwell, Edward, third Baron Cromwell (*c.*1559–1607), soldier. See *ODNB*.

[3] Lecale is a barony situated on the peninsula between Strangford Lough and the Irish Sea. There are twenty-nine depositions taken after the Ulster Rising in October 1641 which relate to what happened in Lecale in and after the Rising: for example, the destruction of Lord Cromwell's property and attacks on his tenants etc. (for example, see the deposition of Robert Kinaston, who swore that 'That the Lord Cromwell had his towne of Downe Patricke, the shiretowne and his house burned, his whole estate in Lecale to the value of 2600 li. per annum or therabouts ouer runne and wasted his cattell and corne taken and burned' (www.1641.tcd.ie, transcript of MS 837, fos 008r–v).

[4] Ardglass is a coastland village within the barony of Lecale.

[5] For the progress of the case, see *CCCD*, 2:951.   [6] Added in a different hand.

[7] Robert Jenner, MP, see n. 1.

29 OCTOBER 1646

Sr

My Lord Cromwell upon the putting of in of his particuler into Gouldsmithes Hall,[8] Knowing what the whole value of his estate amounted unto yearely gave it in att 470li in Generall which was the true value of the whole: lying in Severall Countyes: But not being soe perfect in the particuler values of the severall parcells of his estate haveing trusted it constantly to the mannaging of others, did give in his lands in Staffordshire, Derbyshire and Cheshire at 350li per annum whereas the true value is but 255li: And his lands in Wiltshire but 120li whereas the true value is 215li per annum, both amounting to the sayd summ of 470li for which hee compounded: My Lord desires that hee may have liberty to sett the severall values upon his severall parcells of land all amounting tp the sayd summ of 470li[9] And that hee may have his letters to the severall countyes accordingly;[10] what Favour you shall shew my Lord Cromwell herein you shall obleige[11]

Yor very loveing Freind
Oliver Cromwell

29 Octob: 1646
if it appear that there be such a mistake as is here alleaged lett it be amended as is desired
John Ashe[12]

---

[8] Goldsmiths' Hall was the meeting place of the Committee for Compounding with Delinquents throughout the 1640s and early 1650s. It is in Foster Lane, almost exactly two miles east of the palace of Westminster along the river.

[9] Cromwell himself seems to get the figures muddled here, and the figures for Wiltshire appear to have been reversed. Certainly in his appeal to the Committee in September 1646, which Oliver's letter was intended to support, he says he is putting in 'a particular of mistakes in the former statement, valuing his property at 500 li instead of £350li a year'.

[10] The sequestration committees of every county in which he owned land had to receive a separate order from the Committee for Compounding before it could release the lands.

[11] For the progress of his case, see *CCCD*, 2:941–78.

[12] John Ashe was chairman of the Committee for Compounding. John Ashe (1597–1659), clothier and parliamentarian activist. See *ODNB*.

THE LETTERS, WRITINGS, AND SPEECHES OF OLIVER CROMWELL

1646 10 31[?]

Recalled conversation between Oliver Cromwell and Edmund Ludlow

Date: n.d. (but no earlier that 12 October 1646 and possibly as late as spring 1647).

Source: *Memoirs of Edmund Ludlow Esq; Lieutenant General of the Horse, Commander in Chief of the forces in Ireland, one of the Council of State, and a Member of the Parliament which began on November 3, 1640*, 3 vols. (1698–9), 1:185–6 (later account of conversation)

This is very borderline for inclusion. Ludlow's *Memoirs* are a notoriously difficult text, the manuscript original covering the events of the 1640s and 1650s being lost. A comparison of the sections for the Restoration with the published version of 1698/9 shows that an editor, most probably John Toland, had massively recast them and added material from other sources.[1] Furthermore, we do not know whether or not Ludlow wrote up his *Memoirs* from notes taken at the time of the events they describe, and even the date of the conversation reported here is very uncertain. It appears in the text published in 1698/9 as occurring immediately after the funeral of the earl of Essex, which took place on 12 October 1646, but Samuel Rawson Gardiner thought it fitted much better with Cromwell's bitter mood in March 1647 (at the time of Essex's death, the party Cromwell supported was in the ascendant).[2] And Sir Charles Firth, in his edition of the *Memoirs*, appears to concur with Gardiner.[3] We tend to the earlier date because of its location in the 1698/9 edition.

There is little evidence to support the view that what has come down to us via the heavy 1690s filter represents an accurate memory of a real conversation. In its favour is that it does seem to be a memory personal to Ludlow and not intruded into his narrative and that it gives a very precise and credible venue—'Sir Robert Cotton's garden'—i.e. the large house adjacdent to the Houses of Parliament granted to Sir Robert Cotton in 1622 to allow his large library to be available to MPs and parliamentary clerks (and judges).[4]

Edmund Ludlow was the son of Sir Henry, knight of the shire for Wiltshire in the Long Parliament and one of its most radical members before his death in 1643. Edmund was an

---

[1] E. Ludlow, *A Voyce from the Watch Tower*, ed. Blair Worden (Camden Society, 4th series, 21, 1978), introduction; Blair Worden, *Roundhead Reputations: the English civil wars and the passions of posterity* (2000) chs. 2–4; Blair Worden, 'Whig History and Puritan Politics: The memoirs of Edmund Ludlow revisited revisited', *Historical Research*, 75:188 (2002), pp. 209–37.

[2] Gardiner, *GCW*, 3:321–2 and 322n.

[3] C. H. Firth, *The Memoirs of Edmund Ludlow 1625–1672*, 2 vols., Oxford 1894, 1:145 fn. 1. Firth very faithfully follows the 1698/9 edition apart from capitalisation and italicisation and direct quotes style aside but our edition does follow the first edition.

[4] Sir Robert Bruce Cotton, first baronet (1571–1631), antiquary and politician. See *ODNB*, which says of Cotton's house and garden that it was 'a four-storey building, containing twenty-one rooms, and which adjoined both the House of Commons and the Painted Chamber. Further, another side had a courtyard which led to a passage under the court of requests and into Old Palace Yard. Finally, the other side led into a garden which backed onto the River Thames.'

31 OCTOBER 1646[?]

early volunteer for the parliamentarian cause and served in the earl of Essex's lifeguard before becoming a colonel in Sir William Waller's southern army. He was appointed sheriff of Wiltshire in late 1644 and served the rest of the war clearing his county of royalists but he worked closely with Cromwell in late 1645, not least at the storm of Basing House. In May 1646 he secured his father's seat as knight of the shire for Wiltshire. He was a strong Baptist and had impeccable godly credentials. Although he later (and at the time the *Memoirs* were put down in their final form) bitterly detested Cromwell, there is no reason to doubt that they were close enough in late 1646 for this conversation to have taken place. He was a regicide and was given senior military (and for a while) civilian authority in Ireland. The big and irreparable rupture in his relationship with Cromwell came with the dissolution of the Rump.[5]

[p. 185]
About this time the Earl of Essex having overheated himself in the Chace of a Stag in *Windsor* Forest, departed this Life: His Death was a great Loss to those of his Party who to keep up their Spirits and Credit procured his Funeral to be celebrated with great Magnificence at the Charge of the Publick, the Lords and Commons with a great number of Offices and Gentlemen accompanying him to the Grave.[6] In the mean time I observed that another Party was not idle; for walking one Morning with Lieutenant General *Cromwell* in Sir *Robert Cotton*'s Garden, he inveighed bitterly against them, saying in a familiar way to me; *If thy Father were alive, he would let some of them hear what they deserve: adding farther, That it was a miserable thing to serve a Parliament, to whom let a Man be never so faithful, if one pragmaticall Fellow amongst them rise up and asperse him, he shall never wipe it off. Whereas,* said he, *when one serves under a General, he may do as much Service, and yet be free from all Blame and Envy.* This Text, together with the Comment that his after-Actions put upon it, hath since perswaded me, that he had already conceived the Design of destroying the Civil Authority, and setting up of himself; and that he took that Opportunity to feel my Pulse, whether I were a fit Instrument to be employed by him to those ends.

---

[5] Edmund Ludlow [Ludlowe] (1616/17–92), army officer and regicide. See ODNB.
[6] For a full account see [anon.] *The true mannor and forme of the proceeding to the funerall of the Right Honourable Robert Earle of Essex* (1646) (Thomason / E.360[1], Wing / T2758A).

THE LETTERS, WRITINGS, AND SPEECHES OF OLIVER CROMWELL

1646 12 21

Letter from Oliver Cromwell to Sir Thomas Fairfax

Date: 21 December 1646
Source: BL, Sloane MS 1519, fos 150r–151v (holograph)

Both the letter and the address are in Cromwell's own hand (and bear the trace of a seal now gone). He was sending to Fairfax a petition that was highly offensive to the Army and that had been warmly welcomed by the House of Lords. He was restrained in what he says, especially about appropriate Army responses, but the tone surely is instructive.

———

[fo. 151v]

For his Excellency Sir
Thomas Fairfax Genl.
of the Parlnts. Armies
            theise

Lt. Generall C.
Dec. 21. <u>1646</u>[1]

[fo. 150r]

Sir havinge the oportunitye by the
Major Generall[2] to præsent a few lines
unto you, I take the boldnesse to lett
you knowe how our affaires goe since
you left the towne. wee have had
a very longe petition from the citty,[3]

———

[1] This endorsement is added by another (later?) hand.

[2] Major General Philip Skippon, appointed Lord Skippon under the Protectorate (d. 1660), parliamentarian army officer and politician. See *ODNB*.

[3] *To the right honourable the Lords assembled in high court of Parliament: the humble petition of the Lord Major, aldermen, and commons of the city of London, in Common Councell assembled. Together with an humble representation of the pressing grievances, and important desires of the well-affected freemen, and Covenant-engaged citizens, of the city of London* (Wing / T1664; Thomason / E.366[14]). It was presented to the Lords and Commons on 19 December 1646 and George Thomason noted that he had acquired this printed version of it on 21 December. The Houses published a response the same day, the Lords ordering the petition and representation to the published and expressing that they were 'fully satisfied with the constant and reall expressions of fidelity and good affections of the common council and of the citizens', while the Commons rested content with mandating the Speaker 'to give the petitioners thanks for their constant good affections' and undertaking to consider the contents on Tuesday 22 December.

360

21 DECEMBER 1646

how itt strikes att the Armie, and
what other aymes itt has, you will
see by the contents of itt,[4] as alsoe
what the prævailinge temper is att
this præsent, and what is to be expected from men. But this is our com
fort, God is in heaven, and Hee doth
what pleaseth him. His, and only
his councell shall stand, what ever
the designs of men, and the furye
of the people bee. wee have now
I thinke \almost/ perfected all our businesse
for Scotland.[5] I beleive commissioners will speedily bee sent downe,
to see agreements performed, its
intended that Major Genl Skippon[6]
have authority, and instructions
from your Excellency to command
the northerne forces, as occasion
shalbee, and that Hee have a commission
of Martiall Law. Truly I hope that
the havinge the Major Genl. to command
this parlye[7] will appeare to bee a good thinge every day more and more.
Heere has beene a designe to steale away the Duke of Yorke[8] from my Lord of

[4] The petitioners call for the 'speedy disbanding of the Army', especially because so many officers and soldiers that 'have never taken the Covenant' and who 'are disaffected to the Church government held forth by the Parliament' have 'usurped...the pulpits of godly ministers' and preached 'strange and dangerous errrours [sic]'—*The humble petition of the Lord Major, aldermen, and commons of the citie of London, in common-councell assembled. With an humble representation of the pressing grievances, and important desires of the well-affected freemen, and covenant-engaged citizens, of the city of London, to the Lords and Commons assembled in high court of Parliament. Together, vvith the severall answers of both houses of Parliament to the said petitions and representation* (1646) (Wing | H3533; Thomason | E366[15]).

[5] On 16 December, the two Houses reached an agreement with the Scots to pay part of their arrears in return for which the Scots would hand over the King to them and would withdraw all their troops to Scotland (*JHL*, 8:603, 614). He was duly handed over on 30 January 1647.

[6] See n. 2, above.

[7] 'Parlye' looks the best transcription, but it could just be 'partye' which would clearly change the sense significantly.

[8] James duke of York, second son of Charles I, see James II and VII (1633–1701), king of England, Scotland and Ireland. See *ODNB*.

361

THE LETTERS, WRITINGS, AND SPEECHES OF OLIVER CROMWELL

Northumberland,[9] one of his owne servants whome hee præferred to waite one the

Duke is found guiltye of itt, the Duke himselfe confessed soe, I beleive you will suddenly heere more of itt. I have noe more to trouble you, but prayinge for you

rest

Your Excellencyes most humble servant
Oliver Cromwell.

Dec. 21.

1646.

1647 01 23

Certificate signed by Oliver Cromwell and sent to the House of Commons committee for petitions

Date: 23 January 1647
Source: TNA, SP 28/267, Part 2, fo. 187r (autograph)

This is one of what must have been many certificates for former colleagues signed by Cromwell. It is written by a clerk (and not by his usual clerk) and signed by Cromwell.[1] The various stages of the evaluation of Patricke's claim can be found at TNA, SP28.267, Part 2, fos.186r, 188r–v, 189r. The certificate says that Patricke served from 5 August to 23 September 1643. William Patrick is listed as serving first as lieutenant in the regiment of dragoons raised by Sir Anthony Irby at the beginning of the war, and then for five weeks as captain in Oliver Cromwell's regiment of horse in the Eastern Association army.[2] He was recruited on a day when Cromwell was back in Huntingdon so perhaps he was an old acquaintance. Cromwell left Hull on 23 September and arrived in Boston on 26 September, so it was an odd time to leave the army. If he had been wounded, there would surely have been some evidence of a war pension. It is just possible but surely unlikely that he left

---

[9] Algernon Percy, tenth earl of Northumberland (1602–68), politician. See *ODNB*.

---

[1] The accounts submitted by William Packer, also of Cromwell's regiment (TNA, SP 28/267, Part 2, fos 181r, 183r, 184v /12r and v, 14r, 15v) and Cromwell's certificate (fos 182r/13r) are in the same hand. See **1647 02 10**.

[2] The *Online Directory of Parliamentarian Army Officers*. He may (perhaps unlikely) also be the Lieutenant Patrick who later served in Lawrence Crawford's regiment of foot.

23 JANUARY 1647

because 25 September 1643 was the day the Solemn League and Covenant was ordered to be enrolled and taken by MPs, and to be taken within London. But it would seem a premature leap for that to be Patricke's reason for leaving the army. His demand was, as captain under the command of lieutenant general Cromwell, 5 Aug.–25 Sept., 51 days @ 39s. per day, himself and six horses: £99. 9s. 0d. He claimed that he was owed for service outside the five weeks of this claim another £394. 9s. 0d. The Committee of Petitions referred it to the Committee for Taking the Accounts of the Kingdom, who certified his claim on 16 February 1647.[3]

[fos 188r/19r]
Capt. William Patrick his Accot Certified
No = 129 – B

[fos 188v–189r/19r–20v.]
Account, dated (certified?), 16 Feb. 1646/47
He demands as Captain under the command of Lieutenant-General Cromwell, 5 Aug.–25 Sept., 51 days @ 39s. per day, himself and six horses: £99. 9s. 0d.
Rest due to him: £394. 9s. 0d.

Debtor to his account for money received by him:
Received of Lieutenant-General Cromwell in September 1643: £5.
Pattricke is how he signs his name.

Thes ar to Certifie That Capt Will Pattricke was In Actuall servis as Capt of Horse in my Regemt himselfe And sixe horses From the 5th of August 1643 Till the 25th of September followeinge
Certiffied this 23th of Januarii 1646[4]
Oliver Cromwell

I doe Forther Certiffie that the said Capt Will Pattricke hath Receaved towards his paye due to him onelye Five pounds which was by my order, Certiffied this 23 January 1646
Oliver Cromwell

---

[3] TNA, SP 28/267, Part 2, fos 186r/17r.   [4] i.e. 1647 n.s.

THE LETTERS, WRITINGS, AND SPEECHES OF OLIVER CROMWELL

1647 01 24
Certificate of service of Edward Whalley

Date: 24 January 1647
Source: TNA, SP 28/267/1–4, fo. 96r (autograph)

This is a type of document which many a senior officer in Parliament's service signed: the attestation of the service of a subordinate making a claim for back-pay. It is one of a number of documents in the same volume that Edward Whalley[1] submitted (though this is the only one Cromwell signed): money owing him and his troop as lieutenant colonel from 24 March 1644–1 January 1645 (fos 98r–100r), and an account of his troop's receipts, March 1642–22 August 1643 (fo. 102r).

What gives the document particular interest is that Cromwell is attesting for a long-serving officer in his regiment, who had risen from captain, appointed on 18 February 1643, to lieutenant colonel on 7 Ocober of the same year, and continued as such as long as the regiment remained in the Eastern Association army. After the battle of Gainsborough on 28 July 1643, Cromwell commended Whalley's actions both in the battle itself and in the orderly retreat when faced with the earl of Newcastle's Northern army.[2] Whalley, the son of a Nottinghamshire landowner, was also Cromwell's cousin: his mother Frances was sister of Cromwell's father.

Whalley was to recur as a significant figure in the late 1640s and 1650s. He was given command in the New Model Army of one of the regiments of horse created out of Cromwell's Eastern Association regiment. As well as a significant military career, he was keeper of King Charles I when the latter was a prisoner at Hampton Court, a regicide, and major general of Derbyshire, Leicestershire, Lincolnshire, Nottinghamshire and Warwickshire in 1655–6.

———

This is to Certify, that Colonell Edward Whalley, was in Actuall service for the Parliament in my Regiment, as Captain of a Troupe of horse, himself and six horses from the 18th of February 1642, to the 15th of May 1643, And was in like actuall service as Major to my said Regiment, himself and six horses from the 15th of May 1643, to the seaventh day of October following, And was in like actuall service as Lief[tenan]t Collonell to my Regiment, in the Army of the Right Honorable the Earle of Manchester, himself and six horses, from the 7th

---

[1] Edward Whalley, appointed Lord Whalley under the Protectorate (d. 1674/5), regicide and major general. See *ODNB* and see also the *Online Directory of Parliamentarian Army Officers*.

[2] See above, **1643 07 29**, **1643 07 30**, **1643 07 31**.

364

day of october 1643 to the 2d of Aprill 1645. Given under my hand the 24th of January 1646,

Oliver Cromwell

1647 02 10

Certificate signed by Cromwell and sent to the House of Commons committee for petitions

Date: 10 February 1647
Source: TNA, SP28/267, Part 2, fo. 182r (autograph)

This is another example of a certificate signed by Cromwell (in the same clerk's hand as **1647 01 23**). Packer was to serve in Cromwell's own regiment of horse (and to command it from no later than the battle of Dunbar) until he was cashiered for his opposition to the creation of the Other House in 1657. In March 1644 Cromwell defended him against the attempts of Major General Laurence Crawford's attempts to remove him from Manchester's army for being an Anabaptist (see **1644 03 10**).

This is to Certifie that Capt. Wm Packer[1] was In Actuall servis as Capt of A Troope of Horse him selfe and 6 horses In my owne Regemt in the Armey of the Right Honrll the Earle of Manchester From the 2th of Julii 1644 Till the 2th of Aprill 1645[2] Certiffied the 10th of Februarii 1646

1647 03 07

Letter from Oliver Cromwell to Sir Thomas Fairfax

Date: 7 March 1647 (just possibly 3 March 1648)
Source: BL, Sloane MS 1519, fos 158r–159v (holograph)

Cromwell's holograph letter is endorsed in his own hand as being sent on 7 March 1647 (i.e. 1648 n.s.), but there is also an endorsement, probably in the hand of Fairfax's secretary

---

[1] William Packer (*fl.* 1644–62), army officer and deputy major general. See ODNB.
[2] i.e. from his promotion on the day of the battle of Marston Moor from lieutenant to captain to the day his regiment was incorporated into the New Model Army.

THE LETTERS, WRITINGS, AND SPEECHES OF OLIVER CROMWELL

John Rushworth, dating it 7 March 1646 (i.e. 1647 n.s.). Carlyle, supported by Lomas, preferred Cromwell's dating, presumably on the grounds that it was Cromwell's;[1] Abbott prefers the earlier date and is almost certainly correct.[2] First of all, Cromwell's own dating or events early in the year is more erratic than that of the bureaucratic Rushworth (see **1646 07 31**). More importantly, the letter discusses Cromwell's recovery from 'a dangerous illness' and we know from newsletters at the time that Cromwell was absent from Parliament for several weeks in January and February 1647 suffering from an 'impostume of the head' (an abscess on his inner ear perhaps) and that thereby the Independent party were 'weaker in the House'.[3] Thirdly the postscript about quartering fits naturally with the events of early March 1647. Indeed on 6 March 1647, the Lords had resolved that 'Whereas this House is informed, That the Army under the Command of Sir *Thomas Fairefax* is now either already, or to be, quartered in the Eastern associated Counties: It is Ordered, by the Lords assembled in Parliament, That no Part of the said Army be quartered within the said Eastern Association; and if any of the said Army, either Horse or Foot, be already quartered within the said Eastern Association, that they be forthwith removed', and they sent him a letter to this effect, which is what Cromwell seems to allude to in his postscript.[4] In contrast, quartering was the last thing on the Parliament's mind in the first week of March 1648. One might note that there is a complete dearth of surviving Cromwell letters during the period of his sickness in early 1647 and then a great flurry in March 1647 (including two more to Fairfax in a group of seven either side of his illness), whereas there are letters in the second half of February 1648 that show no evidence of illness. Indeed there is no other surviving letter to Fairfax between October 1647 and June 1648. The letter itself is one of those periodic letters in which Cromwell lays bare his soul. The obvious comparisons are the letters to Mrs St John (**1638 10 13**) and to Valentine Walton (**1644 07 05**).

———

Lt. General Cromwell
March. 7. 1647

For his Excellency Sir
Thomas Fairfax Genl.
of the Parlnts. Armies
         theise

---

[1] Carlyle-Lomas, 1:295–6.

[2] Abbott, *Writings and Speeches*, I:426. Bizarrely he alters the text to read '7 March 1646'.

[3] Abbott, *Writings and Speeches*, I:426, citing Bodl., MS Clarendon 2:439, letter of intelligence 8/18 Feb. 1647; P. Gaunt, *Oliver Cromwell* (1996), pp. 71–2.

[4] *JHL*, 9:67–8.

7 MARCH 1647

Sir it hath pleased God to raise mee
out of a dangerous sicknesse, and I doe
most willingly acknowledge, that the
Lord hath (in this visitation) exercised
the bowells of a Father towards mee,
I receaved in my selfe the sentence
of death, that I might learne to
trust in him that raiseth from the
dead, and have noe confidence in
the flesh. It's a blessed thinge to
dye daylie, for what is there in
this world to be accounted off,
the best men according to the flesh,
and thinges, are lighter then vanitye. I finde this only good, to
love the Lord, and his poore despised people, to doe for them, and
to bee readie to Suffer with them,
and hee that is found worthy of
this, hath obteyned great favor
from the Lord, and Hee that is
established in this, shall (\beinge conformed/ ~~after confor~~
~~mity with~~ to Christ,[5] and the rest of the
bodye)[6] participate in the Glory of
~~the~~ \a/ resurrection, which will answare all.
Sir I must thankfully confesse your favor in your last letter, I see I am not
forgotten,
and truly to bee kept in your remembrance is very great Satisfaction to mee, for I
cann say in the simplicitye of my hart, I putt a high and true valew upon your
love, which when I forgett I shall cease to be a gratefull, and an honest man, I
most humblie begg my service may bee præsented to your Lady,[7] to whom I
wish all happinesse, and establishment in the truth, Sir my prayers are for you
as becomes
Your excellencies most humble servant

[5] Romans 8:29 (KJV).   [6] 1 Corinthians 12:27; Romans 12:5 (KJV).
[7] Anne Fairfax [née Vere], Lady Fairfax.

Oliver Cromwell.

March. 7th. 1647[8]
Sir mr. Rushworth[9]
will write to you about
the quarteringe &
the letter lately
sent you, and
therfore I forbeare.

1647 03 19
Letter from Oliver Cromwell to Sir Thomas Fairfax

Date: 19 March 1647
Source: BL, Sloane MS 1519, fos 152r–153v (holograph)

This letter is in Cromwell's own hand, but the address is in an unrecognised hand. It illustrates the mounting tension between parliamentary leaders and the Army and it throws light on Cromwell's relationship with his commanding officer.

The Committee of the Army, about which Cromwell writes here, was established alongside the New Model Army in the late winter of 1644/5, and was intended 'to consider of recruiting the army according to the new model, and of all things requisite and necessary thereunto; and what else shall conduce to the setting forth and enabling the army to march and do service'.[1]

The Committee reported to the two Houses on all administrative aspects of the Army in war and in peace and by the winter of 1646–7 was supervising the downsizing of the Army, the transfer of large parts of it to Ireland and the demobilisation of the rest, alongside the sleighting of defence works and the streamlining of garrisons, all with scant reference to the men who had won the war.

---

[8] Cromwell's spiritual reflections form the main body of the text, and they reach to the bottom of the page. His personal compliments to Fairfax and his wife follow in the left-hand margin, starting about four lines down the page. The date is at the very top of the margin; squeezed in the top left-hand corner, between the date and the first three lines of the letter, is the PS.

[9] John Rushworth [Rushforth] (c.1612–90), historian and politician. See ODNB. Rushworth was Fairfax's secretary.

[1] There is a lengthy discussion of the Committee of the Army in HoP, Commons 1640–1660.

19 MARCH 1647

[fo. 153v]

For his Excie Sir Thomas Fairfax Generall of the Parliamts army these
Lt. Generall Cromwell.
March. 19. 1646.

[fo. 152r]

Sir this enclosed order I receaved,
but I suppose letters from the
Committee of the Armie[2] to the
effect of this are come to your
handes before this tyme, I think
itt were very good that the
distance of 25. miles bee very
strictly observed, and they are
too blame that have exceeded
the distance, contrarie to your
former apointment.[3] This letter[4]
I receaved this eveninge from
Sir William Massam a member of
the house of commons,[5] which I
thought fitt to send you, his
house[6] beinge much within the
distance of 25. miles of London
I have sent the officers downe,
as many as I could well light
off Not havinge more att præsent

---

[2] *JHC*, 4:51.

[3] The relevant order of the House of Commons on 17 March 1647 reads: 'That this House takes Notice of [the Lord General's] Care, in ordering that none of the Forces under his Command should quarter nearer than Five-and-twenty Miles of this City: That, notwithstanding his Care and Directions therein, that the House is informed, That some of his Forces are quartered much nearer than that; and to desire him to take Course, That his former Orders, touching the Quartering of his Forces no nearer than Twenty-five Miles of this City, may be observed.' *JHC*, 5:115.

[4] The enclosure has not survived.

[5] Sir William Masham (1591–1656). Masham was related to Cromwell by marriage (see **1638 10 13**) but closer to his father-in-law Sir Thomas Barrington of Hatfield Broadoak (Essex). He was a Presbyterian in politics and in religion—being an elder in the Essex Classis (1646–8).

[6] At Otes, in Essex, close by the seat of his father-in-law and mentor, Sir Thomas Barrington.

369

THE LETTERS, WRITINGS, AND SPEECHES OF OLIVER CROMWELL

I rest
Your Ex. most humble
servant

Oliver Cromwell

March. 19.
1646.

⸺◈⸺

1647 03 23
Letter from Oliver Cromwell to Edward Howard, Lord Escrick

Date: 23 March 1647
Source: TNA, SP 19/106, fos 36r–37v (no. 19) [Committee for the Advance of Money: Bills and Papers, March 1646/7] (holograph)

This letter of commendation (in Cromwell's own hand and with his seal still intact) for an old school friend and co-religionist (Thomas Edwards) was addressed to a political ally in the House of Lords. It is one of a pair of letters on the subject, the other being written eight days later to two members of the House of Commons (see below, **1647 03 31**).

Lord Howard of Escrick (d. 1675) was the seventh son of Thomas Howard, first earl of Suffolk. Ennobled in his own right as a client of Buckingham, he was one of the most stalwart attenders of the House of Lords throughout the Civil War, most especially as a member of the Committee of the Advance of Money (which he frequently chaired). He was one of only three peers to join the Rump Parliament after the abolition of the House of Lords.[1] Cromwell's letter was registered in the papers of the Committee for the Advance of Money which had originally been set up to fine those who had not contributed to the voluntary parliamentary 'Propositions' of 1642, but had developed a broader responsibility, alongside the committees of sequestration and composition, for the estates of suspected royalists. As an extension of this, the committee had responsibility for filling vacancies in the 'civil service' created, their previous holders having deserted their posts and joined the King's party.

⸺⸺

My Lord,
Your favors give mee the bouldnesse to

---

[1] Edward Howard, first Baron Howard of Escrick (d. 1675), politician. See *ODNB*.

23 MARCH 1647

præsent the humble suite of this poore man[2]
to your Lordp whose power (as hee tells mee)
may conferr upon him that which Hee
seekes, which is a dividend[3] Clerkes place
in the Prærogative Office,[4] I have had
many promises from mr. Hill[5] of doinge
the man a favor, but I heere Hee is
now out of towne, Sir Nathanniel Brent
knowes him.[6] And truly that which commends
him to the place, is partlye his merritt,
Hee havinge served there as an under
Clerke about sixteene or seaventeene
yeeres, and in all that tyme his be-
havior has beene such, as I beleive the
strictest man, could not detect him.
My \Lord/ beleive mee I would not putt you
to this trouble, did I not knowe the
man, to bee a most religious honest
man, I have knowen him soe neere
this twentye yeeres[7] havinge \~~our br~~/[8] had

[2] 'This poor man' can be identified as Thomas Edwards from the companion letter **1647 03 31** and from Edwards's petition in the papers of the Committee for the Advance of Money, read 7 April 1647 (TNA, SP19/106 fo. 39r). Edwards was born in Huntingdon and schooled there (presumably at the same school as Cromwell). He matriculated at Sidney Sussex College, Cambridge as a sizar on 16 October 1614, but two years ahead of Cromwell. See *Al Cantab.*, available online: venn.lib.cam.ac.uk/Documents/ acad/2016/search-2016.html

[3] Dividend clerk (corrected in the letter of **1647 03 31**). The clerks received one-third of the fee (or dividend) for processing wills (the registrars receiving the other two thirds) (TNA, SP 18/100, fo. 193r [no. 101.i: cited in Gerald Aylmer, *The State's Servants: The Civil Service of the English Republic* (London, 1973), p. 116]. According to his petition, Edwards had been a writer of wills (under-clerk) since 1630 and he was seeking one of the three clerks' positions vacated by men who had deserted London and joined the King's party.

[4] The Prerogative Court of Canterbury was responsible for administering the wills of those who owned property in more than one diocese (and, over time, the wills of many wealthy men and women who preferred to come to it rather than to their diocesan chancelleries).

[5] Mr Hill is almost certainly John Hill, appointed a clerk in the registrar's office of the Prerogative Court on 24 April 1646 (CCAM, 2:685).

[6] Sir Nathanael Brent (1573/4–1652), ecclesiastical lawyer and college head. See *ODNB*. He was master or keeper of the Prerogative Court. See also *A&O*, 1:564–6.

[7] This is an error for thirty years—and actually more if they had 'had much of our education together'. Cromwell corrects this to thirty in his second testimonial letter for Edwards: see **1647 03 31**.

[8] Presumably 'our brother' is intended—'our br' is written above 'havinge' and then struck out.

371

much of our education together, I dare
professe to your Lordp, that I beleive
his modesty, and integritye have kept
him from being præferred heither unto,
Hee havinge soe good a prætence, I hope
Your Lordp will befreind his just desier, and pardon this trouble
and boldnesse to
my Lord
Your most humble and most
faythfull servant
Oliver Cromwell

March 23.
1646.

[fo. 37v]
For the Right \hnble/ Edward
Lord Howard   theise

1647 03 30

Letter from Oliver Cromwell to Sir Dudley North

Date: 30 March 1646 [=1647]
Source: Carlyle-Lomas, 3:245, appendix 8 (later print copy)

Carlyle, revising his original edition of the *Letters and Speeches,* found a later copy of a lost original 'in the possession of the Rev. W.S. Casborne, of Pakenham, Suffolk, a descendant of the North family'. This in turn was lost by 1904 and has not been recovered.

Carlyle notes that Cromwell had dated it as '30th March 1646 [*error for* 1647]'. He is right to do so and to say Cromwell had overlooked the change of year on 25 March. For on 1 January 1646/7[1] the Commons passed an ordinance discharging John Hobart, Esq., as sheriff of Cambridgeshire and Huntingdonshire, appointing Tristram Dyamond, Esq., in his place; and on 2 January 1646/7 the Lords concurred and ordered the commissioners of the great seal to issue Dyamond's commission.[2]

---

[1] *JHC,* 5:36, 1 January 1647.   [2] *JHL,* 8:642, 2 January 1647.

31 MARCH 1647

For the Honourable Sir Dudley North:[3] *These*

30th March 1646

SIR,

It being desired to have the Commission of the Peace renewed in the Isle of Ely, - with some addition, as you may perceive; none left out; only Mr. Diamond,[4] now High Sheriff of the County, and my Brother Desborow,[5] added, there being great want of one in that part of the Isle where I live,[6] - I desire you to join me in a Certificate; and rest,

Your humble servant,

OLIVER CROMWELL.

⸺⸺◦⸺⸺

1647 03 31

Letter from Oliver Cromwell to Henry Darley and John Gurdon

Date: 31 March 1647
Source: TNA, SP 19/106, fo. 38r [no. 20] (autograph)

This is a follow-up letter to **1647 03 23** to Lord Howard and Escrick on behalf of Thomas Edwards who had been to school and university with Cromwell.

---

[3] Sir Dudley North, later fourth Baron North (1602–77), politician and author. See *ODNB*. He was MP for Cambridgeshire in the Short and Long Parliaments, and a deputy lieutenant for the county; see also *HoP Commons, 1604–1629*; *HoP Commons, 1660–1690*.

[4] Tristam (or Tristram) Diamond (Dyamond) appears frequently in administrative records of the 1640s and 1650s as an active committeeman and commissioner (twelve hits in a search on https://www.british-history.ac.uk). It is likely that he was from Upwell in the north corner of the Isle of Ely, for the only Dyamond in the 1664 Hearth Tax, Peter Dyamond, is the largest payer there with eleven hearths (see *Cambridgeshire hearth tax returns, Michaelmas 1664*, N. Evans, ed., British Record Society Hearth Tax Series 1; Cambridgeshire RS 15 (2000), p. 126).

[5] John Disbrowe was born in Eltisley, west of Cambridge, a younger son in a minor gentry family. By 1636 he was a jobbing attorney and in that year he married Cromwell's sister Jane. He was one of the first to volunteer for Cromwell's troop of horse in 1642 and was its quartermaster. In April 1642 he got his own troop and by 1646 was a colonel. John Disbrowe [Desborough] (bap. 1608, d. 1680), parliamentarian army officer and politician. See *ODNB*.

[6] Cromwell had inherited the half-timbered house, 300 yards from Ely Cathedral (known at that time as 'the Sextry') from his mother's brother in January 1636 and until 1647 it was his principal residence (and certainly where his wife and younger children lived), Gaunt, *Gazetteer*, p. 14.

Gentlemen,

I wrote a letter to my Lord Howard[1] onn the behalfe of this bearer Mr Edwards[2] to desier Hee may bee placed in that office to which Hee has beene related neere Seaventeene yeeres. Hee is (I am persuaded) a godly man, I have knowen him above 30[tie]: yeeres, I beleive the reason Hee has not beene præferred is be more because of his modestye, and honesty, then for any other cause. now you will have oportunitye to right him, Hee is a very able clerke, the place Hee desiers is a divident[3] Clerkes place in the prærogative,[4] for which Hee hath so longe served, and from which Hee hath beene soe longe and undulye kept. Hee hath a familye in towne to maintayne [I][5] would not write thus confidently for him, but upon [?kn]owen[6] groundes.

I rest Your humble servant
Oliver Cromwell

Martii ult.[7]
1647

For my Noble freindes Henry Darlye[8] and John Gurdon[9] Esqrs theise

1647 03 31[?]

Letter from Oliver Cromwell to Sir Thomas Fairfax

Date: March 1646 [/47] [?] or possibly much later in the year
Source: BL, Sloane MS 1519, fos 129r–130v (holograph)

This is a holograph letter, complete with Cromwell's seal, but the address and the date are in different hands.

---

[1] See **1647 03 23**, n. 1. [2] See **1647 03 23**, n. 2.
[3] Divident = Dividend (see **1647 03 23**, n. 3).
[4] The Prerogative Court of Canterbury (see **1647 03 23**, n. 4).
[5] There is a tear in the manuscript here, but the top of an 'I' is visible.
[6] The tear has removed what must be 'kn' here.
[7] 'Martii ult[imo]' = 'the last day of March' (Latin).
[8] Henry Darley (c.1596–1671), politician. See *ODNB* (where he is described as 'a leading member of the Independent-dominated committee for advance of money').
[9] John Gurdon (1595–1679), politician. See *ODNB*. He was an East Anglian MP (for Ipswich) and key member of the Committee for the Advance of Money.

374

31 MARCH 1647[?]

The main problem with this letter is its date. Cromwell added no date himself but there is an addition after the address written in a contemporary hand dating it as 'March 1647'. Carlyle dated it as 11 March and links it to a letter from Fairfax to the House of Commons read on that day 'declaring the Reasons that induced him to remove his Quarters'.[1] He might have added that the House read the Lord General's letter immediately after receiving a petition from Essex 'for easing the burden' of having the Army quartered across the county (which may be what Cromwell is referring to when he writes of 'the late petition which suggested a dangerous designe upon the parlmt. in cominge to those quarters'. However, Samuel Rawson Gardiner was 'incline[d] to put the date of the letter a few days later' but does not explain why.[2] But why then would Fairfax or his secretary date it March 1647 when the new year only began on 25 March? Is it possible that this letter relates to the more fraught days at the very end of the month—i.e. the period during which Parliament rejected the Army's petitioning over concerns about its own future and the rights of demobilised soldiers to arrears, pensions for widows and the maimed, and indemnity. On 29 March Parliament denounced the Army's presumption in directly petitioning Parliament ('the Declaration of Dislike') and summonsed the officers it believed mainly responsible to appear before it. On 30 March Fairfax wrote to the House explaining and justifying the meetings of officers at Saffron Walden and on 1 April the Commons accepted his letter and dismissed the officers but ordered them to ensure that the Declaration of Dislike was read to all their regiments. This does not quite fit with Cromwell's allusions, but his reference to the raising of troops 'on the Fast Day' is suggestive. There were Fast Days on 24 February and 31 March, and the latter seems to fit more naturally. And the dramatic change in the tone of Cromwell's remarks seems to fit in with the deterioration of relations at the very end of March. But there are grounds, to be found in notes 7 and 8, for ignoring the added date and placing it much later in the year. For the moment, the likeliest but far from certain date for the composition and delivery of this letter is 31 March 1647.

For his Excie. Sir Thomas
Fairfax, Generall of
the parliamts army

Lt. Generall Cromwell.
March 1646.[3]

---

[1] Carlyle-Lomas, I:253.   [2] Gardiner, GCW, 3:220–1.
[3] This could well be in Fairfax's own hand.

375

THE LETTERS, WRITINGS, AND SPEECHES OF OLIVER CROMWELL

Sir your letters about your new
quarters, directed to the houses, came
seasonablie, and were to very good
purpose, there want not in all
places men whoe have soe much
malice \against the Armie/ as besotts them, The late
petition which suggested a dangerous
designe upon ⸺⸻[4] the parlnt. in cominge to those quarters doth suffi
cient evidence the same, but the{y}
gott nothinge by itt, for the house
did assoyle the Armie from all
Suspicion, and have left you to
quarter where you please.[5]

Never were the Spirits of men
more imbittered then now, suerly
the Devil hath but a short
tyme. Sir its good the heart
bee fixed against all this, the
naked Symplicitye of Christ, with
that wisdom Hee please to give,
and patience will overcom all
this, that God would keepe your
heart as Hee has donn heitherto
is the prayer of

Your excellencyes most humble
servant
Oliver Cromwell

I desire my most humble service
may be præsented to my Lady.

---

[4] There are three letters comprehensively erased here—the first appears to be a 'c'.
[5] This is the sentence which seems to point to an earlier date, c.11 March.

Mr Allen[6] desires col. Baxter[7] somtime
governor of Readinge may be rememberd,
I humblie desier Col. Overton[8] may not bee out
of your remembrance, Hee is a deserving man
and presents hi[s] humble service to you.

Upon the fast { }[9] souldiers were raised (as I heere) both horse and foote neere 200 in Covent garden[10]
t{o} prevent {sectar}ies[11] from cuttinge the presbiterians throats, theise are fine tricks to mock
God with.

1647 05 03a

Letter from Philip Skippon, Oliver Cromwell and Henry Ireton to the 'Colonels or chief officers of the respective regiments'

Date: 3 May 1647
Source: Worcester College, Oxford, Clarke MS 2/3, fo. 20r (contemporary copy)

We have no letters from Cromwell between the clutch of letters in late March and another clutch in early May. In the course of April, there had been rapid polarisation

---

[6] Almost certainly William Allen, a trooper in Cromwell's own regiment and soon to be one of the leading agitators. For his later career, culminating as a colonel and adjutant general in the Irish campaigns of the 1650s, see Firth and Davies, *Regimental History*, 1:201, 244; 2:594–5, 613–16, 629, 638.

[7] Colonel Baxter = John Barkstead [created Sir John Barkstead under the Protectorate] (d. 1662), major general and regicide, *ODNB*, was governor of Reading (1644–6) and he got his own regiment in the summer of 1647. He seems to have been out of military service from March 1646 to June 1647 (see Malcolm Wanklyn, *Reconstructing*, 1:78, fn. 287). If he was not a colonel as governor of Reading, this raises new problems about the dating of the letter.

[8] Colonel Overton = Robert Overton, formerly of Fairfax's own regiment of foot and more recently his deputy as governor of Pontefract. Robert Overton (1608/9–78/9), parliamentarian army officer. See *ODNB*. Although he did not replace William Herbert as colonel of the 11th regiment of foot in the New Model until June 1647, there is evidence that he was called 'colonel' in pay warrants from his time in Pontefract (TNA, E121/4/1/30, entry 96), for which see Wanklyn, *Reconstructing*, 1:91, fn. 401.

[9] Word or words lost in tear—'day' is the obvious missing word.

[10] Newly built in the years before 1642 and therefore a fashionable London suburb.

[11] Words lost in tear. Carlyle-Lomas suggests 'us soldiers' (and Abbott follows suit) but the last three letters are definitely 'ies' not 'iers'. Much more plausible is 'the sectaries'.

THE LETTERS, WRITINGS, AND SPEECHES OF OLIVER CROMWELL

between the Presbyterian majority in Parliament and a clear majority of the officers of the Army and the representatives (adjutators or agitators) of the common soldiers. On 27 April, the *Vindication of the Officers of the Army*,[1] with 151 signatures attached, was presented to the House of Commons by two colonels, two captains and a lieutenant. It defended the Army's right to petition and challenged Parliament's plan to send to Ireland men who had only volunteered for service in England; and to reduce most of the rest without proper provision for arrears, pensions and a statutory indemnity. Three days later sixteen of the adjutators presented an *Apologie*[2] which, in a series of stinging rhetorical questions, made clear that they would not cooperate with the plans of those 'who have recently tasted of sovereignty; and being lifted beyond their ordinary spheare as servants, seek to become Masters, and degenerate into Tyrants' [p. 4]. The three troopers who presented it were interrogated together and individually. After anxious and angry deliberation, the House ordered four of its members, Skippon, Cromwell, Ireton and Fleetwood—described by Woolrych as 'the four officer MPs most likely to command respect'[3]—to go down to Saffron Walden and to quieten the 'distempers' and to promise that an indemnity ordinance was in the pipeline. Three of them arrived in Walden on 2 May (Fleetwood arrived later which is presumably why his name is missing from the letter containing the signatures of the other three). In the days that followed the structure that was to underpin the General Council of the Army was laid down.[4]

Letter sent to the Collonells or cheife Officers of the Respective Regiments.

Sir

Wee desire you upon receipt hereof forthwith to repaire hither your selfe with some Commission Officers of every Troope in your Regiment to give unto Us the best accompt you can concerning the present temper and disposition of the Regiment in relation to some late discontents reported to have been amongst the Souldiers, and to receive from Us an accompt of such things as wee are appointed by the honoble. House of Commons to impart to the Army concerning the Care of that House for their Indempnity and Arreares, you are with the

[1] *The petition and vindication of the officers of the armie under His Excellencie Sir Thomas Fairfax… As it was presented to the House of Commons on Tuesday, Aprill 27. 1647… And read on Fryday, April 30* (Wing / P1745; Thomason / E.385[19]).

[2] *The apologie of the common souldiers of his Excellencie Sir Tho. Fairfaxes army… About which apologie the said armies commissioners were questioned, and imprisoned about two houres, by the House of Commons, the last of April, 1647. for delivering this apologie to their general… Printed May 3. 1647* (Wing / A3558; Thomason E385[18]).

[3] *JHC*, 5:157–8. See also Austin Woolrych, *Soldiers and Statesmen: The General Council of the Army and its Debates, 1647–1648* (1983), p. 65.

[4] For all this, see Woolrych, *Soldiers and Statesmen*, pp. 55–67.

378

said Officers to be here with as much speed as possibly you may, but at farthest faile not to be here on Thursday next We remaine
Your assured freinds
P Skippon   Oliver Cromwell   H Ireton
Walden[5] May 3^d
1647

1647 05 03b

Letter from Philip Skippon, Oliver Cromwell and Henry Ireton to William Lenthall, Speaker of the House of Commons

Date: 3 May 1647
Source: Bodl., MS Tanner 58/1, fos 86r–87v (no. 44) (autograph)

This is a follow-up to **1647 05 03a**, written the same day and read in the House of Commons on 4 May.[1] It is in the hand of a clerk, but the signatures are those of Cromwell and his fellow officers. The original is in the papers of William Lenthall, Speaker of the House. All three signatories were members of the House of Commons as well as senior officers in the Army.

For the honoble. William Lenthall Esqr Speaker of the honoble. House of Comons, in Parl.[2]
from field Marshall Skippon[3] Lieutent. Genll. Cromwell &ca. employ'd to the Armie.
read 4⁰. May.
1647

May 3^d
Sir

---

[5] Saffron Walden, Essex. Still the headquarters of Sir Thomas Fairfax and his Council.

[1] *JHC*, 5:161.
[2] William Lenthall, appointed Lord Lenthall under the Protectorate (1591–1662), lawyer and Speaker of the House of Commons. See *ODNB*.
[3] Philip Skippon was, at this time, commander of the infantry in the New Model and had recently been appointed to lead the parliamentarian reconquest of Ireland and had entered the House of Commons as MP for Barnstaple.

Wee have sent out Orders to summon the Officers of the severall Regiments to appeare before us on. thursday next, to the end wee may understand from them the true condition and temper of the souldiers in relation to the discontents lately represented, and the better to prepare and enable them (by speaking with them, and acquainting them with your Votes) to allay any discontents that may be amongst the[-]⁴ \souldiers/; Wee judged this way most likely to be effectuall to your service, though it aske some time by reason of the distance of the Quarters; When wee shall have any thing worthy of your knowledge, Wee shall represent it, and in the meane time studdy to approve our selves
Your most humble servants
Ph: Skippon   Oliver Cromwell   H. Ireton

3° May 1647

1647 05 08

Letter from Philip Skippon, Oliver Cromwell, Henry Ireton, Charles Fleetwood to William Lenthall, Speaker of the House of Commons

Date: 8 May 1647
Source: Bodl., MS Tanner 58/1, fos 94r–95v (no. 47) (autograph)

This is the letter sent to the House of Commons by the four army officers sent down to the Army (see **1647 05 03a** and **1647 05 03b**). Each of the four signed in person. The letter was read in the House of Commons on 11 May. William Clarke, Secretary to the Army, made and retained a copy which differs in no significant detail from the one that was sent to Parliament except that while three of the signatories are listed by Clarke, he failed to include the fourth signatory, Charles Fleetwood.[1]

The letter is written the day after a meeting of officers from most of the New Model's regimental officers held in Saffron Walden church the previous day, in which the four officers communicated the conciliatory offers made to them by the House of Commons, and all regiments then proceeded to elect or to select representatives both from amongst the junior officers and from amongst the rank and file (the 'adjutators' or 'agitators').

---

⁴ One indecipherable letter erased here.

[1] This copy is in Worcester College, Oxford, Clarke MS 22/3, fos 28v–29r.

8 MAY 1647

[fo. 95v]

To the honoble. William Lenthall Esq Speaker of The honoble. House of Commons in Parl

from the Comrs. imploy'd to the Army. from Walden[2] of 8° May 1647

read xi° May

[fo. 94r]

Sir

According to our Orders sent out of the Officers of the Army, many of them appeared at the time appointed, the greatest fayling was of Horse Officers, who (by reason of the great distance of their quarters from this place, being some of them above threescore miles of) could not bee heere, yet there were accidentally some of every Regimt: (except Col: Whaleys)[3] present at our meeting which was upon friday morning about ten of the Clock.[4] After some discourse offered unto them about the occasion of the meeting, together with the deepe sence the Parlt. had of ~~the~~ \some/ discontents which were in the Army, and of our great trouble also, that it should be soe, wee told them wee were sent downe to communicate the house of Comons Votes unto them, whereby their care of giving the Army satisfaction might appeare, desiring them to use their utmost diligence, with all good conscience & effect, by improving their interests in the souldiers for their satisfaction, and that they would communicate to their souldiers the Votes together with such enforcemts. as they received then[5] from Us, to the end their distempers might bee allayed. After this had been said, & a Coppy of the Votes delivered to the cheife officer of every respective Regt. to be communicated as aforesaid, Wee desired them to give Us a speedy accompt of the successe of their endeavors. and if in any thing they ~~would use~~ \needed/ our advice or assistance, for furthering the work, wee should be ready heere at Saffron Walden to give it them, upon notice from them. Wee cannot give you a full and punctuall Accompt of the particular distempers, with the growndes of them, because the Officers were desirous to be spared therein by us, untill they might make a farther ⊢—⊣ \inquiry/ amongst theyr ~~common~~ souldiers, & see what effect your Votes & their endeavours might have with them. Wee desired as speedy an accompt of this busines as

[2] Saffron Walden, Essex, Army headquarters from 15 April to late May 1647.

[3] Colonel Edward Whalley was Cromwell's cousin by marriage (his mother Frances Cromwell was the sister of Cromwell's father).

[4] i.e. Friday 7 May 1647. [5] A change here: originally 'their' or 'them'.

might well bee, but upon the ~~earnest~~ desire of the Officers, thought it necessary for the service, to give them untill Saturday next, to bring us an Accompt of their busines, by reason the Regimts. lye so farre distant. As any thing falls out worthy of your knowledge Wee shall represent it, and in the meane time studdy to approve our selves

Your most humble servants

Ph: Skippon   Oliver Cromwell   H: Ireton   Charles Fleetwood[6]

Walden. 8. May 1647.

1647 05 09

Letter from Philip Skippon and Oliver Cromwell to the eight regiments of horse who had petitioned them on 28 April 1647

Date: 9 May 1647
Source: Worcester College, Oxford, Clarke MS 2/3, fo. 29v (contemporary copy)

It appears that just two of the four officer-MPs sent down to quieten the Army (see **1647 05 03a/b** and **1647 05 08**) signed this letter[1] and they addressed it to the eight regiments whose petition had been presented separately to Fairfax, Skippon and Cromwell on 28 April and handed over by Skippon (followed by Cromwell on 30 April). Note that it was addressed to the regiments and not to the sixteen 'commissioners' or 'agents' identified in it. This initiative follows on from the meeting of more than 100 officers in Saffron Walden church on 7 May and from Skippon, Cromwell, Ireton and Fleetwood's letter to the Speaker of the Commons printed above (**1647 05 08**). It is not known if the officer-MPs received any reply to this letter. (See also **1647 05 17** and **1647 05 20a/b**.)

---

[6] Skippon's signature is right under the signing off on the right-hand side. Then from left to right (and Cromwell's is even slightly higher than Skippon) Cromwell, Ireton and Fleetwood. All four officers are in *ODNB*.

[1] Given that Clarke's copy of the letter of 8 May omitted the signature of Charles Fleetwood which appears on the original in the papers of Speaker Lenthall, the absence of Ireton and Fleetwood from this copy in Clarke's papers (the signed version not having survived) cannot be guaranteed.

9 MAY 1647

Copie of the Letter from the Officers to the 8 Regiments,
Sir
When wee were in London there were three Letters ~~in London~~ delivered (the one to the Generall the other two to Us all of the same effect) in the name of 8 Regiments of Horse[2] whereof yours is one which importing matter of dangerous Consequence were imparted to the House of Commons wee desire you to Use your best endeavour to enquire where they had their rise and to bring with you when you come on Satturday next the best accompt thereof you can, and soe wee rest
Your very assured freinds
Phillipp Skippon   Oliver Cromwell.

Walden[3] May 9th 1647.

the 8 Regiments are:
The Generall Regiments of Horse,[4]	Colonell Okey's[5]
Lieutennant Generalls[6]	Colonell Butler's[7]
Commissary Generalls.[8]	Colonell Sheffeild's[9]
Colonell Fleetwoods.[10]	Colonell Riche's[11]

---

[2] Eight, that is, out of a total of ten regiments of horse.
[3] i.e. Saffron Walden, Essex.
[4] Regiment of Sir Thomas Fairfax. See also Wanklyn, *Reconstructing*, 1:82 and *passim*.
[5] Regiment of John Okey (bap. 1606, d. 1662). See *ODNB*. See also Wanklyn, *Reconstructing*, 1:81 and *passim*.
[6] Regiment of Oliver Cromwell. For his own regiment at this time, see Wanklyn, *Reconstructing*, p. 83 and *passim*.
[7] Regiment of John Butler, see Wanklyn, *Reconstructing*, 1:82 and *passim*.
[8] Regiment of Henry Ireton (bap. 1611, d. 1651), parliamentarian army officer and regicide. See *ODNB*. Also see Wanklyn, *Reconstructing*, 1:84 and *passim*.
[9] Regiment of Thomas Sheffeild, see Wanklyn, *Reconstructing*, 1:82 and *passim*.
[10] Regiment of Charles Fleetwood, see Wanklyn, *Reconstructing*, 1:82 and *passim*.
[11] Regiment of Nathaniel Rich (d. 1700x02), army officer. See *ODNB*. Also see Wanklyn, *Reconstructing*, 1:143 and *passim*.

THE LETTERS, WRITINGS, AND SPEECHES OF OLIVER CROMWELL

1647 05 15

Oliver Cromwell's contributions to the New Model Army Debate at Saffron Walden

Date: 15 May 1647

Source: Worcester College, Oxford, Clarke Papers, vol. 41, fos 33r–37v (reported speech)

Throughout the period from May to November 1647, the Army resisted attempts by Parliament to disband it, at least until that Parliament had met what the Army considered its legitimate demands (arrears of pay, indemnity etc.) and to ensure that any settlement with the King was worthy of the sacrifice and sufferings of those who had brought about his military defeat. Periodically throughout the summer and autumn months, William Clarke,[1] secretary to the Council of War, kept records of some of the debates in the Council of Officers, Council of War and General Council of the Army. Much later, and mainly it would seem after the Restoration, he transcribed the notes that he and others had made in shorthand. The original shorthand notes and rough drafts have not survived, but his fair copies of his notes for 15 and 16 May, 16 and 17 July and 28 and 29 October and 1 November, and fragmentary record of the debates between 2 and 11 November survived in his papers which were passed, on his death at a naval battle in 1666, to his son who in due course handed them to the newly founded Worcester College, Oxford, where they languished until 'discovered' and edited by Charles Harding Firth in the 1890s.[2] Firth's edition is an eccentric one, since he rearranges sentences and phrases and adds or changes words, often without telling his readers, all in the interests of clarification. From hundreds of other documents in the Clarke Papers, we know that Clarke used a shorthand system adapted from one developed by Thomas Shelton and published in 1634 (new editions 1641, 1647).[3] We can be confident that Clarke made his fair copies from the notes of more than one (probably three) stenographers, comparing and collating them. This is more certain for the Putney Debates of October/November [**1647 10 28** to **1648 11 12**] than for the debates in May or July, but it is more likely than not that this was the case then too. It is also clear that sometimes Clarke attempted to give the fullest version of the recorded words of those engaged in the debates, and that sometimes he only summarised his notes (for example putting them into third-person reported speech). It is likely that he strove hardest to capture the actual language of the senior officers, especially Cromwell, but that is not certain.[4]

---

[1] (Sir) William Clarke (1623/4–66), military administrator. See *ODNB*.

[2] Lesley le Claire, 'The Survival of the Manuscript' in Michael Mendle, ed., *The Putney Debates of 1647: the Army, the Levellers and the English State* (Cambridge, 2001), pp. 19–35.

[3] Thomas Shelton, *Tachygraphy* (Cambridge, 1634, 1641, 1647).

[4] All this is authoritatively dealt with by Frances Henderson, 'Reading and Writing: The Text of the Putney Debates', in Mendle, *Putney Debates*, pp. 36–52. And see also her introduction to Frances Henderson, ed., *The Clarke Papers V: Further Selections from the Papers of William Clarke* (Camden Society, 2006), pp. 1–12.

384

15 MAY 1647

The first two days for which we have a surviving record are 15 and 16 May 1647. 'A convention of officers' met in the parish church of Saffron Walden in North Essex, close to the Army's headquarters. Following Parliament's attempt to divide the Army, sending a large part of it to Ireland and disbanding the rest, which was just the greatest of a series of other provocations (such as an attempt to deny members of the Army any right of petitioning), representatives of the common soldiers and officers had been meeting to draw up regimental petitions enumerating their grievances, and the meetings at Saffron Walden were called to discuss progress with this campaign and to see if the separate regimental petitions could be collated into a single document. Some senior officers, headed at these debates by Colonel Thomas Sheffield, protested at the process and at their exclusion from it.[5]

In what follows, Cromwell's words are transcribed fully and with spelling and punctuation retained; other speeches and explanatory material in Clarke's manuscript are summarised (and placed in italics) so as to contexualise Cromwell's contributions.[6] And in this and succeeding transcripts we will be noting significant errors in the previous transcripts by Sir Charles Firth in the *Clarke Papers*, vol. 1 (for the debates of May and July) and by Firth, and A. S. P. Woodhouse, *Puritanism and Liberty* (1938) for the Putney Debates of October–November 1647.

[fo. 33v]

At the convention of officers at the Church in Saffron Walden, Satturday May 15: 1647

This meeting, chaired by Major General Philip Skippon, reviewed progress in drawing up regimental petitions summarising the grievances of the Army concerning indemnity, arrears and the auditing of accounts, and more generally to report on 'the temper of your several regiments'. After Skippon's introduction,

Lieutenant Generall Cromwell then said, That what the Major Generall exprest was the sence of them all.

Cromwell then made no further contribution as 31 other speeches are recorded. Initially discussion concerns the request from some officers for more time to finalise their reports; but the bulk of the discussion concerns the complaints of Colonel Thomas Sheffield[7] that he had been left in ignorance about the drawing up a list of grievances in his regiment and his complaint that junior officers and even troopers were being allowed to make representations. Ireton's reply is

---

[5] For background and commentary on these debates, see Gentles, *The New Model Army*, pp. 157–64; Woolrych, *Soldiers and Statesmen*, pp. 72–90.

[6] Firth's 'eccentric' edition of the whole content of the Saffron Walden Debates is available in C. H. Firth, ed., *The Clarke Papers*, 4 vols. (Camden Society, 1891–1902), 1:33–79.

[7] For Colonel Thomas Sheffield and the controversies surrounding his resignation in the summer of 1647, see Firth and Davies, *Regimental History*, 1:175–8.

THE LETTERS, WRITINGS, AND SPEECHES OF OLIVER CROMWELL

that since Sheffield had signed up for Ireland and since he had failed to associate himself with General Fairfax's petition against the Declaration of Dislike,[8] *he could not present grievances that he was not a party to. The meeting was then suspended until 5pm the following day.*

———— ∞∞∞ ————

1647 05 16

Oliver Cromwell's contributions to the New Model Army Debate at Saffron Walden

Date: 16 May 1647
Source: Worcester College, Oxford, Clarke Papers, vol. 41, fos 39r–53r (reported speech)

For notes on the nature of this record, and the context for the debates in the parish church of St Mary the Virgin at Saffron Walden, see **1647 05 15**.

Overnight on 15–16 May a committee of seven colonels and two majors had read the various regimental petitions and produced a digest of them, focused on eleven specific grievances, all relating to the soldiers' concerns as soldiers.[1] The afternoon session took the form of a presentation of this digest to the parliamentary commissioners to the Army.

————

Heads of Proceedings in Walden Church, Sunday 16 May, 1647.
Skippon calls on all present to report on 'what distempers you finde in your severall regiments' and also how their regiments 'are disposed' with regard to the service in Ireland. Clarke then records

[fo. 39v]
Lieutenant Generall Cromwell. Although[2]
There then follow 90 speeches before Cromwell is recorded as speaking again. The discussion revealed deep divisions within regiments and between regiments about the process of consultation and whether multiple petitions of grievances could be accepted, and also about the terms

---

[8] For the Declaration of Dislike, see Gentles, *New Model Army*, pp. 150–2 and for its part in the Debates at Saffron Walden, Woolrych, *Soldiers and Statesmen*, pp. 37–8, 55–8.

————

[1] Printed as 'A Perfect and True Copy of the Severall Grievances of the Army', within *Divers Papers of the Army* (1647), pp. 3–6 (Wing / D1709).

[2] At this point, Clarke leaves a four-line gap in the manuscript. Is this an indication of an intention to return to it later, perhaps because the shorthand was unclear?

16 MAY 1647

and conditions under which regiments would undertake service in Ireland. Skippon struggled to keep control of a tense meeting. Finally Cromwell intervened:

[fo. 50r]

Lieutenant Generall: Gentlemen by the Command of the Major Generall I will offer a word or two to you. I shall not need to reminde you what the occasion of this meeting was, and what the bussinesse wee are sent downe about, you see by what has past that it was for Us to Learne what temper the Army was in, and truly to that end were the votes of the Parliament Communicated by you to Us,[3] That you should Communicate them to the Army that soe we might have an accompt from you, that Accompt is received, but it being in writing and consisting of many particulars wee doe not yett knowe what the Contents of those papers are, but this I am to lett you knowe, That wee shall deale very faithfully through the Grace of God with those that have imployed Us hither, and with you also, the further consideration of these businesses will be a worke of time, The Major Generall and the rest of the Gentlemen thinke it not fitt to necessitate your stay here from your severall Charges, but because there may be many particulars that may require further consideration in these papers that are heere represented, Itt is desired that you would stay heere a feild officer at the Least of every Regiment, and two Captaines, for the rest it is desired of you, that you would repaire to your severall Charges, and that when you are there you would renew your Care and dilligence in pressing[4] the severall souldiers under your Commands, the Effect of those votes that you have already read, That likewise[5] you would acquaint them as particularly with those two things that the Major Generall did impart to you, which hee had f in a letter from the Speaker of the House of Peeres,[6] to witt the addition of a Fortnight's pay, a fortnight to those that are to goe for Ireland, and a fortnight to those that doe not goe, and likewise there is an Act of Indempnitie very full already past the House of Commons. Truly, Gentlemen, it will be very fitt for you to have a very great care in the making the best use and improvement that you can both of the Votes and of this that hath been last told you, and of the interest which all of you or any of you may have in your severall

---

[3] For unaccountable reasons, Firth changes this to 'from us to you' (*Clarke Papers*, 1:72).

[4] Firth has 'pressing [on] the severall soldiers' (*Clarke Papers*, 1:72).

[5] At this point Clarke in error repeats exactly the forty words between 'you would repaire…And likewise'.

[6] i.e. Edward Montagu, second earl of Manchester.

387

THE LETTERS, WRITINGS, AND SPEECHES OF OLIVER CROMWELL

respective Regiments, Namely to worke in them a good opinion of that authority that is over both Us and them. If that authoritie falls to nothing, nothing can followe but confusion: you have hitherto fought to maintaine that duty, and truly as you have vouchsafed your hands in defending that, so now to expresse[7] your Industry and Interest to preserve it, and therefore I have nothing more to say to you, I shall desire that you will be pleased to lay this to heart that I have said.

There are 22 more speeches before the day comes to a close. All kinds of difficulties are raised, demonstrating high levels of distrust and a great fear of disunity and Skippon has to intervene to say 'I pray either speake with moderation or else be silent.'

∞∞∞

1647 05 17

Letter from Philip Skippon, Oliver Cromwell, Henry Ireton, Charles Fleetwood to William Lenthall, Speaker of the House of Commons

Date: 17 May 1647

Source: Bodl., MS Tanner 58/1, fos 104r–105v (no. 52) (autograph). There is a near-contemporary copy in the Worcester College, Oxford, Clarke Papers, vols. 2/3, fos 53 r–v

This letter survives in its original form with original signatures in the papers of William Lenthall, Speaker of the House of Commons, and the file copy kept by the William Clarke, assistant secretary to Sir Thomas Fairfax. It was read in the House of Commons on 18 May 1647.[1]

The four officer-MP commissioners report back in a very circumspect way about the escalation of army demands. Every regiment (officers and men) now had two agents or agitators and each regiment had drawn up its own list of demands. In Austin Woolrych's words, 'there was much intercommunication between their agitators but the soldiers in each regiment had minds of their own.'[2,3]

Eventually all the regimental statements would be condensed into a single document (for which see below **1647 05 20**), which was presented to the House of Commons by Cromwell on 21 May.[4]

_____

[7] Firth offers a clarification here that makes sense: 'so [vouchsafe] now to expresse' [*Clarke Papers*, 1:72].

[1] *JHC*, 5:176.   [2] Woolrych, *Soldiers and Statesmen*, p. 83.
[3] *Clarke Papers*, 1:32–84.
[4] For a full context see Woolrych, *Soldiers and Statesmen*, ch. 3.

17 MAY 1647

[fo. 104r]

Sir

Wee having made Some progresse in the businesse you commanded us uppon, wee are bold to give you this Account, which although itt come not with that Expedicon you may expect, and your other affaires require, yet wee hope you will bee pleased to excuse us with the waight of the affaire, in comparrison wherof, nothing that ever yet wee undertooke, was (att least to our apprehensions) æquall, and wherin (what ever the issue nowe,) our greatest comfort is, That our Consciences beare us wittnesse wee have according to our abilities indeavoured faithfullie to Serve you, and the Kingdome. The Officers repaired to us at Saffron-walden uppon Saturday last,[5] according to appointment to give us a returne of what they had in charge from us att our last meeting, which was to reade your votes to the Souldiers under their respective commands for their Satisfaction, and to improve their interests faithfullie & honestlie with them to that end, and to give us a perfect Account of the effect of their indeavours, and a true representacon of the temper of the Armie: Att this meeting wee received what they had to offer to us which were delivered to us in writing by the hands of Some chosen by the rest of the Officers then present, and in the name of the rest of the Officers, and of the Souldiers under their commands, which was not done till Sunday in the Evening,[6] att which time, and likewise \before/ uppon Saturday \wee/ acquainted them all with a Letter from the Earle of Manchester, expressing, that an act of indempnitie large and full had passed the House of Commons,[7] and that two weekes pay more[8] was voted to those that were disbanded, as alsoe to them that undertooke the Service of Ireland and thinking fitt to dismisse the Officers of their Severall commands, (all butt Some that were to Stay heere about further Businesse,) wee have them in charge to communicate theis Last votes to their Souldiers, and to improve their ut most diligence and interest for their best Satisfaction. Wee must acknowledge wee found the Army under a deepe Sence of Some Sufferinges, and the common Souldiers much unsetled, wherof that which

---

[5] i.e. 15 May 1647.   [6] i.e. 16 May 1647.

[7] It was promulgated on 21 May 1647: 'Ordinance granting indemnity to all who have acted by sea or land by authority or for the benefit of Parliament' [*JHL*, 9:201]. For the text see *A&O*, I:936–8.

[8] This was in addition to the six weeks' pay to be distributed at disbandment that had already been voted (*JHC*, 5:155, 26 April 1647). For a full discussion of the nature and extent of arrears of pay at this time, see Ian Gentles, 'The Arrears of Pay of the New Model Army at the End of the First Civil War', *Bulletin of the Institute of Historical Research*, 48 (1975), pp. 52–63.

wee have to represent to you will give you a more perfect view; which because itt consists of many [fo. 104v] papers and needes Some more Method in the Representation of them to you then can bee by [—]⁹ Letter, and forasmuch as we were Sent downe by you to our Severall charges to doe our best to keepe the souldiers in order, wee are not well Satisfied \any of us/¹⁰ to leave the place, nor duty you Sent us too; untill wee have the Significacon of your pleasure to us, to which wee Shall most readilie conforme: And rest:

Your most humble Servants:

Ph: Skippon¹¹ Oliver Cromwell H: Ireton¹² Charles Fleetwood¹³ Walden.¹⁴ May. 17.
1647

1647 05 20a

Letter from Philip Skippon, Oliver Cromwell, Henry Ireton, Charles Fleetwood to William Lenthall, Speaker of the House of Commons

Date: 20 May 1647
Source: Worcester College, Oxford, Clarke MS 2/3, fo. 127v (contemporary copy)

This is the copy retained by William Clarke. The original has not survived amongst Lenthall's papers.

When the House of Commons received the letter from the four officer-commissioners (**1647 05 17**) on 18 May, they responded with speed and some alarm. They resolved 'That Sir Thomas Fairfax General be desired, from this House, that, if it may stand with the State of his Health, that he would forthwith repair to the Army' (as so often at times of political crisis, his health had failed), and they ordered that 'the [four] forthwith send up one or more of themselves to the House, to give an Account of their Proceedings in the Business

---

⁹ Three or four letters heavily crossed out. Perhaps 'this'.
¹⁰ These words are inserted above the surrounding text and in heavy writing not that of the scribe of the rest of the letter, and especially from the form of the 'y' just possibly Cromwell. They clearly subtly change the sense.
¹¹ Philip Skippon, appointed Lord Skippon under the Protectorate (d. 1660), parliamentarian army officer. See ODNB.
¹² Henry Ireton (bap. 1611, d. 1651), parliamentarian army officer and regicide. See ODNB.
¹³ Charles Fleetwood, appointed Lord Fleetwood under the Protectorate (c.1618–92), parliamentarian army officer. See ODNB.
¹⁴ Saffron Walden, Essex.

they are employed in there; with this Intimation, That Field Marshal Skippon do continue there, to promote the Service of Ireland'.[1] This is their response.

Letter from the 4: Officers to Mr Speaker.

Sir

Upon the order you sent Us of the 18th Instant Wee have herewith Sent upp two of our selves (Lieut: Collonell Cromwell and Collonell Fleetwood to give an Accompt to the House of the bussinesse wee are imploy'd in here according to certaine heads by a Report here agreed upon for that purpose by Us all who are.

your most humble servts:

Phil Skippon.[2] Ol: Cromwell   Hen: Ireton[3]   Charles Fleetwood.[4]
Walden[5] May: 20th 1647.

1647 05 20b

Heads of a report signed by Philip Skippon, Oliver Cromwell, Henry Ireton, Charles Fleetwood and which Cromwell delivered to the House of Commons on 21 May 1647

Date: 20 May 1647
Source: Worcester College, Oxford, Clarke MS 2/3, fos 128r–130r (contemporary copy)

On 16 May Colonels John Lambert[1] and Edward Whalley[2] on behalf of a committee of twenty-four officers presented a digest of the regimental statements/petitions to the four commissioners at Saffron Walden. They in turn converted it into this 'heads of a report' and sent Cromwell and Fleetwood up to Westminster with it. There is no record in the

---

[1] JHC, 5:176.
[2] Philip Skippon, appointed Lord Skippon under the Protectorate (d. 1660), parliamentarian army officer. See ODNB.
[3] Henry Ireton (bap. 1611, d. 1651), parliamentarian army officer and regicide. See ODNB.
[4] Charles Fleetwood, appointed Lord Fleetwood under the Protectorate (c.1618–92), army officer. See ODNB.
[5] Saffron Walden, Essex.

---

[1] John Lambert [Lambart] (bap. 1619, d. 1684), parliamentary soldier and politician. See ODNB.
[2] Edward Whalley, appointed Lord Whalley under the Protectorate (d. 1674/5), regicide and major general. See ODNB.

THE LETTERS, WRITINGS, AND SPEECHES OF OLIVER CROMWELL

parliamentary archives or in the papers of William Lenthall, the Speaker, of whether they read out the 'heads' or delivered it in documentary form. The *Commons Journal* simply states that on 21 May 'Lieutenant General Cromwell gave an Account of the Proceedings of the Commissioners employed from this House to the Army'.[3] Giving an account suggests an *oral* report rather than the recitation of a document. At any rate, after that account was given, the Commons responded by pushing ahead with the disbandment of most of the Army, together with some minor concessions in line with the demands of the soldiers.[4] They were to prove insufficient. [5]

So what has survived in the papers of William Clarke was a briefing document but there is no evidence that either it or the digest of the regimental petitions that had been presented to the MP-officers were ever formally presented to the house of commons. The latter was first published, in an unauthorised version (presumably from agitator sources), on 22 May[6] and, by way of rebuke, an authorised version emanating from Army headquarters was published (and by the Army Council's most regular printer at that time, George Whittington), on 27 May.[7] A third version, the one much used by historians—*The Declaration of the Armie*—published on 4 June—is a spurious edition.[8] *A perfect and true copy of the severall grievances of the Army* (27 May) also contained the names of 241 officers. Only fifteen are known to have dissented.[9]

The heads of a Report to be made to the honoble: House of Commons by Lieutennant Generall Cromwell and Collonell Fleetwood[10] in the name of

---

[3] *JHC*, 5:181. For a royalist newsletter report of Cromwell's statement and the Commons response, see *Clarke Papers*, 1:99–100, note 'a'.

[4] For a full narrative of what is known, see Woolrych, *Soldiers and Statesmen*, pp. 91–100.

[5] *JHC*, 5:181–4, for the debates of 21 and 24 May 2015.

[6] This also includes a copy of the notably more radical demands of Nathaniel Rich's regiment: *Divers Papers from the Army* (Wing / D1709; Thomason / E.88[18]).

[7] *A perfect and true copy of the severall grievances of the Army* (Wing / P1472; Thomason / E.390[3]) This contains the allegation (signed by Lieutenant E[dmund] Ch[illenden] that *Divers Papers from the Army* was 'a very imperfect copy of our grievances' and 'was not the Armies' (final [unpaginated] page). *Divers papers* rewords significant sections (especially in articles 1 and 3 and in the peroration) but also omits a whole line in article 3, clearly in error, for it gives the impression that Ensign Nicholls had been imprisoned by the House of Commons without charge and states that he, and not his gaoler, was a soldier who had signed up for Ireland. This is the version included (out of sequence) in the official compendium of documents of the General Council of the Army in late September 1647 familiarly known as the Army Book of Declarations and formally as *A declaration of the engagements, remonstrances, representations, proposals, desires and resolutions from His Excellency Sir Tho: Fairfax, and the generall council of the Army*, pp. 17–21 (Wing / F152A).

[8] Woolrych, *Soldiers and Statesmen*, p. 93 fn. 7. For the Declaration: *The declaration of the armie under His Excellency Sir Thomas Fairfax, as it was lately presented at Saffron-Walden in Essex* (Wing / D642A; Thomason / E390[26]). ESTC incorrectly dates it 30 March, but Thomason dates receiving it on 4 June.

[9] Worcester College, Oxford, Clarke MS 41, fo. 105.

[10] Charles Fleetwood, appointed Lord Fleetwood under the Protectorate (*c*.1618–92), army officer. See *ODNB*.

20 MAY 1647B

themselves and the ther rest of the Officers in the Army and members of that House lately sent downe to the Army whose names are subscribed

Agreed upon and sign'd by them all at Walden[11] May 20th: 1647.

1. That according to the appointment (whereof wee have formerly given Accompt) the Officers mett here againe on Satturday last to returne an Accompt of their proceedings and successes in communicating the Votes and improving the same together with their utmost Interest and power for the satisfaction of the Souldiers and quieting of all distempers as also to give a full Accompt of the temper of the Army in relation to the late discontents appearing therein.

2. That on Sunday Evening wee received a Summarie Accompt in writing agreed upon and signed by about 24 [—] of the Officers and presented to Us by some of the cheife in the name and presence of the rest of the Subscribers which wee have now sent upp.

3. That at the same time from the 8 Regiments of Horse and 8 of Foot now lying within the association the severall Cheife Officers present for the respective Regiments gave Us Accompt by word of Mouth all of them to this effect, That they had Communicated the Votes and done their endeavours according to order and doe find their Souldiers very quiet and in noe visible distemper at present, but having divers greivances sticking upon them which (they said) were contained in the respective papers then given in by them, and all of them did also expressly declare, That the effect and substance of those their Greivances was contain'd in the said Summary then given in except only those Officers whose distinct returns for their severall Charges given to Us in writing are these following which wee have likewise sent upp. Vizt.

    1. One from three Officers of Collonell Lilburnes[12] Regiment for the remaining soldiers of their three Companies only.

    2. One from the Feild Officers and 5 Captaines of the Generalls Regiment of Foote.

    3. One from Captaine Hall[13] for the Life Guard.

---

[11] = Saffron Walden, Essex.

[12] Robert Lilburne (bap. 1614, d. 1665), regicide and deputy major general. See *ODNB*.

[13] Captain Henry Hall, Lord General's lifeguard, see Firth and Davies, *Regimental History*, 1:47–8 and Wanklyn, *Reconstructing*, 1:64, 75, 84.

THE LETTERS, WRITINGS, AND SPEECHES OF OLIVER CROMWELL

4. One from Collonell Sheffeild,[14] his Major[15] and two Captaines.[16]

To that from the Generalls Regiment there was exception made by three Captaines and some other Officers of that Regimt: as also by 7 Souldiers chosen and intrusted by their fellowes of 7 Companies, who declar'd their greivances to be as in the Summarie and have given in a Paper to that purpose which wee have also sent upp.

To that from Collonell Sheffeild there was Exception made by Captaine Rainborrow,[17] and Captaine Evelyn's Lieutennant[18] for their respective Troopes, and by private Soldiers for other Troopes of that Regiment Chosen and intrusted by their fellowes, who brought the hands of all the Souldiers of the Regiment to attest their greivances which (because contain'd (for substance) within the Summarie, wee doe not trouble the House withall) Colonell Sheffeild Repli'd, That hee knew of noe such thing while he staid with that Regiment but the other averr'd it was publiquely agreed on upon the Randezvous after hee was gone.

That wee received also in writing other distinct Accts: from some Officers of Horse and Dragoones lying out of the Association Vizt.

One from two Lieutennants, two Cornetts & a Quarter Master
of Collonel Graves's[19] Regiment.
One from the Major and two Captaines of Dragoones
of the three troopes lying about Holdenby.[20]

---

[14] For Thomas Sheffeild, see Firth and Davies, *Regimental History*, 1:47–8. For his role as leader of those willing to go along with Parliament's plan for disbandment and enlistment for Ireland, see Woolrych, *Soldiers and Statesmen*, pp. 8–93.

[15] Major Richard Fincher (see Wanklyn, *Reconstructing*, 1:82 who also records that Fincher was replaced in June by Oliver Cromwell's younger son Henry).

[16] Captains Gabriel Martin and Robert Robotham. There were two other captains, but one—Arthur Evelyn—was absent, being simultaneously governor of Wallingford, and the other, William Rainborowe, protested at this representation of the regimental position (see below at n. 16 and for all the captains in May 1647 see Wanklyn, *Reconstructing*, 1:82).

[17] William Rainborowe [Rainsborough] (*fl.* 1639–73), parliamentarian army officer and Leveller. See *ODNB*.

[18] Almost certainly this was Stephen Whitehead, a lieutenant who took over Evelyn's troop just two weeks later (Wanklyn, *Reconstructing*, 1:82).

[19] For Colonel Richard Graves, a key ally of Holles in the Army (which is why he commanded the guard over Charles I at Holdenby at this time), see Firth and Davies, *Regimental History*, 1:102–5, 114–15, 163–5; Woolrych, *Soldiers and Statesmen*, 28–9, 41–2, 109–11, 135–6. For a full list of the junior officers in this regiment at the time, see Wanklyn, *Reconstructing*, 1:84, 126–7.

[20] Holdenby [or Holmby] House, Northampton. For the junior officers in Okey's regiment of dragoons, who had been split been duties in Northamptonshire and Shropshire, see Wanklyn, *Reconstructing*, 1:81, 120–1.

20 MAY 1647B

One from two other Captaines of Dragoones for their
two Troopes lying in Shroppshire.

But wee find that these Accompts were made by the respective Officers without the imediate privitie of all their ~~Offic~~ Soldiers or the other Officers and Troopes of the same Regiments, and that they had not since the former meeting here had time to draw out their Troopes from the rest of those Regiments to acquaint them fully with the votes, or gaine a certaine Accompt of them the great distance of all from those of their Quarters not admitting itt to be soe done within the time and therefore wee have given order that the Votes together with what is since added of the Arreares be effectually communicated to them all and a certaine Accompt to be returned from each as soone as may be

5. That from Sir Robert Pies[21] Regiment of Horse (we suppose for the same Reason) we have had noe returne from any Officer yet appearing nor doe we yet heare whether they have received the Votes. The copie whereof for them was (in defect of any Officer of that Regiment at the first meeting) delivered to an Officer of Collonell Graves's Troope for both those Regiments:

6. Wee have also received some other Papers which at present wee thought not necessary to trouble the House withall.

7. That on Monday another Paper was delivered to Us by Lieutennant Collonell Jackson[22] subscribed by himselfe and other officers that discented from the rest to cleere themselves from mistake or misapprehensions in their said discenting which wee have likewise sent.

8. That since the said Generall meeting the Officers (who by consent of the rest had subscribed it) drew up and perfected the Summary have shew'd us, and we have read over.

    1. The particular returnes in writing from the 8 Regiments of Horse and 8 of Foot

       lying in the association out of which the Summarie was extracte

    2. A Request of them in writing sign'd by the

       Officers that brought in the same unto them, desireing

       that they would take the paines to frame and

---

[21] Sir Robert Pye, (c.1622–1701), army officer. See *ODNB*. For a full list of the junior officers in this regiment at the time, see Wanklyn, *Reconstructing*, 1:83.

[22] Lt. Col. Thomas Jackson of Fairfax's own regiment of foot and day-to-day commander of the regiment. Firth and Davies, *Regimental History*, 2:319–21; Woolrych, *Soldiers and Statesmen*, pp. 52, 87–9, 93, 98, 102–5.

perfect the said Summary.

By all which wee find.

1. That those Officers had good ground for what they did in the Summary, the said particular returnes of greivances being full to the heads of the Summary, and many of them exceeding.

2. That whereas many of them for matter or expressions were brought Confused and full of Toutologies Impertinencies, or weaknesses Answerable to Soldiers dialect, they drew the matter of them into some more forme more fitt for view or Judgment.

3. That whereas many of them for matter or expressions were such as might have given greater offence they did by their perswasions with the Inferiour Officers and Souldiers that came with them (intrusted for the rest) bring them to lay aside many more offencive things, and to be satisfied in the heads of the Summarie and therein endeavoured to bring them as Low and to as much moderation as they could.

4. That their end and Reason for going in that method and undertakeing the Summarie seemes (most probably) to be to gaine the precedent effects and to avoid further offence to the Parliament, soe as the Armies tendernesse towards the authoritie & prviledges of the Parliament, and the Parliaments favourable Construction and consideration of the Army might seeme to remove all discontents and prevent any more inconveniencie.

5. That the Officers thus Joyning with the Souldiers againe in a regular way to make knowne and give vent to their greivances hath contributed much to allay precedent distempers to bring off the Souldrs much from their late wayes of Correspondencie and actings amongst themselves, and reduce them againe towards a right order and regard to their Officers in what they doe.

6. That the said severall Returnes doe generally expresse a pationate sense of the scandall concerning the Petition to the King protesting against the thing and the appearance of it amongst them in a great detestation thereof and importunitie for their Clearing therein.

    1. the same particular returnes themselves the said Officers that shew'd them to us desir'd they might keep both for their owne Justification in what they had done and especially because the Officers and Souldiers that brought them being all satisfied in the Summary.

    2. It was their owne request the particular papers might not be produced in [publique to discover the weaknesses or Rashnesse of those that sent them which they are very sensible of.

21 MAY 1647

3. The Officers therefore conceiv'd it might be better (if the Parliament pleas'd) to take noe notice of them.

9. [23] that though (in the charge to the Officers at their first meeting) wee exprest not nor did intend to expect to have any such Returnes of Greivances, but only an Accompt of what effect the Votes with the Officers endeavour's had for quieting of distempers, and to Knowe what distempers had been or should remaine to the End, wee might the better understand how to apply our selves to pay them, and give the better Accompt to the House, Yet now upon the whole matter wee humbly conceive That the way it hath falne into, the Course taken by the said Officers and (admitted by Us (being all upon a Kind of necessitie) as providence hath cast it for preventing of worse) hath hitherto proved for the best, and may (through the goodnesse of God with the Wisedome of the Parliament) be turn'd to a good Issue.

10. Lastly. That what hath been publiquely said or done by Us in the transacting or prosecution of this great affaire hath been with the advice and unanimous consent or with the aloowance and approbation of Us all. All which wee humbly submitt to the Parliaments better Judgment with the good pleasure of God: Phillipp Skippon[24] Oliver Cromwell H. Ireton[25] Charles Fleetwood.[26] May: 20: 1647.

1647 05 21

Speech by Oliver Cromwell to the House of Commons

Date: 21 May 1647
Source: See [A] and [B] below (reported speech)

Following the previous day's meeting at Saffron Walden, Cromwell and Fleetwood returned to London to report on their discussions with the soldiers. On the afternoon of 21 May Cromwell addressed the Commons.

---

[23] A clerical error by Clarke: [7] and [8] are not used. Perhaps two items had been removed by the commissioners from the list delivered by Lambert and Whalley to the Council of Officers?

[24] Philip Skippon, appointed Lord Skippon under the Protectorate (d. 1660), parliamentarian army officer and politician. See *ODNB*.

[25] Henry Ireton (bap. 1611, d. 1651), parliamentarian army officer and regicide. See *ODNB*.

[26] Charles Fleetwood, appointed Lord Fleetwood under the Protectorate (c.1618–92), army officer. See *ODNB*.

[A] BL, Add. MS 10114, fo. 24v, Diary of John Harington. Printed in Diary of John Harington, p. 53.

Cromwell & Fleetwood bring a larg report from the army that al now were quiet but complain of many greveances only, Cap: He: Hall[1] fully acquiest in the Parlt he & those of the life guard.

[B] BL, Add. MS 31116, fos 310–310v, Diary of Laurence Whitaker

This day a report was made by Lieut: Gen: Cromwell from the Army Lyeing in & nere unto Safforne Walden, in which report diverse papers were read Signed by diverse Officers of the Army Containing the Resolucon of the greatest part of theire Regimts wherein they dessiered before theire disbanding an Ordin: to be passed for theire Indempnity for wt they had done in tyme of warr, Allso a Considerable part of theire arreares to be pd them, & a discharge from being pressed to goe Out of the Kingdome

Outcome: The Commons responded by thanking Skippon, Cromwell, Ireton and Fleetwood. It then addressed some of the soldiers' grievances by resolving that their accounts should be audited without delay, that a bill be introduced to allow apprentices who had served in the parliamentarian armies to seek appointments as freemen, that no soldier who had volunteered should be compelled to serve abroad and that a bill be introduced for the relief of maimed soldiers, widows and orphans.[2]

---

[1] Captain Henry Hall. He left the Army in June 1647 and was replaced as a captain in Ireton's lifeguard by Cromwell's eldest surviving son Richard Cromwell (Wanklyn, *Reconstructing*, 1:84. See also 1:64, 75, 142).

[2] JHC, 5:181.

10 JUNE 1647

1647 06 10

Letter from Sir Thomas Fairfax and other officers to the lord mayor, aldermen and common council of the city of London

Date: 10 June 1647
Source: *JHL*, 9:257 (print copy)

This letter from thirteen officers in the New Model—pretty much the leading radicals[1]—to the governors of London survives in a copy in the House of Lords Record Office. It is undated and its reading in the Lords on 11 June 1646 was not the date of composition. Cromwell's name appears immediately under Fairfax's and alongside Ireton's. There must be a strong chance that these two had a major hand in its composition, but nothing more than that can be established about Cromwell's role in its composition. Its very mild language about religion might indeed point elsewhere.

This 'letter', conciliatory but only to a point, was a salvo by the New Model against the leaders of London who were fully behind the disbandment of the bulk of the New Model, the remodelling of the London trained bands through a purge of 'Independents', and the creation of a broad coalition of interests to force through a 'Presbyterian' settlement in church and state. The lord mayor was fully engaged with this 'counter-revolution'. On 8 June he and his colleagues petitioned the Commons repeating a demand that the New Model be disbanded, that they be allowed to recruit additional troops, principally cavalry, to protect the City and for the King to be brought to a place convenient for both the Scottish and English Parliaments. But immediately their plans began to unravel with the refusal of most of the trained bands to serve under new officers, and the Army's friends began to weaken the control of its enemies. Meanwhile, with the King now in the hands of the Army after his removal by force from Holdenby on 4 June, the Army Council met in emergency session and decided to move closer to London—to Royston on 10 June and St Albans on 12 June. And it was from Royston that the calm, polite and unflinching letter was despatched sometime on 10 June. They denied having an agenda beyond security in their just rights as soldiers, but they left the Corporation in no doubt that they would meet force with force. When, the day after receiving this letter, the mayor called out the trained bands and the hastily conscripted 'Reformadoes' and when he ordered all the City's shops to close, he met with widespread resistance. The bands refused to turn out, and almost all the shops stayed open. The Army had won this round of the cold war and on 14 June it

---

[1] The captain general, two lieutenant generals (Cromwell and Thomas Hammond) and the commissary general (Ireton) but not the sergeant major general and head of the infantry (Skippon); seven of the twenty-four colonels plus two majors (Disbrowe, major in Fairfax's own regiment of horse) and Pride (major in the regiment whose colonel, Edward Harley, had just resigned or was about to do so).

399

THE LETTERS, WRITINGS, AND SPEECHES OF OLIVER CROMWELL

moved on to the next stage of its politicisation with the promulgation of the Solemn Engagement of the Army. As it entered St Albans, the Army crossed a Rubicon.[2]

Right Honourable and Worthy Friends, Having, by our Letters and other Addresses, presented by our General to the Honourable House of Commons, endeavoured to give Satisfaction of the Clearness of our just Demands, and also in Papers published by us remonstrated the Grounds of our Proceedings in Prosecution thereof; all which having been exposed to Public View (we are confident) have come to your Hands, and at the least received a charitable Construction from you: The Sum of all which our Desires, as Soldiers, are no other than a Desire of Satisfaction to our Demands as Soldiers, and Reparation upon those who have to the uttermost improved all Opportunities and Advantages, by false Suggestions, Misrepresentations, and otherwise, for the Destruction of this Army, with a perpetual Blot of Ignominy upon it; which we should not value if it singly concerned our own Particulars, being ready to deny ourselves in this, as we have done in other Cases, for the Kingdom's Good. But, under this Pretence, finding no less involved in it than the Overthrow of the Privileges both of Parliament and People, wherein rather than they shall fail in their Designs, or we receive what in the Eyes of all good Men is just, endeavour to engage the Kingdom in a new War, and this singly by those who, when the Truth of these Things shall be made to appear, will be found the Authors of those Evils that are feared, as having no other Way to protect themselves from Question and Punishment but by putting the Kingdom into Blood, under Pretence of the Honour of and their Love to the Parliament, as if that were dearer to them than us, or as if they had given greater Proof of their Faithfulness to it than we. But we perceive that, under these Veils and Pretences, they seek to interest their Design in the City of London, as if that City ought to make good their Miscarriages, and should prefer a few self-seeking Men before the Welfare of the Public: And indeed we have found these Men so active to accomplish their Designs, and to have such apt Instruments for their Turn in that City, that we have Cause to suspect they may engage many therein upon Mistakes, which are easily swallowed in Times of such Prejudice, against Men that have given (we may speak it without Vanity) the most Public Testimony of their good Affection to the Public, and to that City in Particular.

For the Things we insist upon as *Englishmen*, and surely our being Soldiers hath not stripped us of that Interest, although our malicious Enemies would have it so;

[2] For this battle of wills in early June, see any of Valerie Pearl, 'London's Counter-Revolution' in Gerald Aylmer, ed., *The Interregnum: the quest for settlement 1646–1660* (1972), pp. 29–56, esp. pp. 44–9; Woolrych, *Soldiers and Statesmen*, pp. 122–7; and Ian Gentles, *The New Model Army*, pp. 169–74.

400

10 JUNE 1647

we desire a Settlement of the Peace of the Kingdom, and of the Liberties of the Subject, according to the Votes and Declarations of Parliament, which, before we took up Arms, were by the Parliament used as Arguments and Inducements to invite us and divers of our dear Friends out (some of which have lost their Lives in this War); which being by God's Blessing finished, we think we have as much Right to demand and desire to see a happy Settlement, as we have to our Money, or the other common Interest of Soldiers which we have insisted upon. We find also the ingenuous and honest People, in almost all the Parts of the Kingdom where we come, full of the Sense of Ruin and Misery, if the Army should be disbanded before the Peace of the Kingdom and those other Things before mentioned have a full and perfect Settlement. We have said before, and professed now, we desire no Alteration of the Civil Government; we desire not to intermeddle with, or in the least to interrupt, the Settling of the Presbyterian Government, nor do we seek to open a Way to licentious Liberty, under Pretence of obtaining Ease for tender Consciences: We profess (as ever) in these Things (when the State has once made a Settlement) we have nothing to say, but submit or suffer. Only we could wish that every good Citizen, and every Man that walks peaceably in a blameless Conversation, and is beneficial to the Commonwealth, may have Liberties and Encouragements; it being according to the just Policy of all States, even to Justice itself. These in brief are our Desires, and the Things for which we stand; beyond which we shall not go: And, for the obtaining these Things, we are drawing near your City; professing sincerely from our Hearts, we intend not Evil towards you; declaring with all Confidence and Assurance, that, if you appear not against us in these our just Desires, to assist that wicked Party that would embroil us and the Kingdom, nor we nor our Soldiers shall give you the least Offence. We come not to do any Act to prejudice the Being of Parliaments, or to the Hurt of this in order to the present Settlement of the Kingdom. We seek the Good of all; and we shall here wait, or remove to a further Distance, there to abide (if once we be assured that speedy Settlement of Things be in Hand) until they be accomplished; which done, we shall be most ready, either all of us or so many of the Army as the Parliament shall think fit, to disband or go for Ireland. And although you may suppose that rich City may seem an enticing Bait to poor hungry Soldiers, to venture for to get the Wealth thereof, yet, if not provoked by you, we do profess, rather than any such Evil should fall out, the Soldiers shall make their Way through our Blood to effect it. And we can say this for most of them, for your better Assurance, that they so little value their Pay in comparison of higher Concernments to a Public Good, that, rather than they will be unrighted in the Matter of their Honesty and Integrity, which has suffered by the Men they aim at

and desire Justice upon, or want the Settlement of the Kingdom's Peace, and theirs with their Fellow-subjects Liberties, they will lose all; which may be a strong Assurance to you, that it is not your Wealth they seek, but the Things tending in common to your and their Welfare; which that they may obtain, you shall do like Fellow-subjects and Brethren, if you solicit the Parliament for them, and on their Behalf. If, after all this, you, or a considerable Part of you, be seduced to take up Arms, in Opposition to, or Hindrance of, these our just Undertakings, we hope, by this brotherly Premonition, to the Sincerity whereof we call God to witness, we have freed ourselves from all that Ruin which may befal that great and populous City, having hereby washed our Hands thereof. We rest
Your affectionate Friends to serve you,

	Th. Fairefax.
H. Ireton	Oliv. Cromwell
Tho. Rainsborough	Ro. Hammond
J. Lambert	Tho. Hammond
	Rob. Lilburne
	Hardress Waller
Tho. Harrison	Nath. Rich
	Tho. Pride
	John Disbrowe[3]

Directed For the Right Honourable the Lord Mayor,[4] Aldermen and Common Council of the City of London These Haste

1647 06 25

Letter from Oliver Cromwell and John Hewson to Colonel Edward Whalley

Date: 25 June 1647
Source: Worcester College, Oxford, MS 2/7 (LXV), fo. 95r (contemporary copy)

There is a five-week gap between the last of Cromwell's reports as commissioner to the Army and this letter to Colonel Edward Whalley, who was now in charge of guarding the

---

[3] All signatories have entries in ODNB. And their position within the Army at this precise moment can be found in Wanklyn, *Reconstructing*, 1:76–84, a full regimental listing for 31 May 1647 (the only one not being included being Thomas Hammond, lieutenant general of ordinance 1645–9 and before that lieutenant general of ordinance in the army of the Eastern Association).
[4] The lord mayor for 1646–7 was John Gayer (bap. 1584, d. 1649), merchant. See ODNB. Gayer was a member of the Fishmongers Company and heavily engaged in long-distance trading companies.

25 JUNE 1647

King after his 'liberation' from Holdenby House by Cornet Joyce[1] on 3 June, which Cromwell may or not have instigated or at least approved. He had remained in London and Westminster from 21 May to 3 June. Alerted to the fact that the Presbyterians intended to charge him with instigating the seizure of the King, he left London late on 4 June and by stages had moved between Army quarters at Kentford and Newmarket (Suffolk), then Cambridge (6–9 June) and then Royston, St Albans and Berkhamsted (Hertfordshire) before returning to Westminster at the end of the month. He also (with Fairfax) had his first personal interview with the King near Cambridge on 7 June. The seizure of the King triggered a much more general revolt in the Army against the attempts of Parliament to disband most of the regiments of the Army not destined for Ireland.

These were also weeks during which the Army became much more politicised, calling for early elections on a revised franchise and with a redistribution of seats, the Army calling itself 'not a mere mercenary army'.[2] They also demanded that eleven MPs who were seen as responsible for the botched plan to disband the Army without addressing its legitimate demands should be suspended from the House. In early June, the General Council of the Army was set up (consisting of the General Officers and two agitators or adjutators representing junior officers [majors, captains, lieutenants, ensigns, cornets, quartermasters etc.] and two representing the rank and file of each regiment).[3]

The specific context of this letter was the refusal of the Army to move the King to Richmond and to remove itself to at least 40 miles from London: in fact, it moved its headquarters to Uxbridge. In a small climbdown on 24 June, the Commons wrote to the King, copying Fairfax into the correspondence, 'to desire him, for some time, to make a Stay at Royston, or to go to Newmarkett, as he shall think fit, in regard of some Things that are lately fallen out' (a rather unparliamentary euphemism).[4]

The letter from Cromwell and Hewson survives only as a copy in the fair-copy letter books of William Clarke. It is not at all clear why Cromwell, rather than Fairfax, wrote this letter, and what authority he had to write it. And it is very mysterious indeed why it was co-signed by John Hewson.[5]

---

[1] George Joyce (b. 1618), parliamentarian army officer. See *ODNB*. This contains an admirably clear explanation of what *probably* happened when Joyce met Cromwell ahead of his expedition to Holdenby. The next most authoritative analysis of this episode is in Woolrych, *Soldiers and Statesmen*, pp. 106–15.

[2] The key documents are gathered in *A declaration of the Engagements, Remonstrances, Desires and Resolutions from Sir Thomas Fairfax and the General Council of the Army* (1647) (Wing / F152A), discussed in Woolrych, *Soldiers and Statesmen*, ch. V.

[3] Woolrych, *Soldiers and Statesmen*, pp. 118–20.

[4] *JHC*, 5:222 (24 June 1647).

[5] John Hewson, appointed Lord Hewson under the Protectorate (*fl.* 1630–60). See *ODNB*. He had been promoted to command his own regiment in December 1645 and had been one of those chosen by the General Council to present the Army's charges against the eleven Presbyterian members.

THE LETTERS, WRITINGS, AND SPEECHES OF OLIVER CROMWELL

[fo. 95r]

Letter to Collonell Whalley[6] from Barkhamsted

Sir

Having received Yesterdayes Vote from the House which putts the Comrs into the same Capacitie that they were at Holdenby,[7] we hold you free of all further charge save to looke to your Guards that his Majestie make noe escape, and therein you must be carefull and more now then ever. Dor. Hammond and the other of his Majestys Chaplaines[8] (soe much desired) went through this Towne this morning coming towards you, perhapps the Commissionrs will putt you upon it to keepe them from the King soe you are exact only in faithfullnesse to your trust, and that dureing that only, for now you can be as civill as some others that pretend to be more, Lett such distrustfull Carriages be provided for by those Gent who perhapps will incurre some difficulty in the way wherein you have been faulted, we Commend our selves kindly unto you and rest your affectionate freinds & servants

Oliver Cromwell

John Hewson

June: 25: 1647.

---

[6] Edward Whalley, appointed Lord Whalley under the Protectorate (d. 1674/5). See *ODNB*. His second wife was Cromwell's cousin. He had been a major and then lieutenant colonel in Cromwell's own regiment of horse (1643–5) and in the New Model he commanded a regiment made up of veterans of that regiment. He was responsible for guarding the King from early June to mid-November, when the King escaped from Hampton Court. According to Christopher Durston in his life of Whalley in *ODNB*, 'throughout this time Whalley appears to have dealt with Charles with courtesy and fairness; for example, he refused to carry out orders from parliament to remove the king's chaplains without authorization from his commander, Thomas Fairfax.'

[7] It is not clear what this refers to. The nearest thing in the *Journal of the House of Commons* for 24 June, is an order for the commissioners with the King to be told of the letter sent to him inviting him to choose between Royston and Newmarket as a place to stay and advising the commissioners 'that they do observe their Instructions, concerning such Persons as are not to be admitted to have Access to the King'. *JHC*, 5:221–2.

[8] Dr Henry Hammond, (1605–60), Church of England clergyman and theologian. See *ODNB*. The other chaplain was Gilbert Sheldon (1598–1677), archbishop of Canterbury (1663–77). See *ODNB*. Throughout his time with the Scots and then under parliamentary control at Holdenby, Charles had been denied his own chaplains; but from the time of his seizure by the Army until his escape in November, he had the use of his own chaplains.

prethee be very carefull of the Kings secureing and although you have had some oppertunity of putting all upon others that's unacceptable, yet be never a whitt more remisse in your diligence.

1647 06 29

Warrant from Thomas Grey, Oliver Cromwell, Henry Mildmay, Denis Bond, William Ashhurst, F Rous, Thomas Hoyle to Thomas Fauconbridge, receiver general of the revenue

Date: 29 June 1647
Source: BL, RP4986(i) (autograph)

This is a sample of the warrants on which Cromwell was frequently a co-signatory in this case for payment out the sequestered royal revenues to a garrison commander. The transcript is of a photocopy in the British Library after the original had been sold with an export licence and is currently inaccessible. All signatories had been strong war-party men in 1642–6 but some were now distancing themselves from the Army as its confrontation with the Army escalated. The recipient, Thomas Fauconbridge, was receiver general of the revenue from the King's estates. A 'Thomas Fauconbridge of Westminster' was nominated as one of the elders for the eleventh classis of the London Province on 26 September 1646 where he is named as an enforcing elder in the Ordinance regulating exclusion from holy communion.[1]

By vertue of an Ordinance of both Houses of Parliamt: of the xxi[th] day of September 1643;[2] Theis are to will and require you Out of Such Treasure, as now is, or shall be remaining in your hands, to pay unto Captain Thomas Betsworth,[3] Captain of Calshott Castle, & St. Andrewes Pointe[4] the Somme of One hundred Thirtie five pounds, Sixteene shillings, & three pence, for the wages of himselfe,

---

[1] A&O, I:870–4; cf. ibid., 78–94.
[2] An Ordinance for the sequestration of all revenues of the King, Queen, and Prince, in England and Wales, and Berwick-upon-Tweed, with provisions for sequestering any of the Royal officers who may refuse obedience to this Ordinance. JHL, 6:227–9, A&O, I: 299–302.
[3] Not traced.
[4] Calshot Castle (Hampshire) had been one of Henry VIII's device forts, built on Calshot Spit on the Solent near Fawley to guard the entrance to Southampton Water. The garrison was not in the list of those being disbanded at this time, and indeed it was only a year later (25 July 1647: JHC, 5:648), that it was folded into the Southampton garrison.

& the Officers & Souldiers there, according to the Old Establishment for one halfe yeare ended at Midsummer last past 1647. And for So doing This togeather with his Acquittance, for the Receipt thereof, Shall be your Warrant & discharge; And also to the Auditor generall to allow the Same in your Accompt. Dated at the Committee of Lords & Commons for his Maties: Revenew, sitting at Westminster the xxix[th] day of June 1647.

Thomas Grey[5] Oliver Cromwell Hen: Mildmay[6] Denis Bond[7] W Ashhurst[8] F Rous[9] Thomas Hoyle[10] Jnr[11]

To our very loving freind Thomas Fauconbridge Esqr Receivor generall of the Revenew

5 Capt: Betsworth.[12]

1647 07 12
Conversation between Oliver Cromwell and Sir John Berkeley

Date: 12 July 1647
Source: BL, Add. MS 29689, fos 4r–4v (reported speech)

Sir John Berkeley was a veteran diplomat and royalist soldier.[1] He had been sent as an ambassador to Queen Christina of Sweden in 1637–8 to regain Swedish support for the return of the Palatinate to Charles's nephew as part of any peace settlement. He had served throughout the First Civil War in the West Country, latterly as governor of Exeter, and he

---

[5] Thomas Grey, Baron Grey of Groby (1622–57), regicide. See *ODNB*.
[6] Henry Mildmay (*c.*1594–1664/5?), politician and courtier. See *ODNB*.
[7] Denis Bond (1588–1658), merchant and politician. See *ODNB*.
[8] William Ashhurst (bap. 1607, d. 1656), politician. See *ODNB*.
[9] Francis Rous (1580/81–1659), religious writer and politician. See *ODNB*.
[10] Thomas Hoyle (bap. 1587, d. 1650), politician. See *ODNB*.
[11] The last four names are written on the same line left to right. The first three are written vertically, with Grey's name somewhat to the right.
[12] An unexplained (and inexplicable) addition, with an unattached number '5'. Thomas Bettesworth had been captain in Richard Norton's horse regiment in 1643 and in autumn 1644 took part in the siege of Winchester and the second battle of Newbury. He later served under Massey in the Western Association and as a colonel in the Hampshire trained bands: Spring, *Waller's Army*, p. 110 and the *Online Directory of Parliamentarian Army Officers*.

---

[1] John Berkeley, first Baron Berkeley of Stratton (bap. 1607, d. 1678), royalist army officer and courtier. See *ODNB*.

12 JULY 1647

had earned the respect of Parliament's generals by his conduct. At the end of the war he left England for Paris and the household of Henrietta Maria. She in turn, believing him to be someone who could help Charles work out a deal with New Model generals, sent him back to England in July 1647. He was to be one of Charles's closest advisors (not that Charles accepted his advice) in the period down to the King's escape from Windsor and flight to the Isle of Wight in November 1647. Ahead of him lay a long career in royal service after the Restoration, but these months of July to November 1647 were when he was most aware of the *arcana imperii* and twenty years after his death his account of this period was printed.

However, we can be reasonably sure that it was written fairly soon after the events it describes. In April 1651, the secretary of state to the exiled Charles II, Sir Edward Nicholas, wrote to his fellow exile Lord Hatton asking him 'pray to get a sight of Sir John Berkley's relation of that unhappy business of the King's going to the Isle of Wight...I am told that Sir John Berkley intends to print that his relation.'[2] In fact it was not printed until 1699 at the same time as so many memoirs from the 1640s and 1650s, not least the memoirs of Edmund Ludlowe,[3] which drew heavily on Berkeley's memoir. The letter from Nicholas to Hatton makes it clear that *a* version of Berkeley's account of his time with the King in the second half of 1647 existed in manuscript no later than April 1651. Two manuscripts in mid-seventeenth-century hands survive, and both in general and more particularly for the conversations extracted here as **1647 07 12** and **1647 07 15** they differ very little one from another. The one used here, from the British Library, is marginally more likely to be closer to an original.[4] The second version in Doctor Williams Library is annotated to say that one of the owners was given it in 1662 or 1663 in Geneva.[5] The version printed in 1699[6] may have been a version of one of these two, or of a lost further manuscript. Thus there are strong grounds for believing that Berkeley committed his account to paper within three years of the events he describes but we do not know whether he based his accounts of private conversations on notes he took at the time or just from memory.

It is very striking that as the Army leaders began to plan their own peace proposals, it was they who approached Berkeley, just arrived with the King at Caversham, just across

---

[2] G. F. Warner, ed., *The Nicholas Papers: The Correspondence of Sir Edward Nicholas*, 4 vols. (Camden Society, n.s., 40, 50, 57 and 3rd series, 32, 1886–1920), pp. 1, 233.

[3] *Memoirs of Lieutenant General Ludlow. with a collection of original papers serving to confirm and illustrate many important passages of this and the preceding volumes: to which is added, a table to the whole work* (printed at Vevay in the Canton of Bern [Switzerland], 1699) (Wing / L3462).

[4] This version is untitled.

[5] DWL, Morrice MS D, pp. 9–52; and entitled 'Narrative of the transcribers of Sir John Berkley, formerly Governor of Exeter, in the affairs of King Charles I, from the time when he was sent by the Queen from France into England, to the King's attempted escape from the Isle of Wight; written by himself'. See the discussion of provenance in J. S. A. Adamson, 'The English Nobility and the Projected Settlement of 1647', *The Historical Journal*, 30 (1987), pp. 567–602 at p. 577 n.73.

[6] *MEMOIRS of Sir John Berkley Containing an Account of his NEGOTIATION WITH Lieutenant General CROMWEL, Commissary General IRETON, And other Officers of the Army, For Restoring King CHARLES the First to the Exercise of the Government of England* (London, 1699). This conversation appears at p. 16.

the Thames from Reading, on 12 July 1647. The King had declined to meet the Army leaders in person and expressed a willingness to accept Parliament's request that he move to Richmond, something strongly opposed by the Army. This defiance might make the reader cautious about accepting the sincerity of Cromwell's reported words.[7] At any rate, according to Berkeley, 'Two or three hours after my arrival Cromwell sent an Officer to excuse him to me, that he could not wait on me untill ten at night, by reason he was sitting with the Committee of Parliamt,[8] and should not rise till then. He came then accompanyed with Rainsbrough and Sir Hardress Waller: After general discourse I told him the sum of my Instructions from the Queen and Prince, which were to assure them that Her Ma^ty and His Highness were not partiall to the Presbyterians, nor no way averse to them, that I should endeavour to incline His Ma^ty to comply with them, as far as would stand with his Honor and Conscience, and to dispose them to press His Ma^ty no further: His Answer was in these words...'[9]

[NB: There are open quotation marks at the very beginning. Thereafter every line except the last (which is, of course, Berekley's gloss, has open quotation marks at the beginning.]

[fo. 4r.]

"That what ever the World might judge of them, they would be found no seek [fo. 4v] ers of themselves, further than to have leave to live as Subjects ought to do, and to preserve their Consciences; that they thought no men could ~~could~~ enjoy their Lives and Estates Quietly with out the King had his Rights, wch. they had declared in general terms already to the World, and would more particularly very speedily, wherein they would comprize the severall Interests of the Royal, Presbyterian and Independent parties, as far as they were consisting with each other: Wch I understood afterwards to be meant of the Proposals of the Army.

---

[7] There has been very little discussion of Berkeley's part in the July negotiations. Gardiner, *GCW*, 3:316–20 is the fullest contextualisation of this and the following recorded conversation. But see also Austin Woolrych, *Soldiers and Statesmen: The General Council of the Army and its Debates 1647–1648* (1987), p. 153.

[8] i.e. a meeting with the parliamentary commissioners who were resident with the Army.

[9] BL, Add. MS 29689, fo. 4r.

15 JULY 1647

1647 07 15

Conversation between Oliver Cromwell and Sir John Berkeley

Date: 15 July 1647
Source: BL, Add. MS 29689, fo. 6r (reported speech)

This is a follow-up to Berkeley's account of his late-night meeting with Cromwell to open up lines of communication between the generals and a reluctant King. For an account of Berkeley's role in the events of July 1647 and the status of his memoirs as a reliable record, see **1647 07 12**.[1] Although Cromwell and Ireton were leading the charm offensive that would go along with the Heads of the Proposals that would reach their first full form very soon, Fairfax was fully apprised and sympathetic, and it was Fairfax who allowed the King access to his own chaplains, and who 'wrung from the reluctant House of Commons an order permitting him to receive a visit from those of his children who were still in the custody of Parliament (viz. James, Elizabeth, Henry). They spent two days with him at Caversham, and Cromwell was present for part of that time.[2] Berkeley's overall view of Cromwell at this point was that 'in all my Conferences with him I found no man in appearance so zealous for a speedy close[3] as he, sometimes wishing that the King were more frank, and would not tye himself so strictly to narrow Maxims, sometimes complaining of his Son[-in-law] Iretons slowness in perfecting the proposals, and his not accommodating more to his Maties sence, always doubting that the Army would not preserve their good Inclinations for the King' (fo. 6r).

He records meeting Cromwell in Reading as he returned from visiting Charles and his children at Caversham. This is what he remembers Cromwell as saying to him. We do not know how soon after the encounter he committed the words to paper.

[fo. 6r]

he told me that he had lately seen the tenderest sight that ever his Eyes beheld, wch was the Interview between the King and his Children, and wept plentifully at the remembrance of it, saying, that never man was so abused as he in his sinister opinions of the King, who he thought was the uprightest and the most conscientious of his three Kingdoms; that they of the Independant Party (as they were

---

[1] The essentially identical printed version of this conversation can be found in MEMOIRS of *Sir John Berkley Containing an Account of his NEGOTIATION WITH Lieutenant General CROMWEL, Commissary General IRETON, And other Officers of the Army, For Restoring King CHARLES the First to the Exercise of the Government of England* (London, 1699), pp. 27–8.

[2] Gardiner, GCW, 3:319.

[3] The 1699 printed version has 'blow' where the manuscript has 'close'—the only difference other than of spelling or capitilisation between them.

409

called) had infinite Obligations to him, for not consenting to the Scots Propositions in Newcastle, wch would have totally ruined them,[4] which His Ma[ties] Interest seemed to invite him unto, and concluded with me by wishing that God would be pleased to look upon him according to the sincerity of His heart to wards His Ma[ty].

1647 07 16
Oliver Cromwell's contributions to the New Model Army Debate at Reading

Date: 16 July 1647
Source: Worcester College, Oxford, Clarke Papers, vol. 65, fos 93r–105r (reported speeches)

This is William Clarke's transcription (fifteen years later) of the shorthand notes taken by stenographers at the debates of the General Council of the Army at Reading in Berkshire, 40 miles west of London on the river Thames. For some discussion of the status of Clarke's transcripts, see **1647 05 15**. Since the debates in mid-May in the church at Saffron Walden,[1] the Army had refused to disband as ordered by Parliament, more than a quarter of all the senior officers had resigned and left the Army,[2] the King had controversially been taken from Holdenby House by a detachment of troops headed by Cornet Joyce and brought to Army headquarters, and the Army had called for the impeachment of eleven 'incendiary' MPs—but their demand had been kicked into long grass. Indeed, a majority in the Commons was still in favour of using what force they could muster (including the London militia, and such demobilised forces as were congregated in London, lobbying for their arrears [the 'Reformadoes']) to face down dissidents in the New Model. The generals and their allies still hoped that pressure short of an occupation of London would lead to negotiations with the King that would secure the political and religious liberties so many in the Army believed they had fought for, and when these debates at Reading begin, Henry Ireton, John Lambert and others, perhaps in consultation with the commissioners of the

---

[4] Since in most respects the Army's Heads of the Proposals were more lenient than the Newcastle Propositions, this must be a reference to the religious articles – the Army proposing a fairly general liberty for tender consciences as against Parliament's demand for a confessional state with Presbyterianism replacing episcopacy. There is an admirably clear comparison of the main terms in each set of peace proposals 1642–8 in David L.Smith, 'The impact on government,' in John Morrill, ed., *The Impact of the English Civil War* (1991), p. 45.

[1] For the events of 16 May to 15 July, see Gentles, *New Model Army*, pp. 164–84, and Woolrych, *Soldiers and Statesmen*, pp. 91–167.
[2] For which see Kishlansky, *Rise of the New Model Army*, pp. 218–21.

16 JULY 1647

Parliament resident at Army headquarters, were drawing up the document which has come to be known as the Heads of the Proposals and which a week later would to be presented directly to the King and on 1 August would be presented to the Houses of Parliament. There had been a full (but unrecorded) discussion of the Heads at the Council of War on 14 July. When the account of the Reading debates begins two days later, Fairfax is presiding (apparently mutely) and Cromwell appears to be speaking for him and for the senior officers.

As with the other debates, this is a new edition from the original manuscripts and provides a summary of other speeches only. For Firth's eccentric edition of all the speeches, see *Clarke Papers*, 1:176–211.

[fo. 93v]

Att a General Council of War held at Reading 16 July 1647

Chaired by Lord General Thomas Fairfax. Fifty-one officers are listed as attending, but many others, including common soldiers, are recorded as speaking. Cromwell opens proceedings:

Lieutenant Generall Moved for a Committee, Many thinges then nott being fitt for debate, and the Councill of Warre to be adjourn'd till the afternoone.

This is followed by six speeches on whether to accept the proposals without further debate and whether the Army should march immediately on London in support of the proposals. There is dissent, which Cromwell answers:

[fo. 94r]

Lieutennt. General. Marching uppe to London is a single proposall yett itt does nott droppe from Jupiter as that itt should bee presently received & debated without considering our Reasons for I hope this[3] will ever bee in the Agitators. I would be very sorry to flatter them, I hope they will bee willing that nothing should bee done butt with the best Reason, and with the best & most unanimous concurrence and though wee have this desire back't with such reasons, Certainly itt was nott intended wee had noe reason to weigh those Reasons for I thinke wee shall bee left to weigh these Reasons. All this paper[4] is fill'd with Reason. The dissatisfaction in particulars, The dissadvantages of removall from London the advantages of marching towards London, you are ripe for a Conclusion, & get a Conclusion, but <u>lett</u> this bee offer'd to the Generall & the Councill of Warre.

Thomas Rainborow[5] calls for further deliberation, Henry Ireton countering that the Army must not be seen as proceeding simply from self-interest.

---

[3] Firth suggests 'this [temper] will ever' (*Clarke Papers*, 1:178).

[4] This is the 'Representation of the Agitators' printed in *Clarke Papers*, 1:170–3.

[5] Thomas Rainborowe [Rainborow] (d. 1648), parliamentarian army officer and Leveller. See *ODNB*.

411

THE LETTERS, WRITINGS, AND SPEECHES OF OLIVER CROMWELL

[fo. 94v]

Lieutenant. General. I desire wee may withdraw & Consider. Discourses of this nature will I see putt power into the Hands of any that cannot tell how to use itt, of those that are likely to use itt ill. I wish itt, with all my heart in better Hands, and I shall bee glad to contribute to gett itt into better Hands, and if any man or Companie of men will say that wee doe seeke our selves in doing this, Much good may't doe him with his thoughts. Itt shall not putt mee out of my way.

The Meeting att 6. a clock itt is nott to putt an End to this businesse of <u>meeting</u>,[6] butt I must consult with my self before I consent to such a thinge but really to doe such a thinge, before I doe itt,[7] and whereas the Commissary[8] does offer that these thinges were desired before satisfaction bee given to the publique settlement there may be a conveniencie ofbringing in that to the Councill of Warre next sitting if itt bee ready, & thought fit to bee brought in: If these other things bee in preparation wee may bringe them in, that wee may nott bee to seeke for a Councill of Warre if wee had our businesse ready.

After seven more speeches about the need for action against those opposing a just settlement, a committee of eighteen is appointed including three General Officers (including Cromwell but not Fairfax), nine colonels and six adjutators. Clarke's transcript resumes:

[fo. 96r]

Afternoone

Lieutenant.General. If you remember there are in your paper 5 particulars[9] that you insist uppon. Two of them are thinges new, That is to say, Thinges that yett have nott bin at all offer'd to the Parliament or their Commissioners, That is the 2^d and the 4th. The 2^d which concernes the Militia of the Citty, and the 4th, which concernes the Release of those prisoners that you have named in your paper and a Consideration to bee had concerning those that are imprisoned in the severall parts of the K.dome of whom likewise you desire a Consideration might bee had now the Judges are riding their circuites.

---

[6] Here and throughout Clarke's transcription of his shorthand, there are underlinings which appear to be in the same ink. These do not appear to be for emphasis and our sense is—and Frances Henderson, the great expert on Clarke's shorthand, has told us she agrees—that these underlinings represent uncertainty on Clarke's part that he was correctly reading the shorthand symbols. See **1647 07 16** n. 6.

[7] Firth here changes to 'before I do it, [I must consult] and whereas...' (*Clarke Papers*, 1:178).

[8] Henry Ireton (bap. 1611, d. 1651), parliamentarian army officer and regicide. See *ODNB*.

[9] The five are (1) the expulsion of the eleven 'incendiary' MPs; (2) the restoration of London militia to Independent control; (3) a declaration against the enlisting of foreign forces; (4) the release of John Lilburne and other 'political' prisoners; (5) guarantees that those who stayed in the Army would receive as much of their arrears as those who had deserted the Army in recent weeks ('Representation of the Agitators' printed in *Clarke Papers*, 1:170–3).

16 JULY 1647

To the first[10] [we give you] this Account, That uppon your former paper delivered,[11] & uppon the weight & necessity of the thinge there has bin a very serious care taken by the Generall, hee having, as I told you to day referr'd the preparing of somewhat concerning that for the parliament to Col:Lambert & myself and an Account of that has bin given to the Generall at our meeting in the inner Roome, and, if itt please you that which has bin in preparation may bee read together with the Reasons of itt. That paper that now itt is desired itt may be read to you, parte of itt an Answer to a former paper that was sent to the Comrs concerning the excluding of the Reformadoes out of the lines of Communication & the purging of the House of Commons, & the discharging or sending away into Ireland that men that had deserted the Army. The Generall did order a paper to that purpose to bee sent to the Comrs and that paper, that now is to bee read to you of a Reply to the Commrs; and there is an addition of this businesse concerning the Militia with the Reasons to inforce the Desire of itt.

At this point the paper entitled 'An answer of the Commissioners of the Army to the Paper of the Commissioners of Parliament about a speedy disbanding'.[12]

The Papers read

Lieutenant.General. Care taken of all them only two, which are concerning the suspending of the 11. Members & the discharging of prisoners. [fo. 96v] I am commanded by the Generall to lett you know in what state affaires stand betweene us & the Parliament and into what way all thinges are putt. Tis very true, That you urge in your papers concerning that Effect that an advancing towards London may have, & of some Suppos'd \in/Conveniences that our drawing back thus farre may bringe uppon us, butt I shall speake to that presently; our businesses they are putt into this way, and the State of our businesse is this, Wee are now indeavouring as the maine of our worke to make a preparation of somewhat that may tend to a General settlement of the peace of the K.dome and of the rights of the subject That Justice and Righteousnesse may peaceably flow out uppon us. Thatt's the maine of our businesse. These thinges are butt preparatory thinges to that that is the maine, and you soe remember very well that this that is the maine worke of all was brought to some ripenesse. The way that our businesse is in is this, For the redressing of all these thinges, itt[13] a Treaty, a Treaty

---

[10] At this point, Firth inserted three clarificatory words of his own: '[we give you]'.

[11] On the London militia 6 July.

[12] *A declaration of the engagements, remonstrances, representations, proposals, desires and resolutions from His Excellency Sir Tho: Fairfax* (September 1647), pp. 77–8 (Wing / F152A; Thomason / E.409[25]).

[13] *Clarke Papers*, 1:185 adds a word that improves the sense: 'itt [is] a Treaty'.

413

THE LETTERS, WRITINGS, AND SPEECHES OF OLIVER CROMWELL

with Commrs sent from the Parliament downe hither to the End that an happy issue may be putt to all these matters that soe much concerne the good of the K.dome, and therein our good is <u>soe</u> that they must bee finished in the way of a Treatie. The Truth of itt is you are all very reasonably sensible that if those thinges were nott removed that wee thinke may loose us the fruite of a Treaty and the fruite of all our labours; itt's in vaine to goe on with a Treaty, and its dangerous to bee deluded by a Treaty, and therefore I am confident of itt that least this inconveniencie should come to us lest there should come a second Warre, least wee should bee deluded by a longe Treatie your zeale hath bin stirr'd uppe to expresse in your paper that there is a necessity of a speedy marching towards London to accomplish all these thinges. Truly I thinke that possibly that may bee that that wee shall bee necessitated to doe[14] possibly itt may bee soe, butt yett I thinke itt will bee for our honour & our honesty to doe what wee can to accomplish this worke in the way of a Treaty, and if I were able to give you all those Reasons that lie in the Case I thinke itt would satisfie any rationall man heere for certainly that is the most desirable way and the other a way of necessity, and nott to be done butt in way of necessity, and Truly instead of all reasons lett this serve that whatsoever wee get by a Treaty, whatsoever comes to bee setled uppon us in that way itt will be firme & durable, itt will be firme and durable, itt will be conveyed over to posterity, as that that will bee the [fo. 97r] greatest honour to us that ever poore Creatures had that wee may obtaine such thinges as these are which wee are now about, and itt will have this in itt too that whatsoever is granted in that way itt will have firmenesse in itt. wee shall avoide that great objection that will lie against us that wee have gott thinges of the Parliament by force and we knowe what itt is to have that staine lie uppon us, Thinges though never soe good obtain'd in that way, itt will exceedingly weaken the thinges both to our selves & to all posteritie, and therefore I say uppon that Consideration I wish wee may bee well advis'd what to doe I speake nott this that I should perswade you to goe about to Cozen one another, itt was not in the Generall's, nor any of our hearts. That wee that are Commrs should bee very positive & peremptory to have these thinges immediately granted I beleive within the Compasse of that time which your papers mention within soe many dayes, & for the other two thinges that they yett take noe care of, Thats the Members impeached,[15] These are two additionall which will

[14] *Clarke Papers*, 1:185 adds words here: 'wee shall bee necessitated to doe [in the end] – possibly'.

[15] *Clarke Papers*, 1:186 adds '[and the prisoners]' here.

414

16 JULY 1647

bee likewise taken care of to be considered, and answered nott with words & votes butt with <u>content</u>[16] & action for there needes noe more of our representing of them then these papers that have bin read. In Effect there hath bin Consideration had of the matters in your papers & answer given by the way proposed, and if these bee not granted in a convenient time you are yett putt in such a way in taking such a course of <u>doing</u>[17] thinges as you \have/ proposed sooner then that wee could nott have putt ourselves into a posture of doing.[18]

I hope in God that if wee obtaine these thinges in this way wee propose to you & this convenient time that wee shall thinke our selves very happy that wee have nott gone any other way for the obtayning them that which wee seeke to avoide the having of a 2.^{d} warre and the defeating of those that are soe deare to us whose interest ought to be above our lives to us if wee finde any thinge tending that way to delay us or dissappoint us of those honest thinges wee are to insist uppon I hope itt cannott nor shall nott bee doubted that the Generall nor any of us will bee backward for the Accomplishment of those thinges wee have proposed. Itt remaines that you have some short Account as the time will beare of that that has bin soe longe in preparation which is that that tends to the Generall Settlement of that and the Generall hath Commanded the Commrs to let you have a brief State of that.

Captain John Clarke intervenes to stress the urgency of the situation, to oppose a treaty with the Parliament and for direct action.

[fo. 97v]

Lieutenant General. I may very easily mistake that which the other Officer offer'd to your Excy two particulars which might receive retardement or obstruction by carrying them on in a way of Treaties mention'd indeed particulars which were that of the 11.Members and that of the prisoners, and <u>means</u>[19] by those that should goe as the sence of the whole Army hee conceives itt will adde vigour & strength to the desire & make our Desires more easily granted. Present nott only those butt all the rest. If itt bee soe all the rest will bee obstructed if they goe by way of Treatie there may bee perhaps some mistake or in that which I offer'd to you. I thinke Truly there is noe objection lies in that which is said for soe farre as I know & discerne of these thinges & the way of management of them if wee convey to

---

[16] See **1647 07 16** n. 6.   [17] See **1647 07 16** n. 6.

[18] For whatever reason, Firth completely reorganises this paragraph, changing the emphasis and, in small ways, the meaning: *Clarke Papers*, 1:186.

[19] See **1647 07 16** n. 6.

the Comrs and by them to the parliament, as the sence of the whole represented by [fo. 98r] the Agitators to the Generall & assented to by the Councill of Warre and soe becomes the sence nott only of the Armie that is the offended partie butt alsoe the Commanding parte of itt, and wee represent itt to them with that positivenesse that hath bin spoken of to expect an answer within some few dayes, That is to say, soe fast as they can have itt consulted: wee may call this a Treaty butt I thinke itt signifies nothing else butt what that Gentleman speakes of to bee sent uppe to London, To which wee desire an Answer, and expect within soe short a time, and therfore for my parte I thinke they differ in nothing butt in words, and nott in substance. I suppose there are resolutions nott to enter uppon a further Treaty till wee have an answer to these thinges, and if you have patience to heare that which is offer'd you to be acquainted with from the Commissary General I suppose that businesse may bee soe disposed of as that it may bee seene to all the world that itt is an effectuall meanes to procure these thinges to bee granted as marching to London would doe.[20] Therefore I shall desire that if itt please the Generall that the Commissary Generall may by you have an Account of that other businesse.

William Allen,[21] trooper-agitator for Cromwell's own regiment, then intervened, firmly if reverently expressing deep scepticism about the trustworthiness of those Cromwell wishes still to treat with, and calling for an immediate march on London.

[fo. 98v]

Lieutenant.General. If that that I say of the Treaty bee applyed to one thinge which I meane of another then there may happily bee a very great missunderstanding of mee, butt that which I speake of Treaty that relates to those thinges that are prepared for a generall settlement of the K.dome bee applyed to the obtayning of these thinges which are to precede a Treaty is that I have said to you hath bin mistaken throughout and instead of giving mee Satisfaction of that point which stickes on soe with every one of danger & delay butt that which I say of Treatie in answer to that in is offer'd in your paper that wee should obtaine these by positive demand within a circumscribed time & going of the Comrs yett

---

[20] For some reason, Firth omits twenty-eight words here from his edition (from 'as that it maye' to 'London would doe'. He also changes the sense of the next sentence which in his edition reads: 'Therefore I shall desire that if itt please the Generall, that you may have an account of that other businesse by the Commissary General.' In other words, it changes the role of Ireton from speaker to listener. The original is ungrammatical but makes sense!

[21] P. H. Hardacre, 'William Allen, Cromwellian Agitator and "Fanatic"', *Baptist Quarterly*, n.s., 19:7 (1962), pp. 292–308.

16 JULY 1647

using the name will nott offend if wee doe nott the thinges that if wee doe not treate of those thinges.

Give mee leave to offer one thinge to your Consideration which I see you make to bee your ground of marching towards London because itt came in my minde I am sorry I did itt butt this came in my minde, and I would [fo. 99r] nott offer itt to you butt because I really know itt is a truth. Wee are as our friends are elsewhere very swift in our affections & desires, and Truly I am very often judged for one that goes too fast that way and itt is the property of men that are as I am apt to bee full of apprehensions that dangers are nott soe reall as imaginary to bee alwayes making hast and more sometimes perhaps then good speede, wee are apt to missapprehensions that wee shall bee deluded through delay & that there are noe good intentions in the parliament towards us, and that wee gather from the manifold <u>hearings</u>[22] of those words that wee have represented to them. Give mee leave to say this to you for my owne parte perhaps I have as few Extravagant thoughts, overweaning,[23] of obtaining great thinges from the parliament as any man yet itt hath bin in most of our thoughtes that this Parliament might bee a Reformed & purged Parliament that wee might see men looking att publique & common interests only. This was the great principall wee had gone uppon, and certainly this is the principle wee did march uppon when wee were at Uxbridge,[24] & when wee were at St.Albans,[25] and surely the thing was wise & honourable & just and wee see that providence hath led us into that way. itt's thought that the Parliament does not mend what's the meaning of that, That is to say that Company of men that sitts there does nott meane well to us. There is a partie there that have bin faithfull from the sitting of the parliament to this very day, and wee know their interests and have ventured their lives through soe many hazards they came not to the House butt under the apprehension of having their throats cut every day if wee well consider what difficulties they have past that wee may not run into that extreame of thinking too hardly of the parliament if wee shall consider that

---

[22] This is a very difficult word to read: *Clarke Papers*, 1:192 has 'bearing'. It certainly begins 'h' or 'b'—which may be why Clarke in transcribing from the shorthand underlined it. See **1647 07 16** n. 6.

[23] *Clarke Papers*, 1:192 adds a word for clarification: 'overweaning [thoughts] of obtaining'.

[24] The Army moved its headquarters from St Albans to Uxbridge on 25 June 1647 as part of the extra pressure on the House of Commons to suspend the eleven members the Council believed to be its most inveterate enemies.

[25] The Army's Headquarters were in St Albans from 13 to 25 June 1647 and it was from there that it issued *The Declaration of the Army* on 15 June which was the final summation of the grievances that had been the subject of the Saffron Walden Debates in May (**1647 05 15, 1647 05 16**).

417

THE LETTERS, WRITINGS, AND SPEECHES OF OLIVER CROMWELL

their businesse of holding their Heads above water is the common worke, & every other day[26] and to day that which wee desire is that which they have Strugled for as for life & sometimes they have bin able to carry it, others nott, & yet daily they gett ground. If wee see a purged parliament I pray lett mee perswade every man that hee would bee a little apt to hope the best and I speake this to you as out of a cleare Conscience before the Lord I doe thinke that the parliament is uppon the gaining hand and that this worke that wee are now uppon tends to make them gaine more, and I would wish that wee might remember this always that wee, and they [fo. 99r] they gaine in a free way itt is better than twice soe much in a forc't, and will bee more truly ours & our posterities and therfore I desire nott to perswade any man to bee of my minde butt I wish that every man would seriously weigh these thinges.

William Allen says 'we' do not see our friends as a 'gaining parte' but as 'a loosing partie' and repeats his call for an immediate march on London. Commissary General Henry Ireton, in a long speech, supports Cromwell's line and speaks of the full set of proposals that are in hand, if taking too long to complete. He argues against a march on London until all – General, Council, all the agitators—have agreed the heads of a set of proposals. Allen repeats—again at length—the case for an immediate march.

[fo. 102r]

Lieutenant General. This I wish in the Generall that wee may all of us soe demeasne ourselves in this businesse that wee speake those thinges that tend to the uniting of us, and that wee doe none of us exercise our parts to straine thinges & to lett in thinges to a longe dispute or to unnecessary contradictions or to the stirring uppe of any such seede of dissatisfaction in one anothers mindes as that may in the least render us unsatisfied one in another: I doe nott speake this that any body does doe it butt I say this ought to become both you and mee [fo. 102v] that wee soe speake & act as that the End may bee union, and a right understanding one with another, and Truly if I thought that which was last spoken by Mr Allen had bin satisfactory to that End for which hee spake itt I should nott have said any thinge to you, butt for that which hee made to the Commissary[27] of the Parliament's owning of us & what a thinge that was to us, and how much tending to the settlement of the peace of the K.dome what they doe owne[28] to say or to

---

[26] *Clarke Papers*, 1:192 adds this for clarification: 'every other day ['s work] and'.

[27] *Clarke Papers*, 1:202 adds two words for clarification here: 'the Commissary [General's argument] of the Parliament's'.

[28] *Clarke Papers*, 1:202 adds a word here for clarification: 'that they do owne [us]'.

418

16 JULY 1647

thinke itt is butt a titular thinge that & thinke butt in name only I thinke is a very great mistake for really itt did att that time lay the best Foundation could bee expected for the preventing an absolute Confusion in this K.dome and I thinke if wee had nott bin satisfied in that, wee should nott have bin satisfied in any thinge, and[29] to thinke that this is any weighty Argument itt is butt titular, because they suffer scandalous Bookes flocke uppe and downe I would nott looke they should love us better then they love themselves, and how many scandalous Books goe out of them, and wee have given them & the Parliament more to doe then attend scandalous Bookes I hope that will nott weigh there with any man, and I desire wee may putt this debate to a Conclusion or else lett us answer those thinges that are really & weightily objected as truly that was they had given us as reall a Testimonie that they cannot give more. They cannot disowne us without the loosing of all rationall and honest people in the K.dome and therefore lett us take itt as very great & high owning of us lett not us disowne that owning, if any man would by that which was objected wee would have peace a perfect Settlement of all wee see,[30] and wee would march to London to say wee forc't them. Really, Really. Have what you will have, That you have by force I looke uppon itt as nothing I doe not know that force is to bee used, Except wee cannot gett what is for the good of the K.dome without force, and all the Arguments must tend to this that itt is necessary to use force to march uppe with the Army and nott to tarry 4 dayes, wee shall bee baffled, denied, & shall never march uppe if the Argument was not thus, butt still bee patient & suffer even to have the ruine of the K.dome as hath bin imagined & expect a speedy answer which hath bin offer'd and to make that Criticall to us whether they owne us or intend to perfect the settlement as wee expect the K.dome would be sav'd if wee doe nott march within 4 dayes if wee had these thinges granted to us, if these thinges bee granted [fo. 103r] to us wee may march to Yorke. I wish wee may respite our Determination till that 4. or 5. dayes be over till wee see how thinges will bee, Except wee[31] will urge Reasons to shew itt to bee of absolute necessity to all those Ends to determine just now that wee will march \uppe/ to London to morrow or next day I am sorry that wee bee not satisfied with that which hath bin proposed as to this very thinge, and if having had an assurance these thinges were putt into such a way as hath bin

---

[29] *Clarke Papers*, 1:202 adds a phrase here for clarification: 'and [it is a great mistake] to thinke'.

[30] Very difficult to transcribe, a scribble which looks more like 'see'. Firth suggests 'wee seek', which certainly makes better sense [*Clarke Papers*, 1:202]. But it could be one word not two.

[31] Firth silently changes 'wee' to 'you' here [*Clarke Papers*, 1:203]. This improves the sense but is absolutely not what Clarke has transcribed Cromwell as saying.

THE LETTERS, WRITINGS, AND SPEECHES OF OLIVER CROMWELL

offerd to you that you will rest contented with this as att this time Except you will shew us some absolute Reasons.

Major Alexander Tulidah[32] responded to Cromwell, repeating the case for an advance on London (nothing, he says, has in the past 'sett them on the legges…to expedite…the Kingdome's interest' as a march on London.

Lieutenant General. Truly the words spoken by Major Tulidah were with affection butt wee are rationall but I would faine know with what reason or colour of Reason hee did urge any Reason butt only with affirmation of earnest words butt for that Declaration of the Parliament. That the Parliament hath own'd us & taken off that that any man can legally or rationally charge us with. If that uppon his apprehensions or any mans else wee shall quarrel with every dogge in the streete that barkes at us suffer the K.dome to bee lost with such a fantasticall thinge, I desire that nothing of heate or earnestnesse may carry us heere, nor nothing of affirmation, nor nothing of that kinde may leade us butt that which is Truly Reason and that which hath life & Argument in itt. By that which was alledged of our marching to Uxbridge[33] wee open'd those honest mens mouthes to speake for us. This is nott to bee answer'd with reason, butt this is matter of fact, & better knowne to some of us then itt is to Major Tulida or any of you. Tis true there was feare & an awe upon the Parliament by our marching to Uxbridge there was something of that for that those 11. Members were afraid to bee in the House if you will beleive nott that which is a fancie they have voted very Essentiall thinges to their owne purging, and I beleive this if wee will beleive that which is the Truth in Fact uppon that very one vote that was past concerning the putting a Fine or

---

[32] Major Alexander Tulidah is a mystery. Neither Firth and Davies nor Wanklyn include him in their lists of New Model officers but he appeared in the list of officers attending the General Council on 16 July 1647 as 'Adj. Gen. Tulidah', and in his various contributions to the debate as 'Major Tulidah'. The former title might have been conferred by Clarke when transcribing from the shorthand, since Tulidah was appointed (but only briefly) as adjutant general on 19 October 1648 [WCO, Clarke MS 67, fo. 27]. He first appears as a pall-bearer at the funeral of Major Christopher Bethel on 24 October 1645 (*Moderate Intelligencer* no. 35 for 23–30 October 1645, p. 175 (N&S, 419.35; Thomason / E.307[20])) and there survives an order for the settlement of his arrears of £19 12s. on 12 November 1647 (Chequers MS 782/45). He was considered as a possible governor of Hereford in a letter from senior officers to Fairfax in September 1647 (Clarke MS 66, fo. 15v). Lilburne claimed him as an ally (*Rash Oaths Unwarrantable* [1647], p. 35 (Wing / L2167), discussed in John Lilburne (1614–57), Leveller. See ODNB. He was one of those arrested and imprisoned on 20 March 1647 for promoting the Leveller's Large Petition (Woolrych, *Soldiers and Statesmen*, pp. 61–2, 159, Gardiner, *GCW*, 3:256–7). He had also been assaulted by Sir Philip Stapleton during an altercation arising from his arrest. Sir Philip Stapleton (bap. 1603, d. 1647), politician and army officer. See ODNB.

[33] i.e. 25 June 1647 (Gardiner *GCW*, 3:304).

16 JULY 1647

penalty that knew themselves to be guilty and that if they did nott goe out should accuse themselves to be liable to sequestration I believe there will goe 20 or 30 men out of the House of Comons, and if this bee[34] an Effort[35] & Demonstration of the happy progresse, and by that use of that libertie that they have had by our drawing neere, I appeale to any man, & if they shall as I said before disowne us & wee give them noe cause to doe itt, butt pressing only just, and honourable & honest thinges from them, Judge you what can the world thinke of them & of us, butt wee shall doe that whilest wee are uppon the gayning hand that shall really stoppe their mouthes, To open their mouthes in a Title for us. That whilest they are as fast as they can gayning the thinges wee desire if [fo. 104r] wee shall bee soe impatient that whilest they are strugling for life that they are unable to helpe us and gain'd more within these 3 dayes then in 10 dayes for ought I know wee may by advancing stoppe their Mouthes, They will not have wherwithall to answer that middle partie in the House who is answer'd with this Reason you see the Army is contented to goe backward you see the Army is willing to make faire Representations of that they have from us. I professe I speake itt in my Conscience that if wee should now until wee had made these proposalls to them, and see what answer they will give them wee shall nott only disable them butt divide among ourselves and I as much feare that as any thing and if wee should speake to your satisfactions you must speake to our satisfactions though there bee great feares of others I shall very much Question the integritie of any man, I would not have itt spoken.

There follow five short speeches with cornets and a lieutenant speaking for an immediate march and Major John Disbrowe[36] broadly supporting Cromwell and Ireton.

[fo. 104r]

Lieutenant General[37] Truly Sir I thinke neither of these 2 thinges that Gent[38] spoke last are any great Newes. For the one of them, the Listing of Apprentices I

---

[34] *Clarke Papers*, 1:206 changes the meaning here by adding a 'not'—'if this bee [not] an effort', perhaps correcting a transcription error.

[35] Clarke's word here may well be 'Effect' rather than 'Effort'.

[36] John Disbrowe [Desborough] (bap. 1608, d. 1680), parliamentarian army officer and politician. See *ODNB*.

[37] This final section of the day, including the first half of this speech, seems badly garbled. Perhaps the stenographers or the transcribers were tired; perhaps the word order in the shorthand was confusing. Firth in *Clarke Papers* inserts gaps where he thinks words are omitted in three of the speeches and at 'shall bee in the wronge' in this speech, and he moves phrases around to impose more sense, but they represent little more than his guesses (*Clarke Papers*, 1:299).

[38] 'Cornet Spencer' was probably the John Spencer recently promoted from cornet to captain lieutenant in the cavalry regiment of Thomas Harrison (Wanklyn, *Reconstructing*, 1:93).

THE LETTERS, WRITINGS, AND SPEECHES OF OLIVER CROMWELL

doubt they have listed them twice over butt for the other[39] I am sure wee have have heard more then twice over would rejoice to see us come uppe but what if wee[40] better able to consult what is for their good then themselves itt is the generall good of them & all the people in the K.dome That's the Question whats for their good nott what pleases them. I doe nott know that all these Considerations are Arguments to have satisfaction in these thinges that wee have in proposition. [fo. 105r] If you bee in the right, and I in the wronge if wee bee divided I doubt wee shall all bee in the wronge, whether of them will doe our worke lett them Speake without declaring lett us not thinke that this is a greater Argument that they love those that deserted that they have paid them & nott us which was Mr Sexbye's[41] Argument which if itt had weight in itt I should have submitted to it The Question is singly this, Whether or noe wee shall nott in a positive way desire the answer to these thinges before wee march towards London, when perhaps wee may have the same thinges in the time that wee can march. Heere is the strictnesse of the Question.

Three more interventions rehearse previous arguments and then Ireton sums up the case for delaying a march on London.

1647 07 17
Oliver Cromwell's contributions to the New Model Army Debate at Reading

Date: 17 July 1647
Source: Worcester College, Oxford, Clarke Papers, vol. 65, fos 106r–107r (reported speeches)

Overnight Ireton and Lambert were able to produce a version of the Heads of the Proposals in a state to be presented to the General Council. Clarke's account of the ensuing discussion has the appearance of a very abbreviated account of proceedings dominated by Ireton's presentation of a draft of the Nineteen Propositions. Cromwell just makes two short interventions. He is recorded as making the first intervention after the reading of the Propositions.

For a loose transcription of all the speeches, see *Clarke Papers*, 1:211–14.

---

[39] '[T]he King's coming to Maidenhead'.   [40] *Clarke Papers*, 1:209 adds a '[be]' here.
[41] Edward Sexby (*c.*1616–58), parliamentarian army officer and conspirator. See *ODNB*.

422

[fo. 106r]

Att a Generall Councill of Warre at Reading, July 17, 1647

Lieutenant General. That all prejudices might bee removed

The Propositions read

Lieutenant General. Butt you would nott have a Parliament dissolved without the Consent of the Houses in 120 dayes.[1]

Colonel John Lambert:[2] *but they can only meet for longer than 120 days by consent of 'the Counsell of State, and the Kinge'.*

[fo. 106v]

Lieutenant General. They may bee adjourned if the Kinge & Councill of State thinke fitt, itt may bee as convenient to have a Parliament continued whether itt will or noe as to out itt self. If itt does not conclude itt publique, as that itt bee heere read or noe, if there bee any thinge afterwards that shall bee desired to be offer'd for any Addition, The Councill of Warre will meete, & the Agitators send soe many as they shall select to get any alterations butt itt would not bee read heere butt that itt bee passed by with silence.

Henry Ireton and William Allen confirm the need for a committee and Ireton makes a final speech about the role of the proposed Council of State and military (and naval) appointments. This reads like fragments from a larger, unrecorded debate. (It is followed in the MS by several blank pages.)

1647 07 31[?]
Letter from Oliver Cromwell to Sir Thomas Fairfax

Date: 31 July 1647
Source: BL, Sloane MS 1519, fos 144r–145v (autograph)

This letter seems straightforward enough, but it is full of riddles. It appears in this edition both as **1647 07 31** and as **1646 07 31**.

---

[1] Cromwell launches straight into the second clause of the first article of the Heads of the Proposals [the developed version of which, presented to the Parliament on 1 August 1647, are printed in S. R. Gardiner, *Constitutional Documents of the Puritan Revolution* (3rd ed., Oxford, 1906), pp. 316–36]. Has an earlier debate been unrecorded or untranscribed?

[2] John Lambert [Lambart] (bap. 1619, d. 1684), parliamentary soldier and politician. See ODNB.

THE LETTERS, WRITINGS, AND SPEECHES OF OLIVER CROMWELL

It is in the hand of Cromwell's usual clerk and has Cromwell's own signature and his seal is still attached. There is an endorsement in an unknown hand. Both the letter and the endorsement are very clearly dated 31 July 1646. But...

Cromwell is asking Fairfax to support the petition 'of Adj. Flemming' for assistance in an unstated cause. Christopher Flemming had served as a captain under the earl of Essex from the beginning of the wars. By 2 September 1644 he was adjutant of horse, and continued as both captain and adjutant until at least 21 October 1644.[1] He transferred to the New Model, the only officer in his regiment to do so[2] and has been identified as an 'adjutant general' in the New Model at some unspecified point.[3] He left the Army in June 1647 (1647 note), at the time of the mass resignations over the Army's defiance of Parliament's will[4] but he was reappointed as governor of Pembroke Castle in early 1648.[5] There is also evidence that he was very seriously wounded in hand-to-hand combat on 24 May 1645 and 'shot his enemy, yet received a wound himself, conceived then to be mortal'[6] (Firth and Davies, *Regimental History*, 1:103).

So a complicated story. The one year in which it seems unnecessary for Cromwell to write on his behalf is 1646. And yet that is what the letter clearly gives as its date. So why do we find this entry in the Journal of the House of Lords for 24 August 1647 (yes, 1647): 'Adj. Fleming recommended for an Employment. A Letter from Sir Thomas Fairefax was read, recommending Adjutant Fleming for to have some such Employment conferred upon him as he is capable of, inregard, by his Wounds for the Service of the Parliament, he is disabled from his Service to the Parliament in that Way he is in'?[7]

Because of these complexities, this letter is appearing twice in this edition, first under the date given on the face of the letter, and again under the far more likely actual date.

––––––––

For his Excie: Sir Thomas Fairfax, Generall of the parliaments forces
theise
Lt. Gen: Cromwell.
July. 31. 1646
[Seal]

[1] See Christopher Flemming [Fleming] in the *Online Directory of Parliamentarian Army Officers*.

[2] Wanklyn, *Reconstructing*, 1:151.   [3] Wanklyn, *Reconstructing*, 1:164.

[4] As did his colonel (Richard Graves) and all but one of the captains. The major, Adrian Scroop took over as colonel and the one surviving captain, Nathaniel Barton, was promoted to major—Wanklyn, *Reconstructing*, 1:84.

[5] Wanklyn, *Reconstructing*, 1:84 fn. 331.   [6] Firth and Davies, *Regimental History*, 1:103.

[7] JHL, 9:401.

424

20 AUGUST 1647

Sir

I was desired to write a letter to you by Adjutant Flemming.[8] The end of it is, to desire your letter in his recommendation. Hee will acquaint you with the Summe thereof more particulerly what the business is. I most humbly Submitt to your better judgment when you heare it from him. Craveing pardon for my boldness in putting yow to this trouble I rest Your most humble servant

Oliver Cromwell

July the 31th 1646

1647 08 20

Speech by Oliver Cromwell to the House of Commons

Date: 20 August 1647

Source: BL, Add. MS 10114, fo. 26, Diary of John Harington. Printed in Diary of John Harington, p. 58 (reported speech)

On 26 July 1647 a mob of Londoners had invaded both the Houses demanding that the King be invited to return to London. Four days later, the Independent peers and MPs withdrew from Westminster and joined Fairfax's Army, which had advanced to Colnbrook to the west of the capital. On 6 August the Army entered London. With order restored in the capital, the Independent peers and MPs felt able to resume their places in Parliament. The next step was for them to declare void all that their colleagues had passed in their absence. Their majority in the Commons was however still fragile and it was not until a fortnight later that the legislation to effect this completed its passage. During this debate on the subject on 20 August Cromwell and others evidently questioned the conduct of Thomas Gewen, MP for Launceston. A Presbyterian, Gewen had remained at Westminster after 30 July and had assisted in the military preparations against the Army's advance on London.[1] He also remained unrepentant. On 19 August the Commons debated whether to accept an amendment to this bill which proposed to make it explicit that the decisions being

---

[8] See n. 1. Christopher Flemming (or Fleming), who had served in Waller's army as a captain of horse, and subsequently served in the New Model Army as a captain in the regiment of Richard Graves (1645–7), who was replaced by Adrian Scrope (1647). He was seriously injured during the siege of Boarstall House in May 1645 and nearly died (Firth and Davies, *Regimental History*, 1:103). He served in 1646 and 1647 as adjutant general but it is not known when he took up this position. He was killed in a skirmish near Carmarthen in 1648 (Wanklyn, *Reconstructing*, 1:53, 63, 74, 84, 151, 168).

[1] *JHC*, 5:259, 261, 263, 265, 266.

425

reversed were not only now void but that they had been so at the time. Gewen was one of the two tellers for the MPs who unsuccessfully opposed this.

after dinner Mr Clark[2] charg the army Sr Ra: Ashton[3] Lieu: g: Cromwel Sr Ar: Haselrig[4] had chargd Guen[5] who vindicated himself

Outcome: The Commons and then the Lords passed the bill declaring that all the votes, orders and ordinances passed between 26 July and 6 August were void.[6]

1647 09 01
Letter from Oliver Cromwell to John Williams, archbishop of York

Date: 1 September 1647
Source: *Gentleman's Magazine*, vol. 59.ii (1789), p. 877 (later copy)

The original of this letter is lost, and it only survives because it was one of three letters with Welsh connections printed in 1789 in *The Gentleman's Magazine*.[1] The *Magazine* offers no guidance on provenance. It claims to follow mid-seventeenth-century spelling and punctuation and appears to be authentic. However, the placing of the date and the address are rearranged according to late eighteenth-century conventions.

With the exception of the reports of which he was at best co-author as an MP-commissioner to the Army Council in May and June, there is no letter of Cromwell's surviving for any of the months of April to August. It is one of the longest periods of silence in his whole career between the outbreak of the Civil War and his death.

Cromwell's great-great grandfather married the sister of Thomas Cromwell, and his son later changed his name from 'Williams' to 'Cromwell', and Oliver was well aware of his Williams ancestry and on occasion signed himself Oliver Cromwell alias Williams and incorporated the silver lion rampant from the Williams coat-of-arms into his Protectoral arms.[2] Williams is a common enough name and there is no easy way of establishing a link between Oliver Cromwell and John Williams, despite Cromwell referring to him as a

[2] JHC, 5:279.
[3] Samuel Clarke, MP for Exeter (returned as a recruiter MP in 1645). See *HoP Commons, 1640–1660*.
[4] Sir Arthur Hesilrige [Haselrig], second baronet (1601–61), army officer and politician. See *ODNB*. Also *HoP Commons, 1640–1660*.
[5] Thomas Gewen (1575–1660), MP for Launceton (Devon). See *HoP Commons, 1640–1660*.
[6] JHC, 5:280; JHL, 9:397–8.

[1] The general heading given them is 'Original letters of Charles I; O. Cromwell; and Lenthall'.
[2] Most fully and recently discussed by Lloyd Bowen, 'Oliver Cromwell (alias Williams) and Wales', in Patrick Little, ed., *Oliver Cromwell: New Perspectives* (2009), pp. 168–74.

cousin. Cromwell's ancestry is from the south of Wales while John Williams was born in Ruthin, in north-east Wales. Still, there was nothing in Williams's public career that should have made Cromwell willing to do him favours.

Sept. 1, 1647.
My Lord,[3]
Your advises will be seriously considered by us. We shall endeavor our uttermost soe to settle the affaires of Northwales, as to the best of our understandinges does most conduce to most publicke good thereof, and of the whole; and that without private respect, or to the satisfaction of any humor, which has beene too much practised by the occasion of our trou- bles. The drover you mention[4] wilbe secured (as farr as wee are able) in his affaires, if hee come to aske itt. Your kindsman[5] shalbe very welcom to mee. I shall studye to serve him for kindred's sake, amongst whome lett not be forgotten, my Lord,
Your cozen and servant,
OLIVER CROMWELL.

For the Right H'ble my Lord of Yorke, theise.
The Governor of Conway will not
bee forgotten,[6] to prævent his abuse.

[3] As an archbishop, Williams should have been addressed as 'Your Grace' but calling him 'My Lord' was still quite a startling appellation. Episcopacy had been formally abolished and bishops long since evicted from the House of Lords. John Williams (1582–1650) was bishop of Lincoln (1621–41) and archbishop of York (1641–46 [by parliamentarian] or –1650 [by royalist] calculation. He had also been Lord Keeper (1621–5). A bitter opponent of archbishop Laud, he had been promoted in 1641 in an attempt to find a 'modified-episcopacy' solution to the crisis in the Church. He had spent the civil-war years making Conwy Castle into a stronghold, but he had been double-crossed by a local royalist whom he had commended to the King but who seized the castle and brought charges of treason against him. This in turn led him to reach an accommodation with a local parliamentarian commander, Colonel Thomas Mytton (1596/7–1652). For John Williams (1582–1650) archbishop of York, see ODNB. For details of his escape from sequestration and composition, see JHC, 5:59–60 (21 January 1647).
[4] It is not evident who this refers to.
[5] It is not evident who this refers to.
[6] 'The governor of Conway' may be Sir John Owen who had dispossessed Williams in May 1645 and accused him to the King of treason. But it is more likely that it is the man who replaced him as governor when it was surrendered to Parliament in October 1646—Colonel John Carter, who acquired a dubious reputation as 'an odd man who cares not whom he oppresses if it be to his profit' (Calendar of Wynn (of Gwydir) Papers, 1515–1690: in the National Library of Wales and elsewhere (Aberystwyth and London, 1926), p. 313 [no. 1881]). For Carter, see also the Online Directory of Parliamentarian Army Officers, and G. H. Jenkins, The Foundations of Modern Wales, 1642–1780 (Oxford, 1987), p. 39.

THE LETTERS, WRITINGS, AND SPEECHES OF OLIVER CROMWELL

1647 09 14

Letter from Oliver Cromwell to Colonel Michael Jones

Date: 14 September 1647
Source: TCD, MS 844, fos 1r–2v (holograph)

This oblique letter of congratulation is probably a holograph. Certainly, it ends with Cromwell's signature, and is endorsed in Jones's own hand. On 8 August 1647 Michael Jones (at the time governor of Dublin) had won a major victory over the Confederate Irish Army of Leinster at Dungan's Hill (County Meath). There is no reason to think that Cromwell had ever met Michael Jones although they had collaborated at the time of the Naseby campaign when Jones was Sir William Brereton's deputy commander at the siege of Chester. Cromwell struggled with the tone of this letter as his repeated heavy scoring out and replacement of words makes clear.

Cromwell to Jones[1]

Sir

The mutuall interest and ingagement wee have in

the same Cause gives mee occasion, as to congra-

tulate, so aboundantly to rejoyce in Gods gratious

Dispensation unto you and by you. Wee have (both

in England and Ireland) found the immediate

presence and assistance of God, in guideinge and

succeedinge our endeavours hitherto; and therefore

ought (as I doubt not both you and wee desire)

to ascribe the Glorie of all to him, and to improve

all wee receive from him unto him alone

Though it may bee for the present a Cloud may

lye over our Actions, to them who are not ac-

quaynted with the Grounds, of \them/ our [], yet

wee doubt not but God, [] [hand] will cleare

our integritie and Innocency from any other ends wee

---

[1] Michael Jones (1606x10–49). See *ODNB*. Cromwell would have known of him as a commander in Cheshire and adjacent counties, but also as the brother of Henry Jones (by 1647 royalist bishop of Clogher) whose propagandist efforts on behalf of the victims of the rebellion of 1641 had clearly influenced Cromwell's view of Ireland. Cromwell already knew that he was the popular choice of the Army to lead the reconquest of Ireland, something that would require close collaboration with Jones.

428

15 SEPTEMBER 1647

ayme att, but ~~God~~ \his/ Glorie, and the Publique good.
And as you are [-] \an/ Instrumt herein, so wee \shall/
~~{be:}~~ (as becommeth us) upon all occasions give you
your due Honour For myne owne particuular
wherein I may have your Commaunds to serve you, You
shall find none more ready, then hee that sincerely
desires to approve himselfe
Your affectionate freind and
humble servant
Oliver Cromwell
Septbr. 14th
1647

For the hoble Coll: Jones Governor
of Dublin & Comander in Cheife
of all the Forces in L{einster}[2]
these

7[br?]. 14. 47.
Ld gell Cromwell

1647 09 15

Instructions for William Rowe issued by Oliver Cromwell and nine other members of the Committee of Lords and Commons at Derby House for Irish Affairs

Date: 15 September 1647
Source: TNA, SP21/26 pp. 105–7 (autograph)

By 15 September 1647 Cromwell's allies were firmly in control of the English Parliament and negotiations between the Army leaders and their parliamentary allies and the King over the Heads of the Proposals were at a critical stage. Just a week before he had been

---

[2] This is really badly faded. The only letter we can be sure of is L at the start. The likeliest word in our view is 'Leinster' and certainly that seems the right number of characters.

THE LETTERS, WRITINGS, AND SPEECHES OF OLIVER CROMWELL

asked to choose between the Scottish-backed Newcastle Propositions and the Army-generated Heads of the Proposals and he had stated firmly his preference for the latter. In Scotland, fury at what the leading Covenanters saw as English betrayal was leading to open talk of a new Scottish invasion of England. And meanwhile, Ireland remained unpacified and the substantial Scottish armed brigade in the north remained in rather better shape than that which had now been withdrawn from England.

This set of instructions given to William Rowe, Cromwell's scoutmaster, to take letters to key players in Scotland, especially the earl of Loudoun, Chancellor of Scotland, may or may not have been written or influenced by Cromwell—his is the last of ten signatories at least on the copy retained by the clerks of the Derby House Committee; but then Rowe was his man—but it indicates his ongoing concern for events in Ireland and his desire to diminish the ability of the Scots to influence settlement across the kingdoms.

Rowe's mission was a failure. The Scottish army in Ulster was not disengaged and by the end of the year a majority of the Scottish council had determined on a new war with England, this time to rescue the King from the Independent party.

[p. 105]

Instructions for Mr William Rowe[1] Concerning the Letters wch he is by Order of the Houses to carry into Scotland

Whereas you have herewith three Letters of both Houses of parlt delivered unto you one of them endorsed, For the Right Honble the Lord Chancellor of Scotland,[2] and one other of the same [p. 106] Tennour endorsed For the right Honble the Councell of Scotland, And the third endorsed for Right honble the Committee of Estates for the Kingdom of Scotland

1. You are first with all dilligence to make your 47 to Edinburg or where else you shall understand the Lord Chancellor of Scotland to be. And shall deliver unto him the letters directed unto him, And you are to take notice of the tyme of your delivery of the said letters

2. forasmuch as Wee are informed that the said Lord Chancellor is about to come into England you are as you passe to make dilligent enquiry if he be

---

[1] William Rowe was the son of Yorkshire gentleman and served in 1643–4 as secretary to Parliament's commissioners who negotiated the Solemn League and Covenant, and in 1647 with the commissioners who negotiated Ormond's surrender of Dublin. He then became scoutmaster of the New Model and travelled with Cromwell on the Preston campaign. His previous experience made him an ideal person to be Cromwell's courier for his negotiations with Loudoun and Argyll in September 1648 (anon. 'Grant by Edward Bysshe, Garter King of Arms to William Rowe', *Yorkshire Archaeology Society*, 18 [1905], pp. 346–8).

[2] John Campbell, first earl of Loudoun (1598–1662), Lord Chancellor of Scotland. See *ODNB*.

430

15 SEPTEMBER 1647

upon the way & if you should meet him on the way, You are to deliver him the said Letters, & take notice of the tyme as you were before instructed.

3. In case the Lord Chancellor be upon the way & that you have there as aforesaid delivered him your said Letters, you are notwithstanding to repair in all dilligence to Edinburg or where else you shall understand the Councell of Scotland & Committee of Estates to be unto whom you shall deliver the letters directed unto them & you are to take notice of the tyme of your delivery of that to the Councell of Scotland.

4. for that the letters You carry to the Lord Chancellor, & that to the Councell of Scotland are to signifie the dismission of the Scottish Army in Ireland: who at the tyme of their dismission are to have by the Treaty fourteene days pay provided for carrying of them home

[p. 107]
You are therefore to stay at Edinburg till you shall have answere that the said forces will returne home and thereupon with all expedicon you are to give us notice thereof that the fourteene dayes pay may forthwith sent unto them. In case they shall give an answere that shall not be direct either to the comeing away or staying of the said Army in Ireland, You are to send us what answere you shall soe receive. And continue there until you have further Order from us. Given under our hands at Derby House this 15th day of Sept 1647

    Signed
      Northumberland Manchester
      PWharton   WArmyne
      Art Hesilrige Gilb Gerard
  HVane Ol:St John Rob Wallop[3]
      Oliver Cromwell

---

[3] For all signatories, see ODNB: Algernon Percy, tenth earl of Northumberland (1602–68), politician; Edward Montagu, second earl of Manchester (1602–71), politician and parliamentarian army officer; Philip Wharton, fourth Baron Wharton (1613–96), politician; Sir William Armine, first baronet (1593–1651), politician; Sir Arthur Hesilrige, second baronet (1601–61), army officer and politician; Sir Gilbert Gerard, first baronet (1587–1670), politician; Sir Henry Vane, the younger (1613–62), politician and author; Oliver St John (c.1598–1673), lawyer and politician; Robert Wallop (1601–67), politician.

THE LETTERS, WRITINGS, AND SPEECHES OF OLIVER CROMWELL

1647 10 13

Letter from Oliver Cromwell to Sir Thomas Fairfax

Date: 13 October 1647

Source: BL, Sloane MS 1519, fos 160r–161v (holograph)

This letter and its endorsement are in Cromwell's own hand. Nothing more is known about why Captain Middleton was being court-martialled.

———

[fo. 161v]

Lt. Generall Cromwell

Octr. 13. 1647

For his Ex: Sir

Thomas Fairfax

       theise

[fo. 160r]

Sir the case concerninge Capt.

Middleton[1] heeres ill, in asmuch

as itt is delayed (upon prætences)

from cominge to a tryall, itt

is not (I humblie conceave) fitt

that itt should stay any longer,

the souldiers complaine therof,

and their witnesses have beene

examined, Capt. Middleton, and

some others for him have made

stay therof heitherto, I beseech

———

[1] Captain Henry Middleton was a captain in Cromwell's own regiment of horse, having transferred in from the Eastern Association army into the New Model, transferring from Colonel Vermuyden's regiment to Cromwell's at some point after the battle of Naseby in late 1646. According to Wanklyn, who does not give a source, Middleton was 'cashiered in late 1647 for disobedience'. Elsewhere he tells us that Middleton was replaced by his lieutenant in November 1647 (see Wanklyn, *Reconstructing*, 1:52, 62, 73, 83, 94, 107). Perhaps his delayed court martial resulted in his leaving the Army. (See also Firth and Davies, *Regimental History*, 1:200–1). Abbott bizarrely claims that 'Captain Middleton' was Sir George Middleton, subsequently a defector to the cause of Charles II and indeed a spy for the exiled King in the 1650s (Abbott, *Writings and Speeches*, I:509–10). But Sir George was a royalist, albeit one who fought in Ireland (Newman, *Royalist Officers*, no. 969).

your Excellency to give Order
itt may bee tryed on Friday
or Saturday att farthest if
you please \and that soe much may bee
Signifyed to the Advoca{?te}/ [2,3] Sir I pray excuse
my not attendance upon you, I
Scarse misse the house a day, where
its very necessarie for mee to bee.
I hope your Exellency wilbe att
the head Quarter to morrowe, whe{?re}[4]
If God please I shall waite upon
you

I rest
Your Excellencyes most humble
servant
Oliver Cromwell

Putney[5] this 13th
of octobr 1647

1647 10 22

Letter from Oliver Cromwell to Sir Thomas Fairfax

Date: 22 October 1647
Source: BL, Sloane MS 1519, fos 164r–165v (scribal version with signature missing)

Neither the text nor the address of this letter are in Cromwell's own hand and the signature has been cut away. Sir Thomas Fairfax had succeeded his father as governor of

---

[2] Inserted with caret. The paper has been cut at some time after its composition and the 'te' needs to be supplied.
[3] The Judge Advocate of the New Model, its prosecuting officer, was at this time John Mills who replaced Isaac Dorislaus in 1645 (C. H. Firth, *Cromwell's Army* (1902), p. 282).
[4] The paper has been cut at some time after its composition and the 're' needs to be supplied; as only the beginning of the fourth letter is just visible, it is also possible that the word is 'when'.
[5] Putney (Surrey), on the Thames just five miles from the Palace of Westminster. It was at that time Army headquarters.

THE LETTERS, WRITINGS, AND SPEECHES OF OLIVER CROMWELL

Kingston-upon-Hull in 1645 with Lt. Col. John Mauleverer[1] as lieutenant governor, and this letter concerns his proposed replacement by Robert Overton,[2] a local man and a strong religious Independent. He was quickly in conflict with the Presbyterian majority amongst the aldermen, not least following his appointment of the radical separatist John Canne as chaplain in the town in 1648.[3]

[fo. 165v]

To his Excellency Sir Thomas Fairfax

Theise

Lt. Gen: Cromwell.

octb. 22. 1647

[fo. 164r]

Sir

hearing the Garrison of Hull[4] is much distracted in the present Governemt. and that the most faith full & honest Officers have noe disposicon to serve there any longer under the present Governor.[5] And that it is theire earnest Desires with all the faith full & trusty Inhabitantes in the Towne to have Colonll. Overton sent to them to bee your Excies. Deputy over them:[6] I doe humbly Offer to your Excie. whether it might not bee Convenient that Cololl: Overton bee Speedily sent downe, That soe that Garrison may bee settled in safe hands And that your Excie. would bee pleased to send for Colll: \Overton/ & Conferr with him about it That either the Regimt. in the Towne may bee soe Regulated as your Excie. may bee confident That the Garrison may bee secured by them, Or otherwise it may bee drawne out & his owne Regimt. in the Army bee sent downe thither with him, But I Conceive if the Regimt. in Hull can bee made serviceable to your Excy: & included in the Establishemt. it wilbe better to continue it there, then to bury a Regimt. of your Army in that Garrison. Sir The expedicon wilbe very Neccessary

---

[1] John Mauleverer (c.1610–50), army officer. See *ODNB*.

[2] Robert Overton (1608/9–78/9), parliamentarian army officer. See *ODNB*. A local man, he had served as a captain in the garrison regiment in 1642–3. He became a major after the battle of Marston Moor in July 1644 and was given his own regiment in the New Model in June 1647.

[3] 'Hull in the 16th and 17th Centuries', *The Victoria History of the County of the York, East Riding: vol. 1: The City of Kingston upon Hull* (1969), pp. 90–171, http://british-history.ac.uk/report. aspx?comprid+66773 which gives Canne's appointment as 1648.

[4] Kingston-upon-Hull (historically in the East Riding of Yorkshire, currently in Humberside).

[5] The causes of the distractions in Hull in 1647 seem to have centred largely about arrears of pay and failure to pay for quartering (A. Hopper, ed., *The Papers of the Hothams, Governors of Hull during the Civil War* (Camden Society, 5th series, 39, 2011), pp. 161–3).

[6] Overton had been a captain in the Garrison regiment at least in 1642 and 1643 (Hopper, *Papers of the Hothams*, appendix II).

in regard of the present distraccon there, Thus I thought fitt to offer to your Excies. consideracon I shall humbly take leave & subscribe my Self Your E{x}cies {mo}st humble[7] {   }
Putney 22°
Octobr. 1647

1647 10 28
Oliver Cromwell's contributions to the New Model Army Debate at Putney

Date: 28 October 1647
Source: Worcester College, Oxford, Clarke Papers, vol. 65, fos 1r–25v (reported speech)

Between the debates at Reading in mid July 1647[1] and the more famous Putney Debates of late October and early November, much had happened. The Army had finally marched on London and occupied it, and the eleven 'incendiaries' (whom the Army blamed for attempting to force their disbandment and for seeking to deal with the King without reference to the Army's Heads of the Proposals) had fled and had then been formally expelled from the House of Commons. The Army's leaders ('the Grandees') had conducted direct negotiations with the King before handing over the enhanced proposals to the 'purged' Parliament for completion.[2] The General Council of the Army made up of the senior officers and representatives (agitators or adjutators) of both the junior officers and the rank-and-file had continued to have regular, scheduled meetings. No record of what was said and decided at those meetings between 17 July and late October has survived until the meeting that convened in St Mary's Church at Putney on Thursday 28 October and which was to continue, in full session or in committee, until Thursday 11 November.

In the fortnight before the 'Putney Debates', elements in the Army unhappy with the leadership of Fairfax, Cromwell and Ireton produced a document which contained stinging criticisms of 'the rotten studs' in Parliament and of the Grandees, and which called for a much more radical constitutional settlement than that envisaged in the terms currently being finalised. This document, *The Case of the Armie Truly Stated*, was discussed at a General Council meeting on 22 October and referred to a committee. When the Council reconvened on 28 October, however, things had moved on. Five cavalry regiments, unhappy with the way the Grandees were acting, had chosen new agents to represent them and these appeared at the scheduled meeting of the General Council together with two

---

[7] The signature has been cut away taking the 'x' and the 'mo' partly away too.

[1] Above, **1647 07 16** and **1647 07 17**.
[2] For full narratives, see Woolrych, *Soldiers and Statesmen*, chs. VII–X; and Gentles, *New Model Army*, ch. 7.

THE LETTERS, WRITINGS, AND SPEECHES OF OLIVER CROMWELL

'civilian' advisers, both with links to radical groups in the City of London. These were John Wildman, himself an ex-soldier, and Maximilian Petty or Pettus. These men, together with the new agents, were admitted to the meetings in the days that followed. They brought with them a new document—*The Agreement of the People*—which called for radical reform of the constitution and of the composition of future Parliaments, and it was this, rather than the *Case of the Armie Truly Stated*, which came to form the agenda for the next few days.

William Clarke seems to have fully transcribed the debates of 28 October and 1 November from the shorthand notes made at the time, and he partially transcribed the speeches made at a prayer meeting that led into the debates of a committee on which Cromwell served—this was on 29 October. His notes for the rest of the period from 2 November to 11 November are very incomplete and sketchy, but some of Cromwell's contributions are summarised. In general, Clarke (and perhaps his stenographers) seem to have intended to record fully what the generals said and for the most part to have recorded summary accounts of the speeches of those who disagreed with them.[3] What follows here is a full transcript of Clarke's account of Cromwell's interventions together with summaries of the other speeches (in italics below). The aim is both to summarise the course of the debate and to provide a specific context for each of Cromwell's interventions.

There are two supposedly full modern editions of these debates. The first was made in the 1890s by C. H. Firth and the second in the 1930s by A. S. P. Woodhouse.[4] Both are seriously defective and in the case of Cromwell (but not only Cromwell) misleading. Firth partially follows the original spelling but not always, and he completely changes the punctuation. At many points he moves around clauses and phrases, even whole sentences, to make the sense clearer, but sometimes that means that he imposes one of two or more possible meanings. Where the meaning is unclear he also adds (usually, but not always, in square brackets) words to clarify meaning, sometimes tendentiously. This even includes the introduction of the word 'not' to reverse the meaning on the page. Woodhouse modernises the spelling as well as the punctuation but makes many mis-transcriptions and at one point leaves out several lines altogether. Most astonishingly he omits the decisions reached at the committee on 30 October that led to an agreement of all parties on the future franchise. Many authors reliant on the Woodhouse edition have been led into grave error as a result. In every way, the Woodhouse edition is to be distrusted and the Firth

---

[3] For all matters relating to the (lost) shorthand record and Clarke's later conversion of the shorthand notes into his own version, see Mendle, *Putney Debates*, chs. 1–3.

[4] C. H. Firth, ed., *The Clarke Papers. Selections from the Papers of William Clarke*, 4 vols. (1891–1902), 1:226–413 [henceforth *Clarke Papers*]; A. S. P. Woodhouse, ed., *Puritanism and Liberty: Being the Army Debates (1647–9) from the Clarke Manuscripts with supplementary Documents* (1938), pp. 1–124. Both are now freely available online in searchable pdf form from Liberty Fund: for the Firth edition, see http://oll.libertyfund.org/titles/clarke-the-clarke-papers-selections-from-the-papers-of-william-clarke-vol-1; and for the Woodhouse edition, see http://oll.libertyfund.org/titles/woodhouse-puritanism-and-liberty-being-the-army-debates-1647-9. Cromwell's speeches in Firth's edition were reprinted in Carlyle-Lomas as vol. 3, supplement 25, with extensive additional notes by Sophia Lomas.

28 OCTOBER 1647

edition, for all its frailties, is much to be preferred.[5] In this edition we have made a genuine effort to produce a literal transcription of what Clarke took to be Cromwell's words as recorded by his stenographers.

On 28 October, the first day of the debates, there are fifty-two recorded speeches. Exactly half were made by Cromwell (who presided) or by his son-in-law, Commissary General Henry Ireton. Their twenty-six speeches (thirteen each), however, contained almost two-thirds of all the recorded words. Not one of the colonels present spoke on this first day, although Lieutenant Colonel William Goffe did speak three times to call for a prayer meeting to be held. Three junior officers made a total of four speeches, and five trooper-agitators made ten speeches. The assistants to the new agents, John Wildman and Maximilian Petty (or Pettus) made nine contributions, five of them short, including two short interjections during a long speech of Ireton's. Cromwell's speeches constitute about 25 per cent of the total number of words recorded as having been spoken on 28 October.

[fo. 1r]

Att the Generall Councill
of officers att Putney,
28th October 1647.
[rest of page blank]

[fo. 1v]

The Officers being mett, first said,

Lieutenant General Cromwell: That the Meeting was for publique businesses, Those that had any thinge to say concerning the publique businesse they might have Libertie to speake.

After this, the authors of the Case of the Armie Truly Stated *introduce themselves, and Ireton reports back from the Committee appointed the previous week to discuss it. One of the authors, Edward Sexby,[6] a trooper in Sir Thomas Fairfax's regiment of horse, then sums up the aims of* The Case, *saying that there had been too much effort to please a King who intended to cut their throats and too much power left with 'the rotten studs' in Parliament, and he told Cromwell and Ireton to their faces that their 'credits and reputation had been blasted*

---

[5] Several more recent shortened versions have been published. Some, including Abbott, *Writings and Speeches*, I:515–50 (including full texts of all Cromwell's speeches) follow Firth's transcription; others, including D. Wootton, *Divine Right and Democracy* (1986), pp. 285–317 and G. Robertson and P. Baker, *The Putney Debates: the Levellers* (2007), pp. 61–105, follow Woodhouse. Only Gerald Aylmer, *The Levellers in the English Revolution* (1975), pp. 97–130 offers a transcription based on Firth but checked against the original manuscript. Aylmer modernises spelling and punctuation and only includes one Cromwell speech in his selection.

[6] Edward Sexby (*c.*1616–58), army officer and conspirator. See ODNB.

437

THE LETTERS, WRITINGS, AND SPEECHES OF OLIVER CROMWELL

on these two considerations'. Cromwell, chairing the debate in the absence through supposed sickness of Lord General Fairfax, responded:

[fo. 2v]

Lieut Generall I thinke itt is good for us to proceede to our businesse in some order, and that will bee if wee consider somethings that are latelie past. There hath bin a Booke printed, Called The Case of the Armie Stated,[7] and that hath bin taken into Consideration, and there hath bin somewhat drawne uppe by way of Exception to thinges contayned in that Booke, and I suppose there was an Answer brought to that which was taken by Way of Exception, and yesterday the Gentleman that brought the Answer hee was dealt honestly and plainly withall, and hee was told, That there were new Designes a driving, and nothing would bee a clearer Discovery of the Sincerity of intentions, as their willingnesse that were active to bringe what they had to say to bee judgd of by the Generall Officers, and by this Generall Councill that wee might discerne what the intentions were. Now itt seemes there bee divers that are come hither to manifest those intentions according to what was offered yesterday, and Truly I thinke, That the best way of our proceeding will bee to receive what they have to offer, onely this, Mr. Sexby, you were speaking to us two: Except you thinke that wee have done somewhat or acted some what different from the sence & Resolution of the Generall Councill. Truly, That that you Speake to, was the thinges that related to the Kinge and thinges that related to the Parliament, and if there bee a fault I may say itt, and I dare say, itt hath bin the fault of the Generall Councill, and that which you doe Speake you Speake to the Generall Councill, I hope, though you nam'd us two, both in relation to the one, and to the other. And therefore Truly I thinke itt is sufficient for us to say, and Tis that wee say, I can Speake for my self lett others Speake for themselves, I dare maintaine itt, and I dare avowe I have acted nothing butt what I have done with the publique consent, & approbation and allowance of the Generall Councill that I dare say for myself, both in Relation to the one and to the other, what I have acted in Parliament in the name of the Councill or of the Army I have had my warrant for itt from hence, what I have spoken as a Member of the House in another capacitie, that was free for mee to doe, and I am confident [fo. 3r] That I have nott used the Name of the Army, or interest of the Army to anythinge butt what I have had allowance from the Generall Councill for, and thought itt fitt to move the House in. I doe the rather give you this Account

---

[7] *The Case of the Armie Truly Stated* (1647). Thomason acquired his copy on 19 October (Wing / W1268A; Thomason / E.411[9]).

438

28 OCTOBER 1647

because I heare, there are some slanderous Reports going uppe & downe uppon somewhat that hath bin offer'd to the House of Commons as being the sence and opinion of this Armie, and in the Name of this Army, which I dare bee confident to Speake it hath bin as false and slanderous a Report as could bee raised of a man, and that was this. That I should say to the Parliament, and deliver itt as the Desire of this Armie and the sence of this Armie, that there should bee a second Addresse to the Kinge by way of propositions, I dare bee confident to speake itt what I deliver'd there I deliver'd as my owne sence, and what I deliver'd as my own sence I am nott ashamed of: What I delivered as your sence, I never delivered butt what I had as your sence.[8]

Colonel Thomas Rainborow[9] then spoke to exonerate Cromwell from the charge of betraying the Army's interest, and he is followed by Ireton who robustly rejects the charges against himself and Cromwell, and read the report of the Council Committee that had met since 22 October.[10] William Allen, trooper-agitator from Cromwell's own regiment of Horse,[11] then acknowledged that they had seen this report, and he read the agitators' response.[12] Ireton then angrily accuses the authors of The Case *of themselves seeking to set up 'a divided partie or distinct Councill', and in response a soldier referred to by Clarke as 'Buffe-Coat', now agreed to be Robert Everard, one of the new agents[13] introduces their new proposals known as* The Agreement of the People,[14] *and he beseeched the Council to consider it.*

[fo. 6r]

Lieutenant Generall These thinges that you have now offered they are new to us. They are things that wee have nott att all att least in this Method and thus circumstantially had any opportunity to Consider of them because they came to us

---

[8] These rather defensive comments about his speaking in Parliament probably relate to a debate on 23 September in which Cromwell was prominent in speaking to a proposal for a new approach to the King (*JHC*, 5:314). The newspaper reports on the debates of 23 September are well summarised in *Clarke Papers*, 1:230–1n.

[9] Rainborowe [Rainborow], Thomas (d. 1648), parliamentarian army officer and Leveller. See *ODNB*.

[10] The report is not in Clarke's transcript, although he left space on the page for it. The report can be found in Rushworth, *Historical Collections*, 8:849–50.

[11] William Allen is not in *ODNB*. But see Paul Hardacre, 'William Allen, Cromwellian Agitator and Fanatic', *Baptist Quarterly*, n.s., 19:7 (1962), pp. 292–308.

[12] Again, this is not copied out by Clarke, but available in Rushworth, *Historical Collections*, 8:857.

[13] Everard, Robert (*fl.* 1647–1664), religious controversialist. See *ODNB*.

[14] Again, this is not included by Clarke. The first printing is (Wing / A780; Thomason / E.412[21]): *An agreement of the people for a firme and present peace, upon grounds of common-right and freedome; as it was proposed by the agents of the five regiments of horse.* In addition to discussions in many works on the period, it is very thoroughly assessed in P. Baker and E. Vernon, eds., *The Agreements of the People, the Levellers and the Constitutional Crisis of the English Revolution* (Basingstoke, 2012).

439

THE LETTERS, WRITINGS, AND SPEECHES OF OLIVER CROMWELL

butt thus as you see, This is the first time wee had a view of them. Truly this paper
does containe in itt very great alterations of the very Governement of the
Kingdome, Alterations from that Governement that itt hath bin under I believe I
may almost say, since itt was a Nation; I say I thinke I may almost say soe, and
what the Consequences of such an alteration as this would bee, if there were
nothing else to bee Consider'd, Wisemen and Godly men ought to Consider. I say,
if there were nothing else butt the very Weight and nature of the thinges contayn'd
in this paper, and therefore, although the pretensions in itt and the Expressions in
itt a,re very plausible, and if wee could leape out of one Condition into another
that had soe specious thinges in itt as this hath I suppose there would nott bee
much dispute though perhaps some of these thinges may bee very well disputed,
and how doe wee know if whilest wee are disputing these thinges another
Companie of Men shall[15] gather together, and they shall putt out a paper as plausible perhaps as this, I doe nott know why itt might nott bee done by that time you
have agreed uppon this or gett hands to itt if that bee the Way, and nott onely
another & another butt many of this Kinde, and if soe what doe you thinke the
Consequence of that would bee, would itt nott bee Confusion? Would itt nott bee
utter Confusion? Would itt nott make England like the Switzerland Country, one
Canton of the Switz against another, and one County against another, I aske you
Whether itt bee not fitt for every honest Man seriouslie to lay that uppon his
heart, and if soe, what would that produce butt an absolute Desolation, an absolute Desolation [fo. 6v] to the Nation, and wee in the meane time tell the Nation,
It is for your Libertie, Tis for your priviledge, Tis for your Good, pray God itt
prove soe whatsoever Course wee run; Butt Truly, I thinke wee are nott onely to
consider what the Consequences are (if there were nothing else butt this paper)
butt wee are to consider the probability of the Wayes & meanes to accomplish
That is to say, That according to Reason and Judgement the Spiritts & Temper of
the people of this Nation are prepared to Receive and to goe on alonge with itt
and those great difficulties lie in our way in a likelihood to bee either overcome or
removed. Truly, To any thinge thats good there's noe doubt on itt, objections may
bee made and fram'd, butt lett every honest Man consider, Whether or noe there
bee nott very reall objections in point of difficulty, and I know a Man may answer
all Difficulties with Faith, and Faith will answer all difficulties really where itt is,
and wee are very apt all of us to call that Faith, That perhaps may bee butt carnall
imagination and carnall reasonings. Give mee leave to say this, There will bee

[15] Firth and Woodhouse both suggest a 'not' is missing here.

28 OCTOBER 1647

very great Mountaines in the Way of this, if this were the thinge in present Consideration, and therefore wee ought to Consider the Consequences,[16] and God hath given us our Reason that wee may doe this and itt is nott enough to propose thinges that are good in the End butt itt is our Duty as Christians & Men to Consider Consequences, and to Consider the Way, Butt suppose this Modell were an Excellent Modell, and fitt for England and the Kingedome to Receive, butt Really I shall speake to nothing butt that, that as before the Lord I am perswaded in my heart, tends to uniting of us in one to that that God will manifest to us to bee the thinge that hee would have us prosecute, and hee that meetes nott heere with that heart, and dares nott say hee will stand to that, I thinke hee is a Deceivor. I say it to you againe, and I professe unto you I shall offer nothing to you butt that I thinke in my heart & Conscience tends to the uniting of us, and to [fo. 7r] the Begetting a Right understanding amonge us And therefore this is that I would insist uppon, and have it clear'd amonge us: Itt is nott enough for us to insist uppon good thinges, that every one would doe, There is nott[17] 40 of us butt wee could prescribe many thinges exceeding plausible and hardly any thinge Worse then our present Condition, take itt with all the Troubles that are upon us, butt itt is nott enough for us to propose good thinges butt itt behoves honest Men & Christians that really will approve themselves soe before God and men to see whether or noe they bee in a Condition, Whether taking all thinges into Consideration they may honestly indeavour & attempt that that is fairly and plausibly proposed. For my owne parte I know[18] nothing that wee are to consider first butt that before wee would come to debate the Evill or good of this, or to adde to itt or Subtract from itt, which I am confident if your Hearts be upright as ours are, and God will bee judge betweene you and us if wee should come to any thinge you doe nott bringe this paper with peremptorinesse of minde butt to receive Amendements to have any thinge taken from itt that may bee made appeare to bee apparent by cleare Reason to bee inconvenient or unhonest, butt this ought to bee our Consideration and yours saving in this you have the Advantage of us, You that are the Souldiers you have nott butt you that are not[19]

---

[16] This underlining is in the same ink and appears to be the work of Clarke as he transcribed from the shorthand. Looking at all the examples, the greatest expert on Clarke's shorthand and longhand, Frances Henderson, does not think the underlining represents emphasis but a note to himself that the shorthand is unclear and his transcription needs to be checked.

[17] Woodhouse, but not Firth, suggests the addition of 'one in' here which might make better sense.

[18] Difficult to read: 'knew' or 'know', it could be either.

[19] Firth and Woodhouse both add 'soldiers' here.

THE LETTERS, WRITINGS, AND SPEECHES OF OLIVER CROMWELL

you reckon your selves att a loose and att a liberty, as men that have noe obligation uppon you, perhaps wee conceive wee have; and therefore, and therefore this is that I may saye to the officers, both to those that come with you, and to my fellow officers and all others that heare mee: that itt concernes us as we would approve our selves before God, and before Men that are able to judge of us, if wee doe not make good[20] Engagements, if wee do nott make good that that the world Expects wee should make Good, I doe not speake to Determine what that is, butt if I bee not much mistaken, wee have in the time of our danger issued out Declarations, wee have bin required by the Parliament, because our Declarations [fo. 7v] were general, to declare particularly what wee meant, and having done that how farre that obliges or nott obliges that is by us to be considered if wee meane honestly and sincerely and doe approve our selves to God as honest Men and therefore having heard this paper Read this Remaines to us that wee againe Review what wee have engaged in and what wee have that lies uppon us and hee that departs from that, that is a reall Engagement and a reall Tye uppon him I thinke hee transgresses without Faith, for Faith will beare upppe men in every honest obligation, and God does expect from men the performance of every honest obligation and therefore I have noe more to say butt this wee having received your paper wee shall amongst our selves Consider what to doe, and before wee take this into Consideration, itt is fitt for us to Consider how farre wee are obliged, and how farre wee are free, and I hope wee shall prove ourselves honest men where wee are free to tender any thing to the Good of the publique, and this is that I thought good to offer to you uppon this paper.

Cromwell's speech provoked a response from the civilian John Wildman, who strongly endorsed the Agreement of the People, and argued that it is 'the honesty' of the Agreement that needs to come before any obstacles created by pre-existing obligations. This is strongly contested by Ireton, who says that there is no simple way for the members of the Army to absolve themselves from obligations freely entered into, however appealing much of the Agreement was, as he claims it is to him. Colonel Rainborowe complains about his recent transfer out of the Army but says he has come not to lobby about that but to support the Agreement. He addresses the 'difficulties and dangers they had faced', and he argues that all our liberties have been achieved by 'scufflings' with previous kings. Liberties have not been conferred but secured. Like Wildman, he argues that the justness of the terms of the Agreement should be the first thing considered before deciding which Engagments were just or unjust.

---

[20] Both Firth and Woodhouse suggest 'our' is implied here.

442

28 OCTOBER 1647

[fo. 10v]

Lieutenant Generall Truly I am very glad That this Gentleman that spoke last is heere, and nott sorry for the occasion that brought him hither because itt argues wee shall enjoy his Company longer then I thought we should have done
Rainborough:
If I should not be kicked out—
Lieutenant Generall. And Truly then I thinke itt shall nott bee longe enough. Butt Truly I doe nott know what the Meaning of that Expression is, nor what the Meaning of any hatefull Worde is heere for wee are all heere with the same Integrity to the publique, and perhaps wee have all of us [fo. 11r] done our parts not affrighted[21] with difficulties one as well as another, and, I hope, have all purposes henceforward through the Grace of God nott Resolving in our owne Strength to doe soe still, and therefore Truly I thinke all the Consideration is, That amongst us wee are almost all souldiers; All Considerations of Wordes of that kinde doe wonderfully please us: All Words of Courage animates[22] us to carry on our businesse, to doe Gods businesse that which is the Will of God, and I say itt againe I doe nott thinke that any Man heere wants Courage to doe that which becomes an honest Man, & an Englishman to doe, butt wee speake as men that desire to have the feare of God before our Eyes, and Men that may nott Resolve in the power of a fleshly Strength to doe that which wee doe, butt to lay this as the foundation of all our actions to doe that which is the Will of God, and if any Man have a false Deceit on the one hand, Deceitfulnesse, that which hee doth nott intend, or a perswasion on the other hand I thinke hee will nott prosper butt to that which was mov'd by Col: Rainborow, of the objections of difficulty & danger of the Consequences[23] they are proposed nott to any other End, butt things fitting Consideration, nott forged to deterre from the Consideration of the businesse butt in the Consideration of the thinge that is new \to/ [24] us and of every thinge that shall bee New that is of such importance as this is, I thinke that hee that wishes the most serious Advice to bee taken of such a Change as this is soe Evident and Cleare[25] who ever offers that there may bee most serious Consideration I

---

[21] 'affrighted' is underlined but not necessarily contemporaneously with the transcription.

[22] 'animates' is underlined probably as a sign that Clarke was not certain how to transcribe the shorthand (see n. 16).

[23] 'consequences' is underlined probably as a sign that Clarke was not certain how to transcribe the shorthand (see n. 16).

[24] There is an illegible word here.   [25] Firth and Woodhouse both add 'a change' here.

THE LETTERS, WRITINGS, AND SPEECHES OF OLIVER CROMWELL

thinke he does not speake impertinently, and Truly itt was offer'd to noe other End then what I speake, I shall say noe more to that. Butt to the other Concerning Engagements and breaking of them I doe nott thinke that itt was att all offer'd by any Body that though an Engagement were never soe unrighteous itt ought to be kept, noe Man offer'd a syllable or Tittle,[26] for Certainly itt's an Act of Duty to breake an unrighteous Engagement. Hee that keepes itt does a double sin in that hee made an unrighteous Engagement [fo. 11v] and that hee goes about to keepe itt, butt this was onely offer'd that before wee can consider of this (and I know nott what can be more fitly) wee labour to know where wee are, and where wee stand, perhaps wee are uppon Engagements that wee cannott with honesty breake butt lett mee tell you this, that hee That speakes to you of Engagements heere, is as free from Engagements to the Kinge as any man in all the world, and I know itt, if itt were otherwise I beleive my future actions would provoke some to declare itt butt I thanke God I stand uppon the bottome of my owne innocencie in this particular, through the Grace of God I feare nott the face of any Man, I doe nott. I say wee are to Consider what Engagements wee have made, and if our Engagements have bin unrighteous why should wee nott make itt our Indeavours to breake them, yett if unrighteous Engagements itt is nott a present breach of them unlesse there bee a Consideration of Circumstances: Circumstances may bee such as I may nott now breake an unrighteous Engagement, or else I may doe that which I did scandalously, if the thinge bee good, butt if that bee true concerning the breaking of an unrighteous Engagement, itt is much more <u>verified</u>[27] concerning a disputable Engagement, whether they bee righteous or unrighteous. If soe, I am sure itt is fitt wee should dispute and if when wee have disputed them, wee see the Goodnesse of God inlightening us to see our liberties I thinke wee are to doe what wee can to give satisfaction to Men, butt if itt were soe as wee made an Engagement in Judgement and Knowledge, soe wee goe off from itt in Judgement and Knowledge, butt there may bee just Engagements uppon us such as perhaps itt will bee our duty to keepe; and if soe itt is fitt wee should Consider, and all that I said that wee should Consider our Engagements and there is nothing else offer'd, and therfore what neede anybody bee Angry or offended, perhaps wee have made such Engagements as may in the matter of them nott binde us, in some Circumstances they may, our Engagements are publique Engagements.

[26] Firth and Woodhouse add 'to that purpose' at this point.
[27] 'verified' is underlined probably as a sign that Clarke was not certain how to transcribe the shorthand (see n. 16).

444

28 OCTOBER 1647

They are to [fo. 12r] the Kingdome, and to every one in the Kingdome that could looke uppon what wee did publiquely declare, Could read or heare it Read, They are to the Parliament and itt is a very fitting thinge that wee doe seriously Consider of the thinges and that this is that I shall shortly offer, That because the Kingdome is in the danger itt is in, because the Kingedome is in that Condition itt is in, and time may bee ill spent in Debates, and itt is necessary for thinges to bee putt to an issue, if ever itt was necessary in the World it is now, I should desire this may bee done. That this Generall Councill may bee appointed against a very short time, two days, Thursday, if you would against Saturday, or at furthest against Munday, that there might bee a Committee out of this Councill appointed to debate and Considerwith those two Gentlemen, and with any others that are nott of the Army, that they shall bringe, and with the Agitators of those five Regiments that soe there may bee a Liberall & free Debate had amongst us, That wee may understand really as before God the bottome of our Desires and that wee may seeke God together, and see if God will give us an uniting spiritt and give mee leave to tell itt you againe, I am confident there sitts nott a Man in this place that cannott soe freely act with you if hee sees that God hath shutt uppe his Way that hee cannott doe any service in that Way as may bee Good for the Kingedome, butt hee will bee glad to withdraw himself and wish you all prosperity, and if this heart bee in us as is knowne to God that searches our hearts & tryeth the Reines God will discover whether our hearts bee nott clear in this businesse and therefore I shall move that wee may have a Committee amongst our selves[28] of the Engagements, and this committee to dispute thinges with others, and a short day for the Generall Councill, and I doubt nott butt if in sincerity <u>wee are</u>[29] willing to submitt to that light that God shall cast in amonge us, God will unite us, and make us of one heart [fo. 12v] and one mind. And do the plausiblest thinges you can doe, Doe that which hath the most appearance of Reason in itt that tends to change att this Conjuncture of time you will finde difficulties, butt if God satisfie our Spiritts this will bee a ground of Confidence to every Good Man, and hee that goes uppon other Grounds, hee shall fall like a beast. I shall desire this That you, or any other of the Agitators or Gentlemen that can bee heere will bee heere that wee may have free discourses amongst our selves of thinges, and you will bee able to satisfie each other. And really rather than I would have this Kingedome breake

[28] Firth and Woodhouse add 'to consider'.
[29] 'wee are' is underlined probably as a sign that Clarke was not certain how to transcribe the shorthand (see n. 16).

THE LETTERS, WRITINGS, AND SPEECHES OF OLIVER CROMWELL

in pieces before some Company of Men bee united together to a Settlement, I will withdraw my self from the Army tomorrow, & lay downe my Commission. I will perish before I hinder itt.

An unidentified 'Bedfordshire Man' argues against being bound by unjust engagements and argues 'for the change of the government, which is so dangerous, I apprehend that there may be many dangers in it, and truly I apprehend there may be more dangers without it. For I conceive, if you keep the government as it is and bring in the King, there may be more dangers than in changing the government.' Captain Audley urges the immediate appointing of a Committee and Lt Col William Goffe calls for a prayer meeting since 'wee have in some thinges wandred from God…The motion is, that there might be a seeking of God in the things that now lie before us.'

[fo. 14v]

Lieutenant Generall I know nott what[30] Lieut Col: Goffe meanes for to morrow for the time of seeking God, I thinke itt will bee requisite that wee doe itt speedily, and doe itt the first thinge, and that wee doe it as unitedly as wee can as many of us as well may meete together for my parte I shall lay aside all businesse for this businesse either to convince or bee convinc't as God shall please. I thinke itt would bee good that to morrow Morning may bee spent in prayer, and the after-noone might bee the time of our businesse. I doe nott know that these Gentlemen doe assent to itt that to morrow in the afternoone might be the time.

Goffe and Ireton agree to this, Ireton urging that 'the maine thinge is for every one to waite uppon God for the errours, deceits, and weaknesses of his owne heart,' and Goffe says that 'I think we have a great deal of business to do, and we have been doing of it these ten weeks.[31] I say, go about what you will, for my part I shall not think anything can prosper unless God be first [publicly] sought. It is an ordinance that God hath blessed to this end.' It was then 'agreed that the Meeting for Prayer to bee at Mr Chamberlaine's.'[32]

[fo. 15v]

Lieutenant Generall If that bee approved of, that to morrow shall bee a time of seeking the Lord, and that the afternoone shall bee the time of businesse, if that doth agree with your opinion and General Sense, lett that bee first ordered

Ireton claims that Lt Col Goffe's proposal 'hath a very great impression upon me' in his call for a prayer meeting and he issues a general call to bring God into the heart of their deliberations: 'Every one hath a spirit within him—especially [he] who has that communion indeed with

---

[30] Lomas and Woodhouse suggest adding 'time' here.
[31] Since about 20 July—i.e. since the Reading Debates.   [32] Not identified.

446

28 OCTOBER 1647

that Spirit that is the only searcher of hearts—that can best search out and discover to him the errors of his own ways and of the workings of his own heart... But I think the main thing is for every one to wait upon God, for the errors, deceits, and weaknesses of his own heart; and I pray God to be present with us in that. But withal I would not have that seasonable and good motion that hath come from Lieutenant-Colonel Goffe to be neglected, of a public seeking of God, and seeking to God, as for other things so especially for the discovery of any public deserting of God, or dishonouring of him, or declining from him, that does lie as the fault and blemish upon the Army. Therefore I wish his motion may be pursued, that the thing may be done, and for point of time as was moved by him.' This proved decisive and so it was agreed that there should be a meeting for prayer the next morning.

[fo. 15v]

Lieutenant Generall That they should nott meete as two Contrary parties butt as some Desirous to Satisffie or Convince each other.

Maximilian Petty, the civilian, and Robert Everard ('Buffcoate'), making clear that they speak for themselves and not for those who sent them, agree to this, Ireton adding rather tartly that 'I should be sorry, that they should be soe suddaine to stand uppon themselves'.

[fo. 16r]

Lieutenant Generall. I hope wee know God better then to make appearances of Religious Meetings Covers for Designes or for insinuation amongst you. I desire that God that hath given us some Sinceritie will owne us according to his owne goodnesse, and that Sincerity that hee hath given us. I dare bee Confident to speake itt, That that hath bin amongst us hitherto is to seeke the Guidances of God, and to Recover that presence of God that seemes to withdraw from us, and itt seemes as much to us in this as any thinge wee are nott all of a minde, and to accomplish that Worke which may bee for the good of the Kingdome is our End, and for our parts wee doe nott desire or offer you to bee with us in our seeking of God further then your owne satisfaccons lead you, butt onely against to morrow in the afternoone which will bee design'd <u>for the</u>[33] Consideration of these businesses with you, you will doe what you may to have soe many as you shall thinke fitt to see what God will direct you to say to us, that whilst we <u>are</u>[34] going one Way, and you [fo. 16r] another, wee be nott both destroyed. This Requires Spiritt. It may bee too soone to say itt is my present apprehension I had rather wee should

---

[33] 'for the' is underlined probably as a sign that Clarke was not certain how to transcribe the shorthand (see n. 16).

[34] 'are' is underlined probably as a sign that Clarke was not certain how to transcribe the shorthand (see n. 16).

447

THE LETTERS, WRITINGS, AND SPEECHES OF OLIVER CROMWELL

devolve our strength to you then that the Kingdome for our Division should suffer losse, for that's in all our hearts, to professe above any thinge that's worldlie, the publique Good of the people and if that bee in our hearts Truly and nakedlie I am confident itt is a principall that will <u>stand</u>[35] perhaps[36] God may unite us and carry us both one way, and therefore I doe desire you, That against to morrow in the afternoone if you judge itt meete you will come to us to the Quartermaster-Generall's Quarters[37] where you will finde us if you will come timely to joyne with us, at your Libertie, if afterwards to speake with us & then[38] you will find us. *This leads to an extended discussion between Wildman and Ireton about the binding nature of engagements (ie oaths and covenants) — Wildman saying that there is no obligation to honour a sinful engagement, Ireton distinguishing 'sinful' engagements from those between man and man which did need to be honoured. He 'trembled' at the 'endless consequences' of allowing 'that wild or vast notion of what in every man's conception is just or unjust' as a guide to what engagements are binding and which not. Captain Audley picked up on Wildman's suggestion that 'if we tarry long, if we stay but three days before you satisfy one another, the King will come and say who will be hanged first.' Seeing this discussion as an attack on the agreement to delay discussion of the Agreement until after a prayer meeting, Cromwell speaks again:*

[fo. 21r]

Lieutenant Generall. Lett mee speake a Worde to this Businesse wee are now upon that businesse which wee spake of Consulting with God about itt, and therefore for us to dispute the meritt of those thinges I judge itt altogether unseasonable, unlesse you will make itt the subject of Debate before you Consider it among your selves; The businesse of the Engagement lies uppon us, <u>They are</u>[39] free in a double Respect. They made none, and if they did, then the Way out is now, and[40] which all the Members of the Army Except they bee sensible of itt, and att one Jumpe, Jumpe out of all, and it is a very great Jumpe I will assure you:

---

[35] 'stand' is underlined probably as a sign that Clarke was not certain how to transcribe the shorthand (see n. 16).

[36] 'p'haps' is a possible rather than a certain reading of the faded and rushed characters in the manuscript.

[37] i.e. the quarters of 'Mr Chamberlain', otherwise unidentified, named below, see above, p. 444.

[38] Here there is squiggle, possibly one squiggle on top of another, which is illegible; Firth and Woodhouse transcribe it as 'there' but it cannot be that. It might be 'and then'.

[39] 'They are' is underlined probably as a sign that Clarke was not certain how to transcribe the shorthand (see n. 16).

[40] Firth and Woodhouse suggest adding 'it is a way' here.

28 OCTOBER 1647

As wee professe wee intend to seeke the Lord in the thinge, the lesse wee speake in it the better, and the more wee cast ourselves uppon God the better. I[41] shall onelie speake two things to Mr. Wildman in order to our Meeting, Mee thoughts he said, if there bee delay hee feares this businesse will bee determined, The propositions will bee sent from the Parliament and the Parliament and Kinge agree, and soe those gentlemen that were in that minde to goe on in their way will bee cutt off in point of time to their owne disadvantage, and the other thinge hee said was, That these Gentlemen who have chosen Mr. Wildman & that other Gentleman,[42] to bee their Mouth [fo. 21v] att this Meeting to Deliver their Mindes they are uppon the matter engaged in what they have resolved uppon, and they come as engaged men uppon their owne Resolution, if that bee soe, I thinke there neither needes Consideration of the former,[43] for you will nott be anticipated if that bee soe you worke accordingly, and though you meete us yett having that Resolution in your way you cannott bee prevented by any proposition, or any such thinge though wee should have come hither, and we should meete to morrow as a Company of Men that really would bee guided by God, If any come to us to morrow onely to Instruct us, and teach us, and determine how farre that will consist with the Libertie of a free Liberty, or an End of Satisfaction I referre to every sober spiritted Man to think of.[44] I thinke itt is such a preEngagement that there is noe neede of talke of the thinge and I see then if that is bee soe Things are in such an irrevocable way I will nott call itt desperate as there is noe hope of Accomodation or union, Except wee receive the Councills I will nott call itt the Commands of them that come to us, I desire that wee may rightly understand this thinge, if this bee soe I doe nott understand what the End of the Meeting will bee, if this bee nott soe that they[45] will draw any Man from their Engagements further then the Light of God shall draw them from their Engagements[46] and I

---

[41] There is an unreadable corrected squiggle here and a possible 'I' as part of it. It is difficult to see what else is intended.

[42] Maximilian Petty (Pettus). [Maximilian Petty [Pettus], Maximilian (bap. 1617, d. in or after 1661?), Leveller. See *ODNB*.]

[43] Woodhouse suggest 'nor the latter' here.

[44] The preceding sentence is horribly mangled by both Firth and by Woodhouse, the clauses re-arranged, and the second 'Liberty' changed to 'determination'.

[45] Firth and Woodhouse confidently change 'they' here to 'we' with the note 'i.e. Cromwell and the Council. The reporter changes into *oratio obliqua* for a moment.' This is a possibility but it is no more than that.

[46] At this point Firth and Woodhouse have 'I do not understand what the end of the meeting will be. If this be not so, we will [not] draw any men from their engagements further than the light of God shall draw them from their engagements.' This changes a 'wee' to a 'they' and intrudes a 'not' completely changing the meaning without explanation.

THE LETTERS, WRITINGS, AND SPEECHES OF OLIVER CROMWELL

thinke according to your owne principle if you bee uppon any Engagement you are liable to bee Convinc't unlesse you bee infallible if wee may come to an honest & single debate how wee may all agree in one Common Way for publique good if we meete soe wee shall meete with a great deale the more Comfort, and hopes of a good and happy issue, and understanding of the businesse; but if otherwise, I despaire of the Meeting, or att least I would have the Meeting to bee of another Notion, a Meeting that did represent the Agitators of five Regiments to give Rules to the Councill of Warre, if itt signifie this for my owne parte I shall bee glad to submitt to it under this Notion. If itt bee a free debate what may bee fitt for us all to doe with clearnesse, and opennesse before the Lord, and in that sincerity, lett us understand that wee may come & meete soe, otherwise [fo. 22r] I doe verily beleive wee shall meete with prejudice, and wee shall meete to prejudice, Really to the prejudice of the Kingdome, and of the whole Army. Thus if wee bee absolutely resolved uppon our Way and engaged beforehand the Kingdome will see, itt is such a Reall actual division as admitts of noe Reconciliation, and all those that are Enemies to us and freinds to our Enemies will have the clearer Advantage uppon us to putt us into inconveniency, and I desire if there bee any feare of God among us I desire that wee may declare ourselves freely that wee doe meete uppon these Termes.

Rainborowe, Everard and Wildman continue to rail against the non-binding nature of engagements, Everard saying he would break 100 engagements a day 'if afterwards God would reveal himself.' Cromwell responds:

[fo. 23r]

Lieutenant Generall. I thinke clearly you Were understood to putt itt uppon an issue where there is clearly a Case of Destruction, publique Destruction, and ruine, and I thinke this will bringe itt into Consideration whether or noe our Engagements have really in them that that hath publique Destruction & ruine necessarily following or whether or noe wee may nott give too much Way to our owne doubts or feares, and whether itt bee lawfull to breake a Covenant uppon our owne Doubts & feares will bee the issue and I thinke[47] if wee agree to deferre the Debate[48] to nominate a Committee.

---

[47] Firth suggests adding 'best' here and Woodhouse suggests 'it best', both of which appear to make sense.

[48] Firth and Woodhouse both suggest adding 'and' here which does change the sense but quite possibly correctly.

28 OCTOBER 1647

There follow five short speeches about engagements following the same lines as before. Nicholas Lockyer, a trooper, calls for no proposals to go to the King until the General Council has seen what they are.

[fo. 23v]

Lieutenant Generall. The Question is whether the propositions will save us or[49] nott destroy us. This discourse concludes nothing.

Captain John Merriman highlights points of difference between the parties over the King and the 'broken reeds' in parliament, but he argues that all have committed themselves to 'free the people, which you may doe by taking off tythes and other Antichristian yokes'; 'Buffcoat' [Robert Everard] asserts that Wildman is not averse to seeking God and is concerned only over ways and means; and Lieutenant Edmund Chillenden calls on the new agents to join in the prayer meeting (implying their reluctance to do so) and that that will induce in them 'a sweete compliance in communicating Councils'.

Cromwell responds to Everard rather than to Chillenden.

[fo. 24v]

Lieutenant Generall. That which this Gentleman hath moved I like Exceeding well hee hath fully declar'd himself concerning the freedome of their spiritt as to ~~particular~~[50] principles. In Generall they aime att peace and safetie, And really I am perswaded in my conscience itt is their Aime[51] as may bee most for the Good of the people, for Really if that bee nott the supreame good to us under God, (the good of the people) our principles fall. Now if that bee in your spiritts & our spiritts, itt remaines that God onely show us the Way and lead us the Way which I hope hee will, and give mee leave that there may bee some prejudices upon some of your spiritts, and such men that doe affect your way that they may have some jealousies & apprehensions that wee are wedded and glewed to formes of Governement soe that whatsoever wee may pretend, itt is in vaine for[52] to speake to us, or to hope for any Agreement from us to you, and I beleive some such apprehensions as some parte of the Legislative power of the Kingdome[53] where itt may rest besides in the Commons of the Kingdome you will finde that wee are as farre from being particularly engaged to any thinge to the prejudice of this

---

[49] Firth and Woodhouse suggest the addition of 'whether they will' here.
[50] This word is heavily scored out, and this is the most likely reading of what can be made out.
[51] Firth and Woodhouse suggest the addition of 'to act' here.
[52] Firth and Woodhouse add 'you' here.
[53] Firth, Woodhouse and Lomas, in revising Firth, all offer different ways of making sense of this sentence. The simplest and perhaps least interventionist is Carlyle-Lomas 3:362, 'and I believe [also] some such apprehensions as [to] some parte of the Legislative power of the Kingdome'.

451

further then the notorious Engagement that the World takes notice of that wee should nott concurre with you That the Foundation & Supremacy is in the people, radically in them, & to bee sette downe by them in their Representations, and if Wee doe soe[54] how wee may run to that End that wee all aime att, or[55] that that does Remayne, and therefore lett us onely name the Committee.

Lt Col Goffe re-emphasises his confidence in the outcome of a prayer meeting and William Allen expresses his concerns about 'whether these gentlemen[56] have a power to debate; and if they have not, that they may have recourse to them that sent them' to see what powers they will give them, that 'we may offer our reasons and judgment upon the thing, and may act upon that principle upon which we agree.' Otherwise the meeting would be useless, and endless. To this Cromwell, from the Chair, makes a final reply.

[fo. 25r]

Lieutenant Generall. That Gentleman sayes hee will doe what hee can to draw all or the most of them hither to bee heard to morrow, and I desire Mr. Wildman, that if they have any freinds that are of a Loving spiritt that would contribute to this businesse of a right understanding,[57] and I say noe more butt this, I pray God Judge betweene you and us when Wee doe meete whether wee come With engaged spiritts to uppehold our owne Resolutions and opinions, or whether wee shall lay downe our selves to be rul'd[58] and that which hee shall communicate.

Colonel Rainboro ends the day's proceedings by distancing himself from Allen: if they come not with power to 'do' yet they should come with full power to debate.

The following page lists the eighteen members of the Committee to discuss The Agreement *and to report back. Cromwell and Ireton head the list, together with nine colonels, a lieutenant colonel and six soldier-agitators and agents.*

---

[54] Firth and Woodhouse add 'concur, we may also concur' here.
[55] Firth (silently) and Lomas (explicitly) change this 'or' to 'for' which does impose some clarity. Woodhouse adds a whole clause.
[56] Presumably the new agents and their London friends, Wildman and Petty.
[57] Firth and Woodhouse suggest the addition of 'they would come with him' here.
[58] 'rul'd' is underlined probably as a sign that Clarke was not certain how to transcribe the shorthand (see n. 16), and after 'rul'd' Firth and Woodhouse rather intrusively add 'by God'.

29 OCTOBER 1647

1647 10 29

Oliver Cromwell's contributions to the New Model Army Debate at Putney

Date: 29 October 1647
Source: Worcester College, Oxford, Clarke Papers, vol. 65, fos 26r–63v

On the evening of 28 October and the morning of 29 October, the new agents, together with their advisor John Wildman, appear to have gone off to the City of London (about five miles) to confer further, and from there rushed out the most bitter attack yet on the integrity of the generals.[1] Nonetheless, following the prayer meeting on the morning of 29 October, *The Agreement of the People* was read again, and then Cromwell and Ireton welcomed not only the new agents and their friends Wildman and Petty, but a number of their supporters in accordance with Cromwell's promise at the end of the debate of 28 October. Clarke's transcript of the proceedings on Friday 29 October begins towards the end of the Prayer Meeting and then moves, apparently seamlessly, into the meeting of the Committee appointed to discuss *The Agreement of the People*. Clarke names thirteen contributors to the prayer meeting. They are seven senior officers (six of whom had been named to the committee to discuss *The Agreement*, together with one who had not been), together with Robert Everard, one of the new agents, and Maximilian Petty (one of the agents' London friends). The others who spoke were Commissary Cowling and four captains, none of whom had been named to the committee. When the committee itself started to discuss *The Agreement*, there were twenty recorded speakers, including seven of the general staff and regimental commanders, seven junior officers, three troopers, only one of them a new agent, together with Wildman, Petty and Hugh Peter. In terms of the number of speeches over the whole day, sixty-two (a substantial majority) were given by general officers and regimental commanders, fifteen by junior officers, five by trooper-agitators and agents, and fifteen by the London (Leveller?) spokesmen. Over 80 per cent of the speeches were made by members of the Army appointed to the committee on 28 October, but just under 20 per cent were made by men, mainly by junior officers, who had not been appointed to the committee. No-one below the rank of colonel spoke more than three times. Of those appointed to the committee, six of the colonels and all but two of the agitators appear to have made no contributions to the debate. Cromwell spoke four times during the prayer meeting and four more times during the committee discussions, far less than Ireton and Rainbrowe but more, over the day as a whole, than anyone other than those two.

----

[1] There is a full and convincing account of overnight events in Woolrych, *Soldiers and Statesmeni*, 227–32. The embittered pamphlet is *A cal to all the souldiers of the Armie, by the free people of England* (1647) (Wing / W2167). Authorship is normally ascribed to John Wildman.

453

THE LETTERS, WRITINGS, AND SPEECHES OF OLIVER CROMWELL

[fo. 28v]

Putney October 29.1647

Att the Meeting of the Officers for Calling upon God according to the Appointment of the General Councill after some Discourses of Commissary [Nicholas] Cowling, Major [Francis] White, & others.

William Clarke's transcripts offer extended accounts of the meditations of Captain John Clarke and Lieutenant-Colonel William Goffe (who offered a long exegesis of Revelation, especially ch.17) and he recorded that 'Captain Carter prayed' and that Adjutant-General Richard Deane called for a further prayer meeting on the following Monday. After Goffe's meditation, Robert Everard ('Buffcoat') told the meeting that many supporters of The Agreement, together with 'those two friends that were with me yesterday' (i.e. Wildman and Pettus) were at the door, waiting to be admitted. Cromwell replies to him and to Lt-Gen Goffe:

Lieutenant Generall I thinke itt would nott bee amisse that those gentlemen that are come would draw nigher. I must offer this to your Consideration, Whether or noe wee having sett aparte this Morning to seeke God, and to gett such a preparednesse of heart and spiritt as might receive that, that God was minded <u>to have</u>[2] imparted to us and this having taken uppe all our time all this day, and itt having bin soe late this last night as indeed itt was when wee brake uppe, and wee having appointed a Committee to meete together to Consider of that paper, and this Committee having had noe time or opportunity that I know of nott soe much as a Meeting I make some scruple or doubt whether or noe itt is not better,[3] That danger is imagined, and indeed I think itt is, [fo. 29r] Butt bee the danger what itt will, our Agreement in the businesse is much more then the pressing of any danger, soe by that wee doe nott delay to, and that which I have to offer, Whether or noe wee are fitt to take uppe such a Consideration of these papers now as wee might bee to morrow, and perhaps if these Gentlemen which are butt few, and that Committee should meete together, and spend their time together an houre or two the Remainder of this afternoone, and all this Company might meete about 9 or 19 a clock <u>att furthest</u>,[4] and they understand one another soe well as wee might bee prepared for the generall Meeting to have a more exact & particular Consideration

---

[2] 'to have' is underlined probably as a sign that Clarke was not certain how to transcribe the shorthand (see **1647 10 28**, n. 16).

[3] Woodhouse (but not Firth) plausibly suggests the addition of 'to adjourn the debate. I know' here.

[4] 'at furthest' is underlined probably as a sign that Clarke was not certain how to transcribe the shorthand (see **1647 10 28**, n. 16).

454

29 OCTOBER 1647

of thinges then by a Generall loose debate of thinges which our Committee or at least any of us have had any, or att least nott many thoughts about.

Colonel Thomas Rainborowe thought that with everyone gathered, they could go straight into a reading of The Agreement, *and that the Committee could meet privately for an hour or two after that, and Everard too stressed the urgency and the need to move forward, and he was supported by Captain Lewis Audley, who said that 'while we debate we do nothing. I am confident that whilst you are doing you will all agree together, for it is idleness that hath begot this rust and this gangrene amongst us.' Cromwell responded:*

[fo. 29v]

Lieutenant Generall. I thinke itt is True, Lett us bee doing, but lett us bee united in our doing, if there remayne nothing else butt present action I meane doing in that kinde, Doing in that sort, I thinke wee neede nott bee in Councill heere, such kinde of Action, Action of that nature, butt if wee doe nott rightly and clearly understand one another before [fo. 30r] Wee come to Act, if wee doe nott lay a Foundation of Action before wee doe Act, I doubt whether wee shall Act unanimously or noe, and seriously as before the Lord I knew noe such End of our speech the last night, and appointing another Meeting butt in order to a more perfect understanding of one another, what wee should doe, and that wee might bee agreed uppon some principalls of Action, and Truly if I Remember Rightly, That uppon the Delivery of the paper that was yesterday, this was offer'd, That the thinges are now uppon us, the Thinges are thinges of difficulty, The thinges are thinges that doe Deserve (therefore) Consideration, because there might bee great Weight in the <u>Consequences</u>;[5] and itt was then offer'd, and I hope is still soe in all our hearts that wee are nott troubled with the Consideration of the Difficulty, nor with the Consideration of any thinge butt this, That if wee doe difficult thinges Wee may see that the thinges Wee doe have the Will of God in them, that they are nott onely plausible & good thinges, butt seasonable & honest thinges, fitt forus to doe, and therefore itt was desir'd that wee might Consider before wee could come to these papers that wee might Consider in what Condition wee stood in Respect of former Engagements Which however some may bee satisfied with that there lie none uppon us, or none but such as itt's duty to breake, itt's sin to keep: Therefore that was yesterday promised there may be a

---

[5] 'Consequences' is underlined probably as a sign that Clarke was not certain how to transcribe the shorthand (see **1647 10 28**, n. 16).

THE LETTERS, WRITINGS, AND SPEECHES OF OLIVER CROMWELL

Consideration had of them, and I may speake itt as in the presence of God that I know nothing of any Engagements butt I would see liberty in any man as I would bee <u>free from bondage</u> to any thinge[6] that should hinder mee from doing my Duty, and therefore that was first in Consideration, if our obligation bee nothing, or if itt bee Weake I hope itt will receive Satisfaction why itt should be laid aside that the thinges that Wee speak of are nott obliged, and therefore, if itt please you I thinke itt will be good for us to frame our Discourse to what Wee Were, Where wee are, what wee are bound to, what we are freed from to, [fo. 30v] and then I make noe question, butt that this may conclude what is betweene these Gentlemen, in one afternoone I doe nott speake this to make obligations more then what they were before, butt as before the Lord you see what they are,[7] and when wee looke uppon them wee shall see that wee have bin in a wronge way, and I hope itt will call uppon us for the more double diligence in itt.

Colonel Rainboroe complains that he had thought that the Commissioners had been charged to see how The Agreement *would promote justice and righteousness and not to get bogged down in an endless and fruitless discussion of past engagements and commitments or by an analysis of the Army Book of Declarations. Cromwell responded to him:*

[fo. 31r]

Lieutenant Generall I shall butt offer this to you, Truly I hope that wee may speake our hearts freelie heere, and I hope that there is not such an Evill amongst us as that wee could or would exercise our Witts, or our cunning to vaile over any doublenesse of heart that may possibly bee in us, I hope having bin in such a presence as wee have bin this day, Wee doe not admit of such a thought as this into our hearts and therefore if the speaking of that wee did speake before and to which I shall speake againe with submission to all that heare mee, If the declining to consider this paper may have with any Man a Worke uppon his Spiritt through any Jealousie that itt aimes att delay; Truly I can speake it as before the Lord itt is nott \at all/ in my heart but sincerely this is the Ground of itt, I know this paper doth contayne many good thinges in itt, butt this is the onely thinge that doth stick with mee, the desiring to know my freedome to this thinge, Though this

---

[6] 'to any thinge' is underlined probably as a sign that Clarke was not certain how to transcribe the shorthand (see **1647 10 28**, n. 16).

[7] Firth suggests that Cromwell was referring to here, even brandishing, *The Book of Army Declarations* (*Clarke Papers*, 1:290, note a). This is properly entitled, *A declaration of the engagements, remonstrances, representations, proposals, desires and resolutions from His Excellency Sir Tho: Fairfax, and the generall councel of the Army. For setling of His Majesty in His just rights, the Parliament in their just priviledges, and the subjects in their libertiesf and freedoms…*(27 Septembris 1647) (Wing / A780; Thomason / E.409[25]).

456

29 OCTOBER 1647

doth suggest That that may bee the bottome of all our Evills, and I will nott say against itt because I doe nott thinke against itt, though this doth suggest the bottome of all our Evills, yet for all to see our selves free to this all of us as wee may unanimously joyne upon this, Either to agree to this, or to adde more to itt, to alter as wee shall agree, This impediment lies in our way if every Man bee satisfied with itt butt myself, That is the first thinge that is to bee consider'd that wee should consider in what Condition wee stand to our former obligations. That if wee bee cleare wee may goe off cleare, if nott wee may nott goe on, if I bee nott come off with what Obligations are made, if I bee To whatsoever you shall agree upon, I thinke this is my Duty that I should nott in the least study either to Retard your Worke or hinder itt, or to Act against itt butt wish you as much successe as if I were free to Act with you. I desire wee may view over our obligations & Engagements that soe wee may bee free upon honest & cleare grounds if this bee my Desire[8] [fo. 31v] Lieutenant Generall I have butt one Worde to prevent[9] you in, and that is for imminent danger itt may bee possibly soe that may nott admitt of an houres Debate, nor nothing of delay if that bee so, I thinke that's above all Law and Rule to us.

Col. Thomas Rainborowe pleaded that they get straight down to debating The Agreement *and not to be further distracted by discussion of Engagements. Commissary Nicholas Cowling stressed the need for urgency, and a Major White[10] said that particular engagements must always yield to the public good.*

[fo. 32r]

Lieutenant Generall I desire to know what the Gentleman meanes concerning particular Engagements if he meanes those that are in this Booke,[11] (If those that are in this Booke) butt if hee meanes Engagements personall from particular persons, Lett every man speake for himself. I speake for my self I disavowe all and I am free to Act, free from any such

[8] At this point, Clarke interpolated 'Col. Rainborow offering to speak' but Cromwell clearly ploughed on.

[9] In its old and now abandoned meeting, 'to anticipate or act in advance'—its first meaning in *OED*.

[10] Major Francis White had been expelled from the Council on 9 September for saying that there was 'now no visible authority in the Kingdom but the power and force of the sword' and was not formally readmitted until 21 December (Gardiner, *GCW*, 3:362; Gentles, *New Model Army*, p. 230). But it is not possible to find another 'Major White' as he is described by Clarke (e.g. in Wanklyn, *Reconstructing the New Model Army* or in Firth and Davies, *Regimental History*). So presumably Francis White attended in defiance of his ban.

[11] i.e. *A declaration of the engagements, remonstrances, representations, proposals, desires and resolutions* (see n. 7).

White acknowledged that Engagements approved by the General Council of the Army were binding in conscience, which draws a comment from Col. John Hewson. Maximilian Pettus then tried to return discussion to The Agreement. *This led into a major speech by Ireton (1700 words) in which he clarified his own thinking about the binding force of Engagements and then agreed that they should proceed to a new reading of* The Agreement, *further discussion of Engagements being deferred. Major William Rainborow welcomes this. The Agreement is then read. For a considerable time there were exchanges between Ireton and Thomas Rainborow about the extent of the franchise imagined in* The Agreement *(eleven speeches in all), Rainborow arguing for the rights of the poor. Cromwell then intervenes:*

[fo. 39v]

Lieutenant Generall. I know nothing butt this, That they that are the most yeilding have the greatest Wisedome butt really Sir This is nott right as itt should bee, Noe man sayes That you have a minde to Anarchy butt the Consequence of this Rule tends to Anarchy, must End in Anarchy, for where is there any Bound or limitt sett if you take away this, That Men that have noe interest butt the interest of Breathing,[12] Therefore I am confident on't wee should nott bee soe hott one with another.

The debate on the franchise continued, and there are 29 recorded speeches before Cromwell speaks again; with Ireton (10 recorded speeches) taking the lead, initially in cut-and-thrust with Colonel Thomas Rainborow (7) and then with John Wildman (3). There are six other speakers, three of them New Model officers – a Colonel, a Major and a captain – one agitator (Edward Sexby) and two 'civilians', Pettus and the Army Chaplain, Hugh Peter. What prompted Cromwell's next contribution was Sexby's claim that 'we were noe mercenary soldiers' and that they had fought to regain their birthright, including the franchise.

[fo. 49r]

Lieutenant Generall I confesse I was most [13] dissatisfied with that I heard Mr. Sexby speake of any man heere, because itt did savour soe much of will, butt I desire that all of us may decline that, and if wee meete heere really to agree to that which was for the safetie of the Kingdome lett us nott spend soe much time in such debates as these are, butt lett us apply our selves to such thinges as are conclusive, and that shall bee this every bodie heere would bee willing, That the Representative might bee mended, that is, itt might bee better than itt is, perhaps itt may bee offer'd in that paper too lamely. if the thinge[14] bee insisted uppon too limited, why perhaps

---

[12] Firth and Woodhouse suggest that 'shall have no voice in elections' needs to be supplied here.

[13] Six characters are crossed out here so severely as to be unreadable our best guess is ~~satis.~~

[14] 'thinge' is underlined probably as a sign that Clarke was not certain how to transcribe the shorthand (see **1647 10 28**, n. 16).

29 OCTOBER 1647

there are a very considerable part of Copyholders by Inheritance that ought to have a voice, and there may bee some what too reflects uppon the Generality of th Way if wee may butt Resolve upon a Committee if I cannott be satisfied to goe soe farre as these Gentlemen that bringe this paper I say itt againe I professe itt I shall freely and willingly withdraw my self, and I hope to doe itt in Such a manner, That the Army shall see that I shall by my Withdrawing, satisfying the <u>interest of the Army</u>,[15] the publique interest of the Kingdome, and those Ends these men aime att, and I think if you doe bringe this to a <u>Result itt were Well</u>.[16]

Col.Thomas Rainborow dug in; Sexby, who had served in Cromwell's regiment in the early part of the war and was now a trooper in Fairfax's regiment of Horse, very bluntly told Cromwell to his face if he had made his opinions clearer earlier, he would have had fewer men under his command; Captain John Clarke called for a spirit of moderation; and Captain Lewis Awdley thought the debates likely to last until the Ides of March (ie to a day of disaster). Cromwell responded:

[fo. 50v]

Lieutenant Generall. Really for my owne parte I must needes say whilest wee say wee would nott make Reflections wee doe make Reflections, and if I had nott come hither with a free heart to doe that that I was perswaded in my Conscience is my Duty I should a thousand times rather have kept myself away for I doe thinke I had brought uppon myself the greatest sin that I was guilty of if I should have come to have stood before God in that former Duty which is before you, and if that my <u>saying</u>, which I did say and shall persevere to say that I should nott, I cannott against my Conscience doe anythinge, they that have stood soe much for Libertie of Conscience, if they will nott grant that Libertie to every Man butt say itt is a Deserting I know nott what: if that bee denied mee, I thinke there is not that Equality that I profest to be amongst us. I said this, and I say noe more that make your businesses as well as you can, wee might bringe thinges to an understanding, itt was to bee brought to faire composure, and when you have said, If you should putt this paper to the Question without any Qualifications I doubt whether itt would passe soe freely, if wee [fo. 51r] would have noe difference wee ought to putt itt and lett me speake clearlie and freelie, I have heard other Gentlemen doe the like, I have nott heard the Commissary Generall answered nott in a parte to my

[15] 'interest of the Army' is underlined probably as a sign that Clarke was not certain how to transcribe the shorthand (see **1647 10 28**, n. 16).

[16] 'Result it will be well' is underlined probably as a sign that Clarke was not certain how to transcribe the shorthand (see **1647 10 28**, n. 16).

459

THE LETTERS, WRITINGS, AND SPEECHES OF OLIVER CROMWELL

Knowledge, nott in a Tittle, if therfore when I see there is an Extreamity of difference betweene you to the End itt may bee brought neerer to a Generall Satisfaction,
and if this bee thought a deserting of that interest if there can bee any thing more
sharpely _said_[17] I will nott give itt an ill Worde, though wee should bee satisfied in
our Consciences in what wee doe, Wee are told wee purpose to leave the Armie, or
to leave our Commands as if wee tooke uppon us to doe itt in matter of Will, I did
heare some Gentlemen speake more of will then any thinge that was spoken this
way for more was spoken by way of will then of satisfaction and if there bee nott a
more Equality in our mindes I can butt greive for it. I must doe noe more.[18]

_Ireton, Rainborowe and Pettus then all restated their positions, with Ireton making clearer his
commitment to a broadening of the franchise but one much narrower than that envisaged in_
The Agreement. _Cromwell tried again:_

[fo. 52v]

Lieutenant Generall. Heere's the mistake whether that's the better Constitution in
that paper, or that which is, butt if you will goe uppon such a ground as that is,
although a better Constitution was offer'd for the removing of the Worse yett
some Gentlemen are resolved to stick to the Worse, There might be a great deale
of prejudice uppon such an apprehension, I thinke you are by this time satisfied,
That itt is a cleare mistake for itt is a dispute whether or noe this[19] be nott better,
nay whether itt bee nott destructive to the Kingedome?

_There follow ten speeches, two by Ireton, one each from seven officers and one by Pettus which
exposed the fundamental differences between the parties. Cromwell thought he could see a way
forward:_

[fo. 55r]

Lieutenant Generall. If wee should goe about to alter these Thinges, I doe nott
thinke that wee are bound to fight for every particular proposition, servants

[17] 'said' is underlined probably as a sign that Clarke was not certain how to transcribe the
shorthand (see **1647 10 28**, n. 16).

[18] Woodhouse tries to impose order on this speech by adding a lot of words and phrases and
then omits the final ninety words, beginning from 'though wee should be satisfied...'. Firth,
more wisely, adds a footnote: 'the speech is simply a chaos of detached phrases from different
sentences. The argument appears to be, "if you claim liberty to follow your consciences, but will
not grant me liberty to follow mine, there is no equality between us. Though we conscien-
tiously believe that under certain circumstances we ought to resign our commands, you taunt
us as if we were following our wills instead of our consciences, and accuse us of deserting the
cause. Can anything be more harshly said?"' In answer to Sexby's demand for an immediate
vote Cromwell again proposes that the question should be referred to a committee to try to
make a fair compromise (_Clarke Papers_, 1:332, note a).

[19] i.e. _The Agreement of the People._

460

29 OCTOBER 1647

while servants are nott included, Then you agree that hee that receives Almes is to bee excluded.

Robert Everard, speaking for the New Agents, expressed his frustration at the amount of talk and the lack of action, and Colonel Sir Hardress Waller, a New English landowner in Ireland, says that if King and Parliament will not acknowledge the rights of the soldiers, 'we must get them the best way wee can.' Cromwell makes his final contribution of the day:

[fo. 56v]

Lieutenant Generall. I thinke you say very well, and my freind at my back, Hee tells <u>mee that are great feares abroad and they talke of</u>[20] somethinges such as are nott onely specious to take a great many people with, but reall and substantiall, and such as are Comprehensive of that that hath the good of the Kingedome in itt, and truly if there bee never soe much desire of carrying on these thinges, never soe much desire of Conjunction yett if there bee nott Libertie of Speech to come to a right understanding of thinges I thinke it shall bee all one as if there were noe desire at all to meete, and I may say itt with truth that I verily beleive there is as much reallity and heartinesse amongst us to come to a right understanding, and to accord with that that hath the Settlement of the Kingdome in itt though when it comes to particulars wee may differ in the Way, yett I know nothing butt that every honest Man will goe as farre as his Conscience will lett him, and hee that will goe farther I thinke hee will fall back, and I thinke, when that principle is Written in the hearts of us, and when there is nott hypocrisie <u>in our dealinges</u>, wee must all of us, resolve [fo. 57r] uppon this, That 'tis God that perswades the heart, if there bee a doubt of sincerity, itt's the Devill that created that Effect and 'tis God that gives uprightnesse and I hope that with such an heart that wee have all mett withall if wee have nott God finde him out that came without itt, for my parte I doe itt.

Clarke then gives us eleven more speeches, four by Ireton, two each by Rainborow and Wildman and one each by Colonel Sir Hardress Waller, Maximilian Petty and an unnamed agitator. The subjects of each speech are so unrelated to one another, that there is a strong possibility that this is a very partial recording of much longer debates. The subjects include (a) the circumstances in which Engagements can be broken (b) whether or not the Army should be called to a General Rendezvous (c) the negative voice (right of veto) in the King or the House of Lords and (d) the intention of Agreement to protect the people from the King's prerogative and Parliament's privilege.

[20] 'mee that are great feares abroad and they talke of' is underlined probably as a sign that Clarke was not certain how to transcribe the shorthand (see **1647 10 28**, n. 16).

461

THE LETTERS, WRITINGS, AND SPEECHES OF OLIVER CROMWELL

The Committee met again on Saturday 30 October. There is no record in the Clarke manuscripts of the debates but there is a full record of decisions taken.[21] *All record of these decisions was omitted from Woodhouse's edition of the Putney Debates (there is not even a record of their omission) and this has caused chaos in subsequent discussions of the Debates. It is headed 'At the Committee of Officers [sic] appointed to consider of the Agreement, and compare itt with Declaration, Agreed...' Those recorded as present were Cromwell and Ireton, four colonels (including Thomas Rainborowe and John Lilburne's brother Robert), a Lieutenant Colonel (Goffe), a Major (Thomas Rainborowe's brother William), four officer agitators and six soldier agitators. This was hardly a group of those pre-committed to the position articulated by Cromwell and Ireton. They* **'agreed'** *(the word in the manuscript)*

1. *That the Long Parliament would be dissolved on 1 September 1648*
2. *Fresh elections would take place and a new Parliament meet on the first Thursday of April every two years, beginning in April 1649. Each Parliament would sit until the end of September or sooner if it so resolved (but never for more than six months)*
3. *Each Parliament, at its dissolution, would appoint a Council of State and other executive committees to serve for the 18 months until the next Parliament.*
4. *Emergency Parliaments could be called by the Council of State, but only so long as it met 70 days before the next biennial Parliament and was dissolved at least 40 days before that next biennial Parliament*
5. *That there was to be a redistribution of seats to more fully reflect 'the whole body of those that are to elect'. The electorate was to be decided by Parliament before if was dissolved on 1 September 1648 but must include 'all freeborne Englishmen...who have served the Parliament in the late warre for the liberties of the Kingdome, and were in service before the 14th of June 1645',*[22] *or who had given actual and voluntary cause to the Parliament. Contrariwise, all active royalists (defined as those whose property had been seized under the sequestration ordinances) were disqualified from voting or sitting in the next two Parliaments.*

This agreement was accepted and agreed by all parties. When the General Council reassembled two days later on Monday 1 November, the main issues in The Agreement of the People *had been settled.*

---

[21] Worcester College, Oxford, Clarke MS 65, fos 64r–66r. Firth's edition does include a transcript of the records taken [*Clarke Papers*, 1:363–7] but Woodhouse unaccountably omits it. The committee reconvened on 2 November and completed its discussion of *The Agreement*, and its further decisions, all reached *nomine contradictente*, are in ibid., 1:407–9.

[22] i.e. before the battle of Naseby. This is intended to leave unenfranchised all royalist prisoners of law who accepted a draft into the armies of the Parliament as the royalist cause disintegrated in 1645–6.

462

1 NOVEMBER 1647

1647 11 01

Oliver Cromwell's contributions to the New Model Army Debate at Putney

Date: 1 November 1647
Source: Worcester College, Oxford, Clarke Papers, vol. 65, fos 67r–84r

This is the last day of debate for which we have a fairly full transcript. Clarke gives us eighty-eight speeches, but they break down into two phases. In the first, which consists of seventeen speeches, four by Cromwell, there are a variety of speakers. The thirteen speeches other than those of Cromwell are made by ten men, one a colonel (Thomas Rainsborowe), three lieutenant colonels, four officer-agitators and two soldier-agitators (William Allen and Edmund Sexby). After this initial series, there follow another seventy-one speeches, mainly in the form of dialogues between Ireton and Rainborowe and then Ireton and Wildman. Of the seventy-one speeches, thirty-two are by Ireton, seventeen by Wildman and fourteen by Rainborowe. Only five other men spoke: Colonel Titchburne three times, Commissary Cowley twice, and Colonel Hewson, Captains Bishop and Awdley once. During the dialogue phase, most of the speeches—uncharacteristically of the debates as a whole, consist of terse one or two-line statements and one has to suspect that Clarke is offering very brief summaries. At any rate, Cromwell's contributions are confined to the first quarter of the recorded speeches, and two of them are very long, his very last speech the longest recorded speech by anyone across the whole of the debates within the General Council. At the very end, it was resolved that the Council should adjourn until the following day and so from day to day until the proposals (in *The Agreement*) had all been debated and the Council agreed that the committee that had met on 30 October should meet again. Once again, Clarke gives no information about who said what at the committee meeting on 2 November, but he does list the six resolutions that were passed unanimously and reported back to the Council. These limited the judicial power of the Lords and the extent of the royal veto, and considerably expanded the judicial powers of the House of Commons, especially in cases of maladministration. It also removed from Parliament and reserved to the people as inalienable rights freedom of religion, freedom from impressment and guarantees of indemnity for actions during the wars. Finally, the committee also reserved to the people and removed from Parliament any changes in the arrangements for elections approved on 30 October. On 3 November the committee debated parliamentary control of the militia and the replacement of tithes either by a land tax or otherwise by state stipends.

But back on Monday 1 November, it was Cromwell who opened proceedings.

[fo. 67r]

Putney, 1. November. 1647

Att the Generall Council of the Army.

463

THE LETTERS, WRITINGS, AND SPEECHES OF OLIVER CROMWELL

The Lieutenant Generall first moved, That every one might Speake their Experiences as the issue of what God had given in, in answer to their prayers.

Captain Francis Allen expressed 'what experiences hee had received' and then said that the work before them was to take away the Negative Voice (right of veto) from the King and House of Lords. At that point there was an interruption as messengers came to report that Colonel Lambert's troopers had been persuaded by 'two Horsemen, Agitators' to change the regiment's agitators, 'for that the Officers had broken their Engagements'. Captain Carter and Commissary Cowling both reported what they had been given in prayer, Carter that 'he found nott any inclination in his heart as formerly to pray for the Kinge', Cowling that he believed that only the men of the sword had shown a determination to recover rights lost to the people since the time of the Normans, and Lieutenant Colonel Henry Lilburne (Freeborn John's brother) said that the Normans had but augmented the slavery that already existed. He therefore doubted that what his comrades had just said was 'of God'. Cromwell then offers a long meditation on the nature of political power.

[fo. 67v]

Lieutenant Generall.[1] To that <u>which</u>[2] hath bin moved concerning the Negative vote, or thinges which have bin deliver'd in papers, and otherwise, may present a reall pleasing. I doe nott say that they have all pleas'd, for I thinke that the Kinge is Kinge by Contract, and I shall say as Christ said, Lett him that is without sin cast the first Stone,[3] and minde that Word of bearing one with another itt was taught us today, if wee had carried itt on in the parliament and by our power without any thinge is laid on that kinde, soe that wee could say that wee were without transgression I should then say itt were just to cutt off Transgressors butt considering that wee are in our owne actions failing in many particulars, I thinke there is much necessity of pardoning of Transgressors. For the actions that are to bee done, and those that must doe them, I thinke itt is their proper place to conforme to the parliament that first gave them their being, and I thinke itt is considerable whether

---

[1] In the manuscript, this was originally ascribed to 'Lieut Coll [Henry] Lilburne'; but 'Coll Lilburne is heavily scored through and 'Generall' written above both words. Contrariwise the previous speech was initially ascribed to 'Lieut Generall' and the 'Generall' then overwritten as 'Coll Lilburne'. That speech runs: Lieut. 'That hee never observed that the Recovery of our liberties which wee had before the Normans was the occasion of our taking uppe Armes, or the maine quarrel and that the Norman Lawes are nott Slavery introduced uppon us, butt an augmentation of our Slaverie before. Therefore what was by some offer'd, I doubt for those Reasons I have given you, was nott of God.'

[2] Underlinings in the text are almost certainly made by Clarke to indicate his uncertainty about the meaning of the shorthand he is transcribing. See **1647 II 28** n. 6.

[3] John 8:7 (KJV), where Jesus rebukes and challenges the Pharisees who had tried to trap him over the fate of a woman taken in adultery.

1 NOVEMBER 1647

they doe <u>contrive</u>[4] to suppresse the power by that power, or noe, if they doe continue to suppresse them, and how they can take the <u>Determination</u>[5] of Commanding men, Conducting men, Quartering men, keeping Guards without an Authority [fo. 68r] otherwise then from themselves, I am ignorant of and therfore I thinke there is much in the Army to conforme to those thinges that are within their spheare for those thinges that have bin done in the Army, as this of The Case <u>of</u> the Armie truly Stated, There is much in itt usefull, and to bee condescended to butt I am nott satisfied how farre wee shall press: Either they are a Parliament or noe Parliament if they bee noe Parliament they are nothing, and wee are nothing likewise if they bee a Parliament wee are to offer itt to itt. If I could see a visible presence of the people either by Subscriptions, or Number, for in the Governement of Nations that \which/ is to bee look't after is the affections of the people and that I finde which satisfies my Conscience in the present <u>thinge</u>.[6] They were first families where they lived, and had Heads of families, and they were first under Judges, and they were under Kinges when they came to desire a Kinge they had a Kinge first Elective and 2dly by succession: In all these kindes of Governement they were happy, and in all these Governements they were happy & contented with itt, and if you make the best of itt, if you should change the Governement to the best of itt, itt is butt a Morall thinge. Itt is butt as Paul sayes Drosse & Dunge in Comparison of Christ[7] and why wee shall soe farre Contest for Temporall thinges, yett if wee cannott have this freedome wee will venture life & livelihood for itt, when every Man shall come to this Condition I thinke the State will come to Desolation, and therfore the Considering of what is fitt for the Kingedome does belonge to ~~the~~ parliament well composed in their Creation & Election, [fo. 68v] how farre I shall leave itt to the Parliament to offer itt. There may bee care, That the Elections, or Formes of Parliament are very illegall,[8] as I could Name butt one for a Corporation to chuse two, I shall desire, That there may bee a

---

[4] Underlinings in the text are almost certainly made by Clarke to indicate his uncertainty about the meaning of the shorthand he is transcribing. See **1647 II 28** n. 6.

[5] Underlinings in the text are almost certainly made by Clarke to indicate his uncertainty about the meaning of the shorthand he is transcribing. See **1647 II 28** n. 6.

[6] Underlinings in the text are almost certainly made by Clarke to indicate his uncertainty about the meaning of the shorthand he is transcribing. See **1647 II 28** n. 6. At this point Firth and Woodhouse suggest the addition here of 'consider case of the Jews'.

[7] Probably a loose gloss on Philippians 3:8 (in the Geneva and Authorised Version: 'Yea doubtless, and I count all things but loss for the excellency of the knowledge of Christ Jesus my Lord: for whom I have suffered the loss of all things, and do count them but dung, that I may win Christ.')

[8] Woodhouse, inexplicably, transcribes an unequivocal 'illegall' as 'unequal'.

THE LETTERS, WRITINGS, AND SPEECHES OF OLIVER CROMWELL

Forme for the Electing of Parliaments and another thinge that there is noe assurance to the people, butt that itt is perpetuall, which does[9] satisfie the Kingdome as the perpetuity of the Parliament and for other thinges that are to the Kinges Negative vote as may cast you off wholly, Itt hath bin the Resolution of the Parliament and of the Army If there bee a possibility of the Parliaments offering those thinges unto the Kinge that may secure us I thinke there is much may bee said for the doing of it.   [10] As for the present Condition of the Army I shall speake something of itt for the Conduct of the Army, I perceive there are severall Declarations from the Army by calling Rendezvouz & otherwise, and disobligations to the Generalls orders I must confesse I have a Commission from the Generall and I understand that I am to doe by[11] itt I shall conforme to him according to the Rules & Discipline of Warre, and according to those Rules I ought to bee conformable, and therefore I conceive itt is nott in the power of any particular men to call a Randezvous of a Troope, or Regiment, or att least to disoblige the Armie from those Commands of the General, which must bee destructive to us in Generall or any particular man in the Armie, That this way is destructive to the Armie and to every particular Man in the Armie, I have bin informd by some of the Kinges partie, That if they give us Rope enough wee will hange our selves,[12] if wee doe nott conforme [fo. 69r] to the Rules of Warre, and therefore I shall move what wee shall Center uppon if itt have butt the face of authority if itt bee butt an Hare swimming over the Thames hee will take hold of itt rather than lett itt goe.

Lieutenant Edmund Chillenden draws on Providences relating to the Army's march on London at the end of July 1647; William Allen the agitator, reflects on the prayer meetings before the weekend, and at the Grandees' insistence on the binding Engagements had entered into in three specific documents – those of 14 June, 21 June and 18 August,[13] and acknowledges

---

[9] Firth and Woodhouse suggest that a 'not' is missing here.

[10] A clear gap in the MS may indicate something missing here, even though 'As for the present' is on the same line.

[11] Underlinings in the text are almost certainly made by Clarke to indicate his uncertainty about the meaning of the shorthand he is transcribing. See **1647 II 28** n. 6.

[12] Firth and Woodhouse suggest adding here: 'We shall hang ourselves'.

[13] 14 June—*A declaration from Sir Thomas Fairfax, and the Army under his command. As it was humbly tendered to the Right Honourable the Lords and Commons assembled in Parliament... Printed by the speciall appointment of His Excellency Sir Thomas Fairfax, and souldiery of the Army under his command.* St. Albons, June 14. 1647 (Wing / D587).

21 June (probably)—*A copie of a letter sent from the agitators of his Excellency Sir Thomas Fairfax's armie, to all the honest sea-men of England... Dated at S. Albans 21. June 1647. Published by the order and speciall desire of the said agitators* (Wing / C6146).

18 August—*A declaration of the last demands, propounded by his Excellency Sir Thomas Fairfax, and the Councell of his Army to both Houses of Parliament* (Wing / F155).

1 NOVEMBER 1647

their importance. John Jubbes, Lieutenant Colonel in Hewson's Regiment (in his first recorded contribution to any of the Army Debates) calls for consideration to be given to a further purge of Parliament and whether that purged Parliament might not declare the King 'guilty of all the bloodshed, vast expence of treasure, and ruine that hath bin occasioned by all the warres both of England and Ireland.' Lieutenant Colonel Goffe, however, wanted to go back to the prayer meeting, and reminds them of the 'lying spiritt in the mouth of Ahab's Prophetts and the dire consequences of not hearing messages from God. He suggests that there 'hath bin a voice from Heaven to us, that wee have sinn'd against the Lord in tampering with his enemies'. Cromwell is quick to respond, and forcefully.

[fo. 70v]

Lieutenant Generall. I shall nott bee unwilling to heare God speaking in any butt I thinke that God may bee heard speaking in that which is to bee read, as otherwise. Butt I shall speake a Worde in that which Lieut Col. Goffe said, because itt seemes to come as a Reproof to mee, and I shall bee willing to receive a Reproof when itt shall bee[14] in Love, and shall bee given, butt that which hee speakes was, That att such a Meeting as this wee should waite uppon God, and the voice of God speaking in any of us, I confesse itt is an high duty, butt when any thinge is spoken I thinke the Rule is, Lett the rest Judge![15] butt when any thinge is spoken itt is left to mee to judge for my own satisfaction, and the satisfaction of others whether itt bee of the Lord or nott, and I doe noe more, and I doe nott judge Conclusively, Negatively, that itt was nott of the Lord, butt I doe desire to submitt itt to all your judgments whether itt was of the Lord or noe? [fo. 71r] and I did offer some Reasons which did satisfie me I know nott whether I did others, butt if in those thinges we doe speake, and pretend to speake from God there bee mistakes of Fact. if there bee a mistake in the thinge, in the Reason of the thinge, Truly I thinke itt is free for mee to shew both the one, and the other if I can; Nay I thinke itt is my Duty to doe itt: for noe man receives any thinge in the name of the Lord further then the Light of his Conscience appeares. I can say in the next place, & I can say itt heartily and freely as to the matter hee speakes I must confesse I have noe prejudice nott the least thought of prejudice, uppon that ground I speake itt Truly as before the Lord, butt this I thinke, That itt is noe Evill Advertisement to wish us in our Speeches of Righteousnesse & Justice, to referre

---

[14] Underlinings in the text are almost certainly made by Clarke to indicate his uncertainty about the meaning of the shorthand he is transcribing. See **1647 II 28** n. 6.

[15] Probably an allusion to I Corinthians 14:28–9, in the Geneva translation: 'but if there be no interpreter, let him keep silence in the Church, which speaketh languages, and let him speak to himself, and to God. Let the Prophets speak, two or three, and let the others judge.'

467

THE LETTERS, WRITINGS, AND SPEECHES OF OLIVER CROMWELL

us to any Engagements that are uppon us and that which I have learn't in all Debates, I have still desir'd wee should still Consider where wee are, and what Engagements are uppon us, and how wee ought to goe off as becomes Christians, and this is all that I aim'd att, and I doe aime att, and I must Confesse I had a mervailous reverence and awe uppon my Spirit when wee came to speake, lett us speake one to another what God hath spoken to us, and as I said before I cannott say that I have received any thinge that I can speake as in the name of the Lord, nott that I can say that any body did speake that which was untrue in the name of the Lord butt uppon this ground, That when wee say wee speake in the name of the Lord itt is of an high nature.

Following this speech, 'Lieutenant-Colonel Goffe made an apology for what hee had said before.' William Allen opposed setting up the King again: instead 'down with him'. Colonel Thomas Rainborow dissociated himself from this attack on monarchy and the Lords. Edward Sexby said that they had tried to heal Babylon but could not do so, and that they were seeking to set up the power of the King which God would destroy and that this was why they were in the 'straights' that they were in. In the longest recorded speech in the whole of the debates (2,319 words), Cromwell meets this head on.

[fo. 72r]

*Lieutenant Generall[16]   *I thinke wee should nott lett goe that motion which Lieut Col. Goffe made, and soe I cannott butt renew that Caution That wee should take heede what wee speake in the name of the Lord, butt as for what that Gentleman spoke last (butt itt <u>was</u>[17] with too much confidence) I cannott conceive that hee altogether meant itt, butt I would wee should all take heede of mentioning our owne thoughts and Conceptions with that which is of God, what this Gentleman told us[18] that which[19] was our great fault hee alludes to such a place of Scripture, Hee would have heald <u>Babylon, butt</u>[20] shee would nott, The Gentleman applied itt to us, as that itt had bin that men would have heald Babylon and God would nott have had her healed, Truly though that bee nott the intent of

---

[16] The transcription of Sexby's speech leads straight into Cromwell's mid-line. The transcriber, realising his mistake too late, presumably, inserted an asterisk mid-line and in the margin writes '*Lt Gen:'. It appears to be in the same hand as the rest of the text.

[17] Underlinings in the text are almost certainly made by Clarke to indicate his uncertainty about the meaning of the shorthand he is transcribing. See **1647 II 28** n. 6.

[18] Firth adds 'was' here.

[19] Firth adds 'he conceived' here.

[20] Underlinings in the text are almost certainly made by Clarke to indicate his uncertainty about the meaning of the shorthand he is transcribing. See **1647 II 28** n. 6.

1 NOVEMBER 1647

that Scripture, yett I thinke itt is true, That whosoever would have gone about to heale Babylon when God hath determined,[21] hee does fight against God, because God will nott have her heal'd, and yett certainly in Generall to Desire an healing itt is nott evil, Indeed when wee are convinc'd that itt is Babylon wee are going about to heale, I thinke itt's fit wee should then give over our healing, butt I shall desire to speake a word or two since I heare noe man offering nothing as a particular Dictate from God,[22] speake to us, I should desire to draw to some Conclusion of that Expectation of ours. Truly, as Lieut Col: Goffe said, God hath in several Ages used severall Dispensations, and yett some Dispensations [fo. 72v] more eminently in one age than another. I am one of those whose heart God hath drawne out to waite for some Extraordinary, ordinarie Dispensations according to those promises that hee hath held forth of thinges to bee accomplished in the later times, and I cannott butt thinke that God is beginning of them, and yett certainly[23] uppon the same ground that wee finde in the Epistle of Peter, where hee speakes of the Scriptures, To which says hee you doe well to take heede a more sure word of Prophecy than their Testimonies was, To which you doe well to take heede as a Light shining in a darke place,[24] if when wee want particular and Extraordinary impressions wee shall \either/ altogether sitt still because wee have them nott, and nott follow that Light that wee have, or shall goe against, or short of that Light that wee have uppon the imaginary apprehension of such divine impressions, and divine discoveries in particular thinges, which are nott soe devine as to carry their Evidence with them, to the conviction of those that have the Spiritt of God within them I thinke wee shall bee justly under a Condemnation, Truly wee have heard many speaking to us, and I cannott butt thinke, That in many of those things God hath spoke to us. I cannott butt thinke that in most that have spoke there hath bin some thing of God made forth to us, and yett there hath bin severall contradictions in what hath bin spoken, butt certainly God is nott the Authour of Contradictions. The Contradictions are nott soe much in the End as in the way, I cannott see butt that wee all speake to the same End, and the mistakes are onely in the way, The End is to deliver this Nation from oppression & slavery, to accomplish that worke that God hath carried us on in, To Establish our hopes of an End of Justice & Righteousnesse [fo. 73r] in it wee agree thus farre: Further to, That wee all apprehend danger from the person of

---

[21] Firth adds 'to destroy her' here.

[22] Firth adds 'that hee would' and in general seriously rearranges this sentence.

[23] Firth adds 'we do well to take heed' here.   [24] 2 Peter 1:19.

THE LETTERS, WRITINGS, AND SPEECHES OF OLIVER CROMWELL

the Kinge and from the Lords: I thinke wee may goe thus farre further, That all that have spoke have agreed in this to: Though the Gentleman in the Windowe when hee spoke sett uppe, if hee should declare itt, did nott meane all that that worde might import.[25] I thinke that seemes to bee generall amonge us all, There is nott any intention of any in the Army, of any of us to sett uppe the one,[26] That if itt were free before us whether wee should sett uppe one or other, I doe to my best observation finde an unanimity amongst us all, that wee would sett uppe neither: Thus farre I finde us to bee agreed, and thus farre as wee are agreed I thinke itt is of God, butt there are circumstances in which wee differ as in relation to this hen I must further tell you, That as wee doe nott make itt our businesse or intention to sett uppe the one or the other, soe neither is itt[27] to preserve the one, or the other, with a visible danger & destruction to the people, and the publique interest, soe that that part of difference that seemes to bee among us is whether there can bee a preservation:[28] first of all, on the one parte, There is this apprehension, That wee cannott with Justice and Righteousnesse at the present destroy, or goe about to destroy or take away, or lay aside both or all the interest they have in the publique affaires of the Kingdome, and those that doe soe apprehend would straine somethinge in point of security, would rather leave some hazard, or att least if they see that they may consist without any considerable hazard to the interest of the Kingdome that they doe soe farre[29] to preserve them, on the other hand, Those who differ from this, I doe take itt in the most candid apprehension that they seeme to run thus, That there is nott any safetie or security to the [fo. 73v] Libertie of the Kingedome, and to publique interest if you doe retaine these att all, and therefore they thinke this is a Consideration to them paramount the Consideration of particular Obligations of Justice or matter of Right or due towards Kinge or Lords: Truly I thinke itt hath pleased God to lead mee to a true and cleare Stating our Agreement and our difference, and if this bee soe wee are the better prepared to goe,[30] if this bee nott soe I shall desire that any one that hath heard mee declare[31] if hee doe thinke that the thinge is mistated as to our

---

[25] Firth rewrites this and his version may well convey the meaning better: 'Though the Gentleman in the windowe [seemed to deny it] when hee spoke [of] sett[ing] uppe, [but he] if hee should declare itt, did nott meane all that that worde might import.'

[26] Firth adds 'or the other' here.   [27] Firth adds 'our intention' here.

[28] Firth adds 'of them with safety to the kingdom'.   [29] Firth adds 'wish' here.

[30] Firth suggests adding 'on' here.   [31] Firth suggests '[will] declare [it]' here.

1 NOVEMBER 1647

Agreement or difference and I shall goe on, onely in a Worde or two to Conclude that wee have bin about as to the Dispensations of God itt was more particular in the time of the Law[32] written in our hearts that worde within us the minde of Christ,[33] and Truly when wee have noe other more particular impression of the power of God going forth with itt, I thinke that this Law and this speaking,[34] which Truly is in every man who hath the Spiritt of God, wee are to have a regard to, and this to mee seemes to bee very cleare, what wee are to judge of the Apprehensions of men [as] to particular Cases, whether itt bee of God or noe when itt doth nott carry itt's evidence with itt of the power of God to convince us clearlie, our best way is to judge the conformity or Disformity of the Law written within us, which is the Law of the Spiritt of God, The minde of God, The mind of Christ, and as was well said by Lieut Col: Jubbs, for my parte I doe nott know any outward evidence of what proceedes from the Spiritt of God more cleare than this, The appearance of Meeknesse, and gentlenesse, and Mercy, and patience, and forbearance, and Love, and a Desire to doe good to all, and to destroy none that can bee sav'd, and for my parte I say Where I doe see this, where I doe see men speaking according to this Law which I am sure is the Law of the Spirit of Life,[35] I cannott butt take that to bee contrary to this Law, as hee said of the spir- itt of malice, and Envy, and thinges of that nature: [fo. 74r] and I thinke there is this radically in that heart where there is such a Law as leads us against all oppos- ition on the other hand, I thinke that hee that would decline the doing of Justice where there is noe place for Mercy and the Exercise of the Wayes of force for the safetie of the Kingedome where there is noe other Way to save itt and would decline this out of the apprehensions of danger & difficulties in itt, Hee that leads that way on the other hand doth truly lead us from that which is the Law of the Spiritt of Life, the Law written in our hearts and Truly having thus declared what wee may apprehend of all that hath bin said, I shall wish that wee may goe on to our businesse and I shall onely adde several Cautions on the one hand, and the other, and that is this,

1. I could wish That none of those whose apprehensions run on the other hand, that there can bee noe safetie in a Consistencie with the person of the Kinge or the

---

[32] Firth adds 'of Moses than in the time of the law'.

[33] This possibly links 2 Corinthians 3:2 and 1 Corinthians 2:16 (and not, *pace Clarke Papers*, 1:381, note a, Hebrews 8:10).

[34] Firth expands this to '[word] speaking [within us]'.

[35] Firth adds 'I am satisfied. But' here.

THE LETTERS, WRITINGS, AND SPEECHES OF OLIVER CROMWELL

Lords, or their having the least interest in the publique affaires of the Kingdome, I doe wish them, That they will take heede of that which some men are apt to bee carried away by apprehensions that God will destroy these persons, or that power for that they may mistake in. and though my self doe concurre with them, and perhaps concurre with them uppon some ground that God will doe soe, yett lett us[36] make those thinges to bee our Rule which wee cannott soe clearlie know to bee the minde of God, I meane in particular thinges lett us nott make those our rules, That 'this to bee done is the minde of God butt wee must worke to itt, butt att least those to whom this is nott made cleare,[37] Though they doe nott thinke itt probable, That God will destroy them yett lett them make this rule to themselves, though God have a purpose to destroy them and though I should finde a Desire to destroy them, though a Christian Spiritt can hardly finde itt for itt self yett God can doe itt without necessitating us to doe a thinge [fo. 74v] which is scandalous, or sinne, or which would bringe a Dishonour to his Name, and therfore those that are of that minde lett them waite uppon God for such a Way when the thinge may bee done without sin, or without scandall too: Surely what God would have us doe hee does nott desire wee should steppe out of the way for itt, This is the Caution on the one hand that wee doe noe wronge to one or other, and that wee abstaine from all appearance of wronge, and for that purpose avoid the bringing of a scandall to the name of God, and to his people uppon whome his name is Call'd: On the other hand, I have butt this to say, That those who doe apprehend obligations lying uppon them either by a Generall Dcacasuty or particularly in relation to the thinges that wee have declar'd a Duty of Justice, or a Duty in regard of that Engagement that they would clearlie come to this Resolution, That if they found in their Judgements & Consciences that those Engagements lead to any thinge which really cannott consist with the Libertie and safetie and publique interest of this Nation that they would account the Generall paramount[38] the other soe farre as nott to oppose any other that would doe better for the Nation then they will doe, and if wee doe Act according to that minde & that Spiritt, and that Law which I have before spoken of, and in these particular Cases to take these two Cautions God will lead us to what shall bee his way and as many of us as hee shall incline their mindes to, and the rest in their way in a due time.

[36] Firth adds a crucial 'not' at this point. This is a dramatic but perhaps appropriate suggestion.
[37] Firth expands this sentence as follows: 'That 'this [is] to bee done [this] is the minde of God butt wee must worke to itt, butt att least [let] those to whom this is nott made cleare...'
[38] Firth expands this phrase to 'Generall [duty] paramount [to]'.

8 NOVEMBER 1647

Following this speech, Clarke records a further 69 speeches, but none are ascribed to Cromwell.[39] *Immediately after Cromwell finished, Captain Thomas Bishop, speaking for the first time, called for Charles I to be put on trial as 'a man of bloud'. The next ten speeches are sharp exchanges between Ireton and Wildman and the next eleven between Ireton and Rainborowe, and then with interruptions by four senior officers, the remaining speeches are a three-way debate between Ireton, Wildman and Rainborowe. Much of this has the appearance of very brief summary of possibly lengthy speeches. The subject matter is the future role of a King or House of Lords and specifically their 'negative voice' or right of veto over the actions of the House of Commons.*

1647 11 08

Oliver Cromwell's contributions to the New Model Army Debate at Putney

Date: 8 November 1647
Source: Worcester College, Oxford, Clarke Papers, vol. 65, fos 88r–89v (reported speech)

We have fragments of debates on 2 and 3 November (fos 85r–87v) but no evidence of any contribution by Cromwell. On 2 November, the Committee met and unanimously (or with one dissenting voice) approved six resolutions. On 3 November there were reports of restiveness in the Army, and it is said that were there were debates about the militia and tithes (but no account of individual speeches). It was agreed that the length of time during which the King would surrender authority over the militia be set at ten years, and the 'declaratory laws' would take place after that. And it was debated whether tithes would be

---

[39] There is a puzzle. Wildman addressing 'that Gentleman that spake last save one' (i.e. Cromwell) said that 'some did desire to preserve the person of the Kinge and person of the Lords, soe farre as itt was with the safetie or good of the of the Kingedome, and other persons doe conceive, that the preservation of the Kinge or Lords was soe inconsistent with the people's safetie, and that the Law was to be paramount to all.' To this 'Com. Ireton' is said to have made two short speeches. But if Wildman was addressing Cromwell, then these speeches would surely have been by Cromwell not Ireton. And Sir Charles Firth thought so too (*Clarke Papers*, 1:385 note a). Given the uncertainty, we include those two speeches in this footnote not in the text:
[1] 'Sir, I did not speake of the destroying of the Kinge and
Lords – I have nott heard any Man charge all the Lords
soe as to deserve a punishment but a Reserving to them
any interest att all in the publique affaires of the Kingedome.'
[2] 'I said, that some Men did apprehend, that there might
be an interest given to them with safetie to the Kingedome,
others doe thinke, that noe parte of their interest could bee
given without destruction to the Kingedome.'

THE LETTERS, WRITINGS, AND SPEECHES OF OLIVER CROMWELL

replaced by a land-rate or alternatively that the state would buy out the right to tithes from the holders of impropriations and would then make separate provision for ministers. Clarke has no record of any meetings on 4–7 November, but there are passing references to meetings having been held in other sources.[1]

There is more material for Monday 8 November, including summaries of two speeches by Cromwell and two declarations on which he is the first and third (of eighteen) signatories and quite possibly the draftsman.

––––––––

[fo. 88r]

The Lieutenant Generall Spoke much to Expresse the danger of their principles who had sought to devide the Army, That the first particular of that which they Call'd, The Agreement of the people did tend very much to Anarchy, That all those who are in the Kingedome should have a voice in Electing Representatives. *Captain Bray*[2] '*Made a Longe Speech to take off what the Lieut Generall Said, and that what he called Anarchy was for propriety.*'

Lieutenant Generall. Moved To putt itt to the Question, Whether that the Officers & Agitators bee sent to their Quarters, yea or noe.

Resolved upon the Question: That the Generall Councill doth humbly advise His Excellency That in regard the Generall shortly intends a Randezvous of the Army, and forasmuch as many distempers are Reported to bee in the severall Regiments whereby much dissatisfaccion is given both to the Parliament & Kdome therby through some misrepresentations, To the End a Right understanding may bee had & the souldiers quieted in order to their obedience to his Excellency for the Service of the Parliament and Kingedome, Itt is thought fitt to desire his Excellency that for a time the said Officers & Agitators resort to their severall Commands & Regiments to the Ends aforesaid there to Reside untill the said Randezvouz bee over, and untill his Excellency shall see Cause to call them together againe according to the Engagement.

Committee

Lieut Generall	Mr Allen
Commissary General Ireton	Capt Clarke
Sir Hardresse Waller	Mr Lockyer
Col: Okey	Capt Deane

––––––

[1] *Clarke Papers*, 1:440–1, appendix E.

[2] For Captain-Lieutenant William Bray of Robert Lilburne's infantry regiment, see Wanklyn, *Reconstructing*, 1:89–90, esp. fn. 391, Gentles, *The New Model*, pp. 218, 221–4, 229–30, 320, and Woolrych, *Soldiers and Statesmen*, pp. 229, 264–5, 280, 281–5, 293, 293–8, 301, 316, 341–2.

474

11 NOVEMBER 1647A

Col: Titchborne
Col.Hewson
Commissary Stane
Scoutmaster Generall
Col.Rich

Col. Thomlinson
Lt. Col: Goff
Major Rainborow
Lt. Col. Cowell
Com. Cowling

This Committee to draw uppe Instructions for what shall bee offered to the Regiments att the Rendezvous to consider of the late Letter sent to the parliament and what shall bee thought fitt further to bee proposed to them.

[Four] Desires of the Army follow, but the authorship not clear.

1647 11 11a

Oliver Cromwell's contributions to the New Model Army Debate at Putney

Date: 11 November 1647
Source: Worcester College, Oxford, Clarke Papers, vol. 65 fos 91r–v (reported speech)

On 9 November [fo. 90r–v], with General Fairfax presiding, the General Council asked the standing committee 'to take into Consideration, the Engagement Declarations & papers of the Armie, and uppon them to collect a Summarie of those thinges that concerne the Good of the Kingedome, the Liberties of the people, and The interests of the Armie, and further to Consider the Case of the Army Stated, and a paper Commonly Call'd, The Agreement of the people, and to Consider how farre any thinge contained in the same are consistent with the said Engagements and Declarations and Interests aforesaid'.

Also, apparently on 9 November, thirty nine officers, including Cromwell, issued a disclaimer that 'If any by that Letter bearing Date the 5th of November doe make any Construction as if wee Intended that wee were against the parliaments sending propositions to the Kinge, Wee doe heerby declare That itt was noe part of our intentions in the said Letter butt that the same is utterly a mistake of our intention & meaning therin, our Intentions being only to assert the Freedome of parliament.'

At what is a headed 'a second Meeting of the Committee of Officers' on 11 November (we have no knowledge of what happened at the presumed first meeting), Colonel Thomas Harrison 'made a narration concerning some thinges that lay uppon his Spiritt in relation to the Kinge, Lords & the Reserve That the Kinge was a Man of Bloud, and therefore the Engagement taken off, and that they were to prosecute him.' Cromwell replied to this.

[fo. 91r]
Lieutenant Generall answered him by putting severall Cases in which Murther was nott to bee punished, As in the Case of a Man that had kill'd his sonne should get into a Garrison, whether he might raise Warre, or not give Conditions to that place, Stated the Case of David uppon Joab's Killing of Abner, That hee spar'd him uppon two prudentiall Grounds, one, That hee would nott hazard the spilling of more blowd in regard the Sons of Zeruiah were too hard for him.[1]

Ireton intervenes to support Cromwell, who then continued:

Lieutenant Generall That wee doe the Worke when itt is disputable and the Worke of others to doe itt, if it bee as an absolute & indispensable duty for us to doe itt.

The report ends with an unclear statement by Fairfax,[2] and a comment by Commissary Cowling that the King's usurping power 'would have ruin'd us' but that they should 'destroy that and lett his person alone.'

1647 11 11b
Letter from Oliver Cromwell to Colonel Edward Whalley

Date: 11 November 1647

Source: *His Maiesties most gracious declaration, left by him on his table, at Hampton-Court, 11. Novemb. 1647.* (1647), p. 7 (ESTC: R204486; Wing / C2507B; Thomason / E413[15]) (contemporary print version)

On 11 November, Charles I escaped from Army custody at Hampton Court[1] and made his way south, arriving at Carisbrooke on the Isle of Wight on 14 November.[2] He had been under pressure from the Scots to flee, perhaps to Berwick,[3] for some time, and he had

---

[1] The story of the slaying of Abner is in 2 Samuel 2–3, and the final phrase about David recognising that his nephews were too strong for him is at 2 Samuel 3:39.
[2] 'The Generall: That wee doe butt secure the Kinge in the Right of another, and that itt became them soe to order thinges concerning them.'

---

[1] Hampton Court, the palace built by Wolsey and appropriated by Henry VIII is on the Thames close to Kingston and Richmond, about an hour's hard riding from Westminster. The King was in relaxed captivity there from 24 August to 11 November 1647.
[2] Gardiner, *GCW*, 4:13–20; Woolrych, *Soldiers and Statemen*, pp. 267–76; Gentles, *New Model Army*, pp. 219–22.
[3] Berwick, Berwickshire, the very border of England and Scotland, where he would be in England but under Scots protection.

11 NOVEMBER 1647B

made the decision to escape on 3 November and a decision to flee on the 11th on 9 November, perhaps after receiving an anonymous letter warning him that a group of army adjutators were planning to assassinate him. Indeed following angry exchanges in the Council of the Army early on 11 November in which Thomas Harrison[4] was the latest to call Charles I 'a man of blood',[5] Cromwell himself wrote this letter to the guard commander at Hampton Court, Edward Whalley, warning him of an attempt on the King's person. Whalley showed it to the King and assured him that he would keep him safe. Later that day—at 9 p.m., according to Cromwell (see below item **1647 11 11c**)—the King did escape. Whalley was sent by Fairfax to Parliament to report on what had happened, and his account together with the letter that the King had left in his closet and this fragment of Cromwell's letter to Whalley was ordered to be published. Sir John Berkeley,[6] one of those who escorted the King from Hampton Court to Carisbrooke reported that Cromwell's letter to Whalley also included a statement that a radical party in the Army intended to seize the King the following day: 'in prosecution whereof a new guard was the next day to be put upon His Majesty of that party'.[7] This is a more sinister repeat of Cornet Joyce's actions back in June.[8] We include the material immediately around the extract from Cromwell's letter.

------

p. 7]

Novemb. 13.

This day the House of Com. sate till 7. at night, Col: *Whalley* was called into the House, and examined, he confessed he had received a Letter from Lieutenant Gen: *Cromwell* the day before,[9] which he produced, and was read, to this effect:

---

[4] Thomas Harrison. See above, **1647 11 11a**.
[5] Cf. Captain Bishop's impassioned outburst towards the end of the debate on 1 November (see **1647 11 01**).
[6] (Sir) John Berkeley, first Baron Berkeley of Stratton (bap. 1607, d. 1678). See *ODNB*.
[7] Gardiner, *GCW*, 4:16n, citing *The Memoirs of Sir John Berkeley* (1699), p. 54.
[8] Succinctly discussed in George Joyce (b. 1618), parliamentarian army officer, in *ODNB*.
[9] Which day is that? Whalley is speaking in Parliament on 13 November, but he cannot mean the day before that, for that was *after* the King's escape. How can he mean 11 November, for there is nothing in his narrative that relates to 12 November as the day before which the letter was written? So does he mean the day before the escape, i.e. 10 November? That would be the logic of his language and of course that would mean that Cromwell wrote *before* Harrison's outburst in the Army Council on 11 November. The King left behind a letter to Whalley thanking him 'likewise for his civilities, for he had that morning given Charge to the Guards and others to have a care of His Majesty, having likewise had some intimation of an intended attempt that day upon His Majesties Person' (*JHL*, 9:520) which cannot surely mean a message received on the 10th and acted on only the following morning? Perhaps Whalley got slightly muddled in the heat of the moment. 11 November seems the safer date for the letter.

477

Deare Cos.[10] WHALEY, *There are rumors abroad of some intended attempt on His Majesties Person, therefore I pray have a care of your Guards; for if any such thing should be done, it would be accounted a most horrid act, &c.*

1647 11 11C

Letter from Oliver Cromwell to [William Lenthall, Speaker of the House of Commons]

Date: 11 November 1647
Source: Samuel Pecke, ed., *A Perfect Diurnall of Some Passages in Parliament* no. 224 for 8–15 November 1647 (N&S, 504.81; Thomason / E520[5]) (contemporary print version)

At midnight on 11 November, Cromwell wrote a hurried note to the Speaker of the House of Commons reporting the escape of the King from Hampton Court. The letter was read the next day,[1] and caused consternation in the House. The original was lost in the fire of 1834 and this version was printed in *A Perfect Diurnall* three days later, probably a paraphrase and possibly including information gathered by Pecke independently. It is striking that it does not appear in other newspapers published that week. A slightly tidier version, first published in 1680, appears to be based on the version in *A Perfect Diurnall*.[2] Cromwell wrote at the same time to the earl of Manchester as acting Speaker of the House of Lords, but only a fragment survives in the Journal of the House of Lords.[3]

---

[10] Edward Whalley was Cromwell's first cousin: Whalley's mother Frances was the sister of Oliver's father (see Mark Noble, *Memoirs of the Noble House of Cromwell* (2 vols., 1787), 1:37 and 2:143–54).

[1] JHC, 6:356: 'A Letter from Lieutenant General *Cromwell*, of *November* 11, Twelve at Night, was read, signifying the Escape of the King; who went away about Nine of Clock Yesterday Evening.'

[2] J. Rushworth, *Historical Collections*, 5 pts in 8 vols. (1659–1701), 7:781—'A Letter upon Friday, November 12. was read in the House of Commons, from Lieutenant-General Cromwell at twelve a Clock at Night, directed to the Speaker, acquainting him, "That his Majesty had withdrawn himself from Hampton-Court at nine the last Night": The manner is variously reported, and we will say little of it at present, but that his Majesty was expected at Supper when the Commissioners and Colonel Whaley miss'd him: Upon which they entred the Room, and found his Majesty had left his Cloak behind in the Gallery in the private way: He passed by the Back-Stairs and Vault towards the Water-side. He left some Letters up on the Table in his Withdrawing-Room of his own Hand writing; whereof one was to the Commissioners of Parliament attending him, to be communicated to both Houses.'

[3] JHL, 9:519: The Speaker acquainted the House with a Letter he received from Lieutenant General *Cromwell*, 'That the King, with Nine Horses, last Night, went over *Kingston Bridge*.' — actually an error, since he had in fact departed by boat.

19 NOVEMBER 1647

Friday November 12

A Letter was this day read in the house of Commons from Lieueteaut Generall *Crumwell* at 12 of Clock at night, directed to the Speaker, acquainting him with, that his Majesty had withdrawne himselfe from Hampton Court at 9 the last night, the manuor is variously reported, and we will say little of it at present, but that his Majesty was expected at supper, when the Commissioners and Col. Whaley mist him, upon which they entred the roome and found his Majesty had left his Cloak behind him in the Gallery in the privat way he passed by the back stairs & Vault towards the Water side, He left some letters upon the Table in his with drawing Roome of his owne hand writing, whereof one was to the Commissioners of Parliament attending him to be communicated to both houses and followeth in these words. *His Majesties Letter for the Speaker of the Lords* pro tempore, *to be communicated unto the Lords and Commons in the Parliament of England at Westminster, and the Commissioners of the Parliament of Scotland, and to all my other Subjects, of what degree, condition, or calling whatsoever.*

Hampton Court 11 *November* 1647

1647 11 19

Speech by Oliver Cromwell to the House of Commons

Date: 19 November 1647

Source: Diary of John Boys, BL, Add. MS 50200, fos 76–76v. Printed in David Underdown, ed., 'The Parliamentary Diary of John Boys, 1647–8', *BIHR* 39 (1966), pp. 151–2 (reported speech)

This is the first of three speeches[1] of Cromwell recorded in the fragmentary diary of John Boys, since September 1645 recruiter MP for Kent. Of minor gentry stock and leaning towards the radical and pro-Army side of politics,[2] Boys recorded one or more speeches on thirty-seven separate days between 7 September 1647 and 16 May 1648. His summaries of these speeches are written in a mixture of Law French and English.

---

[1] See also **1647 11 23** and **1648 01 03**.

[2] David Underdown, in his introduction to 'The Parliamentary Diary of John Boys' at pp. 141–6 gives a clear biographical summary.

THE LETTERS, WRITINGS, AND SPEECHES OF OLIVER CROMWELL

At Putney on 8 November the General Council of the officers had ordered that the soldiers were to return to their regiments. This was a tactical move designed to manage the demands for a rendezvous. Even before the issue as to whether the soldiers should be allowed to subscribe to the *Agreement of the People* could be resolved, arrangements had to be made to gather them together. The officers' aim was therefore to avoid a single gathering of the entire army, on the assumption that a series of meetings on different dates at separate locations would be easier to manage. The first rendezvous was set for 15 November at Cockbush Field at Ware, Hertfordshire. This became a test of strength between the agitators, led by Thomas Rainborowe, who wanted the troops to subscribe to the *Agreement of the People* and the officers who demanded that they subscribe to their rival *Remonstrance*.[3] When some of the soldiers mutinied, firm action by Fairfax and more especially by Cromwell crushed the resistance. One of the mutineers was executed immediately on Fairfax's orders to demonstrate that such disobedience was unacceptable. The two subsequent rendezvous at Watford on 17 November and at Kingston upon Thames on 18 November passed off smoothly.

About midway through the proceedings of the Commons on 19 November, the Journal of the House of Commons records that 'Lieutenant General *Cromwell* gave the House an Account of the Proceedings at the Rendesvous of the Army; and how that, by the great Mercy of God, upon the Endeavours of the General and Officers, the Army was in a very composed State of Obedience to the Superior Officers, and Submission to the Authority of Parliament.' The House, it would seem unanimously, had 'Resolved, &c. That the Thanks of this House be returned to Lieutenant General *Cromwell*, for his good Service performed to the Parliament and Kingdom, at the late Rendesvous of the Army' which the Speaker duly did.[4] His speech is a rather sanitised account of what had actually happened, at least as recorded by Boys.[5]

---

ce jor L. G. Cromwell fist un relacon del Rendevouz de l'armé. il dist en les tous 3 rendevouzes[6] la appieroient 19 Regimts. & q ils ne fur. duf dessus ne dessoubs lour nuber (comt q le report fust q divs les nubers fur. grandemt encreas), & q nient obstant grand attachemts de corrupter l'armeé & faire grands devisions intr eux, q nient ils fur unanimous & reduce a bon discipline, issint q ils poient bien ees subservient al svice del pliamt & Kdome. Il dist, q là fur destructive dessignes sur les soldats, al eux seducer al l'engagemt, appell, l'engagemt del people. & q

---

[3] *A remonstrance from His Excellency Sir Thomas Fairfax, and his Councell of Warre, concerning the late discontent and distraction in the Army.* (1647) (Wing / F228; Thomason / E.414[14])

[4] *JHC*, 5:363–4.

[5] Woolrych, *Soldiers and Statesmen*, ch. XI; Gentles, *The New Model Army*, pp. 219–26.

[6] The three rendezvous were at Corkbush Field (Ware) on 15 November, St Albans on 17 November and Kingston on 18 November (Woolrych, *Soldiers and Statesmen*, pp. 279–86).

480

19 NOVEMBER 1647

ascuns veloint enfuser ce principle, Qu'ils avoint Conquer le Royaume, & si coe Wm le Conqueror reduc't c al bondage p son Conqueste, ils sent poient maintent reducer c al Liberté p lor conqueste, & doner leyes al Royaume. dist q il fust grnd mercy de dieu, de tielmt allayer les distempers enter eux, q grnd prfession fust ft p tous les soldats a soubmitter al Generall[7] & l'ancient disciplin. Dist ouster, q'estoit maintent en nre poiar al eux gdr en tiel bon ordr, p eux donr satisfaction en cx choses q eux concern coe soldats, & en settling le Kdome. en q (il dist liberalmt) q nous avions trop retardé p debates, autr choses q ne sont del esse del Royaume, (coe le govrnment de l'esglise) q il esperoit q nous \ne/ ser. offends, sils soient nostre remembrances es choses qux concern le Kdome; & q ils avoit cy-devt prsenté en lor pposalls, qu ne fur debar coe Englishmen a replsenter faire hmble & submisse representacon de tiell choses. il dist, q le peuple avoint ft addres al Genrall pr divrs publique affaires, q il avoit transmis al pliamt, & q il & to eux & le \Royaume/ soldats estimeroint q l'armé avoit declyne & fallen fro thr first Faith, if they should Renew those desires to you. (mes ap. Mr Swinfen[8] aiant replie &c. il grantoit, q il tout tiel representacon dt ees ove submission & acquiescens en le determinacon del parliamt & Mr Swinfen aiant dist ascun chose a ce purpos, q n'e safe pr royaume, q ascun poiar dehors enterprend d'es mediators pr le peuple al parliamt, car c e a doner al eux al moins un autorité equal al parliamt. L. G. Cromwell replye, & see d'insinuate q c q fu dist p Mr Sw: did deny al armé a peticon coe Englishmen, mes allowoit petitioning tantm coe subjects. & q tiel apprehension en les soldats vouloit donr grnd discontents, & pr c desiroit le meason a declarer, s'il fus lawfull, q il avoit benefitt & liberty a petitionr coe soldats \Englishmen/ cy-bien q autrs subjects. mes ordr fus enter a ce ppos, q le L. Genrall fus desire d'enformer l'armeé q le meason seroit prest de receiver lor desires & addresses en un pliamtary waye.

this day L. G. Cromwell made a report of the rendezvous of the army. He said in all 3 rendez-vous there appeared 19 regiments and that there were not above nor below their number (although the report was that divers numbers were greatly increased) and that notwithstanding large claims of corrupting the army and making great divisions among them, that, notwithstanding they were unanimous and reduced to good discipline, so that they may be well subservient to the service of the parliament & kingdom. He said that there were destructive

---

[7] i.e. the Lord General Thomas Fairfax.
[8] John Swynfen [Swinfen] (1613–94), politician. See *ODNB*.

designs upon the soldiers to seduce them to the engagement appeal to the engagement of the people and that some wish to infuse this principle. That they had conquered the kingdom and just as William the Conqueror reduced it to bondage by his Conquest, they (sent) may now reduce it to the liberty by their conquest, & give laws to the kingdom, He said that it was great mercy of God, in such way to allay the discontents among them, that great profession was made by all the soldiers to submit to the General & the old discipline. He said further, that it was now in our power to keep them in such good order by giving them satisfaction in 15 things which concern them as soldiers, & in settling the kingdom in which (he said freely) that we had been too delayed by debates, other things that are not of the (esse) of the kingdom, (as the government of the church) that he hoped that we shall not be offended, if they make our remembrances in the things that concern the kingdom; & that they had as before presented in their proposals, that they were not debarred as Englishmen to make humble & submissive representation of such things. He said that the people had made address to the General for divers public affairs, that he had transmitted to parliament, & that he & all them & the kingdom soldiers would esteem that the army had declined & fallen from their first faith, if they should Renew those desires to you. (but after Mr Swinfen having replied &c. he granted that he all such representation must be with submission & acquiescence in the determination of the parliament and Mr Swinfen having said some thing to this purpose, that it is not safe for the kingdom, that any outside power undertake to be mediators for the people to the parliament, for that is to give to them to at least an authority equal to the parliament. L. G. Cromwell responded & seemed to insinuate that which was said by Mr Swinfen: did deny to the army a petition as Englishmen, but allowed petitioning only as subjects & that such apprehension in the soldiers would give great discontents, and therefore desired the house to declare, if it was lawful, that he had benefit & liberty to petition as soldiers, Englishmen as well as other subjects. but order was entered to this purpose, that the L. G. was desired to inform the army that the house would be ready to receive their desires and addresses in a parliamentary way.[9]

Outcome: The Commons then thanked Cromwell 'for his good Service performed to the Parliament and Kingdom'.[10]

[9] The editors are grateful to Ashley Hannay of the Centre for Legal History in Cambridge for assistance with this translation.
[10] JHC, 5:364.

23 NOVEMBER 1647A

1647 11 23a

Speech by Oliver Cromwell to the House of Commons

Date: 23 November 1647

Source: Diary of John Boys, BL, Add. MS 50200, fos 74v–75r. Printed in 'Parliamentary Diary of John Boys', pp. 152–3 (reported speech)

The Commons had obtained a printed copy of *The Agreement of the People* as early as 9 November. It had immediately denounced it.[1] On receiving a second copy on 16 November, it had appointed a committee to investigate the London agitators.[2] The Speaker, William Lenthall, had since received a petition defending the Agreement and condemning the suppression of the mutiny at Ware. He had passed it on to that committee, which now raised the matter in the Commons.[3] After dinner on 23 November, a petition was presented by men with Leveller links making a fresh case for *The Agreement of the People* and protesting at the execution of Richard Arnold for his part in the mutiny at Ware.[4] The House of Commons called in five of those who had come to present the petition and ordered them to be imprisoned. It also pointedly ordered 'That a Letter be prepared and sent to the General, taking Notice of his Proceedings, in the Execution, according to the Rules of War, of a mutinous Person, at the Rendezvous near *Ware*;[5] and to give him Thanks for it; and to desire him to prosecute the Examination of that Business to the Bottom; and to bring such guilty Persons as he shall think fit to condign and exemplary Punishment.'[6] At some point during the debate on the petition, Boys summarised Cromwell's contribution in the following speech.

For the nature of Boys's diary see **1647 11 19**.

———

L. G. Cromwell, conut q al ies il pmettoit cx hmes a faire address a l'armé, espant q thr follies would vanish,[7] but \now/ wn he saw \sees/ they spread, & infected so much, he confesses it high tyme to suppress such attempts. and for a more equall representative, because he saw many honest officers were possest wth it, he gave waye to dispute about it at the Counsell of war, partly to perswade them

---

[1] JHC, 5:354.

[2] JHC, 5:359–60. It can most accessibly found in Don M. Wolfe, *Leveller Manifestoes of the Puritan Revolution* (New York, 1944), p. 237.

[3] JHC, 5:367.   [4] Gentles, *New Model Army*, p. 224.   [5] Ibid., pp. 219–26.

[6] JHC, 5:364.

[7] i.e Lt Gen Cromwell, knowing that 110 men had been permitted to make an address to the army, hoping that their follies would vanish...

483

THE LETTERS, WRITINGS, AND SPEECHES OF OLIVER CROMWELL

out of the unreasonablenes of that representacon thes these London Agents would have, but wn he saw, that they would exclude children & servts, yet such as recd almes they insisted on as persons competent for electors &c. he saw such a dangerous consequences of that, they wch had no interest in estate at all shld be d choose a representacon (& they being the most, were likely to choose those of their own condion) that this drive at a levelling & paritye &c. he could not but disclayme \& discountenance/ such endeavors, & this hath brought so many obloquies upon him & the officers. & he's confident tht most of the Calumnies raised upon the Army have proceeded from that ptie. &c.

———

Outcome: The Commons agreed and condemned the latest petition as 'a seditious and contemptuous Avowing and Prosecution' of *The Agreement of the People* which they had previously proscribed. They also resolved that five men who had organised the petition were to be imprisoned and that Fairfax was to be thanked for ordering the execution of the Ware mutineer.[8] This did not prevent the publication of the petition which within two days had been printed as *The humble Petition of many free-born people*.[9]

———⟨∞⟩———

1647 12 23b

Letter from Oliver Cromwell to Thomas Hill, master of Trinity College, Cambridge

Date: 23 December 1647
Source: Cambridge, Trinity College Archives (TCA), Collections of Thomas Parne: 'Great Miscellany Volume of Papers' ('Volume 3'), No. 7 (later copy)

No original of this letter survives. There are two eighteenth-century copies, one that appears to have maintained the original seventeenth-century spelling and punctuation, whilst the other equally clearly modernised it.[1] In 1849 a Fellow of Trinity, the Rev. J. Edelston, told Thomas Carlyle that the former had been 'docqueted in the hand of one Porter, clerk to Thomas Parne, about 1724' and was entered as 'L. P.Cromwell's Letter

---

[8] *JHC*, 5:367–8.
[9] *To the Supream Authority of England, the Commons in Parliament assembled. The humble Petition of many free-born people* [1647], most accessibly found in Don M.Wolfe, *Leveller Manifestoes of the Puritan Revolution* (New York, 1944), p. 237: the original can be found at Wing / T1725 or Thomason / 669.f.11[98].

---

[1] BL, Harl. MS 7053 fo. 153b.

484

23 DECEMBER 1647B

concerning Sir Dudley Wyatt';[2] but there is no longer any record of either of these statements. There is no reason to doubt that Edelston had seen them. The British Library version looks like a later copy, and quite possibly a copy of the Trinity copy.[3]

There is nothing in the Trinity College version identifying the intended recipient of the letter. The British Library version adds (it looks like a transcriber's gloss rather than something on the document he was transcribing): '[To Mr Thomas Hill, Master of Trinity College, Cambridge]'.[4] This seems very reasonable but may have been a guess then as now. Cromwell is writing on behalf of Sir Dudley Wyatt (1609–51), the fifth child and third son of a Worcester gentleman. He was educated at Christchurch Oxford and Trinity College, Cambridge (scholar 1627, Fellow 1633). In his letter Cromwell claims (possibly simply on Wyatt's word) that he had been in Ireland since 1641 fighting the rebels there. Indeed, the college records do confirm that on 'Jan:3. 1641'[5] 'Granted then to Mr Wyatt allowance for his Commons[6] during his seruice in the employmt: of Ireland for halfe a yea & time of absence during the same. Both time & commons for the whole yeare in case the employmt. continues so longe.'[7] So not for seven years. There is one other mention of him in the records: 'the 20th of April 1643 ... Granted then to mr Wyatt From this day a Twelvemonthes dayes of absence.'[8] So perhaps he was in Ireland during the early part of the wars there. However, there is no record in the Trinity College archives that, even with Cromwell's support, he was ever readmitted to his Fellowship.[9] Cromwell may not have been given the full story. Clarendon tells us that a 'Sir' Dudley Wyatt spent much of 1646 with the Prince of Wales in Jersey and was used a messenger between the prince and his mother, Queen Henrietta Maria. Was this the same man, knighted for his services on dangerous missions? Perhaps he *was* in Ireland but with royalist forces fighting the Confederates and left as the war there resulted in stalemate. In 1649 he was to relocate to Virginia (perhaps being related to Sir Francis Wyatt, governor of Virginia 1621–5 and 1639–42) and he died there two years later. It has not been established what prior connection there was, if any, between Wyatt and Cromwell.[10]

---

[2] Carlyle-Lomas, 1:287*.

[3] The Harleian version was transcribed in C. H. Hartshorne, *The Book of Rareties in the University of Cambridge* (1829), p. 277.

[4] Thomas Hill (d. 1653), college head. See *ODNB*.

[5] i.e. 1642. This is a very early date to rush off to Ireland. The Ulster Rising was on and after 23 October 1641 but English troops did not start to be assembled until March 1642.

[6] i.e. his food and drink allowances.

[7] Trinity College Cambridge Archives: *The Master's Old Conclusion Book, 1608–1673*, p. 170.

[8] Ibid., p. 172.

[9] There is a note on the BL, Harl. MS transcript which adds 'Upon this letter, Sir Dudley Wyatt was readmitted' but there is no indication on what authority this was added.

[10] *Al. Cantab.*; Carlyle-Lomas, I:286–7; Clarendon, *Great Rebellion*, bk ix, para. 143, bk x, paras 2, 11, 37; Eva Scott, *The King in Exile: The Wanderings of Charles II from June 1646 to July 1654* (1905), p. 9.

L. P. Cromwell's letter concerning Sr Dudley Wyott

Sr /

As I am inform'd, this Gentleman the Bearer hereof, in the Year 1641: had leave of his Colledge to travell into Ireland for seaven Yeares, and in his absence, he (being then actually imployed against the Rebells in that Kingdome) was ejected out of his Fellowship, by a mistake, the Colledge Registry being not looked into, to inquire the cause of his non-residence, I cannot therefore but thincke it a just and reasonable request, that he be readmitted to all the Benefitts, rights & Priviledges, wch he enjoyed before that ejection, and therefore desire you would please to effect it accordingly. Wherein yo' shall doe a favour, will be owned by

Yor affeccionate freind & Servant

Oliver Cromwell

Windsor. 23o Decembr.

1647

1647 12 26[?]
Letter from Oliver Cromwell to Robert Hammond

Date: Undated but likely to be 25 or 26 December 1647
Source: NRS, GD40/2/19/1, no. 24 [old no. 17] (Lothian MS) (holograph)

This holograph letter is in the papers of the earls and marquisses of Lothian, now in the National Records of Scotland.[1] It is undated and concerns one of the several attempts that Charles I made to escape from Carisbrooke Castle. But which one? Sir Charles Firth, the first to print the letter, though as a supplement to his edition of the *Clarke Papers*, thought it was 'evidently written between January and April 1648'.[2] Sophia Lomas, working under Firth's oversight ten years later, in 1904, thought it more likely to have been written c.25/26 December 1647.[3] She draws attention to the phrase 'am I forgotten?' at the opening, suggesting that Cromwell and Hammond had been out of

---

[1] William Ker, third earl of Lothian possessed two letters from Cromwell to Hammond, the other dated 13 May 1651 (below, **1651 05 13**). He was in Scotland prior to his appointment as a Scottish commissioner to the Long Parliament in December 1648 so the presence of this letter in his papers does not throw light on when it was written.
[2] *Clarke Papers*, 2:xxv–xxvi.   [3] Carlyle-Lomas 3:382–3, supplement 26.

26 DECEMBER 1647[?]

touch for some time. Cromwell wrote regularly to Robert Hammond[4] in 1648, beginning with a long letter on 3 January 1648 (below **1648 01 03**). This seems fairly conclusive. If it was written *c.*26 December 1647 it would coincide with the King's rejection of Parliament's Four Bills and acceptance of the Engagement with the Scots, which made his escape urgent. But on 26 December Cromwell would have known none of this and his letter appears to be result of naval intelligence about the movement of vessels in and out of Southampton Water.

Deere Robin[5] am I forgotten?
Thou art not, I wishe thee much comfort
in thy great businesse, and the blessinge of
the Almighty upon thee.

This intelligence was delivered this day, viz
that \Sir George/ Cartwright[6] hath sent 3 boates from
Jersey, and a Barque from Sherbrowe[7]
under the prætence of trade under the
name of Frenchmen, but are absolutely
sent to bringe the Kinge (if their plott
cann take effect) from the Isle of Wight
to Jersey one of which boates is returned
back to Jersey which newes but it is
kept very private.

I wish great care be taken. Truly I
would have the Castle well manned,
you know how much lyeth upon itt.
If you would have any thinge more
donn, let your freindes know your

---

[4] Robert Hammond (1620/21–54), parliamentarian army officer. See *ODNB*. He was a cousin of Oliver Cromwell on his mother's side.

[5] The diminutive form of Robert, and the one Cromwell always used in addressing Hammond. As well as being Cromwell's first cousin, Hammond was nephew of the King's main chaplain at Carisbrooke at the end of 1647—Henry Hammond (1605–60), Church of England clergyman and theologian, for whom see *ODNB*.

[6] Not George Cartwright but Sir George Carteret, the King's lieutenant on Jersey and a fervent royalist—Sir George Carteret, first baronet (1610?–80), naval officer and administrator. See *ODNB*.

[7] Cherbourg, Lower Normandy, France.

minde, they are readye to assist and
serve you.

You have warrant now to turne out
such servants as you suspect,[8] doe itt
suddenly for feare of danger, you see
how God hath honored and blessed every
resolute action of thine for him, doubt
not but Hee will doe soe still.

Let the Parlnts. shipps have notice
of Cartwrights designe that soe they
may looke out for him.

I have noe more but rest
your true servant
O Cromwell

For Col. Rob. Hammond
Governour of the Isle
of wight theise att
Carisbrooke Castle
hast post hast[9]

a letter from Lunt
genll Cromwell when
I was in the Isle of Wight[10]

---

[8] This tends to confirm the date of the letter as late December 1647, for on 29 December Hammond expelled three of the King's closest advisers on the Isle of Wight—Sir John Ashburnham, Sir John Berkeley and William Legge (Gardiner, *GCW*, 4:49).

[9] This address and characteristically impatient addendum was also in Cromwell's own hand.

[10] Added in an unknown hand. Is the 'I' Hammond?

3 JANUARY 1648A

1648 01 03a

Speech by Oliver Cromwell to the House of Commons

Date: 3 January 1648
Source: BL, Add. MS 50200, fos 71–71v, Diary of John Boys (reported speech)

On 24 December 1647 commissioners from Parliament had presented their latest proposals for a constitutional settlement to the King. The Four Bills would have given Parliament control of the militia for twenty years, nullified Charles's declarations against Parliament, rescinded all peerages granted by the King since 1642 and allowed Parliament to adjourn to any place it wished. Charles however rejected these proposals four days later. He had received what he judged to be a better offer, the Engagement, from the Scottish commissioners and so had entered into a secret agreement with them on 26 December. The news of the King's rejection of the Four Bills was debated in the Commons on 3 January. Hesilrige[1] opened the debate by moving that no further overtures be made to the King. Sir Thomas Wroth[2] then raised the stakes by making a speech denouncing monarchy in general. John Maynard[3] in contrast argued for further negotiations. Cromwell, who is recorded by Boys as speaking next, may well have been responding directly to Maynard. Apart from Boys's diary,[4] two other sources purport to record what Cromwell said on this occasion.[5] Only that by Boys however carries any real weight.

We still hold to or interest, & tht of the Kdome; true, we declard or intentions for monrchy, & they still are so, unles necessity enforce an alteracon. its grnted the K. hath ~~hath~~ broken his trust, yet you are fearfull to declare you will make no further addresses. Wre will the people kn. to have you? a Not owning of G. in these troubles, hath caused a protraction of the war. To say, thre is a Lyon in the way, ths difficulty, that dangr, & dissatisfaction of the people, ths becomes you not &c. If you declare yors. as you have don, the people will be for you bec they kn thr interest is in you. & if you let thm see, you take care of their Interest, &c. Declare ths so much the rather, bec yor addres last tyme was in a pliamtary waye,

---

[1] Sir Arthur Heselrige [Haselrig], second baronet (1601–61), parliamentarian army officer and politician. See *ODNB*.

[2] Sir Thomas Wroth [Wrothe] (1584–1672), politician. See *ODNB*.

[3] Sir John Maynard (1604–90), politician. See *ODNB*.

[4] Underdown, 'Parliamentary Diary of John Boys' is the best introduction to both Boys and his diary; for some comments on Cromwell's three speeches, see **1647 11 19**.

[5] [C. Walker], *The History of Independency* (1648), p. 43; Edward Hyde, *The History of the Rebellion and Civil Wars in England*, W. Dunn Macray, ed. (Oxford, 1888), 4:281.

wth the English Interest in the head of it. Look on the people you reprsent, & break not yor trust, & expose not the honest pty of the Kdom, who have bled for you, & suffr not misery to fall upon thm, for want of corage & resolucon in you, els the honest people may tak such courses as nature dictates to thm. Remember the late discontents in the Kdome, & the troubles we have bin in in the army for yor service, & have appeased \thm/ upon or Confidences given the soldier, tht upon ~~yor~~ the answr to your late applicacon you would doe wt shld make for the peace of the Kdome. & it behooves us to deale faithfully wth you. ~~de~~ doe not consider dangers on the one hand only but on the other too; are you not denyed safety, wch concerns yor very Being?

Outcome: The arguments by Hesilrige and Cromwell carried the day. The Commons voted by 141 to 92 that they would 'make no further Addresses or Applications to the King'.[6]

1648 01 03b
Letter from Oliver Cromwell to Robert Hammond

Date: 3 January 1648
Source: W. Harris, *An Historical and Critical Account of the Life of Oliver Cromwell, Lord Protector of the Commonwealth of England, Scotland and Ireland* (London, 1762), pp. 509–10 (later print version)

This was the first of six letters printed by Harris, 'in the possession of Thoedosius Forrest, Esq; of George Street, Yorke-Buildings, London'. It appeared again two years later in an edition by Thomas Birch.[1] This in turn was a version in modernised spelling derived from two transcriptions in Birch's own hand in BL, Harl. MS 4186, fos 14r–v and fos 27r–28r. Birch states clearly in his introduction (p. iv) that 'To render this collection as complete as possible, six other letters, which were part of the collection of Col. *Hammond*, are reprinted here from Harris's *Appendix* to his [p. v] *Historical and critical account of the life of Oliver Cromwell.*' Both manuscript copies are very similar to Harris, but there are some differences which cannot be easily explained as simple misreadings of Harris, and Birch also writes at length about the provenance of the six letters as being from Theodosius

---

[6] *JHC*, 5:415–16.

[1] *Letters between Col. Robert Hammond, Governor of the Isle of Wight, and the Committee of Lords and Commons at Derby-House, General Fairfax, Lieut. General Cromwell, Commissary General Ireton &c. relating to King Charles I While he was confined in Carisbrooke Castle in that Island* [ed. T. Birch] (London, 1764), pp. 23–6.

3 JANUARY 1648B

Forrest, secretary to Richard Hampden 'a direct and penult descendant of the Most magnanimous John ship-money Hampden'. According to this account, Hammond had bequeathed between fifty and sixty letters from Army officers during his time in the Isle of Wight to his Hampden cousins. Tragically, all but six had been lent to an Italian diplomat who never returned them.[2] The differences which are hard to account for are annotated below. There can be little doubt that Harris saw the originals, now lost, and Birch *may* have seen them too. But because they are so obviously 'tidied up', the Harris version is the one that should be the proof text here.

The occasion of Cromwell's letter is to update Hammond on major developments in London. On 26 December Charles and the Scots signed the Engagement and two days later Charles rejected the Four Bills, Parliament's most recent peace proposals. He also made an attempt to escape by sea from the Isle of Wight, only a shift in the wind preventing it. Hammond now made him a close prisoner, no longer able to roam freely around the Isle of Wight. On 3 January 1648 the Commons approved the Vote of No Addresses, which forbade anyone to enter into negotiations with the King and also replaced the Committee of Both Kingdoms set up in December 1643 by the Derby House Committee as the executive committee in charge of the defence of England and Ireland.[3]

Deerest Robin,

Nowe (blessed bee God) I can write, and thou receave, freely. I never in my life sawe more deep sense, and lesse will to shewe itt[4] unchristianly, then in that, which thou diddest write to us when wee were at *Windsor*,[5] and thou in the middest of thy tentation,[6] which indeed (by what wee understood of itt) was a great one, and occasioned the greater, by the letter the generall[7] sent thee, of which

---

[2] BL, Add. MS 4136, fos 75r–v.

[3] The best account remains Gardiner *GCW*, 4:27–53.

[4] Birch omits the 'itt' from both his manuscript versions (but includes 'it' in the printed version; but in one of the manuscript versions (BL, Add. MS 4186, fo. 14r) he originally wrote 'Will to behave unchristianly' and then wrote 'shew' above 'behave' (but without 'itt'). It is hard to believe that he mis-transcribed 'shew' as 'behave'. This is the best evidence that he was working from another copy of the original and correcting against Harris.

[5] Windsor was Army headquarters throughout December and on 22 December at a 10-hour prayer meeting of officers and soldiers, agreement was reached to pardon all those caught up in the November mutinies and to press for Rainsborough's appointment as vice admiral (Gardiner, *GCW*, 4:44).

[6] Possibly a reference to his willingness to contemplate assisting the King's escape. On 28 December, the Engagement signed and the Four Bills rejected, Charles planned to get on board a vessel waiting in the Solent to take him to France, Hammond unaccountably left him to himself (Gardiner, *GCW*, 4:49).

[7] Sir Thomas Fairfax.

THE LETTERS, WRITINGS, AND SPEECHES OF OLIVER CROMWELL

thou wast not mistaken, when thou didest challenge mee[8] to be the pener.[9] How good has God beene to dispose all to mercy, and although itt was trouble for the present, yett glory is come out of itt, for which wee prayse the Lord with thee, and for thee, and truly thy carriage has biene such, as occasions much honor to the name of God, and too religion, Goe onn in the strength of the Lord, and the Lord bee still with thee. But (deere *Robin*) this businesse hath beene (I trust) a mightye providence to this poore kingdome, and too us all.[10] The house of comons is very sensible of the Kgs dealinges, and of our brethrens,[11] in this late transaction, You should doe well (if you have any thing that may discover juglinge) to search itt out and lett us knowe itt, itt may bee of admirable use at this tyme, because wee shall (I hope) instantly goe upon businesses in relation to them, tendinge to prevent danger. The house of comons has this day voted as follows. First that they will make noe more addresses to the K. 2. None shall applye to him without leave of the two houses upon paine of beinge guilty of high treason. 3dly, They will receave nothinge from the Kinge, nor shall any any other bringe any thing to them from him, nor receave any thing from the Kinge.[12] Lastly the members of both houses, whoe were of the committee of both kingdoms, are established in all that power in themselves for *England*, and *Ireland*, which they had to act with both kingdoms,[13] and Sir *John Evelin* of *Wilts*[14] is added in the room of Mr Recorder,[15] and *Rath. F. Fienis*[16] in the roome of Sir *Philip*

---

[8] i.e. a letter written by Cromwell and signed by Fairfax, an interesting insight into their relations at this moment.

[9] The Birch versions insert a paragraph break here, perhaps evidence of their access to a different version.

[10] Was the providence that it reinforced the King's duplicity and prepared the way for his trial with more MPs ready to support it?

[11] i.e. our Scottish brethren.

[12] A summary of the Vote of No Addresses, approved by the Commons on 3 January but by the Lords, and only after Army pressure, not until 17 January (Gardiner, *GCW*, 4:50–3). For the full text see, Gardiner, *Constitutional Documents of the Puritan Revolution*, pp. 56–7, available online at http://www.constitution.org/eng/ conpur079.htm, #79.

[13] i.e. the Committee of Both Kingdoms was dissolved so that the Scots were removed, and much the same group of English MPs reconstituted as what became known as the Derby House Committee with the changes specified.

[14] Sir John Evelyn (1601–85). See *ODNB*. Evelyn was one of the tellers for the Vote of No Addresses.

[15] Sir John Glynne (1603–66), judge and politician. See *ODNB*. Glynne had been Recorder of Westminster since 1636 and Recorder of London since 1643. He was one of the eleven members expelled and impeached after the attempted counter-revolution at the end of July 1647.

[16] i.e. Nathaniel Fiennes (corrected in all Birch's versions; the F. Fienes is a failure to recognise two lower case 'f's as a pre-1700 modern equivalent to a capital 'F'. Nathaniel Fiennes, (1607/8–69), politician and army officer. See *ODNB*.

Stapleton,[17] and my Lord of *Kent*,[18] in the room of the Earl of *Essex*.[19] I thinke it good you take notice of this, the sooner the better.

[20]Lett us knowe how its with you in point of strength, and what you neede from us, some of us thinke the Kinge well with you, and that itt concernes us to keepe that island in great securitye, because of the *French*, et. And if soe, where can the Kinge bee better. If you have more force you will suer of full provision for them. The Lord blesse thee, pray for Thy deere friend and servant
O. CROMWELL.

My Ld *Wharton's*[21] Jan. 3d. neere tenn at night,[22] 1647.[23]

For Col. *Robert Hamond* Governor of the isle of *Wight* theise
For the service of the kingdom hast post hast. OLIVER CROMWELL.

1648 02 25
Oliver Cromwell to Richard Norton

Date: 25 February 1648
Source: Harry Ransom Center, University of Texas at Austin, Medieval and Early Modern Manuscripts Collection, CHP Cat 11A (holograph)

All previous versions of this letter have relied on the eighteenth-century transcript in W. Harris, *An Historical and Critical Account of the Life of Oliver Cromwell, Lord Protector of the*

---

[17] Sir Philip Stapleton: he was one of the eleven members expelled and impeached after the attempted counter-revolution at the end of July 1647. He died of a fever, perhaps plague, as soon as he set foot in France.

[18] Henry Grey, tenth earl of Kent (bap. 1594, d. 1651), parliamentarian nobleman. See *ODNB*. He had been one of the commissioners who had taken the Four Bills to the King.

[19] Robert Devereux, third earl of Essex (1591–1646), parliamentarian army officer. See *ODNB*. Essex had died on 10 September 1646 but was never replaced.

[20] Harris has a paragraph here that is not found in any of Birch's versions.

[21] Philip Wharton, fourth Baron Wharton (1613–96), politician. See *ODNB*.

[22] That Cromwell, at the end of such a dramatic day, chose to write to Hammond suggests great urgency and/or concern about his stance.

[23] Birch has this in a different order:
My Lord Wharton's
Near ten at night
3 Jan 1647
This is the fair copy version at BL, Harl. MS 4186, fos 14r–v (and in the printed version). In the other manuscript version, BL, Harl. MS 4186, fos 27r–28r he has the first line break after 'near'. This might again suggest Birch's access to a different version, original or early copy.

THE LETTERS, WRITINGS, AND SPEECHES OF OLIVER CROMWELL

Commonwealth of England, Scotland, and Ireland (1st ed., 1762), pp. 514–15. But our version is from the holograph in the Harry Ransom Library in Texas. It is the first of a long sequence of letters that trace the tortuous marriage negotiations conducted by Oliver on behalf of his eldest surviving son Richard, for the hand of Dorothy Maijor, daughter of the Hampshire gentleman Richard Maijor. There are a total of eleven letters from Cromwell in the period February 1648 to April 1648 (the marriage finally took place in Hursley, the Maijor home parish on 1 May 1649, at the height of the Leveller mutiny).[1] There are several non-Cromwell letters relating to the marriage in a separate collection of papers in the British Library.[2]

For my {N}oble freind
Col. Richard Norton[3]
theise[4]

Original Letter
From
Oliver Cromwell
To
To Coll.Richd Norton
Feb: 25.
1647.[5]

Deere Norton[6]
I have sent my Sonn[7] over to thee, beinge
willinge to answare providence, and although

---

[1] For an account of the marriage negotiations, see Jason Peacey, '"Fit for Public Services": The upbringing of Richard Cromwell', in P. Little, *Oliver Cromwell: New Perspectives* (2009), pp. 241–64, particulary pp. 243–50. There is a good summary in Richard Cromwell, (1626–1712), Lord Protector of England, Scotland and Ireland, in *ODNB*, and another account, strong on the financial aspects, in R. W.Ramsey, *Richard Cromwell: Protector of England* (1935), pp. 3–14.

[2] BL, Add. MS 24861.

[3] Richard Norton, Esq. of Southwick, Hampshire, had served with Cromwell as a cavalry officer in the army of the Eastern Association, as a colonel in the New Model Army, and as a key ally in Parliament after his return as recruiter MP for Hampshire in late 1645: Richard Norton (1615–91), army officer and politician. See *ODNB*.

[4] This endorsement is in Cromwell's own hand, beneath which is a fragment of his seal.

[5] This endorsement is in a later, probably eighteenth-century hand.

[6] An unusually formal address from Cromwell, who normally preferred informality. He knew Norton well enough to dub him 'Idle Dick' later in 1648.

[7] i.e. Richard Cromwell (1626–1712), Lord Protector of England, Scotland and Ireland. See *ODNB*.

I confesse I have ~~lately~~ had an offer of
a very great proposition from a Father of
his Daughter. Yett truly I rather encline
to this in my thoughts, because though
the other bee very farr greater Yett I
see difficultyes, and not that assurance of
godlynesse, yett indeed fairnesse.[8] I confesse
that which is ~~now~~ \tould/ mee of mr M.[9] \concerninge estate/ is more
then I cann looke for, as things now stand.
If God please to bringe itt about ~~and~~ the
consideration of pietye in the parents, and such
hopes of the Gentlewoeman in that respect, make
the businesse to mee a great mercy, ~~if God~~
concerninge which I desier to waite upon God.
I am confident of thy love, and desier all
~~secrecye~~ \thinges/, may be carried with privacie. The
Lord doe his will, thats best, to which sub-
mittinge I rest

Your humble servant
O Cromwell
Feb. 25
1647

1648 03 07

Letter from Oliver Cromwell to Sir Thomas Fairfax

Date: 7 March 1648 (but probably 1647)
Source: BL, Sloane MS 1519, fos 158r–159v (holograph)

This letter was dated by Cromwell 7 March 1647 [=1648], and by the John Rushworth, secretary to Fairfax 7 March 1646 [=1647]. Carlyle-Lomas opted for the later date, Abbott for

---

[8] This second family with whom Cromwell had been warily negotiating is not now known.
[9] i.e. Maijor.

THE LETTERS, WRITINGS, AND SPEECHES OF OLIVER CROMWELL

the earlier date. This present edition thinks the earlier date is the more likely and the reasons are given in item **1647 03 07**.

However, we include the text again here, for the sake of completeness.

———

Lt. General Cromwell
March. 7. 1647

For his Excellency Sir
Thomas Fairfax Genl.
of the Parlnts. Armies
theise

Sir it hath pleased God to raise mee
out of a dangerous sicknesse, and I doe
most willingly acknowledge, that the
Lord hath (in this visitation) exercised
the bowells of a Father towards mee,
I receaved in my selfe the sentence
of death, that I might learne to
trust in him that raiseth from the
dead, and have noe confidence in
the flesh. It's a blessed thinge to
dye daylie, for what is there in
this world to be accounted off,
the best men accordinge to the flesh,
and thinges, are lighter then vanitye. I finde this only good, to
love the Lord, and his poore despised people, to doe for them, and
to bee readie to Suffer with them,
and hee that is found worthy of
this, hath obteyned great favor
from the Lord, and Hee that is
established in this, shall (\beinge conformed/ ~~after confor~~
~~mity with~~ to Christ, and the rest of the
bodye) participate in the Glory of
~~the~~ \a/ resurrection, which will answare all.

496

21 MARCH 1648

Sir I must thanfully confesse your favor in your last letter, I see I am not forgotten, and truly to bee kept in your remembrance is very great Satisfaction to mee, for I cann say in the simplicitye of my hart, I putt a high and true valew upon your love, which when I forgett I shall cease to be a gratefull, and an honest man, I most humblie begg my service may bee præsented to your Lady,[1] to whom I wish all happinesse, and establishment in the truth, Sir my prayers are for you as becomes

Your excellencies most humble servant
Oliver Cromwell.

March. 7th. 1647[2]

Sir mr. Rushworth[3]
will write to you about
the quarteringe &
the letter lately
sent you, and
therfore I forbeare.

1648 03 21

Letter from Oliver Cromwell to the Committee at Derby House

Date: 21 March 1648
Source: Parliamentary Archives, HC/CL/JO/1/32, pp. 275–6. Manuscript Journal of the House of Commons, 10 Feb.–1 Sept. 1648 (entry for 24 March 1648) (contemporary copy)

In this letter to the Committee of Derby House, Cromwell offered to forgo most of the revenues on lands awarded him by a grateful majority in Parliament for his role in the

---

[1] Anne Fairfax [née Vere], Lady Fairfax.
[2] Cromwell's spiritual reflections form the main body of the text and reach to the bottom of the page. His personal compliments to Fairfax and his wife follow in the left-hand margin, starting about four lines down the page. The date is at the very top of the margin; squeezed in the top left-hand corner, between the date and the first three lines of the letter, is the PS.
[3] John Rushworth who was Fairfax's secretary.

defeat of the King. The biggest single grant to him for his service in the New Model (at £4 per day) was a grant of the marquis of Worcester's lands in Monmouthshire and in the Gower Peninsula around Swansea, and he offers here to forgo £1,000 a year out of an estimated revenue of £1,680. This is for an initial period of five years, but he was to retain more than one-third of the revenues and of course the title to the lands long term. His offer to forgo arrears of £1,500 for his service as lieutenant general of the Army of the Eastern Association and as governor of the Isle of Ely, was of course writing off all future revenues as well as the capital sum. It is the only such offer (certainly one of very few such offers) made by any commander in the Parliament's Army. This version is the one taken from the fair manuscript version of the Journal of the House of Commons. It is so tightly bound that the last word(s) of each line on p. 275 are impossible to read and they are supplied here from the eighteenth-century printed version of the Journals with modernised spelling.[1]

⟨Ireland⟩

⟨Lt Gen Cromwell⟩ Sir John Evelyn[2] reported from the Committee of [Lords and] and Commons for the Affaires of Ireland sitting [at] Darby Howse the Offer of Leuitenant Generall Cro[mwell] for the Service of Ireland, which was read & [was in] these words followeing (vizt.) The two Howses of Parliamt haveing lately [bestowed] one thousand six hundred eighty Pounds per Annum [upon] mee & my heires out of the Earle of Worcest[er's estate][3] The necessity of affaires requireing assistance [I do] hereby offer One thousand Pounds Annually [to be] paid out of the Rents of the said Lands, That [is to] say five hundred Pounds out

---

[1] *JHC*, 5:513. We have not followed the capitalisation and punctuation from *JHC* in the insertions in square brackets, which clearly follow eighteenth-century conventions (although an apostrophe has been retained in 'Worcester's estate').

[2] There were two MPs with the same name, this one is certainly Sir John Evelyn (1601–85) and not Sir John Evelyn (bap. 1591, d. 1663/4), for both of whom see *ODNB*. They were nephew and uncle, and they both sat as MP for Ludgershall (Wiltshire), with the former one of Simonds D'Ewes's 'fiery spirits', the other very much a peace party man. The former was a teller for the Vote of No Addresses in early 1648 and the latter a teller against it. The former had also just become a member of the Committee of Both Kingdoms. It is certainly the former that Cromwell is referring to here.

[3] Edward Somerset, second marquis of Worcester (d. 1667), courtier and scientist. See *ODNB*. The reference to the 'Earle of Worcester' is a pointed reference to the fact that Parliament did not recognise titles conferred since the commencement of hostilities. Worcester's father had been made a marquis on 2 March 1643. He succeeded his father on 18 December 1646. In the two previous years (under his own title as earl of Glamorgan), and as a fervent Catholic, he had negotiated a peace with the papal nuncio in Ireland that would have created a Catholic-dominated kingdom in Ireland. Cromwell also secured the marquis's estates in South Wales, for which see Lloyd Bowen, 'Oliver Cromwell (*alias* Williams) and Wales', in Patrick Little, ed., *Oliver Cromwell: New Perspectives* (2009), pp. 180–6. Bowen believes that his claim that the whole estate could be valued at £1,680 was a fair estimate.

of the next Mich[aelmas] Rent & soe on by the halfe yeares for the spa[ce of] five yeares if the warre in Ireland shall soe [long] continue, or that I live Soe long, to be [employed] for the service of Ireland as the Parliamt shall [please] to appoint, Provided the said yearely Rent of [one] Thousand six hundred & eighty pounds beco[me not] to be suspended by warre or other accident Whereas there is an Arrere of pay due unto mee whilest I was Leuitenant Generall unto the Earle of Manchester of about fifteene hundred Pounds Audited and stated; As also a great Arrere due for about two yeares being Governor of the Isle of Ely,[4] I doe hereby discharge the state from all or any Claime to be made by mee thereunto. 21º Martii. 1647. subscribed with his name.
O. Cromwell.

Ordered.
That this Howse doth accept of the free offer of Leuitenant Generall Cromwell testifieing his zeale & good affections to the Service of Ireland and the releife of the distressed Protestants there, and that Mr Speaker doe returne the hearty thanks of this Howse to the said Leuietent Generall Cromwell for his soe free & liberall offer to the good example & incouragement of otehrs liberally to Contribute to soe good a worke.

1648 03 28
Letter from Oliver Cromwell to Colonel Richard Norton

Date: 28 March 1648
Source: Catalogue of the collection of Autograph Letters and Historical Documents formed between 1865 and 1882 by A.Morrison. Compiled and annotated under the Direction of A.W.Thibadeau (second series, 1893–97), 3 vols. (printed for private circulation, 1895) 2:357–8 (later copy)

The original of this letter has not been found (it was part of the collection gathered in the late nineteenth century by Arthur Morrison and sold at auction in 1922). We do, however, have three transcriptions made from the original. They are substantially the same and each fills out in the same way words that (at least in the 1780s) seem to be missing text caused by damage down the right margin. The earliest transcription was in William Harris's eighteenth-century life and letters of Cromwell, and it is modernised in the style

---

[4] He was appointed governor of the Isle in July 1643 and surrendered the position under the Self-Denying Ordinance in April 1645.

THE LETTERS, WRITINGS, AND SPEECHES OF OLIVER CROMWELL

of the times. But it does retain the original address.[1] Carlyle relied on this in his edition, and he thoroughly modernised spelling and punctuation as was his wont. Sophia Lomas, in revising Carlyle for the 1904 edition, consulted the originals, found Harris/Carlyle to be accurate and made no changes, leaving the text modernised.[2] Finally there was a further transcription in a privately circulated edition of autograph letters collected by Morrison.[3] This appears to be a serious late-Victorian attempt to transcribe the original, although the lost letters noted by Harris have been silently expanded.[4] It is this 1895 version which is used as copy text here.

[A.L.S. to Colonel Norton. Dated Farnham, March 28th, 1648][5]

Deere Dick,[6] - It had beene a favor indeede to have mett you heere att Farnham,[7] but I heere you are a man of great businesse – therefore I say noe more. If itt bee a favor to the house of Commons to enjoy you what is itt to mee?[8] But in good earnest when will[9] you and your brother Russell[10] bee a little honest and attend your charge, surely some expect itt, especially the good fellowes who chose you.

---

[1] W. Harris, *An Historical and Critical Account of the Life of Oliver Cromwell, Lord Protector of the Commonwealth of England, Scotland and Ireland* (London 1762), p. 515.

[2] Carlyle-Lomas 1:297–300. The note on p. 298 does not make it certain that Lomas had seen the original, but her note to **1649 02 01** (Carlyle-Lomas 1:411 fn. 3) does make it clear.

[3] *Catalogue of the collection of Autograph Letters…compiled and annotated…by A.W. Thibadeau*, 2:357–8.

[4] A few other things look inauthentic: 'suerly' in the Harris transcription looks more like Cromwell than 'surely' in the Morrison version (reading 'er' as 're' is an easy misreading to make with Cromwell), and it would be uncharacteristic for Cromwell to put a comma in '40000'. 'Its sayd' (Harris) looks more plausible than 'it's sayd'. But overall, the punctuation and abbreviations in the Morrison transcript look right for Cromwell and note the 'r' inserted in square brackets in 'A[r]mie'.

[5] This is in the 1895 edition but is not found in the other versions. A.L.S. is a standard (modern) abbreviation for 'Autograph letter signed'. The Harris edition (fn. 1) has 'For my noble friend Col. *Richard Norton*, theise' which looks authentic.

[6] Note the familiarity of this opening (the letters to Richard Norton before and after this one both begin 'Dear Norton'). See items **1648 02 25** and **1648 04 03**. See **1648 02 25**, n. 3.

[7] Farnham, Hampshire. It is almost a mid-point between Norton's home at Southwick (36 miles from Farnham) and Cromwell's London home (42 miles) or Windsor (Army HQ, 27 miles)—we are not sure where Cromwell was on 27 March other than that he was in one or the other.

[8] A rough tease.

[9] In the following lines, the editor of this version appears to have silently provided letters missing from a torn original, as set out in Harris's earlier transcription: viz—'when wi…' -> 'when will'; 'a lit…' -> 'a little'; 'so…' -> some'; 'wh…chose' -> 'who chose'; 'I glad…' -> 'I gladly'.

[10] Almost certainly Francis Russell (*c*.1616–64), recruiter MP for Cambridgeshire (1645) and colonel in the New Model. He was Cromwell's predecessor as governor of the Isle of Ely. His daughter Elizabeth married Cromwell's younger surviving son Henry in 1653. See Mark Noble, *Memoirs of the protectorate-house of Cromwell: deduced from an early period, and continued down to the present time* (2 vols. 1784), 2:388–92.

28 MARCH 1648

I have met with Mr Maior,[11] wee spent two or 3 howers together last night. I perceave the gentleman is very wise and honest, and, indeed, much to bee vallewed; some thinges of common fame did a little sticke, I gladly heard his doubts, and gave such answare as was next att hand, I beleive to some satisfaction, never the lesse, I exceedingly liked the gentleman's plainnesse and free dealinge with mee. I knowe God has been above all ill reports, and will in his owne tyme vindicate mee. I have noe cause to cumplaine. I see nothinge but that this perticular businesse betweene him and mee may goe onn. The Lord's will bee done. For newes out of the North there is little. Only the mal: partye is pre-vailinge in the Parlnt of S.,[12] they are earnest for a warr, the ministers[13] oppose as yett. Mr. Marshall[14] is returned, whoe sayes soe, and soe doe many of our letters. Their great committee of dangers[15] have 2 malig:[16] for one right; it's sayd they have voted an A[r]mie of 40,000 in Parliament, soe some of yesterdays letters, but I account my newes ill bestowed because upon an idle[17] person.[18] I shall take speedy course in the businesse concerninge my tenants, for which thankes. My service to your lady.[19] I am really your affectionate servant.[20] [O.Cromwell][21]

[11] Richard Maijor Esq, of Hursley, Hampshire, and father of Cromwell's future daughter-in-law Dorothy. For Richard Major (1603/4–1660), landowner. See *ODNB*.

[12] = Scotland.

[13] The principal opposition to the Engagement came from the General Assembly of the Kirk of Scotland, hence almost certainly 'ministers' in the religious sense.

[14] Stephen Marshall was leading divine in the Westminster Assembly. For Stephen Marshall (1594/5?–1655), Church of England clergyman, see *ODNB*. He was part of a delegation sent to Edinburgh to seek to repair the alliance of the two Parliaments in February and March 1648.

[15] The committee of the Scottish Parliament set up to manage the invasion of England in consequence of the Engagement

[16] Malig.= malignant. In England, those royalists whose offences were too serious to allow them to enter into composition (i.e. payment of heavy fines for the recovery of their estates) were called malignants; those thought less culpable and allowed to compound were 'delinquents'. In a Scottish sense, it is presumably used to describe the Engagers, those willing to support the Engagement signed in December 1647 to fight to reinstate Charles to the government of his kingdoms.

[17] Could this be the origin for Cromwell's teasing name for Norton later in the year: 'idle Dick'?

[18] Another rough jibe at Norton's loitering in the country.

[19] He married, in 1636, Anne daughter of Sir Walter Erle of Charborough, Dorset—an MP who had been a key member of the 'middle group' around Pym, and who was now oscillating between support for and opposition to the Army, and therefore someone Cromwell would want to influence, however indirectly.

[20] Both other versions have 'your obedient servant' on a separate line.

[21] The Morrison transcript omits a signature. Harris has 'O. Cromwell' and Carlyle-Lomas have 'Oliver Cromwell'. Harris is surely to be preferred.

THE LETTERS, WRITINGS, AND SPEECHES OF OLIVER CROMWELL

1648 04 03a
Letter from Oliver Cromwell to Colonel Richard Norton

Date: 3 April 1648
Source: Christie's sale catalogue 16392 (New York, 2018) item 87 (contemporary copy or possible holograph)

This letter was twice transcribed from the original but was lost to public view between a sale in the early twentieth century and its reappearance at a sale in New York in 2018 (purchaser unknown). This is an edition based on the high-resolution photograph of the original in the Christie's sale catalogue checked against the transcription made by William Harris and published in 1762 and in a revised edition in 1772 (Harris is known to be a careful and accurate transcriber).[1] There was a further transcription by the ultra-careful Sophia Lomas when the letter was in the Morrison collection (1904) but that was, after her practice, modernised in its spelling and punctuation. The image in Christie's catalogue confirms that this is a holograph letter and contains a number of crossings-out and corrections, most but not all of which can now be identified.

This is the third in a flurry of letters to Cromwell's New Model fellow-officer, Richard Norton, that deal directly or indirectly with the proposed marriage of Cromwell's eldest surviving son Richard to Dorothy Maijor (see also **1648 02 25** and **1648 03 28**). After a lull, negotiations were reopened in early 1649 and the marriage was contracted on 1 May 1649.

—————

Deere Norton[2]

I could not in my last give you a perfect account of what passed betweene mee and Mr. M.[3] because wee were to have a conclusion of our speech that morninge after I wrote my letter to you, which wee had, and havinge had a full enterview of one anothers mindes, wee parted with this, that both would consider with our Relations, and ~~communicates~~ according to satisfactions given there, acquaint each other with our mindes.[4] I cannot tell how better to doe itt,

---

[1] William Harris, *An Historical and critical account of the life of Oliver Cromwell...drawn from the original writers and state papers* (2nd ed., 1772).

[2] Colonel Richard Norton was with Cromwell at the storming of Basing House and, from 1645, governor of Portsmouth and recruiter MP for Hampshire. He was close to Cromwell in the late 1640s and early 1650s. See also **1648 02 25**. Lomas also includes an endorsement not noted by Harris: 'For my noble Friend Colonel Richard Norton: these' but she adds within single inverted commas which normally indicates material added to the copy she has seen.

[3] Presumably Richard Maijor (see next paragraph of the letter and so corrected by Lomas).

[4] The subject being discussed was the marriage of Oliver's son Richard to Maijor's daughter Dorothy, which after disrupted negotiations finally took place on 1 May 1649 at Hursley (Hampshire). For a full account of the negotiations and outcome, see Peacey, 'The Upbringing of Richard Cromwell', pp. 241–64, particularly pp. 243–50 and Stephen Roberts, 'The Wealth of Oliver Cromwell', *Cromwelliana* (1994), pp. 37–40.

3 APRIL 1648A

to[5] receave or give satisfaction then by you, whoe (as I remember) in your last, sayd that if thinges did stick betweene us, you would use your endeavor towards a close. The thinges ~~stuck att~~ \insisted upon/ were theise (as I take itt) Mr.[6] Maior desired 400 li. per annum of inheritance [-][7] lyinge in Cambridgesheire, and Norfolke, to bee præsently setled \and to bee ~~bee~~/, for maintenance, wherin I desired to bee advised by my wife.[8]

I offered the land in Hampsheire \for present maintenane/, which I dare say with copses and ordinarie fells wilbe communi bus annis 500 li. per annum, ~~and~~ besides 500 li. per annum, in tennants handes houldinge but for one life, and about 300 li. per annum some for two lives, some for three lives. but as to this if the latter bee not liked off I shalbe [————————][9] \willing a farther conference bee had/ in the first. In point of jouncture I shall give satisfaction. And as[10] to the settlement of landes given mee by the Parl[iame]nt satisfaction \to bee given/ in like manner, accordinge as wee discoursed. In what else was demanded of mee I am willing (soe farr as I remember any demand was) to give satisfaction.

Only I havinge beene enformed by Mr. Robinson[11] that Mr. Maior did offer[12] upon a former match[13] Offer to settle the Mannor wherin Hee lived, and to give 2000 li. in monie, I did insist upon that, and doe desier itt may not bee with difficultye, the monie I shall neede for my two little wenches,[14] and therby I shall free my sonn from beinge charged with them. mr. maior parts with nothing in præsent but that monie, savinge their board, which I shoulde not bee unwillinge to give them to enjoy the comfort of their societye, which its reason Hee smarte for, if Hee will robb mee altogether of them. Truly the land to bee settled both \what/ the Parl[iame]nt gives mee, and my owne, is very little lesse then 3000 li. per annum all thinges considered, if I bee rightly enformed. And a Lawyer of

---

[5] The 'to' is written over a two-letter word: original letters no longer clear.

[6] Capital 'M' was written over illegible original letters.

[7] Three (?) letters now illegible are crossed out here.

[8] i.e. Elizabeth Cromwell [née Bourchier] (1598–1665), lady protectress of England, Scotland, and Ireland, consort of Oliver Cromwell. See *ODNB*.

[9] A long word (or short words) are crossed out here and illegible.

[10] 'As' is written over another word, almost certainly 'in'.

[11] Almost certainly Nathaniel Robinson, a godly Hampshire minister, for whom see Matthews, *Calamy Rev.*, p. 413.

[12] The word 'offer' is written over the original word, which was probably 'often'.

[13] From here the letter carries on down the left-hand margin at right angles to the main text, carrying on a few lines down in continuous text at the same angle onto the other side of the fold of the letter.

[14] Cromwell at this point had four daughters, two already married (in 1646), Elizabeth and Bridget, and the two not yet married and referred to here, Mary and Frances.

Lincolns Inn[15] havinge searched all the Marques of Worcester writinges,[16] which were[17] taken at Ragland[18] and sent ~~up~~ for by the Parl[iame]nt and this gentleman was appointed by the committee to search the sayd writinges, assures mee, there is noe scruple concerninge the title, And itt soe fell out that this gentleman whoe searched was my owne Lawyer, a very godly able man, and my deere freind, which I reckon noe smale mercy, Hee is also possest of the writings for mee.

I thought fitt to give you this account, desiringe you to make such use of itt as God shall direct you, and I doubt not but you will doe the part of a friend betweene two freindes, I account my selfe one, and I have heard \you say/ mr. Maior was[ ][19] entirely soe to you. What the good pleasure of God is I shall waite, there is only rest, præsent my service to your Lady,[20] to mr. Maior, &r. I rest

Your affectionate servant

O Cromwell

[21]Aprl. the 3ᵈ 1648.

I desier you to carrie this businesse with all privacie, I beseech you to doe soe, as you love mee, lett mee entreat you not to loose a day heerin, that I may knowe mr. Maiors minde, for I thinke I may be att leisure for a weeke to attende this businesse to give and take satisfaction, from which perhaps I may bee shutt up afterwards by imployment I know thou art an Idle fellowe, but prethee neglect mee not now. delay may bee very inconvenient to mee, I much rely upon you. Lett me here from you in two or 3 dayes. I confesse the principall consideration \as to mee/ is the absolute setlement of the mannor wherin Hee lives, which Hee would doe but conditionally in case Hee prove to have noe Sonn, and but 3000 li. in case Hee have a sonn. but as to this I hope farther reason may work him to more

---

[15] This lawyer is probably John Thurloe. For the identification see David Farr, 'Oliver Cromwell and a 1647 Case in Chancery', *Historical Research* 71 (1998), pp. 342–6 at 344–5.

[16] Parliament voted Cromwell lands worth at least £1,680 from the estates of the Catholic marquis of Worcester in 1646 (the grant had been intended to confer £2,500 a year on him [JHL, 8:134]). See also Lloyd Bowen, 'Oliver Cromwell (alias Williams) and Wales', in Patrick Little, ed., *Oliver Cromwell: New Perspectives* (2009), pp. 177–82.

[17] From here the text, still at right angles and to the left of the main text, continues onto the other half of the folded sheet.

[18] Raglan Castle, a late medieval castle, and seat of the earls and marquises of Worcester.

[19] Crossed out, but most likely 'one'.

[20] Anne Norton (b. 1617, d. in or before 1650?), daughter of Sir Walter Erle of Charborough, Dorset (or possibly his second wife Elizabeth [b. c.1612, d. in or after 1655]).

[21] Lomas adds 'London' immediately before the date.

3 APRIL 1648B

1648 04 03b

Warrant signed by members of the Committee for the Affairs of Ireland at Derby House: from Robert Rich, earl of Warwick; Arthur Annesley; William Pierrepont; Oliver Cromwell; Sir John Temple; Sir Gilbert Gerard to Sir Adam Loftus

Date: 3 April 1648
Source: TNA, SP 16/539 fol 161r (autograph)

This warrant demonstrates Cromwell's close involvement with Irish affairs more than a year before he himself accepted the command of the Army of conquest and settlement. He was one of ten members of the Derby House Committee present at a meeting of its sub-committee for Irish Affairs that sought to ensure that the three parliamentary commissioners who were setting out for Ireland were furbished with money for the cash-starved troops there. A separate order was issued by the same men awarding £100 to each of the commissioners to cover their own travel expenses. Cromwell's signature is not his usual one, but other records show that Cromwell was present at the Derby House Committee at that day.[1]

––––––––––

Whereas You have received the Summe of Five thousand pounds from Alderman Andrewes[2] & Mr Maurice Thompson[3] appointed to be the Trears for the Ordinance of 20000 li. per mensem for the reliefe of Ireland[4] These are therefore to will & require You to cause the said money to be transmitted to Bristoll[5] to be there in a readinesse to be transported into Mounster[6] with Col. Wm. Jephson[7] Major: Richard Salwey[8] & John Swinfen[9] Esqrs: who are appointed by both Houses of Parliamt: to goe Comrs: into that Province. The abovesaid money You are there to issue according to Such Warrants & directions as You

---

[1] *CSPD 1648–9*, p. 40.

[2] Sir Thomas Andrewes (d. 1659), financier and regicide. See *ODNB*.

[3] Maurice Thomson [Thompson] (1604–76), merchant. See *ODNB*.

[4] See 'An Ordinance of the Lords and Commons assembled in Parliament, for raising of Twenty Thousand Pounds a Month for the Relief of Ireland (16 Feb 1648)', printed in *JHL*, 10:48–62, which appointed Adam Loftus as treasurer. A further ordinance (*JHL*, 10:173) passed by the Houses on the day of this warrant, 3 April 1648, appointed Andrews and Thompson to be Treasurers of Receipt, working out of Andrews' home in Lyme Street.

[5] Bristol was the principal port for embarkation for those crossing from England to Ireland.

[6] i.e. Munster, the most southerly of the four provinces of Ireland.

[7] William Jephson (1609/10–58), politician and soldier. See *ODNB*.

[8] Richard Salwey (bap. 1615, d. 1686), politician. See *ODNB*.

[9] John Swynfen [Swinfen] (1613–94), politician. See *ODNB*.

505

THE LETTERS, WRITINGS, AND SPEECHES OF OLIVER CROMWELL

Shall from tyme to tyme receive from the said Comrs. or any two of them, hereof You are not to fayle &c for soe doeing this Shall be Your sufficient Warrant Dated at Derby House this 3ᵈ. of Aprill 1648

Warwick[10]
Arthur Annesley[11]   W Pierrepont[12]
O Cromwell   J Temple[13]   Gilbt Gerard[14]

To Sir Adam Loftus[15] Knt: Trear ar Warres for the Kingdome of Ireland.

Ord: of the Com: for th aff: of Ireland at Darby House dat 3°. Apr: <u>1648</u> to send to Bristoll to be readie to be transported for Munstr: with the Comrs: & to be issued there according to their warrt £5000

⟳⟲

1648 04 06

Letter from Oliver Cromwell to Colonel Robert Hammond

Date: 6 April 1648

Source: [A] BL, Add. MS 4186 ("LETTERS BETWEEN COL. ROBERT HAMMOND, Governor of the Isle of Wight, and the Committee…at Derby House, Gen. Fairfax, Lt. Gen. Cromwell, Commissary General Ireton, etc., relating to Charles I…As prepared for the press by Birch), fos 18r–v (later copy). [B] *Letters between Col. Robert Hammond, Governor of the Isle of Wight, and the Committee of Lords and Commons at Derby-House, General Fairfax, Lieut. General Cromwell, Commissary General Ireton, &c, relating to King Charles I. While he was confined in Carisbrooke-Castle in that Island. Now first published* (1764), pp. 40–2 (later print copy)

This letter survives in two related eighteenth-century versions, a rough transcription (the base for our version) and a polished published one. Birch tells us that the original was

---

[10] Robert Rich, second earl of Warwick (1587–1658), nobleman and politician. See *ODNB*.

[11] Arthur Annesley, first earl of Anglesey (1614–86), politician. See *ODNB*.

[12] William Pierrepont (1607/8–78), politician. See *ODNB*.

[13] Sir John Temple (1600–77), judge and historian. See *ODNB*.

[14] Sir Gilbert Gerard (1587–1670), MP and Treasurer at War 1642–5 and member of the Committee of Both Kingdoms 1644–8. He was a fierce Presbyterian and was secluded at Pride's Purge. He was a veteran administrator, having served as clerk of council, duchy of Lancaster 1609–40.

[15] Not identified. He is not however a son of Sir Adam Loftus, first Viscount Ely in the Irish peerage and Lord Chancellor of Ireland, who died in 1643. Viscount Ely had sixteen children but the only one named Adam died in 1618.

506

6 APRIL 1648

destroyed at a fire in the Chambers of 'The Hon. Mr Yorke' on 27 June 1752. His transcription is a copy of a transcription made before the fire by a physician-in-ordinary to the Queen, Dr Joseph Litherland. There are corrections on Birch's transcription which might have been from the original, or (less likely) on Litherland's transcription (why repeat those?) or marks of carelessness by Birch. We have included them with reminders of their doubtful status. Birch has endorsed his transcript: 'Letter from Oliver Cromwell to Coll Hammond in Cypher'. It is not clear which parts were in cypher. The ellipsis towards the end is presumably something in the original which Litherland could not make sense of. It may be single word or a long passage in code.

This letter shows once more how close Cromwell was to Hammond and how much he trusted him with secret intelligence about the King's attempts to escape from the Isle of Wight where Hammond was his guardian.

Dear Robin,

Your Business is done in the House.[1] Your 10 li. by the week is made 20 li.[2] 1000 li. given you; and order to Mr. Lysle[3] to draw up an Ordinance for 500 li. per annum to be Settled upon you & your Heirs. This was done with Smoothness. Your Friends were not wanting to You. I know thy Burden; This is an Addition to it. The Lord direct and sustain thee. Intelligence came to the Hands of a very considerable Person,[4] that the King attempted to get out of his Window,[5] and that he had a Chord of Silk with him, whereby to Slip down: but his Breast was so big, the Bar would not give him Passage. This was done in one of the dark nights about a fortnight ago. A Gentleman with you led him the Way, and slipped down. The Guard that night had some Quantity of Wine with them.

The same party assures, that there is Aqua Fortis[6] gone down from London to remove that Obstacle, which hindred and that the Same design is to be put in execution the next dark Nights. He saith, that Captain Titus[7] and some others

---

[1] On 3 April 1648, the House of Commons ordered the 'Grand Committee for taking the accompts of the whole kingdom be enjoined to sit constantly' to settle the accounts of Skippon, Hammond and other named officers. Later the same day, it was ordered that the £1,000 cash referred to by Cromwell plus the £500 per year (for his service as governor of the Isle of Wight) 'be settled upon him, and his Heirs for ever, out of Papists Estates in Arms, or Delinquents excepted from Pardon, not yet disposed of'. *JHC*, 5:523–5.

[2] [B] clarifies this by putting a semi-colon between '20li' and '1000li' and this must be the sense, surely.

[3] John Lisle, appointed Lord Lisle under the Protectorate (1609/10–64). See *ODNB*.

[4] Identified below, see n. 11.

[5] The faint comma is in a different ink and probably added by Birch to help to make sense.

[6] Nitric acid. An attempt was indeed made to use acid to remove the bar at the window on 28 May. Charles Carlton, *Charles I: The Personal Monarch* (1983), p. 324.

[7] Silius Titus (1622/3–1704), royalist conspirator and politician. See *ODNB*.

507

THE LETTERS, WRITINGS, AND SPEECHES OF OLIVER CROMWELL

about the King are not to be trusted. He is a very considerable ~~Member~~ \Person/[8] of the Parliament who gave this Intelligence, and desired it should be speeded to you. The Gentleman,[9] that came out ~~of~~ \at/[10] the Window, was Master Firebrace;[11] The Gentlemen doubted, are Creslet,[12] Burroughs,[13] and Titus: The time, when this attempt of Escape was...[14] the twentieth of March.

Your Servant

Oliver Cromwell

April 6. 1648.

For Col. Robt. Hammond.

<hr />

1648 04 14

Receipt signed by Oliver Cromwell for one month's pay

Date: 14 April 1648

Source: TNA, SP 16/539, Part 4, fo. 166 (piece 508.i.) (autograph)

A standard receipt but relating to the period after Cromwell had been out of the Army and was limbering up to take a leading role in the Second Civil War. It is accompanied by a certificate of his arrears signed by John Blackwell.[1]

[8] The emendation could be Cromwell's, Letherland's or Birch's. 'The considerable person' has not been identified.

[9] The commas in this and the two following lines after 'Gentleman', 'Window', 'Burroughs' and 'time' are all in a fainter ink and probably added later by Birch to help establish meaning. All appear in the printed version.

[10] The emendation could be Cromwell's, Letherland's or Birch's.

[11] Sir Henry Firebrace (1619/20–91), court official. See *ODNB*; and C. W. Firebrace, *Honest Harry, being the biography of Sir Henry Firebrace, knight (1619–91)* (1932). Firebrace's account is contained within *Memoirs of the two last years of the reign of that unparallell'd prince, of ever blessed memory, King Charles I: By Sir Tho. Herbert, Major Huntington, Col. Edw. Coke, and Mr. Hen. Firebrace. With the character of that blessed martyr, by…John Diodati, Mr. Alexander Henderson, and the author of The princely-pelican* (1702).

[12] The printed version has 'Cresset', but the manuscript appears clearly to be 'Creslet'. The person concerned has not been identified.

[13] Not identified.   [14] The ellipsis appears thus in both versions.

[1] TNA, SP16/539, Part 4, fo. 165r (no. 508).

508

18 APRIL 1648

Aprill xiiii[th]. 1648

Recd then of Sir John Wollaston Kt.[2] & the rest of the Treers att Warre By vertue of a warrant from the right Honoble. the Committee of Lords & Commons for the Armie, Bearinge date the xii°. \&c/ of Aprill instant in full of xxviii°. daies pay for my selfe As Lieutent. generall of the Armie under Coman of his Excy Thomas Lord Fairfax;[3] accordinge to the Establishment of the 3[d]. of November last. the some of Eightie foure pounds the saide pay to Commence the viii[th]. of Aprill instant 1648 I say lxxxiiii li.[4]

Oliver Cromwell

24[5]

Leiut: Generall Cromwell 28 daies pay Aprill. 14. 1648 - 84[6]

1648 04 18

Letter from Oliver Cromwell to Colonel William Kenricke

Date: 18 April 1648

Source: Harry Ransom Center, University of Texas at Austin, HRC 81 (holograph)

This holograph letter (preserved by the Kenrick family until sold in New York in the nineteenth century) is a letter of recommendation for an unnamed civilian, sent to the lieutenant of Dover Castle.

[verso]

For Col: Kenricke[1]

---

[2] Sir John Wollaston (1585/6–1658), mayor of London. See *ODNB*. Wollaston, a goldsmith who had been lord mayor of London in 1643–4 was a treasurer for a whole series of parliamentary revenue streams in the 1640s, including paying the Armies to win the Second Civil War.

[3] Sir Thomas Fairfax had become the third Lord Fairfax of Cameron on the death of his father, Ferdinando Fairfax, a month earlier—on 14 March 1648.

[4] This is bracketed to the side of the text.   [5] Significance of this number '24' is unclear.

[6] Significance of this number '84' is unclear.

---

[1] William Kenrick had been colonel of Aylesford Lathe's Kentish Regiment of Auxiliaries (the *Online Directory of Parliamentarian Army*). He was later to be nominated to serve for Kent in the Nominated Assembly (1653). There is some discussion of his contentious earlier career in Alan Everitt, *The Community of Kent and the Great Rebellion* (1966), pp. 150–1, 216, 234, 239n, 310. Everitt spells him Kenwricke.

THE LETTERS, WRITINGS, AND SPEECHES OF OLIVER CROMWELL

Leifnt. of Dover
Castle[2]   theise

[seal]
[endorsement]
from Left Generall
Crumwell 18ᵈ Aprill
1648

[recto]
Sir this is the Gentleman[3] I
mentioned to you. I am perswa
ded you may bee confident of
his fidelitye to you in the
thinges you will employ him
in~~n~~, I conceave hee is fitt for
any Civill imployment, as havinge beene bred towards the
lawe, and havinge besids very
good partes. Hee hath beene
a Capt. Leifnt. and therfore
I hope you putt such valew
upon him, in civill way, as
one that hath borne such a
place, shalbe thought by you
worthye off. wherby you will
much oblige your affectionate
servant

O Cromwell

Aprl. 18ᵗʰ.
1648

---

[2] Dover Castle, Kent.   [3] He has not been identified.

I expect to heere from you about
your defects in the Castle, that
soe you may bee tymely supplyed.

1648 05 09a
Letter from Oliver Cromwell to Thomas Fairfax, (now) Lord Fairfax

Date: 9 May 1648
Source: BL, Egerton MS 2620, fos 1r–2v (holograph)

This holograph letter (both the letter and the address are in Cromwell's hand) has the postscript written in the left hand margin.

    Cromwell was now marching down to deal with the revolt of disaffected former parliamentarians and royalists in South Wales, a campaign that would occupy him from early May until mid-July. He left Windsor on 3 May and on 9 May was somewhere between Gloucester and Monmouth, so presumably just entering Wales.

For his Excellency
the Lord Fairfax
Generall theise

Lt Generall Cromwell.
May 9 1648.[1]

My Lord
You heere in what a flame theise
westerne partes are, I cannott but
minde Your Excellency that the
enimie are designinge to surprise
many places, and wee shall still
play the aftergame. I thinke itt
of absolute necessitye that some

---

[1] This endorsement is in a seventeenth-century hand.

THE LETTERS, WRITINGS, AND SPEECHES OF OLIVER CROMWELL

men bee putt into Bristoll,[2] ~~Espeilly~~[3]
especially since Chepstow is taken,[4]
with which (as I heere) they hould
correspondency. Sir Bristoll must
have a fixed guarison of foote.[5]
I beseech you recommend itt to the
Parlnt. that it may be donn. ⌐—⌐[6]
their cannott be lesse then 600.
men for itt. Leit Col Rolphe
would bee a fitt man.[7] Hee is
able to give helpe in the businesse
by his Father[8] Skippon his interest[9]
and it would bee well taken if your
Lordp would recommend him, there is
necessitye of Speede in my opinion,
the cittye desier itt. I take leave
and rest
Your Ex. most humble
servant
O Cromwell

[2] Bristol had changed hands three times during the First Civil War—1642, 1643, 1645. As the second city of the kingdom and a major port, it was clearly essential that it remained in Parliament's hands. See Gaunt, *Gazetteer*, pp. 2–4.

[3] Cromwell wavered over this word, writing it, crossing it out, and then rewriting it. Why?

[4] Taken, that is, by the royalists. Chepstow, with its medieval castle, had been a royalist stronghold throughout the First Civil War until overrun in October 1645. In the spring of 1648 it was seized for the King by Sir Nicholas Kemeys and garrisoned with 120 men. Cromwell retook the town on 11 May as he moved down to Glamorgan and Pembroke and he left Colonel Ewer to storm the castle, which he did, after a heavy bombardment. The castle was then slighted.

[5] Cromwell clearly could not spare these men from his own Army expeditionary force. Fairfax is being asked to get authority to send and supply a regiment of foot to garrison Bristol.

[6] Three letters obliterated here, but they may be 'bec', presumably 'because'.

[7] The existing establishment was 250. The governor of Bristol from September 1645 to October 1649 was Major General Philip Skippon but he was always represented by deputies. William Rolfe was the logical person to choose—he was the lieutenant colonel of Skippon's own regiment (and his son-in-law). But the Presbyterian Colonel Edward Doyley had attempted to replace him by force in July 1647, so there is a bit of a back-story here. In fact, Rolph (who was in the Isle of Wight at the time and shortly after this was accused of planning to assassinate the King) was not transferred to Bristol. See Firth and Davies, *Regimental History*, 2:431; *Clarke Papers*, 1:162, *Fairfax Correspondence*, 3:370; Wanklyn, *Reconstructing*, 1:157.

[8] i.e. father-in-law.   [9] Philip Skippon: his interest is as governor of Bristol.

9 MAY 1648B

may. 9th.
1648.

my Lord Lnt. Col. Blackmore[10] is with
mee, Hee is a godly man and a good
souldier I beg a commission to make
him \an/ Adjutant Genl to the Army.
Hee is very able as most ever
were in this Army.

1648 05 09b
Instructions from Oliver Cromwell to Captain Thomas Roberts and others

Date: 9 May 1648
Source: TNA, SP18/100, fos 273r–4v (no. 117.i) (holograph)

These are two holograph sets of instructions or orders from Cromwell on his march through Gloucestershire in May 1648. They were bundled up with a petition submitted by Captain Thomas Roberts to Cromwell when he was Lord Protector (it is in the papers of the Protectoral Council of State and endorsed as 'Received 7 June 1655; read and ordered 13 September 1655'). Roberts makes clear that he had raised a troop of horse and served with Lord Brooke and at the siege of Gloucester in 1643, remaining in arms until December 1646. He answered Cromwell's call for volunteers in May 1648 but did not get the commission that Cromwell asked Fairfax to grant him, 'which being not obtained, your Highnes was pleased to Say if ever the Lord did give your Highnes oppertunity yow would remember your peticonr: & give him further Commaund'. He now returns two signed letters of Cromwell's from 1648 asking Cromwell to honour that pledge and to secure £3,000

---

[10] For John Blackmore's military career pre-1648, see the *Online Directory of Parliamentarian Army Officers*, and for his later career see Wanklyn, *Reconstructing*, 1:45n and 107. Fairfax did not respond to this request. But this is the very moment at which Robert Huntington resigned his commission as major in Cromwell's regiment (and subsequently wrote his excoriating 'Sundry Reasons inducing Major Robert Huntington to Lay Down His Commission'—to be found in [Francis Maseres], *Select Tracts Relating to the Civil Wars in England*, 2 vols. (1815), 1:395–407). On 14 June John Blackmore was appointed major of Cromwell's regiment in his place. He was a still a major in the middle of 1649 (*Clarke Papers*, 2:270–1), but a colonel by 1652. Cromwell's description of him as lieutenant colonel on 9 May relates to his time with that rank in Colonel John Humphrey's regiment in Gloucester before it was disbanded in early 1648 (Wanklyn, *Reconstructing*, 1:45 n.14).

513

THE LETTERS, WRITINGS, AND SPEECHES OF OLIVER CROMWELL

'upwards' in arrears for all his service. It appears that Cromwell ensured that Roberts got his money.[1]

———

Mr Roberts beinge enformed that
diverse Papists and delinquents
doe gather themselves together
upon prætences of Huntinge mee-
tinges, givinge out dangerous Spee
ches, ridinge up and downe
armed to {the}[2] hazard of the
peace of this Kingdom, I doe
desier y{ } \d/ to Authorize you
to gather to you such of your
freindes, and persons well affected
to the Parlnts. cause, and attach
them, causinge them to bee
brought to Glocester, that theie
they may[3] bee secured, untill the pleasure
of the Parlnt. bee farther knowen, ~~And s[ ]~~[4]
I rest,

O Cromwell
May. 9. 1648

[fo. 274r]
I desier you from tyme to tyme

---

[1] He was an ensign in Lord Brooke's regiment of foot in the earl of Essex's army in 1642. In his September 1655 petition he stated that he had served faithfully from the first going out of Lord Brooke and at the siege of Gloucester. He had raised a troop at his own charge, serving until December 1646, and also commanded a troop at the battle of Worcester (3 September 1651). In May 1648 Cromwell authorised him to arrest local papists and delinquents and bring them to Gloucester. The Council of State allowed him repayment of such money as he could prove to be owed, out of his discoveries of concealments which were to be prosecuted by the treasury commissioners: the *Online Directory of Parliamentarian Army Officers*. There is no Thomas Roberts in Firth and Davies, *Regimental History* or in Wanklyn, *Reconstructing*.

[2] There is a hole in the paper here; 'to' is pretty certain (though part of the 'o' is lost); 'the' (which is largely lost) is guesswork.

[3] 'from hereon' is added in left margin.   [4] Illegible beneath erasure.

16 MAY 1648

to give \such/ assistance to Captaine
Thomas Roberts, in Suppressing
insurrections and Tumults, and
apprehendinge Susspected persons
as Hee shall desier from you.
Given under ny hand this
ninth day of May: 1648.

Oliver Cromwell

To all officers {of}[5]
horse and foote
under the Generall
the Lord Fairfax

1648 05 16

Letter from Oliver Cromwell to Captain [John] Crowther, vice admiral of the Irish Seas

Date: 16 May 1648
Source: W. Beamont, ed., *A Discourse of the War in Lancashire*, Chetham Society, 1st. ser., vol. 62 (1864), p. 98 (later copy)

This letter, addressed to a Captain Crowther,[1] gives us our best evidence of how Cromwell kept himself supplied on his march into Wales. What survives is a nineteenth-century transcript of an original which was (in 1864) in Wincham, Cheshire, presumably in the hands of the Townshend family, who had (through marriage) acquired Wincham Hall, once the home of Robert Venables,[2] who served in the New Model from 1648 to 1660, and who was a senior commander in Ireland in the early 1650s and then in the West Indies.

Sir I received both yours this morning and cannot but acknowledge your greate forwardness to serve the publique. I have here inclosed sent you an order for the takeing up of vessells for the transporting of soldiers and the coates of the horses.

---

[5] There is a hole in the MS here, but the top of an 'f' visible.

[1] For some notes on Captain Crowther, see Elaine Murphy, *Ireland and the War at Sea 1641–1653* (Woodbridge, 2012), pp. 46, 58, 157–62, 190.
[2] Robert Venables (1612/13–87), parliamentarian army officer. See *ODNB*.

My men shal be at the water side tomorrow. If they can provide victualls they shall. If not I shall give you notice that wee may bring it out of your vessels.
Sir
I remayne Your very humble servant
OLIVER CROMWELL.

Cardif
May the 16th
1648.

1648 06 09

Letter from Oliver Cromwell to the Committee of Carmarthenshire

Date: 9 June 1648
Source: Harry Ransom Center, University of Texas at Austin, Medieval and Early Modern Manuscripts Collection, CHP Cat 118, openings 125–6 (holograph)

Cromwell's plea for the casting of artillery shells to assist him at the siege of Pembroke shows lots of evidence of haste and agitation in the writing (as we have indicated in the notes). There were then, or certainly were soon afterwards, iron furnaces close to Llanelli in Carmathenshire but there may have been others. This holograph letter survives in a damaged state, and it has been necessary to confirm our reading against that of Sophia Lomas, who inspected it when it was in the Morrison collection in the 1890s.

For my noble freindes the
Committee of Carmarthen
theise.[1]

137 li: 0 0 in 2 bagges[2]

A Letter of Oliver
Cromwells from
the Leaguer[3] before

---

[1] This address, on the verso, is in Cromwell's hand and there are also fragments of his seal.
[2] This appears to be a contemporary note, but it is not possible to say whether or not it is in Cromwell's hand.
[3] Leaguer = Siege. Cromwell began his siege on 24 May. The town surrendered on 10 July.

9 JUNE 1648

Pembrock June 1648[4]
Gentlemen

I have sent this bearer [————][5] to you
to desier Wee[6] may have your Furtherance
and assistance in procuringe some necessaries to bee cast in the iron furnases in
Your countye of Carmarthen, which will the
better enable us to reduce the Towne and
Castle of Pembrooke.

The principall thinges are shells for our
{mor}terpeice[7] the depth of them [8] ~~Fourteen~~ \we desier may be of
   fourteene/ [——————————————][9]\Inces and three quarters of an Inch, /{t}hat[10]
which
I desier att your handes is to cause
the service to be performed \and/ all[11] that
with all possible expedition. that soe
(if itt bee the will of God) \the service beinge donn/ theise poore
wasted cuntries may bee freed from the
burthen of the Armye.

~~If there~~ In the next place wee desier
some \Demmie/ Canon shott,[12] ~~an~~ \and/ some Culveringe \shott/[13]
may with all possible Speede bee cast for
us and[14] hasted too us alsoe.[15]

---

  [4] This endorsement is in a different (the recipient's?) hand.
  [5] This is illegible, not only to us, but to previous editors. The name seems to consist of about twelve letters with a 'K' or 'k' in the middle.
  [6] The first letter was originally an 'H' but then 'W' is written over it.
  [7] There is a hole in the page which surely covers the first three letters of 'mortarpiece'.
  [8] There is a hole in the page. The top of the missing character(s) looks like 'm' but could be 'ir'.
  [9] Several words (c.30 characters) are so heavily crossed out as to be completely illegible.
  [10] There is a hole where the 'h' at the end of 'inch' and the 't' at the beginning of '{t}hat' are. But the top of the 'h' is still visible and the 't' is easily inferred.
  [11] The 'and' is written over 'all' and 'other' seems to have been changed to 'all', but that it is meant to be crossed out. The passage reads best without either 'other' or 'all'.
  [12] The demi-cannon typically had a barrel 11ft (3.4m) long, with a calibre of 6 inches and a shot of 32lb.
  [13] The culverin was a smaller field gun with a 5.5-inch calibre that fired shot of 17.5lb.
  [14] The 'a' in 'and' is clearly written over an 'h'.
  [15] For the manufacture of ordnance during the civil wars, see Peter Edwards, *Dealing in Death: The Arms Trade and the British Civil War 1638–52* (Stroud, 2000), esp. ch. 6.

Wee give you thankes f{or} your care
in helpeinge us with bread and tooles[16]
&c. You doe herein a very Speciall
service to the state, and I doe most
earnestly desier you to continew heerin
accordinge to our desiers in the late
letters, I desier \that copies of/ this paper may bee published thorough out your countye, and the
effects therof observed for the ease of the countye, and to avoyd
~~plun~~ the wronginge of the cuntrie men, Not doubtinge the continewance
of your care to give ~~yo~~ assistance to the publicke in the services wee have
in hand I rest

Your affectionate servant
O Cromwell

The Leaguer before Pembrooke June the 9th. 1648.

1648 06 14

Letter from Oliver Cromwell to [? William Lenthall as Speaker or to some other member of the Long Parliament]

Date: 14 June 1648 (or 16 June 1648)
Source: Samuel Pecke, ed., *A Perfect Diurnall of Some Passages in Parliament* no. 258 [*recte* 256] for 19–26 June 1648, p. 2060 (*sub* 20 June) (N&S, 504.256; Thomason / E.522[44]) (contemporary print copy)

The date on which Cromwell wrote this letter is uncertain. *A Perfect Diurnal* gives it as 16 June, as does *The Perfect Weekly Account*,[1] which offers a precis of the letter (however it probably got its text from *A Perfect Diurnal*). The *Commons Journal* records that 'A Letter from Lieutenant General Cromwell, from Pembroke Leaguer, of the Fourteenth of June 1648, was this Day read'.[2] This is surely more reliable especially as there are many careless

---

[16] Lomas read this as 'water' rather than 'tooles'. That is possible, but much less likely. It looks more like 'too' than 'wa', and the last letter does not really look like an 'r'.

[1] *The Perfect Weekly Account*, no. 15 for 21–28 June, p. 114 (N&S, 533.15; Thomason / E.450[3]).
[2] *JHC*, 5:606–8.

14 JUNE 1648

misprints and uncorrected errors in that copy of *A Perfect Diurnal* (including the issue number and preceding page numbers). Lomas heads her edition of the letter (within inverted commas, which indicates an addition) 'to the Honorable William Lenthall, Esquire, Speaker of the House of Commons'[3] but does not give any indication why she has done so; Abbott has '[To a member of the Committee of Derby House]',[4] again without evidence. The former seems far more likely, but both lack authority.

Letters were this day read in the House from the Leagure before Pembrook, one from Leiut. Gen. Cromwell and of his owne writing, the letters import as followeth.

SIR, All that you can expect from hence is a Relation of the state of this Garrison of *Pembrook* which is briefly thus, they begin to be in extreame want of provision, so as in probability they cannot live a fortnight without being starved, but wee heare that they Mutined about three daies since, crying out shall we be ruined for 2 or 3 mens pleasure, better it were we should throw them over the Walls, it's certainly reported to us that within foure or six dayes they'le either cut his Throat, to wit, *Poyer*,[5] and come all away to us, *Poyer* told them Saterday last, that if reliefe did not come by mun day night, they should no more beleeve him, nay they should hang him, we have not got our Guns, and Ammunition from Wallingford[6] as yet, but how ever, we have scraped up a few which stand us in very good steed, last night wee got two little Guns planted, which in 24 howres will take away their Mills, ther's Poyer himselfe confesses they are all undone, we made an attempt to storme it about 10 dayes since, but our Ladders were two short, and the breach so as men could not get over, we lost a few men, but I am confident the enemy lost more, Capt. Flower[7] of col. Deans[8] Regiment was wounded, and Major Grigs[9]

---

[3] Carlyle-Lomas, 1:313.   [4] Abbott, *Writings and Speeches*, 1:613.

[5] John Poyer, governor of Pembroke, who had been a parliamentarian officer since 1642 but who had many grievances about the way he had been treated and about the course of events. John Poyer (d. 1649), merchant and army officer. See *ODNB*.

[6] Wallingord, Berkshire.

[7] Captain Henry Flower, see Firth and Davies, *Regimental History*, 2:672, 675 and Wanklyn, *Reconstructing*, 1:68 fn. 223 and *passim*.

[8] Colonel Richard Deane, see Firth and Davies, *Regimental History*, esp. 1:422 and Wanklyn, *Reconstructing* 1:87–9, 100–1. Deane, previously Comptroller of the Ordnance, was given command of Thomas Rainborowe's regiment on 29 September 1647.

[9] This is Major George Gregson of Colonel Thomas Pride's regiment. In the attempt to storm the castle, he was reported to have 'by a stone received a dangerous wound to the head', Firth and Davies, *Regimental History*, 1:365. He left the Army in September 1648 (Wanklyn, *Reconstructing*, 1:102 fn. 530).

Leiutenant and Ensigne slaine, capt. Burges[10] lyes wounded and very sick: I question not but within a fortnight we shall have the Towne. *Poyer* hath ingaged himselfe to the Officers of the Towne not to keep the Castle longer then the Towne can hould out, neither indeed can it, for we can take away his water in two dayes, by beating downe a staire Case which goes into a Cellar where he hath a Wel, they allow men halfe a pound of Beef, and as much Bread a day, but it is almost spent, we much rejoyce at what the Lord hath done for you in Kent: upon our Thanksgiving for that Victory [which was both Sea and Laguer] *Poyer* told his men that it was the Prince[11] was comming with reliefe. The other night they mutined in the Towne, last night we fired divers Houses which runs up the Towne still it much frights them, confident I am we shall have it in 14 dayes by starving, I am, Sir,

Your Servant

Leagure before Pembrook June 16 1648

1648 06 17

Letter from Oliver Cromwell to Major Thomas Saunders

Date: 17 June 1648
Source: W. Harris, *An Historical and Critical Account of the Life of Oliver Cromwell, Lord Protector of the Commonwealth of England, Scotland and Ireland* (1762), pp. 507–9 (later copy)

Cromwell's attempt to round up parliamentarian renegades in South Wales was addressed to Major Thomas Saunders, a Derbyshire man who had had a long feud with his commander, Sir John Gell, and was serving in Colonel Francis Thornhaugh's Nottinghamshire

---

[10] Benjamin Burgess, a captain in Thomas Horton's regiment of horse (promoted to that position not as the siege began, *pace A&O*, 1:84–5 but no later than 1 March 1647, Wanklyn, *Reconstructing* 1:82 fn. 318).

[11] i.e. Charles, at this time Prince of Wales. He was in the Hague preparing an invasion force to join with the Scots and other royalist insurrectionary movements. At this point, he was actually planning an invasion of East Anglia, but he may well have been giving false hope to Poyer— see *Colonell Powell and Col. Poyers letter to His Highnesse the Prince of VVales, vvith their declaration, for restoring His Maiesty, the Protestant religion, the lawes of the land, and the liberty of the subject.* April 1648 (Wing / P3045; Thomason / E.436[14]). After the fall of Pembroke, as Poyer faced trial and execution, Prince Charles requested Fairfax to intervene to the end that 'such moderation may be used towards them as becomes souldgers to one another'. But the lord general replied that he was powerless to act since they had 'betrayed the trust...reposed in them to the ingaging the Kingdom againe in War & Blood' (Rushworth, *Historical Collections*, 7:1233).

17 JUNE 1648

regiment in the Second Civil War. After Thornhaugh's death, he was to be promoted colonel over the head of John Hutchinson, a source of much controversy.[1]

The letter survives only in an eighteenth-century transcript in a series which modernises spelling and punctuation but which, where we do have originals, is fairly accurate.

Copy of a letter from O. Cromwell *to (then) major* Saunders *of* Derbyshire, *dated June 17, 1648; superscribed 'For your selfe;' and endorsed in major* Saunders's *hand writing as followeth, 'The* L. *generalls order for takeing 'Sir* Trevor Williams, *and Mr.* Morgan, *sheriffe of* Monmouthshire.'

SIR,

I Send you this enclosed by it selfe, because it's of greater moment. The other you may communicate to Mr. *Rumsey* as far as you thinke fitt, and I have written. I would not have him or other honest men bee discouraged that I thinke itt not fitt at present to enter into contests, itt will be good to yeeild a little for publicke advantage, and truly that is my end, wherein I desire you to satisfie them. I have sent as my letter mentions, to have you remove out of *Brecknokshire*,[2] indeed into that part of *Glamorgansheire* which lyeth next *Munmouthsheire*, for this end. Wee have plaine discoveries that Sir *Trevor Williams* of *Langevie* about two miles from *Uske* in the countye of *Munmouth*[3] was very deepe in the plott of betrayinge *Chepstowe* castle,[4] soe that wee are out of doubt of his guiltynesse thereof. I doe hereby authorize you to seize him, as also the high sheriffe of *Munmouth* Mr. *Morgan*,[5] whoe was in the same plott. But because Sir *Trevor Williams* is the more dangerous man by farr, I would have you to seize him first, and the other will easilye bee had. To the end you may not be frustrated, and that you bee not deceaved, I thinke fitt to give you some caracters of the man, and some intimations how things stand. Hee is a man (as I am informed) full of craft and subtiltye, very bould and resolute, hath a house at *Langevie* well stored with armes, and very stronge, his neighbours about him very malignant and much for him, whoe are apt to

---

[1] R. Slack, 'Colonel Gell and Major Sanders: Internal Feuding among the Parliamentary Forces in Derbyshire during the Civil War of 1642–1646', *Derbyshire Miscellany*, 16:2 (2001), pp. 34–48; Firth and Davies, *Regimental History*, 1:280–5, 288–9, 229–30. There is a very full and characteristically helpful entry on him in the *Online Directory of Parliamentarian Army Officers*.

[2] i.e. Breconshire.

[3] Sir Trevor Williams had a complicated career both supporting and opposing Parliament and he was involved in several 'Peaceable Armies'. He was a great survivor. His home is normally spelt Llangibby, Monmouthshire: Sir Trevor Williams, baronet (c.1623–92), politician. See *ODNB*. Also *DWB*; *HoP Commons, 1660–1690*.

[4] Chepstow Castle, Monmouthshire, ancient home of the marquis of Worcester until its capture by Parliament in 1646. After its capture it had been sleighted and looted and was of little military significance by 1648.

[5] Possibly Anthony or Edward Morgan of Casebuchan or Marshfield, Monmouthshire, for whom see Newman, *Royalist Officers*, nos. 1002, 1003.

521

rescue him if apprehended, much more to discover any thinge which may prevent itt. Hee is full of jealosie, partly out of guilt, but much more because hee doubts some that were in the businesse have discovered him, which indeed they have, and alsoe because hee knows that his servant is brought hither, and a minister to bee examined here, whoe are able to discover the whole plott. Iff you should march directly into that countye and neere him, itts ods hee either fortefyes his house, or gives you the slip, soe alsoe if you should goe to his house and not finde him there, or if you attempt to take him and misse to effect itt, or if you make any knowen enquirye after him, itt will be discovered. Wherefore to the first you have a faire pretence of goeinge out of *Brecknocksheire* to quarter about *Newport* and *Carleon*, which is not above 4 or 5 miles from his house. You may send to col. *Herbert*,[6] whose house lyeth in *Munmouthsheire*, whoe will certenly acquaint you where hee is. You are alsoe to send to capt. *Nicolas*,[7] whoe is at *Chepstowe*, to require him to assist you if hee should gett into his house, and stand upon his guard. *Sam. Jones*, whoe is quartermr to col. *Herbert's* troupe, wil be very assistinge to you if you send to him to meete you att your quarters; both by lettinge you know where hee is, and alsoe in all matters of intelligence. If theire shal be neede capt. *Burge*[8] his troupe now quarteringe in *Glamorgansheire* shal be directed to receave orders from you. You perceave by all this, that wee are (it may bee) a little too much sollicitous in this businesse, it's our fault, and indeed such a temper causeth us often to overact businesse, wherefore without more adoe wee leave itt to you, and you to the guidance of God herein, and rest

Yours

O. CROMWELL

June 17, 1648.

If you seize him bring & lett him bee brought with a stronge guard to mee. If capt. *Nicolas* should light on him at *Chepstowe*, doe you strengthen him with a good guard to bring him.

If you seize his person, disarme his house, but lett not his armes bee imbeziled. If you need capt. *Burge* his troupe, it quarters betweene *Newport*[9] and *Cardiffe*.

[6] Possibly the royalist Colonel Richard Herbert, for whom see **1648 06 18**.
[7] Abbott identifies him (without offering any evidence) as 'Captain John Nicholas, presently made Governor of Chepstow, rose to high rank in the Protectorate', Abbott, *Writings and Speeches*, 1:615.
[8] Captain Benjamin Burgess, for whom see *A&O*, 1:85–6, Wanklyn, *Reconstructing*, 1:82 fn. 318.
[9] Newport, Monmouthshire.

1648 06 18

Letter from Oliver Cromwell to [the Hon. Richard Herbert]

Date: 18 June 1648
Source: Copy in the *Monmouthshire Merlin* for September 1845 (later copy)

This letter was recovered by Sophia Lomas and included as an appendix to her edition of Carlyle.[1] It was copied 'in a very ignorant fashion', she says, by a Newport (Monmouthshire) attorney called William Townshend who misidentified the recipient. The original (now lost) was 'picked up in converting the old Manor House [of St Jillians] into a farm-house'. The letter relates very closely to **1648 06 16**. Lomas says 'address gone, and not conjectural to with any certainty'. We are more content to own the attribution. Richard Herbert, son of Lord Herbert of Cherbury,[2] lived at some point at St Jillians or St Julians.[3] Shortly after this letter (5 or 20 August),[4] his father died and Richard inherited as second Lord Herbert of Cherbury.[5]

Leaguer before Pembroke, 18th June 1648

Sir

I would have you to be informed that I have good report if your secret practices against the public advantage; by means whereof the archtraitor, Sir Nicholas Kemys,[6] with his horse, did surprise the Castle of Chepstow: but we have notable discovery from the papers taken by Colonel Hewer[7] on recovering the Castle, that Sir Trevor Williams of Llangibby was the malignant who set on foot the plot Now I give you this warning by Capt. Nicholas[8] and Capt. Burgess,[9]

---

[1] Carlyle-Lomas, 3:253–4.

[2] Richard Herbert appears within his father's entry in *ODNB*: Edward Herbert, first Baron Herbert of Cherbury and first Baron Herbert of Castle Island (1582?–1648).

[3] For the relationship between the Herberts and St Julians, see Eija Kennerley, 'The Herberts of St Julians', *Gwent Local History* no. 35 (Spring 1973).

[4] The burial register (and a reference in the State Papers) says 5 August, his monument in St-Giles-in-the-fields, London, says 20 August. See the Herbert family entry in *ODNB*.

[5] Herbert had been a royalist colonel and governor of Aberystwyth in the First Civil War and he had just compounded for his estates at one-third their value (*Cal.Comm.Comp. Delinquents*, III:1682); Newman, *Royalist Officers*, no. 719.

[6] Sir Nicholas Kemys of Cefn Mably, Glamorganshire. He died during the Parliamentarian recapture of Chepstow. Newman, *Royalist Officers*, no. 823.

[7] Isaac Ewer (d. 1650/1), army officer and regicide. See *ODNB*.

[8] Abbott identifies him (without offering any evidence) as 'Captain John Nicholas, presently made Governor of Chepstow, rose to high rank in the Protectorate', Abbott, *Writings and Speeches*, 1:615.

[9] Captain Benjamin Burgess, Firth and Rait, *Acts and Ordinances*, and Wanklyn, *Reconstructing*, 1:82 fn. 318.

that if you harbour or conceal either of the parties, or abet Their mis-doings, I will cause your treasonable nest to be burnt about your ears.

OLIVER CROMWELL

1648 06 26
Letter from Oliver Cromwell to Colonel Thomas Hughes

Date: 26 June 1648
Source: NLW, Clenennau letters and papers 631 (contemporary or near-contemporary copy)

Two versions of this letter survive, one an apparently near-contemporary copy not in the hand of Cromwell or his usual clerk, the other claiming to be a late eighteenth-century copy of an original in Moyne's Court, Monmouthshire.[1] They differ in spelling and punctuation and in a couple of small points noted. The letter is notable for the rather harassed, stressed tone suggesting Cromwell is under pressure to end the revolt as soon as possible.

Coll Hughes[2]
Itt is of absolute necessity that Collington[3] & Ashe[4] doe attend the Councell of warre, to make good what they say of Edwardes[5] Lett itt therefore bee your speciall care[6] to gett them into Mounmouthshire. in order thereunto; What Mr Herbert[7]

---

[1] *The Topographer... containing a variety of orginal articles, illustrative of the local history and antiquities of England*, 4 vols. (1789–91), 4:127. Moyne's Court is just two miles from Chepstow.
[2] Thomas Hughes of Cillwch and Matherne, Monmouthshire was a Welsh politician who sat in the House of Commons in 1654 and 1659 and was governor of Chepstow in 1647-8. His brother Charles had been a major in the royalist army of the earl of Carbery in the First Civil War (Newman, *Royalist Officers*, no. 781). He was an active supporter of the Commonwealth. He was on the Parliamentary Committee for Monmouthshire in 1646. See *HoP Commons, 1640–1660*.
[3] Not identified but possibly Captain William Collinson who no later than June 1649 was serving in a regiment (Overton's) that had previously served in the Pembroke campaign in 1648 (Wanklyn, *Reconstructing*, 1:102).
[4] Not identified.   [5] Not identified.
[6] The other version runs 'Lett itt be your especiall care'.
[7] There are three Herberts on the Monmouthshire militia committee at this time (Firth and Rait, *Acts and Ordinances*, I:1136–7): Col. Thomas, Col. William and John). It is not possible to say which of them, if any, this refers to.

& Mr Craddocke[8] hath promised to them in point of indempnity; I will endeavour to have itt performed for them; And I desire yow to certify so much to them for their incouragement; I pray doe this speedily after receyt hereof; And I shall remaine
Your servant
O: Cromwell

June the xxvi[th] 1648.
O Cromwells letter to Col Hughes Governour of Chepstow Castle

1648 06 27
Letter from Oliver Cromwell to the Derby House Committee.

Date: 27 June 1648
Source: James Caulfield, ed., *Cromwelliana. A chronological detail of events in which Oliver Cromwell was engaged; from the year 1642 to his death in 1658* (1810), p. 41 (later copy)

This claims to be a copy of a letter published in early July in *The moderate intelligencer*, but cannot be found there (although this is a precis of what might be this letter). Other letters from this period can all be traced back to the source given and, apart from modernisation, are reliable transcripts.

At this key moment of the siege, Cromwell raises the chimera of an invasion by the more than notionally Protestant Murrough O'Brien, Lord Inchiquin who had been Parliament's Lord President of Munster since 1644, whose troops had massacred the Catholic garrison at the rock of Cashel in the summer of 1647 and who had won a major victory over the Confederates at Knocknanuss on 13 November. But he had felt increasingly marginalised by the parliamentary leadership in London, and was out of sympathy with religious developments and so in May 1648, just in time for news of it to have reached Cromwell, he had changed sides and had made his peace both with the Old English of Munster and with the King himself.[1] It is this which probably explains Cromwell's comments towards the end of his letter.

---

[8] Presumably Walter Cradock, who was certainly at the siege of Chepstow as a chaplain: Walter Cradok (c.1606–59). See ODNB. He was from Trefela, near Usk. The version of this letter in *The Topographer* has 'Mrs' Cradock.

[1] Murrough O'Brien, first earl of Inchiquin (c.1614–74), nobleman and army officer. See ODNB.

THE LETTERS, WRITINGS, AND SPEECHES OF OLIVER CROMWELL

That they within the Town and Castle cannot hold out above 10 days at farthest; that *Poyer*[2] sent out a message to the Lieut.-Gen. admiring that a *David* should be so persecuted by a *Saul*,[3] having been always faithful to the Parliament of *England*, ever since the beginning of these wars; but the honour of Parliament, and their General lying so deep at stake, the Lieut.-Gen. would not admit of any response, or capitulation, though the Governor inclined thereunto. An insurrection was made near the siege, 500 countrymen, horse and foot, joined under the pretence of stopping some passes, that the Lo: *Inchequin* (whom they gave out were near the shore) might not land. A party of the Leaguer horse was commanded out, to the number of 250, who fell upon this pretended well meaning, though royal, party (as seemed afterwards by their commanders) gave no quarter to them, killed 10, wounded many, the rest fled upon the mountains by the sea side; *Pembrook* much discontented hereat.

1648 06 28

Letter from Oliver Cromwell to Thomas Fairfax, Lord Fairfax

Date: 28 June 1648
Source: BL, Sloane MS 1519, fos 180r–181v (autograph)

This letter survives in the original, in the hand of Cromwell's usual clerk and with Cromwell's signature. All interlineations are also in the clerk's hand, presumably taken down as dictated. The postscript is added and has had to be squeezed between the address and date at top of page and signing off at bottom.

Apart from helping us to understand Cromwell's military problems during the siege, the letter contains a passionate appeal to a passage in Isaiah (which immediately precedes one of the most powerful messianic prophecies of the Old Testament—'For unto us a child is born, and unto us a Son is given: and the government is upon his shoulder, and he shall call his name Wonderful, Counselor, The mighty God, The everlasting Father, The

---

[2] John Poyer, a renegade parliamentarian, he was governor of Pembroke Castle and was later (in 1649) executed by Parliament as a traitor.

[3] David and Saul. David rescued Israel by his feats of arms and the once-successful warrior king Saul became so jealous of David that he tried on several occasions to kill the man who had seen off the Philistines, despite the fact that David was by then his son-in-law (1 Sam., chs 18–19). It has to be said that the analogue, at least in Cromwell's recounting of it, is very vague.

28 JUNE 1648

prince of peace'. Isaiah 9:6). After a long period when he did not draw on the bible much in his letters, this launches a much more active scriptural period.

———

For his Excie the lord Fairfax Generall of the Parliaments army these[1]

[remnant of seal]

My lord.

I have some few dayes since dispatch't horse and dragones for the north. I sent them by the way of West'chester,[2] thinking it fit soe to doe in regard of this inclosed letter which I received from Coll. Duckenfeild,[3] requireing them to give him assistance in the way, And if it should prove that a present helpe would not serve the turne, then, I ordered Captaine Pennyfeathers[4] troope to remayne with the Governor, and the rest immediately to march towards Leeds, and to send to the Committee of Yorke or to him that Commaunds the forces in cheife there; for directions whither they should come, and how they shalbe disposed of. The number I sent are, Six troopes, fower of horse, and two of dragoones, whereof three are Coll. Scropes,[5] and Capt Pennyfeathers troope, and the other two, dragoones I would not, by the judgment of the Collonells here spare more, nor send them sooner, without manifest hazard to theise parts. Here it, (as I have formerly acquainted Your Excellency,) a very desperate enemy, who being put out of all hope of mercy are resolved to indure to the uttermost extremity. being very many gentlemen of quality, and men, throughly resolved. They have made some notable sallyes, upon Leifet Coll. Reades[6] quarter to his loss. We are forced to keepe diverse posts, or else, they would have releife or their horse breake away. Our foot ⊢⊣[7] about three or fower and twenty hundred, wee being necessitated

---

[1] There are the remnants of a seal at this point.

[2] Chester, one of the major gateways to Ireland and a royalist stronghold 1642–6.

[3] Robert Duckenfield [Duckenfeild] (1619–89), parliamentarian army officer. See ODNB. He was governor of Chester from 1647 to 1653.

[4] Thomas Pennyfather, who was to die as major in Colonel John Butler's regiment of horse. See Firth and Davies, *Regimental History*, 1:82–4, 86–7. For his earlier career see Wanklyn, *Reconstructing*, 1:54.

[5] Colonel Adrian Scrope (or Scroop). Scrope himself did not command his regiment during the Welsh campaign which was headed by Major Nathaniel Barton: Firth and Davies, *Regimental History*, 1:107.

[6] Thomas Reade who led eight companies of foot out of Robert Overton's regiment sent on the Welsh campaign (Firth and Davies, *Regimental History*, 1:387). He had recently taken the surrender of Tenby (Pembrokeshire).

[7] Too blurred to read, probably a word of three letters.

527

THE LETTERS, WRITINGS, AND SPEECHES OF OLIVER CROMWELL

to leave some in garrisons, The Country, since we sate downe before this place, have made \two or/ three or fowe insurrections, and are ready to doe it every day, Soe that, what with lokeing to them, and dispersing our horsse to that end, and to get us in provisions, (without which we should starve) this Country being soe miserably exhausted, and soe poore, and wee noe money, to buy victualls, That indeed, whatever may be thought. It's a mercy that we have been able to keep our men together in the middest of such necessityes (the sustenance of the force (for the most part) being but breade & water). our gunns through the unhappie accident at Berkly,[8] not yet come to us. (And indeed it was a very unhappie thing they were brought thither) the windes having been alsoe soe cross, that since they were recovered from Sinking, they could not, this place not being to be had without either fitt[9] instrumts. for batterye, except by starving. And truly I beleive the enemyes straights doth increase upon them very fast and that within a few dayes an end wilbe put to this business. which surely might have been before If we had received things wherewith to have done it \but it wilbe donn in the best time/. I rejoyce much to heare of the blessing of God upon Your Excies endeavors. I pray God teach this Nation, and those that are over us and thereof Your Excie and All us that are under you what the minde of God may be in all this and what our duty is. Surely it is not, that the poore godly people of this kingdome should still be made the object of wrath and anger, nor that our necks God would have our necks under a Yoake of bondage for these things that have lately come to pass have been the wonderfull workes of God breaking the rod of the oppressor, as in the day of Midean not with garments[10] much row'led in blood, but by the terror of the lord, who will yet save his people, & confound his enemyes as in that day.[11] The lord multiply \his spirit/ upon you, and bless you, and keep your heart upright, and then though you be not conformable to the men of this world, nor to the their wisedome, yet you shall be pretious in the eyes of God, and he wilbe to yo a sunn[12] & a sheild. My lord. I doe not know that I have had

---

[8] Berkeley, Gloucestershire, close to the Severn estuary and a crossing point to Lydney, Monmouthshire.

[9] It seems that 'fitt' (or 'fit') was written over an original 'full'.

[10] The remainder of the letter is written in the left margin.

[11] This sentence contains a loose paraphrase of Isaiah 9:4–5: 'For thou hast broken the yoke of his burden, and the staff of his shoulder, the rod of his oppressor, as in the day of Midian. For every battle of the warrior *is* with confused noise, and garments rolled in blood; but *this* shall be with burning *and* fuel of fire' (*KJV*, much closer to Cromwell's text than the Geneva translation).

[12] There has clearly been a changing of letters at and around the second letter: 'sunn' is the more plausible, but 'home' just about possible,

10 JULY 1648

a letter from any of your army of the glorious successes God has vouchsafed you. I pray pardon the complaint \because/. I long to rejoyce with you. I take leave & rest.

My lord. Your most humble & faithfull Servan{t}
O Cromwell

before Pemb.
June the 28ᵗʰ 1648

Sir I desire you that Coll. Lehunt[13] may have a Comission to command a troope of horse the greatest part whereof came from the enemy to us, and that you would be pleased to send blank Comissions for his inferiour officers with what speed may be.

1648 07 10

Letter from Oliver Cromwell to John Poyer, governor of Pembroke

Date: 10 July 1648
Source: Robert Ibbitson (publisher), *Perfect Occurrences of Every Dayes Lournall in Parliament* no. 81 for 14–21 July 1648), p. 580 [a misnumbering, *recte* 592] (N&S, 465.5081; Thomason / E.525[7]) (contemporary print copy)

According to the editor of the *Perfect Occurrences* Cromwell delivered this ultimatum to Poyer on 'July 10 at 4.a clock of the afternoon' and his terms were accepted the following day (11 July, see **1648 07 11a**). This copy of the ultimatum was copied to London and appeared in the *Perfect Occurrences* as having been received there on 15 July where they are linked to the six articles of surrender which appear separately as **1648 07 11b**.

Lieutenant Generall *Crumwels* last letter to Col. *Poyer*.[1]
Sir, I have (together with my Councel of war) renued my Propositions, I thought fit to send them to you with those a'terations, which if submitted unto, I shall make good; I have

---

[13] A slip here. Richard Lehunt was at this stage a captain not a colonel (he only got his own regiment in May 1650, while serving in Ireland. In June 1648 he was a captain in Fleetwood's regiment (his career is clearly outlined in Wanklyn, *Reconstructing* 1:61 n.173 and 2:194).

---

[1] John Poyer.

considered your condition, and my owne duty, and (without threatning) must tell you, that If (for the sakes of some) this offer be refused, and thereby misery and ruine befill[2] the poore souldiers and people with you; I know where to charge the blood you spill. I expect your answer within these two houres. In case this offer be refused, send no more to me about this subject. I rest,

Your Servant

Ol. Crumwell.

July 10 at 4. a clock this afternoon, 1648.

1648 07 11a

Letter from Oliver Cromwell to William Lenthall, Speaker of the House of Commons

Date: 11 July 1648
Source: Bodl., MS Nalson 7, fos 141r–v (no. 65) (holograph)

Having taken the surrender of Pembroke, Cromwell sent the terms of surrender to the Speaker of the House of Commons, and enclosed the terms. In Lenthall's own papers there survives a copy with a close attempt at Cromwell's own signature,[1] but what is clearly the original, with corrections and written by Cromwell's usual clerk, with Cromwell's own signature and most importantly with his seal, is in the Nalson Papers.

[Seal]
A lre from
Coll Cromwell
touching the Surrender of
Pembroke Castle with the
Articles upon the Surrendr

---

[2] Clearly a misprint—obviously 'befall', but in this printed version definitely 'befill'.

[1] That version, Bodl., MS Tanner 62/1B fos 159r–v (no. 80) makes several transcription errors, misses out the changes in the Nalson MS version, lacks a seal and is in a hand not associated with Cromwell autograph letters. It is also wrongly dated 'July the 11th 1643'.

thereof[2]
July 11 1648

[address]
For the honble Wm Lenthall Esqr
Speaker to the house of
Commons
these[3]
Sir
The towne and Castle of Pembroke were Surrendred to me this
day, being the Eleaventh of July, upon the propositions which I
send you here enclosed. what armes, ammunition, victuall,
ordinance, or other necessaryes of warre, are in towne, I have
not to notifie you. The Commissioners I sent in to receave the
same not being yet return'd nor like soddainly to be, and I
was unwilling to defer the giving you an accompt of this
mercy, for a day; The persons excepted are such as have formerly
Served you in a very good cause, But being now apostatized
I did rather make election of them, then of those who had alwayes
been for the king judging their iniquity double because they
have Sinn'd against soe much light, and against soe many
evidences of divine presence going along \with/ [4] and prospering
a righteous cause A share wherein In the mannagemt of which
they themselves had a share: I rest
Your most humble servant
O Cromwell

July the 11th 1648

---

[2] This endorsement is in the hand of Lenthall's clerk.
[3] This endorsement is in another hand.
[4] Inserted with caret, probably, but not certainly, by the clerk who wrote out the whole letter.

THE LETTERS, WRITINGS, AND SPEECHES OF OLIVER CROMWELL

1648 07 11b

Articles of Surrender of Pembroke signed by Cromwell and David Poyer

Date: [10 July 1648 or 11 July 1648]

Source: Bodl., MS Nalson 15, fos 194r–195v [no. 93] (unsigned original and not a holograph)

These can be taken as the articles submitted along with **1648 07 10** by Cromwell to Poyer at 4 p.m. on 10 July and signed and delivered by both parties on the following day and despatched to London on 11 July. These articles and the accompanying letter **1648 07 11a** were read in the Commons on 17 July.[1] Two versions of the articles, apparently deteriorated versions[2] of the copy sent to the Speaker, were printed in *Perfect Occurrences* and *A Perfect Diurnall* the following week.[3] The dating in the *Perfect Occurrences* as 12 July is surely a mistake.

———

Articles agreed upon for the surrendr: of Pembrooke Towne and Castle.

1 That Major. Generall Laughorne[4] Collll Poyer,[5] Collll Hump:Mathewes[6] Capt: Phil Bowen[7] and David Poyer[8] doe surrendr: themselves to the mercy of the Parlyamt.[9]

---

[1] *JHC*, 5:637: 'Surrender of Pembroke. Articles agreed upon for Surrender of Pembroke Town and Castle, were this Day read. Resolved, &c. That Symon Browne, the Messenger that brought these Articles for the Surrender of Pembroke Town and Castle, shall have the Sum of Twenty Pounds bestowed upon him, charged and paid by the Committee of Lords and Commons, usually sitting at Haberdashers Hall. The Lords Concurrence to be desired herein. The Messenger, that brought these Articles, was called in; and did affirm the Truth.'

[2] e.g. the first-person form of article 6 has been changed to the third person.

[3] Robert Ibbitson (publisher), *Perfect Occurrences of Every Dayes Journall in Parliament* no. 81 for 14–21 July 1648, p. 580 [a misnumbering, *recte* 592] (N&S, 465.5081; Thomason / E.525[7]); Samuel Pecke (publisher), *A Perfect Diurnall* no. 259 for July 10–16, unpag. but should be pp. [2087]–[2088] (N&S, 504:255; Thomason / E.525[6]).

[4] Rowland Laugharne (*c*.1607–75), parliamentarian army officer and politician. See *ODNB*; and also Newman, *Royalist Officers*, no. 856.

[5] John Poyer. [6] Humphrey Matthews, see Newman, *Royalist Officers*, no. 950.

[7] Philip Bowen, not identified.

[8] David Poyer, presumably related to John Poyer and apparently the only signatory, along with Cromwell, of the surrender articles.

[9] 'Surrender to mercy' means to surrender your life and property into the hands of the victorious party. In the First Civil War this normally meant that a soldier's life would be spared; but not so in the Second Civil War. Poyer, Laugharne and Powell were sent (via Nottingham) to prison in London. All three were condemned to death, but they drew lots to see which one of them should die and the lot fell upon Poyer who was executed by firing squad in Covent Garden nine months later.

11 JULY 1648B

2 That Sir Charles Kemish[10] Sir Hen: Stradling[11] Mr Miles Button[12] Major Pichard[13] Lt Collll Stradling[14] Lt Colll Laughorne[15] Lt: Collll Brabson[16] Mr. Gamage[17] Major Buttles[18] Mr Francis Lewis[19] Major Mathewes Major Hurnish Capt Roch, Capt Jones, Capt Hugh Bowen Capt Thomas Watts and Lt: Young doe within 6 weekes next followinge depart the Kingdome and not to retorne within 2 yeares from the time of their Departure, and if they shall retorne {within the sa}id t{ime of 2} yeares then to have noe benefitt of these Articles.

3 That all Officers and Gent not before named shall have free Liberty to goe to their severall habitacions and therelive quietly submitting themselves to the Authority of Parlyamt.

4 That all private Souldiers shall ~~bee~~[20] have Passes to goe to their severall homes without being stript, or having any violence done to them, engageing themselves to Live quiettly, and peaceably, And that all sicke, and wounded men shalbee carefully provided for till they shalbee able to goe home, and then shall have passes as the former upon the same Engagemt.

---

[10] Sir Charles Kemyss, Newman, *Royalist Officers*, no. 822.

[11] Sir Henry Stradling, Newman, *Royalist Officers*, no. 1376.

[12] Miles Button was a resident of Cottrell in Glamorgan, he was the son of the explorer Sir Thomas Button (http://yba.llgc.org.uk/en/s-BUTT-THO-1634.html). Miles' sister Elizabeth was married to John Poyer (SP16/515/2 f.141). His house appears as a rallying point for the rebel army before St Fagans' (Rushworth, *Historical Collections*, vol. 7, and online at http://www.british-history.ac.uk/rushworth-papers/vol7/pp1097–1134). A Captain Button appears on a list of prisoners taken at St Fagans' (Rushworth, ibid.).

[13] Not identified (possibly Pritchard?).

[14] A Major General John Stradling appears as Laugharne's 'Quartermaster-General' following his capture at St Fagans'? (Rushworth, *Historical Collections*, vol. 7, and online at http://www.british-history.ac.uk/rushworth-papers/vol7/pp1097–1134). He is also listed as a captive in a letter from Thomas Horton (ibid.). He appears on trial at Cardiff in a dispatch of 22 May 1648 (ibid.).

[15] Probably the William Laugharne who appears as a signatory in several copies of a regional royalist protestation of Pembroke and Haverfordwest made at Carmarthen to the earl of Carbery (TNA, SP16/497 fo. 264). Two years later a parliamentarian William Laugharne signed a public faith declaration alongside Rowland Laugharne and John Poyer (TNA, SP18/70 fo. 178).

[16] Not identified (possibly Brabazon?).

[17] Philip Gamage of Newcastle Emlyn. See Newman, *Royalist Officers*, no. 581.

[18] The print versions of the articles have 'Butler', so possibly Hugh Butler of Sadbury, Pembrokeshire. See Newman, *Royalist Officers*, no. 219.

[19] The remaining eight men named have not been identified and are not in Newman's *Royalist Officers*.

[20] This represents a word change and deletion, and is hard to read. This is our best reading.

5 That the Townesmen shalbee free from Plunder and violence, and enjoy their Liberties as heretofore they have done haveing freedome to remove themselves and Families whither they shall thincke fitt, and that Mr Fleetewood[21] shall have the same Libertie And that all Gent and others that have any Writeings concerning their Estates may carry them away and dispose of them as they please.

6 That the Towne and Castle of Pembrooke with all the Armes Amunicion and Ordnance, together with the victualls and Provisions for the Garrison bee forthwith delivered into my hands, or such as I shall appointe for the use of the Parlyamt.[22]

Articles for Surrendr. of Pembroke Towne & Castle   read 17°. July. 1648[23]

1648 07 12

Cromwell's comments written on a letter sent by Roger, Samson and John Lort to the mayor and aldermen of Haverfordwest

Date: 12 July 1648

Source: Pembrokeshire Record Office, Haverfordwest Borough Records, HAM/26 (scribal letter with holograph elements)

Following the fall of Pembroke, one of Cromwell's priorities was to destroy defences so that there would be less expense of time and money in the event of any future revolt. One of the places concerned was the castle at Haverfordwest. The letters on 12 and 14 July explore the options and reach a resolution. The first is from commissioners[1] appointed by Cromwell to 'view and consider what Garrisons and places of strength are fit to be demolished; and we finding that the Castle of Haverford is not tenable for the services of

---

[21] Not identified.

[22] The printed copies of the articles are said to have been signed by Oliver Cromwell and David Poyer. David was the brother of John, the governor. No explanation of this switch is given. David, along with John, appears in article 1.

[23] This endorsement in another hand relates to the reading of the articles in Parliament.

[1] For the three Lort brothers, see *DWB* at 'LORT family, of Stackpole and other seats in Pembrokeshire': http://yba.llgc.org.uk/en/s-LORT-STA-1567.html.

the Parliament'. The letter is addressed to the mayor[2] and aldermen of Haverfordwest. But because 'yet it may be possessed by ill-affected persons' this letter authorised and required the mayor and aldermen 'to summon-in the Hundred of Roose and the inhabitants of the Town and County of Haverfordwest; and that they forthwith demolish the several walls and towers of the said Castle; so as the said Castle may not be possessed by the Enemy, to the endangerment of the peace of these parts'. And they added that they expected a progress report by Saturday 15 July. Cromwell then added a clear instruction:

If a Speedy course bee not taken to fulfil[l] the commands of this Warrant, I shall-bee necessitated to consider of settlinge a guarrison.
O Cromwell

1648 07 14
Oliver Cromwell to the mayor and aldermen of Haverfordwest

Date: 14 July 1648
Source: Pembrokeshire Record Office, Haverford Borough Records, HAM/28 (holograph)

This is a holograph letter. On 12 July, the Lort brothers had written to the mayor and corporation of Haverfordwest as in **1648 07 12**. On 13 July, the mayor and alderman replied saying they had put 'some workmen about it'. But they said it would be very difficult to complete the task properly without powder to blow it up by, to save a lot of time and a lot of money. They ask Cromwell to send 'a competent quantity of powder' from the ships, that he make it a responsibility of the whole county and that they be empowered to levy a 'competent sum of money on the several Hundreds of the County' to pay for the powder and labour. This is Cromwell's reply. He makes no reference to powder. In the event, the instructions in these letters appear only partly to have been carried out, for just one of the four sides of the castle's curtain wall was demolished.[1]

---

[2] The mayor was John Prynne: he signed the letter to Cromwell on 13 July 1648, as transcribed in Carlyle-Lomas, 1:255.

[1] Gaunt, *Gazetteer*, p. 180.

To the Mayor and Aldermen of Haverfordwest

Whereas upon view and consideration with one Roger Lort[2] Mr Samson[3] Lort,[4] and the Mayor[5] and Aldermen of Haverford west it is thought fitt for the preservinge of the peace of this Countye, that the Castle of Haverford west should be speedily demolished,

Theis are to authorize you to call[6] unto your assistance in the performance of this service, the Inhabitants of the Hundreds[7] of Dangleddy,[8] Dewisland, Kemis,[9] Roose[10] and Kilgarren;[11] whoe are hereby required to give you asistance.

Given under our handes this 14th of July 1648,

O Cromwell

Sam: Lort, John Lort[12]
To the Maior and Aldermen of Haverford west[13]

1648 08 02

Overheard conversations involving Oliver Cromwell recorded by Major Robert Huntington

Date: 2 August 1648
Source: Parliamentary Archives: HL/PO/JO/10/1/266 fos 83–91 (Huntington's holograph)

Robert Huntington (c.1616–84) was born and brought up in Suffolk (probably in Battisford) and by 1642 was a merchant in and freeman of Yarmouth (Norfolk). By no later than the

[2] See **1648 07 12**.
[3] Originally Cromwell wrote 'Samuell', and replaced the 'uell' with 'son'.
[4] See **1648 07 12**.
[5] The mayor was John Prynne: he signed the letter to Cromwell on 13 July 1648, as transcribed in Carlyle-Lomas, 1:255.
[6] There are letters crossed out before 'unto' which we think are 'bef' (for 'before'?).
[7] In the seventeenth century there were seven hundreds in Pembrokeshire. The ones listed here are the northern ones. The two not mentioned are the southern ones facing the Bristol Channel: Castlemartin and Narberth (Bert J. Rawlins, *The Parish Churches and Nonconformist chapels of Wales: their records and where to find them Vol. 1, Carmarthenshire, Cardiganshire, and Pembrokeshire* (Salt Lake City, 1987), pp. 389, 491–3).
[8] Dangleddy is more usually given its Welsh name, Daugleddau. See n. 820.
[9] More usually spelt Cemaes. See n. 820.   [10] More usually Rhos. See n. 820.
[11] More usually Cilgerran, see n. 820.
[12] The signatures of the Lorts are not with Cromwell's but placed in a corner of the paper. More endorsements than signatories.
[13] This is also in Cromwell's own hand.

2 AUGUST 1648

autumn of 1644 he was serving as a captain in the army of the Eastern Association and in the cavalry regiment of Colonel Bartholomew Vermuyden. When that regiment was incorporated into the New Model Army, Huntington became its major and two months later the regiment became Cromwell's own cavalry regiment (Vermuyden leaving the Army and returning to the continent of Europe). Huntington thus served under Cromwell in all the major engagements in the last year of the First Civil War. In 1647, he became a trusted go-between as the generals drew up the Heads of the Proposals and presented them to the King, and he was privy to many private conversations amongst the senior officers. He was present at some of their face-to-face negotiations with Charles I. At some point in 1648 he became disaffected with their radicalisation as the Second Civil War unfolded and in June 1648 he suddenly resigned his commission[1] and, possibly in collusion with 'Presbyterian' MPs, he wrote a denunciation of Cromwell and Ireton's actions in 1647 and delivered his 4,000-word document to the earl of Manchester, as Speaker of the House of Lords. If, as seems obvious, it was presented to Parliament and then published on 2 August 1648 (without any authority and by an unnamed printer) with the aim of discrediting Cromwell and Ireton in the eyes of a majority of Parliament it clearly failed.[2]

Huntington addressed his *Sundry Reasons* to the doubtless welcoming ears of Edward Montagu, earl of Manchester that same day, 2 August 1648, and the Lords immediately agreed to have it read and entered into their journal.[3] They agreed to debate it on 3 August, but then deferred the debate until 5 August when they set up a committee of six 'to draw up some Observations upon the said Narrative, to be delivered at a Conference with the House of Commons'. On 8 August Huntington 'had his Oath given him at this Bar; declaring "That what was expressed in his Narrative as to be of his own Knowledge is true, by the Oath that he hath now taken."' There are passing references to it on 11 and 16 August and then silence.[4] And the committee of six never did present it to the Commons. It was a rocket that quickly fizzled out and fell to earth.

There is a full text of the pamphlet in the Journal of the House of Lords, but it is the original, in Huntington's own handwriting[5] in the parliamentary archives themselves, so it this version which is (for the first time) published here. Two slightly different versions were published almost simultaneously with the presentation to the House of Lords and because it was the printed versions which caused a public reaction at the time, we have edited the original against those printed copies. Neither of the two printings was authorised and neither bore the name of a printer. The first[6] is very close in every way to the text

---

[1] Or was ordered to resign. See the gnomic entry in the *House of Lords Journal* on 11 August 1648: 'The General's Discharge of Major Huntington was read', *JHL*, 10:423.

[2] Robert Huntingdon (*c*.1616–84), army officer. See *ODNB*. See also the *Online Directory of Parliamentarian Officers*; and for Vermuyden, see Wanklyn, *Reconstructing*, 1:38, 52, 62, 73.

[3] *JHL*, 10:408–12.

[4] *JHL*, 10:412 and *passim*.

[5] The handwriting of the pamphlet is identical with that in two petitions from Huntington to Cromwell in 1654 (TNA SP 18/68 fo. 73 [Mar 1654] and TNA SP 18/73 fo. 118 [July 1654]).

[6] *Sundry Reasons inducing Major Robert Huntington to lay down his commission*, London 1648 (Wing / H3774; Thomason / E.538[3]).

THE LETTERS, WRITINGS, AND SPEECHES OF OLIVER CROMWELL

printed in the Journal of the House of Lords; the second, from a hostile source, was prefaced by 'some animadversions on Major Huntington's papers' attacking his veracity and personal integrity.[7]

Huntington does not claim to do much more than paraphrase Cromwell and in extracting versions of what Cromwell said at key moments during the Army revolt of 1647 he drifts between what he said and what he meant. In editing the relevant sections of the letter or pamphlet, we have included material directly relevant to the context by the use of underlining.

Huntingdon began by an account of Cromwell's role in May 1647 when he was sent down by Parliament to persuade the Army peacefully to disband—extract [A]. He then discusses Cromwell's complicity in the seizure of the King from Holdenby House in early June by Cornet Joyce—extract [B]. There follows a long section on the debates within the Army in June and July 1647 and the formulation of the Heads of the Proposals and Cromwell and Ireton's desperate attempts to make the King see them and not the Parliament as his real friends amongst his enemies, and it describes the meetings of the officers with the King, at some of which Huntington was present. Extract [C] contains a sense of Cromwell's words as he and Ireton struggled to keep control of the Army at the time of the Putney Debates and it alleges that he helped to facilitate the King's flight from Hampton Court in mid-November, Extract [D] then suggests Cromwell's anger and exasperation with the various obstructions his and Ireton's plans were encountering and some pretty extreme proposed remedies. The final extract [E] is even less an attempt to recapture Cromwell's precise words, but it does claim to summarise what 'he hath most frequently in publick and private' claimed as his principles. This tract is borderline for inclusion in this edition, but does represent important testimony which, as Samuel Rawson Gardiner said in 1893, 'was probably substantially accurate' and which stopped short of convenient invention.[8]

[A]

[Page 2/ fo. 83v]

<u>And Com. Genll. Ireton in further pursuance thereof framed those papers & writings, then sent from the Army to the Parlt & kingdome; saying also to the Agitators That it was then lawfull & fitt for us to deny disbanding till we had received equall & full satisfaccon for our past service. Leiut Genll. Cromwell further adding,</u> That wee were in a double Capacitie, as Souldiers, & as Comoners,[9] And having our pay as Souldiers, we have somthing else to stand upon as Comoners.[10]

---

[7] *Sundry Reasons inducing Major Robert Huntington to lay down his commission.*

[8] Gardiner, GCW, 3:246 fn. 3; 4:175–8.

[9] Thomason / E.458[3] has 'commissioners' for 'commoners'.

[10] Thomason / E.458[3] has 'commissioners' for 'commoners'.

538

2 AUGUST 1648

[B]

[Page 3/fo. 84]

<u>Leiut Gen: Cromwell comeing then from London, sayd</u> That if this had not bene done, the king would have bene fetcht away by order of Parlt, or else Col: Graves by the advise of the Comissioners, would have carryed him to London, throwing themselves upon the favour of Parlt for that service.

[C]

[Pages 11–13/fos 88–89]

...but before this the king doubting what Answer to give sent me to L. G. Cromwell as unsatisfied wth the proceedings of the Army, fearing[11] they intended not to make good what they had promised: & the rather because his Matie understood, that L. G. Cromwell, & Com. G. Ireton agreed wth the rest of the house in some late votes that opposed the Proposalls of the Army they readally[12] replyed, that they would not have his Matie mistrust them, for that since the house would goe so high, They only Concurred with them that[13] their unreasonablenes might the better appeare to the kingdome. And the Leiut Genll: bade me further assure the king That if the Army remained an Army, his Matie: should trust the Proposalls with what was promised to be the worst of his Condicons which should be made for him; And then striking his hand on his breast[14] in his Chamber at Putney, bade me tell the king he might rest Confident & assured of it. And many tymes the same Message hath bene sent to the king from them both, but wth this addicon [15] from C. G. Ireton, that they would purge & purge & never leave purging[16] the houses till they had made them of such a temper as should doe his Mats. busines, And rather then they would fall short of what was promised, he would joyne wth French Spanyard[17] Cavalier or any that would joyne wth him to force them to it.

---

[11] Thomason / E.458[3] has 'hearing' for 'fearing'.

[12] Wing / H3774 has 'severally' for 'readally'.

[13] There are two horizontal lines in the margin against this line, probably added by a reader not by the author.

[14] Thomason / E.458[3] has 'heart' for 'breast'.

[15] There are two horizontal lines in the margin against this line, probably added by a reader not by the author.

[16] Thomason / E458[3] has 'purge and purge and purge, and never leave purging'.

[17] There are two horizontal lines in the margin against this line, probably added by a reader not by the author.

539

THE LETTERS, WRITINGS, AND SPEECHES OF OLIVER CROMWELL

Vpon the delivery of wch Message, the king made Answer, that if they doe they would doe more then he durst doe. After this, the delay of the settlemt of the kingdome was excused upon the Comotions of Col. Martin & Col. Rainsbrough with their adherents; The Leiut Gen. saying that speedy Course must be taken for outing of them[18] the house & Army, because they were now putting the Army into a Mutuny, by having hands in publishing sevrall Printed papers calling themselves the Agents of Five Regmts. & the Agreemt. of the People, although some men had encouragemt from L. G. Cromwell for the prosecucon of those Papers. And hee being further prest to shew himselfe in it he desired to bee excused at the present, for that he might shew himselfe hereafter for their better advantage, Though in the Company of those men which were of different Judgemts he would often say that these people were a Giddy-headed party, & that there was no trust nor truth in them. And to that purpose wrote a letter to Col. Whaley that daie the king went from Hampton Court, intimating doubtfully that his Mats person was in danger by them; And that he should keepe outguard to prevent them, which Letter was presently shewed to the kinge by[19] Col. Whaley.

[D]

[Pages 14–16/fos 89v–90v]

Lt. Gen: Cromwell perceiving the Houses will not answer his Expectacon he is now againe pe uttering words perswading the hearers to a prejudice agt the Proceedings of Parlt againe crying downe Presbiterian Govrmt, setting up a single interest, wch he calls an Honest Interest and that we have done ill in forsaking of it, To this purpose it was lately thought fitt to put the Army upon the choosing new Agitators, & to draw forth of the houses of Parlt 60 or 70 of the Members thereof much agreeing with his words hee spake formerly in his Chamber at Kingston, saying, What a sway Stapleton & Hollis had heretofore in the kingdome & he knew nothing to the Contrary but that he was as well able to governe the kingdome as either of them. So that in all his discourse Nothing more appeareth then his seeking after the Governmt of king Parlt Citty & kingdomes For the effecting whereof he thought it necessary, and delivered it as his Judgemt. That a Considerable party of the Chiefe Cittizens of London & \some/ of every County bee Clapt up in Castles & Garrisons, for the more quiet & submissive Carriage of every place to which they belong. Further saying, that from the raising of the

---

[18] Thomason / E.458[3] has 'outing of them in,' for 'outing of them'.
[19] There is a clear blot over the 'y'.

540

2 AUGUST 1648

late tumult in London there should be an occasion taken to hang the Recorder, & Aldermen of London then in the Tower, that the Citty might see the more they did stirre in oppo siscon, the more they should suffer. Adding that the Citty must first be made an Example. And since that, Leiut Gen: Cromwell was sent downe from the Parlt for the reduceing of the Army to their obedience he hath most frequently in publique & private delivered these ensuing heads, as his Principles from whence all the foregoing particulars have ensued, being fully Confirmed (as I humbly Conceive) by his practise in the transaction of his last yeares buisines.

[E]

[Pages 17–18/fos 91r–v]

And since that Leivt. Gen Cromwell was sent down from the Parliament for the reducing of the Army to their obedience, he hath most frequently in publick and private, delivered these ensuing heads as his Principles, from whence all the foregoing particulars have ensued, being fully confirmed as I humbly conceive by his practise in the transaction of his last yeares bu|sinesse.

1. First that every single man is Judge of just & right, as to the good & ill of a kingdome.
2. That the interest of Honest men is the interest of the kingdome, & that those only are deemed honest men by him that are Conformeable to his Judgemt & practise; may appear in many particulars To instance but one in the Choice of Col. Rainsbroug[20] to be Vice Admirall; Leiut G. Cromwell being asked how he could trust a man whose Interest was so directly opposite to what he had professed, & one whom he had lately aymed to remoove from all places of trust! He answered That he had now received particular assurance from Col. Rainsbrough, as great as could be given by man, That he would be conformable to the Judgemt. & direction of himselfe & C. G. Ireton for the mannaging of the whole buisines at Sea.
3. That it is Lawfull to passe through any formes of Govrnmt for the accomplishing his ends And therefore either to purge the Houses, & support the remaining party by force Everlastingly, or to put a Period to them by force, is very Lawfull & suitable to the interest of Honest men.
4. That it is Lawfull to play the knave wth a knave.

---

[20] A final 'h' is probably lost in the guttering of the manuscript.

THE LETTERS, WRITINGS, AND SPEECHES OF OLIVER CROMWELL

1648 08 04[?]
Letter from Oliver Cromwell to the people of Bristol

Date: Before 18 August 1648 (when George Thomason noted receiving it)
Source: *The declaration of Lieutenant Generall Cromwel concerning the citizens of London, and their high and strange expressions against the army* (1648) (Wing / C7061; Thomason / E.459[24]) (contemporary print)

This is probably but not certainly a document that Cromwell wrote. Given its inflammatory content and Cromwell's political importance, it is unlikely that it did not have his approval—the consequences of complete fabrication would have been too serious. The language is neither clearly Cromwell's but nor is it clearly not his. The publishing history is also unclear: there are three possible 'R.W.'s in late 1648: if it is Richard White, then he is a publisher with good Army connections—he was the publisher of Joshua Sprigge's *Anglia Rediviva* (1647), a celebration of the first two years of the New Model Army; less likely are Robert Wood (who was involved in several parliamentarian newsletters around this time) and Robert Williamson (mainly a royalist printer by this stage). Both Wood and White are plausible candidates and would be men very unlikely to publish a Cromwell letter that they did not think to be genuine.[1]

The context is that with Fairfax still tied down by the siege of Colchester, and Cromwell heading north to reach the Scots, there was need to steady the nerves of the Army's sympathisers in London, where support for the King and for a quick settlement reached a peak at this very moment.[2] It was clearly written while Cromwell was preparing to face the army of the Scottish Engagers. The battle of Preston (17–19 August lay ahead). Thomason received the pamphlet on 14 August, and Cromwell was in Warwick from 26 to 30 July and then moving up through Leicester (1 August), Nottingham (3 August), Mansfield (6 August) to West Yorkshire (8–10 August). If he was the author, it was probably written in this period, and perhaps in the earlier part of it, or at the very end of July.

Whereas I should long since have acquaintted you of the many favours we received from the City of *Bristol*, by the mediation of Mr *Peters*,[3] when we lay befoor Pembrook,[4] they affording us not only a great supply of Beer, but linen for our wounded and sick souldiers, a mercy seasonable and necessary and at this

---

[1] For the extent of White and Wood's involvement in diurnal publishing, see N&S, p. 723 (White) and p. 724 (Wood).

[2] For the counter-revolution in London in July 1648 see Ian Gentles, 'The Struggle for London in the Second Civil War', *The Historical Journal*, 26 (1983), pp. 277–305.

[3] Hugh Peter [or Peters] (1598–1660), Independent minister. See *ODNB*. He was with Cromwell throughout the campaigns of 1648 and was active in promoting the King's trial.

[4] Pembroke: besieged by Cromwell from 24 May 1648 until 11 July.

present sensibly felt; yet in this very poor condition, we can do no more but acknowledge it with thankfull hearts to God, and by promising to hazard our lives in a farther adventure for them, and the Kingdome in this our Northern expedition, much enabled and encouraged by the benefit and remembrance of those former favours, together with the supply of 2500 pare of shooes from Northampton.[5] and the like quantity of stockings from the city of Coventry,[6] and our joy is, that God hath cleared up our way by the appearance of providence in his former assistances, and believe it, Sir,[7] as long as we have life, we shall keep to first principles, though a poor naked despised partie, and die by the sides of our faithfull Officers, in the owning of that only, which God and reason allows, as for those against whom, we now march, it's our opinion, they if Victors, will put no difference betweene Cavaliers Presbyterians, and Independents, but we trust he that hath hitherto gone along with us, will assist us in this enterprize, to blunt some what the edge of their delights, and that they shall reap as those before them, of that stamp; both old and new, will not Englishmen, consider of whom it is said they are the best servants but the worst Masters in the world we grieve for that famous City of London, over whom we never desired to insult, nor marched we through with any such intent, but to let them and the world see and understand, how false their reports were concerning our endeavours to come up and plunder them, but let them know their destruction (if they perish) will be of themselves, not us.[8] And not withstanding all their high and strange expressions against us, who have been instrumentall of more good to them, then to all of the Kingdom, and received the least from them, yet we professe ourselves their servants in the worke in hand: and for you noble Citizens of Bristol you have had wonderful experiences and deliverances, do do not lose them; we appoint no Government to you nor this Kingdom, we shall stoop, we hope as low as the lowest and look no other way upon ourselves, and take no other notice of the workings of providence, then as instruments used by the eternall, since our new modelling, for subduing those who have and would inslave both soul and body

[5] Northampton has been a national centre for shoe manufacture since medieval times. See Peter Perkins et al., 'The Industrial Heritage of Northampton's Boot and Shoe Quarter' (Northamptonshire Industrial Archaeology Group, 2015), pp. 1–15.

[6] Coventry, pre-industrial town in Warwickshire, See Anne Hughes, 'Coventry and the English Revolution', in Roger Richardson, ed., *Town and Countryside in the English Revolution* (Manchester, 1992), pp. 69–99.

[7] Probably this is reference to either the mayor (Sir William Cann) or the deputy governor (Charles Doyley).

[8] See above, n. 2.

to their wils, not Gods and reasons: and so many of uds as shall out live these troubles, you shall see will be willing to resign all kind of power and trust, when such an agreement or settlement is made, as may put us in capacity to live under the worst of shades, free from tyranny and persecution.

1648 08 14
Letter from Oliver Cromwell to [unknown]

Date: 14 August 1648
Source: Museum of London, Tangye MS 706, no. 32 (contemporary copy)

After a month when no communication of Cromwell's survives, we begin a rich seam of letters running down to just before Pride's Purge when silence descends again. This order was almost certainly written on 14 August and this is a copy made the following day. Cromwell himself was never in Leeds. On 13 August he was at Otley, five miles to the north-west of Leeds, but on 14 August he was at Skipton, 17 miles further north and west, and by 15 August had crossed the Pennines and was at Gisburn in Lancashire.[1]

14° Awg: 1648
Whereas I am informed that Leift Swayne[2] Leift to Capt Cooks[3] Troop of Horse hath taken two Horses of great value from Captayne Willm Harrison[4] for

---

[1] Gaunt, *Gazetteer*, p. 226.

[2] Possibly Francis Swain of York, for whom see Andrew Hopper, 'A Directory of Parliamentarian Allegiance in Yorkshire during the British Civil Wars', *Yorkshire Archaeological Journal*, 73 (2001), p. 90, citing TNA, SP16/513/141; SP19/121/20b; SP19/12—but he had long been a captain not a lieutenant. Or just possibly Henry Swaine, who, also as a captain, served in April and May 1645. Henry Swaine was a captain in Sir William Constable's regiment of horse in the Northern army which was temporarily serving under Sir William Brereton in April and May 1649 (Norman Dore, ed., *The Letter Books of Sir William Brereton*, vols. 1–2, Record Society of Lancashire and Cheshire Record Society, 1:177–8, 394–5, 415, 522). Dore thinks—on the basis of there being a Henry Swaine as a commissioner of York in 1652—that he may have been a citizen of York. But he too is a captain long before July 1648.

[3] Quite possibly the William Cooke of New Chapel, Penistone township and parish: see Hopper, 'A Directory', p. 116, citing TNA, SP28/253a/part i/19; CCAM, 647; *Leeds Parish Registers*, 214.

[4] Probably the William Harrison who had been Lord Fairfax's treasurer from 24 November 1642. He also had a commission as captain, probably in Lord Fairfax's own regiment of foot. He later acquired a troop of horse, probably in Lord Fairfax's own regiment of horse. See Jennifer Jones, 'The War in the North: the Northern Parliamentary Army in the English Civil War', University of York (Toronto) PhD thesis (1991), p. 386.

the restoreing whereof hee hath had Lres, or Ordrs from the Superior Officrs NotwithStanding the Sayd Horses are not restored. It is thrfore ordred that they bee instantly delivered to the Bearer for Capt Harrisons use, & that the Said Capt Cooke See this Ordr duely observed.

O: Cromwell.

Leeds.[5] 15. Aug: 1648

This is a true Copie of the Originall which ~~was~~ Capte Cooke read and beesides it was read to him in presence of us whose names are Subscribed
Abraham Burton Tho: Staveley Timothy Hurst[6]

1648 08 17
Letter from Oliver Cromwell to the Lancashire County Committee in Manchester

Date: 17 August 1648
Source: *A copy of Lieutenant General Crumwels Letter, read in the House of Commons. And other letters of a great and bloody fight neere Preston. The Scots army totally defeated by Lieutenant Generall Crumwell.* (1648), (Wing / C7052; Thomason / E.460[17]), (contemporary print)

This letter has a complicated textual history. No manuscript copy, and certainly no holograph or autograph survives, but we have four versions, all contained within pamphlets published more or less simultaneously on 21 or 22 August 1648. There is thus a six-week gap between Cromwell's previous letter, mopping up military operations in Pembrokeshire, to this letter which finds him in the north of England and victorious over the Scottish army under the duke of Hamilton which had crossed over into England on 8 July and occupied Carlisle. With Fairfax fully engaged with the siege of Colchester (which only finally capitulated on 26 August), it was Cromwell who was sent north to head off the Scots. Moving north via Leicester and Doncaster to Wetherby, he joined up with John Lambert, in charge of the Northern regiments and with the artillery train from Hull, and then made a 'lion-spring across the Yorkshire fells' to confront the Scots, who had little prior knowledge of his whereabouts in a running battle lasting three days (17–19 August).[1]

---

[5] A major borough in the West Riding of Yorkshire.
[6] None of the above has been identified.

[1] The clearest account remains Gardiner, *GCW*, 4: ch. LXIV. Gardiner's phrase 'Lion-spring' is at p. 182.

THE LETTERS, WRITINGS, AND SPEECHES OF OLIVER CROMWELL

At the end of the first day, he wrote this letter to the Parliamentarian Committee at Manchester and they in turn forwarded it to London. Four versions of the forwarded letter were printed. It is not possible to work out in which order they were published or which ones were copied from others, but the identity of the printers is likely to be significant.

[Version A]: *Lieutenant General Cromwel's letter concerning the total routing of the Scots army, the taking of four thousand arms, and almost all their ammunition. With another letter written from Manchester to Sir Ralph Ashton, a member of the Honorable House of commons...* Printed for Edward Husband, printer to the Honorable House of Commons, August 22. 1648 (Wing / C7092; Thomason / E.460[16]). This, which attaches Cromwell's letter to one from 'W.L.' (almost certainly William Langston, recruiter MP for Preston)[2] to Sir Ralph Assheton, MP for Clitheroe,[3] was 'ordered by the Commons assembled in Parliament... [to be]forthwith printed and published' by Parliament's official printer, Edward Husband:[4]

[Version B]: *A copy of Lieutenant General Crumwels Letter, read in the House of Commons. And other letters of a great and bloody fight neere Preston...* printed by Robert Ibbitson, in Smithfield, neer the Queenes-head Tavern, pp. 1–3 (Wing / C7052; Thomason / E.460[17]). This does not include W.L.'s letter but does include other newsletters from the north, and was published by Robert Ibbitson,[5] the man responsible for much authorised Army publication. It looks likely to come from an Army source and might just be from a copy provided by Cromwell himself.

[Version C]: *A letter written by Lievt. Gen. Crumwell, to the honourable the committee of Manchester. Being a full relation of the total routing of the Scotch army, neer Preston in Lancashire...* London: printed by I.M., August 21. 1648 (Wing / C7116; Thomason / E.460[6]). This too has different accompanying material, including much greater detail of the casualties, written by an untraceable 'E.S.'[6] and printed by 'I.M.'.[7] This is fairly close to Version [A], and may indeed be a slightly deteriorated version of [A], or printed from the same manuscript copy.

[Version D]: *The overthrow of the Scottish Army: or a letter sent from Lieutenant Generall Cromwell to the committee of Lancashire sitting at Manchester, shewing the utter routing of the Scottish forces.* London: Printed for John Bellamy, 1648 (Wing / C7136; Thomason / E.460[5]). This last version contains, in addition to Cromwell's letter, a short letter from Henry Molyneux[8] to

---

[2] William Langston, recruiter MP for Preston, for whom see *HoP Commons, 1640–1660*. For his distinctive politics at the end of 1648, see David Underdown, *Pride's Purge: Politics in the Puritan Revolution* (Oxford, 1971), p. 175.

[3] For this Ralph Assheton of Whalley, and MP for Clitheroe, who was in Westminster at the time of the letter, see E. Broxap, *The Great Civil War in Lancashire* (2nd ed., 1973), pp. 30–2 and see also *HoP Commons, 1640–1660* and Underdown, *Pride's Purge*, pp. 175–6.

[4] For Edward Husband, see H. R. Plomer, *A Dictionary of Booksellers...1641–1667* (London, 1907), pp. 104–5.

[5] For Robert Ibbitson, see Plomer, *A Dictionary of Booksellers...1641–1667*, pp. 105–6.

[6] It seems to have been written by an officer in the Army, and the only one who has the same initials is Edward Shuttleworth, son of the MP for Preston, Richard Shuttleworth.

[7] 'I.M', probably John Macock, for whom see Plomer, *A Dictionary of Booksellers...1641–1667*, pp. 121–2.

[8] Henry Molyneux. Not identified.

546

17 AUGUST 1648

'Mr Winstanley', probably Captain James Winstanley, a 'Presbyterian' officer in the Lancashire militia,[9] and it was printed by John Bellamy,[10] the leading printer to the London Presbyterians. This version is anomalous in one particular way: it gives Ralph Assheton (not to be confused with *Sir* Ralph) as Cromwell's co-signatory.[11] Since Ralph Assheton, who had been commander-in-chief of Lancashire forces in the First Civil War,[12] was a leading Presbyterian, all this adds up to a version with a Presbyterian slant.

What is the likeliest explanation of the considerable differences between the versions (none really affecting the sense) is that different members of the Lancashire committee made hurried copies of Cromwell's letter and sent their copies to their friends in London. The differences in the additional material in each of versions [A]–[D] change the meaning more than changes in the Cromwell letter-text but it is not possible to say that one version gets us closer to the lost original. Version [A] might seem the safest, since it was authorised by Parliament. But there are a number of ways in which [A] seems a more careless copy and a close comparison between [A] and [B] (the latter an Army source) suggests [B] may be closer to Cromwell's original. Why would someone in the north take standard Lancashire place names and deteriorate them? [B], which has some very phonetic spellings of place names, reads more comfortably as what Cromwell might have written. So it is [B] which is used as the proof text here.

Gentlemen,

It hath pleased God, this day, to shew a great mercy to this poore kingdome,[13] by making the Army successefull against the common Enemy. We lay the last night

---

[9] A James Winstanley was made captain of the 'Yellow' regiment by the militia committee of Lancashire at an uncertain date (TNA, SP28/46, part I, fo. 40r), a damaged document.

[10] Bellamy was an active member of the London Artillery Company and joined the (Presbyterian-controlled) London militia committee in 1645. He was made a colonel of the White regiment of the London militia on 22 August 1646. He was also a printer, much associated with the London Presbyterian caucus. Plomer, *A Dictionary of Booksellers, 1641–1667*, pp. 20–1; Leona Rostenberg, *Literary, Political, Scientific, Religious & Legal Publishing, Printing & Bookselling in England, 1551–1700: twelve studies*, 2 vols. (New York, 1965), 1:97–127; Keith Lindley, *Popular Politics and Religion in Civil-War London* (1997), pp. 191, 193–5, 212, 215, 230, 368.

[11] Broxap, *Lancashire*, pp. 30–2 sorts out the various Ralph Asshetons.

[12] This Ralph Assheton of Middleton, MP for the county of Lancashire and major general of all the forces in Lancashire since 1643, served with Cromwell in the Preston campaign and was subsequently sent off to take Appleby Castle and to disperse dissident elements in the Lancashire militia (Broxap, *Lancashire*, pp. 167–75). For his biography, see also *HoP Commons, 1640–1660*.

[13] 'a great mercy to this poore kingdome' as in [B], [C], and [D]. But in [A], we have 'his great power known'.

547

THE LETTERS, WRITINGS, AND SPEECHES OF OLIVER CROMWELL

at Mr. *Sherburns*,[14] of *Stamerhurst*,[15] about 9 miles from *Preston*,[16] which was within three miles of the *Scots* quarters, we advanced this morning betime[17] towards *Preston*, with a desire to engage the Enemy, and by that time our forlorn[18] had engaged the enemy, we were about foure miles from *Preston*, and thereupon wee advanced with the whole Army; and the Enemy being drawn out upon a Moore betwixt us & the Town, the Armies on both sides ingaged, & after a very sharpe dispute, continuing for three or foure houres, it pleased God to inable us to give the Enemy[19] a defeat, which I[20] hope we shall improve by Gods assistance, to their utter ruine, and in this service your Country-men have not the least share, which wee cannot expresse by[21] particular, having not time to take an accounts of the slain, and the prisoners, but we can assure you we have many prisoners, and many of those of quality, and many slain, and the Army disipated. A principall part whereof (with Duke *Hambleton*)[22] is on the South side of *Ribb*,[23] and *Darwentbridge*,[24] and wee lying with the greatest part of the Army close to them nothing hindring engageing of[25] that part of the Enemies Army but the night; It will be our care that they shall not passe over any Ford beneath the Bridge, to goe Northward, nor to come over betwixt us, and *Whaley*,[26] we understand that three Companies[27] of Col. Generall *Ashton*[28] are at *Whalley*, we have

---

[14] Richard Sherburn of Stonyhurst, scion of substantial gentry family whose main branch had been at Stonyhurst since the thirteenth century. They were a resolutely recusant family.

[15] [B]: 'Stamerhurst'; [A] and [D] have 'Stonihurst', [C] has 'Stanhurst'. Who is more likely to use the common usage at the time (Stonihurst), Cromwell who had never been in Lancashire before or a Manchester copyist? Does this point to [B] as the more faithful copy?

[16] A Lancashire town that served as the administrative headquarters of the duchy of Lancaster.

[17] 'This morning betime': [A] has 'next morning', [C] and [D] have 'betime the next morning'.

[18] 'forlorn' in [A] and [B], 'forlorn hope' in [C] and [D]. A forlorn hope was the Army name for an advance party sent out to confirm the presence of an enemy.

[19] 'the enemy' in [B] and [D], 'them' in [A] and [C].

[20] 'I' in [A] and [B], 'we' in [C] and [D].

[21] 'cannot expresse by' in [B] and [D], 'cannot be' in [A] and [C].

[22] James Hamilton, first duke of Hamilton.

[23] Ribb = the river Ribble. It rises in the Yorkshire Pennines, and flows through Settle, Clitheroe and Preston, before emptying into the Irish Sea. [B] and [C] have Ribble.

[24] The bridge over the river Darwen, which flows south of the Ribble until it joins it at Preston. The town of Darwen was an important river crossing. The other versions of 'Darwain-bridge' are in [A] 'Darwain-bridge', in [C] 'Darwent bridge' and in [D] 'Rible and Darwen bridges'.

[25] 'engageing of': in [A], [C] and [D] we have 'the ruine of'.

[26] Whalley, a large village in Ribble Valley on the banks of the Calder, a tributary of the Ribble.

[27] [A] omits 'three companies of' which appears not only in [B] but in [D]. In [C], we have 'four of'.

[28] i.e. Ralph Assheton of Middleton, MP for Lancashire and commander-in-chief of Lancashire parliamentarian forces since 1643. See above, n. 12.

548

20 AUGUST 1648A

7 Troops of Horse and Dragoons, that we beleeve all at or neer *Clithero*.[29] This night I have sent order expresly to them to march to *Whalley*, to joyne with those Companies that you shall improve of your Country Forces, toward the ruine[30] of those enemies: you perceive by this how things stand, by this means the enemy is broken, most of the Horse being gone Northward, and wee having sent a considerable party at the very heeles of them, and the Enemy having lost almost all their Ammunition, and neer 4000 Armes, so that the greatest part of the Foot are naked: Therefore in order to this work we desire you to raise your County, and to improve those forces for the totall ruine of the enemy, which way soever they goe. And if you shall accordingly doe your part, doubt not of their totall ruine. Wee thought fit to speed this unto you, to the end you may not bee troubled if they shall march towards you, but improve your interest aforesaid. And that you may give glory to God for this unspeakable mercy[31] from

Your humble Servant
OLIVER CRUMWELL[32]
Preston[33] *17 August* 1648.[34]

1648 08 20a

Letter from Oliver Cromwell to Sir Henry Cholmley and Sir Edward Rodes

Date: 20 August 1648
Source: Museum of London, Tangye MS 706, no. 44 ([probable] autograph)

After writing to the Lancashire Committee on 17 August to report his initial victory over the Scots, Cromwell was busy in the follow-up operations, including more substantial engagements with the enemy. By 20 August, the rout was complete, and he wrote two

---

[29] Clitheroe is a parliamentary borough on the river Ribble, upstream from Preston.
[30] In [B] and in [D]: 'you shall improve of your Country Forces, toward the ruine': in [A] this is 'so we may endeavour the ruine'; in [C] 'you shall improve to the ruine'.
[31] [A] and [C] add 'this is all for present' after 'mercy.' [D] follows [B].
[32] The others all have 'Cromwell' not 'Crumwell' and [D] has 'Ralph Ashton' = Assheton as a co-signatory.
[33] 'Preston' appears in [B] but in none of the others.
[34] [A] alone of the versions adds this endorsement: 'For the Honorable Committee of Lancashire, sitting in Manchester. I desire the Commander of those forces to open this Letter, if it come not to their hands.'

549

THE LETTERS, WRITINGS, AND SPEECHES OF OLIVER CROMWELL

letters detailing the scale of his victory. First, he wrote to two MPs currently serving as colonels commanding the Yorkshire troops besieging Pontefract, for them to share with the county committee of Yorkshire sitting in York. The letter to Lenthall written on the same day refers to this letter and so this one must have been written first.

The version we have seems to contain Cromwell's signature. But the text itself is neither in his own hand nor in that of his usual clerk. It is folded as though to be sent but there is no endorsement or address on the back, nor any sign of a seal. Thus, there are puzzles about it. On balance, it seems likely to be an unsent copy.

In the mid-nineteenth century it was owned by William Beaumont of Warrington (where Cromwell was on 20 August) but that may be a coincidence.[1]

Gent

We have quite tyred our horse in pursute of the enimy Wee have killd taken & dissipated all his foote & left him only some horse with whom the Duke[2] is fledd into Dalamore Forrest[3] haveing neither foote nor dragoons They have taken five hundred of them there I meane the Country forces as they sent me word this day they are soe tyred & in such confusion that if my horse could but trott after them I could take them all but we are soe weary we shall scarse be able to doe more then walke after them I beseech you therfore lett Sir Hen Cholmley[4] Sir Edw Rodes[5] Colonel Hacker[6] & Col White[7] & all the Contryes about you be sent \to,/ {} to rise with yow and follow them For they are the miserablyest party that ever was I durst engage my selfe with five hundred fresh horse & five hundred nimble foote to distroy them all My horse are miserably beaten out And I have tenne thousand of them Prisoners We have killd we know not what but a very great number Having done execution upon them att the least 30 miles

---

[1] William Beaumont (1797–1889), a local solicitor, philanthropist and antiquarian, who edited works about the history of Warrington. At some point the letter was acquired by Sir Richard Tangye, collector of Cromwelliana: Sir Richard Tangye (1833–1906), machine tool manufacturer and engineer. See *ODNB*. When his collection was dispersed much of it, including this letter, was acquired by the Museum of London.

[2] James Hamilton, first duke of Hamilton.

[3] Delamere Forest (Cheshire), just a few miles south of Warrington.

[4] Sir Henry Cholmley: see Andrew Hopper, 'A Directory of Parliamentarian Allegiance in Yorkshire during the British Civil Wars', *Yorkshire Archaeological Journal*, 73 (2001), p. 96.

[5] See the sub-entry within Francis Rodes (1530?–88), judge, in *Dictionary of National Biography* (1897)—a fuller account than within the entry for Francis Rodes in *ONDB*; and Hopper, 'A Directory', p. 107.

[6] Francis Hacker (d. 1660), parliamentarian army officer and regicide. See *ODNB*.

[7] Colonel Charles White (a Nottinghamshire man), see Gladwyn Turbutt, *A History of Derbyshire* (4 vols., reprint 1999), 3:1058–9, 1061, 1064, 1097, 1379; A. C. Wood, *Nottinghamshire in the Civil War* (1937), esp. pp. 164–6.

together besids what wee killd in the twoe great feights the one att Preston[8] & the other att Warrington[9] The Enemy was fower & twenty thousand horse & foot in the day of the fight wherof Eighteene thousand foote & six thousand horse And our numbr about six thousand foote & three thousand horse att the utmost This is a glorious day God helpe England to answer his minde I have noe more but beseech you in all your parts to gather into bodyes and pursue them I rest

Your most humble servant

O Cromwell

Warrington this 20 of Aug 1648

The greatest part by farr of the nobility of Scotland are with Duke Hamilton

To the hoble Sir Hen Cholmley & Sir Edw Rodes neare Pontefract[10] Hast Hast

To be comunicated to the Committee of York & Col Bethell[11] & the troops belong to Westmorland under Capt....[12] & Capt Crackenthorp[13] who may spare their attendinge upon provisions and are hereby required to attend the Common service

O Cromwell

1648 08 20b

Letter from Oliver Cromwell to William Lenthall, Speaker of the House of Commons

Date: 20 August 1648

Source: *A full relation of the great victory obtained by the Parliaments forces under the command of Lievt. Gen. Cromwel against the whole army of the Scots* (Wing / F2362) (contemporary print)

This is the longest surviving letter of Cromwell's (2,820 words), more than 200 words longer than his account of the battle of Dunbar (see **1650 09 04**) and 800 words longer than his letter to Robert Hammond during the kingship crisis of November 1648 (see **1648**

---

[8] Preston: a town on the river Ribble in Lancashire. See **1648 08 17**.

[9] Warrington, parliamentary borough on the river Mersey where the Scots were overtaken by Cromwell's pursuing men.

[10] A parliamentary borough in West Yorkshire with a medieval castle occupied by royalists and under siege since April 1648. It held out until March 1649.

[11] Col. Hugh Bethel, see Hopper, 'A Directory', p. 101, citing TNA, SP28/6/473.

[12] Definite blank in the manuscript (a name that had slipped his mind and could not be recalled?).

[13] Captain Crackenthorp: not identified.

THE LETTERS, WRITINGS, AND SPEECHES OF OLIVER CROMWELL

II 25). Cromwell despatched it from Warrington on 20 August and it was read in the Commons on 23 August[1] and sent on to the Lords who read it on the same day.[2] Both Houses ordered it to be printed and Thomason received his copies on 24 August. They are:

[A] *Lieut: General Cromwel's letter to the honorable William Lenthal Esq; speaker of the honorable House of Commons, of the several great victories obtained against the Scots and Sir Marmaduke Langdales forces in the North: where were slain of the Scots party above two thousand, above nine thousand taken prisoners, four or five thousand arms taken, the whole infantry ruined, Duke Hamilton fled into Wales, and Langdale northward, Major General Vandrusk, Colonel Hurry, and Colonel Ennis taken prisoners, who formerly served the Parliament. Ordered by the Commons assembled in Parliament, that this letter be forthwith printed and published. H: Elsynge, Cler. Parl. D. Com., London: Printed for Edward Husband, printer to the Honorable House of Commons, August 23. 1648* (Wing / C7111; Thomason / E.460[24]).

[B] *A full relation of the great victory obtained by the Parliaments forces under the command of Lievt. Gen. Cromwel against the whole army of the Scots, under the conduct of Duke Hamilton. With the numbers slaine and taken prisoners…Ordered by the lords assembled in Parliament, that Lievt Generall Cromwels letter be forthwith printed and published. Joh. Brown Cler. Parliament., Imprinnted [sic] at London : for Iohn Wright at the Kings Head in the old Bayley, 1648* (Wing / F2362; Thomason / E.460[28]).

There are lots of minor differences between the two versions (the House of Lords' [B] version has more careless typographical errors), but the Lords version contains an important addition to the postscript omitted from the Commons' version [A]. It is just possible that the passage was omitted from the latter because of lack of space, but the whole postscript is in a larger typeface than the rest of the pamphlet. So a likelier explanation is that the content of the missing passage—Cromwell speaks of 'our Horse is almost destroyed, and our Foot beaten out of clothes, shoes and stockings'—may have seemed unwise intelligence to give an enemy still in the field. Certainly the Commons acted on Cromwell's pleas for urgent help and ordered the Committee of the Army 'to take care that the Soldiers in the North may be speedily supplied with Shoes, Stockings, Cloaths and other Necessaries, and Recuits'. If the Commons were being prudent, the Lords, perhaps ignorant of what the Commons were doing, were not and included both the whole of Cromwell's text and the order of both Houses for a national day of solemn thanksgiving on 7 September.

For the Honourable *William Lenthall* Esq; Speaker of the House of Commons. These. Haste.

SIR;

---

[1] JHC, 5:679–81.   [2] JHL, 10:452.

552

20 AUGUST 1648B

I have sent up this Gentleman,[3] to give you an accompt of the great and good hand of God towards you in the late victory obtained against the Enemy in these parts. After the conjunction of that party which I brought with me out of *Wales*, with the Northerne Forces about *Knaresborough*[4] and *Weatherby*,[5] hearing that the Enemy was advanced with their Army into *Lancashire*, we marched the next day, being the 13 of this instant *August*, to *Oately*,[6] (having cast off our Traine,[7] and sent it to *Knaresborough*, because of the difficulty of marching therewith through *Craven*;[8] and to the end we might with more expedition attend the Enemies motion) and from thence the 14. to *Skipton*,[9] the 15. to *Gysburne*,[10] the 16. to *Holder Bridge*,[11] over *Ribble*, where we had a Councell of War, at which we had in consideration, Whether we should march to *Whalley*[12] that night, and so on to interpose betweene the Enemy and his further progresse into *Lancashire*, and so Southward, which we had some advertisement the Enemy intended, and since confirmed that they resolved for *London* it selfe; or whether to march immediately over the said Bridge, there being no other betwixt that and *Preston*,[13] and ingage the Enemy there; who we did believe would stand his ground, because we had information that the Irish Forces under *Munroe*[14] lately came out of *Ireland*, which consisted of 1200. Horse and 1500 Foot, were on their march towards *Lancaster*[15] to joyne with them; It was thought that to ingage the Enemy to fight was our businesse; and the reason aforesaid giving us hopes that our marching

---

[3] Identified in the *Commons Journal* as Major James Berry who was given a £200 reward (he was escorted by Edward Sexby who received £100 [*JHC*, 5:680]).

[4] Knaresborough, a market town in North Yorkshire (close to Harrogate and due north of Leeds).

[5] Wetherby, a market town on the Great North Road 12 miles north-west of Knaresborough.

[6] Otley, Yorkshire, five miles North East of Leeds. Otley is 18 miles from Knaresborough.

[7] Train = artillery train.

[8] Craven, a farming region in the Yorkshire Pennines; the area around the market town of Skipton.

[9] Skipton, a market town in the West Riding of Yorkshire, 15 miles from Otley.

[10] Gisburn, a market town in the Ribble Valley on the Lancashire side of the Pennines and 11 miles from Skipton.

[11] Holder Bridge (correctly [as in [A]] Hodder Bridge on the river Hodder), which joins the Ribble at Great Mitton, south of Clitheroe. The march on that day was 15 miles.

[12] Whalley, a large Lancashire village, three miles on the south side of the Ribble on the river Calder.

[13] Preston, a large borough 12 miles to the west of Whalley.

[14] Major General George Monro, a senior officer in the Scottish Covenanter army in the north of Ireland (1642–8) and a veteran of the Thirty Years War. Sir George Monro, of Culrain and Newmore (d. 1694), army officer. See *ODNB*.

[15] Lancaster, the county town of Lancashire and 22 miles north of Preston. But note that [A] has 'was on their march towards Lancashire'. The Scots were far south of Lancaster, so [A] gives the clearer sense.

THE LETTERS, WRITINGS, AND SPEECHES OF OLIVER CROMWELL

on the North side of *Ribble* would effect it; It was resolved we should march over the Bridge, which accordingly we did, and that night quartered the whole Army in the fields by *StonyHurst*-Hall,[16] being Mr. *Sherburnes* house,[17] a place nine miles distant from *Preston*, Very early the next morning we marched towards *Preston*, having intelligence that the Enemy was drawing together there abouts from all his out quarters; we drew out a forlorn[18] of about 200. Horse and 400. Foot, the Horse commanded by Major *Smithson*,[19] the Foot by Major *Pounell*;[20] our Forlorn of Horse marched within a mile, where the Enemy was drawne up in the inclosed grounds by *Preston* on that side next us; And there upon a Moore about halfe a mile distant from the Enemies Army, meet with their Scouts and out-Guard;[21] and did behave themselves with that valour and courage, as made their Guards (which consisted both of Horse and Foot) to quit their ground, and tooke divers prisoners, holding this dispute with them untill our Forlorne of Foot came up for their Justification;[22] And by these we had opportunity to bring up our whole Army. So soone as our Foot [23] and Horse were come up, we resolved that night to ingage them if we could; and therefore advancing with our Forlornes, and putting the rest of the Army into as good a possture as the ground would beare (which was totally inconvenient for our Horse, being all in closure, and myerye ground)[24] we pressed upon them, the Regiments of Foot were ordered as followeth, There being a lane very deepe and ill up to the Enemies Army and leading to the Towne, we Commanded two Regiments of Horse, the first whereof was Colonell *Harrisons*,[25] and next was my owne, to charge up that Lane, and on either side of them advanced the Battle, which were Lievtenant Colonell *Reads*,[26]

---

[16] Stonyhurst House, ancient home of the Sherburnes at Hurst Green, two miles west of Hodder Bridge on the north bank of the Ribble.

[17] See **1648 08 17**, n. 14.

[18] Forlorn = forlorn hope (advance party), a party of men to seek out the enemy's position.

[19] Major George Smithson. See the *Online Directory of Parliamentarian Army Officers*. He was more recently a major in Fairfax's regiment of horse (Wanklyn, *Reconstructing*, 1:164).

[20] Major Pownall. There is no major Pownall (Pownell, Pennell) in Wanklyn, *Reconstructing* or in Firth and Davies. Perhaps he was the Captain Henry Pownall who had been briefly a major in early 1645 but served as a captain after a merger of regiments and at Preston (see the *Online Directory of Parliamentarian Army Officers*).

[21] Out-guard = outpost (*OED*).   [22] 'for their justification' = 'to give them support'.

[23] [A] has 'your foot'.   [24] 'myery' = 'swampy' (*OED*).   [25] Thomas Harrison.

[26] Lieutenant-Colonel Thomas Reade (commanding Robert Overton's regiment in his absence). See the *Online Directory of Parliamentarian Army*, and Wanklyn, *Reconstructing*, many entries via the index.

20 AUGUST 1648B

Colonell *Deanes*,[27] and Colonell *Prides*[28] on the right, Colonell *Brights*[29] and my Lord Generals[30] on the left, and Colonell *Ashton*[31] with the *Lancashire* Regiments in reserve; we ordered Colonell *Thornhaugh*,[32] and Colonell *Twisletons*[33] Regiments of Horse on the right, and one Regiment in reserve for the Lane, and the remaining Hotse [34] on the left; so that at last we came to a hedge dispute, the greatest of the impression from the Enemy being upon our left wing, and upon the Battell on both sides the Lane, and upon our Horse in the Lane, in all which places the Enemie was forced from their ground after foure houres dispute, until we came to the Towne, into which foure Troopes of my Regiment first entered and being well seconded by Colonell *Harrisons* Regiment, charged the Enemy in the Towne, and cleared the Streets, there came no hands of our Foot to fight that day, but did it with incredible valour and resolution, amongst which Colonell *Brights*, my Lord Generall, Lieutenant Colonell *Reads*, and Colonell *Ashtons* had the greatest worke, they often comming to push of Pike and to close firings, and alwaies making the Enemy to recoyle, and indeed I must needs say, God was as much seene in the valour of the Officers and Souldiers of these before mentioned, as in any action that hath beene performed, the Enemy making (though he was still worsted) very stiffe and sturdy resistance, Colonell *Deanes*, and Colonell *Prides* out winging the Enemy could not come to so much share of the action, the Enemy shoging[35] downe towards the Bridge, and keeping almost all in reserve, that so he might bring fresh hands often to fight, which we not knowing but least we should be out winged, placed those two Regiments to inlarge our right wing, which was the cause they had not at that time so great a share in that action; at the last the Enemy

---

[27] Richard Deane (bap. 1610, d. 1653), army and naval officer and regicide. See *ODNB*.

[28] Thomas Pride, appointed Lord Pride under the Protectorate (d. 1658), parliamentarian army officer and regicide. See *ODNB*.

[29] For Sir John Bright.

[30] Lord General Fairfax's regiment was commanded by Lt. Col. William Cowell, who was to die of wounds sustained during the battle of Preston. See Firth and Davies, *Regimental History*, 1:317–29, 359–60, 365; and for Cromwell's letter to Fairfax as his service and widow's rights, see **1648 09 11**.

[31] Colonel Ralph Assheton, MP of Middleton. See **1648 08 17** n. 12.

[32] A. C. Wood, 'Colonel Francis Thornhaugh', *Transactions of the Thoroton Society*, 38 (1934) and available online at http://www.nottshistory.org.uk/articles/tts/tts1934/ thornhagh1.htm.

[33] Colonel Phillip Twistleton. See Wanklyn, *Reconstructing*, 1:52, 62, 73, 83, 94, 106.

[34] Misprint for Horse (as in [A]).

[35] Shoging, a term Cromwell uses several times. The *OED* definition is not especially helpful. Sophia Lomas suggests that 'shog is from the same root as *shock*'; 'shogging', a word of Oliver's in such cases, signifies moving by pulses, intermittently.

THE LETTERS, WRITINGS, AND SPEECHES OF OLIVER CROMWELL

was put into disorder, many men slain, many prisoners taken; the Duke[36] with most of the Scots Horse and Foot retreated over the Bridge, where after a very hot dispute betwixt the *Lancashire* Regiments, part of my Lord Generals and them being at push of Pike, they were beaten from the Bridge, and our Horse and Foot following them, killed many, and tooke divers prisoners, and wee possessed the Bridge over *Darwent*[37] and a few Houses there, the Enemy being drawne up within Musquet shot of us where we lay that night, we not being able to attempt further upon the Enemy, the night preventing us; in this posture did the Enemy and we lie the most part of that night; upon our entering the Towne, many of the Enemies Horse fled towards *Lancaster*, in the chase of whom went divers of our Horse, who pursued them neare ten miles, and had execution of them, and tooke about five hundred Horse, and many prisoners; We possessed in this Fight very much of the Enemies Ammunition,

I beleeve they lost foure or five thousand Armes, the number of the slain we judge to be about a thousand, the prisoners we took were about four thousand. In the night the Duke was drawing off his Army towards *Wiggon*,[38] we were so wearied with the dispute that we did not so well attend the Enemies going off as might have been, by means whereof the Enemy was gotten at least three miles with his reare before ours got to them. I ordered Colonell *Thornhaugh* to Command two or three Regiments of Horse to follow the Enemy if it were possible, to make him stand till could bring up the Army: The Enemy marched away seven or eight thousand Foot, and about foure thousand Horse, we followed him with about three thousand Foote, and two thousand five hundred Horse and Dragoones, and in this prosecution that worthy Gentleman Colonell *Thornhaugh* pressing too boldly was slaiue,[39] being run into the body, and thigh, and head, by the Enemies Launcers, (and give me leave to say, he was a man as faithfull and gallant in your service as any, and one who often heretofore lost bloud in your quarrell, and how his last; he hath left some behind him to inherit a Fathers honour, and a sad Widdow, both now the interest of the Common-wealth)[40] our Horse still prosecuted the Enemy, killing and taking divers all the way, at last the enemy drew up

---

[36] James Hamilton, first duke of Hamilton.

[37] River Darwen, a Lancashire river that flows south of the Ribble until it joins it at Walton-le-dale, upstream from Preston.

[38] Wiggon = Wigan, a parliamentary borough midway between Preston and Warrington.

[39] Slaiue is a misprint for 'slaine' (as in [A]).

[40] On receipt of this letter, the Commons ordered the committee of the Northern Association to 'consider and present some way of Recompense and Satisfaction to the Wife and Children of Colonel Thornhaugh for his gallant service': *JHC*, 5:680.

556

20 AUGUST 1648B

within three miles of *Wiggon*, and by that time our Army was come up they drew off againe and recovered *Wiggon* before we could attempt any thing upon them, we lay that night in the field close by the Enemy, being very dirty and weary, and having marched twelve miles of such ground as I never rod in all my life, the day being very wet we had some skirmishing that nigh;[41] with the Enemy neere the Towne, where we tooke Major Generall *Van Druske*[42] and a Collonell,[43] and killed some principall Officers, and tooke about a hundred prisoners, where also I received a Letter from Duke *Hamilton* for civill usage towards his Kinsman Colonell *Hamilton*[44] whom he left wounded there.

We took also Col. *Hurrey*,[45] and Lieut. Col. *Ennis*,[46] sometimes in your service. The next morning the enemy marched towards *Warrington*, and we at the heeles of them, the town of *Wiggon* a great and poore town, and very Malignant,[47] were plundered almost to their skins by them; we could not ingage the enemy untill we came within three miles of *Warrington*,[48] and there the enemy made a stand at a passe neare *Winwicke*,[49] we held them in some dispute untill our Army was come up, they maintaining the passe with great resolution for many hours, ours and theirs comming to push of pike, and to very close charges, and forced us to give ground, but our men by the blessing of God quickly recovered it, and charging very home upon them beat them from their standing, where we killed about a thousand of them, and tooke (as we beleeve) about two thousand prisoners, and prosecuted them home to *Warrington* town, where they possessed the Bridge which had a strong Barracado and a Worke upon it, formerly made very defensive; as soone as we came thither I received a Message from Lieut. Generall *Baily*,[50]

[41] [A] correctly has 'night'.

[42] For Major General Jonas van Druschke, a Dutchman, see E. M. Furgol, *A Regimental History of the Covenanting Armies* (Edinburgh, 1990), pp. 193–6.

[43] Probably John Innes, for whom see Furgol, *Covenanting Armies*, pp. 253–4 and 323–6.

[44] Probably Lt Col Claude Hamilton, whom we know to have been captured with an arm broken by a musket ball on 17 August (J. Turner, *Memoirs of His Own Life and Times 1632–1670*, T. Thomson, ed., *Bannantyne Club*, 28 [1829]), p. 64. But possibly Lt Col William Hamilton, captured at Winwick on 19 August (Furgol, *Covenanting Armies*, p. 271).

[45] Sir John Urry [Hurry] (d. 1650), army officer. See *ODNB*; and Furgol, *Covenanting Armies*, pp. 240–1.

[46] Colonel Ennis. Not identified.

[47] Wigan was a borough which had long been under the control of successive bishops of Chester, the most recent of whom, John Bridgeman, had a son (Orlando Bridgeman who was one of the most active royalist officers in the area).

[48] A town on the north bank of the Mersey, midway between Liverpool and Manchester.

[49] A large village, three miles north of Warrington.

[50] For William Baillie (d. 1653), army officer, see *ODNB*. Cromwell was unaware that all but 250 of Baillie's men had thrown down their arms and fled and that Baillie had seriously contemplated suicide.

THE LETTERS, WRITINGS, AND SPEECHES OF OLIVER CROMWELL

desiring some capitulation, to which I yeelded, considering the strength of the passe, and that I could not goe over the river within ten miles of *Warrington* with the Army; I gave him these tearms, That he should surrender himselfe, and all his Officers and Souldiers prisoners of War, with all his Armes and Ammunition and Horses to me, I giving quarter for life, and promising civill usage, which accordingly is done, and the Commissioners deputed by me have received, and are receiving all the Armes and Ammunition which will be as they tell me about foure thousand compleat Armes, and as many prisoners. And thus you have their Infantry totally ruined, what Colonells or Officers are with Lieutenant Generall *Bailey*, I have not yet received the List. The Duke is marched with his remaining Horse, which are about 3000. towards *Namptwich*,[51] where the Gentlemen of the Country have taken about 500. of them, of which they sent me word this day; the Country will scarce suffer any of my men to passe, except they have my hand, telling them, They are *Scots*; they bring in and kill divers as they light upon them. Most of the Nobility of *Scotland* are with the Duke, if I had a thousand Horse that could but trot thirty miles I should not doubt but to give a very good account of them; but truly we are so harrased and hagled out in this businesse that we are not able to doe more than walke an easie pace after them. I have sent Post to my Lord *Grey*[52] to Sir *Hen. Cholmley*, and Sir *Edw. Roads*,[53] to gather all together with speed for their prosecution, as likewise to acquaint the Governour of *Stafford*[54] therewith; I heare *Munro*[55] is about *Cumberland* with the Horse that ran away, and his *Irish* Horse and Foot, which are a considerable body; I have left Colonell *Ashtons* three Regiments of Foot with seven Troops of Horse, six of *Lancashire*, and one of *Cumberland* at Preston, and ordered Col. *Scroope*[56] with five Troops of Horse, and two Troops of Dragoons, with two Regiments of Foot, *viz.* Col. *Lassells*,[57] and Col. *Wastalls*[58] to imbody with them, by which I hope they

---

[51] Nantwich, a market town in Cheshire, about 30 miles south of Warrington.

[52] Thomas Grey, Lord Grey of Groby, a peer closely aligned to the Army's interest throughout the political crises of 1647–9.

[53] Cromwell's letter to Cholmley and Rodes is the one given above, **1648 08 20a**.

[54] The longstanding governor of Stafford was Henry Stone, for whom see innumerable references in Dore, *Brereton Letter Books*, vols. 1–2, Record Society of Lancashire and Cheshire Record Society, vol. 123 (1983–4) and vol. 128 (1990) and I. Carr and I. Atherton, eds., vol. 3, Staffordshire Record Society, 4th series, vol. 21 (2007). The Commons wrote to him as governor of Stafford on 14 August 1648 (*JHC*, 5:671).

[55] See above, n. 16.

[56] For Adrian Scrope (1601–60), army officer and regicide. See *ODNB*.

[57] Col. Francis Lascelles. See the *Online Directory of Parliamentarian Army Officers*.

[58] Col. John Wastell. See the *Online Directory of Parliamentarian Army Officers*.

will be able to make a resistance till we can come up to them, and have ordered them to put their Prisoners to the Sword if the *Scots* shall presume to advance upon them, because they cannot bring them off with security.

Thus you have a Narrative of the particulars of the successe which God hath given you, which I could hardly at this time have done, considering the multiplicity of businesse; but truly when I was once engaged in it, I could hardly tell how to say lesse, there being so much of God; and I was not willing to say more, least there should seeme to be any thing of man, onely give me leave to adde one word shewing the disparity of the Forces on both sides, that so you may see, and all the world acknowledge the great hand of God in this businesse; The *Scots* Army could not be lesse than 12000. effective Foot well armed, and 5000. Horse, *Langdale*[59] not lesse than 2500. Foot, and 1500. Horse, in all one and twenty thousand; and truly very few of their Foot but were as well armed, if not better than yours, and at divers disputes did fight two or three houres before they would quit their ground: Yours were about 2500. Horse and Dragoons of your old Army, about 4000. Foot of your old Army also,[60] about 1600. *Lancashire* Foot, and about 500. *Lancashire* Horse, in all about 8600. you see by computation about 2000. of the Enemy slaine, betwixt eight and nine thousand Prisoners, besides what are lurking in Hedges and private places, which the Country daily bring in or destroy. Where *Langdale* and his broken Forces are, I know not, but they are exceedingly shattered; surely Sir, this is nothing but the hand of God, praise onely belongs to him, and where ever any thing in this world is exalted, or exalts it selfe, God will pull it downe, or this is the day wherein he alone will be exalted; it is not fit for me to give advice, nor to say a word what use should be made of this more than to pray you, and all that acknowledge God, that they would onely exalt him, and not hate his people who are as the apple of his eye, and for whom even Kings shall be reproved; in fulfilling the end of your Magistracy, in seeking the peace and welfare of the people of this Land, that all that will live quietly and peaceably may have countenance from you; and they that are implacable, and will not leave troubling the Land, may speedily be destroyed out of the Land; and if you take courage in this God will blesse you, and good men will stand by you, and God will have glory, and the Land will have happinesse by you, in despight of all your enemies, which shall be the prayer, of

[59] For Marmaduke Langdale, first Baron Langdale (bap. 1598, d. 1661), royalist army officer, see ODNB.

[60] In [A], the comma comes before the 'also', slightly changing the meaning.

THE LETTERS, WRITINGS, AND SPEECHES OF OLIVER CROMWELL

Your most humble and faithfull servant

O. Crumwell

20 August.
POSTSCRIPT
We have not in all of this lost a considerable Officer but Colonell Thornhaugh, *and not many Souldiers, considering the service, but many are wounded, our Hors almost destroyed, and our Foot beaten out of Cloaths, Shooes, and Stockings; our Horse will need recruit, and our Foot Regiments need to be recruited also, for they are very much shaken with hard marchings, very much wanting supplyes of money; some of those which were with me in* Wales *not having had any pay since before our march thither.*[61] *I humbly crave, That some course be taken to dispose of the Prisoners, the trouble and extreame charge of the Country where they lye is more then the danger of their escape; I thinke they would not goe home if they might without a Convoy, they are so fearfull of the Country from whom they have deserved so ill; ten men will keep a thousand of them from running away.*[62]

⸎

1648 08 23a

Letter from Oliver Cromwell probably to the Committee at York

Date: 23 August 1648
Source: Packets of Letters from Scotland, and the North of England to Members of the House of Commons [published by Robert Ibbotson, 28 August 1648] (N&S, 480.33; Thomason / E.461[29]), pp. 2–3 (contemporary print)

This short letter exists in two contemporary forms. One, in an apparently mid-seventeenth-century hand survives (via a nineteenth-century collector) and its previous

---

[61] The sixty-two words in [B] from 'almost destroyed' to 'before our march thither' are replaced in [A] by just two words, 'much wearied'.

[62] [B] (but not [A]) concludes: '*Die Mercurii* 23 *August.* 1648. Ordered by the Lords and Commons in Parliament Assembled, That Thursday come fortnight, the seventh of *September* next, be appointed a day of solemne Thanksgiving thorow the whole Kingdome, unto Almighty God, for his wonderfull great mercy and successe bestowed upon the Parliament Forces under the Command of Lieutenant Generall *Cromwell*, against the whole Scots Army under the Conduct and Command of Duke *Hamilton* on the seventeenth, eighteenth, and nineteenth of this present *August* in *Lancashire. Joh. Brown Cler. Parliamentorum.*'

560

23 AUGUST 1648A

history is not known except for a scribbled 'James Greenwood' on the verso.[1] The other is printed in a collection of five letters from officers in the New Model dated between 21 and 29 August plus a list of *c*.300 prisoners taken at the battle of Preston. The manuscript version is riddled with evident small errors and omissions (a rushed transcript?), and since the provenance of the pamphlet is known, and the manuscript provenance is obscure, this edition follows the pamphlet.

Neither copy states to whom Cromwell is writing, but the covering letter to the pamphlet links it closely to a letter from Major General Lambert that was addressed to the committee at York and there is an allusion to just such a letter in Cromwell's letter to the Derby House Committee written later on the same day: 'I have Sente to Yorkshire[2] & to my Lord Gray to Alarame all parts to A prosecution'.

———

Gentlemen

I Have intelligence even now come to my hands that Duke Hamilton,[3] with a wearied body of Horse is drawing towards *Pontefaite*,[4] where probably he may lodge himselfe, and rest his horse, as not daring to continue in these Counties whence we have driven him, the country people rising in such numbers & stops his passage at every bridge, Major Gen. *Lambert*[5] with a very considerable force pursues him at the heeles, I desire you that you would get together what force you can, to put a stop to any further designs they may have, and to be ready to joyne with Maj. Gen.*Lambert*, if there shall be need: I am marching Northward, with the greatest part of the Army, where, I shall bee glad to heare from you I rest Gentlemen

Your very affectionate friend and servant
OL CRUMWELL
Wigan[6] *23 Aug. 1648*

Gentlemen

I Could wish you would draw out whatever force you Have, either to be in his reare, or to impede his march, for I am perswaded if he, or the greatest part of

---

[1] Museum of London, Tangye MS 706, no. 50.

[2] Probably a reference to **1648 08 23b**.   [3] James Hamilton, first duke of Hamilton.

[4] Pontefaite = a misprint for Pontefract (Tangye MS 706, no. 50 has 'Pomfret'). Pontefract is a town with a fortified castle in West Yorkshire. In fact the garrison held out against the New Model until March 1649.

[5] John Lambert [Lambart] (bap. 1619, d. 1684), parliamentary soldier and regicide. See *ODNB*.

[6] Wigan, a parliamentary borough in Lancashire about 14 miles north of Warrington from where Cromwell had also written his letters on 20 August.

those that be with him be taken, it would make an end of the businesse of Scotland

OL. Crumwell

1648 08 23b
Letter from Oliver Cromwell to the Committee at Derby House

Date: 23 August 1648
Source: Bodl., MS Tanner 57/1, fos 229r–230v (no. 116) (autograph)

This letter survives only in its original form. It is damaged in places and 'much injured by mildew and moths'. Many of the words are easy to infer (even if the precise spelling cannot be certain). Sophia Lomas, who saw it with a century less wear and tear and who added some of the worst passages that Carlyle had omitted, seems very careful in inferring missing words (and some are partially missing, not just illegible).[1] Our reading is assisted by the use of ultraviolet lamps and magnification of high-resolution digital images. The letter appears to be in the hand of William Rowe, Cromwell's scoutmaster and has Cromwell's own signature on it (and fragments of his seal).

Leiut. Grall Cromwell
August 23 1648[2]
[seal]
For the right hoble. the Committee of Lords and Commons at Derby house.[3]
these. hast hast[4]
O Crom{well}[5]

Wiggen[6] august the 23th 1648.[7]

---

[1] Carlyle-Lomas, 3:258–60.
[2] This endorsement is in two different contemporary hands.
[3] The Derby House Committee is the name given to the central executive committee of the Long Parliament after the Scots withdrew from the Committee of Both Kingdoms in 1647. It had substantially the same English membership as the Committee of Both Kingdoms and met in Derby House in Cannon Row, Westminster from 1644 to 1650.
[4] The second 'hast(e)' is in a different hand, quite possibly Cromwell's.
[5] Throughout this letter, text in { } brackets is conjectural.
[6] Wigan, a borough in central Lancashire.
[7] This address appears to be Cromwell's own hand.

23 AUGUST 1648B

My Lords & Gen:

I did not (beinge Straighthened with time) Send you an accompt of the great blessinge of god uppon your Army, I trust it is Satisfactory to your Lordshps: that the howse had it Soe Fully presented to them.[8] My Lords it cannot bee Imagined that Soe great a busines as this could bee without Some {lo}sse, Although I {co} nfes v{e}ry Littell Compa{red} with the f weigh{ht}y{n}es of the engagemente, theere beinge o{n} our parte not on hundr{e}d Slai{n}e {y}et many wounded and to our Lit{t}ell {it} is areall we{a}k{en}inge for indeed wee are {bu}t a handfull & I {   }t[9] to your Loships: whether you will thinke fitt or noe {to} recruite our L[o] sse [10] wee havinge but Five poore regtt: of Foott & o{ur} horsse Soe Exceedingly batterd as I never Saw them in all my Life: It is not to bee dowbted: but your ene-myes designes are deep. this blow will make them very angry,: the principles they went uppon ~~wheere~~ \weare/ [11] Such as should A Littell awaken English men: for I have it from very good hands of theyre owne partie that the Duke[12] made this the {   [ ]}mente[13] to his armye that that the Lands of the {   }tye { }'Ge{   }ld keepe Share of them {   }e offic{   }[]yes to theyre private {Sou}ldyers and {   }poss{ } they would b{r}inge {   } theyre F{amil}yes which accordingly is done, in parte theere being a transplantation of many wemen & children & of whole Famylyes in Westmorland & Cumberland as I am Credibly Informed much more might bee Saide but I forbeare I offer it to your Loshps: that monny may bee to pay the Foot & horsse to {some} equallitie Some of thosse that are heere Since 14 dayes before I marched from Windsor[14] into Wales have not had any paye: And amongst the horsse my owne regtt & Some others are much behinde, as longe as this [cost][15] of warr must continue I{wi}sh your Lordhps: [ ] [16]Manage it for the beste {advan}tage & not {   be} wantinge to your Selfes in {what} is necessarye

---

[8] See **1648 08 23a**.

[9] Not legible. Lomas confidently says 'submit'(Carlyle-Lomas, 3:257n), which makes sense and the tail of 's' may just be there. Certainly there appear to be five to seven letters, ending in 't'.

[10] From the spacing and possible wear and tear, it might have been 'losses', but 'losse' is cer-tain, plural hypothetical.

[11] This correction is in Cromwell's hand.

[12] James Hamilton, first duke of Hamilton (1606–49), politician. See *ODNB*.

[13] Space for nine letters. The half-visible word is presumably 'argumente'. Throughout we have left an equivalent number of spaces where letters are lost or illegible.

[14] Windsor, borough and royal castle in Berkshire and headquarters of the Army in the late winter of 1647–8.

[15] This is Lomas's speculation, not verifiable now.

[16] This is illegible but is possibly 'must'; Lomas reads it as 'may', which works better. But for 'may' to be correct there would be a large space before 'Manage'.

which is the end of my offeringe theesse t{hi}ngs to y{o}u, My Lo{rdshipp's} Money is not for Contingen\cys/ { so}¹⁷ as weere to bee wi{sh}ed wee have very many {th}ings to dooe w{hich} {m}ight bee better done if wee had whe{[rewi]}thall our Foot want clothes Showes¹⁸ & Stokins¹⁹ theese [w]ayes & weather have Shattered them all to peeces, that which was the great blowe to our horsse was (besides the weather & incessente marches) our march ten miles to fight with the enemye & A Fight continuinge fowre howres In as dirty a place as ever I saw horsses Stand in and uppon the matter the continuance of this fight two dayes more together in our Followinge of the en{e}mye & Lyin{g clo}sse²⁰ by hime in the myre & { u}ntill att { } wee broke hime att or neere { } a g{ p}artie of our horsse havenge { } miles { }rds Lancaster²¹ who came upp a { } to us and { } wheere with us in all the action theese things I thought fitt to Intimate not knowing what is fitt to aske because I know not how your affaires Stand nor what: you can Supplye. I have Sent maior: Genll: Lambart²² uppon the day I receved this inclosed with above 2000 horsse & dragoones and A bout 1400 Foot in prossecution of the Duke²³ and the nobillitie of Scotland with hime who will I doubt not have the blessinge of God with hime in the bussnes but indeed his horsse are excedinge weake and weary: I have Sente to Yorkshire²⁴ & to my Lord Gray²⁵ to Alarame all parts to A prosecution and if they bee not wanttinge to the worke I See not how many can Escape I am march{ed m}y Selfe bake towards Presto{n a}nd Soe on towards Munroe²⁶ or otherwisse as God Sh{a}ll Directe As things fall out I shall represente them to yow and remayne My lords & Gent:
Your most hum{ble servant}
O Cromwell

---

¹⁷ This is Lomas's speculation, not verifiable now. ¹⁸ Shows = shoes?
¹⁹ Stockins = stockings?
²⁰ Lomas thinks the missing letters are 'ying close'. Since the top of an 'l' is just visible, this is plausible, although that would mean that a short word has been lost between the two words.
²¹ Lancaster, the county town of Lancashire, 30 miles north of where Cromwell is writing from.
²² John Lambert [Lambart] (bap. 1619, d. 1684), parliamentarian soldier and politician. See ODNB.
²³ James Hamilton, first duke of Hamilton, politician.
²⁴ Probably a reference to **1648 08 23a**.
²⁵ See Cromwell's comment in **1648 08 20b**: 'I have sent post to my Lord Grey.'
²⁶ Sir George Monro, of Culrain and Newmore (d. 1694), army officer. See ODNB.

1 SEPTEMBER 1648

1648 09 01
Letter from Oliver Cromwell to Oliver St John

Date: 1 September 1648
Source: BL, Stowe MS 184, fos 145r–v ([probable] holograph)

This—like the letter a decade earlier to St John's wife (**1638 10 13**)—is Cromwell writing for no obvious purpose other than to bare his soul. After many months when bible citation is absent from his writings, it returns here with a vengeance.

The version of the letter presented here is *probably* a holograph. Although the lay-out is unusual for Cromwell (the letter completed on the verso, the address at the bottom not top of the verso, no seal), the handwriting looks to be Cromwell's and it has been folded and has the appearance of having travelled. The British Library cataloguer thought it a copy, perhaps because the other Cromwell letter in the volume is a copy of another letter to St John (**1643 09 11**). There are also two early copies of this letter also in the British Library viz.

[A] BL, Add. MS 33643 fos 57r–v.

[B] BL, Add. MS 4107 fos 13r–v.

The first of these, [A], comes from a late seventeenth-century collection of papers of the Ramsey branch of the Cromwell family—i.e. Cromwell's father's elder brother's descendants (the volume is titled 'Cromwell family correspondence 1617–1661'). It claims to be an exact copy 'even to the letter and very stopps' although its use of dashes to denote new paragraphs and replacement of the word 'and' on five occasions by ampersands is not authentically Cromwellian. Otherwise there are a few minor differences of spelling and punctuation. Version [B] is the one used in previous editions and is a copy made by Thomas Birch (1705 –66), the Whig historian. It modernises spelling and punctuation but otherwise introduces no significant alternative readings and can be disregarded.

Deere Sir
I cann Say nothinge, But Suerly the Lord our God
is a great, and glorious God. Hee only is worthye
to bee feared, and trusted, and his appearances
patientlye to bee waited for, Hee will not fayle his
people. Lett every thinge that hath breath praise
the Lord.[1] Remember my love to my deere brother,

---

[1] Exactly as in the *KJV* of Psalm 150:6.

565

(H.V.)[2] I pray hee make not too little nor I too much
of outward dispensations God preserve us all, that
wee in Simplicitye of our Spirits may patiently
attend upon Him, and lett us not bee carefull
what use man will make of theise actinges, they
shall, will they nill they, fulfill the good pleasure
of God, and wee shall Serve our generations.[3]
Our rest we Expect else where, that wilbe durable. Care wee not for to morrowe, nor for
any thinge, this Scripture has beene of great
staye to mee, reade itt, Isay 8. 10th. 13. 14. reade all
the Chapter.[4] I am informed from good handes that
a poore godlye man died in Preston the day before
the fight, and beinge Sicke neere the hower
of his death Hee desired the woeman that looked
to him, to fetch him a handfull of grasse, Shee
did Soe, and when hee receaved itt, Hee asked
whether it would whither or not now it was
cutt, the woeman Said yea, Hee replyed Soe
Should this Armie of the Scotts doe and come to
nothinge, soe Soone as our's did but apeare

---

[2] H.V. = Henry Vane. This is almost certainly the message Vane is referring back to in 1656 in *The proceeds of the Protector (so called) and his Councill against Sir Henry Vane, Knight* (pp. 6–7) (Wing / P3629): 'The Messuage which in former times you sent me, is in my *Memory still*, it was immediately after the Lord had appeared with you against Duke *Hamiltons* Army, when you bid a Friend of mine, tell your Brother *Vane* (for so you then thought fit to call me) that you were as much unsatisfied with his passive and suffering principles, as he was with your active; and indeed I must crave leave to make you this Reply at this time, that I am as little satisfied with your active, and *self-establishing Principles*, in the lively colours wherein daily they shew themselves, as you are or can be with my *passive Ones*, and am willing in this to joyn issue with you, and to begg of the Lord to judge between us and to give the decision according *to truth and righteousnesse*.'

[3] Echoes Acts 13:36 (*KJV*): 'For David, after he had served his own generation by the will of God, fell on sleep, and was laid unto his fathers, and saw corruption.'

[4] Isaiah 8:10, 13, 14 (*KJV*): '(10) Take counsel together, and it shall come to nought; speak the word, and it shall not stand: for God *is* with us. (13) Sanctify the LORD of hosts himself; and *let* him *be* your fear, and *let* him *be* your dread. (14) And he shall be for a sanctuary; but for a stone of stumbling and for a rock of offence to both the houses of Israel, for a gin and for a snare to the inhabitants of Jerusalem.' See John Morrill, 'How Oliver Cromwell Thought', in J. Morrow and J. Scott, eds., *Liberty, Authority, Formality: Political Ideas and Culture 1600–1900* (2008), pp. 89–111, esp. at p. 94.

or words to this Effect, and soe immediatly dyed. my Service to mr W.P.,[5] Sir J.E.[6] and the rest of our good freindes. I hope I doe often remember you.

yours O Cromwell

Sept. 1st. Knaesburgh[7]

My Service to Frank Russell[8]

and honest Pickeringe[9]

For my Worthye freind
Oliver St Johns Esqr
Solicitor General
Att Lincoln's Inn
Darbie House
Theise

---

[5] W.P. Almost certainly William Pierrepoint (1607/8–78), politician. See *ODNB*. He was a member of the Derby House Committee.

[6] Sir J.E. Almost certainly Sir John Evelyn of Wiltshire, for whom see Sir John Evelyn (1601–85), politician, in *ODNB*. He was a member of the Derby House Committee.

[7] Knaresborough, the Yorkshire borough with a castle occupied by royalists that held out until March 1649.

[8] Francis Russell had fought with Cromwell in the army of the Eastern Association, become a colonel in the New Model and his daughter married (in 1653) Henry, Cromwell's younger surviving son. According to *ODNB*, in the life of Henry Cromwell (1628–74), soldier, politician and lord lieutenant of Ireland, 'Russell was a close friend and comrade in arms of Oliver Cromwell and had campaigned with him in East Anglia and elsewhere during the civil wars, succeeding him as governor of Ely.'

[9] Sir Gilbert Pickering, first baronet, appointed Lord Pickering under the Protectorate (1611–68), politician. See *ODNB*.

THE LETTERS, WRITINGS, AND SPEECHES OF OLIVER CROMWELL

1648 09 02

Letter from Oliver Cromwell to Philip Wharton, Lord Wharton

Date: 2 September 1648
Source: Bodl., MS Rawl. Letters 49, fos 25r–26v (holograph)

The holograph of this letter survives but is in poor condition, with large holes along two of the horizontal folds. The damage was already present when Thomas Birch transcribed it in 1742.[1]

The letter is, at best allusive, but it was evidently to congratulate Philip Lord Wharton on the birth of his third (but eldest surviving) son. Curiously there appears to be an unusually long gap between the birth of Thomas (presumably late August) and his recorded baptism (23 October 1648). But it also appears to refer to the recent death of an earlier child.

My Lord,[2]
You knowe how untoward I am att this
businesse of writinge,[3] Yett a word.
I beseech the Lord make us sensible of this
great mercye heere, which suerlye was much
more then my {   }[4] the house
expresseth, I trust {   }[5] age the
goodnesse of our God) time and oportunitye
to Speake of itt with you face to face. When
wee thinke of our God, what are wee![6]
\Oh/ His mercy \to/ the whole societye of Saincts
despised \jeered/ Saincts, lett them mocke onn
would wee were all Saincts, the best of

---

[1] T. Birch, ed., *A collection of the state papers of John Thurloe, esq.* (7 vols., 1742), I:99.
[2] Philip Wharton, fourth Baron Wharton (1613–96), politician. See *ODNB*. Wharton was a close political ally until they split over the regicide.
[3] This echoes Cromwell's letter [**1644 09 06**] to Valentine Walton.
[4] About sixteen letters are lost to the tear in the MS.
[5] About eighteen letters are lost to the tear in the MS.
[6] This looks like a very rare exclamation mark of Cromwell's, but it could be a very straight question mark.

568

2 SEPTEMBER 1648

us, are (God knowes) poore weake saincts,
yett saincts, if not Sheepe, Yett Lambes,
and must be fedd, wee have daylie
bread,[7] and shall have itt, in despite
of all enimies, theres enough in our
Fathers house, and Hee dispenseth itt
as our eyes {   }[8] behinde
then wee can {   },[9] { }[10] ite wee
for him, I thinke thorough theise outward mercyes (as wee call them) fayth
patience, love, hope all are exercised
and perfected, yea Christ is formed, and[11]
growes up in us \to a perfect man/. I know not how \well/ to destinguish, the difference is
only
in the Subiect, to a worldly man they are outward, to a Sainct, Christian.[12] but I
dispute not.
my Lord I rejoyce in your perticular meryce, I hope that is soe to you, if soe
itt shall not hurt you, not make you plott or shift for the younge Barron[13] to
make
him great. You will say Hee is God's to dispose off, and provide for, and there you
will
leave him. my love to the deere little Ladye,[14] better then the child, the Lord blesse
you both.

---

⁷ 'daily bread': from the Lord's Prayer (Matthew 6:11 or Luke 3:11). The surrounding text *sounds* biblical but does not contain actual quotations.

⁸ About seventeen letters are lost to the tear in the MS.

⁹ About nine letters are lost to the tear in the MS.

¹⁰ Just one or two letters lost to the tear in the MS.

¹¹ Having written so expansively to this point, and just as he reaches the meat of his letter, Cromwell reaches the end of the page and the rest has to be written in very cramped script horizontally in the right-hand margin.

¹² These three letters ('ian') are added in a significant redder shade of ink. Written over a full stop.

¹³ Thomas Wharton, first marquis of Wharton, first marquis of Malmesbury and first marquis of Catherlough (1648–1715), politician. See *ODNB*.

¹⁴ Presumably Wharton's wife, Jane, Lady Wharton (bap. 1618, d. 1658), daughter of Arthur Goodwin MP.

my love and service to all freindes \High/ [—]h and Lowe,[15] If you will my Lord and Lady
Moulgrave[16]
and willm Hill.[17] I am a [ ] truly

Your faythfull freind and humblest servant
O Cromwell

Sept. 2ᵈ. 1648.

[Seal]

For the Right hnble. the
Lord Wharton theise[18]
An original letter of Oliver Cromwells
Sept. 2 1648[19]

1648 09 07

Letter from Oliver Cromwell to Colonel Charles Fairfax [and (but struck out) Col. Henry Currer, Governor of Skipton]

Date: 7 September 1648
Source: Museum of London, Tangye MS 706, no. 73 (autograph)

This letter is in the hand of Cromwell's usual scribe, with Cromwell's autograph signature. It is written as he was rapidly marching on Scotland.

---

[15] These three words are difficult to make out, being written over something else.
[16] Edmund Sheffield, second earl of Mulgrave (1611–58), parliamentarian nobleman. See *ODNB*. This also mentions his wife, Elizabeth Cranfield (1607/8–72), daughter of Lionel Cranfield, first earl of Middlesex.
[17] Possibly William Hill, a Buckinghamshire JP (Carlyle-Lomas 1:354 fn. 3). Lady Mulgrave's father was a prominent Buckinghamshire landowner and (with John Hampden) knight of the shire for Buckinghamshire.
[18] This address is in Cromwell's hand.
[19] This is in eighteenth-century hand or hands.

8 SEPTEMBER 1648

To the hoble. Coll. Charles Fairfax[1] ~~and Coll C[ ]~~[2] ~~(governor of Skipton either of them~~ present

The enclosed peticon[3] comming to my hands I could not but recommend it to you, as being the fittest instrumte to doe them right, being neare to information which will leade you \to/ what wilbe most fitt to be donne I desire therefore you would please to give them their desires in the peticon, as being \in/ my opinion ~~the~~ very just I remaynne

Your very humble Servant

O Cromwell

Duresme[4] 7mber 7th. 48[5]

1648 09 08

Declaration (or remonstrance and resolution) of Lieutenant General Oliver Cromwell relating to Scottish prisoners of war

Date: 8 September 1648

Source: *Packets of letters from Scotland, and the north parts of England*, num. 26, 11 Sept. 1648, pp. 4–6 (N&S, 480.26; Thomason / E.463[8]) (contemporary print)

This printed declaration of Cromwell was said by its London publisher to have been copied from an original of 8 September. It also states that it was first published in York but no copy of that printing has been found. It may well have been written a few days earlier. It was printed in London by Robert Ibbitson, the regular Army printer. The pamphlet contains other letters and gives its date of publication as 11 September. Thomason acquired his copy on 13 September. A second version[1] was printed on 14 September and appears to be

---

[1] Charles Fairfax, uncle of Lord General Thomas Fairfax and an active parliamentarian. Cromwell had stayed with him on the eve of the battle of Marston Moor. Charles Fairfax, (1597–1673), antiquary and genealogist. See ODNB.

[2] The name is particularly heavily struck out. It definitely starts with 'c' and seems to end with 's'. The name is presumably a variant of 'Currer' since the governor at Skipton at the time was Henry Currer, for whom see Joseph Foster, *Pedigrees of the County Families of Yorkshire* (1874), item 273. Skipton is a market town in Yorkshire 15 miles north-east of Leeds.

[3] This has not survived.   [4] Duresme = Durham.   [5] i.e. 7 September 1648.

---

[1] *Blouldy Newes from the Lord Byron in Wales...and the Remonstrance and Declaration of Lieut.Gen. Cromwell...Septemb.14. Imprinted in London for G.H. 1648* (Wing / W2253; Thomason / E.463[15]).

THE LETTERS, WRITINGS, AND SPEECHES OF OLIVER CROMWELL

a slightly degraded version of Ibbitson's version (misspellings, changes to punctuation, words shortened as Parl. for Parliament). So the Ibbitson version is preferred, but there is one significant variant reading which is noted at the appropriate place.

———

A Declaration published by Lieutenant Gen. Crumwell.[2]

Whereas the Scottish Army under the Command of *James* Duke of *Hambleton*,[3] which lately invaded this Nation of *England*, is by the blessing of God upon the Parliaments Forces) defeated and overthrowne, and some thousands of their Souldiers and Officers are now prisoners in our hands, so that by reason of their great number, and want of sufficient Guards and Watches to keep them so carefully as need requires (the Army being imployed upon other Duty and Service of the Kingdome) divers may escape away, and many (both since and upon the pursuit) lye in private places in the Country: I thought it very just and necessary to give notice to all, and accordingly to Declare, That if any Scottishmen (Officers or Souldiers) lately Members of the said Scottish Army, and taken or escaped in, or since the late fight and pursuit, shall be found stragling in the Countreys, or running away from the places assigned them to remain in (till the pleasure of the Parliament, or His Excellency the Lord Generall[4] be knowne) it will be accounted a very good and acceptable Service to the Country and Kingdome of *England* for any person or persons to take and apprehend all such Scottishmen, and to carry them to any Officer having the charge of such prisoners; or (for want of such Officer) to the Committee or Governour of the next Garrison for the Parliament within the County where they shall be so taken, to be secured and kept in prison, as they shall finde most convenient. And the said Committee, Officer, or Governour respectively are desired to secure such of the said Prisoners as shall be so apprehended and brought unto them accordingly. And if any of the said Scottish Officers or Souldiers, shall make any resistance, and refuse to be taken or render themselves, all such persons well-affected to the Service of the Parliament and Kingdome of *England*, may, and are desired to fall upon, fight with, and stay[5] such refusers. But if the said prisoners shall continue and

---

[2] The *Bloudy Newes* version is headed 'The Remonstrance & Resolution of the Right Honorable, and truly valiant, Lieut.Gen.CROMWELL, in behalf of all His Majesties loyall, and free born people of ENGLAND, concerning the Scottish Nation, & their engaging against Religion, King, and Kingdom.'

[3] James, Hamilton, first duke of Hamilton.   [4] i.e. the Lord General Thomas Fairfax.

[5] *Bloudy Newes* has 'slay' not stay, which makes more sense. But if, as seems likely, this version is copied from *Packet of Letters* of 11 September, it remains more likely to be a misprint in *Bloudy Newes*.

11 SEPTEMBER 1648

remaine within the Places and Guards assigned for the keeping of them, that then no violence wrong, nor injury be offered to them by any meanes. Provided also, and speciall care is to be taken, that no Scottishman, residing within this Kingdome, and not having been a Member of the said Army, or such of the said Scottish prisoners, as shall have liberty given them, and sufficient Passes to goe to any place appointed, may not bee interrupted or troubled hereby.[6]

O. Crumwell.

Vera Copia, Septem. 8. 1648.
First Printed at Yorke by Tho. Broad, and now Re-printed.

1648 09 11
Letter from Oliver Cromwell to Thomas Fairfax, Lord Fairfax

Date: 11 September 1648
Source: BL, Lansdowne MS 1236, fos 89r–90v (holograph)

The letter itself is in Cromwell's hand, the address in another (almost certainly Cromwell's usual secretary). Cromwell commends the rights of the widow of one of Fairfax's own officers who had died during or in the aftermath of the battle of Preston. William Cowell was lieutenant colonel in Fairfax's own regiment of foot, having previously served with the earl of Essex (1642–5) and in Harley's regiment in the New Model (1645–7). He had joined Fairfax's regiment in June 1647 but that regiment had recently served with Cromwell in the Preston campaign and had played a leading role in that battle.[1]

---

[6] Bloudy Newes, between the text and the signature, adds: 'This Declaration and Remonstrance being assented to by the Lieutenant Generall, and the rest of the officers of the Army, were commanded to be forthwith published.'

[1] Firth and Davies, Regimental History, 1:320, 325–8, 359–60, 365. William Cowell was a gentleman's son and was apprenticed to the Haberdashers' Company in 1626 and made free of the Company in 1636. He was admitted to the London Artillery Company on 18 August 1640 (K. Bennet, The Cardew Rendle Roll: a biographical dictionary of members of the Honorary Artillery Company, 1537–1908 (2 vols., 2013), 1:582).

THE LETTERS, WRITINGS, AND SPEECHES OF OLIVER CROMWELL

[seals]

For his Excie the lord Fairfax
Genll of all the Parliaments
armyes   these

Lt. Generall Cromwell.
Sept. 11 1648[2]

'Letters in the warr time
tempore Ca: 1: Rs:'[3]

My Lord
since wee lost Leifnt. Col. Cowell,
his wife[4] came to mee neere North
Alserton,[5] much lamentinge her losse
and the sadd condition shee and her
children were left in. Hee was an
honest worthye man, Hee spent himselfe in Yours and the Kingdoms
service, Hee beinge a great trader
in London deserted itt to Serve the
Kingdom. Hee lent much monies
to the state, and I beleive few
out did him, Hee hath a great Ar-
reare due to him, Hee left a wife
and three smale children, but meanlye
provided for, upon his death bed Hee commended
this desier to mee, that I should befreind his
to the Parlnt. or to your Excellencye, His
wife will attend you for letters to the
Parlnt. which I beseech you to take into

---

[2] This endorsement appears to be in the hand of John Rushworth.

[3] This is in a later (late seventeenth-century?) hand.

[4] Almost certainly Mary Cowell (cf. *JHC*, 6:237, grant of pension to 'widow Cowell' on 29 June 1649 and *JHC*, 6:298, and review of pensions to amongst others 'Mary Cowell', 19 September 1649).

[5] Northallerton, North Yorkshire, through which Cromwell passed on 1 September 1648. Gaunt, *Gazetteer*, p. 226.

14 SEPTEMBER 1648

a tender consideration, I beseech you
to pardon this boldnesse to

Your Excellencyes most humble
servant
O Cromwell
Sept. 11th. 1648

1648 09 14
Letter from Oliver Cromwell to [possibly William Armyne MP]

Date: 14 September 1648

Source: A Perfect Diurnall of Some Passages in Parliament and Daily Proceedings of the Army under his Excellency the Lord Fairfax no. 269 for 18–25 September, p. 2161 (N&S, 504.82; Thomason / E.526[8]) (contemporary print)

This is clearly superior to the version used in previous editions.[1]

There is no mention of this letter in the Journal of the House of Commons or the papers of the Derby House Committee, so its recipient is unclear. On the basis of a reference in Cromwell's letter to the latter on **1648 09 20** ('I did, from Alnwick, write a letter to Sir William Armyne about our condition')[2] it seems quite possible that this is the letter, perhaps abbreviated from the one actually sent.[3]

Beginning Munday Septem. 18.

The houses sate not at all this day. From Leiutenant Generall *Cromwell* out of the North by letters *September* 14th. is thus certified.

Monday we marched from *Newcastle*[4] to *Morpeth*[5]: Suesday [*sic*] to *Alnwick*,[6] we left our guns behind us there as knowing we can send for them at pleasure, we have

---

[1] Rushworth, *Historical Collections*, 7:1264.

[2] Sir William Armine, first baronet (1593–1651), politician. See *ODNB*. Armine was a specialist on Scottish affairs.

[3] Abbott, *Writings and Speeches*, 1:650 fn. 115.

[4] Newcastle upon Tyne, a city set within the county of Northumberland.

[5] Morpeth, a market town in Northumberland, 16 miles due north of Newcastle upon Tyne on the Great North Road.

[6] Alnwick, a borough with castle, 18 miles north of Morpeth.

575

sent a strong party of horse with Major Generall *Lambert*[7] towards *Belford*,[8] and with him a summons to *Barwice*,[9] the English Cavaliers under Sir T. *Tildesly*,[10] being about 1500 lye on this side *Barwicke*, as not being suffered to come in. It's beleived they will come in if summoned, *Monro*[11] marcht through with 3000, and is joyned with *Lanerick*[12] having 5000. more. *Argile*[13] lyes at *Hedington*,[14] 12 miles behither *Edenburgh*, with an Army of neare 10000 men, these Scotch parties are upon a treaty, and its beleived, will not fight, they lye within 4. miles one of another, and must either fight or agree. Old *Leven*[15] is possest of *Edenburgh* Castle, *David Leisley*[16] is Lieutenant Gen. to *Argile*. We finde no bread in this County, but shall have Biskit[17] from *Newcastle* till new corne come, which is upon the ground in abundant measure. Leiut. Col. *Ashfield*[18] is with us with six companyes of Major Gen. *Skippons*[19] Regiment. Col. *Ashton*[20] is marched towards *Carlisle*[21] with the Lancashire foot.

Alnwick September 14. 1648.

[7] John Lambert.
[8] Belford, a village on the Great North Road, 15 miles north of Alnwick.
[9] Berwick, a strongly fortified town 15 miles north of Belford, on the Great North Road and marking the Anglo-Scottish border.
[10] Sir Thomas Tyldesley (1612–51), royalist army officer. See *ODNB*.
[11] Sir George Monro of Culrain and Newmore (d. 1694), army officer. See *ODNB*.
[12] Lanerick = William Hamilton, earl of Lanark (later second duke of Hamilton) (1616–51), politician. See *ODNB*. He was the younger brother of James Hamilton, first duke of Hamilton.
[13] Archibald Campbell, marquis of Argyll (1605x7–61), nobleman and politician. See *ODNB*.
[14] Hedington = Haddington, a Scottish burgh in Haddingtonshire [East Lothian].
[15] Old Leven = Alexander Lesley, first earl of Leven (c.1580–1661), army officer. See *ODNB*.
[16] David Leisley = for David Leslie, first Lord Newark (1601–82), army officer. See *ODNB*.
[17] Biskit = biscuit.
[18] Lt. Col. Richard Ashfield, see Firth and Davies, *Regimental History*, 2:430–3, 436–40, 440–1 and the *Online Directory of Parliamentarian Army Officers*.
[19] Philip Skippon. [20] Colonel Assheton = Ralph Assheton MP, see **1648 08 17**.
[21] Carlisle (Cumberland), a cathedral city on the western side of England and just south of the Anglo-Scottish border, had been occupied by Royalists since 29 April 1648. It surrendered to Assheton in early October 1648.

15 SEPTEMBER 1648

1648 09 15

Letter from Oliver Cromwell to Ludovic Lesley, governor of Berwick

Date: 15 September 1648

Source: *The transactions of several matters between Lieut: Gen: Cromwel and the Scots, for surrendring the towns of Bervvick, Carlisle, and all other garisons belonging to the kingdom of England. Together with the reason of Lieut: Gen: Cromwels entring the Kingdom of Scotland*...London, p. 9: Printed for Edward Husband, printer to the Honourable House of Commons, Octob. 2. 1648 (Wing / C7176D; Thomason / E.465[18]) (contemporary copy)

This is the first of a series of letters sent by Cromwell either to those Scottish leaders who had been supporters of the Engagers' army that had been defeated at Preston or to those who had opposed the Engagement and who were now re-establishing themselves in power in Scotland. Dated separately, Cromwell sent all four of these letters, together with ancillary material, to Parliament where they were read in the House of Commons on 28 September and reported to the Lords.[1] The Commons also ordered the bundle of correspondence to be published. The Clerk of the Parliament spared his staff the task of copying the material into the Lords' Journal by attaching the pamphlet to the Journal and it was the pamphlet in slightly modernised form that appears in the printed Journals. This first letter appears in the pamphlet after a wide-ranging review of his options that Cromwell wrote five days later on 20 September (**1648 09 20a**). It is a copy of his summons to the governor of Berwick[2] which Leslie responded to immediately, saying he had to consult with those who had appointed him.[3]

Lieut: General *Cromwels* Summons to the Governor of *Berwick*.[4]

SIR, *Being come thus near, I thought fit to Demand the Town of* Berwick *to be delivered into my hands, to the use of the Parliament and Kingdom of* England, *to whom of right it belongeth: I need not use any arguments to convince you of the justice hereof; the witness that God hath borne against your Army in their Invasion of this Kingdom, which desired to sit in Peace by you, doth at once manifest his dislike of injury done to a Nation that meant you no*

---

[1] *JHC*, 6:37, for the reading of the correspondence and a series of resolutions; *JHL*, 10:516–20 for the reading of the documents in the Lords.

[2] Colonel Ludovick Leslie, a veteran of the Thirty Years War had been quartermaster general of the Armies of the Covenant in England (1644–7) but in 1648 he was governor of Carlisle. After his surrender he withdrew to continental Europe: Furgol, *Covenanting Armies*, pp. 113–14, 156–8, 264.

[3] The text of the reply: 'Much-honoured and Noble Sir, I have received yours, wherein ye desire the Delivering-up of this Town, which I was put in Trust with by the Committee of the States of *Scotland*; wherewith I am immediately to acquaint them, and expects their Order; and in the mean Time rests, Noble Sir, Your humble Servant, Lo. Leslie.'

[4] Berwick-upon-Tweed, the fortified border town between England and Scotland on the Great North Road.

577

harm, but hath been all along desirous to keep Amity and brotherly affection and agreement with you: If you deny me in this, we must make a second Appeal to God, putting our selves upon him, in endeavoring to obtain our Rights, and let him be Judge between us; and if your ayms be any thing beyond what we profess, he will require it; if further trouble ensue upon your denial, we trust he will make our innocency to appear: I expect your Answer to this Summons this day, and rest,

Your Servant,
O.C.

1648 09 16a
Letter from Oliver Cromwell to the Scottish Committee of Estates

Date: 16 September 1648
Source: NAS, PA 7/23/2/58 [formerly S.P. No. 207] (autograph)

The letter is in the hand of Cromwell's clerk and has Cromwell's signature and seal. It is addressed to the Scottish Committee of Estates in Edinburgh. He sent a copy to the House of Commons in Westminster and a copy of that copy was then printed with his other letters of **1648 09 15** and **1648 09 21b** and appeared on the streets of London on 2 October 1648.[1]

[seals]
For the Right Hoble. The Committee of Estates[2] for the kingdome of Scotland these
Cromwells lre to the Committee 18 Sept. 1648[3]
Cromwels Letter[4] 38 84 87[5]

---

[1] *The transactions of several matters between Lieut: Gen: Cromwel and the Scots, for surrendring the towns of Bervvick, Carlisle, and all other garisons belonging to the kingdom of England...*, pp. 10–13 (Wing / C7176D; Thomason / E.465[18]). See **1648 09 15**.
[2] The Committee of Estates is the body made up of members of the nobility, commissioners of the shires and of the burghs who were the executive committee of the Scottish Parliament and continued to serve when Parliament was in recess.
[3] This is added in a different seventeenth-century hand, neither Cromwell's nor his clerk's.
[4] This is added in a different seventeenth-century hand, neither Cromwell's nor his clerk's.
[5] These numbers appear to be contemporary with the letter.

16 SEPTEMBER 1648A

[recto]

Right Honoble:

Being upon my approach to the borders of the kingdome of Scotland, I thought fitt to acquaint you of the reason thereof; It's well knowne how injuriously the kingdome of England was lately invaded by the armye under Duke Hamilton,[6] contrary to the covenant, and our leagues of amity; and against all the engagemts. of love, and Brotherhood between the two Nations; And Notwithstanding the pretence of your late declaration, published to take with the people of this kingdome, The Commons of England in Parliamt. assembled declared the Said armie soe entring; as enemyes to the kingdome; And those of England who should adhere to them, as Traytors. And haveing received Commaunds to march with a Considerable part of their army to oppose Soe greate a violation of faith, and justice, what a witness, (God, being appealed too,) hath borne upon the engagemt. of the two armyes[7] against the unrighteousness of man, not onely your Selves, But this kingdome, yea, and a greate part of the knowne world will, I trust, acknowledge how dangerous a thing is it to wage an unjust warre, much more to appeale to God, the righteous judge, therein? wee trust hee will perswade you better by this manifest token of his displeasure, least his hand be streched out yet more against you, and your poore people alsoe, if they wilbe deceived. That which I am to demaund of you, Is, the restitution of the garrisons of Barwick[8] and Carlile[9] into my hands for the use of the Parliamt., and kingdome of England. If you deny me herein; I must make our appeale to God, and call upon him for assistance, in what way hee shall direct us; wherein wee are, and shalbe, soe farr from Seeking the harme of the wel'affected people of the kingdome of Scotland, that wee profess (as before the lord) That (what difference, (an army necessitated in an hostile way to recover the auncient rights, and inheritance of the kingdome, (under which they Serve,) can make,) wee shall use our indeavour to the utmost that the trouble may fall upon the contrivers, and authors: of this breach, and not upon the poore innocent people, who hve been led, and compelled into this action, as many poore Soules, ~~who~~ now prisonrs.to us, confess. Wee thought our Selves bound in duty thus to expostulate with you; and thus to profess; to th'end wee may beare our integrity out before the world, and may have comfort in God, whatever the event bee: Desireing your answer I rest

---

[6] James Hamilton, first duke of Hamilton.
[7] i.e. at the battle of Preston, 17–19 August 1648.
[8] For the taking of Berwick, see **1648 09 15**.
[9] For the taking of Carlisle, see **1648 09 14**.

Your lopps humble Servant
O Cromwell
Septembr the 16th. 1648

1648 09 16b

Letter from Oliver Cromwell to Archibald Campbell, marquis of Argyll, 'and the rest of the well affected lords, gentlemen, ministers and people now in armes in the kingdome of Scotland'

Date: 16 September 1648
Source: [J. Birch] *A collection of the state papers of John Thurloe*, 7 vols. (1742), 1.100 (later print)

Birch, in editing the Thurloe State Papers in 1742, gives this as 'from the public records of Parliament in the laigh parliament house at Edinburgh'. He also describes it as an original. But it cannot now be found in the National Records of Scotland, and unlike other Scottish correspondence from this time, it was not entered into the Journal of the (English) House of Lords, nor published in the pamphlet *The transactions of several matters between Lieut: Gen: Cromwell and the Scots* (see **1648 09 15**).

Letter from Oliver Cromwell, – *directed thus: For the right honorable the lord marquess of* Argile,[1] *and the rest of the well affected lords, gentlemen, ministers and people now in armes in the kingdome of* Scotland, *present. Orig.*
MY LORDS AND GENTLEMEN,
Being (in prosecution of the common enymie) advanced with the army under my command to the boarders of Scotland, I thought fitt, to prevent any misapprehension, or prejudice that might be raised thereupon, to send to your lordships these gentlemen, coll. Bright,[2] scout-master-generall Rowe,[3] and Mr

---

[1] Archibald Campbell, marquis of Argyll.
[2] Sir John Bright, baronet (bap. 1619, d. 1688), parliamentarian officer and landowner. See *ODNB*.
[3] William Rowe was the son of Yorkshire gentleman and served in 1643–4 as secretary to Parliament's commissioners who negotiated the Solemn League and Covenant, and in 1647 with the commissioners who negotiated Ormond's surrender of Dublin. He then became scoutmaster of the New Model and travelled with Cromwell on the Preston campaign. His previous experience made him an ideal person to be Cromwell's courier for his negotiations with Loudoun and Argyll in September 1648 (anon. 'Grant by Edward Bysshe, Garter King of Arms to William Rowe', *Yorkshire Archaeology Society*, 18 [1905], pp. 346–8).

Stapilton,[4] to acquaint yow with the reasons thereof; concerning which I desire your lordships to give them credence. I remayne.

My lords,

Your very humble servant,
O. CROMWELL.
Sept. 16, 1648.

1648 09 18
Letter from Oliver Cromwell to John Campbell, earl of Loudon, Lord Chancellor of Scotland

Date: 18 September 1648

Source: *The transactions of several matters between Lieut: Gen: Cromwel and the Scots, for surrendring the towns of Bervvick, Carlisle, and all other garisons belonging to the kingdom of England. Together with the reason of Lieut: Gen: Cromwels entring the Kingdom of Scotland to assist the marquis of Argyle.* Octob. 2. 1648, pp. 20–3 (Wing / C7176D; Thomason / E.465[18]) (contemporary print)

This is Cromwell's reply to a letter from Lord Loudoun to Cromwell dated 15 September. In it Loudoun notes Cromwell's presence on Scotland's borders, and assures him that 'the Noblemen, Gentlemen and Burgesses now in Arms, who dissented in [the Scottish] Parliament from the late Engagement against the Kingdom of England' are determined 'co-operate, by contributing our best endeavour with you' to hand back towns in the hands of the Engagers, to ensure a total disbandment of Engager forces, with a rather ambiguous promise 'to observe inviolably the Covenant and Treaties between the kingdoms'. Cromwell's response shows that he was keen to reassure Loudoun, the Chancellor of Scotland, that he was crossing the border simply to 'assist' those Loudoun represented as seeking to end the Engager aggression on behalf of King Charles.[1]

Cromwell's autograph letter has not survived. There are three contemporary copies and one made in 1742 from an alleged original.

---

[4] Not identified.

[1] *The transactions of several matters*, pp. 13–14. This is followed by instructions Loudoun issued to commissioners to ensure the disarmament of the Engagers (ibid., pp. 15–16); the Articles in Treaty between the Two Armies, Falkirk, 15 September (ibid., pp. 16–18); and a gloss on those Articles (ibid., pp. 19–20).

THE LETTERS, WRITINGS, AND SPEECHES OF OLIVER CROMWELL

[**Version A**] is the one reproduced here and comes from the pamphlet[2] produced by the Long Parliament's main printer from a copy of the letter that Cromwell sent up to Westminster from the Scottish Borders. This has the advantage of being an approved official copy.

[**Version B**] is in the National Archives of Scotland and is written with spelling and punctuation following Scottish conventions.[3] Of the two Scottish versions, it is the less careless but is very much using Scottish spelling and idiom and so is clearly not an exact copy. Its provenance before it came to the National Archives of Scotland is unknown.

[**Version C**] is from the National Library of Scotland and is also written with spelling and punctuation following Scottish conventions.[4] It appears to be a more careless transcription with words omitted or in a different order. But there are some important variant wordings and, since all versions are copies of lost originals, we have noted the significant variations below.

[**Version D**] was copied by Thomas Birch in or before 1742, from, he tells us, 'the public records of Scotland in the High Parliament house at Edinburgh'.[5] There is at least one obvious error and several other implausible words so on balance the copy of the copy Cromwell sent to Westminster is the preferred version.

[p. 20]

For the Right Honorable, The Earl of Loudoun Chancellor of Scotland, to be communicated to the Noblemen, Gentlemen, and Burgesses now with the Army,[6] who Dissented from the late Engagement against the Kingdom of ENGLAND.

Right Honorable.

We received yours from Falkirk of the 15 of *Septem.* instant; we have had also a sight of your Instructions given to the Laird of *Gramheats*[7] and Major *Straughan;*[8] as also two others Papers, concerning the Treaty between your Lordship and the Enemy, wherein your care[9] of the In [p. 21] terest of the Kingdom of *England*, for the Delivery of their Towns unjustly taken from them, and desire to preserve the Unity of both Nations, are dearest:[10] By which also we understand the posture

---

[2] Wing / C7176D; Thomason / E.465[18].   [3] NAS, GD188/20/13/13.

[4] NLS, MS 21183, fo. 92.

[5] Thomas Birch, *A Collection of the State Papers of John Thurloe, esq.*, 7 vols. (London, 1742), 1:101–2.

[6] [C] has 'in armes' instead of 'with the Army' and the address appears at the end not the head of the letter.

[7] See the biography of Sir Andrew Kerr of Greenhead, Roxburghshire, first baronet, in the *HoP Commons, 1640–1660*. [C] has 'Laird of Greenhead' not 'Laird of Gramheats'.

[8] Major Archibald Strachan, see Furgol, *Covenanting Armies*, pp. 118, 326–30 and *passim*.

[9] [C] has 'cause' instead of 'cause'.

[10] [C] has 'unity of both nations appeares', [D] has 'union of both nations appears'.

582

18 SEPTEMBER 1648

you are now in to oppose the Enemies of the welfare and Peace of both the Kingdoms; for which we bless God for his goodness to you, and rejoyce to see the power of the Kingdom of *Scotland* in a hopeful[11] way to be invested in the hands of those, who we trust are taught of God to seek his honor, and the comforts of his people. And give us leave to say, as before[12] the Lord who knoweth the secret of all hearts, That as we think one especial end of Providence in permitting the Enemies of God and Goodness in both Kingdoms to rise to the height, and exercise such Tyranny over his people, was, to shew the necessity of the Unity amongst his of both Nations; so, we hope and pray, That the late glorious Dispensation in giving so happy success against your and our Enemies in our Victory, may be the foundation of the Union of the People of God in Love and Amity: and to that end we shall, God assisting, to the utmost of our power endeavor to perform what may be behinde on our part: And when we shall through any wilfulness fail herein,[13] let this Profession rise up in Judgement against us, as having been made in Hypocrisie; A severe Avenger of which, God hath lately appeared, in his most righteous witnessing against the Army under Duke *Hamilton*,[14] Invading us under specious pretences of Piety[15] and Justice: We may humbly say we rejoyce with more trembling, then to dare to do so wicked a thing. Upon our advance to Alnwick,[16] we thought fit to send a good party of Horse towards the Borders of *Scotland*, and therewith a Summons to the Garison of Berwick;[17] to which having received a dilatory Answer, I desired a safe Convoy for Col: *Bright*[18] and the Scoutmaster General,[19] to go to the Committee of Estates of *Scotland*, who, I hope, will have the opportunity to be with your Lordships before this come to your hands, and according as they are instructed, let your Lordships in some measure (as well as we could in so much igno [p. 22] rance of your condition) know our affections to you, and understanding things more fully by yours, we now thought fit to make this return.

The Command we received upon the defeat of Duke *Hamilton*, was, *To prosecute the business until the Enemy might be put out of a condition or hope of growing into a new*

---

[11] [C] has 'hostile' rather than 'hopeful'.

[12] For what it is worth [C] moves the comma, with important shift of sense: 'give us leave to say as before, the Lord who knoweth...'.

[13] [C] has 'when we shall fail thorow our willfullnes' instead of 'when we shall through any wilfulness fail herein'.

[14] James Hamilton, first duke of Hamilton.   [15] [C] has 'partie' not 'piety'.

[16] Alnwick, Northumberland, where Cromwell stayed from 12 to 15 September.

[17] See **1648 09 15**. [C] adds 'and Carlyle' after Berwick.   [18] Sir John Bright.

[19] For William Rowe, see **1648 09 16b**. 'Scoutmaster General' is impossibly rendered in Birch, *Thurloe* as 'Lieutenant General'.

583

Army, and the Garisons of Berwick *and* Carlisle[20] *were reduced:* Four Regiments of our Horse, and some Dragoons, having followed the Enemy into the South parts being now come up, and this countrey not being able to bear us, the Cattel and old Corn thereof having been wasted by *Monro*[21] and the Forces with him, the Governor of Berwick also daily victualling his Garison from *Scotland* side, and the Enemy yet in so considerable a posture, as by these Gentlemen and your Papers we undersstand, still prosecuting their former Design, having gotten the advantage of Sterling-Bridge,[22] and so much of *Scotland* at their backs to enable them thereunto; and your Lordships condition at present not being such as may compel them to submit to the honest[23] and necessary things you have proposed to them for the good of both the Kingdoms; We have thought fit out of the sence of our Duties to the Commands laid upon us by those who have sent us, and to the end we might be in a posture more ready to give you an assistance, and not be wanting to what we have made so large Professions of, to advance into *Scotland* with the Army; And we trust by the blessing of God, the Common Enemy will thereby the sooner be brought to a submission to you, and we thereby shall do what becometh us in order to the obtaining our Garisons; engaging our selves, That so soon as we shall know from you the Enemy shall yield to the things you have proposed to them, and we have our Garisons delivered to us, we shall forthwith depart out of your Kingdom, and in the mean time be more tender towards the Kingdom of *Scotland* in the point of Charge, then if we were in our own Native Kingdom. If we shall receive from you any desire of a more speedy advance, we shall readily yield compliance therewith, desiring often to hear from you how Af [p. 23] fairs stand. This being the Result of the Councel of War, I present it to you as the expression of their affections and my own, who am, My Lord,
Your most humble Servant,
O. CROMWEL.[24]

[20] Carlisle, Cumberland close to the Scottish Border which at the time of writing was still in the hands of the Engagers.
[21] (Major General) Sir George Monro, of Culrain and Newmore (d. 1694), army officer. See *ODNB*.
[22] Stirling Bridge, a crucial crossing point over the river Forth.
[23] [C] has 'just' rather than 'honest'.
[24] [D] adds 'Cheswick, this 18th of September 1648'. Cheswick, Northumberland, is a village five miles south of Berwick.

1648 09 20a

Proclamation by Oliver Cromwell as lieutenant general of the Army in the Scottish Borders

Date: 20 September 1648
Source: *A Perfect Diurnall of Some Passages in Parliament* no. 270 for 25 September–2 October 1648, pp. 2171–2 (N&S, 504.270; Thomason / E.526[11]) (contemporary print)

This proclamation made to his own troops exists in two London printings, one in a pamphlet that gives details of his progress in recent days and is headed by the proclamation;[1] the other in *A Perfect Diurnall*, a newsbook controlled by the Army's friends. There are no significant differences between the versions so the semi-official diurnal version is preferred here.

The Lieut. Generall hath published a Proclamation upon his entring of Scotland, and it is as followeth; Whereas we are marching with the Parliaments Army into the Kingdome of Scotland, in pursuance of the remaining part of the Enemy, who lately invaded the Kingdome of England, and for recovery of the Garrisons of Barwicke and Carlisle;[2] These are to declare, that if any Officer and Souldier under my command shall take or demand any money, or shall violently take any Horses, Goods, or Victuals, without order, or shall abuse the people in any sort, it shall be tried by a Councel of war, and the said person so offending shall be punished according to the Articles of war, made for the government of the Army in the Kingdome of England, which is death. Each Colonell or other chiefe Officer in every Regiment is to transcribe the copy of this, and to cause the same to be delivered to each Captaine of his Regiment, and every said Captaine of each respective Troop and company, is to publish the same to his Troop and company, and to take strict course that nothing be done contrary hereto.[3]

---

[1] *A letter sent from Lieutenant Generall Cromwel to the Marquis of Argyle and Generall Lesley, and his protestation concerning the Scottish forces, under the command of Gen. Monro* ... London, Printed for C. VV. and are to be sold at the Royall Exchange in Cornhill, Thomason date 29 September [1648], pp. 1–2 (Wing / C7106; Thomason / E.465[7]).

[2] Berwick and Carlisle: the Anglo-Scottish border towns held by Scottish troops, Carlisle on the west side of England, Berwick on the east.

[3] For a very similar declaration made by Cromwell at the outside of his Irish campaign of 1649–50, see **1649 08 24**.

Given under my hand, Sept. 20. 1648.
Cromwell.

1648 09 20b
Letter from Oliver Cromwell to the Committee at Derby House

Date: 20 September 1648

Source: *The transactions of several matters between Lieut: Gen: Cromwel and the Scots, for surrendring the towns of Bervvick, Carlisle, and all other garisons belonging to the kingdom of England. Together with the reason of Lieut: Gen: Cromwels entring the Kingdom of Scotland....* London: Printed for Edward Husband, printer to the Honourable House of Commons, Octob. 2. 1648, pp. 3–8 (Wing / C7176D; Thomason / E.465[18]) (contemporary print)

This letter exists only in pamphlet form. For the details see the introduction to **1648 09 15**. It is the last of four letters written over the course of a week and sent up to the Palace of Westminster, read in both Houses and then published in a single pamphlet. This one, to the Derby House Committee, represents an overview of his progress thus far.

To the Right Honorable, The Committee of Lords and Commons at *Derby-house*.[1]

My Lords and Gentlemen,

I did from Alnwick[2] write to Sir *William Armyn*[3] an account of our Condition,[4] and recommended to him divers particular considerations about your Affairs here in the North, with desire of particular things to be done by your Lordships appointment, in order to the carrying on of your Affairs. I send you here inclosed a copy of the Summons that was sent to Barwick[5] when I was come as far as Alnwick; as also of a Letter written to the Committee of Estates of *Scotland*,[6] I mean those who we did presume were convened as Estates, & were the men that

---

[1] Committee at Derby House = the principal executive committee from early 1647, replacing the Committee of Both Kingdoms that had previously met in Derby House and consisting mainly of the same English MPs without the Scottish commissioners.

[2] A town and castle on the Great North Road in Northumberland where Cromwell rested from 12–15 September (Gaunt, *Cromwellian Gazetteer*, p. 226).

[3] Sir William Armine, first baronet (1593–1651), politician. See ODNB.

[4] For what is probably the letter referred to here, see **1648 09 14**.

[5] See **1648 09 15**.   [6] See **1648 09 18**.

20 SEPTEMBER 1648B

managed the business of the War: But there being (as I hear since) none such, the Earl of *Roxbourgh*[7] and some others having deserted, so that they are not able to make a Committee, I believe the said Letter is suppressed and retained in the hands of Colonel *Bright*[8] and Mr. *William Rowe*, for whom we obtained a safe Convoy to go to the Estates of that Kingdom with our said Letter; the Governor of Barwicks Answer to our Summons leading us thereunto:[9] By advantage whereof, we did instruct them to give all assurance to the Marquis of *Argyle*, and the honest Party in *Scotland*[10] (who we heard were gathered together in a considerable Body about Edenburgh, to make opposition to the Earl of *Lanerick*,[11] *Munro*,[12] and their Armies) of our good affection to them; wherewith they went the Sixteenth of this Moneth. Upon the Seventeenth of this Moneth Sir *Andrew Carr*[13] and Major *Straughan*,[14] with divers other Scottish Gentlemen, brought me this enclosed Letter. Signed by the Lord Chancellor of *Scotland*,[15] as your Lordships will see: They likewise shewed me their Instructions, and a Paper containing the matter of their Treaty with *Lanerick* and *Monro*; as also an Expostulation upon *Lanericks* breach with them, in falling upon *Argyle* and his men contrary to Agreement, wherein the Marquis of *Argyle* hardly escaped, they having hold of him, but Seven hundred of his men were killed and taken: These papers also I send here enclosed to your Lordships. So soon as these Gentlemen came to me, I called a Councel of War, the Result whereof was, the Letter directed to the Lord Chancellor, a Copy whereof your Lordships have also here enclosed, which I delivered to Sir *Andrew Car* and Major *Straughan*, with which they returned upon the Eighteenth, being the next day. Upon private discourse with the Gentlemen, I do finde the condition of their Affairs and their Army to be thus; The Earl of *Lanerick*, the Earl of *Crawford-Lindsey*,[16] *Monro*, and their Army hearing

---

[7] Robert Ker, first earl of Roxburghe (1569/70–1650), courtier and politician. See *ODNB*.

[8] Sir John Bright, who had served in the Northern Brigade under his brother-in-law, Major General John Lambert.

[9] See **1648 09 15** n. 6.

[10] i.e. those Covenanters who had refused to take the Engagement and support the Scottish adventure in England which had culminated in the battle of Preston.

[11] William Hamilton, first earl of Lanark, and brother of the duke of Hamilton.

[12] For Sir George Monro, of Culrain and Newmore (d. 1694), army officer. See *ODNB*.

[13] Sir Andrew Ker, lieutenant colonel in the regiment of the earl of Roxburgh. See Furgol, *Covenanting Armies*, pp. 287, 389.

[14] Archibald Strachan (d. 1652), army officer. See *ODNB*.

[15] John Campbell, first earl of Loudoun.

[16] John Lindsay, seventeenth earl of Crawford and first earl of Lindsay [known as earl of Crawford-Lindsay] (1596–1678), politician. See *ODNB*.

of our advance, and understanding the condition and endeavors of their Adversaries. marched with all speed to get the possession of Sterling-Bridge,[17] that so they might have three parts of four of *Scotland* at their backs to raise men, and to enable themselves to carry on their Design, and are above Five thousand Foot, and Five and twenty hundred Horse, or Three thousand; The Earl of *Leven*,[18] who is chosen General, the Marquis of *Argyle*, with the honest Lords and Gentlemen, *David Lesley*[19] being the Lieut: General, having about Seven thousand Foot, but very weak in Horse, lye about six miles on this side the Enemy; I do hear that their Infantry consists of men who come to them out of Conscience, and generally are of the godly People of that Nation, which they express by their Piety and Devotion in their Quarters, and indeed I hear they are a very godly and honest Body of men.

I think it is not unknown to your Lordships what Directions I have received from you for the prosection of our late Victory; whereof I shall be bold to remember a Clause of your Letter, which was, *That I should prosecute the remaining party in the North, and not leave any of them (where-ever they shall go) to be a beginning of a new Army, nor cease to pursue the Victory, till I finish and fully compleat it, with their Rendition of those Towns of* Barwick *and* Carlisle, *which most unjustly, and against all Obligations and the Treaties (then) in force, they surprized and Garisoned against us.*

In order whereunto, I marched to the Borders of *Scotland*, where I found the countrey so exceedingly harrased and impoverished by *Monro* and the Forces with him, that the countrey was in no sort able to bear us on the English side, but we must have necessarily ruined both your Army, and the Subjects of this Kingdom, who have not bread for a day, if we had continued amongst them. In prosecution of your Orders, and in answer to the necessity of your Friends in *Scotland*, and their desires, and considering the necessity of marching into *Scotland*, to prevent the Governor of Barwick from putting Provisions into his Garison on *Scotland* side (whereof he is for the present in some want, as we are informed) I marched a good part of the Army over Tweed yesterday about Noon, the residue being to come after as conveniently as we may. Thus have I given to your Lordships an Account of our present condition and Engagement; and having done so, I must

---

[17] Stirling Bridge, an important strategic bridge on the river Forth, and only crossing place for many miles.

[18] Alexander Leslie, first earl of Leven.

[19] David Leslie, first Lord Newark (1601–82), army officer. See *ODNB*.

21 SEPTEMBER 1648

discharge my duty in remembring to your Lordships the Desires formerly expressed in my Letters to Sir *William Armyne* and Sir *John Evelyn* for Supplies; and in particular, for that of Shipping to lye upon these Coasts, who may furnish us with Ammunition or other Necessaries wheresoever God shall lead us, there being extreme difficulty to supply us by land, without great and strong Convoys, which will weary out and destroy our Horse, and cannot well come to us if the Tweed be up, without going very far about. Having laid these things before you, I rest, My Lords,

Your most humble Servant,

O. CROMWEL.

Norham[20] this 20 of *Septem*. 1648.

Whilest we are here; I wish there be no neglect of the business in Cumberland *and* Westmerland: I *have sent Orders both into* Lancashire *and the Horse before* Pontefract;[21] I *should be glad your Lordships would second them, and those other Considerations expressed in my Desires to Sir* William Armyn *thereabouts.*

O.C.

1648 09 21

From Oliver Cromwell to the Scottish Committee of Estates

Date: 21 September 1648

Source: NAS, PA 7/23/2/59 [formerly S.P. 209] (autograph)

This letter, in the hand of Cromwell's principal clerk, contains additions and corrections in his own hand, at times clearly intended to tone down what he had initially dictated.[1] It is a letter of apology for plundering by troops under his command (but note how careful he is

---

[20] Norham, Northumberland. A village on the south bank of the Tweed, which formed the Anglo-Scottish border. Cromwell stayed at Norham from 19 to 21 September.

[21] Pontefract, West Yorkshire, a town and castle held by the royalists until early 1649.

---

[1] Other versions of this letter are copies/transcriptions from this original: **(a)** T. Birch, ed., *A Collection of the State Papers of John Thurloe*, 7 vols. (1742), 1:103 ('From the public records of Scotland in the laigh parliament house at Edinburgh'); **(b)** *Facsimiles of national manuscripts of Scotland / Selected under the direction of the Lord Clerk Register of Scotland and photozincographed by the Ordnance Survey. Pub. by authority of the Lords Commissioners of Her Majesty's Treasury, under the direction of the Lord Clerk Register of Scotland*, 3 vols. (1867–72), 3:xcix.

THE LETTERS, WRITINGS, AND SPEECHES OF OLIVER CROMWELL

to exonerate the New Model regiments). The reply from the Chancellor of Scotland, the earl of Loudoun was printed in *Moderate Intelligencer* for 5–12 October[2] and is wholly emollient. Both sides want a peaceful resolution at this stage.

For the Right honoble. the Committe of Estates of the Kingdome of Scotland
At Edenburgh[3] these
Right honourable

Wee perceive that there was upon our advance to the borders the last lords day[4] a very disorderly carriage by some horse, who, without order did Steale over the tweed[5] and plundred Some places in the kingdome of Scotland and Since that Some straglers ha[—] have been alike faulty, to the wrong of the Inhabitants, and to our very greate greife of heart. I have been as diligent as I can to finde out the men that have donne the wrong, And I am Still in the discovery thereof and I trust It shall appeare to you that there shalbe nothing wanting on my part that may testifie how much we abhorre Such things, and to the best of my information, I cannot finde the least guilt of the fact to lye upon the regiments of this army. But upon Some of the northerne horse who have not been under our discipline and goverment, untill just that wee came into these parts. I have commaunded those forces away back againe into England, and I hope this exemplarety of justice will testifie for us our greate detestation of the fact, for the remayneing forces which are of our old regiments we may engage for them their ~~abhorre to doe any evill~~ \officers will keepe them from doinge any such/ thinges.[6] And wee are confident that, Saving victuall, they shall not take any thing from the Inhabitants, and in that alsoe, they shalbe Soe farre from being their own carvers; as that they shall Submitt to have provisions ordered and proportion'd by the consent, and with the direction of the Committees & gentlemen of the Country; and not otherwise, If they please to be assisting to us therein. I thought fitt for the preventing of misunderstanding, to give your lopps this accompt; and rest.

---

[2] *The moderate intelligencer impartially communicating martiall affaires to the kingdom of England,* no. 186, pp. 1686 (N&S, 419.186; Thomason / E.467[16]).
[3] Added by Cromwell himself.   [4] Sunday 17 September 1648.
[5] i.e. river Tweed.
[6] The interlineation is in Cromwell's hand and appears to be an attempt to soften the tone of what he is saying.

My lords Your most humble Servant
O Cromwell
Norham[7] the 21th. of Septbr 1648[8]

1648 09 23[?]
Precis of letter from Oliver Cromwell to Archibald Campbell, marquis of Argyll

Date: Between 21 and 25 September 1648

Source: *A letter sent from Lieutenant Generall Cromwel to the Marquis of Argyle and Generall Lesley, and his protestation concerning the Scottish forces, under the command of Gen. Monro*... London, Printed for C.VV. and are to be sold at the Royall Exchange in Cornhill, p. 6 (Wing / C7106; Thomason / E.465[7]) (contemporary print)

This is the precis of a letter Cromwell sent to the military leaders in Scotland, and which he included in the bundle of letters he sent to Parliament and which were read in both Houses and published by them on 28 September. It is undated, but in the sequence must have been written on or after 21 September and before 25 September.

Thomason received his copy on 29 September 1648.

Liet. gen. *Cromwell* having received a message from the Marq. of *Argyle*, sent by the Lord *Lowden*,[1] desiring the assistance of the English Army against *Monro*:[2] he immediatly calls a Councell of War, the results wherof was to give them assistance: and sent a Letter to the said Marq. intimating, that he would be ready to joyn with him against *Monro*, desiring nothing more then the subduing of all such as are enemies to peace and truth; assuring them that in his income he will deny himself and his souldiers that which he would take in *England*, and that the enemy once subdued, and the English towns[3] delivered or gained, he will return: And

---

[7] Norham is (just) on the English side of the Anglo-Scottish border eight miles west of Berwick-upon-Tweed.

[8] This place and date are added by Cromwell himself.

---

[1] John Campbell, first earl of Loudoun, Lord Chancellor of Scotland.
[2] Sir George Monro of Culrain and Newmore (d. 1694), army officer. See *ODNB*.
[3] i.e. Berwick and Carlisle.

desires that the Letter he now sends may be kept as a testimony against him and those under his Command, if they do not, as a brand of their hypocrisie for ever. The Letter was *Signed*,

O. CROMWEL.

1648 10 02a
Letter from Oliver Cromwell to William Lenthall, Speaker of the House the Commons

Date: 2 October 1648

Source: Bodl., MS Tanner 57, fos 330r–331v (contemporary print)

This account of the progress of Cromwell's military and political campaign in Scotland is in the hand of Cromwell's usual clerk, with Cromwell's signature. It is in the papers of the Speaker of the House of Commons, William Lenthall. There is a contemporary copy made for the House of Lords in the Braye Manuscripts in the Parliamentary Archives.[1]

[fo. 330r]

Sir,

I have formerly represented to the Committee at Derby house[2] how farr I have prosecuted your business in relation to the Commaunds I did re-ceive from them, To witt, That I having sent a party of horse with a Summons to Barwick,[3] and a letter to the Committee of estates. which I supposed did consist of the Earle of Lanerick[4] and his participates and a letter of kindness and affection to the Marquess of Argile and the welaffected party in armes at Edenburgh, with

---

[1] HLRO, BRY 3, fos 16–17. It has been used to confirm some readings where the original has blotches. The letter, together with one for the Lord Chancellor of Scotland to Cromwell, was published as (Wing / C7018B; Thomason / E.467[3]): *Lieut: General Cromwels letter to the honorable William Lenthal Esq; speaker of the honorable House of Commons, containing a narrative of his proceedings in the managing the affairs of the Parliament of the kingdom of England in Scotland...London:* Printed for Edward Husband, printer to the Honorable House of Commons, Octob. 10. 1648, pp. 3–6.

[2] The central executive committee of the Long Parliament, 1647–9. The letter he is referring to is **1648 09 20**.

[3] Berwick-upon-Tweed, a fortified town on the Anglo-Scottish border that had been occu-pied by the Scots.

[4] William Hamilton, earl of Lanark.

2 OCTOBER 1648A

Credence to Collonell Brightand Mr. William Rowe Scoutmaister of the army,[5] to lett them know upon what grounds, and with what intentions wee came into their Kingdome, And how, that in the meane time; the Marquess of Argile and the rest at Edenburgh had sent Sir Andrew Carr Layrde of Gramheade,[6] and Major Straughan[7] to me, with a letter and paypers of instructions expressing their good affection to the Kingdome of England, and disclaymeing the late engagemt. together with my answer to the Said letters and paypers, duplicates of all which I sent to the Committee at Derby house and therefore forbeare to trouble you with the things themselves. I thinke now fitt to give yow. an accompt what further progress has been made in your business. The two armyes being drawne upp, the one[8] under Lanerick and Munroe[9] at Sterling and the other[10] under the Earle of Leven and Leifetennt Generall Leslie betwixt that and Edenburgh, the heades of the two armyes being upon treatyes concerning their owne affaires, And I having given (as I hoped) Sufficient Satisfaction concerning the justice of your Cause and the Clereness of my intentions in entring that kingdome, did (upon thursday being the one and twentieth of September and two dayes before (the Tweed being foardable) march over Tweed at Norham[11] into Scotland with fower Regimts. of horse and Some dragones, and Six Regiments of foot, and there quartred, my heades quarters being at the lord Mordingtons house,[12] where. heareing of the Marquess of Argile, the lord Elcoe[13] and Some others were Coming to me from the Committee of Estates assembled at Edenburgh, I went on fryday the two and twentieth of September Some part of the way to wayte upon his Lo[rdshi]pp who, when hee was come to his quarters delivered me a letter of which the enclosed is a Copie, Signed by

---

[5] William Rowe. See above, **1648 09 18**.

[6] Sir Andrew Kerr, laird of Greenhead, Roxburghshire, first baronet. See a biography of him in *HoP Commons, 1640–1660*.

[7] Major Archibald Strachan. See Furgol, *Covenanting Armies* and *passim*.

[8] i.e. the remnants of the Engagers.

[9] George Munro, nephew of Major General Robert Munro, Scottish commander in Ireland, who had brought 2,000 men from that army back to Scotland to fight with the Engagers. See Furgol, *Covenanting Armies* and *passim* but esp. pp. 28–57.

[10] i.e. the army of the un-Engaged Covenanters.

[11] Norham, Northumberland, a market town eight miles south-east of Berwick-upon-Tweed.

[12] At Over Mordington, Berwickshire. For James Douglas, first Lord Mordington (raised to the peerage in 1641). See *The Peerage of Scotland* (Edinburgh, 1834), pp. 176–7.

[13] David Wemyss, Lord Elcho and second earl of Wemyss (1610–79), army officer. See *ODNB* sub. David Wemyss fourth earl of Wemyss (bap. 1678, d. 1720).

THE LETTERS, WRITINGS, AND SPEECHES OF OLIVER CROMWELL

the lord Chauncellr[14] by warrt. of the Committee of Estates,[15] And after Some time Spent in giving and receiving mutuall Satisfaction concerning each [fo. 330v] others integrity and cleareness (wherein I must be bold to testifie for that noble Lord the Marquess, the lord Elcoe, and the other gentlemen with him, that I have found nothing in them but what becomes Christians and men of honor.) the next day it was resolved that the Commaund of the Committee of Estates to the Governr. of Berwick[16] for rendring the towne, should be Sent to him by the Lord Elcoe and Collonell Scott,[17] which accordingly was donne, But hee, pretending that hee had not received the Commaund of that place from those hands that now demaunded it of him, desired libertye to Sende to the Earle of Lanerick engageing himselfe then, to give his positive answer, and intimateing it should be Satisfactory. Whilst these things were in transacting I ordered Major Genll Lambert[18] to march towards Edenburgh with Six Regimts. of horse and a Regim{t} of dragones, who, accordingly did Soe, and quarter'd in East Louthian within Six myles of Edenburgh, the foot lying in his reare at Coperspeth[19] and thereabouts. Upon fryday the 29th of September came an order from the Earle of Lanerick and diverse other lords of his party, requireing the Governor of Barwick to march out of the towne, which accordingly hee did on Satturday the last of September, At which time I entred having plac't a garrison there for your use, the Governor would faine have Capitulated for the English, But wee, having this advantage upon him, would not heare of it. Soe that they are Submitted to your mercy, and are under the Consideration of Sir Arthur Hesilrige, who (I beleive) will give you a good accompt of them, who has already turn'd out the Malignant Maior[20] and put an honest man in his roome. I have alsoe received an order for Carlile,[21] and have Sent Collonell Bright with horse and foot to receive it Sir Andrew Carr[22] and Colonell Scott being gonne with him to require an observance of the Order, there having been a treatie and \an/ agreemt the two partyes in armes in Scotland, to disband all forces except fifteen hundred horse and foot under the Earle of

---

[14] John Campbell, first earl of Loudoun.

[15] And printed after this letter in *Lieut: General Cromwels letter to the honorable William Lenthal Esq.* [Wing / C7018B], pp. 7–8. For full details see below, **1648 10 09**.

[16] Lodowick Leslie. See Gardiner, *GCW*, 4:230.   [17] Not identified.

[18] John Lambert.

[19] Almost certainly Cockburnspath, in Coldingham parish, Berwickshire—see **1650 09 02**.

[20] Maior could represent Major or more probably Mayor (of Berwick?).

[21] Carlisle, Cumberland being now the last Engager garrison in England.

[22] i.e. Kerr. See above, n. 7.

Leven, which are to be kept up to See all remayning forces disbanded, And having some [fo. 331r] other things to desire \ / I ~~am my Self going thitherward this day~~ from the Committee of Estates at Edenburgh for your Service, I am my selfe going thitherward this day, and Soe Soone as I shalbe able to give you a further accompt thereof, I shall doe it. In the meane time, I make it my desire, That the Garrison of Barwick (into which I have placed a Regimt of foot, and shalbe attended alsoe by a Regimt of horse) may be provided for, And that Sir Arthur Hesilrige may receive Commaunds to supply it with gunns and ammunicion ~~fro~~ from NewCastle, and be otherwise enabled by you to fournish this garrison with all other necessaryes according as a place of that importance will require. Desireing that these mercyes may begett trust and thankfulness to God the onely author of them, and an improvemt of them to his glory, and the good of this poore kingdome. I rest Your most humble Servt.

O Cromwell

Barwick this 2^d of October 1648[23]

1648 10 02b
Letter from Oliver Cromwell to Thomas Fairfax, Lord Fairfax

Date: 2 October 1648
Source: BL, Sloane MS 1519, fos 183r–184v (holograph)

This is a holograph letter (although the address is in an unknown hand). A fragment of a seal survives. It throws light on the quality of Cromwell's relationship with the Lord General at this crucial time.

[fo. 184v]

Lt. Generall Cromwell

Oct. 2. 1647.

[fragment of seal]

---

[23] The printed version is included in *Lieut: General Cromwels letter to the honorable William Lenthal Esq.* [Wing / C7018B], pp. 3. Full bibliographical information is at n. 1 above.

[Address]
For his Excie: the lord Generall
Fairfax these

[fo. 183r]
May it please your Excellencye,
I receaved your late directions with
your Commissions, how they shalbe
disposed, which I hope I shall per-
sue to your Satisfaction,

I haveinge sent an account to
the house of Commons concerninge
affaires heere,[1] am bould (beinge
straightned in tyme) to præsent
you with a duplicate thereof which
I trust will give you satisfaction.
I hope there is a very good un-
derstandinge betweene the honest
partye[2] of Scotland and us heere,
and better them some would have.
Sir I begg of your Excellency to
write to Sir A. Hazleridge[3] to
take care of Barwicke.[4] Hee havinge
all thinges necessarie ~~from~~ \for/ the guarrison
att Newcastle[5] which is left destitute of
all, and may bee lost if this bee not
I begg of your Lordp a Commission to bee
Speeded to him.

---

[1] Viz **1648 10 2a**.
[2] Given Cromwell's use of 'honest' to mean the godly as he understood the term, the use here to describe the Covenanting leadership is striking.
[3] Sir Arthur Hesilrige [Haselrig].
[4] Berwick-upon-Tweed, garrisoned town on the Anglo-Scottish border.
[5] Newcastle upon Tyne, of which Heselrige was governor.

I[6] have not more att present but \rest/ ~~presentinge my obed~~ \my Lord/ Your most humble servant

O Cromwell.

Berwick:

Octobr. 2ᵈ.
1648.

1648 10 05

Letter from Oliver Cromwell to the Committee of Estates of Scotland

Date: 5 October 1648

Source: *Lieut: General Cromwels letter to the honorable William Lenthal Esq; speaker of the honorable House of Commons, concerning his last proceedings in the kingdom of Scotland, in order to the establishment of a firm and lasting peace between the two nations: all the enemies forces there being disbanded. With another letter from the Lieutenant General to the Committee of Estates, representing the great damage the kingdom of England hath received from that kingdom by the late invasion*... London: Printed for Edward Husband, printer to the Honorable House of Commons, Octob. 19. 1648, pp. 5–6 (Wing / C7108A; Thomason / E.468[19]) (contemporary print)

This letter needs to be read in the context of his previous letter to the Speaker of 2 October (**1648 10 02a**) and subsequent letter of 9 October (**1648 10 09**), the latter printed with this letter in a pamphlet dated 19 October. The letter on 9 October provides a full context for this letter.

[p. 5]
The Lieutenant Generals Letter to the Committee of Estates of SCOTLAND.
Right Honorable,
I shall ever be ready to bear witness of your Lordships forwardness to do right to the Kingdom of *England*, in restoring the Garisons of Berwick and Carlisle;[1] and having received so good a pledge of your Resolutions to maintain Amity and a

---

[6] The remainder of the letter is written in the left-hand margin.

[1] The subject of several preceding letters.

THE LETTERS, WRITINGS, AND SPEECHES OF OLIVER CROMWELL

good Understanding between the Kingdoms of *England* and *Scotland*, it makes me not to doubt, but that your Lordships will further grant what in Justice and Reason may be demanded: I can assure your Lordships, That the Kingdom of *England* did foresee that wicked Design of the Malignants[2] in *Scotland*, to break all Engagements[3] of Faith and Honesty between the Nations, and to take from the Kingdom of *England* the Towns of Berwick and Carlisle: And although they could have prevented the loss of those considerable Towns without breach of the Treaty, by laying Forces near unto them; yet such was the tenderness of the Parliament of *England*, not to give the least suspition of a breach with the Kingdom of *Scotland*, that they did forbear to do anything therein: And it is not unknown to your Lordships, when the Malignants had gotten the power of your Kingdom, how they protected and employed our English Malignants, though demanded by our Parliament, and possessed themselves of those Towns; and with what violence and unheard of Cruelties raised an Army, and began a War, and invaded the Kingdom of *England*, and endeavored to the uttermost of their power, to engage both kingdoms in a perpetual Quarrel; and what blood they have spilt in our kingdom, and what great loss & prejudice was brought upon our Nation, even to the endangering the total ruine thereof: And although God did by a most mighty and strong hand, and that in a wonderful maner destroy their Designs; yet it is apparent, that the same ill-affected Spirit still remains, and that there are divers persons of great quality and power, who were either the Contrivers, Actors or Abettors of the late unjust War made upon the kingdom of *England*, [p. 6] now in *Scotland*, who undoubtedly do watch for all advantages and opportunities to raise dissensions and divisions between the Nations: Now forasmuch as I am Commanded to prosecute the remaining part of the Army that invaded the Kingdom of *England* wheresoever it should go, to prevent the like miseries; and considering that divers of that Army are retired into *Scotland*, and that some of the heads of those Malignants were raising new Forces in *Scotland* to carry on the same Design, and that they will certainly be ready to do the like upon all occasions of advantage; and forasmuch as the Kingdom of *England* hath lately received so

---

[2] 'Malignants' is a loaded word. In England, all convicted royalists were divided into two groups, the 'delinquents' who were required to pay heavy fines to regain their property, and the 'malignants' who were to be permanently deprived of their property. As the letter unfolds, it is clear that this is the sense in which he is using the term here.

[3] For the debate on the binding nature of 'engagements' (commitments under oath freely entered into) at the first day of the Putney Debates, see above [**1647 10 28**]. Of course, given that those he is speaking of here are those who had signed the 'Engagement' with the King, the word here is full of conscious or unconscious irony.

8 OCTOBER 1648

great damage by the failing of the Kingdom of *Scotland*, in not suppressing Malignants and Incendiaries as they ought to have done, and by suffering such persons to be put into places of great Trust in the Kingdom, who by their Interest in the Parliament and Countreys, brought the Kingdom of *Scotland* so far as they could, by an unjust Engagement to invade and make War upon their Brethren of *England*. My Lords, I hold my self obliged, in prosecution of my Duty and Instructions, to demand, That your Lordships will give assurance in the Name of the Kingdom of *Scotland*, that you will not admit or suffer any who have been active in, or consenting to the said Engagement against *England*, or have lately been in Arms at Sterling or elsewhere in the maintenance of that Engagement, to be employed in any publique Place or Trust whatsoever; and this is the least Security I can demand. I have received an Order from both Houses of the Parliament of *England*, which I hold fit to communicate to your Lordships, whereby you will understand the readiness of the Kingdom of *England* to assist you who were Dissenters from the Invasion: and I doubt not but your Lordships will be as ready to give such further satisfaction, as they in their wisdoms shall finde cause to desire. Your Lordships most humble Servant,

O. CROMWEL.

Edenburgh, 5 Octob. 1648.
For the Right Honorable, The Committee of Estates of Scotland.

1648 10 08

Letter from Oliver Cromwell to William Lenthall, Speaker of the House of Commons

Date: 8 October 1648
Source: Bodl., MS Tanner 57/2, fos 346r–347v (no. 181) (autograph)

This letter is signed by Cromwell but the scribe for the body of the text is uncertain: it *could* be written by Cromwell's usual secretary, but there are variants—e.g. a sort of acute accent extending from or over lower-case 'c's at beginning of words, a squiggle over 'r' in 'For' (line 6)—which make it closer to the hand of William Rowe, Cromwell's scoutmaster. Cromwell's letter reinforces another to the same purpose from the marquis of Argyll.[1]

---

[1] *JHC*, 6:57 (21 October 1648). Argyll's letter is dated 11 October.

[fo. 324r]

Sir

Upon the desire of diverse noble men and others of the Kingdome of Scotland I am bold to become a Suitor to you on the behalfe of the gentleman the bearer Colonell Robert Montgomery[2] Sonne of the Earle of Eglington,[3] whose faithfulness to you in the late troubles may render him worthy of farr greater favour then I shall at this time desire for him. For I can assure you that there is not a gentleman of that Kingdome that appeared more active against the late invaders of England then himselfe. Sir It's desired that you would please to graunt him an order for two thousand of the Common prisoners that were of Duke Hamiltons army, you will have very good Security that they shall not for the future trouble you; he will ease you of the charge of Keeping them, as speedily as any other way you can dispose of them, besides their being in a freinds hands. Soe as there need be noe feare of their being ever imployed against you. Sir what favour you shall please to afford the gentleman[4] will very much oblige many of your freinds of the Scottish nation, and particularly

Your most humble servant

O Cromwell

Dalhousee[5] neare Edenburgh the 8th of October 1648.

[fo. 325v]

[address, in clerk's hand]

For the honoble: Willm Lenthall Esq Speaker of the honble. house of Commons these

from Lieutent. Genll Cromwell recommending Coll Robt [6]Mont gomery to have libe[ ]tie to transporte 2000 Scotts Prisonr

read xxj° Octbr. 1648

Oct 8

---

[2] Robert Montgomery [Montgomerie] (d. 1684), army officer. See ODNB, which claims that Montgomery's purpose was 'to sell them to the king of Spain for service in the Low Countries, but negotiations with both Spain and France proved abortive'.

[3] Alexander Montgomery [Montgomerie; formerly Seton], sixth earl of Eglinton (1588–1661), army officer. See ODNB. Robert was his fifth son.

[4] The Commons did indeed respond as Cromwell desired: see JHC, 6:57 (21 October 1648).

[5] Dalhousie, Midlothian, eight miles south of Edinburgh.

[6] The missing letter, obviously 'r' is obscured by a blob of wax.

9 OCTOBER 1648

1648 10 09

Letter from Oliver Cromwell to William Lenthall, Speaker of the House of Commons

Date: 9 October 1648

Source: *Lieut: General Cromwels letter to the honorable William Lenthal Esq; speaker of the honorable House of Commons, concerning his last proceedings in the kingdom of Scotland, in order to the establishment of a firm and lasting peace between the two nations: all the enemies forces there being disbanded. With another letter from the Lieutenant General to the Committee of Estates, representing the great damage the kingdom of England hath received from that kingdom by the late invasion.* Printed for Edward Husband, printer to the Honorable House of Commons, Octob. 19. 1648, pp. 3–4 (Wing / C7108A; Thomason / E.468[19]) (contemporary print)

This letter was printed, along with Cromwell's letter to the Committee of Estates dated 5 October (**1648 10 05**) and *A Declaration of the Committee of Estates, concerning their Proceedings in opposition to the late unlawful Engagement against England* in a pamphlet printed in London by the House of Commons' usual printer on 19 October (Wing / S1206).

[p. 3]

For the Honorable William Lenthal Esq, Speaker of the Honorable House of Commons.

SIR,

In my last,[1] wherein I gave you an accompt of my dispatch of Col: *Bright* to Carlisle after the rendition of Berwick, I acquainted you with my intentions to go to the head-quarters of my Horse at the Earl of *Wyntons*,[2] within six miles of Edenburgh, that from thence I might represent to the Comittee of Estates, what I had further to desire in your behalf. The next day after I came thither, I received an Invitation from Committee of Estates to come to Edenburgh, they sending to Me the Lord *Kircudbright*[3] and Major Gen. *Holborn*[4] for that purpose, with whom I went the same day, being Wednesday 4. Of this instant *Octob*. We fell into consideration what was fit further to insist upon, and being sensible that the late Agreement between the Committee of Estates and the Earls of *Crawford*,[5]

---

[1] Letter of 2 October 1648 (**1648 10 02a**).

[2] George Seton, third earl of Winton (1584–1650), nobleman and politician. See *ODNB*.

[3] John Maclellan, third Lord Kirkcudbright (died 1664). See Furgol, *Covenanting Armies*, pp. 152, 294, 330–1.

[4] James Holburn of Menstrie. See Furgol, *Covenanting Armies*, pp. 253, 302, 322–4, 326, 333, 354, 386.

[5] Ludovic Lindsay, sixteenth earl of Crawford (d. 1652), royalist army officer. See *ODNB*.

THE LETTERS, WRITINGS, AND SPEECHES OF OLIVER CROMWELL

Glencarn,[6] and *Lanerick*,[7] did not sufficiently answer my Instructions, which was, to disinable them from being in power to raise new Troubles to *England*; therefore I held it my duty, not to be satisfied onely with the disbanding of them, but considering their power and Interest, I thought it necessary to demand concerning them and all their Abettors according to the Contents of the Paper here inclosed;[8] wherein (having received that very day your Votes for giving them further assistance)[9] I did in the close thereof acquaint them therewith; reserving such further satisfaction to be given to the Kingdom of *Scotland*, as the Parliament of *England* should in their wisdom see cause to desire. The Committee of Estates sent to the Earl of *Cassils*,[10] L.*Warriston*,[11] and two Gentlemen more[12] to me, to receive what I had had to offer unto them, which upon Thursday I delivered: Upon Friday I received by the said persons this enclosed anwer, which is the original it self.[13] Having proceeded thus far as a Soldier, and I trust by the blessing of God not to your disservice; and having laid the business before you, I pray God direct you to do further as may be for his glory, the good of the Nation wherewith you are intrusted, and the comfort and encouragement of the Saints of God in both Kingdoms and all the world over. I do think the Affairs of [p. 4] *Scotland* are in a thriving posture, as to the Interest of honest Men, and like to be a better Neighbor to you now then when the Great pretenders to Covenant, Religion and Treaties (I mean D. *Hamilton*, the Earls of *Lauderdale*,[14] *Traquair*,[15] *Carnegy*[16] and their Confederates had the power in their hands; I dare say, that that Party, with their pretences, had not onely through the treachery of some in *England* (who have cause to blush) endangered the whole State and kingdom of *England*, but also brought *Scotland* into such a condition, as that no honest man that had the fear of God, or a Conscience of Religion, the Just ends of the Covenant and Treaties, could have a being in that kingdom: But God, who is not to be mocked or

---

[6] William Cunningham, eighth earl of Glencairn (1610/11–64), royalist army officer. See *ODNB*.
[7] William Hamilton, earl of Lanark.   [8] This letter is above, **1648 10 05**.
[9] *JHC*, 6:35–8.
[10] John Kennedy, sixth earl of Cassillis (1601x7–68), politician. See *ODNB*.
[11] Sir Archibald Johnston, Lord Wariston (bap. 1611, d. 1663), lawyer and politician. See *ODNB*.
[12] Not identified.
[13] *A Declaration of the Committee of Estates, concerning their Proceedings in opposition to the late unlawful Engagement against England* in the same pamphlet as this letter, at pp. 9–16.
[14] John Maitland, earl (and later duke) of Lauderdale (1616–82), politician and judge. See *ODNB*.
[15] John Stewart, first earl of Traquair (c.1599–1659), politician. See *ODNB*.
[16] Presumably David Carnegie, first earl of Southesk (1574/5–1658), nobleman. See *ODNB*.

deceived, and is very jealous when his name and Religion are made use of to carry on impious designs, hath taken vengeance of such prophanity, even to astonishment and admiration; And I wish from the bottom of my heart, it may cause all to tremble and repent (who have practiced the like to the Blaspheming of his Name, and the destruction of his people) so they may never presume to do the like again; and I think it is not unseasonable for me to take the humble boldness to say thus much at this time. All the Enemies Forces in *Scotland* are now disbanded; the Committee of Estates have declared against all of that parties sitting in Parliament; good Elections are made in divers places of such as dissented from, & opposed the late wicked Engagement; and they are now raising a force of about 4000 Horse and Foot, which until they can compleat, they have desired me to leave them two Regiments of Horse, and two Troops of Dragoons; which accordingly I have resolved, conceiving I have warrant by your late Votes to do, and have left Major Gen. *Lambert* to Command them. I have received, and so have the Officers with me, many Honors and Civilities from the Committee of Estates, the City of Edenburgh, and Ministers, with a Noble Entertainment, which we may not own as done to us, but as your Servants. I am now marching towards Carlisle; and I shall give you further accompts of your Affairs as there shall be occasion. I am, Sir,

Your Humble Servant,

Dalhousie,[17] 9 *Octob.* 1648

O.CROMWEL

<hr />

1648 10 28

Letter from Oliver Cromwell to William Lenthall, Speaker of the House of Commons

Date: 28 October 1648

Source: Bodl., MS Tanner 57/2, fos 393r–394v (no. 206) (autograph) (See also fos 391r–392v, no. 205, for Cholmley's own letter)

Cromwell had just taken over command of the siege of Pontefract from Sir Henry Cholmley, cousin of one of Cromwell's officers, Major John Cholmley, who had been killed in action at the battle of Preston. Sir Henry had shown resentment at being replaced,

<hr />

[17] Dalhousie, Midlothian, eight miles south of Edinburgh.

THE LETTERS, WRITINGS, AND SPEECHES OF OLIVER CROMWELL

so maybe there is a gesture of good will and calculation in this intercession by Cromwell on behalf of the father of his late major Cholmley for some compensation.[1]

[fo. 393r]

Sir

I doe not often trouble you in particular businesses, But I shalbe bold now, upon the desire of a worthy gentleman Leifet Col. Cholmley[2] to intreate your favour on his behalfe. the case Stands thus, His Sonne, Maior Cholmley[3] \who\ was kild in the feight against the Scottes at Winnick,[4] was Custome Maister at Carlile. The gentleman merited well from you, Since his death his aged father having lost this his eldest Sonne in your Service, did resolve to use his endeavour to procure the place for a younger Sonne[5] who had likewise been in your Service, and resolving to obtaine my letter to Some freinds about it, did acquaint an under tennant[6] of the place to his Sonne with this his purpose to come to me, to the borders of Scotland to obtayne the said letter which the said tennt. did Say was very well and when the Said leifet. Colonell was come for my letter, This tennant immediately hastens away to london, where hee in a very circumventing and deceiptfull way preferrs a peticon to the house of Commons. getts a referrence to the Committee of the Navy. who approve of the Said man by the mediation of Some gentlemen. But I heare there is a Stop of it in the house. My humble Suite to you is, that if Colonell Morgan[7] doe wayte upon you about this

---

[1] See the resolution of the House of Commons on 20 October, about which Cromwell may have heard just before writing this letter: 'A Letter from Sir Henry Chomley was this Day read, touching the Command in Chief of the Forces at the Siege of Pontefract. Resolved, &c. That a Letter be written to the General; and this Letter from Sir Henry Cholmley inclosed: And that it be recommended to the General, to settle the Business with Respect to Sir Henry Chomley's Honour, and faithful Services; and especially for the Carrying on of the Service' *JHC*, 6:56–7. See also Andrew Hopper, *Black Tom: Sir Thomas Fairfax and the English Revolution* (Manchester, 2007), p. 83. Sir Henry Cholmley's own letter precedes it in the volume: Bodl. MS Tanner 57/2, fos 391r–2v (no. 205).

[2] Almost certainly John Cholmley of Braham, Yorkshire, buried at Spofforth, aged 74, on 27 October 1653, Hopper, *Directory of Parliamentary Allegiance*, p. 119.

[3] Major John Cholmley, whose will was proved at York on 23 December 1648. For the family details of Cholmley of Braham, see J. W Clay, ed., *Dugdale's Visitation of Yorkshire, with additions*, 3 vols. (Exeter, 1899–1917), 2:444–6.

[4] Winwick, in South Lancashire, where some of the later actions of the 'battle of Preston' took place.

[5] Not identified.   [6] Not identified.

[7] Sir Thomas Morgan, first baronet (1604–79), army officer. See *ODNB*. Morgan married Cholmley's daughter no later than 1650.

businesse I (having given you this true information of the State of it, as I have received it) you would be pleased to further his desire concerning leifet Col. Cholmleyes younger Sonne that hee may have the place confer'd upon him and that you would acquaint Some of my freinds herewith. By which you will very much oblige Your most humble Servt.

O Cromwell

Burroughbriggs[8]

Oct 28th 1648

For the Honorable Wm Lenthall Esqr. Speaker to the house of Commons, these.

1648 11 02

Letter from Oliver Cromwell to Charles Fairfax

Date: 2 November 1648

Source: Museum of London, Tangye MS 706, no. 98 (autograph)

This is the first in a short series of letters between Cromwell and Charles Fairfax, uncle of Sir Thomas Fairfax.[1] It is in the hand of Cromwell's usual secretary and is signed by Cromwell himself. It has no addressee but is clearly one of a sequence subsequently acquired by Sir Richard Tangye, and Lomas is surely correct in seeing Fairfax as the recipient of this letter too. Cromwell was moving from place to place finding the right control post for the siege of Pontefract. On 28 October 1648 he was at Boroughbridge (on the Great North Road well to the north of Pontefract); by 2 November, when he wrote this letter, he was at Byram House, 1.5 miles north of Pontefract and by no later than 6 November and until 29 November he was at Knottingley, just over two miles to the north-east of Pontefract.

Sir

Being inform'd by Sir Edward Rodes[2] this evening, that there is a party of the enemyes horse gonne out of Pontefract Castle,[3] and having some apprehension

---

[8] Boroughbridge, North Yorkshire, from where Cromwell supervised the siege of Pontefract over the next month.

[1] Charles Fairfax (1597–1673), antiquary and genealogist. See ODNB.
[2] Sir Edward Rodes. See **1648 08 20a**.
[3] Pontefract, West Yorkshire. Seized by royalist troops on 8 June 1648, it was to hold out until 22 March 1649. It was on the Great North Road, about 17 miles south east of Leeds.

that they will attempt Somewhat upon the horse guard in the parke by coming upon their reare, I desire you that you would Send to their assistance five files of musquetteirs, who will give them time to mount their horses if the enemy shall attempt upon them with horse and foot. I desire you to Send them Commaunder of the guard there this enclosed note, Not having more I rest.

Your affectionate Servant

O Cromwell

Byron[4] No: the 2ᵈ at 8 at night.

1648 11 06a
From 'Heron's brother' to Robert Hammond

Date: 6 November 1648

Source: Lambeth Palace Library, MS 933, no. 68 (one of three contemporary or near-contemporary copies)

This letter has been thought to be by Cromwell since Sir Charles Firth first discovered a copy of it in the Clarke Papers in Worcester College, Oxford in the early 1890s.[1] While he was in the process of editing it for publication, S. R. Gardiner drew Firth's attention to a second copy in the papers of the marquis of Lothian at Newbattle Abbey. This version of the letter (together with other Lothian papers) is now in the National Archives of Scotland.[2] It is that version which Firth published in his edition of the *Clarke Papers*.[3] In a hand different from that of the scribe, the Lothian version calls it 'A letter from L.G.C.', presumably Lord General Cromwell. In yet another hand is added 'Cromwell lost [or last] letters'. In the same collection, are two other holograph letters from Cromwell to Hammond dated December 1647 and May 1651.[4] Because of this and 'from internal evidence' (unspecified), Firth concluded that this was a letter from Cromwell to Hammond. But there exists a third copy of the letter in the Tenison papers in Lambeth Palace library. This muddies the water because a contemporary (not the scribe) has written on this copy, 'this is Will Rowe's letter by a feigned name'. There is further separate endorsement 'Lre

---

[4] Byram is a hamlet close to Knottingley and less than two miles from Pontefract. By the time he next wrote (on 6 November) Cromwell was stationed in Knottingley itself.

[1] Worcester College, Oxford, Clarke MS 1/3 (XVI), unfol.

[2] NAS, GD 40/2/19/1, no. 23 [previously no. 16].

[3] *Clarke Papers*, 2:49–53. Firth (correctly) preferred the Newbattle/NAS version to the Clarke version because it was 'an obviously better text'.

[4] See **1647 12 26[?]** and **1651 05 13**.

6 NOVEMBER 1648A

of Will.Roe'. Rowe, of course, was Cromwell's scoutmaster from sometime in early 1648, and he had been entrusted by Cromwell with a critical mission to Edinburgh in September 1648 (**1648 09 16b**, **1648 09 18**, **1648 10 02**). This third version has a few unimportant divergences from the Lothian version. In most of them, the Clarke version endorses the Lambeth not the Lothian version. On that ground alone, the *text* used here is the Lambeth Palace library version. But deciding whether the author was Cromwell or Rowe (or someone else) is more complicated.

The case for this being a letter of Cromwell's is strong but not watertight. All three copies of the letter are dated from Knottingley, Cromwell's headquarters for the siege of Pontefract. Cromwell wrote regularly to Hammond, calling him Robin, and this letter is of a type with others in the sequence[5] except in one important matter. This would be the only Cromwell letter to Hammond to use a simple cypher (codenames), the author referring in the course of the letter to 'brother Heron' or 'Herne', to 'brother Fountain' and to 'Sir Richard'. Cromwell uses just such a cypher on other occasions. It is clear from those other occasions that 'Brother Heron/Herne' is Sir Henry Vane,[6] a close ally of Cromwell's from the beginning of the Long Parliament until the establishment of the High Court of Justice to try the King (but not thereafter); and Vane was one of the parliamentary commissioners with the King on the Isle of Wight throughout November 1648. Cromwell signs himself 'Brother Fountain' in a letter to Vane written in 1644 and is referred to by the name in a letter from Vane to Cromwell in 1651.[7]

A close comparison of this letter with the long letter Cromwell wrote in his own name less than three weeks later offers ambiguous evidence.[8] This later letter of 25 November is a reply to a letter from Hammond to Cromwell that *could* itself be a reply to this letter, although this remains supposition. There is some overlap in content and wording, perhaps most obviously the reference to the Levellers: 'for what wee would have, how easy to take offence at things called Levellers & runn into an extremity on the other hand, medling with an accursed thing?' (6 Nov.); 'DOEST thou not think, that fear of the Levellers (of whom there is no fear) that they would destroy nobility, had caused some to rake up corruption, to find it lawful to *make this ruining hypocritical agreement* (on one part).' (25 Nov.). More tantalising is how Cromwell on 25 November quotes Hammond as speaking of 'the dissatisfaction you take at the ways of some good men, whom you love with your heart, who through this principle, that it is lawful for a lesser part (if in the right) to force, &c.' This might just be Hammond quoting back to Cromwell the letter of 6 November: 'Are they not a litle justifyed in this, That a lesser party of a Parliat. hath made it lawfull to declare the greater parte a faction & made the Parliat. null & call'd a new one, & To doe this by force & This by the same Mouths that condemn'd it in others.' But note that on

---

[5] See **1647 12 26[?]**, **1648 01 03b**, **1648 04 06**, **1648 11 25a**, **1651 05 13**.

[6] Vane refers to himself twice as brother Heron in letters to Cromwell in 1651 (J. Nickolls, *Original Letters and Papers of State, Addressed to Oliver Cromwell* (1743), pp. 78–9, 84).

[7] Cromwell signs himself 'brother Fountain' in a letter to Vane on 22 April 1644 (**1644 04 22**), and Vane addresses him as 'Brother Fountain' in 1651 (Nickolls, *Originall Letters*, p. 79).

[8] See below, **1648 11 25**.

THE LETTERS, WRITINGS, AND SPEECHES OF OLIVER CROMWELL

25 November Hammond is said to have attributed this phrase not to Cromwell but to 'some men'. The evidence keeps cutting two ways. One straw that does blow in the direction of Cromwellian authorship is the use of the phrase 'wee wayte upon the Lord, who will teach us & lead us, whether to doing or suffering', which is very reminiscent of his phrase in a letter of 1638, 'if heere I may honour my God either by doeinge, or sufferinge I shalbe most glad'.[9]

It is also important but not conclusive that the copy in the Lothian papers ascribes authorship to Cromwell. The volume in which that letter appears is a collection of separates with little in common with one another, documents that had come into the possession of the Lothian family over the late seventeenth and eighteenth centuries but *not* in 1648 or during the Interregnum. The authority of the ascription to L.G.C. cannot be determined.

The case *against* Cromwell's authorship is strong but perhaps less strong. The Lambeth copy is in the Gibson papers: manuscripts donated by Edmund Gibson, Bishop of London, which came to the library upon his death in 1748. The bulk of Gibson's collection came from Archbishop Tenison (Gibson had been his librarian and chaplain): and this was amongst the Tenison collection, in a miscellaneous collection of correspondence from across the seventeenth and into the eighteenth centuries. It is a 'loose' item.[10] How Tenison got hold of it is completely unknown. But that version very firmly ascribes the letter to William Rowe. Even more to the point, the letter is in the hand of William Rowe[11] so he clearly wrote it or himself made a copy. That of course may explain why someone who owned it before Gibson thought it was authored by Rowe. His hand is highly distinctive. But surviving examples of Rowe's writing are rare, and none are in the Tenison/Gibson collection, so that need not be the explanation. Moreover, Rowe as well as Cromwell used this same cypher on other occasions, although Rowe appears to make an error in his use of it twenty-one months later (perhaps a trick of memory years after it was in common use?)[12]

Why would Cromwell, for the only time in a sequence of letters across 1648, sign himself not with his own name but as 'Heron's brother'? This is the *only* letter to Hammond using that cypher. Is that not odd? Why did Hammond not keep it with the other letters from Cromwell across 1648 which were then published together in the eighteenth century? Furthermore since, in the cypher, Cromwell is 'Brother Fountain', why does the author of this letter refer to 'Brother Fountain' in the third person—'especially takeing in some Doubts, that Sir Roger & Bro: Fountayne are also turn'd Presbiterians'? And why not

---

[9] See **1638 10 13**.

[10] For the catalogue entry, see http://archives.lambethpalacelibrary.org.uk/CalmView/Record.aspx?src=CalmView.Catalog&id=MSS%2f929–942%2f933.

[11] 'Copies of papers which passed between the English and Scotch Commissioners in Scotland', more than 6,000 words in Rowe's certified hand can be found in the Main Papers of the House of Lords, At HL/PO/JO/10/1/195.

[12] On 30 August 1650 William Rowe wrote to Cromwell from Whitehall; 'Your brother Fountayne is drawing up a declaration in answere to the Scotts King's, and I must bee his amanuensis all day to-morrow' (Nickolls, *Originall Letters*, pp. 16–17).

608

6 NOVEMBER 1648A

sign it 'Brother Fountain' rather than 'Heron's brother'? But then again, would Rowe have had the degree of familiarity with Hammond to write in such a way? And did he have the status and authority to write in this manner? On balance, probably not.

Much more work needs to be done on Rowe before these questions can be answered. What we can say is that he had moved in exalted circles for some years. In the spring of 1645 he was secretary to the parliamentary commissioners at the treaty of Uxbridge and from that time forward he had been closely involved in Anglo-Scottish relations as a messenger between the two Parliaments (as when he was 'employed to carry a Letter from both Houses to the Parliament of Scotland'), or when he called in by one or both houses to report on meetings with (for example), the marquis of Argyll, Lord Chancellor Loudoun, or the full Parliament. He was also 'Secretary to the Commissioners of both Houses' at Newark in May 1646, as soon as the King had surrendered himself to the Scots. He made at least three visits to Scotland as messenger of the Houses between late 1645 and mid-1647. On 11 November 1645 Lord Wharton presented to the Lords twenty-two documents, all attested by Rowe to be true copies of documents signed by English or Scottish parliamentarians and some of the English documents drafted by Rowe. They all related to '[w]hat passed between the English Scots commissioner in Scotland, concerning the Treaty about the Garrisons on the Borders; to prevent the Scots Army levying Money; Protections; Accompts. &c'. He was the clerk responsible for writing out the proposals of the English commissioners headed by Lord Wharton, but significantly for this item, by Henry Vane (and William Armyne).[13]

But then: where was Rowe on 6 November? We do not know. He was still in Edinburgh as one of Cromwell's two envoys (the other being Colonel John Bright) on 17 October when he wrote a newsletter about events there.[14] He was at Army headquarters at Windsor by 25 November when he is noted as being present at the Council of the Army.[15] So he could have been in Knottingley with Cromwell on 6 November; what would have been more natural than for a man born and brought up in Pontefract[16] to stop over as he travelled down the Great North Road to meet up with his commanding officer at the siege of his home town? But whereas we can be sure Cromwell was in Knottingley that day, we can only speculate that Rowe was there.

Of course, the letter could have been written by another person entirely, clearly someone who had been in a senior position during the Scottish campaign in the autumn of 1648 and who was with Cromwell on 6 November. That rules out, for example, John Lambert. Such a person would also need to know Hammond well enough to use the familiar 'Robin' and to know the cypher. No-one springs to mind.

So this letter must be treated with caution. But there is not sufficient evidence to exclude it from the canon of Cromwell texts. Its comments on Providence, on the religious

---

[13] *JHC*, 4:341–2, 384–5, *JHC*, 5:294–5, *JHL*, 7:690–6.   [14] *Clarke Papers*, 2:42–4.

[15] *Clarke Papers*, 2:278.

[16] Anon., 'Grant by Edward Bysshe, Garter King of Arms to William Rowe', *Yorkshire Archaeology Society*, 18 (1905), p. 347.

THE LETTERS, WRITINGS, AND SPEECHES OF OLIVER CROMWELL

settlement, and its anticipation of Pride's Purge make it potentially a very important letter. But doubts linger.

The content of the letter raises a number of issues. Two men are being addressed: Hammond and Vane. Much of the letter takes the form of a request to Hammond to pass on information to Vane. Why did the author not write to Vane directly since he knew him to be with Hammond on the Isle of Wight? Is he using this as a device to tell Hammond unpalatable truths? Some parts of the letter are very much 'Cromwell' ('Peace is onely good, when wee receive it out of our Fathers hand, Its dangerous to snatch it, most danger-ous to goe against the will of God to attayne it: Warre is good when lead to it by our Father, most evill when it comes from the lusts that are in our Members, wee wayte upon the Lord, who will teach us & lead us, whether to doing or suffering'). But others are not: where (at least before 1654) can you find him speaking of the union of 'Scotts, English, Jewes Gentiles, Presbiterians Indepts. Anabapts'?[17] Would the man who was an architect of the Heads of the Proposals, which had allowed for the restoration of an emasculated episcopacy in a national church of which no-one was required to be a member,[18] ask Hammond to 'tell my Bro: Heron I smyled at his expression, concerning my wise friends opinion, who thinkes that the inthroneing the King with Presbitery brings spirituall Slavery, but with a moderated Episcopacy, workes a good Peace. Both are a hard Choyce: I trust there's noe Necessity of Eyther except our base unbeleife & fleshly wisdome make it soe'?

This is a clearly a really important letter, not least in its apparent prediction of Pride's Purge. But it is a problem letter.

Knottingley Novbr. 6. 1648
Deare Robin

I trust the same spirit that guided thee heretofore is still with thee: looke to thy heart, Thou art where temptations multiply: I feare least our friends should burne their Fingers as some others did not long since, whose hearts have aked since for it: How easy is it to fynde Argumts. for what wee would have, how easy to take offence at things called Levellers & runn into an extremity on the other hand, medling with an accursed thing?[19] Peace is only good, when wee receive it out of our Fathers hand, Its dangerous to snatch it, most dangerous to goe agaynst the will of God to attayne it: Warre is good when lead to it by our Father, most evill when it comes from the lusts that are in our Members, wee wayte upon the

---

[17] See discussion in the introduction to this item.

[18] Gardiner, *Constitutional Documents of the Puritan Revolution*, p. 321 (articles XI and XII).

[19] 'And ye, in any wise keep *yourselves* from the accursed thing, lest ye make *yourselves* accursed, when ye take of the accursed thing, and make the camp of Israel a curse, and trouble it.' Joshua 6:18 (*KJV*).

6 NOVEMBER 1648A

Lord,[20] who will teach us & lead us, whether to doing or suffering: Tell my Bro: Heron[21] I smyled at his expression, concerning my wise friends opinion, who thinkes that the inthroneing the King with Presbitery brings spirituall Slavery, but with a moderated Episcopacy, workes a good Peace Both are a hard Choyce: I trust there's noe Necessity of Eyther except our base unbeleife & fleshly wisdome make it soe: But if I have any Logick it willbee easyer to tyrannize, haveing that he likes & serves his turne, then what you know & all beleive he soe much Dislikes. But as to my Bro: himselfe, tell him indeed I thinke some of my friends have advanced too farre & need make an Honoble. Retreate, Scotts Treatyes haveing wrought some perplexityes & hindering matters from going soe Glyb as otherwise was hoped especially takeing in some Doubts, that Sir Roger[22] & Bro: Fountayne[23] are also turn'd Presbiterians: Deare Robin, Tell Bro: Herne[24] that wee have the witnes of our Consciences, that wee have walked in this thing (whatsoever surmizes are to the contrary) in playnnes and Godly simplicity, according to our weake measure & wee trust our daily busines is to approve our Consciences to Godward, & not to shift & sharke,[25] which were exceeding basenes in us to Doe, haveing had such favour from the Lord, & such manifestacions of his presence & I hope the same experience will keep their hearts & hands from him, agaynst whom God hath soe witnessed, though reason should suggest things never soe plausible: I pray thee tell my Bro: Herne[26] thus much from me, and if a mistake concerning our complyance with presbitery perplex an evill busines (for soe I accompt it, and make the wheeles of such a Chariott goe heavy, I can bee passive & lett it goe, knowing that innocency & integrity looses nothing by a patient wayting upon the Lord: Our Papers are Publique: Let us be judged by them: Answeres doe not involve us, I professe to thee - [27] I desire from my heart, I have prayed for it I have wayted for the day to see Union & right Understanding

---

[20] This is a phrase that can be found throughout the Bible, but most obviously in Psalms 37:9: 'those that wait upon the Lord, they shall inherit the earth'.

[21] 'Herne' in the Lothian and Clarke versions.

[22] Not identified, but clearly a code name.

[23] See discussion in the introduction to this item.   [24] i.e. Sir Henry Vane.

[25] 'shark(e)'= to 'cut or tear'. See *OED*.   [26] Sir Henry Vane.

[27] There's a sort of dash after this: possibly a blurred full stop, possibly just a fill-in to the end of the line. 'I professe to thee' could equally well belong to the preceding or succeeding clauses (despite only being separated by a comma from the preceding clause). It reads better as going with the succeeding one, but is that what was intended? The Lothian version has a comma before and after the clause 'I profess to thee'. The Clarke version has a comma before but no punctuation after that clause.

THE LETTERS, WRITINGS, AND SPEECHES OF OLIVER CROMWELL

betweene the Godly People (Scotts, English, Jewes Gentiles, Presbiterians Indepts. Anabapts[28] and all) Our Br of Scotld. (really the[29] Presbians.) were our greatest Enemyes: God hath justifyed us in their sight, caused us to requite good for evill, caused them to acknowledge it publiquely by Acts of State, & privately, & the thing is true in the sight of the sunn It is an high conviction upon them, was it not fitt to bee Civill, to professe love, to deale with cleernes with them for removeing of prejudice, to aske them what they had agaynst Us and to give them an honest answere, This wee have done & not more, And herein is a more glorious worke in our eyes then if wee had gotten the sacking and plunder of Edinbh, the strong castles into our hands, & made a conquest from Tweed to the Orcades[30] & wee can say through God, wee have left by the grace of God such a witnes amongst them, as if it worke not yet, (by reason the poore soules are soe wedded to their Governamt. yet there is that conviction upon them that will undoubtedly beare its fruit in due tyme: Tell my Bro: Herne[31] I beleive my wise friend would have had a conquest or if not, things putt in a Ballance the first was not[32] unfeazable, but I thinke not Christian & I was comanded the contrary by the two Howses, as for the later by the Providence of God, it is perfectly come to passe Not by our wisdome for I durst not designe it, I durst not admitt of soe mixed soe low a consideracion wee were ledd not (to the prayse of our God bee it spoken) to more Sincere more spirituall consideracons, but as I sayd before: The Lord hath brought it to a ballance if there bee any dangerous disproporcion It is that the honest party (if I may without offence soe call them)[33] in my apprehencion are the weaker & have manifold Difficultyes to conflict withall: I wish our unworthines here cast not the Scale both here & there, the wrong way: I have but one word more to say: Thy friends Deare Robin are in heart & in profession what they were, have not dissembled their principles at all Are they not a litle justifyed in this, That a lesser party of a Parliat. hath made it lawfull to declare the greater parte a faction & made the Parliat. null & call'd[34] a new one, & To doe this by

---

[28] See discussion in the introduction.

[29] The Lothian and Clarke versions omit the 'the' and have it as 'really Presbiterians'.

[30] From the Tweed (Anglo-Scottish Border) to the Orkneys (far North).

[31] See the introduction to this item.

[32] The Lothian version adds a 'very' to 'unfeazible'.

[33] Can Anti-Engaging Scottish Presbyterians, who had so denounced the 'honest' men amongst the Ironsides, now be called 'honest' themselves by Cromwell?

[34] Lothian version has 'call' not 'call'd'.

6 NOVEMBER 1648B

force[35] & This by the same Mouths that[36] condemn'd it in others Thinke of the Example[37] & of the consequence & lett others thinke of it too, if they bee not drench'd too deepe in their owne reason & opinion: Robin Bee honest still: God keepe thee in the midst of snares: Thou hast Naturally a valiant spirit Listen to God & he shall increase it upon thee & make thee valiant for the truth I am a poore creature that write to thee, the poorest in the world, but I have hope in God & I desire from my heart to love his people, and if thou hast oppertunity & a free heart Lett me heare from thee how it is with thee: This[38] bearer is faythfull you may bee very free to comunicate with Him: My service to all my friends & to my Deare Bro: Heron[39] whom I love in the Lord. I rest

Thy true & faythfull friend
Herons[40] Brother.[41]

This is Will Rowes letter by a feigned name
Lr. of Will. Roe.[42]

1648 11 06b
Letter from Oliver Cromwell to Charles Fairfax

Date: 6 November 1648
Source: Museum of London, Tangye MS 706, no. 102 (autograph)

As with **1648 11 02**, this is in the hand of Cromwell's secretary and contains his own signature. This one, clearly a follow-up to **1648 11 02**, is clearly addressed (in the same hand) to Charles Fairfax and modifies Cromwell's request for assistance at the siege of Pontefract.

---

[35] This is an account of how the Covenanters seized control of the Scottish Parliament and began a comprehensive purge of all those who had supported the Engagement with the King.

[36] Lothian version has 'I' rather than 'that'.

[37] A prediction of Pride's Purge on 6 December 1648?

[38] The Lothian version has 'the bearer'.   [39] See the introduction to this item.

[40] The Lothian version has 'Herne's'.

[41] Why 'Heron's brother' when he is known to Vane as Brother Fountain?

[42] Both these endorsements are in a seventeenth-century secretary hand, but *not* in the same hand as the rest of the letter. Is this evidence that this version had been sent in the posts? The paper has clearly been folded up at some stage in its history.

For the honoble: Colonell Fairfax[1] in Pontefract.[2] these.

Sir

I did Order a company of my lord Generalls Regimt[3] to be with the guard of horse in the Parke this night. But finding it fitt to dispose of that company to another place I thought fitt to desire of you, that you would Send Six files of musquetteirs to the guard in the parke this night in the roome of the Other. I shall have occasion alsoe to remove one of the troopes from the guard in the parke to another place, wherefore I desire You that you would only retaine twenty horse of the troope that is to doe duty in the towne, and Send the rest to Strengthen the guard of horse in the parke. I hope within a night or two; now tooles are come; Wee shall not putt yow: to soe much trouble. I rest Sir

Your affectionate Servant

O Cromwell

Nottingley[4] No: 6th 1648

1648 11 09

Letter from Oliver Cromwell to John Morris, governor of Pontefract Castle

Date: 9 November 1648
Source: Worcester College, Oxford, Clarke MS 16, fo. 5r (contemporary copy)

This letter survives in two forms, a copy made at the time by William Clarke, Secretary to the Army (but not with Cromwell in the north) and in a newspaper.[1] The latter also includes John Morris,[2] governor of Pontefract's answer to this summons[3] and tells us that the governor had failed to inform the townsmen that he had

---

[1] See **1648 11 02**. [2] See **1648 11 02**.
[3] i.e. the foot regiment of Sir Thomas Fairfax, which was certainly with him at this time: Firth and Davies, *Regimental History*, 1:328.
[4] Knottingley, just two miles from Pontefract Castle.

---

[1] *The Moderate Intelligencer* no. 191 for 9–16 November 1648, unpag. (N&S, 419.75; Thomason / E.472[11]).
[2] John Morris (c.1615–49), army officer. See ODNB. Morris was a local man.
[3] Sir, I am confident you doe not expect that I should passe my answer before I be satisfied, that the Summoner has power to performe my conditions, which must be confirmed by Parliament, besides the dispute betwixt your selfe, and Sir *Henry Cholmley*, Commander in chiefe by Commission of the Committee of the *Militia* of *Yorkshire*, who, as I am informed,

10 NOVEMBER 1648

received a summons. Cromwell chose this moment to issue his summons after Morris had bungled an attempt to burn down the 'New Hall' at the edge of the town since they could no longer hold it. Cromwell's men extinguished the fire and used the New Hall as a forward point. There are no important differences between the two versions, and this follows the more official 'army' copy.

———

Sir Beeing Coome Hither for the Reduction of this garrison[4] I thought fitt to summon you to deliver ~~this~~ your garrison to mee for the use of the Parliment those gentlemen & soldiers with you may have better Tearms then if you shoold hold it out to extremitie I expect your Answear this[5] &. Rest

Your servant

O: Cromwell

Nov: 9th 1648

to the governor of Pontect:[6] Castle

———

1648 11 10

Letter from Oliver Cromwell to Colonel Charles Fairfax

Date: 10 November 1648
Source: Museum of London, Tangye MS 706, no. 107 (autograph)

This is in Cromwell's secretary's hand and bears his signature, and once again it deals with the stretched resources at his disposal. *The Moderate Intelligencer* no. 191 (see **1648 11 09**) says: 'we are going on with the siege, or blocking up of *Pomfret* to admiration (considering our wants, compar'd with the season, and discouragements from your parts, sufficient to make any Souldiers in the world that fights onely for gelt, to sheath, and be gone).'

———

denyes all subordination to your authority: when my understanding is cleered in this concerning scruple, I shall endeavour to be as modest in my reply, as I have read you in your Summons. Sir, *Your servant*, John Morris. *Pont.* Castle, *Novemb.* 9, 1648. For Lieutenant Gen. *Cromwell.*

4 *The Moderate Intelligencer* has 'place' and not 'garrison'.
5 *The Moderate Intelligencer* has 'this day' and not 'this &c'.
6 i.e. Pontefract (also known as Pomfret).

For the hoble: Col. Charles Fairfax at Pontefract. these
Sir

I have perused your letter. I am very Sorry that your Condicon should be Soe ~~Straight~~ Straite. I pray you Strive with difficultyes as farr as you can, and for my part I will doe what lyes in me to get yow Supplyd. I shall upon this occasion Send expressly to the Committee[1] for a fortnights pay for you, and if I be deny'd, I shall thinke I am not fairly dealt withall. I shall let them know, that I thinke present money & nothing else will keep the men together. And truly, if that my lending of you a hundred pounds for the present will doe you any Service, you shall have it in the morning if you please to Send for it. I have written to Lincolne and Leicester to keep in ~~Ca~~ the Capt Jacksons[2] and the other Companye of foot for a fortnight their officers promised me they should performe duty as before untill they had an answer. I desire you to Send them this enclosed order I {—}[3] take it not ill at all that you give out the word, nor can I take anything ill at your hands, I pray you Still accompt me

Your true & faithfull frend & Servt.
O Cromwell

Knottingley[4] No. 10th 1648

~~I shall desire you to~~ \speed/ ~~send this letter by an express to Yorke.~~

The word is[5]

---

[1] Presumably the Derby House Committee at Westminster.
[2] Captain Jackson: not identified. There are several Captain Jacksons in the pre-New Model Army, but none seems plausible. Wanklyn (*Reconstructing*, 1:161 fn. iii) thinks it may be the William Jackson who had served in the Northern Brigade pre-1647, but that is speculation.
[3] There are three or four letters heavily scored out.
[4] Knottingley, two miles from Pontefract.
[5] An apparently abandoned postscript. This presumably indicates that Cromwell was dictating directly to his secretary.

1648 11 11a
Letter from Oliver Cromwell to Charles Fairfax

Date: 11 November 1648
Source: Museum of London, Tangye MS 706 no. 108 (autograph)

The first of two short notes from Cromwell to Charles Fairfax written on 11 November. It is in the hand of Cromwell's usual clerk and with Cromwell's own signature and seal.

Sir

The bearer has been with me, complaines exceedingly of her poverty, as not able to get victualls for her familye, & yet is forced to maintaine sold: much beyond her ability. I desire that what favour can be afforded here you would doe it. at the desire of
Your humble Servt
O Cromwell

Knottin: No. 11th 1648
For the honoble Col. Charles Fairfax at Pontefract these

1648 11 11b
Letter from Oliver Cromwell to Charles Fairfax

Date: 11 November 1648
Source: Museum of London, Tangye MS 706 no. 109 (autograph)

This is the last in the series of surviving letters between Cromwell and Charles Fairfax, once again written by his usual clerk and signed by Cromwell himself. It shows even more courtesty—compassion—than **1648 11 11a** (although we have no way of knowing which was written first). They appear here as catalogued in the nineteenth century. They could possibly relate to the same woman, 'Mrs Gray'.

Sir,

The bearer Mrs Gray[1] is desirous to goe into the Castle to See a brother of hers who lyes sick in the Castle – I desire you would let her have a drumme & give her your pass to returne within a limitted time I rest Sir Your very humble Servt
O Cromwell

Knottingley No the 11th 1648

For the hoble Colonell Fairfax in Pontefract these

1648 11 13

Annotation by Oliver Cromwell to a letter from Charles Fairfax

Date: [on or after] 13 November 1648
Source: Museum of London, Tangye MS 706 no. 111 (holograph comment)

This very brief endorsement of a letter from Charles Fairfax[1] completes the series of correspondence between them in the early part of November 1648 (above **1648 11 02, 1648 11 06, 1648 11 07, 1648 11 10, 1648 11 11a, 1648 11 11b**). There is one later extant letter, dated 8 May 1652 (below, **1652 07 08**). Of those mentioned in Fairfax's letter, John Morris was

---

[1] Neither 'Mrs Gray' nor her brother have been identified.

---

[1] The text of that letter is: 'Honorable Sir, The bearer herof has an humble sute to present unto yow And this is the case Mr Dawson a Norfolk drover havinge suffered losse to the vallue of 1300 li. by the Enimy in the Castle who tooke from him 267 beasts most of them fatt oxen And he havinge bene permitted to solicit a restitution of all or part Upon good ingagmt to give neither money nor arme nor any thinge for them And havinge prevailed with Morris that the Hydes shalbe returned, And Captaine Oates givinge his faithfull promise that if itt can be proved by good information & credible persons that ani consideration was given for them by the said Dawson or any other by his procurmt or privity that then the said Captaine shalbe responsible for the use of the souldiers that beleaguer the Castle soe much money as shalbe really proved to have bene soe payed for the said Hydes I did therfore \about a Moneth agoe/ (with the consent of all our Officers) order towards his losses that he by himselfe or agents should have free liberty to receive the sayd Hydes or soe many of them as he can procure Provided they were of his owne beasts only & not any other Now yow may please to be informed that ther are about 120 received & the rest are ready but without your allowance I will graunt noe passe some small benefitt may be made of them but if a little longer delayed neither the pore man nor ani other can make anythinge of them Leavinge all to your wisdome I take leave beinge your most humble servant C Fairfax.
Pontfr 13 of 9 br. {164}8'

1648 11 11a
Letter from Oliver Cromwell to Charles Fairfax

Date: 11 November 1648
Source: Museum of London, Tangye MS 706 no. 108 (autograph)

The first of two short notes from Cromwell to Charles Fairfax written on 11 November. It is in the hand of Cromwell's usual clerk and with Cromwell's own signature and seal.

Sir
The bearer has been with me, complaines exceedingly of her poverty, as not able to get victualls for her familye, & yet is forced to maintaine sold: much beyond her ability. I desire that what favour can be afforded here you would doe it. at the desire of
Your humble Servt
O Cromwell

Knottin: No. 11th 1648
For the honoble Col. Charles Fairfax at Pontefract these

1648 11 11b
Letter from Oliver Cromwell to Charles Fairfax

Date: 11 November 1648
Source: Museum of London, Tangye MS 706 no. 109 (autograph)

This is the last in the series of surviving letters between Cromwell and Charles Fairfax, once again written by his usual clerk and signed by Cromwell himself. It shows even more courtesty—compassion—than **1648 11 11a** (although we have no way of knowing which was written first). They appear here as catalogued in the nineteenth century. They could possibly relate to the same woman, 'Mrs Gray'.

Sir,
The bearer Mrs Gray[1] is desirous to goe into the Castle to See a brother of hers who lyes sick in the Castle – I desire you would let her have a drumme & give her your pass to returne within a limitted time I rest Sir Your very humble Servt
O Cromwell
Knottingley No the 11th 1648
For the hoble Colonell Fairfax in Pontefract these

1648 11 13
Annotation by Oliver Cromwell to a letter from Charles Fairfax

Date: [on or after] 13 November 1648
Source: Museum of London, Tangye MS 706 no. 111 (holograph comment)

This very brief endorsement of a letter from Charles Fairfax[1] completes the series of correspondence between them in the early part of November 1648 (above **1648 11 02, 1648 11 06, 1648 11 07, 1648 11 10, 1648 11 11a, 1648 11 11b**). There is one later extant letter, dated 8 May 1652 (below, **1652 07 08**). Of those mentioned in Fairfax's letter, John Morris was

---

[1] Neither 'Mrs Gray' nor her brother have been identified.

---

[1] The text of that letter is: 'Honorable Sir, The bearer herof has an humble sute to present unto yow And this is the case Mr Dawson a Norfolk drover havinge suffered losse to the vallue of 1300 li. by the Enimy in the Castle who tooke from him 267 beasts most of them fatt oxen And he havinge bene permitted to solicit a restitution of all or part Upon good ingagmt to give neither money nor arme nor any thinge for them And havinge prevailed with Morris that the Hydes shalbe returned, And Captaine Oates givinge his faithfull promise that if itt can be proved by good information & credible persons that ani consideration was given for them by the said Dawson or any other by his procurmt or privity that then the said Captaine shalbe responsible for the use of the souldiers that beleaguer the Castle soe much money as shalbe really proved to have bene soe payed for the said Hydes I did therfore \about a Moneth agoe/ (with the consent of all our Officers) order towards his losses that he by himselfe or agents should have free liberty to receive the sayd Hydes or soe many of them as he can procure Provided they were of his owne beasts only & not any other Now yow may please to be informed that ther are about 120 received & the rest are ready but without your allowance I will graunt noe passe some small benefitt may be made of them but if a little longer delayed neither the pore man nor ani other can make anything of them Leavinge all to your wisdome I take leave beinge your most humble servant C Fairfax.
Pontfr 13 of 9 br. {164}8'

10 NOVEMBER 1648

received a summons. Cromwell chose this moment to issue his summons after Morris had bungled an attempt to burn down the 'New Hall' at the edge of the town since they could no longer hold it. Cromwell's men extinguished the fire and used the New Hall as a forward point. There are no important differences between the two versions, and this follows the more official 'army' copy.

Sir Beeing Coome Hither for the Reduction of this garrison[4] I thought fitt to summon you to deliver ~~this~~ your garrison to mee for the use of the Parliment those gentlemen & soldiers with you may have better Tearms then if you shoold hold it out to extremitie I expect your Answear this[5] &. Rest
Your servant
O: Cromwell

Nov: 9th 1648

to the governor of Pontect:[6] Castle

1648 11 10
Letter from Oliver Cromwell to Colonel Charles Fairfax

Date: 10 November 1648
Source: Museum of London, Tangye MS 706, no. 107 (autograph)

This is in Cromwell's secretary's hand and bears his signature, and once again it deals with the stretched resources at his disposal. *The Moderate Intelligencer* no. 191 (see **1648 11 09**) says: 'we are going on with the siege, or blocking up of *Pomfret* to admiration (considering our wants, compar'd with the season, and discouragements from your parts, sufficient to make any Souldiers in the world that fights onely for gelt, to sheath, and be gone).'

---

denyes all subordination to your authority: when my understanding is cleered in this concerning scruple, I shall endeavour to be as modest in my reply, as I have read you in your Summons. Sir, *Your servant*, John Morris. *Pont.* Castle, *Novemb.* 9, 1648. For Lieutenant Gen. *Cromwell*.

[4] *The Moderate Intelligencer* has 'place' and not 'garrison'.
[5] *The Moderate Intelligencer* has 'this day' and not 'this &c'.
[6] i.e. Pontefract (also known as Pomfret).

For the hoble: Col. Charles Fairfax at Pontefract. these
Sir

I have perused your letter. I am very Sorry that your Condicon should be Soe ~~Straight~~ Straite. I pray you Strive with difficultyes as farr as you can, and for my part I will doe what lyes in me to get yow Supplyd. I shall upon this occasion Send expressly to the Committee[1] for a fortnights pay for you, and if I be deny'd, I shall thinke I am not fairly dealt withall. I shall let them know, that I thinke present money & nothing else will keep the men together. And truly, if that my lending of you a hundred pounds for the present will doe you any Service, you shall have it in the morning if you please to Send for it. I have written to Lincolne and Leicester to keep in ~~Ca~~ the Capt Jacksons[2] and the other Companye of foot for a fortnight their officers promised me they should performe duty as before untill they had an answer. I desire you to Send them this enclosed order I {-}[3] take it not ill at all that you give out the word, nor can I take anything ill at your hands, I pray you Still accompt me

Your true & faithfull frend & Servt.
O Cromwell

Knottingley[4] No. 10th 1648

~~I shall desire you to~~ \speed/ ~~send this letter by an express to Yorke.~~

The word is[5]

---

[1] Presumably the Derby House Committee at Westminster.
[2] Captain Jackson: not identified. There are several Captain Jacksons in the pre-New Model Army, but none seems plausible. Wanklyn (*Reconstructing*, 1:161 fn. iii) thinks it may be the William Jackson who had served in the Northern Brigade pre-1647, but that is speculation.
[3] There are three or four letters heavily scored out.
[4] Knottingley, two miles from Pontefract.
[5] An apparently abandoned postscript. This presumably indicates that Cromwell was dictating directly to his secretary.

15 NOVEMBER 1648

a royalist turned parliamentarian turned royalist army officer from Esthagh, South Elmshall, near Pontefract,[2] Captain Thomas Oates was of gentry stock from Batley, south of Leeds, and 16 miles from Pontefract.[3] Dawson the drover has not been separately identified.

Sir I allwaise approve of what
comes from you, And I thinke this to
bee most æquall.

O Cromwell

For the right noble the
hoble Generall Leift Generall
Cromwell the{se} humbly
present Att the heade Quarters

1648 11 15

Letter from Oliver Cromwell to the Derby House Committee

Date: 15 November 1648

Source: *Propositions sent in a letter from Lieu. Gen. Cromvvell and his officers, to the Lords and Commons of the committee of Derby-house. And by them presented to the House of Commons: and by them read, and reffered to a committee. Die Sabbati Novemb. 19. 1648. Ordered by the Commons in Parliament assembled, that this letter from Lieutenant Generall Cromwell, be referred to the committee of the army. to make provisions of the particulars therein desired and mentioned. H. Elsynge, Cler. Parl. D. Com.* (Wing / C7164; Thomason / E.472[24]) (print copy)

This letter of Cromwell's survives only in two probably unauthorised print versions published by Robert Ibbitson, who had close links with the Army. The cover of one of them says that the Derby House Committee referred the letter to the House of Commons who referred it to the Army Committee, but there is no reference to this in the Journal of the

---

[2] John Morris (*c.*1615–49), army officer. See *ODNB*, which recounts the injustices which led to his execution once Pontefract finally surrendered in March 1649.

[3] *Online Directory of Parliamentarian Army Officers.*

619

THE LETTERS, WRITINGS, AND SPEECHES OF OLIVER CROMWELL

House of Commons.[1] The second version, published two days later, was also issued by Ibbitson, and the text of the letter is almost identical, but without any comment on the reception of the letter in Westminster.[2]

This letter, with its anxieties about the shortage of supplies, throws light on several of the preceding letters and also on Cromwell's preoccupations as he prepared for the Irish campaign a few months later. If he had difficulty getting what he needed in Yorkshire, what assurances could he get for his huge challenge in Ireland?

The letter in the pamphlet used as the base version here is also preceded by the following order: 'Ordered by the Commons in Parliament Assembled, That the Lieutenant of the Ordnance, be required to make provisions of, and issue out of the publique stores, two hundred and fifty barrels of pouder, for the service of the siege against Pomfret, and Scarborough Castles, and that they be likewise required, to provide and issue, such cannon bullet and ball, as the Committee of the Army shall give order for.' [pp. 2–3]

[p. 3]

For the Right Honourable the Committee of Lords and Commons sitting at Derby House these present.

My Lords and Gentlemen, So soon as I came into these parts, I met with an earnest desire from the Committee of this County, to take upon me the charge here, for the redusing of the Garison of *Pomfret*.[3]

I received also commands from my Lord Generall,[4] to the same effect.

I have had the sight of a Letter to the House of Commons, wherein things are so represented, as if this siege were at such a passe, that the prize were already gained: In consideration whereof, I thought fit to let you know what the true state of this Garrison is, as also the condition of the Country, that so you may not think my desire for such things as would be necessary to carry on this work, unreasonable.

My Lords,

---

[1] On Saturday 18th (NB the title page incorrectly says Saturday 19th), there is a probably oblique reference as follows: '*Ordered,* That the Officers of the Ordnance do deliver, out of the Stores, the Two Cannons of Seven, with their Equipage, desired by the Committee of the Army for the Siege of *Pontefract Castle*', JHC, 6:81. Yet Cromwell's letter asks for demi-cannon, and the phrase cannons of seven is probably what they sent him, seven inches being the size of the bore of a demi-cannon.

[2] *Packets of Letters from Severall parts of England, to Members of the House of Commons concerning the Transactions of the Kingdome. Brought by the Post, on Tuesday November 21. 1648* (N&S, 480.36; Thomason / E.473[12]).

[3] Pontefract.   [4] Thomas Fairfax, third Lord Fairfax.

620

15 NOVEMBER 1648

The Castle hath been victualled with two hundred and twenty or forty fat Cattle, within these three weeks, and they have also gotten in (as I am credibly informed) Salt enough for them and more. So that I apprehend, they are Victualled for a twelve month: The men within are resolved to endure, to the utmost extremity, expecting no mercy, and indeed they deserve none. The place is very well known to be one of the strongest inland Garisons in the Kingdome, well watered, situated upon a rock in every part of it, and therfore difficult to Mine The walls very thick and high, with strong Towers, and if battered, very difficult of accesse, by reason of the depth and steepnesse of the Graft.[5] The Country is exceedingly impoverished, not able to bear free quarter, nor well able to furnish provisions, if wee had moneys. The work is like to be long, if materials be not furnished answerable. I therefore think it my duty, to represent unto you as followeth, Viz.

1 *That monies be provided for three p. 4] compleat Regiments of Foot, and two of Horse.*
2 *That Money bee provided for all contingencies, which are in view too many to innumerate.*
3 *That five hundred barrels of powder, six good battering Guns, with three hundred shot to each Gun, bee speedily sent down to Hull.*[6]
4 *Wee desire none may bee sent lesse then Demy-Canon.*
5 *We desire also some match & bullet*
6 *And if it may be, we should be glad that two or three of the biggest Morter-peeces with shels may likewise be sent.*

And although the desires of such proportions may seeme costly, yet I hope you will judge it good thrift, especially if you consider that this place hath cost the Kingdome, some hun [p. 5] dred thousands of pounds already. And for ought I know, it may cost you one more, it if be trifled withall, besides the dishonour of it, and what other danger may be immergent, by its being in such hands.

It is true, here are some two or three great Guns in *Hull*, and hereabouts, but they are unserviceable: And your Garisons in *Yorkeshire* are very much unsupplyed at this time. I have not as yet drawn any of our Foot to this place, only I make use of Col. *Fairfax*, and Col. *Maleveries*[7] [p. 6] Foot Regiments, and keep the rest of the Guards with the Horse, purposing to bring on some of our Foot to morrow. The

---

[5] Graft = ditch or moat (*OED*).
[6] Kingston-upon-Hull in the East Riding of Yorkshire, 46 miles from Pontefract.
[7] John Mauleverer (*c*.1610–50), contained within Sir Thomas Mauleverer, first baronet (bap. 1599, d. 1655). See *ODNB*.

rest being a little dispersed in *Lincolne & Nottinghamshires,* (these parts being not well able to bear them) for some refreshment, which after so much duty they need, and a little expect.

And indeed, I would not satisfie my self, nor my duty to you and them, to put the poore men at this season of the year to lye in the field, before we be furnished with Shooes Stockings, and Cloathes, for them to cover their nakednesse (which we heare are in preparation, and would be speeded). And untill wee have Deale boards to make them Courts of Guards, and tools to cast up works to secure them.

These things I have humbly represented to you, and waiting for your resolution and command, I rest

Your most humble Servant

O. Cromwell.

Knottingley 15 Novemb. 1648

1648 11 20a
Letter from Oliver Cromwell to Thomas Fairfax, Lord Fairfax

Date: 20 November 1648

Source: *Severall petitions presented to His Excellency the Lord Fairfax. By the Lievt. Generals Col. Harrisons Coll. Prides Coll. Deanes. regiment. Together with Lievt. Gen. Cromwels letter to his Excellency concerning the same.* [London: s.n.], Printed in the year. MDCXLVIII. [1648] (Wing / C2796; Thomason / E.474[5]) (print copy)

Cromwell's letter to the Lord General was printed, with minor variants, in two pamphlets. The proof text here is undated and without an identifiable publisher. Cromwell's letter is the first item in the pamphlet and is followed by a letter (unsigned as printed) to Cromwell (pp. 2–3), followed by the petitions of the regiments of Cromwell (pp. 3–4), Thomas Harrison (pp. 4–7) and Thomas Pride and Richard Deane[1] (pp. 7–8), all addressed to Fairfax. The letter to Cromwell asks him to forward the inclosed, 'ours and our Soldiers just, most necessary, and (as we hope) modest desires, to his Excellency our much honored General, upon whom, together with your self'. The petitions 'ask that some speedy and effectual course be taken for the discovery, trial and due punishment of [those]…guilty of all the bloods and treasures that hath bin spent in the Kingdoms', and for settlement

---

[1] Richard Deane (bap. 1610–53), army and naval officer and regicide. See ODNB.

20 NOVEMBER 1648A

worthy of the sufferings undergone. Some of them add grievances about quarter and pay. One of them (the petition of Col. Pride and Col. Deane's regiments is more explicit):

1. *That the Parliament be desired to take a review of their late Declarations and Charge against the King. As also to consider his own Act in taking the guilt of bloodshed upon himself, and accordingly to proceed against him as an Enemy of the Kingdom.*

The background is the struggle over *A remonstrance of His Excellency Thomas Lord Fairfax, Lord Generall of the Parliaments forces*,[2] which prepared the way for the trial, probable deposition and possible execution of the King. Fairfax had waivered over presenting this to Parliament, but had finally consented on 16 November, in time for news to reach Cromwell and for this to be his response. Although the date of publication for this version of Cromwell's letter is not given, George Thomason acquired his copy on 30 November.[3]

The other version of the letter includes Cromwell's letter as an afterthought after printing a letter in Fairfax's name calling for a rapid response to the *Remonstrance of His Excellency Thomas Lord Fairfax, Lord Generall of the Parliaments forces*, agreed at St Albans on 16 November and presented to Parliament on 20 November.[4] It too is undated. There is only one significant difference between the two versions, and that is noted below.

For His Excellency the Lord General FAIRFAX.

My Lord,

I find a very great sence in the affairs of the Regiments of the sufferings and the ruine of this poor Kingdom, and in them all a very great zeal to have impartial Justice done upon Offenders; and I must confess I do in all, from my heart, concur with them; and I verily think, and am perswaded, they are things which God puts into our hearts: I shall not need to offer any thing to your Excellency, I know God teaches you, and that he hath manifested his presence so with you, as that you will give glory to him in the eyes of all the World. I held it my duty, having received these Petitions and Letters, and being desired by the Framers thereof, to

---

[2] *A remonstrance of His Excellency Thomas Lord Fairfax, Lord Generall of the Parliaments forces And of the Generall Councell of officers held at St Albans the 16. of November, 1648. Presented to the Commons assembled in Parliament, the 20. instant, and tendred to the consideration of the whole kingdome*. London: Printed for John Partridge and George Whittington; in Black Fryers at the gate going into Carter Lane, and at the blue Anchor in Cornhill, MDCXLVIII. [1648] (Wing / F229; Thomason / E.473[11]).

[3] Ibid., p. 1.

[4] *The demands of his Excellency Tho. Lord Fairfax. And the Generall Councell of the Army, in prosecution of the late remonstrance to the two houses of Parliament as also against those persons who were the inviters of the late invasion from Scotland, the instigators and encouragers of the late insurrections in this kingdom. With Lieutenant Generall Cromwels letter to his Excellency concerning the executing of justice upon all offenders, and the setling of the kingdom upon a due. Safe, and hopefull succession of Parliaments. By the appointment of his Excellency the Lord Fairfax Lord Generall, and his Generall Councell of the Army. Signed John Rushworth*. London : Printed for R.M., 1648 (Wing / D073; Thomason / E.475[10]).

present them to you; the good Lord let[5] his will upon your heart, enabling you to do it; the presence of the Almighty God shall go along with you; This prays,
My Lord,
Your most humble and faithful Servant.
O. Cromwel.
Knottingley Nov. 20. 1648.

1648 11 20b
Letter from Oliver Cromwell to Robert Jenner and John Ashe

Date: 20 November 1648
Source: BL, Sloane MS 1519, fos 186r–187v (autograph)

This is an autograph letter, the main body of which is in the hand of one of his usual clerks. Cromwell here protests to two prominent members of the Committee for Compounding against their granting one of the prisoners Cromwell had taken at Preston permission to enter into composition. In Cromwell's view, this man, Colonel William Owen, was not a 'delinquent' who could be restored to his estate upon paying a fine and taking oaths of obedience but a 'malignant', all of whose property should be retained for the use of the state. In the course of the letter, he makes rather bitter reference to others who have been treated leniently. His sense that those who had restarted the war after God had given Parliament victory in 1646 is very clear in this letter.

[fo. 187v]
For my honord. freinds Robert Jenner[1] and John Ashe[2] Esqrs these

[seal]
Lt. Genl. Cromwell about prisonrs
[effo. 186r]
Gentlemen

---

[5] In the second version of this text (*The demands of his Excellency Tho. Lord Fairfax*), 'the good Lord **let** his will upon your heart' is rendered as 'the good Lord **work** his will upon your heart' (emphasis added).

[1] Robert Jenner, Wiltshire MP and London merchant: see *HoP Commons, 1640–1660*.
[2] John Ashe (1597–1659), clothier and parliamentarian activist. See *ODNB*. Both he and Jenner were secluded from Parliament at Pride's Purge just two weeks later.

20 NOVEMBER 1648B

I receiv'd an order from the Governr. of Nottingham,[3] directed to him from you, to bring up Colonell Owen,[4] or take bayle for his comming up to make his Composicon, hee having made an humble peticon to yow. for the same. I must profess to you, I was not a little astonish't at the thing, If I be not mistaken the house of Commons did voate all those traytors that did adhere to, or bring in the Scotts in their late invadeing of this kingdome, under Duke Hamilton, and not without very cleare justice, this being a more prodigious treason then any that had been perpetrated before, because the former quarrell \on their part/ was, that Englishmen might rule over one another, this, to vassalize us to a forraigne nation. And their fault who have appear'd in this summers business is certainly double to their's who were in the first, because it is the repeticon of the same offence against all the witnesses that God has borne, by making and abetting to a second warre. And if this was their justice, and upon soe good grounds, I wonder how it comes to pass, that soe eminent Actors should soe easily be received to compound. You will pardon me, if I tell you, that if it were contrary to some of your judgmts. that, at the rendition of Oxford, though we had the towne in con-sideration, and blood saved to boot. yet two yeares purchase was thought too little to expiate their offence,[5] But now, when yow have such men in your hands, and it will cost you no thing to doe justice, Now after all this trouble, and the hazard of a second warre for a little more money, all offences shalbe pardon'd. S̶i̶r̶ This gentleman was taken with Sir Marmady Langdale[6] in their flight together, I presume you have heard what is become of him, Let me remember you, that out of this garrison, was fetch't not long since, (I beleive, whilst wee were in heate of action) Colonell Humfrey Mathewes[7] [fo. 186v] then whome,

---

[3] The governor at this time was Captain Thomas Poulton (see his letter to William Pierrepoint, MP dated Nottingham Castle 23 Aug. 1848, Bodl. MS Tanner 57, no. 227).

[4] Col. William Owen of Brogynton, Shropshire: see Newman, *Royalist Officers*, no. 1083.

[5] The surrender of Oxford on 24 June 1646 had been controversial. To save blood and treas-ure, the generals offered all those in the town generous terms, including the right to compound for their estates at the rate of one-tenth (i.e. two years' annual income of their estates), instead of the norm of one-sixth. See F. J. Varley, *The Siege of Oxford: An Account of Oxford during the Civil War, 1642–1646* (Oxford, 1932), pp. 141–6.

[6] Marmaduke Langdale, first Baron Langdale (bap. 1598, d. 1661), royalist army officer. See *ODNB*. He was in Nottingham Castle with Owen. On 21 November he was one of seven English royalists exempted from pardon by the House of Commons and liable to execution. But he escaped from the castle and made his way to the continent. For some background see his letter dated 26 August to Sir Thomas Fairfax in Cary, *Memorials*, II.60.

[7] Col. Humphrey Matthews, taken prisoner at the end of the siege of Pembroke and sent to prison in Nottingham. See Newman, *Royalist Officers*, no. 950.

the cause wee have fought for has not had a more daungerous enemye, And hee not guilty, only, of being an enemy, but hee h apostatized from your cause & quarrell, having been a Colonell, if not more, under you. And the desperatest promoter of the welsh Rebellion amongst them all. And how neare you were brought to ruine thereby, All men that know any thing, can tell, And this man was taken away to Composicon,[8] by what order I know not. Gentlemen, though my sence does appeare more warme, then perhapps you would have it, yet give me leave to tell you, I finde a sence amongst the officers concerning such things as these \even/ to ⊢──⊣ \amazement/.[9] which truly is not soe much to see their blood made soe cheape, as to see such manifest witnessings of God (soe terrible, and soe just,) noe more reverenc't. I have directed the Governr to acquaint the Lord Genll herewith, and rest

Your most humble Servant

O Cromwell

Knottinngley neare Pontefract this 20th of Novemb 1648.

1648 11 25a
Letter from Oliver Cromwell to Robert Hammond

Date: 25 November 1648

Source: *Letters between Col. Robert Hammond, Governor of the Isle of Wight, and the Committee of Lords and Commons at Derby-House : General Fairfax, Lieut. General Cromwell, Commissary General Ireton, &c. relating to King Charles I, while he was confined in Carisbrooke-Castle in that Island* [ed. T. Birch] (1764), pp. 101–13 (later copy)

This is the final document (of thirty-eight, four by Cromwell) in a collection of Robert (Robin to Cromwell) Hammond's incoming and outgoing correspondence while he was in charge of Charles I at Carisbrooke Castle on the Isle of Wight. They were transcribed by Thomas Birch, the editor of Thurloe's letters, at some time before they were 'consumed…in the fire, which proved fatal to a great number of other valuable Manuscripts, in the chambers of the Hon. Mr Yorke, in Lincoln's-Inn, on the 27th of June, 1752'.[1]

---

[8] He was allowed to compound but at the rate of one-third (i.e. one-third of the capital value of all his property), *CCCD*, 3:1855–6.

[9] An original word is so obliterated as to be unreadable and 'amazement' written over it.

---

[1] From Birch's preface to the volume.

25 NOVEMBER 1648A

As with the rest of the letters, the text has clearly been updated to mid-eighteenth-century spelling, punctuation, printing conventions (the large capitalisation of the first word in a number of paragraphs) and there must be some suspicion over italicised passages and phrases: lots of underlining does not look very Cromwellian. And what of the exclamation mark: 'Good by this man! against whom the Lord hath witnessed'? In Cromwell's holograph letters, the exclamation mark is rare.

Hammond had been manifesting indecision about his position for some time (see **1648 11 06a**).[2] He was not so much considering defecting to the King as remaining loyal to the majority in Parliament still committed to a negotiated settlement; and indeed parliamentary commissioners were hammering out terms at Carisbrooke until the morning of 27 November. But already on 22 November, alarm bells were ringing in Windsor. Fairfax wrote to Hammond on that day, requesting him to demonstrate his consent to the terms of the *Army Remonstrance* and ordering him to come up to Army headquarters.[3] But included in the package with Fairfax's letter was an impassioned plea from Henry Ireton begging Hammond to remember that his higher 'affection and trust' belonged to those who represented 'some higher and more public ends' than those of 'the prevailing party' in the Parliament.[4] It might well have taken Cromwell, as he headed south from Yorkshire, three more days to hear of Hammond's wobble. By the time that Cromwell's letter reached Hammond, he had come off the fence. The man sent to persuade him to cooperate or else to arrest him was Colonel Isaac Ewer, who had been Hammond's lieutenant colonel 1645–7 and who had succeeded him as colonel when Hammond accepted the governorship of the Isle of Wight. Following a decisive conversation, Ewer did indeed escort him under armed guard from the Isle of Wight to Windsor.[5] Fairfax had also sent Colonel Ralph Cobbett from headquarters to replace Hammond and to move Charles I initially to Hurst Castle and then to Windsor Castle.[6] A major reason for this was that when Hammond had received the letters from Fairfax and Ireton, Hammond had sent on the former to the House of Commons, seeking their advice.[7] On 27 November the Commons ordered him to stay put and wrote to Fairfax to confirm their order.

Cromwell's letter failed to prevent this private catastrophe for Hammond. It could not have reached him before his arrest. In any event, his career was over.

---

[2] And more generally Robert Hammond (1620/1–54), parliamentarian army officer. See *ODNB*.

[3] Rushworth, 7:1338; *JHC*, 6:88.

[4] *Letters between Col. Robert Hammond, Governor of the Isle of Wight, and the Committee of Lords and Commons at Derby-House: General Fairfax, Lieut. General Cromwell, Commissary General Ireton, &c. relating to King Charles I*, pp. 95–100.

[5] Gentles, *New Model Army*, pp. 276–7; Firth and Davies, *Regimental History*, 1:346–54.

[6] For the complicated manoeuvres in the third week of November, see Gentles, *New Model Army*, pp. 276–8.

[7] Hammond's commission to be governor of the Isle of Wight had been issued by Fairfax in August 1647 but then confirmed a few days later in a Parliamentary Ordinance—see *JHL*, 9:423. The Ordinance clearly stated that he should remain as governor 'until the Lords and Commons assembled in Parliament shall otherwise order'.

The striking thing about this letter is the extent to which it is drenched in biblical allusion. It is not a systematic application of an Old Testament story to the present crisis but a rhetorical *tour de force* aiming to mask a call to disobedience. It draws on seven Old Testament and seven New Testament books.[8]

It has been suggested that in part this is a follow-up to the Brother Fountaine letter (**1648 11 06**), or rather Cromwell's response to Hammond's unhappiness at the question raised there, 'that it is lawful for a lesser part (if in the right) to force, &c.'. If so, this would strengthen the difficult case for seeing that letter as by Cromwell.

[p. 101]

Oliver Cromwell, to Col. *Hammond.*

Nov. 25. 1648

Dear *Robin*,

No man rejoyceth more to see a line from thee, than myself. I know thou hast long been under tryal. Thou shalt be no loser by it. All must work for the best.[9] Thou desirest to hear of my experiences. I can tell thee, I am such a one, as thou didst formerly know, having a body of sin and death;[10] but, I thank God, through Jesus Christ our Lord, there [p. 102] is no condemnation, though much infirmity, and I wait for the redemption;[11] and in this poor condition I obtain mercy[12] and sweet consolation through the Spirit; and find abundant cause every day to exalt the Lord, abase flesh. And herein I have some exercise.

As to outward dispensations, if we may so call them; we have not been without our share of beholding some remarkable providences and appearances of the Lord.[13] His presence hath been amongst us, and by the light of his countenance we have prevailed.[14] We are sure, the good will of him, who dwelt in the bush, has shined upon us;[15] and we can humbly say, we know in whom we have

---

[8] The identification of the biblical allusions follows the study of this letter by Robert S. Paul, *The Lord Protector: Religion and Politics in the Life of Oliver Cromwell* (1955), pp. 406–10. See also John Morrill, 'How Oliver Cromwell Thought', in J. Morrow and J. Scott, eds., *Liberty, Authority, Formality: Political Ideas and Culture, 1600–1900: Essays in Honour of Colin Davis* (Exeter, 2008), pp. 89–112. Cromwell is drawing on both the King James Bible and the Geneva Bible, often intertwined, but the former is the dominant translation he draws on.

[9] Cf. Romans 8:28.   [10] Romans 6:6.   [11] Romans 8 (especially vv. 21–5).

[12] 1 Timothy 1:13.

[13] The best introduction to Cromwell's providentialism is Blair Worden, 'Providence and Politics in Cromwellian England', *Past and Present*, 109 (1985), pp. 55–99; and more generally Alexandra Walsham, *Providence in Early Modern England* (Oxford, 1999).

[14] Psalms 44:3.   [15] Cf. Exodus 3:1–6, Deuteronomy. 33:16.

25 NOVEMBER 1648A

believed,[16] who is able, and will perfect what remaineth,[17] and us also in doing what is well-pleasing in his eye-sight.[18]

BECAUSE I find some trouble in your spirit, occasioned first, not only by the continuance of your sad and heavy burthen,[19] as you call it; but by [p. 103] the dissatisfaction you take at the ways of some good men, whom you love with your heart, who through this principle, that it is lawful for a lesser part (if in the right) to force, &c.[20]

To the first: Call not your burthern sad nor heavy. If your father laid it upon you; he intended neither. He is the father of lights, from whom comes every good and perfect gift; who of his own will begot us,[21] and bad us count it all joy when such things befall us; they being for the exercise of faith and patience; *whereby in the end (James i.) we shall be made perfect.*[22]

DEAR *Robin*, our fleshly reasonings ensnare us.[23] These make us say; heavy. *Sad, pleasant, easy:* Was not there a little of this, when *Rob. Hammond*, through dissatisfaction too, desired retirement from the Army, and thought of quiet in the *Isle of Wight.*[24] Did not God find him out there?[25] I believe he will never forget this. – And now I perceive, he is to seek again, partly through his sad and heavy burthen, [p. 104] and partly through dissatisfaction with friend's actings. Dear *Robin*, thou and I were never worthy to be door-keepers in this service.[26] If thou wilt seek. Seek to know the mind of God in all that chain of providence, whereby God brought thee thither, and that Person[27] to thee: How before and since God has

---

[16] 2 Timothy 1:12.

[17] 'He conflates the "He is able" of 2 Timothy 1:12 with the idea of perfection in Hebrews 12:20–23 (Paul, *Lord Protector*, p. 406 fn. 8).

[18] Hebrews 13:21.

[19] i.e. looking after the King and preventing both his escape and attempts to assassinate him.

[20] This may be a reference to item **1648 11 06a** ('that a lesser party of a Parliament, hath made it Lawfull to declare, the greater part a faction, and made the Parliament Null, and call a newe one, and to do this by force') and bolsters the case for that being a letter by Cromwell and not by William Rowe or anyone else.

[21] James 1:17 et seq.   [22] A free paraphrase of James 1:2–6.

[23] 2 Corinthians 1:12.

[24] Hammond's previous queasiness of conscience over the Army's occupation of London in August 1647 had been very deliberately eased by his commission (31 August 1647) to serve as governor of the Isle of Wight. No-one could have predicted that Charles I would escape from custody and surrender himself into Hammond's charge three months later.

[25] Cf. Psalms 139:7–13.   [26] Psalms 84:10.   [27] i.e. King Charles I.

629

ordered him, and affairs concerning him. And then tell me, whether there be not some glorious and high meaning in all this, above what thou hast yet attained. And laying aside thy fleshly reason. Seek of the Lord to teach thee what that is; and he will do it. I dare be positive to say; it is not, that the wicked should be exalted, that God should so appear, as indeed he hath done. For there is no peace to them:[28] No, it is set upon the hearts of such as fear the Lord, and we have witness upon witness, that it shall go ill with them, and their partakers. I say again. Seek that spirit to teach thee;[29] which is the spirit of knowledge and understanding, the spirit of counsel and might, of wisdom and of the fear of the Lord.[30] That spirit will [p. 105] close thine eyes, and stop thine ears. So that thou shalt not judge by them; but thou shalt judge for the meek of the earth,[31] and thou shalt be made able to do accordingly. The Lord direct thee to that, which is well pleasing in his eye sight.[32]

As to thy dissatisfactions with friend's actings upon that supposed principle, I wonder not at that. If a man take not his own burthen well, he shall hardly others; especially if involved by so near a relation of love and christian brotherhood, as thou art. I shall not take upon me to satisfy; but I hold myself bound to lay my thoughts before so dear a friend. The Lord do his own will. You say; "God hath appointed authorities among the nations, to which active or passive obedience is to be yielded. This resides in *England* in the Parliament. Therefore active or passive, &c."

AUTHORITIES and powers are the ordinance of God. This or that species is of [p. 106] human institution, and limited. Some with larger, others with stricter bands, each one according to its constitution. I do not therefore think, the authorities may do any thing, and yet such obedience due; but all agree, there are cases, in which it is lawful to resist. If so, your ground fails, and so likewise the inference. Indeed, Dear *Robin*, not to multiply words, the query is, whether ours be such a case? This ingenuously is the true question. To this I shall say nothing, though I could say very much; but only desire thee to see what thou findest in thy own heart as to two or three plain considerations: *First,* Whether *Salus Populi*[33] be a sound position? *Secondly,* Whether in the way in hand, really and before the

---

[28] Isaiah 57:21; cf. Isaiah 48:22.   [29] Cf. John 14:26.   [30] Isaiah 11:2.
[31] Isaiah 11:4; cf. Psalms 25:9, Psalms 37:11, Matthew 5:5.   [32] Cf. Hebrews 13:21.
[33] From '*salus populi suprema lex esto*' in Cicero's *De Legibus* (book III, part III. Sub. VIII), a commonplace of parliamentarian political thinking throughout the 1640s, and widely popularised. For example, it was the motto of Thomas Rainborow's regiment.

25 NOVEMBER 1648A

Lord, before whom conscience must stand, this be provided for; or the whole fruit of the war like to be frustrated, and all most [p. 107] like to turn to what it was, and worse. And this contrary to engagements, declarations, implicit covenants with those, who ventured their lives upon those covenants and engagements, without whom perhaps, in equity, relaxation ought not to be. *Thirdly.* Whether this Army be not a law [p. 108] ful power, called by God to oppose and fight against the King upon some stated grounds; and being in power to such ends, may not oppose one name of authority for those ends as well as another? the outward authority, that called them, not by their power making the quarrel lawful; but it being so in itself. If so, - it may be, acting will be justified in *Foro humano.* But truly these kind of reasonings may be but fleshly, either with or against; only it is good to try what truth may be in them. And the Lord teach us. MY dear friend, let us look into providences; surely they mean somewhat. They hang so together – have been so constant. So clear and unclouded. – Malice. Swol'n malice against God's people, now called Saints, to root out their name. And yet they by providence having arms; and therein blessed with defence, and more.

I DESIRE, he, that is for a principle of suffering, would not too much slight this. [p. 109] I slight not him, who is so minded; but let us beware, lest fleshly reasoning see more safety in making use of the principle, *than in acting. Who acts, and resolves not through God to be willing to part with all?* Our hearts are very deceitful on the right and on the left.[34] What think you of providence disposing the hearts of so many of God's people this way, especially in this poor Army, wherein the great God has vouchsafed to appear. I know not one officer amongst us, but is on the increasing hand: And let me say, it is *here in the North, after much patience,* we trust the same Lord, who hath framed our minds in our actings, is with us in this also. And this, contrary to a natural tendency, and to those comforts, our hearts could wish to enjoy with others. And the *difficulties* probably to be encountered with, and enemies, not few, even all, that is glorious in this world, with appearance of united names, titles, and authorities, and yet not terrified, only desiring to fear our great God, that we do nothing against his will. Truly this is our condition. [p. 110] AND, to conclude, we in this Northern Army were in a waiting posture, desiring to see what the Lord would lead us to. And a declaration is put out,[35] at which many are shaken; although we could perhaps have wished the stay of it, till

---

[34] Jeremiah 17:8.   [35] i.e. the *Army Remonstrance.*

THE LETTERS, WRITINGS, AND SPEECHES OF OLIVER CROMWELL

after the treaty: yet. Seeing it is come out, we trust to rejoyce in the will of the Lord, waiting his farther pleasure. Dear *Robin*, beware of men, look up to the Lord. Let him be free to speak, and command in thy heart. Take heed of the things, I fear thou hast reasoned thyself into; and thou shalt be able though him, without consulting flesh and blood, to do valiantly for him and for his people. Thou mentionest somewhat, as if by acting against such opposition, as is like to be, there will be a tempting of God. Dear *Robin*, tempting of God ordinarily is either by acting presumptuously in carnal confidence, or in unbelief through diffidence: both these ways *Israel* tempted God in the Wilderness, and he was grieved with them. The encountring difficulties therefore makes [p. 111] us not to tempt God; but acting before, and without faith. If the Lord have in any measure persuaded his people, as generally he hath, of the lawfulness, nay of the *duty*; this persuasion prevailing upon the heart is faith, and acting thereupon is acting in faith, and the more the difficulties are, the more faith. And it is most sweet, that he, that is not persuaded, have patience towards them that are, and judge not; and this will free thee from the trouble of others actings; which, thou sayest, adds to thy grief. Only let me offer two or three things, and I have done.

DOEST thou not think, that fear of the Levellers (of whom there is no fear) that they would destroy nobility, had caused some to rake up corruption, to find it lawful to *make this ruining hypocritical agreement* (on one part). Hath not this biassed even some good men? I will not say, their fear will come upon them; but if it do, they will themselves bring it upon themselves. Have not some of our friends by their passive principle (which I judge not, [p. 112] only I think it liable to temptation as well as the active; and neither good, but as we are led into them by God – neither to be reasoned into, because the heart is deceitful) been occasioned to overlook what is just and honest; and think the people of God may have as much, or more good the one way, than the other. Good by this man! against whom the Lord hath witnessed; and whom thou knowest. Is this so in their hearts, or is it reasoned, forced in?[36] – *Robin*, I have done. Ask we our hearts, whether we think, that, after all these dispensations, the like to which many generations cannot afford. Should end in so corrupt reasonings of good men; and should so hit the designings of bad? Thinkest thou in thy heart, that the glorious dispensations of God point out to this, or to teach his people to trust in him, and to wait for better

---

[36] Interestingly repunctuated by Gardiner (*GCW*, 4:253) as 'Good, by this man, against whom the Lord hath witnessed; and whom thou knowest! Is this so in their hearts, or is it reasoned, forced in?'

632

25 NOVEMBER 1648B

things, when, it may be, better are sealed to many of their spirits? And as a poor looker on, I had rather live in the hope of that spirit, and take my share with them, expecting a good issue, than be led away with the [p. 113] other. This trouble I have been at, because my soul loves thee, and I would not have thee swerve, nor lose any glorious opportunity the Lord puts into thy hand. The Lord be thy counsellor. Dear *Robin*,

I rest thine,
O. Cromwell.
Nov. 25, 1648.

1648 II 25b
Letter from Oliver Cromwell to Thomas St Nicholas

Date: 25 November 1648
Source: J. Oldmixon, *The history of England, during the reigns of the royal house of Stuart. Wherein the errors of late histories are discover'd and corrected* (London, 1730) (later copy) p. 352.

There are two eighteenth-century versions of this letter, but the second[1] is clearly copied from the first, which in turn says that it had been transcribed from Cromwell's holograph letter. There is a recipient, Thomas St Nicholas, but no address. Carlyle (followed by the ODNB life of St Nicholas) asserts that it was London - but this makes no sense, especially as the son of the recipient, Thomas St Nicholas, was buried two days later in York.[2] Sophia Lomas, in correcting Carlyle, says laconically, without offering evidence, that the address was 'certainly not London. Probably York; possibly Wakefield'.[3]

SIR,

I Suppose it is not unknown to you how much the Country is in Arrear to the Garrison of Hull, as likewise how probable it is that the Garrison will break, unless some speedy Course be taken to get them Money, the Soldiers at this Present being ready to mutiny, as not having Money to buy them Bread, and without Money the stubborn Towns-People will not trust

---

[1] Isaac Kimber, *The Life of Oliver Cromwell, Lord Protector of the Common-wealth of England, Scotland and Ireland* (3rd ed., 1731), pp. 95–6.
[2] Thomas St Nicholas (bap. 1602–68), lawyer and poet. See ODNB.
[3] Carlyle-Lomas, 1:392–3.

them for the Worth of a Penny. Sir, I must beg of you, that as you tender the Good of the Country, so far as the Security of that Garrison is mention'd, you would give your Assistance to the helping of them to their Money which the Country owes them. The Governor[4] will apply himself to you either in Person or by Letter. I pray you do for him herein as in a Business of very high Consequence. I am the more earnest with you, as having a very deep Sense how danger-ous the Event may be of their being neglected in the Matter of their Pay. I rest upon your Favour herein, and subscribe my self, SIR,

Your very humble Servant,
O. CROMWELL.

Knottingley, Nov. 25. 1648.
For my Noble Friend Thomas St. Nicholas, Esq

⸗⸗

1648 11 27

Letter from Oliver Cromwell to [Philip Wharton, Lord Wharton]

Date: 27 November 1648
Source: Pierpont Morgan Library, New York. Department of Literary and Historical Manuscripts, Rulers of England Box 08, Cromwell, no. 01 (autograph)

The letter is signed by Cromwell but written in the hand of a scribe he did not otherwise use. There is nothing in the letter to indicate the identity of the peer to whom Cromwell is writing this letter of recommendation. In a much later pencil comment written below the letter in the current bound volume, he is identified as Philip Wharton, fourth Baron Wharton,[1] with whom Cromwell certainly had good relations in the late 1640s. Since the letter is now glued to a larger blank page, one might surmise that the attribution is on the verso of the document. However, that is not stated and so the attribution is insecure. This is the first time this letter has been printed, being unknown to Carlyle-Lomas and to Abbott.

---

[4] For Robert Overton (1608/9–78/9), parliamentarian army officer. See *ODNB*.

---

[1] Philip Wharton, fourth Baron Wharton (1613–96), politician. See *ODNB*. The pencil note reads 'To Philip Wharton, 4th Baron Wharton, Requesting that certain estates be assigned over to William Sykes.'

30 NOVEMBER 1648[?]

My Lord

My honest good freind Mr William Sykes[2] whose affections to the Parliamt hath beene very great by his volluntary lendinge of large summes of mony to the Parliamt For which he hath beene a great sufferer even from the begininge And in perticuler by the late revolt of Pontefract Castle, who upon there revoltinge came to this Towne and plundered his warehouse caryinge away as I am given to understand by his neighbors betwixt Fowrescore and a hundered Cart load of Merchandize besides other goodes to the vallue as is conceived of a bove one thousand pounds, And whereas divers of the said revolters have estates in or neere Leedes[3] part where of are as yet concealed and the rest under sequestracon, It is the desire of the said Wm Sykes that he may have the said estates assigned over to him to be in his possession till that his losses be repayed, In which I desire your Lop furtherance and assistance[4] which will be an act of great Justice And very much oblidge My Lord Your Lopps most humble servt
O Cromwell

From my Quarters before Pontefract at Knottingley the 27[th5] of November 1648

1648 11 30[?]
Letter from Oliver Cromwell to Thomas Fairfax, Lord Fairfax

Date: Between 25 November and 1 December 1648
Source: BL, Egerton MS 2620, fos 3r–4v (holograph)

This letter, including the address, very unusually for the period, is in Cromwell's own hand and not that of a clerk. It is difficult to date precisely. The *Remonstrance* mentioned at the beginning became available in London on 22 November and in Yorkshire by 25 November (see **1648 11 25**). On 28 November, the day Hammond was arrested and the King began his

---

[2] Not identified.

[3] Leeds, a large market town in Yorkshire, 19 miles from Pontefract.

[4] Wharton was a member of the Committee for Compounding (for his appointment see *A&O*, I:914 [7 February 1647]) and therefore able to respond directly to Cromwell's request.

[5] The date could also be read as 'vi[th] November', but we have followed the catalogue dating. Both are possible.

THE LETTERS, WRITINGS, AND SPEECHES OF OLIVER CROMWELL

journey to London and the day on which Ireton and the Levellers began formal talks at Windsor, Fairfax summonsed Cromwell to leave the siege and Pontefract and come immediately to Army headquarters. So this letter must be written between 25 November and 1 December. There is no evidence to support Abbott's suggestion of 29 November rather than any other day within that period.[1]

[fo. 4v]

For his Excellencye the
Lord Generall Fairfax

theise

Lt. Generall Cromwell. Nov. 1648.[2]

Inc[r].[3]

[fo. 3r]

Sir wee have read your Declaration[4] heere
and see in itt nothinge but what is honest,
and becominge Christians, and honest men
to say, and offer, it's good to looke up
to God whoe aloane is able to sway
hartes to agree to the good and just
thinges conteyned therein. I verylye
beleive the honest partye in Scotland
wilbe ~~not boggle att itt~~ Satisfied in
the justnesse thereof, however it wilbe
good that will Rowe[5] be hastned with
instructions theither, I beseech you
command him (if it seemes good to your
excells: judgment) to goe away with
all Speede, what is tymely donn heerin

---

[1] Abbott, *Writings and Speeches*, 1:707.

[2] This endorsement is in a different, seventeenth-century, hand. Sophia Lomas thinks it is in the hand of William Clarke and this may be correct (Carlyle-Lomas, 3:395).

[3] Also in a different hand and very hard to read. 'Incr' or 'Jut'.

[4] Presumably *A remonstrance from the army, to the citizens of London* (Wing / R983; Thomason / E.473[11])—presented to Parliament on 20 November and printed in time for George Thomason to date his copy 'Novemb.22th' [sic].

[5] William Rowe, Cromwell's scoutmaster. For his mission for Cromwell in Edinburgh, see above **1648 09 18** and **1648 10 02**.

636

2 DECEMBER 1648

may prævent ⊢—⊣[6] misunderstandinges
in them. I hope to waite Speedily upon
you, att least to begin my journye upon
Tuseday. Your owne Regint. wilbe cominge
up. soe will Okey,[7] mine Harrisons[8] and
some others the two Garrisons have mor
enowe (if provided for) to doe that worke
Lambert[9] will looke to them. I rest
my Lord
Your ex.[10] most humble and
faythfull servant

O Cromwell

1648 12 02

'A LETTER from *Lieut. Generall* CRUMWELL To the Citizens of London, Concerning the King's Majesty the Parliament, the City, Army and Kingdome'

Date: 2 December 1648

Source: *The Kings Majesties message to His Highnesse the Prince of VVales. Concerning the Lord Generall Fairfax, and the Army; and his propositions and desires therein, to be communicated to the Right Honorable the Earl of VVarwick, Lord high Admirall of England... And Lieutenant Gen. Crumwels declaration in reference to the King, city, and kingdom: signed O. Crumwel.* (1648), pp. [1]–[2] (Wing / K601; Thomason / E.475[31]) (near contemporary print)

This is another of the letters written in the last months of 1648 where the attribution to Cromwell is far from certain. It is dated from Knottingley, where Cromwell had certainly been from 6 to 29 November, but it is dated from there on 2 December, which looks a little late given he had to cover 185 miles in order to be in Westminster by the afternoon of 6 December. The publisher is uncertain. The only known publisher called 'George Wharton' was noted for publishing royalist almanacs and anti-Independent rants.[1] He was

---

[6] Heavily crossed out and illegible. The best guess of what is written is 'worse'.
[7] John Okey (bap. 1606, d. 1662), parliamentarian army officer and regicide. See *ODNB*.
[8] Thomas Harrison.   [9] John Lambert.   [10] = Excellency's.

---

[1] (Sir) George Wharton, first baronet (1617–81), astrologer and royalist. See *ODNB*.

THE LETTERS, WRITINGS, AND SPEECHES OF OLIVER CROMWELL

in desperate straits in 1648 and if this publication is his, we can place little faith in it. But perhaps he (or an otherwise unknown man of the same name) was publishing whatever scraps he could get, mindful of the censor who had already imprisoned him once. Despite being placed last in the title, Cromwell's 'letter' (in fact a summary in reported speech) appears first in the pamphlet, followed by an account of Charles's rejection on the Army's *Remonstrance* and the replacement of Hammond as the King's custodian by Colonel Isaac Ewer,[2] followed in turn by an account on the debates in Parliament about the Army's Remonstrance, and it closes with an account of the King's final conversation with the parliamentary commissioners as he was being brought up to London. This letter has not appeared in any previous edition of Cromwell's recorded words.

Right Honorable,[3]

Here hath lately been called a Generall Councell of Officers, consisting of the Northerne Brigade, whose results acquiesce and tend chiefly to the safety and preservation of your Honourable City, and to the welfare and tranquillity of our English Nation; as appears by the most excellent demonstration of Lieu. Gen.Cromwell, at the Councell table, in presence of divers Colonels, Lieut. Colonels, Majors, and Captains, who declared, *That he was willing to wade through all troubles and difficulties for preservation of the peace and tranquillity of this bleeding Kingdom , and would sacrifice his life for the peace and liberty of the subject,and for dissipating the dismall cloud of Malingancy, which threatens ruine to all the well-affected within the Nation.* And for the better propagating of the said work, the said Lieutenant Generall (our worthy and ever honored Patriot) hath declared his ardent and zealous affection to his Excellency the Lord Generall: protesting, That he will live and dye with him for the obtaining and faciliating the just Demands and Desires of the Army, specified in their late Remonstrance, and that he doth most freely and really concur with them, for the speedy executing of impartiall Justice upon all Offenders whatsoever; intimating, that he doth verily believe they are things which God puts into the harts both of Officers and Souldiers, and that the great Jehovah in Heaven is pleased to manifest his presence unto them, in pursuing and prosecuting so pious a worke, so much tending to the honour of his holy Name and the peace and tranquillity of all his

---

[2] Firth and Davies, *Regimental History*, 1:352–5.

[3] The final sentence makes it clear the person referred to is the Lord General, Thomas Fairfax.

people on Earth; which declaratory expressions, have presented to his Excellency the Lord Gen. Fairfax, and   signed

O.CROMWEL

Knottingley neer Pontefract 2. Decemb. 1648.

1648 12 08
Certificate signed by Oliver Cromwell

Date: 8 December 1648
Source: TNA, SP 23/207, p. 651r (autograph and seal)

John Kellond of Painsford and Totnes, Devon (bap. 16 May 1609, d. 6 June 1679)[1] was a royalist who submitted a petition to compound to the Committee for Compounding on 14 December 1648.[2] He wished to take advantage of the special terms awarded by Fairfax and Cromwell at the end of the siege of Truro in[3] March 1646, and indeed on 1 January 1649 his fine was set at a rate of one-tenth (two years' income). Cromwell's certificate will have helped him make the case for a reduction in his fine from one-sixth (or higher) to one-tenth. The certificate is in the hand of one of Cromwell's regular clerks and bears his signature and seal.

[p. 651r]

Theis are to certifie that all those whome it may concerne That John Kelland of Totnes in the County of Devon Esqr. was in Cornewall att the tyme of the disbanding of the horse att Truro, and is Comprised within those Articles, and ought to enjoy full benefitt of them Witnesse my hand and Seale this 8th. of December 1648.

O Cromwell

---

[1] For brief comments on Kellond, see the biography of his son (John Kelland), in *HoP Commons, 1660–1690*, 2:670. See also J. L. Vivian, ed., *The Visitations of the County of Devon* (1895), p. 508.

[2] TNA, SP23/207, p. 651r.

[3] For the Truro Articles, see Joshua Sprigg, *Anglia rediviva Englands recovery being the history of the motions, actions, and successes of the army* (1647), pp. 220–8 (Wing/ S5070).

THE LETTERS, WRITINGS, AND SPEECHES OF OLIVER CROMWELL

1648 12 18

Letter from Oliver Cromwell to the master and fellows of Trinity Hall, Cambridge

Date: 18 December 1648

Source: Carlyle-Lomas I:403–4, from a manuscript previously in Trinity Hall, Cambridge and long missing from there (autograph)[1]

This simple letter of recommendation may not be as bland as it sounds. The reason why Cromwell might want the civil lawyer Isaac Dorislaus[2] to have chambers in the Doctors' Commons is that he was a key figure in drawing up the charge against Charles I for his trial a month later.

———

To the Right Worshipful the Master and Fellows of Trinity Hall in Cambridge: These 18th December 1648

Gentlemen

I am given to understand that by the late decease of Dr. Duck,[3] his chamber is become vacant in the Doctors' Commons,[4] to which Dr Dorislaus now desireth to be your tenant: who hath service unto the Parliament from the beginning of these wars, and hath been constantly employed by the Parliament in many weighty affairs, and especially of late, beyond the seas, with the States General of the United Provinces.[5]

---

[1] Alexandra Browne, Archivist at Trinity Hall in 2015, informed us that it is thought to have gone missing before the preparation of a new catalogue of Manuscripts in 1929.

[2] Isaac Dorislaus (1595–1649). He had a stormy career in Cambridge after being appointed Professor of History in Cambridge in 1627 where he advocated, in the view of his Laudian critics, 'republicanism and regicide'. Defended by most of the college heads, he was silenced by the King and spent the 1630s abroad. From 1643 he was judge advocate to the parliamentary armies, and developed the Roman Law process for trial at martial law. For this, see John Collins, *Martial Law and English Laws c.1500–c.1700* (Cambridge, 2016), ch. 5. Dorislaus was indeed one of those who made the trial of Charles to a large degree a trial at martial law. For Isaac Dorislaus (1595–1649), scholar and diplomat, see *ODNB*.

[3] Arthur Duck (1580–1648), civil lawyer. See *ODNB*. Duck was the 'Laudian' chancellor of the diocese of London in the 1630s. Despite this and overt royalism for which he was sequestrated and compounded, he was made a Master of Chancery in 1645 and took part in parliamentary negotiations with the King on the Isle of Wight. He died while attending church on either 12 or 16 December 1648.

[4] Doctors' Commons in Paternoster Row, adjacent to St Paul's Cathedral, was the self-governing teaching body of practitioners of canon and civil law.

[5] According to *ODNB*, Dorislaus was made a judge in the Court of Admiralty in April 1648, and this 'led to his first diplomatic mission, with Walter Strickland, to the States General of the United Provinces concerning privileges being accorded "revolted ships" by Dutch provinces sympathetic with the royalists.' See n. 2.

22 DECEMBER 1648A

If you please to prefer him before any other, paying rent and fine[6] to your College, I shall take it as a courtesy at your hands whereby you will oblige

Your assured friend and servant,

Oliver Cromwell

———— ∞∞ ————

1648 12 22a

Letter from Oliver Cromwell and Henry Ireton to Thomas Harrison

Date: 22 December 1648

Source: Worcester College, Oxford, Clarke MS 2/5 [vol. 114], fo. 150v (contemporary copy)

This is the first of two letters tightening security around the King sent on 22 December jointly by Cromwell and Ireton to the King's guards. They survive as contemporary copies in the papers of William Clarke, Secretary to the Army.

———————

Lre to Col: Harrison.[1]

Sir

Col: Thomlinson[2] is to bee speeded away to Windsor[3] with Instructions to himself Lt.Col. Cobbett,[4] & Capt Merriman[5] for securing of the Kinge answerable to the severall Heads You desire Resolution in, soe soone as hee comes. You may come away & your presence heere is both desired & needed butt before you come away, Wee desire you to appoint 3. or 4. Troopes out of your Convoy (of the surest men & best Officers) to remaine about Windsor, to whome you may assigne Quarters in the next[6] parts of Middlesex & Surrey, advising with the

---

[6] i.e. entry fine, initial fee payable up front on taking up the tenancy.

---

[1] Thomas Harrison. Ireton and Harrison had been together at the Whitehall Debates the previous week.

[2] Matthew Tomlinson [Thomlinson], appointed Lord Tomlinson under the Protectorate (bap. 1617, d. 1681), parliamentarian army officer and politician. See *ODNB*. Tomlinson commanded the troop which guarded Charles I during his trial (to which Tomlinson had been appointed as one of the judges, but had declined to sit) and attended the King to the scaffold.

[3] Windsor, Berkshire, where the King was due to arrive the following day (23 December). He remained at Windsor until his transfer to Whitehall and Westminster on 19 January 1649 for his trial.

[4] Lt. Col. Ralph Cobbett. See Firth and Davies, *Regimental History*, 1:337–9.

[5] John Merriman (Firth and Davies, *Regimental History*, 1:145, 147, 150–1, 154).

[6] This could be 'near' rather than 'next'.

THE LETTERS, WRITINGS, AND SPEECHES OF OLIVER CROMWELL

Governor. therin) and to keepe Guard by a Troope att a time within the Castle & for that purpose to receive orders from Col: Thomlinson & wee desire you alsoe out of the Cheif of the Kinges Servants last allowed (uppon Advice with Lt. Col. Cobbett & Capt. Merriman) to appoint about the Number of 6. (Such as are most to bee confided in, and who may best supply all [ ][7] Officers) to stay with & attend the Kinge for such necessary use & the rest wee desire you to Send away nott as discharged from the benefit of their places butt only as Spar'd from extraordinary attendance This is thought fitt to avoide any numerous concourse which many Servants with their followers & their Relations or Acquaintance would draw into the Castle, and for the said Reason itt is wish't that such of the Servants retained as are least sure & nott of necessity to be constantly in the Kinges Lodginges may bee lodged in the Towne, or the lower parte of the Castle wherin the Governor. is to bee advised with.

Capt Mildmay[8] (wee presume) will bee one of those you'le finde to Retaine, The Dragoones of your Convoy send away to the Quarters formerly intended which (as wee Remember) were in Bedfordshire wee bless by whose providence you are come in so well with your charge wee remaine

Your true freinds to Serve you,

Oliver Cromwell

Henry Ireton

Westmr. Decr. 22 1648.

To Col: Harrison att Windsor, or by the way to Farnham[9] thitherward.

Hast

---

[7] Illegible, probably a deletion, but possibly one word written over another.

[8] Anthony Mildmay (MP for West Looe in the Short Parliament) brother of Sir Henry Mildmay—see *HoP Commons, 1640–1660*.

[9] Farnham, Surrey.

1648 12 22b

Letter from Oliver Cromwell and Henry Ireton to Colonel Christopher Whichcott, governor of Windsor Castle

Date: 22 December 1648
Source: Worcester College, Oxford, Clarke MS 114, fos 151r–v (contemporary copy)

After the arrest of Robert Hammond on 28 November, Charles I was moved to Hurst Castle under the control of Lt. Col. Robert Cobbett and Captain John Merriman. The King remained at Hurst Castle as the drama of Pride's Purge and the Whitehall Debates unfolded in London. Finally, on 15 December the Council of Officers determined to bring him up to Windsor Castle and he was brought slowly up, arriving on 22 December. This letter, from Cromwell and Ireton (but notably not Fairfax) gave very full instructions about how the King was to be kept under close control and arrangements made to inhibit any desperate attempt to rescue him. This is a copy in the papers of William Clarke of the order sent to Colonel Christopher Whichcote, the governor of Windsor Castle and is in his hand.

[fo. 151r]

Sir

Capt Brayfeild[1] of Col: Hewson's[2] Regimt. with his owne & two other Companies of Foote are ordered to come to you, and to receive orders from you for the better securing of the Castle & the person of the Kinge therin You may Quarter them in the Towne & in Eyton[3] (if nott in the Castle) Col: Harrison[4] is alsoe Writt unto to appoint 3. or 4. Troopes of Horse out of his Convoy to remaine neere Windsor, & to Quarter in the next parts of Middlesex & Surrey as you shall advise & keepe Guard by a Troope att a time within the Castle. Itt is thought fittest, That the Horse Guard or parte of itt bee kept within the upper Castle & that att least one Company of Foote att a time bee uppon Guard there, and that the Bridge betwixt the Castles (if you thinke fitt) bee drawne uppe in the night, & kept drawne ordinarily in the daye, Alsoe, That noe other prisoners bee lodg'd in that parte of the Castle besides the Kinge unlesse Duke Hamilton in some close roomes where hee may nott have intercourse with the Kinge, & hee

---

[1] Wanklyn, *Reconstructing*, 1:71 fn. 313, 81, 104.
[2] John Hewson, appointed Lord Hewson under the Protectorate (*fl.* 1630–60), army officer and regicide. See *ODNB*.
[3] Presumably Eton, then in Buckinghamshire, but now in Berkshire, very close to Windsor Castle.
[4] Thomas Harrison.

THE LETTERS, WRITINGS, AND SPEECHES OF OLIVER CROMWELL

rather to bee in Winchester Castle (where Sir Thomas Payton was)[5] if you can safelie dispose of the other prisoners elsewhere butt the Kinge (by all meanes) must bee lodged in the upper Castle in some of the safest roomes, & Col. Thomlinson,[6] Lt. Col. Cobbett[7] & Capt Merriman[8] to have lodginges there, & those Gent of the Army (being about 6. or 7.) who are appointed to attend & assist them in the imediate watching about the Kinge to bee alsoe lodged (if itt may bee) in the upper Castle or att least within the Tower. Some of his allowed servants alsoe (that were of imediate attendance about his person) must necessarily bee lodged in the upper Castle about which Col. Harrison & Lt. Col: Cobbett will advise with you; Col: Thomlinson & with him Lt. Col: Cobbett & Capt. Merriman are appointed to the charge of the imediate securing of the Kinges person (as You[9] will see by their Instructions which which they will shew you) and for their assistance & furtherance therin you are desired to appoint such Guards of Foote for the imediate securing of him, and to guard the roome where hee & they shall lodge as they shall desire and that you order those Guards from time to time to observe the orders of Col: Thomlinson, Lt Coll: Cobbett & Capt Merriman therin, The Horse alsoe (as the imediate Guarding of the Kinge) are appointed to receive orders from Col: Thomlinson, but as to the safe-Guarding of [fo. 151v] the Garrison, all (both Horse & Foote) are to bee att your command. Wee thought this distribution better for your ease & for the leaving you more free to looke to the security of the whole Garrison then to burden you both with itt & with the imediate charge of the kinges person where you have alsoe soe many prisoners to looke to, itt is thought convenient that (duringe the kinges stay with you) you turne out of the Castle all malignant or cavalierish Inhabitants (Except the prisoners) and as many others of loose & idle persons as you can well ridde out, and to stinte the Number of prisoneres servants to the lowest proportion you well can. you are desired alsoe to restraine any numerous or ordinarie concourse of unnecessary people into that parte of the Castle of whose affections & faithfulnesse to the publique there is not good assurance or who have not necessary

---

[5] Sir Thomas Peyton, second baronet (1613–84), of Knowlton, Kent. See *HoP Commons, 1660–1690*. He was imprisoned in Winchester after taking part in the failed rising in Kent in 1648.

[6] Matthew Tomlinson [Thomlinson], appointed Lord Tomlinson under the Protectorate (bap. 1617, d. 1681), parliamentarian army officer and politician. See *ODNB*.

[7] Lt. Col. Ralph Cobbett. See Wanklyn, *Reconstructing*, 1:45, 46 fn. 27, 57, 67, 77, 87, 99.

[8] Captain John Merriman. See Wanklyn, *Reconstructing*, 1:95 fn. 445.

[9] 'You' is written over a word now hidden by the over-writing.

occasions there, and to suffer noe publique preaching in the Chappell or any lie occasion for concourse of people. Tis good the prisoners this while bee strictly kept in & with-held from intercourse or Communication one with another, and that the Guards of the Gates att the upper castle have a list of the kinges allowed servants now retayned & their followers as alsoe of the officers & Gent: of the Army that are to watch the kinge with their servants that those Guards may know whom they are ordinarilie to lett in & the Guards att the outer Gate of the lower Castle to have knowledge of the same List & of all other dwellers & lodgers within the inner part The Lord bee with you & blesse you in this great charge. To his Good pleasure I committ you & itt

Your faithfull friend & servant

Westmr, Dec:22 1648

Oliver Cromwell   Henry Ireton

To Col: Whichcott Govr of Windsor Castle[10] Hast these

1649 01 04

Protection issued by Oliver Cromwell to all officers and soldiers whom it may concern

Date: 4 January 1649
Source: Norfolk Record Office, JER/297 (autograph)

This document orders 'all officers and soldiers whom it may concern' to desist from plundering the home of and foodstuffs belonging to one of Norfolk's most prominent and defiant Catholic families. The context is unknown. The protection is printed on a double sheet folded over: on the back is scrawled: 'Protecsion'.

It is in the hand of Cromwell's usual clerk and bears his signature and seal.

These are to Commaund and require you and every one of you That you henceforth forbeare to molest the person, Seize, take, plunder or carry away any of the horses, Oxen, sheep, Corne, householdstuff; or any other goods whatsoever of or

---

[10] Christopher Whichcote. See the *Online Directory of Parliamentarian Army Officers*. Whichcote never served in the New Model. He served in London trained bands from 1642 to 1645, when he became governor of Windsor, a post he held until deep into the Protectorate.

belonging to Sir Henry Jarneghan[1] of Cossey[2] in the County of Norfolke As you and every of you will ans{w}er the Co{nt}rary at your uttmost perills. Given under my hand & Seale at Whitehall the 4th day of Jan: 1648
O Cromwell
To all officers and soldiers whome this may concern

1649 01 06
Summary of speeches by Oliver Cromwell in the Council of the Army

Date: 6 January 1649
Source: Worcester College, Oxford, Clarke MS 65, fos 134r–v (reported speech)

The Army had been debating the text of what became known as the *Officers' Agreement of the People*[1] which would be offered to Parliament on 20 January 1649. The very first clause would call for the dissolution of Parliament by 30 April 1649 and for fresh elections (subsequent clauses would define who was to vote and what the distribution of seats should be). Clarke's notes on the debate on 6 January 1649 consist of brief summaries of five speeches, three by Henry Ireton and two, more by way of interjection, by Cromwell. The heading given by Clarke is 'Debate concerning the setting of a period to this Parliament by the last of April'. When the Agreement was published a slightly different wording was adopted: 'That to prevent the many inconveniencies, apparently arising from the long continuance of the same persons in supream Authority, this Present Parliament end and dissolve upon, or before the last day of *April*, in the year of our Lord. 1649.'[2]

In his three speeches, Ireton argued (1) that it would be for the greater security 'in case the Army should be forced to remove, when the ill-affected partie may come in again' and that it would satisfy the people's desires for 'a future representative'. Cromwell suggests

---

[1] For the Catholicism of the Jerninghams, see T. B. Tappes-Lomax, 'Roman Catholicism in Norfolk, 1559–1780', *Norfolk Archaeology*, 32:1 (1958), pp. 27–46.
[2] Costessey, Norfolk, just three miles from Norwich.

---

[1] For a discussion of this document, see Ian Gentles, 'The *Agreements of the People* and their political contexts, 1647–1649', in Michael Mendle, ed., *The Putney Debates of 1647: the Army, the Levellers and the English State* (Cambridge, 2001), pp. 156–68.
[2] *A PETITION FROM His Excellency Thomas Lord Fairfax And the General Council of Officers of the ARMY, to the Honourable the COMMONS OF ENGLAND in PARLIAMENT assembled, concerning the Draught of An AGREEMENT OF THE PEOPLE for the secure and present PEACE, by them framed and prepared. Together with the said AGREEMENT presented Saturday,* Jan.20... *tendred to the consideration of the PEOPLE.* (London, 1649) (Wing / F213; Thomason / E.539[2]). It is printed in Don M. Wolfe, *Leveller Manifestoes of the Puritan Revolution* (1944), pp. 333–50.

8 JANUARY 1649

that it would be sufficient for Parliament to set a date when they would dissolve, but Ireton replies (2) that it needs to be written into the Agreement and beyond this Parliament's power to control the form of the election, and just to bring in a new one 'in the old way'. Cromwell's second response is one of surprise. Ireton's final comment (3) is that only by putting this in the Agreement which was to be offered to all the people could a new Parliament in a new form be elected.

[fo. 134r]

Ireton (1)

Lieutenant Generall That itt will more honourable & convenient for them to Putt a period to themselves.[3]

Ireton (2)

Lieutenant Generall Then you are afraid they will do

Ireton (3)

1649 01 08

Warrant appointing the meeting of the High Court of Justice to try the King, signed by Oliver Cromwell and thirty-three others

Date: 8 January 1649
Source: Worcester College, Oxford, Clarke MS 16, fos 69r–v (contemporary copy)

On 6 January, a full calendar month after Pride's Purge, the Commons passed 'An Act of the Commons of England Assembled in Parliament, for Erecting of a High Court of Justice, for the Trying and Judging of Charles Stuart, King of England'.[1] This appointed 135 commissioners for the trial of the King. The list began 'Thomas Lord Fairfax, Oliver Cromwell, Henry Ireton, Esquires, Sir Hardress Waller, Knight, Philip Skippon, Valentine Wauton, Thomas Harrison, Edward Whalley, Thomas Pride, Isaac Ewer, Richard Ingoldsby…'— eight senior army officers[2] but without their military titles. Cromwell was placed second. The Act left all the details of the trial, the when, where and to an extent how, to the commissioners or a quorum of twenty or more of them. Two days later, thirty-three of

---

[3] Cromwell may well be referring to this in his speeches of 4 July 1653 and of 12 September 1654 when he claimed he had long urged Parliament to dissolve itself.

---

[1] A&O, 1:1253–5: http://www.british-history.ac.uk/ report.aspx?compid=56301.

[2] Five of the ten—Fairfax, Skippon, Pride, Ewer and Ingoldsby—are not signatories of the warrant of 6 January. Pride, Ewer and Ingoldsby were, however, regicides.

647

THE LETTERS, WRITINGS, AND SPEECHES OF OLIVER CROMWELL

them, with Cromwell being named third, announced that the trial would commence in the Painted Chamber of the Palace of Westminster two days later. All but three were later to sign the King's death warrant (the exceptions being William Lord Monson, the first named, John Fry and John Weekes [recte Fowke]). In accordance with the warrant, the High Court convened on 10 January and met on most successive days to plan the trial. The King first appeared on 20 January and then daily from 22 to 27 January, the 27th being the day until on which he was sentenced to death.

The surviving copy of this warrant, in the papers of William Clarke, does not contain original signatures and contains what must be transcription errors in the copying of the names of commissioners, as noted.

––––––––

[fo. 69r]

By Vertue of an Act of the Commons of England Assembled in Parliamt, for Erectinge of a high Court of Justice, for the Tryeinge and Judging of Charles Stuarte Kinge of England, Wee whose names are here underwritten (Being Comissionrs amongst others, Nominated in the said Act) doe hereby appoynt that the high Court of Justice Mentioned in the said Act , shalbee holden in the Painted Chambers, in the Palace of Westminster on Wednesday the Tenth day of this Instant Janu by One of the Clocke in the afternoone, & this wee appoynt to bee Notifyed by Publique Proclayminge hereof in the Great Hall at Westminster To Morrow being the Ninth day of this Instant January betwixt the howres of Nine & Eleaven in the forenoone, in Testamony whereof,

Wee have hereunto sett our Hands and seales the eighth of January Ann: Dom: 1648.

Wm Monson[3]	Valentine Walton
Tho: Gray[4]	John Blakiston[5]
O: Cromwell	Gilb. Millington[6]
Sir Gre: Norton[7]	J Hewson
Hen: Ireton	Per: Pelham[8]
Hum: Edwards[9]	Edmund Ludlow[10]

---

[3] William Monson, first viscount Monson of Castlemaine (d. 1673?). See *ODNB*. Attended the trial until 23 January but was not a regicide.

[4] Thomas Grey, Baron Grey of Groby (1622–57), regicide. See *ODNB*.

[5] John Blakiston (bap. 1603, d. 1649), regicide. See *ODNB*.

[6] Gilbert Millington (c.1598–1666), regicide. See *ODNB*.

[7] Sir Gregory Norton, first baronet (c.1603–1652), regicide. See *ODNB*.

[8] Peregrine Pelham (bap. 1602, d. 1650), regicide. See *ODNB*.

[9] Humphrey Edwards (d. 1658), regicide. See *ODNB*.

[10] Edmund Ludlow [Ludlowe] (1616/17–92), regicide. See *ODNB*. Clearly written first as 'Edward'.

8 JANUARY 1649

J: Hutchinson[11]   Col: Barkestead[12]

Hard: Waller[13]   Edw: Whalley[14]

Wm Constable[15]   Jon Okey[16]

J: Lisle [17]   Robt Tichburne[18]

Hen: Martin[19]   Jon Weekes[20]

[fo. 69v]

Henry Smith[21]

Sir Tho: Maulyverer[22]

Jon Fry[23]

Adrian Scroope[24]

Jon Carew[25]

James Temple[26]

A: Garland[27]

Rich: Deane[28]

F. Harrison[29]

---

[11] John Hutchinson (bap. 1615, d. 1664), regicide. See *ODNB*.

[12] John Barkstead, John (d. 1662), regicide. See *ODNB*.

[13] Sir Hardress Waller, (*c*.1604–1666), regicide. See *ODNB*.

[14] Edward Whalley, appointed Lord Whalley under the Protectorate (d. 1674/5), regicide. See *ODNB*.

[15] Sir William Constable, baronet (bap. 1590, d. 1655), regicide. See *ODNB*.

[16] John Okey (bap. 1606, d. 1662), regicide. See *ODNB*.

[17] John Lisle, appointed Lord Lisle under the Protectorate (1609/10–64), regicide. See *ODNB*.

[18] Robert Tichborne, appointed Lord Tichburne under the Protectorate (1610/11–82), regicide. See *ODNB*.

[19] Marten [Martin], Henry [Harry] (1601/2–80), regicide. See *ODNB*.

[20] John Weekes [?recte John Fowke]. If Fowke, then he was appointed one of the 135 commissioners but did not attend the trial or sign the death warrant. See John Fowke (*c*.1596–1662), merchant and politician, in *ODNB*.

[21] Henry Smith [Smyth] (b. 1619/20, d. in or after 1668), regicide. See *ODNB*.

[22] Sir Thomas Mauleverer, first baronet (bap. 1599, d. 1655), regicide. See *ODNB*.

[23] John Fry (*c*.1609–56/7), religious controversialist. See *ODNB*. He attended the trial 20–26 January but did not attend the final sessions and did not sign the death warrant.

[24] Adrian Scrope (1601–60), regicide. See *ODNB*.

[25] John Carew (1622–60), regicide. See *ODNB*.

[26] James Temple (1606–*c*.1674), regicide. See *ODNB*.

[27] Augustine Garland (bap. 1603, d. in or after 1677), regicide. See *ODNB*.

[28] Richard Deane (bap. 1610, d. 1653), regicide. See *ODNB*.

[29] Thomas Harrison (bap. 1616, d. 1660), regicide. See *ODNB*. Written clearly as 'F.Harrison', but must be Thomas, the only Harrison named as a commissioner and a man who had been calling for Charles's execution as early as 5 November 1647.

649

Daniel Blagrave[30]
J Jones[31]

1649 01 29
Death warrant of Charles I

Date: 29 January 1649
Source: Parliamentary Archives, HL/PO/JO/10/297A (there is an online image of the warrant at http://www.nationalarchives.gov.uk/pathways/citizenship/rise_parliament/docs/charles_warrant.htm ; or at http://www.parliament.uk/about/living-heritage/evolutionofparliament/parliamentaryauthority/civilwar/collections/deathwarrant/)

The original death warrant is still in the parliamentary archives in the form a flat parchment containing seals and signatures, and is handwritten in iron gall ink. The signatures of the fifty-nine commissioners who signed the warrant are in seven columns, and Cromwell's name appears third in the first column from the left, under the names of John Bradshaw, and Thomas Lord Grey of Groby, the only member of the House of Lords to sign it. The only other man to sign in that column was Edward Whalley, Cromwell's first cousin. There is an article on 'the Regicides' in ODNB, which contains a full list and an instant link to the lives of each of the regicides.[1]

One hundred and thirty-five men were appointed commissioners for the King's trial. As many as forty-eight never attended and of the eighty-five who did, sixteen dropped out during the proceedings. In all, sixty-seven were present at the end of the four-day trial and were recorded as having stood to signify their assent to the sentence. On 29 January all but ten of the sixty-seven signed the death warrant. Thomas Chaloner and Richard Ingoldsby, two commissioners who were not present at the sentencing, added their names to the warrant, bringing the number of signatories to fifty-nine.[2]

---

[30] Daniel Blagrave (bap. 1603, d. 1668?), regicide. See ODNB.
[31] John Jones (c.1597–1660), regicide. See ODNB.

[1] There is also a very useful and accurate table with links to short lives of all the regicides at https://en.wikipedia.org/wiki/List_of_regicides_of_Charles_I.
[2] For some key works on the death warrant itself. See 'Regicides (act.1649)' in ODNB; C. V. Wedgwood, The Trial of Charles I (1964); A. W. McIntosh, 'The Numbers of the English "Regicides"', History (1982), pp. 195–216; Jason Peacey, ed., The Regicides and the Execution of Charles I (2001).

29 JANUARY 1649

At the high Cort of Justice for the tryinge and judginge of Charles Steuart Kinge of England January xxix[th] Anno Dni 1648.

Whereas Charles Steuart Kinge of England is and standeth convicted attaynted and condemned of High Treason and other high Crymes, And sentence uppon Saturday last \was/ pronounced against him by this Cort to be putt to death by the severinge of his head from his body Of which sentence, execucon yet remayneth to be done, These are therefore to will and require yow to see the said sentence executed In the open Streete before Whitehall uppon the morrowe being the Thirtieth day of this instante moneth of January betweene the houres of Tenn in the morninge and Five in the afternoone of the same day with full effect And for soe doing this shall be your sufficient warrant And these are to require All Officers and Souldiers and other the good people of this Nation of England to be assistinge unto you in this service Given under our hands and Seales

To Colonell Francis Hacker,[3] Colonell Huncks[4] and Lieutenant Colonell Phayre[5] and to every of them.

---

[3] Francis Hacker (d. 1660), parliamentarian army officer and regicide. See *ODNB*.

[4] Hercules Huncks had served in Ireland throughout the 1640s; in October 1648 he was appointed governor of Londonderry and in January 1649 he was still raising a regiment to take with him. See Firth and Davies, *Regimental History*, 2:641–3, 656–7.

[5] Robert Phayre [Phaire] (1618/19–82), parliamentarian army officer. See *ODNB*.

Jo: Bradshawe
Tho: Grey
O Cromwell
Edw: Whalley
H Ireton
Tho Mauleverer

Har: Waller
M Livesey
John Okey
J Danvers
Jo: Bourchier
Pr. Temple
J Hewson

Hen Smyth
John Blakiston
J Hutchinson
Will: Goffe
Tho. Pride
Dan: Blagrave
Owen Rowe
Willm Purfoy

A.Garland
Per: Pelham
Ri Deane
Robert
Tichborne
H Edwardes
Rich Ingoldesby
Will. Cawley
Jo Barkstead
Ad: Scrope
James Temple

Symon Mayne
Edm: Ludlowe
Henry Marten
Vinc: Potter
Wm: Constable
G Fleetwood
J Alured
Robt Lilburne
Isaa Ewer
John Dixwell
Valentine
Wauton

Tho Wogan
Tho. Horton
J Jones
John Moore
Gilbt
Millington
Tho: Harrison
Tho:Scot
Jo: Carew
Miles {Corbett}
Will Say:
Anth Stapley
{Gre Norton}

John Venn
Gregory
Clement
Jo: Downes
Tho Wayte

{Tho Challoner}

VOLUME 1 OMISSIONS

There are far fewer 'omissions' from volume 1 than from volume 2 and volume 3.

The principle of all three volumes is that we would include everything which captured Cromwell's voice and by implication his mind. When in doubt we have included rather than excluded. So we have included most of the documents in which he was one of many signatories even though we had little or no indication of his part in the composition. We have included all letters and public documents (declarations etc.) of which he was sole signatory or stated author. In this first volume, we have included a high proportion (higher than in the other volumes) of standard documents, pro-formas, such as warrants, certificates, receipts, protections and orders (twenty-one in all) because they are important for understanding his growing authority and web of connections. Two documents strain our rules but cannot possibly be omitted—the warrant establishing the High Court of Justice for the trial of the King (**1649 01 08**) in which he might just have had a hand, and the King's death warrant (**1649 01 29**) in which he almost certainly didn't. We list below those we have not included, but we have not had the resources to trawl through the uncalendared tundra of the Commonwealth Exchequer papers where a lot more pro-forma warrants, passes, protections, orders and commissions would undoubtedly be found.

The conventions of the project limit the inclusion of second- and third-hand accounts of conversations between Cromwell and one or more other persons. The general rule was that the conversation has to be recorded by an ear-witness and that there must be some evidence that a record was made close to the time of the conversation. Again, as in the case of Edmund Ludlow's report of a conversation in a garden at Westminster in the aftermath of the funeral of the earl of Essex (we have recorded it as **1646 10 31 [?]**), we have been generous in our interpretation of the rule, and the same is broadly true of the conversations overheard by Sir John Berkeley (**1647 07 15**) and Robert Huntingdon (**1648 08 02**). Less problematic are the sworn statements of two witnesses at the committee investigating his charges against the earl of Manchester in December 1648 (**1644 12 04b** and **1648 12 06**).

Abbott, *Writings and Speeches*, includes as text about thirty fabricated writings, converting notes by clerks of the Commons or its committees relating to documents that they had received (but which no longer survive, having for the most part been destroyed in the fire at the Palace of Westminster in 1834). They are so remote from anything Cromwell actually

OMISSIONS

wrote that we have excluded them, even from the list of omissions. They are Abbott's creations not Cromwell's. Here are three examples:

1. [Abbott 1:347]
To the Committee of Both Kingdoms
Goring has joined with the Princes' forces in Oxford, Saddles are needed for the new troops' [May 4, 1645?][1]

2. [Abbott 1:387]
To William Lenthall, Esq., Speaker of the House of the Commons
Acknowledging the letter from the House of Commons and explaining the condition of affairs in the west which made it necessary to join Fairfax. On the way west he would endeavour to take Langford House. Their orders regarding Donnington Castle would be carried out if they still considered it advisable. Wallop, Oct. 16, 1645.[2]

3. [Abbott 1:608]
To the Committee at Derby House
Desiring powder, ammunition, arms, guns and shot for carrying on the work of reducing Wales; with some intercepted enclosed, and a 'Declaration in the Name of the Gentlemen and Inhabitants of Wales.' Cardiff, May 15, 1648.[3]

What follows is a list of items bearing his signature which, for the reasons given above, have been excluded.

Date	Description	Source	Reason for Omission
1642 12 17	Warrant to Captain Vernon	Carlyle-Lomas 3:314 from source untraced in TNA SP28	Pro-forma
1645 03 17[?]	Speech in Parliament briefly summarised	Abbott 1:334 from *Whitelocke's Memorials* (1732), p. 136	Later construction
1645 05 03	Certificate that troop had been disbanded	Abbott 1:346 unrecovered text in TNA, SP28	Pro-forma
1645 10 10	Requisition of horses from 'Mr Herbert'	Abbott 1:384 from TNA SP16/539 no. 132	Pro-forma
1646 08 18	Protection order for John Heron, disbanded royalist	Abbott 1:411–12 from TNA SP18/186 no. 717	Pro-forma
1646 10 30	Warrant sending men to the Channel Islands	Abbott, 1:418 from TNA SP23/245/73	Pro-forma

---

[1] Source given as the *CSPD* (1644–5), pp. 457, 459. The letter has not survived.
[2] Source given is *JHC*, 4:312. The problem with treating this stump as a 'Cromwell' document is shown by comparing it with the letter written on the same day on the same subject to Fairfax as **1645 10 16**. This one is included as the one which came closest to inclusion of all of them.
[3] Source given is *JHC* 5:566.

654

OMISSIONS

Date	Description	Source	Reason for Omission
1646 12 23	Formal Articles of Agreement with the Scots	Abbott 1:421–4 from JHL 8:614–15	Committee document with no evidence of Cromwell role
1647 06 03[?]	Clarendon's paraphrase-account of a lost letter	Abbott 1:456 from Clarendon, History, 10:89	Third-hand at best
1647 07 18[?]	Fragment of a conversation with French Ambassador, Pomponne de Bellievre	Abbott 1:472 from Memoires of Cardinal de Retz (1859)	Third-hand at best
1647 08 05[?]	Conversation reported to Clarendon	Abbott 1:493 from Clarendon, History, 10:125	Third-hand at best
1647 11 14	Remonstrance signed for but not by senior officers following the Putney Debates	Abbott 1:557–60 from JHL 9:529	Possible but not likely Cromwell input
1647 11 24[?]	Conversation reported to Clarendon	Abbott 1:554 from Clarendon, History, 10:138	Third-hand at best
1647 11 21[?]	Conversation some time in 1649 about the end of all dealings with the King	Abbott 1:564 from 'the Biography of Orrery' in Thomas Morrice, ed., A Collection of State Letters of … Roger Boyle	Third-hand at best First earl of Orrery (1743), 1:219–28
1648 04 08	Receipt for pay	Abbott 1:596 from TNA SP16/539 fo. 508	Pro-forma
1648 04 20	Much later version of a speech at Abbott 1:598–9 re the council of war recorded by William Allen	from William Allen, 'Narrative' in Somers Tracts 6:500.	Tendentious, after the event
1648 08 14b	Order for restitution of horses	Carlyle-Lomas 3:387 from original now lost	Pro-forma
1648 10 24	Commission for John Fenwick as Major	Abbott 1:671 from original now unavailable	Pro-forma
1648 10 25	Precis of order to Colonel Thomas Barwis	Carlyle-Lomas 3:388 from lost original	Pro-forma
1648 11 22	Pass for Sir John Digby and servant to come to and to leave Pontefract	Abbott 1:693 from an original in private hands and now missing	Pro-forma
1648 11 23	Warrant for monthly assessment payments	Abbott 1:693 from HMC 3rd Report, appendix p. 87	Pro-forma

INDEX OF BIBLICAL CITATIONS

This index consists of all the biblical references referred to directly by Cromwell or which have been identified by the editors and given (with comments where appropriate) in the footnotes. The separate indexes for the Old and New Testament are arranged, helpfully for readers, alphabetically by book title, following the titles used in the Authorised (King James) Version, not those of the Geneva Bible, since it is the editors' view that the Authorised Version is the one Cromwell himself knew best.

Old Testament

Book/chapter:verse(s)	vol./page(s)
2 Chronicles 16:9	2:469
Daniel 2	3:464
Daniel 2:44	2:684, 2:704, 2:712
Daniel 3:19	3:513
Daniel 6:8	3:96
Daniel 6:12	3:96
Daniel 6:15	3:96
Deuteronomy 4:34	3:333
Deuteronomy 32:10	3:136, 3:307, 3:332
Deuteronomy 33:16	1:628
Ecclesiastes 2:18–19	3:144
Ecclesiastes 9:10	3:257
Exodus 3:1–6	1:628
Ezekiel 21:27	3:75
Ezekiel 37:1–4	2:432
Genesis 3:15	3:291
Genesis 4:8–9	2:193

Genesis 4:15	3:477
Genesis 25:29–34	2:613
Genesis 34	2:191
Habakkuk 2:2	2:668, 2:690
Hosea 6:1–2	3:231
Hosea 11:12	2:678, 2:690, 2:710
Isaiah 1:26	3:144
Isaiah 2:5	3:323
Isaiah 8:10,13,14	1:566
Isaiah 8:17	2:353
Isaiah 9:4–5	1:528
Isaiah 11:2,4	1:630
Isaiah 21:8	3:470
Isaiah 25:1	3:333
Isaiah 28:5–15	2:307, 2:310
Isaiah 28:13	3:136
Isaiah 28:21	2:667, 2:689
Isaiah 41	2:711
Isaiah 41:2	2:327
Isaiah 41:19–20	2:682, 2:701, 2:711

657

INDEX OF BIBLICAL CITATIONS

Isaiah 42:8	3:146	Psalms 25:9	1:630
Isaiah 43	3:136	Psalms 25:21	3:254
Isaiah 43:21	2:682, 2:702, 2:712	Psalms 27:3	1:16
		Psalms 28:5	3:465
Isaiah 48:22	1:630	Psalms 30:3	2:458
Isaiah 56:10	3:159	Psalms 37:5	3:254
Isaiah 57:20–1	1:630, 3:302	Psalms 37:9	1:611
Isaiah 58:12	3:466	Psalms 37:11	1:630
		Psalms 40:2	2:458
Jeremiah 17:8	1:631	Psalms 40:5	3:71
		Psalms 44:3	1:628
Job 33:14	3:148	Psalms 46:2–5, 7, 11	3:317
		Psalms 46	3:316
Jonah 4:6–7	3:471	Psalms 52:5	3:476
Jonah 4:11	3:477	Psalms 54:6–8	2:728
		Psalms 58:4	3:483
Joshua 5:2–8	3:81	Psalms 62:11	3:148
Joshua 6:18	1:610	Psalms 63:1	1:16
Joshua 6:26	3:377	Psalms 65:5	3:333
		Psalms 68:11–13	2:684, 2:705
Judges 8:20–1	3:138	Psalms 68:15–17	2:685, 2:705
		Psalms 68:22	2:684, 2:704, 2:713
1 Kings 3:26	1:301		
		Psalms 84:10	1:629
2 Kings 2:12	2:238	Psalms 85:1	3:463
2 Kings 10:30	2:451	Psalms 85:1–3	3:462
		Psalms 85:8	3:483
Lamentations 3:29	3:230	Psalms 85:9	3:333, 3:334, 3:463, 3:464
Lamentations 3:41	1:11		
		Psalms 85:10	3:135, 3:334, 3:464
Micah 4:6–7	3:322		
Micah 6:9	3:136	Psalms 85:11	3:464
		Psalms 85:13	3:464
Numbers 11:24–6	2:358	Psalms 85	3:315
Numbers 11:27–9	2:359	Psalms 86:13	2:458
Numbers 14:4	3:294	Psalms 94:20	3:398
Numbers 16:1	2:193	Psalms 106:5	2:484
Numbers 22ff	2:193	Psalms 110:3	2:682, 2:702, 2:712
Proverbs 18:10	3:140	Psalms 118	3:316
Proverbs 28:3	3:138	Psalms 118:23	2:347
		Psalms 118:23–4	2:308
Psalms 2:2	1:301	Psalms 119:134	2:469
Psalms 9:16	3:136		
Psalms 10:11	1:16		
Psalms 16:9	1:16		
Psalms 17:8	3:307, 3:332		

658

INDEX OF BIBLICAL CITATIONS

Psalms 120:5	1:16	2 Samuel 5:3	3:364
Psalms 139:7–13	1:629	2 Samuel 22:29	1:16
		2 Samuel 23:3	2:678, 2:699, 2:710–11
1 Samuel 2	3:334		
1 Samuel 12:3	2:293	Song of Solomon 2:3	3:135
1 Samuel 25	3:376, 3:382		
1 Samuel 31:3–6	2:531	Zechariah 2:8	2:432, 3:136
2 Samuel 3:39	1:476, 2:276	Zephaniah 3:19–20	3:322

New Testament

Acts of the Apostles 1:19	3:479	James 1:2–6	1:629
Acts of the Apostles 2:46	3:254	James 1:17	1:629
Acts of the Apostles 12:21–3	3:147	James 3:17	2:679
Acts of the Apostles 13:36	1:566	James 3:18	3:483
Acts of the Apostles 18:12–17	2:531		
		John 1:5	1:16
		John 1:7–9	1:16
Colossians 3:22	3:254	John 3:19	1:16
		John 5:31	3:85, 3:90
1 Corinthians 2:11	3:465	John 7:49	2:191
1 Corinthians 2:16	1:471	John 8:7	1:464
1 Corinthians 9:7	1:12	John 14:26	1:630
1 Corinthians 11:18	3:483		
1 Corinthians 12:27	1:367	Jude 1:4	3:73
1 Corinthians 13:1	3:312, 3:316	Jude 1:22	3:328
1 Corinthians 14:28–9	1:467	Jude 1:22–3	3:75
		Jude 1:23	3:329, 3:377, 3:382
2 Corinthians 1:12	1:629		
2 Corinthians 3:2	1:471	Jude 5:13	3:72
2 Corinthians 10:4–5	2:353		
		Luke 1:74–5	3:463
Ephesians 4:3	1:301	Luke 3:11	1:569
Ephesians 5:8	3:323	Luke 17:10	2:432
Ephesians 6:5	3:254	Luke 19:12	3:132
		Luke 19:17	3:315
Hebrews 4:16	2:341	Luke 19:27	3:132
Hebrews 10:26–7	3:148	Luke 23:12	3:301
Hebrews 10:31	3:148		
Hebrews 12:1	3:90	Mark 3:25	3:392
Hebrews 12:2–23	1:629	Mark 10:43	2:193
Hebrews 12:23	1:16		
Hebrews 13:21	1:629, 1:630	Matthew 5:5	1:630
		Matthew 6:11	1:569

INDEX OF BIBLICAL CITATIONS

Matthew 7:6	2:194	Revelation (general)	3:295
Matthew 12:25	3:392		
Matthew 25	3:356	Romans 1:32	3:407
Matthew 25:14–30	3:132	Romans 6:6	1:628
Matthew 27:3–8	3:479	Romans 8, esp. vv. 21–5	1:628
		Romans 8:28	1:628
1 Peter 1:23	3:146	Romans 8:29	1:367
1 Peter 2:5	1:11	Romans 8:37	3:522
1 Peter 5:10	3:255	Romans 12:1–21	2:681, 2:711
		Romans 12:5	1:367
2 Peter 1:4	2:239	Romans 14:23	3:421
2 Peter 1:19	1:469		
2 Peter 2:1–16	3:72	2 Thessalonians 2:3–12	3:295
Philippians 1:6	1:16	1 Timothy 1:13	1:628
Philippians 1:8	1:12, 1:465	1 Timothy 1:15	1:16
Philippians 3:8	1:465	1 Timothy 4:1–2	3:72, 3:73
Philippians 3:8–10	2:239	1 Timothy 4:2	3:313
Philippians 3:14–15	3:323	2 Timothy 1:12	1:628–9
Philippians 3:18–19	3:314	2 Timothy 3:1–4	3:72
		2 Timothy 3:5	3:73, 3:314, 3:445
Revelation 3:14–22	3:313		
Revelation 3:15–16	2:531	Titus 1:11	3:159
Revelation 3:16	3:309		

GENERAL INDEX

This index seeks to be a full people and places index to all three volumes and a more focused subject index. In keeping with the underlying principle of this project as a whole, that it seeks to identify Cromwell's voice, the subject index is arranged around words and concepts as Cromwell perceived them. So, there are only a few subject entries relating to the preliminary and introductory material and none to the appendices listing omitted items. The entries have been created not only by a close reading of the texts but by word-searches on more than fifty keywords in Cromwell's political, religious and social vocabulary. Among the surprises are that he never uses the word 'royalist', only uses the word 'puritan' twice (1656, 1658), and that he applies very distinctive meanings to words like 'honest' and 'conscience'. For ease of use, the index to all three volumes (together with the separate index of biblical citations) is included in each of the three volumes. Henry, Oliver and Richard Cromwell are abbreviated HC, OC and RC.

Abbot, Daniel **2**:152, **2**:216, **2**:233
Abbott, Wilbur Cortez **1**:97, **1**:103, **1**:122, **1**:137,
    1:141, **1**:156, **1**:162, **1**:183 n. 1, **1**:189 n. 1, **1**:332,
    1:334, **1**:366
    1937–47 edition **3**:xlviii
    additions to texts **1**:519
    bibliography of Cromwell's writings
        1:xxxvi–xxxvii
    copies of licences **2**:248
    dating of documents **1**:495–6, **1**:636, **2**:297,
        3:16–17, **3**:28
    dating of meetings **3**:459
    edition analysed **1**:xl–xli, **2**:xlii–xliii,
        3:xxxiv–xxxvi
    edition of Cromwell's writings **1**:xl–xli,
        3:xlviii, **1**:xlix, **1**:l
    identification of Captain Nicholas **1**:523 n. 8
    and letters to Popham **2**:58 n. 1
    on Middleton **1**:432 n. 1
    on originals of letters **2**:462
    on RC's marriage deed **2**:40 n. 1
    reconstruction of missing letters **2**:lvi n. 8
    as source for biographies **1**:lii
    as source of letters **2**:228
    on Stapleton **2**:14
    suggested emendations to text **1**:377 n. 11
    versions of speeches **2**:664
Abdy, Christopher (1632–63) **2**:530
Abernethy, Andrew **2**:395, **2**:396–7, **2**:398–401
Abingdon, Oxfordshire **1**:231–2, **1**:234, **2**:535

Abington Pigotts, Cambridgeshire **1**:10
Ackman, Henry **2**:334
Adamson, John **1**:250 n. 4
Adamson, Robert **2**:332
Adbury House, Hampshire **2**:504 n. 2
Adolf John I, Count Palatine of Kleeburg
    (1629–89) **3**:50
Adwalton Moor, Yorkshire **1**:122, **1**:125
Agard, John **3**:14–16
Agnue, Francis **2**:331
Agreement of the People **1**:436, **1**:439–42, **1**:455,
    1:457–76, **1**:474, **1**:482, **1**:483–4
Ainsworth, Henry (1569–1622) **2**:559
Aitzema, Lieuwe van (1600–69) **2**:lxiv, **2**:433–4
Akehurst, Alexander **1**:192
Aken, James **2**:332
Alabaster, William **1**:5, **1**:6
Albemarle, duke of, *see* Monck
Aldermaston, Berkshire **1**:211, **1**:229, **1**:238
Aldermaston Heath, Berkshire **1**:229
Alexander VII, pope (bap. 13 February 1599–d.
    22 May 1667) **3**:299, **3**:472
Alexander, Jean **3**:33
Alexander, William, first earl of Stirling
    (1577–1640) **3**:33
Alford, Sir Edward **1**:46
Alford, Somerset **1**:300
Alfreton, Derbyshire **1**:223 n. 45
Allen, Francis (c.1583–1658) **1**:464, **2**:608, **2**:610
Allen, Richard **2**:333

661

GENERAL INDEX

Allen, William (*fl.* 1642–67) 1:377, 2:596, 3:128–9
   at the Putney Debates 1:439, 1:452, 1:463,
     1:466–7, 1:468, 1:474–5
   at the Reading Debate 1:416, 1:418, 1:423
Allington, Hampshire 2:31–2
Almond, Edward 1:104, 1:112–13
Almond, John 1:66
Alnwick, baron, *see* Percy
Alnwick, Northumberland 1:575, 1:583, 1:586,
   2:289
Alresford, Hampshire 1:259
Alston, Sir Thomas (*c.*1609–78) 3:180
Altham, Sir James 1:14
Altham, Joanna 1:14
Alured, Matthew (bap. 1615, d. 1694) 2:368,
   3:38–9, 3:40–1, 3:300 n. 59
Anabaptists 1:140, 1:170, 1:178, 1:191, 1:234, 1:365,
   1:612, 3:101–2, 3:140, 3:254, 3:280, 3:306–7,
   3:344–5, 3:410–11
Anderson, Sir Henry 1:35
Anderson, Robert 2:333
Anderson, Thomas 2:333
Anderson, William 2:335
Andover, Hampshire 1:62 n. 1, 1:228, 2:45
Andrewes, James 1:112–13
Andrewes, Sir Thomas (d. 1659) 1:505,
   2:559 n. 8, 3:111
Andrews, John (*fl.* 1642–7) 2:633–4
Anglesey, earls of, *see* Annesley
Anglesey, North Wales 2:51–2, 2:550
Annandale, earl of, *see* Murray
Annesley, Arthur, first earl of Anglesey
   (1614–86) 1:505–6
Annis, John 1:110
annual Parliaments, Cromwell speech about 1:19
Antrim, earl and marquis of, *see* MacDonnell
Appelboom, Harald 2:733 n. 6
Appleby Castle, Cumbria 1:547 n. 12
Appletree, Thomas (d. 1666) 2:540
Apsley, Sir Allen (1616–83) 2:660–1
Arbury, Warwickshire. 1:6 n. 1
Archdeacon, James 2:219–22
Archer, Sir Simon (1581–1662) 3:182
Ardfinnan, County Tipperary 2:210
Ardglass, County Down 1:356
Ards, viscount, *see* Montgomery
Argyll, marquis of, *see* Campbell
Arklow, County Wicklow 2:103, 2:113, 2:140, 2:143
armaments, procuring of 1:72, 1:73, 1:89, 1:93–4
Armer, James 2:333
Armine, Sir William, first baronet (1593–1651)
   1:351, 1:429–31, 1:575–6, 1:586, 1:609,
   2:10, 2:24
Armstrong, Sir Thomas (d. 1662) 2:143, 2:144 n.
   28, 2:247
Army Debates (1647), *see* General Council of the
   Army

Army Plot, First, of 1641 1:25–6
Army revolt of 1647: OC's discussions of
   1:365–70, 1:377–402, 1:410–26, 1:428–32,
   1:435–75, 1:480–2
Arnett, Elizabeth 2:479
Arnett, George 2:479
Arnold, Richard 1:483, 2:275 n. 7
Articles of Surrender, *see* Surrender Articles
Arundel, earl of, *see* Howard
Arundel, Sir John (1576–1654x6) 2:443
Arundel/Arundell, Richard, first Baron
   Arundell of Trerice (1616–87) 2:442–3
Arundel, Sussex 1:46
Arwenack, Cornwall 3:209–10
Ashburnham, Sir John (1602/3–71) 1:336–7,
   1:488 n. 8
Ashburnham, William 1:43, 1:67–8
Ashby-de-la-Zouche, Leicestershire 1:118
Ashdown Forest, Sussex 3:65–6
Ashe 1:524
Ashe, John (1597–1659) 1:357, 1:399–402, 1:475,
   1:477, 1:624–6
Ashe, Simeon 1:240
Ashfield, Richard 1:576
Ashhurst, William (bap. 1607, d. 1656) 1:405–6
Ashmole, Elias 1:4 n. 7
Ashtead, Surrey 1:6 n. 1
Ashurst, William 1:217 n. 15, 1:245, 1:247, 1:249
Ashwellthorpe, Norfolk 1:342
Assessment (tax), Cromwell authorises
   continued collection of (1653) 2:644–7,
   2:647–50
Assheton, Sir Ralph 1:546, 1:547, 1:548, 1:548 n. 32,
   1:554–5, 1:576
Association, Oath of (1641), *see* Oath of Association
Astley, Sir Bernard 1:309
Astley, Sir Edward 1:127–8, 1:129
Astley, Sir Jacob 1:127 n. 4
Aston, Sir Arthur (*c.*1590–1649) 2:87–8, 2:92,
   2:94, 2:95, 2:97, 2:104
Aston, Sir Thomas 1:lxi n. 27
Athlone, County Westmeath 2:342 n. 13
Athlone, viscount, *see* Wilmot
Atkins, Sir Thomas (*c.*1589–1668/9) 3:170
Atkinson, Thomas 1:104
Atterbury, Francis, bishop of Rochester
   (1663–1732) 2:527
Atterbury, Lewis (1630/1–1693) 2:527
Audley, baron, *see* Tuchet
Audley, Lewis 1:446, 1:448, 1:455, 1:463
Augustin, Captain 2:415, 2:450
Axtell, Daniel (bap. 1622, d. 1660) 2:66–7, 2:227
   n. 4, 2:255, 2:596
Aylesbury, Buckinghamshire 1:206, 1:207, 1:271,
   2:650
Aylmer, Sir Andrew, of Donadea, second
   baronet 3:156

662

GENERAL INDEX

Aylmer, Gerald **1**:437 n. 5
Ayloffe, Colonel Thomas **1**:188
Ayscough, Sir Edward **1**:130, **1**:132–7, **1**:140
Ayscue/Ascough, Sir George (*c*.1615–72) **2**:lv,
    2:76–7, **2**:560, **2**:727, **2**:729

Backhouse, Peter (bap. 1614/15) **3**:175
Bacon, Sir Edmund, of Redgrave, second
    baronet **1**:107, **1**:143–7
Bacon, Nathaniel **1**:179
Bacon, Nathaniel (bap. 1593, d. 1660) **1**:283–5,
    3:487
Bacon, Nathaniel, of Friston, Suffolk **1**:107 n. 8
Bacon, Nathaniel, of Shrubland, Suffolk **1**:107
Bacon, Sir Nicholas (*c*.1543–1624) **1**:147 n. 15
Baggott, Robert **2**:181
Bailey, William **2**:333
Baillie, Robert (1602–62) **1**:215, **2**:374, **2**:399, **3**:36
Baillie, William (d. 1653) **1**:557–8
Baily, Mr **1**:59
Baily, Patrick **2**:333
Balfour, Sir James, first baronet (1600–57) **2**:448
Balfour, Sir William (d. 1660) **1**:207–10, **2**:651
Ballantine, James **2**:729
Ballinkill, County Laois **2**:215
Ballydoyne Castle, County Tipperary **2**:234
Ballyhack, County Wexford **2**:164
Ballyhendon/Ballyhindon, County Cork **2**:160
Ballyshannon, County Donegal **2**:230
Ballyvolane, County Cork **3**:219
Baltimore, baron, *see* Calvert
Baltimore, County Cork **2**:141
Bampfylde, Thomas **3**:431
Banbury, earls of, *see* Knollys
Banbury, Oxfordshire **1**:205, **1**:227 n. 70, **1**:228
Bandon/Bandonbridge, County Cork **2**:132,
    2:152, **2**:162
Bandon, river **2**:132 n. 5
Bandon Bridge, County Cork **2**:155
Bannockburn, Stirling **2**:471
Bantam, Spice Islands **3**:501
Baptists, *see* Anabaptists
Barbados, West Indies **2**:91, **2**:97, **3**:60–1,
    3:228–9
    transportation of prisoners of war to **2**:96–7
Barbon/Barebone, Praisegod (*c*.1598–
    1679/80) **2**:639
Barebone's (or Barbone's) Parliament (1653), *see*
    Nominated Assembly
Barker, John (*fl.* 1624–70) **1**:85
Barkstead, Sir John (d. 1662) **1**:377, **1**:647–9,
    3:251, **3**:298 n. 46, **3**:488–9
Barnardiston, Sir Thomas, first baronet
    (*c*.1618–69) **1**:112–13, **1**:143–7, **3**:182
Barnes, George **2**:136 n. 1
Barnstaple, Devon **2**:660
Barrière, M. **3**:25

Barrington, Elizabeth **1**:14 n. 4
Barrington, Henry (1592–after 1659) **3**:221
Barrington, Joan, Lady Barrington, née
    Cromwell/Williams (*c*.1558–1641) **1**:14,
    1:178, **2**:759
Barrington, Sir John, third baronet (*c*.1615–83)
    2:759–60, **3**:181
Barrington, Judith, Lady Barrington (d. 1657)
    2:759
Barrington, Sir Thomas, second baronet
    (*c*.1585–1644) **1**:38, **1**:72, **1**:80–1, **1**:130,
    1:154, **1**:155, **1**:162, **1**:163, **1**:165, **1**:169 n. 1,
    1:369 nn. 5 & 6, **2**:759
    letters to **1**:177–8
Barrow/Barrowe, Maurice (1597–1666) **1**:112–13,
    1:143–7, **1**:164–8, **1**:171–6, **1**:283–5
Barrow, Robert **3**:41 n. 6
Barrow, river **2**:119, **2**:121, **2**:124, **2**:127, **2**:142,
    2:152, **2**:230–1
Barry, James, first Baron Barry of Santry
    (1603–73) **3**:193–4
Barry, Robert, Catholic bishop of Cork and
    Cloyne (*c*.1588–1662) **2**:184–9
Barthick, Andrew **2**:334
Barton, cousin **2**:135
Barton, Mr **2**:38–9
Barton, Colonel Nathaniel (1615/16–1672/73) **2**:49
Barton, Major Nathaniel **1**:344 n. 4, **1**:424 n. 4,
    1:527 n. 5, **2**:480
Basing House, Hampshire **1**:208–9, **1**:210,
    1:221, **1**:228, **1**:237, **1**:318, **1**:322, **1**:323–4,
    1:326, **1**:359
Basingstoke, Hampshire **1**:209, **1**:227, **1**:229
Basket, John (*fl.* 1650–7) **2**:600
Basse, Edward (d. 1665) **1**:9, **1**:12 n. 23
Bastwick, John (1593–1654) **1**:24
Bate, George (pseud. Theodorus Veridicus)
    (1608–68) **2**:457–8
Bath, Somerset **1**:346
Bathhurst, John (d. 1659) **2**:515
Battles
    1643: Belton **1**:229
    1643: Gainsborough **1**:129–51
    1644: Marston Moor **1**:196–9
    1644: Lostwithiel **1**:202–3
    1645: Brampton **1**:269
    1645: Naseby **1**:286–9, **1**:294
    1645: Langport **1**:291–4
    1645: Hambledon Hill **1**:295–300
    1648: Preston **1**:545–64
    1649: Rathmines **2**:70–2
    1650: Dunbar **2**:316–39
    1651: Inverkeithing **2**:467–9
    1651: Worcester **2**:485–6, **2**:487–95, **2**:501–2,
    3:85, **3**:393
Baxter, Richard (1615–91) **2**:617 n. 9
Beake/Beke, Richard (1630–1707) **3**:46–7

663

GENERAL INDEX

Beale, Thomas 2:505
Beard, Thomas (c.1568–1632) 1:5–6, 1:9
Beaton, Sigismund 1:151
Beauchamps Court, baron, see Greville
Beaufort, duke of, see Somerset
Beaumaris Castle, Anglesey 3:241, 3:280 n. 8
Beaumont, William (1797–1889) 1:550
Becher, Phane 2:83–4
Bedford, earl of, see Russell
Bedford, Bedfordshire 1:188
   Swan Inn 1:188
Bedingfield, Sir Henry (1581/2–1657) 1:100–1,
   1:102–3
Bedminster, Bristol 1:308
Belasyse, Mary, née Cromwell, Countess
   Fauconberg (bap. 1637, d. 1713) 2:547 n. 13
Belford, Northumberland 1:576
Bell, Robert 1:152, 1:153
Bellamy, John 1:546, 1:547
Bellarmine, Robert, SJ (1542–1621) 1:111
Bellièvre, Pompone de (1606–57) 3:455
Belton, Lincolnshire 1:120
Belvoir, Leicestershire 1:197
Belvoir Castle, Leicestershire 1:95, 1:224,
   1:225
Ben Israel, Menasseh (1604–57) 3:243–4
Benburb, County Tyrone 2:598
Bendish, Sir Thomas, second baronet (1607–74)
   1:113, 2:739, 3:61–2
Bennet, James 2:334
Bennett, Ambrose (fl. 1649–61) 2:551–2
Bennett, Richard (1608–75) 3:226
Bennett, Robert (1605–83) 2:440–1, 2:519–20,
   2:560, 2:637, 2:686 n. 109
Bennett, William (d. 1670) 2:652–3
Benson, Gervase 3:427
Benson, William 1:13
Berkeley, John, first Baron Berkeley of Stratton
   (bap. 1607, d. 1678) 1:43, 1:406–10, 1:477,
   1:488 n. 8, 3:326, 3:329
Berkeley, Gloucestershire 1:528
Berkenhead, Sir John (1617–1679) 1:273
Bernard/Barnard, Robert (1600–66) 1:95–6,
   1:115–16, 1:214, 3:181
Bernard, Manchester 1:115
Berners, Josias (d. 1661x3) 2:663
Berry, Captain-Lieutenant James 1:135 n. 14,
   1:139, 1:145 n. 9, 1:149 n. 13, 2:238
Berry, Major James 1:553 n. 3, 2:311
Berry, Major General James (d. 1691) 1:95 n. 5,
   3:164, 3:165–6
Bert, Thomas 1:104, 1:112–13
Bertie, Montague, second earl of Lindsey
   (1607/8–66) 1:336–7
Bertie, Robert, first earl of Lindsey 1:85
Bertie, Robert, Lord Willoughby de Eresby,
   and third earl of Lindsey (1630–1701)
   2:546

Berwick, Berwickshire 1:476, 1:576, 1:577, 1:579,
   1:583–4, 1:585, 1:588, 1:592, 1:595, 1:596,
   1:597–8, 2:298–9, 2:308, 2:324, 2:325
Best, James 1:45
Best, John 1:65
Betham, Sir William (1779–1853) 3:253
Bethel, Hugh 1:551
Bethel, Slingsby (bap. 1617, d. 1697) 3:121, 3:123 n. 3
Bethell, Christopher 1:293, 1:300–1, 1:312,
   1:420 n. 32
Beton, Captain 2:332
Bettesworth, Peter (d. 1663) 2:504–5
Bettesworth, Thomas 1:405–6
Betts, Nicholas 2:259
Beverning, Hieronymous van (1614–90) 2:714
   n. 2, 2:722–5
Bevis, Peter 3:129 n. 8
Bewdley, Worcestershire 2:490
Bible (general references) 1:133, 1:321, 3:353
   OC supports publication of the Polyglot
      Bible 2:628–9
   and see Scripture (general references)
   for specific citations from, see the separate
      Index of Biblical Citations
Bickerton, James 2:332
Bickerton, Major James 2:411
Biddle, William (b. 1718, MD 1752) 2:439
Biel, East Lothian 2:651
Bilton, George 2:424, 2:442, 2:454, 2:466, 2:506,
   2:507, 2:508 n. 1
Bingham, John (1610–75) 3:178
Binney, Thomas 2:400
Birch, John (1615–91) 1:308, 1:311, 1:312, 3:176
Birch, Thomas (bap. 1608, d. 1678) 2:499–500,
   3:112–13
Birch, Thomas (1705–66) 1:lx, 3:204
   and ciphers 3:223
   copies of letters 1:565, 1:582, 3:327
   identification of recipients of letters 3:234
   letters to Robert Hammond 1:490–1 & n. 4,
      1:492 n. 9, 1:493 nn. 20 & 23, 1:506–7, 1:508
      nn. 8, 9 & 10
   and Thurloe's State Papers 1:580, 1:583 n. 19,
      3:234, 3:259–60, 3:355
   transcriptions 1:568, 1:626–7, 3:238
Biscoe, John (1613–after 1666) 3:217
Bishop, Thomas 1:463, 1:473, 1:477 n. 5
Bishops
   as enemies of 'God his truth' 1:12
   Irish Catholic 2:182–92
   OC hostile comments about 1:36, 1:40–1,
      1:611, 2:690, 3:76, 3:94, 3:140–1, 3:440, 3:464,
      3:478
Bisset, George 2:333
Black, John 2:334
Black Bourton, Oxfordshire 2:557
Blackley, James (d. 1666) 1:32, 1:89, 1:104, 1:112–13
Blackmore, John 1:513

664

GENERAL INDEX

Blackston, Mr 1:249
Blackwater, river 2:156, 2:205, 2:208, 2:210, 2:598 n. 3
Blackwell, John 1:508
Blackwood, James 2:333
Blagrave, Daniel (bap. 1603, d. 1668?) 1:647–50
Blair, Robert (1593–1666) 3:36–7
Blake, General Robert (bap. 1598, d. 1657) 2:140, 2:146, 2:541, 2:595, 2:728 n. 2, 3:196–7, 3:199–201, 3:244, 3:437
  commissions for 3:5–7
  letters to 3:li, 3:lii, 3:lvii, 3:213–14, 3:223–4, 3:284–7, 3:356–62, 3:429–30
  and recall of part of Mediterranean fleet 3:268–71
Blake, Major 3:175
Blakiston, John (bap. 1603, d. 1649) 1:217 n. 15, 1:647–9
Blandford Forum, Dorset 1:295
Blayer, William 2:333
Bletchingdon, Oxfordshire 1:269, 1:274, 1:276 n. 11
Bletchingdon House, Oxfordshire 1:lvii, 1:263, 1:265, 1:266–7
Blewbury, Berkshire 1:231
Block, Captain 2:416–17
Blomefield, Francis 1:112
Blomer, Francis 3:32
Blount, Robert (d. 1656) 2:537–8
Blount, Thomas (1605/6–78) 2:374–5
Boallry, Coronet 1:174
Boally, Samuel 1:174 n. 11
Boarstall House, Buckinghamshire 1:425 n. 8
Bolles/Bolle, Richard 1:330
Bolsover Castle, Derbyshire 1:223
Bolton, Robert 1:193
Bolton, Lancashire 2:497
Boncle/Bunckley, John (fl. 1652–65) 2:570, 2:584–5, 2:740
Bond, Denis (1588–1658) 1:405–6, 2:9–10, 2:541–2
Bonne, François de, duc de Lesdiguières (1543–1626) 3:515
Bonnell, Benjamin 2:733 n. 6
Bonner, Captain 2:332
Book of Common Prayer, Cromwell speaks against 1:38–9
Book-burning, OC speech in favour of 1:54–5
Booth, Sir George, first Baron Delamer/ Delamere (1622–84) 2:602, 3:180
Bordeaux, Antoine de, sieur de Neufville 2:642–3, 3:60, 3:69, 3:80, 3:326, 3:329 n. 41, 3:454–5
Boreman, Captain 2:133
Borlace, Nicholas 2:459–60
Borlase, Sir John (1575/6–1648) 2:117
Borlase, Sir John, the younger 2:117, 2:118
Boroughbridge, North Yorkshire 1:605
Borthick, James 2:332

Borthwick, John, ninth Lord Borthwick (1615/16–74/5) 2:381
Borthwick Castle, Midlothian 2:lxii, 2:381
Boston, Lincolnshire 1:9, 1:123, 1:157, 1:172
Boston, Massachusetts 2:504, 3:186
Boswell, Sir William (d. 1650) 2:433
Boteler/Butler, William (fl. 1645–70) 2:52–4, 2:530–1, 3:65–6, 3:164 n. 8, 3:185, 3:521–2
Bottisham, Cambridgeshire 2:621–2
Boughton, baron, see Montagu
Boulogne, France 3:441
Bourke/Burke/De Burgo, John, Catholic archbishop of Tuam (c.1590–1667) 2:184–9
Bourne, Lincolnshire 1:128
Bowen, Henry 1:311
Bowen, Hugh 1:533
Bowen, Lloyd 1:498 n. 3
Bowen, Philip 1:532
Bowles, Edward 1:286
Bowles, Jonathan (d. 1686) 2:527
Bowreman, Thomas (1614–78) 2:600
Boxford, Berkshire 1:229, 1:230
Boyd, Thomas 2:335
Boyle, Francis, first Viscount Shannon (1623–99) 3:14–15
Boyle, Joshua 2:136 n. 1, 2:137 n. 1
Boyle, Michael, Protestant archbishop of Armagh (1615?–1702) 2:241–2, 2:244, 2:247–8, 2:253, 2:254, 2:255
Boyle, Richard, 1st earl of Cork (1566–1643) 2:133, 2:14
Boyle, Richard, 2nd earl of Cork and 1st earl of Burlington (1612–98) 2:434
Boyle, Robert (1627–91) 3:14–15
Boyle, Roger, first Baron Broghill and first earl of Orrery (1621–79) 2:131–2, 2:138–9, 2:141, 2:146, 2:148–9, 2:150, 2:152, 2:155, 2:161, 2:162, 2:177, 2:204, 2:207, 2:208, 2:241, 2:249, 2:435, 3:210, 3:220–1, 3:435, 3:436–7, 3:450, 3:451, 3:457
  kingship committee 3:413, 3:358–66
Boyne, river 2:98
Boys, John 1:lxi, 1:479, 1:483, 1:489
Brabazon, Edward, second earl of Meath 3:282
Brabson (not identified, possibly Brabazon), Lieutenant Colonel 1:533
Brackley, Northamptonshire 1:280
Bradford, Yorkshire 1:122
Bradley, John (fl. 1626–1665) 1:12 n. 23
Bradshaw, Henry (bap. 1601, d. 1662) 2:498
Bradshaw/Bradshawe, John, Lord Bradshaw (bap. 1602, d. 1659) 2:lv, 2:lxiv, 2:13, 2:420, 2:498 n. 15, 2:614, 3:121, 3:279, 3:437
  letters to 2:91–3, 2:301–5, 2:336–8, 2:431–2, 2:457–8, 2:461, 2:471–4
  and the Engagement (1649) 2:10
  refusal to sign Recognition (Sept 1654) 3:83
  and regicide 1:liv n. 12, 1:650

665

GENERAL INDEX

Bradshaw, Richard (bap. 1610, d. 1685) **3**:121–2, **3**:123 n. 3, **3**:202–3
Brampton/Brampton-in-the-Bush, Oxfordshire **1**:179, **1**:269
Bramston, John **3**:267
Brandley, Captain William **2**:91, **2**:93, **2**:103
Brathwaite, Percivall (d. 1662) **2**:757
Bray, William **1**:474
Brayfield, Alexander **1**:643, **3**:450, **3**:451 n. 15, **3**:452 n. 17
Brayne, William (d. 1657) **3**:264–5, **3**:266–8, **3**:273
Brent, Sir Nathanael (1573/4–1652) **1**:371
Brereton, Peter **2**:414
Brereton, Sir William **1**:224 n. 54, **1**:544 n. 2, **3**:339, **3**:346
Bresbon, William **2**:332
Bresse, France **3**:515
Bret, Mr **2**:279
Brewse, James **2**:335
Brewster, Humphrey **3**:178
Brewster, Nathaniel **3**:204
Brewster, Thomas (d. 1664) **2**:615, **2**:647, **2**:655, **2**:658
Bridge, Tobias (d. after 1672) **2**:423–4
Bridgeman, John, bishop of Chester **1**:557 n. 47
Bridgeman, Orlando **1**:557 n. 47
Bridges, James **2**:493, **2**:494
Bridgewater, earl of, *see* Egerton
Bridgewater, Somerset **1**:293, **1**:294, **1**:295, **1**:511–12
Bright, Sir John, baronet (bap. 1619, d. 1688) **1**:554–5, **1**:580, **1**:583, **1**:587, **1**:592–3, **1**:594, **1**:609, **3**:166
Brinkley, Lawrence **1**:90
Briot, Nicholas (1579–1646) **2**:419–20
Bristol **1**:300, **1**:307–16, **1**:317, **1**:505, **1**:542–4, **3**:lii, **3**:12, **3**:324–5, **3**:504–5
Bristol Castle **3**:114
Bristol, earls of, *see* Digby
Bristol Fort **3**:114
Broad, Thomas **1**:573
Brograve, Hanna **1**:81 n. 1
Brograve, John **1**:81
Brook, Colonel **3**:175
Brooke, Christopher (c.1570–1628) **2**:603
Brooke, Henry (1611–64) **2**:498, **2**:602
Brooke, John (*fl.* 1638–53) **2**:603
Brooke, Lieutenant Colonel John **2**:602
Brooke, Mrs **3**:24–5
Brooke, Robert, second Baron Brooke of Beauchamps Court **1**:85
Broughton, Hampshire **2**:547 n. 12
Broughton, Huntingdonshire **2**:547 n. 12
Brown, John, **2**:334
Brown, John, cornet **2**:332
Brown, Sir John, of Fordell **2**:365, **2**:468
Brown, Robert **1**:176–7, **1**:193

Brown, Thomas **2**:331
Browne, Alexandra **1**:640 n. 1
Browne, Captain **2**:164
Browne, Captain John **1**:192
Browne, John (1580–1659) **3**:181, **3**:289, **3**:324, **3**:339, **3**:346, **3**:351, **3**:355, **3**:359, **3**:390, **3**:419, **3**:423–4
Browne, Major John **2**:338
Browne, Mr **3**:170
Browne, Sir Richard, first baronet (c.1602–69) **1**:263, **1**:264, **1**:266, **1**:278
Browne, Robert **1**:342–3
Browne, Symon **1**:532 n. 1
Browne Ffolkes, Sir William H. **3**:434
Brownlow, Sir William, first baronet (1595–1666) **3**:181
Brownrigg, Ralph, bishop of Exeter (1592–1659) **1**:42
Broxmouth House, Haddingtonshire **2**:321, **2**:326
Broxolme, John (bap. 1583, d. 1647) **1**:132–7
Bruce, Ann **2**:479
Bruce, George **2**:479
Bruce, John **1**:219, **1**:221 nn. 31 & 32, **1**:233
Bruce, Margarett **2**:479
Bruges, Netherlands **3**:295, **3**:507
Bruse, Lieutenant **2**:332
Brussels, Netherlands **3**:507
Bruton, Somersetshire **1**:260
Buchan, John **1**:lii n. 2
Buckingham, dukes of, *see* Villiers
Buckley, Thomas **1**:104, **1**:112–13
Bulkley, Stephen **2**:279
Bullingdon Green, Oxfordshire **1**:232
Bunratty Castle, County Clare **2**:60
Burdett, Sir Francis (1608–96) **3**:180
Burford, Oxfordshire **1**:231, **2**:47, **2**:587
Burgess, Benjamin **1**:520, **1**:522, **1**:523
Burgess, Roger **1**:272–5
Burghley House, Lincolnshire **1**:130, **1**:133, **1**:138, **1**:142, **1**:144, **1**:148
Burgoyne, Sir John **1**:114–15
Burgoyne, Margaret (née Wendy) **1**:114
Burgoyne, Montague **1**:114
Burke/Bourke/De Burgo, Hugh (c.1592–c.1654) **2**:184–9
Burke, Ulick, marquis of Clanricarde (1604-58) **1**:83, **2**:27
Burley, New Forest, Hampshire **2**:547
Burley-on-the-Hill, Rutland **3**:262
Burlington, earl of, *see* Boyle
Burnet, Gilbert, bishop of Salisbury (1643–1715) **2**:lvi, **2**:305–6, **2**:321, **3**:245, **3**:246
Burnett, Henry **2**:67
Burntisland, Fife **2**:400, **2**:437, **2**:462, **2**:475
Burroughs **1**:508
Burroughs, Jeremiah **3**:316 n. 109

666

GENERAL INDEX

Burton, Abraham **1**:545
Burton, Henry (bap.1578, d. 1647/8) **1**:24
Burton, Robert (pseudonym of Nathaniel
  Crouch, c. 1640–1725?) **3**:244 n. 10
Burton, Thomas (*fl.* 1656–61) **2**:559
  diary **3**:67 n. 7, **3**:103, **3**:113, **3**:324, **3**:351, **3**:390,
    3:426, **3**:427, **3**:461 n. 4, **3**:466, **3**:468
  and Humble Petition and Advice **3**:418,
    3:430
Burton, William (inhabitant of
  Cambridge) **1**:104, **1**:112–13
Burton, William **2**:332
Bury, John (*fl.* 1642–52) **2**:534–5
Bury St Edmunds, Suffolk **1**:97, **1**:284
Butler, Daniel **1**:24
Butler, Elizabeth, née Clifford **2**:435
Butler, J. **3**:437
Butler, James, fourth Baron Dunboyne **2**:215
Butler, James, marquis of Ormond, twelfth earl
  and first duke of Ormond, (1610–88)
  1:189–90, **1**:214, **1**:345, **1**:347, **2**:lix, **2**:24, **2**:27,
  2:55, **2**:57, **2**:70, **2**:71–2, **2**:95, **2**:119, **2**:124 n. 2,
  2:126–7, **2**:131, **2**:136, **2**:147, **2**:152, **2**:153, **2**:165,
  2:228, **2**:241, **2**:244, **2**:255–6, **2**:598, **2**:727,
  3:25, **3**:283, **3**:327, **3**:328, **3**:507
Butler, John **1**:383
Butler, Pierce, first Viscount Ikerrin **3**:502–3
Butler, Piers (d. 1652) **2**:203
Butler, Richard, of Kilcash **2**:177, **2**:206, **2**:251–2
Butler, Richard, Viscount Mountgarret **2**:217 n. 2
Butler, Thomas, sixth earl of Ossory (1634–80)
  2:209
Butler, Sir Walter **2**:217–19, **2**:220–1, **2**:222–6,
  2:232, **2**:233
Buttles, Major (possibly Hugh Butler of
  Sadbury) **1**:533
Button, Miles **1**:533
Button, Sir Thomas **1**:533 n. 12
Byram, Yorkshire **1**:606
Byram House, Yorkshire **1**:605
Byrne, Colonel **2**:100, **2**:104
Byrne, James **2**:106 n. 2

Cadiz, Spain **3**:269, **3**:286, **3**:199, **3**:258
Cahir Castle, County Tipperary **2**:212–15, **2**:230
Caishoe/Cassiobury, Hertfordshire **2**:594
Calais, France **3**:441
Calamy, Edmund (1600–66) **1**:190 n. 8, **2**:451,
  3:486, **2**:603–4
Caley, Jacob (1612–80) **1**:107, **2**:640
Callan, County Kilkenny **2**:205, **2**:207, **2**:209–10,
  2:251
Calley, George **2**:335
Calshot Castle, Hampshire **1**:405, **2**:504–5
Calshot Spit, Hampshire **1**:405
Calvert, Cecil, second Baron Baltimore (1605–75)
  3:227

Calvert, Giles (bap. 1615, d. 1663) **2**:530, **2**:647,
  2:655, **2**:658
Cambridge, Cambridgeshire **1**:lv, **1**:lvii, **1**:60–1,
  1:93, **1**:94, **1**:100, **1**:112, **1**:155, **1**:165, **1**:172, **1**:187,
  2:lxiv, **2**:61–2
  Black Bear Inn **2**:277
Cambridge University
  elections of Heads of House at **1**:61–2
  Emmanuel College **1**:61
  Holy Trinity **1**:60–1
  no troops to be quartered in (1652) **2**:549
  OC speaks about the reform of **1**:60–1
  reform of **2**:277
  Sidney Sussex College **1**:371 n. 2, **2**:521
Camel, Collin **2**:334
Cameron, barons, see Fairfax
Camide, David **2**:335
Camil, Duncan **2**:335
Camil, James **2**:332
Camil, Lieutenant John **2**:333, **2**:335
Campbell, Archibald, fifth marquis of Argyll
  (1605x7–61) **1**:346–7, **1**:576, **1**:587, **1**:588,
  1:593, **1**:594, **1**:599
  letters to **1**:580–1, **1**:591–2
Campbell, Ian **1**:xlii
Campbell, John, first earl of Loudoun (1598–1662)
  1:346–7, **1**:430–1, **1**:581–4, **1**:587, **1**:593–4
  letters to **1**:591
Canburn, Patrick **2**:335
Cann, William **1**:543 n. 7
Canne, John **1**:434
Cannon, Henry **1**:275
Cansfield, Sir John **1**:264 n. 14
Cantwell, John **2**:184–9
Cantwell Castle, County Kilkenny **2**:233
Cape St Vincent, Portugal **3**:213
Capel, Arthur, first Baron Capel of Hadham
  (1604–49) **1**:41, **2**:17–18, **2**:232
Capell, Mr **2**:592
Cappoquin, County Waterford **2**:141, **2**:210
Car, Alexander **2**:333
Car, Captain John **2**:332
Car, Captain Lieutenant John **2**:333
Car, Captain Lieutenant Lancelot **2**:333
Car, Lieutenant Lancelot **2**:333
Car, Thomas **2**:334
Carbery, earl of, see Vaughan, Richard, second
  earl of Carbery
Carew, Sir Alexander, second baronet **1**:64
Carew, John (1622–60) **1**:647–9, **2**:626–7,
  2:686 n. 109
Carey, Edward (d. 1657) **2**:662, **2**:663
Carisbrooke, Isle of Wight **1**:476
Carisbrooke Castle, Isle of Wight: Charles I's
  escape attempts **1**:486–8, **1**:491 & n. 6,
  1:507–8
Carleon, Newport, Wales **1**:522

GENERAL INDEX

Carleton, Bigley 2:732 n. 5
Carlingford, County Louth 2:89, 2:102–3
Carlingford, earl of, *see* Taaffe
Carlisle, Cumberland 1:576, 1:577 n. 2, 1:579,
    1:583–4, 1:585, 1:588, 1:594, 1:597–8, 1:603,
    2:279, 2:445
Carlisle, earl of, *see* Hay
Carlow, County Carlow 2:230, 2:341
Carlyle, Thomas (1795–1881) 1:95, 1:103, 1:111,
    1:137, 1:156, 1:177, 1:191 n. 9, 1:283, 1:285, 1:326,
    1:332, 1:366, 1:372, 1:633, 2:613
    1845 edition 1:xxxvii, 1:xxxvii–xxxviii, 3:xlvii
    on authenticity of writings 2:321
    copies of letters 2:521
    dating of letters 1:375, 1:495–6, 2:462
    edition analysed 1:xxxvi–xxxvii,
        2:xxxviii–xxxix, 3:xxix–xxx
    editorial guesses 1:10 n. 16
    identification of recipients of letters 3:234
    letter to Richard Norton 1:501 n. 21
    Letters and Speeches 1:140–1
    and letters to Robert Hammond 1:500
    on location of documents 2:88
    on Mrs Nuttinge's petition 2:22
    on original spellings 2:89 n. 6
    silent changes to documents 1:293 n. 10
    as source for biographies 1:lii
    on Robert Stapleton 2:14
    on storming of Drogheda 2:102
    suggested emendations to text 1:377 n. 11
    versions of speeches 2:664
Carmarthen, Carmarthenshire 1:345 n. 8, 1:425
    n. 8, 1:516–17, 1:533 n. 15
Carmihil, Henry 2:331
Carmihil, John 2:335
Carnecuse, William 2:334
Carnegie, David, first earl of Southesk
    (1574/5–1658) 1:602
Carnwath, earls and countess of, *see* Dalzell/
    Dalyell
Carrick-Bridge 2:483 n. 3, 2:486 n. 6
Carrick-on-Suir, County Tipperary 2:147, 2:148,
    2:152, 2:153, 2:154
Carrickfergus, County Antrim 2:142, 3:33,
    3:266, 3:267
Carstairs, John 2:393
Cartagena, Colombia 3:229, 3:233
Carter, Captain 1:454, 1:464
Carter, John (*fl.* 1647–51) 1:427 n. 6, 2:507–8
Carter, John (*c.*1619–76) 2:498–9
Carteret, Sir George, first baronet (1610?–80)
    1:487
Cartwright, Dr 2:235
Cary, Lucius, second Viscount Falkland 1:48
Caryl, Joseph (1602–73) 3:343 n. 27
Casborne, W.S. 1:372
Cascais Bay, Lisbon 3:223

Case, John 2:485
Case, Thomas (bap. 1598, d. 1682) 2:451
Case of the Armie Truly Stated 1:435–9
Cashel, County Tipperary 2:203, 2:205, 2:209,
    2:210, 2:242
Cassilis, earl of, *see* Kennedy
Castell, Robert 1:104
Castle/Castell, James 2:96, 2:99
Castle, Thomas 1:201
Castlehaven, County Cork 2:141
Castlehaven, earl of, *see* Tuchet
Castletownshend, County Cork 2:141 n. 10
Castle Island, baron, *see* Herbert
Cathedrals, future of, Cromwell's speech
    about 1:28
Catholics
    (normally spelt Catholique when he is in
        Ireland) 2:27, 2:180, 2:185, 2:189, 2:192,
        2:194, 2:198–9, 2:232
    of foreign powers 3:79, 3:261, 3:328
    of 'the people of God' in general 3:352
    see also papists; popish; popery
Caulfeild, William, first Viscount Charlemont
    (1625–71) 2:177, 2:181
Cavalier(s)
    dismissive references to 1:543, 1:576, 1:644
    disparaging references to 1:77, 1:539
    Party in England 3:127, 3:168, 3:206, 3:407,
        3:454, 3:494, 3:497–8, 3:505
    Scottish 1:114
    see also 'Enemy'; Delinquents; Malignants
Cave, Thomas (*fl.* 1644–52) 2:582
Cavendish, Charles (1620–43) 1:120, 1:133,
    1:134–5, 1:139, 1:145, 1:149, 1:151
Cavendish, William, earl (later marquis, duke)
    of Newcastle 1:122, 1:125, 1:126, 1:131,
    1:132, 1:133–4, 1:145, 1:150, 1:156, 1:157, 1:159,
    1:169–70, 1:172, 1:197, 1:223 n. 42
Caversham, Berkshire 1:409
Cecil, William, second earl of Salisbury
    (1591–1668) 1:35, 2:12
Ceely, Thomas 1:332–3
Cemaes, Wales 1:536
Censorship by Parliament of Cromwell's
    letters 1:286–8, 1:305, 1:314–15, 1:315–316
Chaloner, Thomas (1595–1660) 1:349, 1:650, 2:50
Chamberlaine, Mr 1:446, 1:448 n. 37
Chapman, Livewell (*fl.* 1643–65) 2:687
Chapman, William 2:334
Charlemont, County Armagh 2:142
Charlemont, viscount, *see* Caulfield
Charles Emmanuel, duke of Savoy (1634-75)
    3:512, 3:513, 3:514, 3:515
Charles I, king of England 1:lxiii, 1:25, 1:34, 1:42,
    1:44, 1:48, 1:50, 1:169 n. 3, 1:205, 1:234, 1:235,
    1:236–7, 1:271, 1:288, 1:409–10, 2:194, 2:325,
    3:26–7

668

GENERAL INDEX

call for trial of 1:473
conditions of imprisonment 1:404
control of crossing points on Trent 1:130
death warrant 1:650–1
and Engagement 1:491
escape attempts from Carisbrooke
  Castle 1:486–8, 1:491 & n. 6, 1:507–8
escape from Hampton Court 1:476–9, 1:538
escape from Oxford 1:338
and former Army Plotters 1:67
and the Four Bills 1:489, 1:491
guarded by Colonel Edward Whalley 1:402–3
handed over by Scots 1:361 n. 5
at Holdenby 1:394 n. 19
at Hurst Castle 1:627, 1:643
and the Irish rebellion (1641) 1:70
journey to London 1:635–6
and move to Richmond 1:408
negotiations with army 2:661
and Newcastle Propositions 1:345–6
OC on why he was deposed 2:283–4
OC's part in the trial of 1:640–1, 1:641–5,
  1:647–50, 1:650–4
OC's reported attitude towards 1:406–8,
  1:408–9, 1:477–8, 1:486–8, 1:506–8,
  1:538–43, 1:622–4, 1:635–7, 1:637–9
and parliamentary control over militia 1:63,
  1:88
peace settlement 1:336–7
prisoner of Army 1:399
protection granted by 2:730
in Robert Huntington's *Sundry Reasons*
  1:539
seizure from Holdenby House 1:538
sequestration of revenues 1:405 n. 2
and Sir John Berkeley 1:407
surrender at Newark 1:338
suspension of Temple 3:197–8
warrant for trial of 1:647–9
at Windsor Castle 1:627, 1:643
Charles II, king of England, Scotland and Ireland
  (1630–85) 1:35, 1:48, 2:180, 2:194, 2:267,
  2:283–4, 2:325–6, 2:340, 2:451, 2:502, 2:598,
  3:127, 3:443
as Charles Stuart 2:262, 3:137, 3:153–4, 3:155,
  3:283, 3:288, 3:294, 3:337, 3:340, 3:475, 3:505,
  3:506, 3:507, 3:508
covenanted 2:338
in France 3:44
as king of Scots 3:298, 3:496
negotiations with 2:376, 2:574
as Prince of Wales 1:269, 1:292, 1:405 n. 2,
  1:408, 1:520
recognised as king 2:lviii, 2:lix
sequestration of revenues 1:405 n. 2
at Stirling 2:365
and Treaty of Breda 2:386

Charles X Gustav, king of Sweden (1622–60)
  3:49, 3:50, 3:52, 3:448–9, 3:473
Charlestown, Massachusetts 3:16
Chastleton, Oxfordshire 2:500
Chatham, Kent 2:542
Chatteris, Cambridgeshire 1:183 n. 3
Cheevers, John 2:231 n. 9
Cheevers, Nicholas 2:106 n. 2
Chepstow, Monmouthshire 1:512, 2:656
Chepstow Castle, Monmouthshire 1:521, 1:523,
  3:114
Cherbourg, France 1:487
Cherbury, baron, *see* Herbert
Cheshunt, Hertfordshire 2:633
Chester, Cheshire 1:224, 1:278, 1:527, 2:355,
  2:497, 3:20, 3:113
Chesterfield, earl of, *see* Stanhope
Chesterton, Cambridgeshire 1:10 n. 9
Cheswick, Northumberland 1:584 n. 24
Chicheley, Sarah, née Russell (d. 1654) 1:321 n. 12
Chicheley, Thomas (1614–99) 1:321
Chichester, Sussex 1:325
Chillenden, Edmund 1:392 n. 7, 1:451, 1:466
Chipping Norton, Oxfordshire 2:496
Cholmley, John (d. 1648) 1:603–4
Cholmley, John (d. 1653) 1:604
Cholmley, Sir Henry 1:549–51, 1:558, 1:603–4 &
  n. 1, 1:614 n. 3
Christina, queen of Sweden (1626-89) 1:406,
  2:726, 2:731, 2:733, 3:14, 3:27, 3:49, 3:50, 3:52,
  3:100, 3:458
  and Treaty of Uppsala 3:56
Church, Private 2:47
Ciff, Alexander 2:333
Cilgerran, Pembrokeshire 1:536
Civilians, killed at Drogheda 2:91–3, 2:93–101,
  2:101–4
Claiborne, William (bap. 1600, d. 1677) 3:226
Clanbrassill, earl and viscountess, *see* Hamilton
Claneboye, earl and viscountess, *see* Hamilton
Clanrickarde, marquis of, *see* Burke
Clanwilliam, County Tipperary 3:41
Clare, earl of, *see* Holles
Clarecastle, County Clare 2:242
Clarendon, earl of, *see* Hyde
Clarke, Adam 2:84
Clarke, John 1:415, 1:454, 1:459, 1:474–5
Clarke, George 3:41–2
Clarke, Samuel 1:426
Clarke, Colonel Samuel 3:448
Clarke, William (1623/4–66) 1:lii, 1:lxii, 1:386, 1:388,
  1:390, 1:392, 1:397 n.23, 1:422, 2:43, 2:410
  copies of letters 1:lv, 1:380, 1:614, 1:641, 1:643
  copies of speeches 3:351
  copies of warrants 1:648
  fair-copy letter books 1:403
  letters to 3:339

669

GENERAL INDEX

Clarke, William (1623/4–66) (*cont.*)
notes on debate on *Agreements of the People* 1:646
Putney Debates transcriptions 1:liv, 1:lxiii, 1:436, 1:439 nn. 10, 12 & 14, 1:453, 1:454, 1:461, 1:457 n. 8, 1:462,1:463, 1:473, 1:474
Saffron Walden Debates 1:liv, shorthand system 1:384
transcriptions 1:385, 1:410–22, 1:420 n. 32, 1:421 n. 35, 1:436, 1:439 nn. 10, 12 & 14
underlinings in transcriptions, significance of 1:412 n. 6, 1:417 n. 22, 1:441 n. 16, 1:443 nn. 22 & 23, 1:444 n. 26, 1:445 n. 29, 1:447 nn. 33 & 34, 1:448 nn. 35 & 39, 1:454 nn. 2 & 4, 1:455 n. 5, 1:456 n. 6, 1:458 n. 14, 1:459 nn. 15 & 16, 1:460 n. 17, 1:461 n. 20, 1:464 n. 2, 1:465 nn. 4, 5 & 6, 1:466 n. 11, 1:467 n. 14, 1:468 nn. 17 & 20
Clarke, William (merchant tailor) 3:41
Claypole/Cleypole/Claypoole, Elizabeth, *see* Cromwell, Elizabeth (OC's daughter)
Claypole/Cleypole/Claypoole, John (1625–88) 1:181–2, 1:354 n. 6, 2:439, 2:564
Claypole, John (1625–88) 2: 564
Claypole, Wingfield 2:564
Clayton, Randall 2:452–3, 2:564, 2:566
Clements, Gregory (bap. 1594, d. 1660) 3:31–2
Clenche, Edward 1:97–102, 1:104, 1:111, 1:112–13, 1:283
Clergy
Clergy, reformation of 2:274–6, 3:93–4
Presbyterian, in Scotland, OC's relations with 2:292, 2:306–10, 2:329, 2:351–3, 2:355–60, 2:361–2, 3:23, 3:444–5
Roman Catholic, in Ireland 1:111, 2:176, 2:180–3, 2:202–3, 2:213–14, 2:222–3, 2:225–7, 2:230, 2:247–8, 2:255, 2:279–81
Clerke, Robert 1:97–102, 1:104, 1:112–13
Cliffe, John (*fl.* 1627–52) 2:561–2
Clifford, Henry, Lord Clifford 2:435 n. 3
Clifton, Bristol 1:308
Clifton Campville, Staffordshire 2:602
Clinton, Edward, Baron Clinton (1624–57) 3:14–16
Clitheroe, Lancashire 1:548–9
Clobery/Clobury, Major John (1623–87) 2:440–1, 519–20
Clogheen, County Tipperary 2:208
Clonmacnoise, County Offaly 1:xlvii, 2:lxi, 2:182, 2:184–9
Clonmel, County Tipperary 2:lxii, 2:85, 2:148, 2:598
articles of surrender 2:258–9
parliamentary losses at 2:230
siege of 2:liii
Clotworthy, Sir John, first Viscount Masareene 1:49, 1:58, 1:91

Cloughoughter, County Cavan 2:140
Cloughoughter Castle, County Cavan 2:85
Clubmen, Cromwell's dealings with 1:294–9
Cludd, Edward (1603–78) 2:658–9
Clyde, river 2:385
Cobbett, John (d. 1657) 2:489
Cobbett, Ralph 1:627, 1:641, 1:642, 1:643, 1:644
Cochrane, William, first earl of Dundonald (1605–85) 3:63–4
Cockburnspath, Berwickshire 2:301, 2:302, 2:318, 2:319, 2:325
Cockraine, Richard 1:254 n. 1, 1:276
Coghill, Sir Thomas 1:263, 1:267
Colchester, Essex 1:121–3, 1:542, 1:545, 2:232 n. 15, 3:221–2
Cole, William (d. 1674) 3:320, 3:321, 3:322–3
Cole, William (1714–82) 2:439
Coleman, Charles 2:334
Coleman, Henry 1:179
Colepeper, Sir John, first Baron Colepeper 1:38
Coleraine, baron, *see* Hare
Coleraine, County Derry 2:142
Collerwood, John 2:332
Collington 1:524
Collinson, William 1:524 n. 3
Cologne, Germany 3:151
Colquhoun, Sir John, of Luss, second baronet 3:64–5
Colours, captured Scottish, hung in Westminster Hall 2:495–6
Colville, James, second Lord Colville of Culross (s1604–54) 2:210
Combes/Cornes, Richard 2:383
Comerford, James 2:252
Comerford, John 2:227
Compton, James, earl of Northampton 1:264, 1:266
Compton, Spencer, second earl of Northampton 1:85
Compton, Berkshire 1:233
Conant, John (1608–94) 2:424, 2:425, 3:433
Condé, prince de 3:25
Condolence, letters of by Cromwell 1:196–200
Connacht, Ireland 1:84, 3:502
Conscience
liberty of 1:287–8, 1:401, 1:459, 2:188, 2:197, 3:74–5, 3:94, 3:293, 3:462, 3:484
OC's appeals to 1:174, 1:250, 1:315–16, 1:343, 1:381, 1:389, 1:408, 1:418, 1:421, 1:441, 1:451, 1:459–61, 1:465–72, 1:588, 1:602, 1:611, 1:631, 2:28, 2:47, 2:122, 2:129, 2:178, 2:192, 2:211, 2:234, 2:269–73, 2:287–8, 2:308, 2:313, 2:357–8, 2:362, 2:378, 2:286, 2:389, 2:391–2, 2:409, 2:463, 2:532, 2:573, 2:604, 2:613, 2:672, 2:677, 2:694, 2:698, 2:709, 2:716, 2:719, 3:59, 3:73–4, 3:78, 3:80, 3:93, 3:136, 3:140–5, 3:148, 3:245–6, 3:261, 3:297–9, 3:304–10, 3:313–14,

670

GENERAL INDEX

3:321, 3:328–9, 3:354–7, 3:363–5, 3:373–7, 3:395, 3:401, 3:406, 3:409–10, 3:420–5, 3:462, 3:469, 3:472, 3:474, 3:482, 3:491, 3:501, 3:523

Constable, Sir William, baronet (bap. 1590, d. 1655) 1:544 n. 2, 1:647–9, 2:11, 2:743, 2:744, 3:176

Constantinople, Ottoman Empire 2:739, 3:61

Conwy Castle, Caernarfonshire 1:427 n. 3, 2:507–8

Cook, John (1608–60) 2:169, 2:275, 2:450, 2:562

Cook, Mrs 2:727 n. 1

Cooke, Colonel 3:174

Cooke, Thomas 1:111, 1:112–13

Cooke, William 1:544, 1:545

Cooper, Anthony Ashley, first earl of Shaftesbury (1621–83) 2:638, 3:8

Cooper, C. H. 1:13, 1:103

Cooper, Sir Roger 3:167

Cooper, Thomas II (d. 1659) 3:283, 3:284

Coote, Sir Charles, first earl of Mountrath (c.1609/10–61) 2:87, 2:102, 2:126 n. 2, 2:142, 2:760, 3:30

Coote, Chidley 2:230 n. 3

Copinger, James 3:219

Copinger, Robert 3:219

Coplestone/Copplestone, John 3:176, 3:248, 3:250

Corbett, Sir John, first baronet 1:71

Corbetlt, Miles (1594/5–1662) 1:154, 1:156, 3:242

Cork, Munster 1:xlvii, 2:131–3, 2:134–5, 2:137–9, 2:140, 2:141, 2:146, 2:175, 2:204

Corkbush Field, Ware, Hertfordshire 1:480

Cornbury House, Oxfordshire 1:355 n. 10

Costessey, Norfolk 1:645–6

Coston, Nicholas 2:333

Cottenham, Cambridgeshire 1:66, 2:568

Cotton, Anthony 1:219 n. 22

Cotton, John (1585–1652) 2:501–4, 2:544

Cotton, Sir Robert Bruce (1571–1631) 1:358

Cottrell, Captain 2:539

County Down, Ulster 1:356

Courtney, Hugh (fl. 1649–66) 2:178–9, 3:488, 3:489

Courts martial, Cromwell's participation in 1:432–3

Courtstown (now Tullaroan), County Wexford 3:218

Covenant, Solemn League and Covenant
OC's contempt for 2:358–9, 2:360–2, 2:386
OC's relations with the Scottish 1:345–8

Coventry, Warwickshire 1:85, 1:543

Cowell, Mary 1:574 n. 2

Cowell, William 1:474–5, 1:555 n. 30, 1:573, 1:574

Cowley, James 2:227

Cowling, Nicholas 1:453, 1:454, 1:457, 1:463, 1:464, 1:474–5, 1:476

Coxe, Alban (c.1605–65) 1:289, 3:liv, 3:190, 3:337–8, 3:498–9

Crackenthorp, Captain 1:551

Cradock, Walter (c.1606–59) 1:525, 3:204

Craford, James 2:125

Crane, John (1571–1652) 1:86–7, 1:89, 1:90

Crane, Richard 1:309

Crane, William (1608–73) 1:90

Cranfield, Lionel, first earl of Middlesex 1:570 nn. 16 & 17

Cranston 2:450

Crant, Thomas 1:59

Craven, William, earl of Craven (bap. 1608, d. 1697) 3:155

Craven, Yorkshire 1:553

Craw, Robert 2:335

Crawford, earls of, see Lindsay

Crawford, Lawrence (1611–45) 1:187 n. 5, 1:189–90, 1:207–8, 1:214, 1:215, 1:223 nn. 43 & 44, 1:240, 1:365

Crawford, Lieutenant Colonel 2:331

Crediton, Devon 2:555

Creed, Richard 3:175

Creshton, Matthew 2:332

Creslet 1:508

Crew/Crewe, John, first Baron Crew (1597/8–1679) 1:187, 1:232

Crispin, William 3:124 n. 3

Croke, Sir George (d. 1680) 2:527

Croke, Unton (d. 1694) 3:128–9, 3:168

Crompton, Thomas (bap. 1606/7) 3:175

Cromwell, Anna (HC's daughter, b. 1617) 1:14 n. 6

Cromwell, Anne (RC's daughter, 1651–2) 2:462

Cromwell, Anne (OC's first cousin) 2:167–8

Cromwell, Bridget (OC's daughter, bap. 1624, d. 1662) 1:lix, 1:337; see also Fleetwood, Bridget, née Cromwell; Ireton, Bridget, née Cromwell

Cromwell, Dorothy, neé Major (1627–76), wife of RC 2:289–90, 2:346–7

Cromwell, Elizabeth (OC's cousin, b. 1616) 1:14 n. 6

Cromwell, Elizabeth (HC's daughter, OC's granddaughter, 1654–59) 3:518 n. 6

Cromwell, Elizabeth, née Russell (HC's wife, 1637–87) 1:500, 3:256, 3:518

Cromwell, Elizabeth (OC's aunt), see Hampden, Elizabeth, née Cromwell (d. 1664)

Cromwell, Elizabeth (OC's daughter, bap. 1629, d. 1658) 1:lvi, 1:lix, 1:181–2, 1:353–4, 2:439–40

Cromwell, Elizabeth, née Steward (OC's mother, d.1654) 2:63, 2:446–7, 2:522, 2:595 n. 3

Cromwell, Elizabeth (OC's sister, 1593–1672) 2:521–2

671

GENERAL INDEX

Cromwell, Elizabeth, née Bourchier (OC's wife, 1598–1665) 1:180 n. 5, 1:194, 1:503, 2:lvi, 2:lxiv, 2:64, 2:65–6, 2:522, 2:566
  letters to 2:344–6, 2:439–40, 2:446–7
Cromwell, Elizabeth (RC's daughter) (1650–1731) 2:289 n. 6
Cromwell, Frances (OC's daughter) (bap. 1638, d. 1720) 1:xxxvii n. 8, 1:503 n. 14
  marriages 3:335
  see also Russell, Frances, née Cromwell (other married name Rich), Lady Russell (bap. 1638, d. 1720)
Cromwell, Frances (OC's aunt) 1:381 n. 3; *see also* Whalley, Frances (née Cromwell)
Cromwell, Henry (OC's first cousin, b. 1608) 1:8 n. 4, 2:565, 2:596
Cromwell, Henry (OC's son, 1628–74) 1:321 n. 13, 1:394 n. 15, 1:500 n. 10, 1:567 n. 8, 2:565, 2:596, 3:128
  and Charles Fleetwood 3:lx, 3:203–4, 3:446, 3:450–1
  letters to 3:lii, 3:lix, 3:339, 3:342, 3:450–1
  letters to: in Ireland 3:219–20, 3:238–40, 3:253–6, 3:267, 3:283–4, 3:336–7
  letters to: on Remonstrance 3:342–3
  as Lord Deputy of Ireland 3:450, 3:517–19
  marriage 2:546
Cromwell, Henry (OC's uncle) 1:14
Cromwell, Jane (OC's sister) 1:186; *see also* Disbrowe, Jane
Cromwell, Major Richard 1:313
Cromwell, Margaret (OC's sister) 1:lv, 1:14
Cromwell, Mary 1:503 n. 14
Cromwell, Oliver (HC's son, OC's grandson, 1656–85) 3:518 n. 6
Cromwell, Oliver (*c*.1742–1821) 1:13
Cromwell, Oliver (OC's first cousin) 2:161, 2:163, 2:167–8
Cromwell, Oliver (OC's grandson) 3:240 n. 8, 3:256 n. 17
Cromwell, Oliver (OC's son) 1:192, 1:197
Cromwell, Sir Philip 1:8 n. 4
Cromwell, Ralph Lord Cromwell 1:223 n. 45
Cromwell, Richard (OC's great-grandfather) 1:liii
Cromwell, Richard (OC's son, 1626–1712) 1:liv, 1:lix, 1:398 n. 1, 2:lv, 2:lxiv, 2:64–5, 2:134, 2:135, 2:238–41, 2:566, 3:lii, 3:34–5, 3:262–4, 3:417, 3:432–3, 3:439
  birth 1:3
  at Hursley 2:289–90
  as Lord Protector 3:488–9, 3:511
  marriage negotiations 1:494, 1:502–3, 2:lx, 2:3, 2:8, 2:14–17, 2:19–21, 2:30–4, 2:36–41
  OC's complaints about 2:289–90

Cromwell, Robina (1594–1660) (OC's sister) 2:568–9
Cromwell, Thomas (*c*. 1485–1540) 1:liii
Cromwell, Thomas, fourth Lord Cromwell (1594–1653) 1:356–7
Crosby, Sir Piers (1590–1646) 1:59
Crouch, Edward 1:284 n. 15
Crouch, Nathaniel (pseudonym Robert Burton, *c*.1640–1725?) 3:244–5
Crowland, Lincolnshire 1:116, 1:142
Crown, offer of, to Cromwell, *see* Monarchy
Crowne, William (*c*.1617–83) 3:162–3, 3:176, 3:189 n. 7
Crowther, John 1:515–16
Croxton, Thomas (*c*.1603–66) 2:498, 3:178
Cruise/Crewe, Francis 2:383
Cruisetown, County Louth 2:89–90
Crutchly, Thomas 2:lx n. 24, 2:29–30
Cuba 3:233
Cudworth, Ralph (1617–88) 1:66
Cuffe, Maurice 2:133
Cullompton, Devon 1:329
Culme, Arthur 2:85–6
Culross, baron, *see* Colville
Cunningham, George 2:333
Cunningham, Henry 2:333
Cunningham, James 2:333
Cunningham, William 2:332
Cunningham, William, eighth earl of Glencairn (1610/11–64) 1:601–2
Currer, Henry 1:571 n. 2
Curson, Sir John 1:245, 1:249
Curtis, Edmund 2:86 n. 1
Curtis, John 2:591, 2:592
Curzon, Sir John 1:217 n. 15
Custaires, Mr 2:417
Custos Rotulorum, Cromwell's actions as, for Monmouthshire 2:513–14

Dacres, Sir Thomas (1587–1668) 1:41
Dalbier, John (d. 1648) 1:323, 1:325, 1:326
Dalby, Lincolnshire 2:547
Dalegarth, Cumbria 2:5–6
Dalhousie, Midlothian 1:600
Dalzell/Dalyell, Gavin, second earl of Carnwath (1627–74) 3:220
Dalzell/Dalyell, Katherine, dowager countess of Carnwath (d. 1712) 3:220–1
Dalzell/Dalyell, Robert, first earl of Carnwath (d. 1654) 3:220
Danby, earl of, *see* Danvers
Daniel, William 2:469
Daniell, John 2:244, 2:247–8, 2:253, 2:254
Danvers, Henry, first earl of Danby (d. 1643) 1:355 n. 10
Danvers, Sir John (1584/5–1655) 2:11, 3:204

672

GENERAL INDEX

D'Anvers, Joseph **3**:204
Darby, John **2**:274
Darcy, Oliver, Catholic bishop of Dromore
  (d. 1664) **2**:184–9, **3**:327 n. 18, **3**:328
Darley, Henry (c.1596–1671) **1**:82, **1**:373–4
Darwen, Lancashire **1**:548
Darwen, river **1**:556
Daugleddau, Wales **1**:536
Daulton, Vincent **2**:252
Dauphiné, France **3**:515
Daurlmple, William **2**:332
Daventry, Northamptonshire **1**:280, **1**:287–8
Dawkins, Rowland **3**:175
Daws, William **2**:529
Dawson, Mr **1**:618 n. 1
De Carteret, Philippe (1626–72) **3**:162
de Courcy, John **3**:191
de Courcy, Patrick, Lord Kingsale (d. after 1663)
  3:191–2
De Rue, John **3**:161–2
Dean and Chapter lands, disposal of **2**:427–8
  3:81, **3**:312
Deane, Joseph **3**:435, **3**:436
Deane, Richard (bap. 1610, d. 1653) **1**:300–1,
  1:519, **1**:554–5, **1**:647–9, **2**:146, **2**:471, **2**:592,
  2:714, **2**:742–3
  battle of Worcester **2**:488
  commissioner in Scotland **2**:651 n. 2
  and Putney Debates **1**:454, **1**:474–5
Dease/Deise/Dessy, Oliver **2**:184–9
Deeping St James, Lincolnshire **1**:282
Delamere Forest, Cheshire **1**:550
Delinquents defined **1**:598
  comments on **1**:52, **1**:69, **1**:356–7, **1**:514, **1**:578,
  2:45, **2**:70, **2**:689, **3**:198, **3**:312, **3**:372
  see also Malignants; Royalists
Delop, James **2**:334
Denbigh, earl of, see Feilding
Dendy, Edward (bap. 1613, d. 1674) **2**:612 n. 3,
  3:185 n 10
Denguit, John **2**:333
Denham, James **2**:332
Denington, river (river Lambourn) **1**:229
Denmark **3**:78, **3**:79
Denmark, treaty with **3**:79 n. 40, **3**:294–5
Derby, earl of, see Stanley
Derby House, Canon Row, Westminster
  1:562, **2**:9
Derickson, Christiana **3**:447, **3**:448
Dering, Sir Edward, first baronet **1**:54–5, **1**:57, **1**:63
Derry, Ireland **2**:lix, **2**:86
Dethicke, John (d. 1671) **3**:251 n. 1
Devereux, Robert, second earl of Essex
  (1565–1601) **2**:214–15
Devereux, Robert, third earl of Essex (1591–1646)
  1:44, **1**:94, **1**:98, **1**:116–17, **1**:128, **1**:129, **1**:186,

1:202, **1**:203 n. 3, **1**:248, **1**:249, **1**:350, **1**:359,
  1:493, **3**:374
Devizes, Wiltshire **1**:271, **1**:317, **1**:318
D'Ewes, Sir Simonds **1**:lxi, **1**:20, **1**:29 n. 4, **1**:31,
  1:33, **1**:40, **1**:41, **1**:43, **1**:48, **1**:57, **1**:211, **1**:259–60
  on bishops **1**:40, **1**:42
  diary **1**:71, **1**:72, **1**:78 n. 3, **1**:80, **1**:81, **1**:87
  on Dublin **1**:66
  mistake on Army Plotters **1**:68
  on parliamentary privilege **1**:47
  partial reporting of events **1**:86
Dewisland, Pembrokeshire **1**:536
Diamond/Dyamond, Tristam/Tristram **1**:372
Dibdin, Mr **3**:437
Dieppe, France **3**:441
Digby, George, second earl of Bristol (1612–77)
  1:58, **1**:271, **2**:194
Digby, John, first earl of Bristol **1**:23, **1**:48–9
Digges, Edward **3**:225–7
Dillingham, John (fl. 1639–49) **1**:219–20, **1**:238
Dillon, Sir James (c.1600–c.1667) **2**:100
Dillon, Theobald **2**:106 n. 2
Dingle Bay, County Kerry **2**:166
Dinton, Buckinghamshire **3**:46
Disbrowe/Desborough, John (bap. 1608, d. 1680)
  1:186, **1**:200 n. 13, **1**:239, **1**:293, **1**:297–8,
  1:300–2, **1**:310, **1**:373, **1**:421, **3**:129, **3**:341 n. 13
  commissions for **3**:5–7
  conversations with **2**:516–19
  Council member **2**:686 n. 109, **3**:8
  and Humble Petition and Advice **3**:418
  letters from **1**:399–402
  letters to **3**:liv, **3**:164–5, **3**:205–6, **3**:248–50
  and Lord Protector's oath **3**:431
  and Western Design **3**:115
Disbrowe, Jane, née Cromwell **1**:186, **1**:200
Dixon/Dickson, John **3**:228
Dixon, John **2**:334
Dobbins, William **3**:100
Dodson, Lieutenant Colonel William **1**:194,
  1:240
Dodson, Major William **1**:183
Dodsworth, Captain **1**:108–9
Dodsworth, Captain John **2**:589–90
Dogger Bank, North Sea **3**:449
Doncaster, Yorkshire **1**:197, **1**:223, **1**:545,
  2:483 n. 3
Doneraile, County Cork **2**:245
Donn, Elizabeth **3**:271–2
Donnadieu, A. **3**:456 n. 11
Donnington, Berkshire **1**:232, **1**:233, **1**:234,
  1:254–5
Donnington Castle, Berkshire **1**:210, **1**:220,
  1:228, **1**:229, **1**:234–6, **1**:255, **1**:318, **1**:325, **1**:326,
  1:340
Doon Hill, Haddingtonshire **2**:321

673

GENERAL INDEX

Dorchester, Dorset **1**:295

Dorchester-on-Thames, Oxfordshire **1**:233, **1**:234

Dore, Norman **1**:544 n. 2

Dorislaus, Isaac (1595–1649) **1**:433, **1**:640–1

Dormer, Matthew **2**:125

Dorney, John (*c*.1605–58) **2**:573

Doro, river **2**:113

Douglas, James, first Lord Mordington (*c*.1591–1656) **1**:593, **2**:302

Douglas, Robert (1594–1674) **3**:36–7

Douglas, Sir William, of Kirkness (d. 1650) **2**:331

Douglas, William **2**:332

Dove, John (d. 1664/5) **3**:164 n. 6, **3**:184–6

Down Ampney, Gloucestershire **2**:599

Downepatricke, County Down **1**:356

Downes, John (bap. 1609, d. in or around 1666) **1**:47

Downhall, Henry (d. 1669) **1**:3–4

Downing, Sir George, first baronet (1623–84) **3**:lii, **3**:130, **3**:355, **3**:501–2

Downs, Kent **2**:58, **3**:269

Downs, Sussex **3**:269

Doyley, Charles **1**:276, **1**:543 n. 7

Doyley, Edward **1**:512 n. 7

Drainage of the Fens, *see* Fen Drainage

Drake, Sir Francis (bap. 1617, d. 1661) **3**:181

Draper, Thomas (*fl.* 1653–60) **2**:750–1

Driden, Sir John, second baronet (*c*.1580–*c*.1658) **3**:181

Drogheda, County Louth **2**:70–1, **2**:87–8
St Mary's Church **2**:95, **2**:97
St Peter's Church **2**:97, **2**:98
storming of **2**:liii, **2**:lv, **2**:lx, **2**:91–2, **2**:93–104

Drogheda, viscounts, *see* Moore

Drummond, David **3**:236–7

Drumon, Andrew **2**:333

Drury, George **3**:157, **3**:159, **3**:160

Dublin, Ireland **1**:49, **1**:65, **1**:84, **2**:lx, **2**:70, **2**:71–2, **2**:75–6, **2**:80–3, **2**:552
declaration for peace and safety **2**:82–3, **2**:90
proclamation against offences **2**:80–1
Rathmines **2**:57, **2**:71, **2**:251
Ringsend **2**:liii, **2**:75
Trinity College Dublin **2**:543–4

Duck, Arthur (1580–1648) **1**:640

Duckenfield/Duckenfeild, Robert (1619–89) **1**:527, **2**:295, **2**:497, **2**:498, **2**:499

Duckett, George (1684–1732) **2**:641

Duckett, Thomas **1**:104, **1**:162–3

Duffus, lord, *see* Sutherland

Dugard, William (1606–62) **2**:627, **2**:687

Dunalson, Andrew **2**:335

Dunbar, James **2**:335

Dunbar, Haddingtonshire **2**:lxii, **2**:300, **2**:302, **2**:318, **2**:324, **2**:325, **2**:330–6

Dunbarre, Lieutenant Colonel **2**:331

Dunboyne, baron, *see* Butler

Duncan, Robert **2**:332

Duncannon, County Wexford **1**:91, **1**:93, **2**:154–5, **2**:166

Duncannon Fort, County Wexford **2**:142–3, **2**:341

Dunch, Anne, née Major **2**:290, **2**:464 n. 8, **3**:438–9

Dunch, Bridget **2**:583–4

Dunch, Edmund (1603–78) **3**:180

Dunch, Edmund (1613–72) **2**:583–4, **2**:599

Dunch, John (*c*.1630–68) **2**:464 n. 8, **3**:lii, **3**:438–9

Dunch, Mary, née Cromwell (d. 1617) **3**:438

Dunch, Samuel **3**:439 n. 8

Dunch, Sir William (1578–1612) **3**:438

Dundalk, County Louth **2**:70–1, **2**:88–9, **2**:91, **2**:92

Dundas, Walter **2**:lvi, **2**:lxii, **2**:351–3, **2**:355–62
and surrender of Edinburgh Castle **2**:387–96, **2**:398–9, **2**:403

Dundas, Linlithgowshire **2**:471

Dundass, Captain **2**:332

Dundrum Castle, County Tipperary **2**:215

Dunfermline, earls of, *see* Seton

Dungan, Garrett **2**:100 n. 17

Dungannon, viscount, *see* Trevor

Dungan's Hill, County Meath **1**:428, **2**:55, **2**:85

Dungarvan, County Waterford **2**:141, **2**:162

Dunkirk, France **3**:268, **3**:269, **3**:441, **3**:443

Dunkitt, County Kilkenny **2**:234

Dunlop, Robert **3**:liv, **3**:12, **3**:24, **3**:25, **3**:41–2, **3**:106–7, **3**:150, **3**:156, **3**:198
letters not appearing in **3**:210
transcriptions **3**:15, **3**:27, **3**:31, **3**:37, **3**:42, **3**:45–6, **3**:219, **3**:282, **3**:457, **3**:509

Dunnottar, Aberdeenshire **2**:437

Durdham Down, Bristol **1**:308

Durham, County Durham **2**:427–8

Dursey, Severinus **1**:312–13

Durston, Christopher **1**:404 n. 6

Dury/Durie, John (1596–1680) **1**:9, **2**:13 n. 3

Dusseldorf, Germany **3**:303 n. 69

Dutch War (1651–4), *see* Netherlands

Dutton, Anne **3**:lii, **3**:334–5

Dutton, John (1594–1657) **3**:247–8, **3**:334–5

Dutton, William (1642–75) **3**:247, **3**:334–5

Dwight, John (1633x6–1703) **2**:629

Dysart, earl of, *see* Murray

Earnley, Richard **1**:268

East Ilsley, Berkshire **1**:235

Eastern Association
origins of **1**:97–9, **1**:99–103, **1**:105–8
relations with the committees of **1**:126–9, **1**:163–8, **1**:177–8, **1**:184

Eaton, Prestwick **1**:23–4

674

GENERAL INDEX

Eddes, Mr 1:268
Edelston, J. 1:484–5
Edgehill, Liverpool 1:94
Edinburgh, Midlothian 1:576, 1:592–3, 1:601,
    1:609, 2:279, 2:303, 2:307, 2:317–18, 2:324,
    2:337, 2:365–6, 3:444
  Arthur's Seat 2:318
  Committee of Estates in 2:283
  declaration to 2:402–3
  maintenance post-victory 2:354–5
  Market Cross 2:431
  proclamation to, concerning markets
    2:349–51
Edinburgh Castle, Midlothian 2:lxii, 3:301
  articles for surrender 2:398–401
  list of ordnance 2:401–2
  negotiations for surrender 2:387–98
  report of surrender 2:404–5
Edminston, James 2:334
Edmonds, Francis 1:59
Edward, James 2:334
Edwardes 1:524
Edwards, Humphrey (d. 1658) 1:647–9
Edwards, James 1:183 n. 1
Edwards, Thomas 1:370–2, 1:373–4
Edwards, William? 1:69, 1:183
Egan, Boetius, Catholic bishop of Elphin
    (1580?–1650) 2:184–9
Egerton, John, first earl of Bridgwater 1:140 n. 13
Egger, William 2:334
Eglinton, earl of, see Montgomery
Egmanton, Nottinghamshire 2:556
Eillistone, Joseph 1:113
El Puntal, Bay of Cadiz 3:258
Elcho, Lord, see Wemyss
Elderwood, James 2:335
Elect (of God), Cromwell's only known use of
    the term 2:279–83; see also godly
Elections, parliamentary
  (i.e. selection) of members for the Nominated
    Parliament (1653) 2:634–42
  Army calls for fresh 1:462, 1:465, 2:586,
    2:606, 2:618
  of Fellows in Cambridge 1:62
  OC's speeches about 1:42, 1:46, 1:47, 2:675,
    2:696, 3:86, 3:92, 3:142–3
  to Protectorate Parliaments (1654) 3:37–8,
    3:42–3, 3:45–6, (1656), 3:343, 3:395, 3:403–4,
    3:412–14
Elizabeth I, queen of England and Ireland
    (1533–1603) 3:292, 3:474, 3:475
Elizabeth, daughter of Charles I: 1:409
Elliot, William 2:333
Ellis, John (d.1681) 1:60–1, 1:66
Ellis, Thomas 1:66
Ellwood, Thomas (1639–1713) 2:664, 3:158, 3:160
Elmes, Master 1:275

Elphenstou, George 2:334
Elsenham, Essex 1:154
Elsyng, Henry 1:342
Elton, Romeo 3:248 n. 5
Ely, Cambridgeshire 1:liii, 1:lv, 1:13, 1:39,
    1:94, 1:169, 1:172, 1:179, 1:180, 1:181 n. 1,
    1:354 nn. 3 & 6, 2:521; see also Isle of Ely,
    Cambridgeshire
Ely, viscount, see Loftus
Emery, William 2:333
Empson, Thomas 2:303, 2:406
Enderson, Thomas 2:335
Enemy, the, Cromwell's usual word to describe
    royalists
  in England 1:104, 1:112, 1:122, 1:125, 1:147–50,
    1:159–61, 1:169, 1:173, 1:185, 1:207–9,
    1:220–38, 1:241–2, 1:250, 1:261–2, 1:266,
    1:270–1, 1:279, 1:283–4, 1:288, 1:293–4,
    1:300–1, 1:308–13, 1:324–5, 1:331, 1:340, 1:519,
    1:528, 1:529, 1:535, 1:605–6, 3:18, 3:173, 3:177,
    3:179, 3:185, 3:340, 3:507
  in Ireland 2:92–3, 2:95–8, 2:113–15, 2:117, 2:129,
    2:140, 2:142–4, 2:147, 2:152–6, 2:162–6, 2:170,
    2:180, 2:187, 2:188, 2:215, 2:230–4, 2:245,
    2:264, 3:156, 3:283–4
  in Scotland 1:548–9, 1:551–9, 1:564, 1:582,
    1:583–5, 2:302–4, 2:317–18, 2:322, 2:338,
    2:342, 2:445, 2:468, 2:470–1, 2:486, 2:494,
    3:126
  in Spain 3:17–18, 3:269, 3:273, 3:276–7, 3:474,
    3:507
Enfield, Middlesex 1:17 n. 26
Engagement (1649), parliamentary debates on
    2:9–12
  refusers of the 2:277, 2:284
Engagements, binding force of 1:443–6,
    1:448–51, 1:455–8
Engles, Cornelius 2:335
Engley, William 2:333
Enkhuizen, Netherlands 2:257
Ennis, Colonel 1:552, 1:557
Ennis, John 2:334
Enniscorthy, County Wexford 2:114, 2:181
Enniskillen, County Fermanagh 2:246
Ennisnag, County Kilkenny 2:229 n. 5, 2:233
Enos, Walter 2:194
Episcopacy, see Bishops
Epping, Essex 1:17
Eresby, baron, see Bertie
Erle/Earle, Sir Walter (1586–1665) 1:42, 1:58, 1:72,
    1:346 n. 5, 1:501 n. 19
Escrick, baron, see Howard
Esmond, Sir Thomas (d. 1674) 2:113
Esmonde, Laurence, Baron Esmonde of
    Limerick 1:91, 1:92
Esnouf, Simon 3:162
Essex, earls of, see Devereux

675

GENERAL INDEX

Eston, Henry **2**:333
Estwick, Stephen (d. 1658) **2**:632–3
Eton, Buckinghamshire **1**:643
Eton College, Windsor, Berkshire **2**:584–5
Evans, J. Gwenogvryn **1**:127
Evelyn, Arthur **1**:300–1, 302, **1**:394 n. 16
Evelyn, John (bap. 1591, d. 1663/4) **1**:498 n. 2
Evelyn, Sir John (1601–85) **1**:492, **1**:498, **1**:567, **3**:182
Everard, Clement **3**:195–6
Everard, Robert (*fl.* 1647–1664) **1**:439, **1**:447, 450, **1**:451, **1**:453, **1**:454, **1**:455, **1**:461
Everard, Sir Richard **1**:155
Everard, Sir Richard, first baronet (*c.*1590–1660?) **2**:208
Evesham, Worcestershire **1**:207, **1**:270, **2**:494
Ewer, Isaac (d. 1650/1) **1**:512 n. 4, **1**:523, **1**:627, **1**:639, **2**:99, **2**:232–3, **2**:656
commissioner for trial of King **1**:647
Excise, Cromwell and the collection of **2**:510–11
Eyton, Sir Robert **3**:183
Eyton, Sampson (d. *c.*1671) **2**:551–2

Fairdise, John **2**:335
Fairfax, Anne, née Vere, Lady Fairfax (1617/18–65) **1**:348, **1**:355, **1**:367, **1**:497 & n. 2, **2**:267, **2**:268
Fairfax, Charles (1597–1673) **2**:538–9
annotation to letter from **1**:618–19
letters to **1**:570–1, **1**:605–6, **1**:613–14, **1**:615–18
Fairfax, Ferdinando, second Lord Fairfax of Cameron (1584–1648) **1**:122–4, **1**:130, **1**:140 n. 12, **1**:197, **1**:350, **1**:509 n. 3, **2**:538
Fairfax, Thomas, first Lord Fairfax of Cameron (1560–1640) **2**:538
Fairfax, Thomas, third Lord Fairfax of Cameron (1612–71) **1**:lx, **1**:172, **1**:259–60, **1**:262–5, **1**:276, **1**:281–2, **1**:286, **1**:288, **1**:294–9, **1**:300–1, **1**:303–5, **1**:305 n. 2, **1**:317, **1**:318, **1**:326–8, **1**:329 n. 9, **1**:334, **1**:335 n. 2, **1**:337, **1**:339 n. 4, **1**:341, **1**:344–8, **1**:351–2, **1**:355, **1**:360–2, **1**:365–8, **1**:368–70, **1**:374–7, **1**:382, **1**:383, **1**:509 n. 3, **1**:620, **2**:lv, **2**:10, **2**:42 n. 4, **2**:534
and 1647 mutiny **1**:480
in Andover **2**:45
chaplain **2**:533
commissioner for trial of King **1**:647
conversations with **2**:267–73
in Declaration on Scottish prisoners of war **1**:572
on fall of Pembroke **1**:520 n. 11
and King's access to chaplains **1**:409
and King's access to children **1**:409
letters from **1**:399–402, **1**:627
letters to **1**:423–5, **1**:432–5, **1**:495–7, **1**:511–13, **1**:526–9, **1**:573–5, **1**:595–7, **1**:622–4, **1**:635–7, **2**:117–19
and Levellers **2**:lix, **2**:46, **2**:47

in Oxford **2**:47, **2**:48
and Putney Debates **1**:438, **1**:476
and Reading Debates **1**:411
refusal to accept commission **2**:268–9, **2**:272–3
review of regiments in Hyde Park **2**:44–5
and sequestrations, petitions for relief from **2**:459
state of health **1**:390
and Ware mutiny **1**:484
Fairfax County, Virginia **3**:253
Faith, evidence for Cromwell's private **1**:16–17, **2**:73–5, **2**:116–19, **2**:134–5, **2**:439–40, **2**:728–9, **2**:238–9, **2**:240–2, **2**:454–6, **2**:503–4, **2**:564–5
Falkirk, Stirlingshire **2**:364
Falkland, viscount, *see* Cary
Falmouth, Cornwall **3**:209
Family, Cromwell
and hereditary claims **3**:144, **3**:424, **3**:450–2
background **1**:liii–liv
supports distant members of his **1**:364–5, **1**:426–7, **2**:64, **2**:167–8
for particular members (wife, children, sons and daughters-in-law, etc, *see* under their names)
Fanshawe, Ann, Lady Fanshawe (1625–80) **2**:515–16
Fanshawe, Sir Richard, first baronet (1608–66) **2**:515–16, **3**:213
Faringdon, Oxfordshire **1**:lvii, **1**:269, **1**:271, **1**:272–5, **1**:318, **1**:325
Farley/Farleigh Castle, Somerset **2**:583
Farnham, Surrey **1**:324, **1**:500, **2**:3
Farrell, Richard **2**:147, **2**:163–5, **2**:230
Fauconberg, Countess, *see* Belasyse
Fauconbridge, Thomas **1**:405–6
Feake, Christopher (1611/12–82/3) **2**:756–7, **3**:399–400
Feilding, Basil, second earl of Denbigh (*c.*1608–75) **2**:11
Fell, Thomas **3**:182
Fellowes, Sir James (1771–1857) **2**:504 n. 2
Felsteed, George **1**:104
Felton, Nicholas, bishop of Ely **1**:5
Fen drainage **2**:621–2, **2**:657–8
OC speech about **1**:30, **1**:33
Fen Drayton, Cambridgeshire **1**:103–4
Fenton, Sir Geoffrey **2**:133 n. 8
Fenton, Sir William **2**:133, **2**:138, **2**:141, **2**:146
Fenwick, George (*c.*1603–57) **2**:651 n. 2, **3**:181, **3**:241 n. 6
Fenwick, Sir John (*c.*1579–1658) **3**:181
Fenwick/Fenwicke, John (bap. in or after 1593, d. *c.*1670) **3**:241 n. 6
Fenwick, Roger **2**:100, **3**:41 n. 6
Ferdinand II, Holy Roman Emperor and king of Bohemia (1578–1637) **3**:472

676

GENERAL INDEX

Ferdinand Maria, elector of Bavaria (1636–79) 3:472
Fermoy, County Cork 2:159
Ferns, Nathaniel 2:103
Ferns, County Wexford 2:113–14
Ferrall, Richard 2:176–8
Fethard, County Tipperary 2:lxii, 2:202–4, 2:205, 2:209, 2:210, 2:231, 2:244
Fiennes, John, Lord Fiennes (d. in or before 1710) 1:205 n. 1, 1:207, 1:228 n. 76, 1:262, 1:270, 1:271
Fiennes, Nathaniel (1607/8–69) 1:492–3, 2:594, 3:172, 3:270, 3:467
  and dissolution of 1658 parliament 3:490
  kingship committee 3:358–66, 3:384
  speech to Parliament 3:460–1
Fiennes, William, first Viscount Saye and Sele (1582–1662) 1:35, 2:531 n. 2, 2:568, 3:237
Fife, Fifeshire 2:382, 2:400
Finch, John, Baron Finch of Fordwich 1:6
Fincham, Rachel (b. 1605) 2:522–3
Fincham, Thomas (d. 1666) 2:522–3
Fincher, Richard 1:394 n. 15
Finchingfield, Essex 1:9
Finglas, Lieutenant Colonel 2:104
Fining/Fanning, James 2:243
Fiott, Peter (fl. 1646–60) 2:540
Firebrace, Sir Henry (1619/20–91) 1:507 n. 4, 1:508 n. 11
Firth, Charles Harding 1:xxxix, 1:176–7, 1:179, 1:180, 1:184, 1:194 n. 1, 1:358, 1:411, 1:419 n. 30
  additions to documents 1:417 n. 23, 1:418 n. 26, 1:419 n. 29, 1:421 n. 34, 1:436, 3:126, 27 & 28
  changes to documents 1:387 nn. 3 & 4, 1:388 n. 7, 1:412 n. 7, 1:413 n. 10, 1:414 nn. 14 & 15, 1:415 n. 18, 1:416 n. 20, 1:419 n. 31, 1:421 n. 37, 1:436
  on Clarke papers/textual footnotes 3:125
  dating of documents 3:241
  dating of letters 1:486
  discovery of letters 1:606
  edition of Cromwell's writing 1:xxxvi, 1:xxxvii, 1:xxxviii, 1:384, 1:385
  edition of Putney Debates 1:xlvi, 1:436–7, 1:440 n. 15, 1:441 nn. 17 & 19, 1:442 n. 20, 1:443 n. 25, 1:444 n. 26, 1:445 n. 28, 1:448 nn. 38 & 40, 1:449 nn. 44, 45 & 46, 1:450 nn. 47 & 48, 1:451 nn. 49, 51, 52 & 53, 1:454 n. 3, 1:458 n. 12, 1:460 n. 18
  edition of Ludlow's *Memoirs* 3:278–9
  and letter to Robert Hammond signed 'Heron's Brother' 1:xlvi, 1:lxi
  and Putney Debates 1:456 n. 7, 1:462 n. 21, 1:466 nn. 9 & 1 2
  and Putney Debates: additions 1:465 n. 6, 1:468 nn. 17 & 20, 1:469 nn. 21, 22 & 23, 1:470 nn. 26, 27, 28 & 29, 1:471 nn. 32 & 35, 1:472 n. 36

and Putney Debates: expansions 1:471 n. 34, 1:472 nn. 37 & 38
and Putney Debates: suggested additions 1:466 n. 9, 1:466 n. 12, 1:470 n. 30
and Putney Debates: suggestions 1:470 nn. 25 & 31
and Putney Debates: uncertainties in 1:473 n. 39
on storming of Drogheda 2:102
Fishbourne, Richard 1:8–9
Fitch, Thomas (c.1610–66) 2:537, 2:601–2
Fitzgerald, Sir Luke 2:56 n. 4, 2:95 n. 5
Fitzgerald, Major 2:104
Fitzgerald, Pierce MacThomas 2:230 n. 7
Fitzgerald, Richard 2:411–12
Fitzgibbon family (White Knights) 2:208
Fitzharris, Edward 2:208
Fitzwilliam, Oliver, second Viscount Fitzwilliam (d. 1667) 3:14–15
Flamank, Henry (1628–92) 2:604–5
Fleetewood, Mr 1:534
Fleetwood, Bridget, née Cromwell, Lady Fleetwood (bap. 1624, d. 1662) 1:354 n. 3, 2:565, 2:728, 3:204–5
Fleetwood, Charles (c.1618–92) 1:300–1, 1:378, 1:380–2, 1:383, 1:388–97, 1:398, 2:63–4, 2:326, 2:327, 2:486, 2:552–4, 2:563, 2:564–6, 3:30, 3:210–11, 3:242, 3:270 n. 47
  on Matthew Alured 3:39
  battle of Worcester 2:488
  conversations with 2:516–19, 3:241
  Council member 3:8
  and dissolution of 1658 parliament 3:490
  and Humble Petition and Advice 3:418
  letters from 3:336
  letters to 2:561–2, 2:727–9, 2:760–1, 3:li, 3:lii, 3:12, 3:40–1, 3:57–8
  letters to: as Lord Deputy of Ireland 3:37–8, 3:106–8, 3:118–19, 3:150–1, 3:187–8, 3:191–2, 3:193–5, 3:197–9, 3:203–5, 3:214–16, 3:218, 3:282–3
  letters to Lenthall 1:388–91
  letters to: personal 3:lx
  as Lord Deputy of Ireland 3:106, 3:114, 3:446
  on OC's last illness 3:521
  papers of 2:748
  relationship with Henry Cromwell 3:450, 3:451
Fleming, Colonel 2:104
Fleming, Sir Oliver (d. 1661) 2:12–13, 3:458
Fleming, Thomas, Catholic archbishop of Dublin (1593–1651) 2:184–9
Flemming, Christopher 1:344–5, 1:424–5
Flower, Henry 1:519
Floyd, Mr 2:439, 2:440
Flushing/Vlissingen, Netherlands 3:440
Fonmon Castle, Glamorganshire 2:532

677

GENERAL INDEX

Foote, Sir Thomas **2**:263
Forbes, George **2**:331
Forbis, Arthur **2**:331
Forbis, William **2**:333
Ford, Sir Edward (bap. 1605, d. 1670) **2**:749–50
Fordwich, baron, *see* Finch
Forest of Dean, Gloucestershire **1**:260
Forguson, Lancaster **2**:334
Forquer, James **2**:334
Forrest, Theodosius **1**:490–1
Fort Matagorda, Bay of Cadiz **3**:258
Fort Santa Maria, Torre Pellice **3**:514
Fortescue, Richard (d. 1655) **1**:300–1, **3**:229–30, **3**:231–4, **3**:273
Fortescue, William **1**:297 n. 15
Forth, river **2**:472–3, **2**:481
Fortune, Stephen **1**:104
Forty Hall, Enfield **2**:602
Fotheringay/Fothergill, John **1**:285–6
Fountain, brother, as codename for Oliver Cromwell **1**:195–6, **1**:607, **1**:608–9, **1**:611, **1**:628
Fowke, John (*c*.1596–1662) **1**:647–9, **1**:649 n. 20, **2**:630 n. 3
Fox, George (1624–91) **2**:lvii
  conversations with **3**:l, **3**:157–60, **3**:317–19, **3**:350, **3**:520
  on OC's last illness **3**:520, **3**:521
Fox, John (d. after 1662) **3**:209–10
Foxcroft, George (*fl.* 1653–60) **2**:662, **2**:663
Foxton, Mr **3**:170
France
  fear of troops to support King arriving from **1**:51, **1**:236, **1**:255
  Lord Protector's relations with **3**:44, **3**:74–80, **3**:101, **3**:293–5, **3**:305, **3**:316, **3**:325–6, **3**:345, **3**:441–2, **3**:455–6, **3**:474, **3**:441–2, **3**:455–6, **3**:474, **3**:513–14, **3**:515
  see also Mazarin
Franchise, debates on parliamentary **1**:458–62
Francklyn, Deborah (d. 1657) **2**:512–13
Francklyn, John (*c*.1590–by 1645) **2**:513
Francklyn, John (1624–43) **2**:513
Frane, George **1**:184
Franklin, William **3**:208
Frederick William, duke of Brandenburg (1620–88) **3**:472
Free, Edward Drax **1**:114
Freesle, Major **2**:331
Freman, Ral **1**:162–3
French, Nicholas, Catholic bishop of Ferns (1603-78) **2**:111, **2**:184–9
French, Peter (d. 1655) **2**:568–9
Frend, Mr **1**:88
Frome, Somerset **1**:308
Frost, Gaulter/Walter (bap. 1598, d. 1652) **2**:384
Fry, John (*c*.1609–56/7) **1**:647–9

Fry, Major **1**:330
Fryer, Robert **2**:334

Gadley, Hartley **2**:334
Gainsborough, Lincolnshire **1**:124 n. 2, **1**:130, **1**:131, **1**:132–40, **1**:143–6, **1**:148–9, **1**:156, **1**:185 n. 3
Gale, George (1626–95) **2**:555–6
Gallilee, Thomas (d. 1669) **2**:739
Gallilee, Thomas (*fl.* 1652–69) **2**:739
Gallio Annaeanus, Lucius Junius **2**:531
Galway, Ireland **1**:83, **2**:166, **3**:480, **3**:509
Gamage, Philip **1**:533
Gardiner, Samuel Rawson **1**:xxxvii, **1**:208, **1**:214 n. 3, **1**:358, **1**:538, **2**:574
  dating of letters **1**:375
  editing of letters **1**:606
  re-punctuation of letters **1**:632 n. 36
Garland, Augustine (bap. 1603, d. in or after 1677) **1**:647–9
Garrycastle, King's County **3**:31
Garter, Mr **1**:190 n. 8
Garton, Henry **1**:46
Gaudie, Thomas **1**:113
Gaunt, Peter **1**:122
Gawdy, Edward **1**:100–1
Gawdy, Framlingham **1**:lxi n. 29, **1**:68, **1**:80
Gayer, John (bap. 1584, d. 1649) **1**:402 n. 4
Gayler, George **2**:334
Gell, Sir John, first baronet (bap. 1593, d. 1671) **1**:116–17, **1**:118, **1**:123–6, **1**:282, **1**:520
General Council of the Army, debates at (1647) **1**:lvi–lvii, **1**:lxiv–xv
  at Saffron Walden **1**:384–9, **1**:398
  at Reading **1**:410–33
  at Putney **1**:435–75
Gerard, Charles, first earl of Macclesfield (*c*.1618–94) **1**:232
Gerard, John (1632–54) **3**:297 n. 40
Gerard, Sir Gilbert, first baronet (1587–1670) **1**:48, **1**:429–31, **1**:505–6
Gernon, Luke **2**:250–1
Gewen, Thomas (1575–1660) **1**:425–6
Geynau, Thomas **2**:125
Giavarina, Francesco **3**:447, **3**:458–9
Gibbon, Robert (1613–81) **3**:160–2, **3**:174
Gibraltar **3**:258, **3**:284–7
Gibson, Edmund, bishop of London **1**:608
Gifford, Andrew (1700–84) **2**:727 n. 1, **2**:728
Gifford, John **2**:138, **2**:141, **2**:175–6
Gill, George **2**:367–9
Gillespie, Patrick (1617–75) **3**:22–3, **3**:343
Gipps, George **1**:252 n. 2
Gisburn, Yorkshire **1**:544, **1**:553
Gladman, John **1**:297 n. 15
Gladsmuir, Haddingtonshire **2**:302
Gladston, William **2**:333

678

GENERAL INDEX

Glamorgan, earl of, *see* Somerset
Glastonbury, Somerset 1:260
Gleason, Madeleine 1:xl n. 20
Glemham, Sir Thomas (1595–1649) 1:321 n. 15,
   1:348–9
Glentworth, Lincolnshire 1:141
Gloucester, Gloucestershire 1:260, 2:lxiv, 2:572,
   3:lii, 3:503–4, 3:509–10
Glover, Cornelius 2:128
Glynne, Sir John (1603–66) 1:492 n. 15, 3:170–1,
   3:358–66, 3:384
Goad, Christopher (1601–52) 2:531
Goad, George (1603–71) 2:531 n. 2
Goad, Thomas (c.1595–1666) 2:531 n. 2
Goddard, Guybon (1612–71) 3:67, 3:68, 3:69,
   3:82 n. 1, 3:83, 3:109
Goddard, Jonathan (bap. 1617, d. 1675) 2:529–30,
   2:568, 2:569
Godly
   (specific) man 1:374, 1:504, 1:513, 1:566, 2:163,
     2:171, 2:464, 2:535, 3:150
   (specific) woman 3:204
   clergy (ministers) 1:244, 2:284, 2:308, 3:20,
     3:23, 3:26, 3:307, 3:445, 3:472, 3:484
   men 1:11, 1:153, 1:167, 1:440, 2:26, 2:266, 3:140,
     3:208, 3:375, 3:410
   party 1:198, 2:118, 2:294
   people 1:528, 1:588, 1:612, 2:361–2, 2:378,
     2:708, 3:20, 3:23, 3:26, 3:344
   Scots 2:280, 2:288, 2:360, 2:377, 2:502, 3:23,
     3:26
Godmanchester, Cambridgeshire 1:9, 1:258 n. 3
Godrey, Richard 1:18
Goffe, Major General William (d. 1679?) 1:437,
   1:446–7, 1:452, 1:454, 1:462, 1:467, 1:468,
   1:474–5, 2:327, 3:19, 3:175, 3:237–8
Goldenbridge Castle, County Tipperary 2:215
Goldsmith, Daniel 2:505–6
Goldsmith, John 1:lii
Goldsmith, Mr 1:176
Goodsonn/Goodson, William (bap. 1609/10,
   d. in or after 1680) 3:229–31, 3:273, 3:274
Goodwin, Arthur (d. 1643) 1:43, 1:569 n. 14
Goodwin, Robert (c.1601–81) 3:446
Goodwin, Thomas (1600–80) 2:529–30, 2:535,
   2:568, 2:569, 3:68, 3:70 n. 15, 3:71 n. 17, 3:72
   n. 19, 3:81 n. 48
Goodwyn, Robert 1:346 n. 5
Gordon, Lewis, third marquess of Huntly
   (c.1626–53) 2:472
Gorges, Edward, Lord Gorges (d. c.1650)
   2:661 n. 1
Gorges, Jane, née Sproxtoune (c.1584–1665) 2:661–2
Gorges, John (c.1620–96) 3:178
Gorges, Robert 3:343
Goring, George, first earl of Norwich
   (1585–1663) 2:720

Goring, George, Baron Goring (1608–57) 1:260,
   1:269, 1:271, 1:292
Gossage, Mr 3:119
Gothenburg, Sweden 3:13
Gough, Anne 1:127
Gourdon, Alexander 2:334
Gourdon, Captain 2:332
Gourdon, John 2:333
Gourdon, Samuel 2:334
Goure, Dr 3:330 n. 67
Gower Peninsula 1:498
Gowran, County Kilkenny 2:231–2
Grace, John 3:218
Grace, Sheffield (1788–1850) 3:218
Grafton, Oxfordshire 1:281
Graham, James, first marquis of Montrose
   (1612–50) 1:300, 1:345, 1:347, 2:180,
   2:285–6
Grangeforth, County Carlow 2:231
Grannagh Castle, County Kilkenny 2:216, 2:231,
   2:234
Granster, James 2:331
Grant, David 2:334
Grantham, Lincolnshire 1:118, 1:119, 1:144
Grave, William 1:104
Gravelines, Netherlands 3:441, 3:443
Graves, Mr 2:171
Graves, Richard 1:344 n. 4, 1:345 n. 8, 1:394,
   1:424 n. 4, 1:539
Gravesend, Kent 3:46
Gray, James 1:300–1
Gray, John 2:334
Gray, Mrs 1:617–18
Gray, Thomas 2:332
Grayne, William 1:112–13
Great Ockley, Northamptonshire 2:582
Green, Mary Everett 1:xxxvii
Greene, George 3:100
Greene, Giles 3:100
Greene, Joshua 3:216–17
Greene, Thomas 3:216–17
Greenhill, William (1597/8–1671) 3:116
Greenwood, Daniel, as Vice Chancellor of
   Oxford 2:411–12, 2:420–3, 2:500–1, 2:526–7,
   2:529–30, 2:533–4, 2:535–6, 2:539–40,
   2:542–3, 2:551–2, 2:554–7, 2:566–7
Greenwood, James 1:560
Gregory, John (d. 1653) 1:90, 2:564
Gregson, George 1:519–20
Grenville, Sir Richard, baronet (bap. 1600,
   d. 1659) 1:260, 1:269, 1:292
Gresham, Sir Thomas 1:11 n. 17
Greville, Robert, second Baron Brooke
   of Beauchamps Court (1607–43)
   1:78, 2:534
Grey, Henry, tenth earl of Kent (bap. 1594, d. 1651)
   1:493

679

GENERAL INDEX

Grey, Thomas, Baron Grey of Groby (1622–57)
 1:liv n. 12, 1:116–17, 1:123–6, 1:128, 1:161, 1:558,
 1:561, 1:564, 2:10, 2:11
 signatory of king's death warrant 1:650
 signatory of warrant for king's trial 1:647–9
 warrants from 1:405–6
Grey, William, first Baron Grey of Warke (1593/4
 –1674) 1:114, 1:163, 2:10, 2:12
Gridley, Samuell 3:187 n. 3
Griffith/Griffiths, George (1618?–99x1702) 3:327,
 3:330 n. 67, 3:486
Grisons, Switzerland 3:472
Groby, baron, see Grey
Grosvenor, Edward 2:374–5
Guerdain, Denis (d. 1668) 3:162
Guerden, Aaron (c.1602–76?) 1:xlvi n. 31, 3:162
Guibons, Colonel 3:174
Guienne, France 3:25
Guiler, Andrew 2:334
Guise, Elizabeth 2:lxiii, 2:493
Guise, William 2:493, 2:494
Guizot, Francois (1787–1874) 1:lii n. 2, 2:642
Gun, William 2:333
Gurdon, Colonel 2:331
Gurdon, John (1595–1679) 1:217 n. 15, 1:249,
 1:373–4
Gurney, Sir Richard, baronet 1:45, 1:92
Guthrie, James (c.1612–61) 3:36–7
Gutteridge, Elizabeth 2:536
Gutteridge, William (d. c.1650/1) 2:536
Gwells, Robert 1:112–13
Gwilliam, Captain William 1:309
Gwynne, George (c.1623–73) 3:183

Haborn, Robert 2:334
Hacker, Francis (d. 1660) 1:550, 1:651, 2:337,
 2:406–7, 3:157, 3:158, 3:166, 3:175
Haddington, Haddingtonshire 1:576, 2:302,
 2:324–5
Haddock, Sir Richard (c.1629–1715) 2:541–2
Hadham, baron, see Capel
The Hague, Netherlands 2:376
Haily, Andrew 2:334
Hale, Sir Mathew (1609–76) 2:38
Hall, Henry 1:393, 1:398
Hamberton, Robert 2:333
Hambledon Hill, Dorset 1:295, 1:296–7
Hamburg, Germany 3:51, 3:53, 3:202–3
Hamilton, Anne, Viscountess Claneboy
 and Countess Clanbrassill (d. 1689)
 2:761, 3:30
Hamilton, Archibald 2:447–8, 2:450
Hamilton, Claude 1:557 n. 44
Hamilton, Sir George (d. 1676) 2:242
Hamilton, James (d. 1676) 2:242–3
Hamilton, James, first duke of Hamilton
 (1606–49) 1:347, 1:548, 1:550, 1:551, 1:552,

 1:556, 1:557, 1:558, 1:561, 1:563 n. 9, 1:564,
 1:572, 1:579, 1:583, 2:18, 3:402
Hamilton, James, second Viscount Claneboye
 and first earl of Clanbrassil (c.1618–59)
 2:760–1, 3:30
Hamilton, Jane, Viscountess Claneboy
 (fl. 1644–53) 2:760–1
Hamilton, Major 2:304
Hamilton, Mary, Lady Mary Hamilton 2:242–4
Hamilton, Captain Robert 2:332
Hamilton, Robert 2:334
Hamilton, William, earl of Lanark, later second
 duke of Hamilton (1616–51) 1:576, 1:587–8,
 1:592, 1:593, 1:594, 1:601–2, 1:643–4, 2:270–1,
 2:490
 breach of treaty 2:282, 2:283, 2:285
Hamilton, Lieutenant Colonel William
 1:557 n. 44, 2:331
Hamilton, Major William 1:190
Hamilton, Lanarkshire 2:384
Hammond, Henry, (1605–60) 1:404, 1:487 n. 5
Hammond, Mary, née Hampden (bap. 1630,
 d. 1689?) 2:455
Hammond, Robert (1587–1650) 2:232, 2:276
Hammond, Robert (1620/1–54) 1:300–1, 1:320,
 1:325, 2:172, 2:174, 2:534
 arrest of 1:635
 letters from 1:399–402
 letters to 1:xxxviii, 1:xlvi, 1:lx–lxi, 1:486–8,
 1:490–3, 1:506–8, 1:606–13, 1:626–33,
 2:454–7
 and Wharton 2:lxiv, 2:343, 2:483
Hammond, Thomas (c.1600–58) 1:271, 1:300–1,
 1:310–12
 letters from 1:399–402
Hamond, Sir Henry 1:245, 1:247, 1:249
Hampden, Elizabeth, née Cromwell (d. 1664)
 1:342, 2:455
Hampden, John (1595–1643) 1:14, 1:59, 3:374
Hampden, Richard 1:491
Hampton, Charles (d. 1704) 2:530
Hampton Court Palace 1:lviii, 1:362, 1:402,
 1:474–7, 1:474 n. 1, 1:536, 1:538, 3:47, 3:210,
 3:263, 3:438–9, 3:520
Hand, John 1:13
Hanna, Andrew 2:334
Hapton, Norfolk 1:342–3
Harcliffe, John 2:527
Hardwick, Philip, Lord Hardwick 3:355
Hare, Hugh, first Lord Coleraine 1:328
Harington, Sir John 1:lxi n. 29, 1:350, 1:353
Harlakenden, William 1:154, 1:155, 1:156 n. 12,
 1:162–3, 1:165, 1:169 n. 1, 1:179
Harley, Edward 1:399 n. 1
Harman, Nicholas 1:46, 1:47
Harman, William 3:196
Harral, Gilbert 2:334

680

GENERAL INDEX

Harrington, Sir James, third baronet (bap. 1607, d. 1680) **2**:9, **2**:60–1
Harris, William **1**:499–500
  and letters to Hammond **1**:490, **1**:491, **1**:493 n. 20
  and letters to Norton **1**:501 n. 21, **1**:502 & n. 2
Harrison, Edward (1618–89) **2**:559
Harrison, Israell **1**:112–13
Harrison, Thomas (bap. 1616, d. 1660) **1**:320, **1**:554–5, **1**:637, **1**:643, **1**:644, **2**:52–3, **2**:63–4, **2**:424, **2**:444–5, **2**:480, **2**:482, **2**:596–7, **2**:614, **3**:399–400
  Conversations with **2**:267–73, **2**:516–19
  Council member **2**:686 n. 109
  dissolution of Rump Parliament **2**:608–10, **2**:611, **2**:612
  letters to **1**:641–2
  signatory of warrant for trial of King **1**:647–9
Harrison, William **1**:544–5
Harrowden, baron, *see* Vaux
Harry, Edward **1**:55 n. 1
Hartcliffe, John (d. 1676) **2**:526–7
Hartlib, Samuel (c.1600–62) **1**:9, **2**:169, **3**:331, **3**:346, **3**:457, **3**:469, **3**:490–1
Hartopp, Sir Edward, first baronet **1**:117
Hartopp, Sir Thomas **3**:181
Harvey, Charles **3**:159, **3**:520, **3**:521
Harvey, Edmund (c.1601–73) **1**:162–3
Harwell, Oxfordshire **1**:231–2, **1**:232
Haslingfield, Cambridgeshire **1**:114
Hastings, Henry **1**:117–18
Hatfield, John **2**:264–5
Hatfield Broadoak, Essex **1**:369 n. 5
Hatsell, Henry (1609–67) **3**:271, **3**:287
Hatsell, John (1733–1820) **2**:512 n. 4
Hatter, Richard (*fl*. 1651–3) **2**:591
Hatter, Thomas (*fl*. 1647–53) **2**:591–2
Hatton, Christopher, first Baron Hatton (bap. 1605, d. 1670) **1**:407, **3**:43–5
Hatton, Sir Thomas **1**:30
Haverfordwest, Pembrokeshire **1**:533 n. 15, **1**:534–6
Hawking, Cromwell's interest in **1**:6–8
Hay, Archibald **3**:228
Hay, John **2**:332
Hayden, B. B. **2**:604
Haynes, Hezekiah (d. 1693) **3**:125–6, **3**:174
Hazelwood, Thomas **2**:429
Heads of the Proposals (1647) **1**:lxiv–lxv; origins of **1**:410–23
Health, Cromwell's, *see* Illness
Heard, Henry **2**:136 n. 1
Hearne, Thomas **1**:3, **1**:4 n. 7
Heath, James (1629?–64) **2**:586, **2**:606, **2**:607
Heath, Sir Robert (1575–1649) **2**:602–3
Heath, Robert (bap. 1620, d. in or after 1685) **2**:601–3

Heath, Thomas **1**:93
Heatly, Quartermaster **2**:334
Henderson, Frances **1**:412 n. 6, **1**:441 n. 16
Henderson, Robert **2**:395, **2**:396–7, **2**:398–401
Henderson, Thomas **2**:312
Henley-on-Thames, Oxfordshire **1**:256
Henri IV, king of France (1553–1610) **3**:515–16
Henrietta Maria, Princess Henrietta Maria of France (1609–69) **1**:30, **1**:124–5, **1**:127–8, **1**:129, **1**:407, **1**:408, **2**:285
  sequestration of revenues **1**:405 n. 2
Henry, prince, duke of Gloucester (1640–60) **1**:409, **2**:518, **2**:527
Herault, Abraham **3**:162
Herbert, Edward, first Baron Herbert of Cherbury and first Baron Herbert of Castle Island (1582?–1648) **1**:523
Herbert, Edward (d. 1666) **2**:44, **2**:514
Herbert, George (1593–1633) **3**:179
Herbert, Henry (c.1617–56) **3**:181
Herbert, John **1**:524 n. 7
Herbert, Joseph **2**:44
Herbert, Lord, *see* Somerset, Henry, first duke of Beaufort (1629–1700)
Herbert, Philip, first earl of Montgomery and fourth earl of Pembroke (1584–1650) **1**:35, **1**:346 n. 5, **2**:12, **2**:420
Herbert, Philip, fifth earl of Pembroke (1621–69) **1**:331 n. 3
Herbert, Richard, second Lord Herbert of Cherbury **1**:522, **1**:523–4
Herbert, Sir Thomas, first baronet (1606–82) **1**:286, **1**:331
Herbert, Colonel Thomas **1**:524 n. 7
Herbert, Colonel William **1**:300–2, **1**:312, **1**:377 n. 8, **1**:524 n. 7
Herbert, William (c.1593–1651) **1**:56, **1**:524 n. 7, **2**:514
Hereford, Herefordshire **3**:114
Heriot, George (1563–1624) **3**:271–2
Herne, John (b. 1623) **2**:527
Heron, brother, *see* Vane, Sir Henry, the younger (1613–62)
Hertford, marquis of, *see* Seymour
Hesilrige, Dorothy **2**:340
Hesilrige/Haselrig, Sir Arthur, second baronet (1601–61) **1**:34, **1**:62, **1**:217, **1**:219 n. 19, **1**:228, **1**:231, **1**:254–5, **1**:426, **1**:594, **1**:595, **1**:596, **2**:9–10, **2**:318–20, **2**:427, **2**:428, **2**:442, **2**:614, **3**:468
  deposition for Cromwell in Quarrel with Manchester **1**:248–9
  and dissolution of 1658 parliament **3**:490
  and Four Bills debate **1**:489, **1**:490
  letters signed by **1**:429–31
  letters to **2**:339–40
  orders concerning Scottish prisoners **2**:337, **2**:354–5

681

GENERAL INDEX

Hesilrige/Haselrig, Sir Arthur, second baronet (1601–61) (*cont*.)
　proclamation to, concerning Scottish prisoners 2:348–9
　refusal to sign Recognition 3:83
Heume, John 2:333
Heume, Robert 2:334
Heveningham, Arthur 1:293
Heveningham, William (1604–78) 1:283–5, 2:11
Hewet, Sir John, baronet 1:93–4
Hewson, John (*fl*. 1630–60) 1:320 n. 3, 1:329–30, 1:402–5, 1:643, 2:99, 2:227 n. 4, 2:230–2, 2:260, 3:450
　and Putney Debates 1:458, 1:463, 1:474–5
　signatory of warrant for king's trial 1:647–9
Hewson, Thomas 1:24
Heyman, Sir Henry 1:217 n. 15
Heywood, Oliver (bap. 1630, d. 1702) 2:543
Hicks, Mr 2:558–9
Hickson, Mary 3:24
High Laver, Essex 1:15
Hill, John 1:371
Hill, Roger (1605–67) 2:550
Hill, Thomas (d. 1653) 1:484–6
Hill, William 1:570
Hillesden House 1:187, 1:188
Hills, Henry (*c*.1625–88/9) 2:615, 2:647, 2:655, 2:658, 2:687, 3:130
Hinchingbrooke House, Cambridgeshire 1:214
Hinton Waldrist, Oxfordshire 1:278
Hippesley, Sir John 1:346 n. 5
Hispaniola, West Indies 3:xlvii, 3:101 n. 5, 3:230
Hitch, William (b. *c*.1590) 1:181–2
Hitler, Adolf 1:xl–xli
Hobart, Frances Lady Hobart 1:140 n. 13
Hobart, James 1:113
Hobart, John 1:372
Hobart, Sir John, second baronet (1593–1647) 1:97–102, 1:137–42
Hobart, Sir John, third baronet (bap. 1628, d. 1683) 3:181, 3:491, 3:500
Hobart, Sir Miles (b. *c*.1602) 1:lvii, 1:119–20, 1:123–6, 1:129, 1:141–2, 2:522 & n. 5
Hobart, Thomas (d. 1560) 1:142
Hobart, Sir Thomas (knighted 1603) 1:142
Hobart, Sir Thomas (d. 1623) 2:522 n. 5
Hodder, John 2:131, 2:133
Hodges, Thomas 1:61, 1:217 n. 15, 1:245, 1:247, 1:256
Hodges, Thomas (*c*.1611–75) 3:446–7
Hodgson, John (1617/18–84?) 2:298
Hoe, Robert 2:548
Holburn, James, of Menstrie 1:601
Holden, Roger 2:333
Holdenby/Holmby House, Northampton 1:394, 1:402–3, 1:404 n. 8, 1:538
Holder Bridge/Hodder Bridge, Lancashire 1:553

Holdsworth, Richard (1590–1649) 1:42, 1:61
Holl, Augustine 1:105 n. 1
Holland 2:432, 2:451, 3:76, 3:78, 3:79
Holland, Cornelius (1600–71?) 1:217 n. 15, 1:245, 1:247, 1:249, 1:256, 2:11, 2:554–5
Holland, earl of, *see* Rich
Holland, Sir John, first baronet (1603–1701) 3:26–7
Holland, Lincolnshire 1:128, 1:160, 1:161, 1:173
Holles, Anne 3:15
Holles, Denzil, first Baron Holles (1598–1680) 1:30, 1:44, 1:65, 1:75, 1:78, 1:338, 1:350–1, 1:540, 3:15
Holles, John, second earl of Clare (1595–66) 1:338–9, 3:15
Holles, Robert 1:295
Holliburton, George 2:331
Holliburton, Patrick 2:333
Hollister, Dennis (d. 1676) 2:587
Hollister, Ed. 1:55
Holloway, Mr 2:521 n. 6
Holmes, Clive 1:124 n. 2, 1:240 n. 231
Holywell, Huntingdonshire 1:30
Honest
　and party in Scotland 1:507–8, 1:596, 1:612, 2:313, 2:338, 2:391, 2:617, 3:480
　and peaceable inhabitants, in Ireland 2:182, 2:187, 2:191, 2:197, 2:198, 2:201–2
　linked to being 'godly' 1:109, 1:153, 1:167, 1:170, 1:178, 1:212, 1:215, 1:244, 1:258, 1:286–8, 1:341–3, 1:442, 1:636, 2:25–6, 2:368, 2:596, 2:628, 2:635–42, 2:659, 2:668, 2:680, 2:691, 2:701, 2:750–1, 2:757, 3:20, 3:74, 3:161, 3:305, 3:310, 3:314, 3:321, 3:342, 3:348, 3:387, 3:395, 3:422, 3:444, 3:471
　linked to being 'well affected' 1:103, 1:112, 1:401, 1:434, 1:490, 1:541, 2:559, 3:152, 3:249
　with 'godly' or 'well-affected' implied 1:175, 1:195, 1:204, 1:258, 1:264, 1:282, 1:374, 1:389, 1:414, 1:419, 1:421, 1:440–1, 1:461, 1:541, 2:116–17, 2:180, 2:493–4, 2:692, 2:694, 3:85, 3:88, 3:135, 3:217, 3:303, 3:375, 3:376, 3:420, 3:476, 3:482
Honywood, Sir Thomas (1587–1666) 3:174
Hooke, Sir Humphrey (1629–77) 2:265–6
Hooper, John 1:222 n. 35
Hopper, Andrew 1:123, 1:125 n. 11
Hopton, Ralph, Baron Hopton (bap. 1596, d. 1652) 1:298, 2:459
Horner, Sir John (1576–1659) 3:182
Horsea Bridge, Peterborough 1:128–9
Horsey Hill, Peterborough 1:285 n. 5
Horsman, Edward 1:206, 3:175
Horsman, Robert 1:206, 3:175
Horsman, Robert (1615–1713) 3:182
Horton, George 3:130
Horton, Thomas 1:533 n. 14

682

GENERAL INDEX

Horton, Thomas (bap. 1603, d. 1649) 2:128
Hoskins, Sir Bennet/Benedict, baronet
  (1609–80) 3:181
Hotham, Sir John, first baronet (1589–1645) 1:31,
  1:48, 1:64, 1:124
Hotham, John (1610–45) 1:44, 1:50, 1:120,
  1:123–6, 1:127, 1:128
Howard, Charles, first earl of Carlisle (1628–85)
  2:719, 3:180
Howard, Edward, first Baron Howard of Escrick
  (d. 1675) 1:370–2, 1:373–4
Howard, Thomas, fourteenth earl of Arundel,
  fourth earl of Surrey and first earl of
  Norfolk 1:46, 1:47
Hoyle, Thomas (bap. 1587, d. 1650) 1:405–6
Hubbard, William 2:406
Hudson, Robert 1:104
Huett, Charles 2:168
Hugan, Thomas 1:112–13
Huggett, William 2:44
Hughes, Charles 1:524 n. 2
Hughes, Richard (d. 1658) 2:592–3
Hughes, Thomas 1:524–5
Huling, Christopher 2:429
Hull, see Kingston upon Hull, Yorkshire
Humble Petition and Advice, Cromwell's
  response to the offer of 3:345–50, 3:351–4,
  3:355–8, 3:358–82, 3:383–90, 3:390–412,
  3:413–16, 3:418–23, 3:424–6
Hume, Christian, née Hamilton, Lady Polwarth
  (d. 1688) 2:407, 2:409–10
Hume, Patrick, first earl of Marchmont
  (1641–1724) 2:407
Huncks, Hercules 1:651, 2:86
Hungerford, Anthony (c.1608–57) 2:557–8,
  2:583–4
Hungerford, Anthony (fl. 1645–59) 2:175 n. 4,
  2:557
Hungerford, Rachel (d. 1680) 2:558
Hungerford, Berkshire 1:237–8
Hunt, Henry 2:175 n. 4
Hunt, John 1:52
Hunter, John 2:334
Huntingdon, Huntingdonshire 1:liii, 1:lv, 1:93–4,
  1:115, 1:138, 1:157, 1:161, 1:226–7, 1:285, 2:6
  charitable bequest 1:8–9
  St John's Hospital 1:5
Huntington, Robert (c.1616–84) 1:513 n. 10,
  1:536–41
Huntly, marquis of, see Gordon
Hurnish, Major 1:533
Hursley, Hampshire 1:494, 2:19–20, 2:289, 3:439
Hurst, Timothy 1:545
Hurst Castle, Hampshire 1:643
Hurst Green, Lancashire 1:554
Husband, Edward 1:287, 1:546, 1:552
Husbands, Azariah 1:200–1

Hussey, Captain 1:151
Hussey, John 2:184–9
Hutchen, Thomas 2:334
Hutchinson, John (bap. 1615, d. 1664) 1:125,
  1:127, 1:338 n. 1, 1:339 n. 3, 1:521, 1:647–9, 2:11,
  2:589, 2:661
Hutchinson, Lieutenant Colonel (royalist) 1:268
Hutchinson, Lucy, née Apsley (1620–81) 1:xxxvii
  n. 7, 2:589, 2:268
Hutton, Robert (c.1620–80) 2:441–2
Hyde, Sir Edward, first earl of Clarendon
  (1609–74) 1:33, 1:43, 1:251, 1:303, 1:485,
  2:17–18, 2:54, 2:371 n. 4, 3:44, 3:45, 3:213,
  3:327
Hyde, Henry 3:330 n. 67

Ibbet/Ibbot, Robert 1:104, 1:112–13
Ibbitson, Robert 1:546, 1:571–2, 1:619–20
Iconoclasm, Cromwell and 1:181–2
Ikerrin, Viscount, see Butler
Illness, Cromwell comments on, while in
  Scotland 2:425–6, 2:431–2, 2:457–8, 3:580,
  3:581–2
Impeachment
  (of Lord Mayor of London) OC speech
    about 1:92
  planned, of OC 1:240–1
Inchgarvie, Fife 2:474
Inchiquin, earl of, see O'Brien
Indemnity, Committee of 2:662–3
Independents/Independency
  as a group within the Army 1:213
  OC identifies himself as and for 1:212
  relationship of with Presbyterians 1:314–16,
    1:408, 1:543, 3:78, 3:280, 3:306–7, 3:322,
    3:345, 3:411, 3:481; as a 'party' 1:315, 1:433–4,
    3:39, 3:101, 3:321, 3:344, 3:324, 3:410
  as the 'orthodox ministry in England' 3:140
Indonesia 3:501
Ingles, Alexander 2:331
Ingoldsby, Sir Henry, first baronet (bap. 1623,
  d. 1701) 1:313, 2:lvi, 2:305–6
Ingoldsby, Oliver 1:313
Ingoldsby, Sir Richard (bap. 1617, d. 1685)
  1:300–2, 1:312, 1:647, 1:650, 2:464–5, 3:178
Inistioge, County Kilkenny 2:152, 2:216
Innes, John 1:557 n. 43
Innocent X, pope (1644–55) 2:194
Instrument of Government
  implementation of the 3:38, 3:339–47, 3:344,
    3:354
  OC's account of the four fundamentals of
    the 3:94–6, 3:102–4
  parliamentary scrutiny of 3:109–10, 3:133,
    3:142–5, 3:149, 3:153–4
Inverkeithing, Fife 2:496
Irby, Sir Anthony 1:362 n. 1

683

GENERAL INDEX

Ireland
  analysis of OC's writings from 2:liii–lvi
  background to OC's campaigns in 2:lix–lxii
  campaigns in 2:lix–lxii;
  Cromwell speech about 1:49–50, 1:53, 1:56–7,
    1:58–9, 1:65–6, 1:67, 1:69–70, 1:70–1, 1:71,
    1:72–3, 1:76, 1:77–8, 1:83, 1:84, 1:86, 1:87,
    1:91–2, 1:93
  appointment to Council in 3:446–7
  campaigns in Ireland 1649–50 2:75–261,
    passim: *see also* under battles; sieges;
    surrender articles
  continuing concerns with (1651–3) 2:340–1,
    2:434–5, 2:451–2, 2:455–6, 2:509, 2:543–4,
    2:548, 2:548, 2:552–4, 2:564–6, 2:596,
    2:598–9, 2:730–1
  conversation with Ludlow about 2:275–6,
    3:240–1, 3:278–81
  correspondence as Lord Protector with Lord
    Deputy Fleetwood 3:li–liv, 3:12, 3:14–15,
    3:24–5, 3:27–8, 3:30–1, 3:107–8, 3:156–7,
    3:187–8, 3:191–2, 3:210–11, 3:214–15, 3:218–19,
    3:282–3
  demobilised Irish sent to Spain 3:436–7
  English preparations for Irish campaign of
    1649–50 2:50–1, 2:54–5, 2:66–7, 2:68–9
  and the first Ormond Peace (1646) 1:347
  foregoes pay to help fund Irish
    campaign 1:498–9, 1:505–65
  interactions with Adventurers 3:31–2, 3:41–2,
    3:192–3
  interactions with new English settlers 3:150–1,
    3:469
  interactions with Ulster Scots 3:33–4,
    3:106–7, 3:112–14, 3:480
  Irish references in Lord Protector's
    speeches 3:76, 3:80, 3:83
  letters to HC in 3:219–20, 3:238–40, 3:253–4,
    3:283–4, 3:336–7, 3:450–2, 3:457–8, 3:502–3,
    3:509–10, 3:517–18, 3:518–19
  military instructions 3:21–2
  nomination as commander in chief and Lord
    Lieutenant 2:293–9
  OC as an Adventurer in 1:170–1
  OC reluctantly accepts post of Governor
    General of Ireland 2:54–5
  OC speech about 1:49–50, 1:53, 1:56–7, 1:58–9,
    1:65–6, 1:67, 1:69–70, 1:70–1, 1:71, 1:72–3,
    1:76, 1:77–8, 1:83, 1:84, 1:86, 1:87, 1:91–2, 1:93
  OC's attitude to the native people of 2:75–6
  OC's engagement with the affairs of 1:428–9,
    1:498–9, 1:525–6
  OC's exchanges with the Bishops of 2:180–1,
    2:182–202
  OC's involvement in affairs 1:505–6
  OC's responses to rebellion of 1641 in 1:xlii,
    1:42, 1:49–50, 1:53: 1:58, 1:62, 1:67, 1:69–71,

    1:77–8, 1:83–4, 1:86–7, 1:90–1, 1:93, 1:170,
    1:485–6
  OC's role during the Irish crisis of 1647 1:lxii,
    1:368, 1:378, 1:385–91, 3:392 n. 7, 1:401–3,
    1:428–31
  OC's speech about accepting the command
    in 2:23–9
  overview of OC's campaigns in Ireland
    1649–59 2:liii–lvi, 2:lix–lxii
  and parliamentary elections in Ireland
    3:37–8, 3:45–6, 3:403–4, 3:413–14
  Protectoral references to earlier massacres
    in 3:293, 3:303
  report to Parliament upon his return 2:263–4
  role of HC in 3:204
  Scottish troops in 1:189, 1:553
Ireland, Gilbert (1624–75) 2:485, 2:498–9, 3:178
Ireton, Bridget (née Cromwell) (bap. 1624,
    d. 1662) 1:353–5, 2:552
Ireton, Captain (HI's brother) 1:311
Ireton, Henry (bap. 1611, d. 1651) 1:lv, 1:lxii,
    1:lxiii, 1:176–7, 1:200–1, 1:239, 1:300–1, 1:308,
    1:336–7, 1:354, 1:377–82, 1:383, 1:385–6,
    1:388–97, 1:411, 1:412 n. 8, 2:47, 2:177, 2:253,
    2:261, 2:276, 2:534, 2:598, 3:437
  and *The Case of the Armie Truly Stated* 1:435
  commissioner for trial of King 1:647
  death of 2:521
  and Heads of the Proposals 1:409, 1:410–11,
    1:422
  in Robert Huntington's *Sundry Reasons* 1:538,
    1:539
  in Ireland 2:152, 2:207–8, 2:216–17, 2:231
  letters from 1:399–402, 1:627, 1:641–5
  letters to: in Ireland 2:216–17
  letters to Lenthall 1:388–91
  letters to: on Scottish victory 2:340–2
  and Putney Debates 1:437–8, 1:439, 1:446–7,
    1:448, 1:453, 1:458, 1:460, 1:462, 1:463, 1:466
    n. 13, 1:473 & n. 39, 1:474–5
  signatory on warrant for king's trial 1:647–9
  speeches 1:418, 1:423, 1:646–7
  talks with Levellers 1:636
  unsuccessful sieges 2:342 n. 13
Ireton, Thomas 2:612–13
Ironsides, formation of the 1:152–3, 1:156–8,
    1:176–7, 1:179
Isaack, Robert 2:84
Isle of Ely, Cambridgeshire 1:30, 1:115, 1:281–2,
    1:354 n. 3, 1:499
Isle of Man 2:499
Isle of Wight 1:627, 2:51, 2:545–6, 2:600–1
Islip, Oxfordshire 1:263, 1:266

Jack, George 2:334
Jackson, Captain [William?] 1:616 n. 2
Jackson, Thomas 1:300–2, 1:395, 2:57

684

GENERAL INDEX

Jackson, William 1:616 n. 2

Jaffray, Alexander (1614–73) 2:393, 2:416–17

Jamaica 3:xlvii, 3:lvii, 3:101 n. 5, 3:229, 3:231–2, 3:264–5, 3:273–8

James, duke of York, *see* James II and VII, king of England, Scotland and Ireland (1633–1701)

James I and VI, king of England, Scotland and Ireland (1566–1625) 2:238, 3:292, 3:368

James II and VII, king of England, Scotland and Ireland (1633–1701) 1:361, 1:409, 2:518, 2:605, 3:326, 3:329

Jeaffreson, John 3:196

Jenkins, George 2:104

Jenkyn, William (bap. 1613, d. 1685) 2:451

Jenner, Robert (1584–1651) 1:356–7, 1:624–6

Jephson, William (1609/10–58) 1:505, 2:155 n. 10, 3:210

Jermy, Robert 3:175

Jermyn, Henry, earl of St Albans 1:36

Jerningham, Henry 1:645–6

Jersey, Channel Islands 1:487, 3:160–2

Jessey/Jacie, Henry (1601–63) 3:244–5

Jessop, William (bap. 1603, d. 1675) 3:434, 3:459 n. 7

Jocelyn, Torrell 1:97–102, 1:104

John IV, king of Portugal (1604-56) 3:208, 3:213–14, 3:259, 3:260

John of Austria (1629–79) 3:295, 3:302

Johnson, Richard 2:464–5

Johnson, Robert 2:230, 2:232

Johnson, Thomas 1:175 n. 13

Johnston, Alexander 2:334

Johnston, Archibald, Lord Wariston (bap. 1611, d. 1663) 1:232, 1:602, 2:310–11, 2:437–8, 2:447–51

Johnston, Helen, née Hay, Lady Wariston 2:437

Johnstone/Johnson, William 1:175 n. 13

Jones, Captain 1:533

Jones, Edmund (1612–83) 3:182

Jones, Henry, Protestant bishop of Clogher 1:428 n. 1, 2:227 n. 4

Jones, John (c.1597–1660) 1:647–50, 2:11, 2:337

Jones, Michael (1606x10–49) 1:428–9, 2:55, 2:57, 2:71–2, 2:80, 2:85, 2:114, 2:145, 2:146, 2:152
death of 2:161, 2:163

Jones, Philip (1617/18–74) 2:43–4, 3:166, 3:172, 3:222, 3:271
Council member 2:686 n. 109, 3:8
indenture 2:532–3
kingship committee 3:358–66, 3:384, 3:413

Jones, Rice 2:558 n. 5

Jones, Robert 1:55

Jones, Roger, first Viscount Ranelagh (d. 1644) 1:84 n. 2

Jones, Samuel 1:522

Jongestall, Allart Pieter van (1612–76) 2:714 n. 2, 2:722, 2:723, 2:751–3, 2:754–5

Joyce, George (b. 1618) 1:402–3, 1:477, 1:538

Jubbes, John (*fl.* 1643–9) 1:333, 1:467

Jubert, Henry 2:86–7

Juliers, Duchy of 3:298 n. 46

Juxon, Thomas (1614–72) 1:211, 1:213, 1:220

Keayne, Robert 1:9

Kellond, John (bap. 16 May 1609, d. 6 June 1679) 1:639

Kelsey, Thomas (d. in or after 1676) 1:329–30, 3:174

Kelyng, Sir John (bap. 1607, d. 1671) 1:74

Kemmen, John 2:335

Kemys, Sir Nicholas 1:512 n. 4, 1:523

Kemyss, Charles 1:533

Kendall, Jo: 1:154, 1:155

Kenkins, David 1:55 n. 1

Kennedy, John, sixth earl of Cassillis (1601x7–68) 1:602

Kennet, river 1:229, 1:325

Kenrick, William 1:509–11

Kent, earl of, *see* Grey

Ker, Gilbert 2:365, 2:376–9, 2:381, 2:384, 2:385

Ker, Robert, first earl of Roxburghe (1569/70–1650) 1:587, 2:321

Kerkpatrick, Charles 2:332

Kerney 2:479

Kerr, Ann, Lady Lothian (d. 1667) 2:375–6, 2:412–13

Kerr, Sir Andrew, laird of Greenhead, Roxburghshire, first baronet 1:582, 1:587, 1:593, 1:594

Kerr, William, third earl of Lothian (c.1605–75) 1:486 n. 1, 2:376, 2:410–11, 2:412

Ketton, Rutland 1:181 n. 1

Keynsham, Somerset 1:308

Kilbeheny, County Limerick 2:208

Kilcash, County Tipperary 2:206

Kilkenny, County Kilkenny 2:124, 2:127, 2:129, 2:144, 2:148, 2:149, 2:149 n. 1, 2:150, 2:175, 2:207, 2:216, 2:217–27, 2:230 n. 7, 2:232–3
articles of surrender 2:225–7, 2:233
parliamentary losses at 2:229–30

Killgrew, Sir Peter (c.1593–1668) 3:209–10

Killincarrig, County Wicklow 2:113

Kilmacthomas, County Waterford 2:162

Kilmallock, County Limerick 2:241

Kilpatrick, Ensign 2:334

Kilsyth, Stirlingshire 1:300, 2:374

Kiltinan Castle, County Tipperary 2:215

Kimber, Isaac (1692–1755) 2:603–4, 3:245

Kimbolton, Baron, *see* Montagu, Edward, second earl of Manchester

Kinaston, Robert 1:356 n. 3

King, Edward 1:190 n. 8, 1:339

King, Henry, bishop of Chichester (1592–1669) 1:42

King, James, Lord Eythin 1:151

685

GENERAL INDEX

King, Joh[ann]es 1:112–13
King, Sir Robert (d. 1657) 2:158–9
King's Lynn, Norfolk 1:172, 2:355, 3:11, 3:216–17
Kingsale, baron, *see* de Courcy
Kingsclere, Hampshire 1:228, 1:237–8, 1:261
Kingship, offer of, to Cromwell, *see* Monarchy
Kingsmill, Ann (1605/6–62) 2:17 n. 1
Kingston, earl of, *see* Pierrepoint
Kingston upon Hull, Yorkshire 1:64–5, 1:82,
 1:92, 1:125, 1:130, 1:140 n. 12, 1:169–70, 1:172,
 1:433–4, 1:621, 2:58, 2:742
Kingston upon Thames, Surrey 1:480, 3:520
Kingswood Forest, Gloucestershire 3:65–6
Kinnesswood, Kinross-shire 2:479
Kinsale, County Cork 2:93, 2:152, 2:155 n. 10,
 2:162
Kirby family 1:17–19
Kirby, Thomas (father) 1:18–19
Kirby, Thomas (son) 1:18–19
Kirby, William 1:18
Kirkcudbright, lord, *see* Maclennan
Kirwan, Francis, Catholic bishop of Killala
 (1589–1661) 2:184–9
Kitchin, William 2:298 n. 2
Knaresborough, Yorkshire 1:197, 1:553, 1:567
Knight, Isaac (*fl.* 1637–62) 2:533
Knight, Ralph (1619?–91) 3:287
Knight, Thomas (b. 1634) 2:534
Knocks, William 2:333
Knocktoper, County Kilkenny 2:210
Knollys, Nicholas, third earl of Banbury
 (1631–74) 2:571
Knollys, William, first earl of Banbury
 (c.1545–1632) 2:571
Knottingley, Yorkshire 1:605, 1:607, 1:609, 1:614,
 1:637
Knyvett, Thomas (1596–1658) 1:lix n. 21, 1:341–3
Koca Dervish Mehmed Pasha, grand vizier of
 Ottoman Empire 3:62

La Ferté-Senneterre, Henri de(1599–1681) 3:443
La Tour d'Auvergne, Henri de, vicomte de
 Turenne (1611–75) 2:337
Lagerfeldt, Israel Israelson 2:733 n. 6
Laggan, County Donegal 1:76
Lambert/Lambart, John (bap. 1619, d.
 1684) 1:308 n. 18, 1:320 n. 4, 1:391–2, 1:397
 n. 23, 1:413, 1:423, 1:545, 1:561, 1:564, 1:576,
 1:603, 1:637, 2:lvi, 2:337, 2:370, 2:384–5,
 2:450, 2:465–6, 2:482, 2:596, 2:614, 3:liv,
 3:58–60, 3:172, 3:211, 3:270, 3:281
 accused of defending witches 2:451
 authorization for examination of condition
 of Windsor Castle 3:19
 commissioner in Scotland 2:651 n. 2
 conversations with 2:267–73, 2:305–6, 3:241
 Council member 2:686 n. 109, 3:8

and Heads of the Proposals 1:410–11, 1:422
and Humble Petition and Advice 3:418
letters from 1:399–402
letters to 2:519–20, 3:434
occupation of Edinburgh 2:351
possible successor to Ireton 2:552
preparation of letters 3:214–16
victory at Inverkeithing 2:467–9
warrant for pay to 2:508
Lambourn/Denington, river 1:229
Lanark, earl of, *see* Hamilton
Lancaster, Lancashire 1:553, 1:564
Lancaster Castle, Lancashire 2:642
Landbeach, Cambridgeshire 1:110
Land Settlement in Ireland, Cromwell's plans
 for 2:199–202
Langbaine, Gerard (1608/9–58) 2:48
Langdale, Marmaduke, first Baron Langdale
 (bap. 1598, d. 1661) 1:552, 1:559, 1:625
Langford/Longford House 1:328–30
Langley, John 1:108
Langport, Somerset 1:291, 1:292, 1:293, 1:294
Langston, William 1:546
Lanivet, Cornwall 2:604–5
Lansamlett, Swansea 2:44
Lascelles, Francis 1:558
Latimer, John 3:453
Laud, William, bishop of London, archbishop of
 Canterbury (1573–1645) 1:41, 1:166,
 3:299 n. 50
Laugharne, Rowland (c.1607–75) 1:532,
 1:533 n. 15
Laugharne, William 1:533
Laurence, Richard (d. 1657) 2:739
Lavender, Bartholomew 2:lx n. 24, 2:34–5
Lavenham, Suffolk 1:165 n. 5
Law reform
 in Ireland 2:168–70
 OC and 2:274–6, 3:51, 3:77–8, 3:94, 3:132–3,
 3:248–50, 3:252, 3:282, 3:291, 3:310–11
Lawford's Gate 1:308, 1:310
Lawhitton, Cornwall 2:440, 2:519
Lawrence, Henry (1600–64) 2:343, 3:8, 3:171,
 3:177, 3:270 n. 46
Lawrence, Richard (d. 1684) 2:739 n. 1, 3:61
Lawrence, Thomas 1:108
Lawson, Nicholas 2:332
Lawson, Robert 2:334
Lay Preachers in the Army, Cromwell
 commends 2:355–60, 3:74, 3:78, 3:101, 3:403
Lazarus, Armenian Christian/Persian 3:511–12
Le Febvre, Philip 3:161–2
Le Hunt/Lehunt, Richard 1:529, 2:109–10
Le Marinel, Thomas 3:161–2
Lea, James 2:252
Lea, Mathew 2:485
Lecale, County.Down 1:356

686

GENERAL INDEX

Lectureships, puritan 1:8–12
Lee, Dr 1:111
Lee, Major 1:270
Lee, Mr 1:297
Lee, Samuel 1:190
Leeds, Yorkshire 1:544, 1:635
Legge, William (1607/8–70) 1:271, 1:488 n. 8
Leicester, earls of, *see* Sidney
Leicester, Leicestershire 1:117–18, 1:281, 1:542, 1:545
Leich, Philip 2:333
Leighlin Bridge, County Carlow 2:124
Leighton, Alexander 1:22
Leighton, Harcourt 1:286
Leith, Edinburgh County 2:303, 2:417, 2:475, 2:483
  maintenance post-victory 2:354–5
  proclamation to, concerning markets 2:349–51
  and surrender of Edinburgh Castle 2:403
Lemprière, James 3:161–2
Lemprière, Michel/Michael (1606–71) 3:160–2
Lemprière, Nicolas (1611–67) 3:162
Lenaeus, Johannes Canuti, archbishop of Uppsala (1573–1669) 3:50, 3:52–3
Lennox, duke of, *see* Stuart
Lenthall, William (1591–1662) 1:lx, 1:57, 1:60–1, 1:63, 1:115, 1:132–3, 1:156, 1:243, 1:278–9, 1:286–9, 1:305–15, 1:315–16, 1:319–27, 1:328–30, 1:379–82, 1:388–92, 2:lv, 2:lx, 3:103–5, 3:131, 3:368 n. 18
  conversations with 2:516–19
  dissolution of Rump Parliament 2:608, 2:609–10, 2:612
  and Humble Petition and Advice 3:418
  kingship committee 3:358–66, 3:384
  letters from 2:571–2
  letters to 1:388–91, 1:478–9, 1:518–20, 1:530–1, 1:551–60, 1:592, 1:599–605, 1:601–5, 2:61–3, 2:69–70, 2:76–8, 2:93–100, 2:101–4, 2:112–17, 2:126–8, 2:139–45, 2:151–6, 2:161–7, 2:179–80, 2:207–11, 2:217, 2:229–36, 2:265–6, 2:322–9, 2:367–9, 2:384–6, 2:404–5, 2:408–9, 2:427–8, 2:442–4, 2:453–3, 2:459–60, 2:467–9, 2:470, 2:475–6, 2:480–2, 2:485–6, 2:487–91, 2:492–6, 3:103–4, 3:104–5
  and petition defending *The Agreement of the People* 1:483
  recommendations by 2:559
  thanks on behalf of House to army officers 2:50, 2:51
Leopold, king of Hungary/Leopold I, archduke of Austria, Holy Roman Emperor (1640-1705) 3:302, 3:449, 3:472
Lesley, George 2:333
Lesley, Lieutenant Colonel 2:331
Lesley, Norman 2:333
Lesley, Walter 2:332

Lesley, William 2:334
Leslie, Alexander, first earl of Leven (c.1580–1661) 1:197, 1:300–1, 1:576, 1:588, 1:593, 1:594–5, 2:365
Leslie, Andrew 2:410–11
Leslie, David, first Lord Newark (1601–82) 1:197, 1:576, 1:588, 1:593, 2:312–16, 2:321, 2:338, 2:363, 2:415, 2:416–17, 2:449–50
Leslie, John, sixth earl of Rothes (c.1600–41) 3:110
Leslie, John, duke of Rothes (c.1630–81) 2:490
Leslie, John, Lord Newton (d. 1651) 2:379
Leslie, Ludovick 1:577–8, 1:594
L'Estrange, Sir Hamon (1583-1654) 2:738
L'Estrange, Sir Roger (1616–1704) 2:738
Letters, Cromwell's, analysed 1:lvi–lxi, 2:liv–lvvi, 2:lvi–lvii, 2:lxii–lxiv, 3:xli–lx
Levellers 1:lx, 1:484, 1:607, 1:610–11, 1:632, 2:44–5, 2:45–6, 2:50–1, 3:139
Leven, earl of, *see* Leslie
Leverett, John (1616–79) 3:186–7
Lewes, Sir William 1:351 n. 9
Lewis, Charles (1618–80) 2:568
Lewis, Francis 1:533
Lewis, Mr 2:523
Lewson, John 2:334
Liberton, lord, *see* Winram
Liberty/liberties, civil
  and the public interest 1:472
  defence of religion and 2:280–3, 2:293, 2:518, 2:579, 2:581, 2:616, 3:4, 3:73–4, 3:313, 3:364, 3:392, 3:461, 3:463
  English 2:201, 3:97
  from 'bondage' 1:456, 3:394
  from the 'taskmaster' 1:334
  in 'propriety'/ estates 2:76, 2:218, 2:222, 2:246, 2:266, 2:381, 2:400, 2:403, 3:75, 3:139, 3:261, 3:398
  licentious 1:401, 3:299–300, 3:479
  of Parliament 1:203, 1:212, 2:211, 2:389–91, 3:62, 3:343
  of speech, 1:437, 1:461
  of the gospel 2:623
  of the kingdom/country 1:288, 1:440, 1:462, 1:470, 2:698, 2:703, 3:398
  of the subject/people 1:304, 1:401–2, 1:638, 2:366, 3:87, 3:97, 3:281, 3:362, 3:373, 3:375, 3:388–9, 3:399, 3:479
  'to abuse, rob, pillage' 2:82
  to petition 1:482
  to live unmolested and move freely 2:102, 2:202, 2:213–14, 2:226, 2:259
  'true' 3:99
Liberty, religious 2:679–85, 2:700–5
  as discussed by OC 1:610–12
  in England, defended 2:531–2
  OC's limited grant of to Irish Catholics 2:120–2, 2:197–9

687

GENERAL INDEX

Liberty, religious (*cont.*)
OC pleads for 1:314–15, 1:315–16
in Scotland, defended 2:284, 2:313–14, 2:351–3, 3:355–60
Lichfield, Leonard (bap. 1604, d. 1657) 2:740
Lilburne, Henry 1:349–50, 1:464
Lilburne, John (1615?–57) 1:liv, 1:lviii, 1:lxiii n.
   32, 1:190 n. 8, 1:220, 1:222 n. 35, 1:223 n. 40,
   1:239, 1:290–1, 1:339–40, 1:349 n. 2, 1:412 n.
   9, 1:420 n. 32, 2:59 n. 1
vendetta against earl of Manchester 1:339–40
Lilburne, Robert (bap. 1614, d. 1665) 1:349 n. 2,
   1:393, 2:490, 2:591–2, 3:167
   letters from 1:399–402
   letters signed by 3:207
   letters to 3:22–3
   and Putney Debates 1:462
Lilburne, Thomas 1:349 n. 2
Limerick, baron, *see* Esmonde
Limerick, County Limerick 2:341, 2:342 n. 13
Limerick, County Wexford 2:113
Lincoln, William 2:6–7
Lincoln, Lincolnshire 1:133, 1:138, 1:140, 1:156,
   1:169, 1:197, 1:200, 1:223, 1:224, 1:225, 1:226
Lindsay, John, seventeenth earl of Crawford and
   first earl of Lindsay (1596–1678) 1:587–8
Lindsay, Ludovic, sixteenth earl of Crawford
   (d. 1652) 1:601–2
Lindsey, earls of, *see* Bertie
Linlithgow, Linlithgowshire 2:363, 2:364, 2:365
Linsey, John 2:334
Linsey, Mathew 1:113
Lisbon, Portugal 3:223
Lisle, John (1609/10–64) 1:217 n. 15, 1:239, 1:240,
   1:245, 1:247, 1:248, 1:249, 1:256, 1:507,
   1:647–9, 2:11, 2:726
   appointment as Commissioner of Great
      Seal 3:106
   kingship committee 3:358–66
Litherland/Letherland, Joseph 1:507, 1:508 nn.
   8 & 10
Little Shelford, Cambridgeshire 1:111
Littleton, Edward, Baron Littleton (1589–1645)
   1:50, 1:270
Liverpool, Lancashire 2:500, 3:509–10
Livingston, James, of Kinnaird, first earl of
   Newburgh (1621/2–70) 2:661–2
Livingston, Sir John, of Kinnaird, first baronet
   (d. 1628) 2:661 n. 1, 2:662
Livingstone, John (1603–72) 2:386, 3:22–3
Livorno, Italy 3:200
Llanelli, Carmathenshire 1:516
Llangibby, Monmouthshire 1:521–2
Lloyd, Sir Charles 1:317
Lloyd, John 3:257, 3:259, 3:270, 3:285
Lloyd, Jenkin 2:439 n. 4
Lloyd, Walter 1:302 n. 22

Lockhart, Sir William (1621?–75) 3:lii, 3:329–30,
   3:440–3, 3:454, 3:458, 3:459, 3:512–16
Lockyer, Nicholas 1:451, 1:474–5
Lockyer, Robert (1625/6–1649) 2:42
Loftus, Sir Adam 1:505–6
Loftus, Adam, first Viscount Ely (d. 1643) 1:506
   n. 15
Loftus, Adam (d. 1651) 1:71
Loftus, Sir Arthur 2:145
Loftus, Nicholas (1592–1666) 1:71 n. 2, 1:90–1
Lomas, Sophia 1:97, 1:137, 1:140–1, 1:153, 1:156,
   1:165, 1:177, 1:179 n. 3, 1:189 n. 1, 1:263 n. 6,
   1:284 n. 15, 1:285 n. 5, 1:332, 1:366, 1:436 n.
   4, 1:633
   additions to texts 1:519
   and Carlyle-Lomas edition 3:xlvii–xlviii
   and dating of letters 1:486–7, 1:495–6, 2:175
      n. 10
   editing of Cromwell's writing 1:xxxvi,
      1:xxxvii–xxxviii, 1:l
   her edition analysed 1:xxxvii–xxxix,
      2:xxxix–xli, 3:xxx–xxxii
   identification of recipients of letters 3:234
   identification of writers' hands 1:636 n. 2
   insertions in letters 3:435 n. 9
   interpretation of texts 1:516, 1:518 n. 16, 1:562,
      1:563 nn. 9, 15 & 16, 1:564 nn. 17 & 20
   interpretation of words 1:555 n. 35
   letter to Richard Herbert 1:523
   and letters to Robert Hammond 1:500
   on letters to Cardinal Mazarin 3:326
   and letters to Richard Norton 1:501 n. 21,
      1:502 & nn. 2 & 3, 1:504 n. 20
   and Putney Debates' documents 1:446 n. 30,
      1:451 n. 53
   on recipients of letters 1:605
   suggested emendations to text 1:377 n. 11
   transcriptions 3:24, 3:248
   versions of speeches 2:664
Lomax, Gervase 1:177
Lomsden, James 2:331
London and Westminster, cities of 1:liv, 1:204,
   1:227 n. 70
   Balcony Tavern, Covent Garden 1:59
   Banqueting House 3:468, 3:500
   Bartholomew Close 2:274
   Bedford Street 2:521 n. 6
   Carlisle House, Lincoln's Inn Fields 3:167 n. 14
   Chancery Lane 2:516 n. 4
   Charing Cross 3:158 & n. 11, 3:279
   Charterhouse School, Smithfield 2:584–5
   Chelsea 3:47
   Christ Church Greyfriars/Christ Church,
      Newgate Street 3:53–4
   Cockpit, Whitehall 2:liii, 2:439, 2:346, 2:586,
      2:744
   Covent Garden 1:liii, 1:lvi, 1:59, 1:377

688

GENERAL INDEX

Dog Tavern, Royal Exchange **1**:11 n. 17
Drury Lane **1**:liii, **1**:lvi
Ely House/Palace, Holborn **2**:523, **2**:524,
  2:526, **2**:528, **2**:536
Finch Lane **2**:739
Fleet prison **1**:348
Goldsmiths' Hall **1**:356–7, **2**:5, **2**:485, **2**:560
Gray's Inn **1**:8
Haberdashers Hall **2**:513, **2**:523
Hounslow Heath **2**:262
Hyde Park **1**:44–5, **2**:262, **3**:317–18
Inner Temple **1**:8 n. 4, **2**:550, **2**:603
Inner Temple Church **2**:744
Lincoln's Inn **2**:38, **2**:603
Lincoln's Inn Fields **3**:167 n. 14
Mermaid Inn, Charing Cross Road **3**:158
Middle Temple **2**:657
Newgate prison **1**:339–40
Old Palace Yard **1**:358 n. 4
Palace of Westminster **1**:47, **1**:648
Painted Chamber, Palace of
  Westminster **1**:648, **3**:67, **3**:68, **3**:82, **3**:130,
  3:288, **3**:319, **3**:423, **3**:428
Paternoster Row **1**:45, **1**:640
Royal Exchange, Cornhill **1**:11 n. 17, **2**:629–30,
  3:475
St Anne Blackfriars **2**:756, **3**:399
St Bartholemew's Hospital **2**:559 n. 7
St Benet Fink **1**:10
St James's Palace **2**:12, **3**:427
St James's Park **2**:343, **2**:573, **2**:718, **3**:318
St Margaret's **1**:252 n. 2
St Martin-in-the-Fields, Westminster **3**:228
St Mary Magdalen, Milk Street **1**:10 n. 13
St Mary Spital, Spitalfields **1**:5
St Mary's Church, Putney **1**:435
St Olave, Hart Street **2**:560
St Paul's Cross **1**:5–6
St Swithin's Lane **1**:24
St Thomas's Hospital, Southwark **2**:lx n. 24,
  2:29–30, **2**:34–5, **2**:558–9
Soper Lane **1**:299 n. 1
Southwark **2**:lx n. 24, **2**:29–30, **2**:34–5, **2**:509,
  2:558–9
Tower of London **1**:340
Trinity House **2**:541–2
Uxbridge **1**:403, **1**:420
Warwick Lane **2**:524
Westminster **1**:lvi, **1**:lvii, **1**:lx
Westminster Abbey **1**:182 n. 7, **1**:252 n. 2
Westminster Hall **3**:431
Whitehall Palace **1**:lvi. **2**:liii, **2**:439, **2**:346,
  2:586, **2**:744, **3**:468, **3**:486, **3**:490, **3**:500
Withdrawing Chamber, Whitehall
  Palace **3**:486, **3**:490
York House **3**:468
Long, George **1**:47, **1**:48

Long, Major **2**:65
Long, Thomas **2**:227 n. 4
Long, Sir Walter (1589–1645) **1**:48
Long Sutton, Somerset **1**:292, **1**:294
Longford Castle, Wiltshire **1**:326
Longhorn, Lieutenant Colonel **2**:230, **2**:232
Longland, William **1**:318
Longleat, Wiltshire **2**:583
Lort, John **1**:534–5
Lort/Lorte, Roger (1607/8–64) **1**:534–5, **1**:536,
  3:183
Lort, Samson **1**:534–5, **1**:536
Lostwithiel, Cornwall **1**:203
Lothian, earl of, *see* Kerr
Loudoun, earl of, *see* Campbell
Loughlin Bridge **2**:230, **2**:231
Louis II de Bourbon, Prince of Condé (1621–1686)
  2:541
Louis XIV, king of France (1638–1715) **2**:lxvi,
  3:60, **3**:455–6, **3**:512
Love, Christopher (1618–51) **2**:604
Love, Nicholas (bap. 1608, d. 1682) **2**:614
Love, Richard (1596–1661) **2**:22–3
Lower, Thomas (bap. 1633, d. 1720) **3**:158
Lower Bann, river **2**:142
Lowestoft, Suffolk **1**:105
Lowndes, G. A. **2**:759
Lowry, John (d. 1699) **1**:26–7, **2**:61–2
Lowther, Sir John, first baronet (1606–75) **3**:182
Lucerna San Giovanni, Piedmont, Italy **3**:513–14
Lucy, Sir Richard, first baronet (1592–1667) **3**:181
Ludlow/Ludlowe, Edmund (1616/17–92) **1**:xxxvii
  n. 7, **1**:358–9, **1**:647–9, **2**:lvi, **2**:11, **2**:258–9,
  2:267, **2**:512–13, **2**:614, **3**:15, **3**:37
  conversations with **2**:273–7, **3**:l, **3**:240–3,
  3:278–81
  dissolution of Rump Parliament **2**:607,
  2:610–12
  events post-dissolution **2**:626–7
  memoirs **1**:407, **2**:596–7, **3**:278–9
Ludlow, Elizabeth, née Thomas (1629/30–1702)
  2:277
Ludlow, Mr, leaseholder at Hursley **2**:20
Ludlow Castle, Shropshire **3**:176
Luke, John (b. 1632) **2**:527
Luke, Sir Samuel (bap. 1603, d. 1670) **1**:lv,
  1:99–101, **1**:187–8, **1**:205–7, **1**:254 n. 1, **1**:276,
  1:277 n. 13, **1**:279–81, **1**:289, **2**:527
Lumsden, Sir James, of Innergellie (*fl.* 1629–51)
  2:328, **2**:331
Lumsden, William, (*fl.* 1645–50) **2**:331
Lyme Regis, Dorset **1**:332–3
Lynch, Andrew, Catholic bishop of Kilfenora
  (1596?–1681) **2**:184–9
Lynch, Ma. **2**:125
Lynch, Walter, Catholic bishop of Clonfert
  (1593?–1663) **2**:184–9

689

GENERAL INDEX

Lynne, Edward (1570–1655) 1:10
Lynne, John (d. 1659) 2:532 n. 1
Lynne, William (d. 1589) 1:10
Lysons, Sir Thomas 2:493, 2:494
Lytcott, Leonard 2:469
Lytton, Sir Robert 1:85
Lyvett, John 2:147, 2:149–50

Mabbott, Gilbert (bap. 1622, d. in or after
  1670) 2:631, 3:339, 3:346, 3:419, 3:486
MacCarthy, Donough, second Viscount
  Muskerry, first earl of Clancarty
  (1594–1665) 2:165
Maccaulla, Robert 2:332
Macclellan, John 2:332
Macclesfield, earl of, see Gerard
Macdoer, Anthony 2:332
MacDonnell, Randall, second earl and first
  marquis of Antrim (1609–83) 2:180
Macdoughel, Walter 2:334
Mackbey, James 2:333
Mackburney, George 2:333
Mackdoughal, John 2:333
Macke, Edmund 3:184–5
Mackellum, Robert 2:332
MacKiernan, Thomas 2:184–9
Macknab, Patrick 2:333
Macknath, James 2:334
Macknight, John 2:333
Mackworth, Humphrey (1603–54) 2:498, 3:30–1,
  3:162–3
Mackworth, Humphrey (1631–81) 3:188–9
Mackworth, Thomas (1627–96) 3:182
Maclan, William 2:335
Maclellan, John, third Lord Kirkcudbright (died
  1664) 1:601
MacLeod, Rory, laird of Dunvegan 3:236–7
MacMahon, Heber/Ever/Emer, bishop of
  Clogher (1600–50) 2:184–9
Macock, John 1:546 n. 7
Macroom, County Cork 2:204
Macularoy, James 2:332
Macuo, John 2:334
Madole, Hugh 2:332
Madrid, Spain 3:302
Magavile, Jam 2:332 n. 19
Magennis, Arthur, Catholic bishop of Down
  and Connor (c.1611–53) 2:184–9
Mageoghegan, Niall Anthony, Catholic bishop
  of Clonmacnoise (c.1595–1664) 2:184–9
Magil, James 2:332
Maidstone, Kent 2:507, 2:597
Maitland, John, earl (later duke) of Lauderdale
  (1616–82) 1:602, 2:490, 2:651
Maimed and sick soldiers, Cromwell's concern
  for 1:184, 1:204–5, 1:362–3, 1:374–7, 1:398,
  1:424–5, 2:335–6, 2:523–6, 2:528–9, 3:19, 3:57

Major, Ann, neé Kingsmill (1605/6–1662) 2:65,
  2:290
Major, Ann (RM's sister-in-law) 2:65
Major, Dorothy (1627–76) 1:494, 1:502, 2:lx, 2:3,
  2:8, 2:14–17, 2:19–21, 2:30–4, 2:36–41, 2:64–5,
  2:134, 2:135
  letters to 2:73–5
  see also Cromwell, Dorothy, née Major
Major, Gregory (fl. 1645–53) 2:597
Major, John (d. 1630) 2:32 n. 2
Major, Richard (1603/4–60) 1:494, 1:495, 1:501,
  1:502, 1:503, 2:lv, 2:lvi, 2:lx, 2:lxiv, 2:3–4,
  2:7–9, 2:14–17, 2:19–21, 2:30–4, 2:36–41,
  2:64–6, 2:70–3, 2:71, 2:236–8, 3:8
  letters to: from Ireland 2:134–5
  letters to: from Scotland 2:346–7
  letters to: on purchase of land in Essex for
    RC 3:34–5
  letters to: on RC's failings 2:289, 2:462–4
Major Generals (1655–7), Cromwell's defence
  of the 3:237–8, 3:251–2, 3:303–4, 3:310–13,
  3:338, 3:341, 3:344
Maker, Sir Richard 3:491
Malaga, Spain 3:196–7
Malignants
  defined 1:501, 1:662
  discussed 1:556, 1:662–3, 2:285, 2:314–15,
    2:357–8, 2:362, 2:373, 2:378, 2:385–6, 3:163,
    3:298, 3:403
  see also Delinquents; Royalists
Mallow, County Cork 2:162, 2:205, 2:208,
  2:452 n. 1, 2:564
Malmesbury, Wiltshire 2:557
Malvin, Henry 2:331
Malyn, William 2:532 n. 1, 2:620, 2:644
Manby, John 1:66
Manchester, earls of, see Montagu
Manchester, Lancashire 2:556
Mandeville, Viscount, see Montagu, Edward,
  second earl of Manchester
Manhattoes, New Netherlands 3:18
Manhop, William 2:332
Manning, Henry 3:298 n. 46
Mannord, William 2:335
Mansell, Bussy (1623–99) 3:183
Mansfield, Nottinghamshire 1:542
Manton, Thomas (bap. 1620, d. 1677) 3:343 n. 27
Mapperton House, Dorset 3:58
March, Cambridgeshire 1:183 n. 3, 1:201
Marchmont, earl of, see Hume
Marche, William 1:97–102, 1:193, 1:194
Mardyke, Netherlands 3:441, 3:447, 3:454
Margery, Ralph 1:166, 1:167, 1:168, 1:172, 1:173–4
Market Harborough, Leicestershire 1:283,
  1:287–9
Markham, Anthony 3:65–6
Markham, Henry (1602–74) 3:282–3

690

GENERAL INDEX

Marks, Christian **2**:lvii n. 17
Marlborough, Wiltshire **1**:237, **1**:271, **3**:liv, **3**:111–12, **3**:125–6
Marsh, Thomas **1**:193 n. 6
Marsh, Thomas Orlebar (1787–1828) **1**:114
Marshall, Stephen (1594/5?–1655) **1**:9, **1**:252 n. 2, **1**:501, **3**:66–7
Marshfield, Gloucestershire **1**:261
Marston Moor, Yorkshire **1**:196–7, **2**:582
Marten/Martin, Henry/Harry (1601/2–80) **1**:25–6, **1**:337, **1**:647–9, **2**:11, **2**:609, **2**:610 n. 4
Martial Law **2**:380, **2**:417–18, **2**:496–8, **2**:544–5
  in Ireland **2**:79–80, **3**:6
  OC issues commissions of **2**:295–6, **2**:298–300
Martin, Colonel **1**:540
Martin, Gabriel **1**:394 n. 16
Martin, Sir Thomas **1**:60, **1**:99–102, **1**:104–5, **1**:112–13
Martyn, Sir Thomas **1**:110, **1**:162–3
Marvell, Andrew (1621–78) **3**:247
Mary I, queen of England and Ireland (1516-58) **3**:292, **3**:293
Maryland **3**:225–7
Masareene, viscount, *see* Clotworthy
Masham, Sir William (1591/2–1656) **1**:14, **1**:39, **1**:369
Masham, Sir William (1615/16–54/5) **2**:9
Mason, Thomas **2**:498–9
Massachusetts Bay, Massachusetts **1**:9
Massey, Sir Edward (1604x9–1674) **1**:260, **1**:269 n. 1, **1**:293, **1**:329 n. 9, **1**:348, **2**:486
Masson, David **1**:219, **1**:221 n. 31, **1**:233
Mathewes, Major **1**:533
Mathews, George **2**:212, **2**:213–14
Matthews, Humphrey **1**:532, **1**:625–6
Maude, Jonathan (c.1613–84) **2**:543
Mauleverer, Dorcas **2**:408–9
Mauleverer, John (c.1610–50) **1**:433–4, **1**:621, **2**:408–9
Mauleverer, Sir Thomas, first baronet (bap. 1599, d. 1655) **1**:647–9
Maurice, prince palatine of the Rhine (1621–52) **1**:205, **1**:263, **1**:264, **1**:266
Maxwel, James **2**:332
Maye, John **3**:216–17
Maynard, Sir John (1604–90) **1**:489
Maynard, Thomas **3**:213–14, **3**:260
Mayne, Zachary (1631–94) **2**:535–6
Mayo, Christopher **3**:436
Mazarin/Mazzarini, Cardinal Jules Raymond (1602–61) **2**:642–3, **2**:720–1, **3**:lii, **3**:325–30, **3**:441, **3**:454–6
Meadows, Sir Philip (bap. 1626, d. 1718) **3**:259–60, **3**:261
Meath, earl of, *see* Brabazon
Meautys, Henry **1**:162–3

Medals, victory, following Battle of Dunbar **2**:419–20
Medway, river **2**:542 n. 9
Meer, John **2**:333
Mehmed IV, sultan of Ottoman Empire (r. 1648–87) **3**:62
Melbury, Dorset **1**:261
Melcombe Regis, Weymouth, Dorset **2**:545
Meldrum, Sir John (b. before 1584?, d. 1645) **1**:133, **1**:134, **1**:144 n. 4
Mellifont, County Louth **2**:260
Mellish, Captain **2**:36
Melville, Lieutenant Colonel Henry **2**:410–11
Mennis, Thomas **2**:333
Menzies, John (1624–1684) **3**:22–3
Mercers Company of London **1**:8–12
Merriman, John **1**:451, **1**:641, **1**:642, **1**:643, **1**:644
Merrion, County Dublin **3**:14
Mervyn/Mervin, Sir Audley (1603?–75) **3**:240
Messervy, Philip **3**:161–2
Michil, Alexander **2**:332
Middle Wallop, Hampshire **1**:326
Middelburg, Netherlands **2**:257
Middleton, Sir George **1**:432 n. 1
Middleton, Henry **1**:432–3
Middleton, John, first earl of Middleton (c.1608–74) **3**:22–3
Middleton, Mary **3**:517 n. 5
Middleton/Mydelton, Timothy/Tymothy (d. 1655) **1**:81, **1**:154, **1**:283–5
Middleton Stoney, Oxfordshire **1**:269
Midleton, County Cork **2**:450
Mildenhall, Suffolk **1**:97, **1**:98
Mildmay, Anthony **1**:642
Mildmay, Sir Henry (c.1594–1664/5?) **1**:39, **1**:67, **1**:83, **1**:87, **1**:283–5, **1**:405–6, **2**:11
Mildmay, John **2**:140, **2**:141
Milford Haven, Pembrokeshire **2**:58, **2**:68, **2**:71, **2**:146
Militia, Irish **2**:134
Militia Ordinance (1642)
  implementation of **1**:73, **1**:74, **1**:81, **1**:86, **1**:88
  OC speech about **1**:44, **1**:50–1, **1**:59, **1**:63
Militia, reform, of **1**:409–12, **2**:444, **2**:494, **4**:578, **3**:171–8, **3**:337–8, **3**:341, **3**:453–4, **3**:498–9, **3**:503–4, **3**:506–7, **3**:508–9
Millington, Gilbert (c.1598–1666) **1**:647–9
Mills/Mill, Colonel John **3**:340, **3**:342, **3**:343–4
Mills, John **1**:433 n. 3
Milton, John (1608–74) **2**:664, **3**:158
Milward, John **3**:14–16
Mitchell, William (*fl.* 1651–60) **2**:631
Mitchelson, John **2**:381
Moat, Lieutenant George **2**:333
Moat, Major George **2**:331
Molins, William (d. 1662) **2**:662–3

691

GENERAL INDEX

Molyneux, Sir Francis, second baronet (1602–74) 3:182
Molyneux, Henry 1:546–7
Monaldeschi, Giovanni (1626–57) 3:458, 3:460
Monarchy
  offer of the title in 1657 3:340–5, 3:350, 3:351–90, 3:420–3
  OC on the future of 1:463–6, 1:468–72, 1:475–6
  OC said to have proposed restoration of (1651) 2:516–19, 2:574–80, 2:603–4
Monck/Monk, George first duke of Albemarle (1608–70) 2:71, 2:88, 3:25, 2:326, 2:382, 2:396, 2:397–8, 2:399, 2:481, 2:482, 2:592–3, 2:728 n. 2, 3:33, 3:36, 3:114, 3:127, 3:149 n. 62, 3:211–12, 3:236–7, 3:267, 3:301
  commissioner in Scotland 2:651 n. 2
  commissions for 3:5–7
  letters to 3:lii, 3:264–6, 3:355
  notes sent to 3:287
Monmouth, Monmouthshire 1:62–3, 1:210
Monnergain, John 2:333
Monpress, Alexander 2:331
Monro, Sir George, of Culrain and Newmore (d. 1694) 1:553, 1:558, 1:564, 1:576, 1:584, 1:587–8, 1:591, 1:593
Monro, Robert (d. 1675?) 2:598, 3:33
Monson, Sir John, second baronet (1599–1683) 2:300–1
Monson, William, first viscount Monson of Castlemaine (d. 1673?) 1:647–9
Montagu, Colonel 1:308, 1:310, 1:320 n. 4
Montagu, Edward (kinsman of earl of Manchester) 1:257
Montagu, Edward, second earl of Manchester (1602–71) 1:xlvi, 1:l n. 38, 1:lviii, 1:30, 1:67–8, 1:95, 1:115–16, 1:141, 1:163, 1:164, 1:170, 1:171, 1:179, 1:185, 1:188 n. 1, 1:189–92, 1:200, 1:202, 1:203, 1:207–12, 1:258, 1:387 n. 6, 1:478, 1:537, 2:6, 2:540
  clerk's summary of Cromwell's allegations against 1:241–2
  examination of Cromwell's allegations against 1:245
  examination of James Pitsum/Pitson 1:246
  and indemnity/grant of payment 1:389
  letters signed by 1:429–31
  OC's quarrel with 1:214–40, 1:256–7, 1:339–41
  recollection of Cromwell's words 1:242–4
Montagu, Edward, second Baron Montagu of Boughton (1616–84) 2:344
Montagu/Mountagu, Edward, first earl of Sandwich (1625–72) 1:300–1, 1:323–4, 3:30–1, 3:256–62
  appointment as Commissioner of Treasury 3:106
  conversations with 3:241

Council member 3:8
  letters to 3:lii, 3:268–71, 3:284–7, 3:437–8, 3:439–40, 3:447–50
Protectoral Council debate notes 3:58–60
Montagu, George 1:212
Montagu, Henry, first earl of Manchester 1:33
Montagu, Montagu 1:332
Montgomerie, Robbin 2:385
Montgomery/Montgomerie, Alexander (formerly Seton), sixth earl of Eglinton (1588–1661) 1:600, 2:448
Montgomery, dowager Lady Montgomery 3:33
Montgomery, earl of, see Herbert
Montgomery, Hugh 2:332
Montgomery, Hugh, second Viscount Montgomery of the Ards (1598/9–1642) 3:33
Montgomery, Hugh, third Viscount Montgomery of the Ards and first earl of Mount-Alexander (c.1623–63) 2:98, 2:117, 2:127, 2:598–9, 3:33, 3:240
Montgomery, John 2:331
Montgomery/Montgomerie, Robert (d. 1684) 1:600, 2:277, 2:302, 2:304, 2:305, 2:381, 2:415
Montrose, earl and marquis of, see Graham
Moore, Charles, second Viscount Moore of Drogheda (1603–43) 2:260
Moore, Edward 2:55–6, 2:267, 2:458–9
Moore, Henry, third Viscount Drogheda (d. 1675) 2:260
Moore, John (c.1599–1650) 1:lxi n. 29, 1:31, 1:33, 1:55, 1:56, 2:55–7, 2:267
Moore, Major 2:331
Moore, Mary (née Rigby) 2:56 n. 5
Moore, Richard (1627–98) 2:663
Moore, William 3:267 n. 6
Morant, Philip 1:108 n. 3, 1:121
Mordaunt, Henry, second earl of Peterborough (bap. 1623, d. 1697) 2:60–1
Mordington, baron, see Douglas
Mordington, Berwickshire 2:299
Mordington House, Berwickshire 2:302
Morgan, Sir Anthony (1621–68) 2:49–50, 3:339, 3:342–3
Morgan, Anthony/Edward 1:521
Morgan, Edward 1:56
Morgan, Ethelbert (d. 1665) 2:511–12
Morgan, Sir Thomas, first baronet (1604–79) 1:604–5, 3:417–18
Morley, John 1:lii n. 2
Morpeth, Northumberland 1:575
Morris, John (c.1615–49) 1:614–15, 1:618–19
Morris, William 2:311–12
Morrison, Alfred (1821–97) 1:177, 1:499, 1:500, 1:501 n. 21, 3:454–5
Morrison, Elizabeth (1609/10–61) 2:18 n. 4
Mortimer Heath/Common, Berkshire 1:238

692

GENERAL INDEX

Morton, Roger **3**:195–6
Mosse, E. **2**:410–11
Mosse, John **2**:410–11
Mostyn, Ambrose **1**:69
Mostyn, John (1603–75) **2**:550
Mostyn, Sir Roger (1567/8–1642) **2**:550
Mountrath, earl of, *see* Coote
Moyer, Samuel (*c*.1609–83) **2**:663, **2**:686 n. 109
Moyne's Court, Monmouthshire **1**:524
Mulgrave, earl of, *see* Sheffield
Mulgrave, Lady (Elizabeth Cranfield) (1607/8–72) **1**:570
Munster, Ireland **1**:505, **2**:113, **2**:119, **2**:121, **2**:124, **2**:127, **2**:129, **2**:146, **2**:155
Murray, David **2**:332
Murray, James, second earl of Annandale (d. 1658) **3**:106–7
Murray, Cornet John **2**:332
Murray, John **3**:106–7
Murray, John, first earl of Annandale **3**:106–7
Murray, Lieutenant Colonel **2**:331
Murray, William **2**:331
Murray, William, first earl of Dysart (d. 1655) **1**:58–9
Musket, James **2**:334
Musselburgh, Edinburghshire **2**:302–3, **2**:303, **2**:306, **2**:316, **2**:324
Myn, Andrew **2**:334
Mytton, Thomas (1596/7–1652) **1**:427 n. 3, **2**:498

Naas, County Kildare **3**:156
Nalson, John (bap. 1637, d. 1686) **1**:306, **1**:319
3:423, **3**:468, **3**:485
Nantwich, Cheshire **1**:558
Naseby, Northamptonshire **1**:294
Navy
    Commonwealth **2**:594, **2**:600, **2**:653–5, **2**:717
    Parliamentarian **1**:604
    Protectoral **3**:6, **3**:76, **3**:116, **3**:119–20, **3**:209, **3**:225, **3**:256, **3**:437–9, **3**:442, **3**:449, **3**:516–17
Nayler, James (1618–60) **3**:324–5, **3**:341, **3**:343, **3**:344
Needham, Clement **3**:166
Needingworth, Huntingdonshire **1**:30
Needwood Forest, Staffordshire **3**:65–6
Negative Voice, *see* Veto, Cromwell and the royal
Neicen, James **2**:334
Neile, Richard, archbishop of York **1**:5–6
Nelson, Captain John **1**:106–7
Nelson, Lieutenant Colonel John **3**:518–19
Nero (Roman Emperor, AD 54 to 68) **3**:242
Nether Wallop, Hampshire **1**:326
Netherlands
    appeals for peace with **2**:659–60, **2**:715–20, **2**:722–5, **2**:751–5
    Lord Protectors' relations with **3**:501–4

OC issues declarations about naval victories against **2**:652–5
    peace with **2**:645, **2**:654, **2**:660, **2**:715–18, **2**:723–5, **2**:754
    war with **2**:lxvi, **2**:433
Netherwitton, Northumberland **2**:291
Neville, Henry (1620–94) **2**:603–4
Nevis, West Indies **3**:230, **3**:234
New Amsterdam **3**:18 n. 12
New Hall, Essex **3**:262–3
New Ross, County Wexford **2**:111, **2**:119–23, **2**:129, **2**:130, **2**:142, **3**:518
    articles of surrender **2**:124–5, **2**:135–6
New Windsor (now Windsor), Berkshire **2**:554
Newark, lord, *see* Leslie
Newark, Nottinghamshire **1**:124 n. 2, **1**:125, **1**:126, **1**:127, **1**:130, **1**:179, **1**:222, **1**:223–6, **1**:609
    Charles I surrenders at **1**:338
    river crossings **1**:133
Newbattle, Edinburghshire **2**:376, **2**:413
Newburgh, earl of, *see* Livingston
Newbury, Berkshire **1**:204, **1**:205, **1**:211, **1**:220, **1**:221, **1**:228, **1**:229, **1**:231, **1**:233–4, **1**:235, **1**:237, **1**:255, **1**:272, **1**:325, **3**:164
    Shaw's House (Dolman's House) **1**:229, **1**:230
Newbury Field, Berkshire **1**:255
Newcastle, County Down **3**:24
Newcastle upon Tyne, Northumberland **1**:74–5, **1**:346 n. 8, **1**:575, **2**:lvii n. 17, **2**:504, **3**:lii
    letters from **2**:278–9
Newdigate, John (1600–42) **1**:lix n. 21, **1**:6–8
Newdigate, Sir Richard, 2nd Bt. (1644–1710) **1**:6 n. 1
Newdigate-Newdegate, Anne Emily **1**:6 n. 1
Newman, Richard **1**:295–6
Newmarket, Suffolk **1**:283–4
Newport, Monmouthshire **1**:522
Newport Pagnell, Buckinghamshire, **1**:lv, **1**:187, **1**:197, **1**:276, **1**:280
Newry, County Armagh **2**:89, **2**:103
Newton, lord, *see* Leslie
Newton, Robert **1**:112–13
Nicholas, Sir Edward (1593–1669) **1**:5–6, **1**:407, **2**:371 n. 4, **3**:43–4, **3**:66
Nicholas, John (governor of Chepstow) **1**:522, **1**:523, **3**:175
Nicholas, John (son of Sir Edward Nicholas) **2**:371, **2**:377
Nicholas, Robert (bap. 1595, d. 1667) **3**:164 n. 6
Nicholls, Ensign **1**:392 n. 7
Nichols, James **2**:333
Nickolls, John (1710/11–45) **2**:664
Nicoll, Anthony (1611–59) **1**:341, **3**:180
Nicoll, John (*c*.1590–1668) **2**:350, **2**:374, **2**:448
Nieupoort, Willem (1607–78) **2**:714 n. 2, **2**:722, **2**:751–3, **2**:754–5, **3**:501–2
Nix, William **1**:152 n. 4

693

GENERAL INDEX

Noble, Mark **3**:439
Noell, Martin **3**:263
Nominated Assembly (1653)
  announced **2**:628
  OC addresses **2**:664–88, **2**:688–99
  summonses to members of **2**:634–42,
   2:658–9
Nonsuch Park, Cheam, Surrey **2**:534
Nore, river **2**:142, **2**:152, **2**:231
Norham, Northumberland **1**:589, **1**:593
Noris, Thomas **1**:105
Norris, Sir Francis (d. 1669) **3**:182
North, Dudley, fourth Baron North **1**:86–7,
  1:89–90, **1**:239, **1**:243, **1**:277, **1**:372–3
North Queensferry, Fife **2**:468, **2**:471, **2**:474
North Scarle, Lincolnshire **1**:134, **1**:144, **1**:148
North Wichford hundred, Cambridgeshire **1**:183
Northallerton, Yorkshire **1**:574
Northampton, earl of, *see* Compton
Northampton, Northamptonshire **1**:94, **1**:289,
  1:543
Northumberland, earl of, *see* Percy
Norton, Anne (b. 1617, d. in or before 1650?)
  1:501 n. 19, **1**:504
Norton, Sir Gregory, first baronet (c.1603–1652)
  1:647–9
Norton, Richard (1615–91) **1**:195, **1**:196, **1**:239,
  2:3–4, **2**:276, **2**:344, **3**:176
  letters to **1**:493–5, **1**:499–504, **3**:237–8
  and Philip Lord Wharton **2**:483
  skirmish at Odiham **1**:228 n. 80
Norton, Robert (d. 1664) **2**:551–2
Norwich, earl of, *see* Goring
Norwich, Norfolk **1**:105, **1**:153
Nottingham, Nottinghamshire **1**:123–4, **1**:125,
  1:127, **1**:133, **1**:542, **2**:589–90
Nugent, Richard, second earl of Westmeath
  (1626–84) **2**:100, **3**:27–8, **3**:282
Nuttinge, Mrs **2**:22

Oagle, Major **2**:331
Oates, Thomas **1**:618 n. 1, **1**:619
Oath of Association **1**:25–6, **1**:26–7
Oath, Protectoral **3**:3–5, **3**:89–90, **3**:134, **3**:431–2,
  3:484
O'Brien, Barnabas/Bryan/Barnaby, sixth earl of
  Thomond (c.1590–1657) **2**:60–1
O'Brien, Elizabeth, Lady Inchiquin **2**:256–7
O'Brien, Murrough, first earl of Inchiquin
  (c.1614–74) **1**:525, **1**:526, **2**:27, **2**:59, **2**:83–4,
  2:87, **2**:88, **2**:127, **2**:131, **2**:140, **2**:144, **2**:154,
  2:204, **2**:208, **2**:217–19, **2**:241, **2**:249, **2**:255,
  2:452
O'Brien/Ó Briain Aradh, Terence Albert/Muiri,
  Catholic bishop of Emly (1601–51) **2**:184–9
Ockham, Surrey **2**:547 n. 10
Ockham, Sussex **2**:547 n. 10

O'Clery, Thady **2**:184–9
O'Coghlan, Terence **3**:31
O'Connolly, Owen (d. 1649) **1**:49–50
O'Dempsey, Edmund, Catholic bishop of
  Leighlin (d. 1658) **2**:184–9
Odiham, Hampshire **1**:228
O'Dwyer, Edmund, Catholic bishop of Limerick
  (c.1590–1654) **2**:184–9
O'Farrell, Gregory **2**:184–9
Offord Mills, Huntingdonshire **1**:112
Ogle, John **2**:436
Ogle, Sir William **1**:318, **1**:319 n. 2, **1**:320
Ogleby, Captain **2**:332
Ogleby, Robert **2**:334
Okey, Elizabeth **1**:204–5
Okey, John (bap. 1606, d. 1662) **1**:204, **1**:309,
  1:383, **1**:637, **1**:647–9, **2**:383, **2**:469, **3**:39, **3**:300
  n. 59
  dissolution of Rump Parliament **2**:607–8,
   2:609
  and Putney Debates committee **1**:474–5
Old Castletown, Kildorrery, County Cork **2**:208
Oldfeild, Mr **3**:170
O'Molony, John, Catholic bishop of Killaloe
  (1591–1651) **2**:184–9
O'Neale, Moses **1**:256, **1**:257
O'Neill, Daniel (c.1612?–64) **1**:43, **2**:86
O'Neill, Henry **2**:126, **2**:127, **2**:129
O'Neill/Ó Néill, Hugh Dubh/Aodh Dubh
  (c.1605–c.1660) **2**:177, **2**:180–1, **2**:206,
  2:258–9
O'Neill, Major **2**:164
O'Neill/Ó Néill, Owen Roe/Eoghan Rua (c.1580–
  1649) **2**:71, **2**:95, **2**:99, **2**:126–7, **2**:140, **2**:142,
  2:165, **2**:285
O'Neill, Phelim (officer in Ulster Irish
  army) **2**:181
O'Neill, Sir Phelim Roe/Felim Ruadh (1603–53)
  1:76, **2**:181 n. 4, **2**:730
Ongar, Essex **2**:521
Onslow, Sir Richard (bap. 1601, d. 1664) **3**:182,
  3:358–66, **3**:384
Orchard Close, Swansea **2**:533
O'Reilly/Ó Raghallaigh, Hugh/Aodh, Catholic
  archbishop of Armagh (c.1581–1653)
  2:184–9
Orléans, France **2**:411
Ormond, earls and dukes of, *see* Butler
Ormond Peace (1646), Cromwell's discussion
  of **1**:345–8
Orphans of deceased soldiers, concern
  for **2**:523–6, **2**:528–9
Orpin, Edward **2**:495–6
Orrery, earl of, *see* Boyle
Osborn, Allen **2**:333
Osborn, James **1**:353
Ostend, Netherlands **3**:268, **3**:269, **3**:504, **3**:507

694

GENERAL INDEX

Otes, Essex 1:369 n. 6
Otley, Yorkshire 1:544, 1:553
Ottery St Mary, Devon 1:320 n. 3, 1:332
Oundle, Northamptonshire 1:18
Outwell, Norfolk 2:522
Over Mordington, Berwickshire 1:593
Over Wallop, Hampshire 1:326
Overstreet, John 3:57–8
Overton, Richard 2:59 n. 1
Overton, Robert (1608/9–78/9) 1:lviii n. 19,
  1:377, 1:434, 1:634 n. 4, 2:326, 2:468, 2:469,
  2:479
Owen, Sir Hugh, first baronet (1604–c.1670)
  2:51, 2:52, 3:182
Owen, Sir John, governor of Conwy 1:427 n. 6
Owen, John, vice-chancellor of Oxford
  University (1616–83) 2:424, 2:425, 2:526–7,
  2:531, 2:566–70, 2:591 n. 5, 3:28–9, 3:156,
  3:168, 3:178, 3:288, 3:318
  letters to 2:567–70, 2:584–5, 2:740, 2:741–2,
  3:9–10, 3:432–3
Owen, William 1:624, 1:625, 2:551
Oxenstierna, Axel (1583–1654) 3:50, 3:52–3
Oxford, Oxfordshire 1:127–8, 1:187, 1:205 n. 1,
  1:228, 1:229, 1:263–4, 1:266–7, 1:336, 1:625,
  3:167–8
  Charles I escapes from 1:338
Oxford University
  actions as Chancellor of 2:lxv, 2:422–3,
  2:500–1, 2:529–30, 2:533–4, 2:535–6,
  2:539–40, 2:542–3, 2:550–1, 2:554–7,
  2:566–70, 2:584–5, 2:740, 2:741–2
  Brasenose College 2:500
  OC and 2:47–8
  OC elected as Chancellor of 2:420–1
  OC intercedes for Irish convert from
   Catholicism at 2:411–12
  St John's College 1:3

Packe, Sir Christopher (c.1599–1682) 3:101, 3:102,
  3:103
Packer, William (fl. 1644–62) 1:191 n. 11, 1:362 n. 1,
  1:365, 2:621–2, 3:337
Packerell, Richard 1:18
Paget, William, sixth Baron Paget (1609–78) 2:23
Pakenham, Suffolk 1:372
Palgrave, Sir John 1:97–102, 1:127, 1:128, 1:129,
  1:140, 1:141–2
Palmer, Andrew 1:74
Papist(s) 1:62–3, 1:65, 1:79, 1:84, 1:98, 1:101, 1:514,
  2:27–8, 2:165, 2:378, 2:711, 2:719, 3:246, 3:278,
  3:294–301, 3:473, 3:514; see also Popery;
  Catholics
Papworth, Cambridgeshire 1:104
Parham, baron, see Willoughby
Paris, France 1:407
Parker, George 1:59

Parker, Henry (1604–52) 2:90
Parker, Samuel 1:206 n. 2
Parliament, dissolution of (20 April
  1653) 2:603–21, 2:625–6, 2:632–3, 2:669–77,
  2:692–8
Parrie, Archibald 3:228
Parrie, Richard 3:228
Parsons, Sir William, baronet 1:49
Parson's Charity, Ely 1:13
Partridge, John 1:lviii n. 18
Passage Fort, County Waterford 2:154–5, 2:161
Passerini, Philippi 3:458–9
Patrick/Patricke, William 1:362–3
Patterson, George 2:334
Patterson, Robert 1:132
Paulet, John, fifth marquis of Winchester
  (1598?–1675) 1:322
Paulet, Lord William 2:321 n.4
Paulucci, Lorenzo 3:66
Pauncefote, Grimbald 2:598 n. 7
Pauncefote, Tracy (d. 1659) 2:598, 2:599, 2:661
Peachell, Richard (fl. 1653–9) 2:600
Peake, Sir Robert (c.1605–67) 1:324
Peard, George (bap. 1594, d. 1644/5) 1:28
Peck, Francis (1692–1743) 2:636
Pecke, Samuel 1:478
Peckover, Mathew 1:112–13
Peebles, Peeblesshire 2:385
Peeterson, Reiue 2:257
Peke, Edward 3:169
Peke, Thomas 3:169
Pelham, Peregrine (bap. 1602, d. 1650) 1:61, 1:62,
  1:647–9
Pell, Sir Bartholomew (d. 1671) 1:329–30
Pell, John (1611–85) 3:109, 3:331, 3:346, 3:469,
  3:490, 3:510
Pell, Samuel 3:lii
Pellice, river 3:513
Pembroke, earls of, see Herbert
Pembroke Castle, Pembrokeshire 1:344, 1:424,
  1:530–1, 1:532–4
Pendennis Castle, Cornwall 1:347 n. 12, 2:443,
  2:604, 3:209–10
Penington, Isaac (c.1584–1661) 1:20, 2:11
Penn, Margaret (d. 1682) 3:118
Penn, Sir William (bap. 1621, d. 1670) 2:249–50,
  2:594–5, 2:714–15, 3:115–20, 3:158
  commissions for 3:5–7
  letters to 3:li, 3:liv, 3:lvii, 3:115–17, 3:119–20,
  3:124
Pennant, Thomas (1726–98) 1:126–7
Pennard, Glamorganshire 1:69
Pennere, Andrew 2:333
Penney, Norman 3:520
Pennington, Alderman 1:326
Pennyfather, Thomas 1:527
Penrith, Cumbria 2:445

695

GENERAL INDEX

Penruddock, John (1619–55) 3:li, 3:lvii, 3:167, 3:168, 3:205
Penshurst, Kent 2:607
Pentland Hills, Edinburghshire 2:314
Peppard, George (*fl.* 1641–53) 2:730–1
Perceval/ Percivale, Judith 2:452 n. 1
Perceval/ Percivale, Sir Philip (1605–47) 2:452 n. 1, 3:100
Percevall, cousin 1:200
Percivalle, John 3:100
Percy, Algernon, tenth earl of Northumberland (1602–68) 1:75, 1:350, 1:361–2, 1:429–31
Percy, Henry, Baron Percy of Alnwick 1:36
Perkins, Corporal 2:47
Perre, Paulus Van de (1598–1653) 2:714 n. 2
Persevall, James 1:112–13
Perth, Perthshire 2:lxii, 2:382, 2:388, 2:389, 2:476–8, 2:480–1
Peter/Peters, Hugh (bap. 1598, d. 1660) 1:321 n. 14, 1:542, 2:lx, 2:75, 2:751
and Putney Debates 1:453, 1:458
Peterborough, Cambridgeshire 1:128, 1:142, 1:160, 1:202, 1:226–7
Peterborough, earl of, *see* Mordaunt
Petre, William 2:332
Pettit, Richard 1:104
Petty/Pettus, Maximilian (bap. 1617, d. in or after 1661?) 1:435–6, 1:437, 1:447, 1:449 n. 42
and Putney Debates 1:453, 1:454, 1:458, 1:460, 1:461
Petty, William (1623–87) 3:457
Peyton, Sir Thomas, second baronet (1613–84) 1:644
Phayre/Phaire, Robert (1618/19–82) 1:651, 2:108–9, 2:125–6, 2:133, 2:138, 2:140–1, 2:146, 2:204–5, 3:435
Philip (Philip II of Spain), king of England and Ireland (1527–98) 3:293
Philip IV, king of Spain (1605–65) 2:194, 3:288, 3:291, 3:302, 3:429, 3:436
Philip William, Count Palatine of Neuburg 3:295–6, 3:298 n. 46, 3:303 n. 69
Philiphaugh, Scottish Borders 1:300
Philipps, Sir Erasmus, third baronet (*c.*1623–1697) 3:182
Phillips, Edward (bap. 1630, d. in or after 1696) 3:491
Pichard, Major (not identified, possibly Pritchard) 1:533
Pickering, Benjamin 1:252 n. 2
Pickering, John 3:207
Pickering, John (bap. 1615, d. 1645) 1:183, 1:300–1, 1:310, 1:313, 1:320, 1:323, 1:324, 1:332–3
Pickering, Sir Gilbert, first baronet (1611–68) 1:332–3, 1:567, 2:9, 2:345, 2:732–3, 3:271
Council member 2:686 n. 109, 3:8
Pickering, William (1796–1854) 3:456 n. 11

Piedmont, Savoy 3:471, 3:512, 3:513–14
Pierpoint, Francis (d. 1658) 2:589–90
Pierrepont, Robert, first earl of Kingston (1584–1643) 1:131, 2:589
Pierrepont/Pierrepoint, William (1607/8–78) 1:51, 1:505–6, 1:567
Piggott, Sir Richard (d. 1685) 3:180
Pigot, Gervase (1616–69) 2:635–6, 2:658
Pinerolo, Piedmont, Italy 3:515–16
Pitsum/Pitson, James 1:246
Pitts, Mr 1:268
Playford, Anthony 2:429–30
Plumstead, Norfolk 1:142, 2:522
Plunder
OC seeks to prevent 1:589–91, 2:417–18, 2:466
prohibition of and penalties for 2:156–7
references to 1:114, 1:125, 1:177–8, 1:268, 1:296, 1:299, 1:304, 1:322, 1:534, 1:543, 1:557, 1:676, 1:699, 1:709, 2:111, 2:115, 2:130–1, 2:160, 2:189, 2:221, 2:285, 2:299–300, 2:351
Plunkett, Patrick, (1603–79), Catholic bishop of Meath 2:184–9
Poe, William 1:132
Pollard, Hugh 1:68
Pollard, Sir Hugh, second baronet (1603–66) 1:43
Polwarth, lady, *see* Hume (née Hamilton)
Pontefract, West Yorkshire 1:lvi, 1:561, 1:589, 1:603, 1:605, 1:615–16
Pontefract Castle, West Yorkshire 1:620–1
Popery 1:5–6, 2:194–5, 3:309, 3:394, 3:463, 3:471
Popes, actions of, denounced 3:261, 3:293, 3:299, 3:472
Popham, Alexander (1604/5–69) 2:9–10
Popham, Edward (*c.*1610–51) 1:196 n. 8, 2:58–9
Popish
Army 1:125, 2:286, 2:372
Clergy 2:232
Idolatry 3:246, 3:462
Innovations 2:358
Interest 3:313, 3:322, 3:337, 3:513
Interest abroad 2:285, 3:293, 3:295–6, 3:299, 3:480, 3:514
Party in Ireland 2:129, 2:165–6, 2:182, 2:185, 2:245–7, 2:314, 3:303
Portpatrick, Wigtownshire 3:265–6, 3:267
Porter, Captain 1:206
Portman, John (*fl.* 1652–67) 3:488–9
Portsmouth, Hampshire 2:51
Portugal 3:76, 3:78, 3:80, 3:259, 3:260, 3:261–2
Potter, Edward 1:112–13
Potts, Sir John 1:97–102
Poulakerry, County Tipperary 2:234
Poulton, Thomas 1:625 n. 3
Powell, Colonel 1:532 n. 9
Powick, Worcestershire 2:488
Pownall, Henry 1:554 n. 20
Pownall, Major 1:554

696

GENERAL INDEX

Pownell, Philemon **3**:274
Poyer, David **1**:532–4
Poyer, Elizabeth, née Button **1**:533 n. 12
Poyer, John (d. 1649) **1**:519, **1**:520, **1**:526, **1**:529–30, **1**:533 nn. 12 & 15
Prayer meetings, Army **1**:446–8, **1**:451–2, **1**:453–4, **1**:467–9, **2**:625
Preaching, Cromwell speech about **1**:39–40, **1**:55–6, **1**:66, **1**:69
Prendergast, John **3**:24–5, **3**:502
Presbyterians
   approved by OC **3**:101, **3**:280, **3**:307
   as a distinct political party **3**:709
   as a system of church government **1**:401, **3**:94
   distinguished from Independents **1**:213, **1**:408, **1**:543, **3**:78, **3**:306, **3**:410
   ministers in Northumberland and Durham, **3**:322–4
Presbyterian clergy in Scotland, *see* Clergy
Preston, Colonel **1**:293
Preston, Sir Robert **3**:31
Preston, Thomas, first Viscount Tara (1585–1655) **2**:27, **2**:255
Preston, Lancashire **1**:542, **1**:547 n. 12, **1**:548, **1**:549 n. 33, **1**:551, **1**:553, **1**:554–6, **1**:558, **1**:579 n. 7
Price, Hugh **3**:183
Price, Richard **2**:69–70
Pride, Thomas (d. 1658) **1**:300–1, **1**:399–402, **1**:554–5, **1**:647, **2**:326
Prideaux, Edmond (1601–59) **1**:217 n. 15, **1**:245, **1**:247, **1**:335, **2**:301, **3**:185
Prideaux, John, bishop of Worcester (1578–1650) **1**:42
Prince, Thomas (*fl.* 1630–57) **2**:59
Pringle, George **2**:332
Pringle, Thomas **2**:334
Prinne, Mr **1**:88
Prior's Hill Fort, Bristol **1**:310–12
Prisoners of War
   1:264–5, **1**:269, **1**:293–5, **1**:298, **1**:299–300, **1**:324, **1**:412, **1**:548–50, **1**:554, **1**:556–60, **1**:571–3, **1**:600, **1**:624, **2**:70–2, **2**:85–6, **2**:142–4, **2**:153, **2**:164, **2**:180–2, **2**:206, **2**:322–4, **2**:330–5, **2**:335–7, **2**:341–2, **2**:346, **2**:348–9, **2**:354–5, **2**:362–3, **2**:384–6, **2**:393–4, **2**:414–16, **2**:467–70, **2**:489–91, **2**:501–4, **2**:621–2
   exchanges of **1**:571–3, **1**:624–6, **2**:176–8, **2**:180–2, **2**:362–3, **2**:416–17
   OC's complaint about mistreatment of, by the Scots **2**:415–16
   OC's (mis)treatment of **2**:336–8, **2**:348–9, **2**:363
Proctor, Robert **1**:9
Propagation of the Gospel **2**:623, **2**:673–4
Propositions (loans to Parliament, 1642), Cromwell speech about **1**:78–9, **1**:80, **1**:82

Providence, Cromwell's belief in **1**:626–33, **2**:128–30, **2**:321–2, **2**:324–5, **2**:346–7, **2**:664–8, **2**:678–9, **2**:688–91, **2**:699, **2**:705–10
Providence, Rhode Island **2**:531
Providence Plantations, Rhode Island **3**:183–4
Prynne, John **1**:535, **1**:536
Prynne, William (1600–69) **1**:24, **3**:327–8
Pryse, Sir Richard, second baronet (*fl.* 1651–7) **3**:182
Puller, Isaac **1**:283–5
Purdon, Nicholas **2**:139, **2**:141
Purefoy, William (c.1580–1659) **1**:73, **2**:11, **2**:78
Puritan(s), Cromwell's only use of the word **3**:309, **3**:462
Pury, Thomas (c.1590–1666) **2**:572
Putney, Surrey **1**:liv, **1**:433
Putney Debates **1**:lxv, **1**:435–75
Puttick and Simpson, auctioneers **2**:521
Pye, Captain John **2**:601
Pye, John (minister) **3**:320, **3**:321, **3**:322–3
Pye, Sir John, baronet, of Twickenham and Hone (c.1626–c.1697) **2**:601–3
Pye, Sir Robert (bap. 1585, d. 1662) **2**:602
Pye, Sir Robert (c.1622–1701) **1**:272, **1**:300–1, **1**:395, **2**:602
Pym, John (1584–1643) **1**:4–5, **1**:6, **1**:25, **1**:38, **1**:41, **1**:56–7, **1**:59
Pyott, Edward (d. 1670) **3**:318

Quarrel with [earl of] Manchester, its origins **1**:189–92, **1**:202–4, **1**:208
   the Quarrel itself **1**:210–54, **1**:339–41
Quarter, denial of, at Drogheda **2**:91–3, **2**:93–101

Raghill/Reghill Castle, Ireland **2**:205, **2**:208–9
Raglan, Monmouthshire **1**:346
Raglan Castle, Monmouthshire **1**:504
Rainborowe/Rainborow, Thomas (d. 1648) **1**:lxiii, **1**:300–1, **1**:308, **1**:310–12, **1**:313, **1**:408, **1**:411, **1**:480, **1**:491 n. 5
   in Robert Huntington's *Sundry Reasons* **1**:540, **1**:541
   letters from **1**:399–402
   and Putney Debates **1**:439, **1**:442, **1**:443, **1**:450, **1**:453, **1**:455, **1**:456, **1**:457, **1**:458, **1**:459, **1**:460, **1**:462, **1**:463, **1**:468, **1**:473, **1**:474–5
Rainborowe/Rainsborough, William (*fl.* 1639–73) **1**:462, **1**:394 & n. 16
Rainton, Sir Nicholas (1569–1646) **2**:602
Rainton, Nicholas (c.1638–96) **2**:601–3
Ralegh, Sir Walter (1554–1618) **2**:238, **2**:239
Ramsey, Mr **3**:170
Ramsey, Huntingdonshire **1**:8 n. 4, **1**:18
Ranelagh, viscount, *see* Jones
Rankin, Robert **2**:334
Rathmines, Co.Dublin **2**:57, **2**:71, **2**:251

697

GENERAL INDEX

Raven, Jo 1:112–13
Ravenscroft, James 1:51–4
Rawlins, Thomas 1:282
Raymond, John 1:300–2
Reade, Thomas (1612–62) 1:527, 1:554–5, 3:125–6
Reading, Berkshire 1:liv, 1:lxii–lxiii, 1:114, 1:204,
 1:227, 1:229, 1:238, 2:571
Reading Debates 1:410–30
Records, Scottish government, *see* Registers
Redbraes, Berwickshire 2:407, 2:409–10
Redhill Field 1:230, 1:235
Reed, David 2:335
Reformadoes 1:351
Registers, Scottish government, seized by
 Cromwell 2:436–8, 2:447–9
Rehill, County Tipperary 2:205
Reid, Andrew (d. 1658) 2:487
Release of prisoners, Cromwell opposes 1:200–2
Remonstrance, parliamentary (Feb. 1657)
 3:339–45
Remonstrants (or Protestors), as hard-line
 Scottish Covenanters 2:376–9
Reynolds, Edward, bishop of Norwich
 (1599–1676) 2:424, 2:425
Reynolds, Sir John (1625–57) 2:36, 2:113–14,
 2:147, 2:152, 2:153–4, 2:207, 2:209–10, 2:216,
 2:251
Reynolds, Sir Robert (1600/1–78) 1:87, 2:50
Reynolds, Thomas 3:221, 3:222
Rhodes, Captain 3:175
Rhos, Wales 1:536
Ribble, river 1:548, 1:553–4
Rich (d. 1653/4) 1:166
Rich, Henry, first earl of Holland (bap. 1590,
 d. 1649) 1:29, 2:18, 2:60
Rich, Isabella 1:29
Rich, John 2:333
Rich, Nathaniel (d. 1700x02) 1:311, 1:383, 2:49,
 2:261, 2:473, 2:480, 2:482, 3:279
 letters from 1:399–402
 and Putney Debates committee 1:474–5
Rich, Robert, second earl of Warwick
 (1587–1658) 1:505–6, 3:263
Rich, Robert (1634–58) 3:263, 3:335
Rich, Sir Robert 1:93
Richardson, Sir Thomas 1:97–102
Richbell, Jeffrey 1:312 n. 62
Richman, Thomas 2:333
Richmond, duke of, *see* Stuart
Rigby, Alexander (bap. 1594, d. 1650) 1:73
Ringsend, Co.Dublin 2:liii, 2:75
Rinuccini, Gianbattista, archbishop 1:347
Riots, suppression of in the Cambridgeshire
 fens 2:657–8
Ritson, Joseph 2:298 n. 2
Rivers, Sir Thomas, second baronet (d. 1657) 3:182
Roberts, Thomas 1:513–15

Roberts, Sir William (1604–62) 2:523, 3:181
Robinson, John 2:436, 2:442
Robinson, Luke (bap. 1610, d. 1669) 1:346 n. 5, 2:11
Robinson, Nathaniel 1:503, 2:3–4, 2:8
Robotham, Robert 1:394 n. 16
Robson, Robert (d. 1659) 1:26 n. 1, 1:112–13
Roch, Captain 1:533
Roche, David 2:204
Roche, Maurice, third Viscount Fermoy
 (1597–1670) 3:210
Roche, Redmond 2:159–60
Roche, Tibbot 3:210–11
Roche family 2:208
Rochester, earl of, *see* Wilmot
Rochester, Kent 2:542
Rockby, Colonel 2:337
Rocket, John 3:66–7
Rockingham, Northamptonshire 1:128
Rodes, Sir Edward 1:549–51, 1:558, 1:605
Roe, Thomas 1:196
Roger, Sir (codename, not identified) 1:611
Rogers, Christopher 2:47–8
Rogers, John (bap. 1627) 3:488, 3:489
Rogers, Major 3:176
Rogers, Thomas 2:537
Rogers, Wroth (d. *c.*1684) 3:175
Rokeby ,Thomas (d. 1650) 2:328
Rolfe/Rolph, William 1:512 n. 7
Rolle, Henry (1589/90–1656) 2:10, 3:106,
 3:164 n. 6
Rolston, James 2:334
Roman Catholic clergy, *see* Clergy
Roman Catholicism, Hierarchy of 1:20
Romford, Essex 1:15, 1:155
Rood, Edward (d. 1689) 2:530
Roosevelt, Theodore 1:lii n. 2, 1:165 n. 1
Rooth, Patrick 3:57–8
Rooth, Richard 3:124 n. 3
Roots, Ivan 1:xxxix–xl, 3:xlviii
Roots and Branches petition, Cromwell speech
 about 1:20
Roscrea, County Tipperary 2:243
Roslin, Edinburghshire 2:382
Rosse, Lieutenant 2:415
Rosslare, County Wexford 2:114
Roth, Edward 2:227
Rothes, earls of, *see* Leslie
Rous, Francis (1580/1–1659) 1:22, 1:405–6,
 2:555–6, 2:584–5, 3:8
Rowe, Owen (1592/3–1661) 1:196 n. 8
Rowe, Theophilus 3:327, 3:419
Rowe, Thomas 1:196 n. 8
Rowe, Sir William, of Higham Hall 1:162–3
Rowe, William, scoutmaster general 1:580,
 1:583, 1:587, 1:593, 1:629 n. 20, 1:636, 2:163,
 3:327, 3:351, 3:419, 3:424
 instructions for 1:429–31

698

GENERAL INDEX

letter attributed to 1:606–7, 1:608–13
as possible scribe 1:562, 1:599
Rowles, Mary 2:548–9
Rowles, William (*fl.* 1646–52) 2:548
Roxburgh, earl of, *see* Ker
Roy, Henry 2:335
Roy, Robert 2:334
Royal College of Physicians, Ireland 2:544 n. 5
Royalists, a term Cromwell never uses; *but see*
Enemy; Delinquents; Malignants
Royston, Hertfordshire 1:399
Rudderford, James 2:335
Rudderford, Robert 2:332
Rudderford, William 2:332
Rufford Abbey, Nottinghamshire 3:166
Rugeley, John 3:336
Rugeley, Simon (1597/98–1665) 3:336–7
Rumsey, Mr 1:521
Rumsey, Sisley 1:55 n. 1
Rumsey, Walter (1584–1651) 1:56
Rupert, prince and count Palatine of the Rhine
and duke of Cumberland 1:97, 1:98, 1:197,
1:198, 1:205, 1:232, 1:260–1, 1:271, 1:307,
1:313–14, 2:285, 2:314, 2:720, 3:208
Rushworth/Rushforth, John (*c.*1612–90) 1:249,
1:252, 1:281, 1:286, 1:287, 1:306, 1:349–50,
1:365–6, 1:368, 1:495, 1:497, 1:574 n. 2, 3:468
letters to 2:42–3
signatures on behalf of OC 2:278, 2:288,
2:292, 2:295
Russell, Elizabeth (1637–87) 1:500 n. 10, 2:546
Russell, Frances, née Cromwell (other married
name Rich), Lady Russell (bap. 1638,
d. 1720) 3:263, 3:335
Russell, Sir Francis, second baronet (*c.*1616–64)
1:276, 1:283–5, 1:500, 1:567, 2:546, 3:180,
3:518 n. 6
Russell, Francis, fourth earl of Bedford (bap.
1587, d. 1641) 1:30, 1:35, 1:97–102, 1:193 n. 4,
1:199, 1:321, 2:621
Russell, James (*c.*1610–55) 2:662–3
Russet-coated captains, Cromwell's preference
for 1:164–8
Ruthin, Denbighshire 1:427
Rutland, dukes and earls of, *see* Manners
Rycaut, Sir Paul (1629–1700) 3:244
Rye, Mr 2:450

Sabbath observance, Cromwell speech about
1:21
Sadler, John (1615–74) 1:66, 2:168–71, 2:262, 2:263
Sadler/Sadleir, Thomas 2:157–8, 2:233–4
Saffron Walden, Essex 1:liv, 1:lxii, 1:174 n. 11,
1:378, 1:380–2, 1:391, 1:393
New Model Army debate 1:384–8, 1:389
St Mary the Virgin Church 1:386
Saffron Walden Debates 1:384–9, 1:398

St Albans, Hertfordshire 1:94, 1:226, 1:227,
1:399–400, 1:417 nn. 24 & 25, 3:lii
St Aubyn, John 1:303–5
St Christopher, Barbados 2:560
St Christopher's, West Indies 3:195–6
St Fagans' 1:533 n. 12
St Ives, Huntingdonshire 1:liii, 1:liv, 1:3, 1:10, 1:30
St Jago de Cuba, Cuba 3:233
St Jago de la Vega, Jamaica (later Spanish Town)
3:275
St John, Sir Beauchamp (1594–1667) 3:181
St John, Mrs 1:14–17
St John, Oliver (*c.*1598–1673) 1:14, 1:168–9, 1:347
n. 16, 2:10, 2:433, 2:541, 2:627, 3:170, 3:358–9
appointment as Commissioner of
Treasury 3:106
commissioner in Scotland 2:651 n. 2
conversations with 2:267–73, 2:516–19
letters signed by 1:429–31
letters to 1:565
St John, Oliver (d. 1638) 1:15
St John's Hospital, Huntingdon 1:5
St Johnstones, *see* Perth, Perthshire
St Julians, Newport 1:523
St Lawrence, Christopher 2:89–90
St Leger, Sir William 2:257 n. 2
St Nicholas, Thomas (bap. 1602–68) 1:633–4
St Peter's Church, Drogheda 2:97, 2:98
Saints
OC's appeal to those in Scotland who
are 2:278–9
OC finds them divided 2:728–9
OC's term for God's chosen ones, 1:602,
1:631, 2:190, 2:193–5, 2:278–9, 2:286,
2:342, 2:357, 2:361, 2:463, 2:521, 2:678–80,
2:699–702, 2:711, 3:67, 3:315, 3:323, 3:345,
3:377, 3:483
Salisbury, earl of, *see* Cecil
Salisbury, Wiltshire 1:227, 1:260, 1:261–2, 3:164,
3:167
Salmon, Edward (*fl.* 1646–61) 2:742–3
Saluzzo, Marquisate of 3:515
Salway, Richard (bap. 1615, d. 1686) 1:505,
2:726–7, 3:41, 3:61
commissioner in Scotland 2:651 n. 2
conversations with 2:626–7
Sample, William 2:334
Samuel, Sir Richard 1:69–70
Sancroft, William, archbishop of Canterbury
(1617–93) 2:277–8
Sanders/Saunders, Colonel Thomas (1610–1695)
2:49, 2:473, 2:480, 3:39
Sandown Castle, Sandown, Isle of Wight 2:600
Sandwich, earl of, *see* Montagu
Sandwich, Kent 3:151–3, 3:168
Sandys, Miles 1:97–102, 1:183, 1:193, 1:194
Sandys, Sir Miles 1:183 n. 6, 1:193 n. 7

699

GENERAL INDEX

Sanford, J. L. 1:262
Sanford, Theophilus 2:35–6
Sankey/Zanchie/Zanchy, Sir Hierome/Hierom/
Jerome (c.1621–c.1687) 2:48, 2:163–4, 2:215
Santa Cruz, Canary Islands 3:429
Santa Marta, Colombia 3:229
Santo Domingo, Hispaniola 3:234
Santry, barons, *see* Barry
Saul, King of Israel 2:531
Saumur, France 2:411
Saunders, Mary (c.1627–1707) 3:318
Saunders, Thomas 1:520–2, 3:300 n. 59
Savile, Sir George, first marquis of Halifax
(1633–95) 3:166, 3:167
Sawbridge, George 3:69, 3:83
Sawtry, Cambridgeshire 1:liii
Saye and Sele, viscount, *see* Fiennes
Sayers, James 2:333
Scarborough Castle, Yorkshire 1:620
Scariffhollis, County Donegal 2:100, 3:41 n. 6
Scilly Isles 2:451
Scobell, Henry (bap. 1610, d. 1660) 2:610–11,
3:56, 3:345
Scot, Francis 2:333
Scot, James 2:332
Scot, Jonas 3:216–17
Scot, Robert 2:332
Scot, Captain Walter 2:332
Scot, Walter 2:335
Scot, William 2:334
Scotland
analysis of OC's writings from 2:lvi–lvii
civil war in (1644) 1:300
disbandment of its armies 1:22, 1:37–8
discussed in OC's speeches as Lord
Protector 3:139, 3:149, 3:153–4, 3:301, 3:402,
3:480–2
involvement in religious reforms of 1641–2
1:23–4
Kings visit to (1641) 1:33–5
OC's campaigns in (late 1648) 1:577–632,
passim
OC's campaigns in (1650–1) 2:265–491,
passim
OC's continuing engagement with, and letters
to 2:505–6, 2:506–7, 2:511–12, 2:519–20,
2:536, 2:591–2, 2:602–3, 2:651, 2:741, 2:743,
2:748, 3:22–3, 3:36 – 7, 3:38–9, 3:64–5,
3:113–14, 3:211–12, 3:236–7, 3:264–6, 3:272–3
OC's dealings with the government of
1:429–31, 1:578–84, 1:589–92, 1:597–603
OC's discussion of the politics of
(1646) 1:345–8
OC's victory over the Engagers and
occupation of Edinburgh 1:545–60,
1:562–4, 1:571–3, 1:575–8, 1:585–9, 1:592–7
overviews 1:lviii, 2:lxii–lxiv, 3:lvi

and the post-war settlement of 1646–7 1:346–8,
1:360–2, 1:429–32
and the Preston campaign 1648 1:544–64,
1:571–3
reactions to regicide in 2:25–6
relations with, OC speech about 1:62–3
Scots, OC seeks advice on their intentions
(1641) 1:22–5
Scotland, background to OC's campaigns
in 2:lxii–lxiv
Scotland, OC authorises the seizure of lands
in 2:651
support for widows in 3:220–1
Scott, Anna/Anne (1651–1732) 3:110
Scott, Colonel 1:594
Scott, Francis, second earl of Buccleuch
(1626–51) 3:110
Scott, Margaret (d. 1688) 3:110
Scott, Mary (b. August 1647) 3:110
Scott, Peter 1:77
Scott, Thomas (d. 1648) 2:548
Scott/Scot, Thomas (d. 1660) 2:11, 2:54, 2:128–9,
2:145–6, 2:614, 3:83
Scott, Sir Walter 2:298 n. 2
Scott, Sir William 3:110–11
Scottish troops in Ulster, Cromwell speech
about 1:76
Scringer, William 2:331
Scripture (general references) 1:246, 1:532–3,
2:194, 2:239, 2:357–9, 2:678–9, 2:681–2,
2:699–700, 2:710–11, 3:138, 3:196, 3:219,
3:291, 3:305–6, 3:351, 3:355, 3:373, 3:393,
3:492, 3:541
for specific citations from, *see* the separate
Index of Biblical Citations
Scroggs, Joseph 1:113
Scrope/Scroop, Adrian (1601–60) 1:344 n. 4,
1:345 n. 8, 1:527, 1:558, 1:647–9, 2:45, 2:47,
2:295–6, 2:587–8, 2:748–9
Scudamore, Mary 3:335
Scudamore, Viscount 3:335
Searle, Daniel (*fl.* 1616–74) 2:560–1, 3:60–1,
3:228–9, 3:234–5
Seatoun, M. 2:451
Sebirel, Simon 3:161–2
Sedgwick, Obadiah 1:252 n. 2
Sedgwick, Robert (bap. 1613, d. 1656) 3:186,
3:273–4, 3:277
Sedgwick, William (bap. 1609, d. 1663/4) 1:258
Seely, John 2:100–1
Selby, John 1:180 n. 1
Selden, John (1584–1654) 2:627, 2:629
Self-Denying Ordinance 1:249–51, 1:251–3,
1:253–4, 1:256–7, 1:259
Sempery, Thomas 2:250
Seton, Charles, second earl of Dunfermerline
(1615–72) 1:346–7

700

GENERAL INDEX

Seton, George, third earl of Winton (1584–1650) 1:601
Severn, river 2:486, 2:488, 2:490
Severn, Virginia 3:227
Severne, Roger (d. 1679) 2:541–2
Seward, W. 1:202 n. 1, 1:203 nn. 5, 6 & 7
Sexby, Edward (c.1616–58) 1:422, 1:437–8, 3:302 n. 64
  conspiracy 3:283, 3:288
  and Putney Debates 1:458, 1:459, 1:463, 1:468
Seyer, Samuel 3:453
Seymour, Henry (bap. 1612, d. 1687) 3:43–5
Seymour, William, first marquis of Hertford and second duke of Somerset (1587–1660) 1:35, 1:336–7, 3:44
Shaftesbury, Dorset 1:260, 1:295, 1:296
Shaftesbury, earl of, see Cooper
Shakespeare, William 2:195 n. 50
Shannon, river 2:166, 2:249
Shannon, Viscount, see Boyle
Shapcote, Robert (b. 1621, d. before 1690) 3:176
Sharlston, Yorkshire 2:426
Shaw, Berkshire 1:230, 1:239
Shawe Side 1:230
Shawefeild 1:236, 1:248, 1:255
Sheffeild/Sheffield, Thomas 1:300–1, 1:383, 1:385–6, 1:394
Sheffield, Edmund, second earl of Mulgrave (1611–58) 1:570, 2:10, 2:12, 3:218
Sheffield, South Yorkshire 1:223, 1:225
Shelburne, Thomas 2:230–1
Sheldon, Gilbert, archbishop of Canterbury (1598–1677) 1:404 n. 8
Shelford House, Nottinghamshire 1:224
Shelton, Robert (d. 1642) 2:554
Shelton, Thomas 1:384
Shelton, Thomas (fl. 1650–2) 2:554–5
Sherborne, Dorset 1:298, 1:307
Sherburn, Richard 1:547–8
Sherland, Christopher (1594–1632) 1:5
Sherman, Elizabeth 1:9
Sherwood Forest, Nottinghamshire 3:65–6
Shields, Ersby 2:334
Shipton Moyne, Gloucestershire 3:446
Shrewsbury, Shropshire 1:227, 3:113–14, 3:162–3
Shuttleworth, Edward 1:546 n. 6
Sibbald, Captain 2:331
Sidney/Sydney, Algernon (1623–83) 1:271, 1:282, 2:276, 2:607–9
Sidney, Philip, Lord Lisle, third earl of Leicester (1619–98) 2:9–10, 3:8, 3:198
Sidney, Robert, second earl of Leicester (1595–1677) 1:49, 1:70, 2:607–9
Sieges and places stormed
  (1643) Wakefield 1:122
  (1643) Burghley House 1:138
  (1644) Hillesden 1:187–8

(1644) Tickhill 1:223–4
(1644) Newbury 1:228–36
(1645) Bletchingdon 1:265, 1:267–8
(1645) Farringdon House 1:272–5
(1645) Bristol 1:300–18
(1645) Winchester 1:318–20
(1645) Basing 1:322–6
(1645) Longford 1:323–30
(1648) Pembroke 1:516–24, 1:529–34
(1648) Haverfordwest 1:535–6
(1648) Berwick 1:577–8, 1:584, 1:586–7, 1:594
(1648) Carlisle 1:575–6, 1:584, 1:594
(1648) Pontefract 1:603–6, 1:613–19, 1:634–5
(1649) Drogheda 2:91–9, 2:101–4
(1649) Wexford 2:104–8, 2:110–18
(1649) New Ross 2:119–30
(1649) Waterford 2:147–56
(1649–50) Duncannon 2:142–3, 2:154, 2:161–5
(1650) Cahir 2:212, 2:215
(1650) Kiltonan 2:215
(1650) Goldenbridge 2:215
(1650) Dundrum 2:215
(1650) Kilkenny 2:217–27
(1650) Clonmel 2:233–6
(1650) Edinburgh Castle 2:351–62
(1651) Stirling 2:364–5
Simes, Major 2:230, 2:232
Simon, Thomas (bap. 1618, d. 1665) 2:419–20
Sinclare, William 2:334
Sindercombe, Miles (d. 1657) 3:331
Sinnis, William 2:333
Sinnott, Colonel David 2:lv, 2:104–8, 2:110–12, 2:114
Sittington, mother 1:353–4
Skeiper, Captain 2:416–17
Sken, John 2:334
Skippon, Philip (d. 1660) 1:207–10, 1:276, 1:308, 1:311, 1:360–1, 1:377–83, 1:388–97, 1:576, 2:9, 3:154, 3:155, 3:251, 3:252
  and Bristol 1:512
  commissioner for trial of King 1:647
  Council member 3:8
  letters to Speaker Lenthall 1:388–91
  and New Model Army debate 1:385, 1:386–7, 1:388
Skipton, Yorkshire 1:544, 1:553, 1:571 n. 2
Slaney, river 2:114
Sleaford, Lincolnshire 1:179, 1:197, 1:202–4
Sligo, County Sligo 2:166
Slingsby, Arthur 1:293
Slingsby, Robert 1:293 n. 13
Slingsby, Walter 1:293 n. 13
Smallwood, Thomas (d. 1667) 3:65–6
Smith, Captain George 2:332
Smith, George 2:334
Smith/Smyth, Henry (b. 1619/20, d. in or after 1668) 1:647–9

701

GENERAL INDEX

Smith, Major 1:275
Smith, Mr 2:454
Smithick (now Falmouth), Cornwall 3:209
Smithsby, Thomas 1:17 n. 26
Smithson, George 1:554
Smithwick, Henry 2:138, 2:175
Smythe, John 3:468
Smythsby, George 3:116, 3:117
Soley, Thomas 2:492
Sollicitor, Mr 1:326
Somerset, duke of, *see* Seymour
Somerset, Edward, earl of Glamorgan,
    later second marquess of Worcester
    (d. 1667) 1:498, 1:504, 2:43–4, 2:194
Somerset, Henry, first duke of Beaufort
    (1629–1700) 2:439, 2:440
Somersham, Huntingdonshire 1:30, 1:33
Sotheron Estcourt, G. T. J. 3:446
South Molton, Devon 3:164
Southampton, earl of, *see* Wriothesley
Southampton, Hampshire 2:4
Southampton Water, Hampshire 1:405
Southesk, earl of, *see* Carnegie
Spain
    fear of support for Irish Catholics from
        2:194
    Irish exiled troops in 3:108, 3:435–6
    Lord Protector's relations with 3:59, 3:69,
        3:80 n. 44, 3:101, 3:197, 3:223, 3:256–9,
        3:278–80, 3:288, 3:294–7, 3:439, 3:472–81
Spalding, Samuel 1:104, 1:112–13
Spalding, Lincolnshire 1:118, 1:160
Speeches, Cromwell's
    recorded speeches analysed 1:liv–lv, 1:lxi–lxiv,
        2:liv–lvii, 3:xli–lx
    for individual speeches, *see* the list of contents
        in each volume
Speen, Berkshire 1:229, 1:230
Speldhurst, Kent 2:749
Spelman, John (Hunstanton) 1:97 n. 5, 1:99
Spelman, John (Narborough) 1:97–102
Spence, Alexander 2:334
Spence, Joseph 3:245–6
Spencer, John 1:421 n. 38
Spice Islands 3:501
Spittlehouse, John (bap. 1612, d. in or after
    1657) 2:687
Sprigg/Sprigge, Joshua (bap. 1618, d.
    1684) 1:lvii–lviii, 1:299, 1:300, 1:318, 1:319,
    1:321 n. 15, 1:542
Spring, Sir William (1613–1654) 1:102, 1:107,
    1:143–7, 1:164–8, 1:171–6, 1:283–5
Squibb, Arthur (d. 1679/80) 2:663, 3:399–400
Stafford, James 2:111, 2:112–13, 2:115
Stafford, Staffordshire 1:558
Staine/Stane, Richard(c.1608–80) 1:179 n. 3,
    1:180 n. 5, 1:183, 1:194, 2:521

Staine/Stane, William (1610–80) 1:179–80, 1:194
    n. 3, 1:474–5, 2:521, 2:530
Stainer, Charles L. 1:xxxix, 1:xl, 3:xlviii
    his edition analysed 1:xxxix–xl, 2:xli–xliii,
        3:xxxii–xxxiv
Stamford, Lincolnshire 1:117, 1:129, 1:130, 1:160
Stanborowe/Stanbrow, Henry (d. c.1644–6)
    2:594
Stanground/Stoneground Peterborough,
    Cambs 1:285
Stanhope, Philip, second earl of Chesterfield
    (1633–1714) 3:517
Stanley, James, seventh earl of Derby (1607–51)
    2:497
Stanley, John 2:5–6
Stansted Mountfitchet, Essex 1:154
Stapelton, Robert 2:14, 2:15, 2:16, 2:19
Stapilton, Mr 1:580–1
Stapleton, John 1:17 n. 26
Stapleton, Sir Philip (bap. 1603, d. 1647) 1:17 n. 26,
    1:100, 1:165 n. 1, 1:351, 1:420 n. 32, 1:492–3, 1:540
Stapleton, Somerset 1:308
Stapley, Anthony (bap. 1590, d. 1655) 2:11,
    2:213–14, 2:686 n. 109
Starkey, Thomas 1:10
Staveley, Thomas 1:545
Stawell, Sir John 1:53
Stearne/Sterne, John (1624–69) 2:544
Steele, William (1610–80) 2:263, 3:155
Stephens, Nathaniel 1:217 n. 15
Stephens, Richard 2:551 n. 1
Stephens, Thomas (b. c.1624) 2:551–2
Sterling, Robert 1:256, 1:257, 2:242, 2:244,
    2:247–8, 2:253
Sterlyn, James 2:331
Sterry, Peter (1613–72) 1:301 n. 3, 2:756
Stevens, Mr 1:245, 1:247, 1:249, 1:256
Steward, Alexander 2:332
Steward, Arthur 2:332
Steward, James 2:332
Steward, John 2:333
Steward, Joseph 2:331
Steward, Sir Thomas (d. 1636) 1:13, 2:595
Steward, Cornet Walter 2:332
Steward, Walter 2:334
Steward, William (d. 1660) 2:63–4, 2:594
Stewart, John, first earl of Traquair
    (c.1599–1659) 1:602
Stewart/Stuart, Sir William 1:76
Stile, William (*fl.* 1647–60) 2:743–4
Stirke, Captain 2:53
Stirling, earls of, *see* Alexander
Stirling, Sir George (c.1612–67) 2:741
Stirling, Stirlingshire 1:593, 2:317, 2:385, 2:400,
    2:448, 2:480, 2:481
    letters concerning exchange of prisoners
        2:362–3

702

GENERAL INDEX

march to 2:364–5
siege of 2:lxii, 2:363
Stirling Bridge 1:584, 1:587–8
Stoakes/Stokes, John (c.1610–65) 3:511–12
Stockholm, Sweden 3:51
Stokes, Luke 3:234, 3:274
Stone, Henry 1:558 n. 54
Stonyhurst, Lancashire 1:547–8
Stonyhurst House, Lancashire 1:554
Storey/Story, Robert (d. 1652) 1:10 nn. 9 & 13
Story, George 1:9
Storye, Elizabeth 1:10 n. 11
Storye, James (1588–1660) 1:9–12
Storye, Walter 1:10
Strachan, Archibald (d. 1652) 1:582, 1:587, 1:593, 2:lxiii, 2:302, 2:304, 2:365, 2:385, 2:392
letters to 2:376–9
Stradling, Sir Henry 1:533
Stradling, John 1:533
Strafford, earl of, see Wentworth
Strafford, William 2:106 n. 2
Strangways, Sir John (1584–1666) 1:20
Stratford upon Avon, Warwickshire 2:484
Stratton, baron, see Berkeley
Straughan, Robert 2:333
Streater, John (c.1620–77) 2:605–6, 2:607
Streatten, Lieutenant 2:400
Strick, John 2:53 n. 4
Strickland, Walter (1598?–1671) 1:640 n. 5, 2:433, 2:541, 2:726, 2:738, 3:44, 3:271, 3:320, 3:321, 3:511
conversations with 3:241
Council member 2:686 n. 109, 3:8
Strickland, Sir William, first baronet (c.1596–1673) 2:50, 3:181
Stringer, Thomas 2:426–7
Strode, William (bap. 1594, d. 1645) 1:19, 1:49, 1:59
Stuart, James, fourth duke of Lennox and first duke of Richmond (1612–55) 1:336–7
Stubber, Peter 2:79–80
Style, Sir Thomas, second baronet (1624–1702) 3:181
Suckling, Sir John 1:36
Suffolk, earl of 1:346 n. 5
Suir, river 2:147, 2:152, 2:153, 2:208–9, 2:210, 2:215
Sulgrave, Northamptonshire 1:207
Summerall, Patrick 2:400
Surrender Articles
(1645) Bletchingdon 1:267–8
(1645) Langford 1:329–30
(1646) Pembroke 1:532–4
(1649) New Ross 2:124–5, 2:136
(1650) Fethard 2:202–3
(1650) Cahir 2:213–14
(1650) Kilkenny 2:225–7

(1650) 'for the Protestants in Ireland' 2:224–8, 2:253–5
(1650) Clonmel 2:259–60
(1651) Perth 2:477–8
(1655) Jamaica 3:231–4
importance of honouring 1:336–7, 1:348–9, 1:639
Sutherland, Alexander, first Lord Duffus 2:476–7
Sutton, Bedfordshire 1:114
Surrey, earl of, see Howard
Swaffham Bulbeck, Cambridgeshire 2:621–2
Swaffham Prior, Cambridgeshire 1:193 n. 6, 2:621–2
Swain, Francis 1:544 n. 2
Swaine, Henry 1:544 n. 2
Swallow, Robert 1:153
Swallowfield, Berkshire 1:229
Swansea, Glamorgan 2:532–3
Sweden
English alliance with 3:13–14, 3:46–53, 3:54–6, 3:448–9, 3:458–9
English relations with 2:726–7, 2:731–7, 2:744–7
Sweeney, Tony 2:183
Swinstead, Lincolnshire 1:160
Swinton, John 2:392, 2:398–9
Swiss Confederacy 3:295
Swynfen/Swinfen, John (1613–94) 1:481, 1:482, 1:505
Sydenham, John 2:442
Sydenham, William (bap. 1615, d. 1661) 2:545–6, 2:600–1, 2:641, 3:271, 3:343
appointment as Commissioner of Treasury 3:106
conversations with 3:241
Council member 2:686 n. 109, 3:8
Sykes, William 1:635
Syler, Edmund 2:469
Symonds, Richard (b. 1609, d. in or after 1658) 1:62
Symons/Simmonds, Thomas 1:97–102, 1:112–13
Symontoun, William 1:24
Syon House, Isleworth, Middlesex 2:liii, 2:551
Syresham, Northamptonshire 1:206
Syston, Lincolnshire 1:119, 1:131
Syston Park, Lincolnshire 1:130

Taaffe, Lucas 2:119–23, 2:124–5, 2:127, 2:188 n. 35
Taaffe, Peter 2:98, 2:104
Taaffe, Theobald, first earl of Carlingford (c.1603–77) 1:56–7, 2:27, 2:90, 2:98, 2:165, 3:303
Tangiers, North Africa 3:269
Tangye, Sir Richard (1833–1906) 1:550, 1:605, 3:248, 3:263

703

GENERAL INDEX

Tanner, Thomas, bishop of St Asaph 1:156
Tate, Zouch (1606–50) 1:211, 1:213, 1:217, 1:239, 1:240, 1:241, 1:245, 1:248, 1:249, 1:251, 1:254–5, 1:259
Taunton, Somerset 1:291–2, 1:339 n. 2
Tavistock, Devon 1:4–5, 2:605
Taw, river 2:660 n. 2
Tay, river 2:478
Taylor, Austin (1858–1955) 1:165 n. 1
Taylor, Thomas 2:136 n. 1
Tecroghan, County Meath 2:56, 2:95
Tecroghan Castle, County Meath 2:267
Teme, river 2:488
Temple, James (1606–c.1674) 1:647–9
Temple, Sir John (1600–77) 1:505–6, 2:183, 2:238, 3:197–9
Temple, Purbeck 1:275–6, 1:276
Templer/Templar, Dudley (bap. 1627) 3:174
Tenby, Pembrokeshire 1:527 n. 6
Tenison, Thomas, archbishop of Canterbury (1636–1715) 1:608, 3:521
Termonfeckin, County Louth 3:195
Teviotdale, County Roxburgh 2:413
Tewkesbury, Gloucestershire 1:46
Thickness, Ralph (d. 1689) 2:559
Thomason, George (c.1602–66) 1:lviii, 1:119, 1:147, 1:189 n.2, 1:287, 1:290, 1:306, 1:315–16, 1:340 & nn. 3 & 4, 1:360 n. 3, 1:623, 2:307, 3:506
  acquisition of publications 2:510–11, 2:530, 2:615 2:624, 2:687
  and *The Case of the Armie Truly Stated* 1:438 n. 7
  copies of letters 3:327
  copies of speeches 3:130
  copy of proclamation 2:350
  dating of documents 3:69 n. 7, 3:130–1
  and declaration of Commonwealth 2:628
  and Declaration on Scottish prisoners of war 1:571
  and dissolution of first Protectorate parliament 3:130
  and Huntington's *Sundry Reasons inducing Major Robert Huntington to lay down his commission* 1:538 nn. 9 & 10, 1:539 nn. 11, 14 & 16, 1:540 n. 18
  and letter to people of Bristol 1:542
  and possible forged letter to Mazarin 3:328, 3:329, 3:330
  on publication of Cromwell's oath 3:3
  tract pamphlets 2:384
Thomastown, County Kilkenny 2:149, 2:152–3, 2:216, 2:231 n. 9
Thomond, earl of, *see* O'Brien
Thompson, Cornet 2:47
Thompson, James 1:97–102, 1:104, 1:111, 1:112–13
Thompson, Thomas 2:334
Thompson, William 2:47

Thomson, George (bap. 1607, d. 1691) 1:195
Thomson/Thompson, Maurice (1604–76) 1:505
Thornhaugh, Francis 1:520–1, 1:554–5, 1:556
Thornton, Anne, Lady Anne Thornton 2:291
Thornton, John 2:291
Thornton, Sir Nicholas 2:291
Thorpe, Francis (bap. 1594, d. 1665) 3:170–1
Throckmorton, Clement 1:85
Throughton, Mr 3:204
Thurloe, John (bap. 1616, d. 1668) 1:15, 1:504 n. 15, 2:413–14, 2:433, 2:655, 2:658, 2:722, 2:723, 2:746, 3:liii, 3:liv, 3:13, 3:48, 3:486
  and Brayfield 3:450
  copies of letters 3:39, 3:40–1, 3:185, 3:222, 3:226, 3:232, 3:274, 3:320–1, 3:441
  draft copies 3:21, 3:164, 3:165, 3:170–1, 3:199–201, 3:256, 3:259, 3:268–9, 3:284, 3:413
  letters to: from Montagu 3:285
  letter to Pell 3:109
  letters to Henry Cromwell 3:283, 3:239, 3:339
  letters written by 3:225
  OC's comments on parliamentary committee for retrenching forces 3:113
  and possible forged letter to Mazarin 3:328, 3:329, 3:330
  presents letters to Council 3:259
  revisions to letter to governors of English colonies 3:16, 3:18 n. 16
  and Sindercombe plot 3:331
  undated copies 3:166, 3:265
  visit from Whitelocke 3:52
  working drafts 3:213, 3:429
Thynne, Henry Frederick 1:28–9
Thynne, Sir James 1:28–9, 1:31–2
Thynne, Sir Thomas (d. 1639) 1:28–9
Thynne, Thomas 1:29 n. 4
Tichborne/Titchburne, Robert (1610/11–82) 1:463, 1:474–5, 1:647–9, 2:632, 2:651 n. 2, 3:508
Tickhill, Yorkshire 1:197
Tickhill Castle, Yorkshire 1:223
Tickle, John (d. 1694) 2:527
Tillinghast, John (bap. 1604, d. 1655) 3:204
Times, Richard 1:104
Tite, William 1:147 n. 19
Tito, George 3:196–7
Tito, Thomas 3:196–7
Titus, Captain Silius (1622/3–1704) 1:507–8, 2:451
Tiverton, Devon 1:329, 1:332–3
Tobacco Islands, *see* Barbados, West Indies
Toft, Cambs. 1:3
Toland, John (1670–1722) 1:358, 2:274, 3:278–9
Toll, Thomas 1:75, 3:216–17
Tomlinson/Thomlinson, Matthew (bap. 1617, d. 1681) 1:279–80, 1:474–5, 1:641, 1:642, 1:644, 2:42, 2:339, 2:686 n. 109

704

GENERAL INDEX

Tompson, John 2:334
Tookey, Job 1:3
Toovey, C. J. 1:95
Torrente Chisone, river 3:515 n. 13
Totnes, Devon 1:334
Townley, Francis 3:122, 3:123 n. 3
Townsend, Richard (*c.*1618–92) 2:136–7, 2:138, 2:140, 2:141
Townshend, William 1:523
Trenchard, John (*c.*1586–1662) 2:424
Trent, river 1:133
Trerice, baron, *see* Arundel/Arundell
Treswell, Daniel 3:25–6
Trevor, Marcus/Mark, first Viscount Dungannon (1618–70) 2:143, 2:144, 3:240
Trim, County Meath 2:91, 2:92, 2:95, 2:98, 2:247
Trinity College Dublin, nomination of a Provost for 2:543–4
Tromp, Maarten Harpertzoon (1598–1653) 2:727
Troughton, William 3:204 n. 7
Trowbridge, Wiltshire 1:261
Tuchet, James, Lord Audley and third earl of Castlehaven (*c.*1617–84) 2:107, 2:115, 2:117, 2:127, 2:165, 2:216, 2:230, 2:231
Tulidah, Alexander 1:420
Tullaroan, County Wexford 3:218
Turnbull, David 2:227
Turner, Dawson 1:137, 1:140, 1:143, 1:147 n. 19, 1:165 n. 1
Turner, Methuselah 3:32 n. 4
Turner, Mr 3:53–4
Turner, William 1:74
Turnham Green, Brentford 1:94
Twede, James 2:333
Tweed, river 1:590, 1:593
Twells, Robert 1:104, 1:112
Twisleton, George (1617/18–67) 2:498–9
Twisleton, Philip (1602–73) 1:554–5, 2:311, 2:327, 2:511, 3:164–5
Tyldesley, Thomas (1612–51) 1:576
Tynemouth, Northumberland 2:504
Tyrrell, Sir Timothy 3:194–5, 3:343

Underwood, Francis 1:285
United Provinces, *see* Netherlands
Up Park/Uppark House, Harting, Sussex 2:749–50
Uppsala, Sweden 3:51
Upton, Huntingdonshire 1:17–18
Upton-upon-Severn, Worcestershire 2:486, 2:488
Urry/Hurry, Colonel (d. 1650) 1:552, 1:557
Ussher, Elizabeth 3:195
Ussher, James, archbishop of Armagh (1581–1656) 2:412, 2:629, 3:194–5
Uvedale, Edmond 1:329–30
Uvedale, Sir William 1:37

Val Perosa, Piedmont, Italy 3:515
Vale of the White Horse, Oxfordshire 1:272
van Druschke, Jonas 1:557
Vandrusk, Major General 1:552
Vane, Frances (née Wray, 1623/4–79) 1:196 n. 10
Vane, Sir Henry (1589–1655) 1:83
Vane, Sir Henry (1613–62) 1:lv, 1:40, 1:64, 1:65, 1:195–6, 1:219 n. 19, 1:251, 1:326, 1:565–6, 1:607, 1:609, 1:610, 1:611, 1:612, 2:10, 2:63–4, 2:268, 2:320, 2:345, 2:424, 2:425, 2:439, 2:440, 2:509, 2:515
  as brother Heron 1:xlvi, 1:lx–lxi
  commissioner in Scotland 2:651 n. 2
  dissolution of Rump Parliament 2:608, 2:609, 2:612
  letters read out by 2:471, 2:472
  letters signed by 1:429–31
  letters to 2:300–1
  publication of *A Healing Question* 3:278
  summoned to Council 3:279
  trial for treason 2:578 n. 13
Vaughan, Henry 1:269
Vaughan, Howell 3:183
Vaughan, Colonel Richard 1:269, 1:270, 1:271
Vaughan, Sir William 1:190
Vaux, Edward, fourth Baron Vaux of Harrowden (1588–1661) 2:571–2
Vaux, Elizabeth (1586–1658) 2:571–2
Veitch, John 2:417
Venables, Robert (1612/13–87) 1:515, 2:102–3, 2:142, 2:144, 2:760, 3:118, 3:119, 3:120, 3:231–2, 3:273
Venn, John (bap. 1586, d. 1650) 2:758
Vermuyden, Bartholomew 1:271, 1:282, 1:537
Verney, Sir Edmund (1616–49) 2:92, 2:100
Vernon, John (*fl.* 1653–67) 2:596–7
Veto, OC and the royal 1:463–6, 1:492
Vevey, Switzerland 2:273–4
Vicars, John (1580–1652) 1:lvii, 1:112–13, 1:119–21, 1:147, 1:151 n. 21
Villiers, George, first duke of Buckingham 1:48
Villiers, George, second duke of Buckingham (1628–87) 3:262
Vines, Richard (1599/1600–56) 3:67 n. 5
Virginia, North America 3:225–7
Vote of No Addresses (Jan 1648) 1:489–90
Vyner/Viner, Sir Thomas, first baronet (1588–1665) 2:757, 3:53–4

W., R. 1:lviii n. 18
Wade, John (d. in or before 1668?) 3:175
Wadsworth, John 3:207
Wagstaffe, Sir Joseph (bap. 1611?, d. 1666/7) 3:298
Wakefield, Yorkshire 1:122
Walcott, Humphrey 1:283–5
Walker, Henry (*fl.* 1638–60) 1:213 n. 12, 1:220

705

GENERAL INDEX

Walker, Mr 2:622
Walker, Walter 3:511
Wall, Colonel 2:100, 2:104
Wall, Lieutenant 2:206
Wallace, James (d. 1678) 2:331
Wallace, Mr 2:397
Waller, Edmund (1606–87) 3:201–2
Waller, Sir Hardress (c.1604–66) 1:300–1, 1:310,
    1:320, 1:323–4, 1:408, 2:23, 2:24, 2:29, 2:177,
    2:605
    commissioner/signatory for warrant for trial
      of King 1:647–9
    letters from 1:399–402
    and Putney Debates 1:461, 1:474–5
Waller, Sir William (bap. 1598?, d. 1668) 1:195,
    1:207–10, 1:210–12, 1:213, 1:214–15, 1:216,
    1:219 n. 19, 1:220 n. 25, 1:227, 1:228 n. 78,
    1:231, 1:239, 1:245, 1:257, 1:259, 1:260,
    1:339 n. 2
Walley, Charles 1:71
Wallingford, Oxfordshire 1:228, 1:231, 1:233,
    1:234, 1:235, 1:318, 1:325, 1:519
Wallis, John 2:335
Wallis, Peter (fl. 1644–59) 2:548, 3:107–8, 3:435
Wallis, Thomas 2:334
Wallop, Robert (1601–67) 1:429–31, 2:11, 2:114
Wallops, Mr 3:263
Walsh, Thomas, Catholic archbishop of Cashel
    (1580–1654) 2:184–9
Walsham-le-Willows, Suffolk 1:166
Walton, Anna (1622–61) 1:199 n. 11
Walton, Brian, bishop of Chester (1600–61)
    2:628–9
Walton, Margaret (OC's sister) 1:14, 1:197
Walton, Valentine (1593/4–1661) 1:lv, 1:14, 1:51–2,
    1:196–200, 1:215, 1:647–9, 2:11, 2:51
Walton, Valentine (d. 1644) 1:lv, 1:197, 1:198–9
Walwyn, William 2:59 n. 1
Wandesford, Elizabeth (d. c.1635) 2:546
Wandesford, Sir Rowland (d. 1653) 2:546
Wanhap, Francis 2:331
Wanhap, Walter 2:333
Wanklyn, Malcolm 1:215 n. 3, 1:432 n. 1
Wansey, Henry 3:185
Warden, William 2:139, 2:141
Ware, Hertfordshire 1:480, 1:483, 2:275
Wariston, Archibald 2:lvi
Wariston, lord, see Johnston
Warke, baron, see Grey
Warner, Henry 1:190, 1:214
Warren, John 2:100, 2:104
Warren, Thomas 2:136 n. 1
Warrington, Cheshire 1:550, 1:551, 1:557–8
Warwick, earl of, see Rich
Warwick, Warwickshire 1:94, 1:542, 2:483 n. 3
Warwick Castle, Warwickshire 2:493, 2:494, 3:113
Washington, Ad. 1:112–13

Wastell, John 1:558
Waterford, County Waterford 2:140–1, 2:143,
    2:147–8, 2:149–51, 2:153–4
Waterford City, County Waterford 2:341
Waterford Harbour, County Waterford
    2:142 n. 19
Waterhouse, John/Joseph 2:422–3
Waterhouse, Nathaniel (c.1615–63) 2:453–4,
    3:263
Watford, Hertfordshire 1:480
Watlington, Oxfordshire 1:263, 1:266
Watson, Leon 1:300–1
Watson, Mr 1:105
Watson, William 2:335
Watts, Thomas 1:533
Wayer, John 2:334
Weare, James 2:333
Weare, Nathaniel 3:150–1
Weaver, John (d. 1685) 2:544, 3:83
Webb, Abraham 2:366–7
Weekes, John, see Fowke, John (c.1596–1662)
Welbeck Abbey, Nottinghamshire 1:223, 1:224,
    1:338
Welber, William 1:112–13
Welbore, William 1:103, 1:104
Weldon, Ralph (1606–83) 2:597
Weldon, Ralph (bap. 1606, d. 1676) 1:300–2,
    1:307, 1:312
Welles, Walter 1:9, 1:11, 1:258
Wellingborough, Northamptonshire 1:98
Wells, John 2:511–12
Wells, Somerset 1:260
Wemyss, David, Lord Elcho and second earl of
    Wemyss (1610–79) 1:593, 1:594, 3:110
Wentworth, Sir Peter (1592–1675) 1:217 n. 15,
    1:245, 1:247, 1:256, 1:275–7
    and dissolution of Rump Parliament 2:609,
      2:610 n. 4, 2:611
Wentworth, Thomas, first earl of Strafford
    (1593–1641) 1:25, 3:193
Wereton, North Staffordshire 1:224, 1:225
West, Edward 2:509
West, Francis (d. 1652) 2:469
West, John 1:134 n. 6
West, Nicholas 1:193
West, William (1612–70) 2:642
West Ilsley, Berkshire 1:235
West Indies 3:lii
    Barbados 2:91, 2:97, 2:560, 3:60–1, 3:228–9
    Hispaniola 3:xlvii, 3:101 n. 5, 3:230
    Nevis 3:230, 3:234
    St Christopher's 3:195–6
West Looe, Cornwall 2:519
Westby, Henry (d. 1657) 2:264
Westmeath, earl of, see Nugent
Westmoreland, Matthias 3:41
Weston, Henry (1612–66) 2:749–51

706

GENERAL INDEX

Westrowe, Thomas (1616–53) **2**:483
Wetherby, Yorkshire **1**:545, **1**:553
Wexford, County Wexford **2**:lx, **2**:104–17, **2**:129, **2**:143
Wexford Town, County Wexford **2**:92–3
Whalley, Commissarie General **2**:384, **2**:385, **2**:475
Whalley, Edward (d. 1674/5) **1**:135, **1**:136, **1**:140, **1**:145, **1**:146, **1**:149, **1**:150, **1**:262, **1**:381, **1**:391–2, **1**:397 n. 23, **2**:23, **2**:24, **2**:302, **2**:303–4, **2**:326, **2**:327, **2**:516–19, **2**:591, **2**:594, **3**:517
  assurances to Edinburgh clergy **2**:351
  authorization for examination of condition of Windsor Castle **3**:19
  certificate of service **1**:364–5
  in charge of guarding King **1**:402–3
  commissioner/signatory for warrant for trial of King **1**:647–9
  in Robert Huntington's *Sundry Reasons* **1**:540
  injuries to **2**:328
  letters to **1**:402–5, **1**:476–8
  and mutiny of soldiers **2**:42
  signatory of king's death warrant **1**:650
Whalley, Frances (née Cromwell) **1**:364, **1**:478 n. 10
Whalley, Henry (d. 1665) **2**:373–4, **2**:506–7, **2**:545, **2**:760, **3**:517
Whalley, John **3**:517
Whalley, Richard **3**:517
Whalley, Lancashire **1**:548–9, **1**:553
Wharton, Elizabeth (d. 1669) **2**:546
Wharton, Sir George, first baronet (1617–81) **1**:637–8
Wharton, Jane, Lady Wharton, née Goodwin (bap. 1618, d. 1658) **1**:569, **2**:344 n. 7, **2**:484
Wharton, Nehemiah (*fl.*1641–9) **1**:23
Wharton, Philip, fourth Baron Wharton (1613–96) **1**:239, **1**:243, **1**:493, **1**:609, **1**:634–5, **2**:lv, **2**:lxiv, **2**:171–5, **2**:343–4, **2**:546–8
  letters signed by **1**:429–31
  letters to **1**:568–70, **2**:483–4
Wharton, Thomas, first marquis of Wharton (1648–1715) **1**:569
Whately, William (1583–1639) **2**:568
Wheatley, Oxfordshire **1**:263
Wheelocke, Abraham (*c.*1593–1653) **1**:110–11
Whetham, Nathaniel (1604–68) **3**:176
Whetstone, Leicestershire **3**:157
Whichcote, Benjamin (1609–83) **1**:66, **2**:277–8
Whichcote, Christopher (before 1610–64) **1**:643–5, **2**:758, **3**:19
Whitaker, Laurence **1**:lxi n. 29, **1**:211, **1**:341, **1**:398
White, Charles (d. 1661) **1**:338–9, **1**:550, **2**:589, **2**:590
White, Lieutenant Colonel Francis **2**:396, **2**:397–8, **2**:399

White, Major Francis (d. 1657) **1**:457, **1**:458, **2**:46–7, **2**:327
White, Henry **2**:335
White, John, mayor of Clonmel **2**:258
White, John (d. 1669) **2**:571
White, Lieutenant Colonel **2**:181
White, Michael Oge **2**:259 n. 6
White, Mr, of Fulham **2**:629
White, Richard **1**:201, **1**:542
White Fitz Thomas, Michael **2**:259 n. 6
White Knights (Fitzgibbon family) **2**:208
Whitehead, Stephen **1**:394 n. 18
Whitelocke, Bulstrode (1605–75) **1**:249, **1**:326, **2**:lvi, **2**:10, **2**:13 n. 3, **2**:59, **2**:262, **2**:292, **2**:297, **2**:299, **2**:415, **2**:420, **2**:437, **2**:475, **2**:726, **3**:383
  appointment as Commissioner of Great Seal **3**:106
  on committee for liberty of conscience **3**:109
  conversations with **2**:267–73, **2**:516–19, **2**:573–81, **2**:732–7, **2**:744–7, **3**:l, **3**:47–53, **3**:458–60
  dating of meetings **3**:459
  dissolution of Rump Parliament **2**:608, **2**:609–10, **2**:615
  and John Holland **3**:26
  kingship committee **3**:358–66, **3**:384, **3**:413
  letters to **2**:731, **3**:13–14
  and peace with Sweden **3**:79 n. 39
  return from Sweden **3**:46–53, **3**:54–6
Whitelocke, Mary (d. 1684) **2**:732
Whithed/Whitehead, Richard (1594–1663) **3**:182
Whitstone (OC's nephew) **3**:115, **3**:116, **3**:124
Whitstone, Roger **3**:115
Whittaker, Lawrence **1**:131 n. 7
Whittington, George **1**:392
Widdrington, Sir Thomas (*c.*1600–60) **3**:319 n. 1, **3**:345, **3**:468, **3**:486
  appointment as Commissioner of Great Seal **3**:106
  conversations with **2**:516–19
  letters to **3**:324–5, **3**:351, **3**:425, **3**:427, **3**:430–1, **3**:466–7, **3**:484–5
Widman/Widenham, John **2**:138
Widows, war, concern for **1**:398, **2**:523–6, **2**:408–9, **2**:392–3, **2**:512–13, **2**:525–6, **2**:528–9, **2**:536, **2**:594, **2**:633–4, **3**:24, **3**:334, **3**:527, **3**:532, **3**:551, **3**:556
Wigan, Lancashire **1**:561, **1**:562
Wilburton, Cambridgeshire **1**:193 n. 7
Wilby, Suffolk **1**:176
Wilde, John (1590–1669) **1**:92, **2**:10, **3**:182
Wildman, Sir John (1622/3–93) **1**:lxiii, **1**:435–6, **1**:437, **1**:442, **1**:448, **1**:449, **1**:453, **1**:154, **1**:155, **3**:242, **3**:300 nn. 58 & 59
  and Putney Debates **1**:450, **1**:451, **1**:453, **1**:454, **1**:458, **1**:461, **1**:463, **1**:473 & n. 39
Wilkes, Mr **3**:170

707

GENERAL INDEX

Wilkins, John (1614–72) **2**:568, **2**:569
Wilkinson, Henry (1610–75) **2**:424, **2**:425
Wilkinson, John (d. 1650) **2**:48
Wilks/Wilkes, Timothy **3**:125–7
William II, Prince of Orange (1626–50) **2**:433
Williams, John, bishop of Lincoln, archbishop
of York (1582–1650) **1**:3, **1**:426–7
Williams, Morgan **1**:liii
Williams, Roger (*c*.1606–83) **2**:531, **3**:183–4
Williams, Sir Trevor, baronet (*c*.1623–92) **1**:521–2,
1:523, **2**:656
Williams, Sir William, third baronet
(d. 1659) **3**:182
Williamson, Robert **1**:542
Williamson, Quartermaster Robert **2**:334
Willingham, George (d. 1651) **1**:liv, **1**:22–5,
1:34 n. 3
Willoughby, Charles (*c*.1630–94) **2**:228
Willoughby, Francis (1615–71) **2**:228, **2**:600
Willoughby, Sir Francis, fifth Baron Willoughby
of Parham (bap. 1614, d. 1666) **1**:120, **1**:130,
1:133–4, **1**:139, **1**:145–6, **1**:148, **1**:149, **1**:150,
1:156–7, **1**:158, **1**:160, **1**:185, **1**:214, **2**:228, **2**:560
Wilmot, Charles, first Viscount Wilmot of
Athlone **1**:84 n. 2
Wilmot, Henry, first earl of Rochester (bap. 1613,
d. 1658) **1**:43, **1**:67–8, **1**:264, **3**:298
Wilson, John **2**:333
Wilson, Rowland (bap. 1613, d. 1650) **2**:9–10,
2:732 n. 5
Wilton House, Wiltshire **1**:262
Winceby, Lincolnshire **1**:172, **1**:177
Wincham, Cheshire **1**:515
Winche, O. **1**:162–3
Winchester, Hampshire **1**:228, **1**:318–19, **1**:319–22
Winchester, marquis of, *see* Paulet
Winchester Castle, Hampshire **1**:228, **1**:331,
1:644
Winde, James (*fl.* 1649–56) **2**:650
Windebank, Francis (1582–1646) **1**:265 & n. 1,
1:267–8, **3**:28
Windebank, John (1618–1704) **3**:28–9
Winderum, George **2**:332
Windsor, Berkshire **1**:100, **1**:491, **1**:563, **1**:609,
1:641, **2**:77
Windsor Castle, Berkshire **1**:342, **1**:636, **1**:643,
2:261, **2**:758, **3**:19, **3**:279
Wing, D. G. **1**:539 n. 12
Wingfield Manor/Wingfield House,
Derbyshire **1**:223
Winniffe, Thomas, bishop of Lincoln
(1576–1654) **1**:42
Winram/Windrahame, George, Lord Liberton
of Liberton (d. 1650) **2**:328
Winslow, Edward (1595–1655) **2**:662–3
Winstanley, James **1**:546–7
Winter, Samuel (1603–66) **2**:543–4

Winterbourne Heath, Berkshire **1**:236, **1**:255
Winthrop, John (1606–76) **2**:520 n. 6
Winton, earl of, *see* Seton
Winwick, Lancashire **1**:557 & n. 44, **1**:604
Wirley, Sir John **3**:182
Wisbech, Cambridgeshire **1**:127, **1**:129, **1**:140,
1:142, **1**:183
Wise, Edward (1632–75) **2**:551–2
Wise, Thomas (*c*.1603–41) **2**:551
Witney, Oxfordshire **1**:231, **1**:269
Witton Castle, Northumberland **2**:291
Wodderspoon, John **1**:283 n. 1
Wogan, Edward (*c*.1625–54) **2**:164, **2**:176, **2**:177–8,
2:181, **2**:247
Wolfe, Edward **2**:163
Wollaston, Sir John (1585/6–1658) **1**:509, **2**:66–7,
2:79–80, **2**:83–4, **2**:85–6, **2**:108–10, **2**:125–6,
2:423–4, **2**:441–2
warrants for payment **2**:157–9, **2**:175–6,
2:453–4, **2**:465–6, **2**:506–7, **2**:508
Wolseley, Sir Charles, second baronet
(1629/30–1714) **2**:531 n. 2, **3**:8, **3**:358–66
Wolsey, Cardinal Thomas (1473–1530) **2**:195 n. 50
Wood, Alexander **2**:332
Wood, Anthony/Anthony à Wood (1632–95)
2:48, **2**:422, **2**:500
Wood, Lieutenant Colonel **1**:160, **1**:161
Wood, Captain Lieutenant Robert **2**:333
Wood, Robert **1**:542, **3**:4, **3**:130–1
Wood, William (*fl.* 1651–3) **2**:592
Woodhouse, A. S. P. **1**:385
edition of Putney Debates **1**:436, **1**:440 n. 15,
1:441 nn. 17 & 19, **1**:442 n. 20, **1**:443 n. 25,
1:444 n. 26, **1**:445 n. 28, **1**:446 n. 30,
1:448 nn. 38 & 40, **1**:449 nn. 43, 44, 45 & 46,
1:450 nn. 47 & 48, **1**:451 n. 51, 52 & 53, n. 49,
1:454 n. 3, **1**:458 n. 12, **1**:460 n. 18, **1**:462,
1:465 nn. 6 & 8, **1**:466 nn. 9 & 12
Woodstock, Oxfordshire **1**:231, **1**:266–7, **1**:269
Woolnough, Thomas (d. 1675) **2**:530
Woolrych, Austin **1**:250 n. 4, **1**:378, **1**:388
Woolwich, Surrey **3**:519
Worcester, marquis of, *see* Somerset
Worcester, Worcestershire **1**:278, **2**:lxii, **2**:486,
2:487–92
Worden, Blair **2**:274, **3**:241, **3**:278
Wormell, Bartholomew **3**:216–17
Worsley, Benjamin (1617/18–77) **3**:457
Worsley, Charles (1622–56) **2**:608–9, **2**:612, **3**:336
Worsley, Ralph (d. 1694) **2**:556–7
Worthington, John (bap. 1618, d. 1671) **1**:62
Wounded Soldiers, care of **1**:423–5, **1**:533, **1**:542,
2:335–7, **2**:348–9, **2**:523–4, **2**:558–9
Wrath, Mr **1**:17
Wray, Sir Christopher **1**:131, **1**:186, **1**:196 n. 10
Wray, Sir John, second baronet (bap. 1586,
d. 1655) **1**:137, **1**:140–1

708

GENERAL INDEX

Wren, Matthew (1585–1667), bishop of Ely 1:166
Wright, John 1:287
Wright, Laurence (1590–1657) 2:457–8
Wright, Thomas 1:113
Wriothesley, Thomas, fourth earl of
    Southampton (1608–67) 1:336–7, 3:44
Wroth, Mr 1:17 n. 26
Wroth/Wrothe, Sir Thomas (1584–1672)
    1:489
Wyatt, Sir Dudley (1609–51) 1:484–5
Wyeth, Joseph (1663–1731) 2:664

Wynn, Sir Owen, third baronet (*c*.1590–1660)
    2:621, 2:652

York, Yorkshire 1:340
Yorke, Mr 1:626
Youghal, County Cork 2:125, 2:132, 2:133, 2:134–5,
    2:136–9, 2:141, 2:156–7, 2:163, 2:210
Young, Lieutenant 1:533

Zanchy, Jerome, *see* Sankey/Zanchie/Zanchy,
    Sir Hierome/Hierom/Jerome (c.1621–c.1687)